This uniquely comprehensive study explores all aspects of the English business community as it developed between 1590 and 1720. Drawing on largely untapped records of private firms as well as on institutional archives, Richard Grassby describes and explains the economic and technical structure of business in a pre-industrial economy and examines the ways in which social values, demographic factors, the family, the state and religion distributed talent, trained and motivated businessmen and determined their life style.

The important conclusion which emerges from his study is that individual initiative and a fluid social structure largely account for differences in response to economic opportunities between England and other pre-industrial societies. His book offers an empirically based analysis of why men entered business, how they lived and worked and what they achieved, and it will appeal to all who wish to understand the dynamics of pre-industrial growth and the interaction between business and society.

The business community of seventeenth-century England

The business community of seventeenth-century England

Richard Grassby

Published by the Press Syndicate of the University of Cambridge
The Pitt Building, Trumpington Street, Cambridge CB2 1RP
40 West 20th Street, New York, NY 10011-4211, USA
10 Stamford Road, Oakleigh, Melbourne 3166, Australia

First published 1995

Printed in Great Britain at the University Press, Cambridge

A catalogue record for this book is available from the British Library

Library of Congress cataloguing in publication data

Grassby, Richard
The business community of seventeenth-century England / Richard Grassby
p. cm.
Includes bibliographical references and index.
ISBN 0 521 43450 5
1. England – Economic conditions – 17th century. 2. Merchants – England – History – 17th century. 3. Business enterprises – England – History – 17th century. I. Title. II. Title: Business community of 17th century England.
HC254.5.G73 1995
330.941'06 – dc20 94-40285 CIP

ISBN 0 521 43450 5 hardback

SE

To those who have taught me by example that no value system is proof against self-interest and deceit and that the only certainty in human history is that everybody dies.

Contents

Figures

Tables

Preface

This study was begun in 1957 in an academic world which no longer exists. Although some preliminary data have appeared in periodical articles, the author decided to defer publication until sufficient evidence had been accumulated to sustain a general thesis. The central concept was initially influenced by Sylvia Thrupp's seminal work on London and by studies of medieval European history rather than by the Tawney or *Annales* schools. It has benefited over the past thirty-five years from a dramatic increase in the available sources and the introduction of new techniques and ideas. But the questions originally posed, many of which anticipated more recent fashions, have not changed and the structure of the book is essentially the same as when first planned.

This work, which is intended for both the specialist scholar and the general reader, has been conceived as *l'histoire intégrale*. It attempts to define the role of business in seventeenth-century England by focusing on the contribution of specific individuals and by reconstructing the whole environment in which they functioned. Although merchants who were active and often resident in global markets, feature prominently, the book attempts to re-create the whole business community, the majority of whose members operated in the domestic economy and in manufacturing as well as distribution. Its primary objective has been to explore both the origins of wealth and the impact of variable economic performance on individuals and families, to establish what changed and what survived in England as compared with other pre-industrial societies.

The approach adopted is entirely analytical and those who wish to understand the inner workings of a particular business over time might consult the author's biography of Sir Dudley North. A future book will address the use and abuse of theory in explaining how the social and economic structure evolved. The principal aim here is to describe how the system actually functioned and not to produce from thin air or from the scribblings of some defunct economist a model of development. In a perfect world, it would be mandatory for any theorist to sweat over a ledger for six months before he could pontificate about capitalism.

The questions raised extend beyond economics, accounting and business into political, administrative, intellectual, legal, social and literary history. Consequently the book ventures into the subject matter of other disciplines – jurisprudence, sociology, linguistics, the behavioural sciences, demography, theology and philosophy. Whenever ideas and techniques have been borrowed from fields in which the author lacks specialized knowledge, he has cautiously followed what appear to be the best authorities rather than the latest fashion.

The evidence is not adequate to answer every question and this work is not as systematically documented as the author would wish. He is conscious that certain categories of evidence, such as judicial and demographic records, could have been used more intensively to clarify particular points and that some issues and subjects have been treated more superficially than they deserve. Most of the original research on P.C.C. wills was undertaken before the inventories were available for use and a few anachronistic references to material consulted before the extensive reorganization of archives and libraries may have escaped detection. Nor has it been possible to consult some manuscript materials which have come to light in recent years or original material in Scotland and Ireland or many secondary works published after 1992.

The real problem has, however, been the sheer volume of evidence, which can best be appreciated by those who have spent a lifetime working through the records of just one institution. Attention has been focused on private business papers rather than on statistical sources like the Port Books. Given the breadth of the subject and the need for compression, it has also proved impossible to use more than a selection of the records consulted. Indeed almost all the particular examples incorporated in an earlier and much longer version of the present work have been excised, although those with the interest and stamina can resurrect some of them from the notes. Endless lists of names would have strained the patience of readers without constituting hard proof. The desire for completeness also has to be weighed against human mortality. It therefore seemed appropriate to publish the work in its present form and leave others to remedy its defects and omissions.

The period chosen for study stretches from the 1590s to the 1690s, both of which were decades of economic crisis, protracted warfare and structural change. Although the old medieval pattern of trade was evident as late as 1606 and was only finally displaced after Cokayne's Project, the limitations of the short-distance broadcloth trade were exposed by the depression of the 1550s and the fall of Antwerp, and the long-distance trades had clearly emerged by 1600. Another change in economic structure was evident by 1720, when the Bubble paradoxically confirmed the permanence of the financial changes of the 1690s. Specific dates are less significant in economic than in political and military history, since changes usually took at least a generation to be implemented. The choice of period does, nonetheless, create some difficulties, because the conventional and political periodization of the secondary literature is 1540–1640, 1640–60 and 1660–1760. It has proved hard to separate in works which begin in 1660 or 1680 and continue to 1740 or 1780 arguments and evidence which relate specifically to the seventeenth century.

The statistically minded will note with disapproval the use of four-letter words such as 'many', 'some' and 'most'; several untestable assumptions have also been made in the projections. But precise figures have been used whenever possible and relevant, and the potential flaws in all assumptions have been made explicit. To attempt to be precise when the numbers are incomplete would create a parody of statistical method; 'few' simply means that the author has encountered few examples. Generalizations about attitudes and behaviour cannot usually be presented in statistical form; much of the evidence necessarily consists of multiple examples, of which only one or two can be illustrated in the text. The intention here is to illustrate the range of views and habits rather than to assess their proportional importance.

A strenuous effort has, however, been made to indicate where the evidence is thin. There are really three different levels of explanation in the text – certainties (such as the technical structure of business), high probabilities (such as the pattern of decision-making) and plausible inferences which are incapable of demonstration (such as the intensity of religious belief). Some of the conclusions presented can only be tested by reading thousands of documents to acquire an overall sense of what was normal practice.

Only the tip of the iceberg is visible. Many of the businessmen used here as examples could command full-length biographies and on many topics a sentence has to substitute for a book. A more detailed comparison with other countries, both in continental Europe and Asia, would have been an advantage and deflected criticism of Anglocentrism. It was originally intended to include France, the United Provinces and Germany and this explains the occasional forays into foreign territory. But problems of space and time have made this objective unattainable. Nor has any attempt been made to discuss in detail any individual trade or industry, many of which have been the subject of substantial monographs.

During the long period in which this work has been in gestation, several major contributions to business history have been made by other scholars, particularly in the Atlantic and Asian trades, and a prolific literature on urban history has developed. But the majority of studies are either local in scope or concerned with the whole urban community and with political issues. Historians have surprisingly tended to steer well clear of private business papers and to either ignore or misconstrue the business world. One obvious exception is Peter Earle's *Making of the English Middle Class*, which draws on the inventories in the Orphans Court of London. In order to avoid repetition of evidence, much of the material collected by the present author from the same source has been omitted here. The following studies appeared too late for inclusion: I.K. Ben Amos, *Adolescence and Youth* (New Haven, 1994); J. Hatcher, *British Coal Industry* (New York, 1993); M. Zell, *Industry and the Countryside* (Cambridge, 1994); J. Habakkuk, *Marriage, Debt and the Estate System* (Oxford, 1994); J. Barry and C. Brooke (eds.), *The Middle Sort* (London, 1994); V. Brodsky, *Londoners' Migration* (Oxford, 1995).

The argument of the book has not had the benefit of exposure to prior criticism. It has been written in isolation from the scholarly community without the benefit of research assistants and grants and hostage to the need to earn a livelihood. The author would, however, like to acknowledge the encouragement of Barry Supple, Jacob Price and the Cambridge University Press. Ruth Ellen Proudfoot and Jeanne Silvers also provided invaluable help in preparing the MS for publication.

Abbreviations

A. A. G. Bijdragen	*Afdeling Agrarische Geschiedenis Bijdragen*
AD	Archives Départementales
A.H.R.	*American Historical Review*
AN	Archives Nationales
AO	Archives Office
Acc. Hist. Journ.	*Accounting History Journal*
Acc. Res.	*Accounting Research*
Acc. Rev.	*Accounting Review*
Acta Hist. Neer.	*Acta Historica Neerlandica*
Acta Polon. Hist.	*Acta Poloniae Historica*
Add.	Additional
Agric. Hist.	*Agricultural History*
Agric. Hist. Rev.	*Agricultural History Review*
Amer. Archiv.	*American Archivist*
Amer. Ec. Rev.	*American Economic Review*
Amer. J. Econ. Sociol.	*American Journal of Economics and Sociology*
Amer. J. Legal Hist.	*American Journal of Legal history*
Amer. J. Sociol.	*American Journal of Sociology*
Amer. Nept.	*American Neptune*
Amer. Phil. Soc.	*American Philosophical Society*
Amer. Pol. Sc. Rev.	*American Political Science Review*
Amer. Sociol. Rev.	*American Sociological Review*
Anglo Amer. Law Rev.	*Anglo American Law Review*
Ann. Cisalp. Hist. Soc.	*Annales Cisalpines d'histoire sociale*
Ann. Med. Hist.	*Annals of Medical History*
Ann. Rep. Hist. Assoc. Lisbon	*Annual Report of the Historical Association of Lisbon*
Ann. Sc.	*Annals of Science*
Annales	*Annales Economies Sociétés Civilisations*

Antiq. J.	*The Antiquarian Journal*
Arch. Aliena	*Archaeologia Aliena*
Arch. Cambr.	*Archaeologia Cambrensis*
Arch. Cant.	*Archaeologia Cantiana*
Arch. Hist.	*Architectural History*
Arch. J.	*Architectural Journal*
Archaeol. J.	*Archaeological Journal*
Archaeol. Soc.	Archaeological Society
BAO	Bristol Archives Office
B. I. H. R.	*Bulletin of the Institute of Historical Research*, now renamed *Historical Research*
B. J. R. L.	*Bulletin of John Rylands Library*
BL	British Library
BN	Bibliothèque Nationale
B. N. Y. P. L.	*Bulletin of the New York Public Library*
Bapt. Q.	*Baptist Quarterly*
Beds. Rec. Soc.	*Bedfordshire Record Society*
Bengal P. & P.	*Bengal Past and Present*
Berks.	Berkshire
Bermuda Hist. Q.	*Bermuda Historical Quarterly*
Bibliog. Soc. Amer.	*Bibliographical Society of America*
Bibliog. Soc. Univ. Virg.	*Bibliographical Society of the University of Virginia*
Bod.	Bodleian Library, Oxford
Bod. Lib. Rec.	*Bodleian Library Record*
Brit. Acad.	British Academy
Brit. J. Educ. Stud.	*British Journal of Educational Studies*
Brit. J. Eight. Cent. Stud.	*British Journal of Eighteenth-Century Studies*
Brit. J. Hist. Sc.	*British Journal of the History of Science*
Brit. J. Sociol.	*British Journal of Sociology*
Brit. Mus. Q.	*British Museum Quarterly*, now renamed *Bulletin of the British Library*
Bull. Board Celt. Stud.	*Bulletin of the Board of Celtic Studies*
Bull. Brit. Lib.	*Bulletin of the British Library*, formerly *British Museum Quarterly*

Bull. Hist. Educ. Soc.	*Bulletin of the History of Education Society*
Bull. Jamaica Lib. Assoc.	*Bulletin of the Jamaica Library Association*
Bull. Sch. Orient. & Afr. Stud.	*Bulletin of the School of Oriental and African Studies*
Bull. Soc. Hist. Educ.	*Bulletin of the Society for the History of Education*
Bull. Soc. Hist. Med.	*Bulletin of the Social History of Medicine*
Bull. Soc. d'Hist. Mod.	*Bulletin de la Société d'histoire moderne*
Burl. Mag.	*Burlington Magazine*
Bus. Arch.	*Business Archives*
Bus. Hist.	*Business History*
Bus. Hist. Rev.	*Business History Review*
C	Public Record Office, Chancery
C. H. J.	*Cambridge Historical Journal*
C. J.	*Commons Journals*
CLRO	Corporation of London Records Office
CSB	Common Serjeant's Books
CUL	Cambridge University Library
Cahiers d'Hist. Mond.	*Cahiers d'histoire mondiale*
Cal. S. P. (Dom) (For) (Col)	*Calendar of State Papers (Domestic) (Foreign) (Colonial)*
Camb. Bibliog. Soc.	Cambridge Bibliographical Society
Camb. Law J.	*Cambridge Law Journal*
Camd. Soc.	*Camden Society*
Canad. J. Econ. & Pol. Sc.	*Canadian Journal of Economics and Political Science*
Canad. J. Hist.	*Canadian Journal of History*
Ch. Hist.	*Church History*
Ch. Q. Rev.	*Church Quarterly Review*
Cheth. Soc.	*Chetham Society*
Comp. Stud. Soc. Hist.	*Comparative Studies in Society and History*
Congreg. Hist. Soc. Trans.	*Congregational History Society Transactions*
Constr. Hist.	*Construction History*
Cont. & Ch.	*Continuity and Change*
Derby. Arch. J.	*Derbyshire Archaeological Journal*
Devon & Corn. N. & Q.	*Devon and Cornwall Notes and Queries*

Devon & Corn. Rec. Soc.	*Devon and Cornwall Record Society*
Diss. Abstr.	*Dissertation Abstracts*
Dugdale Soc. Occ. Papers (Pub.)	*Dugdale Society Occasional Papers (Publications)*
Durham Univ. J.	*Durham University Journal*
E	Public Record Office, Exchequer
E. E. T. S.	Early English Text Society
E. H. R.	*English Historical Review*
ESRO	East Sussex Record Office
East Yorks. Loc. Hist. Soc.	East Yorkshire Local History Society
Ec. Dev. Cult. Ch.	*Economic Development and Cultural Change*
Ec. H. R.	*Economic History Review*
Ec. J.	*Economic Journal*
Eight. Cent. Stud.	*Eighteenth-Century Studies*
Eng. Lit. Ren.	*English Literary Renaissance*
Essex Arch. & Hist.	*Essex Archaeology and History*
Eur. Hist. Quart.	*European History Quarterly*
Eur. J. Sociol.	*European Journal of Sociology*
Expl. Ec. H.	*Explorations in Economic History*
Expl. Ent. H.	*Explorations in Entrepreneurial History*
Fam. Hist.	*Family History*
Fem. Stud.	*Feminist Studies*
Furn. Hist.	*Furniture History*
GLL	Guildhall of London Library
Genealog. Mag.	*Genealogical Magazine*
Gloucs.	Gloucestershire
Guild. Misc.	*Guildhall Miscellany*
Guild. Stud. Lond. Hist.	*Guildhall Studies in London History*
HCA	Public Record Office, High Court of Admiralty
H. Gbl.	*Hansische Geschichtsblatter*
H. J.	*Historical Journal*
H. L. Q.	*Huntington Library Quarterly*
HMC	Historical Manuscripts Commission
Hakl. Soc.	Hakluyt Society
Harl. Misc.	*Harleian Miscellany*
Harl. Soc.	Harleian Society
Harv. Grad. Mag.	*Harvard Graduate Magazine*
Harv. J. Asiat. Stud.	*Harvard Journal of Asiatic Studies*

Harv. Lib. Bull.	*Harvard Library Bulletin*
Harv. Stud. Class. Phil.	*Harvard Studies in Classical Philology*
Heref.	Hereford
Herts.	Hertfordshire
Hist. Assoc.	Historical Association
Hist. éc. Belg.	*Histoire économique de la Belgique*
Hist. Ec. Ideas	*History of Economic Ideas*
Hist. Educ.	*History of Education*
Hist. Educ. J.	*History of Education Journal*
Hist. Educ. Q.	*History of Education Quarterly*
Hist. Eur. Ideas	*History of European Ideas*
Hist. Mag. Prot. Episc. Ch.	*Historical Magazine of the Protestant Episcopal Church*
Hist. Meth.	*Historical Methods*
Hist. Mon. Comm.	Royal Commission on Historical Monuments
Hist. Pol. Econ.	*History of Political Economy*
Hist. Pol. Thought	*History of Political Thought*
Hist. Res.	*Historical Research*
Hist. Sc.	*History of Science*
Hist. Soc. Res.	*History of Social Research*
Hist. Stud. Aust. & New Zeal.	*Historical Studies of Australia and New Zealand*
Hist. Stud. Univ. of Melbourne	*Historical Studies University of Melbourne*
Hist. & Theory	*History and Theory*
Hist. Tod.	*History Today*
Hist. Work.	*History Workshop*
Hist. Zeit.	*Historische Zeitschrift*
Hunt. Lib.	Huntington Library
Hunts.	Huntingdonshire
IESRO	Suffolk Record Office Ipswich Branch
IHR	Institute of Historical Research
IOL	British Library, Oriental and India Office Collections
Imm. & Min.	*Immigrants and Minorities*
Ind. Arch.	*Industrial Archaeology*
Indian Ec. J.	*Indian Economic Journal*
Indian Ec. & Soc. Hist. Rev.	*Indian Economic and Social History Review*

Indiana Soc. Stud. Q.	*Indiana Social Studies Quarterly*
Inf. Hist.	*Information historique*
Intl Conf. Ec. Hist.	International Conference of Economic History
Intl Rev. Soc. Hist.	*International Review of Social History*
Irish Econ. & Soc. Hist.	*Irish Economic and Social History*
Irish Hist. Stud.	*Irish Historical Studies*
J. Afr. Hist.	*Journal of African History*
J. Amer. Stud.	*Journal of American Studies*
J. Asian Stud.	*Journal of Asian Studies*
J. B. S.	*Journal of British Studies*
J. Barb. Mus. & Nat. Hist. Soc.	*Journal of the Barbados Museum and Natural History Society*
J. Bombay Branch Royal Asiatic Soc.	*Journal of the Bombay Branch of the Royal Asiatic Society*
J. Brit. Arch. Assoc.	*Journal of the British Archaeological Association*
J. Chart. Inst. Ins.	*Journal of the Chartered Institute of Insurance*
J. Chin. Phil.	*Journal of Chinese Philosophy*
J. Cork Hist. & Antiq. Soc.	*Journal of the Cork Historical and Antiquarian Society*
J. E. G. P.	*Journal of English and German Philology*
J. Ec. Behav. & Org.	*Journal of Economic Behaviour and Organization*
J. Ec. & Bus. Hist.	*Journal of Economic and Business History*
J. Ec. H.	*Journal of Economic History*
J. Ec. Lit.	*Journal of Economic Literature*
J. Ec. & Soc. Hist. Orient	*Journal of the Economic and Social History of the Orient*
J. Eccles. Hist.	*Journal of Ecclesiastical History*
J. Eight. Cent. Stud.	*Journal of Eighteenth-Century Studies*
J. Eng. Lit. Hist.	*Journal of English Literary History*
J. Eur. Ec. Hist.	*Journal of European Economic History*
J. Eur. Ideas	*Journal of European Ideas*
J. Eur. Stud.	*Journal of European Studies*
J. Fam. Hist.	*Journal of Family History*

J. Friends Hist. Soc.	*Journal of the Friends Historical Society*
J. H. I.	*Journal of the History of Ideas*
J. Hist. Geog.	*Journal of the History of Geography*
J. Hist. Med. & All. Sc.	*Journal of the History of Medicine and Allied Sciences*
J. Hist. Sociol.	*Journal of Historical Sociology*
J. I. H.	*Journal of Interdisciplinary History*
J. Imp. and Comm. Hist.	*Journal of Imperial and Commonwealth History*
J. Ind. Arch.	*Journal of Industrial Archaeology*
J. Inst. Chart. Ins.	*Journal of the Institute of Chartered Insurers*
J. It. H.	*Journal of Italian History*
J. Law & Econ.	*Journal of Law and Economics*
J. Legal Hist.	*Journal of Legal History*
J. M. H.	*Journal of Modern History*
J. Med. Hist.	*Journal of Medieval History*
J. Med. & Ren. Stud.	*Journal of Medieval and Renaissance Studies*
J. Merion. Hist. & Rec. Soc.	*Journal of the Merioneth Historical and Record Society*
J. Pol. Econ.	*Journal of Political Economy*
J. Pop. Cult.	*Journal of Popular Culture*
J. Psych. Norm. & Path.	*Journal de psychologie normal et pathologique*
JRL	John Rylands University Library of Manchester
J. Rel. Hist.	*Journal of Religious History*
J. Rom. Stud.	*Journal of Roman Studies*
J. Roy. Inst. Corn.	*Journal of the Royal Institute of Cornwall*
J. Roy. Soc. Arts	*Journal of the Royal Society of Arts*
J. Soc. Arch. Hist.	*Journal of the Society of Architectural Historians*
J. Soc. Archiv.	*Journal of Society of Archivists*
J. Soc. Hist.	*Journal of Social History*
J. Soc. Hist. Med.	*Journal of the Social History of Medicine*
J. Trans. Hist.	*Journal of Transport History*
J. Warburg & Court. Inst.	*Journal of the Warburg and Courtauld Institute*

Japan Q.	*Japan Quarterly*
KAO	Centre for Kentish Studies
Kroeber Anthrop. Soc. Papers	*Kroeber Anthropological Society Papers*
Lanc. Loc. Hist.	*Lancashire Local History*
Lancs. & Ches.	Lancashire and Cheshire
Law & Hist. Rev.	*Law and History Review*
Law. J.	*Law Journal*
Law Q. R.	*Law Quarterly Review*
Leics. Hist.	*Leicestershire History*
Lib. Hist.	*Library History*
Lincs.	Lincolnshire
Lincs. AO	Lincolnshire Archives Office
Lincs. Hist. & Arch.	*Lincolnshire History and Archaeology*
Lit. & Hist.	*Literature and History*
Lit. & Psych.	*Literature and Psychology*
Loc. Hist.	*Local History*
Local Pop. Stud.	*Local Population Studies*
Lond.	London
Lond. J.	*London Journal*
Mar. Hist.	*Maritime History*
Mar. Mirr.	*Mariners Mirror*
Maryland Hist. Mag.	*Maryland Historical Magazine*
Med. Hist.	*Medical History*
Med. & Hum.	*Mediaevalia et Humanistica*
Mem.	Memoirs (*Mémoires*)
Mid. Hist.	*Midland History*
Midd.	Middlesex
Misc.	Miscellany
Mod. Asian Stud.	*Modern Asian Studies*
Mod. Phil.	*Modern Philology*
N. & Q.	*Notes & Queries*
N. Y. Hist.	*New York History*
Nat. Lib. Wales	National Library of Wales
New Eng. Hist. & Genealog.	*New England History and Genealogy*
New Eng. Q.	*New England Quarterly*
New Lit. Hist.	*New Literary History*
Norf.	Norfolk
Norf. Arch.	*Norfolk Archaeology*
Norf. Rec. Soc.	Norfolk Record Society
North. Hist.	*Northern History*
Northants.	Northamptonshire

Northants. P. & P.	*Northamptonshire Past and Present*
Notts.	Nottinghamshire
Occ. Psych.	*Occupational Psychology*
Oxford J. Legal Stud.	*Oxford Journal of Legal Studies*
Oxford Rev. Econ. Pol.	*Oxford Review of Economics and Politics*
P. B. A.	*Proceedings of the British Academy*
P. M. L. A.	*Proceedings of the Modern Language Association*
P. & P.	*Past and Present*
PRO	Public Record Office
PROB	Public Record Office, Prerogative Court of Canterbury records
Parlt. Hist.	*Parliamentary History*
Pharm. Hist.	*Pharmaceutical History*
Pharm. J.	*Pharmaceutical Journal*
Phil. Quart.	*Philological Quarterly*
Pol. Q.	*Political Quarterly*
Pol. Sc. Q.	*Political Science Quarterly*
Pol. Stud.	*Political Studies*
Pop. Stud.	*Population Studies*
Post Med. Arch.	*Post Medieval Archaeology*
Proc. Amer. Antiq. Soc	*Proceedings of the American Antiquarian Society*
Proc. Clifton Antiq. Club	*Proceedings of the Clifton Antiquarian Club*
Proc. Hants. Field Club & Arch. Soc.	*Proceedings of the Hampshire Field Club and Archaeological Society*
Proc. Hug. Soc. Lond.	*Proceedings of the Huguenot Society of London*
Proc. Indian Hist. Rec. Comm.	*Proceedings of the Indian Historical Records Commission*
Proc. Leeds Phil. & Lit. Soc.	*Proceedings of the Leeds Philosophical and Literary Society*
Proc. Music Assoc.	*Proceedings of the Music Association*
Proc. Thores. Soc.	*Proceedings of the Thoresby Society*
Proc. Thorot. Soc.	*Proceedings of the Thoroton Society*
Psych. Bull.	*Psychological Bulletin*
Psych. Rev.	*Psychological Review*
Pub. Hist.	*Publishing History*
Q. J. Econ.	*Quarterly Journal of Economics*
Q. J. Roy. Meteor. Soc.	*Quarterly Journal of the Royal Meteorological Society*

Q. J. Speech	*Quarterly Journal of Speech*
R. H. S.	*Royal Historical Society*
RO	Record Office
Rec. Hist.	*Recusant History*
Rec. Soc.	*Record Society*
Ren. & Mod. Stud.	*Renaissance and Modern Studies*
Ren. Q.	*Renaissance Quarterly*
Ren. & Ref.	*Renaissance and Reformation*
Rep.	Report
Res. Ec. Hist.	*Research in Economic History*
Rev. Acc. Hist.	*Review of Accounting History*
Rev. Econ.	*Revue économique*
Rev. Eng. Lit.	*Review of English Literature*
Rev. Eng. Stud.	*Review of English Studies*
Rev. Hist.	*Revue historique*
Rev. Hist. Bordeaux	*Revue d'histoire de Bordeaux*
Rev. Hist. Ec. & Soc.	*Revue d'histoire économique et sociale*
Rev. Hist. Mod. & Cont.	*Revue d'histoire moderne et contemporaine*
Rev. Inst. Sociol.	*Revue de l'Institut de Sociologie*
Rev. Intl Hist. Banque	*Revue internationale d'histoire des banques*
Rev. It. de Sci. Econ.	*Revista italiana di scienze economiche*
Rev. Litt. Comp.	*Revue de littérature comparée*
Rev. Philol. Franc. & Litt.	*Revue de philologie français et litteraire*
Rev. Quest. Hist.	*Revue des questions historiques*
Rev. Soc. Econ.	*Review of Social Economy*
Royal Anthrop. Instit. (Occ. Papers)	*Royal Anthropological Institute (Occasional Papers)*
Roy. Instit. of Corn.	*Royal Institute of Cornwall*
SA	Sheffield Archives
S. E. E. R.	*Slavonic and East European Review*
SP	Public Record Office, State Papers
Salt Lib.	William Salt Library (Staffordshire Record Office)
Sc. & Soc.	*Science and Society*
Scand. Ec. H. R.	*Scandinavian Economic History Review*
Scot. Hist. Rev.	*Scottish Historical Review*
Scot. J. Pol. Econ.	*Scottish Journal of Political Economy*
Shakes. Q.	*Shakespeare Quarterly*

Shakes. Surv.	*Shakespeare Survey*
Sixt. Cent. J.	*Sixteenth-Century Journal*
Soc.	Society
Soc. Biol.	*Social Biology*
Soc. Guérn.	*Société Guérnaise*
Soc. Hist.	*Social History*
Soc. Res.	*Social Research*
Soc. Rev.	*Social Review*
Soc. Sc. Hist.	*Social Sciences and History*
Soc. Stud.	*Social Studies*
Som.	Somerset
South.	Southampton
South. Econ. J.	*Southern Economic Journal*
South. Hist.	*Southern History*
Stud. Bibliog.	*Studies in Bibliography*
Stud. Eight. Cent. Cult.	*Studies in Eighteenth-Century Culture*
Stud. Eng. Lit.	*Studies in English Literature*
Stud. Med. Ren. Hist.	*Studies in Medieval and Renaissance History*
Stud. Phil.	*Studies in Philology*
Suff. Rev.	*Suffolk Review*
Suss.	Sussex
Suss. Arch. Coll.	*Sussex Archaeological Collections*
T. B. G. A. S.	*Transactions of the Bristol and Gloucester Archaeological Society*
T. J. H. S. E.	*Transactions of the Jewish Historical Society of England*
T. L. S.	*Times Literary Supplement*
T. R. H. S.	*Transactions of the Royal Historical Society*
Text. Hist.	*Textile History*
Thor. Soc.	Thoroton Society
Tijd. v. Gesch.	*Tijdschrift voor geschiedenis*
Trans. Anglesey Arch. Soc. & Field Club	*Transactions of the Anglesey Archaeological Society and Field Club*
Trans. Bibliog. Soc.	*Transactions of the Bibliographical Society*
Trans. B'ham A. S.	*Transactions of the Birmingham Archaeological Society*
Trans. Brit. Instit. Geog.	*Transactions of the British Institute of Geographers*

Trans. Caern. Hist. Soc.	*Transactions of the Caernarvonshire Historical Society*
Trans. Camb. Bib. Soc.	*Transactions of the Cambridge Bibliographical Society*
Trans. Cumb. & West. Antiq. & Arch. Soc.	*Transactions of the Cumberland and Westmorland Antiquarian and Archaeological Society*
Trans. Cymm. Soc.	*Transactions of the Honourable Cymmrodorion Society*
Trans. Devon Assoc.	*Transactions of the Devon Association*
Trans. Hist. Soc. Lancs & Ches.	*Transactions of the Historical Society of Lancashire and Cheshire*
Trans. Hunter A. S.	*Transactions of the Hunter Archaeological Society*
Trans. Leics. Archit. & Arch. Soc.	*Transactions of the Leicestershire Architectural and Archaeological Society*
Trans. Lond. & Midd. A. S.	*Transactions of the London and Middlesex Archaeological Society*
Trans. Shrops. Arch. & Nat. Hist. Soc.	*Transactions of the Shropshire Archaeological and Natural History Society*
Trans. Soc. Guérn.	*Transactions de la Société guérnaise*
Trans. Worcs. A. S.	*Transactions of the Worcester Archaeological Society*
ULL	University of London Library
Univ. B'ham H. J.	*University of Birmingham Historical Journal*
Univ. Chicago Law Rev.	*University of Chicago Law Review*
Univ. Penn. Law Rev.	*University of Pennsylvania Law Review*
Univ. Toronto Law J.	*University of Toronto Law Journal*
Urban Hist. Year.	*Urban History Yearbook*
V. J. S. W.	*Vierteljahrsschrift für sozial- und wirtschaftsgeschichte*
WAM	Westminster Abbey Muniments
Warws. Hist.	*Warwickshire History*
Welt. Arch.	*Weltwirtschaftsarchiv*
West. Pol. Q.	*Western Political Quarterly*
Wilts.	Wiltshire
Wm & Mary Q.	*William and Mary Quarterly*
Worcs.	Worcestershire

Yorks. Arch. J.	*Yorkshire Archaeological Journal*
Yorks. Arch. Soc. (Rec. Ser.)	*Yorkshire Archaeological Society (Record Series)*
Yorks. Bull. Ec. Soc. Res.	*Yorkshire Bulletin of Economic and Social Research*

Explanatory notes

Wherever possible, specific documents and texts have been cited, but the volume of evidence has made abbreviation imperative and business records cannot usually be presented according to the scholarly conventions of political, administrative and literary history. When the evidence for a particular point is scattered over hundreds of pages or through numerous documents or when statistical data have been processed, a blanket reference has been supplied without the redundant *passim*.

Printed primary sources have been described by surname of author and short title (even on first citation). For secondary sources, the Harvard system of annotation by author's surname and date of publication has been adopted, though the citations have been placed in the footnotes and not included in the text. In a few cases where the author or editor of a work is not known, the title and date of publication have been substituted.

The bibliography (divided into primary and secondary sources) contains a full description in alphabetical order of all works cited in the notes. It does not, however, supply page numbers for articles or expand those abbreviations which have been listed separately. Nor should it be regarded as a comprehensive bibliography, which would be considerably longer. Where no place of publication is supplied it is London for books published in English and Paris for those published in French.

To avoid monotony, the appellation 'merchant' has been used as a synonym for 'businessman' throughout the text, except in contexts where the distinction between merchant, manufacturer and retailer is important. A definition of businessman is provided in the introduction.

The day of the month has been cited Old Style and 1 January has been taken as the first day of the year. Unless otherwise specified, the term 'seventeenth century' is employed in its literal sense.

Introduction: Questions and sources

> Why should not the knowledge, the skill, the expertise, the assiduity, and the spiritual hazards of trade & commerce, when crowned with success, be entitled to give those flattering distinctions by which mankind are so universally captivated. Such are the specious but false arguments for a proposition which always will find numerous advocates in a nation where men are every day starting up from obscurity to wealth.
>
> (James Boswell, *Life of Johnson*, i. 492, in response to a remark made to Johnson that the English merchant was a new species of gentlemen, a notion borrowed from Steele's *Conscious Lovers*.)

> Merchants carry on their trade in all directions gaining several hundred per cent, in spite of difficulties with customs stations and dangers from robbers, they still carry on. The scholar sits in his room and discourses of righteousness; he has no difficulties with customs stations, no danger from robbers, and his gain might be incalculable, yet he does not set about his work. So the scholar does not give as much thought to making progress as does the merchant.
>
> (Meh Tse, *The Great Value of the Right*, c. 470–390 B.C. trans. by Tompkinson, in *The Social Teachings of Meh Tse*, Trans. Asiatic Soc. Japan, 1927.)

Seventeenth-century England generated astonishing commercial energy. Such vitality in what was still a fundamentally agrarian economy was neither sudden nor unique.[1] It had been characteristic of the medieval cities of Italy, Spain, Germany and the Netherlands, had sustained the prodigious expansion of Europe across the globe in the sixteenth century and transformed the United Provinces into a world economic power. In comparison England was a late starter, whose maritime and commercial potential developed slowly and unevenly. Despite some important early innovations, English businessmen before 1600 were less advanced and sophisticated than their European counterparts, whose control they resisted but whose practices they imitated. By 1720, however, England had emerged as a formidable business nation with its own self-sustaining

[1] The exclusion of agriculture from consideration should not be interpreted as a denial of its importance: see Chalklin 1974: map F.

traditions, able to challenge its more populous neighbours and to compete aggressively in world markets.

Was this acquisition of a distinctive and dynamic economic identity fortuitous or induced? Was devotion to business a coincidence, a symptom, a cause or a result of economic growth? Did a favourable *conjoncture* of economic forces propel Englishmen towards business or did autonomous changes of attitude and purpose generate the ability to recognize and exploit economic opportunities? To answer these questions it is necessary to look at businessmen both as individuals and as an occupational group, to evaluate the role of business as a career, as a path to fortune and as a style of life. Its formal and informal standing in seventeenth-century society must first be defined and clarified and its opportunities, obstacles and cost of entry compared with alternative professions to determine why men chose it as a livelihood. The actual pattern of recruitment must then be ascertained as well as the relationship between business and government and the rate of success and failure.

To account for variations in performance the technical and personal qualities demanded by business have to be reconstructed from the primary records of actual management. In order to determine whether or not an independent *mentalité* and ideology emerged, whether businessmen adapted to or changed their society, it is necessary to consider their aspirations as well as their functions, their wants as well as their needs, to establish why they sought wealth and how they employed it. The quality of life of the business community must be gauged from its religious beliefs and ethical conduct, from its family structure, its pattern of consumption and leisure and its relationship to contemporary culture. Only then can the contribution of individual initiative and social values to economic growth be assessed with any confidence.

Descriptive analysis

The voluminous and diverse literature on the pre-industrial English economy has not, for the most part, addressed these questions. Economic theory has always been reluctant to recognize the human factor, even in dynamic models, because the idiosyncracies and irrationality of individuals have to be subjectively determined. Both classical and neo-classical economics have tended to focus on equilibrium because in a growth economy the fixed parameters become variables. Its objective methodology predicates a uniform, mechanistic and unchanging society, whose members produce, invest and consume according to consistent and utilitarian principles; it was developed to explain changes within the structure of economies rather than changes of that structure. Macro-economic historians, in their search for causal relationships between endogenous economic factors, have usually taken for granted the motivation and skills of the businessmen.[2] Short-term fluctuations and oscillations have been attributed to seasonal, accidental and non-recurrent factors; the secular trends in the economy have largely been explained in terms of comparative advantage in location, physical and technological resources, differential rates of capital formation and investment and the long-term cyclical movements of population, wages and prices.[3] With some notable exceptions, micro-economic historians have studied units of production and consumption rather than the social imperatives of change and the role of individuals.

The complex interaction of variables within an economy requires the explanatory power of economic theory, whose conceptual models cannot be inductively derived from empirical data. They are necessarily based on logical deduction from given postulates.[4] Historical reality is simplified for theoretical purposes by excluding non-rational and non-economic factors. Practitioners of this approach reject narrative description, indeterminate generalizations and intuitive models.[5] Theoretically ordered quantitative data are abstracted from the observable historical record and statistically manipulated and correlated to test the probability of hypotheses and causal linkages or, in limited cases, counterfactual propositions with no basis in reality.[6] Speculative theories can be stimulating even if proved wrong. But the real value of this approach is to make explicit the hidden value judgements which lurk behind descriptive analysis. Facts do not usually speak for themselves; their importance and relevance has to be determined by specific questions.[7]

The operational value of any theory is, however, determined by its assumptions. Economic theory has difficulty incorporating the factors of time and place which are the speciality of the historian.[8] Even when the functional relationships between known and unknown variables can be

[2] Casson 1982: tables 1:1 & 2:3; Kilby 1971: 3; Alford 1977: 122. For a critical view of attempts to 'personalize' economic movements see Day 1987: 163.

[3] Silva 1962: 986; Imbert 1959; Goldstone 1991b: 51ff.

[4] Herlihy 1981: 115.

[5] The New Economic History, for all its virtues, has relied as much on polemic as on mathematics: see Coats 1980; Redlich 1968: 106; Hyde 1962: 4; Himmelfarb 1987: 44; Field 1987: 29.

[6] Coutau-Bégarie 1989; Kousser 1984; Genovese in Veeser 1989: 217; Jann 1983: 147; MacClelland 1975. On the difference between nomic generalizations and probability statements see Hay 1980: 50.

[7] For disparate views see Elton 1977: 201; Postan 1971: 16; Skinner in Laslett *et al.* 1974: 156; Cochran in Gottschalk 1963: 108; Ferrarotti in Bertaux 1982: 26; Supple in Youngson 1972: 30.

[8] Even the *moyenne durée* in Braudel 1979 represents 50 to 100 years and there is no correspondence between the materialist, market and capitalist economies. It is ironic that François Simiand (Cedronio 1987: 99) should have been canonized, whereas Henry Sée has been cast into darkness: see Knight in *Architects and Craftsmen* 1956: 117; Lévy-Leboyer 1970: 77ff; Burke 1978: 156; Forster 1978: 69; Hexter 1979: 94–7; Hale 1980: 115.

determined by single and multiple linear regression, there are usually insufficient constant variables to support a general hypothesis.[9] Historical events are unique and the vocabulary of ideas changes over time.[10] Ex-post arguments, which read history backwards to explain a known result, can easily become self-fulfilling. The most successful applications of theory to economic history as an explanatory tool have involved single issues within a limited period of time.[11] Static systems can be described and explained without paying much attention to individuals or to the chronology of events. But accounting for change requires a different approach. It has proved extremely difficult to account for initial change or to develop credible dynamic models even as tools. Structural historians have not been notably successful in explaining the transition from one system to another or identifying the relationships between parallel systems.[12]

Ever since Marx accorded primacy to economic forces, social factors have been relegated to a dependent role. The concept of profit maximization, despite its limited application in real life, has a simplicity and directness which social and cultural explanations lack. It is easy to verify by self-analysis and from common observation the inducements of financial gain and the compulsion of economic need, whereas the threat of loss of status and pressure to conform are not so self-evident. Although the interdependence of social and economic variables has been widely recognized, it has proved easier to identify the economic reasons for social change than to demonstrate the less precise effect of social factors on economic development.[13] As in the protracted debates over the general crisis of the seventeenth-century economy, the search for an all-embracing long-term explanation of change has been characterized by crude standards of measurement, a neglect of chronology and a general impatience with inconvenient facts.

Social change has either been regarded as a historical necessity or equated with dysfunction.[14] The early sociologists in their zeal to create a science of society substituted determinist mechanisms for individual autonomy and strained and distorted the historical evidence to sustain the credibility of their dogmas.[15] The German Historical School developed from the ideas of the Enlightenment a nomothetic theory of stages of growth, each of which had a unique end and was an abstract paradigm of

[9] Valentine & Mennis 1980; Gould 1969: 200; Supple in Rabb & Rotberg 1982: 199.

[10] Janssens 1974: 36–7; Taylor in Parel 1979: 50–1.

[11] Fishlow 1974: 458.

[12] The two most recent examples are North 1973 and Wallerstein 1980. Their flaws are detailed in Ringrose 1973: 287; Skocpol 1977: 1078; Kellenbenz 1976: 685–92; O'Brien 1982; MacDonald 1979; Sella 1977: 29–32.

[13] Smelser & Lipset 1966; Davis in Harte 1971: 325–6.

[14] Kramnick 1972: 48; Merton 1964: 40.

[15] Hagen 1969.

variables. Organic, cultural and organizational factors were combined in an arbitrary blend of the real and the ideal.[16] Weber did take into account empirical facts, but he still employed them as a pretext for posing questions, not as a validation of a hypothesis; he was more concerned with typology than with history.[17] The prescriptive laws of social systems lack the predictive potential of the descriptive laws of Nature; the process of social evolution is neither uniform, unilinear or amenable to precise classification. Impersonal social forces are no more than the sum of individual actions and there is often little correlation between prescribed and actual behaviour.[18]

Structural theory has superimposed on the contradictions, discontinuities and ambivalence of social evolution a formal and orderly system of roles, often obscured by a baroque terminology.[19] It has tried to describe how a society functions at a particular moment rather than to explain its origins or its development over time.[20] The categories developed to build the model have frequently been vitiated by circular reasoning; social norms have been construed from the opinions and behaviour of those they are alleged to determine. Interest has focused on how conflicts are resolved and equilibrium is restored within a system, not on explaining changes of that system.[21] The once confident and often strident claims of the social sciences have proved fallible and induced disillusionment.

Shorn of its metaphysical properties, the idea of stages of evolution does nevertheless offer a useful framework for the empirical reconstruction of economic history.[22] Social values have had as great an impact on business as political and legal institutions. Individual businessmen had to operate within a social framework which determined their relative goals and constrained their actions. Measured by the short lifespan of any individual, the social system does function as an independent variable which embodies the collective authority of past generations.[23] Social

[16] Hoselitz 1961; H. G. Jones 1975.

[17] On Weber's intellectual ancestry see Collins 1986: 120; Besnard 1970: 109; Roth 1976: 316; Watkins in Feigl & Brodbeck 1953: 723; Ashcraft 1975: 131, 155; Langton 1982: 342, 356; Kolko 1961: 243; Roth & Schluchte 1979. On the rationale for ideal types see Wilson 1971: 115; Roth 1976: 306ff; Gurvitch 1957: 76.

[18] Rothbard 1979: 10, 15; Weinstein & Platt 1973: 45; Popper 1957: 114.

[19] Cochran in Gottschalk 1967: 104–5. Mathematical models such as Gould 1987: 113 simply add to the confusion.

[20] Lévi-Strauss 1963: 12. On the anti-historical bias of sociology see G. S. Jones 1976: 300; Burke 1980a: 78; Abrams 1982: 230–1, 332; 1972: 30; Wilson & Ashplant 1988: 261; Stone 1987: 31, 94; MacFarlane 1977: 650.

[21] Sociologists have attempted to dynamize Parsonian functional theory to account for historical change: see Barber 1957; Parsons 1961: 71–3; Lockridge in Delzell 1977: 61–2; Zagorin 1982: i. 50; H. L. Smith 1982: 30; Cohn 1980: 219.

[22] Gras 1971: chaps. 3–4, 168; Tuma 1971: 20; Herschlag 1969: 662; Reid 1989: 1.

[23] Kroeber & Kluckhorn 1952: 201; Radcliffe-Brown 1957: 53, 71–89.

institutions change very slowly, because the fundamental needs which they serve retain a consistency of purpose and because methods of social differentiation are similar in all periods and vary only in scale and complexity.

With rigorous discipline and with due allowance for the human coefficient, sociological explanations can be validated by inductive research.[24] Formal and informal social institutions, through reinforcing individual actions, can hinder, permit or actively favour economic development; status does define and dictate the roles which individuals perform.[25] The rate of social mobility, for example, is as important as the rate of population growth and is both a cause and a result of economic growth. Trade is culturally determined and the flow of commodities is directed by the value system. The complex interaction of social and economic forces has to be disentangled and the separate elements compared to establish levels of significance and distinguish cause from effect. It is important to isolate the distinctive features, to distinguish absolute from relative differences, to describe the biology as well as the morphology of English society.[26]

Micro-historians have eschewed general issues and concentrated on the sequential development of the economy. English historians have usually disavowed the relentless determinism of closed economic and social models and emphasized what was factually rather than logically prior.[27] Their analysis of economic development has been based on the meticulous assembly of disaggregated evidence and has judged performance rather than substantive properties. The course of change is not teleologically defined, but reconstructed piecemeal like a jigsaw; a general picture emerges by integrating particular facts rather than by applying universal principles.[28] This tradition of scholarship has inclined to generalize from the bottom up and accord more weight to endogenous factors such as property rights and political freedom. It can of course lead to mere cataloguing, and empirical business history has its detractors.[29] But it has the merit of documenting how problems were resolved, step by step, without being influenced by the eventual outcome. It accords priority to process rather than to structure and asks how and when change occurred before asking why it happened.[30]

[24] Malinowski 1960: 67; Znaniecki 1969: 34; Hoselitz 1963: 43–7; Burke 1986a: 446; Perkin in Finberg 1962: 77–9; Barnes 1948: 153; Laslett 1976: 331. Reification and the logic of explanation are perennial problems in the ontology of the social sciences. On new approaches see Razin 1987: 49–50; Chinot in Short 1981: 259ff; Lloyd 1986: 37; Levi in Burke 1992: 110. [25] Herskovits 1955: 160. [26] Hill 1980a; Pococke 1982.

[27] On the drawbacks of this approach see Lukes 1973; Burke 1980a: 530; Koot 1980: 175; Parker 1990. [28] Kuhn 1970: 16–17.

[29] Supple 1961–2: 82–3; Forman & Turner 1978; 1980; Coleman 1987a: 144; Hannah 1983; Wilson 1972: 458; Herlihy 1972: 761. [30] Dray 1957: 161.

Quantitative methods provide an index to measure change and are essential to correct or confirm inspired guesswork. A norm has to be established before the unique can be recognized.[31] An aggregate of particular examples, however thick the description, is no substitute for comprehensive and continuous statistics. But statistical data in the seventeenth century are inadequate, retrospective and tainted; the figures were usually recorded for specific administrative purposes by inefficient and self-interested officials and there are too many exceptions and omissions to warrant firm conclusions. Quantification is more useful for pathology than for diagnosis.[32] The process of simplification and standardization inherent in the manipulation of data can eliminate important variables or distort the significance of a single factor.[33] Conclusions can be unduly influenced by the initial data. Impressionistic history may be inconclusive, but spurious statistics which mask the limitations and subjective character of the sources with arcane technicalities can prove a worse evil.[34] Even reliable data can, moreover, only quantify quantities. The most important questions are usually qualitative and not susceptible to measurement.[35] The arithmetical mean is a statistical abstraction; the real world consists of individuals with separate identities.[36]

Raw quantitative data have been processed here to establish the economic and demographic structure and to document trends in the regional growth and distribution of business income and manpower. Where continuous series of hard figures do not exist, estimates have been made which are consistent with, though not formally demonstrated by, the available data; attention has been focused on relative proportions and orders of magnitude rather than on precise correlation. Although this method can easily deteriorate into porous generalization, it does yield valid assessments, if not hard conclusions.[37] The majority of merchants are recorded only as names in petitions, returns of municipal officers, aliens, exiles, officeholders and Non-Conformists, tax returns and the Port Books, admission registers of apprentices, freemen and schools, charters, poll books and lists of subscribers to joint-stocks or loans to the City Corporation or the Crown.[38] The vital statistics of the business

[31] Dovring 1960: 96; Evans-Pritchard 1961: 4.

[32] 'Studies in quantitative history' 1969: 72–4; Mayr 1976: 28.

[33] Tilly in Lorwin & Price 1972: 114. On the differences between quantitative and serial history see Furet 1971: 153.

[34] Fitch 1984.

[35] Fogel & Elton 1983: 21, 79, 81. Qualitative judgements do, however, depend on quantitative data: see Floud 1973: 3.

[36] Mayr 1982: 55; Wrigley & Schofield 1981: 157.

[37] Gardiner 1952: 95; Hollingsworth in Glass & Revelle 1972.

[38] Several lists of merchants and investors have been printed, but there is only one contemporary directory (1677) of London businessmen.

community have to be painfully reconstructed from genealogical sources, family pedigrees and the visitation and case records of the Heralds.[39]

Like the Great Barrier Reef, the cumulative minute remains of individual careers can, when multiplied over time, suggest the physiognomy and development of the business community. The historian, unlike the econometrician, has to be more of a detective than a mathematician, to rely on an imaginative sense of reality rather than on logic.[40] The patterns which he constructs by induction from a wide spectrum of empirical evidence acquire their final image like a pointilliste painting. Generalizations about the character of the business community must take into account the uniqueness of individuals, the diversity and contradictions of behavour and the authority conferred by contemporaries on what seem in retrospect to be ephemeral or outdated concepts; the image of the business world varied according to the different perceptions of its constituent members.[41] When proceeding by descriptive integration, the quality and reliability of the sources determines the level of probability rather than rigorous statistical evidence.[42]

It is easier to describe the structure of society and the economy than to explain its transformation.[43] The process of business can be confidently reconstructed from the archives, but the evidence for *conjoncture* is much more fragile.[44] The move from the particular to the general always increases the degree of uncertainty; the businessman becomes merely one of many interdependent variables. By emphasizing the antecedent causes of economic change, historians have often argued too narrow and monolithic a case. All pre-industrial societies were subject to similar forces, but they could produce very different results through comparatively small differences of emphasis, combination or omission. No attempt has been made here to construct a rigid explanatory model of development, but each factor has been weighed and compared to establish the leading coordinators.[45]

The businessman

Without a clear definition of business, all propertied families would qualify as participants. Men in non-commercial occupations traded both individually and through agents. Employees of the joint-stock Compa-

[39] Thrupp 1948: xviii; Judges 1938–9: 367; Hall 1951; BL Stowe MS 670, fo. 230. On the sources see Wagner 1960; Kent 1975; Watts 1983; Taylor & Crandale 1986: 47; Price 1992.

[40] Berlin 1961: 17–18; Hayek 1942: 267–91; 1943: 34–63; Hampshire 1983: 79; White 1987: 57.

[41] Hull 1979: 7; Elton 1991: 8; Burke in Bush 1991: 12

[42] Cochran 1964: 35.

[43] Coleman 1972a: 693.

[44] Heers 1969.

[45] Martin 1977: 51.

nies, officers, lawyers, soldiers and physicians dabbled on the side in business and in the private trade.[46] Landowners, gentlewomen, widows and clergymen were as active as merchants in lending money.[47] Some landowners were active, full-time managers, even though business was not their principal function. The late medieval nobility had been involved in war as a commercial enterprise and in the export wool trade.[48] Many of their descendants farmed part of their estates directly, attended local markets and were more than rentiers. The great and some of the lesser landowners participated directly in the extractive, timber and metallurgical industries, in drainage and transportation schemes and in urban development, as extensions of their landholdings.[49] Some were major promoters, particularly of colonial projects and others combined exploration with business.[50] Few, from the courtiers downwards, were completely divorced from the business world.

Tudor and Stuart gentlemen were active in victualling, turned clothiers, captained privateers and employed factors overseas.[51] Sir John Lowther described himself as 'a man of business' and the family combined their coal interests with the Irish and Caribbean trades.[52] Many landed and professional men were also passive investors in a wide range of colonial, industrial and privateering projects and, to a lesser extent, in the overseas commercial Companies and in the stock market.[53] Through Court privileges and patents of monopoly, many landowners acquired financial interests in a wide range of business concerns, mainly speculative, but also sound investments. Although merchants were the primary investors, the gentry invested in joint-stock privateering voyages during the wars against Philip II of Spain, and again in the West Country, during

[46] Dallaway, *Inquiry into Heraldry*, App., pp. xxv–xxxv; Richards 1965: 108.

[47] BL Egerton MS 3054; JRL Clarke MSS 880–920; 'Lancashire miscellany' 1965: 111 ff; Holderness in O'Day & Heal 1989, in R. M. Smith 1984: 436–9; 1970: 81–2, 1976: 178–9, 1975; Brodsky in Bonfield *et al.* 1986: 144; Rosen in Clark 1981; Hughes 1987: 32–3; Collinson 1982: 101.

[48] MacFarlane 1981: 40, 191–6, 148–55; *Paston Letters*, i. 173; Bridbury in Coleman & John 1976: 92–3; Prestwich 1977: 76, 284.

[49] Stone 1964a: chap. 7, app. 17, which revises his conclusions in 1957–8: 14–18; Stones 1984: fig. 7.2; Gough 1932; Donald 1961; Mingay 1963.

[50] Andrews 1984: 18; D. W. Davies 1967.

[51] C. S. L. Davies 1964–5: 240; Willan 1959: 189; Read 1925: iii. 370ff; Skilliter 1977; *Spanish Company*, pp. 14–15; Friis 1927: 245; J. R. Jones in Downs 1953: 193; Cooper 1983: 170–1; R. S. Smith 1961–2, 1967; W. O. Williams 1948: 111; E. D. Jones 1939–40: 84–5; MacHattie 1951: 52.

[52] Beckett 1981: 15.

[53] The social categories employed by Rabb 1967 are too crude and it cannot be assumed that the gentry contributed financially to the Companies in equal proportion to their numbers as investors. His argument in 1964: 61–9 and 1968 that the gentry were primarily interested in passive investment has also been rightly demolished by Ashton 1967: 54–5 and 1969; see also Croft 1975: 21; Hexter 1971: 119–25. On the later period see Bailyn 1964: 35–6 and K. G. Davies 1952a: 300.

the wars against Louis XIV.[54] The entrepreneurial role and gambling instincts of the landowning class did not die with the Civil War and the Company boom of the later seventeenth century turned the stock market into a gambling den. Richard Hill, the stockbroker, had difficulty persuading his investing clients that they would not make great gains in the South Sea Company.[55] Sir John Mere, after losing £33,000 in the Bubble, because of the Duke of Portland, retorted that 'when all trades fail and I want health, I may incline to lead a triflying country life, but until then I shall not indulge myself in that idle way'.[56]

But most of those, who inherited estates, concentrated on agricultural improvement and, like Mere's friend, Old Dickinson, preferred to see 'half a score fat bullocks in a field'. Courtiers and great men were not in any real sense in business and, as Cradocke said, landowners 'are seldome found to be merchants'.[57] Most gentry did not stray far from their estates and, if they invested surplus capital in business, their main income came from rents. They succumbed to patriotism and royal pressure and to the excitement of London affairs when they attended Parliament. But their non-agricultural investments rarely involved direct participation in everyday decisions and, even when families closely monitored the performance of their assets, their interest was more that of an active shareholder than a professional business manager.[58] Landowners often leased their mineral resources to ironmasters instead of exploiting them directly. Peers served as decorative Governors of the great export Companies, which welcomed landed investors, but did not encourage them to assume managerial functions.[59] Heirs to landed estates and professional men were concerned to increase their property and their political and social status. But they were not intimately connected with the mechanics of international and domestic commerce. They did not train as apprentices for a full-time career in business with profit as their main source of income.

The business community has, therefore, been equated with full-time active management by self-employed investors, distributors and producers, who had at least £500 of equity and £1,000 working capital, in all sectors of the economy except for agricultural production.[60] This definition excludes all farmers, some of whom were enterprising marketeers, artisans who never developed their crafts into independent firms, all

[54] Andrews 1964: 16, 62; 1959: 20–2, 32; Senior 1976; Meyer 1981.
[55] Shropshire RO 112/1775, John Ashe to Rich. Hill, 20 April 1720.
[56] Lincs. AO Whichcote MS 2/114/5, John Mere to Thos. Whichcote, 5 Oct. 1728. For another example see Parker 1971: 2, 13–18.
[57] Cradocke, *Expedient Taking Away Impositions*, p. 2; Clay in Thirsk 1978: v. 178–9.
[58] Coleman 1973: 96–8. [59] Chaudhuri 1965: 3.
[60] Minimum capital requirements are discussed in chap. 3. On Scottish and Irish businessmen see Devine in Gordon & Dicks 1983: 97; Smout 1963: 119–20; North in Minchinton 1988: 21; Cullen 1968: chap. 5 and in Butel & Cullen 1986.

salaried employees, even of business institutions, passive investors, occasional participants and amateur speculators.[61] In every craft, a few entrepreneurs rose to become businessmen and the range of occupations was very elastic.[62] A joiner, woodmonger or carpenter in the building trades could sub-contract, leverage his credit and anticipate the market.[63] Many businessmen were of course pedestrian and not innovative, but they can be identified by scale of operations, organization, style of management and commitment of time and energy.

There was a well-established distinction between *negotiator* and *mercator*.[64] Sir Jonathan Atkin, in 1676, distinguished the Dutch word *copeman*, which included all who bought and sold, from *merchant*, 'such as trade & barter commodities'.[65] Molloy, while allowing for some overlap, distinguished between merchants and artificers; he included bankers and exchange dealers among the merchants, but excluded usurers and speculators who bought to resell when prices rose.[66] Defoe distinguished between an 'upper' and 'lower' class.[67] Although a distinction was always made between foreign and internal trade, the word merchant was applied to wholesaling in both.[68] It was usually synonymous with businessman and, by the end of the century, 'man of bisiness or buissness' had acquired its modern economic connotation as distinct from referring to official and personal matters.[69]

Business records

The business history of England has been written primarily from the records of the commercial and industrial Companies and the evidence of

[61] This is a narrower definition than that of Earle 1989a: 4–5, who includes all the small masters as well as some professionals. It also excludes those identified as independent producers by Small 1992a: 793; Lowe 1972: 29–30. The classic definition of differences between businessmen and artisans remains Unwin 1925: 189–91, 228, and 1958: 195–6. The distinction drawn here is between those who had at least a nucleus of working capital and those (both wage-earners and self-employed craftsmen) who were entirely dependent on external finance.

[62] Power in Beier & Finlay 1986: 213 has distinguished 216 occupations in 1666 and Alexander 1989: 53 records 721 in the 1690s. The trades which Sacks 1985: 493 and 1992: 114 identifies as entrepreneurial were entered by 21 per cent of all apprentices.

[63] North, *Lives*, iii. 55; Johnson 1953; Quiney 1979: 277; Colvin 1972: 3; 1954: 3; Woodward 1981; Power 1978; Brett-James 1935: chaps. 12, 15; Louw 1989a.

[64] Rougé 1966: 29; Beneviste 1951: 25.

[65] *Cal. S.P. Col. Ser. West Indies 1675–6*, no. 973.

[66] Molloy, *De Jure Maritimo*, ii. 436. The bankruptcy laws required a precise definition of 'trading': see Billinghurst, *Judges' Resolutions*, pp. 186–7.

[67] Defoe, *Compleat English Tradesman*, ii. pp. vi, 41, 75.

[68] Stow, *Survey*, ed. Strype, ii. 207.

[69] Hunt. Lib. MS 352410; Collinson 1988a: 191. 'Busyness' was a quality originally associated with lawyers: see Tucker 1984: 51. Allestree, *Gentleman's Calling*, had a section titled 'Of Business and Callings'.

government and municipal regulation and protection. But most branches of trade were in the hands of independent partnerships. In order to analyse the success and failure of private enterprise, to see how businessmen organized their affairs day by day, it is essential to have their books of original entry or what Tawney described as 'dull business documents'.[70] The core items are ledgers, journals and correspondence, supplemented by waste books, used for immediate jottings to be entered later, petty cash accounts, sale and order books, abstracts for ready reference and memoranda.[71] To remind them of terms of sale and maturity dates of bills, merchants sometimes used small, portable pocket books carried in leather wallets and made of vellum or card sometimes coated on both sides for reuse.[72] Additional documentation, depending on the type of business, included minutes, charter-parties, indentures, stock inventories, bills of sale, receipts, evidences of property, loans and obligations, contracts and agreements, legal case and tax records, wage sheets and lists of debtors and customers.[73]

Before 1600, few private business papers sources survive and even those of later periods have not always been accessible.[74] Most family businesses did not leave a continous archival record because they survived as a functioning unit for only one or two generations. There are few English archives on the scale of the medieval Datini collection of 125,549 letters and 600,000 pages at Prato, or of the great firms of South Germany, Spain, Portugal, Venice and the northern and southern Netherlands.[75] But the records of small partnerships compare favourably in their variety and abundance with the Archief Brants of Amsterdam, the Insolvente Boldelkamen of Antwerp and the notarial records of Italy and France, Rotterdam and The Hague.[76] The original papers of over 300 businessmen survive before 1720 and new collections constantly come to light. Some papers of English merchants resident abroad have also been

[70] Tawney 1958: 38; Price 1973: xiv.

[71] Entries were usually cross-referenced by number and struck after posting and the waste books were then destroyed. A ledger can be reconstructed from a complete set of journals and vice versa; the two are sometimes confused in the secondary literature.

[72] Edmond 1987b: 108.

[73] Lee 1980; Goldthwaite in Kirshner 1974: 9; *Bristol Merchants and Merchandise*, p. xxii. Retailers sometimes combined a record of transactions with a stock inventory: see Prior 1981: 76. The journals of ship-masters sometimes record commercial transactions: see KAO U.1515/01.

[74] Sutherland 1935: 71.

[75] Lopez & Irving 1955; Melis 1972; MacKenney 1990; Brulez 1959.

[76] Hardenberg 1970: 17–18; Monicat 1955; Daumaard 1955: 227; 1962; Vogler 1979; Kellenbenz 1973: 19–51, 131–49. Private business papers survive in much the same form and for much the same reasons in all European countries. In France, for example, the collections in Paris and in the Archives Dėpartementales of Rhône, Ille-et-Vilaine, Bouches du Rhône, Lot-et-Garonne, Morbihan and Gironde are similar to those in London and English provincial archives.

preserved in the archives of foreign countries and former colonial dependencies.[77]

Landed families sometimes accumulated commercial and industrial papers as a by-product of estate management, but their business archives were usually acquired through a commercial ancestor who had purchased an estate, through intermarriage with business families or through their younger children. The private papers of office holders often document the activities of businessmen; the Salisbury archives, for example, contain the letters of Baptist Hicks.[78] Isolated groups, like naturalized aliens and religious minorities, both gravitated towards business and tended to preserve their records. Some private business papers were also deposited with corporate institutions. They are more common in a regulated Company, like the Levant Company, but the East Indian and African Companies also have examples among their voluminous factory and marine records and correspondence.[79] The actual practice of business is sometimes described in the archives of guilds whose members actively pursued their nominal trade.[80] A handful of private business papers from the 1690s onwards, also survive in the hands of modern banks and firms

[77] John Browne's letter book is in the Revaler Staat Archives and that of E. Poley in the Swedish Royal Library. The town of Stade has the papers of John Morland and Hamburg has material relating to Jeremiah Borland and William Craddock. The Institute of Jamaica has the papers of William Freeman and the De Sausmare MSS are in Guernsey: see Bromley in Jamieson 1986: 144. The notarial records in the Archives de la Gironde have documents relating to the trade of wine merchants and there is material relating to the Papillons in Arch. Nat. V7 27–32/400. The ledger of Robert Gibbs is among the Massachusetts MSS, the accounts of John Winthrop among the Trelawney papers and the account book of George Cornin in the Essex Institute at Salem. The same situation holds true for Spain and Asia: see Kesward in Mollat 1970.

[78] Hicks-Beach 1909: 64; C30/26/52. The names of retailers can also be culled from the accounts of landed families: see Marley 1979: table 1.

[79] The IOL, for example, has numerous private letters as well as a huge collection of ship journals, whose deposit was usually required by charter-parties. See Sutton 1967; Lancaster 1966; Chaudhuri in Cottrell & Aldcroft 1981. The ledgers of the Company before 1664 are, however, missing and the records of sales and re-exports were destroyed in the nineteenth century. On the other hand many Company documents survive among private papers; examples include BL Stowe MS 759; Bod. Rawl. MS C.745–7; C113/34–7. The Merchant Venturers of Bristol has a merchant's account book later used to list charitable gifts: see Ralph 1988: 12, 73.

[80] Normally London guild records relate only to the administration of the corporate property and buildings, market supervision, records of bindings and admissions to the commonalty and livery, quarteridge accounts, elections of officers, minutes of Court, Wardens' accounts, charitable trust administration, legal cases, loans, subscriptions, fines and taxes, and lists of names and addresses. See Cooper 1984. Sometimes, as in the Pewterers, Drapers and Mercers Companies, the archives include wills and inventories, real-estate transactions and the occasional private ledger. The Stationers Company has the business accounts of its corporate stock, as described in Myers & Harris 1985: app. D. Some provincial guilds also have some trading records: see Talbot 1986: 94; Youings 1967; D. M. Smith 1990: 17.

which evolved from family businesses founded in the seventeenth century.[81]

Many of these collections are neither comprehensive over time nor uniform in subject matter. Frequently an essential section of papers is missing or the period covered is too short or discontinuous.[82] Fragmentary account books and isolated venture accounts, bills, invoices, order books and scraps of journals which cannot be related to a ledger, are of limited value.[83] Frequently, it is mainly legal documents which have been preserved – deeds, bonds, acquittances, settlements and depositions. Sometimes only the correspondence survives or the accounts relate simply to public, household and family matters.[84] Even ledgers often contain insufficient data; probate inventories on their own are of limited use. Since incoming correspondence survives more frequently than copies of outgoing letters, more information is often forthcoming about the client than the recipient.[85] Nor can the contents of letters be taken at face value. Goods were disguised to evade prohibitions and taxes, and factors and merchants did not shrink from distorting or evading uncomfortable facts; they entertained half-baked and erroneous opinions, exaggerated their importance and success and used their letters for self-advertisement. Many letters were written hastily and reflect temporary misery or boredom.[86]

Some business papers have been preserved by accident; occasionally the blank pages of ledgers were used for other purposes, including end

[81] In addition to the Bank of England Record Office, Williams & Glynn's has the banking records of Backwell and Child, Coutts Strange the papers of John Campbell and Lloyds some of Thomas Bowrey's papers. See also Cockerell & Green 1976; Pressnell & Orbell 1985: 32. The records of the Staplers survived only because the Company became a dining club: see *Staple Ordinance Book*, p. 2.

[82] Examples include BL Egerton MS 2524, Add. MS 11411; Som. RO, Trollope-Bellew MSS; Berks. RO D/EBUF13; the letters of John Whalley and John Nelmer in the Gloucs. RO.

[83] Typical examples are Bod. Eng. Hist. MS C.63; St John's College, Oxford, MS 254.

[84] Some characteristic examples are Bod. Eng Hist. MS D.156–63; BL Cott. Vesp. F. MS; BL Add. MS 30494; GLL MS 3415.

[85] Duplicate letters occur frequently, because copies were usually sent by different routes in case one was lost. Sometimes mail was deliberately destroyed if the ship used for carriage was on the verge of capture by the enemy. Although personal seals provided some protection against forgery, handwriting was the best proof of authenticity and incoming letters are usually autograph and endorsed with the date and place of receipt and reply. Once a bundle accumulated, they were frequently but not invariably bound in convenient sizes. Outgoing letters were copied into a book, but could subsequently be removed. Occasionally samples of goods were enclosed. The durable paper used for correspondence has in most cases survived both long sea voyages and the passage of time without any deterioration, although some inks have tended to fade.

[86] Deliberate falsification of private accounts, as distinct from unintended errors, seems to have been rare, compared with later periods; see Brief 1991: 17–21; Parker 1991: 1–18; Hanham 1972; Temple 1922: 124–5; Mason 1982.

papers to a book.[87] The majority, however, are not random survivals but inherently biased towards either success or failure and this increases the likelihood of systematic error.[88] Certain areas of business, such as banking, foreign trade and finance, building and publishing are disproportionately represented, because their firms or products had greater continuity. The number of papers also remains small – at best about 1 per cent of substantial businesses – and they are less numerous for the first half of the century.[89]

Nevertheless, it is also true that both the most and the least successful businessmen are represented, that the bankruptcies which forced the deposit of records in the Courts usually occurred in the second or third generation of a business. There is a reasonable probability that a sufficient proportion of material from different sectors has survived to disentangle the truth and to piece together a coherent and authentic account of what actually happened. The extant collections, which frequently include papers deposited by clients, illustrate the affairs of many correspondents who did not leave records of their own and they cover most branches of trade, if only for arbitrary periods. In several cases, it is possible to trace the same venture through the books of several merchants, to see how a deal developed from the viewpoint of all the parties involved. A functional analysis of business operations depicted from the inside, step by step, is much less prone to error than inferences from results and inspires greater confidence than broad conclusions based on external statistical data. The immediate problem for the business historian is the sheer volume and technical nature of the material.[90]

The history of private business can also in part be written from the political and administrative records of the central and local government. Merchants came into contact with the royal administration and Parliament as intermediary agents, taxpayers and as advisors. Businessmen who dealt with the government as contractors, patentees, farmers or

[87] Booksellers' accounts survive in strange forms: see 'Account book of a Marian bookseller, 1553–4' and 'Bookseller's account book, 1545'; 'Cambridge bookseller's accounts'; Morgan 1940: pl. 2; Morgan in Hunt *et al.* 1975: 71; BL Egerton MS 2974, fos. 67–8 and King 1987: 48. The high rate of survival and recovery is explained by the durability of books as commodities and by the zest of bibliophiles.

[88] Floud 1973: 171. The business papers of builders are sometimes preserved among the estate records of institutions or landed families; one example is the day book of Edward Strong who worked on Greenwich Hospital.

[89] A sample spread over a long period and all sectors of the economy is probably more accurate than a sample tied to one source, group or locality.

[90] Although the majority of private business collections are individually manageable in size, a few are extremely bulky and the aggregate number is formidable; thousands of wills and inventories also survive: see Stitt 1973; Moore in Riden 1985: 16. The problem compounds rapidly from the mid eighteenth century: see Blouin 1979; Wilson 1967: 11–12.

monopolists, often left no business papers of their own. But the details of their careers can be traced through the records of the revenue departments, the Army and the Navy, particularly when the Crown had to raise and transfer money for major wars. Diplomatic archives and reports of foreign legations frequently contain commercial correspondence and memoranda and the records of colonial government are of particular importance.[91] Among the State Papers are a few purely private business papers.[92] When Parliament enquired into Company monopolies and economic crises and when the Crown and its regulatory agencies tried to negotiate treaties, frame policy and intervene in the economy, albeit for fiscal reasons, the debates and reports which were generated contain much information about individual merchants.[93] The implementation of policy at every level left a long paper trail of petitions, informations, depositions and transactions.

Usually, official sources, like the fiscal records of the Customs and Excise, only indirectly illustrate the actual process of business.[94] The hope expressed over fifty years ago that the 'countless names which the Port Books record may cease to be merely names' remains unfulfilled and firms usually made entries in the name of only one partner.[95] But they do shed light on the minimum level of commercial investment and turnover, on the relative importance of different commodities and areas of trade and on the numbers, names and marks of merchant investors. The records of direct taxation – the subsidy, the confiscatory measures of the Early Stuarts and the Interregnum, the hearth and poll taxes – do not indicate how fortunes were made, but they do suggest the relative levels and regional distribution of wealth. The vast majority of ordinary merchants, however, particularly those in the domestic and coastal trades, only feature in local and municipal records. These include the great series of shipping records for provincial ports, the registration of licences and oaths, poll books, freedom registers, the administration of tolls, fairs and markets and occasionally some private papers.[96]

[91] One example is Robert Coles: see Higham 1921. Of particular interest are CO1, series 323–5 and 388–91.

[92] The State Papers also contain business papers of foreign merchants as in SP 9/96, 106.

[93] The House of Lords RO has the correspondence of Robert Gray and the journal of Daniel Bonnell.

[94] Carson 1977a: 74–80; 1977b: 429–30; 1971a: 31.

[95] Willan 1967: 54, 192; Woodward 1970b: 210; Andrews 1956–7: 119; Aström 1968; Grimaud 1983: 373; *Boston Port Books*, intro.; Jarvis 1954: xvi–xvii; Stephens 1969b: 206–13; Williams 1955: 17–18; 1988: chap. 1; Stephens 1968: 34.

[96] The private accounts of a framework knitter are among the City's estate records in the CLRO, which also has clutches of ledgers and correspondence, particularly of alien merchants. The Town Clerk of Chester kept drafts of bills and bonds; the accounts of a lead dealer are at the back of a Chesterfield constable's book in the Derbyshire RO and the blank pages of a cloth merchant's accounts were used to record the borough accounts of Ipswich.

Of even greater value are legal records. All the central Civil and Common Law Courts, including the Prerogative Courts before 1640, handled commercial cases; proceedings in criminal cases often concern merchants either as defendants or as victims of theft and fraud.[97] The Court of Admiralty, whose records include pleadings, sentences, depositions, replies and cross-examinations, charter-parties and Mediterranean passes, dealt not only with Prize cases and naval matters but also with all aspects of the shipping industry.[98] Because there was no special court for bankruptcy, the records of bankruptcy proceedings are dispersed. Most cases were handled by commissioners and the judgements recorded on the Patent Rolls, but others were referred to King's Bench, Exchequer, Common Pleas and to Chancery which also handled many debt and partnership cases.[99] The greatest single collection of business papers occur among the Chancery Masters Exhibits only a few of which have been systematically utilized.[100]

Local and municipal courts also have much material. The Commissary Court of Cambridge dealt with Stourbridge Fair, the Mayor's Court of London has papers relating to the European trades and the Mayor's Court of Plymouth has inventories of goods seized or contested.[101]

[97] Many business documents and inventories survive in the Exchequer K. R. Accounts. Various (E101) and the Memorandum Rolls (E159) have cases of Customs fraud; the Special Commissions and Returns into the Exchequer (E178) regarding outlawry, treason, aliens, etc. record many inquisitions into the goods of merchants under the Early Stuarts; E140 and E134 also contain much material on businessmen. Businesses can be reconstructed from Exchequer cases; see Zell 1981: 130; Outhwaite 1966a; Bryson 1975: chap. 4; Aylmer in Fisher 1961: 173. The Court of Requests (REQ 2) also has many papers relating to debts, partnerships, piracy, leases, apprentices, stock in trade, disputes between executors and beneficiaries over business profits, currency and exchange and intestate estates. The Star Chamber, though it dealt with foreign merchants and creditors of the Crown, has fewer business cases; only 6 per cent of plaintiffs were merchants, 1603–25, according to Barnes in Baker 1978: 10.

[98] The Admiralty (HCA) has the records of Oyer & Terminer, Acts, Examinations, Exemplifications, Early Instances, Interrogatories, Libel Series, Letters of Marque and Prize papers; some papers dealing with shipping, goods and contraband have been classified among SP (Supp) 46. See Jarvis 1957–8; Davis 1966; 1967: 16; Mathias & Pearsall 1971; Ruddock 1949; Murray 1937–9; Berckman 1979. The Charter Parties in HCA series 22–4 provide many more business details than the Port Books. An example of a clutch of business papers is HCA 2/560 and 15/17.

[99] The most valuable series are C2, C217 (Petty Bag Office), C52 (certificates of recognizances of Statute Staple) and C67 (Supplement). A few cases were printed, like *The Case of John Goudet* (1698). Some 12,000 cases from 749 Rolls have been indexed by subject: see Beresford 1979: 8–10; Marriner 1980: 357–8; 1978: 4ff. On the legal distinction between bankruptcy and insolvency see Duffy 1980: 283–305; Levinthal 1919; Hoppitt 1987: chap. 2. The bankruptcy dockets (PROB 4) do not begin until 1710. On Chancery see W. J. Jones 1967. In Common Pleas and King's Bench, 80 per cent of the cases concerned debt: see Brook in Baker 1978: 50.

[100] C103–C114. The collections contain much more material than the invaluable indexes would suggest.

[101] Extracts from legal disputes over business matters also occur in private deposits like GLL MS 6372.

Practically every court, even that of the Chancellor at Oxford, heard cases of debt.[102] The Orphans Courts filed inventories and executors' papers, and sometimes the records of charitable trusts founded by merchants contain the original papers of their founders.[103] Relevant material is buried in the records of Quarter Sessions and the petitions from petty debtors under 23 Chas II, c. 20 and 30 Chas II, c. 4., which include the comments of creditors.

Because the Church had jurisdiction over marriage and probate, its archives contain the majority of wills and inventories left by merchants as well as the vital records of births, marriages and deaths.[104] Courts, like the Court of the Arches and the Prerogative Court of Canterbury, heard many testamentary cases of merchants, including suits concerning legacies, insufficient funds in the estate, allegations of tampering, of pressure on testators, insanity or neglect by executors; the plaintiffs' complaints are recorded along with the defendants' answers, the plaintiffs' replies and the decrees.[105] Of interest too are the depositions and proceedings in cases of defamation, adultery, educational provision and prosecutions of Non-Conformists. In a few cases, business papers occur as strays.[106]

Most legal documents involving merchants, however, record the conveyance of property and describe the structure rather than the process of business. Charters, bye-laws, ordinances and customs merely define the rules. The great majority of lawsuits concern payment of debts or broken contracts and relate only to particular disputes. Although the bills of complaint and the defendants' answers shed light on commercial practices, many allegations are boilerplate and court proceedings tend to describe the exceptional rather than the ordinary, when relationships broke down between businessmen.[107] Normally this evidence is inconclusive and the volume and complexity of contested suits is formidable; the printed Reports and Abridgements usually relate only to particular

102 By the seventeenth century, the legal device of registering a debt by a complaint became less common, though the amounts claimed were sometimes exaggerated: see Muldrew 1993: 26.

103 A typical example is GLL MS 3181–4. Legal action by other beneficiaries often ensured that documents would be preserved by executors and trustees: see Stevenson & Salter 1939: 402–8.

104 For the character, distribution and value of probate evidence see pp. 244–6; MacFarlane 1983; Gibbons 1980; Gittings 1991: 51–9; Grace 1989: 18–25; Georges 1988; Carus-Wilson 1954: 77ff; Willan 1953.

105 Slater 1953: 145–6; Marchant 1969. The Consistory Court records are now in the GLRO.

106 The Chapter Library of Bristol has a merchant's journal, 1558–90, Westminster Abbey has the papers of Sir Andrew King, the Court of the Arches has a notebook of 1690 and the parish church of Nantwich has the accounts of the Tench family.

107 Dumbauld 1973: 21.

points of law.[108] The original records are difficult to use selectively because of inadequate indexing; they are usually classified simply by clerk and by the name of parties. The chief value of cases (as distinct from administrative records) lies not in the formal bills and answers, but in the documents deposited as evidence and in the interrogatories of witnesses examined by commissioners.[109]

Literary sources

The literary evidence is extensive, but both its content and context has to be critically assessed.[110] Antiquarian studies, histories of trades, surveys of towns and itineraries of both native and foreign travellers in England all offer vivid impressions of the business community. Geographical works and the travel literature describe the lives of merchants resident in foreign countries.[111] Professional and Puritan diarists, gossip writers, astrologers and doctors, all recorded biographical snippets about merchants. Handbooks on business are a mine of information about the routines of business; they were usually written by professionals and often annotated by their owners.[112] The early newsletters, sheets, diurnals, mercuries and periodicals reported on movements of trade and shipping, commodities and stocks, fraudulent bankruptcies, the latest City news and gossip.[113] Tracts and broadsides written to plead a case sometimes provide details about techniques of manufacture and individuals.[114] Funeral orations of eminent merchants contain much biographical detail.

But most printed literature was subject to censorship and written for sale or for didactic and polemical purposes; it is frequently ill-informed and biased. Denunciatory sermons and precursors of the fictional novel, like Bunyan's *Life and Death of Mr Badman*, describe everyday problems and methods of exploitation. But they were written to set standards of moral behaviour and to promote religious devotion.[115] The Elizabethan and Jacobean dramatists and ballad writers based their characters on real

[108] Holdsworth 1925; Baker 1986. [109] A typical example is Applebee 1979: 50.

[110] Thompson 1972: 49. For a defence of fiction as evidence see Stevenson 1984: 3; Sharpe & Zwicker 1987: 17.

[111] A distinction should be made between travelogues which describe a foreign environment and those which describe the life of English merchants abroad, such as Ovington, *Voyage to Surat*.

[112] One example is the text of Thomas Milles in Bod. MS 913. On the output of manuals see Cole 1957.

[113] Weed & Bond 1940; Clark 1978: 167; MacCusker 1983: 29, 58; 1986; MacCusker & Gravesteijn 1991. [114] *Clothiers Complaint against Blackwell Hall Factors*.

[115] Richard Neave was targeted in Verax, *Knavish Merchant* and the *Complaynt of Roderick Mors* was directed at Henry Brinklow: see Ramsay 1979: 23.

(and usually notorious) members of the crafts and business world of London, but they had little interest in objectivity or accuracy.[116] Prose writers in the seventeenth century satirized and caricatured the merchant or tried to stylize his attributes in a 'Character'.[117] Journalists, like Daniel Defoe, frequently refer to actual merchants but it is often difficult to separate fact from fiction.[118]

For the business historian who is willing to strap on his boots there is also much physical evidence. The monuments and memorials in churches and churchyards, in England and overseas, provide useful genealogical details, if they are used with caution.[119] One Worcester clothier who acted as agent for the Levant Company, was buried in the cathedral, in 1626. The houses of merchants and the public buildings erected by guilds and cities are concrete examples of mercantile aspirations and taste.[120] Although Stuart England had no Holbein and no equivalent to the interior painters of the Dutch Golden Age, topographical and marine paintings, prints, cartoons and woodcuts illustrate the settings and process of business. The character and visual appearance of several eminent businessmen have been captured in portraits and engravings.[121] The furniture, plate, decorative objects, jewels, marks, trade cards and tokens, instruments and tools which survive from mercantile households evoke their style of life and interiors; a few libraries also survive intact.[122]

[116] Deloney's *Pleasant History of John of Winchcombe* is an early example of fictionalized business biography. Despite its outdated thesis, Wright 1958 remains a useful guide to the sources. See also Mish 1952; Gaunt 1978; Davis 1969. For relevant ballads see *Pepys Ballads*: ii. 87–9; *London Prentice Songs*; *Broadside Ballads Restoration*; Hodgart 1950.

[117] On the gradual substitution of argument for precept see Boyce 1947: 288; 1952: 84–5; Murphy 1925; Greenough 1947.

[118] *Mystery of New-fashioned Goldsmiths*. Defoe drops numerous names, but he covered his tracks well; on his *modus operandi* see Rogers 1975; Starr 1965: 31.

[119] The study of monuments has a continuous tradition: see Weever, *Ancient Funeral Monuments*, and the Bradfer-Lawrence MSS in the Norfolk RO. The English Monumental Inscription Society has preserved this evidence in considerable bulk; see Gross 1897: xxxi. The inscriptions in London churches destroyed during the 1940s have largely survived in copies, like those of A. J. Jewers and J. Brewer in GLL MSS 6784, 2879, 3119. The same process occurred after the Great Fire: see Fisher, *Catalogue Tombs London*. Inscriptions in English cemeteries abroad have also been transcribed and published. On the unreliability of inscriptions see *John Isham*, p. cx; Husbands 1980.

[120] On the value of physical evidence see Platt 1973 and 1976.

[121] Portraits and engravings of businessmen survive in the hands of towns, guilds, Companies, colleges and charitable trusts as well as in the families of their descendants, but there is no comprehensive catalogue or a 'merchant hall of fame' as suggested by Rees 1939: 121. Among the few lists are *Bank of England Catalogue*; Nicholl 1851: 474; Fry 1907; *Lond. & Midd. A.S. Report* (1860). On the problems of interpretation see Burton 1989: 216.

[122] Very few merchants' marks have been reproduced for the seventeenth century, though there is a collection formed by J. J Howard in GLL MSS 1106, 7836. Some mark books of craftsmen survive among the archives of the Livery Companies. There are comprehensive catalogues of marks on tradesmen's tokens: see also Manship, *History of Yarmouth*, ii. 98ff.

In a few cases, samples of the actual commodities which they handled or made have been preserved.[123]

In order to put flesh on the bones of merchants, it is necessary, however, to have their private letters and diaries.[124] It is not easy to analyse the character or emotions of merchants.[125] In their published tracts, merchants seldom provide autobiographical details; their motives have too often been postulated without any hard evidence.[126] A small percentage of the business correspondence of merchants does, however, deal with personal matters, and their family correspondence, which often survives because their children married into landed families, relates more directly to courtship, marriage and social life. Often a merchant's will would be prefaced by last reflections before death, by a review of his life and an assessment of his prospects of salvation in the world to come.[127] Deceased merchants were also commemorated by their descendants. William Lawrence wrote a Memorie of his brother Isaac, a Levantine merchant, interspersed with commercial correspondence.[128] Thomas Isham wrote an affectionate life of his father, John, detailing his friendships, illnesses and corpulence.[129]

The majority of surviving diaries are unfortunately emblematic and dominated by concern for spiritual improvement and they often lack individuality.[130] Devout merchants and tradesmen recorded and examined their inner lives and behaviour, but their purpose in writing was to voice their resignation to God's will and to set a moral example.[131] They wanted to regulate their lives according to the Word, to sublimate their painful experiences, give thanks for their good fortune and educate and inspire their families and friends. There was nonetheless an exponential growth of more intimate records during the seventeenth century.[132] The

[123] Phillips 1935; Buisseret 1986; Anderson 1952.

[124] Bailyn 1982: 22; Zeldin 1982: 341; 1976: 243; Febvre 1973: 13.

[125] The prolific but largely unhelpful literature on psychohistory is listed in Lawton 1988: chap. 3; Gilmore 1984: 6–86; Weinstein & Platt 1975: 203–16; Stone in Rabb & Rotberg 1982; Runyan 1982: 208–9; Hayes 1950: 312–17; Harré 1986: 4–9; Stearns 1985: 835.

[126] Psychological explanations of growth, as popularized by MacClelland 1961: 132, 145, are now largely ignored for reasons offered by Flinn in Burns & Saul 1967: 20–6; Davis 1965: 132; Schatz 1965; Waterman 1984: 155; Manuel 1971: 208. For a defence see Sprinzak 1975: 318; Freeman 1976: 824; Tully 1988: 107; Cochran 1947: 82.

[127] A will does not necessarily reflect a testator's thoughts because many were written by spiritual advisors or third parties or conformed to clerical and legal conventions such as those offered in Swinburne, *Brief Treatise Testaments*. See Capp 1975: 49; Richardson 1972a; Coppel 1988.

[128] Lawrence, *Diary*, pp. ix, xiii, 46ff.

[129] *John Isham*, app. 2.

[130] Bunyan, *Grace Abounding*, intro.; for other views see Wright 1932: 159; Watkins 1971: 34–7; Caldwell 1983: 85.

[131] Many may have been lost when the reading public tired of didactic works: see Barrett 1968: 242; Spufford 1979: 408; Hunter 1966: 83; Atkinson 1885: i. 19.

[132] Many diaries of merchants are omitted from Matthews 1950 and 1955.

keeping of memoranda books and secular diaries by apprentices, shopkeepers and merchants became more common as an aid to memory, a leisure activity and a means of self-expression.[133] In the commonplace books, which vary greatly in subject matter, health was a major preoccupation and medicinal precepts alternate with arithmetical tables. William Thomas, for example, jumbled together births, deaths, illnesses, genealogical memoranda, receipts and horoscopes; account books were used for adding family details or even writing poetry.[134]

The diary, which monitored daily performance and expenses and retailed gossip, was a natural extension of the business journal and was sometimes interleaved in almanacks. Many journals contain little more than monotonous accounts of visits, mundane daily routines and the weather. Others chronicle local political, military and social events. Employees of the East India Company kept diaries to defend their reputation when they returned to England or as a basis for travelogues.[135] The daily logs of ship-masters served primarily as records of navigation, though they sometimes include drawings and comments on business transactions.[136]

A few merchants turned their journals into formal memoirs; Benedict Webb, clothier, wrote 'an oration of my Imployments sithence I came to discresyon' and family histories are often disguised autobiographies.[137] All depend on selective memory and some were largely fiction.[138] The motives for writing a life history ranged from religious zeal to a desire for immortality.[139] Some simply wrote to defend their actions.[140] One reader of the autobiography of Charles Doe wrote in the margin of the copy 'mistake not my shop' and claimed that Doe was 'seeking to get a Name above his degree, like the Protestant footman that wrote against the

133 MacFarlane 1970: 5–8.

134 An innkeeper's interpolations are in HLL Almanack 1652–8 (429497).

135 Although mainly preserved in the IOL, they are found in all repositories: see Fitzhugh 1981: 45–6. Many travel diaries included business papers which are sometimes omitted from printed editions: see Sanderson, *Travels*.

136 William Smythe's journal, written on black paper in white chalk, and kept in a japanned painted wooden case is in Bod. Ashmole MS 1809. On pursers' journals see LeGuin 1967.

137 Rawdon, *Life*; Killick suggests in his edition of Sir Marmaduke Rawdon, *Memoirs*, 315ff, that the memoirs of the family were compiled by the nephew.

138 Dunton, *Life and Errors*; Parks 1976. The fictionalized autobiography is a particularly dangerous source, despite the argument of Redlich 1966 that such works convey a correct image, even when they are not objectively true.

139 On the gradual substitution of inductive for deductive thought patterns see Osborn 1960; Shumaker 1954: chap. 1; Morris 1966: 9, 39, 44; Bottral 1958: 8; Ebner 1971: 20; Weinstein 1981: 5–6. Delaney 1969: 98, 168 distinguishes between subjective, objective and outside approaches.

140 Keane, *Apologia*; Pett, *Autobiography*, betrays no emotion and is partly a defence against corruption.

Papists'.[141] The Dissenter, George Boddington compiled his memoirs partly from religious zeal, partly for business reasons and partly 'in respect to the stock from whence I spring'; like many diarists, he edited his thoughts and mentions some 'pages cut out did containe severall passages relating to my self & Family which that nothing therein might be esteemed other wayes then they ought I thought they might better be obliterated'.[142] Fryer wrote to witness the care and providence of God so that 'his Posterity may hereafter be allways sensible of it'.[143] The Recusant, Nicholas Blundell, maintained a comprehensive and richly anecdotal journal because he had an urge to record and a bad memory: 'I shal afterwards have a desire to know on the day of the Month which may be necessarie for me to give account of'.[144]

Diaries and memoirs are valuable because they record thoughts, ambitions and feelings and they evoke pity or indignation in their emotional recollections of past events. By far the best source for the inner life of merchants is the self-questioning and reflective diary.[145] Non-Conformist zeal for the truth generated a respect for self-knowledge; human weakness saved many diaries from the tedium of excessive virtue, rhetorical exhortation and spiritual imitation.[146] The search for personal identity through narrative rather than through meditation gave memoirs a sense of immediacy and development; because they were not fashionable as literature until the eighteenth century, few were polished or coloured by literary ambition and only those of the Quakers were intended for publication.[147] The journals kept by recruits from outside the business world have unusual vitality, because the novelty of their occupation inclined them to identify implicit assumptions and unconscious mental habits and to retail in detail those experiences and decisions which a man bred to trade from childhood would have taken for granted.[148] Just as Puritan diarists invested trivial and routine events with great spiritual significance and thereby describe the obvious and unremarkable in their lives, so younger sons of gentlemen and yeomen, like travellers in foreign countries, thought fit to record the elementary aspects of their environment.

[141] *Collection Experiences Works Grace*; the marginal comments are in the Bodleian copy (Pamph. 167). [142] GLL MS 10823/1, fo. 23. [143] GLL MS 12017.

[144] Blundell, *Great Diurnal*, i. 7.

[145] Wolff 1968: 26. The journal in Bod. Malone MS 2 has little to say about business, but it includes long extracts from Orlando Furioso.

[146] The complete confession was an illusion: see Sharrock in Lawrence 1990: 97; Watkins 1972: 227.

[147] Stauffer 1964: chap. 5; Cohen 1986: 202. Kirkman, *Unlucky Citizen* is virtually an autobiographical novel, but he was a bookseller and professional author.

[148] Lovejoy 1936: 7.

Method of approach

The business community before the eighteenth century has not been ignored by economic historians. Some of the sources have been printed, starting with Hakluyt who included many business letters and documents in his *Navigations*.[149] Samuel Purchas made use of original papers of the East India Company.[150] The great chartered commercial and colonial Companies have been especially favoured, as have private inventories and correspondence.[151] Selections from the Deposition Books have been printed, mainly for the provincial ports. Ledgers and journals are, however, difficult to edit for publication and usually are restricted to specimen pages; other documents have been edited in typescript but never published.[152]

Although the earliest biographies tend to be literary in approach and compiled by amateurs, more recent studies combine technical expertise with a sound appreciation of business problems. Collective genealogies of municipal officers, families and Members of Parliament and the occupational analysis of recent urban and regional histories are also of great value. Modern studies of Companies have been written on a much wider basis than the older Company histories.[153] The history of colonial trade and settlement, particularly in the Caribbean and on the mainland colonies of North America has generated a rich crop of business biographies, though principally after 1690.[154] But the total number still remains quite small and no systematic study of the whole English business community in the seventeenth century has so far been attempted.[155]

'Pursuit of the genus mercator', it has been wisely observed, 'may result in an unreal abstraction or . . . a series of confused images'.[156] Some of the issues which will be considered here, while generating heated debate, have defied analysis and resolution. This is partly because the questions have been imprecisely formulated and predicated on the erroneous

149 iii. 70. The same was true of manuals like Browne, *Marchants Avizo*. See also Barker in Davenport-Hines 1990: 1–7.

150 Massarella in J. R. Jones 1986: 151; Lynam 1946: 56.

151 The three main exceptions are the Russia and Africa Companies and the Bank of England. The out-letter books of the Levant Company up to 1670 are included in the *Cal. S.P. Dom.* Some business documents are included in compilations such as Khan 1978.

152 On editorial problems see *Archives*, 5 (1951), pp. 20–1. An exemplary model is Marescoe, *Markets and Merchants*, which selects 500 from some 10,000 letters.

153 Most modern histories of firms, which claim descent from the seventeenth century, have little early material. A handlist of London business-house histories is in the GLL.

154 One example is Price 1980.

155 Several studies have, however, been made of business elites in French, Spanish, Italian, Flemish and Dutch cities.

156 Carus-Wilson, review of S. L. Thrupp in *Ec. H. R.*, 2 (1949–50), p. 210.

assumption that there is a rule or theory to cover every contingency.[157] There has been a persistent tendency to base answers on a monolithic theory and on misleading analogies; some ideas, despite trenchant criticism, perversely have wielded power in proportion to their degree of error.[158] Historians have oscillated between the microscopic and the macrocosmic.[159] Some have embraced the fallacy of misplaced concreteness; they have studied texts, rather than the whole body of evidence, and have hesitated to generalize about the business world because of lack of evidence. Others have allowed their addiction to all-embracing hypotheses to run far ahead of the facts and their conclusions have been dictated less by their research than by a grand vision. An overstated argument gains in clarity and force what it loses in veracity. The main obstacle to understanding the business community has, however, been the wish fulfilment implicit in any ideology. Preconceived and determinist theories of development, derived primarily from the social and economic problems of the present, have turned history into mythology.

This study reformulates the issues and addresses them with new evidence and from an unfamiliar perspective. The method employed is both descriptive and analytical; it relies not on theory, but on inductive generalizations from observed facts.[160] The structure and functions of business emerge from an empirical description of how businessmen conducted their affairs. Individual performance has been rated and compared to diagnose trends and uncover any patterns, but the interdependence of numerous factors has been stressed rather than a narrow interpretation. The methodology combines a qualitative treatment with as sound a statistical basis as is possible. The degree of uncertainty in the data cannot always be specified.[161] But the quantity and range of accessible sources is much greater than is conventionally assumed and many of the data fall within an acceptable range of confidence.[162] By careful and imaginative use of personal and business papers, it is possible to reconstruct from the ground up the character of the whole business community.

The economic and social changes in seventeenth-century England are viewed here from the perspective of contemporaries as well as with the benefit of hindsight. Growth is seen as more than a simple progression from a primitive to an advanced economy. Full weight is accorded to the inherent restraints of a pre-industrial economy, but attention is also

157 Hexter 1967: 12–13; Zagorin 1990a; King in King & Parekh 1986: 386, 393; Anderson 1991: 62. The classic critique of historians' methods, which has been ignored rather than refuted, is Fischer 1970.

158 Introduction by Beard to Bury 1960; Lukes in Horton & Finnegan 1973: 243.

159 Postan 1971: 139.

160 Bonnell 1980: 171.

161 MacCullagh 1984: 55–62.

162 Jeannin 1968: 854.

directed to other neglected variables in the equation. Although several traditional theories and arguments are rejected, what follows is not intended to be an iconoclastic work. It is always easier to destroy a hypothesis than to replace it and this study seeks to open and not to close doors. Its qualified answers will certainly not be the final word on the subject. But it does seek to burn some dead wood so that new and fertile ideas planted over the years can grow freely and be more visible. Even if some of the arguments prove controversial, by provoking discussion they may raise the level of debate and elucidate better answers.

Part 1

Business as a career

1 The status of business

In England, as in other societies, the elite had to justify its privileges and legitimize its authority. A system of ideas and beliefs, whether explicitly formulated as propositions or implicitly assumed as values, differentiated occupational groups and prescribed and judged their rituals and functions. Social attitudes cannot, however, be determined with any precision, because they have to be culled from ambiguous, didactic and impressionistic literary sources. Contemporary generalizations about behaviour are not *wertfrei* statements of fact, but expressions of opinion, animated by both hope and fear and intended to persuade. Most social observers sought to rationalize prejudices and either to justify or criticize the status quo. They vary in accuracy and authority, according to which interest they represent, whose example they follow and which audience they address. The evidence is so prolific and contradictory that it is possible to construct almost any hypothesis about the respectability of trade by selecting individual examples.[1]

Literary sources are not amenable to statistical treatment. Word counts and 'content analysis' usually suggest 1 per cent inspiration and 99 per cent desperation.[2] Opinion cannot be quantified, because weight is more important than number. It is necessary to allow for qualitative differences between writers of greater perception, objectivity, reliability, knowledge, intelligence and forcefulness. The interpretation and evaluation of texts also raise complex technical questions, such as the tone and structure of language, the influence of style on content, the context of remarks and the use of irony, satire, metaphor, allegory and symbolism.[3] Although the outlook of English society is mirrored in its literature, it is important to

[1] Hexter 1979: 238; Sharpe 1989: 5; Pococke 1972. A typical example of indiscriminate selection is MacVeagh 1981. The volume of printed matter provides an unreliable index of attitudes since output was closely related to economic factors such as the cost of paper.

[2] One such painstaking example is Barber 1957: 333–6.

[3] Knox 1961; Sharpe 1987: 3; Hawthorne 1978: 6. The sheer volume of original material, which is multiplied in geometrical progression by subsequent commentaries, is a major deterrent: see Wentworth 1981. Literary theorists rarely have an adequate grasp of economics and social structure, whereas economic and social historians often underestimate or misunderstand the subtleties of textual criticism.

categorize authors by background and bias and to distinguish descriptions of actual practice from theories of what society ought to be.[4]

The theorists

The diversity and ambiguity of attitudes to business are well illustrated by the courtesy writers and the Heralds. Although they were self-appointed guardians of gentility, their views carry some weight; often lawyers by training they employed a scholarly apparatus and debated points with each other.[5] In the sixteenth century, their principal objective was to expound the virtues of a Humanist education and to discredit military values.[6] But they were also influenced by Greek and Roman hostility towards trade and by the continental jurists.[7] It has been stated that 'a merchant and a gentleman were terms universally held to be mutually incompatible'.[8] The *Institucion of a Gentleman*, in 1555, did assert that 'by continuance of bying and selling, they are not esteemed gentlemen but merchants'.[9] Gainsford gave an evasive reply when asked whether a gentlewoman could let lodgings.[10] Ferne, a common lawyer, took the Romans and French nobles as his model and regarded merchandizing as 'no competent or seemelye trade of lyfe'.[11]

But Ferne also conceded that Genoa and Venice had combined trade with gentility and the general attitude of the conduct books was cool, but not totally dismissive. Westcote defended the numerous Devonshire squires in trade by citing the precedents of Anglo-Saxon England and medieval Barcelona; he rejected the authority of Cicero with a quotation from Dionides.[12] Thomas Churchyard regarded merchants as gentlemen, because they took risks to supply the necessities of life.[13] Peacham, in 1634, used the same argument, though he hedged on the whole question, citing the Ancients and dismissing the precedent of the Italian cities.[14] Richard Blome argued that anyone who 'can live without manual labour or by his wealth can live and bear the port of a Gentleman shall be called Mr and may purchase a Coat of Arms'; but whereas he specifically included working lawyers, physicians and clergy, he excluded the active

[4] For the views of businessmen see pp. 378–80.

[5] Bainton 1936; Ustick 1932a: 153–7; Mason 1935: 295–6; Brauer 1959: 112ff; Curtis 1985; Day 1990: 99.

[6] Kelso 1929: 61–2; Watson 1969: chaps. 1–4; Simon 1966: 254; Noyes 1937: 3.

[7] Hall 1958: 13; Burke 1986a: 240. [8] Stone 1956: 127. [9] Cooper 1983: 54.

[10] Gainsford, *Rich Cabinet*. Sir William Segar, Garter King of Arms, in his *Honor Military and Civil*, pp. 119, 249, denied active merchants the right to precedence and to a trial by arms. [11] Cooper 1983: 68.

[12] Westcote, *View of Devonshire*, p. 52; D'Arms 1980: 85–6.

[13] Churchyard, *Generall Rehearsall Warrs*; Acton 1971: 16, chap. 2.

[14] Peacham, *Complete Gentleman*, pp. 3, 21–2.

merchant; he admitted that the Saxons had ennobled traders 'but onely those by honest Husbandry or plentiful Merchandizing from beyond the sea'.[15] Braithwaite asserted that trade did not diminish the status of younger sons, 'so by God's blessing and their good endeavour, they become many times so well improved, as they need not obsequiously ingratiate themselves to any inferior favour, nor rely on a pensionary supply or any necessitated succour'.[16]

The academic world was much more scornful of business.[17] By the end of the century, the emergence of a monied interest highlighted the political role of trade and generated a debate on the moral value of self-interest.[18] Some philosophers, like Locke, Hobbes and Mandeville, rejected the traditional view that business was morally harmful, but even they had grave misgivings about materialistic values and the profit motive.[19] Harrington might propose to radically restructure society by abolishing primogeniture, but he rejected trade as a proper outlet for younger sons of the gentry.[20] Ever since Plato put tradesmen low in the hierarchy of his ideal Republic, intellectuals had denounced an occupation which they considered beneath them; they shared the high-minded contempt for money displayed by Sir Thomas More.[21] Impoverished scholars, like the younger son Robert Burton, and unsuccessful hunters for preferment were envious and contemptuous of men who rose through business.[22]

Those with stable incomes from benefices or government sinecures frequently identified profit with exploitation and regarded as socially subordinate any who did not service the Crown and the commonweal, the arts and sciences, God and the Church. The values of the business world presented a real threat to those whom society rewarded in status rather than in money. It undermined their claim to moral superiority, based on the deliberate rejection of material advantage and the pursuit of knowledge for its own sake. Milles considered that a gentleman should derive

[15] Blome, *Art of Heraldry*, pp. 253–4; idem, *Britannia*.

[16] Braithwaite, *Turtles' Triumph*, p. 21 and *English Gentleman*, p. 17.

[17] On later manifestations of the same attitude see Ruegg 1986; Rubinstein 1988: 56; Coleman & Mathias 1984: 35–6; 1987: 65; Hayek 1954: 118–19; Chambers 1971: 365; Ashton 1964: 586; Winter 1978; Wright 1987: 29; Raven 1989: 184; Polanyi 1957: 52; Ryan 1981: 90.

[18] Pocock 1986: 108; 1975: 454–6; Hirschman 1976: 129; Pagden 1987: 3, 12.

[19] Locke, Hobbes and Mandeville have all provoked diametrically opposed interpretations. See Gunn 1969: chap. 11; Ashcraft 1987: 146; Tully 1980: 79; Locke, *Educational Writings*, ed. Axtell, pp. 3–13; Seliger 1968: 143; Dunn 1969: 255; Harpham 1985; Levy 1954: 592; Hobbes, *Works*, vi. 168; Sir Keith Thomas in Brown 1965: 204; Madjarian 1982: 554; Spengler 1959: 64; Hayek 1966: 134–5; Chalk 1966: 4–6; Cooke 1974; Horne 1978; Rosenberg 1962: 186, 194; Landreth 1975; Hughes & Williams 1971.

[20] Webster 1974: 68.

[21] More, *Works*, p. 131; on More's commercial connections see Ramsay 1981: 269. Machlud 1976: 79.

[22] Babb 1959: 101.

'reputation onley from his learning or from some office or function which he beareth'.[23] John Evelyn wrote a panegyric to trade and claimed that it had eventually been accepted by the Romans, but his social conservatism made him ambivalent about his own *History of Trades*; he liked merchants in general, but he thought that Child was sordidly avaricious.[24]

It might be expected that those who wrote on economic questions should approve of business. By focusing on colonial expansion and trade rather than on agriculture, they did much to elevate its status and to persuade both Court and Country of its necessity and national importance.[25] The historical geographer, Richard Hakluyt the younger, was a professional propagandist for Empire as well as for his sponsor, the Clothworkers Company. His *Principal Navigations* not only provided a documentary record, but glorified the patriotic and high-minded aims of venture capital, the courage and independence of businessmen and the distinguished historical record of the City.[26] Thomas Mun, in the 1620s, and Henry Robinson, himself a younger son, had strongly urged the gentry to enter commerce.[27] Blanch considered business a more noble profession for the gentry than war.[28] Sir William Petty and Sir Matthew Hale even advocated manual trades for gentlemen.[29] Josiah Child argued that trade was 'not unbecoming Persons of the highest rank'.[30] The *Compleat Tradesman* suggested that gentlemen should become shopkeepers and marry tradesmen's daughters, because it was an easy life and other trades had declined.[31] Although *Britannia Languens* criticized the gentry for regarding business 'as no otherwise necessary ... than to support younger brothers', pamphleteers always felt that the prospect of employment for younger sons strengthened their case, whether they were promoting plantations or attacking the chartered Companies, aliens, the Scots or the calico importers.[32]

23 Milles, *Catalogue of Honour*, p. 79.

24 Evelyn, *Navigation and Commerce*, pp. 11–15; Keynes 1937: 201–2. He did, however, take an apprentice gardener: see *Diary*, iv. 52. On the failure of England to produce a history of trades see Webster 1974: 350.

25 The extraordinary range of works is illustrated by Wright 1944 and Parker 1966. On early exponents of growth see Grampp 1965: chap. 2 and Hoselitz 1961: 3–64.

26 Hakluyt adapted his text under pressure and his advocacy of imperial expansion is implied rather than stated in his *Principal Navigations*; it is clearer in his *Discourse on Western Planting*. See Quinn 1974: 26–7, 1976: 81. On his Company connections and influence see Ramsay 1977: 505; Detweiler 1971; Griffith 1972: 235.

27 T. Mun in *Early English Tracts Commerce*, p. 85; H. Robinson in *Select Tracts and Documents*, pp. 48–9; Jordan 1942: 218–20, n. 29, extends Robinson's remarks slightly by inference.

28 Blanch, *Interest of England*, p. 38; BL Hargrave MS 321, fol. 34v°.

29 Ustick 1932a: 157; Roncaglia 1985.

30 Child, *Brief Observations*, p. 135.

31 N. H. *Compleat Tradesman*, pp. 34–5.

32 *Early English Tracts Commerce*, p. 285; *Discourse Encouraging Mechanic Industry*, p. 21; *Merchant Adventurers Ordinances*, p. 37; *Clothiers Reason Establishing Merchant Adventurers*.

But an interest in economics and political arithmetic did not necessarily lead to approval of private business.[33] The economic pundits distrusted middlemen who were divorced from production and feared that merchants would export bullion, create scarcity and encourage luxury and usury, that they were interested in profit, not in maintaining a favourable balance or full employment, in increasing the royal revenue or providing for the defence of the nation. Thomas Violet maintained 'it is the profit is the Merchant's guide, their goddess'.[34] Worsley, Coke, Davenant and others denounced the corruption of trade and denied that the interest of the nation was identical with that of private business.[35]

The literary world

Character writers such as Thomas Fuller and Samuel Butler produced sympathetic portraits of merchants and emphasized the links between land and trade.[36] Chroniclers and antiquarians, like Camden and John Stow, gave business a lineage and a tradition.[37] The professional travel writers, like Flecknoe, who spread knowledge of a world expanded by commerce, gratefully praised merchants for their invaluable help and noble ends.[38] Popular fiction and ballads defended the prestige and captured the risks and routines of business.[39] Thomas Deloney, a silk weaver, wrote realistic prose romances for artisans and prentices which were bestsellers and boosted morale.[40] Journalists and essayists, like Addison and Steele, seduced by the power of credit, romanticized

[33] Letwin 1963: 85–6. Hostility to capitalism can also be found in all the classical economists: see Coleman 1972a: 11; 1988: 161; Grampp 1948: 333; Winch 1978: 167–8; Harpham 1984. Appleby 1978 argues that the intellectual origins of capitalism can be found in the economic literature of the Later Stuarts, even though Locke nipped this development in the bud. This thesis depends on a rather grandiose concept of ideology and disregards both the political context and the chronology of events. The technical issues which form the core of most treatises are downplayed and individual writers are grouped arbitrarily. For a telling critique see Coleman 1980: 779; for a more opaque judgement see Pococke 1979: 303. [34] Violet, *Humble Proposal*, pp. 11–12.

[35] Davenant, *Works*; Coke, *Treatise*, p. 85; Coombs 1957: 94; Waddell 1958–9: 279; *Britannia Languens*, sect. viii; Rich 1957: 61.

[36] Fuller, *Holy State*, ii. 113–16; Houghton 1938: 82; Butler, *Characters*, p. 149; *Character and Qualifications Merchant*, pp. 9–10; *Character Writings*, p. 78.

[37] Stow, *Survey*, ed. Kingsford, ii. 211; Pearl 1979a; Ashton 1978. Stow was subsidized by the Merchant Taylors.

[38] Flecknoe, *Relation Ten Years*, p. 89; Howell, *Epistolae*, p. 367; Stoye 1952: 452; Davies 1967: 88.

[39] Lodge, *Works*, iv. 5; Sisson 1933. Some oral legends about famous merchants and benefactors, like Peter Blundell, survived: see Prince 1810: 89.

[40] Deloney, *Works*, p. xxxi; Kucher 1940; Lawlis 1960: 243; Margolies 1985: 151–4; on the legendary histories of businessmen see Spufford 1981: 238–44. On works written specifically for artisans see Camp 1924: 115–20. On the self-help literature see p. 171.

business and argued that gentility was determined by behaviour.[41] Defoe, of course, was an unabashed and relentless apologist for the respectability and importance of business, though he was prone to deviousness, prolixity and exaggeration and defended the shopkeeper rather than the merchant.[42]

The popular fiction aimed at apprentices was in fact escapist and short-lived.[43] Most men of letters were not particularly interested in business, which they rarely understood and which they associated with moral weakness, philistinism and exploitation. Poets might occasionally be adventurers and employ commercial metaphors, but they patronized the merchant and put him in his place.[44] Milton considered that ministers should ply a trade, so 'they would not then so many of them for want of another trade, make a trade of their preaching'; but this reflected his opposition to tithes rather than his support for business.[45] Dryden, in his assault on the Whigs, denigrated the whole merchant community: 'In Gospel phrase, their Chapmen they betray; their shops are Dens, the Buyer is their Prey'.[46] Swift campaigned repeatedly and ruthlessly against the merchant interest; angered by their political influence and social pretensions, he condemned them for thinking 'the world to be no wider than Exchange Alley'.[47] Even Addison and Steele had aristocratic tastes and views; they ridiculed merchants' wives and regarded business as a living for the mediocre; plain-dealing was merely one virtue to add to those of sensitivity, manners, education and taste. Scurrilous Grub Street hacks, like Ned Ward and Tom Brown, were more realistic in their depiction of business life, but they discredited the cosy image which the business community sought to project.[48]

[41] *Spectator*, i. 294; *Guardian*, no. 76; *Tatler*, iv. 72; Steele, *Conscious Lovers*; Smithers 1968: 467–8; Blooms 1971: 11–27. Much nonsense was spouted about credit, which is taken too seriously by Pococke 1986: 99.

[42] Defoe, *Compleat English Tradesman*, i. 316–17 and *Review*, ii. 10. For different interpretations see Earle 1976: 168; Shinagel 1968: 99, 125–6; Sutherland 1950: 46; Dijkstra 1987: 54; Watt 1967: 40; Reeves 1966: 64–71; Ellis 1969; Hearne 1967; 102–3; Ayers 1967: 407; the standard Marxist analysis is summarized by Wojcik 1979: 5–34 and more subtly by Hill 1980a: 19–20. For a convincing thesis that pride was the basis of Defoe's passions see Novak 1962: chap. 2; 1963: 155; MacDonald 1976: 23–4. Rogers 1972–3: 170, 185 regards the *Tour* as a non-martial epic expressing an hyperbolic vision of the nation's business character.

[43] Salzman 1985: 109. Stevenson 1984: chap. 9 and in Malamud 1980: 287, rightly points out that prentices were accorded chivalric qualities and that the genre was soon replaced by more sophisticated comedy. But the argument, p. 285, that middle-class practices preceded the bourgeois virtues is confused and misconceived; for a better interpretation see Slack 1984: 223–4. The chivalric themes may reflect the numbers of gentlemen apprentices: see Burke 1977: 156–8.

[44] Davis 1955; Goreau 1980: 185; Bernong 1991: 349; Young, *Poetical Works*, ii. 342.

[45] Milton, *Prose Works*, vii. 306. [46] Dryden, *Works*, ii. 48; Winn 1987: 367–8.

[47] Swift, *Prose Works*, ix. 117, 244; Ross 1941: 34–5; Miller 1970; Pope, *Prose Works*, ii. 159; Reichard 1952: 429; Downie 1979: 193.

[48] Browne, *Amusements*, p. 21; Troyer 1946; Pollak 1989: 11.

Elizabethan playwrights often treated citizens as sympathetic characters. Dekker and Heywood were in some respects dramatic journalists and they depicted London life realistically in gross slang without sentiment or grandiloquence.[49] Their portrayals of intriguing rakes, rich widows, shrewish wives and prodigal sons were clearly tailored for audiences of apprentices and tradesmen, even if they could not easily afford the price of a ticket.[50] Thomas Dekker's citizens were moral, affable, humble, generous and considerate.[51] Thomas Heywood's *Four Prentices of London*, in 1594, glorified London tradesmen as adventurers and was very popular.[52] In the *Child of Bristow*, a squire even puts his son to trade after making money from usury, and in *Eastward Ho* one of the characters was a gentleman turned tradesman. Minor dramatists also churned out plays which glorified the prentice and no doubt many young men could identify in their fantasy life with these fictional characters.[53] Even after 1660, elements of this tradition are visible in Shadwell.

Nevertheless, the avarice, corruption and hypocrisy of business was daily pilloried on the stage and often tarred with a Puritan brush.[54] Beaumont and Fletcher satirized Heywood's apprentices and Thomas Dekker's citizens and turned the legends of London into burlesque.[55] Thomas Middleton directed his animus towards the usurer and he rejected the escapist culture of the Court.[56] But he hardly expressed a citizen ethos; in the *Young Fine Gallants*, he made the woollen draper, Epehesias Quomodo, a social climber and scoundrel, like Volpone.[57]

The subject matter of drama and comedy also changed. Domestic, homiletic and realistic tragedy was replaced in the Jacobean repertory by epic characters in bloody and sensational tragedy and tragicomedy.[58] The social and sexual inferiority of the citizen was a staple vehicle of Restoration Comedy, whose conventions survived until Queen Anne.[59] Congreve, Vanbrugh and Farquhar reflected not only the hedonism of the Court, but also hostility towards business as a source of new wealth and social pretension.[60] A telling argument of the campaigners against the stage was that it vilified merchants. One of Aphra Behn's characters was a gentleman, sent as a factor to France, who loudly laments how 'we basely bind our youngest out to slavery, to lazy Trades, idly confined to Shop or

[49] Schelling 1908: i. 207–8; Gibbon 1980: 9–11; Knights 1937a.

[50] For different views on the theatre audience see Harbage 1968; Cook 1981; Gair 1982: app. 1; Butler 1984: 141–79, app. 2.

[51] Gregg 1924; Jones-Davies 1958: 207–10; Wright 1958: 623–4; Hunt 1968. The social analysis in all these works is rather crude.

[52] Heywood, *Dramatic Works*; Boas 1950; Clark 1931: 251; Grimelet 1957.

[53] Vallans, *Honourable Prentice*; Barton 1978: 175.

[54] Holden 1954: 151.

[55] Appleton 1950: 13; Finkelpeare 1990: 83.

[56] Heinemann 1980: 172.

[57] Barker 1958: 47; Middleton, *Triumph of Honor*.

[58] Adams 1943: 190–1.

[59] Loftis 1959: 2, 45, 77; Fujimura 1952: 201; Underwood 1957: 152; Lynch 1926. The term itself is challenged by Hume 1976: 10.

[60] Rodway 1972: 39.

Merchants Books, debasing of their Spirit'.[61] The businessman was not considered an appropriate subject for tragedy until Lillo in 1731.[62]

The theatre is not a reliable source for social attitudes, because it was principally a means of entertainment, dominated by personal idiosyncrasies. The content and range of plays were largely determined by those who patronized the theatre.[63] The dramatist could not ignore, as Bentham put it, 'the passions of those on the pleasure of whom he depends for his success'.[64] He was not a social scientist and had to cope with censorship, to follow dramatic conventions, to develop character and to work within the framework of standardized plots. But the theatre did accurately describe the social and moral ambiguities of business. Shakespeare exposed the contradictions both within and between aristocratic, business and spiritual values.[65] Elizabethan and Jacobean Comedy did more than satirize the acquisitive instinct; it played on the tension generated by genuine conflicts of function and approach. By subverting conventional morality, it ultimately reasserted the fundamental harmony between business and society.[66] By ridiculing the citizenry, the Restoration playwrights unintentionally recognized their importance. In England, *mésalliance* was a subject for comedy, not tragedy.

Churchmen

The views of churchmen about business are not easy to ascertain. There were many traditions of preaching and sermons were better suited to narrative than to analysis.[67] Less than 3 per cent of sermons delivered were ever printed and the more celebrated preachers from prosperous parishes are over-represented. Several bishops were related to or friendly with merchants and those clergy who were presented to City benefices or employed by the commercial Companies and guilds were predisposed to extol the virtues of business.[68] Price scoured Scripture to find appropriate

[61] Behn, *Works*, iv. 327. She was well acquainted with merchants: see Mendelson 1987: 146.

[62] Lillo, *Merchant of London*. Lillo was apprenticed to a goldsmith in 1697: see Burgess 1967: 426; Harmard 1965; Brashear, 1969; Wellwarth 1970: 96.

[63] Beljame 1948: 56–7; for different views on the Restoration audience see Avery 1966; Knights 1937a: 132.

[64] Stonex 1916: 190.

[65] Ferber 1990: 431–64.

[66] Leggatt 1973: 3, 150–1, 1988; Hutson 1989: 8; Barton 1978: 166; Wells 1981: 37; Salinger 1987: 150; Honigmann 1986: 14. It is currently fashionable to interpret early plays in terms of simplistic, abstract modern theories of capitalism and the market, which often betray ignorance of economic principles and which would have bewildered contemporary dramatists. See Agnew 1986: 27–31; Bruster 1990: 207–10; 1992: 4, 11; Haynes 1992. An extreme example of this genre is Killeen 1976: 214, who argues that a capitalist theatre developed in rivalry with the actor-manager and that 'thematic potent' can be discerned even when there is no specific evidence in the literature.

[67] Owst 1961: 353, 414–25; Blench 1964: 244, 308; Mitchell 1932.

[68] MacLure 1958: 130; Catcott, *Antiquity of Merchandise*. Preachers were flattered by invitations to preach at major events: see Josselin, *Diary*, p. 258.

texts and interpreted them liberally. Citing Matthew 13.45–6, he likened the Kingdom of Heaven to a merchant, which was 'translated by some *mercator*, by some *negotiator*', the former an itinerant and the latter a sedentary merchant.[69] William Pemberton described St Paul as 'that experienced merchant'.[70]

John Donne, the orphaned son of a prosperous Londoner, used commercial metaphors and maritime imagery; in a famous sermon to the Virginia Company, he blessed the harmony of land and trade: 'as Merchants grow up into worshipful Families and worshipful Families let fall branches amongst Merchants againe'.[71] Immanuel Bourne, preacher at St Christopher's near the Exchange, asserted that 'Heaven defends trade' because it enlarged the Kingdom of Christ and provided benefactions for churches and universities.[72] Thomas Cooper, in a sermon delivered before the Grocers, when they visited their free school at Oundle, acknowledged the need for business morality and consideration for the public interest. But he also asserted that it was lawful to desire riches 'if necessarie & sufficient, if they fit our callings as persons, if desire submitted to God's pleasure and if accompanied by prayer to God'.[73]

Support for business among the clergy was not limited to those with financial ties to the business community. In their defence of property, some acknowledged that wealth was a test of virtue and others recognized the missionary value of foreign trade and colonization. One preacher expressed sympathetic views about trade, even though his sermon was primarily a conceit for Court consumption.[74] Bishop Reynolds drew confusing analogies between the virtues of business and religion.[75] The 'merchandizing' of religion was a popular theological vogue, particularly after the Restoration, and Dissenting ministers had to treat their congregations, who paid their stipends, as volatile consumers.[76] 'The Lord will not only call you to an account for the principall of the talents of honour and greatness', said Fairclough, 'but for the interest also'.[77] John Collinges dedicated his *Weavers' Pocket Book* to those aldermen of Norwich who had made fortunes; Gataker argued that gain was better than stealing.[78] Attention was usually focused, however, less on the inherent

[69] Price, *The Marchant*, pp. 13, 20.
[70] Pemberton, *The Godly Merchant*, p. 5.
[71] Donne, *Sermons*, iv. 277.
[72] Bourne, *Godly Man's Guide*. Bourne had a benefice worth £136 p.a. in the 1650s: see O'Day 1976: 110, 114.
[73] Cooper, *Worldling's Adventure*, pp. 62, 67; he recognized that callings 'depended upon the custome and fashion of the time'.
[74] Wilkinson, *Merchant Royall*, p. 15.
[75] Reynolds, *Works*, iv. 432.
[76] Ashwood, *Heavenly Trade*, epistle; Bagshaw, *Trading Spiritualised*; Schlatter 1940: 161–7; Dunn 1906: 45–50. Islam also borrowed extensively from commercial terminology, as did Erasmus: see Torney 1892; Todd 1987: 126.
[77] Fairclough, *Saints' Worthiness*, p. 31.
[78] Schlatter 1940: 182–3; Gataker, *God's Eye*, p. 23.

value of business than on the charity, piety and sense of public service of individual merchants. Bishop Sprat was untypical of the clergy when he claimed after the Civil Wars that 'traffic and commerce have given mankind a higher degree than any title of nobility, even that of civility and humanity itself'.[79]

Business was, moreover, a marginal issue in most sermons and treatises. Churchmen were more interested in debating the mystery of the Trinity than the mystery of the new-fashioned goldsmiths. The Anglican Church, with its agricultural base, often just ignored the business world and regurgitated inherited attitudes.[80] Its popular voice, as expressed in the Saint Paul's Cross sermons, neither understood nor trusted business.[81] Exhortations to industry and thrift were accompanied by universal condemnation of covetousness and by grave warnings about the corrupting influence of money and the sharp practices of merchants.[82] Fear of private interests exploiting the public combined with fears of the social upheaval and instability caused by economic change. Crowley attacked the social ambitions of merchants 'for why should they be gentlemen'.[83] Anglican apologists, particularly after 1660, were also concerned with the pretensions of citizens and the association of trade with radicalism. The author of an extreme panegyric on the dignity of labour considered that the gentry should run the country, because they could not do mean work.[84] Some believed that God had given the gentry wealth to free them from business.[85] The more spiritually minded clergy regarded material wealth as a fleeting illusion and a path to sin; business distracted men from their religious duties, was unfair to third parties and undermined the status quo.[86]

Although Presbyterians and Sectarians were less rooted in agricultural society and although Covenant theology was analogous to commercial contracts, Non-Conformists still had a multiplicity of contradictory attitudes.[87] Some, like John Knox, were willing to accept that wealth was a sign of Providence and a blessing of God, which should not be despised.[88] Nehemiah Grew urged the gentry to find in trade 'a durable satisfaction beyond that of any vaine and transient pleasure'.[89] But William Perkins considered that social change could not be justified by

[79] Sprat, *History Royal Society*, p. 408; Knoll 1993: 209; Pococke 1985.
[80] Stevenson 1974; Clark *et al.* 1979: 36.
[81] MacLure 1958: 134; Dyke, *Counter-poyson against Covetousness*; White 1944; 1931.
[82] Tennison, *Excellency of Public Spirit*.
[83] Crowley, *Works*, p. 89; Edgeworth, *Sermons*, p. 288. [84] *Saint Paul Tentmaker*, p. 12.
[85] Schlatter 1940: 119, 122. [86] Godwyn, *Trade Preferred*.
[87] Zanet 1980: 115. The numerous strands in the enormous literature of Protestantism are conveniently summarized by Georges 1961: 165–70.
[88] Knox, *Works*, i. 40–5, 294ff; BL Add. MS 4460. [89] Hunt. Lib. MS 1264, fo. 147.

private necessities, only by the common good, that co-operation was to be preferred to self-interest.[90] The millenarian writers proclaimed the ultimate destruction of the business community; Winstanley would have made buying and selling a capital offence.[91] Calamy insisted that a man should strive only to support his family at its original social level without 'loosening all the bonds of society and setting People together by the Ears'.[92] The Quakers opposed accumulation, because inherited wealth led to idleness and defence of property by military action; in their heroic period they reduced their trade from fear of avarice.[93] Even when Puritan reformism metamorphosed into Dissent, it remained hostile towards covetousness and never developed a coherent attitude towards business.[94] Ministers of every denomination tended to look down on trade, because their prestige, moral superiority and authority were threatened by the assumptions of business, which valued the world above the spirit.[95]

The gentry

Both the Court and the country gentry had grave misgivings about business. These stemmed partly from fears of political radicalism and social mobility and partly from indebtedness to merchants. George Whitston, in 1584, claimed that the 'mortal envie betwixt these two estates' originally derived from 'the cruell usage of covetous merchants in hard bargains gotten of gentlemen'.[96] Bacon advised James I to 'put off the person of a merchant and contractor and rest upon the person of a King'.[97] Sydenham Poyntz thought 'to be bound an apprentice that life I deemed little better then a dogs life and base. At last I resolved ... to live and die a soldier.'[98] Exile and loss of power during the Interregnum made the Restoration gentry more suspicious of business, which was associated with Dissent, republicanism, land taxes, usury, utilitarianism, pretension and moral repression.[99] Clarendon, in his *History of the Rebellion*, displays Royalist suspicion and distrust of *parvenus*. Thomas Violet drew hysterical pictures of disloyalty and conspiracy in the City, and Culpeper attacked the upstarts, 'these modern meteors' who outshone the peerage and gentry and threatened the Crown.[100] Matthew Wren supported

[90] Perkins, *Works*, ed. Brewart, p. 464; *English Puritanist*, pp. 192, 196; Preston, *Remedy against Covetousness*; Steele, *Religious Tradesman*; Scott, *Christian Life*.
[91] Alsop 1989: 97; J. C. Davis 1976: 83.
[92] Calamy, *Sermon Salters Hall*, pp. 5–6.
[93] Grubb 1930: 59–60; Pike, *Life*, p. 389.
[94] Eisenstadt 1968: 163, 174; Knappen 1963: 412–22.
[95] Kearney 1970: 143–4; Best 1982; Miller & Johnson: chap. 5.
[96] Wright 1958: 21.
[97] Bacon, *Works*, iv. 371; his antipathy to merchants is evident in his *New Atlantis*.
[98] *Relation of Sydenham Poyntz*, p. 45.
[99] Marion, *Prophetical Warnings*, p. 77; Seaward 1989: 326.
[100] Violet, *Humble Proposal*, p. 3; Culpeper, *Tracts Concerning Usury*, p. 25.

Hobbes against Harrington and asserted that cash had become more important than land, that foreign trade would raise London at the expense of the gentry.[101] Country gentlemen, like Sir Richard Cocks, resented the effective exemption of business from direct taxation.[102] MacKenzie condemned those who sacrificed 'many of their years by living in such places as Scanderoon, exchanging life itself for money'.[103]

Much of this hostility stemmed from ignorance, indifference, and old-fashioned snobbery which Gervais Holles ascribed to French influence.[104] Thomas Wilson bemoaned the fate of younger sons, but he did not consider trade as a solution. Henry Belasyse considered business a 'low employment': 'to be apprentise in a shop, sitt bare head, sweep the shop and streets is the life of thousands'.[105] According to Pepys, Lord Sandwich, when 'he became a perfect Courtier' said that 'he would rather see (his daughter) with a pedlar's pack at her back so she married a gentleman rather than a Citizen'.[106] George Saville alleged that 'the first Mistake belonging to business is the going into it . . . men make it such a point of honour to be fit for business, that they forget to examine whether Business is fit for a Man of Sense'.[107] Sir Thomas Baines considered that merchants should be ranked among the nobility, as in Genoa and Venice, that 'rich men withdrawing their stock is some disadvantage'; but, as late as 1676, he still asserted that 'the being made an apprentice according to our custom is a blott at least in every man's scutchion'.[108]

Business was, nevertheless, widely tolerated as a necessary evil. The gentry consistently lobbied for commercial openings for their younger children.[109] In the 1621 Commons, Sir Thomas Low reminded the House that 'merchants be most gentlemen's sons and younger brethren'.[110] Status was to a large extent in the eye of the beholder. Gervais Holles proudly wrote of his merchant ancestor, Sir William: 'for my owne part I shall ever esteeme it more honor to be descended from a merchant than from any other civil profession whatsoever'.[111] Streynsham Master was satisfied to learn from his sister that 'the oldest writings my father has show us all ways to be gentilmen'.[112] Younger sons, like Slingsby Bethel and Marmaduke Rawdon the younger, strongly supported their chosen occupation; Osborne recommended the gentry to take to trade or embassies as a safe form of tourism.[113] Edward Bohun believed that trade was an

[101] Wren, *Considerations on Oceana*, pp. 14–15, 85–9.
[102] Hayton 1988: 243; Ailesbury, *Memoirs*, ii. 60.
[103] MacKenzie, *Moral History Frugality*, p. 47.
[104] *Holles Family Memorials*, p. 18; Ascoli 1930.
[105] Belasyse, *English Traveller's First Curiosity*, p. 204.
[106] Pepys, *Diary*, i. 269.
[107] Halifax, *Works*, p. 19.
[108] *HMC Finch*, ii. 29–33, iii. 31.
[109] Ashton 1967: 54–5.
[110] *Parliament Commons Debates 1621*, iii. 429, 443.
[111] *Holles Family Memorials*, p. 19.
[112] Master 1874: 62.
[113] Bethel, *Interest of the Princes*, pp. 3–5, 8; Osborne, *Advice to a Son*, p. 59.

instrument of civility as well as of prosperity.[114] The gentry rarely lived up to the high standards of the conduct books, just as they were never as worried about acquisitiveness as the intellectuals. They recognized the wealth and power of commerce and considered that their participation would civilize it.

The law

England had a few formal legal barriers to entering business.[115] Tradition prescribed that courtesy lords should not trade and new peers did come under pressure to discontinue their traffic. The ranking of social groups in England was defined by the Statute of Additions and the nobility had some exclusive rights.[116] The clergy were forbidden to trade in merchandise by a statute of Henry VIII. A property qualification for apprentices had been created by an act of 1405–6; faced with rapid social change, Thomas Cromwell, Sir Nicholas Bacon, Edward VI, Sir Thomas Chaloner, George Whetstone and Cecil all toyed with limiting purchase of land by merchants.[117] A proposed bill of 1562 would have drastically curtailed overseas trade.[118] The Tudors discouraged social mobility and elevated agriculture above commerce in the interests of defence, food supply and social order.[119]

But the Statute of Additions was interpreted from the fifteenth century onwards so as to permit gentlemen to enter misteries; both common and civil lawyers concurred in asserting that gentility was confirmed by reputation, even though the Heralds insisted on arms.[120] The land market remained free and efforts to regulate labour and freeze employment were directed mainly at the lower orders. Even the reactionary programme of 1559 did not exclude gentlemen from trade; the Statute of Artificers, with exemptions for London and Norwich and special provisions for towns like Exeter, permitted all those 'of the yerely value of three pounds of one estate of inheritance or freehold' to apprentice their sons to a merchant.[121]

[114] Bohun, *Diary*, pp. 133–4. The notion that God had distributed natural resources unevenly so as to encourage communion between men was of great antiquity and a standard theme of the Augustan era: see Haynes, *Great Britain's Glory*, 1; Viner 1962: 274–5.

[115] Holdsworth 1924–6: v. 285–6; Dugdale, *Origines Juridicales*.

[116] Bush 1983.

[117] *Edward VI Chronicles*, pp. 161–2: the proposed ceiling on land purchase is unclear; Elton 1973: 127; *Tudor Economic Documents*, i. 326; *HMC Salisbury*, i. 162–3; Bush 1975: 61–2; Ferguson 1965: 383; Whetstone, *Mirror for Magistrates*.

[118] Elton 1986: 72, 254, 263.

[119] R. D. W. Jones 1970: 170–2; Walter & Wrightson 1976: 30; Loach & Tittler 1980: 84.

[120] Cooper 1983: 49, 62.

[121] *Tudor Economic Documents*, i. 348, 357; Carus-Wilson 1954–66: i. 169; Woodward 1980: 40, 42.

The Courts upheld the status of business and gradually recognized a distinction between artisan and merchant. In 1634, Star Chamber ruled in favour of a gentleman, that it was 'no disparagement nor stain to him to have been a woollen draper as long as he carries himself honestly and with integrity'.[122] By 1700, it could be argued in King's Bench in a prosecution under the Statute of Artificers that 'a merchant is not within the letter neither is he within the meaning of the Law because he is of a superior order and degree of Men'; although the defence did not stand, Justice Dobbins thought the statute should be repealed.[123]

There remained an ambiguous distinction between business and 'base and mechanical arts'.[124] Merchants who turned gentlemen could be rejected by the Court of Chivalry, as in the case of Stepkin versus Dobbins in 1638.[125] John Ferrar regarded the Apostles as gentlemen constrained to servile works.[126] Fitzherbert's *Grand Abridgment* of 1516 cited the case of Estopell 47 Mich. 25. Hen. VII, which implied that merchants could not be gentlemen. Doderidge cited this case and also quoted Cicero's famous attack on trade, but he concluded that the gentry could enter business as long as their profits returned to the land and so long as they did not undertake common buying and selling.[127] Henry Parker's son had his pedigree questioned by Dugdale, but his status was allowed.[128] Anglo-Saxon law had regarded a merchant who thrice fared over the sea as thegnworthy, a precedent which was much cited in the seventeenth century; in late medieval and early Tudor England, gentility could be acquired through service and important merchants enjoyed rough parity with gentlemen.[129]

The law of arms allowed merchants who lived nobly to bear arms, which could always be acquired through inheritance, purchase and grant.[130] John Philpot, Somerset Herald, the second son of a gentleman of Folkestone and a relation both of the Oxindens and of Thomas Milles, the Customer, had himself served an apprenticeship to a London woollen draper in 1611.[131] The Heralds were also prepared to bend the rules for their fees. Sir William Segar and Ralph Brooke were sent to the Marshalsea for giving the hangman of London a coat of arms.[132] Edward

122 Aylmer 1974: 119. Coke also judged that the trade of mercer did not derogate and that reputation was sufficient grounds for gentility: see Sayer 1979: 8–10.

123 Hobbs v. Young in *Modern Reports, King's Bench, Third Part*, p. 315.

124 Squibb 1959: 176–7; Ridley, *View Civil Ecclesiastical Laws*.

125 *Heraldic Cases, Reports 1623–1732*, pp. 30–3.

126 Ferrar, *Blazon of Gentry*.

127 Doderidge, *Honours Pedigree*, pp. 150–2. The author died in 1628, but this work was first published in 1642.

128 Styles 1978: 170.

129 Runciman 1984: 15. The Aztecs likewise gave a merchant dying in a caravan a warrior's funeral: see Soustelle 1959: 48. Mohl 1933: 181.

130 Wagner 1939: 118–19; Thrupp 1948: 260–1, 279, chap. 7; James 1978: 64–5.

131 London 1947: 28, 41–6.

132 Birch, *Court James I*, i. 86; Day 1987: 67.

Bysshe, Garter Principal King of Arms gave Robert Abbott, the scrivener, arms in 1654 'both for his good conversation & prudent behaviour reputed worthily deserving', even though Bysshe was a usurper and Abbott a Royalist.[133] Although families were disclaimed at the Visitations, it was usually for obvious usurpation or failure to appear; the Heralds had only moral sanctions and the Marshall's Court fell into disuse.[134]

The most serious issue was whether apprenticeship extinguished gentility. In 1584, a gentleman did a pirouette on the stomach of a sleeping apprentice, crying 'there little better then roogs that took upon them the name of gentleman'.[135] Sir Thomas Smith had called the apprentice a 'vera servitus', because he could not leave service or marry or employ his own capital and was liable to whipping for idleness and refractoriness.[136] Smith attacked Polydore Vergil for confusing apprenticeship with slavery, but apprentices could easily be equated with involuntary migrants. Those admitted through charity or with insignificant premiums could be treated like indentured servants.[137] It is true that younger sons had frequently entered service in great households, but their lives were usually comfortable and they were presumed to derive their status from their lord.[138]

Binding, on the other hand, abrogated important rights and introduced serious overtones of servitude. In some respects, a master acted *in loco parentis* and was held responsible for unruly prentices.[139] An apprentice ranked low in the household and could be disciplined and made to undertake the most menial tasks, including cleaning, carrying water, emptying slops, weeding the garden, housework and running errands. Henry Norris was made to clean shoes and walk to market with a hand basket; Marmaduke Rawdon served at table as did the 'young men' in the

133 Abbott 1956: 36, citing a MS of the College of Arms.

134 Styles 1978: 144; *Dugdale's Nottingham and Derbyshire Visitation Papers*, p. 95; Ashman 1988: 74; Ramsay 1969: 46; Bedell 1990: 36; Sayer 1979: pp. 9–10. James Lane, draper, disclaimed himself: see Ryland 1888.

135 Manning 1989: 202.

136 C. S. L. Davies 1966: 536, 542–3; Ogg 1955: chap. 3. The City and the guilds, as well as masters, could administer corporal punishment: see Girtin 1958: 96. On the mutual borrowings of Smith and William Harrison see Dewar 1970: 927.

137 Some judges questioned the legality of indentured servitude and the distinction between servant and prentice was often blurred: see Galenson 1981: 6, 78; Merrick 1969; Beckles 1981. Some prentices emigrated as indentured servants and there are similarities between both forms of indenture: see Main 1982: 98–9; *Rich Papers*, p. 143; Seybolt 1917: 13. The social origins of immigrants is a controversial subject: see McGrath 1954: 29–30; Clark & Souden 1988: 164, 188; Wareing 1981; 1976: 20; 1978: 199; Souden 1978: 34; Tate & Ammerman 1979: 92; Emmer 1986: 34; A. E. Smith 1947: 16–17, 39, 67–88, 309; Ballagh 1895: 38–41; Morgan 1971b: 197.

138 Neale 1950: 25; *Health to Gentlemanly Profession*, p. 115; Starkey 1987: 191.

139 Schochet 1969: 417; Lindley 1983: 54.

guilds at Livery dinners.[140] Apprentices frequently complained that they were treated worse than the servants and some masters deliberately humiliated them.[141] Daniel Newcombe was frightened by malicious tales into thinking that his master's household 'would then use him at their pleasure'.[142] An apprentice not only worked for his master without pay, but his services could in theory be sold to others.[143] He lacked independence which was the criterion of political rights. It was no coincidence that the Levellers, some of whom were younger sons who had been apprenticed, should debate so fiercely the nature of freedom and bondage.[144]

It is not, therefore, surprising that Braithwaite could write 'thou art at liberty and yet imprisoned and in more intolerable servitude' or that Chamberlayne should copy the views of Sir Thomas Smith and William Harrison and refuse in 1669 to support apprenticeship.[145] Braithwaite, however, was more accommodating and Chamberlayne admitted that it was no longer judged 'a stain and diminution', that ' of late' sons of Baronets, Knights & Gentry and even one son of an Earl had entered business. His remarks of 1669 were omitted from the 1704 edition of his work.[146] Stow emphasized that apprenticeship was a civil contract, not a form of bondage, and the author of *The Cities' Great Concern* argued that gentility slept during an apprenticeship.[147] His viewpoint was praised by

[140] Rawdon, *Life*; Kirkman, *Unlucky Citizen*, p. 36; *Norris Papers*, pp. 11–12; GLL MS 12017; *John Isham*, pp. xv, xcviii. The Mercers were exempted from carrying water: see Stow, *Survey*, ed. Strype, ii. bk 5.

[141] On the widespread use of household servants as casual labour in rural society see Kussmaul 1981.

[142] Newcombe, *Autobiography*, pp. 177–8, 183; he was particularly timid and eventually ran away. Simon Forman was beaten by both his mistress and the maids and retaliated: see his *Autobiography*, p. 6. In contrast, Thomas Busbridge liked his master and told his sister 'were bound over Wednesday last and I ware not ashamed at all': see Fletcher 1975: 337–8.

[143] Dunlop 1912: 57: Prideaux 1896–7: i. 118. The Cutlers Company once refused to cancel an indenture even at the request of the master: see Girtin 1975: 181, 195–6. In minor trades, prentices were often transferred involuntarily, but at the higher levels their contract rights were usually honoured and parents and Companies were consulted in decisions: see Ben Amos 1988: 42.

[144] Aylmer 1970: 76; Webster 1974: 101–3; Thirsk 1969: 369–70; Schenk 1944: 74.

[145] Braithwaite, *Survey of History*, p. 314; Chamberlayne, *Angliae Notitiae*, pp. 66, 434–6, 445, 478–80. Chamberlayne had strong personal prejudices and was prone to report hearsay as fact. He confidently asserted that buggery had been introduced into England by the Lombards, a notion which he may have borrowed from the third part of Coke *Institutes*.

[146] On the various editions see Arnett 1937: 25–6; Hughes 1926: 367–8.

[147] Stow, *Survey*, ed. Kingsford, ii. 331–2. *The Cities' Advocate*: this was originally published in 1629 and reprinted in 1674 with a different title. Noyes 1937: 62–6 correctly identifies the author as Edmund Bolton, a gentleman in prison for debt. For other attributions see Kelso 1929; Fuller, *Worthies*, p. 283.

Thomas Fuller and by Thoresby, who asserted the equality of gentry and merchants.[148]

The underlying problem was that budding merchants were lumped together with handicraftsmen and paupers. Persistent efforts were made to differentiate wholesaling from retailing, but in practice they overlapped in most towns. What determined the status of an apprentice was the standing of his master and the precise conditions of his binding. Increasingly masters contracted both with the apprentice and with his parents; indentures covered a specific period and could be cancelled with the consent of both parties. Students at the Inns or Universities were also subject to discipline; rich parents, like Cranfield's father, paid others to perform the servile offices.[149] As Defoe later pointed out, the inflation of apprenticeship premiums and the evolution of indentures into more businesslike contracts increased the status and independence of apprentices.[150]

Other societies

The apprenticeship of cadet gentlemen was singled out as a peculiarity of England by French social observers, like Savary, Eon and Mayerne, who attributed this fusion of noble and bourgeois to the proximity of the sea and the absence of legal barriers.[151] But England was not unique in regarding business as a respectable occupation for the well born. A business elite had evolved in the city-states and commercial empires of the Ancient World; the Arab nomads of the Diaspora despised agriculture and preferred banditry and commerce, as did the landless knights of medieval Europe.[152] The Knights Templar were important bankers and the Teutonic Order functioned like a commercial house.[153] Nobles and burghers were inextricably mixed in medieval Flanders, Venice, Genoa, Florence, Lucca and Siena.[154] English writers hostile to gentlemen apprentices claimed that the practice had spread from Italy, like the pox.[155]

148 Fuller, *Holy State*, ii. 48–9; Jacob, *City Liberties*, p. 152; Walker, *Historical Discourses*.

149 Prestwich 1966: 50.

150 Defoe, *Compleat English Tradesman*, i. 20; Stephens, *Relief of Apprentices*, p. 8.

151 Eon, *Commerce honorable*; Savary, *Parfait Negoçiant*; Mousnier 1951; BL Egerton MS 1680, fo. 187; Ascoli 1930: i. 388; Perry 1977: 96.

152 Pirenne 1958: 45–50; Renouard 1968: 426–37.

153 Piquet 1938; Postan & Rich 1963: iii. 30–4; Bordonove 1963.

154 Lestocquoy 1952: 57, 68, 103; Lane & Riemersma 1953: 59; Sapori 1970; Berengo 1965; Blanchard 1901; Hale 1973: 346–7, 371–2; Hughes 1975: 5.

155 Moryson, *Itinerary*, bk 2, 111, cited Italian examples with approval, but the *Italian Relation England*, pp. 24–6, denounced the practice. Attitudes reflected the substantial Italian presence: see Ruddock 1951; Bratchel 1979; 1980.

The Sevillian nobles in the sixteenth century responded to commercial opportunities in the New World; they intermarried with merchants and were defended by contemporary writers.[156] The bourgeoisie of Castille and Catalonia lived in close contact with the *hidalgos*.[157] In sixteenth century Lithuania, the nobility participated in foreign trade, encouraged by exemption from duties.[158] In Bohemia and Hungary, many landed families became urbanized and 70 per cent of the trade of Gdansk, in the early seventeenth century, was in the hands of gentlemen.[159] In the North German states and cities, a few nobles were involved in business.[160] Marseilles had special arrangements for the Provençal nobility in the Levantine trade and the Breton and Norman ports attracted some *gentilhommes*.[161] Jean Jacques d'Espie left home after an unhappy childhood and, once cut off from the family estate, entered trade; officers like the Bégons operated like large-scale merchants.[162]

The European nobility did not merely live on rents from land.[163] Indeed more landowners farmed their estates directly than in England. They often marketed agricultural produce and were active in mining and industrial projects, building and land speculation. French and Italian families entered the wine trade and local industries in regions like Nevers and Dauphiné.[164] In Russia they were involved with manufacturing and in Sweden active in the export copper trade.[165] For centuries, war, privateering and colonization had been treated like a business. In Germany war became a major service industry and, in France, nobles became privateers and some *gentilhommes* made a profession of duelling.[166] In

[156] Lapeyre 1955: 118–20; Pike 1965; 1966: 38–9, 159; Elliott 1971: 75; Schwartz 1979.

[157] Ribalta 1985; MacKay 1977: 127; Thompson 1979: 344; Amelang 1982; Wright 1969: 67.

[158] Loewe 1973: 33–4.

[159] Pachs 1966: 1213, 1230; Zajaczkowski 1963: 94; Burke 1985: 105–6; Bog 1971; Zaniewicki 1967; Earle 1974: 138–40; Federowicz 1976: 97, 361; 1982: 150–2; Freudenberg 1977: 8, 16; Zimanyi 1987.

[160] *International Conference Economic History* 1960: 496–510; Kellenbenz 1953–4; 1965; Beutin 1963; Lütge 1966: 376–8; Geiger 1976; Cowan 1984.

[161] AD Bouches du Rhône, ser. B. 3330, fo. 199; Masson 1896: 360; Bergasse & Rambert 1954: iv. 497, v. 111; Marchetti, *Discourse sur le négoce* and *Explication des usages et coutumes*; Mollat 1952.

[162] Tournier 1912: 516–29; Bézard 1932: chap. 9; 1931: 89–118; Dubois Rouray 1936.

[163] *Expl. Ent. H.*, 6 (1953–4): 78–160; 8 (1955): 246; 2nd ser. 1 (1968–9): 43–47; Rich & Wilson 1977: v. 447–57; Greenfield 1986. It is difficult to obtain an overall picture because the evidence is scattered and incomplete and passive investment is not always clearly distinguished from active management.

[164] Gueneau 1919: 334–5; Déyon 1967: 294–7; Gascon 1971; Léon 1953: i. 60; Dion 1959: 480–3; Forster 1961: 19–23; Morazé 1957; Maidy 1885; Gervais 1870–3.

[165] Zaozerskaza 1965: 188–222; Kirchner 1955: 246; Raeff 1983: 185, 219; Bushkovitch 1980: chap. 3; Gerschenkron 1962: 62; Fuhrmann 1972: 114; Rieber 1982: chap. 1; Baron 1980: viii. 503; Oden 1960; Roberts 1973: 123; Malowist 1959; Jeannin 1969; Banac and Bushkovitch 1983.

[166] Redlich 1964–5: ii. 271; 1956; 1958; 1957; Barker 1982: 13–16; Peju 1900; Benneton 1928: 79.

Portugal, the *conquistadores* were allowed to trade in bullion and slaves as a by-product of the Crusade against the Moors and younger sons played a major role in the colonization of the Americas and the Asian trades.[167] The French nobility were also involved in colonial settlement in the Atlantic and Caribbean, though not on a large scale.[168] Landowners also participated in business as passive investors through third parties. Like the Roman *equites*, the notables of the Italian and German medieval cities had financed trade as sleeping partners.[169] Courtiers were encouraged by their monarchs to finance pet commercial enterprises.

In most pre-industrial societies, however, the elite distanced themselves from business. In the urban civilizations of the Ancient World, the liberal arts and urban and landed property were the favoured sources of income.[170] Rome was an agricultural and plunder economy without a proper credit structure and the *optimates* devoted their efforts to war, politics, law and literature.[171] In Catalonia, Valencia and Portugal, the landed nobility disdained business.[172] Most of the minor nobles in Germany resided in poverty on their estates and the Polish nobility, though mobile, largely ignored trade.[173] The French *financiers* were mostly newly ennobled and maintained a low profile.[174] Only a tiny minority of nobles were active businessmen in Franche-Comté and Beauvais at the end of the sixteenth century or in Bordeaux, Nantes and Toulouse in the eighteenth century.[175] The *noblesse* focused instead on education to compete with their rivals in the professions.[176] The rulers of Brandenburg Prussia, like the Russian Tsars, turned the nobility into an administrative and military class; they prohibited entry into trade in return for restrictions on purchase of noble land by merchants.[177] The higher nobility which controlled the southern and eastern Netherlands was predominantly military and administrative.[178]

[167] Boxer 1969: 320; *Lettres marchandes*, pp. xxxv, lxviii; Verlinden 1970: 113–57; Boyajian 1993: 172. [168] Debien 1952: 138–40; Merle & Debien 1954.

[169] Pirenne 1953: iii. 283, iv. 440–4; Coornaert 1930: 362, 411, 445; Tracy 1985: chap. 5; Wee 1962: 364–6.

[170] French 1964: 155; Finley 1970: 23; A. H. M. Jones 1955; Hasebroek 1933: 162; Garnsey *et al.* 1983: 131ff; Rawson 1982.

[171] For differences of view among classical scholars see Duncan-Jones 1990: 46; Patterson 1980: 154; Abrams & Wrigley 1978: 74; Brunt 1967: 1094; 1971: 220–37; 1983; Badiane 1968; Syme 1986: 72; A. H. M. Jones 1974; Brown 1967: 341–2; D'Arms 1981: chap. 3; Finley 1985; Garnsey *et al.* 1983: 85–8; Wiseman 1971: app. 4; Jaher 1973: 42.

[172] Elliot 1963: 36–9; Casey 1979: 138–9; Mauro 1958: 235–7; 1983; Magalhaes-Godinho 1969. [173] Dworzaczek 1977: 147; Federowicz 1976: 36.

[174] Martin & Bezançon 1913: i. 204–5; Bonney 1981: 278–9; Shennan 1969; Dessert 1979: 464; 1984; Mousnier 1974: 110.

[175] Richard 1950: 185–8; Forster 1960: 118; Febvre 1911: 362–5; Goubert 1959.

[176] Motley 1990.

[177] Martiny 1938; Malowist 1957: 45–7; Carsten 1954: 170–3; Rosenberg 1958; Crummey 1983; Hellie 1978: 119–21; Esper 1967: 138; Meehan-Waters 1982: 10–11, 19–20.

[178] Rosenfeld 1959: 10; Wilson 1970: 13–15; Vries: 137–9; Nierop 1993: 34; Cauwenberghe 1975; Janssens 1975.

Even when there was a high level of mobility, entrepreneurial talent flowed into administration. Commercial capital was sunk into passive investments in real estate and the private and state loan markets. Businessmen purchased legal and municipal offices to acquire status, security and fiscal exemptions. This process was of great antiquity, as evidenced by the Later Roman Empire, but it became more prevalent during the sixteenth century.[179] In the fifteenth century, Andrea Barbarigo was apprenticed on the quarterdeck of a merchant galley and the Venetian patriciate combined business, war and administration.[180] But Barbarigo withdrew into office and the Venetian nobles consolidated their fortunes, closed their ranks to merchants and rigidified into a steadily diminishing caste.[181] In Genoa, the landed nobility became a closed estate and the commercial aristocracy became more financiers than traders.[182]

Florence had originally functioned like a corporation of private shareholders, but, in the fifteenth century, it developed into a territorial patriciate which, though based on civic humanism rather than on chivalric values, created a more aristocratic and less pluralistic society.[183] In the Kingdom of Naples, a similar process occurred and in the Netherlands, merchants retired from business when they entered the patriciate.[184] In Spain, although there were differences between Castille and Aragon, capital moved constantly from trade into the *censos* and *juros*, even though the rate of return fell.[185] Even the Sevillian nobles eventually invested their American profits in land, entailed their estates and turned toward Church and Office.

This retreat from business partly reflected a decline in economic opportunities as growth contracted.[186] The yield from urban property, land and government loans was often higher and more certain than trade. But it also reflected greater social rigidity. The medieval European

[179] A. H. M. Jones 1964: ii. 871, 1066. [180] Lane 1944: 13–18.

[181] Lane 1987; J. C. Davis 1962: 18–20, 26–8, 126–7; Berengo 1956; 1962; Hale 1973: 372; Burke 1974: 103–8; Finlay 1980; Pullan 1971: 573; 1964: 145.

[182] Heers 1961: 538–43, 561; Renouard & Lopez 1958; Pike 1966: 2–7, 14, 151; Lopez 1937: 429–31, 447–8; 1938.

[183] Litchfield 1986; Richards 1932; Berner 1972; Stephens 1983; Butters 1986; Becher 1967; Silva 1964: 480–91; Martinez 1963: 30–3; Goldthwaite 1968: 251, 273; Litchfield 1969a: 699, 717–18.

[184] Caracciolo 1966; Labot 1977: 45; Boxer 1962: 32–6, 312; Vries 1984; Krantz & Hohenberg 1975: 46; Barbour 1950: 140–1; Parker 1977: 48–50.

[185] Pérez 1981; Jago 1973: 230; Ringrose 1983: 312–13; Lohmann-Villena 1968; Gerbet 1970; Ortiz 1963; Salomon 1964: 290–1; Mathers 1988: 395.

[186] For different views see Grierson & Perkins 1956: 191–203; 1986: introduction; Luzzatto 1937: 54–6; Renouard 1949: 253–4; Sapori 1955: 577–95, 705ff; Braudel 1949: 622; Barbieri 1940; Sella 1979: 39–40, 79–81; Clark 1985: 164–5; Martines 1979: chap. 6; Soly 1975: 47; Herlihy 1974: 645; Phillips 1983: 282; Zlatar 1975: 113–30; Rapp 1979: 290; J. C. Davis 1975: 30–1.

nobility had been fluid and mobile. In the eleventh and early twelfth centuries, landless knights and younger sons of the nobility had been commercial entrepreneurs; only gradually did heredity replace valour in France.[187] The Flemish nobility was ill defined and closely associated with the trade of the cities; in the Northern Provinces, the burgher oligarchy was recruited from the merchant community.[188] By the sixteenth century, however, throughout Europe the nobility had developed a similar nomenclature and hierarchy and was more coherent, sophisticated and self-conscious of its privileges and interests.[189] The aristocrats were more clearly differentiated from the petty nobles. In Holland, the old commercial oligarchy was superseded by the unique Regent class, which ranked above the local nobility.[190] Blood and race assumed a great importance in continental Europe. Although the *gentilhomme* and *hidalgo* cannot simply be identified with idleness, it was widely thought that the deference of inferiors and the stability of society was best secured by separation of functions.[191] It was apprenticeship which Montesquieu later blamed for the fall of monarchy in England.[192]

This was reflected in tighter legal controls. Roman and Justinian law had proscribed business for the elite on the grounds that money corrupted and that the plebs would be subject to unfair competition; Roman senators had been prohibited from owning ships. In the seventeenth century, French nobles tried to defend themselves against competition from merchants, lawyers and officeholders by turning the custom of derogation into written law and enforcing it through enquiries into usurpation of nobility.[193] This particular manifestation of the 'feudal reaction' carried through into the eighteenth century despite its harmful impact on the poorer nobles.[194] In Denmark, even the customary sale by nobles of the surplus produce of their demesne was increasingly restricted.[195] In Piedmont, despite the burden of supporting younger sons,

[187] Perroy 1962; Salmon 1975: 94–5; Schalk 1986.

[188] Lestocquoy 1952: chap. 5; Postan & Rich 1952: ii. 294–7, iii. 17; Perroy 1961.

[189] Pirenne 1953: 165–7; Brooke 1964: 112–17.

[190] Sayous 1940; Mousnier 1968; Dijk & Roorda 1976; Marshall 1987: 162; Frijhof 1981.

[191] Garcia-Valdecasas 1958: 71; Elliot 1989: 233–4; Wright 1969; Giner 1968; Thompson 1985: 403–6; Peristany 1965; Vives 1969: 416–18; Maravall 1979; Chaunu 1984: 163; Oliveira 1971: 9.

[192] Montesquieu, *Esprit des Lois*, book 5, chap. xxi; Richelieu, *Testament Politique*, pp. 22–3.

[193] AN E.2664; Archives de la Seine I B^6/36; Belle-Guise, *Traité de la noblesse*; Wood 1980: 41–2; Constant 1973; Deyon 1964; Richard 1960: 24, 31; Grassby 1960 and references cited there; Bush 1988: 86–7; Goubert 1966: 66–7; Larmour 1966; Huppert 1977: chap. 8. On the differences between *noblesse* and *gentilesse* see Ranum 1979: 135.

[194] Goodwin 1953: 65–70, 93–105, 180; Kamen 1971: 134–8; 1984: 99; Woolf 1970: 526–8; Cooper 1983: 120–2; Labatut 1978: 128.

[195] Jorgensen 1963: 76; 1957; Petersen 1968: 1251; 1967; Dahlerup 1963; Christianson 1981: 300.

the nobility tightened ranks in the 1680s.[196] Businessmen approved of these prohibitions, because they feared competition from the privileged orders, and with some justification. In eastern Europe, the exemptions of the nobility destroyed the urban communities.

The fiscal consequences of losing their privilege of tax exemption acted as a major discouragement to noble participation in business. In fourteenth century Catalonia, *hidalgos* had been active in trade, because they enjoyed no fiscal exemptions.[197] Because the Prussian nobles, in contrast to those of Brandenburg, were not exempt from taxes, they energetically marketed foodstuffs despite their antipathy to the towns. The French Crown and its ministers did sporadically encourage participation and prohibitions could always be circumvented.[198] But even in Brittany, where special arrangements were made for the smaller nobles, the recherchés after 1660 reduced the business activities of the nobility.[199] Although the Spanish Crown removed legal obstacles to manufacturing in 1682, an aristocratic resurgence threatened entrants into business with loss of status until the late eighteenth century.[200]

The same situation prevailed outside of Europe. Islam had originally been a religion of itinerant merchants with strong egalitarian overtones. Mecca had been a merchant republic and the caliphs invested in trade; the elite of the Gold Coast traded with Europeans.[201]. But in the seventeenth century the elite Arab and Turkish families eschewed commerce.[202] In India, a Sanskrit work of the fifth century regarded business as honourable, and the Court nobility are said to have been in business in the seventeenth century, but their participation was relatively minor.[203]

In China, the merchant class of the Chhun Chhiu period was given the name of the old Shang dynasty and was probably composed of the old nobility; officials did trade through third parties and the exemptions from taxes and labour services enjoyed by the degree-holding gentry were curtailed by the Ch'ing government in the late seventeenth century.[204]

196 Woolf 1964–5: 280; Nicholas 1978.

197 Lourie 1966: 74–5; Treppo 1972; Curillier 1970; Heers 1963: 214–27; Amelang 1986; Carrère 1967; Roth 1959: 248.

198 Esmonin 1913: 229–31. Custom permitted the status of noble to lie dormant and it could always be restored by *lettres de relief*.

199 Locke, *Travels in France*, pp. 23, 94–5; Meyer 1960: 1251; Delumeau 1969.

200 Herr 1958: 97; Phillips 1979: 59–60; Kamen 1980: 263; Callahan 1972; Chaunu 1967: 167.

201 Kea 1982: 122, 205.

202 Lammens 1924; Wolf 1951: 350–6; Holt *et al.* 1977: ia. 33–6, iib. 525; Lowry 1987: 80; Watt 1967: 7; Richards 1970: 27; Brunschvig 1962: 45–6; Gotein 1966: 22; Cook 1970: 217–18; Inalcik 1969: 119–20; Lebib 1969: 91–2; Faroqhi 1984: 120; Levy 1962: 255.

203 Chandra 1966: 320–1; 1959: 96–7; Prakash 1985: 229–34; Ali 1966; Chaudhuri 1985: 212–14; Kurman 1981–3: i. 182–3; Subrahmanyam 1990a: 370–2; Hasan 1991: 356.

204 Needham 1954: i. 93; Skinner 1977: 341, 456, 462–3; Twitchett 1963; Marsh 1961; Metzger 1973; Levenson 1967; Wakeman 1985: 94, n.22; Kessler 1976: 155–7; Esherick & Rankin 1990.

The *Shen-Shih* or *Shen-Chin* in China are not strictly comparable with the European gentry, because they were identified by education and theoretically selected by merit. But formal lineage organization and venality were still exploited to support kinsmen and frustrate the examination process.[205] Confucianism was hostile to business and the elite were prohibited from trading, which as an occupation ranked lower than farming.[206] In Tokugawa Japan, *samurai* were transplanted from the land into the towns; a few entered trade and individual merit received some recognition.[207] But nobles who wished to put their sons into business paid merchants to adopt them.[208]

English society undoubtedly shared prejudices which were deeply rooted in all pre-industrial societies. Capitalist functions are inherent in any system of exchange and the conflict between the mechanism of the market and communal organization has a very long history.[209] Most Utopias envision perfectibility as the reverse image of a pecuniary culture. Trade was associated with free-thinking and freedom of choice, with a wider consciousness and a relative morality, with individual rights and constant change, all of which threatened social homogeneity. There is no objective means of assessing the depth or breadth of hostility to business, which evoked both fear and contempt. Judged by the quality of observer rather than by the quantity of comment, the majority of those who articulated their views seem to have shared a common distaste for an occupation whose acknowledged criterion was profit. They devalued business in order to trumpet the virtues of their own profession.

But there was no clear consensus of opinion on social norms; contemporaries often acted on unexpressed assumptions which were taken for granted. Attitudes diverged markedly both within and between different occupations and were continuously revised. It is difficult to determine precisely which should be regarded as dominant and how far commentators tailored their views to their audience and to changing circumstances. The debate over gentility and trade was clearly linked with economic recession and genteel unemployment; it resurfaced in each generation. In England, however, it represented a social commentary on an established

[205] For different views on the Chinese gentry see Beattie 1979: 11, 154, 183; Elvin 1973: 248–9, 291–2; Chang 1955; 1962; Ho 1959: 143–4; 1964: 77, whose data does not altogether support the conclusions drawn from it by Eberhard 1962: 178; Kracke 1947: 122–3; Levenson 1958–65; Bary 1970: 158; Hsu 1949: 770; Bielenstein 1980: 132.

[206] Brook 1981: 172; Chan 1982: 84; Fairbank 1953: i. 52.

[207] T. C. Smith 1973: 154–5; Dore 1962; Le Play 1956; Marvyama 1974; on relations between the *chonin* and the *samurai* see Hauser 1974: 4, 10; Bellah 1957: 34, 49; Kakagawa 1977: 89.

[208] Hall 1961: 41; T. C. Smith 1960: 97–102; 1959; Hall 1968: 191; Harley & Yamamura 1977: 325. On the disputed later role of the *samurai* see Hirschmeier 1964; Yamamura 1968: 145, 153; 1971: 378ff; 1974; Cain & Uselding 1973: 181.

[209] Heers 1974: 653.

practice, whereas in France it reflected political efforts to modify the rigidities of re-feudalization.

The *dignitas* of business did not depend on formal theories or hereditary status, but on the relative utility of its function compared with other occupations. Recognition of its importance was fortified by the visible and impressive growth of trade and credit, but it preceded as well as followed the social and political innovations and reversals of the seventeenth century. Although businessmen were generally disliked, it was conceded that society depended on them. The vehement denunciations of conservatives only demonstrated their inability to discredit acquisitiveness. Law and convention influenced goals but did not determine behaviour.[210] English government and society were unwilling, and probably would have been unable, to enforce external sanctions against those who did not fulfil the customary role that their position in society prescribed. Pervasive snobbery only underlined the absence of effective social barriers. Business evoked respect rather than admiration, but it was neither prescribed nor proscribed.

[210] Namier 1961: 35.

2 Obstacles to entry

The status of business depended in part on the economic advantages which it was presumed to offer. How realistic were the opportunities and what obstacles to entry might act as a disincentive? How numerous were the accessible openings and what did it cost to enter? How did business compare with alternative careers?

There was more than one route into business. Despite the Statute of Artificers, the rural and suburban textile, metal and food trades and the transportation industry could often be entered without apprenticeship.[1] Although some mariners were formally apprenticed, it was also possible to just join a ship, rise to mate and master and act as supercargo and agent for merchants in the international and coasting trades. There was constant friction between Trinity House, which served as a guild for shipmasters, and the merchants; fishermen battled over monopolistic rights.[2] But pursers and masters of colliers and merchantmen with their right of free freight moved unobtrusively from carriage into shipowning and dealing and from privateering into normal commerce and even planting.[3] Carriers and drovers assumed banking functions.[4] Professional men moved sideways into business.[5]

Entry was also possible through acquiring stock in Companies or via commercial posts. Every trade and Company could be entered by redemption and favour; children of freemen could enter by patrimony.

1 Westerfield 1915: chap. 7, 359–60; Chartres 1977b: chap. 4; Willan 1967: 50–1; Vanes 1977: 18; Stern 1979: 229–30; Sutherland 1974: 66; Brent 1975: 44; Davies 1956: 254.

2 Croft 1983: 258–63; Gragg 1991: 108–9; *Hull Trinity House*, pp. xi, xxix; Scammel 1972: 397; Jackson 1978: 19.

3 Scammel 1970: 144–53; Woodward 1978: 234; Goodman 1974: 28; Luetic 1978: 280; Tittler 1977a: 44; Davis 1962: 118–21; McGrath 1954: 291–3; 1975: 40–1; *Bristol Merchants and Merchandise*, pp. 28–9; Mundy, *Travels*, p. xxx; Claypoole, *Letter Book*, p. 4; A. S. E. Jones 1968: 247–8; Mann 1982: 223; Fairchild 1954: 24; N. J. Williams 1988: 205; *Welsh Port Books*, p. xli; Lewis 1966: 22–3; *Blakeney Maritime Trade*, p. 35; Frank 1984: 172; Anderson 1989: 145; G. Williams 1974: 69; Andrews 1991: 40, 91, chap. 4; *Portsmouth Borough Sessions Papers*, p. xxv; Norwood, *Journal*, p. 16; *Petty–Southwell Correspondence*, p. 216; Fitzmaurice 1895; chap. 1; Coxere, *Adventures*, pp. 3–4, 108.

4 Davies 1971: 18–19, 27–30; Colyer 1988: 289–90; Dodds 1952: 23; Edwards 1981: 85.

5 Dewhurst & Doublet 1974: 107.

But the main method was through apprenticeship to a master in the appropriate trade. A Freeman of London could legally practise any trade.[6] It is true that, in 1633, a committee of the Court of Aldermen excluded crafts from the liberal provisions of the Custom of London, which had been upheld in Tolley's Case of 1614; Common Council endorsed this policy in 1634, as did the Crown. But rights of patrimony effectively destroyed the equation of Company and trade; the Aldermen, who fundamentally represented the merchants, consistently resisted efforts by craftsmen to enforce demarcation. The number of openings was therefore effectively determined by the number of potential masters.

Numbers

It is extremely difficult to calculate the number of active businessmen. A simple directory of names can be assembled from a number of sources, but the latter do not clearly distinguish between merchants and artificers or indicate type of business.[7] The enterprising merchant, like William Cotesworth, 'dealt in any thing I cd gaine by', but the division of labour between businessmen steadily widened.[8] The bulk of artisans and tradesmen became both more dependent on the middlemen dealers and more specialized. In some crafts, production, processing and distribution could be combined into a real business; metal workers and clothworkers could elevate themselves into ironmongers and clothiers.[9] A shipwright could become a shipbuilder, a carpenter a timber merchant, a cloth finisher a dealer, a bookseller a paper merchant and a glazier a distributor.[10] In the Manchester cloth and linen trades, production was combined with distribution and in the specialized metal trades of the Midlands, craftsmen were genuinely independent.[11] Enterprising glovers, horners, maltsters, bakers, cheesemongers, butchers, wine coopers and textile factors pre-purchased in bulk and played the market.

But many crafts, like pottery, offered no such opportunities in this period and most prentices, including those taken by the Great Companies of London, remained simple artisans.[12] In 1641, 350 merchants were listed in the wine trade, but of these seventy-two were too poor to tax; of 752 Orphans' estates, 1666–75, only forty-one were General Merchants

[6] Medlycott 1977: 45; Aldous 1989; Hadley 1976: 28; Jacob, *City Liberties*, p. 152; Louw 1989a: 93. The Custom had originally been intended to allow the exercise of *related* trades and justified on the grounds that trade was 'liable to casualties'.

[7] See pp. 7–8.

[8] Ellis 1981a: 118.

[9] Leader 1901: 12; Francois 1966: 234; Manders 1973: 55.

[10] Pett, *Autobiography*, p. lxxiv; Youings 1968: 97; Eltringham 1953: 18; Alford & Barker 1968: 87–8.

[11] Willan 1980: 63.

[12] Weatherill 1971: 48, app. A; Rappaport 1989: table 7; Woodward 1981: 33.

as were only thirteen of ninety-five Welsh migrants to London.[13] In the Jacobean Drapers Company, only fifty-one out of 257 liverymen were merchants, in the Merchant Taylors only eight-six compared with 252 bachelors and in the Haberdashers only twenty out of forty-four Assistants.[14] Although some bachelors were dealers and some liverymen small masters, the proportion of merchants is roughly indicated by the ratio of liverymen to yeomen; 66 to 32 in the Ironmongers, 81 to 690 in the Girdlers, 39 to 108 in the Cutlers, 75 to 400 in the Stationers, 90 to 373 in the Goldsmiths and 136 to 2,106 in the Drapers.[15] London merchants exercised financial control over the country glassworkers and Midland nailers; the cutlers were subordinated to the ironmongers.[16]

It is also difficult to enumerate businessmen who resided in market towns, tiny ports and the countryside or the sworn brokers and jobbers who brought parties together in shipping and many trades.[17] It is easy to overcount, because the same men operated in several guilds and Companies, and the active merchants cannot easily be distinguished among the freemen from retirees or those who never practised their trades. Thousands of small men appear in the Port Books, but they participated only occasionally; of 326 names in the Petty Customs accounts, 1547–8, 80 per cent do not recur.[18] The number of businessmen clearly fluctuated over time and between regions and towns depending on the level of economic activity.

On the other hand, those who lived abroad or who never took their freedom can easily be omitted. Elbing had seventy-one residents, reduced to fifty and then to twenty; Hamburg had 148 residents, 1601–8, over 100 in 1620, 35 in the 1650s and 40 in 1691.[19] There were 158 resident English merchants in Teneriffe between 1600 and 1730 and 50 in Leghorn.[20] Lisbon had around thirty, Dublin forty, the Spanish ports at least twenty and Port Royal forty-nine.[21] The English Church in Amsterdam had 450 members in 1623 and 200 in 1705, though this included women, apprentices and servants; there were 50 factors, 1611–20.[22] At least 820 merchants died abroad between 1605 and 1700.[23]

In London, one indicator is the number of freemen and liverymen. By

[13] Crawford 1977: 128; E. Jones 1981: 463.
[14] Johnson 1914–22: iii. 87, 325; Clode 1888: i. 327; Archer 1991a: 50.
[15] Welch 1916–23: ii. 303–4; Prideaux 1896–7: i. app; Nicholl 1851: 301; Smythe 1905: 124; Blagden 1958a: 3.
[16] Godfrey 1976: 167; Latham 1941: 19–35.
[17] R. Downs in Marriner 1978a: 171. The bonds and petitions of brokers are in the CLRO.
[18] Whetter 1974: table 13; Ramsey 1958: 369–71.
[19] Ehrenberg 1895: 201; Lingelbach 1904: 279; Fedorowicz 1980: table 4; Zins 1973: 13, 76.
[20] Steckley 1980: 343; Barbour 1928: 554.
[21] Sims 1965: 221; Phillips 1982: 794; West 1954: 708; Zahedieh 1986a: 588.
[22] Carter 1964: 116–17.
[23] See table 10.1.

the mid seventeenth century the number of freemen has been put at 30,000 and was probably around 25,000 in the 1640s and 20,000 by the 1680s.[24] The receipts from freemen fines in the 1630s suggest an annual enrolment of some 1,800 per annum, and, during the 1670s, it was around 2,100, though numbers were arbitrarily increased by a stay of prosecutions and by waiving of charges; enrolment thereafter declined and, by 1700, the number of freemen was probably 12–15,000.[25] In Elizabeth's reign there were probably 2,500 liverymen who represented 10 per cent of householders.[26] By 1640, the number of liverymen eligible to vote had risen to 4,000 and by 1710 to 8,200.[27]

Other sources shed some light on absolute numbers. Throughout the sixteenth century, tax assessments suggest that the number of London merchants hovered around 1,000, of whom approximately one-half were prosperous and 100–200 were wealthy.[28] The Port Books for 1587–8 contain 2,195 entries, of which 80 were aliens, and 486 stand out in the subsidy returns of the 1590s.[29] By 1604 there were probably 1,000 merchants trading from London.[30] In 1606, 219 Merchant Adventurers exported cloth and in 1640, 103; some 500 entered the Levant Company between 1600 and 1640.[31] Between 1601 and 1660, some 217 great and 958 lesser merchants of London left charitable benefactions.[32] Between 60 and 100 London merchants traded with New England and the number of tobacco traders rose from 175, in 1634, to 264 in 1627–8 and 330 in 1640.[33] In 1640, 1,090 Londoners were listed as potential subscribers to a loan and in 1647, 900 subscribed a total of £200,000; in 1641, the number of wealthy lenders was, however, put at 172.[34]

In 1660 there may have been 1,000 liveried merchants and, in 1666, 3,000 were said to frequent the Exchange.[35] The number of bankers was thirty-two in 1672, forty-five in 1677 and twenty-four in 1725.[36] In 1676, there were 346 members of the Levant Company, plus 46 licensed to trade, of which 156 sent out goods in 1675 and maybe one-quarter were regularly active; by 1710, the number may have fallen to 200.[37] In the

[24] Pearl 1979b: 14, 30. [25] Kellett 1957–8: 389; McHattie 1951: 65.
[26] Thrupp 1948: 43–5; Childs 1978: 49; Archer 1991a: 258.
[27] Pearl 1961: 50; Speck 1975: 253; Krey 1985: 41; Hirst 1975: 94.
[28] Cornwall 1988: 68; *State Papers Henry VIII*, viii. 184; Lang 1963: 281; Allen 1828: ii. 343–429; Willan 1953: 10; Ramsay 1978: 535; GLL MSS 2942, 2859; Ramsay 1975: 49; 1986: 63; Reddaway 1963: 185. [29] BL Lans. MS 683, fos. 61–3.
[30] J. R. Jones in Downs 1953: 188. [31] Brenner 1993: 24, 70 n.12, 74.
[32] Jordan 1960a: 48–9, 71–4, 316. [33] Taylor 1938: 367; Nettels 1934: 157.
[34] 'London, list of principal inhabitants, 1640'; Pearl 1961: 121; SP 28/350/2.
[35] *HMC Fleming*, 42; Jordan 1960a: 49.
[36] D. M. Joslin in Carus-Wilson 1954–66: ii. 341; Horsefield 1982: 524; Melton 1986b: 33–4, 47–8, app. iii; Richards 1929: 87; Judges 1931; Heal 1935.
[37] Anderson 1989: 72; Wood 1935: 38.

1670s, the number of tobacco importers rose to almost 600; seven firms controlled 30 per cent of the supply and a further 30 per cent was in the hands of small retailers.[38] The London Directory of 1677 lists 1,953 major merchants and bankers, of which some two-thirds were in foreign trade.[39] By 1685–6, 298 merchants imported goods from Jamaica to London.[40] In the Port Books for 1695–6, 1,339 merchants are listed, evenly divided between all geographical areas and including 215 colonial traders; but only 210 exporters and 489 importers shipped more than £500 in goods.[41]

The Orphans' inventories suggest that London freemen with over £5,000 of equity capital increased slowly to around 1,000 by mid-century; those with £1–5,000 probably numbered around 4,140 and lesser merchants with £500–1,000 a further 3,200; in 1693, 10,379 paid 4s. in the £ on stock and 30.4 per cent of 11,469 houses had residents who paid the surtax.[42] The number of full-time overseas merchants probably fluctuated around 1,000 with an equal number of occasional participants. The ratio of overseas to domestic businessmen cannot be stated with confidence, but it was probably 1:4.[43]

Numbers in the five major provincial towns were much lower. Bristol, which rose by 1700 to become the second-ranking port in the realm, admitted 293 merchants and 537 large-scale dealers between 1607 and 1651, when the freemen numbered 2–3,000.[44] Between 1600 and 1699, 657 merchants were admitted and the average number was around 150; the Society of Merchant Venturers admitted 343, 1619–99, and including domestic businessmen, probably had 150 members.[45] Bristol also had 467 tobacco and 402 sugar importers, in 1672, and 202 and 316 respectively in 1702; 85 merchants supplied indentured servants to the Chesapeake.[46] In Exeter, the merchants trading to France admitted sixty-nine mercers and grocers, including thirty-six apprentices; in 1662, there were fifty exporters and, in the 1670s, some 19 per cent of 1,000 freemen were merchants.[47] The Newcastle Merchant Adventurers admitted 936 freemen during the century and York admitted 181 merchants, 1575–1600, who represented one-tenth of the freemen.[48] In Norwich, where half the

[38] Price & Clemens 1987: 2–4, 10. [39] Goss 1932: 25. [40] Zahedieh 1986a: 213.

[41] D. W. Jones 1988: 262; Clark & Slack 1972: 350; Krey 1985: table 4.8.

[42] See table 8.1. Alexander 1989: 54, table 1. The number of dealers appears to have been between 4,366 and 5,498 and the number worth over £500 between 2,900 and 3,052, but the data as presented are unclear.

[43] M. J. Power in Beier & Finlay 1986: table 27 lists 125 merchants and 386 dealers in 20 parishes.

[44] Sacks 1985: 468, table 2, apps. ii–iv; Holman 1979: 92; Stephens 1974: 161.

[45] McGrath 1975: 45; 1955: x; Minchinton 1962: xii; Ben Amos 1988: 63.

[46] Price & Clemens 1987: tables 6A, 10A; C. J. Horn in Tate & Ammerman 1979: table 5; Sacks 1987: table 2. [47] Stephens 1954: 139; Youings 1968: 93; Patten 1978: 154.

[48] *Newcastle Merchant Adventurers' Records*, p. xxiv; Palliser 1979: table 4.

freemen were in the textile industry, only 100–200 freemen qualified for the Shrievalty in the 1640s; in 1645, 95 paid a tax of 9s. and 203 paid 5s.; in 1665, 74 paid 16s. and 217 paid 10s.[49] The total number of businessmen with equity of at least £500 in the premier provincial towns was probably around 1,000, one-quarter of whom probably had capital of £1,000 or above.

Any estimate of the numbers of businessmen in the twenty-three small ports and county towns and over 800 other market centres through the country must remain, as was once said, 'provocative rather than conclusive'.[50] There were 84 Shrewsbury Drapers in 1608, 113 in 1625 and 61 in 1665; 15.8 per cent of the freemen were merchants and 5.3 per cent of those on the frankpledge lists.[51] Ipswich, Gloucester and King's Lynn had around 70 merchants apiece in the 1620s and 1630s and there were 196 merchants at Great Yarmouth.[52] Out of 116 merchants at Hull, twenty-two to thirty were substantial.[53] Twenty-seven merchants of Tudor Chester exported cloth, but only two in any quantity; in the province of Chester, 1701–20, 12.4 per cent of 285 male testators were listed as merchants.[54] Liverpool had thirty to fifty tobacco importers, 1678–99.[55] Leeds had thirteen merchants among its burgesses and thirty firms in a population of 6,000.[56] Buckinghamshire, Norfolk and Yorkshire, between 1490 and 1660, produced 535 merchant and 789 tradesman charitable testators.[57] The total number of businessmen worth at least £500 in the lesser towns and the countryside is largely guesswork, but it was probably around 1,000.

Some data do not differentiate between London and the provinces. The subscription lists of commercial and colonial Companies, 1575–1630, list 3,810 merchant investors and 123 merchant knights.[58] Between 1660 and 1700, some 450 were admitted to the Eastland Company and the major exporters to the Baltic from London and Ipswich ranged from 118 to 134 and numbered in total 397 for the whole period 1581–1624.[59] Between 1606 and 1660, 1,304 English merchants traded to Virginia, but 1,062 made just a single venture and only thirty were really active; between 1627 and the end of the 1630s the number of importers rose from 139 to some 300, but 10 per cent dominated the trade; between 1670 and 1725,

[49] Evans 1979: 22; 1974: table 8.

[50] Rich 1949–50: 255; P. Corfield in Coleman & John 1976: 223; E. A. Wrigley in Rotberg & Rabb 1986: table 1. It is impossible to count the clothiers, manufacturers and middlemen who did not reside or function in towns. On the low levels of provincial wealth see pp. 249–52.

[51] Mendenhall 1953: 85; MacInnes 1988: table 1.

[52] Willan 1967: 45–6; Talbot 1986: table 2.

[53] Gillett: 162–4; Davis 1964: 12.

[54] Poole 1962: app. 2; Lowe 1972: 74.

[55] Price & Clemens 1987: 29.

[56] Fraser 1980: 18; Kirby 1985: 48–9.

[57] Jordan 1961b: 81, 203, 210, 420.

[58] Rabb 1968a: 27, table 3.

[59] Hinton 1959: app. C; Federowicz 1980: 56.

signatories to petitions numbered 261 for the Virginia trade, 74 for New England, 45 for New York and 20 for Maryland.[60] Of 71 merchants trading to Spain, in 1576, 10 were substantial.[61] The names of 263 merchants occur in Russian sources for the century.[62] Between 1609 and 1650 approximately 400 men described as merchants proved their wills at Canterbury every decade and approximately 500 between 1650 and 1700, of whom approximately two-thirds came from London and its environs.[63] In England and Wales, 7,787 tokens were issued by 6,575 tradesmen during the century and the number of shopkeepers has been estimated at 2,151 to 2,683.[64] There were 270 apothecaries in the 1670s and 380 by 1700.[65]

Both the absolute and relative numbers of active merchants are uncertain and open to dispute. Gregory King estimated, in 1688, that there were 2,000 major and 8,000 lesser merchants; on other occasions he mentions 10,000 tradesmen, shopkeepers and vintners worth £3,000 and also 10,000 merchants, tradesmen and artificers in or within twenty miles of London inhabiting houses worth £30 p.a. 'whereof the merchants, brokers to merchants are above (500) 400'. King's occupational classifications are highly ambiguous; he never specifies whether he excludes part-timers, retirees, young factors and prentices. His numbers also vary; in 1709 and 1711, he put merchants, vintners, brewers and innkeepers at 151,000.[66] But King's 10,000 is close to an estimate projected from the London Orphans' inventories of 5,350 substantial and 5,000 lesser businessmen for the whole country. It is also consistent with the Canterbury probate evidence, if it can be assumed that at least one-half of testators described by their craft were businessmen and allowing for the fact that many chose to prove their wills elsewhere.

After 1690, longer life expectancy and expanded economic prospects may have raised numbers, but the number of businessmen appears to have remained fairly constant for most of the century and not to have increased proportionately to the growth of foreign trade. The Canterbury evidence suggests a minimum of 800 substantial businessmen before

[60] J. Horn in Tate & Ammerman 1979: 90; Olson 1983: 366–7; Pagan 1979: table 4.

[61] P. Croft in Adams & Rodriguez-Salgado 1991: 253.

[62] G. M. Phipps in *Study of Russian History* 1986: 31.

[63] See table 10.1 and its footnote.

[64] Willan 1976: 85–7; Dickinson 1980 puts the number at 14,000 including 3,000 for London.

[65] Roberts 1962a: 370; 1962b: 505–6.

[66] King, *Two Tracts*, pp. 30–1 and 'Notebook 1679–80'; Barbon, *Apology for Builder*, p. 24; *Seventeenth-Century Economic Documents*, p. 799; Cooper 1983: 439; Holmes 1977: 297–8, 303; D. V. Glass in Hollaender & Kellaway 1969. The phrase 'merchants and tradesmen by land and sea' was a copyist's slip. Lindert 1987: 388 and 1986: table 1, estimates 26,321 merchants and 101,704 shopkeepers; if by merchants he means businessmen, these estimates do not square with the available evidence.

1630, an increase of 25 per cent to 1,000 in the 1630s and then a levelling off until at least 1680.[67] Any increase probably occurred in the domestic trade and at the middling and lower levels. Businessmen always represented a small percentage of the freemen and a tiny percentage of the urban population, maybe 1.25 per cent in London and 1.1 per cent in the five major provincial towns.[68] In Sheffield, 1700–04, there were only seventeen merchants in a population of 1,629.[69] If the number of businessmen was 10,350 and each on average took one apprentice every six years, that would imply around 850 openings at the top end of business every year in London and a further 542 at the lower end; in the provinces the numbers would have been 42 and 292 respectively.[70]

Restrictions on entry

Entry into business was controlled by cartels and by lines of demarcation. In rare cases, the size of a trade was limited by statute: in 1697, the number of stockbrokers was set at one hundred and, though restrictions were later lifted, registration and sureties were still demanded.[71] Before the Civil War, many domestic industries were monopolized by royal patentees, though licences could often be purchased from the grantee or dispensation from an impecunious Crown. Usually, however, it was the export Companies and the guilds who used the monopolistic powers conferred by their charters to exclude non-members from their areas of trade.

As soon as cloth superseded wool exports, the Merchant Adventurers adopted the same restrictive policies as the Staplers; a stint of goods was imposed, though it was not enforced after Cokayne's Project.[72] The Merchant Adventurers of London clashed constantly with their provincial branches over the stint, the price of composition for impositions and

[67] See table 10.1. The increase in the number dying dates from the 1650s, but these men would have entered business some twenty years earlier.

[68] Beier & Finlay 1986: table 13; P. Corfield in Clark & Slack 1972: 305; Everitt 1968a: 118.

[69] Buckatsch 1948–9: 146.

[70] It has been assumed that every businessman on average had at least one prentice and that he would seek a replacement one year before a term expired. Labour-intensive businesses certainly had a higher intake: see Johnson 1914–22: iii. 195, app. 19; Rappaport 1989: table 4.5; Evans 1974: 56; Ben Amos 1991a: 168; Glass in Glass & Revelle 1972: table 3; P. E. Jones 1974: 57. Few of these entrants could have expected to rise above the level of artisan.

[71] Cope 1978: 2. By 1698, the jobbers had moved to Change Alley and the stock market had developed margin and options trading through brokers: see Houghton, *Collection of Letters*, no.99; Jeake, *Astrological Diary*, pp. 246, 249; Dickson 1967: 495, chap. 20; Vega, *Confusion de confusiones*. At least a dozen full-time stockbrokers can be identified.

[72] Lingelbach 1903: 10, 13. Other trades also had a stint: see E. Kerridge in Anderson & Latham 1986: 139.

the entry fees imposed on those trading to Germany.[73] The Levant Company controlled the volume of trade through regulations and the provision of General Ships. London tried to freeze out the outports and excluded Bristol from the chartered Companies. In turn, ports like Hull tried to exclude Londoners from their backyard in the northern seas. Lilburne and *Britannia Languens* attacked the monopolistic Companies as major obstacles to younger sons.[74] After 1660 and particularly after 1688, the export oligopolies, with the exception of the Levant and East India Companies, were shorn of their exclusive privileges.[75] For much of the century, however, they limited opportunities for outsiders in key markets.

Paranoid about competition, business institutions compartmentalized functions and discouraged vertical integration.[76] The export Companies and the provincial ports attempted to restrict membership to 'meer merchants' or 'one that hath used only merchandising to forraign parts'.[77] The retailers and tradesmen suspected that the better-capitalized wholesalers would engross merchandise in their warehouses and deal directly with the consumers at wholesale prices; the import merchants were concerned that artificers would form a majority in the guilds and that retailers would employ their own factors, hold their stock and undercut prices.[78]

The main defensive tactic was however a limit on the number of entrants. Applicants could be reduced by imposing age limits and required skills, but the usual method was to establish a quota of apprentices per member, weighted in favour of senior members.[79] The Merchant Adventurers and Eastland Companies limited a master to one apprentice for seven years and then to two for the next thirteen years.[80] This was ostensibly to safeguard quality of training, but in reality to reduce competition when the demand for commodities was limited. In a depression, as was pointed out in the 1620s, 'to ad more persons to bee

[73] Parker, *Free Trade*, p. 22; *Newcastle Merchant Adventurers' Records*, i. pp. 6–29, ii. pp. xxiv, 43, 95–6; *Eastland Company Acts*, pp. 28, 49.

[74] Gibb 1947: 82; Aylmer 1970: 122; *Early English Tracts Commerce*, p. 336; McKeon, 1975: 108.

[75] *Seventeenth-Century Economic Documents*, p. 528.

[76] The rules varied between towns and Companies. See MacCaffrey 1958: 137; D. M. Palliser in Clark & Slack 1972: 91; M. G. Davies 1956: 98; M. Reed & A. Rose in Clark 1981; Fieldhouse 1978: 173.

[77] SP 105/153, fo. 37; PC 2/45, fo. 171; BL Add. MS 9265, fos. 23, 31; *Spanish Company* 1973: 83–7; Willan 1953: 3; *Bristol. Records Merchant Venturers*.

[78] Kramer 1927: 109–16; Lipson 1931: ii. 221; *Seventeenth-Century Economic Documents*, pp. 21–3.

[79] The Staplers had excluded those worth £40 p.a. in land if they were older than 17: see *Staple Ordinance Book*, p. 134. In some guilds, the Wardens scrutinized apprentices before their indentures were enrolled at Guildhall; in others they had to be presented within one year of enrolment: see *Skinners' Records*, p. 256.

[80] Hinton 1959: 56; Hatcher & Barker 1974: 195–6.

marchants adventurers is to put more sheepe into one and the same pasture which is to sterve them all'.[81] The Merchant Adventurers of Exeter, which had a monopoly of foreign trade, limited participation to those who had been apprenticed to an ancient merchant or who had eighteen years' experience.[82] Even rights of patrimony were abridged, as in Exeter in the 1590s.[83] The established businessmen preferred most apprentices to remain as unfree journeymen.[84] The Stationers held down the number of master printers and, in 1700, there were still only 331 printers and booksellers in England.[85] Until 1640, the freemen of the Clothworkers numbered 2,100, but most were consigned to the yeomanry and, though the latter could be licensed to employ journeymen, the period of apprenticeship was raised to ten years.[86]

In practice, these attempts to control access were never uniformly successful. Restrictions on numbers of apprentices were not enforced by the middle of the century. Whatever their regulations prescribed, the Companies lacked the resources to effectively discipline their own members, quite apart from mariners and interlopers; 7.9 per cent of shortcloths were illegally exported to Germany in 1598 and eight merchants traded outside the mart town.[87] Although a monopoly, the organization of the Levant Company was less restrictive than those of the Eastland and Russia Companies.[88] The East India Company which alternated between outright prohibition and restriction, allowed retired factors and seamen to trade as free merchants in return for a percentage of their business; the country trade was entirely private after 1667 as was the re-export of Indian goods.[89] Although most merchants diversified their interests when their traditional trade faltered, new opportunities were largely developed by new groups of entrepreneurs.[90] When successful, however, innovators became equally exclusive. Other merchants specialized by commodity rather than area and created their own niche.[91] Despite periodic efforts to institutionalize trade with the American Plantations, the Caribbean, France and Spain, these areas remained relatively open and unregulated and cheaper to enter.[92]

[81] BL Add. MS 34324, fo. 195, cited by Gould 1954–5: 88; *Seventeenth-Century Economic Documents*, p. 20; D. M. Palliser in Clark & Slack 1972: 112.

[82] Cotton 1872: 60, 160; MacCaffrey 1958: 136–59; *Seventeenth-Century Economic Documents*, p. 433.

[83] Cotton 1872: 61; George 1936: 167–95.

[84] Thomas 1977: 4.

[85] Plant 1974: 64, 134.

[86] Girtin 1958: 10–11, 239.

[87] Baumann 1990: 42; Federowicz 1980: 63.

[88] PC 2/55, fo. 159; *Select Charters Companies*, p. xi; Rowland & Manhart 1924: 172; Wood 1935: 95.

[89] Watson 1980a: 74–7; Gillespie 1920: 171–2; Chaudhuri 1978: 132; Wretts-Smith 1963: 118.

[90] Brenner 1993: 60.

[91] Croft 1987c: 12.

[92] *English Adventurers*, pp. 89–90; Sheridan 1974: 263.

In the provincial ports, the volume of foreign trade was often insufficient to support a whole business, and, despite strenuous efforts in ports like Bristol to exclude retailers and artisans, it was inevitable that overseas merchants would engage in the domestic trade and vice versa. One-third of the shareholders of the first joint-stock of the East India Company were domestic tradesmen and goods could be 'coloured' or capital employed through third parties.[93] In York, Bristol and Chester, retailers invested in foreign cargoes and, in 1607, 12 per cent of exports to Spain were sent by domestic wholesalers.[94] Booksellers travelled abroad to buy and handled an infinite variety of retail goods as well as serving as bankers and property developers.[95] Fifteen Exeter tuckers entered foreign markets between 1670 and 1700 and the Midland ironmongers had world-wide interests.[96] Domestic and foreign trade were closely interconnected and the redistribution of imports like tobacco, sugar, drugs and spices was a major factor of growth.[97] The provisioning of merchant and naval ships and of the Plantations linked rural production with foreign markets and by the end of the century England had become a grain exporter.[98]

Opportunities were most numerous in the domestic trade, whose volume was four times greater than international trade.[99] Silkmen, salters, grocers, harberdashers, woollen and linen drapers and leather-sellers distributed the raw materials for manufacturing. Entrepreneurs experimented with advance purchase and sales through sample; itinerant agents scoured the countryside and the regional fairs acting for sedentary merchants in London. The grain trade in the early part of the century was open to young men and numbers increased to 420 in 1615 and 481 in 1638, though this changed at the end of the century.[100] London had always been an internal distributive centre and half the Jacobean aldermen were in the domestic trade.[101] Wholesalers increasingly contracted directly with producers and London was unique in having specialized large-scale middlemen in the food and fuel markets. By 1700, full-time 'warehousemen' serviced both merchants and retailers and the metropolitan area had become a major shipbulding, transportation and processing centre with some large workshops.[102]

[93] Carus-Wilson 1934: 176; Willan 1953: 45; Robbins 1969: 96.

[94] Taylor 1968: tables 1 & 2, 10–14; Lowe 1972: 56.

[95] Plant 1974: 95–6; *Rhodes Memorandum Book*, p. 31; Pollard 1978: 14; Bennet & Clemens, *Notebook*, pp. 24–5; M. Harris in Myers & Harris 1985: 18; Cave 1899: 3; G. H. Jenkins in R. R. Davies 1984: 164; Morgan 1978: 7–8; Parks 1976: 26, 133; R. Thompson in Allen & Thompson 1976: 39.

[96] Youings 1968: 94; Rowlands 1977: 52; 1975.

[97] Wake 1979; Travers 1990: 67–8; Truxes 1989: 15.

[98] Ormrod 1985.

[99] Willan 1976: chap. 4; Everitt 1969; J. A. Chartres in Thirsk 1971: iv. 469–95, 501–2; D. E. C. Eversley in E. L. Jones & Mingay 1967: 213; Chartres 1977b: 10–11 rates the internal trade at 21 per cent of National Income.

[100] F. J. Fisher in Carus-Wilson 1954–66: i. 59.

[101] Lang 1963.

[102] James 1956: 364–76; A. L. Beier in Beier & Finlay 1986: 142–51.

Provincial England had a high volume of inter-regional trade in domestically produced foodstuffs, fuel, raw materials and manufactured goods.[103] Towns, like Worcester, Gloucester and King's Lynn lived on the distributive and coastal trades rather than on foreign markets. The textile industry produced primarily for the English market.[104] It is easy to overlook the importance of the metal, glass, soap, brewing and leather industries; the coal trade was highly organized with several layers of middlemen.[105] Bristol had substantial distributors and processors, as in the soap and sugar industries.[106] Provincial mercers and drapers discounted bills and sustained the credit and remittance system. Despite corporate restrictions, the more dynamic provincial towns grew at the expense of their less enterprising rivals.

Nor could retailing be wholly divorced from wholesaling. Although defined as direct sale to the consumer, it was really a question of scale. The service trades all overlapped and most of those who kept a shop also dealt wholesale.[107] In Bristol, Exeter, Liverpool and Southampton there was no clear line.[108] Specialization certainly increased and the standing shop and product differentiation became more common, particularly in London and the major towns.[109] Inns began to emerge as rival centres of business.[110] But the timing of sales was still linked with regular urban markets; retailers still bought at fairs and usually derived some of their income from agriculture.

Nonetheless, business was concentrated in a few hands. Although the great merchants usually had multiple interests, most trades were controlled by family networks. In the sixteenth century a tiny minority of merchants had dominated the export trade of London, Bristol, Chester, Exeter, Newcastle and Yarmouth.[111] Maybe 12 per cent of the business community in the first half of the seventeenth century controlled 44 per cent of the cloth exports in the German, Levant and Spanish trades; in 1606, twenty-six out of 219 exported nearly half the cloth.[112] In the Eastland trade, there were five important merchants, forty-eight regular

[103] Kingman 1978.

[104] Bowden 1962: 49–53; Ramsay 1965: 102–4; 1982; Kerridge 1985; Coleman 1969a; Pilgrim 1959: 39–44; 1940; Allison 1961: ii. 69; Ponting 1971: chaps. 4–5; Mann 1971: 18–21. [105] Nef 1932: i. 440. [106] Sacks 1987: table 8.1.

[107] BL Harl. MS 2104, fo. 34; Hunt. Lib. MS 1264, fo. 157; Stow, *Survey*, ed. Strype, i. 287.

[108] *Southampton Assembly Book 1609–10*, ii. p. xxx; *Bristol Merchants and Merchandise*, p. xxi; Latimer 1900: 473; W. G. Hoskins in Bindoff *et al.* 1961: 171–2.

[109] Bergier 1980: 120; D. Davis 1966: 103; Priestley 1985a; Clark 1984; Holderness 1972: 37; Shammas 1990: table 8.4.

[110] Clark 1983: 8; J. A. Chartres in Havinden 1973.

[111] Ramsay 1985: 159; Poole 1962: 79; Clark & Slack 1972: 91; N. J. Williams 1988: 216.

[112] Friis 1927: 77–81, 232ff; Ramsey 1961–2: 9, 138–9; Wheeler, *Treatise of Commerce*, pp. 339, 377; B. Dietz in Knecht & Scarisbrick 1978; 191, 203.

exporters and seventy-five minor participants.[113] At Archangel, a small ring of twenty great merchants controlled half the total imports and there were only seventy-six medium-size merchants and 167 small importers who together had only 7 per cent of the trade.[114] The Swedish trade was dominated by thirty English and Scottish purchasing agents.[115] Only twenty-six Hostmen were admitted in Newcastle, 1600–59, and there were only twenty Lords of Coal.[116] The Virginia trade was dominated by 10 per cent of the merchants and concentration increased after 1686; there was a core of 20 merchants in the Bristol slave trade.[117] In the East India Company, after 1660, stock changed hands mainly between existing shareholders and, in 1691, eight men controlled the Company.[118] The overall trend was towards greater specialization by commodity, by export or import and by area.[119] Paradoxically, an increase in the volume and complexity of foreign trade reduced the number of major players.

The vacancy rate in business reflected the attitudes and interests of individual merchants. Some made a business out of training apprentices and they profited from premiums and cheap labour. In boom years or in the aftermath of plague, they increased their intake. But when business contracted and competition stiffened, many voluntarily declined to exercise their rights. They refused offers or deliberately charged high premiums, because they felt unable to discharge the responsibility of providing business, when busy with other commitments or as they grew older and less active.[120] What places were available were usually reserved for relatives and friends; the guild system was a gerontocracy and patrimony and family preference gave all Companies and trades an hereditary character.

Costs

Direct entry into business for those who were not sons of freemen was deliberately discouraged by high redemption fees. The Merchant Adventurers of London, in 1608, charged £200 and double impositions for five to seven years.[121] A Proclamation in 1634 set the fine at £50 (£25 for the outports), but in 1643 £100 was authorized and £50 for outsiders; after the Restoration it was further reduced in stages until by 1688 it was only

113 Hinton 1959: 57, 116–18.
114 Aström 1963: i. 159, 189–92, 224–5, apps. 9–11.
115 H. Rooseveare in Minchinton 1988: 30.
116 Howell 1967: 20.
117 Pagan 1979: 259–60; Price & Clemens 1987: 12; Price in Greene & Pole 1984: 38; *Bristol Africa and Slave Trade*.
118 K. G. Davies in Carus-Wilson 1954–66: ii. 284, 289.
119 Hinton 1959: 57; D. W. Jones 1988: 272; Price & Clemens 1987: 20, 24.
120 *HMC Var. Coll.*: ii. 172.
121 *Discourse for Enlargement Foreign Trade*, p. 27.

40s.[122] Although entrance fees were temporarily reduced during the 1620s, the Levant Company charged £25–50, the Eastland Company charged £20 (reduced in 1670 to 40s.) and the Russia Company £50 plus an extra £50–60 for trading to Narva.[123] Despite opposition in Parliament, these survived until late in the century. Even the joint-stock Companies had property qualifications. In the early years of the East India Company, the freedom could be acquired with £100 of stock, by redemption for £50 or by apprenticeship for 50s.; but by the 1630s, it took £2,000 to become a Director.[124]

Entry by redemption into the freedom of both cities and guilds varied enormously in cost. The City of London charged £20, though this was often reduced or waived; Liverpool charged from £6 13s. 4d. to £25, Northampton £15–20 and Leeds £50 by the end of the century.[125] The Cutlers of London charged only £2 in 1614 and 15s. in 1675.[126] But the Grocers charged £30, the Glovers £10 and the Haberdashers £20, reduced to 40s. in 1699.[127] The provincial guilds also charged high redemption fees; in Bristol, the Merchant Taylors of Bristol asked £30 and the Merchant Venturers £20–30; in Colchester, the Clothiers imposed fees of £15–60 until 1715.[128]

The majority of new recruits entered by apprenticeship – 229 out of 372 in the Levant Company.[129] Apprentices faced three entrance fees, to their Livery Company, to the City and to their chartered Company, when applicable. The Livery Company fees were not too onerous, though they varied according to the importance of the trade and there were several petty charges. Many fees had been fixed in guild ordinances in the early sixteenth century and were regulated by statute. Fees for binding and presentation varied from 2s. 4d. to 6s. 8d. together with from 4d. to 4s. 6d. for the Clerk, who often drew up the indenture, and from 4d. to 1s. for the Beadle.[130] The fee for taking the freedom of a guild varied from 2s. to £1 3s. 10d. with a payment of around 3s. 6d. for the Clerk and sometimes a present, such as a silver spoon.[131] Fees did rise in the seventeenth century: the Butchers charged only 3s. 4d. until 1638, when £2 was authorized.[132]

[122] *Merchant Adventurers' Ordinances*, pp. 26–8, 35; BL Hargrave MS 321, fo. 94v° argued that throwing open the trade would be unfair to those parents who had invested money in their children. Ashton 1979: 155.

[123] GLL MS 1174/2; SP 105/155, fos. 389, 404; Hinton 1959: 56; Zins 1973: 117–19; North 1984; Aström 1963: i. 159, 183–4, 189–92, 224–5; Croft 1987a: 129.

[124] Chaudhuri 1965: 33, 59.

[125] Chandler 1960: 39, 351; R. G. Wilson 1971: 35.

[126] Welch 1922: ii. 66, 70.

[127] Archer 1991b: 99.

[128] Fox 1880: 95; McGrath 1975: 44; Burley 1957: 129; Cresswell 1936: 59.

[129] Brenner 1993: 70.

[130] Clode 1875: 208–9; Consitt 1933: 134; Dummelow 1973: 15.

[131] Crawford 1977: 77; P. E. Jones 1938: 45; *Masons' Records*, p. 139.

[132] P. E. Jones 1970: 23; Welch 1916–23: ii. 62; Watson 1963: 101; Plant 1974: 139–43; Clode 1892: 15; *Founders' Wardens' Accounts*, p. xxxix.

The provincial guilds sometimes stipulated a dinner on taking the freedom, a piece of plate or a contribution to repairs of the Hall.[133] The Merchant Venturers of Bristol charged 4s. 6d. and in Exeter 5s.; the Mercers Company of Lichfield, £1 plus 3s. 4d. for the Clerk.[134] The combined fees in many trades could amount to three guineas and £3–5 in the Chester leather trade.[135] The cost of admission to the freedom of London was not exorbitant – 4s. for freedom by apprenticeship, 18d. by patrimony and 15s. 4d. for translations.[136] But merchants trading overseas still resented the obligation.[137] Freedom by service in a provincial town cost from 3s. 4d. upwards; it was 4s. 6d. in Bristol, 6s. 8d. in Liverpool and 20s. in York.[138] The regulated Companies also charged moderate entrance fees for prentices; it was 20s. in the Levant Company and 12s. 6d. in the Russia Company.

The major expense for an apprentice was the premium paid to his master. This had originally been a bond or present and it was the labour which prentices could supply which still interested the small masters.[139] But those destined for business were treated more as pupils than servants.[140] Indentures were increasingly negotiated between parent and master and regarded as contracts which specified the form of instruction and even the terms of foreign residence. Indentures began to include provision and charges for schooling and even instruction abroad in languages for one to two years.[141] Sometimes part of the premium was allocated to a merchant resident abroad, who assumed the duties of supervision.[142]

It is difficult to generalize about the level of fees because they were fixed by individuals and not by institutions and because there is no continuous series of returns for all trades for the whole century. It was not until 1709 that there was a legal obligation to record the premium and references to fees in indentures and correspondence do not always make clear the nature and importance of the business. Premiums were sometimes adjusted downwards to the means of parents and reduced for friends and kinsmen or if a prentice served a longer term or earned for his master.[143] A merchant whose reputation and attentiveness and powers of patronage were not rated high would not attract applicants unless his qualifications

[133] *Bristol Soapmakers' Proceedings*, p. 208.
[134] Cotton 1872: 17, 60; Russell 1893: 124.
[135] Holman 1979: 91; Woodward 1967: 92; McGrath 1975: 401.
[136] On the mandatory rules see Kellett 1958: 385.
[137] Anderson 1989: 70.
[138] *V.C.H. York* 1961: 183.
[139] Ramsey 1958: 384.
[140] Dunlop 1912: 181, 196, 210.
[141] *Southampton Calendar Apprentices*, p. xxii; *Norris Papers*, p. 10.
[142] An alternative method was for the surrogate master to enjoy a percentage of profits on the prentice's capital: see Bright 1858: 181.
[143] Nat. Lib. Wales Wynn MS F.iii.18.

were reflected in lower fees. There is no doubt, however, that the level of premiums rose dramatically and continuously.[144] The cost reflected the supply of masters, which remained constant, and the demand for places, which was increased by pressure on all forms of employment and by expectations of profit. Successive editions of Stow illustrate the process; by James I's reign premiums had risen to £20–100 and 'sometimes £100 and now these prices are vastly enhanced to £500 or £600 or £800'.[145] By the early eighteenth century, Defoe put premiums at £2–300 in the country and £500–1,000 in London.[146]

The inflation of premiums was most severe in those areas of London's foreign trade, like the Levant, which were popular with the gentry. The usual rate was £2–300 in the first half of the century, £3–400 by the 1670s and £1,000 by the end of the century.[147] Blanch, in 1698, attacked Child's assertion that fees had increased by one-third during the previous twenty years.[148] But he accepted that the cost was high and he attributed it to better opportunities and training; the 'scarcity of good places' was a consequence of fewer principals, more foreign commission agents and more younger sons.[149] The Levant was not typical of all foreign trades and some parents secured a bargain.[150] But in the early seventeenth century, the German and Dutch traders could command £2–400 and the Mediterranean traders £4–600.[151]

The export trades of those provincial towns which expanded were certainly less crowded and less costly. In 1625, the Exeter merchants trading to France asked £10 for eight years.[152] Bristol seems to have low fees of about £100 excluding sureties rising to between £150 and £210 by the eighteenth century.[153] In Liverpool and the North, £130 sufficed in the 1700s, though premiums later rose to £4–500.[154] The maritime and coastal trades were even more reasonable.[155] Despite variations in costs,

[144] Winchester 1955: 223–5; S. L. Thrupp in Postan & Power: 256; Yonge 1951: 26.

[145] Stow, *Survey*, ed. Strype, ii. 329; on Strype's additions see Morrison 1977: 47.

[146] Defoe, *Compleat English Tradesman*, i. 20, 147.

[147] Ambrose 1931–2: 240–7; Berks. RO D/EZ56/1, letters 21 and 24 April 1701; Lincs. AO Heathcote MS 1/11; Brenner 1993: 70 n.50; Grassby 1994: 24; Anderson 1989: 101; GLL MS 10823/1; Bod. Ashurst MS DD Ashurst C.1, letter 12 July 1680; Woodbridge 1969: 784; Holmes 1967: 166 citing M. Ransome; the figure of £11,000 in the text must be a misprint.

[148] *East India Company's Reply* (1681): 15; *HMC Lords MSS 1695–7*, ii. 42–3; *Norris Papers*, p. 10.

[149] Blanch, *Interest of England*, pp. 56–7; W. E. Minchinton in Aitken 1965: 23.

[150] *Wynn Papers Calendar*, p. 80; SP 46/83, no.44; D. R. Hainsworth in MacGregor & Wright 1977: 67; Marescoe, *Markets and Merchants*, p. 100; Sutherland 1962: 3.

[151] Bod. Dep. MS C.23, fo. 11; Berks RO D/ED F 41; R. Davis in Fisher 1961: 126; Hainsworth 1988: 156.

[152] Stephens 1954: 139; Croker, *Life*, p. 302.

[153] *Bristol Merchants and Merchandise*, p. xi; Yarbrough 1980: table 3.3; Ben Amos 1988: 62–3 shows lower levels of £2–14.

[154] Hughes 1952a: i. 104–6; 1952b: 55; Wilson 1981: 80.

[155] N. J. Williams 1988: chap. 5, 200–3.

all branches of foreign trade nevertheless became more expensive to enter.[156]

The domestic trades were much cheaper. Since they had less prestige, they attracted fewer candidates who could afford high premiums.[157] In London and the provinces, the usual level was £10–20 for craftsmen and £70–100 in trades with real business potential, though some masters could charge £300.[158] Apothecaries paid £40–50; although they could also acquire their freedom through purchase and patrimony, some evidence of capacity to handle medicines and of knowledge of anatomy was required.[159] In Bristol, premiums ranged from £34 to £250, but they averaged £100 plus sureties rising to £150–200 by 1700.[160] In 1681, it was said that the shopkeeping trade could be entered for £50–60 in a country town compared with £100 in London.[161]

There were also other charges. Sureties for good behaviour were more frequently demanded and for larger sums. Bonds were posted for 6.1 per cent of Bristol indentures and in some trades £1,000 bonds were demanded by the end of the century, although sureties could be offered by more than one guarantor.[162] Any cash deposited was returned, but the master received the interest. One pamphleteer condemned those who 'make a kind of trade of it to take great sums of money with apprentices' and wanted Parliament to prohibit sureties.[163] Some costs for tuition were incurred before an apprenticeship. By 1722, the cost of a commercial education was quoted at £26 per annum for boarding, three guineas for

156 Stephens, *Relief of Apprentices*, p. 7.

157 Nethercot 1938: 32–3; Edmond 1987a: 25.

158 Simpson 1961: 116–17; Oglander, *Commonplace Book*, p. 235; Cliffe 1969: 45; Plummer 1972: 76; Blagden 1960: 248–9; Finberg 1957:170; Healey 1992: 21; Josselin, *Diary*, pp. 530–2; Seaver 1985: 236; Welch 1922: 61; *Sussex Apprentices*, pp. 111–13; Plant 1974: 151; McDonald 1964: 24–5. Campbell, *London Tradesman*, lists a wide range of premiums; Burnby 1983: 27, 94–5; Thomas 1971: 11–13; Priestley 1985a: 190–4. Apothecaries and surgeons frequently overlap in the records: see Whittet 1964: 259. Although the apothecaries needed a sophisticated knowledge of botany and chemistry to make up medicines and resembled the modern general practitioner, they were closely associated with the grocers and, as suppliers of drugs, were in effect retailers who served an apprenticeship in a shop. They have therefore been classified as businessmen and not with the professions.

159 Cameron & Wall 1963: i. 77, 80; Copeman 1968.

160 ULL MS 554, indenture; Lincs. AO Whichcote MS 21/18; IESRO HE/30, will of William Blois, 6 Feb. 1671; Wilson 1971: 23–4, table 4; *Wiltshire Apprentices*, p. xiv; *Sussex Apprentices*; *Bedfordshire Apprentices*, p. 148; *Leicester Register Freemen*, pp. 382, 388; Burley 1958–9: 290; Stout, *Autobiography*.

161 *Trade of England Revived*, p. 30; Wadsworth & Mann 1931: 33, 73–4; Aikin, *Description Manchester*, p. 182; *Newcastle Hostmen Records*, p. liv; *Leicester Register Freemen*, pp. 382, 388; Burley 1957: 34; *Wiltshire Apprentices*, p. xiii; Barnet 1968: 23; Lane 1988: 17; Pelling 1982: 495; 1983: 5–8.

162 Archer 1991b: 50; Anderson 1989: 68–9; Ben Amos 1988; Holman 1979: 89; Hall 1957: 124; 1965: 119; McGrath 1985.

163 Stephens, *Relief of Apprentices*, pp. 2–3.

writing and arithmetic and three guineas for merchants' accounts.[164] Books and transportation were also necessary and expensive.[165]

Before 1650, apprentices were often treated like children who received their food, lodging and replacement clothing from their masters or received wages in lieu of apparel.[166] Thereafter, however, parents often had to pay for clothing, laundry and medical expenses, though practice varied considerably and provincial apprentices were sometimes sent to London without any maintenance.[167] Special apparel was a particular bone of contention and some parents paid extra to exempt their children from menial tasks; additional pocket money and gifts were necessary to avoid a sudden drop in a prentice's standard of living. It is often difficult to determine if maintenance was included in the premium quoted, because separate provision became so common.[168]

The cost of entering business was directly related to fashion, prospects and competition for places. It would be wrong to conclude that it was so universally high that no propertied family could afford to place one younger son at least in the domestic trade. Theoretically a father could discharge his responsibilities by one capital payment which he could borrow or even pay in instalments. But high premiums were a disincentive and whereas at the beginning of the century the major trades were within reach even of minor gentry families, by the end those trades which were most acceptable were reserved for the wealthy and connected or for sons of established merchants. Even merchants had difficulty finding the premium.[169] Charities only provided funds for artisan apprentices.

The money invested in an apprenticeship could also be lost. If an indenture was broken, the premium was forfeited.[170] A master could also fail financially and disappear into hiding or prison or emigrate.[171] Sometimes a master had himself neglected to take his freedom.[172] If a prentice died before the end of his term, a master was usually contractually obliged to return a proportion of the fee.[173] If a master died, his widow or son could take over or the prentice could be turned over to a new master; sometimes the executors made a financial settlement with the parents. But frequently prentices were discharged and set adrift; masters omitted to enrol their indentures and replaced them with new pren-

[164] Watts, *Essay Forming Man of Business*, p. 9.
[165] Plant 1974: 238–47; Johnson 1950: 83–112.
[166] Dunlop 1912: 180, 196; Stephens thought that servants were better off with wages and maintenance; SP 46/85, no.66.
[167] Claypoole, *Letter Book*, p. 186; Fowkes 1965: 451. [168] SP 46/84, no.93.
[169] ULL MS 553, letter Aug. 1675; Melton 1986a: 146; Cressy 1976a: 310; Barlow, *Journal*, p. 15. [170] Newcombe, *Autobiography*, p. 76.
[171] *Yorkshire Diaries*, ii. 24; J. M. Price in Davenport-Hines 1989; *Norris Papers*, pp. 10–12.
[172] Stephens, *Relief of Apprentices*, p. 8; Bacon, *Works*, vi. 269; Keynes 1966: 131.
[173] Bod. Dep. MS C.23, fo. 11.

tices.[174] The pressure on places made the safeguards against dishonesty and irresponsibility of little effect. Once the premium had been paid, there was no certainty of recovery at law. Even gentlemen prentices were also subject to physical abuse, though this was more characteristic of poor children put to artisan trades; in the hierarchy of the household, junior prentices could be bullied by their seniors as well as by the mistress and maids.[175] Hundreds of cases were brought before the Wardens of guilds, at Quarter Sessions and in the municipal, Common and Civil Law Courts and in Chancery.[176] Prentices sometimes won their case, but justice was uncertain when the jurors and sometimes the judges were businessmen.[177]

Seven years was laid down as the minimum period of service by the Custom of London and the Statute of Artificers; eight was usual and some guilds, like the Stationers, and some Companies, like the Eastland Company, insisted on even longer terms.[178] In the Weavers Company, one-half served seven, one-third eight and one-tenth nine, with an average of eight years.[179] The long terms had no educative justification, but they delayed manhood and protected the old against the young. They reflected the fact that an apprentice was most valuable to his master in his final years, when he had learned the business; masters would sue for loss of service and they sometimes as a favour remitted residues of terms in their wills.[180] Apprentices did often begin to earn before their service was complete.[181] But restrictions on trading before taking the freedom, even in partnership with a master and towards the end of a term, were enforced by fines and expulsions.[182] Business did not offer congenial conditions of

174 Stephens, *Relief of Apprentices*, p. 11.

175 For examples of brutality see *Newcastle Merchant Adventurers' Records*, i. 241; Beier 1978: 215–21; Kirkman, *Unlucky Citizen*, p. 148; Grubb 1992: 105.

176 Cotton 1872: 157–8; REQ 2/C1/3, case of Henry Fawcett, C2 Jas I/L. 18/39, William Lucas v. James Kicker; GLL MS 12017; Bohun, *Privilegia Londinium*, pp. 337–74; *Southampton Assembly Books 1609–10*, p. 98; S. R. Smith 1981: 457; Pape 1938: 286; *Western Circuit Assizes Orders*, no.803; Rushton 1991: 97; Seaver 1989: 50–6; Earle 1989a: 92–6, 100–2; Fletcher 1988: 218. Of 269 cases in the Lord Mayor's Court, 1641–71, 23 concerned gentlemen prentices: see P. Seaver in Kunze & Brautigam 1992: 135–6.

177 *Newcastle Merchant Adventurers' Records*, i. 199–200.

178 Hinton 1959: 56; *York Mercers*, p. 274; Cotton 1872: 172; Lingelbach 1903: 10–12. An average length of service was 7.5 years, though gentlemen served longer because they began younger. See Rappaport 1989: 321, table 8.9; Earle 1989a: 359; Ben Amos 1991: 166; Evans 1979: 10; Rappaport in Rappaport *et al.* 1991: 252 n.36.

179 Plummer 1972: table 4.1.

180 Thomas 1977: 12–14, 25: seven appears to have been a popular number and twenty-four a much invoked age. Baker 1990: 518.

181 Woodward 1969: 296 points out that the Statute of Artificers permitted payment for prentice labour, though it was probably pocketed by the master; *Southampton Calendar Apprentices*, pp. xx, 41.

182 Peele 1939: 213; Lancs. RO MD DDB, Barcroft MSS; Cotton 1872: 17, 60; *Newcastle Merchant Adventurers' Records*, pp. 183, 190, 199.

work and it required a period of unpaid training equivalent to one-quarter of a man's life.

Alternative careers

The alternatives to business divided broadly into vocations, like the Church and medicine with their academic enclaves, which required some intellectual or moral training, and practical professions, like the law, arms and public office, each of which had a body of specific knowledge which required specialized training and administrative talent.[183] Although not dependent on formal learning, all were career-oriented, based on education at the Universities and Inns of Court and directed to the service or command of others. The private sector and the quasi-public joint-stock Companies also generated administrative posts.

The second oldest profession continuously expanded in size and importance. The bench and bureaucracy of the Common Law Courts and Chancery offered the most tempting prizes to the ambitious, but careers could also be made by civilian advocates, proctors and registrars in the ecclesiastical courts and the Court of Admiralty. Increased recourse to litigation, particularly in the central courts, created more business for those in private practice, for the barristers who pleaded, the 'mechanical' attorneys who, though officers of a court, handled process, and the solicitors who co-ordinated suits.[184] Opportunities for experienced lawyers also existed in the county and municipal courts and in the diocesan administration; several became town clerks or recorders.[185] Legally trained administrators, engrossers and record-keepers were required by charities, trusts and private estates for drafting indentures, mortgages, contracts and conveyances.

Many gentlemen who entered the Inns between 1590 and 1639 were simply finishing their education and had no intention of earning their living from the law.[186] But 2,293 were called to the Bar and 450 were practising in 1638; although the number of active barristers later dropped to 338, the upper bench at any one time probably numbered around 500.[187] After a slack period in the middle decades, 1,996 were enrolled between 1660 and 1689; admissions then declined except for the two Temples.[188] The number of attorneys rose from 1,050 in 1606 to 1,750 in 1646; in the first half of the century there were probably 1,000 at any one time in Common Pleas and King's Bench together with 430–450

[183] Charlton 1969: 41; Hoskins 1946: 358; F. J. Fisher in Harte 1971: 15; Pares 1954: 16–17; Holmes 1981. [184] Brooks 1986: chap. 4.
[185] Dyer 1965–6: 134; Ashley, *Case Book*; Mathew 1951: 153. [186] Ives 1964: 79.
[187] Prest 1972: table 13; 1986: table 1.1; J. H. Baker in Prest 1981: n.17.
[188] W. R. Prest in Prest 1981: fig. 3; Lemmings 1985: 150; Lucas 1976: table A.6.

officers.[189] By 1690, their number had risen to at least 2,000 and, by 1729, there were said to be 2,236 attorneys of Common Pleas, 893 in King's Bench and 1,700 solicitors in Chancery; 1,500 clerks were articled 1680–1730 and, by 1730, there were some 3,129 attorneys in London and 418 in the provinces; the total lower branch probably numbered over 4,000.[190] There may also have been around 200 civil lawyers, excluding office holders, but only 41 practised; between 1603 and 1625 there were 1,250 counsel in Star Chamber.[191] The whole profession grew, but different branches developed at different rates, the civil lawyers declining and the attorneys multiplying throughout the century.

The Reformation reduced openings in the Church. Despite efforts to create Protestant monasteries after 1660, the religious orders no longer offered permanent maintenance for younger sons and unmarried daughters.[192] At the lower levels, there was always a shortage of good livings and they were reduced by pluralism, despite periodic efforts at reform.[193] But the number of livings above the poverty line did slowly increase, thanks to innovations like Queen Anne's Bounty, and the ejection of Presbyterians after the Restoration created more benefices for the Anglican gentry; municipalities, Companies and individual laymen also supported lecturers, preachers and chaplains.[194] The Church had both a parochial and a collegiate structure; the number of College Fellows alone was probably 900. The total number of livings, including the cathedrals and the Universities, has been put at 12,000, reduced by plurality to 11,000.[195] In 1710, the effective number worth at least £50, allowing for plurality, was probably around 4,000; after 1663, there were also some 1,400 Dissenting ministers, most of whom could not rely on continuous support from their 'gadding' congregations.[196]

Although the total number of medical practitioners has been put around 1,000 in the first half of the century, the number of university-trained physicians was probably around 100 in the first half and 200 in the second half of the century.[197] Only 123 testators out of 27,000 wills between 1653 and 1656 described themselves as doctors and of these only twenty-nine had degrees.[198] The number of registered physicians, including several aliens, was around 50 in 1628, 136 in 1695 and 110 in

189 Brooks in Baker 1978: 53; 1986: 29, table 6.1.
190 Holmes 1982: 322; W. Prest in Prest 1987: 74.
191 Levack 1973: 203; T. G. Barnes in Baker 1978: 25.
192 Knowles 1948–59: iii. 229; Chesterton 1967. 193 Daeley 1967: 49.
194 Green & Cross in O'Day 1981: 86, 249; Clark 1980: 76; Heal 1980: 220.
195 Green 1981: 98; Holmes 1982: 152.
196 *Valor Ecclesiasticus*; Donagan 1984: 90–2. See also p. 260.
197 Bloom & James 1935; Raasch & Wall 1962: 14, puts the total number at 814, but this includes apothecaries and surgeons and excludes Non-Conformists and those free of other guilds but practising medicine. 198 Clarkson 1975: 145.

1705; in 1687, the number of Fellows of the College of Physicians was doubled to 80.[199]

Government steadily centralized and expanded in size and in responsibilities. Before the Civil War, the fiscal exigencies of the Crown restricted the growth of bureaucracy and the abolition of the Prerogative Courts eliminated some positions.[200] But from the 1650s onwards, the organs of government grew continuously to meet the demands of war, to collect new sources of revenue and to administer overseas possessions. The number of posts multiplied even faster, after 1688, spurred by the new taxes imposed to pay for the French Wars and by the increased borrowing capacity of the government. Ancient institutions like the Treasury, Customs and Admiralty expanded and new institutions developed, like the Navy Board, Excise, Salt and Stamp Offices, the Post Office and the Board of Trade. Even the diplomatic service had an increase in posts after 1689.[201] Although London dominated, there was also some growth in local government and, once the Plantations ceased to be proprietary, new posts were created in the colonial administration.[202]

Salaried government administrators only numbered 600 in major and 600 in minor offices during the reign of Charles I with a slight expansion during the Interregnum.[203] By 1690, there may have been 3–4,000 office holders in central and local government earning more than £100 and probably another 4,000 in the £50–100 salary range.[204] Many departments still remained small: there were only forty-nine employees of the Inland Department of the Post Office in 1700.[205] The major growth occurred in revenue departments, such as the Customs and Excise, which had some 2,500 posts in London and 500 in the provinces by 1688; the Excise rose from 1,313 in 1690 to 2,247 by 1708. The size of the Court fell from 1,450 in Charles I's reign to 950 under George I. Only eighty men were admitted to the diplomatic service between 1689 and 1702, and only 136 between 1702 and 1714; only fourteen consulates were controlled by the government.[206]

The growth and defence of empire also required a permanent military and naval establishment. England was slow to join the military revolution in Europe which institutionalized war as an impersonal, expensive, large-

199 Cook 1980: table 6; Birken 1987: 204–5.

200 Reid 1921: 248–56; Richardson 1961; P. Williams 1958.

201 Barbour 1928: 550–6; Hatton & Anderson 1970; Bell 1990: 3–4.

202 Parry 1954.

203 Aylmer 1959: 235–6; 1971: 259, 272, chap. 3; 1973: 176–7, 189, 337.

204 Baugh 1965: chap. 3; Brewer 1989: table 41. The growth is well illustrated by successive editions of Chamberlaine's *Anglia Notitia*. Holmes 1982: 255, 320 puts the number, including technicians, much higher at 11–12,000 in the 1720s.

205 Hemmeon 1912: 27.

206 Lachs 1965: 63–5, 159–61, chap. 5; Horn 1961: chap. 3; Barbour 1928: 578.

scale activity, organized, financed and controlled by the state. The Tudor army was both a feudal and a national body.[207] Until the 1640s, regular military employment at a living wage could only be found as mercenaries in foreign armies and wars or in overseas Companies.[208] Memories of Cromwell's army acted as a brake on development and, even after the threat of military absolutism receded after 1688, there were fears that the Army would become a system of outdoor relief for idle gentlemen.[209] Under Charles II and James II the number of standing regiments was only increased by one and the number of officers from 344 to 613; under William III, however, numbers rose to 3,600, though they fell to 2,000 with peace.[210] A standing navy was always politically acceptable, but it increased slowly in size and then only in wartime.[211] Cromwell's navy commissioned only thirty-seven captains and 150 in hired ships.[212] The real growth occurred during William III's wars; between 1702 and 1712, 695 naval officers were admitted and numbers rose to 1,000.[213]

Employment in the households of the great also survived the attenuation of noble retinues; the great estates still needed secretaries, treasurers, chamberlains, librarians and estate managers.[214] Corporate institutions of every kind from the Church to the guilds and charitable institutions, all needed full-time administrators at every level as registrars, receivers of revenue, accountants and general managers as well as more lowly book-keepers and junior clerks. The City of London employed around 500 up to the 1640s and 2,700 by 1725.[215] The regulated commercial Companies usually chose their Governors from retired merchants or politically connected outsiders, but they maintained a small staff of consuls and chancellors. The Russia and Eastland Companies took a few apprentices, who were sent out with diet and lodging to learn the trade, but they also employed agents, clerks, lawyers and lobbyists as well as commercial agents; posts like that of the Secretary of the Merchant Adventurers at Hamburg were really administrative.[216]

The joint-stock Companies, both commercial and colonial, had always attracted younger sons.[217] They had a broad range of personnel both in England and abroad, including secretaries, accountants, commanders, physicians, surgeons, soldiers, clerks, teachers and craftsmen, who were

207 Goring 1975: 195; Cruickshank 1961: 154–5; Brodsky 1988: 6.

208 Cecil, *Certaine Precepts*, p. 11; Palmer 1902: 277; Campbell 1925.

209 Miller 1946: 308; Schwoerer 1974.

210 Childs 1976; 1980; 1987: 77. The number commissioned was higher.

211 Penn 1912; Ollard 1969; Tedder 1916.

212 Capp 1989: 155; Milford 1990: 35–6.

213 Baugh 1965: 98.

214 Neale 1948: 9; Sheffield Archives, Barker MSS; Mayo 1922: 27–9. For the estate stewards see pp. 120, 261.

215 Foster 1977: 54, 149, app. 2.

216 Willan 1956: 32–8, 278; Aström 1963: 184; Firth 1907: 21; Jordan 1942: 213; Baumann 1990: table 20.

217 *Ferrar Papers*, pp. 20, 67.

distinct from the merchants, factors and warehouse-keepers who managed the trade. The Royal Africa Company and the Hudson's Bay Company had relatively few positions.[218] But the East India Company, with its residences on both the east and west coasts of India and its agents in Persia, offered more opportunities. Even before the territorial expansion of the eighteenth century, it operated like a petty state and assumed a military and diplomatic role. Its employees, whatever their disregard for Company ordinances, were not independent businessmen, but Company servants employed by the shareholders. In 1630, there were only 141 East India Company servants in India, but 291 servants were sent out in 1658 and the total number of servants fluctuated around 200.[219] Domestic industrial Companies, like the Mines Royal, also hired full-time salaried managers.[220]

The professions, both old and new, expanded in scope during the century along with the economy. But numbers fluctuated and growth was discontinuous and uneven; some branches grew at the expense of others. The total number of positions paying at least £50 per annum, an income equivalent to a businessman with £500 equity, probably numbered a little over 11,000 in the first half of the century and a little over 27,000 by the end of the century.[221]

Requirements for entry

Some institutions restricted entry by imposing qualifications and attempting to monopolize knowledge; written tests and references made their appearance. The law was a monopolistic profession protected from competition by its technical complexity and mystique as well as by the use of Court hand, Latin and Norman French. In order to prevent an excess of pleaders, only utter barristers examined before the Bench and called to the Bar were allowed after the 1590s to practise in Westminster Hall. Attorneys and solicitors, who were apprenticed, were excluded from the Inns as early as 1556, though they continued until 1640 and the issue was not settled until 1681.[222] The localities controlled the number of lawyers

[218] K. G. Davies 1957: 163 lists only twenty. The Hudson's Bay Company usually hired on four-year contracts: see *Hudson's Bay Company Letters Outward 1688–96*, pp. 14, 103, 114.

[219] Watson 1980a: x; Bod. Rawl. MS A.303, fos. 145–6, D.747, fos. 139, 164, 169; IOL Home Misc. 78, nos. 2, 64, fo. 681; Hunter 1961: ii. 11, 164; D. K. Bassett in Bromley & Kossman 1960: 83; Strachey 1916: app. B. The total numbers in Asia rose to 1,000 between 1668 and 1690, but many of these were not employed by the Company.

[220] Rees 1968: ii. app. 1.

[221] See table 2.1.

[222] Bellot 1910: 143; Robson 1959: app. 5, who does not distinguish legal officers from practising lawyers; Birks 1960: 119, 191; Hector 1966: 66.

Table 2.1. *Estimated openings in the professions, 1600–40 and 1680–1720*

	1600–40		1680–1720	
	No.	Ann. intake	No.	Ann. intake
Law (upper branch)	500	25	500	25
Law (lower branch)	1450	73	4000	200
Estab. Church	4000	200	4000	200
Dissent. churches	—	—	500	25
Major govt office	600	30	4000	200
Lesser offices	600	30	4000	200
Local govt	1000	50	3000	150
Physicians	100	5	200	10
Army and Navy	500	25	4600	230
Business instit.	400	20	500	25
Private instit.	500	25	1000	50
Court	1450	73	1000	50
Total	11100	556	27300	1365

Note: The upper branch of the law includes barristers, advocates and holders of legal offices. The lower branch includes attorneys and solicitors, but not scriveners or notaries. Business institutions include the joint-stock Companies in foreign trade and domestic industry. Private institutions include managers employed by private estates, charities, trusts and the Church. Local government includes salaried offices in London and the provincial towns. Posts paying less than £50 p.a. have been excluded. Vacancy rates have been calculated on the assumption that the average tenure of an incumbent was twenty years. Most of the figures, in particular those for private and business institutions and local government, are only offered as rough estimates. Holmes 1982: 16 puts the total at 35,000 in 1680 and 55–65,000 in 1730, excluding apprentices, ship-masters, the royal household and naval dockyards and the joint-stock Companies, but including schoolmasters, apothecaries and surgeons and many officials earning less than £50 p.a.

who were permitted to practise in their courts. But the Inns declined as teaching institutions and, although the Universities assumed many of their functions after 1680, a degree did not really provide quality control.[223] The Bar did not enforce a high standard and barristers were admitted both *ex gratia* and by dispensation.[224] There was little formal control of either the numbers or qualifications of attorneys.

The minimum qualification in the Church was outward orthodoxy, but during the century strenuous efforts were made to exclude those who lacked a university education.[225] Some academic ability was desirable for senior posts in the Universities. Responsible public offices usually required political and religious orthodoxy and some evidence of adminis-

[223] Knafla 1969: 240; Bland 1978. [224] Lemmings 1990: 74, app. 1.
[225] Jenkins 1982: 168; Owen 1959: 70; R. O'Day in O'Day & Heal 1976.

trative ability. An examination was introduced by the Treasury for collectors of customs in 1689 and the excisemen were carefully trained.[226] The Navy introduced an examination for lieutenants in 1677. The East India Company vetted petitioners and those recommended for its posts and initially preferred experienced merchants.[227]

A few physicians were apprenticed, but it was essentially a graduate profession.[228] The College of Physicians recruited primarily from Oxford, Cambridge and Trinity College, Dublin and it insisted on conducting its Fellowship examinations in Latin arguing that a gentleman's education was essential to strengthen character.[229] But its monopoly was infringed by the right of bishops to license medical practitioners in the provinces and, after 1676, it had to accept graduates of continental Universities; it was also willing to license outsiders for money. Rose's Case, in 1704, did not resolve demarcation disputes with the apothecaries; its main impact was to disallow the taking of fees for advice by the Physicians, though they could still accept honoraria.[230]

The cost of entry varied considerably within and between professions. The law had no scholarships, though it was possible to defray expenses by helping friends with private counsel. Admission fees and entry fines varied according to the Inn.[231] Dinners had to be kept, books bought and fees to servants and officers and sureties could amount to £10–40.[232] The cost of maintaining a student at an Inn steadily inflated. In the early seventeenth century, it took £40 per annum, in 1660 £50, in 1680 £80 and in 1700 £100 upwards.[233] The time factor was also a deterrent. It took at least seven years at an Inn after Moots before an inner barrister became an utter barrister; a regulation of 1615, confirmed in 1664, stipulated a further three years of exercises and probation, though this was difficult to enforce. Sometimes the whole process could take twelve years and the average barrister had invested at least £1,000 and up to £1,500 by the time that he practised.

A civil lawyer had the cost of his doctorate and fees at Doctors' Commons which included an entrance fee of £13 6s. 8d. and 10–20 shillings per annum.[234] Attorneys could be apprenticed for £30–80 for much of the century and premiums were always lower in the provinces;

[226] Jarvis 1977a: 522.
[227] Massarella 1990: 90, 140. The system was formalized in 1697: see Marshall 1970: 9.
[228] Cook 1987. [229] Hamilton 1951–2: 141–61; Root 1969.
[230] Cook 1990: 554; Ellis 1965: 198; Clark 1964: i. 16.
[231] *Gray's Inn Pension Book*, i. pp. xxxii, xxxix. [232] Prest 1972: 36–8.
[233] Cliffe 1969: 43; Keeton 1965: 40; Lemmings 1985: 162; Lucas 1976: 241; Duman 1980; Hughes 1952b: 48; 1952a: i. 77–82; Lemmings 1990: 24.
[234] Levack 1973: 21; Squibb 1977.

living costs during service, which lasted six to seven years, could amount to £20 per annum.[235] Admission to an Inn of Chancery ranged from £5 to £6 13s. 4d. Premiums gradually rose to £60–150 and by the early eighteenth century could reach £2–300 in London.[236] Proctors paid £70–100 and those who became clerks to judges or common solicitors had to train for five years.

The Church was cheaper to enter, since the primary cost was a university education. This cost £20 per annum in 1600, £30–40 per annum by 1650 and £50–60 later, plus the cost of books; the outlay could rise to £100 per annum.[237] A living could be acquired through purchase of an advowson or grant of next presentation; the price depended on the age and health of the incumbent, but was usually one year's income.[238] Other costs, like First Fruits, also reduced income from the benefice at the outset.[239]

Entry into office by appointment had no premium and no financial outlay for special training, though some form of higher education was desirable and sureties of £1,000–30,000 were required by certain offices, as in the Ordnance.[240] A graduate of a university or an Inn could begin as a private secretary to a magnate or diplomat and progress to royal service.[241] But entry through purchase or patrimony required family capital. In the 1630s, prices of major offices varied from £3,000 to £6,000, though they were often a sound investment for children.[242] After the Restoration, they ranged from a clerkship in Chancery or Secretaryship of State at £6,000 to a clerkship of the Privy Council at £1,250 and a Searcher or Warden of the Fleet at £1,000.[243] Increased salaries and strong demand raised both the price and resale value of offices as well as the profits of sub-leasing, though litigation was a nuisance.[244] The number of venal offices was, however, limited because new royal creations had been restricted by the judges, in 1587, as an infringement of property rights and because, in England, offices were sold by the individual rather than by the state and did not confer tax exemptions.[245]

235 Brooks 1986: 157, 243.
236 Lane 1977; G. L. Andersen in Harris 1969: chap. 3; Belcher 1986; Finberg 1957: 179.
237 Sykes 1967: 194; Lyman 1935: 29; Stone 1974: 43; 1964a: 71.
238 Bucks. RO, Calendar of the Archives of Major R. H. Way, ii. 16.
239 D. R. Hirschberg in O'Day 1981: 223; Best 1964: 13–19; Heal 1973: 216; O'Day 1975a.
240 Tomlinson 1979: 98.
241 Barnett 1969; A. G. R. Smith 1968: 481, 503; Miller 1963: 11–13; Osborne, *Advice to Son*, p. 73; Jancey 1955–6: 145.
242 Bell 1953: 35–8; Aylmer 1971: 225.
243 *Early English Tracts Commerce*, p. 379; Vale 1956.
244 Barnard in Lloyd-Jones *et al.* 1981: 216; Potenger, *Private Memoirs*, pp. 42–3.
245 D. Bitton in Rabb & Seigel 1969. A few offices did confer tax exemptions: see Aylmer 1971: 173.

Institutions in the private sector could be entered at minimal cost. It was not necessary to own any stock to enter the East India Company and servants automatically acquired their freedom and usually entered as writers. Between 1662 and 1694, the Hudson's Bay and East India Companies even took on a few apprentices, notably the Bluecoat boys, as well as captains who acted as supercargoes; by 1675, however, only the Accountant-General's Department took clerks with indentures.[246] The initial cost of admission consisted of £5 for the freedom and a bond for good behaviour, which in 1674 was raised to £500 for a writer, £1–2,000 for a factor, £2,000 for an Agent at Fort St George and £5,000 for a Presidency.[247] High sureties of up to four times the annual stipend were also demanded of consuls and treasurers by other Companies. Despite exile for up to twenty years and a high death rate, whatever was saved on an apprenticeship premium could be invested in the private trade.[248]

In the Army, the purchase of a commission was lower than the cost of a mercantile apprenticeship, except in smart regiments like the Foot Guards.[249] In Anne's reign, an ensign in a regiment of the line required £150–200; a company could be bought for £250, a regiment for £4–500 and a company of Guards for some £1,600.[250] The cost of entry into the Navy was also low. Orphans and, after 1661, cadet volunteers were taken on at the age of thirteen to sixteen as captains' servants or midshipmen and, after five year's service at sea, could become lieutenants. In 1676, the system of instruction was improved and the category of volunteers was introduced to encourage the gentry 'to breed up their younger sons'.[251]

The cost of a medical education was not exorbitant, though it could rise to £50, and serious students went abroad to train at universities like Montpellier and Leiden. Degrees could also be purchased. In the early seventeenth century, admission to the College of Physicians cost £11 3s. 4d. with a subscription of £4 in the first year and £2 thereafter; election to a Fellowship cost £5 11s. 8d. plus wine and sweetmeats. The fees were doubled for those without an Oxbridge degree.[252] Since it took some six years before a Physician was ready for private practice, he probably had to invest up to £1,000 by the end of the century.[253]

Access to the job market depended, however, as much on patronage and nepotism as on money. The law was in many respects a dynastic profession and entry always cost less for sons of lawyers.[254] Although there was considerable competition between younger sons for vacant

[246] Foster 1924: 88; Morse 1926: i. 77; Rich 1958: 296. [247] Master, *Diaries*, i. 193.
[248] Love 1913: i. 173–5, ii. 67; C109/10. [249] Childs 1976: 38, 45.
[250] Scouller 1966: 126, 138–9, app. G.
[251] Ehrmann 1953: 138–43; J. D. Davies 1991: 16; Oppenheim 1896: i. 152, 226; Tedder 1910: 60. [252] Keynes 1966: 35. [253] Allen 1946: 115ff.
[254] Dugdale, *Origines Juridicales*, p. 210.

clerkships by 1650, some posts became almost hereditary.[255] In the Church, the prosecution of family connections accelerated after the prohibition on marriage was lifted. Of 3,850 church livings subject to rights of impropriation, lay patrons controlled some 1,200.[256] For the career administrator, patrimony and patronage were more important than purchase. In the Household, a few posts were venal but most fell to peers and their kin.[257]

Many salaried municipal offices could be purchased and often passed through the same family.[258] The directors of the East India Company could nominate relatives to posts and there was constant importuning for factorships and writerships; dynasties of East Indian servants began to emerge.[259] Before 1689, 97 per cent of the officer corps in the Army consisted of gentlemen and the latter were preferred as naval officers even during the Protectorate. Although the Crown owned the ships and although private patronage was usually exercised responsibly in wartime, captains chose the new recruits and often preferred their kin.[260] Eldest sons outnumbered their younger brothers at the Inns before 1590 and after 1660 and, except for the Interregnum, they obtained the lion's share of public appointments.[261]

[255] Cockburn 1969: 317–25; 1977: app. 7.

[256] W. T. MacCaffrey in Bindoff *et al.* 1961: 101, 123–4, 181; 1968; Hirschberg 1980: 111.

[257] Beattie 1967: chaps. 6–7.

[258] Kellett 1952: app. 4; Deakin 1980: 23.

[259] Parkinson 1937; Hedges, *Diary*, ii. p. cccclviii; Gill 1961: 18–20; Love 1913: ii. 67; Fitzhugh 1983.

[260] Baugh 1965: chap. 3.

[261] Aylmer 1959: 235.

3 Funding and risk

When an apprentice finally gained his freedom, he still had to establish an independent business. How much capital did he need to set up on his own and what sources could he tap? What hazards did he face and how far could they be reduced? How did his prospects of advancement compare with someone who chose a profession or other career?

Capital requirements

The minimum amount initially required varied according to the type and area of business. Commerce required relatively little fixed capital; established markets with a sound credit structure demanded a smaller outlay, as did the short-haul and carrying trades which had greater liquidity and a faster turnover.[1] Several successful merchants began with modest stakes and merchants who earned commission as factors could manage with less equity.[2] The European trades nevertheless demanded deep pockets of £2,000–5,000.[3] In 1689, a third share of a two-year partnership in the wine trade in Malaga was £2,451.[4] Substantial reserves were needed to offer the credit which was essential for sales, to weather seasonal fluctuations, delays and losses.[5] Factors could not survive without trading on their own account; principals expected their commission agents to advance funds against goods, often without adequate security, and sought to circumvent the cost of middlemen by breaking up shipments into smaller units.

Long-distance trades tied up capital for several years; stock could be immobilized waiting for the Spanish fleet and greater risks demanded

[1] Willan 1959: 208. [2] Papillon, *Memoirs*, p. 14.

[3] *HMC Salisbury*, ii. 320; Baumann 1990: 164, table 21; *Bristol Documents Illustrating Trade*, p. 25. [4] GLL MS 10187.

[5] There is no sure way of determining what was considered an adequate reserve, which could be short-term (cash), medium-term (stocks and loans) and long-term (real estate). Charles Marescoe's cash reserves represented 5 per cent of his assets: see Marescoe, *Markets and Merchants*, p. 117.

greater assets. A factor starting in the Levant trade needed at least £400 and an independent merchant at least £1,000.[6] A voyage from Bristol to the Atlantic required £3–4,000 and a working plantation £4,000.[7] The West Country merchants claimed that they could not compete with London because they had limited working capital and were dependent on quick returns.[8] Even in the joint-stock Companies, £1,000 was usually needed for the private trade, though some managed with less.[9] Most areas of foreign trade required an initial investment of at least £500 in the first half and £1,000 in the second half of the century; a fully-fledged business was capitalized at £5,000.[10]

Many of the domestic trades demanded a smaller initial outlay, though practice varied enormously. Capital expenditure could be reduced by focusing on inventory and by leasing rather than owning business premises.[11] The minimum level set by many guilds and by the City for setting up shop, though still onerous for a journeyman, was only £20 and sometimes less.[12] An ironmonger just needed a steelyard, scales and a stout table and could set up even in London for £40–50. A mercer in the provinces could stock a small shop for £15–25 and an apothecary for £50, though a full-time shopkeeper really needed £50–100 in the provinces and from £100 upwards in London.[13] A tanner could manage on £60–90 and a clothier could start with £30–40, but a safe minimum in the textile trades was £100.[14]

More substantial capital was, moreover, essential to cover the overheads of a major domestic business, to maintain a variety of stock, advance credit and deal wholesale in volume. One merchant of Lynn had 330 debtors at his death; even a shopkeeper was obliged to give his customers up to six months to pay and to hold as much as £1,000 in inventory,

[6] Anderson 1989: 99; Grassby 1994: 94; GLL MS 5105, fo. 31; BL Stowe MS 219, fo. 220; Berks. RO D/EZ5/B1, fo. 37, B2 letter 2 April 1701; C104/44, letter June 1684; Hedges, *Diary*, i. p. cviii.

[7] *Bristol Africa and Slave Trade*, p. xviii; Zahedieh 1986a: 208.

[8] *Seventeenth-Century Economic Documents*, p. 448.

[9] Collett, *Letter Book*, p. 91; C109/10; Watson 1980a: 60.

[10] The surtax level was set at £600, in 1692, with another tax bracket at £300. The Pewterers required £300 for its Livery in 1685 and £500 in 1689: see Welch 1902: i. p. viii; Luttrell, *Parliamentary Diary*, pp. 142–3. In 1697, the Court of Aldermen decreed a minimum of £1,000 for the Livery of the great Companies and £500 for the lesser ones.

[11] Mendenhall 1953: 87; Papillon, *Memoirs*, p. 14; Earle 1989a: chap. 4.

[12] Ramsey 1961: 384; Thrupp 1935: 140; Sherwell 1937: 191.

[13] Berger 1981–2: 45; Stout, *Autobiography*, pp. 19–21; Roberts 1962b: 505–6; 1964: 370; Poynter & Bishop 1951: xvi; Yonge, *Diary*, p. 205.

[14] Dyer 1972: 121; Warws. RO CR 314, no. 123; Burley 1958–9: 290; Raines 1903:11; *Seventeenth-Century Economic Documents*, pp. 185–6; *Harl. Misc.*, xi. 54; Cornish, *Thomas Firmin*, p. 5; Chalklin 1965: 180, 209.

because it took time to replenish stock.[15] A silk thrower only needed £5 for an apprenticeship, but he needed £400 to set up a business, as did the Shrewsbury Drapers.[16] To rise above the level of artisan in the pewter, book, silk and drapery trades took at least £500 and the working capital of a successful firm was at least £1,000 per partner.[17] The coastal trade required an equity of at least £2–300.[18] The shipbuilding, construction, glass, tanning, soap, sugar, brewing and coal industries needed even heavier investment, not so much in fixed assets as in raw materials, building space and wages. A sugar house took £5–10,000, a hosiery mill at least £1,000 and a glassworks £5,000.[19] Philip Foley started with £4,702 and the Foley partnership of five individuals had £39,000; even then there was no cash reserve and the firm had to borrow and assign debts.[20] Campbell's estimates, in 1747, of working capital in the different domestic trades can be taken as representative of most of the seventeenth century and he postulated an unlimited figure for a general merchant.[21]

Connection

Capital of this magnitude could not normally be accumulated by saving wages, profits or commissions; a handful worked their way up from manual trades or in the Plantations, but only at the lower levels or when firmly established could a business be self-financing.[22] Start-up capital had to be acquired by outright grant. Young merchants relied on parental provision and the generosity of relations, both living and dead.[23] Usually they received a lump sum when they came of age or advances against their portion, as allowed by the Custom of London.[24] Provision took many forms, including goods, credit, tools and even land in England and New England which could be sold to acquire investment capital.[25] Some parents bought the freedom for their sons and put them in a partnership,

[15] Wray, 'Account book', p. 117; Berger 1980: 128; Muldrew 1993: 27; Willan 1976: 81; D. W. Jones 1988: table 8.5. Debts owing could constitute as much as one-half of gross assets in inventories, but usually ranged from 20–30 per cent. Earle 1989a: 106–23, tables 4.4, 4.6, calculates that 35.72 per cent of the assets of his sample of Londoners were in trade credits, though the latter cannot easily be distinguished from private loans in inventories. For East Anglia and the Midlands, Holderness 1976b: 162 , calculates 18 per cent.

[16] Stern 1956: 30; Mendenhall 1953: 87.

[17] GLL 12017, fos.22–3; J. M. Price in Dunns 1986: 365; Simpson 1961: 116–17; Lang, 1971: 245, 253; Warws. RO CR 314; R. G. Wilson 1971: 23.

[18] N. H., *Compleat Tradesman*, pp. 32, 37; Jeake, *Astrological Diary*, pp. 63, 128.

[19] Smout 1961: 248; Chapman 1972: 20, 36; Godfrey 1976: 171.

[20] Schafer 1971; *Foley Stour Valley Ironworks*, pp. 35–6.

[21] Campbell, *London Tradesman*, pp. 331–40.

[22] *Wynn Papers Calendar*, nos. 896, 964, 1023. [23]Kirby 1986: 161.

[24] Ellis 1981a: 180; Dewhurst 1975: 67; *Compleat Solicitor*, p. 452.

[25] Harris 1960: 65; I. F. Jones 1938–9: 12.

allocating what they saved on a premium as working capital. Some prentices acquired dowries by marrying the daughters or widows of their masters or partners, though Cranfield eventually had to support his father-in-law.[26] They could also inherit property in their own right, though that usually occurred late in life.[27]

Capital could sometimes be acquired through a master. Apprentices originally received a lump sum and double apparel at the end of their term, but this practice became less common.[28] Masters did, however, employ or take their prentices into partnership and sometimes set them up, particularly if they had no sons.[29] Others left bequests, often in return for their help in winding up their estates.[30] Charles Horsley obtained the residue of the goods of Henry Riddel who died at Elbing; John Lygerd entrusted his servant Richard Marshal with £1,000, his warehouse, stock and ships, and charged him to liquidate and pay the proceeds plus 5 per cent to his children.[31] Sir Thomas White, who had himself benefited from a bequest from his master, left his apprentices a substantial sum in cloth, which was to be paid back over ten years 'if his widow did not wish to trade'.[32] Sometimes a young man would run his late master's business for the surviving widow.[33] Prentices also moonlighted at other jobs. Roger Lowe and Edward Terrill acted as scriveners and George Boddingon as a bookkeeper: 'Mr Henry Haswell, an East Cuntries merchant lodging at my father and wanting a bookeeper, I undertook . . . for 30 li. p. Annum, my desire in so doing being to attain a full knowledge of that trade and help to save my Expenses'.[34]

Additional funds could be acquired from sleeping or active partners. Factors could pool their resources or attract venture capital from friends and relations in return for a share of the profits; Jonathan Priestley's aunt financed him at '12d p £' and repayment of loans from relations could be delayed with less likelihood of prosecution.[35] Financiers acted as intermediaries between conservative investors and speculative investments. Sir

[26] Bod. Rawl. MS 1483; *HMC Sackville*, ii. 75; C114/55; SP 105/152, fo. 19; Dawe 1950: 16, 19; Ramsay 1978: 536; *Yorkshire Diaries*, i. 20; Tawney 1958: 11. See also p. 305.

[27] Hill 1904: 128.

[28] *Southampton Calendar Apprentices*, table C; Brigden 1986: 48 n.67; Webb 1960: 31.

[29] Lowe, *Diary*; Simpson 1961: 178.

[30] *Printers Abstracts from Wills*, p. iv; *Stationers Company Court Records*, p. 53; Currer-Briggs 1969: 832; Murray 1988: 384.

[31] *Durham Wills*, iii. 168; *North Country Wills*, p. 126.

[32] Stevenson & Salter 1930: 384, 399, 401; White later changed his will twice.

[33] *Southampton Calendar Apprentices*, p. xxviii; Ellis 1981a: 5.

[34] GLL MS 10823/1, fos. 38, 41–2; Wharton 1979: 29; *Bristol Records Church of Christ*, p. 5; Hayden 1970: 349.

[35] Harris 1953: 22, 35; *Yorkshire Diaries*, i. 14; Watson 1980a: 123; Burnby 1983: 54; Willan 1976: 142; Plummer 1972: 26.

William Russell borrowed at 7 per cent to lend to the Crown at 8 per cent and the West Country fishermen in the Newfoundland trade borrowed at 25 per cent from moneylenders, who themselves borrowed at 10 per cent from local lenders.[36] Long-term general partnerships were rare until the eighteenth century, but short-term associations were standard in both foreign and domestic trade and in shipowning.[37] Indeed partnerships and syndicates with saleable shares were much more common than incorporated joint-stocks in the coal industry, in government finance and in enterprises which depended on a royal patent. A grocer who took his East India dividend in pepper was really investing in a syndicate.

Informal networks of associates linked by a common trade or background also emerged, as in the sugar, slave and jewellery trades or in the Tobacco Adventure to Russia; marine insurance remained in the hands of partnerships, despite attempts in the 1600s to establish an Office of Assurance and a proposal, in 1719, to adapt the charter of the Mines Royal.[38] Merchants formed partnerships in England and abroad with foreign merchants who sought to circumvent restrictions on trade by aliens, though this was prohibited in some towns.[39] A few guilds had their own internal joint-stocks, most of which failed; the distribution of both materials and profits was governed by seniority and was usually contentious.[40]

Capital could be raised by conventional loans on bond or by putting up bonds rather than cash in joint ventures.[41] Mun and Malynes noted that merchants traded in excess of their equity, using the funds of retired merchants, widows and orphans.[42] But most short-term credit was obtained from commercial suppliers, by delaying payment for goods advanced and through bills of exchange. In 1707, one writer claimed that one-sixth of the nation's trade was in the hands of men worth £500–1,000,

[36] Ashton 1960a: 255; Hicks-Beach 1909: 85; Innis 1954: 34; Davis 1973b: 238.

[37] Formal partnership agreements are uncommon among business papers, though letters of attorney sometimes define the relationship and agreements surface occasionally in legal depositions and probate records: see KAO Dodwell MSS U.47/15, U.145/C1/563 K, fo. 56, U.593; E178/5455; C105/29; Lincs. AO Trollope-Bellew MSS; Devon RO Lee MSS; Berks. RO Craven MSS; *Bristol Documents Illustrating Trade*, pp. 117–18; REQ 2/ BA 312; Earle 1989a: 111, 139; Price 1993: app. A.

[38] Morgan 1978: 9; Wright & Fayle 1928: 31, 45, 66; Pares 1960: 5; 1956–7: 255; 1950: 163ff; Sosin 1983: 40; Richardson 1985; Dunn 1976: chap. 13; Sheridan 1974: 284–6; Thoms 1969a: 5–7; Samuel 1982: 25.

[39] *Bristol Documents Illustrating Trade*, p. 21; Arasaratnam 1966: 89.

[40] Welch 1902: ii. 68, 92; Myers 1983: 82; Fisher 1936: 145–6; 1990: 43ff; Young 1913: app.; Unwin 1904: 53–6; Cameron 1963: 82; Pollard 1978: 48; Blackmore 1986: 18–20.

[41] Kerridge 1988: chap. 3 and in Anderson & Latham 1986 demonstrates the early importance of bills obligatory and the high ratio of book debts in inventories. See also Price 1980: chap. 6; 1989: 273–4, 278–81; Anderson 1970: 90; Godfrey 1976: 172.

[42] Malynes, *Maintenance Free Trade*, 23. Selling annuities was a device used by corporations in England but not with any frequency by individuals.

who secured 500 per cent credit from the greater tradesmen and in turn financed their own sales.[43] A comparison of the total value of English exports and imports with estimates of total wealth and paid-up capital suggests the extent to which working capital was borrowed; the debt of the Hudson's Bay Company, in 1695, equalled its liability on issued capital and the same was true of the East Indian and African Companies.[44] Private ledgers suggest that working capital was at least twice and sometimes three times equity capital. A major problem, however, was that the period of time required to realize cash proceeds from sales was longer than the term of most loans; short-term credit could finance a quick turnover, but not permanent inventory.[45] Some loan funds for beginners were available from charitable foundations and municipal institutions in most towns at rates as low as 2½–4 per cent.[46] The Quakers apprenticed their children to Friends in the domestic trade and sometimes provided cheap funds, though they also charged market rate to established merchants.[47] In London, £24,000 in loan funds was available at market rate and £43,942 at under 3 per cent interest. Some bequests were intended for merchants and excluded handicraftsmen; Robert Rogers provided £20 for artificers and £100 at 6.75 per cent for Merchant Adventurers. But the maximum loans provided, as in the Sutton and Drapers bequests, was only £100–200 and the average loan was £30–70 spread over three to four years.[48] The Aldersey charity at Chester offered only £25 at 6 per cent for seven years and the Elkington trust at Northampton only £10.[49]

Although the London funds could support some 400 young men at modest levels, some of the loan charities never reached those for whom they were intended. They were often commandeered by established merchants, who believed that charity should begin in their homes.[50] Borrowers usually entered into a conditional bond with sureties, but the documents could be lost and it was often difficult to recover the principal; the legal charges of enforcement could exceed the interest.[51] Corporations appropriated funds and the Warmouth charity at Newcastle, although

43 Dickson 1967: 30; Defoe, *Compleat English Tradesman*, i. 46.

44 *Hudson's Bay Company Letters Outward 1688–96*, liv. See also pp. 256–7.

45 Malynes, *Lex Mercatoria*, p. 365.

46 CLRO Rep. 79, fo. 328; *Eastland Company Acts*, p. xxxvi; Jordan 1959: 172–7, 267; 1961: 272, 102, 106, 429; 1960: 172–7; James 1948: 158; *Compleat Solicitor*, p. 452; Dyer 1972: 116; Cotton 1872: 126–8; T. Jones 1909–30: ii. 118; Mendenhall 1953: 112; Woodward 1967: 93–4; Taylor 1949: 106; Leonard 1900: 232–5; Adam 1951: 90; Halcrow *et al.* 1952: 76; Wilson, *Discourse upon Usury*, p. 120.

47 Lloyd 1950: 40, 171.

48 CLRO Rep. 79, fo. 328.

49 *Northampton Records*, ii. 308; *Chester City Minutes*, pp. xxxii–xxxiii.

50 Powell, *Tom of All Trades*, p. 204; Moies in Clark 1981: 160; Woodward 1965: 98–9, 201; Berger 1981–2: 46; Roper 1962: 384; Archer 1991b: 81.

51 Johnson 1920: iii. 174; Cox 1975: 63; R. Myers in Myers & Harris 1985: 10–11; H. G. Jones 1969: 28; Smyth 1905a: 244.

founded in 1647, made its first loan in 1674.[52] When the rate of interest fell, loan funds which stipulated a high rate to provide income for the poor, had no takers.[53]

There were other sources of cheap capital. The East India Company factors in Persia used the Company's stock as well as local capital to finance their private partnerships.[54] Executors could make temporary use of capital in their hands and City notables could borrow cheaply from the Chamber at 5 per cent, raised to 7 per cent in 1624, and from the Orphans Fund at 4–7 per cent; in 1633, £130,000 was available and, in 1666, £239,000.[55] Rates were usually under 5 per cent, when the market rate was 10 per cent, and though loans required recognizances and lasted only during the minority of the orphans, some £1 million was borrowed between 1560 and 1682. In Exeter in 1639, £11,846 was available in small amounts of under £300 and only $1^2/_3$ per cent was paid on the larger loans.[56] Exchequer tellers and businessmen who acted as collectors of revenue could also temporarily appropriate cash deposits.[57] Livery Companies and towns had always been able to borrow below the legal maximum rate of interest from the innumerable trusts, widows, retirees and charitable foundations looking for safe investments.[58] The East India Company could borrow at 6 per cent even in the early seventeenth century.

The cost of money was, however, a major deterrent for a young merchant who did not have adequate collateral or security of income and was considered a poor risk; he could not borrow on bond and had to rely on trade credit.[59] The usury laws provided little protection, since maximum limits could easily be evaded by overvaluing goods advanced or by deducting a premium from the principal. Novice businessmen had to pay double the rate of a corporation or a non-commercial borrower and there was a finite limit to the credit which principals were prepared to advance.[60] Good years pushed interest rates high and encouraged over-trading; in bad years, there was no reason to borrow.[61] Borrowing on

[52] Rees 1923: 125; Howell 1967: 316. [53] Youings 1968: 138.

[54] Palmer 1933–4: 43.

[55] Wren 1948: 50–1; Carlton 1974a: 14, 85; Kellett 1963: 221; Brydges, *Continuation History Willoughby Family*, pp. 132, 136; Masters 1975: 10.

[56] Carlton 1971: 32–3; 1973: 314. Before 1657, the rate on Orphans' money was as low as $1\frac{2}{3}$ per cent. [57] Alsop 1979a: 42.

[58] Roover 1974: 345; Homer 1963: tables 10, 12; BL Egerton MS 917, fo. 89; Ramsay 1975: 230; Campbell 1976: 112; *Southampton Assembly Books*, ii. p. xxviii; Kellett 1963: 221–6; Richards 1929: 107; Welch 1902: 89; Sievekin 1907: ii. 223–4; Goldthwaite 1968: 245.

[59] Crowley, *Way to Wealth*, pp. 41–2; Wilson, *Discourse upon Usury*, pp. 27–9; Burgon 1839: i. app. 6.

[60] SP 110/16, letter 25 Aug. 1684; Fideler & Mayer 1992: 173. The Crown also had to pay a 'reward' or 'gratuity' above the legal maximum: see Nichols 1987: 44.

[61] Mun in *Early English Tracts Commerce*, p. 179; *Seventeenth-Century Economic Documents*, p. 410, suggests a rate of 4.5 per cent for land and 8 per cent for personalty.

bottomry for speculative investments could cost 30 per cent.[62] Merchants in the Levant and India could borrow from local merchants or other factors, but only at rates of 12–25 per cent.[63] There was a paper-thin margin between the rate of interest demanded for risky investments and the profit which could, on average, be expected.[64]

Most novices suffered therefore from inadequate capitalization; many were apprenticed to craftsmen because their families could not afford to provide them with stock.[65] Large, established firms had greater borrowing power and, if they managed their cash flow properly, had greater liquidity. Sons of merchants usually received adequate provision and they could be trained more cheaply and enter by patrimony.[66] But merchants rarely entrusted their sons with more than a fraction of the family's capital and their bequests often overestimated the value of their estate. Sir Josiah Child advocated partible inheritance, as in Holland, as a means to provide capital for younger sons in trade. But partible inheritance in a large family in fact reduced individual portions and its importance as a source of capital was challenged by Blanch.[67] Some entrants from outside the business world did receive adequate financing.[68] But few could run up an overdraft of £67,662, like the son of Richard Hoare, and usually funds were less than needed or promised.[69] Children were often placed in business precisely because family assets were limited or illiquid. Parents underestimated the need for capital and expected their financial outlay to be limited to the cost of education and binding.

The fate of a new entrant also depended too much on his master, whose support and business were essential even after he had acquired his freedom. Factors who failed to raise venture funds were dangerously dependent on the reputation and level of investment of their masters. In order to secure a foothold, it was essential to secure principals. But merchants preferred to entrust their affairs to experienced men whom they knew well and increasingly they bypassed their own factors.[70] They preferred to employ their own relations as a safeguard against financial failure, dishonesty and disloyalty.[71] If they had to take a chance on a raw

62 Cell 1969: 11; J. Gilchrist in MacMillan 1977: 15; Rink 1986: table 7.1; BL Add. MS 22846, fo. 120. 63 Watson 1980a: 96–100. 64 Cook, *Unum Necessarium*.

65 Hill, *Interest United Provinces*; Morison, *Itinerary*, pp. 101, 111; Gibb 1947: 82; Bangs, *Memoirs*, p. 11; Newcombe, *Autobiography*, p. 173.

66 Willan 1953: 50, 130; Cokayne 1873: 103.

67 Blanch, *Interest of England*, p. 90.

68 Laslett 1948a: 153; *Yorkshire Abstracts Wills*, pp. 51, 66, 80, 133, 137, 165; Dalleson & Scott Robinson 1883–7: 152–3; Blundell, *Diary 1702–28*, pp. 39–40, 46; Keeler 1954: 603; Anderson 1989: 88, 90; Hollingshead 1990: 86; Kirby 1985: 37.

69 Hoare 1955: 6; Fletcher 1975: 37; Willan 1979: 208; Gay 1939: 406, 423; Vann 1979: 360; *Wynn Papers Calendar*, pp. xvi, 175, 190, no. 896.

70 C104/44, letter 12 Aug. 1686; K. G. Davies 1952a: 92–9; Penson 1924.

71 See also pp. 330–1.

youth, they gave priority to their own kin, to whom they acknowledged an obligation to help. Business was exceedingly clannish and often restricted to members of the same Livery Company. Speed of advance was closely connected with membership of a Great Company and apprenticeship to an important merchant; the surnames of masters and prentices in the registers of London, Norwich, Bristol and Shrewsbury are frequently the same.[72] Sometimes parents chose to pay to apprentice their sons to a major Company even though they could enter a lesser Company by patrimony.

Although business revolved around the extended rather than the nuclear family, merchants were interrelated in every trade and an organization chart of any firm reads like a genealogy. In the Levant Company, the active traders of the 1630s were the grandsons of the founders.[73] Kinship was the basis of many partnerships; client lists and correspondents were passed on between generations. Family networks were solidified by religious affiliations, city office and local nationalism. Sons and nephews served as factors for their fathers and uncles all over the world, often linking different areas of trade. In the Heathcote family, Sir Gilbert was in London, Samuel in Danzig and the tobacco trade to Russia, George, John, Josiah and William in the Caribbean and Caleb in New York; the Wyche family had three merchants in England, three in Turkey, one in Spain, one in the East Indies and one in Russia.[74]

Children from landed families had connections which sons of yeomen lacked.[75] Some gentlemen in business did their best to employ their relations and other gentlemen.[76] Maurice Wynn acted as agent for his father and Marmaduke Rawdon as factor for his uncle in the Canary and French wine trades.[77] Richard Newdigate represented his eldest brother in London, a common practice in the lead trade.[78] William Whaley, the godson of squire Helyar, was taken as an apprentice by Cary Helyar, in 1664, and inherited half a sugar plantation when his master died.[79] John Paige acted for his father-in-law while John Priestley provided his two younger brothers with stock and commissions.[80] Nicholas Blundell pushed his brother, Richard, into the Preston guild and helped him in Liverpool.[81]

72 Rappaport 1989: 31, 341; 1983–4: 119–20; Sacks 1985: 672, table 4; Yarbrough 1980: 114. In Norwich, there was no particular advantage in having a magistrate for a master: see J. T. Evans 1974: 56.

73 Brenner 1993: 72.

74 Fox 1926: 6; Heathcote 1899: 65–9; Mundy, *Travels*, iii. app. B, iv. 151; Rutman 1965: 182, 191; Clarke 1940: 102; Bailyn 1955: 87ff; 1953: 380 and 1959: 73; Wilson 1960: 28; Pares 1950: 32; 1960: 76; C104/44, letter 12 Aug. 1682; Sheridan 1974: chap. 13; Marambaud 1973: 132; Davis 1962: 90, 159–60; Bridenbaugh 1968: 471; Ellis 1981a: 33; Roberts 1965: 149; Meroney 1968: 238; Hall 1949: 143.

75 Carroll 1968: 92, 103.

76 *Oxinden Letters*, pp. 40, 117.

77 Rawdon, *Life*, pp. 17, 65.

78 Larminie 1987: 37; Westerfield 1915: 246.

79 Bennet 1964: 53–76, 113.

80 *Yorkshire Diaries*, i. 26; Sitwell, *Letterbook*, pp. vii, xxii, 142.

81 Blundell, *Diary*, pp. 39, 46.

Immigrants from the counties exploited their regional connections and formed their own associations, dining together in London.[82] But entrants without relatives in business had few contacts and less access to capital and advice; they had to build an entirely new client base without the benefits of family patronage and referral. Heigham Bright acquired business through his brother, but he bitterly complained that his correspondents neglected to offer him commissions, that there was 'no living upon the air'.[83] Even well-connected men, like Michael Blackett, had difficulty building up their businesses and kinsmen often evaded their responsibilities.[84]

Risk

All worldly affairs, wrote Malynes, were subject to inconstancy: 'to be rich and to become poore or to be poore and to become rich is a matter inherent to a Merchant's estate'.[85] A major catastrophe could damage the infrastructure of the economy.[86] The Great Fire of London destroyed £8 million of property; £25,000 of cloth was lost at Blackwell Hall and John Joliffe personally lost £20,000.[87] Some natural disasters, such as earthquakes and volcanic eruptions, were geographically restricted, but drought, excessive cold, storms, flood and fire were common occurrences. Although an individual merchant was not directly affected by long-term demographic and climatic change, he was subject at regular intervals to severe short-term crises, which could be caused by poor harvests, plague, war and currency problems. Trade was depressed during one out of every two years between 1571 and 1641 and recessions reached crisis levels during the 1590s, the 1620s, the 1640s and the 1690s.[88]

Even in a prosperous economy, weather and temperature randomly determined the availability of goods, the speed and timing of transportation and the condition and market value of perishable cargoes.[89] The global market was highly volatile with sharp fluctuations in prices caused by glut and scarcity; many trades depended on a single staple commodity and on a particular season.[90] A business could be ruined by a realignment of channels of distribution and by protective barriers, by adverse exchange rates, by the renaissance of old rivals or the emergence of new

[82] Dawe 1950: 19; Morgan 1978: 5, 7, 10; Locke 1916: 119–22; Vanes 1982: 3. Earle 1989a: 90–1 notes that only a minority had family and geographical links.

[83] Bright 1858: 188–9. [84] CUL Add. MS 91C; KAO U.119/C4, Feb. 1704.

[85] Malynes, *Lex Mercatoria*, p. 221. [86] Stratton 1969; BL Sloane MS 811.

[87] *HMC Sackville*, ii. 102; Reddaway 1940: 74–5; Johnson 1920: iii. 275; Bell 1923: 227.

[88] Scott 1910–12: i. 261, 464–7; Ashley 1962: 143–4, 178; Wilson 1957: 148–9; J. P. Cooper in Aylmer 1973b: 135; Taylor 1972: 260; Coleman 1977: 66, 137; Minchinton 1969: 10; J. R. Jones 1979: 138; D. W. Jones in Butel 1979: 159. [89] *Bolton Letters*, p. 46.

[90] P. Musgrave in Cottrell & Aldcroft 1981; Steakley 1980: 338.

opponents. When demand slackened, goods had to be sent on consignment without firm orders. The value of inventory could be reduced by changes in fashion or political events. Success only encouraged others to imitate and a competitive advantage could be eroded by changes in technology and design which produced better and cheaper goods. Only one coal pit in two was profitable and two-thirds of the Companies founded between 1690 and 1695 had disappeared by 1698. Ill-informed markets were governed by rumour and the whole financial structure was vulnerable to panic and loss of confidence; the patents boom bankrupted several merchants.[91] The chain of credit was only as strong as its weakest link and it is the vulnerability of businessmen which explains why they regarded bankrupts with a mixture of sympathy and hostility.

Merchants who lived as resident aliens in countries with corrupt and arbitrary regimes and with different religions, faced political coups, rebellions, confiscation and requisition, interrogation as heretics and massacre by lynch mobs.[92] When travelling, they could be poisoned by foreign competitors, captured by pirates and murdered or enslaved, kidnapped by mutineers, imprisoned, often under harsh conditions, by foreign governments as spies or hostages.[93] Even in self-governing settlements overseas, they lived behind fortifications; factors were expected to defend their ships and goods and some died in the attempt.[94] The records of Trinity House and the Admiralty Court provide a vivid record of irresponsible ship-masters, poorly maintained and overladen ships, undisciplined and mutinous crews.[95]

Heavy losses were suffered by individuals in the numerous wars of the century. Some 390 ships were lost, 1625–30, 700, 1672–3, 4,000, 1688–97 and some 3,250 during the War of the Spanish Succession; the *Johannah* went down with £70,000 in specie and the loss of the Levant fleet in 1693 was catastrophic.[96] Even when war was undeclared or when England remained neutral, naval protection could not eliminate privateers and pirates, which were most dangerous in local waters. The indirect effects of war at sea were also serious – shortages of transport and seamen, higher costs, delays, embargoes and detaining of ships. Masters were tempted to run ahead of convoys to beat the competition. One pamphleteer thought that the disruptions of wartime 'ought to be allowed to pass instead of his

[91] Bod. Rawl. Lett. MS 66, fo. 110; Macleod 1986: 562, 566.

[92] Foxe, *Acts and Monuments*, viii. 513–16; Aström 1963: i. 130.

[93] *Trinity House Deptford Transactions*, p. 58; Knight, *Relation Several Years' Slaverie*; Watson 1980a: 226; Paige, *Letters*, p. xi; Crump & Shortal 1935: 46.

[94] McGrath 1954: 293; Johnston 1971: 400; Strachey 1916: 127.

[95] HCA 1/60; *Trinity House Deptford Transactions*, p. 114; Andrews 1991: chap. 3.

[96] GLL MS 10823/1, fo. 22; K. G. Davies 1957: 207–9; Lenman 1990: 49; Clark 1923; 1952; Barlow, *Journal*, i. 355; Clarke 1940: 106.

Quota to all publick Taxes'.[97] Land warfare was even worse, as pillage and disruption were more widespread. During the Civil Wars in England there was considerable destruction of property and Thomas Priestley had to travel on business in hired convoys.[98]

Merchants who dealt in cash and goods were also particularly vulnerable to fraud, theft and pilferage by dishonest servants, apprentices, warehousemen, ship-masters, professional thieves and confidence tricksters.[99] The worst risk was, however, the bankruptcy and misfortunes of third parties.[100] It was impossible to ascertain with complete certainty the true financial position of any client and it was extremely difficult and time-consuming to recover debts.[101] Despite efforts to reform and strengthen the law, fraudulent bankruptcy remained an insoluble problem and there was no real protection against genuine failure.[102] Every merchant was far too dependent on the integrity, competence and reliability of his factors, agents, partners and clients; retailers could be ruined by customers who failed to pay their debts.[103] Receipts had to come in faster than payments were made.

The greatest hazard which every businessman faced, however, was premature death; contemporary diaries and correspondence are filled with announcements of illness and untimely deaths. Longevity was crucial to success, because a fortune accumulated over time and older merchants had greater experience. Itinerant and overseas merchants were particularly exposed to infectious diseases, like cholera, typhus, yellow fever, malaria, dysentery and tuberculosis.[104] Two-thirds of the factors in Persia died within two years and in India, as Ovington put it, two monsoons were the age of man; the average annual mortality rate for adult males in the West Indies was 33 per 1,000 compared with 23 for rural Massachusetts.[105] It was merchant shipping which carried the pandemic diseases; the cemeteries in commercial outposts all over the world bore silent witness to careers cut short. Approximately 20 per cent of merchants whose wills were proved at Canterbury died abroad or at sea, though many of these would have lived a normal span.[106]

[97] C. K., *Some Seasonable Thoughts*, p. 71.

[98] *Yorkshire Diaries*, i. 23; Porter 1986.

[99] *Southampton Examinations 1634–9*, p. 98; GLL MS 5105; Sharpe 1984: 5, 104, 119, 175; Beattie 1981: 114, 175–6, table 4.9; Cockburn 1977: 52, 64–5; Shoemaker 1991; Pugh 1978: 137; V. C. Edwards in Ives & Manchester 1983: 91. Crime could be regarded as a business in its own right: see McMullan 1984: 119, 157.

[100] Lowe, *Diary*, p. 60; Stout, *Autobiography*, pp. 8–9.

[101] Paige, *Letters*, p. 71.

[102] It is often difficult to know who suffered more, the debtor or the creditor. See *Companion for Debtors*; *Imprisonment of Men's Bodies for Debt*; Duffy 1986.

[103] N. H., *Compleat Tradesman*, p. 31. The Crown was the worst offender, though it could issue letters of protection from creditors: see Mason 1985: 93.

[104] Willan 1959: 27; Biraben 1975–6: i. 127–9, 375, 449.

[105] Ferrier 1970: 193; Galenson 1985: 231.

[106] See table 10.1; Morse 1926: i. 48.

Even in England, although they were diseases of the young and poor and could be countered by preventative measures, plague and influenza disrupted business and death could strike arbitrarily at any time.[107] It was not mere rhetoric for the preachers to urge good accounting on those who might die at any moment.[108] The demographic characteristics of businessmen are uncertain because, except for studies of the magistrates of some towns, the data accumulated for the century has not yet been classified by occupation.[109] London was not as healthy as the countryside and average life expectancy was 21–36, though there were substantial differences between parishes; 84 per cent of five-year-olds reached 20 and 75 per cent of those reached 50.[110] Life expectancy at birth for the whole population fell to 32 between 1625 and the 1690s.[111]

Merchants resident in England are unlikely to have fared worse than the norm, though the advantages which they enjoyed in living conditions and nutrition probably had little impact.[112] Although mortality was high in infancy and childhood, those who survived to take their freedom could expect to live to around 50.[113] Tudor prentices could expect 29.2 years of life after their freedom and the life expectancy of the children of the Elizabethan aldermen of London at age 5 was 50.[114] In Norwich, the average age at election was 46 for sheriffs and 48 for aldermen, whose life expectancy was 63; in Glasgow the average age at death of donors was 56.5 and in Barnstaple it was 63.4.[115] But there were arbitrary and significant differences within and between families. The average age of the Mousehole Carys was 37 and that of the Bideford and Hampshire Carys was

[107] Appleby 1988: 162; Slack 1971: 476; 1985: chap. 12; Shrewsbury 1970: 486–7; Dyer 1978: 309–13; Doolittle 1975: 333; Hollingsworth 1971: 144; Palliser 1973: 56. Moore 1993: table 3. [108] N. H., *Compleat Tradesman*, p. 237.

[109] Studying elite groups is convenient, but unfortunately biased, because those who had survived to the age at which admission was normal were more likely to be long-lived.

[110] Brodsky (Elliott) in Outhwaite 1981: 90; 1980: 14; Finlay 1981: tables 5, 16; E. A. Wrigley in Bynum & Porter 1991: 134.

[111] Wrigley 1969: 86; 1981: 230–1; Dublin *et al.* 1949: chap. 2; Alter 1983: 40–1. For the Quakers, 1651–99, it was 29: see Vann & Eversley 1992: table 3.13. Hollingsworth 1969: 23, 216; Weir 1989: 107.

[112] Appleby 1975b: 19; Livi-Bacci 1983: 298; Drummond 1958: 128–31, 157–60; Riley 1987: xiii, 30.

[113] BL Harl. MS 7021; D. V. Glass in Glass & Revelle 1972: 14; Rappaport 1988: 118 puts the life expectancy of Tudor apprentices at 54 when they took their freedom, though only one-third lived to 60. In Leeds the average age at death was 48–52: see Kirby 1983: 140. Even in the fifteenth century, northern merchants who survived to their twenties lived to 50–60: see J. H. I. Kermode in Clough 1982: 12. Earle 1989a: 310, fig. 11.3 has a median of 44.5 for his whole sample and 52 for the merchants. The age of gravity was usually regarded as 50–70.

[114] Private communication from Malcolm Kitch. Rappaport 1989: 7.

[115] Smout 1968: 61; Trease 1972: 46; Evans 1974: 57 and 1979: 55.

64.5.[116] Some of the most successful merchants lived into their seventies and eighties and one Aleppo factor lived to be 97.[117]

Good health, which was a constant preoccupation, was as much a matter of luck as of self-preservation. Temporary incapacity and fatigue as well as chronic disability could devastate an otherwise sound business.[118] Smallpox was declining, though still a real threat, but respiratory and venereal diseases, ulcers, liver complaints and parasitic infestations were common among merchants.[119] Even those ailments which did not kill, like the stone, the ague, paralysis and failing eyesight, skin troubles like ringworm, rheumatism, vitamin deficiency, hernias, bad teeth, improperly knit fractures, intestinal parasites and disorders, sciatica and back pains, could undermine attention to business and force retirement. Cotesworth and Liddell were chronically ill and Thomas Pengelly had to suspend his business because of the ague.[120] Sir William Turner suffered from continuous bouts of gout, colic and stone and once passed a stone the size of a grain of wheat.[121] James Bovey had to retire at 32 to the country where he lived on chicken and studied law and philosophy.[122] Failing health at the end of a merchant's life could also create problems. When Priestley's father's strength failed at 40 and he could not attend Hall and the Exchange, he took a coach home to die: 'I heard him say he had enough of this world'.[123]

Businessmen were also subject to random accidents. Several terrifying accounts of sea journeys occur in merchant journals and although youngsters constituted the majority of casualties, the older were not spared.[124] Merchants were crushed by their own merchandise when packing, caught in explosions, scalded, thrown from horses, run over by coaches, engulfed in sudden fires or drowned when fording rivers; Nicolas Herrick was urged 'to make your book of reckoning perfect for we be all uncertain when it shall pleased God to call us' and indeed he fell

[116] Harrison 1920: 691, plate 9.

[117] At least twenty-five examples could be cited from private business papers. The median age of Jacobean aldermen was 71.3: see Lang 1963: 280; Anderson 1989: 93; Hammer 1978: 24.

[118] Diamond 1967: 561 mentions that Schumpeter in discussion regarded this as the most important single factor.

[119] *Portledge Papers*, p. 30. On death from disease see Brett-James 1929–33; MacFarlane 1970: 170–71; Porter 1989: 12–13; Beier 1987: chap. 5.

[120] Bod. Add. MS C.267, fo. 8.

[121] GLL MS 5105, fo. 4.

[122] Aubrey, *Lives*, ed. Clark, p. 112.

[123] *Yorkshire Diaries*, ii. 201.

[124] *Admiralty Court Deposition 1637–8*; PCC indexes; Kirby 1986: 169; Oosterveen 1970: 117 shows a rate of 1 per cent in 3,060 burials.

from a window to his death.[125] James Boddington was nearly killed while stacking galls in his father's cellar and all his family had close shaves.[126] John Richards tired of keeping the East Indian warehouse and set out for India as a factor with his family and some bullion he had saved, but he died from a fall aboard ship on the fifth day after leaving the Downs.[127] Even sedentary merchants were exposed to physical assault and violent death in brawls, riots and robberies.[128] Any business was also vulnerable to the sudden death of principals and clients. When a debtor died, repayment was uncertain: 'I am sorry it was not followed while he lived', explained one factor, 'but now tis too late'.[129] Recovering the debts and assets of those who died abroad was even more difficult.[130]

Both external and internal risks of course varied in frequency and severity.[131] Many of these everyday hazards were faced by the whole population. Landowners and professional men could also lose their assets; their estates could be confiscated and their houses could burn down.[132] Merchants were less liable to die at sea than mariners, since they did not usually travel on tiny ships of 26–35 tons.[133] Shipping losses from wreck and seizure can be exaggerated and convoys were effective; the East Indian ships had a loss rate of only 6 per cent per annum.[134] Risk could be spread among partners and shareholders and hedged by insuring ships and cargoes at rates as low as 2–4 per cent in peacetime; houses could be covered against fire after 1681 and their contents after 1708.[135] Speculative ventures could be combined with staple trades and a safety net was provided by kinsmen and by religious fellowship. Ill fortune did not usually strike all merchants at the same time or with the same force; high mortality created more opportunities for the survivors. War simply directed trade into new channels and offered new markets, high prices and

125 *Southampton Calendar Apprentices*, p. xxii and *Book Examinations*, iii. 43; GLL MS 10823/1; Rawdon, *Life*, p. 44; Bowles 1918: 31; BL Harl. MS 7021; Nichols, *Leicester*, ii. 616. Miraculous escapes were of course reported as a sign of Providence by the religious: see Taylor 1945: 138–9; Heywood, *Autobiography*, ii. 230–303; Youings 1968: 97. Causes of accidental death are listed by Forbes 1971: chap. 6 and 1976: 413–14; Clarkson 1975: chap. 6.

126 Verney MSS, letter 19 April 1660; GLL MS 10823/1, fo. 57; Rawdon, *Life*, p. 44.

127 Hedges, *Diary*, ii. p. cclxxiii.

128 Cocks, *Diary*; SP 110/13, letter John Heath; Smythe, *Obituary*, 29; Sanderson, *Travels*, i. 18; Ellis 1981a: 215; J. A. Goring in Knecht & Scarisbrick 1978: 216; Applebee 1979: 54.

129 Bod. Rawl. Lett. MS 66, fo. 49.

130 Bod. Ashurst MS C.1, fo. 73.

131 On the different categories of risk see Knight 1921: 43; Hayek 1978; Discoll & Rizzo 1985: chap. 5; Coornaert 1970: 582.

132 On the incidence of house fires see Porter 1973 and E. L. Jones 1984: tables 1–2. The Grocers were able to recover their plate, though melted, after the Great Fire and Simon D'Ewes' father recovered £500 in gold when his office burned down: see Heath 1869: 23; D'Ewes, *Autobiography*, i. 211.

133 *Southampton Book Examinations*, vi.

134 Davis 1962: 318; Krishna 1924: 254.

135 GLL MS 3041/1, fo. 72.

quick profits for some.[136] Opportunity was directly related to instability and one man's loss was another's opportunity. Indeed a high level of bankruptcy was one indicator of a vigorous and expanding economy.[137]

There was, however, no way of rationally managing risk, because it was not possible to calculate probability accurately.[138] 'If one could forsee ... it wld be an Easey matter to get an estate', remarked Cotesworth.[139] Insurance was still regarded as bad luck and cowardice.[140] Merchants frequently underinsured and policies provided limited protection.[141] Although they lacked a proper statistical basis, premiums still had to reflect the degree of risk and rates escalated as high as 20–25 per cent in wartime, when the need for coverage was greatest, and the insurers often collapsed.[142] Active and sleeping partners still bore unlimited liability and the joint-stock Companies and shipping syndicates called on their shareholders for additional funds.[143]

It was no consolation for anyone who suffered reverses to know that some of his fellows would prosper. It is not surprising that merchants should invest in real estate, which was infinitely safer than business. The Italians, observed Lewis Roberts, 'are loath to trust God with their estates at sea, when they may have the same safe on shoare'.[144] Frequently a merchant was assailed from all directions at the same time. George Warner, for example, faced a reduction in purchasing power because of war and civil disturbances which lowered prices and restricted credit; meanwhile his cloth deteriorated in storage in the summer heat, one of his debtors drowned and, when a ship ran aground in Kent, his goods were washed ashore and taken by the country people.[145]

All businessmen were therefore subject to specific and continuous

136 On the complex calculations of gain and loss from war see Andrews 1991: 147; Kepler 1973: 221; Clark 1923: 127–8; D. W. Jones in Israel 1991: 399, 402; D.W. Jones in Butel 1979: 159.

137 Hoppitt 1987: chap. 2; Lloyd 1978: 307.

138 See p. 174.

139 Ellis 1981a: 5, 41.

140 *Southampton Book Examinations*, ii. 53–4; CUL Add. 91C, fo. 120v°; Gravil 1968: 73–5.

141 Shammas 1975: 10 n.13; Kepler 1975: 48–50; MacGrath 1954: 286–7; Bod. Rawl. Lett. MS 66, fo. 110; BL Add. MS 70223, letter 20 July 1694; Essex RO D/DU 457/7, letter 2 Dec. 1665; BL Add. MS 24107, fo. 149; Halperin 1945: 8.

142 There is abundant information on rates in private business papers, such as the Bowrey MSS at Lloyds; BL Add. MSS 5222; Lincs. AO, Pearson–Gregory MSS; GLL MS 10823/1; Paige, *Letters*, p. xxix; Cruttenden, *Atlantic Merchant Apothecary*, p. 37; *Aufrère Papers*, p. 29. The best series is in Marescoe, *Markets and Merchants*, app. E, table A.7. See also Davis 1956: 318; 1962: 88, 318; Barbour 1929: 585, 590–2; Ward 1978: 200, table 2; Posthumous 1946: lxiv; Trenerry 1926: 272; Grassby 1994: 84; Dunn 1972: 211.

143 Cooke 1959: 77–9; Patterson & Reiffen 1990: 167; K. G. Davies 1957: 341–7; Pennington 1973: 151.

144 Roberts, *Merchant's Map Commerce*, preface.

145 SP 46/84, nos. 86–7, 281.

risks, even though their degree of exposure was higher in new ventures and the impact on individuals was arbitrary. Disinvestment could be slow and difficult and it was the wealthy and active who frequently went bankrupt.[146] Providence was always on the lips of merchants, because fortunes gyrated wildly and bad luck could ruin the ablest and richest.[147] 'Well might this place be termed the Change', wrote Thomas Fuller.[148] Too much depended on choice of trade and timing of entry. Merchants had no control over unpredictable events and most were not cushioned by abundant resources against disaster. When Sir John Morden founded his college, in 1695, he intended it for the relief of honest and poor merchants who had been impoverished by ill fortune. Young merchants had to trust 'upon day' and if they failed, they were thrust into the squalid, frightening world of the bankrupt, the criminal and the social outcast.[149] At best they faced disgrace and pauperism, at worst the living death of the Counters sustained by food and clothing brought by kinsmen.[150]

Once a business was established, profits could grow to cover overheads and enable some capital to be accumulated. Money and reputation attracted more business and cheaper funding. Every business had its point of take-off, after which it matured and became self-generating. But new entrants were trapped in a vicious circle. Too many of them competed for too few opportunities. Their shortage of capital, aggravated by high premiums and by negligent or incompetent masters, forced them to either withdraw or to take dangerous chances which could ruin them. Their high rate of failure, in turn, made it harder for them to find principals, partners and masters. Any young novice faced higher risks and lower expectations of profit than a seasoned trader and he could not expect to attain financial independence quickly or easily. Child's estimate of ten years to build up a network of customers, accumulate profits and attain self-sufficiency is close to the truth.[151] In Powell's words, business 'requireth greate stock great experience in Forraine estates And great hazard and adventure at the best'.[152]

146 C. B. Phillips in Riden 1985: 46. See also p. 252.

147 Gill 1961: 11. Although gradually Providentialism became secularized and vestigial, a greater stress on secondary causes and on free-will did not eliminate feelings of helplessness. See Bec 1967a: 1207–9, 1212–13; Boiteux 1968: 142.

148 Fuller, *History of Worthies*, ii. 336.

149 Stow, *Survey*, ed. Strype, ii. 25; Rogers 1971: 454.

150 Bagwell, *Distressed Merchant*; *Humble Representation upon Perpetual Imprisonment*; Harris, *Œconomie of Fleet*, pp. 82–4; Pitt, *Cry of Oppressed*; M. Harris in Myers & Harris 1985: 195. Debtors, although mixed with other offenders since there were no individual cells, were the main occupants of Ludgate, Newgate and other prisons.

151 Friis 1927: 92–3.

152 Powell, *Tom of all Trades*, p. 162.

Office and the professions

Business was not alone in requiring start-up capital. Some active barristers delayed taking chambers and were consequently fined by the Inns. But usually those who had been called had the expense of renting a chamber – £80–100 per annum together with entry fines, though these were at the discretion of the Treasurer. Half-chambers could be rented, but they had to be furnished at a cost of £10–20 and general maintenance of £20–50 per annum had to be found as well as travelling expenses on circuit; presents of wine were expected on advancement to the Bench.[153] The purchase price of legal offices was related to their income: D'Ewes' father paid £5,000 for a clerkship which brought in £1,400 per annum.[154] But they still represented a major investment; a lesser judicial post cost £2,000–6,000 and a major judgeship £5,000–17,000. In contrast, an attorney could set up for £100, though a place in a sheriff's court could cost £1,200.[155] Employees of Companies and office-holders also needed capital if they wished to engage in private trade.[156] Army officers had to supply equipment and advance money to their troops.

Office automatically generated income according to a pre-fixed stipend. Payment in kind and by daily allowances survived in departments of state, the Army, the diplomatic service and the Church and provided some protection against inflation. The emoluments of royal officials before 1640 included clothing, gifts, benefices, board and lodging, licenses and grants of executorships. Some officials, like the clerks of Assize were paid per diem, which really made them journeymen. But there was a persistent trend towards payment in money and by annual salary, though paid in instalments. The clergy preferred to commute their tithes, which they exploited more efficiently in the later part of the century and compounded to reduce the cost of collection.[157] One by one the major institutions monetarized. The House of Commons appointed its first salaried Clerk in 1645, and gradually eliminated fees for Bills and payment by grants of benefices and gratuities.[158] The Admiralty reduced payment by perquisites in 1665 and the Cromwellian reforms in the Ordnance Office were retained when it became salaried and civilian in 1683.[159] Although the East India Company initially paid commissions and a share of profits, it introduced salaries as early as 1609.[160]

153 Lemmings 1990: 23; North, *Lives*, p. 30; his grandfather also gave him £20 p.a.
154 D'Ewes, *Autobiography*, i. 177.
155 Brooks 1980: 249; *Yorkshire Diaries*, ii. 208.
156 C109/19; Love 1913: i. 173–5; Bod. Eng. Hist. MS C.156, fo. 95.
157 Evans 1970: 26; *Warwickshire Ecclesiastical Terriers*; Pruett 1978: 74–5; Leatherbarron 1982.
158 O. C. Williams 1954: 17–18.
159 Walton 1894: 723.
160 Chaudhuri 1965: 83–4.

The real profits of office, nonetheless, came from fees. The salaried law officials and judges made their money from fees and *douceurs* from suppliants and the Chancery Masters utilized funds deposited in Court; law clerks supplemented their low wages by extortion and by taking a percentage of damages. Barristers took honoraria and retainers; attorneys and solicitors relied entirely on fees, which steadily rose during the century, and indulged in related banking, broking and investment transactions on the side.[161] The clergy supplemented their stipends by offerings, fees, gifts and obits, teaching, chaplaincies and preaching.[162] The poorest ministers sometimes farmed or kept alehouses.[163] Consuls sold passports, extracted fees from ship-masters and indulged in private trading. Teachers ran private schools to supplement their formal income.[164]

Since neither the Crown nor other public bodies could raise the revenue to pay their servants properly, it was assumed that they would recompense themselves by charging consumers of their services; bribery served as a commission or brokerage fee.[165] Most officers, from the Customs and Ordnance to the prisons and the Post Office, made their real income by exploiting the inefficiencies of the system. The Elizabethan Court of Wards put £2 million into private hands and, despite reforms, some £590,000–760,000 in fees was extracted by government servants in the 1630s.[166] In the Farms, private contractors could line their pockets by anticipating revenue for the Crown at a discount.[167] Even under direct management, Paymasters and Receivers profited handsomely from manipulating tax revenues and providing essential banking services.[168] A relatively honest career administrator, like Pepys, still took his fees and in six years as Secretary of State Daniel Finch acquired £50,000.[169]

Ever since the Hundred Years War, the Army had been treated as a business as much as a profession.[170] The regiment was an unlimited Company and a professional officer was virtually self-employed; he bought and could resell his commission, and earned his income by contracting for supplies, collecting pay and allowances for ghost troops

161 G. L. Andersen in Harris 1969; *Somerset Assize Orders*, p. xvii.

162 M. L. Zell in O'Day 1981: 8; Stieg 1982: 148.

163 Tyler 1969: 91; Hart 1958: 125; B. A. Holderness in O'Day & Heal 1981: 204.

164 Horne 1952: 14.

165 Hurstfield 1973b: 161. A distinction was made between the fees of office and those privately enjoyed by an officer: see J. D. Alsop in Haigh 1984: 101.

166 Aylmer 1971: 249; Hurstfield 1973a: 279–80, 343–8; Bell 1954: 35–8, 44; Braddock 1975; D. Thomas 1977: 72.

167 Ashton 1957: 167.

168 Tomlinson 1975: 56, 72–4.

169 H. J. Habakkuk in Plumb 1955: 145; Pepys, *Diary*, v. 1.34; Poole 1966: 37–9.

170 Keen 1965: 15, 242; Childs 1976: 30–9, 44–5, app. H.

and cheating his men on their rations.[171] His pay bore little relation to the price of commissions, but through corruption a Company could yield £400 per annum and a colonelcy £200–600 per annum. In the Navy likewise, low pay was supplemented by passengers, false musters, prize money, fees for convoys and, until 1686, by freight money on bullion and valuable cargoes; naval officers frequently alternated with the merchant service.[172]

Employees in the private sector did not rely on their salaries. A steward had his commission on leases and independent trade.[173] The Clerks of City Companies received fees on sealings and for drawing up indentures; the Clerk of the Merchant Adventurers at Exeter was paid for drawing up charter-parties.[174] Agents and officers of the export Companies could receive a share of profits, the right to take apprentices or the right to private trade; Sir Edwin Sandys wanted to introduce high salaries in the Virginia Company.[175] The East India Company paid minimal salaries, though it did provide free transport and board and lodging in India.[176] Consequently factors and their wives, chaplains and surgeons all ignored Company prohibitions and traded for themselves and on behalf of relatives, sailors and principals in England; they also double-charged and embezzled Company funds. There was never a clear line between Company servant and independent businessman: Humphrey Walcott was apprenticed to James Carbonel of Cadiz, in 1691, but he ended as a servant of the Africa Company.[177]

All offices of profit had drawbacks. Sometimes the overheads of patronage exceeded the profits of office. The salaries of many posts were totally inadequate or had been fixed at pre-inflation levels: the stipends of college fellows and schoolmasters were often restrained by the terms of the endowment or by college statutes.[178] The solution adopted by incumbents was pluralism, which was essential in the Church and common in all branches of law and government.[179] Blathwayt at his peak was drawing from plural offices £4,415 in salaries, though he normally received about £2,000 per annum after deductions for fees, sub payments

171 Walton 1894: 392, 447–50, 455, 635, 644–91; B. Williams 1932: 16; Cruickshank 1946: chap. 9; Fortescue 1910–30: i. 318–20.

172 Walker 1938: 21; Routh 1912: 152.

173 Coleman 1963: 183; Hainsworth in Prest 1987: 160–5; Hainsworth 1993; Melton 1978; Martin 1979; J. V. Beckett in Chartres & Hey 1990: chap. 3.

174 Cotton 1872: 60.

175 Willan 1953: 33–8; Aström 1963: 184; Lingelbach 1902: 31; Farnell 1963–4: 448; Dering, *Parliamentary Diary*, p. xi; Nat. Lib. Wales Wynn MS F.iii.18; H. C. Williams 1958: i. 189.

176 *Reasons Humbly Offered against the East India Trade*, p. 3; K. G. Davies 1957: 163, 252–6.

177 Shropshire RO Walcott & Bittersley MSS.

178 Winstanley 1935: 279–91; MacConica 1986.

179 Mitchinson 1962: 188–9.

and the cost of patents.[180] Thanks to the recurrent financial crises of the government and the sloth of the Exchequer, salaries were frequently in arrears; pensions and salaries had to be suspended in 1681, and soldiers had to wait for their pay even in wartime. The allowances to diplomats for equipage, plate and diet often did not cover their expenses; they had to compensate by engaging in business and stockjobbing or exploiting their diplomatic privileges.[181] The East India Company paid half of a servant's salary in England and often in arrears.

Employment was irregular in the Army and Navy and those who survived combat in wartime became economic casualties in time of peace 'like chimneys in summer'. Half-pay in the Army was introduced in the 1660s but was only regularized in the 1690s, and in 1715 only 449 officers were so supported; in the Navy it dated from 1668 but was not regularized until 1694.[182] There was also limited provision for retirement and for dependants. Although payments in the Army were made from a contingency fund after 1661 and extended in 1672, pensions really date from 1697; in the Navy the operative date was 1674.[183] In the Church, the income from a benefice stopped with death.[184] Even the bishops had problems providing for their children and surviving family, as they had high expenses and only enjoyed their revenues for life.[185] Formalized pensions for civil servants, as distinct from *ad hominem* grants, were not introduced until the end of the century; the Excise had adopted them by 1687 and the Customs and Salt Office by 1713.

There were always insufficient posts at the higher levels.[186] Although new ranks were introduced, like King's Counsel, the number of judges and legal officers in England remained constant: there were only eight Common Law judges and four Barons of the Exchequer plus the Chancellor and the Master of the Rolls and forty serjeants.[187] Only fifty-two judges were appointed between 1603 and 1642 and only forty-seven barristers became serjeants, 1648–60; one in five reached the Bench.[188] There were only twenty-six sees, twenty-four deaneries and twenty-six archdeaconries; forty-one episcopal vacancies occurred between 1603 and 1625. The Treasury had only twenty to twenty-five officials in the 1680s. There were few ambassadorships and they were usually filled by men of substance. Even after 1689, the main expansion occurred in the revenue departments and the armed services and in the middle and lower

[180] Jacobsen 1932: 2, 435–8; Webb 1968.
[181] Lane 1927: 95–9; Horn 1959; 1932: 22–46; Bell 1980: 122; Haley 1986: 293; Bale 1981: 18.
[182] J. D. Davies 1991: 53–5.
[183] I. Roy in Prest 1987: 201; Ehrmann 1953: 139–40.
[184] Sykes 1934: 147–57, chaps. 4–5; Aylmer, *Asheton's Proposal*; Naish, *Diary*.
[185] Giles Fletcher Elder, *English Works*, p. 394; Hembry 1967: 256–8; Hill 1956: 26.
[186] Elton 1976: 214.
[187] Foss 1848–64: vi. 13, 41.
[188] Prest 1986: 135.

ranks, like clerkships in Chancery and the Exchequer. All the professions had a hierarchy and a preference for age and seniority, but they lacked a clear and consistent career structure. There was no personal rank in the Navy until after the Restoration and soldiers were appointed to command at sea.

Patronage and connection were as important to advance a career as to secure entry. Promotion in government was haphazard and depended on influence rather than on skill; political interference and nepotism were rampant. The spoils of office whether in government or the law did not necessarily fall to those with the greatest learning, training and talent.[189] A barrister known and connected to a judge had a much better chance of having his motion accepted.[190] Merit or piety sometimes carried weight in the Church, but it was virtually impossible to obtain preferment without family and political connections.[191] Patronage and corruption were rife in the Army and Navy, except during the Interregnum, and led to inefficiencies in both administration and command. Promotion in the East India Company was determined by favouritism in India as well as in England. Physicians needed to move in the right social circles to secure wealthy patients. Members of all professions intermarried, though networks of kin were more common than hereditary transfers from father to son.[192]

All the professions competed fiercely for preferment and for private clients. The Common Law lawyers found that their market was saturated after 1660; the volume of business declined and there was internal fighting between Courts for business; the Civil Law Courts were threatened by prohibitions and the number of civilians fell by half.[193] The attorneys took work away from the scriveners, who had combined legal, clerical and business talents and who had themselves taken business from the notaries public.[194] The physicians had to compete not only with the apothecaries but with empirics, unlicensed providers and midwives: although they tried to avoid payment by results, some contracts were conditional and they had to cater to the consumer.[195] It took good timing and luck for a naval officer to secure prizes. Progess was also slow; it took twenty to twenty-five years to rise to a captaincy in the Navy and ten years to rise from utter barrister to the Bench.

Nor did incumbents enjoy complete security. The Church was torn by

[189] W. J. Jones 1971: chap. 2; Lemming 1990: chap. 8; Peck 1982.

[190] Veale 1970: 46.

[191] Stone 1964a: 71; Cross 1960; Pruett 1975: 213; O'Day 1975a: 260; Beddard 1967: 35.

[192] Collinson 1982: 115; M. Hawkins in Beier *et al.* 1989: table 7.9.

[193] C. W. Brooks in Baker 1978: table 1; Levack 1973: chap. 2.

[194] H. C. Gutteridge in *Cambridge Legal Essays* 1926: 132; *Scriveners Company Papers*; *Bristol Inhabitants in 1695*, p. xv.

[195] Beier 1987: 256; Cook 1980: chap. 1; Pelling 1987.

political and religious turmoil and the reforming spirit within and outside the Church challenged tithes and discredited the comfortable abuses of the past. The 1640s introduced disorder, uncertainty and the prospect of expulsion; the bishops faced impeachment, sequestration and imprisonment; the Laudian clergy were repressed and 1,479 were deprived.[196] Slingsby Bethel thought that the Dissolution and the poverty and insecurity of the Church had driven gentlemen into trade.[197] In 1662, 1,760 Presbyterians were ejected from the Church and had to turn to teaching or keeping coffee houses; non-jurors were in turn ejected after 1688.[198]

The high offices of state were hostage to political swings and all offices were subject to tests of religious belief. Office-holders were happy to retain the Penal Laws, because they reduced competition.[199] Judges were purged, as were military officers during the Civil Wars and under James II.[200] Party conflict created a spoils system: Charles Davenant lived in poverty while out of office from 1689 until 1703.[201] Offices were only inheritable if a reversion had been granted for life. From the sixteenth century onwards, the Crown had tried hard to prevent transfer without royal consent, to reduce political pluralism and to discourage the performance of duties by under-clerks and deputies rather than by the titular holders.[202] Life tenure and reversionary interests were indeed eliminated in a significant number of departments of state in the late seventeenth century. Offices were converted to tenure by pleasure and, except in Chancery, this became mandatory after 1668. Residual interests had been largely eliminated by 1685, when an old rule was enforced that offices held *durante bene placito* should terminate and be renewed on the death of the Sovereign; this was made statutory in 1707.

A career structure did, however, slowly develop in government service. Public administration had over the centuries been slowly modernized in successive spasms of reform.[203] The bureaucrats had struggled with the courtiers and magnates who sought to profit from royal favour and office.[204] Although government had never been really open to talent, it had always depended on a hard core of competent administrators some of whom rose from the ranks.[205] During the seventeenth century, the nucleus of a professional civil service with a more formal organization

[196] Shaw 1900: ii. 193; James 1941; King 1968: 530–1; Green 1979: 525, 531; F. Heal in Heal & O'Day 1977: 113.
[197] Bethel, *Interest of Princes*, p. 5.
[198] Whiting 1931: 126, 469; Matthews 1934; A. Bosher in Nuttall & Chadwick 1976: 34–5. They did not, however, enter business.
[199] J. R. Jones 1972: 66.
[200] Childs 1980: 73.
[201] Waddel 1958–9: 280–5.
[202] Slavin 1965: 46; Aylmer 1959: 259.
[203] Tout 1934: ii. chap. 7; Elton 1961: 81.
[204] Slavin 1966: chap. 8; W. J. Jones 1967: 168; Young 1979; Hill 1988: xi.
[205] Hurstfield 1967: 30.

appeared. A secretariat emerged from the cluster of secretaries to individual officers.[206] After the Restoration, the Treasury, the Customs, the Army and the Navy were put into commission and the Farms were discontinued. The Treasury, from 1667 onwards, developed a clear hierarchy with differentiated functions, assigned duties and systematic record-keeping; the clerks developed an *esprit de corps* and were better paid and promoted by seniority.[207] The Ordnance Office standardized and doubled salaries; even the Exchequer introduced some reforms.[208] The diplomatic service made tentative steps towards professionalization and differentiated between ambassadors, envoys and secretaries.[209] The lesser offices provided first steps on the ladder of preferment.[210] It became feasible for ambitious men to rise from clerks to secretaries: the richest man in Restoration England, Sir Stephen Fox, started as a pageboy at Court.[211] A new, sophisticated and cultivated type of government servant emerged – though the old ways were slow to die.[212]

The same upward mobility was true of the professions. The law served as a ladder to political and administrative office. Those who failed to reach the highest judicial office could prosper in intermediate posts, as Benchers of their Inn or Masters of Requests and Chancery.[213] Although a division of labour was created between advocates and mechanics and despite efforts to restrict entry to gentlemen, barristers were drawn from all social groups and even clerks could rise. One-third of those who chose to practise were promoted; able and aggressive younger sons could rise fast.[214] The Lord Chief Justices over the century were drawn from a cross-section of society.[215] In the Church, graduates could start as chaplains, tutors and stipendiary preachers and climb through preferment. Although the Jacobean bishops were unusually diverse in origin, the episcopate was never monopolized by one social group.[216] The standing Army which emerged from the Interregnum, although still confused with the Navy, had a better defined hierarchy, including staff officers from 1685, scales of pay and regulations governing the sale of commissions.[217] The Navy benefited from greater professionalism during the Commonwealth; Officers Instructions clarified the structure of command.[218] In wartime it was always possible to rise from the ranks.

206 Jensen 1976: 29.
207 Baxter 1957: 139, 177; Roseveare 1973: 44; W. A. Aiken in Aiken & Henning 1960: 212.
208 Tomlinson 1974: 60, 66; Ball 1990: 88.
209 Quiller 1961: chaps. 4–5; Lee 1968: 126; Horn 1961: 43; Lachs 1965: 160.
210 Richardson 1953: 16–17. 211 Clay 1984. 212 Jacobsen 1932: 20.
213 Holdsworth 1902–16: vi. 432; Foss 1870.
214 Keeton 1965: 499; Prest 1986: 82, 144. 215 Campbell 1874: ii. 193.
216 G. Alexander in Ives *et al.* 1978; Kennedy 1962: 179; Heal 1980; Simon 1965; Fincham 1990: 19; Ravitch 1965: 318–19; 1966: 123–4, tables 6–10.
217 Bruce 1980; Glover 1980. 218 Lewis 1939: chap. 4.

Preferment was a game of snakes and ladders embracing several different professions. The author of *Of the Russe Commonwealth* took a Doctorate of Civil Law, served as Assistant to the Remembrancer of London and wrote letters for £50 per annum, later increased to £100; he then bought his freedom of the Haberdashers, obtained the lease of a parsonage and the Treasurership of St Paul's and ultimately served as a diplomat in the negotiations concerning the Merchant Adventurers and the Hanse.[219]

The classic career structure emerged in a business institution, the East India Company.[220] By 1658, the Company already had the nucleus of 'Civil Servants', a term which was to become synonymous with bureaucracy after the reforms of Cornwallis.[221] After 1669, it established a proper hierarchy with promotion by seniority and length of service; after 1675, regular grades of salary in four main classes defined the conditions of service.[222] Merit was often rewarded and it was quite possible to go out to India as a writer and return as head of a factory. There was supposed to be a five-year interval between promotions, but high mortality reduced that to three. John Hicks went out to Fort St George as an apprentice at £5 per annum, was made factor in 1676 at £20 and rose to be Secretary and a major figure in the factory, before he was expelled for fraud.[223] The other joint-stock Companies had similar structures, though their salaries were lower.

Both the Church and public office eventually acquired institutional security. The Church survived inflation, spoliation and revolution and was re-established in 1660 albeit under lay control.[224] Most ordinands eventually acquired a benefice.[225] An incumbent enjoyed life tenure and a stable, if low, income. As Roger North put it, 'The advantage you of the clergy have of other professions which lean upon perpetuall competition ... what you gett is a settlement in all events and even a rich wife falls short for she may die.'[226] Office was equally stable. Good behaviour was hard to disprove and, in practice, the Crown could not alter the unconditional nature of life tenure.[227] The same offices were frequently passed on from one generation to the next; all departments of state and their provincial branches had their dynasties. The middling offices were less political and,

219 Giles Fletcher Elder, *English Works*, 22–4, 44–6; Grassby 1958: 96.

220 Fryer, *New Account East India*, i. 89–90, 216–17; Bod. Rawl. MS A.303, fo. 145; D.747, fos. 139, 164; *East India Company Factories 1618–69*, xi; *1670–84*, vol. I, 1670–77, i. p. vii, ii. pp. vi, 143.

221 Chaudhuri 1965: 75, 83; Furber 1951: 338–9; O'Malley 1965.

222 *East India Company Factories 1618–69*, vol. XIII, 1668–69, x; *1670–84*, vol. I, 1670–77, ii. p. 273; *East India Company Court Minutes 1671–3*, ix. 82; Foster 1926: 211–12.

223 Hedges, *Diary*, ii. p. cclviii; *East India Company Factories* vol. I, *1670–77*, i. p. vii.

224 Green 1978: 177.

225 C. Cross in Thirsk 1970: 81; Pruett 1978: 54.

226 BL Add. MS 32501, fo. 77.

227 Sainty 1961: 151–2, 165; 1965: 464.

when the party furore of the 1690s had subsided, there were fewer political purges and greater continuity. The Crown refused to give any party a monopoly of office and the distribution of offices bridged the political division between executive and legislature.[228]

The potential rewards of business cannot easily be compared with the professions, because each had a different career path and a fluid structure which inhibits compilation of a reliable, composite index of earnings.[229] Future income depended on promotion and consisted of a confused medley of perquisites, gratuities, salary and the profits of private contracting, all of which were reduced by concealed costs. Industry, ability and patronage all played their part. Some entrants tried several professions and failed in all of them. The professions were not equally lucrative and were primarily geared to support a basic standard of living, not to serve as financial escalators. Although there were profits for the unscrupulous, the Army was best suited to those with a private income who regarded combat as a duty or as a leisure activity.

The professions were fundamentally divided by levels of risk. Barristers paid as much for their training as a merchant and, like the physicians, functioned in a competitive market. Public office and benefices in the Church, on the other hand, had lower starting costs and much greater relative security and regularity of income. The joint-stock export Companies offered the security of a minimum income and subsistence combined with the prospect of private trading and corruption. A fully salaried and pensioned Civil Service had not yet emerged, but conditions of employment did stabilize and officials enjoyed greater independence with less danger of dismissal. Although some posts were subject to purges and suspension, incompetence was rarely fatal. Incumbents could afford to be lazy and less persistent, because they suffered no monetary loss when they failed at their tasks. Those who sought a life of leisure could purchase a minor office, employ a deputy and still secure a modest income.

[228] Dering, *Parliamentary Diary*, pp. 39–40; Aylmer 1965: 60; Western 1972; Reitan 1966: 322; 1970: 587; Miller 1983: 491; C. Roberts in Baxter 1983: 205; Plumb 1967: 145, 189; Rubini 1967: 30. [229] See pp. 259–61.

4 Necessity and choice

What ultimately determined the flow of recruits into business as compared with other forms of employment? The incentive for sons of artisans and husbandmen is self-evident. Their entry can be regarded as betterment migration, which always accompanied the desperate migrations of the poor and unemployed. The children of propertied families were also pushed rather than pulled into business. Their need for employment was generated by demographic and inheritance patterns, family ambitions and financial imperatives. But they had a wider range of alternatives. In order to understand why they should choose business, it is necessary to examine closely the actual process of selection.

Primogeniture

The first priority of landed families was to guarantee the male succession, which required a reservoir of sons, since adoption of heirs was virtually unknown. The English chose to pass property between members of the elementary family rather than seek heirs among distant males in the collateral line.[1] But unilineal descent and vertical inheritance is much more difficult to sustain than lateral or bilateral inheritance.[2] The rate of extinction in the male line among landowners was remarkably high.[3] Only 30 per cent of the eldest sons of peers reached maturity; in a family with three sons, there was a chance of 1 in 8 that none would survive.[4]

There are some signs that births did cease, through abstinence or possibly artificial controls, once the male succession was assured.[5] 'The conspicuous consumption required in the reputable maintenance of a child', as Veblen put it, 'is probably the most effective of the Malthusian

[1] The English favoured 'divergent devolution' and estates were divided among surviving daughters rather than allowed to descend to a collateral male heir: see Goody 1976; Holdsworth 1923: iii. 114–16. [2] Goody 1975: 3; 1970; 1990: 427–8.

[3] Hollingsworth 1977: table 3; Stone 1962: app.; MacFarlane 1973: app. B; Walter & Laslett in Wachter 1978: 134; Cliffe 1969; Roebuck 1980: table 30; Beckett 1977: 572; Wrigley 1969: 102; Seldon 1981.

[4] Hollingsworth in Glass & Eversley 1965: 374; Wrigley 1973a: 727.

[5] Wrigley in Ranum 1972: 83; 1969: 72–4; Morrow 1978; MacLaren 1984: chap. 3.

prudential checks'.[6] Sir Patience Ward's father 'having had six sons & one Daughter by a second wife did frequently say if he had another son he would call him Patience'.[7] When ten of William Blundell's children survived, he remarked that 'this is not the way to grow rich'.[8] However, because death in infancy and adolescence was so common and unpredictable, it was inadvisable to limit births, and by the time that an heir had survived the most dangerous period of his life, several other children had been born. Although overall fertility was falling, some families were consequently weighed down with a numerous brood of children, half of whom were daughters who needed portions.[9]

The survival of the landed class depended on the transfer through inheritance of property rights. It was the notion of reversion, that service created rights for descendants, which had always been the *raison d'être* of noble families. To prevent morcellation of estates, primogeniture was essential, but this practice did not appear in Europe until the end of the twelfth century and its incidence varied considerably.[10] Estates could also be concentrated by abstinence from marriage.[11] But younger sons constituted a persistent social and political problem in all the European states. The debate on the *noblesse commercante*, which resurfaced at intervals of roughly a generation, recognized the severity of the problem.[12]

Even in England, the victory of primogeniture was by no means certain.[13] The extended kin network, rather than direct descent, determined succession during the Middle Ages; the law of inheritance was only slowly clarified.[14] Gavelkind or equal division survived in some counties like Kent as late as the seventeenth century, though it only applied in cases of intestacy.[15] Borough English or ultimogeniture endowed the youngest,

[6] Veblen 1935 : 113. [7] BL Add. MS 4224, fo. 33; Bramston, *Autobiography*, p. 19.

[8] Blundell, *Cavalier Letters*, p. 79.

[9] Hollingsworth in Glass & Eversley 1974: 370–5; 1965: 29, 32–4, 45, 56–7, tables 21, 23; Stone 1984: figs. 3.5, 8.

[10] Boutruche 1963: 285–94; Lewis 1968: chap. 3, 205; Génichot 1962; Yver 1966; Pillorget 1979: 102–3; Elliott 1963: 36–8; Kluchevsky 1951: 101–10; Roberts 1964–5: ii. 36–7, 60; 1967: 216–17.

[11] Peller 1947: 52–3; Davis 1975: chap. 6; Litchfield 1969a; Zanetti 1972: chap. 4; Herlihy in Abrams & Wrigley 1978; 1969: 1348; Hurwich in Beier *et al.* 1989: 45; Hopkins in Finley 1974:118–19.

[12] Hecht 1964: 267–89; Jouanna 1968; Lucas 1973; Rouray 1936; AD Loire-Inf, C.894, fo. 91v°; Bibliothèque Municipale Grenoble T 1410–14; Goubert 1969: i. 146, 158, 168.

[13] Bloch 1961: 195; Denholm-Young 1937: 265; Miller 1952; Kenny 1878: 48, 132; Maine 1906: 225; Rawson in Finley 1976: 85–6; Schulz 1954; MacFarlane 1973: chap. 4.

[14] Rosenthal 1984: 90; Holt 1972; Milsom 1976: 181; Coward 1971: 214–15; Jefferies 1979.

[15] Dodwell 1967: 59–60; L. B. Smith 1976: 538; Homans 1937; Scammel 1974: 528–9; Pollock & Maitland 1968: ii. 270; Hoskins 1954: 87; Williams in Roderick 1960: 32; MacCulloch 1986: 30; Hayami 1983: 5; Bettey 1982: 49; 1975; Thirsk 1965: 17–18; Fieldhouse & Jennings 1978: 135–8; *Bedfordshire Visitations*, p. 81; Roake 1970: 73; Baker 1964: 19; Warnicke 1974: 60; Taylor, *History Gavelkind*; Chalklin 1965: 18, 195; Everitt 1961: 47; Elton & Mackay 1897.

though he did not necessarily become the sole heir.[16] The principle of 'two sons and one heir' often prevailed and estates were held in common rather than divided.[17] Although practice varied among different American colonies, entails could be barred there and inheritance law favoured just a double portion for the eldest.[18] There was also a tradition in England that purchased land and land inherited through the mother should be utilized for younger sons and that whatever was available for the younger children should, if possible, be shared equally between them, male and female.[19] Sir Edward Coke advised landowners to 'lay up yearly a 3d part for provision and preferment for younger children'.[20]

In 1540, English landowners gained permanent control over the distribution of their estates.[21] The Statute of Wills restored the right of devise for feudal tenants over two-thirds of their land, a right which was made comprehensive by the abolition of wardship in 1646.[22] Fathers could now determine their own heirship strategy and occasionally disinherited disobedient eldest sons, though this was said to bring bad luck to the new heir.[23] Some families continued to give all their children some land.[24] Entails had been used to provide for younger sons before Uses emerged and provision was also made in buildings.[25] Grants of land were, however, normally for life or tail male, the land by various devices ultimately reverting to the rightful heirs of the grantor.[26] Primogeniture was favoured by landowners as early as the fifteenth century; by the seventeenth century it predominated and was increasingly adopted by urban families.[27]

16 Raftis 1980: 200–24, discusses the ramifications of Borough English.

17 Goody in Goody *et al.* 1976: 35.

18 Haskins in Flaherty 1969: 242; Shammas 1987: 154–6; Alston & Schapiro 1984: table 1; Shammas *et al.* 1987: chaps. 1–2; Keirn 1968: 554–7; Auwers 1978: 137; Quitt 1988: 647; J. M. Smith 1959: 108–9; Greven 1970: 131.

19 Cooper in Goody *et al.* 1976: 21–3.

20 Warburton 1929: app. 6, 323.

21 Cecil 1895; Bean 1968: 293–4, 304; Simpson 1961: 179.

22 Thorne 1959; Ives 1967: 696; Roebuck 1978; Hawkins 1982; Bellamy 1989: 134–9.

23 Aubrey, *Remaines Gentilisme*, p. 107. In Shropshire, on the other hand, there was a superstition that partible inheritance brought bad luck: see Gough, *History of Myddle*; Hey 1974; MacFarlane 1979: 85, criticized in *Mid. Hist.*, 2 (1987); Hainsworth 1988; Beckett 1980: 133–4.

24 Coward 1983; Lloyd 1968: 50–2; Hughes 1974: 161–2; Hughes 1987: 34; Fitzwilliam, *Correspondence*, p. vii; *Salusbury Correspondence*, p. 15.

25 Cornwall in Chalklin and Havinden 1974: 56; *Durham Wills*, ii. 7; *North Country Wills*, p. 126.

26 Swann 1986: 73–6, 148; Reresby, *Memoirs*, pp. 53, 106.

27 Rosenthal 1991: 12; Wrightson & Levine 1979: 98–9. On inheritance customs in business families see pp. 368–70, and Horwitz 1984: 223ff. Bilateral descent created both a patrilinear and a bilateral kinship system which was ego-centred but not strictly speaking a system of primogeniture.

Provision

The greater families and the newly arrived often wished to demonstrate their wealth by endowing their children.[28] By the second half of the seventeenth century, they no longer had to rely on accumulated savings or land.[29] Improvements in the long-term mortgage market and the introduction of the equity of redemption allowed them to borrow more easily and safely.[30] By the eighteenth century, sophisticated methods were at hand to provide in advance for younger children and not leave them to the devices of a temporarily embarrassed father or an unsympathetic elder brother.[31] Estates could be leased to trustees for long terms and younger sons could obtain portions out of capital, when married or of age, as well as an annuity or rent charge. The strict settlement and settlements on the marriage of the mother or eldest son permitted the interests of younger sons to be balanced more fairly in family conclave free of immediate pressures.[32] The strict settlement did, however, conflict with primogeniture and divide wealth, because it accorded priority to the raising of portions and limited the ability of a father to penalize his younger sons.[33]

The majority of younger sons received either a monetary portion or an annuity or a rent charge; sometimes both capital and income payments were combined.[34] One convention was that a younger son should receive the equivalent of one year's income from the estate as his portion.[35] An annuity could be a general charge on the whole estate, but more commonly it was tied to a particular piece of land or urban property or represented income from an office or living.[36] Provision of this kind was sometimes sufficient to create an independent income; William Percy lived for thirty-eight years in lodgings at Oxford on £145 p.a. provided by

[28] Cooper 1983: 150, 212–15; Bernard 1987.

[29] Habakkuk in Goodwin 1953: 9; 1950: 16–17; G. Williams 1974: 94.

[30] Habakkuk 1950: 18–20; Stone 1962: 182; Ward 1991: 33; Turner 1931: 24–37; Jessup 1965: 20, 110. [31] Larminie 1987: 32, 37.

[32] For the lengthy and convoluted debate on the efficacy of the strict settlement in determining shares and timing of transfer and on differences between marriage and family settlements see English & Saville 1983; 1980; Beckett 1977; 1984: 21; 1986; Bonfield 1979; 1986: 41; 1988; 1983: 104–14; 119; Spring 1983; 1986; 1988. Although disagreement remains both about the law itself and the relative importance in practice of *ante mortem* endowment through marriage settlements and *inter vivos* transfers compared with *post mortem* bequest by will, there seems to be a general consensus that the strict settlement was chiefly employed after 1700, as a substitute for entail, and that in the seventeenth century parental discretion remained wide. [33] Bonfield 1983a: 306.

[34] Habakkuk 1979: 199; 1981: 13; *Wentworth Papers*; Ferris 1965: 107; Cholmely, *Memoirs*, p. 7; Finch 1956: 28, 58; *Flemings in Oxford*, p. 453; Evelyn, *Diary*: i. 12; Rowlands 1977: 49; Hughes 1987: 33; *Yorkshire Wills*, p. 51. [35] Habakkuk 1969: 136.

[36] A life interest was usually calculated as seven years' purchase, though life expectancy at 21 was much longer: see Clay 1981: 29; *Mosley Family*, p. 8.

his father and eldest brother.[37] But, in most cases, the income was intended to supplement earnings; the portion, combined with an education, was intended for setting up in a career and in lieu of a settlement.[38]

Most families, however, had to exercise financial restraint. In the seventeenth century, they could no longer expand their estates at the expense of the Crown and Church and their expenses, both discretionary and unavoidable, often outgrew improvements in income.[39] An increase in the size of portions relative to jointures – maybe two to three times between 1650 and 1710 – benefited a gentleman on marriage, but made daughters more expensive and reduced the available resources for younger males.[40] In large families with daughters to place and country houses to emulate, there was little to spare. The basic costs of maintaining and bringing up children were a burden in themselves, quite apart from any future provision.[41] Although endowed schools were often free or charged reduced fees for younger sons, education was still expensive.[42]

Even eldest sons could face financial difficulties, if their children matured before they inherited the family estate. Generosity towards younger sons increased the burden of debt and could lead to a financial crisis and forced sales.[43] John Winthrop migrated to New England in 1630 in part because '3 eldest sons are come of age'.[44] Better estate management was one solution, but, in poor agricultural areas, the land was often insufficient to support even those who inherited.[45] The financial circumstances of the poorer gentry deteriorated even faster as a result of delinquency and heavy borrowing during the Interregnum and of land taxes and falling rent rolls at the end of the century.[46] Large and impoverished gentry families had no choice but to send their children into the professions or apprentice them.[47] Sir John Oglander put his son to a mercer for reasons of economy; Streynsham Master went out to India in the 1650s because his family, formerly knights with estates, had decayed even in the main branch.[48]

[37] Dodge 1944: 97–106.
[38] Adair 1969: 29; Cliffe 1969: 44–5; Wrightson in R. M. Smith 1984: 328–9; Larminie 1987: 35.
[39] The original storm over the gentry, 1540–1640, tended to ignore younger sons.
[40] On this controversial subject see Outhwaite in MacKendrick & Outhwaite 1986; Cooper 1983: 222–3; Erickson 1990: 30–1; Hainsworth in Frappel 1979.
[41] Stone 1962: 686–7.
[42] Oldham 1952; Cranston 1957: 23–4; Sargeaunt 1898: 101; O'Day 1982: 32–3; Carlton 1973: 313.
[43] Habakkuk 1980: 203; Cross 1967: 35; 1966: 85; Gay 1939: 423; Doran 1988; Stone 1973: 155; Feiling 1955: 3. [44] *Winthrop Papers*, ii. 126; Dunn 1962: 202.
[45] Everitt 1965: 67–8; Habakkuk 1978; M. G. Davies 1978; Mimardière 1964.
[46] Broad 1970: 189, 196–7.
[47] MacCaffrey 1958: 251; GLL MS 10823/1; Crouch, *Posthuma Christiana*; G. P. Jones 1967: 187–8. [48] Oglander, *Commonplace Book*, p. 235; Master 1874: 60–2.

Before the eighteenth century, many younger sons fared poorly.[49] Several of the gentlemen who eventually became Jacobean aldermen received tiny portions of £40 and one received his provision in livestock.[50] The richer gentry of Warwickshire provided annuities of £150 and portions of £500–1,000, but many families in Lancashire, Shropshire, Kent and Warwickshire could only provide trifling annuities of under £50 per annum and sometimes under £10.[51] All propertied and professional families had the same problem.[52] Yeomen families increasingly provided their younger sons with money rather than livestock and sometimes the younger children inherited a larger share of the personalty.[53]

Territorial ambition was probably even more damaging to younger sons. Changes in the ratio of population to land during the sixteenth century reinforced primogeniture and made parents reluctant to allocate portions of their estates even temporarily to their younger children. In the seventeenth century, the preservation, expansion and consolidation of the estate through marriage and inheritance became an absolute priority.[54] Sir Matthew Hale recognized that equal partition was the rule before the Conquest, but that was 'found to be very inconvenient' and it was better that younger sons enter business or the professions.[55] All landed families, whatever their relative rank and economic position, concentrated their assets on their heirs. 'If I shall leave my Land . . . equally devided amongst my children . . . then shall the dignitie of my degree the hope of my house be quite (as Issue extinct) buried in the bottomless pit of oblivion.'[56] To a serge trader: 'he that hath many children values nott any one soe high as he yt hath butt few especially daughters who by politick men are looked on as cumbers to a family & thers little regard to them where thers ye designe & hope of makeing an onely child great that shall be a Living monument of ye fathers care wisdom & riches'.[57] Both the successful and those struggling to survive chose to maintain their line at the expense of their younger children.[58] The thankless role of the younger son was to insure the family against failure of heirs without becoming a financial burden.[59] Even those families which displaced their less fortunate counterparts through efficient management, Court favour and office, did not wish to

49 Brereton, *Letters and Accounts*, p. 15.

50 Lang 1974: 40.

51 Blackwood 1978; 13, table 6; Hughes 1987: 34–5; Meredith 1965: 57; Mendenhall 1953: 91; London 1947: 27; Larminie 1984: 7; Young 1986: 6; Turner 1965–6: 256.

52 MacFarlane 1970: 48.

53 Howell 1983: 267–8; Raftis 1990: 86, 96; Thomson in J. C. Davies 1957: 416; Johnston 1971: 33.

54 Thirsk in Goody *et al.* 1976: 190, 233.

55 Hale, *De Successionibus*, pp. 36–8.

56 *Health to Gentlemanly Profession*, pp. 198–9.

57 Cruwys, *Diary*, p. 262.

58 Habakkuk 1965: 150; Blackwood 1976: 66–73; Cooper in Flood 1979; Wren, *Considerations on Oceana*, pp. 14–15, 86–9; Ferris 1965: 105–6.

59 Stone 1977a: 88.

distribute their gains among their younger children, who were apprenticed and expected to make their own way.[60]

Many younger brothers matured before the marriage of the eldest and after their fathers had died. A younger son whose father remarried had to compete with step-brothers and, if orphaned without any settlement, was at the mercy of his eldest brother.[61] Many heirs faithfully protected the wishes of their fathers and the interests of their younger brothers, even to the extent of endangering the estate.[62] But they were often accused of neglect and self-indulgence in conspicuous consumption. A considerable literature during the Interregnum espoused the Roman principle of equal division and argued that primogeniture neither gave younger sons an independent income nor the means to earn their livelihood.[63]

The fate of a younger son depended therefore on affection and circumstances. During the seventeenth century, an increasing number of younger sons, particularly those from cadet branches, could expect little income – at best a pittance of a life interest – and no real property. The most that families were willing and able to provide was an education, training and assistance in placement. Expenditure on their younger children was primarily intended to improve their range of choice and chances of success in a career rather than to provide a private income for leisure. Parents were unwilling to support their children indefinitely and expected them to achieve financial independence, though they usually tried to supplement their earnings. Thus the majority of younger sons of gentry families had a chronic need for salaried or self-employment. Primogeniture ensured that only the eldest could be a rentier and he might still compete in the job market with his younger brothers. However much social convention might identify the gentleman with a man of leisure and independence, younger sons had, like Gulliver in Swift's parable, to make their own way and earn their own income.[64]

[60] *John Isham*, p. xiii; Finch 1956: 28–58; Lowther, *Correspondence*, p. xiv; Davis 1967a: 6–13.

[61] Wilson, *State of England*, p. 24; Roberts, *Younger Brother*; *Warwickshire Quarter Sessions 1690–96*; Page, *Jus Fratrum*; *Vindication of Degree of Gentry*.

[62] Newcombe, *Autobiography*, p. 5; Nicholls 1992: 312.

[63] Thirsk 1969: 360–3; Lawrence, *Diary*, p. xi; Aylmer 1975; Frank 1955: 12–13; Veale 1970: 217; Scott 1988a: 59. The patriarchal theorists had problems with Biblical law which enjoined a double portion for the eldest: see Daly 1979: 75–6; Filmer, *Patriarcha*, intro. Bohun, *Preface and Conclusions*, sect. 68, attempted to reconcile primogeniture with the right of alienation. On the controversial question of Locke's views on inheritance see Gautier 1966; Wood 1984: 80. The classical economists uniformly opposed primogeniture: see Miller 1980: 566, 570; Shelton 1981: 96.

[64] MacKeon 1987: 338–40; Crossman, *Young Merchant's Calling*, updated by Crouch, *Apprentice's Companion*.

Concepts of gentility

Even in a developing economy, heredity continued to carry great weight. In England, all children inherited their family's status and the primacy of descent was emphasized by families struggling to protect their social position against *nouveaux riches*.[65] Wealth was certainly necessary to retain status in the long run.[66] Gentility remarked one courtesy book 'is but a Non ens'; 'wealth denominates it and wealth maintains it'.[67] But wealth was conveniently regarded as vulgar, when separated from genteel values. Birth was a much better defence against mobility than wealth, because what wealth and political favour had created, wealth and numbers could destroy. In Markham's view, no doubt attached to gentility 'by acquisition of descent'.[68] Although lineage had formerly defined social and political loyalties, status in England always attached to the individual through primogeniture rather than through the kinship group.[69]

Nature, however, has a way of disrupting the best-laid conventions; failure of heirs constantly undermined the transfer of status by descent. Consequently gentility had to be associated more with specific military functions and the capacity to govern.[70] Early medieval society had rigid categories, but considerable fluidity in practice, because contemporaries had little awareness of the past or of social change.[71] The title *miles* and the concept of knighthood were borrowed from military adventurers to differentiate the higher degrees of society.[72] In the fourteenth century, the development of tail male and paradoxically of Enfeoffments to Uses distinguished the gentry from the nobility.[73] Institutions reinforced the notion of perpetual succession. Whereas gentility had formerly derived from a man's lord, it was now presumed to follow from posts of responsibility. Prominence in the private sector never conferred the status automatically attached to public offices, which, though they could

[65] It is not entirely clear how far status was inherited by the non-armorial urban gentry; see Wagner 1983: 125–6.

[66] Squibb 1959: 173–9; *Lowther Family Estate Book*, p. 201.

[67] *Gentleman's Companion*, pp. 1, 3.

[68] Markham, *Book of Honour*, p. 58.

[69] James 1973: 56–7; Wagner 1983: 124–7, 137–9; MacKinley 1980; Given-Wilson 1987: 19; Watson 1960: 56. Sir Henry Maine's famous phrase 'from status to contract' is usually cited inaccurately and out of context; in fact he was describing the origins of the family and of feudalism not an exchange economy. See Maine 1906: 353.

[70] Tatlock 1950: 298; Mathew 1968: 104–5; Denholm-Young 1937; Keen 1965: 254; Naughton 1976; Morrill 1974: 72; Powicke 1962; Bennett in Harper-Bell & Harris 1986.

[71] Duby 1967: 5–6.

[72] Thrupp 1948: 272–5; Duby 1968: 7; Keen 1984: 250.

[73] MacFarlane 1973: 273–4; 1965: 337–45; 1968: 259; Denholm-Young 1969: 5; Moreton 1991: 261; Payling 1992: 70.

be manipulated to validate new money, were dominated by the same families.

Nobility was more than rank; it was considered an outward sign of greatness of spirit, which descended through blood, though theoretically it was manifested by valour. The concept of a nobility of virtue predated the Renaissance, though earlier versions embraced military functions rejected by the Humanists.[74] In fifteenth-century London, *gentilesse* represented an ethical code; younger sons had a dual status and described themselves both as merchant and gentleman.[75] The poorer gentry not surprisingly preferred to base their status on character rather than on wealth.[76] In Wales, a distinction was maintained between *bonheddig* and *uchelwr*.[77] Because they enjoyed no exemptions from taxes in England, gentlemen could be recognized as such simply by reputation.[78]

One criterion employed was style of life which, in England unlike the continent, preceded the grant of arms. Streynsham Master's sister confirmed that the Masters were ancient gentry because they had always lived nobly and kept threescore men in blue coats.[79] Even strenuous efforts by the Heralds could not stem the inflation of titles and the Visitations became less a matter of registering true arms than of recognizing a right to be styled Gentleman or Esquire.[80] Conservatives regarded the Courtesy Books as threatening because they showed new men how to attain through imitation the trappings of gentility.[81] Gentility might have been defined in terms of distinctive skills and attributes: merit and performance, what a man could do rather than what he was. But utility, creativity and intelligence were usually excluded as criteria, because they were randomly distributed, individualistic and potentially more threatening than the infusion of new wealth to those special genetic attributes which were assumed to justify the hereditary principle.[82]

Some tried to resist *nouveaux riches* by identifying gentility with the rejection of profit and abstention from work. But it was difficult for a family to both maintain an appropriate level of consumption and simultaneously isolate itself from the process of acquisition. In practice, social approval followed closely behind profits. Rentiers and salaried men still expected the maximum return on their property and their educational investment. The social position of those without independent incomes

74 Charlton 1965: 78–9.

75 Thrupp 1949: 236–9; Hanham 1985: 3.

76 Davril 1954: 52–3; Williams 1967: 178; Council 1973: chap. 1.

77 J. G. Jones 1989: 128; 1983: 281.

78 Sitwell 1902: 103; Selden, *Table Talk*, p. 50; Berkowitz 1988: 19.

79 Master 1874.

80 The property qualification for gentility was low: £5 p.a. in the 1520s and £10 p.a. or £300 in movable property by the seventeenth century: see Cornwall 1988: 11; Wagner 1967.

81 Staves 1989: 127.

82 Viner in Miller 1970: 93; Jouanna 1976; Devyver 1973: chap. 8.

was defined more by their level of responsibility and earnings than by the nature of their occupation. If younger sons suffered some loss of status, it was because they did not inherit the patrimony, not because they entered business. The real division in English society was not between business and other walks of life or between professional etiquette and concern with profit. It was between those who had to earn and those for whom all activity was a leisure occupation.[83]

The major economic and social divisions were both vertical and horizontal; they lay within as well as between the professions. Each was ranked as a separate unit in a vertical hierarchy of trades and occupations. But each also had a graduated hierarchy with its own elevators, which corresponded to the ranks of society, and numbers decreased and incomes increased at each upward step. The distance between the top and bottom of any occupation, distinguished usually by education and salary, was greater than that between the same level of different occupations.[84] English society was not a legally constituted system of estates but a cluster of social and economic groups which applied different standards in different localities.[85] The Poll Tax, for example, employed horizontal economic and vertical social criteria. Aldermen and Sheriffs of London were taxed at the same level as knights bachelor, judges in Admiralty and Probate, town clerks and doctors of physic.[86]

English society was both ascriptive and prescriptive. Social categories certainly hardened from the sixteenth century onwards and efforts to differentiate may have been more effective in the eighteenth century.[87] The Crown also asserted its authority as arbiter of the social order.[88] But the elasticity of the social structure, whose criteria for differentiation constantly shifted in absolute and relative importance, reflected both a need to accommodate the expansion of the upper class and a contrary tendency towards oligarchy. Social facts were retrospectively accepted and synthesized with traditional rules of conduct and habits of thought into new norms. Theories of gentility emerged which enabled the landed interest to justify its privileges and to adjust to economic change and social mobility.

[83] The persistent tendency to equate gentility with regularized play (whether constructive or frivolous) is well illustrated by Lee 1969: 366, 380; E. Jones 1982: 22; Carradine 1978: 463; Cain & Hopkins 1986: 505; Shapin 1991: 326. The emphasis on deliberate unproductivity can be reconciled in part with the practical utilitarianism of many gentlemen by the concept of discretionary roles and by the argument that their labour was undertaken by choice, not by necessity. The same argument justified the interest in and practice of mechanical arts by some gentlemen: they had amateur rather than professional status.

[84] Lipset & Zetterburn in Bendix & Lipset 1960: 503.

[85] Wrightson in Bonfield *et al.* 1986: 189–90.

[86] 12 Car. II, c. 9; see also Laslett 1987: 42; Cooper 1983: 49.

[87] See p. 384.

[88] James 1978: 22–3.

English society was permissive, but it imposed tough standards of acceptability. Instead of relying on birth, wealth and conspicuous consumption, on outward signs of rank or legalistic formulas, gentility was increasingly defined in terms of personal qualities whose elusive nature infuriated social climbers and which provided the best defence of the established elite against the values of new men. New wealth was accepted only when its owners thought, lived and reacted like gentlemen; inequalities of status became a subject of subtle discrimination.[89] Individuals were judged by their willingness and ability to assimilate.[90]

Social conventions were too diverse and contradictory in their formulation to legitimize a generalized and paramount system of values or beliefs, which, through punishment and rewards, could enforce conformity of behaviour among the elite.[91] Contemporary social observers not surprisingly failed to schematize an ambiguous reality. Their contradictory explanatory systems reflected a society which was riddled with anomalies and prone to ambivalence and dissonance. Without an institutionalized pattern of conduct or an effective mechanism of social control, it was hard to define and neutralize deviance or to socialize individual aspirations. Honour depended as much on self-perception as on social behaviour.[92] For the socially ambitious, nothing succeeded like success. Status derived from such a wide variety of factors that it effectively depended on acceptance rather than on formal rules. England did not have a shame culture, reinforced by external sanctions; it was closer to a guilt culture, based on conscience and conviction, in which actions were suppressed or prohibited by less visible precepts internalized in the individual.

Acceptable employment

There were of course restrictions on the tasks which a gentleman could perform without losing face. There is a perverse tendency, and not just in agrarian societies, to value occupations in inverse ratio to their utility, because conspicuous abstention from labour demonstrates the ability and wealth to pursue economically unproductive leisure. Manual work as undertaken by the labouring masses for daily wages, including most craft skills if practised for gain, was unacceptable.[93] Despite efforts to convince

[89] Namier 1961: 13–14; Wagner 1983: 153–4. A telling example of the strength of the gentlemanly code is provided by E. Jones 1953: 164. When Jung unintentionally made a slip, Freud remarked 'a gentleman should not do such things even unconsciously'.

[90] Marshall 1958: 92; Letwin 1981; Sitwell 1902: 64–5; Lea 1966: 635; Hobsbawm & Ranger 1983: 10; Wagner 1961; Cressy 1976a: 36.

[91] Gerschenkron in Robinson 1987: 269.

[92] Jouanna 1968: 623.

[93] Smith, *De Republica Anglorum*, pp. 39–40, 72. In Jamestown, genteel colonists refused to undertake manual work: see Morgan in Breen 1976: 28. Locke optimistically recom-

the gentry that industry was a duty, in the 1660s and 1670s, the rejection of mechanic trades remained a *sine qua non* of status.[94] But it was as much the low incomes as social prejudice which discouraged gentlemen from entering the minor trades, and their low status in turn reflected the quality of their entry. Even a non-manual occupation, like schoolmastering, which produced an income comparable to the minor clergy and sometimes enforced celibacy, was generally regarded as unsuitable.[95]

There was real concern that a gentleman might carry wares on his back from door to door, like a porter or pedlar. The 'shopkeeping trade', declared one advocate, 'is esteemed creditable enough for the preferment of the best men's sons in the kingdom next unto the Nobility but so is not the Pedlar's trade'.[96] Richard Mulcaster included physicians, lawyers and the clergy among the nobility and gentry and distinguished them from the commonalty; the latter he divided into 'marchauntes' and 'manuaries' or 'those whose handiworke is their ware and labour their living'.[97] A strenuous effort was made in both contemporary literature and in real life to distinguish between foreign and domestic trades and between wholesaling and retailing.[98] Merchants denounced hawkers and chapmen who were not apprenticed and provided competition.[99] The London Aldermen were displeased with Baptist Hicks, later Viscount Camden, when he kept shop after he had been knighted.[100] The role of middleman was elevated and white-collar business – banking, finance, wholesaling – was ranked above manufacturing and transport, which were too close to the masses who produced the necessities of life. A distinction was drawn between managing an enterprise, like dyeing or soap boiling, and performing manual and processing tasks, which convention wrongly assumed that anyone could perform.

Such distinctions were, however, hard to sustain and confusion was generated by the complex links between different economic sectors, each

mended that gentlemen and scholars work with their hands for three hours per day: see *Thoughts concerning Education*, p. 255.

94 The distinction between gentleman and mechanic also had political implications: see Nietkiewicz 1989: 34.

95 Orpen 1979: 86–7; 1977; Feyerhaven 1976: 115; Cressy in Prest 1987: 146; Anglin 1980: 70; Vincent 1950: 54, 161, 169–71; O'Day 1982: 172, 178. There were of course great variations in incomes which could reach £100 p.a.: see Dyer 1966; Kissack 1975: 31; Hill 1951: 32–4.

96 N. H., *Compleat Tradesman*, p. 45.

97 Mulcaster, *Positions*, p. 197.

98 BL Add. MS 9365, fos. 22, 31.

99 *Seventeenth-Century Economic Documents*, pp. 21–3, 420–1; Shammas 1990: 237. Innkeeping and butchery were not considered suitable trades for aldermen of York: see Palliser 1979: 110.

100 Burgon 1839: i. 287. Hicks' clients, however, included the Royal Household and the wife of Sir Robert Cecil looking for a bargain; when Hicks went courting, he thought it advisable to emphasize that a mercer did not necessarily sell a yard of silk: see Hicks-Beach 1909: 84, 89. 101 Court 1953: 38.

of which overlapped. In some trades, those who used their hands were the more prosperous.[101] Sooner or later, a merchant had to feel a piece of cloth or put his hand into a barrel of fish. The retailer, even in the luxury service trades, had to deal directly with the consumer. The surgeons, although their functions had been separated from the barbers in 1605, still had to wash clothes and bodies. In general, business was rated by wealth and scale of enterprise, not by specific function; Mulcaster conceded that whatever the function of merchants and manuaries 'their distinction is by wealth'.[102] Any occupation entered by the gentry was soon validated by their participation.

A younger son could remain as a tenant farmer on the estates of his own or other families or manage property in the Atlantic colonies. Cadet branches settled on the land and sometimes adopted intensive farming and overshadowed the main line.[103] In aristocratic families, a younger son could serve in the Commons as a political agent for his father or eldest brother.[104] Sons could emigrate to Ireland, the Caribbean and America.[105] Sir Humphrey Gilbert had suggested settling Ireland with younger sons, who could obtain grants of land during the successive confiscations of the century.[106] In the Leeward Islands, Barbados and Jamaica, planters combined landowning and trade and created a local aristocracy.[107] Virginia was strongly promoted for younger sons and, although the majority of Atlantic emigrants were of humble origins, gentlemen moved from overcrowded Barbados to Carolina.[108] *In extremis*, a cadet could and sometimes did become a gentleman of the road.[109]

The arts provided few openings and they usually had to be combined with a royal office. There were no barriers to becoming a musician,

[101] Court 1953: 38 [102] Harris 1969.
[103] Everitt 1965: 67; Ferris 1965: 104. For estate management see p. 75.
[104] Wither 1943: chap. 1, 53; *Parliament, Protests Lords*: i. 130; Holmes 1967: 178–9; MacHattie 1951: 31. [105] Miller 1985.
[106] Gillespie 1985: 149, 232; Clark 1987; Boyle, *Works*; Thirsk in Goody *et al*. 1976: 186.
[107] Pares 1950: 25; Dodd 1952: 48; Page 1976; Chandler 1979; Farnie 1963: 209; Sheridan 1961; Scammel 1989: 63; Gay 1928–9: 153.
[108] On the controversial subject of gentleman emigrants to the southern colonies see Wright 1940: 47; Waterhouse 1975a: 262, 280; Quinn 1976: 81, and in Quinn 1982: 128; Hakluyts, *Original Writings*, p. 282; Bailyn 1964: 35–6, 110; 1986: 149; Salerno 1979; Campbell and Bailyn in J. M. Smith 1957: 67; Cressy 1987: 15; Fairchild 1954: 8; Diamond 1958; *Trelawney Papers*; Gemery 1980: 205, 230; Wagner 1983: 286–91; Wertenbaker 1922: 75; 1959: ii–iii, 24; Fischer 1989: 225; Quitt 1988: 631; Mesnard 1973, and in Greene & Pole 1984: 127; Breen & Foster 1973; Breen 1976: 11, 15, 196; Clemens in Aubrey *et al*. 1977: 163–5; Galenson 1978–9: 522; 1970: 91; N. H. Davies 1949: 74. Emigrants sometimes improved their status through 'shipboard mobility': see Reavis 1957: 418–21.
[109] A relation of the Verneys was hanged for highway robbery. See *Verney Memoirs*, iv. 289–95: 'I have no great news but only that I thinke to die next weeke.'

though few sons of merchants and gentry chose this as a career.[110] In the seventeenth, unlike the eighteenth century, architecture was a marginal occupation subject to the whims of patrons.[111] A few gentlemen did become artists, but copying, restoring and decorating was regarded as a craft and yielded little income.[112] As the theatre developed into a business, professional players gradually acquired more regular work, board and lodging, retainer fees and even a share of profits, but actors remained serving-men.[113] Some younger sons took up the pen; several became professional dramatists, but they earned no more than a curate or schoolmaster and had low status.[114] By the end of the century, professional journalists and Grub Street hacks could earn £60–300 per annum, but writing usually had to be combined with an office or bookselling.[115]

The respectability of any occupation was in part determined by whether entry was through apprenticeship or through a liberal education, which was identified with reason and the rejection of mechanical arts.[116] Because surgeons, solicitors, attorneys and apothecaries were apprenticed, they were more questionable than physicians or barristers.[117] Lawyers, officers and physicians wished to distance themselves from the merchants, whom they considered their inferiors.[118] Gradually a classical education became the hallmark of the Church, the law and office and served to distinguish the professions from business.[119] This process was, however, slowed by several factors. In the second half of the century there was a reaction against institutionalized learning and formalized instruction, reflected in part in the decline of admissions to the Inns and to the Universities by those not intending to enter the law or the Church.[120] Supporters of vocational education, like Sir William Petty, attacked the grammar schools for their parrot-like repetition of 'heteroclitous nouns and verbs'.[121] Some Puritans recommended that manual skills be taught

[110] Woodfill 1950: 166. [111] Beattie 1967: 156; Colvin 1978: 29; Rogal 1974.

[112] Buckeridge, *Art of Painting*: 399, 408, 414, 425; Everitt in Chalklin & Havinden 1974: 177; Edmond 1978–80: 104, 119–20; Rogers 1983: 7, 9.

[113] Nungezer 1929; Bentley 1984; Wickham 1963: ii. 115–17; Limon 1985; *Henslowe Papers*; Forse 1990: 165–6, 178–9; Bradbrook 1961: 111; Bentley 1968: 62.

[114] Bentley 1971: 43–6; Gayley 1914: 12; Albright 1927: 10.

[115] Markham, *English Housewife*, p. xi; Miller 1959: chap. 1; Saunders 1967: chap. 5; Congreve, *Letters*, pp. 82–5; Ewald 1956: 9; Mumby 1949: 118–19.

[116] Axtell 1970; Kearney 1970: 169. [117] Chamberlayne, *Angliae Notitiae*, p. 484.

[118] Poynter & Bishop 1951: xxvii.

[119] Jansen & Stone 1966–7: 219; Ong 1959; Clarke 1959: 45–6; Molen 1974: 129. Aylmer in Custance 1982: 288 found no Old Wykehamists in business, but for one example see MacNamara 1895: 436.

[120] Stone 1974: 37, 48, app. 4, tables 1A, 2. [121] Petty, *Advice of W.P.*, p. 15.

alongside the liberal arts so that learning would not become an invidious distinction and reinforce the privileged hierarchy.[122]

The distinction between brain and hand was more apparent than real. Training was not standardized and much of the knowledge transmitted was irrelevant or incorrect. It was the empirics in medicine who had the most to offer patients.[123] Most practising lawyers, doctors and clergy taught themselves informally by reading and observation, through experience on the job. The lowest rungs of all the professions, like the assistant curates or chaplains in the Church, were similar to apprenticeships; barristers had originally been called apprentices-at-law.[124] Indeed the institutions which regulated the law and medicine closely resembled the old guilds with their oaths, initiations, searches and rules of practice.[125]

All the professions rose in status and developed clearer hierarchies during the century. Barristers automatically became esquires and status was conferred by seniority rather than by birth or title.[126] Even though reformers hotly campaigned against the parasitism, inefficiency and abuses of the law and its practitioners, even though landowners often felt trapped in its web, the lawyers were too vital to propertied society to be ignored. Their prestige was also enhanced by massive enrolment at the Inns by all levels of the landed gentry.[127] The civil law attracted an even higher proportion of younger sons.[128] Attorneys and solicitors also gained recognition and attracted as many eldest as younger sons, though their status was no higher than businessmen.[129] In 1683, *The Complete Solicitor* saw no reason why 'a man of brisk parts (though formerly against his inclination perhaps or by some urgent necessity put to a Trade) may not as well set up as a Solicitor'.[130]

The Church was a time-honoured sanctuary for those who wished neither to fight nor to labour.[131] Sons of gentlemen and merchants were sometimes repelled by the clerical odour. Anti-clericalism was reinforced by zealous reformers among the clergy, both Laudians and those Puritans who stressed the ministry of the word and preaching rather than simple pastoral duties.[132] The uniqueness of the priesthood was undermined by

[122] Schlatter 1954: 183. [123] Cook 1986: 260. [124] Ives 1983: 17–18.

[125] The ability of professional bodies to retain their monopolistic authority, in stark contrast to the guilds, is not easily explained. The crafts were, however, too numerous, decentralized and in competition with each other; they also lacked a common body of essential technical knowledge which could be uniformly applied and tested.

[126] Ives 1964: 79–80; 1959–60; Johansson 1966; Levack 1973: 12–13, chap. 2; Prest 1972: chap. 2. [127] Prest 1986: 93; Lemmings 1985: 154–6.

[128] Levack 1973: 11; in Prest 1981: table 5.2.

[129] Brooks 1986: 276, table 11.4; *North Country Diaries*, ii. 177.

[130] *Complete Solicitor*, preface.

[131] Bill 1965–6: 96–7; Heath 1969: 135–6; Le Neve, *Fasti Ecclesiae*.

[132] Tyler in Cornish 1967: 91–3; Kearney 1970: 143–4.

clerical marriage and lay control was firmly established.[133] There was a large proletariat of poor vicars and curates, fed by the grammar schools, who did not enjoy the status of the senior hierarchy.[134] But the Jacobean bishops were respected and the decline in clerical status has been exaggerated.[135] The acid test was the quality of entry. The number of sons of gentlemen entering the Church, 1600–40, tripled in Oxfordshire and Worcestershire; 16.5 per cent entered the diocese of Bath and Wells before the Civil War and they held livings comparable in value to sons of clergy.[136] After 1660, the gentry once more dominated the episcopate and the status of the middling clergy rose; 15–25 per cent of the Leicestershire clergy came from the gentry and 25–35 per cent from professional families, chiefly clergymen.[137] In Warwickshire they represented 10 per cent in 1662 and 30 per cent by 1700.[138]

Public office conferred automatic status even on those low in the hierarchy and clearly ranked as 'genteel employment'.[139] Even the posts of scavengers who emptied cesspools attracted acquisitive gentlemen. 'Persons of gentle parentage and some social credit', wrote a Victorian editor with surprise, 'were glad to earn their living by avocations that are now-a-days regarded as unsuitable for persons of quality'.[140] The East India Company attracted the cream because it resembled a department of state.[141] William, the younger brother of the 1st Lord Monson, became a factor at Fort St George and Gerald Aungier, second son of the 2nd Baron Longford, started as a factor at Surat in 1661.[142] Cooke wrote several letters recommending Oglethorpe, whom he described as a hopeful young gentleman, whose father was his very good friend. The lad had insisted on an Indian career and his father agreed, 'with some Reluctance ... and more of my Lady's, for the young Gentleman had a large prospect of great advantage by continuing here, being one of the Duke of Gloucester's Bedchamber and a particular favourite of the Princess's now our Gracious Queen'.[143]

The profession of arms had originally provided the prime justification

[133] Trinterud in Trinterud & Hudson 1971: 34–9.

[134] Chamberlayne, *Angliae Notitiae*: 232, 385, 387; Owen 1959; 1960: 184.

[135] Collinson 1982: 39–42. On the controversial debate on status see Barrie-Curien 1988: 460; Brook 1945–7; Mayo 1922: 28–9; O'Day 1979: chap. 1; Styles 1978: 130; Namier 1939: 137; Best 1964: 13–21; Wagner 1983: 162–3, 186; Hart 1958: chap. 7; 1968; 1955; Heal 1981; Tyler 1967.

[136] Stieg 1982: 81; Green 1981: 73, 82.

[137] Pruett 1978: 35–8.

[138] Morgan 1970: 5.

[139] Ward 1955: 28–9; Carpenter 1992: 90.

[140] *Middlesex Records*, iv. pp. xxxiii–xxxv. He might have recalled that the Emperor Vespasian, if Suetonius is to be believed, did not hesitate to draw rents from the public urinals on the grounds that money has no odour. The actual work was, of course, performed by deputies.

[141] BL Add. MS 22849, fo. 77.

[142] Lincs. AO, catalogue of the Monson MSS.

[143] BL Add. MS 22851, fo. 111.

for noble privilege and status and, although England never had a distinctive *noblesse d'épee*, the desire to demonstrate military prowess and fighting quality had tempted generations of gentlemen to seek glory in war.[144] Popular fiction related stories of prentices leaving their shops to serve as archers in the Hundred Years War.[145] The Navy always enjoyed a higher status than the merchant marine and recruited younger sons of gentlemen, except during the Interregnum, though there was continual conflict between them and the tarpaulins.[146] Physic had the status of a learned profession and attracted several younger sons of gentlemen.[147] In the seventeenth century, out of sixty-six Fellows of the College of Physicians, one was the son of a knight and sixteen were gentlemen. But the physicians were ridiculed on the stage and they had to struggle to obtain social recognition.[148]

In practice, the professions differed from business in degree rather than in kind. Lawyers exploited the demand for regulation and formalization; even those who had salaried offices charged fees and ran their practices as a business.[149] The physicians controlled medicine as a business monopoly and the apothecaries were really retailers of medicines. The professional soldier was as much a contractor as a fighting man; the naval officer was separated by a thin line from the ship-master and privateer. The traffic in ecclesiastical livings, like the purchase of commissions, made the Church an institution in which business aptitude brought results. Preaching was a calculated performance and declaratory skill was cultivated by imitation of the stage.[150] Public office was still closer to a private business corporation than to a civil service. The sale of office, low salaries and the identification of office with private property, turned officers into businessmen.

As the author of *The Cities' Great Concern* wrote, 'I cannot but confess that in the common repute of the World, there are several other ways whereby men may arise to Wealth & Honour, as the sword & the gown, yet I think ... that strictly taken those very ways and methods are in effect Trades & Mysteries, the End of all being Emolument & Profit'.[151] Most of the accusations levelled against trade, against the acquisitive concern for private profit and disregard for the public weal, could be levelled just as easily against any of the professions which still lacked a code of public

[144] Clark 1958: 98; 1962: 43; Best 1982: 13–14. [145] Vallans, *Honorable Prentice*, p. 2.
[146] Capp 1989:175–6; Gibson 1800–2: 1.
[147] Pelling 1983a: 27–8; Porter 1987; Axtell 1978: 158; Munk 1878: 103, 180, 231; Roach 1965: 217; Dewhurst 1966: 4. [148] Birken 1987: 205; Silvette 1967: 196.
[149] Roper 1953: 11. [150] Donagan 1984: 85.
[151] Bolton, *Cities' Advocate*, preface.

service. All were private trades and the means of acquiring a competence, through fees rather than salaries, were similar.[152]

The determining factors

The aspirations of gentlemen did not necessarily correspond to their actions, which always provide the acid test of fundamental beliefs.[153] All families sought to preserve and improve their status, but in practice there was little correlation between prescribed and actual behaviour. Genteel families did not just perform roles imposed by birth or allocated by convention.[154] Without external sanctions, social values became subjective and indeterminate; they conditioned, but did not determine either means or ends. Given a wide spectrum of opinion, gentlemen could choose to accept and follow those interpretations of the normative order which best suited their purposes. Despite efforts by the professions to ground their status on inherent self-worth, their prestige depended heavily on participation by the gentry with their independent status based on birth. Necessity and not the ideal of rentiership determined actual decisions; families had to balance viable alternatives with conflicting obligations.

By insisting on primogeniture, it was inevitable that the most deeply rooted concept of the gentleman as a man of independence and leisure could not apply to the younger children. Whatever the pundits said, the needs of families dictated some relaxation of older theories of compatibility and some status discrepancy. Some compromise was essential between the old ideal of a static, hereditary society and the need to accommodate new demographic and economic forces. Eldest sons living off rents were bound by the prescribed rules, ideals and responsibilities of landownership. But younger sons, who received no rewards by right and who were obliged to earn their own livelihood, could not embrace a disinterested life style. Once the principle of paid employment had been accepted, they had to produce as well as consume, unless they could obtain a sinecure.

Occupations were compared and rated in a clumsy fashion according to their perceived reputation and their association with educational institu-

[152] See pp. 258–62. The identification of the professions with the notions of duty and service by Tawney 1921: 91–2 is a much later development. See Reader 1966: chap. 12; Perkins 1989; Mathias in Coleman & Mathias 1984: 152–4; Dingwall & Lewis 1983; Jackson 1970. Some would deny that even the modern professions are altruistic: see Johnson 1972; Riesman 1982: 106.

[153] MacIntyre in Laslett & Robinson 1962: 54.

[154] On the difference between planned action and ideal patterns of behaviour see Firth 1964: 36.

tions and with the great and prosperous.[155] There was, *ceteris paribus*, a general order of preference. It was common to put the first or an only younger son into a profession and it was both traditional and fashionable for parents to rank the upper levels of the Church, the law and office higher than business. The professions were more closely related to the upbringing, education and social skills of the gentry and did not usually require residence abroad. Much depended on the number of children. Sir William Wentworth advised that 'if there be many of them let one be prentise to a marchant'; John Green had sixteen children and so the sixth went into business.[156]

The exact order of merit of occupations varied according to taste and period. Professional families often put their own children into business and the attractiveness of the Army and the Church fluctuated over the century.[157] A family benefice or a military commission were usually more popular than provincial business, but to many parents the status of a successful merchant was higher than a naval officer on half-pay or a minor official. The decisions of fathers and mothers were based on rational interests rather than on prejudice.[158] Profit did not carry any social stigma and it was family background rather than occupation which determined status; what mattered was the relative social position and opportunities for advancement of alternative careers.[159]

Financial considerations always dominated.[160] As Hobbes observed, 'all men naturally strive for honor & preferment but chiefly they who are least troubled with caring for necessary things'.[161] Indeed, prestige was closely tied to earning power. The economic resources and responsibilities of a family, in relation to the number and life expectancy of its children, dictated the type as well as the necessity of employment. All occupations required an initial capital investment; opportunity cost also had to be considered and this required comparison of alternatives. The known charges of setting up had to be weighed against the supposed return and the expected opportunities for advancement. The relative costs of training had to be related to the level and security of future income. Maybe a rent charge or an annuity was better than investing a large sum in an apprenticeship, which might lead nowhere and would be

155 Jessup 1965: 108–9. The argument of Kearney 1970: 158 that merchant wealth destroyed the social superiority of the Universities is unfounded.

156 *Wentworth Papers*, p. 21; Greene, *Diary*, p. 386.

157 North, *Discourse Study Laws*, pp. 3–6.

158 Wives and of course widows were often given discretion to place the younger children: see Hughes 1987: 38.

159 Jonson, *Works*, viii. 504; Bourdieu 1972: 1123–4.

160 Schuyler 1931: 264; Mandeville, *Fable of Bees*, i. 58–9.

161 Cited by Thomas in Brown 1965: 191.

wasted if a child died young. A desire for security made salaried positions more attractive than careers which depended on fees or profits. An expensive career for an elder child might require the cheapest possible career for the youngest. Some parents cast their bread upon the waters hoping that their children through successful careers and marriages would return their investment with interest and bring money back into the family, though usually their financial outlay was irrecoverable. But the primary objective of all parents was to settle all their children financially for life at the minimum cost to the estate.

Parents, however, often lacked the knowledge to make informed choices. It was no easy task to balance conflicting claims, to weigh the pros and cons of each alternative. Parents had to learn and follow complex procedures for placement, which varied among different careers. Good timing and adequate information about the condition of particular trades were essential to selecting a business. Yet many gentry families had no knowledge of how to select a master or negotiate an indenture.[162] Parents could consult printed advices, like one published in 1676; Kirkman suggested that they investigate the number of prentices made free by a prospective master as well as his religion.[163] A few positions were advertised and some gentlemen acquired a business library.[164] But no comprehensive guide was available until 1747. Parents had to depend for advice on relations, friends, fellow countymen in the City, business associates, scriveners and the writing-school masters; astrological help was often sought.[165] Optimism and ignorance frequently misled them into thinking that trade would generate wealth in boom or slump.[166] Many parents wisely sought to have their cake and eat it. They favoured salaried positions which could be combined with private trade while providing a hedge against the high risks of business.

All forms of livelihood, including business, also retained a hereditary character and particular families were disproportionately represented. The number of brothers and close relations over several generations in the same profession or trade is quite striking, though it also reflects the relatively small size of propertied society. Connection often dictated choice and was essential to enter the great Companies and find important masters.[167] Preference was always given to those careers which permitted the family to use its influence in a competitive world. Family traditions of employment were perpetuated, because patronage carried more weight

[162] Defoe, *Novels and Selected Writings*, xiii. 9; M. G. Davies 1978: 92.
[163] *Seventeenth-Century Economic Documents*, p. 287; Kirkman, *Unlucky Citizen*, pp. 146–8.
[164] Levy 1982: 28; Wright 1940: 266.
[165] Starr 1967: 21; Thomas 1971: 373–5.
[166] *Spectator*, 24 March 1711.
[167] *Oxinden Letters*, pp. 39–40; Frank & Einsley 1971: 147; Sheridan 1951: app. 4; Shropshire RO, Walcott & Bitterley MSS, case of Humphrey Walcott.

than merit and because those already entrenched could help their kin with advice, accommodation, loans and referrals.[168] England was not a meritocracy, selecting candidates objectively by examination. It was a system of 'sponsored' rather than 'contest' mobility. Each family strove for preferential treatment and wished to perpetuate its advantage by continuity. At the same time, parents tried to distribute their children between different professions.[169] This spread minimized the risk of failure and entailed, in a large family, that at least one son would enter business.[170]

Political and religious affiliations could also eliminate whole sectors of employment. Devout parents insisted on devout masters.[171] The choice of Recusant families was permanently restricted and their children had to seek employment abroad.[172] Any family estranged from the government or its chief ministers was obviously excluded from office and favour. Those who opposed the Laudian Church and the Stuarts before and after the Civil War or who supported them during the Interregnum were deprived of many outlets.[173] Puritan magnates exploited their family rectories and the law and medicine, but they also put their children into trade.[174, 175] Health and conditions of work were also taken into account; occupations which had a low life expectancy were less popular.[176] John Fryer had to change his trade because he had a rupture and could not carry goods on his back or turn the wheel.[177] Hooke was apprenticed to Peter Lely, but could not stomach the smell of paint and so he was sent to Oxford.[178] Chubb became a glover, but his eyesight was too weak and so he was put to a chandler.[179]

The Church was attractive because the duties to be performed were not heavy or effectively enforced, particularly in sinecures, and the family name could be preserved. The law and minor offices, on the other hand, could be rejected for their boring routines; the clerical duties of copying and inspecting evidences offered no real challenge to an energetic young man. The Army and Navy might be eliminated as both tedious and hazardous. In peacetime garrison duty was debilitating and there were restrictions on leave, whereas combat and disease while on campaign endangered both life and limb. Conditions of service at sea were likewise hard and mortality was high, though it depended on the area of ope-

168 Cressy 1986. 169 Gough, *History Myddle*, pp. 137–9.

170 James 1974: 177; Markham 1870: 12; Roberts 1968: 1.

171 Newcombe, *Autobiography*, p. 173.

172 Miller 1973a: 50; Parker 1972; Aubrey, *Lives*, ed. Dick, p. 114; Murphy 1986: 24. In Ireland, however, families weakened by the Penal Laws lacked the resources to set up their children in business: see Cullen in Cullen & Smout 1977:170.

173 Ramsey 1930: 118; Pares 1950: 10; Keeler 1954: 102–3; *Yorkshire Diaries*, p. 21.

174 Ferris 1965: 106; Cliffe 1984: 107–8. 175 Souers 1931: 14.

176 Chamberlain, *Letters*, i. 3; Notestein 1956: 35. 177 GLL 12017.

178 Rostenberg 1989: 238. 179 Chubb, *Posthumous Works*.

rations. Physic appealed to the scholarly and scientific-minded, but all medical practitioners faced the risk of contracting disease; conditions of work for surgeons were unpleasant and required strength.

A major consideration was the 'difference of wits' or the aptitude and disposition of the child.[180] In judging the abilities of their children, parents had to rely on personal knowledge and their performance at school. Their careers were effectively determined when they reached the relatively early age of entry into either a university or Inn or an apprenticeship.[181] The skills, temperament and qualifications conventionally associated with and demanded by each profession had to be taken into account, and placing the mediocre was often a major problem. Francis Le Piper was intended for trade like his brother, 'but his Genius leading him wholly to designing', he was allowed to become an artist.[182] Any tendency towards dissoluteness also had to be considered. Lord Lonsdale advised Sir John Lowther that Whitehaven would suit his son, Christopher, as it was 'out of harm's way'.[183]

The law was thought to require a meticulous approach, a flair for making subtle distinctions and 'a quaint and studious Temper'.[184] It certainly required knowledge, industry, subtlety of mind and luck, but the intellectual demands were flexible and different levels of ability could be accommodated.[185] A little education and a sense of vocation was increasingly expected in the Church. It was an obvious choice for the pious and learned; men like Isaac Barrow preferred poverty in a university to prosperity in business.[186] But an ambitious cleric also had to master the intricacies of the ecclesiastical machinery of appointment and administration rather than the niceties of theology. Service in a household or at Court required 'extravagances of form and feature'.[187]

Office demanded no formal qualifications and Westcote argued that younger sons 'by means of their travel and transmigration' were particularly well qualified.[188] But offices which carried real duties demanded administrative skill as well as a taste for political intrigue. Even estate management required an education and preferably some legal, surveying and accounting skills, though integrity was almost as important. The Navy had always demanded greater technical skill than the Army, though

[180] Jonson, *Works*, p. viii. 504; *Petty–Southwell Correspondence*, p. 105; Harrington, *Political Works*, p. 304 recognized that the majority 'must be unto the mechanics'; Perkins, *Works*, cited by Berry 1974; Steele, *Religious Tradesman*, p. 23.

[181] This was normally 16–18, though it was flexible and decisions might be taken when the child was 13–14. See Stone 1977a: 9; 1980; 1974: table 6, graph 8; Cressy 1979; Molen 1976: 207–26.

[182] Buckeridge, *Art of Painting*, p. 453.

[183] Lowther, *Correspondence*, p. 295.

[184] Brewster, *Essays on Trade*. p. 44.

[185] Namier & Brooke 1964: i. 105.

[186] Aubrey, *Lives*, ed. Clark, i. 88.

[187] Lysons 1860: 31.

[188] Westcote, *View of Devonshire*, p. 51.

land warfare was slowly becoming more of a science and mathematical aptitude was needed for gunnery and fortifications.[189] The basic skills were less demanding than trade and some, like horsemanship, were second nature to country gentlemen. The Army provided real competition for business, because it demanded much the same qualities – courage, stamina, organizing ability and risk-taking.[190] Since medical knowledge was so limited, the intellectual demands of physic could easily be met.

Because there was no objective means of assessing capacity for business, its skills were usually underestimated.[191] Hudibras thought that 'Country gentlemen always design the least hopeful of their Children to Trades and out of that stock the City is supplied with the sottish ignoramus which we see it perpetually abounde with'.[192] It was generally agreed that business was more suitable for those who showed little interest in learning.[193] According to Lady Gardiner, 'a profetion is of more advantage to a younger brother, who if hee has not larning had better bin a marchant then a courtyare'.[194] John Speidel's father was intended 'to have become a merchant, but what with great losses and my father's extraordinary love to music and mathematics he was diverted'.[195]

Children were sometimes given a trial run and there was always a probationary element to apprenticeship. An initial decision was not final, because careers were not yet rigidly compartmentalized. The successful and the failed could move horizontally between professions and change careers in mid-stream. It was possible to begin as a clerk and switch to diplomacy or war, to move both ways between trade and office.[196] Thomas Raymond was sent to his uncle in London, but he disliked the 'long waits and short meals' and since he had 'neither money nor courtesie' he joined the English army in the Netherlands.[197] Parents sometimes chose to recognize the tastes and vocational preferences of their children.[198] Gervaise Disney's father 'perceiving me to decline learning, gave me my choice of any trade'.[199] In the 1630s, John Langford considered religious factors and the number of vacations and cited the text 'Go stand in the

[189] Lewis 1939: chap. 6; Owen 1938: 13–14.

[190] *Gentleman's Magazine* (1732), pp. 1014–15.

[191] *Oxinden Letters*, p. xxiv. [192] Butler, *Characters*, p. 149.

[193] Travers 1977: 167. [194] *Verney Letters*, p. 89.

[195] Lincs. AO Monson MSS, Misc. Books 21, Life of John Speidel.

[196] Harbage 1935· 3. [197] Raymond, *Autobiography*, pp. 9, 26; Plummer 1972: 88.

[198] Ben Amos 1988 overstates the case for children acting for themselves, which depended on the level of trade; spiritual autobiographies also tended to be written by the more independent. See Cliffe 1969: 44; *HMC Fortescue*, i. 18; Dalton 1915: 6; Williams 1913: i. 24; Forman, *Autobiography*, p. 6; *Yorkshire Diaries*, ii. 197–8; Norwood, *Journal*; Wilson 1972: 143.

[199] Disney, *Remarkable Passages*, p. 29; in fact his first two choices were refused and he became a heraldic painter; Grassby 1994: 26.

market place (though idle) that I may be hired into that Vineyard.'[200] Ellis Lloyd, orphaned with £80, was sent to London to be apprenticed, but the lad would only serve a Welshman.[201]

It would be unwise to state categorically what determined the ultimate choice, when few details of individual decisions survive.[202] Although financial settlement was a universal objective, the range of possibilities was broad and they could be combined in different ways; complex emotions also governed the placing of children. Practice varied between regions and changed over time under the pressure of fashion and events. Ignorance and prejudice sometimes prevailed and parents did not always allocate careers in a rational way. Marmaduke Rawdon was intended for the ministry and a scholarly career, but his father feared that he might go blind from reading too many books and so he was put to trade.[203] Dorney declined to specify the 'cogent reasons' why the fifth son of his family was put to trade, though a scholar and religious, whereas the eldest was put to the law and the Church.[204] Usually, however, in both landed and urban society, choice of career reflected the particular circumstances, interests, priorities and needs of each family. The final decision always remained a family responsibility, which was treated with great seriousness. The value system conditioned what men desired and ranked motives in a preferential order, but it was parents who determined the future of their children.[205]

The demographic imperative

Choice was often limited by factors outside their control, the most important of which was supply and demand. There are few reliable statistics for younger sons, who have generally been ignored and it is difficult to allocate an appropriate multiplier of sons per family; the proportion of elder to younger sons, the rate of survival and the interval between generations remain uncertain variables.[206] Estimates of the size of households by historical demographers vary and are not always

[200] BL Add. MS 28009, fos. 48–66: Deliberations by John Langford, 1632.

[201] *Wales, Calendar Letters*, pp. 115–16.

[202] Contemporary memoirs and family histories invariably record the careers of all the children but usually do not specify the reasons for particular choices. Career choices were nonetheless a frequent topic of discussion and gossip: see Isham, *Diary*, p. 97.

[203] Rawdon, *Life*, pp. 1–2; Trosse, *Life*, p. 57.

[204] Dorney, *Divine Contemplations*, p. 2.

[205] Sociologists and anthropologists have been forced to modify their concept of institutionalized value systems and to recognize the individual factor in social transfers: see the introduction to Medick & Sabean 1984.

[206] Goldstone 1991a: 118 alleges that the number of younger sons increased twice as fast as the number of gentry families, but he does not present any hard evidence.

categorized by occupation and status; but mean household size seems to have ranged from 4.64 to 6.63 persons.[207] Gregory King assumed eight heads per gentry family, but this included all members of the household.[208]

The peerage produced 50 per cent more children every generation until 1650; a fall in fertility then reduced the number of children from 5 to 3.5 per married unit with an average rate of childlessness of 18.6 per cent of all persons married and high mortality in middle age; the mean family size for cohorts fell from 5 to 4 between the periods 1625–49 and 1675–99.[209] In a stable population, sixty out of every hundred men will be eldest sons. In the seventeenth century, only 25 per cent of marriages in the whole population produced more than two sons and there was a 0.65 probability of a child dying before his father; 20 per cent of men who married left no surviving child and 20 per cent only left daughters.[210] Among gentry families in Lancashire before the Civil War there were 1,000 younger sons to 774 eldest.[211] There may, however, have been fewer younger sons among the whole gentry after 1640; in Glamorgan the number of children per family fell from between 3.85 and 5 to between 2.58 and 3.6.[212] It seems safe to assume, allowing for daughters, that on average no more than one younger son survived to maturity.[213]

Although some counties have been studied intensively, there is no definitive figure for the overall number of gentry.[214] The population as a whole certainly increased in the sixteenth century and levelled off during the seventeenth century with fluctuations around an equilibrium until the mid eighteenth century.[215] The growth of gentry families was not, however, determined just by fertility rates and by the rate of survival to maturity, but also by an increase of new families claiming gentry status.[216] Numbers increased drastically during the sixteenth century, maybe by a

[207] Laslett & Wall 1972: 154, 192, tables 1:10, 13, 4:4, 10, 15; Laslett 1969; 1983: 72. The mean size of gentry, clerical and yeomen families was 5.62. Goose 1980: table 7 puts the mean household size of the gentry in Cambridge at 8.63 and the mean number of children at 4.67. [208] King, *Two Tracts*, p. 48.

[209] Hollingsworth 1965: 25, 45, 65, 72, tables 32, 36; Chambers 1972: 51.

[210] Wrigley 1987: 199–202, 206–7, table 8.3; Clay 1968: 505; Goody 1973: 16–18.

[211] Blackwood 1970: 322. [212] Jenkins 1983: table 3; Clay 1981: 32.

[213] Aylmer 1974: 259; Laslett & Harrison in Bell & Ollard 1963: 166, 171, 176, 182; Laslett 1972: table 4.16.

[214] Everitt 1968b: 65, 33; Ferris 1965: 104–5; Mousley 1958–9: 467; Watts 1975: 63; Jenkins 1983: 32; G. Williams 1974: 315; Bedell 1990: table 1; Cliffe 1969: 10, 28; Blackwood 1978: table 8, app. 1; Everitt 1961; Morrill 1974: 15.

[215] Wrigley 1981: table A 3.3; Palliser 1982b; Thrupp 1948: 231; 1965; Payling 1992: 64. Gottfried 1978: 227, shows from 14,000 wills and 5,000 other testamentary documents, that only 50 per cent of all families had a surviving son and only 20 per cent both a son and a daughter. [216] Stone 1958: app. 1.

factor of three. Between 1560 and 1589, there were 2,000 grants of arms and a further 1,760 between 1589 and 1639.[217]

One estimate for the early seventeenth century suggests 160 peers, 1,400 baronets and knights, 3,000 squires and 15,000 armigerous gentry; another for 1633 puts the baronets and knights at 1,500–1,800, the esquires at 7–9,000 and the gentry at 10–14,000.[218] Gregory King estimated that there were 1,400 baronets and knights, 3,000 esquires and 12,000 gentry.[219] Robert Glover's compilation of arms in the late seventeenth century numbered about 11,000 coats.[220] By the early eighteenth century, however, the number of country gentry families may have declined, though the Land Tax commissioners, in 1702, numbered 32,000.[221]

Thomas Wilson, in 1600, estimated 500 knights, 16,000 esquires and 'I cannot speak of the (number) of yonger brothers albeit I be one of the number'.[222] Chamberlayne postulated 16,000 younger sons, in 1669, and Petty a median of 10,000 families worth about £800 per annum, each of which had one younger brother who needed £200–300.[223] If, estimating conservatively, there were 16,000 gentry families during the seventeenth century, this would imply, assuming a generation is thirty years, that around 533 younger sons reached maturity every year, distributed unevenly between individual families. If there were 10,350 business families, 80 per cent of which, allowing for celibacy and infertility, produced one child in every generation who did not become a rentier, there would also have been some 276 sons of businessmen entering the job market each year. As the professions expanded, the children of incumbents would also have increased; if there were 20,000 such families, 80 per cent of which had at least one son, they would have produced a further 533 job-seekers. That would amount to some 1,342 candidates for employment each year, not counting children from yeomen families, alien and Scottish immigrants, returned colonials and eldest sons of gentlemen.

The growth of the professions, striking though it was, lagged behind the growth of prospective applicants. According to Gregory King in

217 Beckett 1980: tables A. 3, 5, 6; Stone 1964a: app. 2.

218 Stone 1965: 24; Aylmer 1975: 330–1, table 35.

219 In his notebook, King estimated 1,500 knights and baronets, 3,000–3,800 esquires and 13,000–20,000 gentlemen: see *Seventeenth-Century Economic Documents*. Discrepancies in his calculations are discussed by Mathias 1957–8: 32 n.1; Holmes 1977. Lindert 1980; 1982–3: 388 by regression analysis from burials raises King's figures to 15,000 gentlemen. See also Glass in Glass & Eversley 1965; Le Roy Ladurie 1979.

220 Papworth 1961: intro.; the number in 1874 was about 50,000. Sayer 1979: 12, puts the number of agnatic families at 8,000 in 1660.

221 Holmes 1980a: 297.

222 Wilson, *State of England*, p. 241.

223 Chamberlayne, *Angliae Notitiae*; Petty, *Economic Writings*: i. 312–13.

1688, there were 10,000 officers, 10,000 lawyers, 10,000 clergy, 16,000 in the sciences and liberal arts and 9,000 in the armed services.[224] But the number of posts which provided an income of £50 or higher was probably some 11,100 in the first half of the century and some 27,300 by the end of the century compared with 10,350 in business.[225] The number of vacancies, moreover, was much smaller, even though it is almost impossible to establish with any precision, because it depended on the death rate of incumbents and the rate of promotion and turnover.[226] Without distinguishing between rich and poor livings, the Church, before 1640, may have taken in 550 per year.[227] Barristers were called at the rate of 40–50 per year between 1590 and 1639.[228]

If the average working life of a professional or officer was twenty years, there may have been some 556 annual vacancies in the first half and 1,365 in the second half of the century, compared with 800 major and 825 minor openings in business.[229] It is pressure of numbers which explains the periodic efforts by the gentry to restrict entry into the Church, the Army and the Inns of Court.[230] The campaign of the 1680s against the exclusiveness of the East India Company was in part driven by excess demand and limited places.[231]

Families with wealth, influence and able, well-educated children had no problem and some contemporaries were sceptical about underemployment. Christopher Wase wrote caustically that 'all trades think themselves overstocked, some have fancied the World to be so, that if men did not in Wars kill one another, they must eat one another'.[232] But most were not so sanguine. Bacon noted the surplus of educated young men and Sir Edwin Sandys in 1604 argued that 'nothing remains fit for them, save only merchandise . . . unless they turn servingmen'.[233] Apologists for younger sons emphasized the relative decline in opportunities compared with the

224 *Seventeenth-Century Economic Documents*, p. 780. King's total of 55,000 in his tables correlates with Holmes 1982. In his notebook (Cooper 1983: 439), King however lists 2,000 clergy worth £50–60 per annum, 400 Doctors of Divinity, Law and Physic and 2,000 lawyers, which are closer to the estimates adopted here of positions worth more than £50 p.a. Even if the higher figure were correct, it would not seriously weaken the present argument. 225 See table 2.1 and p. 60.

226 Contemporaries did have to estimate length of tenure in order to calculate the value of benefices and offices; see BL Add. MS 22781, fos. 36–7.

227 Curtis 1962: 31; 1959: 300 puts the number at 327–427, based on an average tenure of thirty years: see also Usher 1910: i. 241; Stone 1964b: 74. That conclusion has been successfully challenged by O'Day 1979: 9, 20, 31 and Green 1981: 90, 95 who argue that the average period of tenure was twenty years. 228 Prest 1986: table 1.1.

229 See table 2.1 and p. 58.

230 Lucas 1962: 465–73; *Welbeck Catalogue Letters*, p. 192, app. 1; Reresby, *Memoirs*, p. 146; Ogg 1967: 146, citing Clarendon MS 109; Peck 1986: 59.

231 *East India Company Factories 1670–77*, iv. p. xv; Sutherland 1957: 20.

232 Wase, *Considerations Concerning Free Schools*.

233 *English Economic Documents*, pp. 445–6.

past.[234] Eachard thought that the Church had filled with younger sons who were too stupid for the law and could not find openings in business.[235] The *Trade of England Reviv'd* thought that younger sons could not expect more than one year's revenue for their patrimony and that the Inns and Universities could only accommodate one-third of their number.[236] Petty wrote that office, the Army, the Navy, the Church, law and physic, and service in noble households, could not, by 1690, accommodate more than 3,000 of 10,000 younger sons, and that the remainder would have to depend on trade.[237] Many younger sons had leisure thrust upon them and needed indefinite support from their families; they often had no choice but to remain as unwanted additions to their elder brother's household.[238]

The business sector had always been larger than any single profession and it maintained this differential. Although the numbers of those seeking employment and the vacancy rate for different occupations can only be broadly estimated, the relative orders of magnitude are fairly clear. The professions could not absorb all younger sons of gentlemen. On a strict cost-benefit analysis, business was not necessarily the best choice, but it offered indispensable openings and opportunities for growth. That is why demand for places inflated apprenticeship premiums. The overall distribution of children between different forms of employment was in the long run determined more by opportunity than by family preference. In the final analysis, parents were obliged to select for their children what they could afford from the best options which were available.

234 Roberts, *Younger Son*; Waterhouse, *Gentleman's Monitor*, pp. 72–5; Sharpe 1974: 42.
235 Eachard, *Grounds Contempt of Clergy*.
236 *Seventeenth-Century Economic Documents*, p. 29.
237 Petty, *Economic Writings*, i. 312–13; BL Add. MS 22781, fos. 36–7, temp. Chas II.
238 Blackwood 1976: 66, 69 concludes that only some 10 per cent of younger sons were gainfully employed, though he could only find information on 480 out of 1,000.

Part 2

Paths to fortune

5 The pattern of recruitment

Who entered business in the seventeenth century? What were the social and geographical origins of new recruits and which sectors of the economy did they prefer? Did entry vary over time and how important was birth order? Individual indentures, sureties and references to apprenticeship occur frequently in private archives. Bindings were recorded voluntarily until 1709, when the Apprenticeship Act imposed a stamp duty on premiums and, by making enrolment compulsory, created the first national record of apprenticeship.[1] The primary statistical sources for recruitment are therefore the apprenticeship and freedom registers of towns, guilds and Companies. The former indicate intent and the latter actual entry.

The overall pattern of recruitment is clear. A comparison of the apprenticeship and freedom registers reveals a high wastage rate. In mid-Tudor London, only 41 per cent completed their apprenticeships and became householders; given a probable mortality rate of 9 per cent during their term, the effective rate of completion was probably 65 per cent.[2] In early Stuart London, 40 per cent of the Carpenters, 44 per cent of the Masons, 38 per cent of the Drapers, 27 per cent of the Cordwainers, 45 per cent of the Goldsmiths, 42 per cent of the Merchant Taylors, 50 per cent of the Poulterers and 41 per cent of the Stationers took their freedom.[3] Approximately 50 per cent in Bristol, Chester, Coventry and Newcastle

[1] The returns from the apprenticeship duty are in PRO IR and have been published for some counties; masters who were not freemen are included but after 1750 few details of parentage are recorded. Although numerous bonds and indentures have survived by accident, most apprenticeship registers remain in manuscript and are often incomplete. See Cooper 1984; Watts 1983; Gollard 1989; Phythian-Adams 1971; Ashworth 1969; Feather 1979: 96; D. M. Smith: 1990: 14. Unless otherwise stated, all percentages which follow in the text have been calculated by the author.

[2] Rappaport 1983; 1989: 311.

[3] Curtis 1964 points out that printers had higher completion rates, as their entry was more strictly controlled. P. E. Jones 1976: 16; 1937: 44, 68; Clode 1888: i. 217; Alford & Barker 1968: 73, as revised by Lang 1969: 84; Sale 1990: 145; S. R. Smith 1972. This failure to reach the freedom was not a recent development: see Swanson 1988: 46.

also fell by the wayside.[4] In Norwich, only 17 per cent of migrants remained as freemen and only 21 per cent at Salisbury.[5]

This does not necessarily imply a high rate of failure. Some prentices died or changed profession and cancelled their indentures. Some masters died and their prentices were not turned over; 6.5 per cent of the Bristol apprentices, 1600–43, lost their masters through death and 20 per cent were released on economic grounds.[6] Others just dropped out, often returning to their home counties. Many simply neglected to take their freedom to avoid quarterage, particularly when overseas. Others were discouraged by lack of capital and opportunity from setting up on their own in business and they worked instead for their former masters as wage labourers. A higher proportion of gentry apprentices in Newcastle, Shrewsbury, Bristol and London took their freedom, compared with children from non-business families, and in mid-Tudor London half of them entered the Livery.[7] But overall one-half of those who began training never practised as merchants.

Although most entered business through apprenticeship, a significant minority entered by redemption, patrimony and marriage. The freeman registers of Liverpool and Lincoln show many admitted by purchase, though in London, Yarmouth and Norwich, admission by purchase became less common in the seventeenth century.[8] Roger Mallock bought his way into the Exeter trade and this was the method followed by established businessmen who wished to branch out into additional trades.[9] Entry by patrimony varied considerably between towns and periods. In Elizabethan York, 36 per cent entered by patrimony and in Bristol 203 of 657 merchants, admitted between 1600 and 1699, and one-quarter of the Merchant Venturers chose this route.[10] In London, on the other hand, only 9 per cent of prentices in Tudor London entered by patrimony and 4 per cent by redemption; 84 per cent of the London aldermen, 1600–09, acquired their freedom by apprenticeship.[11] Under James I, 1,171 were freed by apprenticeship in the London Drapers Company compared with 217 by patrimony and 61 by redemption; between 1660 and 1688, the numbers were 1,142, 184 and 117 respecti-

[4] Clark & Souden 1987: 94; Berger 1982: 44. [5] Clark & Souden 1987: 270.

[6] Ben Amos 1988: 64; 1991: 162, tables 1, 3; Sacks 1985: 469; Holman 1979: table 5.

[7] Rappaport 1989: 678; Sacks 1985: 678.

[8] Poole 1962: 265, table 1, app. 2; Pound 1981: 50, 54; Lang 1963: 85; Hill 1956: 88. Twelve times as many Vintners entered by redemption as by patrimony (1435–1535), but only six of the Jacobean aldermen entered by redemption: see Crawford 1977: 70.

[9] Stephens 1960: 280.

[10] MacGrath 1955: x; 1975: 44; Sacks 1985: table vi; 1987: 123; Palliser 1979: 128, 153. The same was true of Chester and Liverpool: see Chandler 1965: 39.

[11] Ramsay 1978: 527; Rappaport 1989: table 8; Kahl 1956: 18. After 1681, about 12 per cent entered by patrimony: see Medlycott 1977: 45.

vely; in the Pewterers, only 2 per cent entered by patrimony and redemption and in the Turners 8 per cent falling to 4 per cent.[12] Of 156 mayors of Norwich, 1620–90, 89 had been apprentices.[13] In the Eastland Company, although sons followed their fathers, only 27 of 246 members entered by patrimony.[14] Most merchants, if they put their children to business, chose to apprentice them and gentlemen also preferred this method to redemption.

The limitations of the sources

Enrolments of apprentices have the disadvantage of both great volume and irregularity and they are scattered, imprecise and incomplete. The total number of registered apprentices in London certainly grew from around 2,100 in the fifteenth century to 28–40,000 in the 1600s; numbers fell during the Civil Wars and after recovering at the Restoration declined again after 1690; estimates vary from 11,000 in 1690 to 23,800–32,640 in 1700.[15] The average annual intake has been put at 1,485 in the 1550s, 4–5,000 in the 1600s, 1,250 in the 1650s, 1,850 in 1690 and 1,939–4,000 in 1700. Numbers fluctuated considerably between Companies, but the decline in enrolment was fairly uniform. In the 1630s the Grocers were taking in 154 per year and in the 1690s 59 per year and the same trend is visible in the Weavers and the Butchers.[16] But these figures may simply reflect greater freedom of trade and a decline in enforcement as the authority of the guilds weakened in the face of Common Law hostility.[17] Even when the guilds had a clear economic function, the mandatory requirement of the freedom had been resisted as repressive; when only high costs and onerous duties remained, many chose to opt out. Widespread evasion of registration in the suburbs and in towns where trade decayed creates serious deficiencies in the evidence.[18]

Since parents of apprentices were classified either as gentlemen or by their trades, it is also difficult to identify precise origins. The names of some fathers were omitted and often a widow or executor was listed. Social descriptions were often ambiguous and supplied by the prentice. The ubiquitous description 'Gent.' was a vague and elastic term employed indiscriminately in formal documents.[19] Although a more serious historical approach to heraldry developed after 1550, few contem-

[12] Johnson 1914–22: iii. 32, 96; Hatcher & Barker 1974: table 13; Seaver 1985: 234.
[13] Evans 1974: table 2. [14] Aström 1963: part 1, 190.
[15] Conflicting estimates are provided by Hollaender & Kellaway 1969: 385–6, table 9; Beier & Finlay 1986: 15; Finlay 1981: 248, table 3.7; S. R. Smith 1972: 197; Schwarz 1987: 20–2.
[16] Kahl 1956: 18; Plummer 1972: 78; P. E. Jones 1970: 15.
[17] Kellett 1957–8: 381–7; Pearl 1979b: 8. [18] Dobse 1973: 15, 21.
[19] Morrill 1974: 15; Stone 1975: i. 44; Ripley 1976: 121.

porary pedigrees were accurate.[20] The Visitations of the Heralds sometimes give occupations, but the investigators were usually not local men and their findings were incomplete.[21] They do not even clearly distinguish between gentlemen and esquires, a title which had originally referred to younger sons of barons, eldest sons of knights, royal creations and heirs of male heirs, but which was adopted by doctors of law and divinity, officials, judges, sheriffs and JPs.[22] On the other hand, gentility was sometimes voluntarily disclaimed, when merchants were faced with composition for knighthood or status-based taxes.[23] Squireens and armigerous copyholders frequently tried to void a status which imposed the obligations of office.[24]

Yeoman and husbandman were status and not occupational categories.[25] Many farmers were also clothiers and a thin line divided the prosperous yeoman with a manor from the impoverished gentleman. The Temples rose to gentry status on the wealth generated by grazing and the export trade in wool.[26] As Sir Thomas Smith said, gentlemen were 'good cheape in England' and he himself was the younger son of an Essex sheep farmer: his elder brother farmed and a younger brother was a London Draper.[27] William Harvey's father called himself a gentleman rather than a yeoman, when his sons became celebrated.[28] Many younger sons of gentry were accorded yeoman status and, when they enrolled as prentices, they may have discreetly omitted their genteel status. To distinguish the status of such men is laborious and often impossible when there is no complete guide, particularly to younger sons of families below the rank of baronet.[29]

Because businessmen were simply described by their craft, it is also difficult to distinguish those who financed and controlled output from craftsmen who, though technically self-employed, were in practice wage-earners.[30] It was also common for successful businessmen, like Thomas Revett, to conceal their origins and upgrade their status; famous mer-

[20] Fox 1956.

[21] The Visitations ended in 1686 and their erratic reliability is discussed by Styles 1978: 143; Squibb 1978: 3–4; Wagner 1939: 6; 1951: 205; Sayer 1979: 8. The county returns printed by the Harleian and local record societies are nonetheless a mine of information. Wales is covered by Dwynn 1846, but the Welsh relied on their poets rather than on the Heralds: see J. F. G. Jones 1989: 128.

[22] Brydall, *Jus Imaginis*, p. 52; Harper-Bell & Harris 1986; Saul 1981: 252–3; Squibb 1981: 42–3; Phillips 1970: 41–2. Walker, *Historical Discourses*, pp. 310–11, thought that 'riches and usurpations' were 'the best titles that most men have'.

[23] Leonard 1978; Roberts 1977: 50; Kirby 1985: 33.

[24] Ferris 1965: 105. Gentlemen would enrol at Oxford as plebeians in order to qualify for lower fees.

[25] Harte 1971: 199.

[26] Temple & Heritage, *Account Book*, pp. 246–7; Bettey 1978.

[27] Smith, *De Republica Anglorum*, p. 71; Dewar 1964: 10.

[28] Keynes 1966: 128; Morgan 1978: 4.

[29] Some information is also buried in Clay 1894 and Walker 1936.

[30] Kenyon 1958: 58; Unwin 1904: chap. 3.

chants, like Sir Josiah Child, were ascribed a genteel background by posterity.[31] Thomas Middleton's father was a London bricklayer with a modest estate who married a Londoner, but he boasted a coat of arms with an ape passant with a collar and gold chain.[32]

The gentry expanded faster than the population as a whole and many of those described as gentlemen in the seventeenth century would not have been recognized as such in the sixteenth century. Numbers were swollen by elevation through intermarriage, service and professional occupations, rather than through arms. In Warwickshire, only thirty-seven out of ninety-four gentlemen were armigerous.[33] The parents of apprentices in the urban registers who were described as gentlemen were often officers in local government, lawyers, physicians or clergy; in 1689, it was decreed that all mayors, aldermen, sheriffs and commissioners of Bristol should rank as esquires.[34] Many of these new 'urban gentry' were, however, younger sons of landed families, like the father of Sir Gilbert Heathcote.[35] To confuse matters further, some Visitations, like that of London in 1633–5, describe them as merchants, whereas second-generation merchants, upgraded through municipal office or knighthoods, are described as gentlemen.

The freeman registers also have flaws.[36] Many apprentices neglected to take their freedom and not all freemen were active in trade. Ipswich has no surviving freeman rolls and those for Chester, Exeter, York and Leicester usually list masters, but only the names and status of parents when entry was by patrimony.[37] London presents peculiar difficulties. Most of the freeman registers before 1688 have not survived and the actual business of a freeman was frequently different from the guild of which he was free.[38] A combination of trades and diversification was often necessary for survival; translations were only enforced in certain Companies, like the Stationers.[39] Of 528 freemen of the Drapers, only twenty-five were drapers: four were clothworkers, six merchants, one hundred and sixteen tailors and forty-six silkmen.[40] Of the Livery of the Vintners Company in 1641, thirty-two were tavern-keepers, but five were haberdashers, two linen drapers and one a silk dyer or salter.[41] The master of George, son of Henry Malbou, gentleman, was described as a barber chirugien, wax chandler and painter.[42] George Whittingham was free of the Cooks Company, but in fact was a cloth merchant and clockmaker.[43]

31 Morant, *History Essex*, i. bk 2, 30. 32 Barker 1958: 1–2. 33 Styles 1978: 163.
34 Brooks 1986: 261; *Bristol Inhabitants 1696*, p. xii.
35 Heathcote 1899.
36 Woodward 1970–1: 91; Pound 1981: 52–3; Patten 1970–1: 50; Clark & Slack 1972: 274.
37 There are also few records of apprenticeship for Ipswich after 1651: see Hutchinson 1964. 38 This may only have began in the 1570s: see Rappaport 1989: 91.
39 Patten 1977; Fox & Butler 1979; Lavin 1969: 222; Earle 1989a: table 9.4.
40 Johnson 1914–22: iii. 93, app. 10. 41 Crawford 1977: 128. 42 Alsop 1979a.
43 Barder 1983: 28.

After 1712, London abandoned efforts to enforce the freedom on overseas merchants. By the eighteenth century, admission to the twelve great Livery Companies of London became more of a social honour and political franchise than a right to trade and was secured without apprenticeship; many major figures were not even citizens.[44] The same was true of other towns. Half of the freemen admitted to Chester and Preston, and to Winchester between 1680 and 1700, many of them by favour, ranked as esquires or above, but they had no intention of entering business.[45]

There is no watertight solution to these problems, but they can be reduced in size. It was mainly in the craft trades that evasion was common; the higher levels of business continued to recruit through apprenticeship. The registers of bindings therefore provide a reasonably comprehensive record of entry into business and they have survived in sufficient numbers for most towns. In the first half of the century, social descriptions in formal documents are fairly accurate. Although there are too many names in apprenticeship lists to be individually traced, the status of gentleman was not so devalued that the clerks who compiled the admission registers would passively accept spurious claims by individuals. In some cases, as in the Shrewsbury and Bristol registers, marginal notes by the clerk show that he had doubts about particular applicants. Sons of peers, baronets and knights are easily recognized and the armorial gentry and their junior branches can usually be identified in local records. The urban gentry, moreover, has a rightful claim to be considered part of the elite.[46] Businessmen can often be distinguished from the craftsmen and their real from their nominal trades by the institutions to which they belonged, from the Port Books, the records of the Hearth, Poll and Marriage taxes, from livery lists, wills, burial registers and from other business sources.[47]

Numbers and status

The proportion of recruits with genteel status was remarkably high. In the early seventeenth century, some 500 of 750 migrants to London from

[44] Kahl 1956: 17–19; Jacob, *City Liberties*.

[45] Clark 1981: 162, 183; Clark & Slack 1972: 279.

[46] For a contrary view see Stone & Everitt 1965: 62 and Stone & Stone 1984. The latter well illustrates the confusion created by overlapping definitions. At different times, depending on which argument they are advancing, the Stones both merge and separate the peerage and gentry; by p. 281, younger sons of the gentry are classified as upper middle-class with gentry connections who, after retirement from running the Empire, become parochial gentry. Bush 1984: 11 treats the nobility and gentry as a single group, but is ambiguous about the professions. Tawney 1978: 87, 99 rightly regarded the professional men and the gentry as one group, though he wrongly considered the commoners as a proto-bourgeoisie in opposition to the aristocracy. Here, gentleman have been identified by acceptance, not by their right to arms or by the form in which they held their assets. Although status corresponded closely to wealth, the two did not always coincide.

[47] Beier & Finlay 1986: 213, table 13.

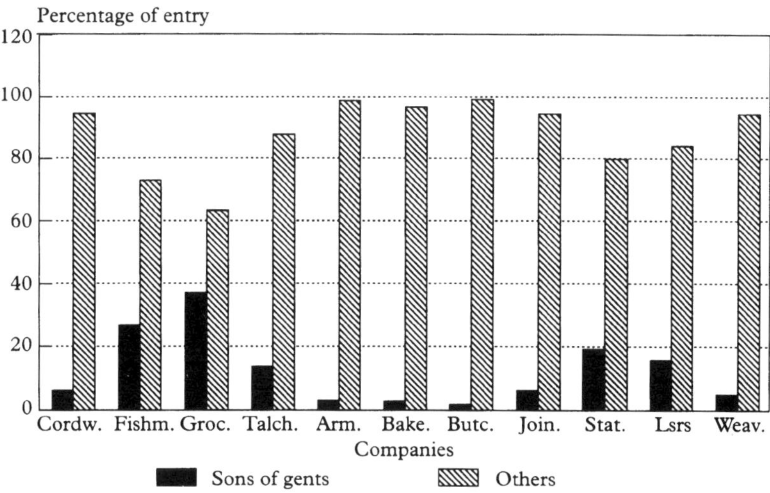

Fig. 5.1. The social origins of London apprentices, principally 1630–60. (*Source*: Grassby in Thomas & Pennington 1978, Lang 1963, MacKenzie 1958, Plummer 1972, S. R. Smith 1973a.)

the upper levels of society came as apprentices.[48] Between one-quarter and one-third of 140 Jacobean aldermen were sons of knights or gentlemen and mainly younger sons, though these fall to 17 per cent when the lesser merchants are included.[49] In the Visitation of 1633–5, of 849 whose occupations were given, 696 were in business compared with 35 at Court, 67 lawyers, 14 officers of the City of London, 29 in medical trades and 4 churchmen; 785 or 91 per cent were younger sons.[50] In eleven greater and lesser Livery Companies, mainly between 1630 and 1660, an average of 15 per cent of all apprentices were sons of gentlemen and 3 per cent of esquires, compared with 23 per cent from yeomen families.[51] One-fifth of those bound to the Stationers Company were of gentry stock.[52] Of 4,387 apprentices to the Leathersellers, between 1629 and 1673, 139 were sons of knights, esquires and baronets and 562 sons of gentry. Of 1,096 apprentices to the Weavers Company, 1655–64, 49 or 4.57 per cent were of gentry origin.[53] Of 375 citizens of all trades who left orphans, 1665–1720, one-quarter were sons of gentlemen.[54] In the Skinners Company,

[48] Finlay 1981: 67.

[49] Lang 1962: 7–8; 1974: 38–40 identifies the social origins of only 89 of his sample of 140 and the percentages change according to whether the aldermen-elect or just those who took their seats are included.

[50] Grant 1962: 199–200; *London Visitation 1633, 1634 and 1635*; *London Visitation Pedigrees 1664*.

[51] See fig. 5.1; S. R. Smith 1972: 199–200; 1973: 151; GLL MS L.37/55; 76/3; 11593/2/3.

[52] MacKenzie 1958; 1961; Myers 1983.

[53] Plummer 1972: tables 4:5, 4:6.

[54] Earle 1989a: 86.

1604–94, there were 261 gentlemen, 165 esquires, 64 knights and baronets and one son of a peer.[55]

Of the Restoration aldermen and Common Councilmen, 34 per cent have been identified as gentry, 5.2 per cent as esquires, 2.3 per cent as soldiers and 3.4 per cent as knights; taking just the aldermen, 27 per cent were of gentry origin.[56] In 1690, of the 1,850 who took the freedom of London, 179 or 10 per cent were sons of gentlemen.[57] Between 1691–1700 and 1711–13, the proportion of gentlemen apprentices rose from 14.9 per cent to 17.9 per cent, from third to first place.[58] Between 1694 and 1714, nine out of sixty-two aldermen were sons of gentry and more came from professional families and would count as urban gentry.[59]

The same was true of the provincial towns in the South, East and North. In the declining port of Southampton, between 1610 and 1710, 1 per cent of all apprentices were sons of esquires and more than 12 per cent sons of minor gentry.[60] Tudor Rye, Colchester and the Surrey and Sussex towns recruited from the local gentry and there were at least eleven gentlemen at Lynn and six at Yarmouth.[61] In Norwich, on the other hand, although gentlemen featured among the magistrates, only 2.2 per cent of approximately 6,000 apprentices between 1510–1720 were described as sons of gentlemen; of 990 freemen, between 1548 and 1713, only 25 or 2.5 per cent were listed as gentlemen, though a tax roll of 1660 named 21 as esquires and 41 as gentlemen; 106 freemen, mostly younger sons and including 13 merchants, were recorded in the Visitation.[62] In Chester, only 1 per cent of prentices taking the freedom, 1600–39, were sons of gentlemen, and none, 1640–59, but 5 per cent fell into this category, 1660–89, and 10 per cent, 1690–1720.[63] In the Newcastle Merchant Adventurers, between 1600 and 1720, 47 per cent of the apprentices and 57 per cent of the freemen by apprenticeship were sons of gentry; 26.2 per cent of apprentices to hostmen between 1603 and 1715 also fell into this

[55] Calculated from Cokayne 1896, excluding citizens, aldermen and clerks.

[56] Woodhead 1965 contains the biographical details, but not the social tables in 1963: 49, apps. 4–6. The social categories are rather broad.

[57] Hollaender & Kellaway 1969: 387–8.

[58] Beier & Finlay 1986: 246.

[59] Horwitz 1987: app. A; Krey 1985: 143.

[60] See table 5.1; *Southampton Third Book Remembrance*, p. xv; Patterson 1966.

[61] Mayhew 1989: 107, 113; Morant, *History Essex*, i. 110; Sutherland 1962: 6; Stephenson 1977; Pritchard 1960: 408; Brent 1981; Clark & Slack 1976: 119–20; A. H. Smith 1974: 16; Patten 1979: 158; Clark & Souden 1987: 98, show that 17 per cent of Yarmouth migrants were apprenticed to merchants.

[62] Clark & Slack 1972: 272, table 18; Evans 1974: 55–6, tables 8–9; 1980: 6, 21, 34, tables 2, 5; Allen 1951: 61–70; Sayer 1979: 12.

[63] See fig. 5.2.

Table 5.1. *Social origins of Southampton apprentices, 1610–1710: parental occupations as percentage of total*

Occupation	1610–20	1620–31	1631–38	1638–48	1648–69	1670–83	1683–1710
Esquire	0	1	0	3	2	1	0
Gent	6	14	15	15	20	8	8
Clerk/Minist.	5	2	6	2	6	2	0
Yeoman	18	22	20	13	7	9	22
Husbandman	18	12	11	5	3	4	0
Merchant	9	19	9	22	16	17	18
Craft/tradesman	30	27	34	26	25	51	30
Labourer	3	0	1	1	0	1	0
Sailor	2	2	2	3	1	0	2
Widow/other	9	1	2	10	20	7	20

Source: Southampton Calendar Apprentices, p. xxxi. Tabulated from enrolments in the General Register.

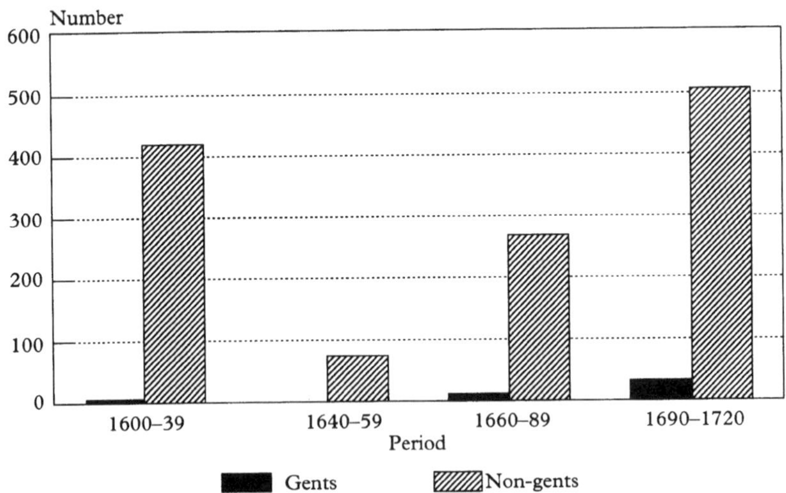

Fig. 5.2. Freedom through apprenticeship: Chester, 1600–1720. The gentry are under-represented, because those described as widows and by their municipal office have been excluded and there are gaps and other irregularities in the Rolls: see Woodward 1967: 66. (*Source: Chester Rolls of Freemen 1392–1700.*)

category.[64] York, Halifax, Leeds, Hull and Liverpool also had their share of genteel recruits.[65]

The same was true of towns in the West and Midlands. Most of the Exeter mayors in the sixteenth century had well-established pedigrees and only one was of mean parentage; the Subsidy Roll of 1629 listed eight esquires, four doctors of law or medicine and thirty-four gentlemen.[66] In Bristol 23 per cent of those apprenticed to merchants and 6–8 per cent of those entering all trades came from the gentry.[67] Of the 109 admitted between 1653 and 1699 to the Society of Merchant Venturers, 28 or 26 per cent were sons of squires and gentlemen.[68] In Gloucester, 40 per cent of

[64] See tables 5.2 and 5.3. Howell 1967: 19–20.

[65] *C.J.* xvi, 11 Feb. 1709; Read 1972; Francois 1966: 233; Wilson 1971: 14–15; Burt & Grady 1985; Kirby 1985: 135; *V.C.H. Yorkshire, East Riding* 1969: i. 150; MacNamara 1895: 437; Surfield 1986; Palliser 1979: 21, 101, 132; Chandler 1965: 37; Morton 1889: 150; Mullett 1972: 32.

[66] Hoskins 1963; Bindoff *et al.* 1961: 168; *Exeter in Seventeenth Century*, app. 1; MacCaffrey 1976: 259; Stephens 1960: 280–2; 1957; 1969.

[67] See table 5.4. The Bristol indentures are not systematically recorded after 1659: see Jones 1938–9; Goodman 1974: 28; *Bristol Merchants and Merchandise*; Sacks 1985: table 8; 1987: table 16; Salerno 1979: table 3; Ben Amos 1988: 62, n.15; 1991: 230, 235; Holman 1975. For Gloucester and Worcester see Ripley 1976 and Talbot 1986.

[68] *Bristol Records Merchant Venturers*; MacGrath 1975: 40–1.

Table 5.2. *Social origins of apprentices and freemen of the Merchant Adventurers of Newcastle, 1600–1720*

	Appr.	Gent	Esq.	%	Adm. appr.	Adm. patr.	Gent	Esq.	%
1600–40	416	135	22	38	14	10	0	4	29
1641–60	260	113	14	49	143	61	60	7	47
1661–89	393	169	23	49	192	23	100	17	61
1690–1720	254	127	13	55	152	91	89	6	63
Total	1323	544	72	47	501	185	249	34	57

Note: The figures have been tabulated by the author. Columns 2 and 6 are totals of all apprentices enrolled and admitted. Of those listed as esquires, two were sons of baronets. The number of gents admitted is expressed as a percentage of all freedoms by apprenticeship, i.e., excluding those by patrimony and redemption. Esquires represent 13 per cent of all genteel apprentices and 14 per cent of all genteel freemen.
Source: Newcastle Merchant Adventurers' Records (Surtees Soc., 101, 1899).

Table 5.3. *Enrolment of hostmen of Newcastle, 1603–1715*

	No. admitted	No. gents	% gents
1603–40	9	2	22.2
1641–60	49	7	14.3
1661–88	96	14	14.6
1689–1715	163	60	36.8
Total	317	83	26.2

Note: The freeman registers list trade but not social origins and are incomplete and erratic. Between 1603 and 1715 approximately 126 were made free by apprenticeship and many entered by patrimony.
Source: *Newcastle Hostmen Records* (Surtees Soc., 105, 1901).

apprentices were sons of gentry, yeomen and businessmen.[69] In Leicester, between 1600 and 1720, 22 or 18 per cent of the mayors were described as gentlemen, mainly in the mercery and haberdashery trades; of 614 freemen, between 1660 and 1689, excluding MPs and honorary freemen, 16 or 2.6 per cent were sons of gentlemen, 7 of whom were younger sons.[70] In the Shrewsbury Drapers Company, between 1572–1715, 42 per cent of apprentices were sons of gentlemen; 38 per cent of all freemen admitted, between 1572 and 1657, and 14 per cent of the bailiffs of Shrewsbury also fell into the same category.[71]

Only five guilds in fifteenth-century London had excluded women; daughters could be apprenticed in London if unmarried, and were entitled to freedom by patrimony, though this right could be lost by marriage to a non-freeman.[72] Katherine Wetwood was freed by patrimony after the Master and Wardens of the Merchant Taylors and two silk weavers swore that she was a virgin.[73] Of 4,293 apprentices to the Stationers, 1641–1700, 51 or 1 per cent were female and 79 or 4 per cent of 1,740 booksellers and printers; one was admitted by patrimony.[74] A handful of women were apprenticed in the Companies of Cutlers, Weavers, Glass-sellers, Scriveners, Gunmakers and Basketmakers; five entered the Drapers between 1660 and 1688 and more entered the Girdlers.[75] But only 73 women were apprenticed in mid-Tudor London

[69] Clark *et al.* 1979: 169. [70] Calculated from the freemen lists.
[71] See fig 5.3 and table 5.5. These figures have been calculated from Peele 1939 and combined with those of Mendenhall 1953: apps. B, C, and 1951: 165; the registers are less reliable before 1608. [72] Girtin 1964: 165. [73] Welch 1902: 92.
[74] Morgan 1978: 2.
[75] Welch 1916–23: 58, 65; Johnson 1914–22: iii. 321; Young 1913: 282; Smyth 1905a: 128; Ronald 1978: 87; *Scriveners Company Papers*, p. xi; Blackmore 1986: 22; Plummer 1972: 62, table 12.8: women were not allowed to work looms.

Table 5.4. *Social origins of apprentices to Bristol merchants, 1600–30 and 1670–90: parental occupations*

Occupation	1600–30	%	1670–90	%	Total	%
Gentlemen	88	23.3	50	22.1	138	22.9
Husbandmen	24	6.4	5	2.2	29	4.8
Mariners	11	2.9	7	3.1	18	3.0
Mercers	10	2.7	3	1.3	13	2.2
Merchants	70	18.6	57	25.2	127	21.1
Vintners	11	2.9	4	1.8	15	2.5
Yeomen	37	9.8	16	7.1	53	8.8
Others	126	33.4	84	37.2	210	34.8
Total	377	100	226	100	603	100

Note: Apprentices to all trades: additional data. Sacks 1935: table VIII finds that 211 or 7.8% of 2,734 prentices, 1626–36, were sons of gentry. Ben Amos 1988 lists 1,517 prentices, 1600–48: 88 or 5.8% were sons of gentry, 40 or 2.7% sons of merchants, 210 or 13.9% sons of tradesmen and 48 or 3.2% sons of professionals.

Salerno 1979 lists 6.1% of Wiltshiremen apprenticed at Bristol, 1600–29, as sons of gentry and 13.2%, 1630–58. Holman 1979 lists 7% of all apprentices, 1675–1726, as sons of gentlemen

Source: (main table) *Bristol Merchants and Merchandise*, app. B.

Table 5.5. *Social origins of Shrewsbury Drapers' apprentices and freemen, 1572–1715*

	Admissions	Gents	% gents
Apprentices			
1572–1608	78	14	17.9
1609–1640	171	74	43.3
1641–1659	147	80	54.4
1660–1688	154	58	37.7
1689–1715	77	35	45.5
1572–1715	627	261	41.6
Freemen			
1572–1607	77	11	14.3
1608–1657	203	87	42.8

Note: The figures for freemen and for apprentices, 1572–1608, have been taken from Mendenhall. The other figures have been calculated by the author from Peele's lists. Of 247 apprentices categorized as gent (1609–1715) 39 or 15.8% were sons of esquires.
Source: Mendenhall 1953; Peele 1939.

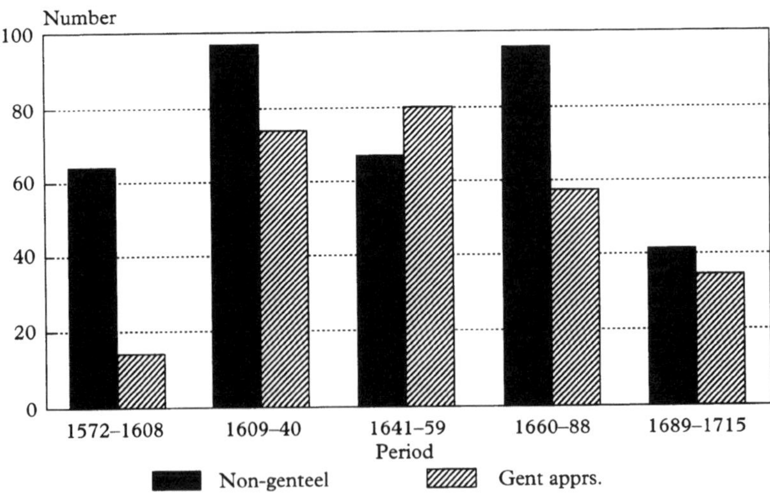

Fig. 5.3. Enrolments of Drapers' apprentices: Shrewsbury, 1572–1715. (*Source*: Peele 1939.)

and none occurs among 8,000 examples in fifteen Companies, 1598–1619.[76] In 1690, only twenty-three were admitted to the freedom, of which fourteen were poor seamstresses and one was admitted as a bookbinder, cooper, draper, exchangewoman, goldsmith, haberdasher, ironmonger, skinner and victualler.[77] Women were never full members who voted, joined the Livery or held office; rights were restricted to wives and daughters of existing freemen.[78]

They were also accepted as apprentices in provincial towns, like Coventry, Bristol, York and Southampton. In Bristol, some daughters of merchants, gentry and professionals were apprenticed to mercers, drapers, grocers and haberdashers; but few became merchants and they mainly entered the crafts or retail trades.[79] John Whitson of Bristol founded the Red Maids School for forty daughters of decayed or dead freemen and they were bound as apprentices to the schoolmistress to learn spinning and sewing.[80] In York, few women were indentured, but in Southampton 10 per cent of prentices were women and one French-speaking widow was in the cloth business.[81] The daughter of a Gloucestershire gentleman became a seamstress and a few women became silk throwsters, but only daughters from poorer families were apprenticed as artisans.[82] Spinsters exercising a trade or craft were the exception in propertied society. There are some signs that numbers also declined during the seventeenth century compared with earlier periods, as in Oxfordshire; where there was a shortage of openings and when the guilds declined and Custom weakened, there was more discrimination by male artisans. But the evidence that women were deliberately reduced to housekeeping status is not conclusive.[83]

In Misson's opinion 'it is very rare for Peers to put their younger sons out apprentices as 'tis said they used to do' and indeed this was characteristic only of the lesser barons and the Scottish and Irish peers.[84] A few sons of spiritual peers became merchants. Maurice Abbot, the celebrated London merchant, was the third son of an archbishop, who was himself the second son of a clothworker.[85] But sons of baronets and knights were more common. Sir William Blackett put his second son Michael into trade and John Trolloppe, younger son of the 3rd Baronet,

[76] Rappaport 1989: 37; Brodsky 1980: 14.

[77] Hollaender & Kellaway 1969: table 8. [78] Charles & Duffin 1985: 57.

[79] Ben Amos 1991: 228–34, table 2. [80] Bridenbaugh 1968: 350.

[81] Willen 1984: 217–18. *Southampton Calendar Apprentices*, p. lxxvi.

[82] Dale 1932–4: 327; Carter 1975: 197.

[83] Thwaites 1984: 38; Prior 1985: 17, 103, 107; Hanawalt 1986: xv.

[84] Misson, *Mémoires*, pp. 7–8; Muralt, *Lettres sur Anglois*; Berks. RO D/ED/ F 41.

[85] Welsby 1962: 4; L. B. Smith 1953: 12. On the other hand only one out of seventy-eight sons of Elizabethan bishops entered business: see Berlatsky 1978: 12.

became a London linen draper.[86] Sir Nathaniel Barnardiston, Sir John Wynn, Sir Robert Filmer, Sir Edward Wiseman and Sir William Gostwick of Willington all apprenticed their children and Sir John Reresby apprenticed two of his younger brothers.[87] Knighthoods were, of course, conferred by the Crown as a fiscal expedient and were relatively easy for merchants and municipal officers to obtain; after 1660, knighthood became a civil status.[88] Esquires were even more common, representing 3 per cent of all apprentices in London, 1 per cent in Southampton and 5.4 per cent in Newcastle; of 247 genteel apprentices to the Shrewsbury Drapers, between 1609 and 1715, 39 or 15.8 per cent were sons of esquires.[89]

The great majority of genteel recruits from the country came, however, from the middling and parochial gentry, some bordering on yeoman status, even if they could genuinely claim former grants of arms. They were often grandsons of armorial families or younger sons of cadet branches which had entered business or the professions.[90] Maybe half of all genteel recruits were sons of established businessmen and professional men, gentrified by office and occupation, purchase and education, acceptance and manner of life.[91] Sir John Banks drew equally for his prentices on both the country and the urban gentry; in Bristol, 1626–36, of 548 apprentices to major businessmen, 11 were urban gentlemen and 39 sons of esquires and country gentlemen.[92]

Although many sons and kinsmen of merchants and urban tradesmen did follow their fathers into business, it is clear that business depended on migration from the countryside.[93] Entry into business accelerated down the social scale. The percentage of sons of husbandmen and yeomen, however, tended to fall in London during the century and sons of the more prosperous rural and urban craftsmen constituted the majority of recruits to the lower levels of business. The high cost of entry closed major Companies, like the Mercers and Drapers, to the poor. Although the social base of business did narrow during the century, it nonetheless remained broad. Business recruited its managers not just from its own members but from the whole of propertied society in proportion to their numbers at each social level.

86 Lincs. AO, Trollope-Bellew MSS.

87 Finberg 1956: 95; Reresby, *Memoirs*, p. 54; Weigall 1975: 103; Laslett 1948a: 528–31.

88 Shaw 1906; the exceptions were the Garter and the Bath. The unwarlike knights had always outnumbered the fighters: see Denholm-Young 1965: 149.

89 See tables 5.1, 5.2 and 5.5.

90 B. Williams 1913: i. 2–4; Harris 1987–8: 107.

91 It is difficult to provide hard statistics for the comparative numbers of country and urban gentlemen in apprenticeships, particularly since both recruited from each other.

92 Coleman 1963: 28; Sacks 1983.

93 Campbell 1960: app. 2; Cornwall 1967.

Regional distribution

Apprenticeship registers usually specify the residence of parents and thereby the geography of recruitment. London depended for its growth on migration and its catchment area was the whole nation; similarity of economic structure made migration easy.[94] Some provincial towns, like Worcester, York and Ipswich, exported children to London, though this was less common in the more prosperous outports, like Bristol.[95] In mid-Tudor England, London recruited 54 per cent of its apprentices from the North and Wales, which probably represented a mass betterment migration from upland and pastoral areas to the lowland zone.[96] But, during the seventeenth century, as some provincial towns expanded, London began to turn inwards. The Jacobean aldermen came mainly from nearby counties, though only 16–20 per cent came from the City itself.[97] Four-fifths of the Stationers and 26 per cent of the Leathersellers came from the City, Middlesex and the South. The percentage of entrants from the Home Counties rose from 19 per cent, 1570–1640, to over 31 per cent, 1640–90.[98] In the 1630s and 1640s, 41 per cent of those apprenticed to eight Companies came from London and the South.[99] Between 1655 and 1664, 279 of 1,100 weavers came from London and a further 181 from the Home Counties.[100] Between 1660 and 1689, 25 per cent of the aldermen came from London and 20 per cent from the South East.[101] Although it remained dominant and continued to draw on all counties, London increasingly relied on its own urban craftsmen and on its hinterland and adjacent counties.[102] In 1690, 70 per cent of London apprentices still came from outside the City.[103]

Other towns also drew primarily on their hinterland and neighbouring counties and it was usually sons of propertied families who travelled the greatest distance.[104] Southampton drew 56 per cent, Norwich 57 per cent and Sheffield 15 per cent of its prentices from their own population and the rest from nearby counties. Between 1675 and 1726, 47 per cent of Bristol apprentices came from outside the city, principally from Gloucestershire, Somerset, Devon, Shropshire, Wiltshire and the Welsh counties, though a few also came from the Home Counties, presumably

[94] Wrigley 1991: 118; Spufford 1973–4; Rappaport 1989: fig. 3.4; Finlay 1981: tables 3.5, 3.6. [95] Dyer 1972: 182, 188; Paige, *Letters*, p. x; Sacks 1987: 30.
[96] Ramsay 1978: 529, table 1; his figures cover all trades. [97] Lang 1974: 31.
[98] Grant 1962: table 1; Girtin 1958: 7; Finlay 1981: 64, tables 3.5, 3.6.
[99] Smith 1972: 199. [100] Plummer 1972: table 4.4. [101] Woodhead 1965.
[102] Wareing 1980: 242; 1981: 356–7; Jordan 1960a; Warburton, *London and Middlesex*, pp. iv–v.
[103] Beier & Finlay 1986: 230–4, fig. 5. [104] Clark & Souden 1987: 279.

because they had been unable to find a London master.[105] Chester attracted not only Cheshire gentlemen, like Sir Thomas Browne, but also William Jewetts from Yorkshire and William Edwards from Flintshire.[106]

Throughout the country, however, distant migration became less common. The drawing power of any town depended on the opportunities which it offered; shifts in migration reflected relative population density and wealth.[107] York attracted few from outside the county; it had little industry apart from the lead trade and, although the number of freemen by apprenticeship remained steady at 500 per decade, the number of haberdashers, merchants and mercers declined.[108] Smaller towns within the London orbit, like Canterbury, could not compete for high-class recruits.

Most counties in the North and East sent some gentlemen into business. Bedfordshire, between 1711 and 1720, had twenty-four gents and three esquires out of 432 apprentices, of which fourteen went into commerce. The gentry of Berkshire, Kent, Hertfordshire, Northamptonshire, Leicestershire, Suffolk and Buckinghamshire made their contribution.[109] Sons of Derbyshire gentlemen mainly entered the Liverpool trades, but some, like the Bludworths, went to London; of forty-four families, three had trading and ten industrial interests.[110] The same was true of Lancashire, Cheshire and Northumberland.[111] Ralphe Hartley of Manchester went to London; his eldest son was squire of Strangeway, but his second son became a London merchant and all his three daughters married London citizens.[112] Yorkshire sent many apprentices to Newcastle, which was usually hostile to uplanders, and also to York, Norwich, Ipswich and Yarmouth [113] In Cumberland, Westmorland and the Lake District, on the other hand, despite business connections between landowners and the German miners at Keswick, trade seems to have been primarily an avenue of advancement for yeomen.[114] In Scotland, lairds'

105 *Bristol Merchants and Merchandise*, app. A; Yarbrough 1979: table 10; Sacks 1983: tables 4, 7; Holmes 1980a: 87–8.

106 Chetham, *Life*, i. 6–8, 50, ii. 42–4; Stephens 1968; Woodward 1970c; *Wales Calendar Letters*, p. 6.

107 Clark & Slack 1972: table 1.

108 Clark 1979; Lovett *et al.* 1985; Watts 1975; Dyer 1979c; 1991; Coleman & John 1976: 226–32; Goose 1982b; Everitt 1975: 130; *V.C.H. City of York*: 166–7, table 5; Palliser 1985; 1978; Johnson 1949: table 1.

109 Finch 1956: 24, 56; *Oxinden Letters*, pp. xxiv, 117; Chalklin 1965: 209; Everitt 1966: 41–3; 1968: 63; Laslett 1948b: 153; A. G. Davies 1988; Fleming 1979; Barron 1906: 63–6, 218.

110 Blundell, *Diary*, p. 39; *V.C.H. Derbyshire*, ii. 346; Moore 1899: 77; Keeton 1967: 42–50; Newton 1966: 3.

111 Blackwood 1976: 66–73; 1978: 18, table 8; Wadsworth & Mann 1931: 73; Hughes 1952a: i. 104–9, 164–6.

112 Dugdale, *Visitation Lancaster*, part 2, p. 131; Aikin, *Description Manchester*, p.182.

113 Fraser & Emsley 1978: 119–23; Cliffe 1969: 10, 49, 61, 84–5; Rawdon, *Life*, pp. xi, 155.

114 Bouch & Jones 1961: 84–5; Marshall 1975a; MacGregor & Wright 1977: 69.

sons like Walter Gibson, entered business in Glasgow; in Edinburgh, Hugh Montgomery, the younger son of a baronet was apprenticed to the sugar and iron trades.[115]

The same was true of the South and West. The Dorset, Somerset and Sussex gentry produced a few merchants, like Denis Bond in Dorchester and George Gollopp in Southampton.[116] The Shropshire and Wiltshire gentry went into the clothing trades and those of Gloucestershire into a variety of enterprises extending to the tobacco colonies.[117] A few Cornish gentlemen like Jonathan Rashleigh of Fowey, Samuel Enys and John Eliot of Port Eliot entered business.[118] The gentry of Herefordshire, Staffordshire, Worcestershire and Warwickshire were more active, though not in Coventry.[119] Recruitment from the poor Welsh gentry was continuous; families in South Wales employed factors on a small scale and sixty-five became merchants between 1550 and 1603.[120] In Ireland, the gentry of Galway and Waterford sent their children into foreign trade.[121] Counties were not economic regions and it was those in close proximity to major centres of distribution and with the most gentry families that made the greater contribution.[122] But no region was completely insular.[123]

The contribution of aliens, both naturalized subjects and those acting under special licence, was also significant. Although the preponderance of Hansards, Castilians and the Italian merchants had disappeared by the seventeenth century, they retained a strong presence.[124] Foreign merchants sent their children to be apprenticed in England and learn the local technology.[125] There were 230 Dutch merchants in 1617, of which fifty-six had been born in England and thirty-five were wealthy; some were free of the City.[126] Half of the population of Colchester in 1571 were foreign immigrants and 5,650 aliens were resident in England by 1583.[127] Many of the successive waves of Protestant immigrants, like the German miners and the Walloons in Norwich, were not merchants, but artisans who

115 Smout 1967: 67; 1969: 171–5; Gordon & Dicks 1983; Devine 1975: part 1; Houston & Whyte 1989: 46; Lynch & Spearman 1988: 273; Stewart 1881: 45.

116 Ferris 1965: 107; Tittler 1985a; Keeler 1954: 110, 189; Fletcher 1975: 37; *Shiffren Archives*, pp. ix, xi, xv.

117 Ramsay 1968: 412, app.; Moir 1957–8; Finberg 1957; *Shropshire Visitation 1623*, p. xiii; Thirsk 1984: 291.

118 Rowse 1941: 77; Whetter 1974: 154; Scartlebury 1978.

119 Styles 1978: 132; Farr 1968; Hughes 1987: 16; Kidson 1958; Johnston 1978: 200.

120 Dodd 1952: 1–3, 47; *Chirk Castle Accounts*, ii. p. viii; Stephens 1977: 282; *Welsh Port Books*, p. xli; W. O. Williams 1967; Griffiths 1953–4: 198, 336; M. I. Williams 1978; Owen 1988: 132–5; G. Williams 1974: iv. chap. 2; *Haverfordwest. Calendar Records*, p. 67; Lloyd 1968: 84–7; Jenkins 1983: 37.

121 Cullen & Smout 1977: 170.

122 Holmes 1981.

123 Everitt 1969; Holmes 1980a.

124 Ives *et al.* 1978: 203; Ramsay 1986: 63; D. W. Jones 1988: table 8.3; Ruddock 1951; Lloyd 1982; 1991: chap. 6; Childe 1978: 216; Cobb 1978: 609; Bratchell 1984; 1982; 1980; 1978: 52–3.

125 Ehrenberg 1895: 251; Prynne, *Diary*, p. 144.

126 Grell 1989: 44–6, 153, app. 7.

127 Goose 1982a: 262–3; Ormrod 1973.

introduced new technologies.[128] Only 23 per cent of 7,113 ranked as householders and, in 1593, only 208 of 1,040 were merchants.[129] The retailers and craftsmen were regarded with fear and envy by native businessmen and they were subject to restrictions.[130] In 1576, a London merchant revived as a fiscal project the old custom of hosting strangers; in 1619, 160 aliens were accused of illegally exporting bullion and eighteen were fined £140,000 in Star Chamber, later reduced to £60,000.[131]

Since the Jews were not exempted from the freeman's oath required for retailing until 1697 and could not purchase land until 1718, they became dealers and middlemen in new industries and trades.[132] By 1680, there were maybe 450, of which only forty were prosperous and only six wealthy.[133] Some Huguenots were of noble origin or former soldiers and the elite merchants of La Rochelle went to Bristol.[134] But as refugees, they were often destitute when they arrived, like the Palatines at the end of the century.[135] In 1680, the Threadneedle Street church had only twenty-three merchants and forty-one related trades.[136] But some immigrants became important financiers under both James I and William III; the Huguenots and Jews developed commercial networks throughout Europe and the Spanish and Portuguese Empires.[137] There was also some back migration from the Atlantic colonies of merchants like Thomas Fowle, David Yale and Richard Lee; the stepson of the Deputy Governor of Massachusetts became an Islington goldsmith.[138] Italian, German, Walloon, French, Dutch, Jewish, Huguenot and Scottish immigrants, though they represented at most 10 per cent of the business community, nonetheless constituted an important segment.[139]

Birth order

Since the apprenticeship registers do not specify the position of an apprentice in his family, this has to be reconstructed from individual

128 *Norwich Accounts Strangers' Goods*; Vane 1984; Richwood 1984: 124; Gwynn 1975–6: 434; 1983; 1985; Scouloudi 1937–41: 48; Cottrett 1991: 16.

129 *Aliens, Returns of Strangers*, p. 90; Scouloudi 1987: 47–51; Pettigree 1986: 11, 296.

130 Statt 1990: 49–53.

131 *Yarmouth Assembly Minutes*, p. 83; Grell 1987: 370–1.

132 Roth 1964: 192–3; Wolfe 1934: 134; Israel 1989a: 242; Hyamson 1928; *Bevis Marks Records*, p. 25; Abrahams 1937: 80–3; Woolf 1974: 51; Diamond 1973: 140, 146; Arnold 1970; Samuel 1982: 27–31; Grell 1991: 237–8.

133 Pollins 1982: 43, 62.

134 Mayo 1970: 439; Caldicott *et al.* 1987: 131.

135 Sundstron 1976: 234; Thorp 1976: 572–3.

136 Harden & Scouloudi 1971: app. 1.

137 Judd 1971: 354; Fortune 1984: 37, 81, 95–7; Acres 1934–7: 243.

138 Cressy 1987: 204; J. M. Smith 1959: 93–4; Stout 1974: 394; Sachse 1947–8: 255; 1956: 118–19; Rutman 1965: 191.

139 Finlay 1981: table 3.8; Wyatt 1952–8: 91; Woodward 1977a; Smout 1963; Neave 1988; Kierner 1991: 10; Matthews 1974: 270–1; Chartres & Hey 1990: 307; Carter 1975: 87–90; Carswell 1960: 6.

examples. Eldest sons of gentlemen did enter business.[140] Both the elder and younger brothers of the Hoare and Blundell families were in business together; Nicholas Blundell advanced money for Richard, who was apprenticed to Mr Houghton of Liverpool and sent as a family factor to Virginia and to trade on his own account.[141] But usually it was the younger children and often younger sons of younger sons. The third son of the second son of Mosley III of Manchester became a clothier despite his inheritance of land.[142]

The high percentage of orphans in the registers also suggests that the youngest child was often apprenticed to trade. There was a high rate of orphanage throughout propertied society.[143] In the Butchers Company of London, 1585–9, 29 of 144 prentices were orphans and in the Weavers Company 624 out of 1,100; 25 per cent of those bound to the Fishmongers and 20 per cent bound to the Stationers were orphans.[144] Half the London aldermen in the fifteenth century and a quarter between 1580 and 1614 fell into this category; 40 per cent of 1,439 apprentices in the late sixteenth, and 49 per cent of eighty in the early seventeenth century were orphans.[145] In Bristol, 15 per cent of prentices were orphans, 1542–65, 19 per cent, 1675–76, 24 per cent, 1695–6 and 34 per cent in 1705–06.[146] The same was true of Ipswich and Norfolk and the number of orphan apprentices rose as high as one-quarter in Southampton, though it declined towards the end of the century.[147] Apprenticeship was clearly a popular and convenient option for widows and heirs with dependent sons and brothers. Sometimes children were illegitimate, like Henry, bastard son of Sir Henry Killigrew, who was apprenticed to a Truro merchant.[148] Gerard Legh, a Draper, was the son of a bastard of a cadet family from Cheshire.[149]

But there was no obvious order of preference between younger sons. Sometimes it was the second son who entered business and the youngest who entered a profession.[150] The Jacobean aldermen were equally divided between second, third and fourth children with a slight preponderance of the second.[151] Many examples could be given of third, fourth and fifth

[140] Barcroft, *Memorandum Book*, p. 55; Lancs. RO DDB/58–60; Keeler 1954: 110; Rawdon, *Life*, p. xi; Porter 1968: 57.

[141] Blundell, *Great Diurnal*, pp. 39–40; Hoare 1932: 5.

[142] *Mosley Family*, p. 13 and pedigrees; Willan 1980: 57.

[143] *Somerset Sale of Wards*, p. xxviii; Bell 1953; Cliffe 1969: 128–30; Holman 1975: 41; Laslett 1974: 12; 1977: 162–3; Carlton 1974a: 66, 80; Grubb 1992.

[144] Jones 1976: 14–15; Plummer 1972: table 4.7; Blagden 1953: 3.

[145] Thrupp 1949: 312; Lang 1963: 280; Boulton 1990: 338.

[146] Holmes 1980a: 43–4; Yarbrough 1980: n.7; Holman 1975: 89.

[147] Lancs. RO DDB/58–60; Ketton-Cremer 1944: 82; Webb 1960.

[148] Whetter 1974: 155; Laslett 1980: 54–5, suggests an overall rate of bastardy, exclusive of pre-nuptial pregnancies, of 14 per cent, but does not break this figure down by social group.

[149] Nichols 1863: 108.

[150] Mathew 1948: 57.

[151] Lang 1963: 8.

sons.[152] It is possible that the richer families sent the youngest, whereas the poorest sent their elder.[153] But there was great variety in practice and no consistent allocation of occupation by seniority within the family. The conventional view that business was relegated to the youngest and usually the fifth son is not upheld by the evidence for the seventeenth century.[154]

Large families, moreover, frequently consigned more than one son to trade.[155] Edward Bohun sent one son to America as a merchant and one to Hudson Bay, and another was apprenticed to a leatherseller.[156] Sir George Sondes apprenticed his fourth, fifth and youngest sons.[157] When the first entrant was successful, it is not surprising that other brothers should follow and help each other.[158] George Ravenscroft, a second son, entered the glass business by importing mirrors from Venice, where his brothers John and Francis were resident merchants.[159] Once the initial decision had been made, there was no compelling reason to stop at one. Participation in specific areas of trade often became a family tradition and more than one generation was involved.[160] Sir Robert Chester of Royston put one son to a grocer in Bishopsgate and his numerous grandsons by his second and third sons went into the sugar trade.[161] Several branches of the Jeffries and Lowther family were in business as were Marmaduke Rawdon's father and his uncle.[162]

Distribution by trade

Every sector of the economy which could support an independent business attracted sons of gentlemen. Private and public banking, exchange and bill buying and selling, brokerage, the farming of taxes and government contracting were usually entered later in life by established businessmen with capital and political connections.[163] Some parents purchased patents of monopoly or licences for their younger sons in the early Stuart period.[164] Scrivening was a path to a financial career and

[152] Keeton 1967: 42–50; Laslett 1948: 153; Nicholls, *History of Leicester*, ii. 388; Keeler 195: 102–3. [153] Mathew 1948: 69 n.1. [154] Namier 1961: 9.

[155] Whitelocke, *Liber Famelicus*, pp. vi, 11; Spalding 1975: pedigrees; Reresby, *Memoirs*, pp. 22, 54; Dawe 1950: 8; Bramston, *Autobiography*, p. 21; *Norris Papers*, pp. xvii–xviii; *Oxinden Letters*, pp. xxiv, 117; Tucker 1961: 10; Nat. Lib. Wales Wynne MS 489, 5830; Lincs. AO, Nelthorpe MS; Prideaux, *Letters*, p. 146; Sitwell, *Letter Book*, pp. vii, xxiii; Willan 1959: 201–5; Harrison 1920: plate 8. [156] Bohun, *Diary*, pp. 29, 87.

[157] Chalklin 1965: 209; *Harl. Misc.*, x. 54; Everitt 1965: 68; 1960: 17–19; *Suffolk Tears*.

[158] Bindoff *et al.* 1961: 249–381; *Bowles Family Records*; *Smythe Family Correspondence*.

[159] Rendel 1975: 102.

[160] Cussans 1877–81: iii. 122; Palliser 1985: 95, 116; Raines & Sutton 1903: i. 6–8, 35–6, 42–6; Finch 1956: 24, 56; Earle 1989a: 90. [161] Sheridan 1951: p. xviii, app. 4.

[162] Keeton 1967: 50; Rawdon, *Life*, pp. xi, 315; Hainsworth 1988: 156.

[163] Richards 1965: app. 4; Boyce 1958: 2–3, 14.

[164] Carus-Wilson 1954–66: ii. 203; Price 1906: apps. B, D, F; Godfrey 1976: 75.

sixteen gentlemen were apprenticed, but the average annual entry into the Scriveners Company was only five.[165] Humphrey Shalcross, the famous usurer and younger son of a gentleman, began as a scrivener.[166] Francis Meynell was apprenticed to a London goldsmith, as were the Dingleys of Kent and Richard Nelthorpe.[167] Charles Duncombe was apprenticed to Alderman Backwell and Richard Hill apprenticed his nephew Thomas to bankers in Amsterdam.[168] Speculative trading in stocks and lotteries gradually became a specialized business, but the early jobbers, like John Hopkins and John Blunt were of obscure origins.[169]

The primary preference was for large-scale merchandising. In London, it was the Great Companies which had a high percentage of gentleman apprentices; in the 1550s, 75 per cent of gentleman apprentices were bound to Liverymen and, between 1639 and 1660, they numbered 27 per cent of the total entry of the Fishmongers and 37 per cent of the Grocers compared with only 2.7 per cent of the Bakers, 1.3 per cent of the Butchers, 1.5 per cent of the Braziers and 6.3 per cent of the Joiners.[170] In Bristol, between 1532 and 1565, fourteen of forty-six gents were apprenticed to *mercatores*; gentlemen constituted 11.3 per cent of merchant apprentices and 548 of 2,852 apprentices, 1626–36, were apprenticed to entrepreneurs.[171] The Northamptonshire gentry were bound to goldsmiths, drapers, stationers, tobacconists, chandlers and ironmongers.[172]

Foreign trade attracted three-quarters of the Tudor genteel apprentices and all branches were entered in the seventeenth century, though they were not equally popular and much depended on market conditions.[173] Because the long-distance trades were both more glamorous and offered the prospect of foreign residence, many recruits were attracted towards the London-based regulated, monopolistic Companies in the Netherlands, Germany, the Baltic and the Levant.[174] The Merchant Adventurers during its period of prosperity had a solid quota of gentlemen.[175] The most popular choice was, however, the Levant Company. Although the lists of Company freemen are not classifed by social origins, it is clear that the proportion of gentlemen was always high.[176] Areas outside the monopolistic Companies were not, however, ignored. France, Spain and Portugal, Leghorn, Scandinavia and the Canaries all attracted the better sort of apprentice.[177] Roger Mallock participated in

[165] *Scriveners Company Papers*, pp. 52–62; Steer 1973: 38. [166] Beloff 1939: 688.
[167] Abbott 1941: 18; Chalklin & Havinden 1974: 179; Finberg 1956: 95; Sale 1990: 146, shows that fifty-seven sons of gentry or 22.8 per cent became goldsmiths; Lincs. AO, Nelthorpe MS 4/21/2. [168] Jancey 1955–6: 156. [169] Cope 1978.
[170] See fig. 5.1. [171] Sacks 1985. [172] Everitt 1965: 68.
[173] Rappaport 1989: 300, 305, table 8.5. [174] Rabb 1963: 173–4.
[175] Wheeler, *Treatise of Commerce*, p. 317; MacIntyre 1956: 185; *Ferrar Papers*, p. 67.
[176] Grassby 1994: 23; Anderson 1989: 67, 74, 86.
[177] Rawdon, *Life*, p. 196; *Bolton Letters*; Sheridan 1974: 82–3; Prynne, *Diary*, p. 87.

the wine and cloth trade to France and Spain as well as in Newfoundland cod trading and in retailing.[178] Thomas Maynard was apprenticed at La Rochelle and became a factor for Rowland Hill in the Portuguese trade.[179] The coastal and internal carriage of goods was a business of small men, but shipping attracted a few gentlemen. In Ipswich, six gentlemen were apprenticed to mariners, presumably to learn navigation.[180] Bryan Blundell went to sea at thirteen, was a ship-master by 1696 and then became a merchant and ship-owner.

As the Caribbean and American trades expanded, they also became increasingly attractive.[181] The majority of emigrants to America were not, of course, merchants.[182] But Walter Tocknell sent his genteel apprentice to transport indentured servants to America.[183] Maurice Thompson emigrated to Virginia in 1617 and became involved in a wide range of business activities from ship-owning and land speculation to tobacco and privateering.[184] Wilfrid Hudleston visited Barbados and was in the Virginia tobacco trade as well as the Baltic, Whitehaven and Irish trades.[185] William Pynchon, an Essex country squire and Puritan, sold his estate, emigrated to Massachusetts and became successful in the fur trade.[186] Sir Perceval Willoughby sent his errant son, Thomas, to Newfoundland as a remittance man.[187] Networks of kinsmen bridged the Atlantic.[188] William Vaughan, son of Sir Roger, was apprenticed to Josiah Child and sent to New Hampshire.[189]

Although a division of labour gradually emerged between merchants and planters in the Caribbean, the two functions still overlapped.[190] Peter Hay went out to Barbados as a receiver for his kinsman, the Earl of Carlisle, but acquired a plantation and became a merchant.[191] Cary Helyar went out to Jamaica in 1664 and dealt in slaves before becoming a cacao and sugar planter.[192] Christopher Jeaffreson was apprenticed in England and opened a shop in St Kitts selling English goods, though he later returned to England.[193] Many settlers in Maryland and Virginia had been apprenticed in England.[194] The gentleman planters of Virginia, like

178 Stephens 1968: 280–1. 179 Shaw 1989: 150. 180 Webb 1960: 30.

181 Wilkinson 1958: 104; *English Adventurers*, pp. 89–90; Quitt 1988: 655; Steele 1986; Altman & Horn 1991.

182 For net migration figures see Wrigley & Schofield: table 7.11. See also chap. 4, n.108.

183 Clark & Souden 1987: 164. 184 Pagan 1979: 260; Greene 1988: 13.

185 G. P. Jones 1967: 189; Price 1992: 19. 186 Morison 1930–2.

187 Cell 1965: 621. 188 *Trelawney Papers*; Dunn 1972: 208; Bailyn 1953: 313; 1959: 59.

189 Hodgdon 1918: 11.

190 Zahedieh 1986a: 215; Bridenbaughs 1972: 320; Thoms 1969a: 78; Clemens *et al.* 1980: 95. 191 Campbell 1974: 85, 88.

192 Bennett 1964: 53–4, 74–6; 1966: 113ff; Dunn 1972: 213.

193 Jeaffreson, *Papers*, i. 61, 95–6.

194 'Kennon family' 1905–6: 132; Johnson 1981: 15; Carr & Jordan 1974: 136–51, 162, 282; Blundell, *Diurnal*, p. 39.

William Byrd II and Robert Carter, were as active in trade as the merchants of New England.[195] By the eighteenth century, younger sons of Antigua planters were acting as agents for their families in London.[196]

Most of the better sort of apprentices probably remained, however, in England in the inland and coastal wholesale commodity trades, distributing foodstuffs, minerals and imports. In Jacobean London, 73 of 140 aldermen, including many sons of gentlemen, were in the domestic distributive trades; gentlemen after 1680 entered a wide cross-section of trades.[197] Walter Stanhope entered the inland trade, as did the Ishams who founded their business on mercery or Thomas Rutter who became a haberdasher.[198] John Stratford entered the tobacco trade as well as dealing in soap, cloth and Baltic goods.[199] Many gentlemen became Stationers and publishing was combined with other trades and professions; Moses Pitt speculated in building and seamen's tickets as well as in atlases.[200] Apprentices who chose their local town had to follow the dominant trades of the region. Younger sons of the Derbyshire gentry went into the lead trade both in London and the provincial ports.[201] Those apprenticed in Newcastle went into the coal as well as the Baltic trades.[202] In sixteenth-century Bristol, 9.3 per cent of gentlemen apprentices were mercers and 8.9 per cent grocers; the Daubeneys moved from grocery to sugar baking.[203] The food and livestock trade attracted the lesser gentry of Wales and Leicestershire and a few even became drovers.[204]

Except in years of depression, gentlemen also entered the sprawling textile industry as clothiers and merchants. In mid-Tudor London, thirty-six out of fifty gentleman apprentices entered the clothing trades, all of which continued to attract recruits.[205] This was equally true of the provinces.[206] Scions of Wiltshire families were prominent among the factors at Blackwell Hall and Lancashire gentlemen became linen drapers.[207] Between 1542 and 1565, 9.2 per cent of gentlemen apprentices in Bristol were drapers and at least four gentlemen entered the textile

195 Wright 1940: 26, 46; 1947: 40; 1957: 7–11.
196 Sheridan 1960–1.
197 Lang 1963: 78, 96, table 3; 1971: 244; Earle 1989a: 87.
198 Wilson 1967: 13; Styles 1978: 128.
199 Chalklin & Havinden 1974: 81.
200 Plant 1974: 150–1; Plomer 1968: 41, 70, 215; Phelps 1978; Morgan 1978: apps. 2–3; Myers & Harris 1985: 193; Tyacke & Wallis 1973: 69.
201 *V.C.H. Derbyshire*, ii. 342–7; Dias 1981: 41–2.
202 Dietz 1986; Cameron 1970; Nef 1932: ii. 5, 40, 86; Liddell, *Letters*, p. x.
203 Yarbrough 1980: table 2.2; Hall 1965: 113–16.
204 W. O. Williams 1948: 106–8; *V.C.H. Leicestershire*: 88.
205 Mendenhall 1953: 218; BL Hargrave MS 321, fos. 100–3; Friis 1927: 99, 102, 245; Griffiths 1954: 116; Aikin, *Description Manchester*, p. 182; Spufford 1984.
206 Flinn 1962: 32; Keeler 1954: 110.
207 *V.C.H. Wiltshire*: 164; Ramsay 1965: 31, 41; Wadsworth & Mann 1931: 73; Willan 1979: 178.

trades in the seventeenth century.[208] In Shropshire, many gentry became linen and woollen drapers and served as middlemen between the London merchants and the Welsh producers.[209]

Although most gentlemen preferred the role of wholesaling middleman, they also engaged in retailing and resold goods in small quantities directly to the consumer. The Gloucestershire gentry handled cheese, stockings, salt, soap and flax.[210] A few became upholders, who acted as pawnbrokers and dealers in second-hand goods.[211] Sir Christopher Lowther told his father that at Whitehaven 'I know none yet who doth not retayell.'[212] Others entered service trades; several gentlemen kept inns and bowling alleys.[213] A surprising number, except in Norwich, became apothecaries and surgeons; of 223 prentices, 1710–13, forty-three were sons of gentlemen and esquires, as were 20 per cent of the barbers, 1631–60.[214] The seventh son of Nicholas Mosley of Ancoats in the 1660s was apprenticed to an apothecary and died of a fever.[215]

Nor was manufacturing and processing ignored. In fifteenth-century Derbyshire, a younger son without provision could become a scythe-maker and gentlemen were apprenticed to the Hallamshire cutlers.[216] In Bristol, between 1532 and 1542, sons of gentlemen became cordwainers, coopers, fletchers, cappers, bakers, weavers, tailors, cofferers, shearmen, butchers and tuckers; between 1542 and 1565, they constituted 7 per cent of the whittawers, 4 per cent of the skinners and 8 per cent of the dyers; in the seventeenth century, 24 per cent of gentleman apprentices were bound to a craft and 20 per cent to the leather trades.[217] In Chester, between 1558 and 1625, four out of 106 apprentices to shoemakers were sons of gentlemen, as was one glover and one tanner.[218] John Sanderson descended from a Yorkshire gentry family, but his father was a London hatter.[219] Griffin Ameredith was a tailor before becoming a draper as was Pepys' father before he inherited the family estate, when his elder brother died.[220] The youngest half-brother of Sir George Sondes became a journeyman, though he received a supplementary allowance of £20 per annum.

The heraldic devices on the token issues of tradesmen, like Thomas Jeynes of Tewkesbury or William Hopton of Stroud, suggest descent

[208] Yarbrough 1980: table 2.2. [209] Sacks 1985: table 2.
[210] Thirsk 1984: 265, 295. [211] Walton 1973: 51.
[212] Lowther, *Commercial Papers*, p. 23.
[213] *Chirk Castle Accounts*, p. viii; Edwards 1972; Goose 1986: 175; Everitt 1985: 184.
[214] Burnby 1983: 96; Prest 1987: 109; Miles 1986: 202; S. R. Smith 1972: 205; Barnett 1968; Pelling 1982. On the barbers as retailers see Riden 1985: 108.
[215] *Mosley Family*, p. 21. [216] Wright 1983: 47–50; Leader 1905–6: 3–7.
[217] Ben Amos 1991a: 235–6; 1988: 64; Yarbrough 1980: table 2.2.
[218] Woodward 1967: 95. [219] Sanderson, *Travels*, pp. x–xi.
[220] MacCaffrey 1976: 251; Pepys, *Diary*, i. p. xix.

from the gentry.[221] Among the twenty-five men styled gentleman, admitted to the Freedom of Norwich between 1548 and 1713, one was apprenticed to a hatter, one to a London merchant, ten to worsted weavers, one to a baker, one to a hosier, four to tailors, one to a periwig-maker and one to a carpenter.[222] The returns under the 1709 Act for Wiltshire, Surrey and Sussex also confirm entry into a broad range of crafts, though by this period the description 'gentleman' was more loosely applied. In Bedfordshire, between 1711 and 1720, the trades which they chose included wheelwright, upholsterer, joiner, stone-cutter, peruke-maker and clockmaker.

Most sons of gentlemen and established merchants were, however, deterred by the marginal status and limited business opportunities of the basic handicrafts. Many tradesmen were skilled artisans who marketed their own product, but they operated on too small a scale and had a low ratio of capital to labour. Those gentlemen who did participate were often indigent or orphans. Although certain crafts, like wig-making, seem to have been popular, few entered the minor Companies of trades.[223] In London, none entered the Butchers, Bakers or Paviours Companies and only one is recorded as an apprentice in the Masons Company.[224] Only three of forty-one apprentices to the Joiners Company, 1625–1700, were sons of gentlemen and few became carpenters, painter-stainers or potters.[225] Although some became booksellers and publishers, few became printers, who were, in contrast to France, regarded as mechanics. In Tudor Bristol, 7.1 per cent of gentry prentices became brewers, who gradually converted a household function into a business; but brewing did not attract the better sort until the eighteenth century.[226] Retailers and shopkeepers were drawn predominately from the rural and urban craftsmen.[227] The better sort of apprentice was always less evident in manufacturing towns, like Worcester and Norwich, and most prominent in prosperous commercial entrepots such as Newcastle, Shrewsbury, Exeter, Bristol and, especially, London.

221 Gray 1965: 103–5; Berry 1988: chap. 2.

222 Pound 1966; Sayer 1975: 170; Gurney-Read 1989.

223 Neither the apprenticeship registers nor the official histories of the lesser London Companies suggest significant participation by children of the gentry.

224 P. E. Jones 1972: app. 5; Knoop & Jones 1935: 20; 1932; Thrupp 1933: 142; Welch 1909: 40.

225 Crawford 1987: fig. 6; GLL MS 5667–9; Surry 1981; Weatherill 1971: 140; Alford & Barker 1968: 84; *Carpenters Company Records*, i. 23, 34; Goodman 1972; Airs 1975: 149.

226 Mathias 1959: 23–8; Rapp 1974: 380; Haselgrove 1989.

227 Lincs. AO, Inventories 169/97, 172/202, 173/252; Barleys 1959.

Periodization

Participation by the gentry in business was not a recent innovation. Minor Somerset families sent their sons to Bristol in the fourteenth century and the famous Richard Whittington was the third son of a knight.[228] Landed families were involved in the medieval wool trade.[229] Fifteenth-century Bristol, Colchester and Southampton recruited some gentlemen and London attracted recruits from as far away as Yorkshire.[230] The younger son of Lord Berkeley was in trade in the fifteenth century and the Greshams, the Springs and the Verneys moved in both directions between town and country.[231] Of 132 apprentices to the Skinners, between 1496 and 1515, who finished their time, 17 or 13 per cent were sons of gentlemen from many different counties, compared with 24 yeomen and 130 husbandmen.[232] Richard Hakluyt's father was a Skinner from Herefordshire gentry stock who placed several sons in business.[233]

There does not seem to have been any marked increase in the numbers of trading gentlemen in the sixteenth century, either in absolute terms or as a percentage of all entrants. Many of the genteel pedigrees which Tudor merchants compiled, like that of the Ishams, were bogus. In London, between 1551 and 1553, only 6 esquires and 42 gentlemen out of 881 admitted to all trades became freemen by apprenticeship.[234] Only one merchant of the Russia Company in 1555 was the son of a gentleman.[235] But the Visitation of London in 1568 does reveal an inextricable mix of gentry and commercial families and many younger sons of younger sons; of 204 families, 57 came from areas outside of London, though not all were practising merchants.[236] William Stump, the famous clothier, came from the Gloucestershire gentry and George Needham's father was a *generosus* of a cadet Derbyshire family.[237] Isham took a gentleman as an apprentice and the younger sons of the Hough branch of the Mosley family went into business in Manchester and in London.[238] In Bristol, 15 per cent of apprentices, 1532–42, and eighty-three or 3.4 per cent of all

[228] Penn 1986: 183; Carus-Wilson 1954: xxix, 79; Hollaender & Kellaway 1969; Breslow 1977: 135; Tibbetts 1977: 13.

[229] *Stonor Letters*, p. xxxi; Power 1941: 111; Lander 1980: 25.

[230] Thrupp 1948: 211, 218, 227, 231, 243–4, 280, 389–92, table 21; G. A. Williams 1963: 14–15; *London Plea and Memorandum Rolls*, ii. p. xxv; Britnell 1986: 210; Clough 1982: 37.

[231] J. Smith, *Berkeley Manuscripts*, ii. 83; Burgon 1839: i. app. 1; Cornwall 1964–5: 466; Cox 1982; Albertson 1932: 50.

[232] Veale 1966: 95, 191.

[233] Parks 1928: app. 2; *Original Writings Hakluyts*, i. 15.

[234] Ramsay 1986: 538, table 2; 1957: 10; Rappaport 1989: table 3.5 calculates 50 out of 771; Butcher 1974.

[235] Willan 1955: 13–14, 72; 1959: 194, 208.

[236] *London. Visitation 1568*.

[237] *Mosley Family*, pp. 4–5; *John Isham*, pp. xxii, xcvi; Ramsay 1986; Reddaway 1966: 291–2; Rowse 1950: 249.

[238] Yarbrough 1980: table 2.1; Vanes 1982; 1977; Sacks 1985: 119.

apprentices, 1542–65, were gentlemen; recruitment was brisk in York, Lynn and Yarmouth.[239] Exeter drew heavily on the gentry for its mayors and Hugh Aldersey, third son of a Cheshire gentleman, became Mayor of Chester in 1541.[240]

In the seventeenth century, as contemporaries noticed, entry increased in volume and regularity, even though the population stabilized.[241] There were of course variations between towns and trades and fluctuations between decades. But enrolment by gentlemen in the major Companies of London was continuous from the 1630s to at least 1690.[242] In Southampton, gentry outnumbered yeomen and husbandmen by 2 to 1, between 1648 and 1669, and the peak years were 1620 to 1669, with a decline thereafter.[243] In the Shrewsbury Drapers Company, entry by the Welsh gentry increased threefold after 1609, compared with 1572 to 1609, and there was an acceleration of activity between 1640 and 1689.[244] In Bristol, there was little variation between the 1620s and the 1670s and 1680s, though entry into the Merchant Venturers increased dramatically during the Civil Wars. The Newcastle Merchant Adventurers had a stable entry throughout the century with a slight increase between 1660 and 1689. The absolute numbers of gentlemen who were hostmen increased steadily throughout the century with a substantial leap between 1689 and 1715.[245] In Norwich, both the total number of apprentices and the number of gentlemen decreased after 1660. But Liverpool enrolled many more gentlemen after 1690, as the port expanded.[246]

Entry into business is harder to track after 1690, because guild regulation declined and foreign trade became more open.[247] Social terminology became so diluted that masters of apprentices were increasingly described as gentlemen. The comments of Defoe and others suggest that the early years of the eighteenth century did not bring any radical change.[248] Ackers' *London Directory* of 1749 still shows entry by the minor gentry and the Braund family apprenticed several sons.[249] Bristol, between 1711 and 1747, had ten gentlemen and esquires out of fifty-three entrants and David Hume was apprenticed there; Hull, Liverpool, Whitehaven, Leeds, the Lincolnshire towns and Glasgow continued to

[239] Needham, *Politics Merchant Adventurer*, p. 3.
[240] Bindoff *et al.* 1961: 8–9; Hoskins 1976: 98; *Lancashire Wills*, ed. Piccope, p. 71; Sutton 1986. [241] BL Egerton MS 627, fo. 64.
[242] There is no evidence of a decline after 1660 as argued by Stone 1965.
[243] Table 5.1; Patterson 1966. [244] See fig. 5.3 and table 5.5.
[245] See figs. 5.4 and 5.5
[246] Moore 1899: 77; Clemens 1976: 211.
[247] No systematic attempt has been made to collect data after 1720.
[248] Defoe, *Compleat English Tradesman*, i. 306ff; Trevelyan 1930–4: i. 32–3.
[249] Sutherland 1962: 3, table 1; Chaloner 1949–50: 158.

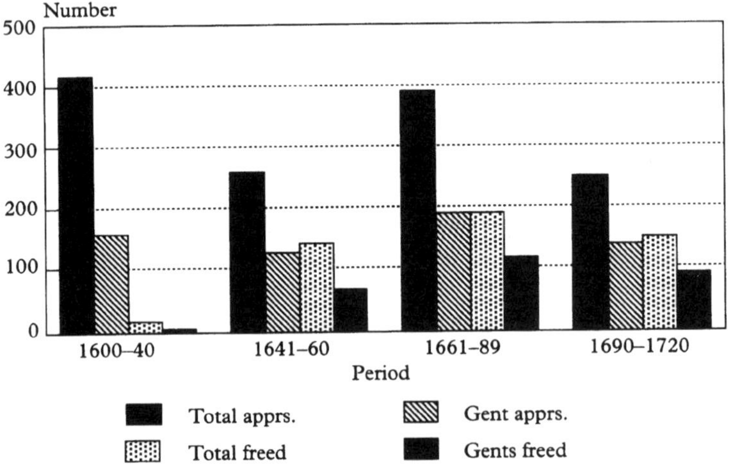

Fig. 5.4. Apprenticeship and freedom admissions: Merchant Adventurers, Newcastle, 1600–1720. (*Source*: *Newcastle Merchant Adventurers' Records*.)

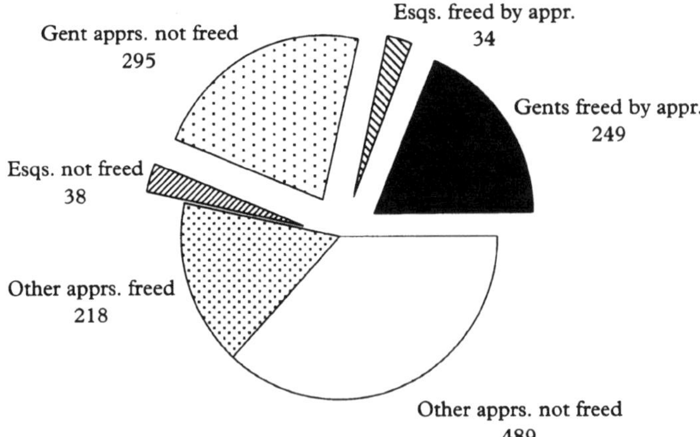

Fig. 5.5. Freedom through apprenticeship: Merchant Adventurers, Newcastle, 1600–1720. (*Source*: *Newcastle Merchant Adventurers' Records*.)

recruit from this source.[250] In Shrewsbury, a third of the drapers were still gentlemen, though the number of merchants declined.[251] In Newcastle, the proportion of gentry to other groups only fell from 40.6 per cent to 36.3 per cent between 1691–1720 and 1721–40; the proportion of gentleman hostmen actually increased. The returns under the 1709 Act do not suggest a dramatic change.

But there are several indications that both the absolute and relative numbers of gentleman apprentices, particularly in the lesser trades, declined in the eighteenth century, as the population expanded.[252] The scholarly debate over the gentility of trade in the mid eighteenth century assumed, like Gibbon, that prior to the growth of the professions 'the mercantile profession was more frequently chosen by youths of a liberal race and education'.[253] Between 1738 and 1763, the proportion of London aldermen of gentry origin fell to 22 per cent.[254] In the seventeenth century, however, as many sons of gentlemen were in business as sons of merchants, though they were outnumbered by sons of yeomen and craftsmen.[255] If gentlemen represented approximately 6 per cent of all

[250] Minchinton 1957: app. G; Butel 1979; Chalklin 1974; Cannon 1981: 15; Jackson 1972: 104–5; Hughes 1952a: i. 164–6; Devine 1975: part 1; Clemens 1976: 211–12; Wilson 1971: 25; Roebuck 1980: 51; Mossner 1954; Holderness 1974: 565.

[251] MacInnes 1988: 62.

[252] Aitken 1965: 24, 53; Sedgwick 1976; Namier & Brooke 1964: i. 104–5, 131–2; Habakkuk 1940: 17.

[253] Gibbon, *Memoirs*, pp. 7–10, 12, 16, 199–200; his source for the previous century was probably the *Lives of the Norths* listed in Keynes 1940: 208; *Gentleman's Magazine* (1732), p. 1021; (1733), pp. 1014–15; (1737), pp. 717–36; BL Stowe MS 993, printed in 1750 as *Treatise on Trade*.

[254] Rogers 1979: 443.

[255] This conclusion, which was outlined by the author in Thomas & Pennington 1978, has been challenged by Stone & Stone 1984: 234–9 as a 'bold' and 'extravagant' claim which 'is not supported by the evidence'. The Stones do not present any contrary data, but instead reject the hard evidence of enrolments on the grounds that the parents of apprentices were 'pseudo gentry'. Their own 'sociological definition' of gentlemen is entertaining, but idiosyncratic and subjective, excluding all those who would be 'at a loss if anyone had challenged them to a duel'. In fact, a significant proportion of prentices descended from families who would qualify as gentry even on this restrictive definition. The Stones, drawing largely on evidence cited by the present author, then advance the contradictory argument that the high costs of entry into business excluded all but the wealthier gentry; gentlemen 'certainly would not have stooped to anything lower' than the Levant Company. Not only is this statement false, but the few examples, casually cited, are drawn indiscriminately from different periods. The analysis in general proceeds without any real understanding of the basic structure of business; an Elwes is described as a 'businessman of some sort in London'. In some cases the evidence cited in the notes flatly contradicts the text. These errors may be just unintended consequences of careless scholarship and hasty composition, but they also seem to reflect impatience with any evidence that conflicts with a pre-conceived thesis. Faced with the inconvenient prospect of social miscegany between the landed interest and business community caught *in flagrante delicto*, the Stones fall back on the classic response of unequivocal denial.

apprentices, 80 per cent of whom probably remained as artisan-tradesmen, then at least 30 per cent of the business community would have been drawn from the country and urban gentry.

Although they represented a small percentage of the whole genteel population, this widespread and consistent participation had great significance.[256] Apprenticeship was a much more radical social step than passive investment by heirs to estates, because it cut the children off from landed society and put them on an equal footing with City merchants, with whom they lived and served their time. It involved them for life in the details of business management and required that their income would come from profits rather than from rents or salaries. It was particularly noteworthy that the urban gentry and newly elevated families whose status was more flimsy, like the Knapps, should be as willing to put their children to trade as the ancient gentry.[257] The scale and regularity of apprenticeship of younger sons by the gentry distinguished England clearly from other pre-industrial societies.

[256] Perkin 1969: 60–1. [257] *Knapp Family Memorials*, pp. 315, 329.

6 Skills and motivation

Business demanded both innate and acquired skills. It is not easy to define expertise, because every commodity and area of trade had its own *modus operandi* and organizational structure.[1] Founding an independent business was different from running an established firm or from management of a joint-stock Company.[2] The popular and inventive contemporary handbooks on how to succeed alternated between clichés and commonsense.[3] Henry Audley's amoral ten rules for thriving provide insight into the loan and property markets, but they are less relevant to the shipping industry or the commodity trades.[4] Despite increasing specialization, most merchants employed a minimal staff and therefore required personal knowledge of the whole process of production, distribution and sale.

Unrelenting and persistent motivation was also a *sine qua non*. The origins and relative importance of different traits of character are, however, difficult to establish. Innate talent cannot clearly be distinguished from acquired drives and there is no sure way of determining whether hypermotivation was inner-directed or dependent on external approval.[5] What is certain is that the art of merchandising cannot simply be equated with a particular *Geist*.[6] The stereotypes of businessmen in sociological models are abstracted uncritically from literary sources rather than from empirical evidence and they are constructed by crude psychological reductionism.

[1] *Norris Papers*, pp. 10–12.

[2] On differential performance: see Finch 1956: intro. by H. J. Habakkuk, p. xiii.

[3] Self-help books ranged from authentic manuals to superficial digests of maxims such as Trenchfield, *Cap for Grey Hairs* and Brittaine, *Humane Prudence*. This genre should be distinguished from the popular legendary histories of celebrated businessmen, discussed by Spufford 1981: 238–44, and the almanacks discussed by Capp 1979: 115–16. It is dangerous to extrapolate an ethos from the manuals as suggested by N. Z. Davis 1960: 45.

[4] *Way to be Rich*. [5] Riesman 1954: 201; 1976: 118.

[6] Weber's spirit of capitalism (sometimes relabelled as *Unternehmungsgeist* even though there is a fundamental difference between entrepreneurship and the work ethic) has survived repeated empirical refutation because it is an abstract concept in which historians want to believe: the latest disciple is Otsuka 1982. Shadwell, *Works*, p. 189 equated 'entreprennants' with witty fops.

Innovation and risk

Entrepreneurial initiative and a propensity to innovate were vital.[7] The potentialities of new markets, products, knowledge and methods could not easily be inferred from pre-existing facts and a businessman had to choose as well as act, to search and reorganize, to implement new ideas and look ahead. Since he certainly could not predict the future, he had to act on intuition, hoping to be proved right later, to experiment with alternatives to ingrained habits and fixed routines which were inherently limited. Direct personal intervention, energy, ingenuity and inspiration were needed to appreciate and seize opportunities.[8] The market was *ad hoc* and could only temporarily be controlled by coercion. Since no settled branch of trade was likely to sustain its growth and prosperity forever, merchants were obliged to adapt and improvise.

Examples of innovation and risk-taking are not hard to find in mining, the metal and textile industries, high finance and even cabinet-making.[9] The financial innovations of the 1690s combined imagination and virtuosity with acute intelligence. A merchant had to be audacious and willing to make mistakes, to know when to take chances and when to withdraw and cut his losses. 'Every milk sop can swim in hot baths', wrote Scott, 'but he is the man that can endure violent tides and still swim afloat'.[10] 'People that will not run to hazard must be content with small gains', wrote Heigham Bright.[11] Many investments were purely opportunistic and not based on planning; the immediate chance had to be seized and merchants had to fly by the seat of their pants.[12] Some were compulsive gamblers and backed the most threadbare schemes.[13] Boredom, greed or a desire to have a fling could tempt even sober men, like William Stout, into weak investments. Security was a relative term and all trades carried risk.[14]

The importance of innovation should not, however, be exaggerated; few business methods were qualitatively different from the past. Most projectors were temperamentally unable to judge the value of their ideas and often ruined themselves.[15] It was often sufficient to borrow and adapt current ideas to new circumstances, to co-ordinate and refine existing

[7] See pp. 409–12. [8] Rabb 1974: 678–9; Doerflinger 1986: 164, 355.

[9] *Seventeenth-Century Economic Documents*, pp. 206–8; Moir 1957: 263; Thirsk 1988: 136; *Bowles Family Records*, p. 54; Swann 1986: 176; Flinn 1962: 33; Melton 1986a: chap. 6; Jeake, *Astrological Diary*, pp. 68ff; Symonds 1955: 27.

[10] Scott, *Essay on Drapery*, p. 24. [11] Bright 1858: 190. [12] Pollet 1973: 27.

[13] Dickson 1954: 331; Quinn in Cronne *et al.* 1949: 76; Mandrou 1969: 209–10.

[14] Knight 1921: 43; Hayek 1977; O'Driscoll & Rizzo 1985: chap. 5; Coornaert 1970: 582.

[15] R. Davis 1965: 15.

methods.[16] Merchants were more likely to survive if they were hard-headed and stuck to the trades in which they had started and which they knew well. Their degree of specialization was determined by personality as well as by economic factors. Some could not resist the temptation to extend their interests or refuse any opportunity to turn a profit. Others declined to own ships because the benefits were not worth the trouble.[17] Technical limitations, nostalgia, inertia and family pride reinforced conservatism.

Minimization of risk was as important as maximization of profit; venture capital had to be related to total assets.[18] Even bold merchants deplored speculative mania; they managed rather than invested in the lotteries.[19] Cautious exploration of all opportunities was more effective than reckless adventurism, which usually failed. Government finance and commodity futures were a gamble and it was dangerous to leverage credit; the early Stuart financiers usually limited their investment in any one syndicate to £5–15,000. Necessity is the father of caution as well as the mother of invention; as Sir John Temple commented, 'it is as much vertue to keep as to gett'.[20] Many merchants played safe, protected their market through cartels and monopolies and were less interested in growth than in survival. 'He that resteth upon gains certain shall hardly grow to great riches', wrote Bacon; 'and he that puts all upon adventures doth oftentimes break and come to poverty'.[21]

As business grew more complex, its organization became more rational and systematic. Merchants needed to prioritize their objectives clearly, to sustain a diversity of multiple interests and to act on facts rather than hope. Rigour of mind, a grasp of essentials and methodical attention to detail were essential to achieve even a limited measure of control over the numerous variables; Liddell was credited with 'a head and Genius for business'.[22] Merchants based their decisions on their accounts.[23] The flow of goods and capital had to be co-ordinated by multilateral exchange with the volume of cargo space and with the realities of demand. The Foleys built a complex, but flexible and integrated, system of operating divisions.[24] 'The orders I have made', wrote Ambrose Crowley III, 'are

[16] The English successfully imitated the Dutch: see Kooy 1931; Ormrod in Krantz & Hohenberg 1975: 42 and in Coleman & Mathias 1984: 89ff.

[17] Dietz 1991: 11; D. W. Jones in Slack & Clark 1972: 335.

[18] Bruchey 1960: 497; MacCloskey 1976 and in Galenson 1989: 48.

[19] Ewen 1932; Kindleberger 1978a: 29.

[20] Hunt. Lib. Stowe MSS, no. 5.

[21] Bacon, *Works*, iv. 4, vi. 462.

[22] Ellis 1981a: 119.

[23] Bristol RO MS 105311, 15 Feb. 1675/6.

[24] *Foley Stour Valley Ironworks*, part 1, p. xii; part 2, p. xiii.

built upon such a rock that while I have my understanding it shall bee out of the power of satan and all his disciples to destroy them'.[25]

During the century, the commodity and capital markets became better integrated and the information system improved in quality and speed; knowledge of the quantities of goods in transit and of price currents allowed merchants to match supply and demand more effectively and protect themselves against unscrupulous agents.[26] Cheaper paper and the printing press standardized and unified data in a fixed objective form.[27] As early as 1580, a commission of London merchants was set up to standardize insurance by time and distance and by 1692 Lloyd's list had appeared; Peter Brugge reported political news so that its effect on Exchequer bills and stock values could be calculated.[28] A forward market in Indian indigo was developed as well as an advance payment system to equalize prices in India.[29] A major feature of business correspondence was news about the standing of creditors and debtors.

But knowledge of the market was too incomplete and dated for merchants to forecast trends. Even the joint-stock Companies with their greater reserves were unable to cope with fluctuations and manage risk.[30] The dissemination of news and facts through print did not change habits overnight and often just reinforced old ways and fallacies. The principle of uncertainty could be rationally conceived, but probability could only be calculated imperfectly.[31] Insurance premiums and prices had to be set and adjusted on the basis of rumour and by intuition rather than by logic.[32] Timing was the name of the game and this required commonsense and quick thinking rather than creative genius. The arrival of slave ships in the Caribbean, for example, had to coincide with the sugar harvest. Heigham Bright's uncle was wont to say that 'when it rained porridge he was without his dish' and 'the difficulty is to hitt it nicely'.[33]

Passion, greed and fear often carried greater weight than rationality or cognitive skills.[34] Profits were exaggerated or anticipated to bolster morale; stubbornness, petty jealousies or hatred could precipitate rash actions and delay withdrawal. Some merchants procrastinated: Samuel

[25] Flinn 1962: 65; *Crowley Law Book*, p. 59.

[26] Price 1954–5: 241–6; Neal 1988: 165–6; MacCusker 1985: 8–9; 1978: 324–6; Wright & Fayle 1928: 7–9; W. D. Smith 1982: 1004; Chaudhuri & Davies 1979: 152; Carson 1971b: 177; Steele 1980: 110, 219.

[27] Eisenstein 1979.

[28] Kepler 1979: 268; MacCusker 1991: 427; *Eliot Papers*, p. 56.

[29] Chaudhuri 1985: 200; 1978: 143.

[30] K. G. Davies 1957: 348–9.

[31] Shapiro 1983; Alchan 1950: 215–16; Hald 1990; Daston in Kruge *et al.* 1987: 244–5; Hacking 1975: 5; Shackle 1961: chap. 7; Pearson 1978: 126; David 1962: 98. Maistrov 1974 argues that probability developed from business and not from gambling.

[32] Flinn 1962: 25; BL Stowe MS 745, iii, fo. 145. For a brave attempt to tabulate returns and risks, 1698–1708, see Neal 1990: table 3.

[33] Bright 1858: 190.

[34] Arrow 1974: 3; Keynes 1934: ii. 162.

Jeake suffered agonies deciding when to sell even though 'the Sun and Jupiter were in exact conjunction to a Minute'.[35] Others acted on impulse: Roger Lowe knew from personal experience that 'nothing werser to a man then over hastiness especially in hot concernments'.[36] But decisions still had to be made speedily on inadequate information. Rawdon 'did seldome trust to the benefitt of a latter gaine, but did allwayes endeavour to taike time by the foretop'.[37] Business management remained informal, flexible and subjective.

The art of merchandizing

The one term conspicuous by its absence in studies of the pre-industrial economy is salesmanship.[38] Yet it was crucial, because vent was the overriding preoccupation of every merchant and it was always easier to buy than to sell. The volume of sales was not only determined by price, quality and demand, but by the flamboyant talents of the hustler. A resourceful marketeer could make money in a declining market, whereas an incompetent salesman could turn a silk purse into a sow's ear. In order to predict what would sell, a merchant had to anticipate as well as recognize trends in supply and demand, to take account of seasonal fluctuations, and be aware of relative prices and patterns of trade. Whaley went to Jamaica with fine cloth which he could not sell and neglected to bring linen and brandy which was in demand.[39] To understand the market also took discriminating judgement and an awareness of volatile desires, prejudices and foibles, the ability to measure and satisfy 'other mens fancies and opinions and errors'.[40] A merchant had to select the right location for his premises, to match output to fashion.[41]

The priority of every businessman was to buy cheap and sell dear. Each tried by ingenuity and collusion to obtain advance information, to obtain the best bargain and corner the market. Whenever a price had to be agreed, as buyer or seller, lessor or lessee, producer or distributor, borrower or lender, the ancient and varied skills of bargaining came into play. Barter remained common, even in the eighteenth century, though transactions were still recorded in monetary terms.[42] Competition by price, service and credit was a harsh reality in every trade; there was continuous rivalry between members of the same factory and between servants of different Companies.[43] Endless stratagems were contrived to

[35] Jeake, *Astrological Diary*, p. 243. [36] Lowe, *Diary*, p. 40.
[37] Rawdon, *Memoirs*, p. 196.
[38] Lowell called this the 'oldest of the arts': see Cole 1957: 50. [39] Bennet 1966: 114.
[40] *Petty Papers*, i. 192; Robinson 1963; E. L. Jones in Cain & Uselden 1973: 200–1; Deyon 1972: 28–9; *Bankes Family Records*, p. 2. [41] Kusamitsa in Berg 1991.
[42] Jensen 1963:13. [43] Temple 1923:109–10.

force down prices when the export merchants bought from the producers or the retail tradesmen from the import merchants.[44]

Weakness and ignorance were as liable to be exploited in a middleman as in the consumer; unwary merchants could be caught by con-artists and disreputable brokers 'like conies in the hay'.[45] In a competitive and dishonest world, even acquaintances had to be chosen with care. Good fellowship usually flourished in prosperous years and declined in hard times. Sir Christopher Lowther was warned not 'to trust Bradelow or anie other that are soe duble handed all of them'.[46] George Boddington in his first venture used 'one had been my school fellow' but he had to confront his agent when the latter conveniently disowned knowledge of the investment.[47]

Although all businessmen played the same tricks and employed both the hard and the soft sell, each had his own rhythm and style; every trade had its own special needs and peculiar mannerisms and even facial and bodily gestures.[48] The street skills of selling by parcel to individual consumers differed both from selling raw materials and finished goods in bulk in the wholesale market and from the marketing of financial services.[49] Because there was still no mass consumption market in inessential goods, advertising was limited. Guilds, Companies and towns regulated the days and hours of sale to prevent undercutting as much as to ensure quality and supply, but the Custom of market overt in London created relatively free exchange. Companies issued prospectuses and purveyors of patent medicines and books pioneered the art of publicity; wants were created and exploited orally and visually, through street cries, the display of goods and signs and increasingly through broadsheets, printed trade cards, hand-bills, newspapers and books.[50]

The shape and direction of any business was also determined by connection. Contacts had to be continuously nursed and extended both at home and abroad.[51] The first priority of a young factor was to cultivate prospective principals and rustle up business; even important and responsible masters could not, on their own, usually generate sufficient commissions to fully employ an apprentice, once out of his time. Business operated in a face-to-face society. It was essential that a merchant penetrate the inner coteries of the relatively compact business world,

[44] BL Add. MS 4159, fo. 98; French 1972: 245.
[45] Greene, *Notable Discourse Coosenage*; Aydelotte 1913: 164; *Defence of Conny Catching*, pp. 361–2, 376; Campbell 1961: 89–90; Buckeridge, *Journal*.
[46] Lowther, *Correspondence*, p. 7.
[47] GLL MS 10823/1, fo. 38.
[48] Wheeler, *Treatise of Commerce*, pp. 2–3.
[49] Scott, *Essay on Drapery*, p. 23.
[50] Ewald 1956: 10–11, 111; Richardson 1930: 384–5; 1936: 1022; Walker 1975: 117; Whitford 1967: 513–15; Elliott 1962; Newman 1983; Laroon, *Criers and Hawkers*; GLL MS M8; Heal 1924: 498; 1947.
[51] GLL MS 6645, bundle 2.

move in the right circles and persuade the major players to use his services. To find cargo space or insurance or to transfer by bill required knowledge of people.[52]

One way of building up a clientele was to frequent the walks of the Exchange, the Customs House and the wharves at the right hours, patronize the right taverns and coffee houses and serve in offices in the guilds and the City.[53] Robert Livingston proposed himself as a correspondent and Joseph Cruttenden pushed hard for business.[54] Circles of intimates formed in the Livery and the overseas Companies; bargains were sealed over a bottle in the garden.[55] Heigham Bright thought that Mark Winn gave him an order because he had observed 'my sober deportment in London'; Thomas Firmin's 'words and manner of address were so pleasing', as an apprentice, that customers preferred to deal with him rather than his master.[56] Because every businessman was at the same time a debtor and creditor, indebtedness, far from creating a subordinate relationship reinforced connections and confidence. The inns served as distribution centres and as business offices for merchants.[57] Religious and ethnic affiliations were also vital. As Mr Money-Love observed, 'by becoming religious' a man 'may mend his market, perhaps get a rich wife ... and far better custome to his shopp'.[58] Friendship could also be exploited to obtain favours and priority.[59] In their wills, merchants frequently listed their close friends and distributed legacies in remembrance.[60]

Importuning was as much the stock-in-trade of the factor as of the place-hunter. There was a thin line between courteous flattery and obsequious hypocrisy. 'I desire you a merry Xmas and a prosperous New Year with many following', wrote one factor, 'and hope you will be so kind as to give me your further orders'.[61] Thomas Pitt sent a present of cloth to Sir Henry Johnson, when the latter was elected to the Court of the East India Company, adding 'Sir, I assure you 'twas made up and markt, before any news of alteration ... 'tis ye account of pure friendship and old acquaintance'.[62] A young merchant had to swallow his pride and conscience and tolerate in silence the humiliation, faults and offensive opinions of those whose support he needed. But once he had earned a reputation, he acquired business by referral and could let the world beat a path to his door.

52 Byrds, *Correspondence*, i. 104. 53 *Harl. Misc.*, i. 377.
54 Leder & Carosso 1956: 22; Cruttenden, *Atlantic Merchant Apothecary*, p. 7.
55 CUL Add. MS 91C, fo. 13. 56 Bright 1858: 175; Cornish, *Thomas Firmin*, p. 3.
57 Chartres 1972: 27. 58 Bunyan, *Life Mr Badman*.
59 Kress Lib. MS 787, letter 7 March 1710.
60 BL Add. MS 5489 is an extreme example of this tendency.
61 Holroyd, *Letter Books*, p. 32. 62 Hedges, *Diary*, i., p. ccii.

No merchant could direct all his affairs in person, particularly as his business grew. Control from the top, when letters exchanged just between England and the Baltic took five weeks, could be self-defeating.[63] He was obliged perforce to depend on intermediaries, who acted as his eyes and ears both at home and abroad. He had to select and trust his bankers, shipmasters, husbands and commission agents and be prepared to give them power of attorney and to delegate discretionary responsibility.[64] In the textile and coal trades, syndicates entrusted their capital and subcontracted to middlemen. Those who put out raw materials had to supervise carefully to prevent delays and embezzlement. The distances which separated principal from agent often generated a sense of helplessness, complaints and differences of opinion.[65]

Judgement of character therefore really counted. A merchant had to assess the relative strengths and weaknesses of his competitors, the trustworthiness as well as the credit of his clients. Sir John Barnard advised young men to understand the temper and disposition of their associates and to study their faces.[66] Aggressiveness, self-righteousness and litigiousness could backfire. A merchant had to know when to give preferential treatment and when to refuse sureties for third parties, when to compound for bad debts and when to be impervious to complaints and pleas, when to be rigorous and when to bend. Debtors had to be chased without provoking their collapse. Since independent contractors constituted its middle management, a business firm had to solicit intelligence and advice from its correspondents and factors while discouraging them from independent marketing. Prospective associates could be tested and appraised in small transactions before their services were fully utilized, but the selection process and subsequent supervision was often conducted through correspondence and referral without any meeting between the parties. A principal had to ensure that his factors obeyed his instructions and gave him priority; he also needed substitutes, should they prove unsatisfactory. A fair-minded merchant who nursed and coaxed his factors secured better performance than a peremptory principal who bullied, cheated or dissembled. It was important to retain control without giving offence.

Formal skills

Even though every merchant drew on his internal resources for his strategic inspiration and acquired his tactics by experience, there was a

[63] Zins 1971: 301.

[64] In the seventeenth century there is no real equivalent to the Directions printed by Price in Davenport-Hines & Lieberman 1986: 136.

[65] A typical example of an angry exchange is Bod. add. MS C.26, fos. 16–17; *Norris Papers*, pp. 10–12.

[66] Barnard, *Present for Apprentices*, pp. 54, 61.

hard core of knowledge which had to be learned by rote. The professional teachers, in the hope of improving their status and attracting pupils, enthusiastically prescribed a curriculum which would have graced a nobleman on the Grand Tour.[67] But the fundamental techniques, as detailed in contemporary handbooks, were essentially the same as in fourteenth-century Italy.[68]

Some branches of business could be conducted orally or from memory; merchants sometimes used their marks rather than signatures to authenticate documents.[69] A few manufacturers, small-scale merchants and even some usurers were unable to write.[70] Some of the aldermen of Yarmouth were illiterate and tradesmen elected to Livery companies were sometimes excused from office because they could not sign their names.[71] Gilbert Wright, Master of the Salters, employed William Lilly as a scribe.[72] Business, however, normally required the ability to write as well as to read and the rate of literacy among the urban tradesmen was in fact high.[73] Only 2 per cent of the Ironmongers signed their oath with a mark in the 1580s and some guilds, like the Goldsmiths, made literacy a condition of binding and tested applicants.[74] Only 1 per cent of 145 merchants in the North were unable to write and thirteen out of fifty-seven merchants in Ireland.[75] Information, instructions and remittances were usually transferred by correspondence; any transaction which might be the subject of dispute was committed to writing, if only to a wastebook. Charles Marescoe wrote fifty letters per day in five languages.[76] Sir John Banks advised his apprentice not to talk too much, to count everything and to keep a diary.[77]

Scriveners and some businessmen preferred the fluent secretary hand,

[67] Watts, *Essay on Proper Method*; Wallis 1983: 52.

[68] The best introduction to business skills is provided by historians of medieval Italy: see Bec 1967a: 383–7; Fanfani 1951: 344–5; Sapori 1955: i. 66–7, 84–7; Lopez 1958: 502. There is no glossary of seventeenth-century terms comparable to Edler 1934; the best general secondary guide before the eighteenth century is Jeannin 1957: 97–117. Examples of commonplace books include Hanham 1979: 109; Bradford MS 10/2; BL Harl. MS 5769; Winchester 1955: 227; *Blundel's Diary*, p. 42. Annotations by John Tempest of Roberts' *Merchant's Map Commerce* are in Leeds University Libraries, Brotherton MS LTQ. Carpenter, *Most Excellent Instrument* had blank pages for scribbling.

[69] Anthropological linguists have wrongly assumed that record-keeping leads to a mechanistic way of thinking: see Goody 1968: 64.

[70] Flinn 1962: 27, 123; one son was, however, considered a liability because of his poor handwriting. Woodward 1965: 213; Phillips in Chaloner & Ratcliffe 1977: 21; Kirby 1983: 29; Goring in Ives *et al.* 1978: 213.

[71] Cressy 1980: 112, 124–5, 130–6, tables 5.2, 6.1–6.6, 7.3 and 1974: 235 puts illiteracy at 15 per cent among country and 10 per cent among urban tradesmen; Moran 1981: 7; Fisher 1936: 9.

[72] Wood, *Atheniae Oxonienses*, i. 36. Clark in Clark *et al.* 1979: table 7.

[73] Houston 1982a: 209; 1982b: 92.

[74] Rappaport 1989: 298, table 8.4; Cooper 1984: 342; Hare 1984: 372.

[75] Houston 1982a: tables 3–4; Canny in Canny & Pagden 1987: 117.

[76] Marescoe, *Markets and Merchants*, p. 77.

[77] Coleman 1963: 65.

because they wanted to cram as much as possible into a minimum space, but the round hand and the Italian or Roman hand in its simple sloping form without flourishes became much more common, because it was prettier, faster and easier to read.[78] Thomas Hill recommended 'an Italian hand being most in use and best for all languages'.[79] Accuracy was essential when posting and letters had to be written quickly often in poor light while remaining neat and legible, neither 'crampt like a Scrivener's boy nor scrawling long Tails like a Wench at a Boarding School'.[80] Apprentices regularly practised their penmanship and copied letters and accounts for their masters, although clerks increasingly assumed this function. Copyists were expected to be correct on their first entry; the East India Company instructed its factors to keep their cash books 'without blotting, scraps or interlining'.[81] Shorthand could also be learnt, but was rarely used.[82]

Some hands were virtually illegible and Stout wrote very slowly because he was left-handed.[83] But most merchants wrote clearly and often doubled as scriveners.[84] Contemporaries recommended that a merchant's style be direct, unambiguous, informal, unemotional, plain and brief in contrast to the rhetorical and metaphysical conceits which still weighed down the sermons even of Ramists and Non-Conformist preachers.[85] Josiah Heathcote was known as a 'man of few words' and James Bankes recommended 'in any company be very silent and use few words'.[86] But many letters were still written too hastily or marked by effusiveness, irrelevance, fussiness and floridity of metaphor.[87]

Business did not require a sophisticated knowledge of mathematics. Goods could be weighed and sized by eye or by standard containers, like the barrel. One skill which had been hard to master became obsolete. In the sixteenth century Roman numerals were still used by merchants in

[78] Woodbridge 1969: 7; Heal 1931: xvii, xxxv; Jenkinson 1926: 216–17; Schultz 1943: 385; Dawson & Skipton 1966: 9; Heaton 1960. Whalley 1969: 30, 39 has illustrations of commercial hands.

[79] KAO U.145/C1, letter Thomas Hill, 20 Sept. 1661; Lincs. AO, Monson MS, Misc. Books 21; Bod. Dep. MS C.23, fo. 1.

[80] *Character and Qualifications of a Merchant*, p. 7.

[81] *East India Company Letters, 1600–19*, p. 322.

[82] Watson 1899: 260; Butler 1951. Petty had two clerks, one of whom took shorthand: see *Down. Survey History*.

[83] Webb 1955: 210; Stout, *Autobiography*, p. 72.

[84] Jeake's calligraphic exercises are in the Rye Museum. He used shorthand to express concerns about questionable transactions: see Jeake, *Astrological Diary*, p. 60.

[85] Howell 1956: 390–2; Mitchell 1932: 270–1.

[86] Heathcote 1899: 69; Hall in Sheels 1985: 308; *Bankes Family Records*, p. 1.

[87] Business has been blamed for a decline in standards: see Robertson 1942: 65. One example of how a poorly written letter could create problems is Newcombe, *Autobiography*, pp. 193–4.

conjunction with the abacus and the counting-board with its bone and metal jettons; notched tallies continued in use at the Exchequer and in some shops.[88] By the seventeenth century, however, the overwhelming superiority of the zero had standardized arabic cyphers; precision became increasingly important. John Wallis initially learned mathematics from his brother who was training to be a merchant.[89] Mathematical tables and ready reckoners were used to calculate compound interest and annuities, the value of land and leases, and rebates and discounts.[90] Both contemporary comments and surviving accounts suggest, however, that low standards of arithmetic remained a problem.[91]

Anyone in foreign trade had to be proficient in speaking and writing several languages. Latin was still used by scholars, scientists, lawyers, apothecaries and clerks of towns, guilds and the Customs; some businessmen cited tags, read the classics and indulged in occasional compositions.[92] Isaac Lawrence was credited with a 'neat stile', a knowledge of antiquity, a perfect oral command of Latin, French and Italian and a working knowledge of other languages.[93] But as Locke said, Latin was 'necessary for a gentleman but useless to a merchant'.[94] Modern European and Oriental languages were more relevant and some countries required that transactions be recorded in the native tongue. Some merchants were polyglots: James Bovey spoke seven languages. Every area of trade had its own lingua franca – Italian in the Mediterranean and demotic Low German in the North – but merchants also communicated with their foreign clients in their native languages.[95] 'Be sure to study and perfect ... the French tongue', advised Thomas Hill; 'the Dutch you must necessarily learn'.[96] John Jones of Maes-y-garnedd used English in his business and Welsh in his spiritual correspondence.[97]

When sorting and selecting for purchase or sale, merchants needed a specialized knowledge of an enormous range of commodities.[98] In order

[89] Wallis, *Life*, i. p. clxvi.

[90] The basic mathematics required by business is illustrated by Purser, *Compound Interest*; Leybourn, *Platform Guide*; Hodges, *Enchiridion Arithmeticon*; Collins, *Introduction Merchants' Accompts*; Hatton, *Merchant's Magazine*. Thomas 1987: 116–17; Wingate, *Arithmetique*; Turner 1973: 52.

[91] Bod. Aubrey MS 10, fo. 35; Aubrey, *Idea of Education*, p. 103; Hunter 1975: 50–1; Locke, *Educational Writings*, pp. 268, 319–20; Pollexfen, *Discourse of Trade*, p. 49; N. Yorks. RO ZCG; West Yorkshire Archives Service, Leeds NH 2183A; Lancs. RO DDCA 1/46.

[92] *Northampton Records*, ii. 314. Until the seventeenth century, Latin served as a lingua franca, according to Brinsley, *Ludus Literarius*, and it is found in some business accounts.

[93] Lawrence, *Diary*, p. 46.

[94] Locke, *Thoughts Concerning Education*, p. 255.

[95] Ramsay 1975: 217.

[96] KAO U.145/C. 1, letters 6, 20 Sept. 1661.

[97] Dodd 1952: 6.

[98] Browne, *Marchant's Avizo*, pp. 22–5; Roberts, *Merchant's Map of Commerce*, chap. 9; Willan 1959: chap. 1.

to recognize flaws and assess quality, durability and value, some familiarity with not only the raw materials but also every stage of the process of production was required. Mastery of the numerous and intricate variations in standards of weight and measure, in England and overseas, was also essential to detect shrinkage, wastage and fraud and to equalize differences in volume and size.[99] Storage, packing, loading, stowage and transportation differed according to the shape and fragility of the commodity and according to whether carriage was by land, river or sea.[100] A merchant had to deter pilfering and breakage, to expose deceitful packing and to know the practices and fees of the carters, watermen, wharfingers, lightermen, porters and warehousemen.[101]

To secure cheap and safe shipment of exports and imports, it was important to know the geography of markets and the relative freight costs by different sailing routes, the itineraries and reputation of ships for hire and their masters, port and wharf charges and any relevant political and naval news.[102] Factors who travelled supercargo even had some training in navigation, because they occasionally assumed maritime functions.[103] The merchant or factor supervising loading or discharge had to be familiar with local regulations and brokerage fees, groundage, anchorage, lastage, lighterage, cranage, the procedures for consignment and receipt, Customs dues, the formalities of declaration and clearance, and how to deal with dishonest and incompetent petty officials. The marks on each item of cargo had to be compared with invoices and bills of lading, three copies of which were usually made, one each for the consignor, consignee and purser.[104] Scriveners, notaries and attorneys increasingly took over the drafting of charter-parties, contracts, indentures, insurance policies and official documents.[105] But the businessman still handled much of the paperwork and he needed to know the local procedures of each market, the tricky process of forward buying or sales by candle and the conventions of bargain and sale.[106]

The borrowing and remittance of funds was even more technical. The complexity of financial instruments can be gauged from the voluminous

[99] For differences in weight and measure see Kisch 1965; Zupco 1985; Doursther 1840; *Select Tracts and Table Books*. Printed pocketbooks superseded the abstracts of reckonings and memoranda kept by earlier merchants.

[100] Crofts 1967; Chartres 1977b and 1980. Goods between decks were subject to pillage on capture, but those below hatches were sealed: see Salisbury 1966: 331.

[101] MacGrath 1954: 292; Norman 1935; Stern 1968: chap. 1, 68–71; Humpherus 1874–86: i. 320–3; Chartres 1980a.

[102] Vance 1990.

[103] MacGrath 1954: 23; Webb 1955: 20–9; Farrington 1991: i. 531; Vanes 1977: 15.

[104] Malynes, *Lex mercatoria*. Disputes over incomplete deliveries were common: one example is REQ 2/308/27.

[105] Gutteridge in *Cambridge Legal Essays* 1926: 132.

[106] Sale by candle was a variant of the Dutch practice of sale by clock: see Chance 1971: 295.

contemporary handbooks.[107] Each area of trade had its own money of account, conversion rates and symbols and there was a bewildering mixture of coins in circulation with fluctuating intrinsic, face and exchange values. A merchant had to know how to write, assign and draw on credit instruments, to split and match them geographically. The most important of these were inland and foreign bills of exchange, but they included other types of loan and methods of payment, such as bottomry bonds, mortgages and several categories of government paper and promissory note.[108]

Henry Parker asserted that the licensing of factors without breeding 'is to send men naked into battle'.[109] That the unskilled merchant was a danger both to himself and to others was not just a convenient argument to defend a monopoly. Merchants in every area of trade complained about 'raw young men' who were reckless, who overpaid and sold too cheaply.[110, 111] The high degree of skill required by trade was frequently underestimated by gentlemen who mistakenly put their least intelligent children into business.[112] As Waterhouse remarked, younger sons 'run into it without fear or wit and know not when to leave it'.[113] In the professions, the worst consequence of incompetence was slower promotion, whereas in competitive trades, ignorance and poor judgement led to failure. Business was no game for amateurs.

Law and accounting

Merchants needed more than a passing acquaintance with foreign and international law to settle disputes which arose outside England. Every country presented them with different rules and practices but recovery of debts was a universal problem.[114] International trade was governed by a body of maritime, mercantile and insurance Custom, as well as by the conventions of war and neutrality.[115] Despite inevitable conflicts of jurisdiction, the guiding principles of commercial law were, if not universal, fairly uniform throughout the maritime nations of Northern Europe and the Mediterranean and had a common origin in ancient and medieval codes.

A major problem in England was the diversity of jurisdictions. Business was regulated by Common Law in King's Bench, Exchequer and

[107] Blount, *Several Forms Instruments*; Marius, *Advice concerning Bills of Exchange*.

[108] Roover 1953: 113; 1974: 221, 230; Rosegaard 1910: 56–8.

[109] Parker, *Free Trade*, p. 13.

[110] Raleigh, *Works*, vii. 367; BL Stowe MS 132, fo. 289.

[111] Barbour 1928: 554; BL Lans. MS 152, fo. 51; Muchmore 1971: 481; Federowicz 1980: 58–9.

[112] BL Add. MS 42613, fo. 225.

[113] Waterhouse, *Gentleman's Monitor*, p. 207.

[114] Malynes, *Lex mercatoria*, p. 223.

[115] Keeton 1960: chap. 17.

Common Pleas, by statute, by secular Civil Law in Admiralty and the ecclesiastical courts of probate, by the customary law of the diverse municipal courts, by the case law of the Customs and other government departments, by the bye-laws of chartered corporations, by the equitable jurisdiction of Chancery and the Lord Mayor's Courts, and by Special Commissions, like those for insurance and bankruptcy.[116] Before the Civil War, prerogative courts, like the Court of Requests, provided another forum. Practically every court heard cases of debt.[117]

It was vital, therefore, that a merchant have sufficient legal expertise to comprehend his contractual rights and obligations and the machinery of probate. He had to know the appropriate procedures for sealings, the correct form of bills of debt, conditional bonds, acquittances and assignments, to be able to weigh the risks of issuing and acting under letters of attorney.[118] Problems could arise from factorage and partnerships.[119] Because businessmen lent on mortgage when title to land was not registered, they had to be sufficiently abreast of property law to ascertain how far land was encumbered.[120] Some branches of business spawned endless litigation: Ingram had as many as twenty-five suits in the courts at the same time.[121]

Specialists, like Sir Thomas Pengelly, did emerge within the legal profession to meet the specific needs of business; attorneys often worked with their clients against the legal bureaucracy. The real costs of litigation fell and independent debt collectors would wheedle and threaten for a percentage of what they recovered. But professional assistance was still expensive and merchants had to determine their own legal options and liabilities. The functions of the attorney and the factor originally overlapped, and many merchants undertook para-legal work as public notaries and scriveners, represented themselves and served as judges in the municipal courts and as executors, arbitrators, trustees and commissioners of bankruptcy.[122]

By far the most important single skill was casting accounts.[123] A merchant's books constituted the vertebrae of his business and served as title for his heirs. Ledgers and correspondence were produced as evidence of transactions in the Admiralty Court and Chancery to settle disputes

[116] Steckley 1978: 172; Wynne, *Leoline Jenkins*, pp. lxxxii–xcix. [117] See pp. 216–18.

[118] For the forms of action and statutes governing debt see Dumbauld 1973: 19; Milsom 1969: 216–17; Kiralfy 1951: 189–90; Simpson 1966: 399–422. See also p. 215.

[119] Price in Davenport-Hines & Lieberman 1986: 19ff; Munday 1977.

[120] Shipley 1973. [121] Upton 1961: 56–7.

[122] Carus-Wilson 1954: 83; Lincs. AO Ancaster-Heathcote MSS; GLL MS 11896, papers of Sir John Mead; Jeaffreson 1878: i. 190; Brooks 1986: 99; 1984: 274–5.

[123] The hostility towards accounting as a vocational subject surfaced later. On Marshall's view that it 'fills the mind without enlarging or strengthening it' see Kadish 1989: 233.

over sales and prices.[124] In Bohun's opinion, 'one shall not wage law against a Merchants Book'.[125] An entry in the vendor's hand of a debt was accepted as evidence of non-payment by the buyer until deleted.[126] Crafty merchants would sometimes delete their journal, but not their ledger, which could be produced if the payor died.[127]

The Companies employed professional accountants and duplicated records; merchants increasingly employed clerks as cashkeepers at £20–30 per annum.[128] Indeed suits against bookkeepers became more common in the courts.[129] But merchants were always their own accountants and often kept a secret book; even ship-masters and pursers had to be proficient.[130] Accounting in partnerships was particularly complex, because costs had to be allocated and profits distributed between participants whose interest could vary from a single joint venture to a percentage of the whole business.

The primary role of bookkeeping was to record and categorize transactions according to a preconceived structure. The raw data was stored in particularized ledger accounts for individual ventures, commodities, factors and clients. Subsidiary books for cash and bills were opened to lighten the journal and entries were abbreviated when posted to the ledger, but few ledgers had a single collective trading account. Doubtful debts were usually accounted for separately, but written off only at death. The perpetual stock inventories constituted a permanent record which could be compared with actual goods during regular stocktaking. They served to track movement and to prevent and uncover losses and fraud, though outright embezzlement was more characteristic of the great Companies than of small firms. Bookkeeping developed as a system of charge and discharge for verification and audit; its primary function was to report and vindicate the responsible officer, not to depict a true financial position.[131]

Humphrey Chetham and William Stout were meticulous and exact in their accounts, as was Richard Archdale, though he could not account for

[124] REQ 2/296/69; Saltzman 1931: 169–70; Ruddock 1951: 95; Duncan 1971: 151.

[125] Bohun, *Privilegia Londini*, p. 78. This Custom was not necessarily recognized by the Common Law Courts: see *New York Lord Mayor's Court*, p. 31.

[126] The debtor sometimes struck out the entry on payment: see Webb 1962: 110.

[127] BL Add. MS 32519.

[128] *Hudson's Bay Company Minutes 1671–84*, p. 40; there are many examples among the inventories in the CLRO CSB.

[129] One example is REQ 2/302.

[130] For an example in 1609 of an advice to pursers see BL Cotton Charters and Rolls, iii. 13; Roe, *Journal*, p. 465.

[131] Edwards 1960: 447. Three examples are *Founders Company Wardens' Accounts*, p. xi; *London Chamberlain's Accounts*, pp. xvi, xxxviii; *Banbury Corporation Records*, p. 187. The system dates back to Mesopotamia: see the clay tablets from Ur III printed in Snell 1980: 53. Even the Foleys used a system of charge and discharge: see Hammersley in Smout 1979: 70–2.

£142 'withall my Indeavours'.[132] But the accounting periods in many books were not clearly defined and the posting was sloppy, retrospective and uneven. Tooley's accounts were erratic, though his main ledger has probably been lost, and Humphrey Shalcross and Myddelton were little better.[133] Lowther was highly dissatisfied with the accounts which Richard Wiberg kept in Ireland, as was John Pynchon with John Crow.[134] A few merchants, like Ingram and John Pitt, did not even keep proper books, but recorded their activities 'upon loose papers' or the equivalent of backs of old envelopes.[135] In some cases, like that of Thomas Forster, the books were so disorganized that it was impossible to value the estate.[136]

Accountancy developed very slowly. In contrast to simple bookkeeping, it is an integrated system with a theoretical base in which each entry expresses a complete idea.[137] The income statement juxtaposes revenue and expenditure as the balance sheet juxtaposes liabilities and assets; both are combined into a financial statement. Transactions can be analysed to determine how a business has progressed to its current position, to calculate relative rates of return, project into the future and determine policy. A merchant can overspend, overpay or misprice his wares if he is unaware of his real cash position and liabilities or the true cost of acquiring and maintaining his goods. To secure control, assets have to be treated methodically, capital clearly separated from revenue and credits and debits balanced regularly.

Medieval Italian firms had employed subsidiary ledgers with control accounts and depreciation allowances, but the first English handbooks, when double-entry and cost accounting methods spread from Italy and Antwerp, treated these innovations in a diverse and casual manner.[138] Double entry was practised in a crude and inconsistent fashion by some sixteenth-century merchants, but others, like Thomas Howell, kept their

132 Berks. RO D/EDB2, transferred to the GLL in 1989.

133 Webb 1962: 105; Beloff 1939: 688; E. D. Jones 1939–40: 85.

134 Lowther, *Correspondence*, pp. 114–16; *Pynchon Papers*, p. 43.

135 Hedges, *Diary*, i. p. xc; C107/20; Upton 1961: 172, 175.

136 SP 105/176, fos. 399, 427; IOL G/4017, 155, estate of George Woolaston.

137 Jeffreys 1967: 50–2; Littleton 1961: 25–8; 1933: chap. 6; Pollard 1965: 257. Although the adjective 'rational' is usually reserved for double-entry systems, it has been used to describe William de la Pole's accounts by Fryde 1988: 25. Early bookkeeping was often ingenious, but, like the roman numeral, it was inherently limited as a tool.

138 Peele, *Maner and Fourm* and *Pathe Way to Perfectnes*; Mellis, *Brief Instruction*. Roover 1974: 120 shows that double entry developed quite early in Italy from the bill of exchange and was diffused first through the *libro di mercantura* and then through printed manuals; Wee 1967:1089; Lane 1944: 164–8; Goldthwaite 1972: 433. Double entry was not widely practised in the Netherlands: see Houtte 1977: 207; Samuel 1982: 14–15; Wee 1972.

books 'in such forme as noo man can understand yt but hym selfe'.[139] By the seventeenth century, accounting had moved from description to rules; verbs like 'debit', became labels and Thomas West kept his accounts in the third person.[140] Businessmen paid more attention to the effect of dead stock on yields, factored in the actual and opportunity cost of capital, grasped the concept of irreducible expenditure and were capable of complex calculations when valuing land and leases.[141]

A few merchants balanced their books in a rudimentary manner, closed their particular accounts through profit and loss and attempted to calculate their overall rate of return.[142] Ironmasters compared the profitability of different forges, valued capital equipment, estimated production costs and recorded capital growth.[143] Richard Archdale graded his debts and balanced his profit and loss account annually and his stock account triennially.[144] John Winter, Henry Hunter and Sir William Turner regularly balanced their profit and loss accounts and valued their assets.[145] The East India Company sought to establish the profit and loss for each voyage and prescribed annual balancing; the Hudson's Bay Company produced a profit and loss statement in 1694.[146] Clayton not only kept double-entry accounts, but used standardized forms for bills and orders to pay.[147] By the end of the century, annual statements of assets became more common, like those of Henry Phill who valued the 'totall of all the real and personal estate'; Richard Hoare produced balance sheets which valued all deposits and stock at market value.[148] Charles Marescoe kept double-entry accounts, but not on an annual basis, and Sir Charles Peers even kept a double-entry journal.[149]

Sometimes a bastard form of double entry was employed, as by George Warner, Richard Ashe, Thomas Myddelton and Charles Blunt.[150] Sir Thomas Cullum estimated his gains by comparing the inventories of

139 Winchester 1955: 228–9; Smythe, *Ledger*, pp. 12–14; Yamey 1959 and in Baxter & Davidson 1962: 18–34; Ramsey 1958: 81, in Littleton & Yamey 1956: 247–54 and in *Produzione Commercio* 1976; *John Isham*, p. ciii, chap. 11, and review by B. S. Yamey in *Accountancy*, 74 (1963), 228; Connell Smith 1950–1: 370.

140 West, *Accounts*, p. 76.

141 Habakkuk 1952: 125; Lowther, *Commercial Papers*, p. 187.

142 Examples include N. Yorks. RO ZCG 6 (Cholmeley); Lancs. RO DDCA/1/46 (Pooley); Lincs. AO, Massingberd of Gunby MSS (Meux).

143 Crossley 1966: 272–4; Edwards *et al.* 1990: 61ff; *Foley Stour Valley Ironworks*, part 2, pp. xv, 3, 113.

144 Berks. RO D/EDB2, now in GLL.

145 *Trelawney Papers*, pp. 181ff, 290ff; Berks. RO D/EZ5/B5; GLL MS 5105.

146 IOL Home Misc. MS 1511, Rules for Accompts, 1664; Home Misc. 11/257 has an example of poorly kept books. Wretts-Smith 1963: 105; Scott 1910–12: ii. 388; Chaudhuri 1978: 80; Rich 1958: 324; Horsefield 1957.

147 Melton 1979: 93.

148 C111/127; Hoare 1955: 179–80.

149 Yamey 1968: 639–41; Marescoe, *Markets and Merchants*, p. 11.

150 SP 46/85/3; C114/164–5; C107/20/3; E. D. Jones 1939–40: 85.

successive years, excluding wages and bad debts; after balancing, he carried any surplus to his stock account. Stout did not use double entry or annual inventories, but he had his own method of measuring accumulation. Shershaw Cary kept his stock separate from his profits and distinguished between private and business expenses, though he only calculated percentage profits on individual ventures.[151] A most extraordinary case is that of Thomas Cony, who recorded an inheritance of goods and land and fifty-seven years later added up his total income from all his assets, deducted his expenses and costs of his children and calculated his net accumulation.[152]

Most businessmen worked by rule of thumb and followed their own idiosyncratic style rather than the precepts of the handbooks.[153] Balancing was usually infrequent and inaccurate and often no attempt was made to ascertain why accounts were out of balance.[154] Thomas Bowrey did not bother to frame annual statements and even Francis Child and Sir John Banks cast up irregularly.[155] Many merchants, like Weddell, transferred balances only when there was no more room on the page.[156] Although it is always possible that they performed this task outside the ledger, few calculated their net yield on capital; imprecision led to disputes between partners.[157] In most cases, profit and loss accounts were rudimentary; Thomas Jeffery used his for wages and Henry Hunter to record expenses.[158] Fixed assets were not depreciated or revalued or properly distinguished from current assets; revenue was confused with capital and personal with business expenditure. Sometimes assets were carried forward at cost and any net income (receipts less payments) posted to profit and loss; sometimes they were carried forward at original cost plus expenses less receipts or revalued and the new value carried forward, any difference being posted to profit and loss. Major costs were often overlooked and little attention was paid to the period of time when assessing returns.[159] Calculation of profit did not even approach a minimum level of accuracy. Corporations, like government departments, still lived by the agricultural calendar. The Africa Company did not account properly for income and expenditure and the East India Company did not have annual balance sheets until 1704; poor accounting may

[151] Bristol AO 105/311. [152] Cony,'Household Book', pp. 22–31.
[153] Yamey *et al.* 1963: 184–8, 190ff; Littleton & Yamey 1956: 252; Yamey 1949: 109–12.
[154] SP 105/176, fos. 399, 427; SP 46/85/3; C114/64; C111/127; Roseveare in Minchinton 1988: 40. [155] Bowrey, *Papers*, p. 119.
[156] West Yorkshire Archives Service, Leeds NH 2183A.
[157] GLL MS 6372; REQ 2/309/44; Ramsey 1958: 342.
[158] Berks. RO D/EZ5/B5; Devon RO G1/6/1.
[159] Murray 1930: 52–9, 217–70; Solomon 1952: 112; Chambers 1966: 78–9; Garnier 1954: chap. 1. The opponents of usury had distinguished between 'gayne of wares' and 'sellyinge tyme therein': see Wilson, *Discourse upon Usury*, p. 309.

have been partly responsible for bank failures.[160] The joint-stock accounts of the Stationers were chaotic.[161] Seventeenth-century merchants were still in what might be termed the household stage of accountancy.[162] They kept books to combat fraud, to define ownership and obligations to creditors and factors, to ascertain the status of debtors and losses, to track revenue and expenditure, to prevent fraud and to administer estates after death; not to value assets, test solvency, prepare budgets, rationalize inventory or provide quantitative data.

Businessmen wanted to know what they were worth and to define their liabilities, but they had little interest in projecting future potential from past performance or in analysing transactions in order to reorganize, improve and control their businesses. The informal structure of a small family partnership did not require sophisticated methods. What mattered was accuracy and completeness of record, rather than creative accountancy. In the seventeenth century, a business was seen as a succession of unrelated ventures. Modern accounting developed in response to the different needs of corporate and industrial enterprises, which function in a continuum.[163]

Education

Some of the basic skills of business were acquired through formal education, which was considered part of a son's provision. Responsibility for primary education from four or five years to seven or eight was often assumed by a family member and the spelling books were written for artisans to teach each other; children were also sent to village dames, the local parson or a petty school.[164] Some could read and write and handle basic arithmetic before they went to a grammar school.[165] Others taught themselves late in life; a Mayor of Taunton was not literate until he was twenty-six.[166] Private tutors were occasionally engaged, as for John

[160] Chaudhuri in Blusse & Gaastra 1981: 43–4; Scott 1910–12: ii. 388; Usher 1943; Riemersma 1968: 50; Glamann 1958: 244. It is possible that the Dutch Companies confused capital expenditure and working costs and therefore miscalculated their profits. The Sun Fire Office did not introduce double entry until 1890.

[161] Blagden 1957: 167ff.

[162] The same was true of French merchants; see AD Bouches du Rhône IX B 171–B 175 and XXXIX E. 35, 47; AD Rhône B. Fonds Carcenac & Corbière and Fonds Vitte.

[163] On the slow growth of cost accounting see Tucker 1960; MacKendrick 1970: 48, 67; Solomon 1952: 12; Brown 1968: 115; Lee 1975: 35; Johnson & Kaplan 1987: 205–6; Bloom 1980.

[164] Schulz 1943: 385, app. 3; Curtis 1964: 60; Spufford 1979: 417; Jenkinson 1926: 216–17; Baldwin 1943: chap. 1; Michael 1987: 16.

[165] Children first learned to read print, then script and then how to write: see Thomas in Baumann 1986: 100; Brydges, *Continuation History Willoughby Family*, p. 117.

[166] Barlow, *Journal*, p. 29; Tryon, *Memoirs*, p. 10; Fontaine, *Mémoires*, pp. 209ff.

Sanderson, who was withdrawn from school after being subject to barbarous treatment, and learned accounts at home.[167] A foreign education was sometimes considered: Thomas Pitt, in 1701, wanted his two younger sons, William and Thomas, to be educated at an eminent school 'or else send 'em to Holland to the reformed Jesuits at Rotterdam for their writing, language, arithmetic and marchand accompts'.[168] But the most common institution of secondary education was the inexpensive and socially comprehensive grammar school. The final stage before apprenticeship was a spell in an advanced commercial arithmetic school.[169]

A few examples will suffice. John Priestley went to school for writing and arithmetic and was then apprenticed to a local cloth merchant; he was sent to London to be a factor at Blackwell Hall before returning to a partnership with his master.[170] Thomas Gwyn of Falmouth was taught to read at four, went to a local Latin school at eight, and was then exchanged with the son of a merchant at Rochelle at fourteen to learn French.[171] George Boddington, grandson of a Warwickshire landowner, was sent first to reading school, where he made slow progress; then he was 'put to Latin School at 9, at 12 put into Greek ... at 13 could wright the characters from a copy with exactness but my Memory being not good and my father apprehending I would not make any great use of learning put me to a wrighting school and having made a small progress therein and Arithmetic about the yeare 1661 set me to his business in the packing trade and wrighting his letters and keeping his cash'; in 1663, after proving his diligence, someone 'came home and taught me merchants accounts in which I became proficient'.[172]

Some endowed grammar schools did not cater only for scholars and clerics, but taught also writing and mathematics and occasionally accounts.[173] Christ's Hospital taught mathematics and navigation for the Navy after 1673 and added a writing school for 300 boys in 1695. Of 155 pupils at Bristol Grammar School, 1710–17, 53 were destined for trade or the sea.[174] Reformers, like Mulcaster, Aubrey and Locke, campaigned against the education of 'counterfeit gentlemen' and proposed to bring the curriculum closer to business by teaching useful knowledge and accounting.[175] Sir John Lowther wanted arithmetic and shorthand taught

[167] Sanderson, *Travels*, p. 2.

[168] BL Add. MS 22844; Hedges, *Diary*, i. p. lxix; C110/87, memorial, 1702; *HMC Fortescue*, i. 5, 13, 18. They eventually went to Meures Academy near Soho Square.

[169] GLL MS 12017.

[170] *Yorkshire Diaries*, i. 19.

[171] Whetter 1974: 154–5. He later taught other merchants.

[172] GLL MS 10823/1, fo. 38.

[173] Vincent 1969: 74, 98, 201–2; Bridenbaugh 1962: 329. A school exercise book is reproduced in Myers & Harris 1985: 17; Lambert 1806: iii. 34.

[174] Orme 1989: 21; Morgan 1985: 223–6; Hill 1951.

[175] Mulcaster, *Positions*, p. 193; Bod. Aubrey MS 10, fo. 36; Molen 1974: 128.

at his school; the boarding school run by the Quaker, William Jenkins, taught both Latin and accounts.[176] Pollexfen was conscious that his works were difficult to read 'for want of School learning (and because trades Men have special words and ways of writing)' and he wanted the schools to prepare gentlemen for business.[177]

But none of these schemes made any headway and the syllabus of the grammar schools remained irrelevant to business. Vernacular subjects were taught and were often determined by the master, not by the statutes of the school. But the curriculum consisted primarily of Latin and occasionally Greek, Hebrew and history, together with a heavy diet of religious instruction.[178] Modern languages, geography, mathematics and natural science were usually excluded.[179] The Humanists had dismissed vocational subjects and sought to convert a belligerent nobility into an aristocracy of virtue.[180] Theoretically, by studying the classics and rhetoric, by parsing and composition, children could learn how to reason; but in practice, they just memorized the rules of grammar as a prolonged puberty rite.[181] 'We continue to squeeze all the sapless Papers and Fragments of antiquity', remarked *Britannia Languens*, 'whilst the Notions of Trade are turned into Ridicule'.[182] Although their harsh discipline probably hardened children to face the world, the grammar schools catered to the social and personal needs of the leisured.[183]

The commercial writing schools, in contrast, were purely utilitarian institutions which taught not only the three Rs, but also double-entry bookkeeping, geometry and even astronomy, surveying and navigation.[184] Often the course of instruction, which was both practical and thorough, would only last a few months and was highly specialized. London with its large immigrant population had always had open schools run by lay masters for business and languages.[185] In Bristol, the Merchant Venturers ran their own writing school and the Dutch in London had their own commercial schools and provided scholarships to Leiden.[186] Instruction in business skills became a speciality of teachers like John

[176] Wallis & Robinson 1975: 263; Braithwaite 1919: 531.
[177] Pollexfen, *Discourse of Trade*, preface, pp. 46, 49.
[178] O'Day 1982: chap. 4; Cressy 1976a: 30; 1975: 130; Watson 1908: 530–1; Bennett 1970: 136–7, 161.
[179] Lambley 1920: 240; Dunlop 1912: 179, 196; *Blundell's Diary*, p. 42; Watson 1899: 259; 1909: xxxvi, 228, 324–6; Thomas 1987: 109.
[180] Humanism may have driven men out of business in Italy: see Roover 1963: 365; Renouard 1968: 400; Charlton 1965: chap. 9; Caspari 1954: 7; Lehmberg 1960: 83.
[181] Curtis 1964: 56; Moran 1979: 38.
[182] *Early English Tracts Commerce*, p. 357.
[183] Watson 1908: 53; Vincent 1950: introduction.
[184] There were at least forty-five mathematics teachers and seventy writing masters in London: see Taylor 1956: 9–10; Heal 1931: xvii, xxxv. On rivalry between the scriveners and schoolmasters at York see Palliser 1982a: 103; Clark 1949: 79.
[185] Anglin 1983: chap. 4.
[186] MacGrath 1975: 215–17; Grell 1989: 114.

Goodwin, who was 'eminent in educating youth in making them fit for merchants and trade and not a stranger to the mathematic'.[187] These teachers, who also wrote most of the handbooks, were drawn from several quarters, including former elementary schoolmasters, young merchants, moonlighting bookkeepers and scriveners and mathematicians who were often unwilling to admit that they had descended to business instruction.[188] John Kersey, whose prospectus included Italian double-entry accounting, surveying and navigation, told Sir Ralph Verney that he taught mathematics, not business.[189]

A few dreamers envisaged academic business schools. Gresham and Petty proposed institutions of higher education with a broad philosophical as well as a practical base which would graduate students in commerce.[190] William Dell wanted the Universities to teach languages, arithmetic and geography.[191] Brewster thought that university men made better leaders, but that their training was too narrow; he proposed to give young men five years' theoretical and practical training and £1,000 starting capital.[192] A few merchants did attend Oxford or Cambridge or an Inn before entering the business world.[193] A legal training was certainly useful for a merchant, but the subject matter of the Inns was too esoteric for businessmen, the cost was high and the tuition offered was hardly inspired.[194] The Universities taught mathematics, but their deficiencies as teaching institutions were such that they were hard put even to train clergymen.[195] Samuel Taylor was elected scholar of St John's, Oxford, but went instead to Smyrna as a merchant.[196]

The main problem was that education was imbued with values antipathetic to business. Pedantry, snobbery, licensed amateurism and religiosity, particularly when combined, proved unassailable obstacles to educational reform even during the Interregnum and after the Toleration Act.[197] The Dissenting Academies served as both schools and universities, but they were intended primarily to train ministers and their syllabus

[187] Lincs. AO Monson MS, Misc. Books 21; Watson 1900: 170–2.
[188] Taylor 1956: 114; Dafforne, *Apprentice Time Entertainer*; Bridges, *Vulgar Arithmetique*; Hodder, *Hodder's Arithmetic*.
[189] Watson 1909: 324–6; Verney, *Memoirs*, iii. 356.
[190] *Petty Papers*, i. 12; *Harl. Misc.* vi. 15; Redlich 1957: 38–9; Cole 1957: 5; Turnbull 1947: 51; Greaves 1979: 49; Capkora 1978.
[191] Dell, *Right Reformation*.
[192] Brewster, *Essays on Trade*, preface, vi; Everitt 1969: 43.
[193] Jordan 1942: 39; Sheridan 1951: app. 18; Foster in Jaher 1973: 125; Newdigate 1961: 8; BL Add. MS 4224, fo. 33; *HMC 14th Report*, app. 9, pp. 487–8.
[194] Prest 1967: 35; 1972: tables 10–11; Hasler 1982: 5.
[195] Charlton 1960–1: 38; Feingold 1984: 215.
[196] *Merchant Taylors School, Register*, p. vii.
[197] SP 105/109, no. 129; Cowie 1949: 52.

reflected that goal.[198] The numbers enrolled in educational institutions may have expanded, but the system remained fundamentally conservative. The sons of merchants who went to the Universities and Inns entered the Church and the law, not business.[199] The traditional division between the academic and the business world could not be bridged. Although it was recognized that businessmen were more than just clerks or artisans, there remained a fundamental gulf between the gentlemanly ideal of a liberal education and the vulgarity and stigma of a manual apprenticeship.[200] The emphatic rejection of utility even degraded arithmetic, geometry and astronomy, because they had practical applications.[201] The Universities and the Inns were designed to educate for leisure not for business.

One important substitute was the printed word. In addition to the moralistic works targeted at prentices, there was a veritable library of technical manuals on every conceivable subject – computational texts, glossaries, topographical and language dictionaries, atlases, writing handbooks, foreign phrase-books, legal formularies and anthologies of trades, some of them published in pocket size.[202] Sample documents and forms superseded the formularies of precedence formerly used by notaries. The literature on accounting expanded continuously.[203] Foreign guides could also be consulted for local practices, laws and information on currencies and exchange rates.[204] Many of these works were just omnivorous potboilers by professional scribblers, like Giles Jacob; George Peele, clerk at Christ's Hospital, larded his advice on commercial arithmetic with dialogues and verse.[205] But most manuals were orthodox and practical and were reprinted frequently; changes in technique can be detected by comparing editions.[206] Their length and lack of excitement is an important reminder of the dull but necessary routines of business.

198 Cragg 1957: 186–7; Hans 1951: chap. 1, 38–41; MacLachlan 1931: 21, 29; Wardle 1967: 432–3.

199 Holmes 1977: 95.

200 Lucas 1962: 456, 473.

201 Costello 1958.

202 Lambley 1929: 240; Bennett 1965: ii. 136–7, 161; Wright 1958: chap. 10; Hornbeak 1934: 3–32.

203 They are listed with reissues in the Kress Library catalogue and by Thomson & Yamey 1968; Yamey & Bywater 1982 and Parker 1980. See also Reeves 1960; Parker 1982; Vanes 1987: 19–22.

204 Each European country produced its own business literature on which English authors drew. Examples include Laporte, *Guide des négocians*; Ricard, *Traité général du commerce*; Gobain, *Le Commerce en son jour*; Desagulier, *Traité Général*; Marperger, *Der allzeit fertige Handels Korrespondent*.

205 Horne 1952: 7–8; Peele, *Minor Works*.

206 Roover 1949.

Training

In fact, the lessons of the classroom were less important than experience on the job in an apprenticeship. The great majority shared the view of William Petyt that pen men were unsuited to trade. When a Huguenot refugee approached the borough of Taunton to learn carding and said that he had been apprenticed to books, there was a spontaneous outburst of laughter.[207] The writing schools could teach the basic techniques, but it was by imitating the example of their masters and through contact with the everyday routines and problems of the real world that apprentices learned how to function.[208] Even those who could enter by patrimony often served an apprenticeship.[209] The great majority of businessmen, who were apprenticed young at seventeen to nineteen, started at the bottom among the undereducated tradesmen and were not fed, like university graduates, directly into the professional mills.[210]

The weakness of the system was that the transfer of skills depended too much on the quality of instruction of a particular master.[211] Blanch claimed that there were matters 'too secret to be taught to an Apprentice' and Josiah Child recommended that apprenticeship be abolished.[212] Diligent and dutiful masters were hard to find; parents outside the business world frequently selected badly owing to ignorance or the need to economize. Many of those who charged low fees were incompetent, negligent, dishonest or indifferent.[213] They used their prentices as cheap labour and errand boys, taught them little and dumped bad goods on them. Failure to provide an education was as common a complaint as physical maltreatment; the courts and the guilds heard many such cases.[214] The correspondence between parents and their children is replete with horror stories of such masters. Henry Norris claimed that his master had pocketed £5, but paid a scrivener only 8s. to teach him arithmetic and accounts for a few months; he was also farmed out to a merchant in Smyrna at a fraction of the premium which his father had paid.[215] The level of training was neither uniform nor consistent.

No doubt, the master was sometimes the victim and the apprentice the wrongdoer. Sanderson accused his prentice of extravagance, whoring,

[207] Fontaine, *Mémoires*, p. 235. [208] Curtis 1964: 60; Dunlop 1919: 179, 196.
[209] Ward, *Lives of Professors*, i. 6.
[210] Orphans were sometimes bound at fourteen or fifteen and the age of entry varied between London and the provincial towns. Brodsky 1993 has calculated an average age of 18.9 for 232 apprentices. [211] Tryon, *New Method Educating Children*, p. 83.
[212] Blanch, *Interest of England*, p. 57.
[213] Stephens, *Relief of Apprentices*; Hodges 1953: 15.
[214] *Warwickshire Quarter Sessions*, ix. 89; *Yorkshire West Riding Quarter Sessions*, p. 222; Pinchbeck 1973: i. 223–31; GLL MS 12017. [215] *Norris Papers*, pp. 10–12.

fighting, impudence, dishonesty, lying, conspiracy and assault, but it was Sanderson's quarrelsome and melancholy nature which was probably to blame.[216] Gentlemen prentices often treated their masters disrespectfully and zealous converts upbraided them for their spiritual shortcomings; Defoe thought that the inflation of premiums gave prentices a sense of self-importance and some of the accusations of embezzlement, carelessness and giving credit without authority must have been true.[217] Many masters were conscientious and gave their apprentices a solid start. Henry Stanford, when he feared a breach between England and Spain in 1702, sent his apprentice home so as 'not to expose his tender years ... to the Natives of this Country'.[218] As parents became more involved, the prentice was more protected; guilds and municipalities did intervene and examine masters and apprentices. The East India Company trained its employees and even employed teachers of Oriental languages with limited success.[219] At its best, the system did provide an opportunity to learn and a solid grounding in practical skills for the ambitious prentice.

A budding merchant had a different training from a craftsman.[220] He began by keeping the petty cash and was then allowed to make the monthly entries in the journal under the supervision of his master; ultimately he graduated from bookkeeping to posting to the ledger.[221] At the same time, he cut his teeth by collecting debts and handling the wharfingers or by travelling with his master's wares.[222] In 1641, George Warner sent his servant, Edward Halford, to Starkey to help in the packinghouse and learn languages and accounts. He suggested that Halford write up the sales weekly, copy the journal monthly and 'what else he shall think needful'.[223] Most prospective overseas merchants were sent abroad as a factor or supercargo and learned from foreign merchants, with whom they lodged, as well as from exposure to the international market.[224] Cranfield began by visiting the fairs to buy and Paul Bayning began as a cape merchant.[225] Young men frequently went into partnership with a more experienced merchant and most partnerships had one dominant member who usually carried the business.[226] Sir Paul Pindar

[216] Sanderson, *Travels*, pp. 24–31; the apprentice seems to have prospered. Another example among many is Lincs. AO, Ancaster MS 9/A/9a–q, letter from Thomas Mitchell at Leghorn.

[217] Defoe, *Great Law Subordination*, p. 13; Rees 1933: 120; Clarke 1940: 52; Cliffe 1984: 108; Kunze & Brautigam: 138, 149.

[218] Bod. Dep. MS C.23, fo. 1.

[219] Keeling & Bonner, *Journal*, p. 119; Chaudhuri 1965: 82; Furber 1977: 299. Boxer 1957: 134 shows that the Dutch had similar problems.

[220] Beloff 1942: 39; MacFarlane 1970: 210.

[221] *Wynn Papers Calendar*, pp. 81–2.

[222] *Portsmouth Borough Sessions Papers*, p. 72.

[223] SP 46/85, no. 66; SP 46/84/93, 10 Aug. 1641; Claypoole, *Letter Book*, p. 186.

[224] Morse 1921: 199–203; *English Adventurers*, pp. 72, 129; Applebee 1979: 36.

[225] Croft 1983: 252–4.

[226] Bright 1858: 186.

was apprenticed at seventeen to a firm of Italian currant merchants in Lombard Street and a year later went to Venice as a commission agent where, at the end of his time, he traded on his own account.[227] The north-eastern merchants sent their apprentices to the Baltic and Holland, those in the south to Germany and Holland, and the western merchants to France and Spain.[228] Sir Richard Hoare's son went to Genoa, Amsterdam and Hamburg and was forced to write and speak French and Dutch by Mr Hall, a merchant friend.[229]

The art of merchandising could only be learned by making mistakes, by trial and error.[230] Merchants both taught themselves and each other; several successful businessmen were never apprenticed.[231] A merchant needed commonsense and astuteness rather than rational cognitive skills, insight rather than calculation, practicality rather than cleverness and discriminating judgement rather than formal knowledge.[232] Better accounting, tighter controls and greater knowledge might have improved business decisions, but it is doubtful whether greater sophistication in technique would have made much difference. The basic skills were related to need and never became redundant. The merchant was a man of action whose marketing depended fundamentally not on logic or intellect, but on instinct, experience and flair, keenness and vigour. Business was still more of an art or craft than a science.

Commitment

Knowledge is not an imperative to action and a merchant had to be willing as well as able.[233] Business demanded singlemindedness, intensity and steadfastness of purpose; a merchant had to accept responsibility for his own economic salvation. Hunger is more visceral than dreams of glory or salvation, but necessity by itself is an inadequate incentive; those ensnared in poverty can easily become resigned, apathetic and fatalistic. Some merchants were defeatist and just abandoned the struggle; the

227 Goss 1933: 238.

228 BL Cotton MS Otho E. viii, fo. 41; *Newcastle Merchant Adventurers' Records*, i. p. xxiv; Riden 1987: 193; Trosse, *Life*, p. 62; Healey 1992: 21; Burley 1957: 328; Byrds, *Correspondence*, introduction; Donnen 1931: 75; Patten in Clark & Souden 1987: 99; Wilson 1971: 209; Kirby 1986: 155; Moir 1957: 257.

229 Woodbridge 1969: 784–5.

230 Whether business was a learned skill or an acquired art provoked the same debate in contemporary handbooks as in the modern literature on business schools and professional management. See Johnson 1964: 142.

231 ESRO 145/11. Jeake bought a copy of the *Accomptant's Guide* for 5s; *Bankes Family Records*, p. 3.

232 Thomas Isham described his father as 'a wise man though altogether unlearned'; see *John Isham*, p. 72. Defoe, *Complete English Tradesman*, ii. chap. 2.

233 Kardiner 1939: 463; S. Pollard in Melling & Barry 1992: 147.

initiative to terminate an indenture often came from the apprentice and many just ran away.[234] A merchant needed a driving, obsessive personality. Richard Norris sent his son to sea, because he was thought diligent, prudent and industrious in accounting: 'if he seems to have any defect it is want of spirit'.[235] 'Resolution', as Fuller put it, 'hath driven success before it'.[236] A businessman had to be self-directed, to lead not to follow; it was persistence which enabled the English merchants in Sweden to overcome local obstructionism.[237] One explanation for business success is the dynamism, enthusiasm and will-power of self-made men who founded, managed and identified with their businesses.

To function efficiently, a merchant needed to accumulate beyond his capacity to consume. Because business was both personal and governed by profit, merchants were by definition economic individualists. 'The chief end of business of trade', wrote Barbon, 'is to make a profitable bargain'.[238] The great majority of contemporary portraits of businessmen emphasize their greed: 'his money is his Ultima Perfecta the very Ratio formalis of his Soul . . . tantalous like he is never satisfied'.[239] Defoe, while travelling in Norfolk, described, 'every man busy on the main affair of life, that is to say, getting money'.[240] Although universally condemned for cold bloodedness, a businessman was expected to be ruthless in pricing and debt collection. Property was valued above persons because capital was easily exhausted, whereas human labour was replaceable. As the Quaker, Sir John Barnard, put it, 'in case of property men alter their very nature' and 'our very friendships are but a barter of service'.[241] The term 'adventurer' was applied to those who adventured their property, not to those that risked their lives.

Once the basic necessities of food and shelter had been met, it was wants which sustained motivation; a little whet the appetite for more. Utility pulls and ambition pushes.[242] The drive for wealth may be rationally pursued, but the end is conditioned by a mixture of non-rational goals and motives.[243] A businessman needed an objective beyond mere survival, a commitment to self-improvement and advancement.[244] The required level of reinforcement increased with age. The young, travelling factor on the bottom rung of the ladder needed less encouragement than the comfortable, sedentary merchant, who had less reason to exert himself. What distinguished men like Edward Colston, Cranfield, Sir Josiah Child

234 Ben Amos 1988: 55, 63; Fletcher 1988: 219. 235 Poole 1962: 69.
236 Fuller, *Holy State*, ii. 48. 237 Malone 1977: 279, 386.
238 Barbon, *Discourse of Trade*, p. 6; Jeaffreson, *Papers*, i. 246.
239 *Harl. Misc.*, iv. 225; Stoughton, *Arraignment of Covetousness*, p. 11; Ward, *Reformer*, pp. 17–18. 240 Defoe, *Tour*, i. 72. 241 Barnard, *Present for Apprentice*, pp. 25, 38.
242 Kroef 1961: 41. 243 Lauterbach 1959: 135; Kardiner 1945: 107, 163.
244 Kaldor in *International Congress Underdeveloped Areas* 1954; Lofthouse 1976.

and Sir John Banks was that they continued to strive even when they were rich.[245] They were driven by ego to engage in predatory competition for control of resources and distribution of rewards.

The acquisitive spirit is not, however, a universal dictate of reason and its strength has always varied in intensity and scope. All cultures maximize satisfaction and have business relationships. But some have had no clear concept of personal gain or deferred wants; they have adopted the gift as their method of exchange, deliberately rejected private possessions and refused to identify wealth with status.[246] Merchants did not simply seek to maximize their profits or operate in a vacuum. They were often more interested in security and regularity and continuity of income than in the highest possible yield. They sought to shelter themselves from economic forces in a competitive world through the family and familial institutions, like the guilds and Companies. Unlike an industrialist, a merchant was not constrained by fixed assets which would have to be written off in the event of withdrawal and he could easily turn rentier. Even Defoe recognized the curse of Midas: ''Tis time to leave off and have done, 'tis Time to leave labouring for the World, when he has the World, as they call it, in a string'.[247] Quaker merchants were enjoined to resist the temptation 'to think of a higher Trade and a finer House'.[248] Andrew Pitt set a limit to his fortune and retired after thirty years; the successful Joseph Pike deliberately restrained his efforts and 'never inclined or strove to be rich'.[249]

As Spinoza and Halifax pointed out, 'all men certainly seek their self-advantage but seldom as reason dictates'; profit was not self-justifying and self-interest could be both an end and a motive.[250] The individualism of the Chesapeake was different from that of New England.[251] Frequently, businessmen did not know what they wanted. A diversity of alternative goals made it difficult to define self-interest and channel effort

[245] Prestwich 1966: 53–7, 93, 587.

[246] Herskovits 1952: 24, 42, 205; Dermigny 1964: i. 60; Hobson 1954: 28–9; Evans-Pritchard 1962: 27. The intellectual gymnastics to which disciples of Polányi (Polányi *et al.* 1957) will resort to deny the ubiquity of markets and economic self-interest are well illustrated in the debate over how New England became a capitalist economy: see Mutch 1980: 862; Perkins 1989: 166–7; Nash in Greene & Pole 1984: 236; Breen 1986: 481.

[247] Defoe, *Compleat English Tradesman*, i. 284; Defoe takes an opposite line in his *Essay on Projects*, p. 7; Dijkstra 1987: 175.

[248] Rigge, *Brief and Serious Warning*, p. 10; *Constancy in the Truth*, pp. 235–6.

[249] Lloyd 1950: 77; Braithwaite 1919: 501.

[250] Spinoza, *Political Works*, p. 93; Downie in Skinner 1976: 160; Anspach 1972: 182; Godelin 1966; Heilbronner 1956: 20–2; Hollander 1977. Rational self-interest is of course assumed by neo-classical economic historians: see Shepherd & Walton 1972: 9; Fieldes 1968: 169.

[251] Breen 1980: 109. Staves 1990: 223 argues that bourgeois culture is schizophrenic, but this diagnosis better fits the inherent contradictions between Marxist theory and the real world.

in one direction. Social and family pressures were also influential.[252] Most merchants did not wish to be alienated from or rejected by their own society. Property was acquired in order to emulate others and achieve temporal fame. Sir Thomas More and Hobbes thought that the driving passion was pride and not acquisitiveness.[253] It was ambition rather than greed, miserliness or physical indulgence, which kept the rich and successful in the counting-house.

The restless, preoccupied striving of the merchant, in this world rather than the next, reflected an intense desire to excel; he wanted to see evidence of personal accomplishment and have the satisfaction of exercising skill and ingenuity. A businessman also needed a romantic sense of adventure to counter the boredom and monotony of routine; several identified vicariously with the exploits of the Elizabethan seadogs.[254] Business could be an exciting sport, which made the adrenalin flow, as well as a prosaic source of income.[255] A merchant functioned best if he made an emotional investment and identified business with life, if he derived pleasure from making events happen. 'It is my duty and function to be fervent in my vocation', said the merchant in *Westward Hoe*.[256] Thomas Pitt was pleased with his son, Robert, 'for he sticks to business and loves it'.[257]

A businessman also had to master anxiety and fear. Heigham Bright was 'melancholy but not such a degree as to doe me an injury'.[258] Mental stress could lead to apoplexy, melancholy and madness or to gambling mania. William Gilbert was called in to examine Rowland Lee, who had fallen into distraction.[259] Several businessmen fitted the dire image projected by the medieval preachers – so tormented 'that at night they have no rest ... they have dreams of plenty and money brok sleep'.[260] Although depression from high stress was fairly common, madness was fairly rare and only five out of 1,000 prentices and seven merchants between 1570 and 1600 are known to have committed suicide.[261] When it occurred, it was usually prompted by exposure of fraud or the disgrace of financial failure: Jeremy Sambrook junior, accountant to the East India

[252] For a definition of property see Goody 1962: 287.

[253] Thomas in Brown 1965: 190; Colman 1972: 135; Lamb 1974: 682; More, *Works*, p. 188.

[254] Niccholl, *Discourse of Marriage*, p. 182.

[255] Ellis 1981b: 119. On competition as a game see Knight 1935: 65; Neumann & Morgenstern 1944; Piaget 1971: 104–5.

[256] Dekker, *Dramatic Works*, ii. 331.

[257] C110/81, letter 1 Feb. 1700.

[258] Bright 1858: 188.

[259] *Character of Honest Merchant*, p. 6; Hunter & McAlpine 1963: 65.

[260] Owst 1933: 352; Sanderson, *Travels*, p. 18. Merchants occasionally reported dreams about money and debts: see *Eliot Papers*, i. 74.

[261] Stevenson 1987–8: 225, 249, 267; MacDonald & Murphy 1990: 270, 427, table 7.1; MacDonald 1981: 87, chap. 3, table 2.4; 1986: 75. To avoid forfeiture, verdicts on suicides were usually 'non compos mentis'. E178/7099 is one example of an inquisition into the goods of a merchant who had killed himself.

Company, Sir Stephen Evance, James Milner, Alderman Hoyle and Sir Randolph Knipe were numbered among the casualties and Sir Basil Firebrace made an attempt.[262]

Self-reliance and toughness were vital to survival; losses, including loss of life, had to be accepted with equanimity.[263] Merchants who resided abroad needed the inner resources to withstand loneliness and isolation in the distant outposts of Turkey, India or Japan.[264] The long delays, ennui and physical discomfort which had to be endured while travelling by sea or living in tropical climates cannot easily be appreciated.[265] Although the Companies, concerned about the corrupting effects of contact with debauchery and heresy, attempted to create the routines of English society in the factories, there was little choice of company and much contention.[266] The same sense of isolation occurred even closer at hand, in the Baltic, Spain or the Canaries.[267] The families of merchants frequently did not know where they were and news from abroad was slow and intermittent. Many, like Thomas Hill who died at Lisbon, never saw England again.[268] Businessmen had to ignore pain, separation and the possibility of sudden death and concentrate on their task.

It was precisely because they were not masters of events that they organized meticulously and were determined to maximize their advantage. Their self-centredness, ruthlessness and callousness sprang in part from insecurity. Fear, suppressed by self-discipline, could reinforce assertiveness and generate aggressive risk-taking.[269] But fear of the unknown could also lead to nihilism and existentialism; motivation could easily be undermined by uncertainty. 'The burned Child', George Sitwell repeated, 'dreads the fyre'.[270] Persistent self-doubt led to indecisiveness, lethargy and submission before events. Fear of falling behind could cause foreboding and provoke defensive strategies designed to minimize failure.

In business, as in religion, success itself could produce adverse reactions. On the one hand, it could breed self-indulgence, vanity and supreme egotism; on the other hand, it could aggravate personal insecurity.[271] Achievement could evoke remorse for exploitation or awake a latent sense of justice or provoke regret at sacrificing alternative styles of life for

262 SP 9/247/54, 1677; Le Neve, *Pedigrees of Knights*, p. 435; Morrill *et al.* 1993: 223.

263 On attitudes to death and disease see Wunderli & Broce 1989: 275; Beaty 1970: 217; Porter 1987.

264 Farrington 1991; Masters 1988: 79.

265 Kupperman 1984: 239.

266 Hedges, *Diary*, ii. p. cccvi.

267 KAO U.119/C.4, Masters correspondence; SP 110/14, letter 1 Sept. 1689; SP 437, correspondence of Prestwick Eaton; Mathew 1951: 172–5.

268 Hill 1904: 122.

269 Namier 1962: 178; Atkinson 1957: 371 makes an interesting distinction between strong achievement motivation, which assumes intermediate risks, and fear of failure which pursues either safe or speculative courses.

270 Sitwell, *Letters*, p. 124.

271 Rothenberg 1975: 62 discusses predestinarian dualism. See also Cohen 1986: 110.

business; many 'seem prosperous yet cannot obtain the jewel of internal peace'.[272] Disillusionment could follow the accumulation of wealth while the conflict between acquisitive and traditional values could create *anomie*. Old age, *Selbstunsicherheit* and affective longings could also undermine business dynamism, create doubts and engender passive responses or withdrawal. Many grew weary of business, disinvested, settled for lower yields, institutionalized their profits and sought a quieter life at a lower output of energy.

In the face of cold reality, a merchant could easily doubt himself. Those who sustained the courage of their convictions and a sense of superiority, who believed that they would prevail, were the fittest in a Darwinian struggle for survival. Optimism about the future was crucial; 'when Buissnes is at worst, it must be better'.[273] Inflated assurance and wishful thinking could, of course, be dangerous; many merchants muted self-criticism and just believed what they wanted to believe.[274] 'Foolish hopes', wrote Steele, 'are more fatal than groundless fear'.[275] It was important to recognize, accept and learn from reverses and not attempt to conceal them by false rationalization, to recognize the magnitude of problems, but not to condone failure. When John Pynchon regretted a purchase, he wished that 'I would have been asleep'.[276] A businessman needed confidence in his own judgement rather than the advice of others.

Merchants continued to trade under adverse conditions, either because they could not disinvest or because they hoped for better times. Indeed they could not have functioned if they had accepted that they were completely at the mercy of events; they had to entertain the illusion that they could weight the odds and succeed. 'If my expectation of Gold fails me', wrote Pettit, 'tis but the error of the whole world, who still are Deluded with hopes of more then ever they obtained, it is only the part of a wise man to guide his hopes soe neare as may be within a Probability of attainment, but whether mine are Soe or noe only my selfe and time can explain'.[277] Businessmen chose not to dwell on the risks, which they either ignored or neglected to calculate. They assumed that they would gain on the swings what they lost on the roundabouts.

Nature and nurture

The inner qualities required for business are hard to catalogue because they were so diffuse and contradictory. They certainly included a capacity

[272] Hirschman 1977: 59; Gwin, *Journal*, p. 43; Robinson 1972: 62.
[273] *Bolton Letters*, p. 133. [274] Keynes 1939: 162.
[275] Steele, *Religious Tradesman*, p. 54. [276] *Pynchon Papers*, p. 42.
[277] IOL Factors Record Misc. XV, letter to John Child; BL Add. MS 43730, fo. 19.

to inspire trust and leadership, a sanguine temperament, humour, discretion, commonsense, compromise, stamina, tolerance, alertness, patience, tenacity, a methodical approach and the ability to concentrate.[278] Each trait of personality was, however, double-edged and subject to attrition, reversal and excess. The model merchant embraced the middle state eulogized by so many preachers between Napoleonic dreams and fatalism, between aggression and inertia, between certainty and doubt, between resolve and stubbornness, between recklessness and cowardice, between firmness and laxity, between procrastination and haste, between excess of confidence and failure of will. A merchant had to be well adjusted and able to weather success as well as failure. This required stability of temperament and the ability to adapt constantly to new circumstances. The ideal merchant neither embraced his own society too closely nor distanced himself too far. He was neither obsessed by profit, nor distracted from his main purpose. His self-assertiveness was balanced by recognition of the claims of others in society.

Personality certainly acted as an autonomous factor. Children who were either introverted and inclined toward meditation and reflection or who were too impulsive or passionate, were both unlikely to develop the necessary practicality, self-control and self-direction.[279] Genetic inheritance is too random to serve as an explanation for differences in aptitude. But businessmen do seem to have selected themselves and to have been born, not made.[280] Behaviour is, however, conditioned and reinforced positively and negatively by environment. Although upbringing can only develop existing potential, child-rearing and schooling during adolescence do inculcate behaviour patterns and reinforce motivation.[281]

Children were definitely stimulated by the example of their parents. The nuclear family seems to have instilled self-help and a desire for achievement, though size of family and birth order were also major factors. Children were detached from their families early in life when they were sent away to school or apprenticed; although relations frequently served as masters, fathers did not usually fulfil this role.[282] Competition was also encouraged between boys at school.[283] Their characters were therefore formed both by their masters and by their own peer group of

[278] Flinn 1962: 25; BL Stowe MS 745, iii. fo. 145. [279] Christensen 1989: 689–709.

[280] Tawney believed that men had no inherent propensity to barter or seek profit; see Wilber 1974: 257. For a corrective see Chapman 1980: 55–6.

[281] Erikson 1963: 112; Strout 1968: 284, 296. Although the evidence and methodology employed by MacClelland 1961 and 1969 and by Atkinson 1957 and 1958 are faulty, their thesis is not inherently implausible. See Vannerman in Ayal 1973; Beier 1975: 243; Locke, *Thoughts on Education*, pp. 133, 145, 236; Burton, *Anatomy of Melancholia*, p. 284.

[282] In Bristol only 1.9 per cent of boys were apprenticed to their fathers, 1542–65: see Yarbrough 1979: 68. [283] O'Day 1982: 52–3.

fellow apprentices and factors. In his upbringing, a merchant had several examples to imitate and follow.

Personality is also culturally determined. Exclusion from traditional society did help to generate independent attitudes and drive.[284] The overseas merchant, although he sometimes took his culture with him, was also subject to alien influences and was freed from cultural restraints. Younger sons had a special incentive to make their own way; they shared the values of the picaresque heroes of fiction and the alien immigrants.[285] Robert Burton and Donaldson thought that the cult of idleness among the gentry led to boredom and melancholia and made them unfit for business.[286] But the ambitious and conscientious son of a landed family was probably better fitted for commerce than many sons of merchants and professional men with inherited wealth.

Success in business depended on reciprocity between multiple and contradictory methods and objectives. What were virtues in one context were vices in another, particularly if taken to extremes. Mastery of technique was vital, but it was no substitute for judgement of men; planning and calculation were important, but flexibility and resilience in the face of changing circumstances were equally required. Self-interest was a useful trait as long as it was not socially destructive. Insecurity was a valuable incentive, if it did not create too much anxiety and discourage risk-taking. Competitive instincts discouraged complacency, but many ventures depended on co-operation.

Acquisitiveness by itself could not guarantee success. The high failure rate is an important reminder that making money was not simply a question of determination. But neither necessity nor opportunity alone could produce the will to succeed. Individual egotism was essential, though the best incentive was self-respect and the satisfaction of exercising talents. An epitaph on Fraunces Benison, in verse, listed as his distinguishing qualities audacity, linguistic ability, diligence, honesty and benevolence.[287] Because it was so personal, business was a viable prospect only for those who had the right temperament and who could master a variety of difficult skills.

284 Perkin in Finberg 1962: 77–9.
285 Finch 1956: xix; Pirenne in Bendix & Lipset 1966: 502; Thirsk 1969: 360.
286 Burton, *Anatomy of Melancholia*, p. 439; Simon 1964: 505; Gardiner 1977: 388.
287 Awdeley, *Epitaph*.

7 Politics and government

What were the political principles and affiliations of merchants and can they be credited with an independent and coherent agenda? Did they do more than defend their economic interests and how significant a role did they play in national and regional politics? It is not easy to reconstruct the political views of the silent majority who did not take part in the theoretical debates over the constitution or formulate an ideology; the evidence is strongly biased towards the committed. Participation in government is much easier to assess. Businessmen were the primary managers of the quasi-public chartered Companies and they served alongside professional administrators in a variety of government offices at both the central and local levels. Which branches of government did they find particularly attractive, how relevant were their business methods and experience and what influence could they exert on policy?

Political ideology

Businessmen were to be found on both sides of every controversy and a minority positioned themselves at each extreme of the ideological spectrum. National issues spilled over into the overseas factories and urban communities. Merchants identified liberty with property rights and opposed arbitrary actions by the executive; they favoured the rule of law and government by Crown in Parliament and they resided 'where they are most secure'.[1] But property was a term with many meanings and businessmen disagreed about the most appropriate division of power and responsibility between competing institutions.[2] Their political loyalties were not just determined by their occupation, wealth or type of trade; on the great issues of the day, the business community divided vertically and not horizontally.[3]

[1] Reynell, *True English Interest*, p. 60.

[2] Property was a juridical and not an economic term and no concept of absolute property rights existed: see Tully 1980: 131; Dickinson 1977: 89–90; Aylmer 1980; Pococke 1986: 56.

[3] Farnell 1977: 658. Brenner 1993 argues that political factions can be identified with particular areas of trade, but the connections are too elastic to sustain his argument.

Before the outbreak of the Civil War, many merchants participated in the efforts within and outside Parliament to defend the status quo against the innovations of the Crown. A few, like Henry Robinson, even theorized about the constitution; Henry Parker entertained the notions of popular consent and Parliamentary sovereignty.[4] Because taxation of trade by the Early Stuarts raised fundamental constitutional questions, merchants were inevitably drawn into the debate; the case of ship-money was engineered by the Providence Island Company.[5]

The City always sought a harmonious relationship with the Court; the London Aldermen and the great merchants who benefited from monopolies, domestic concessions and revenue franchises were natural allies of the Crown. But royal actions, such as the licensing of Cokayne and Sir William Courteen, angered the export Companies, which shifted their allegiance after 1625, though they rallied round at the abyss.[6] The City was alienated from the Crown by conflict over local issues such as royal interference in the suburbs and royal exactions in the Ulster Plantation.[7] It was the refusal of the City on sound economic grounds to raise money to fight the Scots which precipitated the recall of Parliament in 1640. A majority of businessmen supported the early actions of the Long Parliament and the assault on Strafford.

When the intransigence of Charles forced a choice between military resistance and forfeiting the gains of 1640–1, 72 per cent of the merchant MPs supported Parliament.[8] But neither London nor provincial merchants flocked to the Parliamentary cause.[9] Norwich split evenly between King and Parliament and Hull had its Royalist merchants.[10] The Grocers refused to take down their royal arms during the Interregnum and Sir Abraham Reynardiston was deposed as Lord Mayor, in 1649, because he refused to make public the Act abolishing monarchy.[11] Others were driven back into the Royalist camp during the 1640s by growing political and religious radicalism. London was frequently blamed for the Civil War, but it took an internal revolution in the City to put the Parliamentary Puritans into power.[12]

The majority of merchants adopted a neutral, non-doctrinaire position until they were forced to commit themselves. They sought regularity and consistency of government and did not welcome the disruption created by

[4] Judson 1949: 409; Jordan 1942: 2, 213; Firth 1907: 21; Mendle 1989: 515.

[5] Sharpe 1978: 264–5; Bond 1977.

[6] Ashton 1964: 586.

[7] Moody 1939: 271, 366, 385; Barnes 1970: 340; *Stuart Proclamations*, ii. no. 234; Smuts 1991: 149.

[8] Antler 1972: 155; Brenner 1993: table 7:1 is unable to identify the political affiliations of the majority of export merchants.

[9] Pearl 1961: 283, apps. 1–2; Howell 1979; Richardson 1992: 25, 52.

[10] Gillett & MacMahon 1980: 175–6.

[11] Heal 1869: 19.

[12] Pearl 1961: 277; Malcolm 1981: 301.

the aggressiveness of either Crown or Parliament. A factor wrote to his principal in 1642: 'God send us good news and unite the King and Parliament.'[13] Royalist merchants were reluctant to leave London and their businesses, in 1642, and many stayed and suffered financially; Sir Andrew King paid to return from exile in 1648. It is not surprising that the *Humble Petition and Advice* should be introduced by a Merchant Adventurer or supported by a Coventry draper like Robert Beake.[14]

Radicals did emerge once the conflict escalated, even among the prosperous merchants, and they were not confined to London.[15] A hard core of merchants, many of them younger sons of gentlemen, subscribed to the model of the 'Commonwealth', as exemplified by the Venetian and Dutch Republics; twelve merchants were regicides.[16] But only a minority of businessmen were active in Common Council and most of the radicals did not emerge from the established magistracy or from the chartered Companies. The Levellers included small businessmen such as John Lilburne; Winstanley was a failed businessman.[17] The Fifth Monarchists and Muggletonians exploited the insecurity of self-employed tradesmen.[18] But the great majority of merchants rejected radical views and few actively supported the Protectorate. Republicans, like Bethel, considered that 'arbitrary government (that must be maintained by the sword) . . . are altogether inconsistent with and enemies to trade and Commerce'.[19] A more practical reason was Cromwell's lack of interest in economic questions.[20] Many of the new leaders were connected with the business world, but the Protectorate neglected business interests.

The business community generally welcomed the Restoration to which even convinced Cromwellians, like Sir Patience Ward, conformed.[21] The influence of the republicans waned and many went into exile.[22] Echoes of the 1640s could still be heard: Samuel Lewys, in 1663, was accused of saying that the King would leave like his father because of the Hearth Tax.[23] The London Whigs of the 1670s were substantial businessmen who drew on the radical civic ideology and political tactics of the 1640s.[24] A few businessmen were attracted to new radical sects, like the Quakers, but the latter were quietist in politics. Memories of the 1640s, however, kept many merchants in the Stuart camp, though fears of economic

[13] SP 46/84, no. 252, 20 Sept. 1642. [14] Elliott 1981: 171.

[15] Grant in Fisher 1989; the radicals who came to power in London in 1649 are listed by Farnell 1967: 24; Andrews 1991: 58; Pearl 1961: 177–89; Kirby 1970: 103–4, 117.

[16] Sachse 1973: 83–4; MacIntosh 1982: 204; Whitbrook 1938–9: 151; Elliott 1984: 129.

[17] Gibb 1947: 20–2, 82; Gregg 1961; Davis 1976: 92–3; Alsop 1979b: 73; Dalton 1991: 973.

[18] Dow 1985: 33. [19] Bethel, *Observations on Letter*, p. 16; MacHenry 1984: 258.

[20] Prestwich 1950: 120.

[21] Cromwell, *Writings and Speeches*, iv. 803; Behrens 1941: 53–4, 71.

[22] Walker 1948: 123; Ramsey 1949: 206. [23] Harris 1987: 61.

[24] Krey in Harris 1988: 16, 134, 137.

competition could be combined with anti-Popery in their attitude towards France.[25] In Norwich the grocers switched from Parliamentary Puritanism to Royalist Anglicanism, as did the Moore family in Liverpool which had supported the execution of Charles I.[26]

During the Exclusion Crisis, apprentices were to be found in Tory as well as Whig mobs in London; some 40 per cent of the liverymen in the 1680s, particularly in the lesser Companies, were Tory.[27] Because a major political priority for Dissenting merchants, after 1662, was toleration, it sometimes made tactical sense for them to support the Crown rather than Parliament. Business played a minimal role in the events of 1688, which was an aristocratic coup with foreign help and not a bourgeois revolution.[28] James made a last-minute personal appeal to London merchants, but it is doubtful whether he seriously intended to rely on the urban magistrates rather than the gentry.[29]

After 1688, although party labels are inexact, business was split fairly evenly between Whigs and Tories; the domestic merchants, small-scale manufacturers and old-monied men tended to be Tories and the financiers Whigs, but there was no clear division; a minority in every business institution belonged to the other party and businessmen frequently crossed party lines.[30] Whig radicalism declined in London in the 1690s and the alliance of big business and landed grandees in the Junto jettisoned revolutionary principles except for religious toleration and the Protestant Succession; the Tories became the radical party and inherited the mantle of the Old Whigs.[31] There were few Jacobites among the merchants who were bound to the Hanoverian Succession by the Financial Revolution.

Throughout the century, merchants of every political and religious persuasion were prepared to act on their beliefs. In London, political consciousness was created in the guilds, Companies, ward clubs, shops and taverns.[32] Several merchants risked their property and freedom by opposing both the Early and Later Stuarts. Bates, Vassal and Chambers suffered heavy financial penalties and others were imprisoned by the Court of Aldermen for refusal to pay their assessments towards royal loans. In 1628, there were substantial merchants among those who broke into the Customs warehouse and released goods which had been seized.[33]

Probably egged on by their masters, apprentices during the Interreg-

25 Miller 1985: 53; Priestley 1956: 211. 26 Evans 1979: 193; Morton 1889: 157.

27 Harris 1987: 164. 28 J. R. Jones 1972: 11, 15, 137, 254; Speck 1988: 7.

29 Beddard 1988: 34.

30 Holmes 1987: lii, 169; Mullett in C. Jones 1987: 133; Krey 1985: 32, 126, 153–7, 167, table 4.1; Speck 1970: app. B; MacHattie 1951: 297.

31 Krey in Schwoerer 1992: 215, table 12/1–2; Goldie 1980: n.23; Miller 1985: 67.

32 Pearl 1979b: 6. 33 Popofsky 1990: 30, 59; Woodward 1967: 88.

num joined the London mobs which agitated both for radical measures and against the New Model Army.[34] They served in the Civil War on both sides.[35] John Taylor, son of a gentleman and a Bristol apprentice, fought for the King and was killed at the siege of Bristol.[36] Samuel Priestley left his apprenticeship to fight with Fairfax; when his mother tried to dissuade him, he replied, 'if I die it is in a good cause' and he did succumb to a fever, after rescuing a wounded man in water.[37] Nehemiah Wharton wrote a gripping account to his former master of his military experiences in the Army.[38] Apprentices continued to participate in political demonstrations after the Restoration. One was hung, drawn and quartered in 1668 and five were pilloried in the 1670s.[39] But demonstrations often served as an antidote to boredom; apprentices probably participated with the same youthful ebullience that led them to riot against aliens or whorehouses on feast days.

Mature merchants also risked their lives. Sir Alexander Davison died in defence of Newcastle during the Civil War.[40] Sir Marmaduke Rawdon left his business to join Charles at the age of sixty-one, in 1643, raised a regiment of foot and died during the siege of Faringdon.[41] Robert Abbott was involved in a Royalist plot in 1643 and two merchants were hanged in Bristol for planning to betray the city.[42] Merchant ship-masters struggled to run their business and serve in the Navy of the Interregnum.[43] Alderman Henry Cornish was hung, drawn and quartered for his role in the Rye House Plot in which several merchants were implicated.[44] Others were executed and transported for involvement in Monmouth's Rebellion.[45]

Some merchants certainly wanted a share in power and even those without such ambitions could not ignore politics without endangering their livelihood. The chartered Companies were bound to the Crown and Privy Council; a glass manufacturer could not avoid the battles over patents. The merchants were divided over Bate's Case because they were anxious to avoid trouble.[46] Since the central administration generated a market for goods and services, businessmen had actively to nurse their Court connections. Those who benefited from grants of monopoly,

[34] S. R. Smith in Slack 1984; Clark 1976a: 372; Burke in Reay 1985a: 53; Harris 1989: 478; *Remonstrance of Apprentices*; *Vox Juvenalis*, p. 2; Lindley 1983: 110; Manning 1988: chap. 8.

[35] Gentles 1983: 290; S. R. Smith 1972: 576; Farr 1968: 8; Gough, *History of Myddle*, p. 11.

[36] *Bristol Deposition Books 1643–47*, pp. 254–5.

[37] *Yorkshire Diaries*, ii. 25–6.

[38] *Letters from Subaltern Officer*, pp. 310–34.

[39] MacInnes 1982; Harris 1989: 17–19, 234–41.

[40] Hall 1933: 261.

[41] Rawdon, *Memoirs*, pp. 315–16.

[42] Abbott 1956: 36; Carlton 1992: 170.

[43] Capp 1989: 197.

[44] Milne 1951: 97; Ashcraft 1986: chap. 8.

[45] Earle 1977: 203; Little 1956: 228; Clifton 1984: 269–71; Pinney, *Letters*, p. 19.

[46] Croft 1987a: 537–8.

lenders to the Crown, tax-farmers and office-holders were inextricably bound to royal government.[47] Even after the Farms were abandoned, government contractors for the armed services were closely linked with loan and debt management; great merchants, stockholders and Company directors could hardly ignore City politics or the colonial lobbies. To a businessman, politics, whether through the Crown or Parliament, was the pursuit of profit by other means just as foreign policy was an instrument of trade.

The business community was consistently divided into 'ins' and 'outs'. It was impossible to regulate and protect trade without benefiting one economic group at the expense of another. A merchant's attitude to monopoly was naturally dictated by his chance of acquiring one; the shopkeepers and tradesmen could be attracted to political radicalism as a means to assert their independence of the merchants.[48] Those excluded from the inner circles of government or from the London-based chartered Companies were prepared to oppose the central government. In London the old division between merchants and financiers became even more pronounced after 1688.[49] Opposition groups were bound by kinship and every businessman owed allegiance not to the nation, but to his own Company, industry, town and area of trade. When merchants entered regional and national politics, it was to defend their particular economic interests rather than to promote a cause. They had orders of priority and personal preferences rather than passionate enthusiasm. The merchants and financiers who came to the fore under the Protectorate were practical men and many of them survived to be numbered among the business elite of the Restoration. Businessmen often preferred to maintain a low profile and refrain from political comment.[50]

English politics alternated between periods of consensus and moments of crisis in which personalities and particular issues came to the fore.[51] But there was no permanent political division between business and landed society; the majority of disputes occurred within the business community and involved distribution of rewards. Merchants would resist any government, institution or party which threatened their lives and property, but their fealty did not extend to embracing one absolute truth. Businessmen were natural Trimmers with a disdain for political ideology, willing to function under any regime which did not actively persecute them and opposed to confrontational politics. There were more turncoats and time-servers than martyrs.

[47] Ashton 1979: 156. [48] *Advice to Liverymen London*, p. 7.
[49] Woodhead 1965: apps. 4, 6–7. [50] GLL MS 5105, fo. 41; Sharp 1989: 14.
[51] Scott 1988a: 466.

Interests

The business community was an amalgamation of many competing interests which could not all be satisfied. The shippers focused on volume, the merchants on value, the artisans on labour-intensive goods; the export merchants wanted freedom to export raw materials and unfinished cloth, the wholesalers freedom to import goods directly; domestic producers wanted a captive market for their products. London fought with the outports and the Companies fought both with the independent traders and with each other, since monopolies were defined by geography, not by commodities.[52] The Merchant Adventurers feared that the Spanish merchants would ship direct to the Baltic, the Levant Company that the Merchant Adventurers would import Levantine goods from the Netherlands. Competition from London was a threat to the northern ports in the Baltic trade and to the West Country in the trades with Newfoundland, France and Spain. The concessionary syndicates were split, particularly after the 1624 Statute of Monopolies, between domestic manufacturing and foreign trade. By the end of the century there were three gangs of export merchants representing the old Companies, the new institutions and the unincorporated traders.[53]

The whole business community did, however, share a common interest in fiscal questions. As highly liquid dealers in money and goods, merchants were particularly vulnerable to taxation, legal or illegal, and they sought to minimize their exposure and to divert the burden. They were as much opposed to Parliamentary as to unconstitutional levies.[54] Ship-money was opposed, less on constitutional grounds, than because it was feared that it would become a permanent tax.[55] The business lobbies simply exploited constitutional anxieties.[56] The Aldermen of Norwich agreed to the Forced Loan because they thought that ship-money would be even costlier.[57] The business community was slow to raise funds to support Parliament when the war finally came.[58]

The usual strategy, which was not uniformly successful, was to transfer the tax burden to landowners and consumers.[59] Although merchants always argued that lower customs would increase trade and therefore revenues, they proved unable to prevent continuous increases; the landed interest ensured that the Excise rather than assessments on land would replace Purveyance.[60] In the 1670s, business faced a real threat that interest would be taxed and a subsidy laid on stock-in-trade; the Aid of

[52] Ashton 1979: 86. [53] Price 1961a: 313. [54] Croft 1987a: 528.
[55] Ashton 1979: 64, 129, 199. [56] Russell 1979: 62. [57] Cust 1987: 131.
[58] Fletcher 1981: 251. [59] BL Add. MS 41613, fos. 10–11.
[60] Aylmer 1957–8: 91–2; O'Brien 1988: 17, 24, 28; O'Brien *et al.* 1991: 396; Beckett 1985: 286; Beckett & Turner 1990: 378, 387.

1688 seriously attempted to tax non-landed capital and income and the poll taxes of the 1690s targeted wealth as well as status.[61] But the business community proved adept at avoiding direct taxes; fear of inquisitorial methods and disclosure of debts spared personalty from effective assessment.[62] The gentry preferred to stomach a land tax, because they controlled the organs of local government which was responsible for assessment and collection.[63] There was, however, less agreement on means than on ends. Each individual or group wished to transfer taxes to trades in which they had no interest. The monied interest which, when the chips were down, always supported the government of the day, depended for their profits on a high and regular revenue stream.[64]

The attitude of businessmen to war was ambivalent. On the one hand, they were reluctant to sacrifice strength and security abroad to domestic political considerations; it was widely held that world trade was finite.[65] An aggressive and often xenophobic faction noisily rejected neutral rights and the freedom of the seas and advocated the exclusion of aliens and war against the Dutch.[66] Merchants always needed political help abroad against local rulers and they expected protection from foreign competitors both at home and abroad through direct intervention by the Privy Council and by legislation like the Navigation Acts, which replaced the privileged Companies as instruments of economic policy and made England an entrepot for colonial staples.[67]

There was a thin line between economic competition and open warfare and, in the long run, naval conflicts did determine the allocation of markets. Merchants armed their ships and provided private convoys; towns maintained naval ships and merchantmen helped to suppress Bacon's Rebellion.[68] But the business community expected the state to clear the seas of pirates and privateers and to assist and protect their interests and concessions abroad. The inability of the Early Stuarts to defend trade was a major source of grievance, though Charles I did modernize the Navy with ship-money; protection improved after the Restoration, but it still proved inadequate during the Nine Years War.[69]

[61] Dering, *Parliamentary Diary*, pp. 37–40; Brooks 1982: 53; Alexander 1989: 51; Kennedy 1913: 41; Faraday 1976: 105. Leases were taxed at 5 per cent on a notional income which was equivalent to a 6 per cent return on the value of property, excluding household goods and debts.

[62] Merchants were of course subject to the land tax on property owned in towns as well as in the country. See Ward 1953: 27–8; Brooks 1974: 283–5.

[63] Brewer 1987: 100. [64] Hill 1971: 411. [65] Knorr 1963: 20. [66] Irwin 1991: 1312.

[67] Harper 1939: 280; Davis 1966: 302, 306–8; Baumier 1977: 345; *Bristol Great White Book*, pp. 95–6; Federowicz 1980: 58.

[68] *Law of the Sea Documents*, p. xxv; Johnson 1986: 418; Ramsay in Scott & Kouri 1986: 454; Swales 1977: 674; *Rye Shipping Records*, p. xlv.

[69] Quistnell 1988: 173; Hornstein 1991; Crowhurst 1977: 46–7; Pearsall 1989: 112–13; Johnston 1971: 400–4; Bruyn 1979: 82, 88; Fissel 1991: 145.

In every war, declared and undeclared, merchants fitted out ships for privateering, which was a rationalization of piracy and an acknowledgement of the limitations of government.[70] Of the 406 ships granted letters of marque during the Nine Years War, 77 per cent were owned by merchants.[71] Even though privateers gave security in return for their commission, there was no real system of control and many grounds for conflict with the Navy.[72] Privateering was always conducted as a private business, usually organized in joint-stocks.[73] It often merged imperceptibly with the covert trade in contraband and with interloping and provided essential employment for merchant shipping and capital in wartime.[74] Merchants also traded with buccaneers and dealt in prize ships and confiscated goods.[75] It is difficult to determine whether these activities were symbiotic with trade, exploration and colonization or whether they disrupted normal and fundamentally more important trades.[76]

On the other hand, international trade generated a cosmopolitan pacifism and many believed that the flag followed trade.[77] It was taken for granted that war was built into the system, but few envisaged trade as a form of aggression.[78] Merchants had been cool towards the early voyages of exploration because they were costly and unprofitable and, although influenced by Dutch success, they were slow to embrace militant imperialism.[79] Companies were reluctant to bear the cost of military and naval action and they preferred to support diplomatic efforts. The East India Company, except for one ill-fated military adventure by Josiah Child, cooperated with and relied on the protection of local rulers.[80]

England profited from neutrality and its strategic position during the war between Spain and the United Provinces, when Dover became an

[70] Pénotu-Daemon in Tracy 1991: 217.

[71] Kepler 1973: 220 corrects Rabb's overestimate of Elizabethan and Jacobean privateers. Meyer 1981; Clark 1923: 47, app. 3; D. W. Jones in Clark & Slack 1972: 324; Ramsay 1986: 144; Andrews 1974a: 5. [72] Andrews 1972: 532; 1991: 139; Hill 1977: 351.

[73] Andrews 1964: 26; Stevens 1969: 97; Powell 1930; Lloyd 1981; Meyer 1981: table 2.

[74] Croft 1989: 300; Zahedieh 1986a: 575; Andrews 1974a: 244; 1974: 5; 1978: 194; Gerhard 1960: 154–5. [75] Senning 1983: 205; Buisseret & Pawson 1975: 31, 78.

[76] The positive view is expressed by Wernham 1980: 86; Andrews 1984: 35; Scammel 1989: 18; Bromley 1987: 343; the negative view by Croft in Adams & Rodriguez-Salgado 1991: 239; Battick 1972: 82. Meyer 1983: 444–5; 1981: 268 points out that the annual average value of prizes was less than 0.5 per cent of the total value of foreign trade.

[77] Roberts, *Trades Increase*, p. 16.

[78] There was little economic analysis of war: see Silberner 1939.

[79] Adams, *Brief Relation*, pp. 12–13; Canny 1973; Cullen in Cullen & Stout 1977; Webb 1979: xvi; MacCusker in Andrews & Quinn 1978: 160; Condon 1968: 34. On the debate over whether the Dutch pursued profit or power see Ashton in C. Jones *et al.* 1986: 160; Syrett 1954: 543.

[80] Chaudhuri 1978: 6, 47, 117. For an alternate view see Watson 1980a: 81; Basset in Bromley & Kossmann 1960: 83. The Hudson's Bay Company was more territorial: see Gough 1970: 42.

entrepot, and one argument for free ports was that they would draw the Dutch to England; the large resident English community in Holland suffered from hostilities.[81] The Anglo-Dutch wars were sectoral and primarily about power. The Navigation Act of 1651 was intended to protect English shipping and enhance naval strength, but not to generate a war; although the Second Dutch War did reflect inability to compete, merchants still benefited more from peace.[82] As Coke rightly pointed out, trade could be defended, but not won by war.[83] The foreign and colonial policy of the government often conflicted with the interests of merchants who feared embargoes and the economic consequences of war and were quite prepared to trade, even in armaments, with foreign enemies and to colour goods and ships.[84]

The attitude of businessmen to government intervention at home was equally ambivalent. Freedom was interpreted as an exclusive right and all wanted privileges and exemptions from statutes. English merchants were unwilling to compete with Ireland; only Papillon argued against the cattle bills.[85] In principle, they supported regulation of the domestic economy, whether through the Privy Council, Parliament or the municipalities, and complained about lax enforcement.[86] Businessmen expected the central government to standardize weights and measures, unify the market, maintain internal peace and order and secure property rights. They recognized that strong expansive government was both a cause and a result of economic stability.

At the same time, businessmen wanted to reduce interference in their affairs to a minimum and preferred that action be taken only at their request.[87] They had no compunction about smuggling or evading any regulations which conflicted with their interests by 'a little art in making a small alteration'.[88] The prohibition in urban markets of forestalling and engrossing was widely ignored and there were endless squabbles between merchants, consuls and searchers; the Norwich merchants colluded with the clothworkers.[89] Tolerance of authoritarian state control was predicated on the assumption that most rules would be selectively enforced,

[81] Kepler 1976: 4, 109, 147; Taylor 1972: 237; Sprunger 1982: 392.

[82] Cooper in Aylmer 1973b: 135; Price in J. R. Jones 1979: 126–30; Taylor 1972: 260. The passing of the 1651 Act cannot be ascribed just to one group: see Farnell 1977: 654.

[83] Coke, *Reasons Increase Dutch Trade*, epistle; Wilson 1957: 15.

[84] *Law of Sea Documents*, p. 138; *Bristol Documents Illustrating Trade*, p. 6; Clark 1923: 66; Croft 1989: 281, 302; Sprunger 1982: 386.

[85] Sosin 1985: 39; Barnard 1973: 63; Edie 1970: 47; Ogg 1955: chap. 3.

[86] Cooper 1983: 204–7; Endrei & Egan 1982. [87] Hirschman 1970: 3–5.

[88] Ramsay 1952: 143–4; 1959: chap. 6; Harper 1939: 140–5, chap. 11; Williams 1961: 82–8; Bridenbaughs 1972: 324; Kammen 1970. For an example of how goods were concealed in chests see Ramsey 1898: 62.

[89] *Norwich Mayoralty Court Minutes*, p. 163; Archer 1991a: 202–3.

primarily against the lesser men. Although controls over food supply and apprenticeship were largely discontinued after 1660, the scope of government actually increased and the bureaucracy became more efficient. Freedom from heavy-handed interference and adequate representation in government therefore became more critical issues.

Merchants and tradesmen played little part in the legalistic debates over whether the Crown should govern by proclamation or statute.[90] But they formed the bulk of litigants in Common Pleas and King's Bench and they were even more prominent in the local courts, initiating suits to collect and settle debts.[91] Consequently merchants had a special interest in the consistent and uniform enforcement of clear and practical laws; many campaigned to make the judicial system more responsive to business needs, but, despite the presence of two merchants on Hale's commission in 1652, little was achieved even during the Interregnum.[92] Businessmen pressed the courts to address more fully the pressing issues of liability and recovery. Many, like Child and Petty, considered that the laws of England were cumbersome and irrelevant.[93]

Some progress was achieved through piecemeal legislation and improvisation by judges.[94] Chancery and Exchequer took over from the Church Courts areas of probate and provided better procedures and equitable remedies against the rigidity of the common law, which took no account of particular circumstances.[95] The Statute of Frauds in 1677 attacked perjury and the Statute of Distribution in 1670 dealt with intestate succession. Acts of 1696 and 1705 recognized the practice of not enforcing the exact terms of conditional and penal bonds. The common law did not absorb borough customs, the law-merchant or international and civil law, but from the 1650s onwards it did treat mercantile Custom as a matter of fact and thereby create commercial law.[96] In the 1690s, the responsibilities of the endorsers of a bill of exchange were gradually clarified.[97] The law of contract slowly began to emerge from assumpsit; the action of trespass upon the case to recover debts was enlarged by an action based on wrong occasioned by a breach of an oral agreement.[98] The courts both

[90] *Stuart Proclamations*, i. p. vi.

[91] Brooks in Baker 1978: table 1; 1986: 60, 70; Lemmings 1990: 175; Muldrew 1992: 27–30, table 1.

[92] Cottrell 1968: 691; Shapiro 1975a: 310 and 1980: 360.

[93] BL Add. MS 30323, fo. 29v°; *Petty–Southwell Correspondence*, p. 59.

[94] Stump 1974: 26ff.

[95] W. J. Jones 1967: 442–7.

[96] Baker 1979; 1986: 306, 367; Calvert 1965: 16; Holdsworth 1956: i. 470–3, 526–44; 1914; Freund *et al.* 1907–9: i. 327, iii. 44–5; Sanborn 1930: 14–16, 108–11; Sutherland 1934: 150ff; Mackinnon 1936: 33.

[97] Holden 1951: 247–8; 1955: 30–70. According to one theory, modern capitalism begins with assignability and contract: see Commons 1968: 253.

[98] Milsom 1969: chap. 3; Atiyah 1979; Simpson 1979: 547; Ibbetson 1983: 316; 1982; Palmer 1989: 49; Spelman, *Reports*, ii. 286.

made the repayment of loans more flexible and facilitated the collection of debts.[99]

Nevertheless, through most of the century, the law fell far short of business needs. Although Coke opposed monopolies, his legalism retained obsolete rules and he supported several restraints on trade and opposed the Bankruptcy Act of 1624.[100] It was often difficult to enforce contractual obligations; rivalry between competing courts delayed the settlement of disputes.[101] Theft was not a felony but a civil offence which had to be prosecuted by individuals; forgery of paper, including Exchequer bills was not made a felony until 1696.[102] The number of indictments fell and only 10 per cent of those convicted were executed; the increase in capital crimes after 1688, inflated by the need for separate Acts, only underlined the inability of law enforcement to control crime; frustration generated recourse to new methods such as transportation.[103]

The common law remained cocooned in medieval legal precedent and still thought in terms of classes of persons rather than individual entrepreneurs.[104] It was slow to recognize that customs between merchants could originate a legal duty and had difficulty apportioning responsibility between principals and agents. Partnership and factorage disputes had to be settled by invoking the law of debt or relations between masters and servants.[105] To sue a multiple partnership, it was necessary to sue in the name of each partner. Common law followed words rather than intentions; fictitious pleadings had to be employed to consider contracts made overseas. Intricate procedural rules bogged down debt cases in King's Bench and Common Pleas; despite the use of juries of merchants, the courts could not keep pace with changing commercial practices.[106] The litigant had to face multiple actions in different courts, blocking measures and inconsistencies of decision by different judges. The failure to establish a registry of land made it complicated and expensive to authenticate title when granting mortgages.[107] Many of the business estates left to charity raised thorny legal problems for the beneficiaries.[108]

Before the Civil War, merchants could turn to the Prerogative Courts, like the equity Court of Requests, which offered faster decisions.[109] They

99 Muldrew 1993: 36; Henderson 1974: 298ff.

100 White 1979: 123, app. C; Holdsworth in Vinogradoff 1913: 310.

101 Blundell, *Cavalier Letters*; Albyn, *Appeal to God*.

102 Ogg 1955: 106.

103 Beattie in Cockburn & Green 1988: 226; Herrup 1984: 822, 829; Cockburn 1977: 131; Sharpe 1984: 71; Hay 1975: 13; Langbein 1983: 96, 119–20. A few merchants opposed capital punishment for religious reasons: see Zaller 1987: 133; Davison *et al.* 1992: 55–8.

104 Spelman, *Reports*, p. 38; Ogilvie 1958: 13, 92–3.

105 Postan 1973a: 17–21, 68–70.

106 Francis 1983: 91–6, 136.

107 Shapiro 1975a: 311; Thorne 1985: 202.

108 Ralph 1988: 25.

109 REQ 2, bundle 387, BA 312; BL Add. MS 34218, fo. 95v°.

could also resort to the civil law in the Admiralty Court, which accepted written evidence, downplayed precedence and had a summary process.[110] Admiralty law recognized the validity of mortgages on ships, bottomry contracts and the negotiability of bills of exchange; creditors were permitted to proceed *in rem* against a ship and seize it as collateral. The Admiralty Court benefited from an ordinance of 1648 and branched out into all the overseas territories.[111] But it failed to extend its jurisdiction over all maritime contracts and the opposition of the common lawyers reduced it to adjudicating disputes on the high seas and prizes after the Restoration.[112] Losers in Admiralty could obtain prohibitions, even after sentence and appeal; by 1669, affreighting and insurance cases had been pre-empted by the Common Law Courts which were ill equipped to handle them.[113]

Merchants could also fall back on Custom and the law-merchant in the municipal courts, whose diffuse rules had largely been borrowed from the continent and, because they were not properly codified and digested, were more flexible. Freemen had the right to sue and be sued in their local courts, which included courts of equity, such as the Orphans Court and the Court of Requests for small debtors.[114] The Staple Court of Bristol applied the law-merchant and relied more on sureties and pledges than on imprisonment for debt.[115]

The remedies for both creditors and debtors were nonetheless limited. Sanctuary for debt was a problem throughout the century; in Hull it extended to the roof overhang of a burgher's house.[116] Although the Whigs secured its abolition in an Act of 1697, further legislation was still required.[117] Planters and local debtors in the colonies stripped their property before declaring bankruptcy and were protected by their legislatures.[118] The Bankruptcy Act of 1576 empowered the Lord Chancellor to appoint commissioners, who could apportion assets between creditors. But the commissioners could be sued for wrongful action and the process was slow and could only be initiated by creditors, who could not enter a house or warehouse or seize choses in action. Some debtors lived in the Rules and continued to conduct their business. On the other hand the debtor was also handicapped; even after his property had

110 BL Add. MS 5489, fos. 38–9, 83; Steckley 1978: 172–3; Roscoe 1924: 25–6, chap. 3. See also p. 184.

111 Crump 1931: 167; Johnson 1963: 32–3. New York relied in part on Dutch law and an Act of Assembly in 1684 made debts assignable.

112 Roscoe 1924: 16–18; 1931: 10–13.

113 Yale in Jenkins 1975: 98.

114 Atkinson 1963: chap. 9; Winder 1936: 372; P. E. Jones 1943; Carlton 1974a: 135–6.

115 *Bristol Staple Court Books*, pp. 82–3, 91.

116 Gillett & MacMahon 1980: 114.

117 Hertzler 1971: 476–7.

118 K. G. Davies 1957: 321; Harlow 1926: 315; Higham 1921: 157.

been distributed, he was still liable for the remainder. The Statutes of 1677 and 1680 permitted debtors in gaol to petition for discharge, but only if their estate was under £10 and all their creditors agreed.

It was not until 1705–6 that a statute addressed the difference between fraud, negligence and misfortune or between short-term cash-flow problems in an otherwise sound business and long-term insolvency.[119] Merchants could now continue to trade on licence under sureties, pay in instalments or compound with their creditors, obtain a certificate of discharge and retain 5 per cent of their assets or £200, whichever was less. A commission of bankruptcy put all creditors on an equal footing and forced compliance. The commissioners had power to seize, examine, imprison and investigate property; assignees valued and liquidated assets which were then distributed by the commissioners. The receivers were designated as trustees responsible to Chancery while debtors secured additional means of release from prison.

The difficulty remained that creditors acting in conjunction had to initiate; four-fifths of all creditors had to agree before a certificate of composition could be granted. Although improved, it was still a long and expensive process. Creditors still had to proceed without any priority of claim against the body of small debtors who did not qualify under the Act, such as those who owed less than £100 to one creditor. On the one hand, a vindictive creditor could stifle the process; on the other hand, debtors could put their creditors in jail by frivolous suits. Suspicion of fraud was so endemic that imprisonment was often considered the only remedy to secure payment and prevent flight. Creditors were still inadequately protected against fraudulent bankruptcy and honest debtors were too heavily penalized.[120]

Financial instruments eventually acquired legal recognition, but not until the eighteenth century. Because they were not sealed, insurance policies could not be enforced at common law until 1720. Insurers had to rely on commissioners appointed by the Lord Chancellor, which proved an ineffective process, or on arbitration under the law-merchant.[121] An attempt, in 1601, to introduce continental merchant tribunals proved abortive.[122] The common law regarded inland bills as single transactions and did not recognize their negotiability until 3 & 4 Anne c. 9; promissory notes (sealed bills of obligation) could be assigned, but the bearer could not sue the debtor until the Promissory Notes Act of 1704, and the rules of

[119] Goodinge, *Law against Bankrupts*; Hoppit 1987: chap. 3; Marriner 1980: 357–8; Duffy 1980: 286–7.

[120] N. H. *Compleat Tradesman*, pp. 29–30; W. J. Jones 1979; Duffy 1980: 285–6; Cohen 1982: 155.

[121] Kepler 1975: 50–3; Freund *et al.* 1908: iii. part V, 44–5; W. J. Jones 1959: 53–5.

[122] Sutherland 1934: 150, 156.

the law-merchant were only adopted in 1710.[123] Although the repayment order acquired a fiduciary role, Exchequer tallies were not assignable.[124]

The primary concern of merchants was *celeris justitia*; complex cases could drag on for more than a decade.[125] Businessmen were less interested in sealings and considered that the lawyers were too rigid and the meaning of the law obscure.[126] The lawyers, in turn, criticized merchants for relying too much on Custom and for drawing up slovenly agreements.[127] Merchants were usually willing to proceed through arbitration and actively sought to create tribunals for this purpose.[128] The guilds, Trinity House and the independent churches provided arbitration procedures and were sometimes referred cases from other courts.[129] John Locke explored the possibilities 'of some method of determining differences between merchants by referees that might be decisive without appeal'.[130] But arbitration awards were not made enforceable in the King's Courts until 1698 by 9 & 10 Wm III c. 15. which regularized current informal procedures.

Power base

The power of the overseas merchants rested on the charters of their Companies which conferred the right to fine, imprison, judge and tax. The regulated Companies operated mainly as pressure groups and cartels which provided both a protective umbrella and an entrée into municipal politics. They fiercely guarded their prerogatives and even a municipal Company, like the Merchant Venturers of Bristol, could raise and employ fighting ships.[131] The joint-stock Companies were miniature states with considerable political clout. Businessmen bought Company stock to exercise patronage and power as well as for investment purposes; they did not undertake the onerous task of running Companies just for the modest stipends.[132] By refusing to issue new shares and by amassing one-quarter of the stock, thirty men controlled the East India Company in 1681; only 180 out of 550 held enough stock to even qualify for election to the Court of Committees.[133] Although the other joint-stock Companies were not so tightly held, they were all run by the principal shareholders; when the

123 Holden 1955: chap. 3; Horsefield 1977; 1983: xiii. 124 Nichols 1971: 98.
125 Malone 1972: 394. 126 Carter 1901: 242.
127 Robinson, *Certain Proposals*, preface.
128 On the frequency of arbitration see Roberts and Sharpe in Bossy 1983: 11–13, 185; W. J. Jones 1959: 279.
129 *Trinity House Deptford Transactions*, p. xiv; Carter 1964: 170.
130 Bourne 1876: 355–8. 131 Morgan in Kiralfy 1985: 51.
132 Horwitz 1978; Sherman 1976: 331; Rich 1958: 89. The East India Company paid its Governor £200 in gratuities and its Deputy Governor £100 plus 9s. per attendance after 1673. 133 Wretts-Smith 1963: 95–6.

Hudson's Bay Company trebled its stock to attract small investors, it raised the voting qualification to £300.[134]

The privileges of the chartered Companies could be and were revoked by either Crown or Parliament; the Commons was consistently opposed to monopolies. The colonial and some of the minor Companies were in fact dissolved; the Bermuda Company was liquidated in 1684 after a leading shareholder started proceedings against the Charter.[135] Conflicts within the Companies mirrored conflicts at Court. The great merchants needed royal support to defend their privileges and exemptions against both their own rank and file and rival cartels from other sectors of the economy. This constant struggle divided loyalties and drained time and energy.

Successful businessmen were automatically elected to the governing bodies of city corporations. The guilds in London, except for some democratic experiments during the Interregnum, had by convention wholly oligarchic, though not hereditary, constitutions.[136] Life tenure and self-election, nomination or co-option by existing members ensured that the guilds would not be run by artisans; by the end of the century, the yeomanry organization had disappeared. In London, the Corporation was reluctant to absorb the suburbs, because it feared that this would weaken its oligarchic control. Common Council could attack but, except in the 1640s, not effectively counter the executive authority and veto powers of the Court of Aldermen. The democratic proposals to reform the City constitution in 1689–90 ran out of steam and the Whigs settled for oligarchic control.[137]

London maintained a balance between oligarchy and mobility during the century.[138] But power had always rested on wealth rather than on economic function; only the rich could afford the considerable costs of office.[139] The property qualification for a Sheriff of London was £10,000 in 1631 and for an alderman £10,000 in 1640 rising to £15,000 by 1711; the cost of holding major City offices ranged from £1,000 to £4,000 and the fines for exemption from £500 to £1,000.[140] In the major guilds, a Warden had to spend £80–100 or pay a fine of £20–30.[141] The rotation of offices and appointment by seniority also restricted the governing elite to those with both age and experience.[142] The same was true of the provincial

[134] *Hudson's Bay Company Letters Outward 1688–96*, p. l. [135] Dunn 1963: 487.
[136] Plummer 1972: 50. [137] Krey 1985: 32, 64, 71; Dickinson 1988: 141.
[138] Pearl in Lloyd Jones *et al.* 1981: 120.
[139] Reynolds 1977: 76; Nightingale 1989: 33; Archer 1991b: 65. The same was true of Scotland: see Houston & Whyte 1989: 15. In Philadelphia some sons of merchants chose to be craftsmen: see Nash in Dunns 1986: 342.
[140] Wunderli 1990: 4; Kirby 1970; Beaven 1908–13: i. 57, 77, 149.
[141] Manningham, *Diary*, p. 42. [142] Archer 1991a: 47.

towns. Norwich and Oxford remained open, thanks to high mortality and turnover; the aldermen of Gloucester were drawn from the tradesmen.[143] But it still took wealth to either enter or escape civic government; the fine for a Sheriff of Norwich was £20–50 before 1660 and £50–100 thereafter. In Bristol, York, Newcastle, Lancaster and Exeter, access to power was effectively restricted to merchants.[144] Whatever municipal constitutions might prescribe, most towns were dominated by particular families connected by business and marriage.[145]

Most businessmen stood stiffly for the liberties, immunities and franchises of their cities, even though they disagreed as to whom should be represented.[146] Most towns incorporated at great expense in order to protect themselves from outside interference, and though a charter was a revocable grant, they acquired a degree of autonomy.[147] At the city level, the issues which dominated the national political scene were fought out on a smaller scale usually superimposed on local economic and political grievances.[148] The new men who came to power during the Interregnum were as conservative as the old guard. The leaders of Newcastle served all parties and regimes, and several towns, like Worcester, adopted a neutral stance.[149] As in academic politics, the battle was often most heated when no major issue was at stake.

Businessmen acquired unpaid responsibility for the proper functioning of municipal government under that peculiar mixture of centralization and decentralization which characterized English government.[150] The Aldermen of London had both executive and judicial authority and even had a potential militia force in the trained bands.[151] They supervised the courts and the prisons, administered the Poor Law and charities, the sewers and the municipal estates, collected and disbursed revenue (usually in combination with Common Council), safeguarded the supply of water and fuel, stored grain (until 1666), maintained bridges, wells, ditches and fortifications, dealt with epidemics, and regulated the crafts and trades.[152] They also disseminated information for the government, supplied troops, reviewed national legislation, regulated prices and raised

143 Evans 1974: 40, 65; 1979: 5, 33, 54, 62, 319, table 12; Harris 1978: 25; Ripley 1976: 122.

144 Sacks 1986a: 88; Stephens 1954: 139; Howell 1967: 40; *V.C.H. City of York* 1961: 179; Palliser 1979: 93, 106; Mullett 1983: 71.

145 Kirby 1986: 128; Hughes 1987: 275; Wilson 1971: 162; *Worcester Chamber Book*, intro.; Clark in Smith & Tyacke 1979; Berger 1981–2: 49; Mullett 1975: 65 and 1972: 31; Clemens 1976: 216; Cotton 1889; Sheenan in Brady & Gillespie 1986: 101; Tittler in Loach & Tittler 1980: 91.

146 Levin 1969.

147 Tittler 1977b: 40; Bond & Evans 1976: 119; Lea 1991: 61.

148 Clark 1977; Howell 1980: 24; 1984: 7, 34; in Morrill 1982: 73–6; Johnson in Clark & Slack 1972: 205; Evans 1979: 190, 321.

149 Hughes 1987: 275.

150 Forster 1983; Kenyon 1986: 415.

151 Allen 1972: 288–9; Harris 1989: 21.

152 Foster 1977.

loans and taxes for the Crown often at the price of great unpopularity. New municipal institutions, like the Bridewells, took over some functions of the Church Courts.[153] The same was true on a smaller scale of the provincial towns. The Mayor's Court of Norwich handled all cases brought before Quarter Sessions except for manslaughter, murder and sudden death.[154]

The magistrates contributed their time to public service in rotation.[155] In London, overseas merchants served as Chamberlain and Under Chamberlain and constituted one-fifth of Common Councillors in the 1690s.[156] The normal progression was from freeman to liveryman to office first in a Livery Company and then in the City, crowned by a knighthood or baronetcy. The Livery Companies, which were the centre of London politics, handled disputes over trade, apprentices and debts and adjudicated between members and even within families. Some aldermen took an interest in parish affairs.[157] Municipal administration was not depersonalized and businessmen accepted that their rights as citizens had reciprocal duties.

The quality of government varied considerably. London failed to control development and the suburbs grew haphazardly without any overall direction.[158] By 1694, the City was bankrupt, though ultimately saved by the coal duties.[159] Some provincial towns, like Exeter, were run like chartered Companies to make money; communal services were farmed out to private enterprise.[160] But in other cities, particularly in London, municipal government was broadly based and often enlightened. Attendance at both the Court of Aldermen and its committees was surprisingly high.[161] The Court continued to meet during the plague, though one reason may have been the unwillingness of the Aldermen to relinquish power.[162] Although conflict always simmered beneath the surface, stability and order were maintained without force through successive crises.[163] The main problem may have been too much, not too little government.

The primary concern of businessmen was to defend regional economic interests.[164] The charters of guilds and towns gave them authority over

153 Snyder & Hay 1987: 68. 154 Evans 1979: 59.

155 Full-time administrators increasingly assumed the greater burden. As early as 1520, the Drapers appointed a salaried Renter Warden to improve their accounting: see Cooper 1984: 339.

156 Masters 1988: xxxiii; Beattie in Cockburn & Green 1988: 242.

157 Priestley 1956: 208. On the considerable work involved even at the parish level see Boulton 1987: 271–4.

158 Reddaway 1940: 221–43; Power 1985: 385; Berlin 1986: 24. 159 Doolittle 1983: 461.

160 MacCaffrey 1958: 178, 281. 161 Foster 1977: 81. 162 Slack 1985: 264–5.

163 For different views see Pearl 1979b; Lindley 1991: 989; Archer 1991a.

164 Morrill 1976.

many branches of domestic production and distribution. The Livery Companies, particularly in technical trades like gun and clock making, exercised their right of search until the end of the century and fined and seized goods; the London Goldsmiths did a search at Newcastle, in 1635, and the Stationers profited from the sale of confiscated books.[165] The merchants of Dartmouth regulated the fishing industry.[166] The civic community was often little more than an economic organization of businessmen interested in excluding non-freemen, acquiring special privileges and making profits. But fundamentally towns were united rather than divided by economic interests.[167] The politics of London maintained a balance of power between the overseas Companies and the domestic traders.

Since business required personal attention, merchants were reluctant to fill posts which did not carry high salaries or provide useful connections and leverage. Many opted out of the Livery because of the cost of dinners and because it made them eligible for office. They increasingly sought to evade the burden of local administration either by buying exemption or resorting to subterfuges such as residing outside municipal jurisdiction. In London, half of those elected Alderman under James I paid £100–800 to be exempt; under Elizabeth twenty-one fined off as Aldermen and seventy-one refused the Shrievalty.[168] Aldermen left the Court rather than serve as Lord Mayor. After 1672, the shortage of candidates was such that the City, although it needed the income from fines, made men serve and jailed them if they refused.[169] The same was true of other towns, like York.[170] Many eminent businessmen never held any major municipal office and the lesser merchants were even more reluctant to sacrifice time and money.

Businessmen were always vulnerable to political coercion; the Aldermen collected ship-money because they had little choice. After the Restoration, the attack on the charters forced many merchants to take an active role. London was in real danger until 1688 and the City refused to surrender its Charter in 1683 because that would have given the King control over City lands and offices.[171] Those whose religious affiliations or political sentiments made them a target for persecution and discrimination had to defend themselves as best they could through influence in

[165] Hetell in Myers & Harris 1985: 52; Gill 1980: 2; *Scarborough Records 1641–60*, p. 143.

[166] Russell 1950: 82.

[167] Cust 1992: 8.

[168] Lang 1974: 42–3; Ramsay 1975: 36; Archer 1991a: 21; Foster 1977: 61; Hicks-Beach 1909: 87.

[169] Wunderli 1990: 14, 5 n.25. The rate of fining does not in itself indicate indifference; in London it could actually accelerate promotion. See Johnson 1969: 145; Kermode 1982: 197.

[170] Palliser 1979: 205; *V.C.H. City of York* 1961: 176.

[171] Doolittle 1982: 14.

local government against the hostility of an Anglican Parliament. Dissenters evaded the Corporation Act and served in municipal office, as did aliens.[172] But many merchants chose to ignore national issues and mainly squabbled amongst themselves. Prosperity generated complacency and political indifference: as Sir Robert Atkins said of the Aldermen of Bristol, 'since they grew rich and full of trade and Knighthood . . . they have been miserably divided'.[173] As the danger of royal absolutism receded, so did the need for corporate protection against the state.

Before 1640, economic legislation was initiated more through the Council than in Parliament, though government bills were usually amended; 49 per cent of Elizabethan proclamations dealt with economic issues.[174] After 1660, Parliamentary legislation replaced the royal prerogative. In the great economic debates of the century – on monopolies, the crises of the 1620s and the 1690s, the rate of interest or the treaty of 1713 – businessmen participated fully both in the Commons and its committees, which consulted and co-opted outsiders.[175] The provincial merchants consistently resisted the political influence of London and they entered Parliament to promote or block legislation. Merchants from London and prosperous ports like Exeter and Bristol were active in the Commons, but many others absented themselves from sessions and neglected to vote on issues of policy.[176] Parliament sometimes resembled a share-holders' meeting; in 1585, only one member turned up for a committee on London apprentices.[177]

Periodically, pamphleteers argued for greater representation of merchants on the grounds that the gentry were ignorant of trade and unqualified to levy taxes on 'the trading part'.[178] Originally the boroughs had returned merchants.[179] But outsiders who were more efficient at self-promotion had at an early period invaded the boroughs and had clipped the political wings of the merchants.[180] The Property Qualification Act of 1711 excluded from the Commons all but the richest businessmen who had bought freehold land or urban hereditaments, though it was never properly enforced. Merchant families controlled a few borough seats through local connections and by purchase of land. One MP from Hull was always a merchant and twenty of thirty-one Bristol MPs were Merchant Venturers; York alternated between gentry MPs, 1660–80, and

[172] Grell 1989: 50, 81; Mullett 1983: 63; Evans 1979: 320.
[173] Seyer 1821: ii. 520; Howell 1967: 336–8.
[174] Elton 1986: 235, 261; *Proclamations Tudor Queens*, table 2.
[175] Seaward 1988: 446; Coleman in Coleman & John 1976: 192–3.
[176] Dean & Jones 1990: 153–7; Burton *et al.* 1968: 12. [177] Loach 1991: 144.
[178] *Seventeenth-Century Economic Documents*, pp. 408, 411; Gunn 1968: 50.
[179] MacKisack 1932: 104; Roskell in Cam 1960–61; 1954: 49–53; Barron 1990: 366.
[180] Loach 1991: 117; Kishlanski 1986: 14, 32.

merchants after 1690.[181] In the 1710 election, 81 per cent of the London Livery voted and, in 1713, 92 per cent; a tradesman stood at Hastings and beat the son of Lord Ashburnham.[182] But other towns, like Worcester and Exeter, kowtowed to the gentry or preferred to select their members from local country families.[183]

London only had four seats and businessmen were always a minority in the Commons. In Elizabethan Parliaments, 414 merchants were elected in comparison to 1,163 gentlemen, 197 officers and 140 servants of great men; the percentage of merchants, excluding sons who had often entered other professions, declined from 17 per cent to 13 per cent.[184] The Addled Parliament had forty-eight lawyers compared with forty-two merchants.[185] The Long Parliament had thirty-one merchants, of whom eleven had seats outside of London, and twenty-three members of City Companies as well as twenty-seven sons of tradesmen.[186] Business representation increased only marginally during the Interregnum.[187] The Rump had more merchants, but they were still outnumbered; Barebones Parliament had nine merchant-gentlemen and twenty-three merchant-professionals.[188] The Protectorate Parliaments had a similar quota of merchants and financiers and Richard Cromwell's Parliament had about twenty.[189]

Between 1660 and 1690, there were 173 merchant MPs compared with 277 lawyers; they represented 9 per cent in 1660, 7 per cent in 1667, 10–12 per cent in 1679–81 and 8 per cent in 1685.[190] In the Parliament of 1701–2, although 40 per cent were in business or the professions, there were still only 43 merchants, 18 others connected with trade and 12 bankers out of 513 members, as compared with 350 esquires, (20 of whom had mining and industrial interests), 50 servicemen and 62 lawyers.[191] In the 1710 Parliament, there were only fifty-seven merchants, bankers and manufacturers, of which two-thirds were from London and connected with the great trading Companies.[192] The back benches of the Commons were dominated numerically by the country gentry,

Those who did not seek or could not obtain political appointments still tried to exert influence through informal contacts. Merchants often preferred to promote their policies indirectly through petitioning, bribery and the distribution of printed pamphlets, which often skilfully

[181] Gillett & MacMahon 1980: 160; Clark 1978; MacGrath 1975: 32; *V.C.H. City of York* 1961: 122. [182] Krey 1985: 249; Speck & Craig 1975: 253; Speck 1970: 4.
[183] Wanklyn 1979a; 1979b; Dyer 1972: 214.
[184] Neale 1950: 151–2, 313–17; Hasler 1982: 20. [185] Moir 1938: 57.
[186] Keeler 1954. [187] *Stafford Committee 1643–5*, p. xxii.
[188] Worden 1974: 30–3; Woolrych 1982: 167. [189] Ashley 1962: 7.
[190] Henning 1983: i. 541. [191] Walcott 1956: 21–31, app. 1; Speck 1980.
[192] MacHattie 1951: 10; Speck & Craig 1955.

manipulated statistics as propaganda.[193] Each Company and economic interest had its own political lobby which, depending on whether it was defending or attacking a grant, informed and badgered Parliament as well as the Privy Council, Star Chamber and the Exchequer. The London guilds were particularly active and the Goldsmiths reviewed proposed legislation.[194] The East India Company had an effective lobby from the beginning and hired an artist to depict the massacre at Amboyna.[195]

Projectors targeted particular members, friends in the House and specialist committees to obtain sponsors for private bills; merchants testified in person before Parliament and petitions presented there were forwarded to the committees of the Privy Council and appropriate government departments. Pressure groups raised funds, hired lawyers, nurtured officials with gifts, feasts and honorary freedoms and paid professional pamphleteers.[196] The presence of MPs from the clothing constituencies on committees increased the success rate of bills after 1688.[197] Lobbying was not confined to London. Few towns offered legislative programmes, but every Parliament was inundated with provincial petitions.[198] The Exeter and Bristol merchants defended their interests against both London and other ports in the West Country.[199] The American colonies had organized lobbies as early as 1649.[200]

The motives of petitioners were of course suspect and their criticism resented by those in authority. Only the Crown could arbitrate between competing pressure groups in the interests of political stability and social harmony. Many Companies tried, but few succeeded, in having their charters confirmed by Parliament. Most private bills stuck in committee and were lost or vetoed thanks to the opposition of vested interests.[201] The government often decided to favour the least likely lobby and never conceded all that was asked.[202] Both legislature and executive were, nonetheless, responsive to complaints, pleas and advice.

Economic policy

A substantial proportion of the contemporary literature on economic problems was written by practising merchants.[203] Although certain concepts and ideas persisted, a great variety of competing arguments and

[193] Needham, *Politics Merchant Adventurer*.

[194] Archer 1991: 137; 1981: 43; Dean 1981: 547–8; 1989: 349; Green 1974: 56–7; Prideaux 1896–7: i. 272. [195] Sherman 1976: 340, 352; Hall 1960: 36; Horwitz 1977: 4.

[196] Keirns 1988: 246. [197] Davison *et al.* 1992: 13

[198] Elton 1986: 240, 250, 267; *Parliament Proceedings 1626*, pp. iii. 167–9; Tittler 1989: 63; Cresswell 1930: 67–8; Youings 1968: 103. [199] Stephens 1954: 152.

[200] Olson 1987: 364–8; Bailyn 1964: 155–6; Olson 1992: 28, 55–6.

[201] Elton 1986: 235. [202] Wilson 1969: 143–6.

[203] Bindoff 1944: 70; R. D. W. Jones 1970: 143.

explanations emerged and business writers tried to build and improve on the work of their predecessors. The questions which they asked and their reasons for asking them are often of historical significance, even though their answers usually have little relevance to modern economics.

A major drawback was that merchants regarded the economy from a narrow and self-centred viewpoint. They wrote to defend their trade and city in the same spirit that the theologian wrote to defend his Church. An ale-house keeper would 'with a grave air complain that trade was not sufficiently encouraged, when he meant the trade of ale drapery and smoking tobacco'.[204] Businessmen tended to recite a litany of particular grievances in broadsheets or ephemeral pamphlets, often in personal terms, and objective analysis was the exception.[205] Provoked to write by recessions, war and internal rivalries, businessmen focused on short-term, single issues rather than on structural problems and they often made specious claims to advance their private agendas.[206]

As middlemen, merchants tended to underestimate the role of agriculture and industry and they contributed relatively little to value theory.[207] The specific policies which they advocated as remedies for problems were based on practical experience, not on an integrated, coherent, general theory. Some political arithmeticians, like Petty, came from the business world and John Graunt may have developed his statistical methods from the practice of double entry.[208] But most businessmen were more concerned with the practical effects on their profits of government policy than with analysing the economic assumptions which underlay regulations; they showed little interest in nor aptitude for system-building. Although they leaped from the particular to the universal, their prognosis of events was usually a projection of what they hoped would occur. Immersed as they were in immediate problems and routine transactions, it is not surprising that they failed to adopt a rational, deductive approach to political economy, which was ultimately developed by moral philosophers and not by businessmen.

Normative concepts can, however, never be eliminated from economics and at least merchants knew how the market actually functioned. They had an economic incentive to try to identify the forces which determined the flow of goods and capital. Some did write comprehensive treatises and their substantial contribution and influence in part explains why Adam Smith should exaggerate the systematic nature of their

[204] *Some Thoughts on Interest*, pp. 65–6.
[205] Wilson 1963; Grassby 1994: chap. 10.
[206] Roover 1957: 82–3; Supple 1976: 197; Gould 1955: 121ff; 1958: 62–4; Muchmore 197ι 500–5; Buck 1977. [207] Bowley 1973. [208] Kreager 1988: 136.

thought and label it 'mercantilist'.[209] They entertained many correct and sophisticated ideas and advocated some sensible proposals. Monetary and balance of trade theory developed from their constant preoccupation with foreign currencies, the exchange and payment for imports; the regulatory system and the protectionist and colonial theories which emerged were a product of competition for world business.[210] Even the demands of lobbying gave rise to new and better arguments. The defenders of bullion exports to India popularized the notion of multilateral balances; the defenders of Company monopolies contributed to knowledge of prices and costing; those who needed cheap money initiated the debate on the rate of interest.

Like other propertied men, merchants feared and distrusted those who lived on the margin of subsistence, but, as the economy prospered, they increasingly regarded poverty as an opportunity for reform rather than as a threat.[211] Indeed, they were more sympathetic than many outside the business world towards the poor, the incapacitated and the involuntary unemployed.[212] Subject to unpredictable fluctuations in the marketplace, they did not automatically blame the victims of economic distress or equate poverty with crime. They adopted a businesslike attitude towards the problem of vagrancy and they contributed to the extensive debates on the reform of the Poor Law. Most merchants preached the virtues of hard labour and only a few glimpsed the significance of underemployment.[213] But their interest in labour costs stimulated far-reaching discussions on the structure of wages and their experience of marketing slowly shifted attention from supply to demand.[214]

The unique English Poor Law depended on the expertise of local men.[215] In London, the Aldermen regarded the parish and not the city as the appropriate administrative unit.[216] In an effort to contain the poor-rate and to distribute welfare more equitably, town governments intro-

[209] Andrews 1934–8: iv. 31; Johnson 1937: chap. 7. The bogus concept of 'mercantilism' is still retained by historians of economic thought, even though it has been systematically demolished by economic historians. See Allen 1970: 391–3; Coates 1973: 488; Wiles 1974: 56ff.

[210] Perotta 1991: 302; Wilson 1958: 10; Lowry 1974: 437–8; Cole 1961: 127.

[211] Slack 1974: 367; 1988: 39, 53, 188; Riis 1986: 24; Beier 1985: chap. 6; 1974; Pound 1976: 128; Kent 1981; MacMullan 1982: 321–3.

[212] Wilson 1969. Attitudes to poverty and unemployment were probably more liberal after the Reformation than among the canonists: see Tierney 1959: 132.

[213] Coleman in Carus-Wilson 1954–66, ii. 283–4, 302–3; Coates 1960–1; Brown in R. Smith 1984: 419–20.

[214] Wiles & Coates in Walter 1974: 79ff; Furniss 1920: chap. 6; Wermal 1939: chap. 1; Meek 1950: 16–17; Pauling 1957: 63–4; Johnson 1932a; Gregory 1921: 39, 45.

[215] Slack 1980: 7; 1989: 21; Marshall 1937–8; Taylor 1976: 45–52; Oxley 1974: 19–20.

[216] Power 1984: 377.

duced the corporations of the poor, merged parishes and experimented with various projects to set the poor on work.[217] Norwich forbad charitable alms and its scheme functioned well until overwhelmed by Flemish immigrants.[218] Many of the workhouse schemes were designed by merchants who treated the poor as a business problem requiring investment; their experiments did, however, run into opposition and sabotage from other merchants who were afraid of economic competition.[219]

The towns mixed voluntary and compulsory charity. The amount contributed privately roughly equalled that raised by taxation up to 1650 and the London Livery Companies alone provided £14,000 per annum.[220] But private charity was often administered for legal reasons by semi-public bodies and the poor-rate was indispensable and levied consistently, even during the Interregnum.[221] The problem of poverty was certainly not solved or fully understood, but it was contained. The system of relief worked by both helping the temporary and the chronic poor and by freeing children from taking care of their elders.[222]

The main protagonists of the merchants were the career officials and advisors who were often free-thinking intellectuals; most of the political arithmeticians held government posts.[223] Their ideas and methodology owed more to administrative procedures, experimental science and government accounting than to experience of business. The daily work of officers of the Customs, Excise and Treasury required some acquaintance with statistics.[224] The civil servants positioned themselves as mediators between an ignorant gentry and a self-interested business community. Locke corresponded with several merchants and discussed their ideas, but, like Adam Smith, he fundamentally distrusted businessmen.[225] The obvious bias of so much advice from merchants and the association of many with opposition to the Court, limited their influence on policy. The government tended to follow the advice of its professional servants, because it feared that merchants would always pursue their private profit. The Crown concluded that a strong bureaucracy was necessary to control the business lobbies and defend the public interest, which was usually identified with the state and with greater efficiency in government.

[217] Styles 1978: 192–3; Slack 1988: 192; 1989: 26, 30; Leonard 1900: 277–81; Coats 1976.

[218] Pound 1962: 150.

[219] Cary, *Essay Towards Regulating*; Sherwin 1950: 41; Haines, *Complete Memoir*, p. 65; Belasco 1925: 167; Beier in Beier *et al.* 1989: 238; MacFarlane in Beier and Finlay 1986: 262; Pearl in Thomas & Pennington 1978: 232.

[220] Slack 1988: 171.

[221] Pearl in Lloyd-Jones *et al.* 1981: 130; MacIntosh 1988: 232–5; Herlan 1978: 46; 1976–7: 50, 197; 1978: 50–1.

[222] Arkel 1987: 46–7; Tronrud 1985a; Slack 1988: 53.

[223] Davenant, *Works*, i. 98; Letwin 1963: 100.

[224] Greenwood 1948: 35.

[225] Vaughn 1980: chap. 3.

Office

Successful businessmen were not averse to the profits of office, which they sometimes purchased as an investment and exploited ruthlesssly.[226] Merchants were mainly attracted to revenue offices and the Londoners often ousted local men.[227] The legal and illegal income from major posts often exceeded that from trade; even minor posts offered perquisites, exemption from regulations and access to useful information. Although Danby restricted the use of short-term funds by the Excise Farmers, all receivers of revenue benefited from a cash float. Even after the Exchange Office was created in 1667 to transfer tax returns by bills, the government's cash flow depended on the services of merchants. London aldermen could borrow cheaply from the Chamber and the Orphans and secure beneficial leases and inside information.

Many offices, however, had heavy maintenance and entertainment costs and were held for dignity rather than for profit. It was vanity and social ambition which attracted businessmen to the elaborate ceremonials of municipal office and which led them to imitate the self-importance and bureaucratic pretensions of the committee men. Even a minor office was prestigious within a regional context. The distinction of a knighthood was conferred to reward those who served in public office, not to recognize success in trade. In some cases, merchants also had a service ethic and a genuine desire to contribute to the public weal. The successful were sucked into political office and they often served in thankless posts from duty and loyalty rather than for self-advantage.

Businessmen were frequently deterred from holding offices, because they were so time-consuming. A London alderman had two Court meetings a week plus endless committees, visitations of hospitals and social and judicial functions, not counting his duties in his ward and co-option by royal and Parliamentary commissions and committees.[228] Livery Courts met eight times per year and the Board of Trade, between 1675 and 1696, met on average thirty-nine times per year. Even though permanent officials usually handled the basic work, the combined duties of sitting on the Courts of a Livery Company, the City and several overseas Companies were formidable.[229]

Some managed to combine a business with office.[230] But a young, active

[226] Aylmer 1974: 117, 238; Sharpe 1984: 156; Robinson 1948: 11–15; Ashley in Ollard & Tudor-Craig 1986: 205; Willcocks 1946: 150; Gillett 1970: 140–8; MacCusker 1985: 9; *Wynn Papers Calendar*, pp. xvi, 174–5, 338, 348, 479, 830, 964, 973, 1017, 1024; Ketton-Cremer 1944: 82.

[227] Levine 1973: 485; Coleby 1987: 103.

[228] Foster 1977: 89 gives some percentages of time absorbed by different duties.

[229] Bieber 1919: 89; Woodhead 1965: 15; GLL MS 11741/2; *Norwich Court of Mayoralty Minutes 1630–31*, p. 113.

[230] *Blakeney Maritime Trade*, p. 19; Friis 1927: 235–6.

merchant, if he wished to have a public career, had either to delegate control over his business or turn usurer and he was often unwilling to make this sacrifice.[231] Born administrators, like William Popple, therefore tended to leave the business world and join the ranks of full-time officers.[232] Those who had inherited a fortune or older merchants who had retired from business could enter politics as full-time participants.[233] Because promotion in the guilds was by seniority, the older merchants served in more offices.[234] The Council of Trade consisted chiefly of 'men wealthy and at their ease'.[235]. The urban magistrates were predominately businessmen, but they cannot be identified with the whole business community; the rulers of Elizabethan London can be divided into an elite, notables and leaders.[236]

By calling in merchants to debate problems and propose solutions, the Crown could sound out the reaction of the business community. The royal administration could not afford to waste the talents of merchants who had demonstrated their high calibre, often in print.[237] The Crown needed their technical advice on the drafting of economic policy and their practical knowledge of affairs. The committees set up by both the Privy Council and Parliament to examine the causes of depressions, to regulate foreign trade, to promote employment or to reform the currency, all relied on the advice and experience of merchants as was amply demonstrated in the 1620s.[238] Businessmen were appointed to the regulatory and advisory boards for trade and the plantations and they were expected to defend royal policies in their occupational constituency.

Given the administrative weakness of the monarchy, responsibilities had to be franchised to private enterprise, which often benefited from the royal power of dispensation. The Crown, though it undermined its own policies by fiscalism, wished to encourage investment by merchants through co-operation; it lacked the power to coerce and could only respond to crises.[239] Policy usually followed rather than directed economic development and syndicates interposed themselves between the Court and the consumer.[240] A major reason for bringing merchants into government was their ability to anticipate revenue. The Customs had long served as the basis for royal borrowing. The reliance by James on individual financiers, often of alien origin, was unusual; Elizabeth had used groups and corporations and, after 1640, specialized financiers replaced individual lenders as the major source of government loans.[241]

[231] Rappaport 1989: 271. [232] Robbins 1967: 19; 1982.
[233] Walcott 1956: 162. [234] Earle 1989a: 381; Archer 1991a: 47.
[235] Davenant, *Works*, i. 52. [236] Foster in Jaher 1973: 118; 1977: 103, app. 1.
[237] Peck 1982: chap. 7; Roberts 1985: 7. [238] Supple 1957: 243.
[239] Roberts 1967: 172; Farnell 1963–4: 454; Thompson 1966: 163–4; Supple 1957: 228–9.
[240] Ashton 1979: 23. [241] Outhwaite 1971b: 259.

But merchants became Parliamentary financiers during the Civil War and officers were still expected to provide cash, even after the abolition of the Farms.[242]

The operational experience of merchants was vital to implement policy and collect Customs efficiently at rates of duty which did not kill the golden goose. Occasionally merchants were appointed to a major department, but they usually served in revenue posts in England and the colonies or acted as Ordnance Paymasters and Receivers.[243] During the Interregnum, when many incumbents were excluded as politically unreliable, new businessmen entered the Navy, the Customs and the Treasury, sequestered delinquent estates, raised loans and administered the Excise.[244] The foreign residence and connections of merchants also made them useful as colonial agents, diplomatic couriers and spies and they helped to negotiate treaties which had commercial clauses.[245]

Even judged by the administrative standards of the day, the record of businessmen in government is uneven. Much of their advice was ill informed or poorly reasoned and tended to reflect the interests of one group. Negligence and absenteeism was common and there was mismanagement and peculation at the highest financial levels; Cranfield 'as a merchant . . . palliated a bribe with a bargain'.[246] Accustomed to informality and personal control, merchants were sometimes reluctant to delegate authority and were often outmanoeuvred by the bureaucrats.[247]

Nevertheless their experience of Company management often proved relevant and useful. Merchants had a concern for detail, a consistency of purpose and the ability and knowledge to expose the impracticality of many policies. Some of them should be included among that newly emerging corps of professional appointees who served at the will of the Sovereign and who constituted the nucleus of a more independent and objective royal bureaucracy. As government assumed direct responsibility for commercial diplomacy and revenue collection, businessmen were translated from independent contractors into civil servants.

Policy-making, however, remained firmly in the hands of the landed interest which monopolized executive offices. Ministers who were knowledgeable about trade were rarities on the Privy Council; even Cromwell's

242 Meekings in Hollaender & Kellaway 1969: 346; Western 1972: 103.

243 Sachse 1947–8: 273; Glasgow 1970: 16; Aylmer 1974: 63, 93, 177 shows that fifty-seven merchants were in royal service under Charles I; Hoon 1938: 409.

244 Andrews 1991: 59; Aylmer 1973a: 247–8.

245 Szeftel in *Russian Institutions* 1975: xiii. 339–41; Phipps 1990: 257–8; 1983; in Hartley 1986: 34; Taylor 1968: 16; Lachs 1965: 165; Andrews 1974a: 6; Wood 1935: 88; MacLachlan 1940: 20–1; Evans 1923: 141; Haynes 1992: 19; Howell, *Epistolae Ho-Elianae*, pp. xxvii–xxviii; Stoye 1952: 374–5; Woodbridge 1969: 784. Sometimes they spied for the enemy: see Loomie 1963a: 178–9; Grant in Grant *et al.* 1989: 94.

246 Prestwich 1966: 208–11; Young 1979: 70.

247 Cain 1987: 13–14.

Council of State was dominated by landed men and very few merchants became accredited ambassadors.[248] The subordination of business is well illustrated by the history of the Councils of Trade and Plantations. The Council established in 1650 reflected the unusual influence of merchants in the Rump.[249] But, when reconstituted after the Restoration, it had to face opposition from the outports as well as from Parliament, which had its own standing committees.[250] Some merchants advocated a Parliamentary body, but, as was pointed out, a permanent body was needed.[251] The 1669 Council had only eleven identifiable merchants, most of whom were 'well versed in trade but not traders themselves'.[252] Later Councils and the Board of Trade included eminent merchants and stockholders, but they usually had some stake in government finance and were always outnumbered by courtiers and officials.[253] John Whiston campaigned for wider representation, but a project, in 1695, to have elected representatives of merchants failed.[254] After 1696, when Parliament was more involved, provincial merchants were still effectively excluded and party politics dominated; after 1707 many members were placemen with short tenure.[255]

The relationship between the Lords of Trade and businessmen was equivalent to that between academic administrators and teaching faculty. From Bacon to Downing, bureaucrats disliked merchants and thought them inferior.[256] Neither the Court nor the Country was prepared to delegate control of shipping and trade to merchants or had any intention of sharing political power with the City.[257] Benjamin Worsley thought that trade was too serious a matter to be left to merchants and Sir William Coventry told Charles II that letting merchants into the Navy would be costly and would jeopardize security.[258] As Nathaniel Harley wrote to his brother, 'I know also very well . . . that you look upon Merchants only as a Useful sort of knaves . . . and yet you wont let us alone but will be meddling with what you think a disgrace to you to understand'.[259] A commercial government did not replace feudal monarchy, as John Miller suggested in the eighteenth century.[260]

248 Bell 1990. 249 Worden 1974: 30–2. 250 Lees 1933: 150.

251 *Seventeenth-Century Economic Documents*, p. 411.

252 Thornton 1956: 7, 148; Bieber 1919: app. D.

253 Laslett in Yolton 1969: 141–3; Lees 1939: 45–7; Andrews 1934–8: iv. 281–4; 1908; Rich 1957: 49–52, 63; Steele 1968: 11–15. The same was true of the Chambres de Commerce in France, though the Conseil de Commerce did have provincial representation: see Archives de la Chambre de Commerce de Marseille A. 12; Schaefer 1983: 256.

254 Whiston, *Causes Present Calamities*.

255 Steele 1968: 12–15; Sosin 1985: 235; Olson 1980: 39.

256 Roseveare in Coleman & Mathias 1984: 149; Viner 1958: 224.

257 J. R. Jones 1978. 258 MacKeon 1975: 113.

259 BL Add. MS 70223, letter 3 April 1696; Halifax, *Works*, p. 159.

260 Lehman 1960: 122–3.

When merchants and gentlemen were at loggerheads in the early colonial Companies, the greater financial power of the merchants often prevailed and the courtiers were effectively excluded from real power in the commercial Companies. But the business community was unable to challenge effectively the political supremacy of the landed interest. The English state was of course an amalgam of power networks.[261] Businessmen did exploit their power base in the cities to thwart the policies of the central government and resist the Crown. The Land Banks failed because the gentry lacked experienced representatives.[262] But merchants were obliged to co-operate with landowners in order to prosecute and defend their interests; power depended on perception.[263] Businessmen were a useful conduit for ideas, but they neither decided nor implemented policy. The warring cliques within and between Companies, towns and regions tended to cancel each other out and the landed gentry could divide and rule. There were too many conflicts of interest within the business community to sustain unity of purpose or to identify it with a coherent set of principles.

In a century of revolutions, when government and trade were so closely connected, businessmen could not stand aloof from politics. But many had only a marginal interest in power and their preferences varied with temperament, wealth, religion and age. If they entered the political arena it was an individual choice; the greatest businessmen were not necessarily the most active politically.[264] Although merchants knew how to play the game of urban politics, most were absorbed by business and were politically naive; they lacked the specific skills, the time, the cohesion and the numbers to compete with the professionals who pursued politics and intrigue for its own sake. Few entered that circle of great men who ran the country and set the tone of political life. Whatever their ambitions and claims, merchants had to settle for profit and influence rather than power.

[261] Man 1986: 6–7. [262] Rubini 1970: 705–7.
[263] Sharpe 1989: 9; Farnell 1977: 644. [264] Foster in Jaher 1973: 129, 131–3.

8 The measure of success

The dream of rags to riches was perpetuated by periodic reprints of legendary histories of businessmen.[1] It was widely assumed in pamphlet wars and family correspondence, as it was in the Commons of 1621, that 'the raysing of many good families from small beginnings and the recovery of many decayed houses of the Gentry' could be ascribed to trade.[2] Lewis Roberts argued, in 1641, that gentlemen 'should by all likelihoods benefit themselves more in one yeare by a well governed traffick at sea, then peradventure at Court by ten years waiting and solicitations'.[3] After 1660, several observers regarded business in general and London in particular as a primary source of capital accumulation for new men.[4]

To Bacon an estate was a pond and trade a spring, but he added that there were many ways to riches and all of them were foul; it was through patents of monopoly, wardship, usury, legal trickery and marriage that men like Audley acquired wealth.[5] Was business in fact an effective channel of upward mobility? To answer this question, it is necessary to establish the origins, scale and distribution of wealth (both capital and income) within the business community. Only then can the success of children from within and outside the business world be compared and the social impact of commercial wealth be assessed.

The rate of return

All businessmen acted as agents and earned commission without pledging their own capital. The normal rate in the Spanish, East Indian, Baltic, Teneriffe, Portuguese and Leghorn trades was 2–2.5 per cent; in the

[1] *Way to be Rich*; BL Stowe MS 993; Piper in Brown & Fishwick 1972; Bolton 1990: 73.

[2] Bolton, *Cities Advocate*, pp. 51–2; *Reasons against East India Trade*, p. 3; Defoe, *Review*, ii. 9; *Parliament Commons Debates 1621*, vii. 258; BL Hargrave MS 532, fo. 94v°; Gillespie 1920: 29; BN Anc. franc. MS 18592, fo. 681.

[3] *Select Tracts and Documents*, p. 85; Molloy, *Jure Maritimo*, ii. 430–1, 436; Bellers, *Writings*, p. 7.

[4] Locke, *Works*, ii. 8, 95; Kearney 1970: 144.

[5] Imray 1968: 25; Tibbetts 1977: 13; Barron in Hollaender & Kellaway 1969: 199.

Netherlands in the 1620s it was 2 per cent, falling later as low as 1.5 per cent.[6] In the domestic market, Robert Gray took 2.5 per cent and Michael Blackett 1.5 per cent; William Cotesworth paid 2 per cent of the selling price with an additional 0.5 per cent for transfers by bill.[7] Scriveners and brokers usually charged 1–2 per cent and sometimes as little as 0.5 per cent.[8]

Some trades did have higher rates. East India factors charged 5 per cent or double the officially sanctioned rate, when 'consignments compensate Emoluments'.[9] The consul at Algiers charged 5 per cent plus consulage, and 2–3 per cent for handling plus 1.5 per cent on sales was a common rate in the Caribbean and in New York; in Port Royal, the factors charged 10–15 per cent of the selling price and Joseph Cruttenden's rate rose from 3 to 10 per cent if he held goods for a year.[10] In the Chesapeake tobacco trade, receivers received 5–10 per cent, though commissions fell to 2.5 per cent during the century.[11] The brokers at the Back Hall, Bristol, charged 5 per cent and factors also increased the effective rate by overcharging, accepting kickbacks, inflating their expenses and trading on the cash float from sales.[12] On the other hand expenses could absorb two-thirds of gross commissions while competition between agents allowed principals to negotiate rates: Arthur Sharpe offered to 'do twice as much for ½ the money'.[13] Nonetheless, rates fluctuated within standardized parameters and remained consistently low.

It is extremely difficult to calculate 'clear gain' or the normal return on capital.[14] Both contemporary ledgers and later studies usually calculate the gross profits on particular transactions and not the yield on the total

[6] BL Lans. MS 152, fo. 177; Ruddock 1951: 100; Browne, *Marchants Avizo*, pp. 26–45; Connell-Smith 1950–1: 368; Willan 1959: 31; Holroyd, *Letter Book*, p. 10; SP 46/87, fos. 300–14; Smout 1960a: 125; Dow 1965; Paige, *Letters*, p. xi; K. G. Davies 1952b: 94; Pares 1960: 32; 1950: 34; Shaw 1989: 107; Price in Tracy 1991; Barbour 1928: 554; Steele 1986: 377; Clarke 1940: 103; Samuel 1982: 18; Chaudhuri 1965: 75; Morse 1926: i. 31, 74; Grassby 1994: 95; Riden 1987: 195–6, 202–4; in Minchinton 1988: 38; Aström 1963: i. 123, 149.

[7] Ellis 1981a: 37; Willan 1976: 137; CUL Add. MS 91; Marescoe, *Markets and Merchants*, pp. 19–21, 99, 102 documents a standard rate of 2 per cent of cost F.O.B. on exports and 2 per cent upwards on imports, depending on the services provided.

[8] Gay 1939: 427; Melton 1986a: 151, 246. Jeake paid 4d. in the £ on bills and 0.75 per cent brokerage on East India stock: see Jeake, *Astrological Diary*, p. 66.

[9] BL Add. MS 22844, fo. 24; Fryer, *New Account*, p. 217.

[10] Zahadieh 1986: 582; Cruttenden, *Atlantic Merchant Apothecary*, p. xviii, xxi; Bromley 1987: 41; Armour 1980: 39–40; Price in Solow 1991: 301.

[11] Menard 1980: 149; Clemens in Clemens *et al.* 1980: 38, 94; R. B. Davis 1963: 226; Price 1992: 30, 49, table 2.

[12] Ralph 1988: 112–13; WAM MS 11689, letter 4 Nov. 1672.

[13] Claypoole, *Letter Book*, p. 189.

[14] *Sidney Ironworks Accounts*, p. 27. Evidence cited in Grassby 1969: 724–31 has not been repeated here.

equity of a business over a long period of time.[15] The chief factor in Persia was informed that 'I expect the foote or grosse account that I may judge of the whole Profitt and Losse'.[16] But merchants rarely calculated their net return on capital.[17] Isolated ventures are not representative and they have to be aggregated to iron out fluctuations and equalize good and bad years.[18] Occasionally a commodity might double or treble on sale, but mark-ups were usually one-third of prime cost in the domestic trade and one-half overseas. Gross profit on sales must not be confused with net returns. It is easy to be misled by enthusiastic claims that, for example, English goods in New York yielded 'generally 100 p cent advance above the first cost and some of them 200, 300 yea 400'; Robert Livingston in New York in fact made around 21 per cent and 60 per cent of Joseph Cruttenden's mark-up of 75 per cent was eaten up by the Exchange.[19] The early East India Company could market pepper at three times the price it paid in Asia, but the initially high profits from Asian spices did not last and the factory in Japan found that it took a year to sell its wares.[20] The profit on sales in the contraband trade in slaves to Spanish ports from Jamaica was 75 per cent gross, but 25 per cent net.[21]

Returns on capital had never exceeded 25 per cent; before 1600, in Italy, the Levant, Flanders and England, they ranged from 10–20 per cent.[22] The gross profit on cloth sales of the Merchant Adventurers was 20 per cent at Antwerp in 1554 and 31 per cent in the 1560s and 1570s.[23] In the first half of the seventeenth century most of the joint-stock Companies lost money; the Russia Company fluctuated between profits of 7–9 per cent and a loss of 30 per cent.[24] The early East Indian voyages netted between 8 and 13 per cent on the cost price of shares, when allowance is made for delays in winding up terminal stocks; the first joint-stock yielded 7.25 per cent per annum and the overall return for investors in 1617 was probably 24.5 per cent.[25] One merchant made 24.4 per cent in the European trade in 1641–2 and Richard Archdale averaged 7.7 per cent in the 1630s, William Hoskins 6.8 per cent gross in the 1650s and William

[15] See pp. 187–8; Tucker 1968: chap. 2. Some historians have employed unclear or erroneous methods to calculate profit rates. See Bogucka 1971: 82; Jeannin in Braudel 1973: 276. [16] Roe, *Journal*, p. 465. [17] See pp. 198–9.

[18] Pares 1956: 143; Marshall 1961: ii. 621.

[19] Miller, *New York Considered*, p. 45; the author's calculation from data in Leder 1961: 9; Cruttenden, *Atlantic Merchant Apothecary*, p. 28.

[20] Massarella 1990: 128; Farrington 1991: i. 553; Disney 1977: 245–6.

[21] Zahedieh 1986a: 585, 591.

[22] Goldthwaite 1968: 248; Roover 1974: 64–8; Fryde 1983: xiv. 324; Kedar 1976: 63–5; *Cely Letters*, p. xxi; Hanham 1982: 146–8; Chiat & Reyerson 1988: 35; Ashtor 1975; 1983; Ball 1977: 118; Smythe, *Ledger*; Ramsey 1958: 367; 1976: 388.

[23] Bauman 1990: 145, 162. [24] Willan 1956: 156, 211, 216.

[25] Chaudhuri 1965: 212–17, tables 2, 8, 9.

Atwood 12 per cent.[26] The Spanish trade, however, yielded modest returns and in the Guernsey stocking trade the normal mark-up was only 10 per cent on cost.[27]

In manufacturing and the domestic wholesale trade, the rate of return also varied. Sir Thomas Cullum in his partnerships seems to have made between 11.4 and 15.3 per cent.[28] Christopher Lowther, in 1634, calculated that he had gained 20 per cent before 'interest to be deducted for my uncle ... Mr Foster and my mother'; he aimed at 30 per cent, pricing candles bought at 3½d. at 4½d. since 'they will sell the faster and there will be gain enough'; on the other hand he was willing to accept 10 per cent on a transaction in cloth, though not an offer of 5 per cent 'clear profit'.[29] Wool dealers made 9–10 per cent and some clothiers in Lancashire made 16 per cent on sales over several months.[30] John Stratford made £1,200 on an outlay of £2,000 in two years.[31] Ironworks could yield a gross profit on production cost of around 35 per cent and the Hochstetters made 11–12 per cent on cost in the Cumberland copper industry.[32] The gross profits on brewing were around 26 per cent and the coal shippers may have made up to 25 per cent.[33]

In the retail trade, Robert Gray of London made around 13 per cent on wine sales, but his profits on cloth were much lower; Abraham Rodes of Manchester had a mark-up of 26 per cent and although his net profit was 17.3 per cent at one point, it fell to 5.6 per cent; Wray marked up his goods by one-third.[34] The gross profit margin in the retail book trade was 15 per cent, less the cost of binding and carriage; dividends on the English stock of the Stationers Company were 12.5 per cent before 1640.[35]

Literary sources reinforce the evidence of business papers. When calculating the balance of trade in 1614–15, 20 per cent was added to the Customs valuation for merchant's gain and shipping and this was the rate suggested by Cranfield who in his own business seems to have made around 16 per cent.[36] Campaigners against usury thought that 10–12 per cent was a normal and reasonable return on trade.[37] The Magazine of the Virginia Company was limited to 25 per cent, though the Company claimed, in 1623, that 25 per cent was too low in relation to risk; the Plymouth court also considered that 25 per cent was reasonable 'without

[26] C107/20; C109/19; Berks. RO D/ED B2; ULL MS 265.
[27] Taylor 1968: 9; Priaulx 1961: 219; Grant in Fisher 1989: 97.
[28] Simpson 1961: chap. 3. [29] Lowther, *Commercial Correspondence*, pp. 9, 32, 188.
[30] Bowden 1962: 84; Lowe 1972: 62. [31] Thirsk 1984: 295.
[32] *Seventeenth-Century Economic Documents*, p. 301; Hammersley 1973a: 13.
[33] Clark 1983: 106; Nef 1932: ii. 71, 88, 93. [34] Willan 1976: 41, 110, 131–3.
[35] Pollard 1978: 16, 23; Ferguson 1976: 37–8; Blagden 1960.
[36] *Seventeenth-Century Economic Documents*, p. 456; Friis 1927: 81; Prestwich 1966: 63.
[37] George 1957: 465; *Seventeenth-Century Economic Documents*, pp. 7–8.

adventure or long forbearance in one and the same place'.[38] In the 1620s, it was alleged that a round trip to Newfoundland from the West Country could net 13 per cent.[39] Sir Matthew Hale envisaged a 4 per cent return for an investor in cloth production.[40]

After 1660, profit rates appear to have drifted downwards. So long as confidence was maintained up to the 1690s, the average return on Africa stock was probably 7 per cent on the face value of issued capital and 3–4 per cent for new purchasers.[41] The dividend of the Hudson's Bay Company was 8 per cent.[42] East India Company shareholders benefited from earnings (net of interest) on working capital raised through the issue of bonds and their return was probably around 10 per cent, though this depended on when they bought their shares and whether they took their dividends in goods. The actual return to an investor in 1681–2 was 15 per cent and Jeake made 12 per cent on his East India Company stock.[43] The price–earnings ratio, 1661–91 ranged from 4.92 to 19.47 and at a nominal price of £100, the yield was 6.62 per cent compounded annually; in 1709–10, on a nominal capital of £3.2 million, net profits were 11.1 per cent of which 8.3 per cent passed to shareholders.[44] Licensed and illegal private trading and usury in India, on the other hand, could generate huge returns for lucky, able and unscrupulous men, if they could find a way of transferring their ill-gotten gains to England without arousing suspicion.[45] The private trade in India could yield 40–45 per cent on sales and justify borrowing capital at 18–20 per cent; the Chinese trade returned 11 per cent.[46]

Sir Dudley North made only 3.25 per cent in the Levant trade, but some merchants earned 10–12 per cent and the same was true of the Atlantic wine trades.[47] The slave trade was clearly profitable for individuals, if not for the Africa Company, though its performance is a subject of much dispute.[48] The returns from the sugar trade depended heavily on good management; plantations owned by absentees made no money, but the net return on a well-managed plantation unencumbered by debt could be 10.3 per cent, excluding capital appreciation.[49] Although the pioneers

[38] Brenner 1993: 98; Menard 1980: 143; Johnson 1932a: 222.
[39] Bridenbaugh 1968: 228. [40] Hale, *Works*, p. 530.
[41] K. G. Davies in Carus-Wilson 1954–66: ii. 280.
[42] *Hudson's Bay Company Letters Outward 1688–96*, p. lv.
[43] Jeake, *Astrological Diary*, p. 72; Wretts-Smith 1963: 93.
[44] Chaudhuri 1978: 433–60, table A.22; Neal in Tracy 1990.
[45] Watson 1980a: 92, 100–5; Quiason 1966: 49.
[46] Gillespie 1920: 171–2; Bhattachanya 1954: 143–4; BL Add. MS 32518, fos. 192–203, 255–6; Yogev 1978: 108. [47] Grassby 1994: chap. 5; Steckley 1980: 348.
[48] Gemery & Hagedorn 1979: 14, 352; Klein in Tracy 1990: 300; Anstey & Hair 1976: 60–90; Rawley 1981: 155–6; Davity 1985; Temperly 1977; Stein 1979.
[49] Zahedieh 1986a: 209, 222; Dunn 1973; Pares 1956: 143; 1950: 320; Sheridan 1965: 20; 1968: 294–5; 1951: 312; Thomas 1968: 431.

in Barbados may have made 40–50 per cent in special circumstances, profits subsequently fell to 5–6 per cent and in Jamaica to 10 per cent.[50] The tobacco plantations could produce a return of 20 per cent, though the smaller planters had thinner margins.[51]

In Europe, Maynard put the maximum rate in the Portuguese trade at 11 per cent, though Madeira wine could be sold at 55 per cent above cost in the West Indies.[52] The tobacco adventurers to Russia averaged 5.9 per cent over twenty-four years.[53] Duarte showed gross profits of 10 per cent in the jewellery trade.[54] Charles Marescoe's profits on different ventures varied from 8 per cent to 42 per cent, but Leonara made 10 per cent in 1670–3 and George Richard commented that 'the proffits are so small now a days'.[55] In Stockholm, English merchants made 14.5–15 per cent on their voyage accounts, but gross margins on iron were only 1.84 per cent and 4 per cent on deal.[56] Frederick Herne made about 8 per cent in shipping in the 1680s and 1690s.[57] Henry Phill's profits fluctuated between 19 and 32 per cent and Peter Du Cane around 22 per cent, but both had income from stocks and financial dealings.[58] Although it was said of the Irish trade, in 1685, that 'the return is 9[l] or 10[l] p. 100', turnover was slow and profits seems to have been closer to 5 per cent.[59] In Scotland, James Ker after deducting losses and overheads made 20 per cent over three years.[60]

In the domestic economy, a colliery was lucky to return 6 per cent and the return at Tarbuck in the 1690s was under 10 per cent.[61] The Foleys in the Stour Valley did not make more than 6 per cent after paying interest at 6 per cent, though there was some capital appreciation.[62] The capital of Whitson's sugar house grew from £800 to £4–6,000 over twenty years at a simple annual rate of some 30 per cent, but this increase may not simply represent retained earnings.[63] The coal trade seems to have hovered around 10 per cent and the shipping industry between 10 and 20 per cent.[64] Investors in the quays of London distributed one-third of revenues.[65] The Wiltshire clothiers usually made 10–14 per cent and Samuel

[50] Ward 1978: 200, 205.
[51] Menard *et al.* 1983: 190; Wertenbaker 1922: 91; Clemens in Clemens *et al.* 1980: 157.
[52] Shaw 1989: 107; Duncan 1977: 50. [53] Price 1961a: 87.
[54] Samuel 1982: 18.
[55] Marescoe, *Markets and Merchants*, pp. 60, 92, 99, 115, 205, 552, tables 5, 9–10, 13–14, 19–20, 26. [56] Roseveare in Minchinton 1988: 35–8.
[57] GLL MS 6372. [58] C111/127; Essex RO D/DDC A1.
[59] Pinney, *Letters*, pp. 19, 79; Cullen 1968: 209–11. [60] Smout 1963: 86–7.
[61] Ellis 1981a: 74; Langton 1979: 120.
[62] *Foley Stour Valley Ironworks 1668–74*, pp. xvii, 3. [63] Hall 1944: 1ff.
[64] Hughes 1952a: 162; Dietz 1986; GLL MS 6372; R. Davis 1962: chap. 17; Hausman 1977: 460; Wardle 1938; Brulez 1981: 82–3; Bruijn in Tracy 1991: 182; Richard 1976: 523; Steensgaard 1965: 160; Andrews 1991: 30–1. [65] Chartres 1980a: 34.

Jeake made 4.6–8.9 per cent.[66] Stout took some losses in foreign ventures, but his gross return, given his high rate of accumulation, must have been at least 16 per cent.[67] Roger Lowe's master may have made 24 per cent on individual transactions.[68]

In the first half of the seventeenth century, the average return on a mixture of safe and risky investments was probably of the order of 10–15 per cent, comparable to yields from farming.[69] After 1650, the average rate may have fallen to 8–12 per cent. Thomas Manley put it at 15 per cent at the end of the 1660s, but Child put it at 8–9 per cent, Brewster at 5 per cent and Pollexfen and Davenant at 6 per cent.[70] The poll taxes assumed a 6 per cent rate of return on inventory and a set of instructions for an eighteenth-century commercial traveller assumed a rate of 9 per cent.[71] Mark-ups and prices had of course to be high to cover interest, damage, delays and losses on returns.[72] Contemporary articles of agreement assume a higher rate than 6–8 per cent and a small businessman, with £500–1000 equity, would have been hard put to survive on 10 per cent, as Richard Steele realized.[73] But the actual income of a small master would have been greater than the net return on his capital, since the value of his product included his own labour; drawings by partners would also be against gross profits.

'Quick returns and small gains' was a much cited maxim and Edward Stephens supposed that a merchant could raise his earnings to 20 per cent 'by frequent returns in the year'.[74] But this policy could rarely be followed because the time period between the purchase of goods and receipts from sales was necessarily long; profits were seriously reduced by the cost of uncollected debts and greatly extended credit. The cost of running a business and reaching the final consumer was also high; in Jamaica expenses reached 23.4 per cent of the sale price not including freight from London.[75] Merchants therefore often settled for low volume at high margins sustained through restrictive practices and protective barriers.

[66] *Wiltshire Textile Documents*, p. xx; East Sussex RO 145/11.

[67] Stout, *Autobiography*, pp. 25–8, 95, 106.

[68] Willan 1976: 90.

[69] Thirsk 1978: v. 118, tables 13, 17–18, 21.

[70] Keirn & Melton 1990: 167; Child, *Brief Observations*; Davenant, *Works*, ii. 23–4; Brewster, *Essays on Trade*, p. 47; Pollexfen, *England East India*, p. 21.

[71] Calculated by the author from *Instructions Commercial Traveller*, p. 140. Wilson 1971: table 6, shows returns of 4.8 per cent in the 1750s and Spooner 1983: 5 puts the profits on the bullion trade in 1747 at $\frac{1}{16}$ per cent. There is a strong presumption in classical, neo-classical, Marxian and Keynesian models that profits will ultimately fall to zero without technological innovation: see Robinson 1958: 181; Missowski 1982; Rosenberg in Skinner & Wilson 1975: 388; Mill 1911: iv. 4; Hicks 1969: 33.

[72] Cruttenden, *Atlantic Merchant Apothecary*, pp. 109–11.

[73] Steele, *Religious Tradesman*, p. 82; Earle 1989a: 139.

[74] BL Add. MS 22843, letter 25 Aug. 1701; Stephens, *Relief of Apprentices*, p. 7.

[75] Buisseret & Pawson 1975: 78.

Competition and limited demand imposed a ceiling on prices and thereby profits, though the relevant factors varied between different trades.[76] In shipping what mattered was efficient utilization and deployment and the rate of depreciation.[77] It cost almost as much to refit as to build a ship; to obtain cargoes, a merchantman had to turn round fast and be in the right place at the right time. Overseas merchants, like shippers, needed return cargoes which could double their profit on the same capital outlay. The fall in freight costs benefited the merchant (though not the ship-owner) as did safer seas and more efficient marketing through entrepots. But these advantages were shared with other competitors and the increase in the volume of staples and their consequent fall in price benefited the consumer more than the merchant and producer.[78]

It is unlikely, therefore, that fortunes were created by profit inflation.[79] The average annual real return on capital invested was much lower than contemporary optimism suggested and it did not increase proportionally with the volume of business. Higher rates could often be extracted by enterprising merchants in a stagnant or falling market with a slow turnover than in a rapidly developing, but overcrowded trade. Overinvestment always threatened to reduce the marginal efficiency of capital and the rate of profit may have declined in tandem with the rate of interest. A falling rate of return per transaction also benefited the bigger merchants who could practise economies of scale.

Indeed it appears to have been usury rather than commodity profits which sustained business incomes. The interest on goods sold on credit and on raw materials advanced to planters, clothworkers, miners and artisans exceeded the statutory maximum rate and generated higher profits than sales for ready money.[80] Jeake made 12–17 per cent on his bottomry loans.[81] The normal interest on loans to landowners on mortgage and to corporations on bond hovered around 5–6 per cent after 1660. But short-term loans to the Crown yielded 5–10 per cent between 1660 and 1688 and 6–8 per cent between 1688 and 1697; the difference between the statutory maximum rate of interest and that obtained from the Crown was at least 4 per cent and it could rise as high as 9 per cent, though the rate was related to the branch of revenue used as security and the expected period of repayment.[82] In the 1690s, government loans were both better

[76] See pp. 91–2. [77] Scammel 1972: 403, 405–6.

[78] Menard in Tracy 1991: 274.

[79] The thesis of Hamilton 1929 and Keynes 1930: ii. 152–63 has been effectively demolished by Gould 1964–5: 262–4 and Felix in Floud 1974: 135–6, though it has been revived in a new guise by Wee 1978: 58ff.

[80] Parker in Parker 1965a: 153; Pares 1960: 32; 1950: 33; Zahedieh 1986a: 213 n.33; Lewis 1966: 217–24; Whetter 1974: 163; Sanford, *Letter Book*, p. 47.

[81] ESRO 145/11. [82] Nichols 1985: 250.

secured and yielded 7–14 per cent, though the rate subsequently fell.[83] The anticipation and collection of revenue for the Crown, Church and private corporations was much more lucrative than conventional trade.

In theory, the differential between interest and profit rates, adjusted for risk, does not seem to have been sufficient to attract capital into active industrial and commercial ventures.[84] But there were always two rates of interest – one for secure and one for speculative loans. The former were often lower than the maximum permitted rate and the latter always commanded a premium.[85] So long as expectations of profit were high, merchants would invest.[86] Few were, moreover, in a position to compare the returns of business with other investments, because gain was indeterminate and there was no conventional minimum level of profit to use as a benchmark.

Business profits did contribute to capital formation. Although it took him five years to accumulate his first thousand in the drapery trade, Sir Thomas Cullum thereafter accumulated £1,000 annually.[87] Richard Hill, a London cordwainer with a stake in most foreign trades, progressed, with some help from an office, from £588 in 1633 to £7,811 in 1660; Charles Marescoe doubled his capital between 1664 and 1667.[88] Merchants usually accumulated little in their early years, however, and there were great variations between trades and decades. The richest had diversified portfolios, both because trade could not accommodate all their capital and because they wished to hedge against risk. Although rentier income rapidly compounded, the rate of accumulation must have been constrained when capital was held in low-yielding passive investments or in plate, coin and household effects. Even those with high incomes often had heavy commitments, in particular provision for their children. The rate of accumulation and saving must rarely have reached King's estimate of 20 per cent for the greater and 15 per cent for the lesser merchants.[89]

The problem of valuation

Business estates are difficult to assess, even when the ledgers survive. Because seventeenth-century accounting usually made no provision for

[83] Dickson 1967: chaps 3–4.

[84] *Early English Tracts Commerce*, p. 563; Papillon, *Memoirs*, p. 14; Barbour 1950; Habakkuk 1952–3: 27; Smith, *Wealth of Nations*, i. 114.

[85] Thrupp 1948: 123; Korner 1980.

[86] Bright 1858: 179.

[87] Simpson 1961: 141, 177.

[88] BL Add. MS 5488; Hill 1907: 146–51; Marescoe, *Markets and Merchants*, p. 25.

[89] King, *Two Tracts*, p. 31; Piquet-Marchand 1965; Deane & Cole 1967: 259–60; Pollard & Crossley 1968: 125; Minchinton 1978. R. Davis 1967a: 14, 23 modifies his earlier view of the role of commercial capital.

overheads or amortization of liabilities, it is usually impossible to value a business accurately except on death or liquidation. Even then, a simple monetary sum at one point of time cannot adequately portray the multidimensional character of a business or its progression through the life cycle of the owner.[90] Cranfield at his height was worth £102,400 with an income of £25–28,000 but, at his death, his assets had fallen to £76,500.[91] Valuations by merchants often include optimistic estimates of future earning power and they frequently overestimated the value of their charitable bequests. Their credit balances were inflated by a reluctance to write down doubtful debts as desperate as they aged.[92] Many delegated to their executors the task of calculating their net worth, assisted perhaps by a rough calculation made prior to their decease.

Business operated in a continuum and the working capital of a merchant, while he was alive, was inflated beyond his net assets by his reputation and included goodwill and his own managerial skill. Wealth was not a fixed stable quantity, but depended on the liquidity of the market, the conditions of trade, on investor confidence, the number of buyers and the demand for goods. Although merchants held real estate as a reserve, they had few fixed assets and their retained earnings were invested primarily in inventory and in credit to customers, both of which were subject to market risk, depreciation and default and which could often only be converted into cash below historic cost because of an unfavourable exchange rate, difficulties of collection or forced sale. Executors' accounts suggest that great fortunes shrank when an estate was wound up, usually over several years; many debts had to be written off and the actual proceeds from sales fell far short of their book value.[93]

The records of taxation and landownership are even more circumscribed. The value of land held by merchants can be established at purchase, but their holdings were usually too piecemeal to be quickly traced through title deeds, surveys and transactions in the courts. By the seventeenth century, the subsidy assessments had become quotas apportioned by local commissioners.[94] The General Aid of 1689 directly taxed stock and goods, as did the poll taxes of the 1690s which had their origins in the 1640s and in the subsidy of 1671 and which were administered through the commissioners for the Aid. But it proved impossible to adequately determine net worth in personalty for direct taxation; it was

90 Grassby 1970b: 106. 91 Prestwich 1966: 53–7, 93, 419–20, 587.

92 Sir Thomas Cullum wrote off his bad debts in three stages.

93 West Yorkshire Archives Service, Yorks. Arch. Soc. Grantley MSS, no. 323 (89a), accounts of Richard Gwyn, 1670; *Lincoln Probate Inventories*, p. lxxx.

94 On the subsidy as a representative source see Webb 1962: 113, 142; Hoskins 1976; *Sussex Lay Subsidies*, p. xxiv; Cornwall 1963: 93; 1976; 1988; Pound 1966: 5; *Exeter in Seventeenth Century*; Kitching 1989: 185; GLL MS 3283, 2942.

easier to tax land and consumption.[95] Like the Hearth Tax returns, the poll taxes suggest the relative differences of wealth between regions and individuals, but they do not accurately assess the absolute worth of individuals.[96] Charitable bequests are a reliable guide only when they represent a stated percentage of an estate.[97] Although the Port Books suggest scale of investment, they do not clearly distinguish between principals and agents or reveal the equity of a business.

The best evidence is provided by wills and inventories, particularly when combined.[98] Most large-scale merchants with property in more than one diocese in the southern Province and those dying overseas had their wills proved and their inventories exhibited in the Prerogative Court of Canterbury; under the Protectorate all probate was concentrated there.[99] Inventories were made obligatory by 21 Hen. VIII, c. 5, but their survival is largely accidental with major gaps, as during the Interregnum. Their total volume is still formidable as well as their average length: in Sussex one in four survive and Lincolnshire has 8,000 between 1669 and 1690.[100] The most comprehensive collection for businessmen is that of the Orphans Court of London. Most inventories calculated the net value of personal estates by listing all assets, including sperate, doubtful and desperate debts owed to the deceased.[101] But those presented to the London Orphans Court also deducted debts owed by the deceased, the furniture of the widow's chamber and funeral and administrative charges.[102]

95 The returns of the 1694 Act have been used by Krey 1985 and by Beattie in Cockburn & Green 1988: table 8.6. But they are unreliable because of underassessment: see Faraday 1976: 105–7; Alexander 1989: 51; GLL MS 11311, 11316.

96 Meekings 1951: app. 3; Horn 1981.

97 The data in Jordan 1960a is of limited use because the methods of valuing estates are not explained, individual cases are rarely documented and the data is aggregated into tables whose medians and averages are invalidated by inflation.

98 On inventories as a source see Kitch in Beier & Finlay 1986; Zell 1984: 109–11; Thirsk 1955: 72; Raymond 1986; Simpson 1985; Marshall 1980: 503–4; Shammas 1977: 686–7; Cox & Cox 1984: 133–45; Riden 1985; Overton 1977; Porter 1976; Gilbert 1980; Rubinstein & Duncan 1974; *Lichfield Probate Inventories*, pp. 5–9; Garrard in Woude 1980; Smedt 1973. Editions of inventories are usually arbitrary selections and doubtful debts are sometimes included in the net totals: see *Worcester Probate Inventories 1545–1614*, ii. 12.

99 For probate procedures and repositories see Camp 1974; Zell 1979: 72. Sometimes inventories are catalogued separately from the court records; strays and copies also occur in municipal, state and private archives: see GLL MS 666; Nottingham Univ. Lib. Archives Dept., Mellis of Hodsock MSS; West Yorkshire Archives Service, Yorks. Arch. Soc. Grantley MSS, no. 323 (89a); Warws. RO, Bridge House deeds; E154/3/34–5/40; REQ 2/299; 2/397/60; 2/307.

100 Kenyon 1958: 67. Unless they have been indexed, the inventory rolls of businessmen cannot be singled out in large collections.

101 Other categories included debts beyond the sea and debts by specialty, i.e. obligations under seal securing the debt. The category of separate debts occurs, which may be a conflation of sperate; a typical example is Gage 1822: 115–16.

102 On the exclusions see Burn 1842: iv. 414–20, 570–80.

It is important to recognize the limitations of both wills and inventories as evidence for wealth. The devices employed by lawyers to circumvent inconvenient aspects of the law of succession can easily distort the assets of testators in wills.[103] Since any wealthy businessmen was likely to hold real estate, the omission of freehold real property in inventories seriously understates their total wealth; although it is dangerous to generalize from individual examples, the personalty of a businessman rarely represented more than two-thirds of his estate and frequently only one-half.[104]

Inventories also omit gifts and transfers before death, such as prior distribution of dowries and portions, and sometimes bequests in wills. The majority of inventories in local archives relate to the lesser men of property rather than to merchants. The Orphans' inventories exclude bachelors and the arrangement of entries, usually grouped in estates of the same value, and several incomplete accounts suggest that items were bound together hastily every decade and that many loose papers were lost.[105] They are sometimes carelessly compiled or fail to give detailed descriptions of stock; leases and chattels are often undervalued and cheap items omitted.

An inventory alone can give a false impression of the real business of the testator.[106] It is not always appreciated that the omission of debts owing by the testator invalidates the great majority, even though these liabilities can sometimes be picked up from the administration accounts.[107] The majority of business estates had a high level of doubtful debts which tended to accumulate quietly over a lifetime.[108] It is also difficult to distinguish advances against purchase or credit on sales from conventional loans. Even in the Orphans Court, the problem of valuing debts is often insoluble. Sperate debts, which had good security or were easily enforceable at law, would normally have been recovered, but executors were often overly pessimistic when classifying debts.[109] Sir Joseph

[103] Liverymen would, for example, hold property for their Companies.

[104] Bank stock and some shares may have been treated as realty: see Godolphin, *Orphans' Legacy*; Rudden 1985: 44. New England was unique in including real estate (though not usually debts owed) in inventories, though each American colony had different practices. See Hanson-Jones 1982: 278; 1977: 18, 21; Main 1975: 92; 1982: app. C; *Yorkshire Abbotside Wills*, p. 53; Foster in Jaher 1973: 130; Stevenson & Salter 1939: 141; GLL MS 10187; Woodhead 1966: 30, 54.

[105] CLRO CSB II; Earle 1989a: table 4.6

[106] D. W. Jones 1988: 282, for example, describes Sir William Turner as a shopkeeper. See also Price 1876: 147.

[107] A few provincial inventories include debts owed by the testator: see *Yorkshire Probate Inventories*, pp. 105–17, 136–7; *Lancashire Probate Records*, pp. 8–9; Riden 1985: 41; Menard 1974: 170; Spufford in Chartres & Hey 1990: 143, 151–3.

[108] Fisher 1936: app. 10.

[109] The proportion of doubtful and desperate debts varied. They represented around one-third in the London Orphans' inventories whereas in Worcester 29 per cent of debts were secured and 2 per cent desperate: see Johnston 1978: table 4; Holderness 1976b: 104; Dechêne 1974: 206.

Sheldon and Sir Thomas Rich had huge sums on loan to corporations and individuals on the security of land, houses and bonds, and yet these debts were classified as doubtful or desperate. Richard Wyche, a Skinner, had £4,697 in doubtful debts including several Levantine and Russian investments and £3,000 in the East India Company, some of which must have been realized.[110] The estate of Charles Marescoe recovered £15,180 out of £19,550 doubtful debts.[111]

Additional payments into Orphans' estates often exceeded the original sum declared in Court and assets must have been received after the final return filed within a year. The executors of Alexander Hosea were still collecting debts fifteen years after his death.[112] It is also possible that the Common Serjeant deliberately classified assets as doubtful and desperate. After 1581, he was entitled to a commission on their collection and he could hold receipts for his own use for one year. But it would still be risky to assume that a large proportion of doubtful and desperate debts were ever collected. Hugh Wood's sperate and doubtful debts in 1684 were assessed at £3,538, mainly in goods, but only £1,920 were recovered. Only £117 of John Badcock's debts of £923 were collected.[113]

These problems cannot be brushed aside, but there are compensating factors. Testators sometimes list and value assets in detail in their wills. In the Orphans Court of London, executors were obliged to exhibit inventories of the total estate to prevent testators from evading the Custom by transfers before death. Executors were bound by recognizances to provide accounts of the collection of debts and the inventories were often drawn up by neighbours and relatives, who knew the trade of the deceased and the value of commercial goods. Valuations, when they can be checked, are encouraging.[114] It was easier to appraise commercial inventory than to value heavily encumbered landed estates. Until 1693, the London Court of Orphans closely supervised executors and made it extremely hard to conceal funds. All business assets, including property abroad and held in partnership, were listed as well as unexpired terms of leases, stocks and personal effects. Inventories had to be drawn up within two months of death and all charges on the estate met before winding up the estate, so that the executors' accounts are both immediate and thorough.

110 Bod. Rawl. MS A.414, fos. 12v–13; a typical example is Bevys, 'Inventory', pp. 213–40. Carlton 1971: 26; 1974: 45–7 establishes that doubtful debts were collected in forty-eight of fifty-seven estates, 1662–3, and suggests a collection rate of 60 per cent. If this was uniformly true, it could mean that the net figures in tables 8:1–5 would have to be increased by as much as 50 per cent and they must be taken as minimum figures. It is, however, preferable to present the hard data from the formal record rather than to adjust upwards by an arbitrary percentage.

111 Marescoe, *Markets and Merchants*, p. 5.

112 Plummer 1972: 262.

113 Vaisey in Riden 1985: 102.

114 GLL MS 6666.

The structure of wealth

At the apex of the London business community was a tiny handful of tycoons with personalty in excess of £100,000, which was a conventional figure for the plutocrat and was called a plum.[115] Between 1600 and 1660, at least ten men were worth over £100,000 at some point in their careers.[116] It was these men that James Howell had in mind when he boasted that the London aldermen could buy a hundred burghers of Amsterdam.[117] Between 1660 and 1720, at least fifteen businessmen were worth over £100,000, including nine aldermen, 1694–1714.[118]

Beneath the unimaginably rich were the very rich with £30,000 to £100,000. At least twelve fell into this category before 1660 and, between 1660 and 1689, at least 11 aldermen and Common Councillors of London were worth over £50,000 as were fourteen of the directors of the South Sea Company.[119] Twelve aldermen, 1694–1714, left £50–100,000. In the second half of the century, there were at any one time probably forty businessmen with assets of more than £30,000.[120]

Beneath the very rich were the mere rich with £20–30,000; a conventional target for the ambitious businessman was £20–25,000 and private business papers reveal at least ten in this bracket.[121] Of 140 Jacobean aldermen, fifty-five or 39.3 per cent were worth more than £20,000, excluding land.[122] Eighty-two of the aldermen, 1694–1714 left £20–50,000. In London, active businessmen in this category probably numbered around sixty and represented approximately 0.3 per cent of the freemen.

A fourth category consisted of the prosperous with between £10,000 and £20,000 who qualified to be Sheriffs of London. Seventy-eight of the Jacobean aldermen fell into this category and 117 of the aldermen 1694–1714; Londoners in this bracket who left orphans averaged fourteen in

[115] Ailesbury, *Memoirs*, pp. xxv–xxvi.

[116] Grassby 1970a: 221–9; Shipley 1975a: 241; 1976: 467; Ashton 1979: 39.

[117] Howell, *Londinopolis*, p. 389.

[118] Horwitz 1987: 272, 275–7, table 10; Price 1980: 21; Clay 1978: 213, table 5; CLRO CSB, box 40; D. W. Jones in Clark & Slack 1972: 334, 329; Coleman 1963: 190; Letwin 1963: 37.

[119] House of Lords RO, South Sea Company Papers; *South Sea Company Particulars of late Directors*, pp. 248–57. Because a levy on the estates was proposed, the inventories certainly understate their value.

[120] See table 8.1. This projection depends on the following assumptions which are open to challenge: 1. That the number of freemen in London was 20,000; 2. That the wealth of the whole body of freemen was distributed in the same relative proportions as for those who left orphans; 3. That the net estates of inventories were neither increased by subsequent recovery of debts nor decreased by distribution of assets during the lifetime of the testator.

[121] Defoe, *Compleat English Gentleman*, pp. 263–4; Marshall 1976: 216.

[122] Lang 1963: 300; 1974: 31.

Table 8.1. *Personal assets of businessmen,* c. *1688: estimates of capital and income (£)*

Brackets ('00s)	No.[a]	Median capital	Median income	Tot. cap. ('000s)	Tot. inc. (000s)
London					
Over 300	40	50000	3000	2000	120
201–300	60	25000	1500	1500	90
101–200	300	15000	1500	4500	270
51–100	600	7500	750	4500	450
41–50	350	4500	450	1575	157.5
31–40	400	3500	350	1400	140
21–30	1000	2500	250	2500	250
16–20	900	1750	175	1575	157.5
11–15	1500	1250	125	1875	187.5
7.5–10	1600	775	78	1240	124.8
5–7	1600	600	60	960	96
Subtotal	8350	—	—	23625	2043.3
Provinces					
Major towns	250	1500	150	375	37.5
	750	750	75	562.5	56.25
Lesser towns	1000	750	75	750	75
Total	10350	—	—	25312.5	2212.05

Note: [a] Projected from the percentage of estates in each financial bracket in the Common Serjeant's Book, assuming a population of 20,000 freemen.

each generation. Many other examples can be found in wills and business archives.[123] This group probably represented 1.5 per cent of the London freemen or some 300 men.

A fifth category consisted of the comfortable who had £5,000 to 10,000. The evidence of charitable bequests suggests a median estate for the greater London merchants of £3,345 under Elizabeth, £10,167 under the Early Stuarts and £7,060 during the Interregnum; the average estate of 569 testators over the whole period was £5,815.[124] In London this bracket represented maybe 3 per cent of the freemen or some 600 men.[125]

Businessmen with net assets of between £500 and £5000 constituted the bottom and basic category. The median estate of the philanthropic tradesmen, 1600–60, was £1,007 and the average of tradesmen was £588.[126]. Of the merchants in a sample from the Orphans' inventories between 1694–1720, 50 per cent had less than £5,000.[127] After 1660, this group probably numbered a little over 7,300.

The small masters and artisans, chapmen, factors, provision dealers, skilled tradesmen, small builders and shopkeepers, who were worth less than £500 and bore the brunt of recessions, numbered approximately 40 per cent of the London freemen.[128] Of the households within the walls, 73 per cent were not liable for the 1695 surtax which was charged on £600 personalty or realty yielding £50 per annum.[129]

In the provincial towns, there were no tycoons, but several left more than £10,000.[130] Tax returns consistently reveal a few exceptionally rich men in each town.[131] Many more were in the £5–10,000 bracket.[132] In 1640, seven merchants of York traded in goods worth £4,000 and four merchants at Whitehaven were worth £4,000 and one above £20,000.[133] Charles Yarwood of Macclesfield had money and goods worth £9,226, though £5,000 was in sperate and doubtful debts about which the testator was clearly uncertain.[134] One yarn-master in Essex was worth over £5,000 and a Mayor of Taunton was said to have £7–8,000.[135] A Hull merchant in

[123] C109/19; C111/127; Essex RO D/DDc/A1; BL Harl. MS 7497.

[124] Jordan 1960a: 108, 114, 338, 341, 350; 1959: 336.

[125] Alexander 1989: 53 puts the number of rich taxpayers in 1692–5 at 20 per cent and the very rich at 5 per cent. The Orphans' evidence suggests that 5 per cent of businessmen had in excess of £10,000 and 20 per cent in excess of £3,000.

[126] Jordan 1960a: 321; 1959: 336. [127] Earle 1989a: 35.

[128] Blackmore 1986: 219–20; Leathersellers Company, Court Minutes, 27 May 1678.

[129] Jones & Judges 1936; *London Inhabitants within Walls*, pp. xxi, xxxv, table 3.

[130] Moore 1899: 99–100; Stephens 1960: 280–1; Poole 1962: 116; MacHattie 1951: 74–7; Lancs. RO DDH/P 39 no. 24; Ramsay 1965: 31; Raines & Sutton 1903: i. 276, app. 2; Howell 1967: 14–16.

[131] Bridenbaugh 1968: 177; Ffoulkes 1969: 75; *Bristol Company Soapmakers*, p. 185; Palliser 1979: 137. [132] MacGrath 1970. [133] Hall 1933: 266; Watts 1978: 356.

[134] Spufford in Chartres & Hey 1990: 142.

[135] Fontaine, *Mémoires*, p. 210; Hunt 1983: 148–51.

the 1630s had £5–6,000 and several Newcastle merchants had turnovers of £3–5,000; Yorkshire had its wealthy clothiers, like Matthew Wilson who left £6,654 including £3,354 in desperate debts.[136] The average estate of the provincial merchant donors was, however, only £1,428 and outside of London, anyone above £5,000 would have been considered rich.

The majority of businessmen in the provinces fell into the bottom category of £500–5,000; the few who do appear in the records of charitable bequests averaged £235.[137] One-quarter of the Shrewsbury Drapers had £1,000 plus land and in Chester two were worth over £1,000 and two over £500.[138] In Elizabethan Manchester, there were two clothiers over £1,000 and two worth £500–1,000 and three Lancashire linen drapers had over £1,500.[139] In the seventeenth century, clothiers could reach £1,500, but very few in Chesterfield and Manchester were worth £3–4,000 before 1690, and the northern inventories reveal that most left under £500.[140] In Tudor York, the majority of businessmen had £400–1,000 with a handful over £2,000; the merchants of Stuart Leeds had up to £5,000.[141] In Newcastle and Hull, the substantial domestic and foreign merchants ranged over £1–2,000.[142]

Some Midland mercers, hosiers and metal manufacturers had £1,000, but most were below £100.[143] In Gloucestershire, four estates were above £2,000, three clothiers were worth over £1,000 and four £500–1,000, and some mercers and maltsters £500–750.[144] In the City of Gloucester, 1540–1640, some aldermen had £3,000, one brewer £2,000, a grocer £1,884 and a mercer, £5–6,000, but the average was £766; between 1660 and 1740, only two had over £1,000 and five £500–1,000.[145] In Bristol, estates ranged from £1,000 to £2,000; the average personalty of the Merchant Venturers was £919, though one had £2,047 and three £4,000–4,500.[146] In Tudor Worcester, a few clothiers had £500–1,000 and in Worcestershire, 1699–1716. there were five inventories over £1,000.[147]

In Ipswich, between 1583 and 1714, only 1.4 per cent of 222 inventories were over £1,000, 0.9 per cent, £751–1,000, and 11.5 per cent over

136 Howell 1984: 2; Cross 1976: 25; *Yorkshire Probate Inventories*, p. 117.
137 Jordan 1961b: 240, 279; 1959: 337.
138 Mendenhall 1953: 92, 118; Woodward 1967: app. B; Alldridge 1983a: 2.
139 Willan 1980: app. 2; Lowe 1972: 54–6.
140 Aikin, *Description Manchester*, p. 182; *Lancashire Wills*, pp. 15, 43; Wadsworth & Mann 1931: 73; Marshall 1975a: 213.
141 Kirby 1986: 160–1; Palliser 1979: 141–3; 1978.
142 Hall 1933: 261–3.
143 Rowlands 1977: 53; 1975: 49; Clark 1931: 64; Gill 1952: 60; *Dudley Probate Inventories*; Newton 1966: 9.
144 Ripley 1984: 173, table 3; *V.C.H. City of Gloucester*, iv. 77, 84.
145 Clark in Clark *et al.* 1979: 177, 257; Ripley 1976: 121; 1980: 143, 151.
146 *Bristol Merchants and Merchandise*, p. xxii; MacGrath 1947: 94–5.
147 Johnston 1978: table 2; Dyer 1972.

£250.[148] In Norwich, Henry Fawcet left £3,000 excluding land, two stuff-makers left more than £1,000 and the mercers and drapers were prosperous; but only one linen weaver left more than £500.[149] Colchester had its rich clothiers, but most were below £500.[150] Cash bequests in Reading wills ranged from £735 to £2,370 and averaged £1,000.[151] Thomas Johnson of Gainsborough, Lincolnshire, had £3,450, and Samuel Jeake in Rye over £2,000; Canterbury had one silkman worth over £1,000 and Southampton at least one merchant worth £2,000.[152] In Leicestershire and Northampton, a few mercers reached £1,000 and one £3,684; in 1635, an upholsterer had £1,358.[153] In Petworth, a tobacco merchant reached £935, but only 10 per cent of all inventories, mainly of glovers and mercers, had more than £500.[154]

In Exeter one-third of the merchants had £3,000 upwards, though many left under £1,000.[155] One Staverton merchant was worth £1,700 and a Totnes clothier £1,112, but the majority of Devonshire inventories reveal more modest estates.[156] In Cornwall, one potter and pewterer died worth £2,298, but only two Cornish merchants were worth over £1,000.[157] James Ashe, a Somerset clothier had a turnover of £4,000, but only four Somerset clothiers, in 1685, had over £400.[158] One Cardiff tanner was worth £900, but that was exceptional.[159]

The provincial inventories reveal that most estates were below £500 and mainly below £100, though with some upward movement during the century.[160] They included some merchants, but most were tradesmen and craftsmen.[161] A small sample of inventories from fourteen counties, 1580–1700, puts the median for merchants at £1,084, mercers at £280 and the majority of trades much lower.[162] Only five out of 127 chapmen were

[148] Reed in Clark 1981: 116–17; *Ipswich Probate Inventories*, p. 3.

[149] Evans 1985: table 4.2; Allison 1960: table 1; 1961: table 3.

[150] Burley 1957: 121–2.

[151] Goose 1984: table 3.

[152] Rothstein 1989: 42; *Southampton Probate Inventories 1561–75*, p. 37; *Lincoln Probate Inventories*, table 4.

[153] *V.C.H. Leicestershire*, iv. tables 1–11; 'Northampton mercer's inventory', p. 317; Thirsk 1971: iv. 489.

[154] Kenyon 1958: parts 1–2.

[155] Stephens 1959: 133; Hoskins in Bindoff *et al.* 1961: 163, 172; MacCaffrey 1958: 263; Portman 1966: 110–11; Bevys, 'Inventory', pp. 213–40.

[156] *Devon Inventories*, pp. 38–44, 98.

[157] Whetter 1974: 166; Douch 1969: 69.

[158] C107/20; Clifton 1984: 26.

[159] M. I. Williams in G. Williams 1974: 82; Owen 1962: 107.

[160] IESRO MS HE 30; Lowe, *Diary*, p. 134; Griffiths 1937; Talbot 1986; Woodward 1967: app. B; Barleys 1959; Allison 1960; *V.C.H. Leicestershire*, iii. tables 1–11; Surfield 1986; Dyer 1978; *Telford Yeomen*; Dyer 1979c; Horn 1981: 91–3; Cowell 1984; Weatherill 1986: tables 5–6; Martin 1982: 37; Husbands 1981: table 1; Woodward 1981: table 2; *Banbury Wills*, table 1; *Haverfordwest Records*, p. 8; West, *Accounts*, p. 74; *Lincoln Probate Inventories*, pp. xlix, lxi, lxv, table 5.

[161] Poole 1962: 701.

[162] Cressy 1987: tables 4, 6, 9. Although 2,879 provincial inventories were sampled, the major centres of business activity do not seem to be adequately represented. A larger sample is explored by Weatherell 1988: table 8.1, but the median figures conceal important differences between occupations and individuals.

worth more than £50.[163] The situation in Scotland, Ireland and the Plantations was similar. Thirty out of 400–500 of the Glasgow merchants were substantial men and a similar proportion of the Edinburgh merchants.[164] The losses claimed by Irish merchants in the 1641 rebellion were in the hundreds rather than the thousands.[165] The average worth of forty-nine merchants in Port Royal was £1,789.[166] Philadelphia had five merchants worth over £2,500, but most were under £500.[167] In the north Chesapeake, only 1.6 per cent had more than £1,000; in Maryland only 0.7 per cent had over £1,000 and £800 was considered a fortune.[168] New England was even poorer, though assets were unevenly distributed; in Boston, the average magisterial estate was £1,363 and 15 per cent were prosperous.[169]

The rate of attrition was also universally high, even among those who took their freedom. There was a rapid turnover of names in the Port Books, though many of these would have been occasional investors; of 239, 1604–6, 110 had disappeared by 1609.[170] Stout's apprentice and his nephew failed. At least 20 per cent of testators in the Orphans Court of London had no assets at death. Many of these were undoubtedly small masters who never had more than minimal capital, but 7.97 per cent were businessmen whose debts exceeded their assets or who had failed.[171] It was extremely common for merchants to seesaw between poverty and wealth and even aldermen of London fell on hard times.[172] Other fortunes disappeared completely through speculation, political changes and shady dealing.[173] Sir Paul Pindar died insolvent at the age of eighty-four and his executor committed suicide after trying to handle the estate; the son of Sir John Wolstenholme went bankrupt in 1650.[174] Often, in Thomas Mann's metaphor, a fortune was like the light of a star, shining brightly when it was already dying or extinguished.

Wealth and connection provided no guarantee against future losses or bankruptcy.[175] Several of the great financiers and bankers failed and of

[163] Spufford 1984: fig. 1. [164] Smout 1969: 170; 1968: 66; 1963: 290; Lynch 1981: 16.
[165] Goodbody 1978; Canny in Andrews *et al.* 1979: 88. [166] Zahedieh 1986b: 588.
[167] Nash in Dunns 1986: 354, table 19.2; Goodfriend 1992: 71, table 4.
[168] Land in Breen 1976: 237; Lane 1972: 114–16; Bridenbaugh 1938: 40; Nash in Greene & Pole 1984: 265.
[169] Hennetta 1965: 79, table 1; Main 1983: 13; Shammas 1980: 7; Wall 1972: 32; Allen in Allen & Thompson 1976: table 3; Anderson 1975: 161, 171.
[170] Taylor 1968: 12. [171] See fig. 8.1.
[172] Wardle 1938: 181; Platt 1902; Le Neve, *Pedigrees Knights*, p. 57.
[173] Evans 1974: 63; Beaven 1909–13: ii. 181, 186, 188; Andrews 1991: 5; Gentles 1978: 308; Ingram 1978.
[174] Goss 1929–33: 238, 247, 255; Habakkuk 1980: 203.
[175] The commissions of bankruptcy in the Patent Rolls (Supplement C67) have yet to be properly explored.

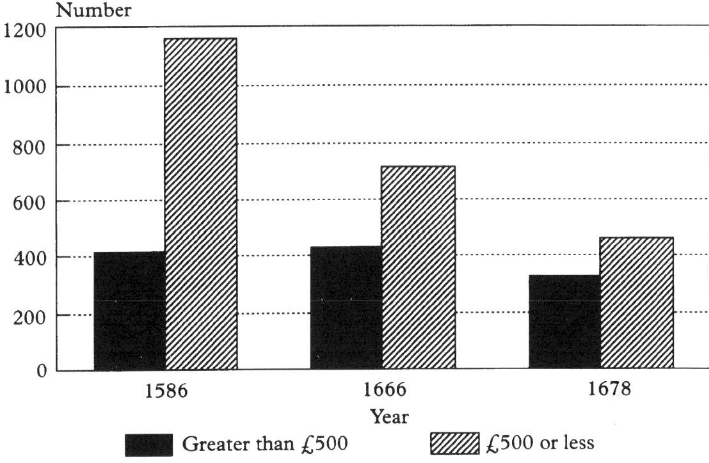

Fig. 8.1. Personal wealth of London freemen, 1586–1614, 1666–77 and 1678–93. (*Source*: CLRO, Common Serjeant's Books, Court of Orphans' inventories.)

ninety-three goldsmith bankers, 1670–1700, only five survived.[176] Merchants in the overseas Companies, planters, shipbuilders, ironmasters, textile manufacturers, insurance underwriters and sons of successful merchants all fell by the wayside.[177] Oliver Heywood's father, a fustian merchant, accumulated a debt of £1,200 and was 'often forced to skulk in holes and flee'; the same was true of Defoe.[178] After 1690, the rate of bankruptcy increased. There were 150–200 commissions of bankruptcy annually between 1710 and 1730, compared with 50 in the 1650s, and a preponderance of merchants; the actual bankruptcy rate was 1–2 per cent, but the effective rate allowing for years spent in business was probably 10–15 per cent.[179] The average annual number of bankruptcies was 45 (1691–1700), 207 (1701–10) and 174 (1711–20) and the failure rate was of course higher than the rate of legal bankruptcy; the casualties numbered 59 linen dealers and 116 mercers in the 1700s.[180] Every town and sector of

[176] Richards 1928: 340; 1965: 25; Clark in Abbott 1941: 17; Ramsay 1975: 59; Defoe, *Compleat English Tradesman*, i. 95; Melton in Myers & Harris 1985: 66–7; Dewhurst & Doublet 1974: 110–18.

[177] GLL MS 11896; Firebrace 1932: 236; Willan 1954: 268; Anderson 1969: 486; Sheridan 1851: xvii–xviii; Dietz 1991: 11; Goring in Ives *et al.* 1978: 215; MacNamara 1895: 437–8; Youings 1968: 98; Whetter 1974: 160; Paige, *Letters*, p. xxiv.

[178] Heywood, *Autobiography*, pp. 20, 22, 24–7; Sutherland 1950: 28, 33, 40–6.

[179] Horwitz 1987: 296; Earle 1989a: 129; Price 1987: table 4.

[180] Hoppitt 1987: tables 1, 10, app. 1.

the economy had its decayed men, and no businessman was immune from bankruptcy.

It is dangerous to generalize about the whole English business community over a century, because the distribution of wealth and population between towns and regions changed continuously.[181] But there was a permanent, qualitative difference between London and the provincial towns. The average value of probated estates in London, 1699–1700 has been put at £1,898 compared with £170 for merchants and £154 for shopkeepers in the West Midlands.[182] A major reason for the massive migration to London was that it offered financial opportunities which did not exist elsewhere. There were also some signs of improvement. In the sixteenth century, the lesser men do not seem to have benefited from economic growth; it was the rich who tended to become richer. But, in the seventeenth century, more were able, on a modestly ascending scale, to leave the world with a little more than they had entered.[183] The percentage of London freemen in the £500–5,000 bracket rose from 23 per cent between 1586 and 1614 to 36 per cent between 1678 and 1693. After 1690, longer life expectancy may also have helped; the median fortunes of those leaving orphans in London rose from £1,353 to £2,076.[184] The structure of wealth was pear-shaped and the total assets of the middling merchants equalled those of the very rich.

Wealth remained unequally divided, however, and the successful often rose at the expense of weaker brethren. Despite mobility and dispersal through inheritance, inequality was built into the structure.[185] Only 5 per cent of London freemen were rich and 20 per cent were comfortable.[186] In the 1692 poll tax, 83.4 per cent of a sample of the adult population of London were rated below £300; 10.1 per cent paid a surtax of 1s. and 6.5 per cent paid £1.[187] It is clear that the median assets of businessmen, adjusted for different levels of activity and allowing for variations between different decades, regions and trades, were modest.[188] The great majority of small masters traded on the capital of others, as wage-earners in practice if not in theory, and just kept their heads above water. Few made their fortune and those who received no financial help from their families either secured a competence or failed.

181 Schofield 1965; Husbands 1987; Cornwall 1988: 24, 29; French 1992: 28.

182 Lindert 1981: 663. 183 Willan 1959: 201–3. 184 See figs. 8.1–8.3.

185 Earle 1989a: 310; Lindert & Williamson 1980. Probate evidence is of course retrospective; a merchant who died in the 1660s would have made his money during the Interregnum.

186 See fig. 8.2. The proportion of wealthy business families in all towns seems to have remained fairly constant at 5 per cent, even though absolute wealth increased. See Hoskins 1976: tables 2.1, 3, 8; Dyer 1972: 176; Peck 1982: 73.

187 Glass in Hollaender & Kellaway 1969: 375, tables 1, 7; Krey 1985: 335–7.

188 Carter 1934–5: 100–1; Cornwall 1962–3: 63; Blanch, *Interest of England*, p. 61.

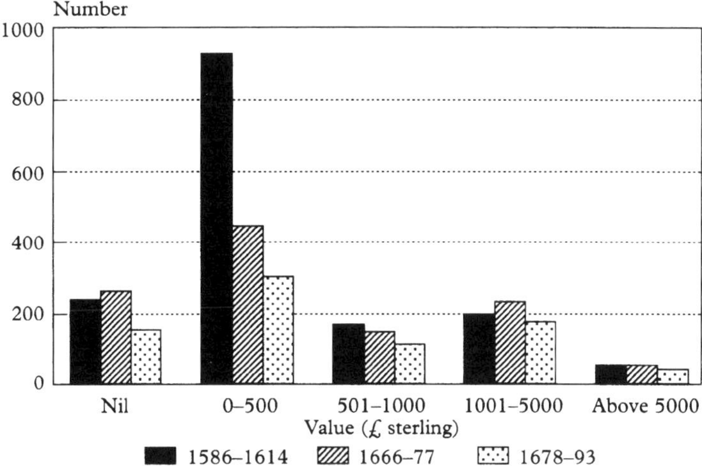

Fig. 8.2. Net personal estates of London freemen, 1586–1614, 1666–77 and 1678–93. (*Source*: CLRO, Common Serjeant's Books, Court of Orphans' inventories.)

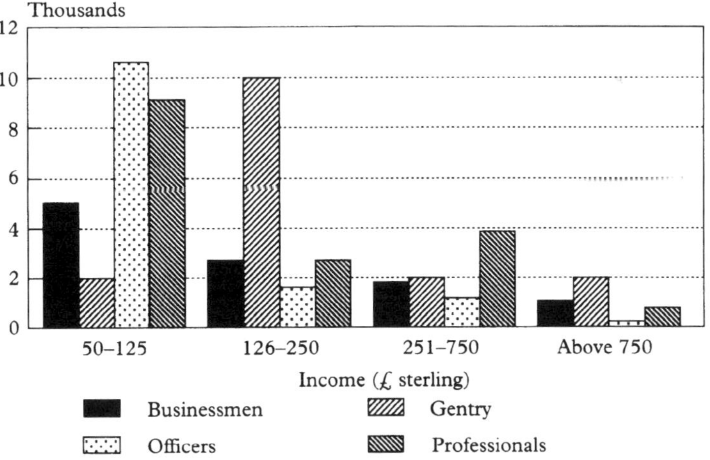

Fig. 8.3. Comparison of occupational incomes, *c*. 1700. The professions include the law, the Church, physic, the Army and the Navy. (*Source*: References cited on pp. 54–60, 131–4, 258–62 and tables 2.1, 8.1.)

The total capital of the business community, *circa* 1688, can be tentatively projected from the Orphans' inventories as some £25.3 million.[189] This estimate is consistent with various contemporary estimates which were made to calculate the yield from taxes and the volume of currency in circulation.[190] Dering, in 1671, challenged an estimate of £25 million for stock-in-trade, after deductions for debts and household stuffs, and considered that £20 million 'above debts' was closer to the truth.[191] In 1688, Davenant put the value of stock, including livestock, at £88 million and stock-in-trade at £15 million; in 1695, he suggested £11 million, after excluding the 'fictitious wealth' of tallies, bank bills and goldsmith notes.[192] King estimated 'actual' stock at £25 million in 1600 and assumed that £1 million of capital financed £3 million of goods in circulation. In 1688, King put 'actual' stock at £86 million of which £33 million was in commodities for exchange and consumption and £28 million in coin, jewels and household stuff; exports and imports combined totalled £11.5 million, financed by £4 million of business capital; in 1690, he reduced stock-in-trade to £26.5 million and, in 1695, raised it to £30 million.[193] In 1690, Petty put the capital required to drive the whole trade of England at £30 million.[194] Although estimates vary considerably during the century, total revenues from land were probably four times higher than aggregated profits from business.[195]

Around £8 million is alleged to have entered the joint-stock exploratory, colonial and commercial Companies, 1575–1630, but most of this evaporated; £1,889,212 was bequeathed to charity, 1480–1660 by 7,391 donors.[196] Loans by businessmen to 121 peers before the Civil War totalled around £1.5 million and another £1.3 million was borrowed during the Interregnum to pay delinquency fines.[197] The shipping

[189] See table 8.1. It must be emphasized that these projections relate primarily to the period 1660–88 and that they almost certainly underestimate the level of wealth; the provincial figures are largely guesswork. The purpose of this exercise is to test contemporary estimates against the evidence of inventories. The same fortune is inevitably duplicated in the records through redistribution and inheritance within and between families.

[190] These estimates were projected from receipts of taxes and therefore reflect assessed rather than actual wealth.

[191] Dering, *Parliamentary Diary*, pp. 40, 58.

[192] Davenant, *Works*, i. 375 and *Two Manuscripts*, pp. 26, 91.

[193] King, *Two Tracts*, pp. 61–2; *Seventeenth-Century Economic Documents*, p. 789.

[194] Petty, *Economic Writings*, i. 106, 112, 311–12.

[195] Aylmer 1974: 236, 331 puts total revenues from land at £6 million, in 1633, whereas Dering estimated £12 million and Petty £8 million.

[196] Rabb 1968a: 66–8, table 5. Table 6 estimates that £5 million was invested in trade outside the joint-stock Companies, but both the evidence and methodology are open to objection. Jordan 1960a: 20; Pollard & Crossley 1969: 151.

[197] Stone 1964a: 545; Habakkuk 1965: 150; Roseveare 1991: 3, 21; D'Ewes, *Journal*, ed. Coates, pp. 42–4, 56.

industry is thought to have absorbed £2.5 million by the 1680s and the rebuilding of London £10 million.[198] Foreign trade was financed by £5.6–7 million in the last decade of the century, when its value was £12–13 million.[199] The taxed stock of London dealers, 1692–5, was £535,000 and that of London manufacturers £106,000.[200] In 1672, 741 shareholders had invested over £480,000 in the East Indian and African Companies; by 1688, joint-stock capital amounted to £630,000 and by 1695, £1,312,049 of the £4.25 million of nominal or issued capital of 140 Companies had been raised; by 1703, total paid-up capital, plus loans to Companies on bond, was around £10 million.[201] By 1720 it had reached £50 million, though public stocks were of course held by passive investors outside the business world and the assets of the great Companies included government debt.

A minority of merchants prospered disproportionately from the growth of overseas trade and their wealth was visible and concentrated in family networks. Unlike many landowners and salaried professionals they had disposable capital as well as income.[202] Business assets were mobile and liquid; although only a minority of businessmen hoarded cash, they did favour short-term loans, leases, joint-stocks and revolving credit.[203] In the domestic economy, commercial wealth financed the credit system and manufacturing and served as a substitute for industrial capital. The financial power of merchants far exceeded their net resources and they were indispensable when landowners or governments or consumers wished to anticipate revenue.

On the other hand, a preference for liquidity made business assets transitory. Sooner or later, a merchant felt a need to stabilize his gains and to secure his family; this could only be achieved by institutionalizing his assets which were thus absorbed into the traditional social structure. However uncertain the overall numbers, it is clear that the business community could not through either numbers or scale of wealth rival landed society. Mercantile wealth was inherently fragile, as Adam Smith illustrated by citing the example of the Hanseatic towns. Land provided the best collateral for financing ventures and the primary source of wealth was still the agricultural sector.[204]

198 R. Davis 1962: 389. 199 Davis in Carus-Wilson 1954–66: i. 258–67.

200 Alexander 1989: 54.

201 Scott 1910–12: i. 335–6, 370–1, 394, 439; K. G. Davies in Carus-Wilson 1954–66: ii. 286, 298–9; Chaudhuri 1978: 416; Holmes 1967: 153.

202 Habakkuk in R. R. Davies *et al.* 1984: 191.

203 The proportion of plate and coin in inventories, even after partial liquidation, is consistently modest, though hoards did emerge during fires and plagues; see Wilson 1927: 157. 204 R. Davis 1967a: 14; John 1961: 189; Smith, *Wealth of Nations*, i. 426.

Comparative incomes

In order to compare business with other groups in society, it is necessary to translate the personal assets of businessmen into income, since the professions were rated by their salaries and fees and landowners by their rent rolls. This was attempted by Gregory King who probably worked from tax assessments based on the rental value of houses. But it is unclear whether his figures are gross or net, what he considered the rate of return, how he calculated his averages, and whether he included bankrupts.[205] His estimate of £200 per annum for the lesser merchants is too high, whereas that of £400 for the great merchants is certainly too low; the £45 per annum which he accords to the shopkeepers is closer to the truth.

There is no foolproof method of determining business incomes, since different types of asset had a different yield; at the lower levels, income was determined as much by input of labour as by capital invested.[206] The working capital of active merchants was usually twice their equity, so that the net rate of return on their own capital should be increased by the difference between their profit rate and the current rate of interest. Since net profits from trade ranged from 8–12 per cent on equity, active businesses could probably earn an additional 2 per cent in the late seventeenth century. Allowing for losses and bad debts and for the fact that household assets did not produce income, it seems safe to put their average overall return at 10 per cent. Samuel Jeake, who combined trade with usury, stock speculation and urban property, earned £100–165 per annum on a little over £2,000.[207] Those with assets above £20,000 held a high proportion of their assets in low-yielding investments or depreciating assets like leases and annuities and so their average income was probably closer to 6 per cent.[208] Cullum's income at death was £2,335 on assets of £43,805. At these rates, the tycoons would have enjoyed incomes of £6,000 upwards, the very rich between £1,800 and £6,000, the mere rich and the prosperous between £1,000 and £1,800, the comfortable between £500 and £1,000 and the bottom rank of businessmen between £50 and £500; if these estimates are reasonably accurate, total business income would have been a little over £2.2 million.[209]

The landed interest divided into similar income categories, although they reflected differences in wealth between regions, and hard data is only

205 For his various drafts see pp. 133–4.

206 It has been assumed that the lesser merchants did not earn additional income on borrowed capital because their debt was short-term and offset by equivalent credit advanced to their customers.

207 ESRO 145/11.

208 Active merchants in London tended to hold their reserves in public stocks rather than mortgages after 1660: see D. W. Jones 1989: 282; Earle 1989a: 367.

209 See table 8.1.

available for particular counties.[210] In 1633, the income of 7,000–9,000 esquires has been put at £500 per annum, that of 1,500–1,800 knights at £800 per annum and that of 10,000–14,000 gentry at £150.[211] In 1641, 121 peers had a gross rental of only £1,094, but the mean net landed income of the peerage was £5,040 per annum and it later increased to an average level of £5,000–6,000.[212] The landed gentry divided into at least four financial brackets.[213] The Exeter merchants had higher incomes than the smaller landed families of Devon; the clothiers of Wiltshire were as wealthy as many squires.[214] But only the tycoons had the capital to buy a great landed estate. When land sold for twenty times its gross annual yield, £20,000 was needed to purchase even a middle-range landed estate and there were probably no more than a hundred merchants with that amount of capital. The landed interest also had the advantage of numbers. By the end of the century there were possibly 1,000 substantial merchants enjoying incomes corresponding to some 2,000 peers, baronets and knights. There may have been around 1,750 merchants with incomes comparable to 2,000 esquires and upper gentry, 2,650 lesser merchants with incomes comparable to 10,000 lesser gentry and 4,950 minor merchants with incomes comparable to 2,000 parish gentry.[215]

Fleetwood contended that the law raised two-thirds of new families and an increase in barristers' fees did raise incomes from the hundreds to the thousands after 1650.[216] But there were three levels of income – under £200, £200–1,000 and £1,000 upwards; the average was probably £150–400 before 1660 and £400–500 thereafter.[217] The clerks in Chancery, Star Chamber and Common Pleas made from £800 to £5,000 per annum, but the lesser offices yielded £30–100; attorneys made £30–100 per annum in fees and left estates ranging from £621 to £2,000.[218] Incomes from private practice and office varied considerably between different courts; barristers earned little in their early years and many lawyers just made a competence and were dependent on small briefs, on fees from sealings and

210 Cornwall 1964–5: 471; Newton 1966: 3; Blackwood 1976: table 1; Cliffe 1969: 426–32; Beckett 1977: 572; Watts 1975: 63; Ward in Wanklyn 1979a: 19–20; Everitt 1966: table 3; Chalklin 1965: 191; Jenkins 1983: tables 7–8; G. Williams 1974: 82; Habakkuk 1940: 3; Mingay 1963: 20–3; 1976.

211 Aylmer 1974: 236, 326–31, table 35.

212 Stone 1964a: app. 9; 1973.

213 Cooper 1983; Keeler 1954: 26; Stone 1965: 22; Cliffe 1984: 107.

214 MacCaffrey 1958: 263–5; Stephens 1958: 53–4; *Wiltshire Two Taxation Lists*, p. xix.

215 See fig 8.3. The distribution of income within each category is only approximate and may require revision when the structure of the professions is more fully investigated.

216 Fleetwood, *Chronicon Preciosum*, p. 158.

217 Lemmings 1990: 154–5; Prest in Baker 1978: table 4; 1986: 148–56; Ives 1964: 80; Clark 1977: chap. 9.

218 Brooks 1986: 37, 228–37, 243–58, table 11.5; Sutherland & Shaw 1937: 168–72.

certificates and on minor offices.[219] Many lawyers in the Long Parliament made under £500 per annum; in 1659, the lawyers and legal officers were put at £250 per annum and Sir Matthew Hale claimed that he could not provide for his six children on the £500 per annum which he earned.[220]

Clerical incomes, which included payments in kind, fees and perquisites, improved with agricultural prosperity and reforms in the Church.[221] Vicars and rectors in the richer towns and counties and the cathedral clergy could reach £100 per annum and a handful of the better endowed livings, particularly if held in plurality, could yield £150–500 per annum; the rich became richer and there was a threefold division as in the law.[222] In the 1640s, even lecturers could earn £50 per annum and the typical parson after 1660 made £70 per annum.[223] Some of the poorest livings were improved through Queen Anne's Bounty.[224] Nevertheless, in 1704, 5,082 of 9,180 livings were worth less than £50 per annum; 44.5 per cent of the personal estates of Warwickshire clergy were under £100.[225] A clergyman paid direct taxes and William Watson alleged that he sacrificed £20,000 in the Farms to continue as Archbishop.[226] Dissenting ministers suffered from even greater uncertainty; they earned up to £150 per annum, but usually the range was £20–50.[227]

Before 1640, the legal income of the royal officers is difficult to calibrate. Fewer than 100 Tudor officers made more than £100 and formal incomes under Charles I were in the hundreds; when realistic salaries were introduced during the Interregnum, they ranged from £150 to £6,000 per annum.[228] After 1660, a tripartite structure of income emerged.[229] Major officers received £1,000 upwards and salaries in the middling ranks ranged from £200 for Chief Clerks to £400 for the Warden of the Mint to £800 for a Secretary.[230] At the bottom, in both London and provincial

[219] Bod. Tanner MS 287; Levack 1973: 12–13, chap. 2; Burrell, *Journal*; Brereton, *Letters*; Cole, *Rod for Lawyers*, p. 321; Whitelocke, *Liber Famelicus*, p. 30; Veale 1970: 46–7.

[220] Keeler 1954: 25; Cole, *Rod for Lawyers*, p. 8.

[221] Pound 1986a: table 2; Cross in O'Day & Heal 1981: table 6.

[222] Heal & O'Day 1977; Stieg 1982: 147, table 5.14; Heal in O'Day & Heal 1976: 107.

[223] Seaver 1970: 190, table 2; Pruett 1975: 209–13; Pruett 1978: 176; *Book of Valuation Preferments*; Evans in C. Jones 1987: 223.

[224] Best 1964: 68–70; Savidge 1955: 8–9; 1964: 52, 79.

[225] Hill 1956: 108–13, 144–5, 202–4; Usher 1910: i. chap. 10; *London Inhabitants 1638*; Dodd 1952: 41; G. Williams 1962: 283; Coate 1933: 329; Erlington 1965: 86; Hudleston 1978; Clark 1980; Savidge 1964: 8–10; Paterson, *Pietas Londinienses*; Cragg 1960: 125–6; Tyler in Cuming 1967: 90; Salter 1976: table A.

[226] Sykes 1957: i. 11.

[227] Watts 1978: 342.

[228] Braddock 1975: 46; MacCaffrey in Bindoff *et al.* 1961: 111; Aylmer 1959: 234; 1974: chap. 4, 204–10, 221–3, 435; 1973: 107–8; Stone 1967: 282.

[229] Haward, *Charges Issuing Forth*; Arnett 1937.

[230] Evans 1920: 513; Thompson 1932: 147; Leftwich 1930: 192; Yolton 1969: 139; Aiken in Aiken & Henning 1960; Collinge 1978; Ruddock 1940: 168–9, 171; Horowitz 1968: 15; Clark 1938: 7; Baxter 1957: 17–18, 139, 150, 172, 231–9; BL Add. MS 18795; Tomlinson 1979: table 1; Craig 1946: 170; Beattie 1961: 18, 51, 153, chap. 6; Anderson 1989: 276; Barbour 1928: 562.

government, the junior officers earned from £5 to £60 per annum.[231] Most clerks at the Treasury made £40–50 per annum and under-clerks in most institutions made £25 per annum. Half of the office holders, in 1690, and possibly 90 per cent of public employees, in 1725, were paid under £100.[232]

In the private sector employees received bonuses, fees, clothing allowances and favourable leases as well as salaries; clerks and book-keepers earned £10–30 per annum, estate stewards £20–40, Clerks of Companies £10–40 and general managers and salaried agents of firms £15–80 per annum.[233] The regulated Companies paid their Secretaries and Chancellors £150–200, as well as offering gratuities and trading rights, but the basic staff received £50 per annum.[234] The joint-stock Companies all had complex salary scales ranging from £10 to £300 per annum.[235]

The pay of officers in the New Model Army and the Restoration Army was modest and, though it increased after 1689, it still ranged from £85 to £140 per annum.[236] The monthly pay of a captain in the Cromwellian Navy was £14 for a third rate and £7 for a sixth rate; after the Restoration the captain of a fourth rate made £126 per annum, though salaries doubled after 1694.[237] A few wealthy physicians were evident in all periods at Court and in London; the celebrated could command up to five guineas a visit as well as gifts in kind, concessions and annuities and some physicians took a percentage of the profits of selling medicines.[238] But their income was unpredictable and the average fee was probably around 10s. a visit (the old angel).[239] Symcots was not wealthy and Claver Morris earned £100 per annum rising to £2–300.[240] It is difficult to determine farm incomes because the evidence consists primarily of inventories of personalty. Some yeomen who owned land and who combined manufacturing with agriculture could earn £100–500 per annum, but the mid-

[231] Hoon 1938: chap. 4; *Boston Port Books*, p. xxx; *Liverpool Customs*, pp. xvii–xix; Carson 1970: 33; Austen 1978: 44; *Norfolk Lieutenancy Journal*, p. 149.

[232] Baugh 1965; Holmes 1982: 256.

[233] CLRO CSB II has many examples; Hall 1965: 123–4; Marescoe, *Markets and Merchants*, p. 4; Coleman 1963: 183; Hainsworth 1985; Melton 1978; Martin 1979; Fitzwilliam, *Correspondence*, p. xv; Rowlands 1977: 52; Godfrey 1976: 25; Cotton 1872: 60; Archer 1991a: 53; MacGrath 1975: 4.

[234] Willan 1956: 33–8; Aström 1963: 184; Lingelbach 1902: 31; Farnell 1963–4: 448; Dering, *Parliamentary Diary*, p. xi; Nat. Lib. Wales Wynn MS F.iii.18; Price 1961a: 85; SP 105/152, fo. 292; Wood 1935: 28, 217.

[235] Willan 1956: 53; *Hudson's Bay Company Letters Outward 1680–87*, pp. 14, 103; Hedges, *Diary*, i. p. ccclviii; Foster 1924: chap. 6; Love 1913: i. 393; Bhattachanya 1954: 142–3; IOL Home Misc. MS 78, fo. 1; Bruce 1818: ii. 216–17, 374–8.

[236] Childs 1976: app. H; 1987: 67–72; Gentles 1991: 47.

[237] Ehrmann 1953: 142; Capp 1989: 168, 174; J. D. Davies 1991: 51.

[238] Rawcliffe 1988.

[239] Lane 1973: 86; Wilson 1927: 20–1.

[240] Claver, *Diary*, pp. 14, 26, 53–4; Pelling 1987; Raasch 1965; Poynter & Bishop 1951: xxvi–xxvii; *Norwich Indentures Apprentices*, p. 2.

dling farmers ranged from £40 to £50 and the majority had estates comparable to artisans and tradesmen.[241]

Each level of business had a corresponding category within each profession and within landed society. Earnings varied enormously and basic salaries were always supplemented by fees, perquisites and subsidiary business activities. Although there were regional variations, opportunities for accumulation were similar in all occupations. The self-employed had a less secure income than the officials and beneficed clergy, but Donaldson underestimated the discretionary income of landowners.[242] If the merchants benefited from the expansion of the economy, the landed interest also benefited from agricultural improvement and the professions benefited from the growth of the bureaucracy and service industries.

The sources of wealth

The eighteenth-century biographer of Thomas Sutton observed that he had made his fortune before 'the Indian wealth dispersed through Europe, the Public Funds Paper Credit and other modern Methods have given some Persons Opportunities of amassing Prodigious Riches'.[243] Under the Early Stuarts, syndicates of businessmen did, however, raise great fortunes by franchising licences and monopolies.[244] After 1660, the tycoons profited from financial manipulation of stocks and credit; the gains which they realized in all the joint-stock Companies were made at the expense of other investors rather than from trading profits.[245] Property development, as the urban population swelled, offered lucrative opportunities to speculative builders and to specialists in real estate transactions.[246]

Lending to the Crown, whether as principal or broker, tax-farming and provisioning for war were also important channels to great wealth from the Hundred Years War onwards.[247] When the Farms were discontinued, short-term loans to the Crown, the discounting of tallies, Exchequer Orders and Navy Bills and contracting for the armed services continued to provide outlets for financiers.[248] After 1688, the revolution in public

[241] Campbell 1960: 162–4, 217–19; Thirsk 1978: v; Hoskins 1963: 151–5, table 5; *Kirkford Inventories*, pp. 81, 102; *Essex Farm Inventories*; *Devon Inventories*; Marshall 1980: 503; *V.C.H. Leicestershire*, ii. 201; Hoskins 1950: 132; *Oxfordshire Farm Inventories*, pp. 7–8, 12; Barley 1955: 293.

[242] Donaldson, *Undoubted Art Thriving*, pp. 76–7, 114, 119.

[243] Bearcroft, *Thomas Sutton*, p. 77.

[244] Ashton 1960a: 35; Keynes 1966: 433; Jordan 1960a: 362, 337, 153.

[245] Holmes 1967: 156. [246] Melton 1977: 41.

[247] MacFarlane 1952: 115; Postan 1964; 1942; *Cal. S. P. Dom. 1591–4*, p. 64.

[248] Coleman 1963: 38.

finance and global warfare created ever greater opportunities. The rate of accumulation achieved by Paymasters and Treasurers was both faster and on a different scale from than that of ordinary merchants.[249] London merchants were not only major stockholders in the Companies, but also invested heavily in both the short- and long-term government debt, advancing money against the land and poll taxes.[250] Although government finance required specialized skills, staying power and connections, banking the state was the fastest road to fortune.

The private East India trade was notoriously lucrative and raised several from obscurity.[251] But every sector of international trade and every commodity had its quota of successful merchants. North-west Europe, Spain and Portugal remained the heart of the trading system, but exports were reinforced by the re-export of goods from the Levant, East Indies and the Atlantic and Iberian colonies.[252] Sugar, slaves, tobacco, wine, timber, ore and grain all founded new families.[253] Sixteen out of twenty-five of those who left £10,000 upwards in London, 1694–1714, were overseas traders; resident factors overseas and the middling merchants could make £5–10,000.[254]

The coasting trade, shipping and the wholesale domestic trades distributing foodstuffs, raw materials, finished goods and imports, also put some businessmen among the rich. Wholesalers had to carry as extensive an inventory as an overseas merchant and on a permanent basis. A few climbed into the £30–40,000 bracket, but £10,000 was the limit for the great majority. Among the Orphans' inventories, 1694–1725, were four wholesalers with over £10,000 and six with £5–10,000; the median estate for mercers was £2,250, for tavern-keepers £1,025, for grocers £922 and for haberdashers £903; a cheesemonger could leave £3,603.[255] John Donne's father made £4,000 in ironmongery and John Leman, Lord Mayor, was in the dairy trade.[256] Several book distributors functioned on a large scale; Thomas Bennett left £9,000 in cash as well as freehold

249 Jancey 1954–6: 145–7. 250 D. W. Jones in Clark & Slack 1972: 338.

251 Hedges, *Diary*, i. 152, ii. pp. ccxxi, cclv–cclvii, app. A; Dalton 1915: 6; Morse 1926: 77; C110/87, letter 19 Feb. 1700; Hoskins 1963: 9; Beaven 1909–13; Ketton-Cremer 1944: 82; Jordan 1960a: 336, 115; E. D. Jones 1939–40: 84–5; Lincs. AO Nelthorpe MS 4/21/2; Yonge, *Diary*, iv; Lancs. RO DDB/58–62; Sheridan 1951: xxi; Keeler 1954: 103, 321, 327; Scartlebury 1978; Price 1961a: 13; Keeton 1967: 50; BL Add. MS 4224; Priestley 1956: 208–12; Collett, *Letter Book*, p. 91; *East India Factories 1670–77*, i. pp. iii, vi–vii; Aungier 1924: 147–51, 165–8, 185–7, 204–8.

252 D. W. Jones in Butel 1979: 167; Dietz in Beier & Finlay 1986: 130, table 10.

253 D. W. Jones 1989: table 9.5; C107/161; Grassby 1994: 113–14; Buisseret 1975: 79; K. G. Davies 1952: 106, 366; Farnie 1963: 209; R. Davis in Carus-Wilson 1954–66: ii. 270 ff; Dunn in Greene & Pole 1984; 1969: 17; Zahedieh 1986a: 588; Price 1992: 51.

254 Earle 1989a: 51; CLRO CSB.

255 Earle 1989a: 31–3, 213, 346, tables 2.2, 4.3; *Yorkshire Diaries*, ii. 21–4.

256 Whitlocke 1955: 23; C110/42–3; Weinstock 1986: 317.

property.[257] Two Cambridge printers had £500–1,000 and two over £1,000 and John Field left £2,115.[258] Ship-masters could acquire estates in the thousands particularly if they were involved in privateering.[259]

The major manufacturing, shipbuilding, construction and processing industries also were financial elevators.[260] Some industries like brewing, sugar refining and soap boiling required more capital than the commodity trade. Although a few were in the £10–20,000 category, the usual range even for the successful was, however, from £5,000 to £10,000; there were clothiers worth £1–5,000 in every region.[261] The Fullers, gunmakers to the Navy, drew an annual income of between £700 and £1,500 from the Ordnance, and the Anchor Brewery in the 1690s yielded £800 per annum.[262] Even at the lower levels estates could rise above £500. In Norwich 4.4 per cent of the weavers had over £2,000 and 5 per cent £1–2,000.[263] Thomas Chappell, tucker and merchant, left £1,303 in cash, £753 in good debts and £300 in stock.[264] A skilled glassmaker could command £135 per annum and shipwrights and mast-makers could accumulate £500–1,000.[265] The profitability and importance of any craft or trade varied according to locality, since most towns and regions specialized in particular services and types of manufacture. Men of substance emerged among the tanners of Worcester, the nailers and smiths of Dudley and Sheffield, the leather trades of Chester and the maltsters, millers and butchers of the country towns.[266]

The service and retail trades were also important. In Walsall and Birmingham, by 1700, the drapers and innkeepers were as rich as the ironmongers and the local gentry.[267] A Wigan mercer could accumulate £1,300, a rural grocer in Yorkshire £481 and an innkeeper of Newmarket £560.[268] A tobacconist of Honiton left £1,823 in 1690 and a mercer in Wootton under Edge £1,377.[269] William Stout with his mixture of retailing and general trade reached £5,000 and in Stafford the retailers were the wealthiest occupational group.[270] Roger Lowe is, however, more typical of the provincial shopkeeper; he earned £20–30 per annum and left £60. The net estates of apothecaries could exceed £2,000, though

[257] Bennett, *Notebook*, p. 5. [258] *Cambridge Printers' Wills*; MacKittrick 1990: 502.

[259] *Trinity House Deptford*, p. 74; Andrews 1991: 45–6, 49–50; Bromley 1987: 462; Anderson 1988: 146.

[260] Moore 1899: 99–100; Poole 1962: 116; MacHattie 1951: 74–7; MacGrath 1947: 94–5; Cornish, *Thomas Firmin*, p. 46; Colvin 1978: 19.

[261] Willan 1959: 196; BL Add. MS 22184; Lloyd 1975: 67–95; Ramsay 1965: 31; Raines & Sutton 1903: i. app. 2, 276. [262] *Fuller Letters*, p. x; Clark 1980: 183.

[263] Priestley 1985a: 188; Vann 1969a: 70. [264] Youings 1968: 70.

[265] Godfrey 1976: 186; IESRO GB 1/8/1–2; Power in Corfield & Keene 1990: 114.

[266] Woodward 1967: app. B; Hoskins 1950: 115. [267] Rowlands 1977: 53.

[268] Bagley 1958: 65; May 1984: 38; Bumstead 1985: 165.

[269] Hampshire, 'Inventory', p. 243; Lindley 1902: 149–52. [270] Adey 1974: 164.

most were less.[271] Despite regulation of their charges for attendance and delays in receiving payment, sales of drugs increased with greater affluence and a wider range of products.[272] Surgeons could, however, make as little as £3–5 per annum rising to £30–50.[273] Although Thomas Hobbs left £4,500, when Charles II touched for the King's evil, he gave his surgeon only 11s. 9d. and James II halved this monetarization of the royal power of healing.[274]

The real money was always in financing and distribution; a drover could raise himself to £30,000 by becoming a banker.[275] Wholesaling was usually more lucrative than retailing; the processing of raw materials and distribution of commodities rather than artisan production.[276] As Thomas Fuller wrote, 'except he hath some outlets ... into wholesale and merchandising, mere artificers cannot heap up much wealth'.[277] In London, merchants were assessed 16 per cent higher than the group immediately beneath them and dealers outnumbered manufacturers in the tax assessments of 1692–5 by 45 per cent to 33 per cent.[278] Financial dealing was, however, never totally divorced from the commodity trade; usury was a natural extension of acting as middleman between producer and consumer and many of the government financiers began as merchants.[279] Contractors to the Navy usually had a commercial interest in shipbuilding and in the import of timber and naval stores from the Baltic.

The most important businessmen straddled all sectors of the economy and, despite an increasing division of labour, they still sustained a diverse mixture of financial and commercial interests. Entrepreneurs moved from the domestic into foreign trade and from the latter into finance, even in the provincial towns. In illiquid markets, merchants had to take goods in payment and therefore engage in additional commodities. The merchants of Leeds were involved in loans, coal mines, navigation, leases of tithes, fee farm rents and the receiving of the land tax.[280] Great fortunes sometimes had their origin in humbler beginnings and ultimately wealth reflected entrepreneurial ability rather than type of business.[281]

[271] C104/130–131; C114/59L; Martin 1980; Trease 1964: 143; Burnby 1983: 18–19, 126–8.

[272] Rowe & Trease 1971: 18; Roberts 1962a: 505–6; 1964: 370; Matthews 1962; 1974; Ellis 1965; Berger 1982; Steele 1977.

[273] Wilson 1927: 21, 85.

[274] Kirk, *London 1689–90*, pp. 656–7; Barlow 1980. The certificates for numbers of persons touched are in E407/85 (i) and AO 3/1193/3; Morris 1972: 204.

[275] Prest 1987: 174; Rubenstein 1993: 34.

[276] Goose 1984. For different views on the comparative importance of merchants and manufacturers in London see Dietz in Beier & Finlay 1986: 133–4; Earle 1989a: table 2.1; Alexander 1989: 57; Smout 1979.

[277] Fuller, *Holy and Profane State*, p. 121.

[278] Alexander 1989: 55–9.

[279] Wee 1963; Rich & Wilson 1977: v. 356; Coleman 1963: 8; Ashton 1979: 25–7; 1960: 89–96; BL Add. Coll. 5853; Lincs. AO, Ancaster-Heathcote MSS; *HMC 13th Report*, vi. 17.

[280] Kirby 1986: 161.

[281] Dawe 1950: 8.

Many examples could be cited of men who started with little and died rich.[282] A few raised themselves from the bottom in the food, clothing and building trades in London, the provinces and the New World.[283] Even a scavenger, like Thomas Rowe, could accumulate an estimated £2,000 in carts.[284] But these were exceptional success stories and maybe one in seven prospered.[285] Most businessmen toiled and worried throughout their lives without ever breaking out of their financial bracket. The lion's share of profit went to those with the most capital, not to those who took the most risks. It was extremely difficult for a business, given the opportunities and methods which were available, to grow fast without initial capital. The greatest fortunes were made in the second and third generations as assets compounded in geometrical progression. The first generation of the Alderseys of Chester, a cadet branch of a gentry family, left only £729, but the third generation left around £3,000, acquired in both the retail and overseas trades, from farming, marriages and legacies.[286] The sons of the rich had a decisive advantage in both the commodity and the marriage market.[287] The richer clothiers could weather depressions because they could afford to take lower profits and hold stock.[288] The majority of successful businessmen were related, if only distantly, to well-established families.

Some historians have detected greater difficulties for advancement after the Restoration, but in fact it was equally hard in all periods for men to rise above the economic station into which they had been born.[289] In Tudor London, only three outstanding men and a handful of substantial merchants emerged out of an intake of 1,100 apprentices.[290] Even an able merchant was limited by his life cycle; those who reached maturity could expect only twenty-five years between starting their careers at 25 and dying at 50.[291] Because the conditions of trade and opportunities for profit changed continuously, a merchant could not simply follow a formula, but had to perpetually readjust and diversify. There were also limits to the time and energy which one man could devote to personal supervision.

It is impossible to quantify the relative success of those who did not come from business families, because the great majority of businessmen lived and died in obscurity. It is much easier to document entry into business than the subsequent history of merchants and their descendants. The surviving evidence focuses on the most and the least successful.

[282] Kirby 1986: 157; Spufford 1984: 46–7; Ellis 1981a: 9; Grassby 1994: 94; Heathcote 1899: 105.

[283] Essex RO GB1/8/1–2; Quiney 1979; Prynne, *Diary*, p. 156; Gruenfelder 1991: 168.

[284] Earle 1989a: 77.

[285] This was also true of America: see Porter 1931.

[286] Woodward 1965: 188–90.

[287] GLL Stocken Collection.

[288] Swain 1986: 144.

[289] Larminie 1987: 36.

[290] Ramsay 1978: 536, 539.

[291] Main 1983: 159–60; Earle in MacKendrick & Outhwaite 1986: 39, 60–1.

Family genealogies tend to ignore younger children who did not found new estates and families. Individual examples of success are not hard to find.[292] Several new families were founded or restored to wealth by a younger son.[293] It was Gabriel Goodwin, the London merchant, and not his eldest brother, a clerk to the Signet Seal, who bought the manor of Kilmerton for £5,400, in 1659, to keep it in the family.[294] Many more, however just obtained a competence.[295] Younger sons among the Jacobean aldermen left small legacies and others invested in the wrong ventures with the wrong partners.[296] Far from founding county families, many younger sons sank to yeoman status.[297]

Although a higher proportion of gentlemen than of other social groups took their freedom, many never reached even that stage through early death or inability to continue, since it is unlikely that they stayed in service as journeymen. Many of the London freemen in the Orphans Court who died with no assets were esquires. Horace Rossiter failed in Smyrna and William Whaley died a failure in the Jamaica sugar business.[298] Those who were unsuccessful had to fall back on family charity.[299] Some who failed in business transferred to other professions and careers, found an office, took up soldiering or entered politics.[300] Overcrowding in foreign trade and a decline in profits may have accelerated this movement in the eighteenth century. Marriage and inheritance were moreover, at every level, the primary factor in capital accumulation.[301] Most younger sons probably had a better chance of making their fortune through marriage and failure of heirs than through trade. A low rate of success was equally true of all entrants into business. Although sons of businessmen had the advantage of better connections and often more capital, the overall impression from the surviving evidence is that success was not determined by social origins. Given favourable conditions of trade, it was

292 Hall 1965: 117; Powicke 1920; *Wales Calendar Letters*, p. 26; Bramston, *Autobiography* p. 19.

293 Finch 1956: 14–16, 24; *John Isham*, p. xiii; Nichols, *Leicester*, ii. 388; *Mosley Family*, pp. 7–21; Willan 1980; Fletcher 1975: 37; Holderness 1976a: 149–50; Blackwood 1976: 72; Beckett 1986: 23; Bruer, *Life*, ii. 93; Hollaender 1957: 33ff; Currer-Briggs 1969: 205.

294 Som. RO, Hylton MSS, Accounts of Gabriel Goodman.

295 Turner 1965–6; Isham 1962; Grassby 1994: chap. 5.

296 Lang 1963: 57; Mundy, *Travels*, i. pp. xvii–xviii; Coleman 1963: 8, 28; Rawdon, *Life*, p. 65; Harrison 1920: 692.

297 Stone & Stone 1984: 281.

298 GLL MS 10823/1; Bennett 1966: 123.

299 Lawrence, *Diary*, pp. xi–xiii.

300 Gay 1939: 406; Bushell 1967; Howell, *Epistolae*, pp. xxvii–xxxi; Bramston, *Autobiography*, p. 22; *Norris Papers*, pp. xx, 10–11.

301 See p. 305; Verney, *Memoirs*, i. 15; Broad 1983: 196; Quitt 1988: 655; *Wales Calendar Letters*, p. 24; Wordie 1982: 16; Richmond 1981; Burnby 1983: 107; Anderson 1988: 74, 83; Wake 1953: chap. 5; Rivington 1981: 187; Sheridan 1974: 82–3; Dawe 1950: 19, app. 11; Woodward 1965: 202; Ferris 1965: 109; Pepys, *Diary*, i. pp. xv–xvi; *Lancashire Record Office Report* 1966: 27; MacIntyre 1956: 184ff; *Fuller Letters*, p. ix.

individual talent which determined who would outperform the competition and rise above the rank and file. Sometimes one son would succeed, when his brothers or father failed.[302]

The sources of wealth did not change fundamentally in the seventeenth century, though their relative importance reflected innovations and adjustments in the economy. Business, like the law and office, did found new families, but only a tiny minority of entrants rose to the top in any occupation and successful businessmen usually diversified their capital beyond their original trade.[303] The great fortunes rested on many foundations, on a combination of financial dealing, shrewd marriages, public office, family legacies and government favour. The ladder of advancement was essentially the same for all families. But there were differences of emphasis and of approach between the climbers and the established. The gentry absorbed commercial capital and businessmen acquired real estate through intermarriage. But the gentry relied for advancement on the lottery of death, marriage and inheritance and used their status and power to create further wealth, whereas businessmen created wealth in order to purchase influence and prestige.

[302] Price 1963: app.

[303] Everitt 1957: 38; Hoskins & Finberg 1952: 81–2; English 1990.

Part 3

Life styles

9 Religion and ethics

Business in the seventeenth century was often equated with heresy or irreligion. Traders were suspect because they had both the opportunity and the means to challenge dogma and credulity; they were mobile, self-employed, literate, individualist, competitive and less wedded to the communal traditions of an agrarian society. Heresy did spread through commerce; although few notable businessmen had been prominent among the Lollards and Protestant martyrs, they may have found it easier to avoid prosecution.[1] Anyone who chose his own path to God put himself at risk. What were the religious affiliations of businessmen and what proportion chose a creed other than that prescribed by the state? How intense were their beliefs and in what ways did they attempt to serve God and avoid sin? How strong was their philanthropic drive and what moral standards did they recognize and follow in their personal lives and in the conduct of their affairs?

Denomination

Business had its quota of Catholics, who were most common in counties heavily populated with Recusants.[2] Children of Catholic landed families which could not afford to grant them annuities had to choose between business, medicine, service in foreign armies, the priesthood or monasteries abroad.[3] Basil Scarisbrick became a merchant, until he inherited the Ecclestone estate, whereas two of his brothers became Jesuits. In Ireland, the Catholic gentry were barred from purchase of land, the Army and the

[1] Haigh 1987: 5; Lake & Dowling 1987: 2–4; Dickens 1959; Aston 1984; Hudson 1988: 130; Loach 1986: 218; *Lisle Letters*, i. 473; Houlbrooke 1979: 319; Brigden 1989: 121, 125, 287, 411, tables 3–4, 6.

[2] G. P. Jones 1967: 187; Leatherbarron 1943; Blackwood 1977; Ward 1971; *Lancashire Record Office Report* 1966: 27; Aveling 1966; 1976; 1967; Foster 1978; Elliott 1984; Meredith 1965: 56–7, 80; Goring in Ives *et al.* 1978: 219.

[3] Haigh 1975: 88; Leys 1961: 173; Walsh & Forster 1969: 41; Newman 1979; Bossy 1962: 47–8; Dures 1983; Hibbard 1980; O'Dwyer 1980; Guilday 1914.

guilds; they either had to emigrate or engage in trade and usury.[4] Recusant merchants usually specialized in trade with Catholic countries, such as Spain and France, where they had an advantage over Protestants who were subject to periodic persecution; they often settled and married abroad and maintained links between the continent and Catholics in England.[5] Catholic merchants were, however, also to be found in Protestant countries and in England.[6] Of the merchant MPs in Elizabeth's Parliaments, 4.3 per cent were Catholic; of the 1,582 suspected of popery in 1680 in London and Westminster, few were in the City itself, but there were at least nine merchants.[7]

A larger minority of businessmen were non-conforming Protestants.[8] Before the Civil War, Calvinist Presbyterianism was primarily a clerical movement whose hostility to episcopacy was tempered by the realization that tithes offered the only satisfactory financial basis for a settled ministry. London parishes with wealthy merchants tended to be Presbyterian and merchants may have favoured the conservative Presbyterian policy of orderly reform in civic and ecclesiastical government.[9] But more were numbered among the 'sincere sort' who just wished to purify some aspects of the Established Church and who were driven by the threat of the Counter-Reformation to make a counter-revolutionary response to Arminianism, which had destroyed the consensus of Humanist reforms in the Church.[10] Merchants were certainly to be found among this group in Bristol, Yarmouth and Newcastle.[11]

During the 1640s, however, the unity of opposition to the Laudian innovations in the Church could not be sustained; some businessmen, like Isaac Pennington, became radical Independents while others, like Sir Thomas Cullum, ended as Royalist Presbyterians.[12] Substantial busi-

[4] Wall 1958–9: 97–8, 104–9; Cornish 1982; Walton 1978: 99; Whiteman *et al.* 1973: 22; Murphy 1987.

[5] *Spain and Jacobean Catholics*; Loomie 1963a; MacLachlan 1940: 20; 1972: 165; Shaw 1989: 30; Le Neve, *Pedigrees Knights*, p. 177; Keeton 1967: 44–5, 50; Duncan 1977: 54–8, 135.

[6] IESRO, Marnock MSS, 1/13/6, 1–2; Knox 1962: 42; Aveling 1970: 97.

[7] Hasler 1982: i. 31; Miller 1973a: 16, 23–4.

[8] The many different factions within English Protestantism were defined as much by their politics as by their theology; the term Anglican only acquires a clear meaning after 1660 and there was no coherent body of thought called Puritanism. Except when otherwise specified, all those who challenged the official Church before 1640 have been described as Puritans and those excluded after 1660 by the Clarendon Code as Dissenters or Non-Conformists. See Bradley 1982: 24; Kaplan 1976; Tyacke 1987: 245; 1991: 753; George 1968: 98; Finlayson 1973: 222; 1983: 6; Cust & Hughes 1989: 19.

[9] Liu 1986: 197, 204–6; Mahoney 1979.

[10] Lake 1982: 292; 1988: 7–8; Zaller 1986: 619; Coward in Newitt & Roberts 1986; Liu 1978: 132; Todd 1987: 21.

[11] Cross 1976: 236.

[12] Williams 1955: 8–9; Pearl in Aylmer 1973b: 34, 56; 1961: 177–9; Gentles 1983: 300.

nessmen were also members of gathered churches.[13] Some of the merchants who emerged in the Leveller movement were religious as well as political radicals and Winstanley was a failed businessman.[14] William Kiffin, a wealthy cloth merchant, interloper and an alderman of London, was a Particular Baptist pastor, as were James Jones and Samuel Clarke.[15] A few even joined the fringe sects: at least thirteen wholesale traders and thirteen retailers were Muggletonians and Freemasonry may have made an occasional convert.[16]

The godly merchants traded with Protestant countries, such as Germany and the Netherlands, financed Puritan settlements in the New World and emigrated to Ireland and the Atlantic and Caribbean colonies.[17] After 1662, the Clarendon Code and the enforcement of tithe payments drove those who 'look a squirt on the Mitre and the Crown' from office and the professions.[18] Business was open to all and self-employment generated fewer points of friction with authority.[19] Although Dissenters probably numbered, by 1715, only one-twelfth of the population, Dissent was disproportionately represented in London. They constituted 15–20 per cent of the electorate, 35 per cent of Company directors, 32 per cent of importers, three-eighths of the aldermen, 27 per cent of holders of short-term debt and 25 per cent of bank subscribers.[20] It also proved hard for the Established Church to compete in the provincial towns with Dissenters.[21] In addition there was a substantial community of alien Protestant immigrants and refugees.[22]

Puritan businessmen came from all levels of society, including the gentry.[23] Henry Ashhurst, apprenticed to a draper at fifteen, shunned whores and the theatre, read godly books and invested his inheritance in a partnership.[24] Sir Patience Ward's family were 'reckoned Puritans' because they wished to abate altars and he 'was designed from his cradle for the Ministry', but orphaned, young and disillusioned with Cambridge he entered the London business world in 1646.[25] There were certainly wealthy businessmen in all the Independent churches which Roger Williams interestingly compared to the Levant and East India Compa-

13 Tolmie 1977a: 40, 104, 114–15; Ramsey 1949: 4.

14 Mulligan 1983: 170; 1977: 74.

15 White 1983: 129; Kiffin, *Life*, pp. 28–30; Kiffin, *Remarkable Passages*, pp. 2, 23; Whiting 1931: 126; *Bristol Records Church Christ*, p. 29.

16 Reay 1976: 46; Hill *et al.* 1983: 51; Jacob 1981: 116–18; Castells 1931.

17 MacIntyre 1963: 15–17, 37–9; Bailyn 1955: 9–14; Banks 1961: 42–50; Morrison 1930–2; Bridenbaugh 1968: 173; Claypoole, *Letter Book*, pp. 3–4.

18 Violet, *Humble Proposals*, p. 13.

19 *Warwickshire Ecclesiastical Terriers*.

20 Holmes 1967: li; Krey in Beier 1989: 465; 1985: tables 3.3–3.8; Horwitz 1987: 275.

21 Spurr 1992: 230; Prideaux, *Letters*, p. 167; Liu 1986: 197, 202.

22 See pp. 157–8.

23 Cliffe 1988; 1984; *Leicester Roll Mayors*, p. 90.

24 Baxter, *Faithful Souls*.

25 BL Add. MS 4224, fos. 33–7; Whiting 1939: 245–6.

nies.[26] The early Quakers certainly attracted some men of property and many later Friends became prosperous merchants in the Atlantic and domestic trades. Bristol Friends included ten merchants, eight of them Merchant Venturers, seven grocers and seven dealers and manufacturers; travelling ministers needed an independent income and were well positioned to engage in the internal trade.[27]

But the Quakers came primarily from lower down the social scale and from the countryside as well as the towns; only 10 per cent of Friends in Bristol and 15 per cent in London had been called merchants and, between 1650 and 1699, only 23 per cent were wholesalers.[28] All the sects mainly attracted the lesser tradesmen, shopkeepers and artisans. Muggleton was a former tailor and most of the Baptists were tradesmen and came from the 'meaner sort'.[29] Businessmen were also substantially outnumbered by other occupations among all branches of Dissent, which had the same occupational distribution as the population as a whole.[30] In Warwickshire, few Baptists and only 1.5 per cent of the Catholics were merchants; 12.3 per cent of non-Anglicans were merchant/professionals and 18.7 per cent traders.[31]

The majority of merchants were nominal members of the Established Church who accepted bishops and Anglican ceremonies and doctrine.[32] A few were Laudians and several of the London elite contributed to Laud's rebuilding of St Paul's; several Laudian bishops were sons of merchants.[33] Many of the London apprentices were moderate in their religious views and rioted against the Quakers; sons of Anglican-Royalist families were forced into business during the Interregnum and became a powerful force in Restoration towns.[34]

Both Catholics and Dissenters wore their religion like coat armour; English society was polarized by faith, not by occupation.[35] One contemporary commented that 'so natural is it for men to paint God in colors suitable to their own fancies that I do not wonder at trading persons who hate ceremonies'.[36] But a career in trade did not necessarily lead to or follow from membership of a particular denomination. Business cannot be identified with one type of personality or with one church; Nicholas

[26] Watts 1978: 271, table 5; Homans 1940; Hurwich 1977: 17, table 3; Woodhouse 1966: 267; Krey 1985: 94–6.

[27] *Bristol Minute Book Mens' Meeting*, pp. xxvi–xxviii.

[28] On the debate over social origins see Hurwich 1970: table 1; Anderson 1979: table 1; Reay 1981: 61, 67, app. 2; 1985: 20–3, tables 1–3; Vann 1969: 91, tables 1, 6; Vann & Eversley 1992: table 2.5; Cole 1956: 106, 112–13; Everitt in Thirsk 1970: 186.

[29] Reay 1976: 49; Tolmie 1977b: 9; Betteridge 1976: 214.

[30] Hurwich 1976: 49, 54, tables 2–4.

[31] Wilkes 1991: 101.

[32] Barry in Harris 1989: 165.

[33] Clarendon, *Life*, i. 24; Ashton 1979: 5; 1989; Welsby 1962: 32.

[34] S. R. Smith 1973a: 327; Horle 1982: 3–4; Pinkus 1992: 13.

[35] Harris 1989: 51.

[36] Pett, cited by Vince in Melitz & Winch 1978: 163.

Barbon did not become an entrepreneur because he was the son of a Baptist leather merchant.[37] Success in business was not determined by the particular beliefs of any group but by their communal organization and connections; the Quakers, for example, allocated prentices at meetings and were said to 'buy only of their own tribe'.[38] 'Trade is not fixt', as was aptly remarked, 'to any species of Religion'.[39]

Intensity of belief

Membership of a church is not of itself evidence of either faith or piety. Because it is mainly the devout who committed their views to paper, it is extremely difficult to assess the level of spiritual concern within the whole business community. The preambles to wills are a treacherous source for religious mentality.[40] Some sought atonement in the love of God and aspired to perfection; others worshipped a demanding God and the nagging of conscience constantly reminded them of their unexpiated sins. Because Puritans believed that sin lay in the individual heart, not in the institutions of society, they recognized no division between the world and the spirit or between religious and secular callings.

Merchants often underwent a personal conversion in their youth; from the Reformation onwards, anxious, inadequate and disoriented adolescents in search of a personal identity and self-knowledge appear to have been particularly susceptible to charismatic preachers and to the idea that they were called to the elect.[41] A high percentage of Quaker converts were younger sons whose future was opaque.[42] Richard Norwood left his apprenticeship to be a soldier, lusted after maids, read vain books and kept bad company; but then he fell into a depression, read Augustine and was converted at the age of twenty-six.[43] Benjamin Bangs, apprenticed to a shoemaker, had a visitation at twelve.[44] William Davenport lived a dissolute life until nineteen, when 'one day as I was walking by my self & considering of my Estate me thought I saw my self hanging over a bottomless Pit by a small Cobweb & every blast of Wind did so shake me'.[45] Edward Terrill, in 1656 at the age of nineteen, when rumours of the end of the world were circulating, attended a meeting of Friends and 'no sooner had sat down and beheld the people but these words darted into my breast This is the way, walk in it'.[46]

It was not only the young who were converted.[47] But mature merchants

[37] Tyacke in Smith & Tyacke 1979. [38] N. H., *Compleat Tradesman*, p. 34.
[39] BL Add. MS 22781, fo. 12. [40] Higgs 1991: 99; Sheppard 1983: 55; Cross 1987: 237.
[41] Bridgen 1982: 48–9; Walzer 1965: 308; Watkins 1971: 227. [42] Vann 1969a: 91.
[43] Norwood, *Journal*, p. 15. [44] Bangs, *Memoirs*, p. 10.
[45] Doe, *Collection Works of Grace*, p. 3. [46] *Bristol Records Church Christ*, p. 6.
[47] Haigh 1975: 144–5.

were driven less by spiritual anxiety than by dissatisfaction with a church which legitimized the presumptions of landed society; the preachers did not all dwell on despair and Roger Lowe worried about his business, not his salvation.[48] Conversion was an emotional experience rather than an intellectual process, a sense of elation upon entering into grace from a state of helplessness.[49] But the beliefs even of those who felt unable to conform were often inherited rather than reasoned or inspired. Most Puritan merchants were either born into a godly household or apprenticed to a godly master. The differences of faith among the London merchants trading to Virginia were replicated in the colony.[50]

A few merchants were certainly zealous to an obsessive degree. Some expressed their faith, their doubts and their anxieties in their ledgers.[51] On their death-beds and when they wrote their own wills, merchants sometimes bared their souls and often hedged their position in the eternal futures market; 'no other honours remain for me to aspire to', wrote John Whitson 'than the honour of the saints in heaven'.[52] Preoccupation with salvation and introspective self-analysis was probably more characteristic of Calvinists and the sects; the Quaker converts expressed their innermost feelings in an ecstatic incantatory style.[53] But there were also fierce uncompromising Anglican merchants who did not consider their religion a compromise or a matter of social and political convenience; Colston's gravity was such that the preacher at his funeral felt obliged to defend him against charges of enthusiasm.[54]

Merchants took risks by distributing seditious and heretical books; several suffered for their faith or went into exile whether under Mary Tudor or James II.[55] The fines imposed on Conventiclers were extremely heavy, though unevenly inflicted; in Bristol, £16,440 was levied on 191 Quakers and in Suffolk, £33,000.[56] When resident in Catholic countries, they faced sequestration, legal chicanery and difficulties in securing a proper burial.[57] Bulstrode Whitelocke's grandfather, who died at twenty-seven on a business trip to France, was buried in a vineyard because he refused the sacrament of extreme unction.[58] A Restoration Tory, like Sir Robert Jeffries, preferred to lose office rather than become a Catholic.

The insecurities of business generated a demand for comfort, solace and guidance. The diary of a wig-maker began: 'Nothing good in me,

[48] Sommerville 1976: 37. [49] Cohen 1986: 13. [50] Olson 1983: 375.

[51] Berks. RO D/ED B 21; GLL MS 5105, 5109; *Yorkshire Diaries*, ii. 20.

[52] Whitson, *Pious Meditation*, p. 14.

[53] Wee in Ollard & Tudor-Craig 1986: 153; Cope 1956: 736; Higgins 1980: 102.

[54] Garrard 1852: 476.

[55] Walker 1948: 111, 123; Ferguson 1972: 194; Garrett 1938: 7–8.

[56] Horle 1988: 268; Harris in Harris *et al.* 1990: 226; Greaves 1990: 139.

[57] Shaw 1989: 3, 127. [58] Whitelocke, *Liber Famelicus*.

spare me for thy mercy.'[59] It was extremely common to record deliverances; businessmen, like the Puritan theologians, were preoccupied with the role of chance and free-will.[60] Whatever their denomination, merchants put their faith in Providence and dedicated their ledgers.[61] An unshakeable belief in grace could lead to spiritual pride; Pryme noted with amusement that a predestinarian shoemaker, who confidently clipped coin openly, was caught and hanged.[62]

Nonetheless, businessmen felt that they were hostage to fortune and there was a running debate as to whether the godly should adopt a fatalistic attitude or keep their powder dry.[63] The Quakers were more self-confident than the Puritans, who could rarely resist the temptation to blame the victim and attribute his fate to personal shortcomings.[64] Businessmen needed to know how to exercise judgement while following God's will and whether their decisions had any impact on their fate. 'I must say', confessed Thomas Papillon, when he was outmanoeuvred, 'I have found it no easy thing complacently to submitt to the will of God'.[65] Merchants sought explanations for disasters and debated whether they were signs of God's displeasure, exhortations to strive harder or purely arbitrary events. When enemies of the true faith were afflicted, this was invariably seen as God's judgement.[66]

As they watched their friends, associates and relations of all ages fall victim to early mortality, it is not surprising that businessmen were as preoccupied with *certitudo salutis* as with their economic salvation. The mourning rings bequeathed by George Skevington were engraved with 'the myrmaide with death striking her with his dart and the words ... make yourself readye to followe me'.[67] Although they were children of God, they could not be sure that they were among the elect. George Boddington would not leave London during the Great Plague, as he did not wish to miss the 'powerful preaching' of Mr Nosse and he rode unconcernedly through the stricken streets, 'looking on the Plague to be the Arrows of the Almighty'; but even he wilted, when the wife of a member of his congregation suddenly died.[68] In the course of the century, however, the concern with trivia became less obsessive and the notion that Providence determined every personal event weakened.[69]

Superstition frequently gained the upper hand, because businessmen

[59] Bod. Rawl. MS C.861.

[60] Todd 1986: 701; Worden 1985: 98; Martingdale, *Life*, pp. 3–5; Seaver 1985: 50–66.

[61] The phrase 'in the name of God and profit' is found as early as the thirteenth century: see Roover 1974: 72.

[62] BL Harl. MS 6842, fo. 289; Pryme, *Diary*, p. 104.

[63] Whitelocke, *Diary*, p. 804. See also pp. 96–8.

[64] Vann 1969a: 21.

[65] Papillon, *Memoirs*, pp. 49, 335.

[66] Crosfield 1913: 132–3.

[67] Ramsey 1958: 448.

[68] GLL MS 10823/1, fos. 16, 22, 46.

[69] Harvey 1979: 511; Donagan 1985: 392.

wished to anticipate the future. Astrologers were consulted by merchants anxious about their ventures, by marine insurers, and by tradesmen who wished to set up shop.[70] Although uneasy about resort to magic, Samuel Jeake, the son of an evangelical preacher, cast horoscopes to help him decide when to speculate in futures and when to build a new storehouse.[71] The apple and oyster women spat on coins.[72] The melancholic, quarrelsome, sweating astrologer and bookseller, Thomas Jones the Stargazer, built up a huge distribution network for his almanacks.[73] Pagan remedies were frequently sought for medical problems and, in 1573, the wife of a Southampton merchant was accused of witchcraft.[74] Conventional religion was often insufficient to explain the discrepancy between effort and reward; witchcraft was the reverse side of Providence and the idea persisted of living in the last stage of the world.[75]

But businessmen usually avoided extremes. Intensity of feeling was regarded as dangerous madness and formal observance was preferred to the agonies of the questioning spirit; the sectarians attracted much ridicule and the later Quakers expanded their original perception of inspiration to include intellect and memory.[76] In the tumult of everyday affairs, merchants were primarily concerned with the practical consequences of conscience, not with saving souls. Bland and undogmatic, they preferred to repress fervour and turn belief to practical use. Banks, a moderate Presbyterian, used Puritan language in his advices, but his religion was formulaic and dispassionate.[77] Religious enthusiasm and big business did not mix and there was more interest in the pastoral than in the evangelical or the prophetic. There were probably as many cynics as bigots.

Although the evidence for observance is spotty, there is little doubt that some merchants took Boyle's injunction seriously and worshipped regularly, both in public and private.[78] Puritans and Non-Conformists preferred example to precept and conducted a personal dialogue with God in their diaries; meditation replaced the Catholic confessional while fasting, images and the cult of saints smacked of popery.[79] Many traditional rituals and ceremonies and the ancient rhythms of ordinary and extraordinary prayer remained, however, in the Anglican liturgy;

70 Bod. Ashmole MS 84, fo. 9v°; 178 fo. 74v°; Lawrence, *Diary*, p. xiii; Thomas 1971: 338; Ehrenberg 1955: 240–1; Lopez 1969–70: 40–1.

71 Jeake, *Astrological Diary*, pp. 13, 74–5; Perceval 1893: 374; Allison 1987: 130–2.

72 Aubrey, *Remains Gentilisme*, p. 86.

73 Curry 1987: 253; 1989: 157; Hetherington 1975: 275–9; Jenkins in R. R. Davies *et al.* 1984: 164, 174.

74 *Winchester Consistory Court Depositions*, p. 25.

75 Webster 1982: 98.

76 Reay 1978: 206; Bynum 1985: 81; Kirk, *London 1689–90*, p. 490.

77 Coleman 1963: 146, 171.

78 Boyle, *Works*, i. pp. cviii–cix.

79 Watkins 1971: 1–2, 9; Haynes, *Diary*, pp. 187–269

Parliament was quite prepared to manipulate the Lenten fast to help the fishing industry.[80] Merchants baptized and catechized their children and special services were held for apprentices; annual communion was common, though it was easier to attend church in the towns.[81] Businessmen ran their households in a godly manner, prayed for rain, recorded their readings of the Bible and sermons, conducted family services, sang divine praises and even preached.[82]

Usually, however, the dictates of religion were not followed rigorously, but as time and routines permitted. As the preachers frequently complained, business crowded out devotion and spiritual reflection; a merchant would 'stay a whole yeare at a Mart rather than one hour at a Sermon'.[83] To Bunyan, 'the man that penny wise and pound foolish, this is he that loseth his good Sheep for a half pennyworth of tarr that loseth a soul for a little of the world'.[84] Dryden's remark about breaking the Sabbath for gain was directed at Slingsby Bethel. Church attendance declined during the century and the success of those forced into business by their non-conformity depended on channelling all their energy and fervour into business.

Several merchants had an intellectual interest in and a sophisticated knowledge of theology and its application to real life. They annotated and criticized prolix and pedantic sermons and they debated points of Scripture in their journals alongside their entries of debts and rents.[85] John Blackeston, a Newcastle mercer, gave a parson a lesson in divinity before the High Commission and a London pewterer wrote a theological treatise.[86] Merchants were a primary market for devotional literature and collected the works of professional theologians.[87] Richard Cocks, when in Japan, asked for a copy of Augustine's *City of God* as well as for commercial and historical works.[88] The factors in Aleppo were reluctant to hear the same old tired sermons and their correspondence sometimes touched on religious questions; Levantine merchants visited the Holy Places and studied the archaeology of early Christianity.[89]

But businessmen were usually prepared to accept the doctrines which they had been taught as self-evident truths. For most of the century, rational scepticism was regarded with unease, because of fears that it

80 J. H. Davies 1970: ii, chap. 6; Erswicke, *Brief Note Fish Days*; Hambrick-Stowe 1982: 101, 179–80.
81 Boulton 1984: 136, 148.
82 J. H. Davies 1948: 280; Papillon, *Memoirs*, p. 306; Thoresby, *Diary*, pp. 25–7; Lowe, *Diary*; Bebb 1935: 493; Hedges, *Diary*, i. pp. cccv–cccxviii.
83 Bourne, *Godly Man's Guide*, p. 20.
84 Bunyan, *Life Mr Badman*, pp. 42, 106.
85 Bod. Rawl. MS D.114, diary 1711–12.
86 Seaver 1970: 43; Bod. Rawl. MS C.765.
87 White 1931: 16.
88 Wright 1943: 59–62; *East India Letters 1601–11*, p. 419; Cocks, *Diary*, p. 118.
89 BL Add. MS 24107, fo. 130v°.

would lead to atheism.[90] By the end, the terrors of Hell had diminished, millenarianism was in retreat and a more rational, Latitudinarian theology had developed.[91] Businessmen were always more interested in practical devotion than in credal controversy and inclined towards the simplistic ideas of primitive Puritanism. They did not participate on any scale in the debates over a mechanical universe or the relativity of morals.[92]

The business community did support the maintenance of a godly and preaching ministry. Several were active in their parishes and by purchase of impropriations and the exercise of rights of presentation in England and overseas, they raised the standard of the clergy; they often co-operated with the bishops and during the Interregnum placed Anglicans.[93] The hotter Protestants supported lecturers and preachers throughout the country both during the struggles within the Church under Elizabeth and the Early Stuarts and after the ejections of 1662.[94] The early colonizing Companies had a spiritual purpose and the churches of the overseas Companies provided asylum for all groups out of favour, whether Elizabethan Presbyterians, like Udall and Cartwright, or Anglicans émigrés during the Interregnum.[95] Merchants in Hull, Lincoln, Beverley, Norwich and York supported Puritans against the Church hierarchy, though the funds subscribed were often inadequate.[96] Non-Conformist merchants allowed conventicles in their homes and the richer helped to pay the fines of the poorer.[97] The commercial Companies responded to pressures to propagate the Gospel along with trade; the New England Company's mission to the Indians was financed by subscriptions from merchants.[98]

Merchants were willing to support ecclesiastical discipline as essential to preserve social and moral order. It was widely assumed that religious instruction moulded moral character; compulsory and communal worship were thought necessary to preserve the identity of Englishmen when living and trading among barbarians, heathen and papists. The guilds hired preachers and attended divine service before their meetings and feasts. The East India Company regarded orthodoxy and prayers as an

[90] Fletcher in Sheils 1984: 163, 185, 202, 233, 245.

[91] Worden in Sheils 1984: 213; Spurr 1988: 82; Walker 1964: 30; Cragg 1957: 35, 59.

[92] Jacob 1977: 543, 568.

[93] *Church of England, Activities Puritan Faction*, pp. xi–xii; Collinson in Prestwich 1985: 208; Richardson 1972a: 128–33; Whitney 1963: 317. Lecturers performed a variety of functions and were often orthodox: see Collinson 1982: 174–5, 182.

[94] Seaver 1970: 52, 92, 158; D. A. Williams 1955: 7; Bate 1908: 94; Greaves 1975: 166.

[95] Rose 1975: 147; Bosher 1951: 60; MacDonnell 1909: 168; Sprunger 1982: 24, 382, chaps. 2, 9.

[96] Marchant 1960: 126; Evans 1979: 97; Sheils in Heal & O'Day 1977: 163.

[97] Brochett 1962: 40.

[98] Kellaway 1961: 17–18, 57–8.

antidote to drunkenness, disloyalty and dishonesty as well as a defence against contamination.

But many merchants, like Henry Parker, leaned more towards Erastianism than towards righteousness. Self-made businessmen were always cool towards a centralized Church and the pretensions of clerics and they were hostile to interference in their affairs by enthusiasts of any religious persuasion.[99] Before 1640 the Church Courts had been a nuisance, though never a real obstacle, and there were squabbles with the Church over turf in most towns.[100] After the Reformation, merchants were unwilling to endow the Church; only fifty-two churches replaced the eighty-seven in London before the Great Fire.[101] The hostility of merchants towards the Church did not diminish until lay control was successfully asserted and the clergy had lost both the administrative power and the will to impede business.

In all denominations, there were businessmen who passionately defended their churches and campaigned energetically against rival faiths. Edward Colston excluded Non-Conformists from his charities and stipulated rigorous worship in his almshouses, 'to revive the primitive zeal for the Church government as by law established'.[102] There was particular hostility to the Socinians and Quakers.[103] Anti-popery feeling ran high among merchants, some of whom had personally witnessed Catholic atrocities on the continent.[104] But it was strongest among tradesmen and artificers and may in part be explained by the congestion and pluralism of the capital.[105]

Toleration remained a dirty word and behind the Penal Laws lay a desire to convert and save souls; Protestants still felt vulnerable and distrust and fear of Rome was more deeply rooted than radical ideologies.[106] The desire for religious uniformity sprang from a yearning for social homogeneity; although there were many religions, it was commonly assumed that there was only one system of values.[107] Persecution therefore continued even when there was no political threat.[108] The Toleration Act indulged but did not accept differences; there was no notion of doctrinal development and each denomination insisted on a single, immutable divine truth and pretended that it had recovered the true faith.[109]

[99] Goldie 1983: 62.

[100] In 1578, Marcus Simpson, who had received 10 per cent interest 'of their own good will' had to read the 15th Psalm as a penance: see *Ecclesiastical Court London Act Books*, p. 166.

[101] Higgs 1991: 92; Cross 1982: 234; Willan 1953: 60; 1980: 104; Phillips 1973: 139; J. H. Davies 1948: ii. 24.

[102] Wilkins 1920: 64.

[103] Anderson 1977.

[104] Underdown 1992: 42–3.

[105] Kenyon 1972: 237–40.

[106] Sheils 1984: 163; Scott in Harris *et al.* 1990: 120.

[107] Russell 1990: 63.

[108] Gunn in Knoll *et al.* 1992: 167.

[109] Spurr 1988: 327; Zakai 1991: 440.

Freedom of conscience was consistently advocated in self-defence by the persecuted. A minority of merchants rejected the need for uniformity in religion and Henry Robinson embraced a form of religious relativism. The struggles between Arminians and Calvinists and the diversity of doctrines which characterized the Interregnum weakened assertions that there was only one path to God. There was much support within the business community for the economic argument that 'easing of tender Consciences ... is that which increaseth the Trade and Grandeur of an Nation'.[110] Monopoly in religion was equated with monopoly in trade. The debate over the admission of the Jews was conducted, after 1660, mainly in economic terms.[111] Missionary efforts were half-hearted; the preachers attacked the slavers who imperilled the souls of their slaves by refusing baptism and encouraging immorality.[112] Merchants who had lived abroad without domestic restraints tended to become more open-minded towards other religions.[113] They were exposed in their regular business to the beliefs and rituals of the Jews and Moslems in Ottoman Turkey, to the ceremonies of the pantheistic Indians and the animal sacrifices of the Chinese merchants.[114] William Popple favoured a rational, non-credal religion, after personally experiencing persecution in Bordeaux.[115]

Slowly but surely, business secularized the predestinarian spirit and stiff-necked opposition metamorphosed into Quietism and Occasional Conformity.[116] Puritan theology was based on a Manichean antithesis which required an Anti-Christ; but its adherents were too closely linked with established society to reject the status quo and their initial reformist vigour was sapped by respectability.[117] Once alternative churches were legally defined and the sects became denominations with established norms, Dissent became a political and economic interest group of related families rather than a belief system. Non-Conformist congregations had always had a hierarchy with discriminatory seating based on wealth. Once the heroic period passed, there was much backsliding, compromising and indifference.[118] The Protestant merchants in Spain and in Ireland were happy to co-operate with Catholicism.[119] Papillon continued to victual

[110] Ent, *Grounds of Unity*, p. 8; Coke, *England Improvement*, Apology to the Reader; Corbet, *Discourse of Religion*, p. 25; Jordan 1932–40: iv. 340–6; *Seventeenth-Century Economic Documents*, p. 70.
[111] Rabb 1979: 29; Samuel 1988–90: 167; Katz 1987: 7, 225–9.

[112] Godwin, *Negros' and Indians' Advocate*; *Trade Preferred*. He considered that Christian slaves would be more obedient.
[113] Pailin 1984: chap. 6.

[114] Morse 1926: i. 163; Hunter 1975: 209; Wheeler, *Journey into Greece*, pp. 61–2.

[115] Robbins 1982: 12; Goldie 1992: 571.
[116] Keeble 1987: 221.

[117] Collinson in Grell *et al.* 1991: 55; Greaves in Knorr 1977: 273; in Cole & Moody 1976: 11; 1983: 542.
[118] Haller 1938: 123–4; George 1976: 486.

[119] Croft in Adams & Rodriguez-Salgado 1991: 228; 1972: 258, 265; Canny 1975: 54.

the Navy, even though he realized that it could be used against his spiritual brethren; a Presbyterian alderman could be a stalwart of his local Anglican parish.[120] Dissenters obtained false sacramental certificates to remain in city government.[121]

Wealth, expediency and the desire for social integration inclined successful businessmen towards the Established Church and some business families were a hotchpotch of several faiths.[122] Even among the Quakers, success reinforced other pressures to conform to mainstream society.[123] Merchants, wrapped up in their affairs, were content to delegate responsibility for keeping the faith to the professional ministers. However successful radical Protestantism had been in reducing the division of labour between clergy and laity, the demands of business made it difficult for each merchant to be his own priest and strive wholeheartedly for his own salvation. The privatization and separation of religion eroded belief and the practice of faith became just a leisure activity.[124]

Philanthropy

Both orthodox Churchmen and the religious radicals claimed that usurers and merchants ground the faces of the poor. The philanthropy of businessmen certainly did not begin with the Reformation, though there was a surge in the 1570s, and it is doubtful whether overall donations increased in real terms or per capita.[125] The proportion of estates given to charity declined under the Early Stuarts and fell even further later in the century; donors were also heavily concentrated.[126] Private philanthropy could not replace the poor-rate and public provision for widows, the elderly and orphans; Tooley's charity needed supplementation from a general collection.[127] Nonetheless, merchants were committed to every kind of philanthropic endeavour. Some just had humanitarian impulses; they wanted the satisfaction of helping the less fortunate and became

[120] Papillon, *Memoirs*, p. 100; Earle 1989a: 245.

[121] IESRO, Eye Borough Records, Court Papers, bundle B/22; Flaningham 1977.

[122] *London, Characters of Lord Mayors*, p. 515.

[123] Tolles 1948: 324; Raistrick 1950: 42–4, 58, 338–48. The Hutterites followed the same path; see Klassen 1964: 95.

[124] Collinson in Sheils & Wood 1986: 253; Sommerville 1992a: 186.

[125] Bridgen 1984: 104; Jennings 1977: 279; Archer 1991b: 167.

[126] Dyer 1972: 242; Archer 1991b: 74.

[127] W. K. Jordan has documented extensive giving by merchants and many gifts of land would have appreciated, but his aggregated monetary figures are invalidated by inflation. See Hadwin 1978: 113–17; Coleman 1978: 120; Gould 1978; Beier 1983: 14–15, 22; Herlan 1976: 50–1, 182–3; Pound 1986c: 68–71, table 1; Rogers 1972: 40; *Ipswich Poor Relief*, p. 18. On the top-heaviness of donations see Feingold 1983; Everitt 1962–3: 379.

professional fund-raisers.[128] Although they could ruthlessly defend their property rights, merchants, unlike the political arithmeticians, did not simply value mankind in monetary terms. They were not saints, but they were not indifferent to suffering or to their social responsibilities.

Their philanthropy cannot, of course, simply be explained by human kindness. Many considered charity to be a religious duty, as enjoined by preachers who argued that the justification of riches lay in their use.[129] Usury had been accepted by the theologians when the interest income went to charity as a free gift.[130] Many took seriously Jeremy Taylor's assertion that 'no man is a better merchant than he that layes out his time upon God and his money upon the Poor'.[131] Samuel Jeake gave '1/10 of clear profit to alms' for necessitous persons and another businessman kept his account with God in double entry.[132] Many bequests showed more interest in spiritual and moral improvement than in economic betterment; the endowments of universities were intended to provide a learned clergy.[133] Elihu Yale's epithet in Wrexham churchyard speaks volumes: 'Much good, some ill he did, so hope all even; And that his soul through mercy is gone to heaven.'[134] As Brown cynically observed, 'when you have got an estate, then tis time enough to think of compounding your sins with heaven by building a hospital according to the laudable and ancient practice of the city'.[135]

Religious injunctions were reinforced by fraternal tradition. By ancient custom, one-third of a personal estate was designated for charity and the medieval convention of bequeathing property to a guild survived the Reformation.[136] The Livery Companies provided an essential service for benefactors, because perpetual trusts were prohibited under Common Law.[137] Between 1600 and 1688 there was an increase in the number of charitable trusts, though they thereafter declined, to be replaced by philanthropic associations.[138]

Benefactions also reflected gratitude for success and insurance against failure.[139] To seal a bargain, it was customary to deposit one or two *denarii*, 'which they call God's penny which is then given in alms'.[140] Sir Matthew Andrews left money for education 'by a vow upon a shipwreck' and Sir John Morden founded almshouses for retired and impoverished

[128] Jordan 1960a: 54; Owen 1964: 17–18; Twigg 1987: 81.

[129] Bourne, *Godly Man's Guide*, 40.

[130] George 1957: 467.

[131] Taylor, *Holy Living*, p. 3.

[132] ESRO 145/11. The French Reformed Church kept its accounts in double entry according to Cottrett 1991: 253; Watkins 1972: 21.

[133] Wilson 1969: 87; Haytor 1990: 67

[134] BL Add. MS 19101, fo. 28.

[135] Brown, *Amusements Serious*, p. 175; Burton, *Anatomy of Melancholia*, p. 83.

[136] Brandon, *Customary Law London*, p. 2; MacCaffrey 1958: 267.

[137] Ramsay 1985: 160.

[138] Kahl 1960: 23; Slack 1989: 52.

[139] Deloney, *Works*, p. 110.

[140] Magno, *London Journal*, p. 146.

merchants in the Levant trade in which he had prospered.[141] Charity benefited the donor as much as the recipient. Hobbes defined pity as that 'which he thinks may happen to himself' and Graunt perceptively observed that 'we ease ourselves when we think we ease them with whom we sympathize'.[142] The world of business was too capricious for men to ignore their less fortunate fellows or the obligations of friendship.[143]

The level of philanthropy was also determined by the life cycle, liquidity of assets and marital status. Merchants did sell food cheaply to the poor and make gifts during their lifetime and sometimes they risked more than money by smuggling enslaved Englishmen out of Turkey. But the great majority of charitable benefactions were bequeathed at death and Timothy Burrell cited Seneca: 'Ingratum est beneficium quod diu inter manus dartis haesit.'[144] The transfer of funds was also facilitated by the fact that business assets were more mobile than landed estates. The most important factor was the absence of direct heirs.[145] By founding a charity, a childless merchant could perpetuate his name; Whitson's daughter died in childbirth and his nephew was a coxcomb, so he gave his fortune to pious uses.[146] To a lesser extent, the same principle guided widows, who constituted forty-two out of sixty-nine female donors in London.[147] It is noticeable that only a small percentage of Orphans' estates after 1680 went to charity, though this may also have reflected changes in the Poor Law and the introduction of charity schools.[148]

Walwyn argued that Protestants were less generous than Catholics; the Puritans were inclined to deprecate the joy of perpetual almsgiving.[149] Charity was increasingly calculated more deliberately; the poor were defined as a separate group and beneficence was given a particular object.[150] Charitable objectives were, however, extended rather than truncated and the bulk of relief was still directed towards individuals; much casual almsgiving, both in person and through poor-boxes occurred, though it cannot be documented.[151] Merchants set up funds to redeem captives and free imprisoned debtors, to provide pensions, food, clothing, fuel and almshouses for the aged and impotent poor and for decayed merchants and prisoners. Nonetheless, there was a change in emphasis. Businessmen endowed educational institutions, dowries for

141 Vincent 1969: 72; Joyce 1982.
142 Hobbes, *Works*, vi. 461; Graunt, *Natural and Political Observations*, p. 12.
143 Hirschman 1986: 117.
144 Burrell, *Journal*, p. 162.
145 Unfortunately W. K. Jordan does not provide statistics of marital status for his charitable donors, but the major benefactions came from bachelors. See Cornish, *Thomas Firmin*, p. 20; Kirby 1983: 43; Archer 1991b: 72; Webb 1962: 152.
146 Garrard 1852: 315; Aubrey, *Brief Lives*, ed. Dick, p. 317.
147 Jordan 1960a: 291.
148 Earle 1989a: 318.
149 Baugh in Baxter 1983: 73; Schenk 1944: 79.
150 Slack 1988: 22.
151 Kirby 1986: 167; Slack 1988: 168; Beier in Clark 1981: 84; Cross 1987: 25.

poor maids and loan funds for beginners in business; the lesser merchants gave more to apprenticeship schemes and municipal betterment.[152] The Quakers attempted to recover the cost of their redemption of captives and the workhouses which they established for the poor were constructive rather than palliative.[153] The changes which occurred in the direction of giving reflected a search for long-term solutions to poverty.[154] They were, however, inspired as much by Humanism and by new needs and concepts of the state as by Protestant theology.[155]

Merchants were acutely aware of the scale of poverty, because they lived cheek by jowl with the poor, and they participated in the continuous debate among both laymen and theologians of all persuasions over the best method of relief.[156] The preachers, concerned that poverty bred sin, favoured spiritual charity whereas businessmen feared disorder and adopted a more secular, practical and utilitarian approach.[157] Merchants targeted areas where the most needy were concentrated and refined the distinction between the idle and deserving poor. Many of the schemes to set the poor to work originated in and were supported by the business community.[158]

Benevolence served as one justification for the unequal distribution of property which, though essential to achieve growth in the long term, generated moral doubts in a poor society. Voluntary giving was preferred to a compulsory poor-rate, because it conferred 'worthiness' or redeeming value on private enterprise.[159] Although Burnet in his funeral oration on Houblon claimed that 'he took care to manage them so secretly that often the persons knew not whence their relief came', most merchants wanted to be seen to be charitable.[160] They needed social recognition more than the landed interest.[161]

Self-denial

In England, the self-denying ordinances of thrift, chastity and obedience had for centuries been a commonplace of proverbs and apprenticeship indentures; they had been routinely invoked by rulers, pamphleteers, employers, schoolmasters and parents as well as by moralists and theologians of every denomination.[162] At the end of the century, they were enshrined in the 'moral revolution' sought by the conservative Anglican

[152] Jordan 1960a: 76. [153] Lloyd 1950: 39. [154] Thomson 1965: 181–4, 195.
[155] Slack 1989 15, 24, 27; Wood in *Property its Rights* 1915: 148; Pullan 1976: 19; MacGee 1976b: 229–31. [156] Slack 1988: 22.
[157] Newton 1966: 28; MacGee 1976b: 37. [158] See pp. 227–8.
[159] Coats 1976: 246; Wilson in Riis 1986; Stow, *Survey*, i. 117; *Essex Town Meetings*, p. xii.
[160] Houblon, *Pious Memoirs*, p. 44. [161] Rosenthal 1972: 131–3.
[162] Greaves 1981b: 354, 646–7; Tilley, *Dictionary Provers*; Blench 1964: 309–14.

Societies for the Reformation of Manners, which had extensive support from the business community.[163] Those cut off from polite society often adopted these precepts in a rigorous form as a badge of self-respect and in order to legitimate their function.[164] But these injunctions were also incorporated into contemporary handbooks on gentility and the advices written for gentlemen, when they came of age.[165] Maxims of this kind had defined behavioural expectations in many different cultures and religions long before they received the imprimatur of Protestant theology.[166] The whole propertied class recognized the value of making a virtue out of necessity.

The intentions of those who preached these virtues differed considerably. Behaviour can only be virtuous if it is practised without regard to consequences, but financial advice sells better than morality.[167] The economic consequences anticipated by businessmen were feared by the theologians, who were anxious to subdue Original Sin, not to promote business.[168] The ecclesiastical courts fought a losing battle against vices which were offensive to laymen, because they undermined productivity, whereas the preachers directed their heavy artillery against vices, such as covetousness, luxury, vanity in appearance and the servility of debt, which they considered offensive to God.[169] Repression of natural instincts through moral self-discipline was intended to subordinate the world to the spirit, not to unleash economic individualism. Even those who opposed the Established Church had a collectivist mentality.[170]

'An abundance of frugality and circumspection' was certainly essential to accumulate capital.[171] A merchant starting in business depended on savings or on borrowed capital and had to meet his overheads on a smaller turnover.[172] Because most costs were fixed, it was important to save on living expenses by eschewing extravagance in dress, food and drink;

[163] Bahlman 1968: 69; Spurr in Harris *et al.* 1990: 40; Curtis 1976: 48; Woodward, *Account Societies Reformation*, p. 60; Bod. Rawl. MS D.1312.

[164] Skinner in Tully 1988: 117.

[165] Smythies, *Advice to Apprentices*; Trenchfield, *Cap of Grey Hairs*; Slingsby, *Diary*, pp. 217–18; Peacham, *Art Living London*, p. 89; Hunt. Lib. MS NH 1264, fos. 145–7; George in Eisenstadt 1968: 170; 1961: 165–70.

[166] C. S. L. Davies 1966: 540; *Constitution and Canon*. For similar maxims in other countries see Courtin, *Traité de la paresse*; Gotein 1956–7: 586. In Japan, the economic virtues were combined with a refined love of pleasure – literary, aesthetic and sexual: see Veda 1956: 25; Saikakaku, *Japanese Family Storehouse*, p. xii and *Life Amorous Woman*, pp. 8–10; Takenaka 1969: 161; Bellah 1957: 126.

[167] Milles 1969: 240; MacIntyre 1984: 185.

[168] Kocher 1953: 19; Worden in Sheils 1984: 201.

[169] Phillips, *Life and Death Rich Man*; Preston, *Remedy against Covetousness*; Rogers, *Sermon Preached Trinity House*; Burton, *Christian's Heavenly Treasure*; Dyke, *Counter-poyson*; Sydenham, *Rich Man's Warning Peece*; Stoughton, *Arraignment of Covetousness*; Braithwaite 1919: 510–5.

[170] Solt 1967: 25–8.

[171] Bod. Eng. Hist. MS C.156, fo. 95.

[172] Helleiner 1951: 106.

bankruptcy was frequently blamed on extravagance.[173] 'Let not thy expenses be equalled with thy gaines', counselled Browne, 'for either sickness, naughtie debtors, let of trade, and misfortunes by the sea or land, may soon overthrow thee'.[174] The merchant was traditionally contrasted with the rentier as a saver and not a spender.[175]

But thrift could degenerate into avarice and even endanger health and reputation; uncompromising asceticism suffocated enterprise.[176] Calvin disapproved of Diogenes who 'observing a child drinking out of his hands he cast away the cup'.[177] The obsession of the Dutch and Scots with frugality and cleanliness was a common target of English jokes.[178] The line between prudence and covetousness was thin: 'Frugality', wrote MacKenzie, 'has two Capital Crimes Avarice and Luxury'.[179] There was an old distinction between *luxuriae* (extravagance), *avaritia* (greed) and *ambitio* (power); any extreme behaviour was expected to have adverse consequences.[180] Capital was accumulated through growth and the mechanism of credit was more important than personal austerity.

As the preachers remonstrated, overindulgence in food and alcohol, particularly in hot climates, consumed an estate, endangered health, impaired judgement and reduced interest in and capacity for work.[181] Ale-houses and taverns tempted apprentices and even God-fearing masters who struggled against 'a longing desire for drink'; James Howell applauded the introduction of coffee, which he considered better for apprentices in the morning than beer or ale.[182] Drunkards appear regularly in the proceedings of the Consistory of the English Reformed Church in Amsterdam.[183] Sobriety was certainly a virtue, but a temperate indulgence of the palate also relieved tedium, stimulated activity and created a mellow atmosphere for negotiation. The patronage of clubs, inns and coffee-houses was essential to gather intelligence; sociability was frequently measured by a willingness to drink heavily.[184]

Playing cards and throwing dice were usually equated with keeping ill company and often proved a path to ruin.[185] Public and private lotteries

[173] *Seventeenth-Century Economic Documents*, p. 104.
[174] Browne, *Marchant's Avizo*, p. 55.
[175] Hume, *Writings Economics*; Carter 1962: 34. [176] Helleiner 1951: 100.
[177] Calvin, *Institutes*, book iii, chap. 10, 720–1; Laertius Diogenes, *Lives Eminent Philosophers*, ii. 231. [178] Haley 1988: 117; Shashko 1966–7: 261.
[179] Bradford, *Honest and Dishonest Ways*, p. 16; Vaughan, *Golden Grove*, i. 2; Preston, *Sin's Overthrow*; Crodacott, *Vanity of Mischief*; MacKenzie, *Moral History Frugality*, p. 4.
[180] Flecknoe, *Relation Ten Years*, p. 132; Philip, *Diaries*, p. 240; Berry 1989: 611.
[181] Dod & Clever, *Godly Form Household*, p. 77.
[182] Ashton 1983: 12–15; *Manchester Collectanea*, p. 178; Roberts 1962a. Alcohol and opium were the only available drugs. [183] Carter 1964: 180.
[184] Defoe, *Poor Man's Plea*, p. 9; R. T., *Art Good Husbandry*, i. 386–7; Baxter, *Christian Directory*, i. 274–5. [185] Croker, *Brief Memoirs*, p. 303.

were both common and periodically suppressed because of corruption and their ill effects on merchants and gentlemen.[186] William Perkins thought that to 'winne other mens money' was 'worse than usury'.[187] But gambling could be a harmless distraction and merchants commonly indulged without harming their business; indeed commodity speculation, insurance and the premium business had their origin in wagers.[188] Swearing, particularly invoking the name of God in vain, was universally denounced and the guilds fined members for this offence.[189] Even jesting was added to the vices of lying, cheating, stealing and idleness.[190] But many businessmen were known for their salty language while cursing was often an integral part of the process of bargaining. It did little harm, providing that it did not offend customers or serve as a substitute for rational argument. The temptations of the numerous brothels and 6d. whores were potentially more dangerous.[191] There is certainly some evidence in diaries of sexual repression which could combine with hypocrisy in an explosive mixture.[192] The moralists reminded their sinful audiences that sexual promiscuity and dissipation brought disease in its wake.[193] Mandeville might joke that 'a hale robust constitution is esteemed a mark of ungentility' but he recognized that 'whoring of itself disposes the mind to such a sort of indolence as is quite inconsistent with industry'.[194]

Chastity may indirectly have fortified the acquisitive instinct. Implicit, but rarely conscious in the arguments of those who castigated womanizing, was a more modern thesis, that repression of the sexual drive was conducive to business.[195] It was commonly thought that excessive indulgence in food and drink led to sexual lust which made man an animal incapable of rational conduct. Evelyn hinted darkly that 'covetousness seldom goes unaccompanied with other secret and exterminating vices'.[196] But contemporaries saw only the visible connections between self-denial and business behaviour. The pleasures of the flesh only

[186] Ewen 1932: 108–9; Ashton 1969: 2. [187] Perkins, *English Puritanist*, p. 222.

[188] KAO U.145/C1, letter Thomas Hill, April 1660; Ehrenberg 1963: 244.

[189] On the distinctions between swearing by, that, to and at, see Hughes 1991: 4; Beake, *Diary*, pp. 112–14. [190] Disney, *Remarkable Passages*, 34.

[191] Merchants did suffer from venereal diseases: see Lindeboon 1950: 72. But the claims of Andreski 1987: 26 should not be taken too seriously. [192] Wolff 1968: 26.

[193] Heywood, *Autobiography*, ii. 266; Schafer 1971: 205.

[194] Mandeville, *Modest Defence Public Stews*, pp. 3–4, 19.

[195] Hobbes, *Behemoth*, ii. 516. Defoe, *Matrimonial Whoredom*, iii. 85 makes the point explicitly. The argument is conveniently set out by Fromm 1932: 272–4 and is discussed by Cominos 1963: 240; Taylor 1958: 161, chap. 8. It is characteristic of Sombart that he should immediately recognize the significance of Freud's early work: see 1913: 256. Most historical applications of Freudian theory do not bother to offer any evidence: see for example Carroll 1981: 466. [196] Evelyn, *Public Employment*, p. 102.

interfered with business if they were indiscreet and obsessively pursued.[197]

The work ethic

The Anglican apologists emphasized the dignity of labour even more than the Puritans and it was the anti-clerical, John Locke, who produced the most far-reaching definition of work.[198] But perceptions of industry were subtle and varied in different strata of society; although the dramatists targeted the apprentice, the labour theory of value was directed primarily at the lower orders.[199] Several businessmen consistently advocated a compulsive attitude to work and rejected the cult of leisure; Peter Mundy advised 'better doe something to noe purpose then be idle, having at present spare tyme'.[200]

Diligence and regularity of application was emphasized because so many of the essential chores were tedious and repetitive.[201] A more rapid pace of change in the seventeenth century made merchants more aware of the passage of time and its effect on profits.[202] The work habits of older merchants could be broken; but it was primarily apprentices who displayed a natural indolence and aversion to routine and a fondness for idle chatter and sports, Sabbath pastimes, newsmongering and light literature. In their autobiographies, most merchants confessed to lapses during the ferment of adolescence.[203] Sons of landed gentlemen were thought to be particularly at risk and some did indeed dress flamboyantly, fornicate, break their indentures, absent themselves without leave and incur dismissal.[204] But many gentlemen became model merchants and children of other social origins were just as inclined towards libertinism and leisure.[205] Sir Richard Hoare closely supervised his son, John, who nonetheless drank, swore, whored, gambled, fiddled his accounts, dressed expensively and died young.[206]

[197] Mandeville, *Free Thoughts Religion*, pp. 8, 12.

[198] Wenzel 1960; Febvre 1948: 27–8; Hundert 1972: 6; Sommerville 1981: 70; 1976: 37; Seaver 1980: 52.

[199] Schelling 1908: i. 208; Starr 1965: 193; Wagner 1985: 49–52.

[200] Pares 1950: 67; Mundy, *Travels*, i. p. xxiii; *Yorkshire Diaries*, ii. 20.

[201] GLL MS 10823/1, fo. 38; Reeves 1956: 95–101; Hale, *Works*, i. 529; Hedges, *Diary*, i. pp. cviii, 78; Markham, *Hobson's Horse-load*; Wilson 1957: 128.

[202] MacCullagh 1987: 46; Landes 1983: 89 points out that clocks denote movement, whereas work signals the continuous passage of time.

[203] GLL MS 12017.

[204] Chamberlayne, *Angliae Notitiae*, p. 481; Sena 1973: 304; *Newcastle Merchant Adventurers' Records*.

[205] Rawdon, *Life*, p. 196; *Yorkshire Diaries*, i. 371; Wadsworth & Mann 1931: 74; GLL MS 10823/1, fo. 44; Donaldson, *Art of Thriving*, p. 114; Lincs. AO I B/48–50, letter 22 Jan. 1705; Diamond 1969: 572–3; Blanchard 1978: 14; Morgan 1971b: 609.

[206] Woodbridge 1969: 784, 788.

Even after the Reformation, England still had seventy-nine non-working days including twenty-seven holy days; Thomas Watts claimed that England lost 'one Fourth of the Year in Vacation'.[207] Ambrose Crowley III never took a holiday, but the London prentices petitioned to have their 'Popish' holy days restored during the Civil Wars and an Ordinance of 1647 did substitute every second Tuesday in the month.[208] Their attitude is not surprising, when it is considered that their hours of work stretched from 6 a.m. to 9 p.m. six days a week and that some holy days provided for the temporary reversal of authority.[209] Although saints' days certainly disrupted trade, particularly in foreign countries, they were not reduced in England for economic reasons.[210]

The prohibition of Sunday retailing neither began with the Reformation nor ended with the Restoration.[211] Sabbatarianism had continental origins, though the Dutch adopted a more secular approach.[212] The Sabbatarian movement was a late-Elizabethan conspiracy used as a theological football to justify two different visions of the Church, and its economic value has often been misunderstood.[213] The persistent efforts to mandate observance, both at home and abroad, were intended to set aside time for meditation, religious exercises, visiting the sick and improvement of mind, not for work, amusement, rest or leisure. Sabbatarian restrictions in fact restricted production in the drink trades.[214]

Religion provided goals for work and Puritan discipline was an inversion of popular culture; but a clothier did not refuse to attend a church ale because he was a capitalist.[215] The flow of business was usually slow, irregular and seasonal and determined by climate and daylight.[216] Merchants did not have a large staff to manage and control and their functions and routines had a different time frame from post-industrial societies.[217] Public clocks were now installed in town halls as well as churches, but until the invention of the balance spring revolutionized the watch, portable timepieces were inaccurate.[218] The compulsive need to

[207] Watts, *Essay Man Business*, p. 18; Lithgow, *Rare Painful Peregrinations*, p. 127; Robinson, *Certeine Proposals*, p. 37; Cressy 1989: 7; Ryder, *Diary*, p. 52.

[208] Greene, *Diary*, pp. 108–9. [209] Thomas 1978: 5.

[210] Olearius, *Travels*, p. 249. [211] Whitaker 1933: 120, 152–8, 182, 195.

[212] Woodcock 1952: 80–7; Rordorf 1968: 296; Collinson 1983: 437; Grell 1989: 76.

[213] Hill 1964; Greaves 1981a: 33; Parker 1988: 6–7. [214] Wilcox 1946: 142.

[215] Firth 1944: 97; Hearnshaw 1954: 135; Collinson 1988a: 152.

[216] Boulton 1989: 43; Cole 1959: 292. It is difficult to determine how many hours were allocated for sleep, but it was probably eight to nine; businessmen usually retired at 9 p.m. and rose at 5–6 a.m.

[217] Thomas 1964: 60; Thompson in Walter 1974: 42; Seaver 1980: 53. Leisure preference owes as much to lack of reward as to cultural factors: see Persson 1988: 5.

[218] Landes 1983: 92–4, 128; Epstein 1988: 259–60; Gurvich 1964: 36; Tittler 1985b: 45. There is little evidence to support the claim of Pococke 1975: 440 that time became dynamic.

work was the exception, rather than the rule.[219] Few internalized or would even have understood the ethic of work for its own sake, as an end rather than a means. To St Thomas *industria* meant enterprise; contemporaries distinguished between working to sustain life and working to accumulate, which was more suspect.[220] Play was not necessarily frivolous, but an integral part of the structure.[221] A workaholic without ability could be a liability to himself and his fellows. What mattered was concentration and shrewdness rather than mindless toil.[222]

Although the prudential virtues conferred respectability on businessmen, their main function was through exhortation and example to teach each new generation of young men to respect authority, resist temptation and master their environment.[223] Work habits had to be justified and leisure preferences countered by moral propaganda and enforcement either in the family or in the guild. The godly, according to Baxter, 'blew the coals among foolish apprentices', who were stubborn, delinquent adolescents inclined towards rebellion and confusion.[224] Still regarded as innocents, though more mature than infants, their play and passions had to be rationed and controlled by coercion until they had learned self-discipline.[225]

Sermons probably had little effect, because their dry technicalities and declamatory wordiness were not really suited for conversion and instruction; they were often written for publication and intended to elevate the academic standing and career of the preacher.[226] What business needed was neither Calvinist theology nor apocalyptic visions, but muscular Christianity.[227] Moral terrorism certainly played some part in repressing and displacing qualities antagonistic to business. But Puritan theology never distinguished morality from tradition and oscillated between external discipline and exploiting the moral anxieties of the self. The inculcation of appropriate norms was achieved primarily through traditional education and socialization and by sublimating aggressive egotism in symbolic rituals. It was apprenticeship which fulfilled the role of a boot camp. The long hours, hard stools, lack of heat and poor diet, the restrictive dress and hairstyles and the menial tasks of sweeping the shop and carrying slops served to break down anti-social attitudes, to instil

[219] Weber became ill when he was forced to be idle: see Bendix 1959: 26; Mitzman 1970: 171–2.

[220] Hill, *Exact Dealer*, p. 2; Gordon 1975: 185; Gill 1935: 78–9; Bushman 1967: 23–4; *Vanity Mischief*; *Shirburn Ballads*, p. 44.

[221] Huizinga 1955: 200; Cohen 1953: 312–22.

[222] BL Add. MS 28009, fo. 48v°; Mustazza 1989: 176; Ellis 1981a: 119.

[223] Cochran 1973: 1–10.

[224] Baxter, *Reliquiae Baxterianae*, p. 39.

[225] Ben Amos 1988: 42–3; Dunlop 1912: 182; Yarbrough 1979; Steven in Fletcher & Steven 1985; Erickson 1963a: 157; Inkeles & Smith 1974: 1–10.

[226] Haigh 1977: 46.

[227] Léonard 1961: ii. 293; Lamont 1979: 319; Samuelsson 1961: 43.

humility and respect for elders and institutions and to prepare adolescents for adult life.

It was, moreover, the instinct for self-preservation, rather than legal and moral prohibitions, which was ultimately most successful in suppressing unproductive appetites. Through trial and error, a young merchant discovered, sometimes too late, what was compatible with business. Some of the prudential virtues were suited to artisans, others to successful merchants whose priority was the preservation of their gains; all could become vices, if practised too rigidly. The key to survival was temperance and moderation. The wise merchant chose a *via media* between overborrowing and undertrading, between patience and hot-headedness, between pointless frivolity and stultifying seriousness, between an obsessive search for purity and the self-indulgence which led to dissipation. Sober intentions alone did not suffice; self-control simply created the necessary conditions in which other talents could be exercised. Many devout tradesmen never raised their businesses above subsistence level. A business fortune was not the baggage of virtue and only time and skill could translate godliness into gain.

Honesty

Of greater importance were the rules which governed relations with third parties. The word 'business' in many circles was synonymous with corruption, opportunism and deceit.[228] Distrust of businessmen, at every level, had roots in agrarian hostility towards middlemen and was exaggerated by fear, ignorance and prejudice. But it was reinforced by actual experience of double-dealing. In the slippery world of government contracting and Court finance, in the narrow oligarchies and monopolies which dominated whole trades, integrity was often overwhelmed by greed; when abroad, merchants could ignore the conventions of age, rank and morality.

In a competitive and often merciless world, businessmen had to look out for themselves and could not afford to be too squeamish or forthright. There are many vivid contemporary descriptions of the seamy world of con men, broken merchants and fraudulent bankrupts.[229] The Deposition Books of ports and proceedings in Admiralty and Chancery give the superficial impression that all businessmen connived, bribed and lied; 'that which a man is bred up in', remarked Selden, 'he thinks no cheating'.[230] As Thomas Pitt remarked, ability in a merchant was always

[228] Grampp 1950–1: 144.

[229] Lodge, *Works*, iv. 5; Fennor, *Counters' Commonwealth* in Judges 1930: 459, 466–7; Kirkman & Head 1935.

[230] Selden, *Table Talk*, p. 129.

preferable to honesty.[231] Attempts by both the central government and the municipalities to control regrating and forestalling failed consistently; buyers were cheated by false weights and measures, deceptive packaging, substandard goods, watered milk and wine, and price extortion.[232] Scott might advise 'trading justly', but he also describes how drapers could darken their shops and practise flattery and dissimulation.[233]

In the retailing of necessary commodities, businessmen cornered markets and exploited scarcity, fire, flood, plague and harvest failure; marketing abuses in the coal and horse trades were notorious.[234] Wholesale dealers cheated the small artisans and consumers who in turn did their best to turn the tables by delaying payment and by fraudulent bankruptcy.[235] In the book trade, authors, publishers and booksellers plagiarized without scruple, exploited medical and political fears and catered to the demand for scandal and titillation.[236] The corrupt practices of the smaller dealers were vividly described from experience by orthodox preachers and by champions of the humble, like Bunyan.[237] A prolific popular literature on cheats and rogues exposed the connection between crime and the retail trades; the Quarter Sessions records illustrate the conflict which accompanied the everyday exchange of goods.[238] The weakest did go to the wall and the Devil took the hindmost.

The sacramental universe had not yet been replaced by an ego-oriented society.[239] To the preachers of all denominations, the marketplace was a battlefield, where the Devil drove and the innocents were slaughtered. Tillotson considered that it was unethical for a seller to take advantage of ignorance, necessity and weakness, even when the market was open.[240] But it was easier for Anglican mystics, like Thomas Traherne, to reconcile business with religion than it was for the more old-fashioned, totalitarian Non-Conformist preachers who still believed in the unity of action and belief.[241] Where Calvinism was able to establish a theocracy in New England, the ministers revived the just price and used ecclesiastical discipline and neighbourly pressure to protect the consumer against the middleman.[242] The philosophical roots of individualism lie more in Latitudinarianism than in sectarianism.

Radicals and Puritans bemoaned the absence of plain-dealing and the

231 Hedges, *Diary*, i. p. ciii; BL Harl. MS 6842, fos. 36, 289; BL Add. MS 22849, fo. 69.

232 Ponko 1964–5: 33.

233 Scott, *Essay Drapery*, pp. 20–2.

234 Willcox 1946: 206; MacArthur 1928: 78; Nef 1932: ii. 33, 104–5; Edwards in Thompson 1983: 114.

235 MacGrath 1954: 291–2; Sanderson, *Rod for Naylors*, p. 62.

236 Redlich 1966.

237 MacLure 1958: 134f; Bunyan, *Life Badman*, p. xxxi.

238 Chandler 1907: 102; *Knaving Merchant*.

239 Boas 1966: 621.

240 Schlatter 1940: 194, 211.

241 Love, *Scriptural Rules*; Breen 1966: 286.

242 Bailyn 1955: 20–2, 43; Johnson 1932a: chap. 7; Roover 1958; Gilchrist 1969: 59–62, 116–17. For a different view see Foster 1971: app. C.

oppression of fellow Christians; 'for matters of buying and selling the earth stinks with much unrighteousness'.[243] Several agreed with Bunyan that it was unethical 'to sell his commodities for as much as he can'.[244] The Quakers believed that there was a just price and that both borrower and lender suffered moral loss; according to the instructions of 1675, none were to trade 'beyond their ability nor stretch beyond their compasse'.[245] Insolvency was stigmatized as moral failure and the English Reformed Church expelled bankrupts until they settled.[246]

An absolute code of ethics, however, created more problems than it solved.[247] A business could not be conducted simply on equity capital; retrenchment was often impossible without further undermining its credit.[248] Indeed naivety and ignorance often led Quakers into bankruptcy.[249] Disputes between Friends could be reconciled by arbitration, but competition could not be eliminated in the marketplace and they could not reconcile their ethics with the retailing of superfluous commodities; the distinction between brewing and distilling was arbitrary and they could not opt out of naval protection.[250] In fact, Friends charged each other the market rate of interest and even invested in privateering.[251] It was not their antiquated morality that made them prosperous, but their risk-sharing, high credit rating and fair pricing which pleased customers and facilitated transactions.[252] The key injunction was not to 'owe no man anything but love' but 'that they use few words in dealing and keepe their worde in all thyngs'.[253]

The logic of the market confounded all theology. The principles of commutative or distributive justice could not determine real value or define what was an adequate profit or a fair price. Exceptional circumstances sometimes required that prices be related to elemental needs; a reluctance on the part of consumers to test the market allowed sellers to

243 Alsop 1989: 97, 107.

244 Ames, *Conscience*, p. 236; Bunyan, *Life Badman*, pp. 118, 123; Hammond in Newey 1980: 126.

245 *Gainsborough Monthly Meeting First Minute Book*, p. 43; Fox, *Warning to All Merchants*. However convenient a set price might be for retail customers, it represented an attempt to bypass market forces and, despite the misleading claims of Sacks 1989: 316, was incompatible with normal business dealings.

246 Fox, *Line of Righteousness*, p. 7; *Epistle to Shopkeepers*. Fox was not above settling old scores: see his *Journal*, i. 50, 395. Although Rom. 13:8. was cited frequently by all denominations, views on bankruptcy differed considerably. To Wilkinson, *Debt Book*, pp. 3–7, two negatives in Greek did not constitute an affirmative; see also Carter 1964: 175.

247 Tolmie 1977b: 11.

248 Santer, *Practise of Bankrupts*; Hoppit 1990: 305ff.

249 Stout, *Autobiography*, pp. 8, 90; Lloyd 1950: 37–9.

250 Grubb 1930: 31, 88, 146, 175.

251 Dewhurst & Doublet 1974: 109; Kunze 1989: 569.

252 Price in Dunns 1986: 384; Fitzwilliam, *Correspondence*, p. 177.

253 *Bristol Minute Book Friends*, p. 43.

formalize prices in certain trades. But the just price was usually equated with market price unless there was evidence of monopolistic practice.[254] Even controlled markets had to respond sooner or later to price adjustments whether through supply and demand or bargaining.[255] A universalistic morality of business was a chimera, because relations between buyers and sellers could not be governed by an absolute moral code. By mid century, the debate over usury was conducted in economic and not theological terms; Milton saw no difference between usury and rent.[256]

There was, moreover, no obvious basis for compromise, because the practice of business was fundamentally incompatible with personal, familial and social values.[257] Profit drove business, not generosity or compassion; the labour theory of value was inapplicable to financial operations, where profits reflected the degree of risk, skill and luck.[258] The exploitation of vanity, greed and incompetence could not clearly be distinguished from the exploitation of ignorance and personal misfortune.[259] Oaths raised complex questions as to what constituted an obligation. Middlemen had to maintain stocks and could not sell immediately. A merchant might wish to follow a godly course, but he had to proceed by bargain and contract, which usually favoured one party.[260] Milton bitterly blamed the fall of the saints on the expediencies of business.[261] But the role of merchants was to initiate and satisfy human wants, not to follow theological definitions of need and obligation. The market was a place set apart. The concept of the stewardship of wealth and of salvation by charitable works could not paper over the fundamental dichotomy between individual enterprise and social morality which was clearly exposed during the debate over Mandeville.[262]

It was inevitable that this ethical vacuum would create a double standard of morality, that religion would be effectively divorced from business.[263] To Thomas Dekker, 'the worldling wasteth his nights and weareth out his dayes in tying his conscience full of knots to pull up riches'.[264] One possible solution was casuistry, whether implied or

[254] Noonan 1957: 82–8; Roover 1974: 290, 331; Finley in Finley 1974: 35; Wilson 1975: 73.

[255] Seaver 1985: chap. 5.

[256] *Milton and his Commonplace Book*, p. 154; MacDonald 1987: 355–9; Ellis 1970: 41.

[257] Taylor, *Holy Living*.

[258] Wood 1950: 160; Rüstow 1945: 114; Weisskopf 1951: 200.

[259] Scott, *Essay Drapery*.

[260] Zaret 1985: 10, 188 rejects the notion of the stewardship of wealth and argues that covenant theology borrowed from business, but this is based on a misreading of the evidence.

[261] Milton, *Works*, v. 147–8.

[262] Monroe 1975: 142; Goldsmith 1976: 478; Chalk 1966: 15; Bredvold 1962: 15–16; Horne 1978: 71; MacFie 1967: 81, 113; Billet 1976; Winch 1992: 103; Culpeper, *Necessity Abating Usury*, p. 10.

[263] Tawney 1944: 188–92, 238.

[264] Dekker, *Non Dramatic Works*, p. 21.

conscious.[265] Anglican casuistry was more honest and less authoritarian than its Catholic equivalent, and was both therapeutic and personal.[266] That last great Scholastic work, the *Christian Directory* practised it on a grand scale; Baxter accepted that price was determined by the market, but argued that no party to a bargain should exercise an unfair advantage.[267]

Some rejected casuistry in favour of autonomy of judgement and the golden rule.[268] Thomas Fuller took 'our Saviours whole-sale rule whatsoever ye would have men do unto you, do you unto them' and he was echoed by the eminently sensible Richard Steele.[269] Businessmen rarely had the time to weigh moral issues before making decisions and they usually followed habit and convenience. The theocrats in England and New England had to bend before economic forces and accept an uneasy co-existence with business.[270] Economic development owed nothing to the ideas of the Puritans, but at least they did not constitute a major obstacle, because the preachers leaned towards an ethic of intention and endless aspiration and did not lay down a precise set of behavioural rules.[271] Growing confidence weakened misgivings about usury and the economic teachings of the Church became irrelevant.[272] Ultimately the doctrine of the harmony of interests emerged to bridge the gap; the automatic and unintended benefits of competition replaced the ideal of reciprocal help.

Interest and conscience

The gradual evolution of a double standard did not, however, render business morality superfluous. Even cynics and sceptics were reluctant to envisage a marketplace driven by ego, like Hobbes' State of Nature, in which Natural Law was the law of survival. A framework of obligation was, in fact, crucial to the functioning of business. The business community was always conscious of the harm generated by fraud, when practised by its members, even though it was more tolerant towards cheating the consumer. If merchants only followed profit, asked Daniel

265 Barbour 1964: 9; Starr 1971: 32; Richetti 1975: 6–7.

266 Perkins, *English Puritanist*, pp. x–xiv; Zagorin 1990b: chap. 10; Holmes 1981: 44, 57; Wood 1952: x, 101; Catheart 1969: 3092A; Slights 1981; Leites 1974; Phillips 1959; Rose 1975: chap. 6; Roover 1974: 290.

267 Baxter, *Christian Directory*, vi. 306–9; Dr William's Lib. Baxter MSS, Treatises, iv. 281–315, lecture for merchants at Pinners Hall, 2 Sept. 1679.

268 Leites in Leites 1988: 125.

269 Fuller, *Holy State*, p. 116; Steele, *Religious Tradesman*, pp. 95–6.

270 Haffenden 1974: 123; Heyrman 1984: 19.

271 Dunn 1969: 217. Sommerville 1992a argues that Protestantism desacralized culture and marginalized religion, but it was more a victim than an instigator of change.

272 Riemersma 1952: 25; Coleman in King & Parekh 1986: 274.

Cooper, where would they stop?[273] Ethical indifference threatened the basis of contracts; bankruptcy could initiate a chain reaction of failures.[274]

The secular law did provide remedies for creditors and enforce contracts.[275] But it was slow, costly, uncertain and a last resort.[276] 'I wish with all my heart you were once rid of him', John Aylward was advised, 'for its very uneasy to have to do with litigious persons'.[277] Dishonesty might pay in evading customs, ignoring government regulations and exploiting the weaknesses of the administration; concealment of the truth was part and parcel of bargaining.[278] But businessmen distinguished between cheating and acceptable sharp practice. They commented unfavourably on the low ethical standards of foreign merchants which were more of an obstacle to exchange in countries like Russia and China than linguistic, political and religious barriers.[279] Anyone whose money passed through the hands of a third party depended on the latter's honesty; a dishonest factor was 'a double infliction by obliging them to sue either a Beggar or that which is worse a naughty man'.[280]

There was clearly a limit to Machiavellian principles.[281] Accuracy of description was essential in the despatch and receipt of goods; speaking and writing the truth reduced the need for defensive regulations and quickened the conduct of business.[282] 'I account plain dealing a jewell', wrote George Sitwell; 'the first commodity a young tradesmen sets to sell', it was remarked, 'is his own honesty'; 'Falsehood and Deceit in Trade may set out briskly, like a Cockneigh upon a Gallop in a Morning, but it always flags in the afternoon.'[283] The whole structure of credit depended on 'mutual trust among private men'.[284] Normal transactions would have been impossible if merchants had not kept their word, honoured their bills, bonds and marks and acted in good faith.[285] A bill or

[273] Tawney 1958: 64. [274] Fleetwood, *Two Sermons*, p. 28.

[275] See pp. 214–18; Guth in Guth & MacKenna 1982: 81; Parry 1967.

[276] Ewald 1956: 132–3; Parks 1976: 3, 106.

[277] Bod Eng. Lett. MS C.192, letter 12 Oct. 1699.

[278] Defoe, *Compleat English Tradesman*, ii. 205–9, 229, 234, 348.

[279] Kirchner 1966: 236–41; Woodbridge 1969: 789.

[280] Bagnall, *Steward's Last Account*; Strong, *Trust of Steward*; Molloy, *De Jure Maritimo*, p. 443.

[281] BL Add. MS 22781, fo. 12; Malynes, *Lex Mercatoria*, p, 22; Milles, *Misterie of Iniquity*.

[282] *Plain Dealing*.

[283] Sitwell, *Letterbook*, p. 149; *Yorkshire Diaries*, ii. 171; *Vulgar Errors Censured*; *Interest England Considered*, p. 20; Yarranton, *England's Improvement*, p. 6; Burley 1961: 26.

[284] C114/55, letter 6 Oct. 1664; Temple, *Observations United Provinces*, p. 101; Coole, *Honesty Truest Policy*.

[285] *Grand Concern of England*, p. 51; Briscoe, *Discourse on Money*, p. 130; Sheridan, *Discourse of Rise Parliaments*, p. 225. The expression 'my word is my bond' apparently dates from the eighteenth century: see MacKendrick *et al.* 1982: 214; on changes in the meaning of honesty see Skinner 1974: 296.

promissory note was only as good as the person on whom it was drawn; yet 'a small script of two or three lines', boasted a pamphlet, 'passes over the World for thousands of pounds'.[286] Many commercial agreements were extraordinarily casual and rested on personal bond; obligations were incurred on a nod or hands were struck 'for confirmation of bargains, grants or covenants or promises and suretyship'.[287] To preserve his credit, a merchant had to eschew 'doubleness of tongue', perform his covenants, punctiliously pay his debts, maintain accurate books and not overtrade.[288]

The importance of honour and reputation cannot be overestimated. 'A goodword behynde your back may avantage you more then a long sayling ... and an ivel worde lykewise may do you more hurte then a losse of a shippe.'[289] Isham and Malynes both cited the Flemish proverb, 'goods lost, nothing lost, credit lost, much lost, soul lost, all lost'.[290] Sincerity was highly valued and a London brewer was dismissed as having 'noe reputation for keeping his word'.[291] Defoe distinguished beween financial credit and moral reputation, but he considered that they were mutually reinforcing.[292]

Reputation was so highly regarded that 'tis no unusual practise for merchants to disturb one another in the same trade by whispered stories to officers without any foundations'.[293] Michael Blackett was furious when he heard that rumours of his unreliability were being spread by his enemies around the coffee-houses of London.[294] Thomas Papillon cited the 15th Psalm to the wife of an alderman, who had accused him of taking bribes.[295] Malicious gossip and defamatory rumours were, like written libels, actionable at both civil and common law, though jurisdiction gradually passed to the latter.[296] Although accusations of dishonesty and bankruptcy were actionable *per se*, the courts became so overloaded that they construed words like 'bankrupt' and 'knave' as innocent when used adjectively or in the heat of passion and insisted on proof of financial

[286] Lee 1869: ii. 330; *Character and Qualifications Merchant*, p. 5.
[287] Bulwer, *Chinologie*, p. 105; Aubrey, *Remaines of Gentilisme*, p. 56. The conventional handshake seems to have been largely confined to greetings. Verbal contracts did of course lead to disputes in the courts: see Caesar, *Ancient State Court of Requests*, p. 97.
[288] Defoe, *Compleat English Tradesman*, ii. 275–92.
[289] G. C. M. Smith 1936: 41.
[290] Malynes, *Lex Mercatoria*, p. 221; *John Isham*, p. 172.
[291] Coole, *Miscellanies*, p. 6; *London Characters Lord Mayors*, p. 516.
[292] Defoe, *Review*, iii. 145–8; Sutherland 1950: 42–4.
[293] Kress Lib. MS, Woollen Collection, *For Bill against Clandestine Trade*.
[294] CUL Add. MS 91 C, fo. 119v°. [295] Papillon, *Memoirs*, pp. 1–2.
[296] Marchant 1969: 61, 72–4, 244; Milsom 1969: 341–4; Plucknett 1956: 493; Ingram 1987: table 12; Prideaux 1896–7: i. 78.

damage as distinct from insult.[297] Many were handled by municipal and guild courts or by arbitration.[298]

Business depended to a large extent on a self-enforcing morality.[299] Most merchants were not so foolish as to cheat those from whom they sought repeat business or who supplied essential services. As Selden, Grotius and Hobbes all argued, the ethics of business behaviour were dictated by rational self-interest and fear of anarchy.[300] Richard Steele pointed out that 'not only duty and conscience but present interest obliges men to the exercise of probity'.[301] Conformity to accepted standards and transactions within extended families and within the fraternity of the guild were also enforced by shame, loyalty and self-respect.[302] Merchants had a basic sense of fairness to others, which may have been reinforced by the code of honour characteristic of officers and gentlemen.[303] This was the criterion applied by arbitrators and it was later to be refined by moral philosophers into a theory of other-regarding sentiments.[304]

The obligation to perform promises did not, however, just rest on mutual interest. Compliance was buttressed by an appeal to moral principle and to personal conviction.[305] Children were brought up on stories of how apprentices who stole came to a sticky end.[306] Breaches of accepted etiquette aroused moral indignation and economic interests were couched in the terminology of self-righteousness.[307] When John Brown of Barbados denied his debt, the creditor responded: 'if I had lost 5 times as much money providentially I could have born it patiently, but this is plain cheating'.[308] Moral character was the ultimate guarantor of agreements. Perjury was not a felony and all recognized the sanctity of marks and oaths, which had not yet been superseded by written con-

[297] Libel carried more serious penalties and truth was no defence, whereas hairsplitting definitions of slander weakened the impact of the law. See W. R. Jones 1971: 279–80; Holdsworth 1924: 304; 1925: 406; MacDonald 1944: 184. Two alternative remedies were the Herald's Court and the duel: see Clark 1958: 38. Sometimes false actions for slander were employed: see *Winchester Consistory Court Depositions*, p. 25.

[298] Bossy 1983: 186; Clode 1888: i. 212.

[299] Buck 1977: 68.

[300] For variant interpretations of Hobbes and Locke see Warrender 1961: 319; Watkins 1965: 326; Kavka 1986; Myers 1983: 4; Sampson 1990: 735; Tuck 1979: 100; Leyden 1982: 82; Colman 1983: 21–2, 237.

[301] Steele, *Religious Tradesman*, p. 80.

[302] Eberhard 1967.

[303] Wright 1940: 178; J. D. Davies 1991: 51; Oakeshott 1962: 294; Ogg 1955: 37; Shapiro in Hunter & Schaffer 1989: 285.

[304] Taylor 1989: 28–9; Myers 1972: 165; Taylor 1955: 30; Eisenach 1981: 130.

[305] Guth in Guth & MacKenna 1982: 84–5; Daube 1969: 58.

[306] Sloane 1955: 38.

[307] Leeds University Libraries, Brotherton Coll. MS Tr U, fo. 15.

[308] Bod. Rawl. Lett. MS 66, fo. 12.

tracts.[309] Theft was regarded as sinful because it was a breach of trust.[310] Miscreants in the Grocers Company were made to repent on their knees, as in the ecclesiastical courts.[311]

The efficacy of religious belief as a moral cement depended on the individual conscience, which could be clouded by hypocrisy. Conspiratorial and unscrupulous businessmen, like Arthur Ingram who was at once self-righteous, self-pitying and subservient, managed to convince themselves that they were always in the right, no matter how avaricious and ruthless their actions.[312] But merchants did consult their conscience daily to discipline and review their actions.[313] John Child wrote to his friend, the interloper John Petit: 'You do well to take law and equity for your guide and with them let conscience come in, who will tell you that not only the light of nature but Holy Writ will have us be obedient to authority.'[314] Dishonesty was abhorred because of its economic consequences, but those consequences were also expected to follow from an immoral action.[315] Oliver Heywood thought that his father 'sinned in changing his calling, in too eager pursuit of the world in unfaithful dealing, in not keeping his word, in pleasing himself with hope of riches'.[316] Bankruptcy, like poverty, was often regarded as the wages of sin. [317]

The friction and tension between selfishness and social values, between business necessity and conscience created unease, ambivalence and doubt. The aggressiveness and obsessiveness of merchants may have been fuelled by social guilt.[318] Francis Rogers could write 'the not giving 6d to the maid has caused me much uneasiness then getting 6s could do me good'.[319] The most effective sanctions were not those of the ecclesiastical and secular courts, but the values internalized in the individual during adolescence through the example and instruction of parents, masters and preachers. It was the self-imposed obligations of conscience which upheld impersonal contractual relationships and maintained stability in business.

[309] Robbins 1972: 305; Hill 1964: chap. 11; Herrup 1987: 2; Heward 1972: 9; Atiyah 1971: 3; Mitchell 1904: 102; Cowell 1984: 68. Thomas Pitt exploited fear of damnation to extract a debt from a dying man: see Hedges, *Diary*, ii. p. xciv.

[310] Fletcher 1975: 474; Brooks in Baker 1978: 57; Gough 1950: chap. 7.

[311] Rees 1923: 119. [312] Upton 1961: 38, 258. [313] Nicholls 1870: part i, 12.

[314] IOL Factory Records Misc. xvi, letter 12 Dec. 1682; Strachey 1916: chap. 4.

[315] On the internalization of social values see Walzer 1965: 106; Evans-Pritchard 1937: 117ff; Kardiner 1963: 441.

[316] Heywood, *Autobiography*, p. 23; *Yorkshire Diaries*, ii. 21.

[317] Hoppit 1987: 162. [318] Erickson 1966: 52. [319] Rogers, *Diary*, p. xxvii.

10 Family structure

The households of businessmen served as units of both production and consumption; the family was their principal instrument for protecting and transferring property and for social advancement. Some historians have argued that patriarchy and lineage were challenged during the seventeenth century by a new ideal of the family based on the nuclear household and more closely geared to the needs of a capitalist society.[1] It is alleged that individualism redefined relationships between husbands and wives, between parents and children and between kin. The 'bourgeois' family is contrasted with the 'aristocratic' family and credited with different attitudes towards domesticity and childhood, with greater affection and less regimentation.[2] Protestantism is assumed to have sacralized collective egoism and property in the family and de-emphasized the community, to have transformed tribal brotherhood into universal otherhood.[3]

The concept of the 'bourgeois' family is a preconceived model. It rests in part on legal formulations, but has primarily been abstracted from Protestant sermons and homiletic and didactic tracts. In fact, the Reformation did not usher in drastic change and men of all religious denominations and social backgrounds agreed on the fundamental principles of the family, many of which derived from the Pauline Epistles.[4] The 'Family Instructors' were aimed as much at the gentry as the merchants.[5] The advice literature was interested in defending and promoting an ideal and sought to reform an institution which had proved inadequate; the numerous works can be read either as complaint or as exhortation, but their meaning is often ambiguous and they cannot be assumed to describe actual practice.[6] The catechisms did, however, spread commonplace ideas and convey the assumptions and values which underlay family organization and justified everyday practice. The practical handbooks on

[1] Stone 1977a; 1981: 83.

[2] Wrightson 1982: 107; Wilson 1980: 142; Sommerville 1992a.

[3] Nelson 1969: 139–63; Eister 1974: 95; Morgan 1966: 1ff; Leites 1982: 394.

[4] K. M. Davies in Outhwaite 1981: 59–60; 1977: 577.

[5] Curtis 1981: 420.

[6] Collinson 1988a: 81.

household administration, which were extremely popular and numerous, addressed more directly the realities of family life.[7] The journalists and hack writers were interested in sales; they targeted a specific audience and tailored their advice to suit the prejudices and aspirations of their readers.[8]

If literary sources are not viewed in context, half-truths can be elevated into myths. In order to define the distinctive characteristics of the business family, it is necessary to reconstruct from private and judicial records, diaries, commonplace books, family correspondence and household accounts the actual routines of domestic life. To understand how the system functioned, it is important to examine and respect the variable and often eccentric characters of individuals.[9] Were there in fact significant differences between landed and business families in their demographic patterns, their attitude to marriage and women, courtship and child-rearing? Did the Family Instructors offer an alternative to traditional ideals and how far were they adopted by the business community? Why did merchants marry and procreate and how did they handle their wives, children and relatives?

The marriage market

Matrimony was rationally appraised in economic and social terms, because the kinship group was remodelled and reinforced by marriage and a wrong choice could jeopardize the future of a whole family. Even the best of alliances raised problems of child-rearing and could be strained by the addition of new kin. Beauty and sentiment usually took second place to rank, religion and wealth. Given a choice, most merchants preferred a woman with some education and social sense and practical household skills. But they had to compromise between several conflicting objectives and responsibilities.[10]

The literature of romance obviously had a market and was more than pure fantasy.[11] Some merchants, like Marmaduke Rawdon, Roger Lowe and Robert Pitt did fall in love.[12] Some of their womenfolk also followed their hearts. Jane Lewknow committed adultery and eloped; Alderman Spurstow's daughter married 'one Boyle who taught her to play on the Organ who was tryed and cast for haveing two wives'.[13] Sir Robert Vyner's infatuated daughter stole away and married; the daughter of Sir

[7] Sommerville 1992a: 16. [8] Powell 1917: chap. 4.
[9] N. Z. Davis 1975: 266. [10] MacFarlane 1985: 214, 297.
[11] Spufford 1981: chap. 7. It is difficult to gauge sensibility as display of affection was stylized and codified: see Elias 1989.
[12] Rawdon, *Life*, pp. xvi, 78; Forman, *Autobiography*, p. 9; Lowe, *Diary*, p. 37; Lever 1947: 28. [13] Marescoe, *Markets and Merchants*, p. 9; Woodcock, *Papers*, p. 74.

William Cony married her footman who beat her, took her money and ran away.[14] George Boddington allowed his daughter, Sarah, to marry Ebenezer Collier, an undesirable suitor, because he was genuinely afraid that she would die of love.[15]

But merchants could not be slaves to their passions and infatuation was universally condemned as folly; 'I acknowledge a Beauty to be a Fortune but money (is) very well termed the jewel of conjugal affection'.[16] It was inconceivable, when the interests of the whole family were involved, that children could be allowed to exercise complete freedom of choice. Parents had less control over those sons who were financially independent and not heirs to the estate, who could marry down more easily than daughters.[17] Some daughters also had independent portions bequeathed to them by their grandfather or other relatives. But parents and guardians still assumed a preponderant role and their formal consent to marriage was still required.[18] Children who disobeyed and flaunted convention could be disciplined and disinherited.[19] Under Judd's law in London, a daughter could lose her entitlement if she married without consent or became a whore.[20] Runaway matches with fortune-hunters and clandestine Fleet marriages were the exception.[21]

In the towns, access in the normal course of life to prospective partners was fairly easy, though men always had an advantage.[22] Courtship could be long-term, since an apprentice could not marry until he was free and financially independent. Marriage was often deferred even longer until the groom could support a family and satisfy the parents of his proposed bride.[23] Suitors employed a wide range of tactics including trickery.[24] Baptist Hicks adopted the line that 'it is not money that you shoot at but the man' whereas a widowed wig-maker relied on a low-key approach through serious conversations.[25] Courtship was, however, usually a formal and unemotional procedure arranged in the initial stages through intermediaries, who were often kinsmen or friends of the family since many brides had lost their fathers.[26] Marriage brokers were sometimes employed, when the immediate contacts of a family proved inadequate, with corresponding allegations of malpractice and suits.[27] Only after the business terms had been agreed were the couple espoused and gloves,

[14] Heywood, *Autobiography*, iii. 263; Aubrey, *Lives*, ed. Dick, p. civ.
[15] GLL MS 10823/1, fo. 30.
[16] Mendelson 1979: 128; SP 110/16, letter 23 Aug. 1689. [17] H. L. Smith 1982: 28.
[18] Wrightson 1982: 76. [19] *North Country Wills*, p. 183.
[20] Carlton 1971: 27. [21] Brown in Outhwaite 1981: 119–20; Wrigley 1973a.
[22] MacFarlane 1985: 293. [23] Papillon, *Memoirs*, pp. 33–8; KAO U.1015/C13/4–6.
[24] Philip 1983: 7. [25] Hicks-Beach 1909: 89–90; Harrold, *Diary*, pp. 194–7.
[26] Woolley, *Gentlewoman's Companion*, pp. 256–7.
[27] Bingham 1938: 31; *Chancery Reports Cases*, p. 31: Glanville v. Jennings.

rings and vows exchanged; then the banns were read, if a formal church ceremony was chosen, though marriage in private ceremonies under licence became increasingly common.[28]

A business approach to marriage had always been characteristic of all levels of propertied society. Men expected to come out ahead financially in any marriage and caution money carried more weight than virtue.[29] Thomas Povey would have married a poor woman 'had my fortune rendered me capable of making my own election', but his individual whims had to be suppressed, because marriage involved posterity and friends.[30] The correspondence of merchants, like that of the gentry, is dominated by discussions of advantageous marital prospects.[31] Rumours soon reach the provinces, for example, that John Jeffreys, the tobacconist, had died worth £300,000 without any family and that another Alderman had left an only daughter.[32]

Defoe defended commercial marriages on the grounds that building a business was more worthy than marrying for lust.[33] Marriage and remarriage certainly offered an important source of working capital and a device for merging businesses.[34] Prentices and factors consistently married into the families of their masters and principals; established merchants acquired additional working capital through dowries.[35] Widows were a common target; Aubrey's godfather, John Whitson, allegedly married his master's widow after she 'bad him broach the best Butt in the Cellar for her'.[36] The incompetent hypochondriac, Richard Blundell, married a rich widow who took him home to Maryland.[37] The marriage market was, however, a complex and unpredictable lottery.[38] Large portions did not come easily; a bride's parents expected to do as well by the bargain as the prospective groom and his family and they made sure that an adequate jointure was obtained as well as provision for future children.[39] The ultimate economic value of a wife depended not just on her monetary dowry, but on prior settlements and mortality rates within

[28] Boulton 1991: 15, 22; Houlbrook 1985: 344.

[29] Loftis 1950: 45; Woodcock, *Papers*, p. 84; Phillips & Tompkinson 1927: 68–9.

[30] BL Add. MS 11411, fo. 80, letter 3 May 1659.

[31] Pinney, *Letters*, p. 80; KAO U.145/18, correspondence of Thos Hill; U.119/C4, letter 9 Aug. 1700; GLL MS 505, 507; CUL MS Dd vii 26, fo. 38, letter 16 June 1677; N. Yorks. County RO ZK 11126, ZCG/6, Strickland of Cholmeley MSS; Northants. RO 2575(a); Univ. Nottingham Mellish MS ME 144–83.

[32] *Portledge Papers*, p. 49.

[33] Defoe, *Matrimonial Whoredom*, iii. 62, 65, 69.

[34] Keeler 1954: 30; Whitelocke, *Liber Famelicus*, p. vi.

[35] Brenner 1993: 122; Reddaway 1963: 187; Price 1875: 23; Mendenhall 1953: 23, 51, 91; Willan 1959: 218; *Norris Papers*, pp. v, xx; GLL MS 10823/1; Devon RO, Exeter City Muniments 61/6/1.

[36] Aubrey, *Lives*, p. 317; Burn 1842: ii. 416.

[37] Blundell, *Diary*, pp. 41–8.

[38] Outhwaite in MacKendrick & Outhwaite 1986; Seddon 1981. See also p. 267.

[39] BL Add. MS 22187, fo. 175.

her family. Competition was severe and younger sons were less desirable than heirs of lower station.

Merchants traditionally relied on mercantile Custom rather than on formal settlements; John Verney claimed that 'joyntures of land (if at all) [was] but rarely to be found amongst young Tradesmen, for Tradesmen trust & they that marry Tradesmen must trust them'.[40] Some businessmen refused to invest in low-yielding assets, and, under the Custom of London as well as under common law, a widow was always entitled to her third. But settlements between merchants as well as when marrying into gentry families became increasingly common and land was acquired for daughters' portions. Even in lesser families, the appraisal of suitors was a complex process of investigation and haggling; for those with status and wealth, marriage was a major operation, negotiated over a long period of time with lawyers in atttendance.[41] Litigation over the provisions of marriage settlements became more common; breach of promise suits occurred among tradesmen, particularly in the 1670s, though thereafter the volume of marriage contract litigation declined.[42] Dowries were often paid in instalments and fell into arrears.[43]

During the seventeenth century, merchants of all persuasions adopted the language of trade when discussing matrimony.[44] Even at the lowest level, a husband had his price.[45] Maurice Wynn, although he rejected an offer from his father of a bride worth £200 per annum on the grounds that he was not prepared for matrimony, was willing to accept a bride worth £300 per annum, if she could speak English, as the price of returning home from his factorage in Germany.[46] The father of Nathaniel Pinney advised him not to expect £800 from a woman of country breeding, 'thinking I should overstand my Market'.[47] Phoebe Crowley was only allowed to marry a man considered too poor, because of a shortage of prospective husbands.[48]

Although property was the overriding consideration, marriage remained the normal method by which business families elevated their social station. Although the Court of Wards disparaged intermarriage with burghers, city and country had always intermarried and this process was accelerated as the availability of land declined.[49] Sometimes the

[40] BL Verney MSS, letter to Robert Townshend, 24 Oct. 1659; Earle 1989a: 196 documents joyntures among only 15 per cent of his sample.

[41] SP 46/83, nos. 46, 50, 53, 60, 64; Houlbrook 1985: 343.

[42] Ingram 1987: 184, 192–4; Gillespie 1944; Stone 1990: 86; Dering, *Parliamentary Diary*, p. xiv.

[43] Larminie 1984: 5.

[44] Habakkuk 1950.

[45] Will of Robert Rogers.

[46] Nat. Lib. Wales, Wynn MSS, nos. 1083, 1088.

[47] Pinney, *Letters*, p. 80.

[48] Flinn 1962: 29; Martindale, *Life*, p. 16.

[49] Habakkuk in Bromley & Kossmann 1960: 170; Hurstfield 1973a: 139–40.

groom was a merchant and the bride a gentlewoman.[50] The sons of the Norwich and Chester magistrates and of the London aldermen married younger daughters of the gentry.[51] But younger sons of gentlemen also married into commercial families and merchants could best advance socially through well-portioned daughters.[52] Baronets frequently married the daughters and granddaughters of City notables; in the Restoration decades, 60 per cent of aldermen's daughters married gentlemen and the proportion was one-third between 1694 and 1714.[53] It was possible, though uncommon, for a merchant family to reach the peerage through their daughters over several generations.[54] But only the tycoons had the resources to infiltrate the aristocracy and only 4 per cent of the peers, 1540–1659, married daughters of merchants.[55] Businessmen were frequently accused of selling their daughters for social ambition, but Sir William Hewitt preferred an apprentice for his daughter rather than the Earl of Shrewsbury. The successful merchant on the other hand was frequently targeted by impecunious landed families. Sir John Moore in his dotage was approached by a mother who listed those of her acquaintance in their eighties who had married young girls and claimed 'I doe believe my daughter can like you as well as a younger man.'[56]

Disequilibrium between supply and demand limited, however, the frequency of intermarriage between town and country. The great majority of marriages and remarriages occurred within business society, at similar social and economic levels, and they were intended to cement businesses, fortify regional and political networks and sustain the oligarchic control of towns, Companies and trades. Most merchants selected their wives from the families of their masters, fellow Liverymen and business associates. The Elizabethan notables of London married mainly within the City; of the London aldermen, 1600–29, thirty-nine out of sixty emigrants to the City married daughters of citizens and 8 per cent married masters' daughters or widows.[57] Two-thirds of the London

[50] T. Jones 1909–30: ii. 118; *Conway Letters*, p. 3; Woodward 1965: 204; Evans 1974: 57; Hedges, *Diary*, pp. ccxlix, ccliv; Flinn 1962: 33. [51] Horwitz 1987: 270, 272.

[52] Cook 1991: 42.

[53] Woodhead 1965; Henning 1983: i. 21; Cokayne, *Complete Baronage*; MacHattie 1951: 76–7; *V.C.H. City of York*, p. 180; Prest 1986: 121.

[54] *Onslow Family Memoirs*, p. 911; Hexter 1961: 76–9.

[55] Stone 1962: 628–33; Thomas 1972.

[56] GLL MS 507, letter from Frances Gresley, 28 Feb. 1693.

[57] Foster in Jaher 1973: 132; 1977: 99–100; Lang 1963: 346. Although it is clear that the business community was closely interrelated, it is not easy to discern the marriage preferences of those who did not belong to a self-defining group, like the aldermen, because the standard genealogical and matrimonial records, like *Westminster Allegations Marriage Licences*, provide only occupational descriptions. Before any overall pattern can be reconstructed, it is necessary to identify from other sources the type of business and importance of each groom and his bride's family.

aldermen, 1694–1720, married daughters of Londoners; twenty-seven of their daughters married gentlemen and twenty-one Londoners.[58] In the early eighteenth century, 40 per cent of London notables married daughters of businessmen.[59] Only a few of the Leeds merchants were sufficiently wealthy to marry into the gentry and though some ventured as far as York and London, most married local girls; the Bristol merchants married daughters and widows of freemen.[60] A substantial minority of merchants also married servants in their households.

Overseas merchants sometimes found Dutch, German and Spanish wives and procreated outside the English Church; they even married Indo-Portuguese women in India and Armenians in Persia and, in 1679, there were numerous half-castes in the English factories on the Coromandel coast.[61] In England, business families also intermarried with the French, Walloons and Dutch and sometimes with Catholics; a Bill to prohibit marriage with foreigners received one reading in the Commons.[62] But overseas residents rarely returned to England with their foreign wives and the majority of marriages occurred between partners of the same faith, whether inside or outside the Established Church; every religious group was interconnected by marriage. Merchants, like the county gentry, operated within a network of kinship and married their neighbours.[63] Urban dynasties, as in Bristol, were excessively in-bred and when they looked beyond the city, merchants married country cousins.[64]

Family size

It is difficult to generalize with confidence about the demography of the business community.[65] Although much statistical evidence has been compiled from parish registers and marriage bonds on the frequency and age of marriage and on the size of families, businessmen are not usually separated in the data from the mass of the urban population.[66] Hundreds of particular examples can be cited from private papers and genealogies, but the overall picture relies heavily on the evidence of wills and on studies of manageably sized elite urban groups, like the aldermen. Average and median figures cannot do justice to significant differences in fertility and mortality between different trades, families and financial

[58] Horwitz 1987: 270, 272; 1984: table 6. [59] Rogers 1979: 445, 450.

[60] Kirby 1985: 33; 1986: 156; Sacks 1985: 686.

[61] Croft 1972: 252; Shaw 1989: 107; Appleby 1979: 40; Hakluyts, *Original Writings*, p. 8; Carter 1964: 29; Zins 1973: 103–4; Anstey 1905; Spears 1932: 12–13; Aström 1963: i. 130.

[62] Pettigree in Grell 1991: 87; Grell 1989: 50; Elton 1986: 239; Aveling 1966: 172.

[63] Cholmely, *Memoirs*, pp. 57, 80; Courthop, *Memoirs*, p. 114; Everitt 1968a: 67.

[64] Chambers 1966: xv.

[65] The conclusions here may need revision as demographers turn their attention to occupational analysis: see Wrigley 1973b: 22. [66] Outhwaite 1973: 56.

categories.[67] Businessmen tended to produce either too few or too many offspring; many merchants who died young slip through the cracks.

Nonetheless it is clear that a significant minority, including some of the most visible and richest merchants, never married. Of the Tudor Merchant Venturers of London who left wills, 7 per cent do not mention widows, and 4.1 per cent of Bristol householders were bachelors.[68] In London parishes with a higher proportion of substantial households, in 1695, only 28.8 per cent were married and 14.8 per cent were bachelors over twenty-five.[69] The average rate over the century, if wills proved at Canterbury are a satisfactory indicator, was at least 6 per cent.[70] The frequency of celibacy was determined by survival to maturity and by place of residence.[71] But it was also a matter of personal preference. Sanderson thought that the price of a dowry was too high: 'I looke not after any, better liking a free single life then with more welth to be subjected to woomens humours.'[72]

The timing of marriage was determined by occupation. A minority of apprentices were stricken from the registers because they married, often because they needed to legitimize children, but most waited until they had acquired their freedom in their late twenties.[73] They had to defer setting up a household until they had achieved financial independence in their business. The average age of applications for marriage licences in early Stuart London was 26.7 and the average age of first marriage for those above the average level of craftsmen was 27.5, though this average is distorted by the high percentage of widows.[74] Very few married in London in the later seventeenth century under twenty-five, which was also the median age of first marriage for merchants in Leeds; the Quakers married between twenty-seven and thirty.[75] Foreign residence caused a further postponement. The Merchant Adventurers and the East India Company allowed its employees to bring out their English wives and this practice was common in the Caribbean and Atlantic colonies.[76] But marriage was generally discouraged abroad and prohibited in some areas, like the Ottoman Empire.

There is some evidence that the wives of businessmen, in their first marriages, were younger than their husbands; the mean age of marriage

[67] Anderson 1980: 30; 'Colloquie démographie historique' 1969: 1423–5.
[68] Ramsey 1961: 373; Holmes 1975: 41; Harrison 1920: pl. 8.
[69] *London Inhabitants within Walls*, pp. xxx-xxxv, tables 4–5; Glass 1968: tables 4; Finlay 1981: 139–40; Wrigley & Schofield 1981: 258–65; Weir 1984: 346; Schofield 1984: 10; 1985: 14; Baker 1977: 259.
[70] See table 10.1.
[71] On life expectancy see pp. 93–5.
[72] Sanderson, *Travels*, p. 255.
[73] Rappaport 1983–4: 117; Earle 1989a: 110; Wilson 1988: 81.
[74] Elliot in Outhwaite 1981: 83–4, table 11.
[75] Earle 1989a: table 7.1; Kirby 1986: 156; Vann & Eversley 1992: table 3.12.
[76] Baumann 1990: 149.

Table 10.1. *Nuptiality and residence of businessmen, 1605–1700*

	Married		Bachelors			Died abroad	
	no.	%	no.	%	Total no.	no.	%
1605–19	445	97.2	13	2.8	458	44	9.6
1620–29	400	99.8	1	0.2	401	23	5.7
1630–34	113	89.7	13	10.3	126	30	23.8
1635–39	147	83.5	29	16.5	176	39	22.2
1640–44	97	82.9	20	17.1	117	24	20.5
1645–49	162	91.5	15	8.5	177	35	19.8
1650–60	644	98.9	7	1.1	651	105	16.1
1661–70	380	94.8	21	5.2	401	108	26.9
1671–75	202	89.4	24	10.6	226	62	27.4
1676–85	547	90.3	59	9.7	606	152	25.1
1686–93	437	96.3	17	3.7	454	91	20.0
1694–1700	387	91.9	34	8.1	421	107	25.4
Total	3961	94.0	253	6.0	4214	820	19.5

Note: This table has been constructed from the indexes to wills proved in the Prerogative Court of Canterbury. Only testators named as merchants, members of overseas Companies, aldermen and those known from other sources or from the scale of their bequests to qualify as businessmen have been included. Those listed simply as knights, esquires, gentlemen, apprentices, factors or by their craft (including clothiers, ironmongers, haberdashers, linen drapers, fishmongers, merchant tailors, vintners, goldsmiths, grocers and mercers, who alone totalled 1,435 betweeen 1660 and 1671) have been excluded, because the businessmen among them cannot be unequivocally identified. The numbers are deflated in the 1640s by the administrative dislocations of the Civil Wars and inflated in the 1650s by the centralization of probate at Canterbury, on which see Kitching 1976: 285. Many merchants, who did not hold property outside their localities or who left orphans are recorded in other diocesan or municipal courts. Earle 1989 only found wills for half his sample of 375 from the Orphans Court of London and for 80 per cent of those who died testate. It is also impossible to distinguish between those permanently and temporarily abroad. Only those specifically described as unmarried have been listed here as bachelors even though it is clear that different compilers did not calendar marital status consistently; from 1620 to 1630 and from 1653 to 1660, it appears to have been ignored completely. Consequently all the figures here must be regarded as minimum numbers.

for London-born daughters was 20.5.[77] A few were extremely young, at least when espoused; Samuel Jeake, after some hard bargaining, married Elizabeth Hartshore, in 1680, when she was thirteen years eight months and the match was consummated.[78] Jefferys of Exeter remarried in his early sixties a woman of twenty-seven.[79] But more typical is the son of a gentleman grocer who married at twenty-five the daughter of a fishmonger of seventeen or Sir John Banks who married at twenty-eight a woman of eighteen.[80] This age difference would help to explain the large number of widows, who constituted 22 per cent of Londoners between 1598 and 1619.[81] Second husbands of widows in London were sometimes younger than their brides, but it is uncertain whether women had more husbands than husbands had wives.[82]

Although widows with young children needed a substitute father, they often faced real opposition to their remarriage from relations who feared the influence of new kin; sometimes they had difficulty establishing that their husbands had died overseas and husbands frequently restricted their choices in their wills.[83] There was a constant fear that 'every body would be riding a Widow as they say and breaking into her jointure' and remarriages may have declined.[84] On the other hand, widows often had to remarry to continue the business, to avoid poverty and to extend their family; one-third of 208 widows of Tudor aldermen of London remarried.[85] There was a high rate of remarriage, often after their wives had died in childbirth, among those merchants who had long and prosperous lives and who profited handsomely from second dowries.[86] Of the aldermen of Tudor York, twenty-seven married at least once, nineteen twice and one three times.[87] William Lilly's master at sixty-six married as his second wife a woman of seventy: he was interested in her estate and 'she married him for considerations he performed not'.[88]

A few business families had ten to twenty children, usually combined from several marriages.[89] In Elizabethan Norwich and Exeter, the median

[77] Elliot in Outhwaite 1981: 86, table 2.
[78] Perceval 1893: 147, 278; Jeake, *Astrological Diary*, 1988: 36. [79] Youings 1968: 97.
[80] Elliot in Outhwaite 1981: 85; Coleman 1963: 188.
[81] Elliot in Outhwaite 1981: table 11. [82] Loschky & Krier 1969: 445.
[83] MacFarlane 1985: 231–5; Carter 1964: 164; Jordan 1960a: 281; MacIntosh 1991: 295; Glass 1968: 581–92.
[84] Wycherley, *Plays*, p. 499. A majority of widows did not find second husbands because there was a shortage of men: see Carlton 1978: 119, 127; Boulton 1990: 341; Todd in Prior 1985: 65, 83. [85] Ben Amos 1990: 240; Rappaport 1989: 40.
[86] In the whole population, 30 per cent of all marriages were of widows and widowers: see Wrigley & Schofield 1981: 258–9. The rate of death in childbirth has been put at 6.7 per cent, though it was a cumulative risk: see Crawford in Fildes 1990: 47; Cornish, *Thomas Firmin*, p. 20. [87] Palliser 1979: 122. [88] Lilly, *Life*, p. 9.
[89] Foster 1977: 72; Lang 1974: 40; Hexter 1961: 56; Barron 1906: 218; Cox 1897 : 59; Lyman 1935: 5; Gent, *History Hull*, pp. 36, 41; *Lancashire Archivist's Report* 1963: 21; Langdale 1937: 9.

number of children per household among the whole urban population was 4.25 and 4.7 respectively.[90] But the majority of business families in the seventeenth century had one to three surviving children.[91] In Bristol, one-third of households with married couples had one child, 27.3 per cent two children and 19.3 per cent three children.[92] The returns of the 1695 tax in London suggest a median of 1.46 children per house in the richer parishes, but all occupations are included.[93] The average number of children born to fifty-seven aldermanic families in the late seventeenth century was 4.75; 2.5 survived infancy and 1.9 to maturity.[94] Between 1694 and 1714, only thirty-eight of sixty-two London aldermen were survived by at least one son, twenty-three by two sons and three by daughters.[95]

High infant mortality always compensated for a high birth rate; all towns depended on natural increase in the countryside to sustain their population level.[96] In late Elizabethan London, 42 per cent of men had no surviving children; even in wealthy London parishes only three out of five survived to the age of fifteen and the Quakers lost 22.5 per cent of their infants.[97] It was common for younger brothers to inherit, because of the premature death of the eldest. Parents frequently outlived all their sons and, in the early eighteenth century, 45 per cent of the London elite did not have male issue.[98] On average, there were five births per family among the Aldermen of Leeds, 1660–1700, but one-quarter had only one surviving son and 29 per cent died without male heirs; in Norwich, 131 mayors at the time of their death had 168 sons living.[99] The same was true of émigré communities, like Barbados.[100]

Even when the rate of child mortality declined, a fall in fertility prevented any increase in the number of sons.[101] Although more males were born in London, more females seem to have survived.[102] Merchants may have employed some method of birth control, but they were usually preoccupied with producing sufficient heirs, not with limiting chil-

[90] Pound 1962: 140–3; Styles 1951: 37.
[91] Mundy, *Travels*, i. app. B; Martin 1977; Dyer 1965–6: 118 n.3.
[92] Holmes 1975: 41. [93] Glass 1969: tables 1–3.
[94] Personal communication from Malcolm Kitch, 23 Oct. 1968.
[95] Horwitz 1987: 272. [96] Wrigley in Glass & Eversley 1969: 86.
[97] Ramsey 1961: 373. The names of heirs were, however, frequently omitted from wills. On failure of heirs see Miskimin in Miskimin 1977: 218; Thrupp 1948: 200–4, 312, as revised by G. A. Williams 1963: 316, 345; Saul 1981: 82; Gottfried 1982: 248; Finlay 1979: 38; Vann & Eversley 1992: 241; Papillon, *Memoirs*, p. 46; Dawe 1950: app. 2; Anderson 1989: 77; Flinn 1962: 42.
[98] Hughes 1952a: i. 9–10; Fairchild 1954: 48; Riden 1987: 193; Rogers 1979: 450; Hughes 1986; WAM no. 10337. [99] Kirby 1985: 167; Evans 1974: 58.
[100] Dunn 1974: 71.
[101] Keczynski in Hogben: 290–312; Glass in Glass & Eversley 1965: 164; Finlay 1979: 32.
[102] Herlan 1980: 117; Thompson 1974: 163–4.

dren.[103] The use of wet nurses should theoretically have increased the frequency of pregnancy, though breast-feeding also probably reduced infant mortality.[104] But the frequency of births was determined principally by the lifespan of the husband and the number of years in which his wife (or successive wives) could bear children. The rich had better health and a more nourishing diet. But they married late and within a narrow circle, thus increasing the chance of infertility as well as genetic diseases.

The mean household size for tradesmen and craftsmen has been put at 4.72 with 2.94 children.[105] In Dissenting families, the number of residents over sixteen was as low as 2.3, but most business households were inflated by apprentices and lodgers and could reach six or more persons.[106] In Southwark, the mean household size was 4.2–4.3 and among the victuallers of Romford it was 4.0 (of which 1–2 were servants), but there were great variations.[107] A Coventry mercer's household could reach 7.4 persons, but at Worcester the mean size for tradesmen and craftsmen was 4.77 with 2.03 children; in King's Lynn it was 4–4.5 and in Poole it was 5.06.[108] At Chester, in the 1640s, the mean household size of freemen was 3.6, though it fluctuated with age and type of business; merchants had a mean of 5.9 with 3.69 adults.[109] In Colonial Bristol there were 5.72 persons per household.[110]

It is presumptuous on the available evidence to relate occupation to family size. But a merchant who married in his late twenties might expect on average to have four to five infants born, of which two or three, and not necessarily the sons, would survive to maturity.[111] The average in London was 4.18 children born of which 3.4 survived; although 35 out of 379 freemen had more than 7 children, 31 were childless and 56 had no surviving children.[112] In general, it seems probable that merchants had fewer children than farmers or artisans.[113] Like the gentry, business families had difficulty reproducing themselves through male descent.

Sexual morality

Contemporary dramatists and ballad writers often contrasted the merchant with the gentleman, as either inhibited or hypocritical.[114] Graunt

[103] Wrigley & Schofield 1983; Wilson 1984; Schnucker 1975: 666.
[104] Campbell 1989: 364. [105] Laslett 1972: tables 1.6, 13, 4.15–16.
[106] Patten 1971b: 23; *Compton Census*, app. G; Finlay in Beier & Finlay 1986: 46; Goose 1980: 373. [107] Boulton 1987: 123–4; MacIntosh 1984: tables 2, 4.
[108] Roy & Porter 1980: table 6; Tittler 1985a: 96; Houlbrooke 1984: 24; Cooper 1985.
[109] Alldridge 1983a: 44, table 4. [110] Demos 1968: 44. [111] Prouty 1942: 5–6.
[112] Earle 1989a: 230; Horwitz 1984: 235, table 12.
[113] Cowgill 1970b:108; 1967: 6, 68; Schochet 1969: 419. See also pp. 131–3.
[114] Middleton, *Chaste Maid Cheapside*, p. xlvii.

and Gregory King found one explanation for the low birth rate in London in the greater intensity of business.[115] Devout merchants oscillated between desire and aversion. The Presbyterian, Ambrose Barnes, drank buckets of cold water to cool the wanton flame and rejected a gentlewoman's love from concern for his business.[116] One East India Company factor went so far as to apply a 'douche of molten lead' to resist the attractions of the Hindu women.[117] Francis Rogers wrote in his diary: 'Find by a retired indolent life, I lye more exposed to some vice then [I] believe shall be by a more bustling & sociable way. My frailties invincible which [I] hope may be reduced by a marriage state.'[118]

Apprentices who had just reached sexual maturity were not surprisingly prone to fornication, which was often cited as cause when an indenture was voided.[119] Although prentices made a habit of burning down brothels on feast days, they patronized those establishments and were inclined to impregnate housemaids; Gervaise Disney confessed that he lusted after maids and visited whorehouses before his conversion, though he added that he was only guilty in his heart.[120] A brothel in the Steelyard catered exclusively for merchants and one brothel keeper was free of the Grocers.[121] Madam Cresswell named Sunday, Prentices' day, and businessmen were said to provide more regular business than the gentry.[122] Puritan diaries make it clear that the hormones were active, no matter what a merchant's background. Norwood recorded when he masturbated and George Trosse admitted that he had been introduced to this vice by a servant; Wallington had his first lustful thoughts at the age of eight.[123]

The canon lawyers had anticipated that merchants, when separated from home and family, would be more tempted to sexual sins; medieval factors were expected to report on their sex lives.[124] The tropics and freedom from the restraints of English society in territories overseas stimulated unconventional behaviour. Natural children and bigamy were comparatively common overseas, though bigamy became a felony in 1604 unless one party was absent for seven years or under age.[125] Cases of adultery, bigamy and even incest enliven the official correspondence of the East India Company.[126] In 1680, a factor in Madras went mad, when Mathew Vincent, the chief of the Bengal Council, apparently seduced his

[115] King, *Two Tracts*, p. 28; Petty, *Economic Writings*, p. 374; Graunt, *Natural Political Observations*, p. 24.
[116] M. R., *Memoir Ambrose Barnes*, p. 229.
[117] *East India Letters Received 1600–17*, pp. xix–xx.
[118] Rogers, *Diary*, p. xxviii.
[119] Yarbrough 1979: 70.
[120] Burford 1976: 172; Emmison 1973: 5; Disney, *Remarkable Passages*, pp. 33–4.
[121] Archer 1991a: 213, 232.
[122] *Whore's Rhetoric*, pp. 62, 117.
[123] Weller 1988: 45–64; Delaney 1969: 59.
[124] Roover 1974; Origo 1957: 127.
[125] Carter 1964: 120; Sisson 1933: 71.
[126] Hedges, *Diary*, i. pp. cclxxiv, ccxix.

wife.[127] In Japan, the merchants lived with local women and had children.[128] Levantine factors kept women slaves in their houses and Mr Cope begat children 'by a Woman he kept very privately'.[129]

Although it was mainly tradesmen who appeared as defendants in cases of immorality and defamation heard by the Church Courts, some businessmen certainly compartmentalized their sex lives.[130] Gossips and those offering advice on marriage assumed that husbands would be tempted to find additional sensual satisfaction.[131] Arranged marriages fortified a natural temptation to adultery, which was tolerated by the laity for men and practised primarily by the husband.[132] John Temple appears to have been more than an acquaintance of the wife of Dr Pickering; Aubrey claimed that Thomas Sutton seduced the young wife of an old rich brewer to the Navy.[133] A mercer of Portsmouth, in 1664, was found with the daughter of a former Mayor in a wheatfield and a witness was offered £5 to hold his tongue.[134]

Some kept mistresses and many more resorted to prostitutes, like the celebrated Mrs Lueson.[135] One haberdasher had an affair with the daughter of an attorney and Agnes Brown slept with the apprentice; some tradesmen may have let their wives practise as whores.[136] A tailor was accused of using his wife to entice lovers and then blackmailing the victims.[137] Richard Cocks brought back pornographic literature from Japan; the domestic production of erotica became a new business for publishers after 1660 and at least ten businessmen were collectors.[138] If Ned Ward is to be believed, London teemed with insatiable wives, prentices and merchants; he accused businessmen of sharing the licentious and dissolute tastes of the nobility, but not their style.[139]

One sign of extra-marital affairs is the existence of bastards. Businessmen were frequently accused of fathering children, usually on their maidservants, and the Heralds were sometimes asked to conceal illegitimacy.[140] Bastards were noted in wills and occur frequently in guild

[127] Lever 1947: 15, 22–5; *East India Factories 1618–69*, pp. xiii. 281, *1670–77*, iv. 228.
[128] Massarella 1990: 231–7. [129] Arup 1907: 253; C104/44, letter 1 Oct. 1685.
[130] Sharpe 1980a: 17; L. W. Smith 1977: 282. [131] Raleigh, *Works*, viii. 559.
[132] *London Jilt*, p. 100; MacFarlane 1985: 241.
[133] Anderson 1989: 107; Aubrey, *Lives*, ed. Dick, p. 291.
[134] *Portsmouth Borough Sessions Papers*, p. 29.
[135] Aubrey, *News from New Exchange*, p. 5. [136] Archer 1991a: 124.
[137] Gent, *History of Hull*, p. 121. Another odd case is REQ 2/295, B.73.
[138] Massarella 1990: 126; Foxon 1963: 27; Thompson 1979: 206. Flandrin 1977: 207 ascribes the growth of pornography to repression, but offers no real evidence.
[139] Ward, *Modern World Disrobe'd*, pp. 54–61; *London Spy*, pp. 34–5; *Reformer*, pp. 20, 55, 62; Roberts 1989: 91.
[140] Ingram 1987: 270; *Middlesex County Records*, iii. 161; Dugdale, *Life Diary*, letter cxxxii, p. 357.

records, usually because their natural fathers had tried to apprentice them contrary to regulations.[141] William Cotesworth's housekeeper had a child and she was named as his wife in his will.[142] It was not only the men who strayed. The licentious zest with which widows of merchants married their apprentices had always struck foreigners.[143] Dekker and other dramatists depicted City women with excessive appetites and the misogynic literature reflected fear of both female sexuality and infidelity.[144] The Court wits liked to imagine citizens' wives dreaming of their attentions.[145] Impecunious gentlemen penned bawdy letters, threatening to spread scandal if credit was not granted to them.[146] The strong, earthy women of Cheapside could, however, hold their own in raillery and repartee with the gallants outside their shops.[147] Ned Ward mentions a woman forced to marry an old merchant for money who kept a young wine cooper as prentice as well as a fencing-master.[148]

Regular sex within marriage was counselled by the preachers and not just for procreation; Whateley suggested prayer before intercourse to keep interest alive.[149] The range of taste seems to have been wide; Defoe's mixture of moralizing advice and lascivious detail was aimed at the citizenry and described, albeit circumspectly, many sexual variations within marriage.[150] Unusual practices do occasionally surface; Sir William Turner, President of Bridewell, was alleged by the ballad-mongers to relish the flogging of women.[151] Despite allegations that there was a homosexual subculture in London, documented cases of unnatural offences among merchants are rare compared with those among mariners, though they would have been concealed, since buggery was a felony after 1534.[152] Apprentices sometimes slept in the same bed as their master which may have encouraged abuse; one possible case is that of Peter Leigh who brought a charge of slander when he was accused of having syphilis.[153] Richard Finch merchant of London was charged with abusing his servant by whipping him naked.[154]

141 Peele 1939: 8; *Newcastle Merchant Adventurers' Records*, p. 29; *Southampton Assembly Books 1609–10*, p. 98; G. C. M. Smith 1936: 20. The English do not seem to have adopted the Italian practice of using bastards as business manpower: see Bratchel 1983: 114; *Smyth Family Correspondence*, p. xi; Shipley 1975a: 230, 243.

142 Ellis 1981a: 201.

143 *Italian Relation of England*, pp. 24–6.

144 Dekker, *Dramatic Works*, iv. pp. vii, 9–11; Sharpe 1980a: 81, 87; Rogers 1966: 126–9.

145 *Roxburghe Ballads*, iii. 369–71; *Broadside Ballads Restoration*, nos. 10, 57; Fennor, *Counters' Commonwealth*, p. 453.

146 Ward, *London Spy*, p. 109.

147 Shadwell, *Works*, p. 200.

148 Ward, *London Spy*, p. 5.

149 Schucking 1929: 39; Leites 1986: 12; Johnson 1970: 102; Wood 1966: 76; Whateley, *Bride's Bush*, p. 43.

150 Pollock 1987: 483; Defoe, *Matrimonial Whoredom*, iii. 162–9; on Defoe's personal escapades see Novak 1970: 40.

151 *Bagford Ballads*, i. 496; O'Donoghue 1929: 12, 156; Cowie 1973: 356; Maré 1958: 81–2.

152 Trumbach 1977: 15; Holdsworth in Freund *et al.* 1908: ii. 297; BL Add. MS 24107, fo. 175.

153 Addy 1989: 146.

154 Bray 1988: 50.

The Family Instructors do not accurately reflect the moral conduct of the whole business community, in which, though signs of outward depravity were rare, healthy appetites of every kind were indulged according to wealth and individual taste. Fear of disease, of bastardy and of loss of reputation were probably more effective in curbing libertinism than the periodic campaigns to reform manners. The sexual peccadilloes of businessmen may have been more discrete than those of gentlemen about town, but if immorality was the badge of gentility in some quarters, many merchants would have earned their coat armour.

Husbands and wives

Women were subordinated by convention and by law. A husband had absolute common-law rights over his spouse's personal property and the income from her real estate, though this was gradually modified, as well as responsibility for her debts.[155] With some variations of emphasis, in both England and the colonies, women could have separate estates and pin money established by premarital contracts under equitable jurisdiction; they could also hold property in trust.[156] Widows were entitled to a dower of one-third, unless this had been superseded by a jointure, as well as some furniture and personal effects. As a widow or in a second marriage, a woman had more opportunities to exercise independence.[157]

Women were allowed to run independent businesses. A spinster or widow could trade as feme sole under the Custom of London and so could a wife, providing that it was in a separate trade.[158] Similar provisions existed in other boroughs and in the colonies.[159] Quaker women were conspicuously active as were those who resided in Scotland, India and cities overseas, like New York.[160] Scattered examples do occur in England.[161] Although women were usually restricted to bindery in the book trade, Frances Hall at Oxford was an enterprising businesswoman who printed almanacks on handkerchiefs.[162] Women gravitated not surprisingly to the distributive, garment and food and lodging trades and were active in brewing, baking and innkeeping.[163] Most brothels were also run by madams and Ned Ward claimed that retailers doubled as whores.[164]

[155] Kenny 1879: 97–8; Prest 1991: 182; Erickson 1990: 21–39; Cross 1987: 86.
[156] Cioni 1985: 280; Salmon 1986: 88; Harris & MacNamara 1984: 29; Okin 1983: 125; Carr & Walsh 1977: 556.
[157] PROB 11/444/77; Prior in Chartres & Hey 1990: 211.
[158] Jacob, *City-Liberties*, pp. 114–15.
[159] Prior in Prior 1985: 103; Ulrich 1982: 41.
[160] Brailsford 1915: 15; Spear 1932: 13; Archdeacon 1976: 63–4; Houston in Houston & Whyte 1989: 122.
[161] Carus-Wilson in Postan & Power 1933: 245; Welch 1916–23: i. 59; Wright in Hanawalt 1986: 115; Johnson in Clark & Slack 1972: 256.
[162] Petter 1974: 23–4.
[163] Forbes 1980: table 2; Erlington 1966: 168; *Kingston Apprentices*, p. xi; Champness 1966: 125; Clark 1983: 79.

Many also practised in the healthcare trades as midwives and empirics.[165] Sometimes wives became full partners; Pepys thought that the wife of John Bland was 'as good a merchant as her husband'.[166] Many more traded as their husbands' agent, while he was away; with their unmarried daughters, they helped to keep the family shop, raise credit and sell retail.[167]

Independent women in business were, however, rare; very few were free of the major Companies of London or occur in the Port Books.[168] Only a handful traded in their own right, while their husbands were alive, and the practical manuals for women did not include accounting; indeed Scott advised a citizen not to tell his wife about his business.[169] Few examples occur of women helping their husbands with their accounts. Only 2 per cent of 32,000 prentices in Tudor London were bound to women and no wife of a freeman admitted that she worked for a living.[170] Only five out of fifty women among the testators in the Orphans Court had businesses and they were mainly small shops.[171] Participation by women was principally focused on home-based activities and varied with their life cycle.

Widows were much more prominent in all the towns. They often exercised their right to take over the family business when their husbands died, in such varied trades as pin-making, iron, grain, linen, coal, publishing and milling.[172] With some exceptions, a widow could transfer the freedom to a new husband; she often traded jointly with him as well as with her sons and daughters.[173] In the book trade, 58 per cent of female members were widows of former printers and 6 per cent were daughters.[174] A widow (or daughter) could also marry her late husband's (or father's) apprentice.[175] Frequently apprentices were bound over and

164 Ward, *Comforts of Matrimony*, p. 57; Burford 1976: 172.

165 Crawford 1984: 69.

166 Pepys, *Diary*, v. 266; Bury, *Elizabeth Bury*, pp. 187–8. A few account books like those of Sarah Fell and Elizabeth Sneyd (Staffordshire RO, Salt Lib. MS 37136) have survived as well as occasional correspondence, like that of Mrs Livingston discussed by Biemer 1987: 183.

167 Hemphill 1982: 168; Ulrich 1982: 42, 46; G. P. Jones 1967: 189; Parks 1976: 20, 37; Roberts in Corfield & Keene 1991: 93; Boulton 1991: 82; Hutton 1984: 357; Elliot in Outhwaite 1981: 91; Coxere, *Adventures by Sea*; Pares 1950: 9; *Henslowe's Diary*, p. xxii; Brodsky 1980: 142.

168 Rappaport 1983–4: 112; Clark in Clark & Souden 1987: 269; Willan 1938: 49; *Welsh Port Books*, p. xli.

169 Tilney, *Brief Discourse Marriage*; Scott, *Essay on Drapery*, p. 34; Hull 1982: 66–7.

170 Earle 1989a: 338–9; Rappaport 1989: 41.

171 Earle 1989a: 171–4.

172 Staffordshire RO, Salt Lib. HM 37/36; Berger 1982: 40; Clark 1919: 25, 305; Evans in Riden 1985: 66; Kunze 1989: 568; *V.C.H. City of Gloucester*, iv. 108; Willan 1980: 60; Swain 1986: table 8.1; Stone 1992: chap. 9; Tyacke 1978: xv, xx; Bell 1989: 46; Todd in Prior 1985: 70; Emmison 1980: 157.

173 Bennett 1985: 157.

174 Schwoerer 1986: n.32; Rostenberg 1965: ii. 423.

175 Prior in Prior 1985: 98; Marescoe, *Markets and Merchants*, p. 5.

eventually presented by the widow who sometimes took on new apprentices.[176] Widows were increasingly appointed as sole executrixes instead of sharing this task and control with relatives.[177] This required expert knowledge of their husband's business and of debt collection and consequently some pamphleteers advocated the training of wives in accounting.[178]

Usually, however, widows were passive investors. They liquidated their husband's business and then either invested in urban real estate or lent on pawn, mortgage or bond.[179] Widows occur among the listed members of the Eastland and North West Companies and among subscribers to the early Russia Company, with investments they inherited; they constituted a minority of shareholders in the Africa and East India Companies.[180] In 1685, 20 per cent of East Indian bonds were held by women and they also held shipping shares, lent to the Hudson's Bay Company and held 5 per cent of Bank stock.[181] Twenty-three out of 1,300 subscribers to the 1689 loan to William of Orange and 12 per cent of Vyner's clients were widows and spinsters.[182] Widows represented a high proportion of small-scale lenders both in the countryside and the towns.[183] In the Orphans' sample, 10–20 per cent of households were headed by widows and 6.4 per cent had money out on loan.[184]

There were certainly many poor widows, but that was because their husbands were poor or because their children had inherited. An important minority had substantial funds. Before 1660, 1,100 donated to charity and 69 left estates with a total value of £85,611; 260 gave £68,303.[185] Ann Goodeere left £1081 and of those who paid surtax in 1692, 7.7 per cent were widows.[186] Widows with rich husbands and either young or no children were women of property and, unlike their landed counterparts, their assets were liquid. Indeed, since many wives of businessmen outlived their husbands and were appointed executrixes and since business assets were mainly personal, the aggregate capital which they controlled at any time probably exceeded £1.7 million. Daughters and single women who did not receive large inheritances were certainly restricted in their business options. But the limited participation of widows in active business was more a question of personal choice. That so

[176] ULL MS 554; *Chester Council Minutes*, p. 60. [177] Earle 1989a: 369.
[178] *Advice Women London*, p. 3; this tract was written by a daughter who kept the household accounts. Cotton, *Ornaments Daughters Zion*, p. 82; Clark 1919: 39; Applebee 1979: 50.
[179] Wright in Charles & Duffin 1985: 112; Goldberg 1992: 162–3.
[180] Zins 1971: 117; Willan 1953: 55; K. G. Davies in Carus-Wilson 1954–66: ii. 279; Shammas 1975: 106; Price 1992: 157.
[181] Rich 1958: 317; Dickson 1967: table 38; Scammel 1972: 397.
[182] GLL MS 40/35; Roseveare 1991: 19. [183] Holderness 1976b: 102.
[184] Earle 1989a: 168. [185] Jordan 1960a: 29.
[186] Glass in Hollaender & Kellaway 1969: table 5; *Ipswich Probate Inventories*, p. 110.

many declined to assume the role of businesswoman reflects their age, their need to acquire a secure income for themselves and their children and possibly a distaste for the burdens of entrepreneurship.

Marriage was civil death, because the family was still patriarchal and there could only be one head; a widow when she assumed control of the household did so as a substitute father.[187] In Platt's Case it was decreed that a prisoner of the Fleet who married a woman guardian had to be released, because a husband could not be in the custody of his wife.[188] A husband could prevent his wife leaving his house and could despoil her estate; the legal husband was the father of all the children in the household.[189] The wife's role was still seen as 'loving subjection' and compared to breaking in a horse.[190] The Puritan preachers might view husband and wife as jointly responsible, but in fact marriage, allowing for age differences, was usually an unequal partnership between functional equals.[191] The advice literature usually enjoined a passive role for all women who, even if they were assertive in business, were expected to be obedient at home.[192] Relationships within the family were different from those between men and women.

Marriage was for both partners a commitment for life. Although it could be annulled and although the Court of Arches could grant separations *a mensa et thoro*, these methods of escape were rarely employed because they conflicted with both contractual obligations and with canon law; even a blameless wife ended up with little alimony.[193] Divorce with the prospect of remarriage was only possible if the marriage had not been consummated, if the parties were too closely related or if it had been imposed by force; a private Act of Parliament was required after 1669. Mortality sometimes had the same impact as divorce, but some business marriages lasted for twenty years and in Leeds there were several which lasted thirty-six years.[194]

Many merchants dominated not only their own wives, but those of their children. Wife-beating was generally condemned, but some argued that the law allowed for proper discipline; physical assault and forms of mental cruelty are well attested by legal proceedings and by private correspondence. Defoe describes a fictional shopkeeper who vented the frustration, created by subservience to his customers, by beating his wife.[195] Several cases of wife abuse by English merchants came before the Dutch Church, which was less tolerant of such behaviour.[196] The husband of George

[187] Swinburne, *Treatise Spousals*, p. 48; Stanley 1979: n.51; Ulrich 1982: 8.
[188] Vaughan, *Reports*, p. 243. [189] MacFarlane 1985: 242; Freke, *Diary*, p. 3.
[190] Whateley, *Bride's Bush*, pp. 22, 43; Michel 1978: 58–9.
[191] Gouge, *Domestical Duties*, pp. 255–6. [192] Amussen 1988: 119–21.
[193] Stone 1990: 4. [194] Kirby 1985: 169. [195] Defoe, *Compleat English Tradesman*.
[196] Carter in Dorsten 1974: 108–9; 1964: 62, 162.

Boddington's daughter, Sarah, beat her to put pressure on her father for handouts and gave her no money for housekeeping; she eventually had to go into hiding with her children.[197] George Churchouse, a failed Goldsmith who lived off his wife's uncle, hated his wife and treated her like an apprentice; she sued him for cruelty and obtained a separation.[198] One innkeeper did murder his wife, in 1686, with a male accomplice, but this was unusual and there was little crime within the family.[199] At the same time, many husbands were henpecked by scolds and shrewish wives, who were as popular a subject for City dramatists as the faithful, but persecuted, helpmate and the prodigal, but repenting son. Some wives were extremely aggressive towards their servants, apprentices and even customers in the shop. The complaint of the apprentices, in 1641, that their mistresses have 'gotten such predominancy over us' was probably a satire, but many serious cases of abuse did come before the courts.[200]

Financial disputes, differences of social background, sickness and incompatibility of temperament often led to friction and bitterness between husband and wife.[201] Paul Bayning struggled hard to put away his second wife and resigned as alderman to avoid the Mayoralty, because he did not wish her to be styled Lady Mayoress.[202] John Thomas went to India and was alleged to have gone insane and anxious to be 'as far as he can from his wife'.[203] John Richards burnt his will before the eyes of his unpredictable, violent Italian wife.[204] Loose living aroused sexual jealousy and remarriage generated unflattering comparisons between present and past partners; widows were ignored because widowers preferred virgins as new wives.[205] Thomas Pitt doubted his wife's fidelity and loyalty while his son Robert declared, 'I make it noe distinction between women that are reputed ill and such as are actually soe'; Mrs Pitt in turn dismissed the informers who had spread scandal about her as 'little sneaking ... and great fat gutted rascally friends'.[206] Families could also be divided by religion. George Boddington's father was 'a great stickler' for the Restoration, but it was with great reluctance that his mother allowed her son to watch, through her legs as she stood with her back to

197 GLL MS 10823/1, fo. 31.

198 Ingram 1987: 184.

199 Sharp 1981: 42; Wiener 1975: 49.

200 S. R. Smith 1978–9: 316; *Seventeenth-Century Economic Documents*, p. 234; Forman, *Autobiography*, p. 6.

201 *John Isham*, p. xcvi; Fletcher 1975: 34.

202 Chamberlain, *Letters*, i. 113–14; Gillespie 1944: 429, 432.

203 Hedges, *Diary*, i. p. cclxxxiv; Welch 1916–23: ii. 59

204 Richards, *Country Diary*, p. 100.

205 Carlton 1978: 122. On the other hand it is possible that men preferred older women as less sexually demanding: see Michel 1978: 44.

206 C 110/81, Memorandum, 1702; 110/ 87, letters 1699, 1701; *HMC Fortescue*, i. 5, 23; Hedges, *Diary*, i. pp. lxxvi–xcvii; Lever 1947: 14–28, 59; BL Add. MS 22244; B. Williams 1913: 25.

the door, the King's entrance into London: 'She said what manner of Man is he. I said a black gowned man on which she turned about on her toe & said weeping ... I have sent you forth to serve other Gods & wept.'[207]

A wife had clearly defined responsibilities and was kept fully occupied by the regular and endless chores of managing an urban household.[208] The arduous task of child-rearing fell mainly on her shoulders, even though wet and dry nurses were employed. In addition, she usually had to keep the household accounts, supervise cooks and maids, purchase and stock the food and fuel, clean, heat and light the house, arrange menus, bake, brew and preserve, and doctor her husband and children.[209] The wife normally selected the servants and guarded their moral and physical welfare, did the mending with her daughters, and supervised everything from killing vermin to hospitality.[210]

The wives of businessmen enjoyed considerable freedom of movement and leisure time.[211] There were business households, heavy with piety, where the women sat in silence in the corner knitting. But many wives entertained themselves with their families and female friends – playing parlour games and cards, producing needlework, walking, telling stories, writing letters, reading fiction, memoirs and periodical journalism and attending plays. Tom Browne describes the City ladies' visiting days, when they met to discuss religion and cuckoldry, sermons, politics, gallantry and cooking recipes, 'coquetry and preserves, jilting and laundry'.[212] Some were keen gardeners and flower arrangers, though the more circumscribed gardens and orchards of town houses demanded a different approach from those of country houses.

The wives of the business elite were literate and educated and they increasingly took part in conversation with their husbands' guests and sang and played the virginals in mixed company.[213] Although 'most in this depraved later age think a woman learned enough if she can distinguish her husband's bed from another', a few turned to literature and scholarship or were known for their wit.[214] It was often alleged that the social aspirations of merchants were really those of their wives, that they accepted offices to give their wives precedence.[215] When the women of the household went out for a christening, funeral, civic ceremony or Sunday worship, they adapted their hair and clothes to the prevailing style and

207 GLL MS 10823/1.
208 Markham, *English Housewife*, chap. 5.
209 BL Add. MS 30494, Accounts of Anne Archer; Add. MS 32456, Accounts of Rachel Pengelly.
210 MacMullen 1977.
211 Platter, *Travels in England*, pp. 181–2. For the leisure activities of their husbands see chap. 11.
212 Browne, *Amusements*, p. 66.
213 Cressy 1980: 119–21, 147.
214 Woolley, *Gentlewoman's Companion*, which has exotic recipes; Kirby 1985: 167; Nadelhaft 1982: 556; *Yorkshire Diaries*, i. 21.
215 BL Egerton MS 921, fo. 109; Hunt. Lib. MS 1264, fo. 14.

wore their jewellery. The literature on deportment, like that on housekeeping, grew rapidly during the century. Above all, there was the pleasure of gossip and matchmaking.[216]

Contemporary dramatists and novelists often implied that a businessman's interest in money and his contractual approach suffocated emotion and deprived family relationships of affection.[217] Sir William Temple thought that in a business society, like the Netherlands, 'all appetites and Passion seem to run lower and cooler'.[218] Merchants were said to concern themselves exclusively with facts and efficiency, to sacrifice the delicacy of inner feelings to the needs of the moment. But the mercenary aspects of courtship did not eliminate the emotional basis of marriage. Although love was not the primary reason for marriage, it was akin to heightened religious sensibility and often became an end.[219] Close attachments, based on mutual esteem, friendship, companionship and intimacy, often formed between partners.[220] When separated, husbands and wives exchanged tender letters; the expression of affection in wills cannot just have been a formality.[221] George Pease, when asked in 1619 why he had left his estate to his friends and not his wife, replied that his wife was one of his friends.[222] Merchants did not normally separate their business premises from their place of residence and they probably spent much of their time in the company of their wives. Private correspondence suggests that the aggressiveness and sternness of the merchant at his business was not carried through into his relaxed family circle.[223] Each couple had to resolve on their own the everyday problems of cohabitation.[224] There was no standard format. The quality of any marriage – whether it was a friendly partnership of equals or a tyrannical regime – depended on personality, not on the occupation of the husband.

Child-rearing

Like the rest of propertied society, merchants accepted the patriarchal order and their authority as parents was justified by appeals to Divine and Natural Law.[225] The head of the household was supreme and the children were regarded as inferior and subject to rule until they acquired economic independence.[226] Merchants maintained the same control over their

[216] Rye 1865: 72.
[217] Vernon 1962: 381; Eisenstadt 1968: 113; Defoe, *Matrimonial Whoredom*, iii. 71–8; Backscheider 1986: 236. [218] Temple, *Observations United Provinces*, p. 105.
[219] Collinson 1988a: 80. [220] Mendelson 1979: 127–9.
[221] Larminie 1984: 9; C110/87, letter 19 Dec. 1699.
[222] *London Calendar Wills Hustings*, pt 2, ii. 743. [223] C109/19.
[224] Osborne, *Letters*, p. 121. [225] Nichols, *History Leicester*, ii. 616.
[226] Powell 1917: chap. 4.

children as over their servants and apprentices and they expected obedience, affection and respect from their offspring. But they often put the interests of their children first and they invested substantial time, energy and money in rearing and providing for them.[227]

Some of the handbooks visualized parenthood as a conditional trust; the notion that children should be allowed to develop as individuals co-existed with the contradictory emphasis on social integration.[228] Childhood had long been recognized as a separate state with special needs, but it is not certain how far contemporaries acknowledged the modern concept of adolescence as a stage between youth and adulthood in which self-control is acquired without loss of self-esteem.[229] One conventional division was between childhood (seven to fourteen), youth (fourteen to twenty-eight) and manhood (twenty-eight to fifty).[230] Far from maturing early in a harsh environment, adulthood was delayed by economic and social restrictions. The rite of passage for a young businessman was obtaining his freedom rather than his marriage, though the two usually came together. There were no prosperous households headed by youths, as in Renaissance Florence.[231]

Primary education still took place within the family, often through the mother.[232] Merchants did not usually employ private tutors, but sent their children to local schools. Social values were internalized through moral indoctrination and mental terror rather than through physical devices like swaddling.[233] Nurture did reinforce nature and it was the family rather than the state, the Church or the educational system which integrated a child with adult culture. The diaries and autobiographies of merchants testify to the durable impact of childhood experiences. The instruction provided at home was intended, like an apprenticeship, to promote character and prepare children for survival in a harsh world. In a society in which original sin was an article of faith and which was ruled by the rod, it is not surprising that parents should impose their values and beliefs on children through harsh discipline and isolation from temptation.[234] There was a persistent fear of spoiling or 'cockering' and some cases of child abuse, though the accounts tend to be one-sided.[235] A significant percentage of reported suicides were youngsters of seven to

[227] Todd in Goldberg 1992: 77.

[228] Ozment 1983: 177. There is no foolproof way of distinguishing changes in sentiments from the same sentiments expressed in different language: see Earle 1989a: 235; Tilly & Cohen 1982: 145.

[229] Keniston 1971: 342; Demos 1971: 316; Wilson 1980: 142; Erickson 1959: 68; Hareven in Cuisenier & Segalen 1977: 340; Pearson 1958: 89.

[230] S. R. Smith 1974–5: 495.

[231] Herlihy in Miskimin *et al.* 1977: 24.

[232] GLL 21107, fos. 13–14; MacConica 1977: 125.

[233] Illick in Mause 1974: 331; Earle 1989a: 208.

[234] M. R., *Memoir of Ambrose Barnes.*

[235] Prideaux, *Letters*, p. 146.

twenty-one, often retaliating against their parents or masters to shame them.[236]

Although a London fishmonger did murder his two children in 1621, after bringing a mistress into the house, this was exceptional.[237] Servants were actually beaten more than children. Although children in the larger households of rich and busy merchants were brought up by the servants, there was less privacy in the smaller urban house and children may have had closer contact with their parents, which could be a blessing as well as a curse. Authoritarianism, bad temper, austerity and repression were diluted by a surprising degree of kindness, protectiveness and affection; merchants recollected their childhood (albeit with selective memories) as warm, happy and sheltered with an abundance of toys and pets.[238] Fathers were often putty in the hands of their children; Nathaniel Cholmely sacrificed £1,000 so that his daughter could marry her dancing-master.[239] Henry Whichcote fulminated against his son's 'base promises of your diligence', but he still sent £500 with a threat that this would be his last handout.[240]

Merchants proudly recorded the day and hour of births; baptism was a public event celebrated with feasting in the presence of relatives and godparents. Tradesmen appear to have been more successful than the gentry in raising infants.[241] Some mothers may have bonded by breast-feeding their infants; the preachers certainly recommended this practice and others feared that harmful qualities could be transferred by wet-nurses.[242] But in prosperous families surrogate mothers and nurses were widely employed.[243] The development from infancy to manhood was watched closely. Parents recorded in writing the date of weaning, which was considered a more significant passage of life than puberty, as well as when infants cut their first teeth, when they graduated from crawling to walking and when their sons were put into breeches.[244]

Siblings were not necessarily treated equally. Frequently a mother or father had a favourite child, who was often the youngest or the most competent, despite the adoption of primogeniture.[245] The pain of sepa-

[236] Murphy 1986: 259ff; MacDonald 1986: 72.

[237] Sharpe 1981: 42; Hoffer 1981: 42.

[238] It has been argued incorrectly that children were treated from infancy as adults because of their low life expectancy: see Aries 1967: 371–3; Snyder 1965; Plumb 1975; Rawdon, *Life*, pp. 1–3; Healey 1992: 22.

[239] Cholmely, *Memoirs*, p. 7; *Euing Collection Ballads*, no. 191B.

[240] Lincs. AO I B/48–50, 27 Dec. 1714; Butler, *Characters*, p. 149.

[241] MacLaren 1978: 381.

[242] Berry 1974: 577.

[243] On the rituals and hazards of nursing see Newall in Fildes 1990: 128; Mause 1974: 331; Clark 1989; Fildes 1988:149–50; 1986: 90, 163; 1989.

[244] The age of weaning ranged from one year to nineteen months: see Pollock 1983: table 10; Crawford 1986: 35–9; MacFarlane 1970: 88–90. Ledgers were often used to record births, marriages and deaths.

[245] Houlbrooke 1984: 126.

ration and the anxiousness of both parents about the welfare of their children is evident in their correspondence and in the exchange of gifts. 'I am now deprived of the dayly sight of all my sonnes', wrote the mother of Thomas Hill, in 1657; she urged him to be virtuous 'so the Comfort I reape by you may reward me for ye Care I had of you when you lay in your cradle'.[246] When a child had to be sent away, Henry Newcombe wrote that the 'sad cries of his poor mother I shall not quickly forget'.[247] Although death was regarded as a test of strength and although parents did not grieve for long over infants, they did not usually regard them as expendable. Bereavement always created a profound sense of loss and was not necessarily accepted with quiet resignation; there was widespread anxiety about safeguarding the future of survivors.[248]

A high proportion of merchants' children were orphaned before attaining their majority.[249] This was mainly due to the late age of first marriage but also to delays of paternity when widowers remarried.[250] Premature death broke up families and reduced the influence of the biological parents.[251] Although parents died most frequently when their offspring were no longer infants, many children must never have known their fathers as adults; overseas merchants were sometimes separated from their children for long periods. The remarriage of a surviving partner also put children under the care of a step-parent and generated tension. Leonara Marescoe sent her daughter from the house when she objected to her mother's remarriage, and appropriated her children's portions by stealth.[252] The estates of orphans or stepchildren were often milked by their stepfathers or guardians, though business families were spared the worst excesses of wardship.[253]

Children acquired at an early age a degree of autonomy. Occasionally, they were boarded away at school or sent to the households of friends and relations at puberty.[254] But most left home when they were apprenticed, which was quite different from fostering. Children of poor artisans often learnt their trade at home, but prospective businessmen were usually bound to masters outside the family.[255] Children did not always respond as their parents hoped. Spoiled favourites, intended for the gentry, interpreted their role more enthusiastically than their parents intended, frittered away their inheritance in wild living and died young.[256] 'They

[246] Hill 1904: 122. [247] Newcombe, *Autobiography*, p. 184.
[248] Crawford in Fildes 1990: 23; Houlbrooke 1989: 14, 76.
[249] See p. 159. [250] Mendel 1978: 245. [251] Bennett 1962: 2.
[252] Marescoe, *Markets and Merchants*, p. 5.
[253] Brydges, *Continuation History Willoughby Family*, pp. 124, 136; Woodcock, *Papers*, p. 75; Garrison 1977: 112.
[254] MacCracken 1983; Wall 1978: 191; Laslett 1948a: 150.
[255] Mayhew 1991: 225. [256] *Yorkshire Diaries*, ii. 21–4.

know such ways of spending their Fathers were wisely ignorant of, but those of saving are as distant from their inclination as the search for America was to Europeans a thousand years ago.'[257] The common literary theme of the prodigal son was by no means confined to the gentry; the ballads often reached a note of melodramatic savagery in retailing the sins of citizens' sons.[258]

Conflict between generations was inevitable. Defoe had problems with his children despite his sermonizing in his Family Instructor.[259] Dominant parents often interfered even in the adult lives of their offspring; some children, once free, reacted strongly against the rigour of their upbringing and the values of their parents. It was possible for a son in conjunction with his mother to take control of a business from an incompetent father.[260] But the patriarchal spirit usually made it difficult for sons to change and improve a business while the father was still alive and active.[261] The young usually deferred to their elders, not because they were awed by their greater wisdom, but because their parents had the property.[262] Since fathers commanded authority through their power of bequest and since their security in old age depended on retaining control of the family estate, they were reluctant to distribute too much during their lifetime. Many children and grandchildren remained dutiful and affectionate, as their parents aged, but other heirs waited with impatience and ingratitude, like vultures, for their parents to die.[263]

Daughters had a dependent status and some merchants took a close interest in the marriages not only of their daughters, but of their daughters-in-law.[264] The role of the mother is less clear, though it is noticeable that women frequently picked daughters as their executrixes.[265] Although the education of sons was for practical reasons given preference over that of daughters, businessmen frequently schooled their daughters for more than childbearing.[266] The primary concern of most daughters was a good husband, because the social status of a wife, though subordinate, was infinitely better to that of dependant in another household. Mary Masters wrote sadly to her brother, reluctantly admitting her age and that she was 'only happy in the Love of her good brother and still a maiden born May Monday ... O sad 1634'.[267] Joyce Jeffries, a gentlewoman turned usurer, fell back on her cats, dogs and birds and 'paid a

[257] *Citizen's Companion*, p. 139. Frequently the prodigal son was assumed to have a covetous miser for a father: see Ward, *The Reformer*, pp. 19, 138.
[258] *Roxburghe Ballads*, iii. 36–41.
[259] Curtis 1981: 411.
[260] PROB/183 Romney, will of Samuel Tuffles.
[261] SP 110/113, letter from John Heal, 21 April 1671.
[262] Thomas 1977: 37.
[263] GLL MS 6645, letter 16 May 1715.
[264] BL Add. MS 22186.
[265] Amussen 1988: 92.
[266] Pollock 1989a: 236–9; WAM MS 9977, nos. 10, 139.
[267] Master, *Diaries*, p. 62. She was later twice married.

man on February 14th to be her Valentine'.[268] To the image of starving widows and orphans in contemporary propaganda was added that of dowerless daughters, who, if deprived by the financial recklessness or meaness of their parents, were 'debauched for want of Husbands'.[269] In fact, parents strained their resources to provide adequate dowries and secure their daughters and granddaughters good marriages, often at the expense of their younger sons.[270]

A major reason for marriage was the procreation of heirs to give property a descent.[271] The perpetuation of a family through the male line required luck and numbers, because it depended on random factors. Biological hazards – sickness, death and deficiencies of character – could easily frustrate the most conscientious father. Often sons lacked the personality and talent to either take over the business or to pursue alternative careers and they had to be invalided out or found sinecures.[272] Of Ambrose Crowley's sons, one had itchy feet and wanted to go to sea rather than into the business and another was considered too idle and stupid.[273]

Neither a strict nor a lax upbringing could guarantee loyalty or commonsense; siblings usually had little in common with each other or their parents.[274] Although commercial talent tended to skip generations and surface somewhere in the family tree, it was randomly distributed and not necessarily transmitted from father to son. A large family could reduce the risk by allocating responsibility according to ability. Some children grew up fast and learned the business before their parents died. But it was harder to compensate for the wastrel and the incompetent in a commercial family.

Kinship

Merchants in London generally lived in nuclear families and separate households; it was unusual for grandparents or parents to cohabit with their married children.[275] Indeed widows and widowers in old age often suffered from loneliness; Elias Pledge was desolate when his son was apprenticed to a Dutch merchant.[276] It was a two-generation world. Lineage loyalty and hospitality declined and mobility led to frequent physical separation. Bequests suggest that paternal relatives were preferred to maternal ones and godparents declined in importance.[277]

[268] Griffiths 1933–5: 23, 200. [269] *Broken Merchant's Complaint*, p. 12.
[270] Fletcher 1975: 26; Marescoe, *Markets and Merchants*, p. 4.
[271] For a different view see MacFarlane 1985: 321.
[272] GLL MS 10823/1; Coleman 1963: 26–32. [273] Flinn 1962: 25–7.
[274] Davis 1967a: 17. [275] Wall in Wall *et al.* 1983: 493.
[276] Houlbrooke 1988: 196; S. R. Smith 1976: 125. [277] Bossy in Greyerz 1984: 200.

Individuals often chose 'fictive kin' as companions on the basis of friendship and personal interests; neighbours helped each other and sometimes could be intrusive.[278] The importance of 'affinity' is evident from the distribution of commemoration rings at funerals.

But the household must not be confused with the family, which was a living organism and was both nuclear and extended.[279] Different generations and relatives of business families tended to live in close proximity, although the frequency of communication reflected both temperament and place of residence. The bonds of kinship, though flexible, remained strong and embraced all economic and functional groups; the business family operated within a bilaterally extended, dense, tribalistic network.[280] Although immediate relatives received priority, 'cousinage' bridged the oceans and obligations were recognized without any sanctions.[281] Even when it was impractical to meet regularly in person, qualitatively useful advice and support was furnished by regular correspondence, which was often warm and uninhibitedly affectionate.[282] Bequests to distant relations, cousins and nieces reveal a strong sense of family; relatives as well as friends and neighbours were chosen as witnesses and overseers of wills. Younger sons of gentlemen, who joined the business community, retained their status and connections with their blood kin.[283] Property was constantly redistributed within the extended family.

Family members were often a financial burden and there were drawbacks to nepotism.[284] Relatives who had neither talent nor interest often had to be advanced and there was continual dissension.[285] Merchants who made loans to or provided sureties for kinsmen often regretted the obligation.[286] Children of wealthy businessmen could fall into the hands of greedy relatives and be sent abroad while the guardian milked the estate.[287] The family in the seventeenth century was bedevilled by conflict between affection and interest, between social pretension and peace of mind, between personality and tradition. Children increasingly resented

278 O'Hara 1991: 40.

279 Wall in R. Smith 1984: 479; Haveren 1975: 242; Berkner 1975: 729, 738; Morgan 1966: 150–60; Schneider & Gough 1961: 2; Casey 1989; Greven 1966: 255; Trumbach 1978: 5, 11; Wheaton 1975; Wrightson 1981: 156; Harris 1983: 146; D. S. Smith 1973.

280 Hurwich in Beier *et al.* 1989: 60; Wolfran 1987: 21–6; Nichols, *History Leicester*, ii. 616; Houblon, *Pious Memoirs*, p. 44; Boulton 1987: 255–6, 291.

281 Cressy 1986: 47–8, 67; 1987: 286–7.

282 Wheaton 1975; BL Lans. MS 241, fos. 341v°, 365.

283 For the contrary, but erroneous, argument see Houlbrooke 1984: 41, 48–9; Stone 1977a.

284 GLL MS 6645, Henry Morse to George Radcliffe, 28 March 1715; a similar example is in REQ 2/390/595, 5 Chas I.

285 GLL MS 4096–7, 1714–15.

286 BL Add. MS 11411, fo. 16, 15 Nov. 1655; G. P. Jones 1967: 188.

287 Anderson 1989: 88.

having to subordinate their instincts and interests to the hereditary principle, to remain under parental authority after they had reached maturity. As property became more openly the basis of family life, so individual greed tended to supersede family loyalty. The demand for privacy clashed with the corporate needs of the family; the ambition of children, forced by primogeniture to assume a precarious independence, conflicted with patriarchal principles.[288] When the interests of the extended kinship group diverged from those of the nuclear household, the latter increasingly prevailed and co-operation between branches of a family could no longer be guaranteed.

The main cause of friction was property, which simultaneously bound together and divided families. John Aylward's brother took his wife and son to law 'who hee pretends hath rob'd him of 1000 New Crownes'.[289] The settlements contracted at marriage normally provided for most contingencies, as far as the property of husband and wife were concerned, specified provision for the children and protected all parties in the event of remarriage. But uncertainties remained and conflict was inevitable when so many parties could claim an interest through kinship. Acrimonious disputes over executorships and the distribution of legacies were endemic. Even careful drafting of wills could not eliminate ambiguity; an absence of direct heirs created many opportunities for lawyers and gold-diggers. Business estates were particularly prone to disruption, because merchants often died abroad or left stocks of money and goods, which could easily be stolen or transferred into the wrong hands.

Daughters complained that their dowries were too small to attract good husbands; relatives remonstrated when they felt that they were likely to be ignored in a will.[290] In scores of cases, a breach betweeen a father and his eldest son led to disinheritance, for the will was the ultimate sanction of parental power.[291] Strife also erupted between siblings, though it was equally common for children to educate and support each other.[292] Because many elder brothers provided diligently for their brothers, there was little resentment; primogeniture bound the nuclear family together and younger sons received money and assistance in their careers in exchange for respecting the rights and succession of the eldest.[293]

Kinship remained the basis of business.[294] Family cartels, reinforced

[288] Tuck 1980: 134.
[289] Bod. Eng. Lett. MS C.192, letter from St Malo, 23 Dec. 1702.
[290] Lever 1947: 59.
[291] Gray 1965: 108; *V.C.H. Middlesex*, v. 161; *John Isham*, p. xliii; Quitt 1988: 633, 641; Willan 1953: 50; *Yorkshire Diaries*, ii. 26.
[292] *Lincolnshire Archivist's Report* 1968–9: 112–13.
[293] Larminie 1984: 32; Pollock 1989b: 28; Hurwich in Beier *et al.* 1989: 44.
[294] See pp. 89–91.

by intermarriage, preserved secrecy, circulated advice and linked different sectors of the economy. The family provided patronage, capital, and initial commissions and offered insurance against misfortune.[295] It could corner a market more effectively than a simple partnership or a syndicate of individuals under contract. The family provided a support system from cradle to grave. The conjugal couple was not alienated from the kinship network and individuals recognized a collective responsibility. Those who had no wives or children of their own found substitutes among the families of their relatives, acting as godfathers, attending christenings and bestowing presents and legacies.[296]

The family was 'too often a Commonweal of Malignants'.[297] Kin were so divided by differences of wealth and rank and so loosely organized that they constituted complex clusters of interests rather than a formal kinship system. Personality conflicts and sibling rivalry divided loyalties and created blood feuds. The internal needs and obligations of the family often conflicted with the prosecution of external business. But it presented a united front to the world and had a structure which was designed to withstand these strains. Even business Companies treated and described their members as a family.[298] At the very least, marriage provided a home where the stress of business could be forgotten, where affection and common pleasures could be indulged and where children could be cherished and moulded to perpetuate the character and achievements of their parents. Within the flexible structure of the family the businessman could find comfort, reassurance and emotional stability.

The bourgeois family

Old patriarchal assumptions and values came under fire during the century.[299] There was a growing tendency to justify parental control more in terms of mutual interest than by appeal to inherited authority. A change of attitude was more likely to occur in cities, where there was greater mobility and social interaction, easier access to the printed word and a higher concentration of people and Non-Conformists. It is also possible that tension within the family structure may have been more prevalent in urban society, where family members had more intimacy, but less freedom. The pattern of late marriage did tend to identify the family with property rather than with honour; the nuclear family facilitated capital accumulation.[300] In some respects, business families resem-

295 GLL MS 6645, letter to George Radcliffe, 28 May 1715.

296 WAM, nos. 10, 337; Aubrey, *Lives*, p. xxiii; Gough, *History of Myddle*, pp. 118–19.

297 Pope, *Prose Works*, ii. 160; Halifax, *Works*, p. 250.

298 Hobbes, *Leviathan*, p. 129; Schochet 1975: 66.

299 Troeltsch 1931: ii. 809.

300 Goody 1986; Chambers 1972: 58.

bled self-perpetuating corporations with their own capital and shareholders.

But the distinction commonly made between the 'bourgeois' and the 'aristocratic' family is a false dichotomy. The reaction against the 'traditional' family in favour of individual responsibility and choice cannot be identified with business. Those families which were attracted by Puritan radicalism had different standards of value, whether they came from the gentry or the commercial world; pressure for greater reciprocity was felt throughout propertied society.[301] The family had to adjust to economic change, but its structure was neither a cause nor a result of some abstraction called capitalism, which has tended to supersede in debate the less amorphous, but chronologically imprecise, process called industrialization.[302] The emphasis on personal autonomy and separate rights from childhood onwards may have helped to generate a work ethic, but it was equally compatible with bonding, the transmission of fraternal values and gentrification.[303]

The traditional rituals of family life remained largely intact. Women remained second-class citizens; convenience and habit continued to preserve the patriarchal principle. Although the interests of parents and children did not always coincide, respect for elders remained a powerful force and younger sons expected to support themselves. The business family was founded as much on patrimony and on the kinship group as was the landed family. Merchants socialized their children to regard its survival as more important than their interests as individual members. It was widely recognized that the family existed to protect property and that property existed to protect the family. Few were unaware that marriage was an essential channel of mobility and the fastest road to wealth.

Both gentlemen and merchants shared the common human ambition for immortality through procreation and favoured impartible inheritance. Even when a great estate and title were not at stake, the incentive to perpetuate the line remained strong. Business families had a similar demographic pattern to the landed gentry and faced the same problems of raising and training their successors. All families were at the mercy of birth and death rates and the ratio of male to female offspring. Every child represented a long-term investment and had an opportunity cost. Sons who secured wives with large portions could transform the financial position of a whole family and conversely bad marriages or an excess of daughters could impoverish an estate. Daughters who were physically or

301 Schochet 1969: 437.

302 MacFarlane 1985: 70–1, 85, 335; 1987: 140. On the difference between modernization and industrialization see Wrigley 1977: 81.

303 Quitt 1988: 643, 649 tries both to have his cake and eat it.

socially unattractive had to be bought husbands or else accepted as a charge for life upon the estate. All sectors of propertied society inherited the same basic family structure and shared the same objectives – increase and consolidation of the family estate, social advancement and continuity in the male line.

The family as an institution was riddled with contradictions and its members held inconsistent beliefs at the same time. But it was too essential in both town and country to be seriously challenged; it remained the repository of social wisdom and the basic administrative unit and was to provide a model for those institutions which were ultimately to usurp many of its functions. Property was vested in the family which provided the only safety net against failure.[304] The nuclear family was actually more dependent on its members than the extended family; businessmen combined the self-reliance of the former with the dutifulness of the latter.[305] Blood was thicker than the ink on contracts and, in the last resort, the group solidarity of family networks was stronger and more effective in securing social stability and economic efficiency than the paternalism of Church and state or the self-sufficient individualism of the business world.

[304] Goody 1962: 287.
[305] The business family indeed fits all the categories devised by Stone 1977a.

11 Consumption and leisure

Social commentators in the seventeenth century identified merchants with specific and inherent qualities which business was thought to both attract and reinforce. Some attempted to encapsulate from observation of actual behaviour the essence of the man of business; others were interested, not in realistic portrayal, but in denigrating the trading fraternity and validating the innate superiority of the landed gentry. The image of the man of business tended to oscillate between two opposing caricatures. On the one hand, there was the parsimonious and self-righteous critic of pleasure and display, more interested in getting than spending, sober, economical, austere and simplistic. On the other hand, there was the socially ambitious *nouveau riche*, anxious to emulate his superiors, subservient to but aping the nobility, pretentiously claiming tastes and interests which were alien to him.

Historical sociologists, to ground their theories of capitalism and Puritanism, have also indulged in wishful exercises in descriptive psychology and constructed a composite *Idealtyp* of the merchant. Their profiles exclude characteristics like sentimentality, melancholy and passion, which are considered irrelevant or antagonistic to his function, and make no allowance for differences between particular individuals or for ambivalent feelings in the same person. It is therefore important to clarify and calibrate the distinctiveness and homogeneity of the business community. The real character of businessmen must be inferred from how they lived, not equated with theories of what they ought to have been.

Was trade a way of life rather than simply a means of making money?[1] What were the objectives and desires of merchants and did they have a consistent pattern of behaviour? How did new recruits adapt to business and did they enjoy in old age the fruits of their labours? To distinguish the exceptions from the norm, it is necessary to aggregate many individual examples of how merchants indulged their wants and cultivated their minds.

[1] Bailyn 1953: 384.

Houses and contents

Businessmen who wanted spacious homes had to move outside the City. Country houses sometimes came with a landed estate and the tycoons often built or improved and landscaped mansions in the same manner as the gentry.[2] The majority of country houses owned by businessmen served, however, as suburban retreats from the noise, smells, dirt and congestion of London.[3] Villas and weekend cottages in villages became increasingly popular, after 1660, and their fastidious gardens and fish-ponds represented an approximation to the universal ideal of country life.[4] 'I see', wrote Richard Hill to Aylward, 'you have provided you a country house at hamsted'.[5] Henry Powell leased a three-storey house in Clapham with a barn, brewhouse, garden and a field with sheep; Leppington's partner retired to Highgate Hill and there were twelve London merchants and directors of the Bank at Woodford.[6] In York, merchants commuted from country houses; Denis Bond of Dorchester had a country house and farm as well as a house on South Street.[7] In 1624, half of the Gloucester aldermen had country houses; Christopher Cary abandoned the Key of Bristol and moved to Stony Hill.[8]

Only the rich could, however, afford country homes and many of them continued to reside in the City. Most of the Jacobean aldermen of London and thirty-one of thirty-seven, who were elected 1687–1700 and alive in 1693, lived within the walls.[9] Some inhabited great mansions, like the four-storey Renaissance house with a marble portico, ornate facade and ornamental gate of Sir Paul Pindar in Bishopsgate or the Cokayne house acquired by Eliab Harvey.[10] But few businessmen were smitten by the building mania of landowners. The City, the guilds, the Crown and landowners owned much of the freehold of London. Investment in urban real estate remained a specialized business and the lesser merchants

[2] Papillon, *Memoirs*, p. 69; Airs 1975: 86; Tawney 1958: 278; Summerson 1955: 227; *V.C.H. Middlesex*, v. 157, 161; Coleman 1963: 51, 124; Lloyd 1931: 215; Hoare 1955: 36; Tipping 1920: part 3, i. 299, ii. 179, 208.

[3] Carter 1975: 85; Røstvig 1962; Warnicke 1984: 60; Porter 1968: 74; Ralph 1947: 18.

[4] Defoe, *Tour*, i. 158; Earle 1989a: 374 in his sample found twenty-nine with country retreats. A substantial number of London philanthropists lived in rural parishes: see Jordan 1960a: chap. 4; Tipping 1920: part 3, ii. 69, iv. 195; Milbourne 1888: 89; Blair 1975: 303; B. Williams 1913: i. 12; Lever 1947: 33; Plummer 1972: 262; Gill 1961: 12.

[5] Bod. Eng. Lett. MS C.192, 27 May 1700.

[6] Dawe 1950: 28–9; *Woodford* 1950: app. 1.

[7] Palliser 1978: 114; Underdown 1992: 52.

[8] Clark in Clark *et al.* 1979: 174; Ripley 1976: 121; PROB/Eure 118.

[9] Stone 1984: 251.

[10] Goss 1933; 223; Hugo 1862: plate 2; Keynes 1966: 433; *Quiet Conquest* 1985: no. 418; Jacobsen 1932: 46.

preferred long leases; the larger houses were usually rented on a temporary basis by those holding City office.[11]

Except for public and communal buildings, most City properties were small in scale, durable and functional.[12] Building styles in London were determined by pressure on space and the exigencies of water supply and light. Before the Great Fire, the houses in the courts and alleys were narrow-fronted with four to five storeys, usually with two rooms on each floor, a yard at the back, warehouses, stables and gardens, cellars and garrets.[13] After the Fire, however, building regulations prescribed a broader and more uniform construction as well as brick.[14] By the end of the century, speculative builders were mass-producing unit houses to match different categories of wealth and status.[15] Difference in rentals suggest that there were four main classes, standardized by size, quality and location with standard ceiling heights, balconies and doorways. The median number of rooms in the Orphans' inventories was seven for those with assets of less than £5,000 and nine for those in the higher bracket.[16] The norm was five bedchambers or four plus a parlour.

Set back from the street with inner courtyards, herb and vegetable gardens, stables and sometimes coach-houses, the mansions of the great merchants, topped by poles, had three to four stories plus a garret, extensive cellars, a kitchen and separate brewhouse, a great parlour and counting house, galleries with collated apartments and an increasing number of private rooms, including nursery rooms, for retiring and sleeping; a typical example of around 1670 is 34 Great Tower Street.[17] A Levant merchant had a five-storey house in Leadenhall Steet, 59 feet deep with a shop or counting house, panelling and shutters and a garden 60 × 30 feet.[18]

Both the open hall, which was difficult to heat, and communal stairways, which offered little privacy, were discarded during the century; cheaper glass and more versatile windows combined with more mirrors and candles to improve interior lighting.[19] Sometimes there was a house of office, but usually residents depended on commodes and close-stools which were emptied into a drain or out of the window. Rooms acquired a more specialized function. The bedroom remained the major room, but

[11] Jones in Clark & Slack 1972: 336; Alford & Barker 1968: 127; Marescoe, *Markets and Merchants*, p. 3.

[12] Sheppard 1966; there are numerous studies of Company Halls such as Metcalf 1977.

[13] Kingsford 1925; Garrett 1977; Brown 1986: 572–4, 587–9, table 2; Barley in Foster & Alcock 1963: 479–501; Kelsall 1974.

[14] Knowles 1972: chaps. 3–4.

[15] Summerson 1970a: 17–19, 29, 42; Brett-James 1929–32: 112, 137.

[16] Earle 1989a: tables 8.1–8.2; P. E. Jones & Judges 1936 suggest an average of 6.1 per house within and 5.1 outside the walls and 7–8 in business households.

[17] Bell 1920: 87; 1910: 437; *Historical Monuments Commission London* 1929: iv. 185–6.

[18] Metcalf 1984: 97.

[19] Crossley 1972: 424; Schofield 1984: 144–8, 158–62.

the dining room was upgraded and the parlour, which had in the past contained a bed, became a separate sitting, withdrawing or living room and was decorated and better furnished.[20]

Business, in contrast to other professions, made no distinction between home and work. Retailers needed street frontage along busy thoroughfares and the domestic residences of wholesalers were usually near the waterfront. The main entry was often through the shop, though that could also be placed in the rear, and the kitchen and dining room were on the first floor.[21] Those who employed artisans sometimes accommodated them in the rear and many shops were workshops. Goods were stored in the basement or in attached or adjacent warehouses.[22]

In the provincial towns, many more physical examples have survived into the twentieth century. Every region and town had its local standardized style of construction and materials and many buildings in use dated from the sixteenth century or earlier.[23] After 1660, some provincial towns, like Whitehaven and Warwick, were substantially replanned and rebuilt by the gentry as well as by merchants; finer materials and less cluttered, classical styles and designs with better light, ventilation and circulation replaced the vernacular architecture.[24] The size and stratification of floors depended on trade as well as on wealth; innkeepers, maltsters, grocers and retailers had larger houses, and warehouses were sometimes integrated with the house.[25] Provincial town houses, many of which were enlarged during the century, were usually two rooms thick and two to three stories high with a great chamber and withdrawing rooms and private areas for storing valuables. The usual format was a hall or living room, a parlour or sleeping room on the ground floor and sometimes a buttery and workshop with guest chambers and bedchambers above. The shopkeepers usually used the whole ground floor for business and lived above, with a kitchen in the basement and the servants in the attic.[26]

The guild and market halls and the private homes of York and Hereford had elaborately carved timber structures with movable shutters on the shops.[27] In Leeds the wealthy merchants had brick residences with splendid facades and courtyards and warehouses near the market.[28] In Hull, the medieval houses were replaced by new buildings, sometimes

[20] Corfield & Priestley 1982. [21] Dawe 1950: 29. [22] Flinn 1962: 33.
[23] Dyer 1981; Wood-Jones 1963; Bunskill 1987.
[24] Borsay 1982: 12; 1977; E. L. Jones & Falkus 1979: 193; Machin 1977: 55, graph 3; Collier 1991: 89, 93. [25] *Goods of Forefathers*, table 12. [26] Girouard 1990: 122.
[27] Crossley 1951: 151–6; Palliser 1982a: 97; *Yorkshire Probate Inventories*, p. 139; *Telford Yeomen*; *Beddle Wills*, p. 168; Fieldhouse 1978: 262, 282–4.
[28] Beresford 1985–6: 52; Wilson 1971: 195; Kirby 1985: 47; 1986: 158.

more than once.[29] In Liverpool, Manchester, Shrewsbury, Newcastle, Worcester, Exeter, Southampton, Poole, Ipswich and the Midland towns, prosperous businessmen enlarged their domestic space and divided it by function.[30] Bristol merchants had timber-framed houses with narrow entrances, lofty halls and gardens, cellars and warehouses, a shop on the ground floor with rooms above for plate cupboards and sometimes a fore and back court and a compting house.[31]

A residence was, of course, a symbol of status. Harrison thought that for 'neatness and curiosity the merchants do far exceed all others'.[32] Lavish ornamentation in London compensated for shortage of space and included elaborate facades and door cases, intricate ironwork and wood carving, decorative cornices, friezes and frescoes in modelled plaster, oak and deal wainscoted panelling, Dutch tiles and marbled chimney-pieces.[33] The factories abroad had to conform to local conditions, but they were usually built and furnished to impress.[34] The houses of most businessmen were, however, simple and functional; they resembled a meeting house rather than the parish church. Emphasis was usually placed on comfort rather than on luxury; curtains were installed and coal-burning fireplaces multiplied to reduce the cold and draughts.

The wealthy always tended to cluster around particular streets and the location of housing was strongly influenced by occupation.[35] The West End of London developed separately during the century under aristocratic patronage; merchants were increasingly differentiated from the gentry and professional men by their place of residence.[36] But the City was less segregated than the suburbs up to 1695. Gentlemen sometimes lodged with merchants and rich and poor lived side by side without rigid zoning; in Southwark too, there was a mosaic of neighbourhoods.[37] In Shrews-

29 Gillett & MacMahon 1980: 160, 187. Grimsby, however, according to Prynne, *Diary*, p. 153, had 'scarce a good house'.

30 Chandler 1965: 40; Willan 1980: chap. 7; Fraser & Emsley 1978: 123; Rowlands 1975: 114; Dyer 1972: 160; *Banbury Wills*, p. 84; MacCaffrey 1958: 267; Gandy, 'Inventory', pp. 1–5; Portman 1966: figs. xiv, xvii; Cotton 1872: 46; Taylor 1974: 63ff; Beamish *et al.* 1976: 121; *Southampton Probate Inventories 1447–1566*, p. xv; *Ipswich Probate Inventories*, p. 5; Crummy & Moyer 1976; *Tudor Market Rasen*.

31 Fuller, *Worthies*, iii. 113; Hunt 1887: 108; Carus-Wilson 1954: 75; Fitch 1965; Pritchard 1922; Hirst 1927: 208; Girouard 1990: pl. 152; MacGrath 1975: 30.

32 Harrison, *Description of England*.

33 Summerson 1955: 2–4; Harris 1960; Dutton 1948: pl. 56.

34 Eeckaute 1965: 332–5; Wretts-Smith 1920; Baumann 1990: 147–8; Strachey 1916.

35 Alexander 1984: 53.

36 Smuts 1991: 123; Brett-James 1935: chap. 6. On the debate over residental and spatial distribution see Carr 1990; Power in Beier & Finlay 1986: 218–22; E. Jones 1980: 132, fig. 4.

37 Pearl 1979a: 7; Finlay 1981: 79; Boulton 1991: 167, 290–3; 1986: 7, 11; Barratt 1953: 322.

bury, trade determined location of residence and the wealthy lived in the centre of town.[38] But in Bristol and Worcester, rich and poor commingled and public spaces were accessible to all.[39]

Every merchant's house had its counters, desks, stools, shelves and chests, its seals, scales, candles, paper, quill pens, ink, sealing thread and wax, ledgers and journals.[40] Shops became more formalized; they were enclosed and glazed and fitted with banners, chests, display boards and counters.[41] The interiors of the guild halls and Company headquarters were similar; the Hudson's Bay Company purchased a deal table, $7\frac{1}{2} \times 3 \times 8$ feet together with chairs and a green cloth carpet for its meetings.[42] Every corporation had its collection of silver plate, usually benefactions and often used in rituals, which was held as a reserve and sold in hard times.

The volume and variety of domestic furniture continuously expanded – tables, hanging and hand mirrors, chests with half or full drawers raised on short legs, cupboards, dressers, open linen cupboards, standing and hanging presses, Oriental screens, couches, cabinets and escritoires, leather-covered, upholstered and Turkey chairs.[43] Lemuel Leppington had six bedrooms with fifty-seven chairs and sixteen tables as well as glass lanthorns.[44] Furniture became lighter and more delicate in the course of the century, as oak gave way to walnut and greater use was made of veneers, cane and filigree; the gate-leg and oval table developed from the joined table and a greater variety of folding and side tables emerged for specialized functions such as playing games or writing accounts; new fabrics, styles and techniques were imported or imitated from Europe and the East.[45] Furniture was upholstered in silk and velvet, rather than leather, with wool or horsehair padding and softened by loose cushions with embroidered coverlets. Sofas and wickerback, rush-bottomed and cane-seated chairs began to replace solid wood settles, benches and stools and, though still not sprung, were turned and had more comfortable shapes. Beds were major pieces of furniture with slender carved pillars, overhead testers, headboards, canopies, curtains and fringes of silk or fine cloth.

[38] Hudson 1983; Forrest 1911: 51ff.

[39] Dyer 1972: 178; Barry in Reay 1985a: 79.

[40] The volume of data in inventories is overwhelming, but changes in living standards cannot be assessed with precision. Monetary valuations can be quantified and visible items, like books and clocks, are easily segregated, but most descriptions, such as 'chair', are too vague for clear identification. Inventories tend to confirm the obvious, that richer businessmen lived up to their incomes. See Weatherill 1988: 8; Husbands 1980–1: 209; Garrard 1980: 55–81; Pardailhé-Galabrun 1988.

[41] Archer 1991b: 26.

[42] *Hudson's Bay Company Minutes 1671–84*, p. 194.

[43] CLRO, CSB 2.

[44] Dawe 1950: 28–9.

[45] Marley 1979: 334; Chinnery 1979: 451; Gloag 1964: 62–8.

In the more prosperous households of London, the range and quality of accessories also broadened and the stock of weapons declined.[46] Carpets were still used mainly to cover furniture, but Oriental rugs and mats covered the boarded floors.[47] Window curtains of serge or linen became more common, as did feather mattresses and flock bolsters, damask and diaper linen napkins and finer quality towels, sheets, pillows and tablecloths, porcelain, clocks and watches.[48] Of 300 inventories in the Orphans Court, 1672–1725, 81 per cent had curtains and 41 per cent china.[49] Any business household of substance had an extensive collection of jewellery and gold and silver plate, much of the latter in daily use for lighting and serving.[50] Silver and glass replaced pewter for drinking as pewter replaced wood for eating; copper and brass replaced tin. Purely decorative items like stained cloths and tapestries also became more frequent and wallpaper evolved from paper hangings glued to canvas.

In the provinces, inventories also reveal greater comfort, more books, clocks and pictures and even coffee-pots and red chairs.[51] John Welston, alderman of Doncaster, had a dining room with two mirrors, twelve pictures, a posset pot, a case of glasses and Delft plates.[52] A Norwich Goldsmith had a high child's chair, a great chair, the *Acts and Monuments*, eleven pictures and a backgammon board.[53] Wainscot panelling replaced hangings in York and Leeds and there was more glassware and even functional heirlooms.[54] The lesser merchants, however, still furnished their homes sparsely.[55] What is remarkable, even in the poorer households, is the sheer volume of utensils in everyday use – fire tools, pots, pans and scales, roasting spits, ovens, endirons, chafing dishes, washing tubs, water cisterns, basons, ewers and chamber pots, wooden trenchers, spoons, knives (some steel) and even forks.[56]

Merchants had easy access to fine craftsmanship and they could acquire a sophisticated knowledge of specialist items such as Venetian glass, jewellery or musical instruments.[57] By purchasing the best that they could afford, they undoubtedly acquired many objects of beauty and elegance. A painted panelled room at 5 Botolph Lane, in 1696, created a fantastic

[46] Thornton 1984: 36, 62; 1978: 326. The best survey of household furnishings and domestic life, although drawn mainly from examples of landed families, remains Hole 1953. [47] Impey & MacGregor 1985: 277.

[48] Most of these were probably thirty-hour and lantern clocks, although pendulum long-case clocks were produced in greater numbers in London after 1680.

[49] Weatherill 1988: 8; Hill 1904: 128.

[50] BL Lans. MS 1156. For types of plate see Taylor 1964; Oman 1962: 15–17, 77.

[51] Kenyon 1958: 67; Willan 1980: 118; Gray, 'Inventory', pp. 80–8; *Lichfield Probate Inventories*. [52] *Yorkshire Probate Inventories*, p. 139. [53] Levine 1973: 486.

[54] Kirby 1983: 159; 1986: 29. [55] *Ipswich Probate Inventories*, p. 5.

[56] Hampshire, 'Inventory', pp. 243–5.

[57] The range of luxury items available is well illustrated by Edwards 1972: 85–9.

private world with theatrical scenes of Amazonian Indians, flanked by Indian cabinets, porcelain and wallpaper.[58] Evelyn describes the house of Mr Bohun in Kent, which had carved wainscot, pictures by Streeter, Indian 'cabinets of all elegancies', Japanese screens, a pendulum clock enclosed in the curious flower work of Mr Gibbons in the middle of the vestibule, and lavish gardens.[59]

Furnishings did absorb surplus income and offered a means of transferring wealth as well as a form of conspicuous consumption; plate served as a liquid reserve.[60] The contents of the houses of rich merchants often exceeded £1,000 in value. But the average proportion of assets held in household furnishings seems to have been around 10 per cent; plate rarely exceeded £500 and was usually under £100.[61] In Gloucestershire, 24 per cent of assets constituted stock in trade, 8.5 per cent plate, 31.5 per cent credits, 12 per cent leases and 21.3 per cent household goods.[62] There was little change in the inventoried value of domestic goods, even of the rich, during the century. In contrast to the gentry, merchants had a marginal interest in interior decoration and were less inclined to express their status through domestic artifacts. Their taste was usually conformist, functional and unrefined.

Comfort and display

Forms of dress advertised status and personality and visibly conveyed respect in an hierarchical society.[63] Clothes displayed or disguised occupation, age and region, obscured physicial deficiencies and poor hygiene, implicitly expressed dissent or explicitly showed deference. Although the formalities of hat honour were gradually relaxed, hats were worn to symbolize rank and authority rather than for warmth or protection.[64] Extravagance of habit was consistently reproved for social and religious as well as for economic reasons; convention and etiquette imposed formal constraints. A blacksmith's wife who ventured out in a gown appropriate to the wife of a merchant was hooted at by the people of Ludlow.[65]

Apprentices were supposed to be better clothed than the servants and provision of their double apparel, that is both working clothes and Sunday best, was a major issue to be negotiated in their indentures. Blue

[58] Croft 1962–72: i. 46, plates 90–1. [59] Evelyn, *Diary*, 31 Aug. 1671, 30 Jan. 1672.
[60] Dyer 1966: 135.
[61] Portman 1966: 101–10. Weatherill 1988: tables 5, 6.2 breaks down domestic goods into categories and notes few decorative items, but the sample relates to every occupation and income group and the median figures in table 8.1 conceal major differences between businessmen and others. [62] Ripley 1984: table 3.
[63] Thirsk 1990: 83; Buck 1976.
[64] Corfield 1989: 66ff; *Bristol Ordinances 1506–98*, p. 105. [65] Wedgwood 1955: 54.

cloaks in summer and blue gowns in winter were the conventional garb with flat round caps and collarless shirts, but inexpensive russet and white fabrics were also worn.[66] Every guild laid down standards which combined sobriety with respect for elders.[67] The Merchant Adventurers of Newcastle prohibited silk garters, girdles and points, jersey stockings, corked shoes, velvet-lined hats, cloaks and daggers and long hair which was a chronic bone of contention everywhere.[68] Three outfits could be acquired for £10–20, but prentices often managed to dress more expensively.[69] Merchants were expected to maintain a minimum standard; mercers dressed up, since it was their trade, and cutlers were fined if they appeared in the Hall in their aprons.[70] A decorous attire was a three-piece suit (including waistcoat) with shirt, drawers, stockings and shoes. Outer clothing was normally woollen or worsted and underclothing was linen with a nightgown for sleeping.[71]

The congestion and impersonality of London, however, encouraged and allowed greater pretence; once the sumptuary laws ceased to operate after 1604, sartorial fluidity and fads could freely express both actual and imagined mobility.[72] Businessmen did not have a uniform and they could not be as readily identified from their appearance as clergymen or lawyers.[73] One of the curiosities of English society was that social groups were distinguished more by fabric than by style. Some merchants could not resist the human impulse to cut a dash.[74] Despite complaints and ridicule, they ostentatiously wore whatever hats, cloaks, breeches, boots and richly patterned silk shirts and hose were in fashion.[75] Like the lawyers, they liked to dress up and parade in their scarlet ceremonial robes of office and they squeezed the spread of middle age into fabrics and shapes intended by the tailors for the gilded striplings of the Court. Merchants imported Oriental gowns and Turkish costumes, adopted the periwig and could greet company wearing a turban.[76] An interest in

[66] Hands & Scouloudi 1971: 10.
[67] Sherwell 1889: 171; Nicholl 1851: 133; P. E. Jones 1976: 24.
[68] *Newcastle Merchant Adventurers' Records*, i. 20–7; Mendenhall 1953; Hatcher & Barker 1974: 189; Plummer 1972: 95. [69] GLL MS 12017; Ryder, *Diary*, p. 8.
[70] Welch 1923: ii. 208. [71] Earle 1989a: 284.
[72] Baldwin 1926: chap. 6; Kent 1973: 51, apps. 1–5; Harte in Coleman & John 1976: 137. Sumptuary laws were often manipulated to protect sales, as when the hosemakers opposed the wearing of boots, and they failed in the Commons in part because the gentry feared that they would be included.
[73] Brooke 1972: 83; Nevinson in Bird *et al.* 1978. There are very few illustrations of everyday outer or underclothing in handbooks such as Cunningtons 1967; Ribeiro & Cumming 1989: 114, 120. Some street costumes are however illustrated in Laroon, *Engravings and Drawings*, and on maps such as Allen, *Caveatt*.
[74] Deloney, *Works*, p. 238.
[75] For fashionable styles see Cunningham 1966: 12; Hall 1970: plates 7–9.
[76] Pepys, *Diary*, 21 Nov. 1666; Cruttenden, *Atlantic Merchant Apothecary*, p. 6.

outward appearances did not, however, extend to washing the body, though public baths appeared in London.

Others businessmen deliberately dressed soberly as a form of inverted pride. 'The Citizen', wrote Corbet,' may ... retaine a grave habit to themselves in which they may sufficiently express their wealth'.[77] Most merchants just stuck to the basic essentials and maintained a demure appearance; they did not wear swords or spurs or adopt the finery of the Court. When resident abroad, they often dressed down to make themselves less conspicuous. Clothes and ready money only represented 3.66 per cent of Worcestershire inventories and, in the London Orphans' inventories, businessmen had from £30–100 invested in their wardrobes.[78]

Apprentices were often poorly fed, but merchants certainly overindulged and probably prematurely destroyed their stomachs, both at home and abroad.[79] Consumption increased with prosperity and a wider range of choice. Excess eating and drinking was not confined to the lavish Company feasts and celebrations of holidays, public events, christenings, marriages and funerals; huge bills of fare were recommended even for fasting days and these habits were unwisely followed in the tropical Caribbean.[80] In India, the factors roasted buffalo on Christmas Day and indulged in dinners of sixteen courses followed by brandy and punch.[81] 'None can outdo a merchant in good eating if he makes it his business', remarked a French visitor.[82] The main, and usually huge, meal was taken at noon; breakfast consisted of bread and porridge and supper, at seven to eight in the evening, of bread and cheese and pies.[83] Quantity was more evident than gastronomic quality, though merchants had easy access to imported delicacies and rarities.[84]

A traditionally heavy diet of bread, meat (game, beef, lamb and poultry), fish (often dried or salted cod, mackerel and herring) and green vegetables, was supplemented by heavy puddings and imported currants, citrus fruits, nuts and vegetables.[85] The only physical evidence from a cesspit in a Tenby merchant's house suggests a diet of seafood, meat and eggs, local grains and plants, figs and grapes.[86] It was not a perfectly

[77] Corbet, *Discourse Religion England*, p. 471. [78] Johnston 1978: 206; Earle 1989a: 94.

[79] Barlow, *Journal*, p. 18; Drummond 1958: 128–31, 157–60.

[80] May, *Accomplisht Cook*; Simon 1953; Dunn 1972; chap. 8; Buisseret & Pawson 1975: chap. 8. Price, *Compleat Cook* suggests a wide range of puddings, pastries and pies and rich desserts.

[81] Ovington, *Voyage Surat*, pp. 386–9; Mundy, *Travels*, i. p. lii; Rawlinson 1920: 129.

[82] Firth 1932: 216. [83] Fenley in Lennard 1931: 214–34.

[84] BL Add. MS 30494 provides a shopping list for an aldermanic family in the 1600s.

[85] One of the most comprehensive studies of the eating habits of merchants, though it relates to the mid sixteenth century, is Winchester 1955: chap. 5.

[86] Murphy *et al.* 1989: 246–62.

balanced diet, but there were no gross nutritional deficiencies. George Warner received artichokes from his factor and stocked a variety of cheeses and preserves as well as liquor and claret.[87] Sir Andrew King purchased Malaga wine, liquorice wine, brandy, beer and ale, mutton, lambs' heads, chicken, partridges, pigeons, tripe, rabbits and fish, olives, beans, asparagus, cauliflower, mushrooms, spinach and sprouts, currants, oranges and lemons, raspberries and walnuts, bread, butter, cream, sugar and eggs, amounting to £126 14s. 5d. over nine months.[88] The businessman began his day with a glass of mum or sack and ended it with a glass of brandy and a pipe of tobacco. Although Portuguese wines eventually ousted canary, French claret remained the favourite drink, despite heavy taxes and prohibitions.[89] Small beer, as distinct from ale, was a necessary substitute for water until the introduction of coffee and chocolate; the taverns provided ample opportunity for carousing.[90]

A laden table was a symbol of prosperity.[91] Communal eating had a social symbolism and the tradition of hospitality continued in the City. The Quarter, Livery, Court and Election Feasts of the City Companies were competitively extravagant: boar, venison, quail, sturgeon, geese and larks were washed down with expensive wines. Samuel Butler inveighed against the alderman who 'dispatches no public affairs until he has throughly dined upon it and is fully satisfied with QuincePye and Custard'.[92] When entertaining royalty or visiting celebrities, feasts were even more elaborate.[93] Indeed the cost became so burdensome that doubts arose in some Companies and communal dinners were suspended in time of plague, war and depression.[94]

The households of businessmen were swollen by apprentices, clerks and journeymen or by lodgers who were unrelated to the family. Apprentices were sometimes used as domestic servants, but, except in the poorer households, a distinction was usually maintained between personal attendance and service.[95] Status in the city did not mandate a large retinue and urban households were more concentrated and did not, like country houses, require a large establishment of live-in servants with a supervisory steward. The loose tongues of servants could be a problem for businessmen and wages were higher in the city; a trained upstairs maid cost £2–3 per annum and a footman £2–6. But houses still had to be

[87] SP 46/83, nos. 46, 50, 53, 60, 64, 67, 100.
[88] WAM MSS 54, 114.
[89] Francis 1972: 99; Pijassou 1974: 149.
[90] Pagan 1985: 367.
[91] On changing attitudes to hospitality see Heal 1990; *Ferrar Papers*, p. 621.
[92] Butler, *Hudibras*, p. 109; *Original Letters English History*, iii. 37–8. There is abundant information on the menus of Livery dinners in histories of the Companies; a typical cycle of feasts is given by Girtin 1975: 178.
[93] Clode 1875: 164–81; Edie 1987: 125.
[94] Archer 1991b: 125–30.
[95] Pinchbeck & Hewitt 1969: 26; this draws heavily on the work of Dunlop and Aries.

cleaned, beer brewed, fuel and water carried, the garden weeded, refuse emptied, fabrics mended, silver polished, the household served and the clothing laundered twice a week. The rich averaged six to seven servants, but the usual complement was one or two women and one man.[96] Bachelors employed housekeepers to run their households and they were sometimes as independent and refractory as a strong-willed wife.[97]

The horse and carriage became the predominant status symbol.[98] Only the rich could afford the cost of maintaining private transport in the city. London horse prices increased from £16 to £40 after 1660 and both animals and vehicles depreciated fast; in addition there was the cost of fodder, saddlery, stable boys and postillions.[99] Many merchants travelled by the public stages which linked most areas of England or hired a horse, which was faster than a coach; despite a real improvement in the roads, the sea and rivers still provided the easiest form of transport.

The business community considered that personal dignity and family honour demanded a splashy exit; a cheap burial implied pauperism. Funeral rites separated the kin from the deceased and bound the family to the community; they confirmed the transfer of property, consoled the bereaved and upheld hospitality.[100] Wentworth advocated a Christian and seemly burial which would cause no annoyance to the living, but he hedged on the question of banquets.[101] Some merchants suffered from a fear of improper burial; Samuel Newton, alderman of Cambridge, 'dreamed methought I digged my own grave but I said this is not deep enough'.[102] Normally the corpse was dressed for burial and lay at home in a handsome open coffin. The woollen shrouds legislated by Parliament and the black drapery provided important business for the textile industry, as tombstones did for the masons. A great attendance in procession following the hearse bearing the escutcheons of the deceased was still considered a mark of respect and was secured by distribution of mourning gloves, hatbands, cloaks, rings and money for the poor.[103]

Non-Conformists consistently attacked the idolatry of tomb portraits and some merchants in their testaments insisted upon an economical burial.[104] The Orphans Court of London, in 1543, imposed on executors a maximum limit of 5 per cent for estates under £1,000 and 2 per cent above £1,000, but it proved difficult in practice to curb expenditure.[105] The

[96] Earle 1989a: table 8.4. [97] GLL 5105.

[98] Ward, *London Spy*, p. 16; BL Lans. MS 1156; Garrard 1852: 471; Thompson 1870: 16; Hoare 1955: 30; Milbourne 1888: 94. [99] Nockolds 1977; Parkes 1925: 61.

[100] Goody 1962; Houlbrooke 1989: 77. [101] Wentworth, *Office of Executors*, p. 187.

[102] Newton, *Diary*, p. 118. [103] Llewellyn 1991: 86, 93.

[104] Heriot, *Last Will*; GLL MS 5105, fo. 52. The median figures in Gittings 1984: 14 relate to all occupations and the sample largely excludes London and businessmen.

[105] Carlton 1974a; CLRO, Journals 15, fo. 34.

executors of Thomas Cony defended their disbursement of £784 on the grounds that he was 'a merchant of the staple and a gentleman of good accompt and great acquaintance so that as well for the credit of the said deceased as themselves they were compelled to bury him according to his calling'.[106] The obsequies of the London tycoons could exceed £2,000 and the merchants of Lancashire and Bristol could be just as extravagant in proportion to their wealth.[107]

A funeral was still an important convivial social occasion, accompanied by music and feasting; Thomas Hill left instructions that the day of his burial be one of civility among his friends.[108] The deceased was eulogized and the mourners wore special coats and hats; night burials were a spectacle.[109] In Turkey, factors were buried with cannon salutes from the ships, because the ringing of bells was forbidden, and with a feast for the mourners.[110] The memory of greatness was preserved by an epitaph and a stone monument or brass plaque; tycoons were interred in elaborate tombs.[111] The overseas factories had their own cemeteries; 'our burying place', wrote Streynsham Master, 'is large and spacious and is adorned with several great and many handsome tombs and monuments'.[112] When Thomas Pye died, no tombstone could be procured at Scanderoon and a stone inscription was therefore ordered from Leghorn.[113]

The format of funerals did, however, change during the century; the dead were more segregated, the clergy played a smaller role and the Protestant abolition of Purgatory eliminated the need for intercession through prayer.[114] Originally, members of a fraternity were fined for non-attendance at burial services; they accompanied the coffin, which was lit by torches and wax tapers and covered by the embroidered hearse-cloth of the Livery from the Hall to the church where bequests by the deceased were distributed to friends, apprentices, guild members and the poor, and a sermon was preached.[115] The professional undertaker, however, emerged and private family funerals gradually superseded communal wakes with doles to the poor; testators, though they still favoured their own parish, became less concerned about the actual place of their

[106] Lincs. AO 8/75.
[107] Hugo 1862: 17; Bearcroft, *Thomas Sutton*, 113; MacGrath 1949: 102.
[108] Hill 1904: 133. [109] Taylor 1983: 92, 99.
[110] Wood 1935: 247; Anderson 1989: 113.
[111] Notestein 1954: 23. Brasses became less common, though one of George Coles and his two wives dates from 1640: see 'Northampton mercer inventory', p. 315; Stephenson 1977: 282; Lysons, *London and Environs*, iii. 429.
[112] Hedges, *Diary*, i. p. cccvii. Bod. Rawl. MS B.376, fo. 35; Ovington, *Voyage Surat*, p. 405; Bellasis 1931: 146; Mundy, *Travels*, i. 149; Oliver, *Monumental Inscriptions of Barbados*; Gray 1945: 496–7. [113] Sheffield Archives MS EM 1285(b).
[114] Houlbrooke 1989: 12; Wrightson in Walker & Schofield 1989: 164–5; Litten 1991.
[115] Webb 1962.

burial.[116] Burial practice varied enormously according to wealth, religion and taste, but costs in London did fall. Although they ranged from £5 to over £700, the funerals of businessmen worth above £5,000 cost between £150 and £300.[117]

Recreation

Physical exercise was often brutal and violent and largely confined to the more boisterous apprentices, who consistently ignored the provisions of their indentures and City prohibitions on dancing and fencing. They engaged in wrestling, running, shouting, brawling, cudgel play and fencing with sword, back sword and dagger until the latter was replaced by boxing.[118] Archery became a leisure activity.[119] The disciplinary records of the guilds and city courts are peppered with fines for misdemeanours; apprentices were sent to Bridewell for riotous living and regularly indulged in outbursts of violence on Shrove Tuesday.[120] Noisy and rowdy behaviour was also characteristic of the trading gentlemen of Shrewsbury; in Newcastle they knocked on doors and windows.[121] Like the young bloods from country estates, prentices gambled with dice and cards, watched bull and bear baitings, rat and cockfights and attended executions.[122] A provincial shop assistant, like Roger Lowe, neglected his duties and ate out with friends, fished, hunted and attended horse races, drank and gambled.

As town-dwellers, businessmen lived under congested conditions and at one remove from nature, but their households included working and racing horses, dogs and cats as well as parrots and canaries. John Harrison cut holes in his house 'for the free passage of cats'.[123] The East India Company reprimanded its factors for keeping a pet tiger which ate one goat per day.[124] The relative closeness of the countryside allowed merchants to fish, fowl and hunt with comparative ease: woodcock could be shot in Conduit Mead and duck in modern Belgravia; sparrow-hawks were flown in Shepherd's Bush.[125] Some overseas merchants were keen hunters and the factors at Smyrna rode twice a week to hounds. Although the Tudor passion for falconry declined, as guns became more effective, merchants imported rare hawks, like gerfalcons, and several were keen

[116] Wrightson in Walter & Schofield 1989: 164; Harding 1989: 124.
[117] Earle 1989a: table 11.1. [118] Ashton 1937: 240.
[119] *Middlesex County Records*, iii. 27. [120] Lindley 1983: 110; Manning 1988: 193.
[121] Mendenhall 1953: 102.
[122] *Newcastle Merchant Adventurers' Records*. i. 25; Boulton 1901: chap. 5; Lennard 1931: 72. [123] Thomas 1983b: 107–9.
[124] Hedges, *Diary*, i. p. ccclvii; Foster 1926: 82, 91.
[125] Bramston, *Autobiography*, p. 108; Brett-James 1935: 450–1.

falconers in England, the Levant and India.[126] In general, however, merchants had less interest than the country gentry in field sports. The game laws, initiated in an Act of 1605, tightened in 1671 and consolidated in 1692, declared game to be private property and largely restricted hunting to those who owned land.[127]

Businessmen took advantage of the public and communal entertainment available in the cities. They could bowl, frequent the baths, stroll in the parks, visit Bedlam and view the Crown Jewels and the zoo at the Tower or the heads on Temple Bar.[128] Coffee-houses and inns served for recreation as well as centres of business, news and mail drops.[129] The numerous fairs lasted for several days with shows, raffles, lotteries and firework displays, and the whole business community could escape into a carnival atmosphere. The citizens had their own jigs and danced in Cornhill on Mayday and at Whitsuntide and at Livery functions. The river was the centre of life, and sailing and cruising were popular diversions.

Both the City and the guilds had seasonal processions and pageants which commemorated their trade and benefactors and marked the change of officers.[130] Although reduced by the Reformation, many holy days survived and they were supplemented by secular festivals – royal birthdays, marriages, births and entries, anniversaries of victories and deliverances.[131] The English émigré communities, which were usually excluded from the local population, likewise celebrated Guy Fawkes Day and the Restoration. The great merchants followed the London season, which was identified by the law terms, and during the Long Vacation from August to October they retired to the country or took the waters at the numerous spas which developed within range of the City at Lambeth, Islington and Tunbridge.[132]

The City fathers were always suspicious of the theatre, which was out of bounds to pious merchants and impecunious apprentices.[133] The best playhouses moved to fashionable locations and wealthy Cavaliers became the chief patrons of dramatic Companies. The Restoration theatre catered

126 Aubrey, *Lives*, ed. Dick, p. 317; Houghton 1942: 214; Pepys, *Diary*, ii. 401; D. W. Davies 1961: 148; Routh 1912: 281; Berry & Crummey 1968: 323; BL Add. MS 70223; Zeuner 1963.

127 Kirby 1931: 239–59; 1933: 240–62; Munsche 1981: 3–5.

128 Colsoni, *Guide de Londres*; Mullett 1946.

129 Clark in Pennington & Thomas 1978: 49; Lillywhite 1965: 602–17; Coke, *England's Improvement*, p. 45.

130 London guild ceremonies are well documented in the numerous histories of City Companies. On the provincial towns see Barry in Reay 1985a: 71–3; Corry & Evans 1816: i. 472; Latimer 1900: 312–15.

131 Cressy 1989: chap. 1; 1990: app. B; Strong 1958: 87, 109–11; Halfpenny 1959: 19.

132 Ward, *Reformer*, p. 138.

133 Ashton 1983: 4–5; Barish 1981; Cook 1981.

less to the City than the Jacobean theatre and celebrated decadent passions rather than morality. But there was no clear division between the private playhouses catering to the gentry and those which catered to the populace. Many theatres were built and managed, often in joint-stock syndicates, by businessmen.[134] The Jacobean and Caroline stage had its merchant patrons.[135] The Presbyterian jeweller, Elliana Swanston, even took to the boards.[136] The City pageants with their elaborate tableaux were also outdoor theatre; in contrast to the continental towns, the London shows were performances rather than processions and, although primarily intended for the masses, were also appreciated by businessmen.[137] There were also itinerant companies of players who toured the provincial towns and performed at fairs.

Businessmen also relaxed by exchanging gifts, gossip and jokes with their friends, clients and relations in their homes, in taverns and on the Exchange.[138] According to Baptist Hicks, the entertainment of friends was 'very pleasing and comfortable, when more serious affairs are not impeded thereby'.[139] Pepys loved to talk to merchants and listen to their stories. Birdcages, toys and games are mentioned in inventories and businessmen played cards, dominoes, backgammon and billiards: Robert Haynes of Exeter paid 23s. in London for an inlaid chessboard with black and white pieces.[140] Ned Ward's shopkeeper had the following routine: he rose at 5 a.m., had breakfast, instructed his apprentice on the duties of the day, went to hear the news at his coffee-house, dined at noon, took a nap, visited the Exchange and Lloyd's, returned to his shop, then went to his club to talk with his friends, then back home to a light supper and bed at 9 p.m.[141]

Some merchants had green fingers.[142] In addition to the kitchen garden with its fruit, vegetables and herbs, the formal flower garden became a fixture. Foreign seeds were imported and Dutch methods borrowed; specialized suppliers appeared after the Restoration.[143] Flowers were displayed on balconies and in basons in houses and were planted in the squares and walks. Thomas Fairchild advised the merchants that small gardens would 'prepare their understanding to enjoy the country when their trade and industry has given them Riches enough to retire from

[134] Schelling 1908: ii; Wickham 1963: ii. 115–19; Hotson 1928: 99, 289; Harbage 1952: 24; Murray 1910; Edmond 1987a: 3–4; Lodge, *Works*, i. 2.

[135] Bentley 1941–68; Harbage 1941: 64, 77; Nungezer 1929: 343; Forse 1990: 173–4.

[136] Pepys, *Diary*, 7 April 1665.

[137] Burke 1977: 153, 158; Leinwand 1982: 137ff; Klein 1991: 26. See also p. 367.

[138] On the social significance of jesting see Thomas 1977: 77.

[139] Hicks-Beach 1909: 86.

[140] Hayens, *Diary*, p. 46.

[141] Ward, *Wealthy Shopkeeper*; Troyer 1946: 133.

[142] Wilkins 1920: 37; Heriot, *Last Will*; GLL MS 5105, fo. 52; Cornish, *Thomas Firmin*, p. 156.

[143] Harvey 1972: 48, 65.

business'.[144] Merchants imported and introduced new plants; Edward Colston had an orange tree, Sir John Shaw built an orangerie and aviary, and Nicholas Lete introduced the double yellow rose from Syria.[145] Bristol gardens had beehives and the notables of Leeds had their home gardens.[146]

Although all were bound by the natural seasons, the routines of urban life were different from those of the country, which revolved around ploughing and harvest, hunting and Quarter Sessions.[147] A metropolitan culture divided the London from the provincial merchant, as it divided polite society from the backwoods gentry. The density and heterogeneity of the population of London permitted greater flexibility in patterns of behaviour and gave image greater importance than substance. But businessmen did not have a uniform life style. Sea life and every trade had its own routines.[148] Life abroad both as sojourners in émigré communities or as settlers in the plantations had a different tempo and was not subject to the same conventions as regional and metropolitan England.[149] Although expatriates usually took their culture with them, several went native and had to adapt to their environment; there was no racism or cult of European superiority in Asia as there was in America.[150]

Intellectual pursuits

Contemporary littérateurs derided merchants for their lack of sensibility and sensory acuteness, their narrow perspective and their disregard for mature contemplation. Businessmen often failed to challenge the ideas, assumptions and explanations which they inherited. But respect for convention and a lack of interest in high culture was just as characteristic of other occupations.[151]

The respect of businessmen for learning predated the social and economic pressures which forced the gentry to embrace education from the sixteenth century onwards.[152] A few businessmen were educated at the Universities and Inns; London had Gresham College and City merchants bestowed £135,000 on Oxford and Cambridge, 1485–1640.[153] Others, like Petty, taught themselves. The reciting of texts by heart at

[144] Fairchild, *City Gardener*, p. 6.
[145] Thomas 1983a: 227–8; Rohde 1924: 70; BL Verney MSS, letter 23 Jan. 1661/2.
[146] Vanes 1982: 22; Kirby 1986: 132.
[147] Vale 1977: chap. 17; Brailsford 1969.
[148] LeGuin 1967.
[149] Spear 1932: 14; Rawlinson 1921; Aungier 1924: 185.
[150] Gale & Lawton 1969; Main 1982; Massarella 1990: 237, chap. 6; Mauro in Tracy 1990.
[151] Locke, *Educational Writings*, p. 319.
[152] Stone 1964b.
[153] Buck, *Third University*. Gresham College declined, however, as it could not change its statutes: see Adamson 1980: 13–25.

school did not, however, incline merchants to a serious appreciation of literature. The learned merchant was the exception and many were all too conscious that they lacked a literary education.[154] Campion in his funeral oration to Sir Thomas White thought it odd that a businessman should endow a college.[155] 'A life of trade', wrote Sir John Barnard, 'is almost incompatible with study and contemplation'.[156]

Urban culture was still predominately oral, though the printing press, introduced to England by a Merchant Adventurer, had standardized communication, encouraged introspection and made memory less important.[157] Business, which depended on regular correspondence, developed a specific and vigorous prose style which had considerable influence.[158] Concerned as they were with content and with ease and brevity of communication, merchants prized simplicity and practicality.[159] Some were gifted linguists and lexicographers, who mastered and translated European and exotic languages: Thomas Bowrey produced a Malay dictionary and John Scattergood a Sino-Portuguese dictionary.[160] Heigham Bright declared that 'he'll stand in need of a little Philosophy during the summer season'.[161] Streynsham Master wrote that in India 'we have much more Discourse of Religion, philosophy, the government of the Passions and affections, and sometimes of history then of trade and getting money for ourselves'.[162] A glover's apprentice and tallow chandler could become the sage of Salisbury.[163]

Businessmen exchanged books, read widely and both published and circulated their views in manuscript.[164] They contributed markedly to early statistical and economic analysis; but their subject matter also included politics, religion, philosophy, natural science, educational reform, memoirs, history and archaeology.[165] Merchants took an active part in the Society for Antiquaries, helped to preserve archives and modernized the writing of urban history.[166] Ralph Thoresby neglected business for his antiquarian and religious pursuits; Humphrey Warley

154 Nedham, *Politics Merchant Adventurer*, pp. 25–7.
155 Stevenson & Salter 1939: 116. 156 Barnard, *Memoirs*, p. 34.
157 Velay-Vallantin in Chartier 1989: 129–30; Baumann in Baumann 1986: 18.
158 Wilson 1960: 64–6; R. F. Jones 1930: 1005; Purver 1962: 99; Slaughter 1982; Kearney 1970: 46. 159 See p. 180.
160 IOL Eur. MS A.33, E.192. For translations and the absorption of foreign words through trade see Yule & Burrell 1907; Burn 1938; Sergentson 1935; Worth 1954: 312–14; Barlow, *Brief Survey Geography*; Bryant 1986: 49; Cioranescu 1963.
161 Bright 1858: 176. 162 Hedges, *Diary*, i. p. cccvi.
163 Bushell 1967: 6. 164 Thompson 1870: 15; Love 1987.
165 Tully, *Narrative Siege Carlisle*, p. 110; Stevenson 1984: app. B; Hodgen 1964: 418; Anderson 1989: 234; GLL MS 17145; Elliot 1981: 170.
166 Cain 1987: 7; Fussner 1962: 212.

was apprenticed to a tinner, but became an Assistant Keeper of the Bodleian.[167] A few merchants moved in literary circles; Isaac Walton was a linen draper and George Lillo a working jeweller.[168] The City had its poets, a tradition continued after the Restoration by Winstanley, and several merchants were amateur poets.[169] Gerard Malynes was well read and wrote in elaborate allegories; William Popple preferred literature to business, was a proficient Latinist and wrote poetry.[170]

Many businessmen were sedentary and became more reluctant to face the strain of travel as they grew older. But even the domestic traders moved outside their immediate locality at some point in their lives. Overseas merchants travelled to remote areas of the world before such journeys became routine.[171] They feature prominently among the travel writers of the period and they approached each new world with restless curiosity, even though some were contemptuous of alien ways and guilty of ethnocentrism.[172] Through travel and often long-term residence abroad, they had to confront other cultures. Even in the colonies of settlement, they exchanged ideas with less-developed communities; in the European settlements and some areas of strategic occupation in the Middle East and Asia, they were exposed to the demonstration effect of civilizations sometimes more advanced than their own.[173]

They were also interested in natural science and took advantage of their residence abroad to experiment, collect, and observe phenomena. Scientific manuscripts, exotic birds, fabrics, plants and animals were brought back to England.[174] In certain fields, such as navigation, dyeing and mathematics, merchants had a practical as well as an intellectual interest.[175] They were less affected by the prejudice against technology characteristic of the virtuosi and the amateur gentleman scientists.[176] Several were connected with the Royal Society which became a fashion-

[167] Thoresby, *Diary*; Thoresby, *Ducatus Leodiensis*, p. vii; Atkinson 1885–7: i. 19; Wilson 1988: 80; *Reliquiae Hearnaniae*, p. 303.

[168] Smiles 1884: 126.

[169] Bergeron 1967; SP 46/83; GLL MS 3386; Wharton 1979: 21.

[170] Robbins 1982: 6; Sanderson 1943; Lowe, *Diary*.

[171] Hakluyt, *Principal Navigations*, v. 204–5; Munter & Grose 1986: iv.

[172] BL Add. MS 10130; Surrey RO, Guildford Muniment Room, Bray MSS (540) 85/15/1; Arasaratnam 1986; Adams 1983: 58; Pagden 1986: 1; Steensgaard in *Intl Cong. Ec. Hist. X* 1990.

[173] Gillespie 1920.

[174] Birch, *History Royal Society*, iv. 328; Wheler, *Journey into Greece*, p. 199.

[175] Webster 1975: 352, 389; Taylor 1954: 89. The Merton thesis always depended on the links between science and transportation rather than with business: see Merton 1949: 611.

[176] The running debate on the relationship of scientists to craftsmen illustrates the tenuous links between business and science. While it is clear that contemporary scientists had a broad range of interests, they were fundamentally non-utilitarian and there was a real distinction between theoretical and applied science. See Houghton 1942: 56; Hopper 1976: 264; Kearney 1970: 143–4; Hall in Clagett 1959: 21; Pérez-Ramos 1988: 291; Jardine 1975: 237.

able club for businessmen with a high annual subscription of £2 12s.[177] Science was linked with national enterprise and an effort was made to recruit merchants, several of whom became active members in the 1680s and 1690s.[178]

The Royal Society, however, was dominated by Anglican university-educated gentry; only 7 per cent were merchants and tradesmen before 1700.[179] Many businessmen, who have usually been ill defined in the debate over the origins of the Scientific Revolution, were conservative, indifferent to science or without influence.[180] Mathematics and a mechanistic world-view had little to do with economic production; the slide rule was more useful to engineers than to mathematicians.[181] Science was primarily an intellectual exercise closely associated with the Universities and not connected with the Utopian idealism of men like Hartlib; the amelioration of society was seen as a moral and not a technical problem.[182]

A few merchants, like Sir Richard Gough, amassed important collections of books and manuscripts on every subject from patristic studies to pure science and technology, history, literature, theology, law, botany and the classics.[183] Authors dedicated their works to City magnates.[184] Levant merchants had access to the thriving antiquarian markets of Constantinople and Cairo.[185] Four libraries of merchants were sold at auction between 1673 and 1723 and the books and manuscripts of Thomas Povey passed to William Blathwayt.[186] Benjamin Furley, Thomas Craddock and Jacob Turner were real bibliophiles; Thomas Britton, a small coal-merchant, hunted for books on Saturday afternoons.[187] When merchants founded schools, they sometimes added a library with chained books, like Humphrey Chetham or Alderman Godfrey Lawson.[188] Lewis Roberts gave his patristic and classical library to Jesus College, Oxford and Sir Paul Pindar his Arabic and Persian manuscripts to the Bodleian Library.[189] Some of the guilds and the overseas factories

[177] Hunter 1982: 8–10.
[178] Kargon 1963: 338; Greenfield 1987: 107; Mulligan 1981: 346.
[179] Hunter 1982: 24–8.
[180] Mulligan *et al.* in Webster 1974: 232, 336, 368, table 1; Hunter in J. R. Jones 1979: 186; 1982; Shapiro 1975a: 136.
[181] Hadden 1988: 279; Hall 1965: 335; Bennett 1986: 25; Feingold 1983; Ross 1975: 66. For an opposite view see Jacob 1975: 171.
[182] Hall in Mathias 1972: 34, 44, 48; Gascoigne 1985: 422.
[183] Reeves 1956: 95, 101; Beecheno 1919: 76.
[184] Bennett 1970.
[185] Galland, *Journal*, p. 25; Oates 1986: 293.
[186] Gloucs. RO, Dyrham papers, D.1799/e 247, deed of sale, 8 Nov. 1693/4.
[187] Walker 1948: 112; Irwin 1958: 183; Cave 1973; Anderson 1989: 80.
[188] Fraser 1980: 18; Kirby 1986: 160; Kelly 1966: 72–4; Streeter 1931: 265.
[189] Hardy 1899: 61; CUL MS Dd. 312, letter from Thomas Davis to James Usher; Wood 1935: 88.

had their own extensive libraries, often stocked by gifts from factors.[190] Robert Redwood of Bristol provided a building and endowment for his books and Norwich had a library.[191]

The substantial financial outlay required for even a small library did not deter even modest tradesmen.[192] Copies of Josephius, antiquarian and historical works, meditations on religion, a description of the sex life of bees, and poetry were interspersed with the business correspondence and accounts of one London merchant.[193] Not surprisingly, many merchants were interested in cartography and collected maps; Daniel Thomas, mercer, had 740 books, models, globes, telescopes, maps and atlases.[194] The stock of Robert Horne, a bookseller at the entrance to the Royal Exchange, suggests what was in demand.[195] Thomas Bowrey had the works of Josiah Child, Thomas Hobbes, sermons, travels, the *Lex Mercatoria*, bibles, pamphlets, plays, statutes, law books and mechanical exercises.[196] Provincial merchants were just as comprehensive in their interests and John Cary even made manuscript copies of works which interested him.[197]

The frequency and size of merchant holdings must not, however, be exaggerated; only 14 per cent of Chester will-makers mention books.[198] The libraries of merchants do not generally compare with those of the clergy, lawyers and gentry. Before 1640, bibles and religious works are most in evidence; there were few histories or ballads or works of literature.[199] John Isham treasured his account books, but he was no scholar and it was his blind son Thomas who became a bibliophile; the same was true of the Rawlinsons.[200] Richard Archdale reinforced the bindings of his ledger with the printed pages of Cicero.[201] Many inventories do not list books at all, though it has to be remembered that they were primarily concerned with value, as represented by size and quality of bindings, and almost certainly omit ephemera and unbound, less valuable sheets. The interest of many merchants also inclined towards vocational subjects and entertainment. Handbooks and economic tracts, often in pirated editions, took pride of place.[202] Almanacks were common because

190 CUL MS Mm vi. 50, fo. 51; Ramsay 1957: 61–2; Fox 1880: 104; SP 105/145, fos. 157–64; Spear 1932: app. C. 191 Bridenbaugh 1968: 349.

192 CLRO, CSB 2; *Liverpool in Reign Anne*, p. 151; Plant 1974: 45; 'Bookseller's account book', p. 145. 193 BL Lans. MS 241, fos. 55ff. 194 Earle 1989a: 296.

195 Advertisement appended to the 1674 edition of Collins, *Introduction Merchants' Accompts*. 196 Anstey 1931.

197 Chilton 1979: 127; MacCaffrey 1958: 271; Portman 1966: 9–40; Cruttenden, *Astrological Diary*, pp. 42–5; BL Add. MS 5540; Lindley 1962: 146–7; Underdown 1992: 46.

198 Richardson 1974.

199 Stone 1978: 96, 103, table 4.4; Barry in Reay 1985a: 67; Upton 1921: 267–78.

200 Hallan 1967: 439; Gordon 1970: 282–3; Milbourne 1881: 93.

201 Berks. RO D/ED B 2. 202 Lowther, *Correspondence*, p. 133.

they included mathematical tables and information relevant to business.[203] Businessmen provided a natural market for ephemeral journalism – the newsletters, periodicals, jestbooks, tracts and ballads with their sensational accounts of monsters, accidents and trickery.[204]

Theology was dominated by the professional clergy; drama and *belles-lettres* by the landed interest. Merchants did not interact as closely with scholars and intellectuals as the Florentine businessmen of the Renaissance and there was no civic Humanist tradition.[205] Nonetheless, a few with talent and active minds were able to gain admission to the intellectual cliques; their interests were identical with those of other scholars. The direct and indirect contribution of businessmen to the advance of knowledge, given their small numbers and more restricted leisure, was proportionately as great as that of landed society, where learning was frequently despised and only a minority became poets, philosophers and wits. There was no qualitative cultural revolution in the educational system.[206] Although sometimes disenchanted with bookishness, merchants followed intellectual fashions and in some respects their exclusion from the traditional paths to knowledge allowed them greater freedom of expression; a few displayed sufficient curiosity and learning to qualify as universal scholars.

The fine arts

The business elite sometimes chose fashionable architects and foreign styles for their private residences and municipal buildings and churches, though the Royal Exchange illustrates how slowly new ideas were adopted.[207] Inigo Jones' design for Covent Garden piazza and the terraces in Lincoln's Inn Fields served as a prototype for the mansions of Sir Robert Vyner and John Lawrence.[208] Dutch influence was also pervasive, as evident in Eltham Lodge built by Hugh May for Sir John Shaw.[209] Native architects from Wren downwards were dependent on the business community, because English towns and guild Halls were built by private wealth, not by state patronage.[210] The houses of London merchants were generally sober and well proportioned with subdued decoration, though the great inns had a flamboyant design.[211]

Architectural innovation was also characteristic of some provincial towns which adopted planned development with wider streets and squares at the end of the century. King's Lynn constructed three

[203] Blagden 1958a. [204] Wilson 1960: 22. [205] Bec 1967b.
[206] Charlton 1965: 167; Russell 1977: 745. [207] Latimer 1900: 403.
[208] Tipping 1920: 407. [209] Louw 1981: 12; Haley 1988.
[210] Whinney & Millar 1957: 153; Harrison 1920: 543, 691. [211] Chartres 1977c: 25.

symmetrically planned public buildings around the old Customs House in the early seventeenth century to attract business and later erected a Merchants Exchange; private buildings successfully incorporated Dutch styles.[212] Henry Bell, merchant and architect of Lynn and Northampton, was a virtuoso who went on a Grand Tour.[213] Structures specifically designed for commerce were often more than functional, like the covered walks of the Tolzey in Bristol.[214]

But houses were usually built by local craftsmen; the design and decoration of their exteriors and interiors tended to be pompous, conventional, clumsy and crude. London had fewer public buildings than the continental towns and, with the exception of Cheapside, its streets were narrow enclosed private spaces; the shops and houses built between 1615 and 1675 lacked harmony and had a bastard style which has been described as 'artisan mannerism'.[215] Sir William Turner, to set an example for the rebuilding of London, put up a robustly ornamental house in Cheapside which was vigorous, but lacked elegance and polish.[216] In Whitehaven, the merchants resisted Lowther and Gilpin's plans for a square because they could conceive of open space only as a trading area. There were noticeable differences between the City and the new developments to the west, undertaken by landowners.[217] The houses of merchants were usually conservative and platitudinous imitations of the country-house architecture of Pratt and May.[218]

Some overseas merchants dealt in paintings and antiquities and mixed business with pleasure. They acted as agents for landed collectors in the markets of Amsterdam and Italy, where paintings were abundant and cheap. Sir Thomas Roe bought for Arundel and Buckingham in the 1620s; Sir John Shaw imported paintings for the King in parcels of fifty, including a Tintoretto self-portrait, a Vandyke and a Breughel the Elder.[219] Thomas Hill visited the Duke's Gallery in Florence and confessed 'my esteeme of pictures'.[220] When the City of London proved unable to sustain its monopoly of public sales and auctions, art dealers emerged in the 1680s and booksellers sold prints and paintings on commission.[221] But painting was still regarded as a manual craft whose

212 Borsay 1982: 4; Parker 1971.
213 Colvin & Wodehouse 1961: 47.
214 MacGrath 1975: 30.
215 Summerson 1970a: 155–70; Brett-James 1935: 42–3; Allen 1937: ii. 95; Tittler 1985b: 40; 1991; Edie 1966–7.
216 Summerson 1955: 43 concedes that the City became less philistine after the 1760s. Collier 1991: 32.
217 Power in Knecht & Scarisbrick 1978.
218 Summerson 1970a: 50–3; Whinney & Millar 1957: 225.
219 Bod. Eng. Hist. MS C.44, fos. 7–8.
220 Hill 1904: 131.
221 Robertson 1990: 406; Pears 1988: 57–60, 71, 77.

primary function was copying, decorating carriages and figureheads and illustrating arms.[222]

A few merchants were serious collectors who acquired the works of major artists. Thomas Dytson had a Hobbema and William Cartwright, actor and bookseller, acquired a formidable collection which he bequeathed to Dulwich College.[223] Cranfield, Sir Joseph Sheldon and Sir Richard Hoare built up substantial holdings and Sir Francis Child had forty-nine paintings.[224] The East Anglian merchants commissioned local artists and Henry Bell had a collection of art books as well as paintings.[225] Inventories of the more prosperous businessmen demonstrate that many had paintings on their walls.[226] In Tudor England religion was the most popular subject, but scenes of battles and women spinning and portraits of English and foreign rulers also featured.[227] During the seventeenth century, the subject matter broadened: John Freeman had fourteen paintings in his London house including one Dutch piece, two prospects, three landscapes, three pictures of 'Fowel', one hunting and one battle scene.[228] Not all purchasers were connoisseurs; the lesser merchants acquired what pleased them and what they could afford. Pictures were bought to fix over doors and fill in space; many of those mentioned in inventories would have been 'painted cloths', hangings, engravings or prints.[229]

The great majority of paintings were portraits of record and were not intended as works of art; Daniel Thomas, mercer, had six portraits in his house.[230] All the guilds commissioned or were given portraits of their officers and royalty; most of the portraits of merchants which still survive were painted to commemorate charitable donors or public servants.[231] Sir Hugh Myddelton was painted alongside a waterspout and Lady Myddel-

[222] Edmond 1978–80: 72–128. The inventory of an artist's supply shop is in CLRO CSB, Box 27. [223] Gage 1822: 166.

[224] Prestwich 1966: 90; Price, *Compleat Cook*, p. 13; Ogden 1955: 86–7; Woodbridge 1969: 786. Buckeridge dedicated his *Art of Painting* to Robert Child whose collection is inventoried in GLC RO Acc. 1128/107/177.

[225] Edmond 1987b: 109; Colvin & Wodehouse 1961: 61–2.

[226] ULL MS 553, letter 1 Aug. 1675; BL Add. MS 23199, fo. 28 ; Whinney & Millar 1957: 10; SP 110/16, letter 2 June 1684; 105/153, fo. 194; Woodward 1967: 105; CLRO CSB inventories; Marescoe, *Markets and Merchants*, p. 120.

[227] Foister 1981: 270–6, based on 613 inventories, 1417–1588.

[228] BL Lans. MS 1156. [229] Levine 1973: 480; Fieldhouse 1978: 284.

[230] Earle 1989a: 295.

[231] For some reproductions of portraits see Peele 1947–8: 240; Goss 1933: 240; Brett-James 1962: 793; G. C. M. Smith 1936; MacInnes & Whitehead 1955: 307; Price 1875: 18; Heathcote 1899: 104; Clode 1888: ii. 315–16; Reid 1966:, plate 1; Suckling 1848: 183; Woodbridge 1969; Stevenson & Salter 1939: 386; Heath 1869; Milbourne 1888: 93–5. Portraits of business ancestors of landed families, like Sir Thomas Cullum and Sir Thomas Kytson, were also preserved in country houses: see Farrer 1908: 147, 178.

ton sent the portrait to hang in the parlour of the Goldsmiths Company.[232] A copy of Kneller's portrait of Sir William Turner was made by Charles Beale for £5 to hang in Bridewell.[233] The tycoons favoured fashionable and expensive portraitists; Cornelius Jansen painted Sir Abraham Reynardson and his wife and Sir Henry Myddelton; Lely painted Elias Harvey and Kneller painted Sir Patience Ward, who was displeased with the result.[234] Sir Robert Vyner commissioned Michael Wright to paint his whole family.[235] But most portraits were mechanical stereotypes by hack artists and record rank rather than fleshing out the character of the subject. They invariably show businessmen against a conventional and stylized background without the intimate details of the counting house found in some Dutch and German works.[236]

Merchants also patronized the plastic arts. The Hamburg Company put up a Roman figure in white marble on the Exchange, which also received gifts of statues from the Fishmongers and Skinners. A bust of Thomas Evans, Master of the Painter Stainers, was commissioned from Edward Piero and one of William Dobson was displayed at Hull.[237] The tombs of merchants were also enhanced by sculpture. Sir Rowland Hayward's monument included his two wives and eight children; Baptist Hicks' baroque tomb at Chipping Campden, probably designed by the Flemish sculptor Jan van Ost, was raised on Doric columns.[238] Sir Thomas Smythe's monument had a canopy on Corinthian columns with an effigy and illustrations of navigational instruments and cargoes.[239] Some aldermanic monuments managed, however, to combine the worst features of every style and period.

Among the Levant merchants were many devotees of the classics and the Orient who collected relics of Byzantium and dug for statues at Smyrna.[240] They found antiquities for aristocratic patrons and rarities for themselves.[241] Their cabinets of curiosities were filled with inscriptions, coins and novelties. Aaron Goodyear, a London merchant, presented the Bodleian Library, in 1681, with a model of the Holy Places; the collections of the East India Company were one of the sights of London.[242] Daniel Sadler sold 'one cherry stone whereon is engraved 124 faces' to John Parson at Speed's coffee-house in Moorgate for £350.[243] A few merchants

232 Aubrey, *Lives*, ed. Dick, p. 198; Prideaux 1896–7: 159.
233 O'Donoghue 1929: 12, 156.
234 Clode 1892: 66; Strong 1969: i. p. ix; Sakula 1980: plate 2; Fry 1907: 72, 80.
235 Waterhouse 1953: plate 67.
236 Yamey 1989: 20; Donald 1989: 756.
237 Gent, *History Hull*, p. 58; Whinney & Millar 1957: 254.
238 Kemp 1980: 94; Jay 1933: 521; Esdaile 1946: 105–6.
239 Spurling 1955: 18.
240 SP 110/10, letter 6 Sept. 1688; Tavernier, *Six Voyages*, part 1, 33.
241 Howarth 1984: 11–13; MacGreggor 1983: 29, 34–5, 84.
242 Impey & MacGreggor 1985: 61–2, 257.
243 West Yorkshire Archives Service, Leeds, Bilton Park MS no. 272, 10 Aug. 1688.

had artistic sensibility, but they were usually indiscriminate collectors of ephemeral artifacts.[244]

Music, both religious and secular, was a primary interest of businessmen.[245] It was not unusual for them to play more than one instrument and to sing.[246] Song-books and scores were avidly collected for use; Thomas Hill, while in Italy, applauded the singing of the castrati and the choirs and collected 'books of airs'.[247] An astonishing number of factors and merchants took their instruments abroad with them, including harpsichords, and played them regularly.[248] Even shopkeepers like Roger Lowe were keen practitioners and every kind of instrument is met in inventories.[249] Sir William Turner's nephew was unaware of amendments by Henry Purcell in his twelfth edition and was ridiculed for being out of date.[250] Some merchants became impresarios; Thomas Britton, a small coal merchant of Clerkenwell, organized concerts in the 1670s.[251] Music featured in the guild and City dinners, waits and ceremonies, in the inns and on the city streets; even women could participate.[252]

It is always difficult to make objective judgements about aesthetics; accusations of poor taste often constitute the last line of defence of an embattled elite. Cultural snobbery has always followed those who are more interested in the mechanics of production than in art and design.[253] The art world became increasingly commercialized and cosmopolitan in England during the seventeenth century, but urban patronage did not unleash a creative explosion as in the Italian Renaissance or in the Dutch towns.[254] There is some truth in the common accusation that the English business community had no style. Merchants were not renowned for their patronage of the arts and they seem to have lacked elegance, imagination, vigour and originality. Standards of taste were set by the landed interest or rather by the artists which the aristocracy patronized and to whom they turned for advice. Business did not, as in Holland, develop its own symbolic domestic architecture. In most cases, merchants simply followed the example of landed society, adjusted where necessary to urban conditions and often after what was borrowed had ceased to be

244 Clarke & Foote 1936: 28. 245 Westrupp 1942: 22. 246 Mackerness 1964: 63.

247 Hill 1904: 124; Pepys 1965: 578; Tilmouth 1972: 143–9.

248 SP 110/16, letters 4 May 1690, 30 March 1689, 15 Feb. 1688/9.

249 Lowe, *Diary*, p. 11; Portman 1966: 110; *Banbury Wills*, no. 286; Earle 1989a: 296 found that one-tenth of his sample had musical instruments.

250 GLL MS 5301/A, fo. 37. 251 Hawkins, *General History Music*, pp. 790–3.

252 Woodfill 1969; Austern 1989: 430.

253 Coleman 1959. Two equally vacuous and incomprehensible attempts to link art with the marketplace are Bunn 1980: 303–4 and Fumenton 1991.

254 Ashton 1964: 139; Hauser 1951: i. 204, 465–8, ii. 558. Investment in culture may be inversely proportional to the intensity of the business spirit: see Holmes 1973: 114; Martines 1979: 174, chap. 6; Chambers 1971; Lopez in *The Renaissance* 1953; Goldthwaite 1994: 210.

fashionable. The business community made no real attempt to create a rival tradition.[255]

Business and pleasure

Vanity and ambition tempted some rich businessmen to pursue the life style of the elite and thereby enhance their dignity and publicize their success. They sought to enjoy the social returns of conspicuous consumption and their extravagance revived those fears of invidious comparison which in the past had provoked sumptuary legislation.[256] On the other hand, self-righteousness, inverted snobbery and repression persuaded others to disavow the cult of leisure as a badge of status, to regard frivolous consumption as the work of the Devil. The less prosperous either lived above their income and station or made a virtue of necessity. The behaviour of the majority of businessmen fell somewhere between these two extremes. They were preoccupied with the hard labour of earning a living rather than with gracious living. Even when they no longer needed to postpone consumption, most lived in quiet civility rather than in aristocratic splendour. Their leisure activities were not intended to while away time, but to better their lives.

It is difficult to quantify their standard of living. Household accounts, diaries and probate inventories reveal a great diversity of interests and a wide range of expenditure.[257] Although a persistent trend to save is evident, it cannot be said with any certainty that a standardized proportion of disposable income was allocated to personal consumption. A businessman of substance was expected to maintain a certain standard of display and to bear the cost of municipal office. Since taxation had a negligible impact, merchants enjoyed considerable discretionary spending power. London was a centre of consumption and Robert Herrick observed that 'those who do live best live nothing like to citizens of London'.[258] Rent was the largest single item and a fixed cost which, at £50–60 for a shop and up to £200 per annum for a large house, was much more burdensome in London. Wages and fuel (another major item) were also higher in the City, but food and imports were cheaper and there was less domestic space to maintain.

Leonara Marescoe consumed £1,500 per annum and the annual expenditure of the tycoons could exceed £2,000.[259] The usual range for a

[255] For a different view see Hill 1980a: 51; 1986: iii. 6.

[256] Lovejoy 1961: 129–229; Mandeville, *Fable of Bees*, introduction; Bowman 1951: 1–5.

[257] Business accounts often record minute details of daily outgoings, but do not break down large items of extraordinary expenditure.

[258] Thompson 1870: 14; Bog in Abel *et al.* 1966.

[259] C111/127 fos. 140, 162; Grassby 1994: 191; Marescoe, *Markets and Merchants*, pp. 152, 206; Clay 1978: 257.

rich merchant was £600–800 per annum and many of the prosperous kept their household expenditure below £500 per annum; in several cases it absorbed 10 per cent of income.[260] At lower levels of wealth, it took a higher proportion of income to support a more modest standard of living. The widowed Giles Pooley boarded out his daughter and lodged with an associate for £20 per annum plus £8 for clothes and 3s. per month for laundry and mending.[261] All businessmen had to cut their cloth according to their means.

Their quality of life certainly improved, but it depended on age, marital status, religion, family background and fashion. The life of an apprentice, unless supplemented by parental contributions, could be very hard.[262] In the early stages of his career, a merchant had to adopt Benthamite rather than Epicurean principles and devote himself wholly to survival. Whether living abroad as a factor or tied to an urban shop, his options were circumscribed. By the time that he was mature and financially stable, his habits of work and leisure had rigidified; success and marriage brought new time-consuming responsibilities and ultimately his capacity to profit from leisure was reduced by old age. Throughout his life, his needs, tastes and aspirations were conditioned by his environment and current expectations.

Many disillusioned writers dwelt on the futility of human desires and achievements. 'Happiness', wrote Donaldson, 'doth not consist in the having of abundance of this World's good things . . . a Person following a Plow or driving a Cart all day and going home to his course fare and mean Cottage at Night, may have as much satisfaction as the greatest Peer or Prince'.[263] This Utopia of agricultural simplicity and serenity does not exactly square with the poverty, disease and insecurity that was the lot of ploughmen and carters. But it does illustrate contemporary awareness that wealth did not necessarily bring satisfaction. The transitory nature of earthly pleasures was, of course, the stock-in-trade of the preachers who harped on the 'beggars in the midst of their riches'.[264] Since the qualities which brought success in business were not necessarily those which enriched private lives or enlarged human experience, business could smother the capacity for pleasure. John Pinney made a 'religion of his accounts' which satisfied his intellectual and emotional needs.[265] The natural instincts of a merchant could atrophy from lack of use and the demands of the marketplace could generate frustration and discontent.[266]

[260] WAM MSS 54, 114; Simpson 1961: table 4; Ellis 1981a: 4.

[261] Willan 1976: 123.

[262] Earle 1989a: 100–2; *John Isham*, p. xcviii; Beier 1978–9: 216.

[263] Donaldson, *Undoubted Art Thriving*, pp. 57–8.

[264] Younge, *Prevention Poverty*, p. 14.

[265] Pares 1950; Barbu 1960: 189–92 argues unconvincingly that this was peculiarly English.

[266] Hostility to the business world reflected fears that the legitimate emotional needs of the family and community would be frustrated: see Taylor 1955: 35.

Those bent on creating new wealth could easily confuse means with ends and embrace a shallow materialism.

Culture and personality are not a pair of opposites, but functions of each other.[267] The upbringing of many merchants did not prepare them for a life of independent leisure. 'Minds that are altogether set on Trade & Profit', asserted one commentator, 'often contract a certain Narrowness of Temper and at length become incapable of great and generous Resolution'.[268] Some were just men of simple, worldly tastes who were concerned more with the practical than the profound. They had no sense of beauty and no curiosity. Others, because of their religious background, looked on drama and art as either devoid of utility or a temptation of Satan. Many just lacked finesse, refinement and wit, focused on their accounts and eschewed intellectual endeavours. Not every merchant could reconcile freedom with responsibility or achieve an identity of life and spirit. It was often their children or grandchildren who inherited their money and entered the cultural mainstream.

Business had, however, a bustling pace which produced its own excitement and pleasure; many participants led purposeful and satisfying lives. They never chose to rival the gentry in triviality and decadence, but they displayed spontaneity, a capacity for self-expression, gentleness, sympathy and playfulness. Very few were misers and most used their wealth at least to pursue happiness. Although prone to complacency, excessive seriousness and self-deception, many were well-travelled and versatile men with breadth of mind and knowledge. When isolated in alien cultures beyond the reach of sea power, some achieved a serenity of life which eluded them in England.[269] Businessmen were both too diverse and too similar to men of other vocations to be defined in terms of a preconceived model with consistent attributes. In fact, they displayed contradictory characteristics – complacency and self-criticism, pride and humility, sincerity and hypocrisy, insensitivity and compassion, stubbornness and opportunism. Puritan values and individualism were also characteristic of a broad cross-section of propertied society. There were boring, intense, greedy and desiccated gentlemen, just as there were charming, relaxed, quarrelsome and effete merchants.

Sprat considered that men of trade had a 'flegmatic imagination'; Locke thought that 'recreation belongs to people who are strangers to business and not wearied with the employment of their calling'.[270] Those without independent means were obliged to give first priority to the demands of

[267] Baumann in Baumann 1986: 20. [268] *Present State of War*, p. 30.

[269] BL Add. MS 24107, letter from Sir Charles Hedges; HCA/13 Examinations 23, Interrogatories.

[270] Sprat, *History Royal Society*, pp. 67–71, 396; Hundert 1972: 16.

their occupation, not to their artistic or intellectual interests. The greater insecurity and personal nature of business made greater demands on time and energy than did the formal duties of lawyers, parsons and government officials. However intense their desires, merchants had little opportunity for mature reflection and self-improvement.

The dividing line between work and leisure may, however, have been more apparent than real.[271] Landowners preoccupied with advancing their families and estates hardly approached the Aristotelian ideal of civility as defined by the courtesy literature. In government, the amateur could imperceptibly acquire professional qualifications; even those without businesses or estates to manage had Quarter Sessions and Parliament to attend. Relatively few men enjoyed both a troublefree income from passive investments and freedom from the conventional duties imposed by high status. Even fewer had the intellectual interest and ability to turn their privileges to full advantage.

The great merchants certainly had a distinctive life style both in London and in provincial cities like King's Lynn, Bristol and Newcastle.[272] Like other professions, business had its peculiar rituals and patterns of behaviour, its special needs and routines. But it was the urban environment, rather than the occupation, which created the difference. There was no alternative, self-contained and schematic mode of consumption and leisure peculiar to the business community; indeed, each financial level had exact parallels in other occupations and segments of society. During the century, the landed and business communities moved even closer together. Gentlemen who came to live in the City during the season adopted the habits of the permanent residents; merchants who moved out to their country houses during the summer or in retirement adopted the patterns of rural life. The life styles of all men of property were increasingly determined more by wealth, temperament and place of residence than by social origins or source of livelihood.

[271] The ceremonial duties of the leisure class were also a mandatory form of work: see Brown 1959: 256.
[272] Bradfer-Lawrence 1929: 1555.

12 A symbiotic culture

Some historians have argued that England during the seventeenth century developed into a possessive market society, in which labour was a commodity, property rights were absolute, values were determined by the market and relationships were governed by impersonal contracts.[1] Others have traced this process back to the early Middle Ages.[2] Although neither the timing nor the course of this development is ever defined with any precision in the model, business is accorded a primary role in creating a capitalist culture. New groups do of course emerge in all societies and develop as independent subsystems with their own explicit or implicit ideologies, which define new objectives, introduce different modes of conduct and establish new criteria of significance. To what extent did the Stuart business community follow this pattern and serve as a catalyst for change? Did businessmen share similar expectations, set themselves apart and develop their own value system?

The city

The role of business had originally been formalized by urban institutions and it was citizenship which conferred on the man of business the status of burgher.[3] The medieval English cities, like their continental counterparts, had celebrated their emancipation from feudal society by glorifying their citizenry.[4] Until the middle of the seventeenth century, the cohesion of the urban community was reinforced by public display in the streets, churches and Livery halls, by pageants, processions, ceremonials and regular feasts.[5] Ritual dramas, like the Corpus Christi play cycle, functioned as symbols of solidarity; the solemn ceremonies of election and the

[1] Polányi 1957: 70; MacPherson 1962: 3–4, 162; Laslett 1964: 150.
[2] Pollock & Maitland 1968: 688; MacFarlane 1978: 198.
[3] On the origins of the term 'bourgeois' see Canard 1913: 35; Corcoran 1977: 479; Corcia 1978: 227; R. Williams 1983: 37–8; Thomas in Brown 1965: 186.
[4] Britnell 1991: 31.
[5] R. Smith 1962: chaps. 10–11; Luttrell, *Brief Relation*, i. 224–6; Withington 1920: ii; Crawford 1977: frontispiece.

swearing-in of officers were tangible expressions of citizenship. Playwrights, antiquarians and popular writers extolled the generosity, vitality and uniqueness of the urban community.[6] The chronicles of towns were written by merchants or town clerks and, after 1640, became historical and topographical; better record-keeping reinforced corporate memory.[7]

London defended its privileges against both Crown and Church.[8] The Lord Mayor sat wearing his hat and sword in the presence of the Bishop of London; high office in the City was regarded as the pinnacle of fame.[9] Local and regional patriotism also inspired and commanded adherence in the provincial towns, whose new city halls symbolized autonomy and authority.[10] Although life still revolved around the parish, York, Bristol, Leeds, Chester, Gloucester and Coventry (but not Warwick) had a corporate pride and resisted the influence and claims to superiority of their local gentry.[11] 'I am a citizen of no mean or obscure city', declared one orator who compared Gloucester to Rome.[12]

The corporate bodies which governed London and its trades upheld the dignity of individual members of the commonalty. In the guilds, freemen found mutual respect and a common sense of identity, reinforced by communal rituals rather than by contractual obligations.[13] Members dined together, pensioned widows and employed each other as business associates and executors; brethren were required not to cheat each other and to accept arbitration by the guild, even in domestic disputes, rather than sue in the courts.[14] Norwich required its aldermen to accept arbitration and dismissed them if they moved outside the city.[15] Civic culture was transmitted through apprenticeship and shared by all.

The incorporated commercial Companies, which were superimposed on the old guild structure, also sought to maintain harmony between their members and emphasize their mutual economic interests.[16] The factors of the Levant and East India Companies shared a camaraderie abroad and they dutifully acted as executors and maintained contact with each other after they returned to England.[17] Apprentices, though they belonged to an age-specific peer group, did not constitute a homogeneous estate, because they were passing through a temporary phase in different trades

[6] Heywood, *Three Pageants*, p. 56; Wright 1958: 121–34, chap. 2; Fussner 1962: chap. 8; Thoresby, *Ducatus Leodiensis*; Palmer, 'Business diary', pp. 202–5.

[7] Clark in Fraser & Sutcliffe 1983: 111–14; Barry in Reay 1985a: 871; Dyer 1977; Archer 1991a: 36; GLL MS 3454.

[8] *Stowes Memoranda*, p. 133; Tittler 1987: 487; Nashe, *Works*, ii. 83.

[9] Scott, *Essay on Drapery*, p. 8.

[10] Tittler 1991: 128, 158.

[11] Clark 1984: 8–9; Sacks 1986a: 77; Kirby 1986: 173; Hughes 1987: 16–17; Palliser 1979: 295.

[12] Riley 1976: 121.

[13] Brigden 1984: 94–5.

[14] Girtin 1964: 165; Sherwell 1937: 169; Warnicke 1974: 66.

[15] Evans 1979: 60–1.

[16] Meroney 1968: 228–42.

[17] Anderson 1989: 113.

with different career prospects; but craft solidarity was real.[18] Guild loyalty did, however, have to compete with the localism of ward, parish and neighbourhood where there was regular face-to-face contact.[19]

Civic patriotism had, on the other hand, always been weaker in England than on the continent. The towns claimed only modest rights and they displayed no strong desire to assert their power against the gentry. It was principally the lesser and more united crafts which identified with the city and its traditions; the oligarchs disliked the popular rituals which legitimized the system.[20] The distinction between town and country was, moreover, always blurred in England; textile and metal manufacturing was largely located in the countryside and Birmingham was really an industrial village.[21] The smaller towns were primarily markets for their rural hinterland and many urban residents, even in London, had agricultural interests and observed agrarian rituals, like Mayday; guild restrictions, the high overhead of maintaining urban institutions, and corporate responsibilities drove entrepreneurs to escape municipal jurisdiction.[22]

The unity of the medieval city had always been challenged by external trade and was easily shattered in ports, like Bristol.[23] After their golden age in the sixteenth century, the London Livery Companies steadily lost ground; some were simply too large for intimacy and others abandoned ceremonies like the passing of the crown and garlands.[24] The London pageants with their infighting between guilds over precedence became, after 1664, stale and less extravagant and their moral message was lost on the populace.[25] In the provincial towns, the interest of members in their guilds declined.[26] The miracle plays ceased in York in the 1570s and those of Coventry fell victim to a pluralistic society and a wider world; public drama was privatized and professionalized and no longer assuaged the tension of mobility in a hierarchical structure.[27] Some rituals were revived or invented, like the Godiva festival at Coventry or the ceremonies of Leeds; Norwich borrowed the London Lord Mayor's Show.[28] But they now had purely entertainment value.

The high turnover in the guilds and city offices of London, Oxford and Norwich always restrained the development of a self-perpetuating patriciate.[29] Since tax exemptions could not be acquired in England through

[18] Stevens in Slack 1984: 230–1; Clawson 1980: 381.
[19] Boulton 1986: 1–2; 1987: 228–33, 261. [20] Reay in Reay 1985a: 71.
[21] Because towns were centres of manufacturing, the term 'pre-industrial city' is ambiguous: see Dyer 1991: 59; 1979: 68, table 1; Burke 1975: 16; Gill 1930; Clarkson 1989: 26.
[22] Palliser 1978: 116; *Exeter in Seventeenth Century*, p. 33. [23] Sacks 1987: 4, 159.
[24] Nevinson 1974: 74; Archer 1991b: 136.
[25] Fairholt 1834–44: 97; S. Williams 1959: 11; Klein 1991: 24; Bradbrook in Coleman 1981: 66. [26] Dyer 1972: 151; *Newcastle Company Shipwrights' Records*, p. 18.
[27] Phythian-Adams 1979: 126, 276–8; James 1986: 38; 1983: 24.
[28] Sharpe 1987: 84; Kirby 1986: 141. [29] Reynolds 1977: 78.

purchase of office, no hereditary *noblesse de cloche* developed, which might have transformed successful merchants into a contra elite. More significantly, the city ceased to be identified exclusively with the business community. Even though the metropolis and the major towns expanded as centres of distribution, they acquired at the same time an increasingly important role as centres of political and legal administration and as resorts of leisure. Even the smaller towns became more pluralistic and cosmopolitan and counted among their residents members of the professions and those who had no direct connection with production and exchange.[30] Although most gentry lived on their estates and were prone to fulminate against the corruption of cities, the numbers of resident urban gentry grew and landowners were the primary consumers of urban services.[31]

The unity of the business community was more apparent than real. Differences of economic interest and function between merchants and craftsmen had always plagued the guilds and provoked political struggles.[32] The corporations were too closely linked with particular interest groups to act for the whole community. Those who speculated in stocks and government finance differed from merchants whose profits came from commodity sales. The tycoons had more in common with the great landed families than with either the middling businessmen or the minor gentry. The merchants, in turn, had more in common with the professions than with the mass of poor tradesmen and artisans. The business world was fragmented at both the urban and regional level and, in the conflicts which continually arose, each clique sought external support.

The polarization of wealth in the cities broke down vertical loyalties.[33] Although the financially successful could always rise to the top of the hierarchy, business had clear social boundaries.[34] The seating arrangements in the Halls and churches, the order of service at feasts and in processions, the wearing of gowns and robes, all reflected wealth, age and family.[35] Civic ceremonies upheld the principle of stratification rather than a sense of community.[36] Loyalty and obedience was reinforced through secular rituals like the Lord Mayor's Show which symbolized the honour and authority of the magistrates and Livery, not of the whole commonalty.[37] The elite liked to pretend that the community was united, but the ideal of brotherhood was hard to sustain when apprentices and yeomen were excluded from many of the rituals.[38]

The wealthier business families wished to publicize their success and

[30] Rose in Clark 1981: 177–8. [31] Pound 1966: 61.
[32] Swanson 1988; 1989: 165. [33] Cooper 1986: 38; 1992: 287.
[34] Burrage & Corry 1981: 391. [35] Tittler 1992: 223. [36] Sacks 1986a.
[37] Berlin 1986: 20. [38] Archer 1991a: 76; 1991b: 122.

distance themselves both from the mass of poor and from the tradesmen.[39] Even though they could suffer downward mobility through failure in business, merchants were hesitant about sharing the same value system as those whom they regarded as their inferiors. Although there were periodic infusions of new blood at the highest levels, citizens were segregated by economic function.[40] As urban society became multidimensional, businessmen could no longer claim to be the natural leaders of the whole community and there was no single reference group which could define the position of every citizen in a clear hierarchy. English cities lacked the sense of undifferentiated solidarity characteristic of the Dutch patriciates. The goals of urban residents became too diverse; the status quo might suit those who had arrived, but those who had still to make their fortune had an interest in destabilization. Those symbolic rituals, which still survived and which were evoked as nostalgic memories by John Stow, reflected past achievements rather than current needs.[41]

Mercantile custom

Business had always been differentiated from landed society by the fundamental distinction between realty and personalty.[42] Real property was bequeathed by will, passed direct to an heir and was equated with political independence; personalty, which included all chattels and most business assets, was bequeathed by testament and embodied individual, male ownership.[43] Landowners had acquired freedom of devise in the Province of Canterbury, but it was customary in towns and in the Province of York to limit the rights of the testator to ensure an equitable division of personal property between all the children.[44] Under the Custom of London, a merchant only had power to bequeath freehold land acquired during his lifetime and one-third of his personal estate, if his widow or any children survived him; the children were entitled to one-third, equally divided, the widow to one-third (and one-half if no children survived) as was the practice in the case of intestacy.[45]

[39] Palliser 1979: 134. [40] Sharp 1980.
[41] Phythian-Adams in Abrams & Wrigley 1978: 183–5; Pearl 1979a: 133.
[42] The distinction was never absolute: see Aylmer 1980: 96; Pollock & Maitland 1968: ii. 114, 117; Giesey 1977: 276.
[43] Pococke in Malamud 1980: 347; 1986: 64, 112; Postan 1935–6: 5; Spelman, *Reports*, p. 218.
[44] Alexander 1923–7: 419–28; *Testamenta Leodiensia*, app.; Watson 1989; Blackstone, *Commentaries*, ii. 492.
[45] Carlton 1971: 28–9; Glanville associates the Custom with the primeval belief that belongings were needed in the after-life. Vinogradoff (Crump & Jacob 1951: 292) cites a tenth-century Russian chief who had one-third of his arms and apparel and his favourite wife and dog burnt with him on his pyre. See also *Borough Customs*, p. xcvi; Hart 1930: 49–52; Swinburne, *Brief Treatise*, pp. 105–6; Sheehan 1963: 292–4, 306.

That merchants, both in London and the provinces, voluntarily divided their personalty equally is evident from testaments; William Cokayne even instructed his executor to show his books to the children.[46] As late as the 1690s, Joseph Collett and Edmond Sherman followed 'the laudable Custom of the City of London' and some merchants continued to prefer the Custom to settling a jointure on trustees.[47] The Court of Orphans of London enforced the Custom vigorously until the late seventeenth century and forced executors to set aside wills and settlements; the King had to intervene, in 1637, on behalf of the Prerogative Court of Canterbury, which had granted administration to Sir William Craven's eldest son.[48] Bristol and Exeter also adopted similar rules and the Custom was followed in the Province of York and in the American colonies.[49]

Merchants, however, increasingly tried to consolidate their estate in the hands of one heir.[50] The eldest invariably received all the lands of the family and the younger children had to be content with a few urban rents, some commercial stocks, shipping shares, some liquid capital and perhaps the lease of a warehouse.[51] The richer merchants began to adopt the forms of settlement utilized by the gentry.[52] Anthony Abdy followed the Custom for his personalty, but entailed lands on his eldest son; Samuel Ibbetson provided in his will that land left to his younger children would revert to the eldest.[53] Josiah Browne tied up his land in strict settlements 'to have the same continue in my name and blood, so long as it shall please God to permit the same'.[54]

Businessmen increasingly tried to escape the Custom, which limited their freedom of devise and divided their assets; as early as 1581, a private bill was introduced to abolish partible inheritance in Exeter.[55] For freemen who lived outside London, the Custom became a nuisance and freehold land was acquired to circumvent it.[56] Between 1660 and 1694,

[46] BL Harl. MS 1231, fo. 5v°, 38v°; *London Consistory Court Wills 1492–1547*, p. xxi; Willan 1953: 54, 57; 1959: 196; Heyward, 'Will', p. 129; Steer 1964: xi; *Bristol Tudor Wills*, p. 73; Cokayne 1873: 10; Shipley 1975a: 164; Souers 1931: 14; Levine 1973: 488; Youings 1968: 69; *Yorkshire Abstracts Wills*, p. 165.

[47] GLL MS 3547; Collett, *Letter Book*, p. 225; MacCaffrey 1958: 267; Lincs. AO Ancaster MS 91/D/11.

[48] P. E. Jones 1943: 357.

[49] Bristol RO 04426; *Bristol Great White Book*, p. 9; Hoker, *Description Excester*, pp. 460–71; *Lancashire and Cheshire Wills*, ed. Piccope, p. 172; *Testamenta Leodiensia*, app.; Swain 1986: 74; Carr in Land 1977: 45; Narrett 1993; *North Country Wills*, p. 183; *Lancashire and Cheshire Wills*, ed. Earwaker, p. 172; Kirby 1983: 42; Stephenson 1977: 282.

[50] Warnicke 1984: 65.

[51] Ramsey 1958: 407; Leathersellers Company will of George Humble; Reddaway 1963: 187; Carlton 1971: 25; Willan 1980: 95; Price, *Compleat Cook*, p. 7; Wilson 1988: 77; Willan 1959: 196.

[52] Erickson 1990: 30; Sisson 1933: 78.

[53] Bramston, *Autobiography*, p. 106; Wilson 1988: 82.

[54] Wadsworth & Mann 1931: 75.

[55] Elton 1986: 298.

[56] CLRO CSB iv, fo. 293v°.

only 56.1 per cent of testators followed the Custom and up to 1725, 26.2 per cent of London notables followed, 12.8 per cent waived and 61 per cent ignored the Custom.[57] Those who observed tradition tended to be younger, poorer and still active in business. The courts and the legislature recognized this change of attitude.[58] Chief Justice Hide was of the opinion that a freeman of London who discontinued his connection with the City and died, leaving his children and estate in the country, should be left to his own devices.[59] The Court of Orphan's powers were seriously abridged by 5 & 6 Wm & Mary c. 10, which removed the obligation of executors to pay Orphans' money into the Chamber. The Custom was abolished in the Province of York in 1692, in Wales in 1696 and in London in 1725. This rejection of partible inheritance removed a major difference between the business world and landed society.[60]

Continuity

If business was to acquire a separate identity, it was necessary for family firms to sustain a continuous existence over time. Genealogies, pedigrees, family histories and biographical dictionaries document a few business and artisan dynasties. There were many families which lasted for three and a few for four or five generations; the Childs and the Hoares spanned three centuries.[61] Only in the fifth generation did William Blois of Ipswich quote the text of Isaiah, 'In that day shall thy cattel feed in large pastures.'[62] Certain trades had an hereditary flavour.[63] Many merchant families had several sons in business often distributed between different geographical sectors.[64] A young man would join a family partnership, his predecessor would move up to head of the firm and the oldest partner would retire and send a son in his place; successive generations provided continuous representation in foreign ports and factories.[65] Businesses

57 Horwitz 1984: 226, 232–7, table 2; 1987: 280; Doolittle 1983: 48.

58 Carlton 1974a: 135.

59 Swinburne, *Brief Treatise*, pp. 105–6; Brandon 1845; Bohun, *Privilegia Londini*, pp. 186, 315, 323; Calthorpe, *Reports Special Cases*, p. 46; Pulling 1854: 185.

60 Goldthwaite 1968: 271.

61 Price in Dunns 1986: 369; Harford 1909: 33; Locke 1916: i. 119–51; Pollard 1954; Straker 1960: 162–5; Lang 1974: 31, 34; Willan 1953: 71; GLL MS 10822; Clarke 1973; Hoare 1955: 22; Hoare 1883; Durtnell 1974: 71; Houblon 1907: i. 335, 340; Jordan 1942: 380; Harrison 1920: 502, 540, plates 7–8; 1918: app. 2; Price 1962: 401; Hall 1949: 111–12; Rogers in Harte & Ponting 1973: 142; Power in Corfield & Keene 1991: 110; Ransome 1964: 236–47; Plummer & Early 1969; Barty-King 1991.

62 IESRO Acc. 787.

63 Latimer 1900: 409; Herringham 1932: 575–89; Keynes 1966: 130–1; *Wiltshire Textile Industry Documents*, p. xiii; Mann 1956–7: 253; Flinn 1962; *Foley Stour Valley Iron Works*, p. xiii.

64 Thoresby, *Ducatus Leodiensis*, pp. 2–5; Keeler 1954: 90–1; West Yorkshire Archives Service, Leeds, MS NN 2926; Fraser 1935: 231; King, *Staffordshire Pedigrees*, p. 145.

65 Lefroy 1980: 240; Ufford 1983: 13.

clung to the same location and passed on the premises within the family.[66] Declining trades were often treated like family possessions which could not be alienated or dissolved; capital was borrowed at high rates rather than admit new partners. Half of the London notables between 1660 and 1725 followed their father's occupation and every provincial city had its oligarchy of prominent families, reinforced by intermarriage.[67]

Businessmen normally educated at least one of their children for business. Sometimes it was the eldest who assumed control and the younger sons migrated to other businesses.[68] Thirteen of the Jacobean aldermen of London were eldest sons and, between 1694 and 1714, eighteen eldest sons of aldermen entered business, compared with thirty-six younger sons.[69] Even when a son inherited a landed estate, he sometimes remained in business.[70] It was more common, however, for business families to perpetuate themselves through younger sons and relations rather than through direct male descent.[71] Younger sons of gentlemen apprenticed their younger children to trade even when they had prospered and when the eldest returned to the gentry.[72]

But the three-generation cycle, first noticed by William Caxton, was still evident and it coincided with the period usually prescribed to acquire gentility by style of life.[73] 'We always begin young men here', wrote Josiah Child, whereas in Holland 'it holds from generation to generation'.[74] The ordinary tradesmen had little choice but to remain in their calling, but the grandchildren of prosperous merchants seized the opportunity to improve their status by leaving business.[75] Only nine leading families of York survived even for three generations and there was no continuity in Leeds or Norwich.[76] Only two of the twenty-five Shrewsbury families who served as Bailiffs lasted more than three generations.[77] Both the Oxfordshire and the Berkshire Knapps had members in business for

[66] Bennett 1988: 118; Reddaway 1963: 188.

[67] Horwitz 1984: table 7; Hall 1933: 104, 137; Welford 1895: iii. 37; *East Anglian Pedigrees*, pp. 15, 188; Roebuck 1980: 24; R. Davis 1964: 62, 26; Calvert 1978: 180; Clay 1894–6: ii. 779; MacHattie 1951: 292; Gent, *History of Hull.*

[68] Sheridan 1951: xviii, app. 4; Foster in Jaher 1973: 125, 135; Ellis 1981a: 180.

[69] Horwitz 1987: 272–6.

[70] Keeler 1954: 103, 321, 327; Scartlebury 1978.

[71] *Durham Wills*, p. 160; IESRO Acc. 787; GLL MS 10822; West Yorkshire Archives Service, Leeds MS NH 2926; Shropshire RO MS 224, letter to William Sharpe, 12 Oct. 1664; Lincs. AO, Holywell MSS, will of Sir Abraham Reynardiston; Barron 1906: 64–6; *London Visitation 1633–5*, ii; *London Visitation Pedigrees 1664*; *Dorset Visitation*, p. 43; Keeler 1954: 346–7; Harrison 1920: 699.

[72] *John Isham*, p. xc ; Raines & Sutton 1903: i. 3–9, 35–6; Reeves 1956: 95; Brunton & Pennington 1954: 58; Le Neve, *Pedigrees Knights*, pp. 191–2.

[73] Caxton, *Prologue*, p. 152.

[74] *Seventeenth-Century Economic Documents*, p. 73.

[75] Hoskins 1956: 8–9; Leland, *Itinerary*; Childs 1978: 189; G. A. Williams 1963: app. A; MacClenaghan 1924: 62, 68; Smythe, *Correspondence*, p. xii; Smythe, *Ledger*; *North Country Wills*, p. 183; Dawe 1950: 53.

[76] Palliser 1979: 154; Kirby 1986: 34; Evans 1974: 58.

[77] Mendenhall 1953: 165.

several generations, but the family finally succumbed to the law.[78] Those who settled in the West Indies often moved from trade into planting to enjoy the pleasures of landownership hoping eventually to return to England; the merchants of Philadelphia failed to perpetuate themselves.[79] Even alien immigrants, like the Huguenots, turned rentier in the second generation.[80] Several families moved not from clogs to clogs but from gentry to gentry in three generations.[81]

Demographic factors were partly responsible for the absence of urban dynasties in England compared with the continent.[82] Many businessmen had no male heirs or they died before their children matured.[83] Samuel Heathcote wrote to Locke, 'I am a Merchant myself and if it please God that I live so long, I intend to make them so too'; but his early death put two of his sons into the gentry.[84] Even when a male heir survived to maturity, he often had no capacity for or interest in business.[85] Another factor was the risk involved in transferring personalty. Businessmen could fall back on relations and the Livery Companies as executors; the Orphans Court protected the estates of minors more effectively than the Court of Wards. But the incidence of fraud was still such that testators were advised to distribute their property during their lifetime.[86] Wily partners could conceal books and thwart honest executors.[87] Even when the family assumed responsibility for liquidating an estate abroad, it was a hard task.[88] A dishonest executor could easily strip the personalty of an estate.[89] The decline of ecclesiastical jurisdiction, in the face of common law hostility, gave executors a free hand until Chancery assumed this responsibility and obliged them to account properly for their actions.[90]

If a merchant had no child or relative sufficiently competent and experienced to administer complex and scattered commercial interests, he had to liquidate his business and acquire safe, easily managed, institutionalized investments with a troublefree income before he died or was incapacitated by ill-health.[91] Merchants frequently had widows and orphans to consider, and they often wished to enjoy more leisure as they grew older.[92] Landed families, of course, also suffered from failure of

[78] *Knapp Family Memorials*, iii. 315, 329. [79] Nash in Dunns 1986: 337.
[80] Carter 1975: 85; 1959: 319.
[81] Mingay 1963: 106; Finch 1956; Browning 1944–51: i. 3–5; Parks 1928: 57; Northants. RO, Cokayne MS 2562, 2592–6, 2611, 2807, 2821–2, 2902, 2923, 3218, 3234; MacCaffrey 1958: 259–60; Barron 1909: 218.
[82] See pp. 312–13. For a different view see Hammer 1978: 20, 25–6.
[83] Jancey 1955–6: 143–7. [84] Locke, *Correspondence*. [85] See pp. 326–8.
[86] Holdsworth 1963: iii. 594; Roebuck 1979: 71–2.
[87] Sheffield Archives MS Pye 7 (b); REQ 2/299/13; Appleby 1979: 49; Anderson 1989: 88.
[88] Bright 1858: 202; Addy 1992: 84–5. [89] REQ 2/307/Rep. 15.
[90] Keeton 1958: 13. See also p. 214. [91] D. W. Jones 1988: 282.
[92] Some typical examples are C109/19; Simpson 1961: 116–17; Burley 1958–9: 291.

heirs and minorities, but the greater liquidity and fragility of commercial fortunes made them particularly vulnerable.[93] A business was too personal to be transferred as a unitary asset and management could not be separated from ownership and control.[94]

Land

That most substantial businessmen in all periods owned some land is evident from the Victoria County Histories and from numerous regional and urban studies, charitable bequests, family histories and private business papers. In every county, business wealth metamorphosed into land through purchase or marriage; the merchants of London, Newcastle, Exeter, Bristol, Gloucester, York, Leeds and Hull all had landed property.[95] Every county had its quota of landed families of mercantile origins.[96]

Although this process can be illustrated by hundreds of particular examples, the precise acreage owned by businessmen remains uncertain and, given the scale and complexity of the sources, the exact distribution of landownership will probably never be firmly established.[97] Of the Elizabethan elite, 85 per cent mention lands in their wills, but only 59 per cent of the notables and 67 per cent of the leaders had land outside London.[98] Half of the Jacobean aldermen acquired land for security and to endow their heirs; nineteen held more than five manors.[99] The surviving private records of businessmen suggest that between one-quarter and one-third of their assets consisted of land or urban property before the 1690s. Of the Orphans' sample after 1680, 50 per cent of the merchants and 25 per cent of all testators had land, though they were mostly smallholdings and some rich men had no real estate.[100] Business-men only owned a small percentage of the total acreage of England, but

[93] Hawkins 1982: 64; Bell 1953: 135–7; Hurstfield 1973: 332; Thompson 1990: 58; Daunton 1988: 270–1.

[94] Partible inheritance did not necessarily force the dissolution of firms; see Jackson 1972: 107; Hirschmeier & Yui 1975: 62.

[95] Hoskins in Bindoff *et al.* 1961: 166–70, 185–6; 1956: 9–12; Grant 1962: 200; Woodhead 1965: 52; Whetter 1974: 251; Hall 1933: 139, 266; *Durham Wills*; Macintosh 1991: 116; Hall 1957: 133; MacGrath 1949: 95; Clark 1981: 6; Wilson 1971: 17; Bouch & Jones 1961: 86; *Hornsey Court Rolls*; Bedell 1990: 36; Beckett 1977: 572.

[96] Macintosh 1977; Barnes 1961: 11, 20–1; Gleason 1969; Gage 1822: 106; Cliffe 1969: 462; *Mosley Family*, pp. 7–21; Willan 1980.

[97] The sheer volume of parchment has forced historians to sample or specialize by region and has precluded any authoritative overall survey of this question. For some illustrative examples see Heathcote 1899: 79; Coulton 1989: 97; Hicks-Beach 1909: 95; Webb 1962: 146; *Bankes Family Records*, p. vii; Mingay 1976: 6; WAM MS 54; Lancs. RO DDW; Anderson 1989: 86; Rowlands 1977: 49.

[98] Foster in Jaher 1973: 125.

[99] Lang 1974: 42.

[100] Earle 1989a: 153; D. W. Jones 1988: app. 2.

few landed estates did not absorb profits from trade and, as mortgagors, merchants had a substantial secondary interest in landed property.

Land was, however, often purchased without any intention of acquiring a country estate. A minority of merchants were active as middlemen in the market in confiscated land after the Dissolution and, during the Interregnum, others provided bridge financing and speculated without intending to hold their purchases permanently. Of the Adventurers in Irish land in 1642, 74 per cent were merchants and tradesmen.[101] Londoners and provincial merchants paid out over £251,000 for bishops' lands.[102] Less than 7 per cent of Crown lands passed to merchants and usually to those with interests in the locality; but four-fifths of Crown land in Northamptonshire was bought by London merchants for resale.[103] Merchants also bought 31 per cent of confiscated Royalist lands.[104] Speculation in real estate under more normal political circumstances followed naturally from participation in the mortgage market.[105]

Most of the real estate held by businessmen was adjacent to or within the towns in which they resided and consisted of small, scattered parcels and plots of three to twenty-five acres, which often served as home farms and country residences.[106] Only a tiny minority of businessmen, who already moved within polite society, had the financial resources to acquire an integrated estate and set up their eldest sons as country gentlemen; it was extremely difficult to accumulate sufficient capital in one lifetime and newcomers usually began modestly.[107] Indeed, many businessmen did not even acquire the freehold of their residences and business premises and they preferred to invest in leases of property to acquire an annuity.[108] The majority had no choice but to live and die in their places of business. The merchants of Exeter and Worcester had ambitions to join the country gentry, but few could afford to abandon their occupation.[109]

The scale of involvement fluctuated with conditions in the land market. Merchants were more active before 1640, because the fiscal needs of both the Crown and private landowners generated a high turnover of properties; land offered opportunities for capital gains as well as a hedge against inflation and attractive returns in income.[110] In the latter part of the century, participation by merchants declined as the land market shrank, rents fell, taxes increased and the price of land rose.[111] Although land

[101] Bottigheimer 1971.
[102] Gentles 1980: 589; Gentles in Gentles & Sheils 1981: table 3; Habakkuk 1978: 205.
[103] Gentles 1976: 208–9, 217; 1973: 622–6; Outhwaite 1971a: 31.
[104] Thirsk 1952–3: 206; Wheaton 1907: 243. [105] Martin 1980: 438.
[106] Beckett 1984: 12; Habakkuk in Bromley & Kossman 1960: 166–7; Habakkuk in Abel *et al.* 1966: 119–28; Rowlands 1977: 50. [107] Habakkuk 1981: 213–15.
[108] Newton 1966: 9. [109] MacCaffrey 1958: 260; Dyer 1972: 187.
[110] Habakkuk 1940: 511; Allen 1988a: table 3.
[111] Habakkuk in Plumb 1955: 144–6; Allen 1988a: 49; Clay 1974: 174, 180–1.

continued to come on to the market, thanks to the long-term effects of the Civil Wars and the land tax, legal innovations protected landowners from forced sales and enabled them to carry debt more easily. Competition from peers and gentlemen eager to extend and consolidate their estates also increased the number of buyers.[112] After 1690, prospective purchasers had to delay withdrawal from business because their capital was immobilized, but demand was simply dammed and, after 1717, tycoons purchased major estates.[113] The London aldermen continued to acquire land between 1690 and 1720 and London merchants were active in the Lincolnshire land market.[114] In the North-east, the coal industry fused landownership and trade.[115]

For most of the century, land offered the only safe form of passive investment. Although a landed estate was subject to outside interference before the abolition of the Court of Wards and liable to confiscation in extreme political circumstances, in practice it enjoyed security of title and physical permanence.[116] It is not surprising therefore that merchants should acquire land to provide for their widows and minors, to satisfy marriage settlements, to provide daughters' portions, and to endow their charities.[117] It also came in by accident or indirectly, through gifts, legacies and marriage, through forfeiture for debt and as payment for services rendered to the Crown. Land was a sound economic investment and was regarded during the seventeenth century primarily as a convenient means of income.[118] Country estates, when properly managed, could provide a return which approached that of the commodity trade; Irish merchants would not invest in industry, only in land.[119] Merchants sometimes balked at the low yield, but they could apply business techniques to estate management.[120] Urban land provided opportunities for building speculation; houses, when let to small tradesmen, yielded a more secure income than lending at interest.[121] Real estate could also serve both as collateral for loans and as a means of holding reserves against

[112] Habakkuk in Bromley & Kossman 1960: 159–60, 172–3.
[113] Habakkuk 1980: 214.
[114] Horwitz 1987: table 3; Holderness 1974: 574–5; Holderness in Wanklyn 1979b: 33–4; Rogers 1979: 448.
[115] Hughes 1952a: i. 79.
[116] Habakkuk 1952: 43; Davies 1978: 91; Allen 1988a: 35; Thirsk 1971: v. tables 13, 17–18.
[117] Essex RO D/DDC/A7; Gouge, *Serious Warning*, p. 27.
[118] Habakkuk 1981: 210; Primatt, *City and Country Purchaser*; Leybourne, *Platform Guide*.
[119] Roebuck in Mitchison & Roebuck 1988: 42.
[120] Thirsk in McGrath & Cannon 1976: 151–2; Wilson in Ward & Wilson 1974.
[121] Roebuck 1979: 36; Palliser 1978: 117. Hoskins 1963 found that merchants responded to increased demand for housing by subdividing urban property. Frequently, investment in real estate was an extension of, rather than an escape from, business, but only private papers can reveal the overall financial strategy.

losses in trade. Frequently it offered an escape from a declining trade or town.[122]

Some merchants regarded landownership as a route to Parliament and others as a route to the gentry; Maurice Wynn considered that it was better to keep sheep than to trade.[123] 'Men of all occupations and Trades', wrote Hartlib, 'toyl and labor with great affection but to get Money and with that Money ... but to purchase land'.[124] 'We that are merchants', wrote Child, who acquired an immense estate, 'can so easily turn Gentlemen by buying lands for less than twenty years purchase, let no Man expect that, if we thrive, we will drudge all our days in Trade, or if we would, to be sure our sons will not'.[125] William Penn said that he would rather have a country estate worth £100 per annum than £10,000 as a merchant.[126] Only by immobilizing his wealth in an inalienable landed estate, in which legal devices limited the improvidence of the life tenant, could a merchant preserve his labours and perpetuate the family name. Thomas Revett eschewed civic honours and concerns and concentrated on building an estate around the manor of Chippenham.[127] Often London merchants wished to re-establish roots in their home counties; Bankes, a London goldsmith, bought land in west Derbyshire 'that by God's good wyll and pleasure doth advance my name'.[128]

The purchase of land was not necessarily driven by social ambition: 'I hope its not presumed I intend att these years of Discression to turn country squire', wrote Pinney.[129] Merchants retreated to the country to escape the fiscal and administrative burdens of the City and to offer their wives and children peace and security; Thomas Sutton only left London when he was old.[130] Many of the country houses of the town oligarchs were more suburban than rural, appendages to city life rather than centres of an estate with pretensions to manorial lordship. Although his son did eventually enter the Kentish gentry, Thomas Papillon bought Acrise Place as a good investment and because it was near to his relations.[131]

Businessmen often acquired land without intending to change residence or abandon their trade; the attractions of politics and urban life were sufficient to keep all but 18 of 140 Jacobean aldermen from returning to their home counties.[132] It was possible to combine the management of a

[122] *Bristol Documents Illustrating Trade*, p. 8.
[123] Nat. Lib. Wales, Wynn MS 1088.
[124] Hartlib, *Directions by Gentleman to Son*, epistle.
[125] Child, *Brief Observations*, pp. 158–9.
[126] Dunn in Dunn & Dunn 1986: 38.
[127] Ramsay 1978: 535.
[128] Bankes 1943: 56–7, 74, 88; GLL MS 5105.
[129] Pinney, *Letters*, p. 80.
[130] Reddaway 1963: 187; Bearcroft, *Thomas Sutton*, p. 12.
[131] Papillon, *Memoirs*, ii. 37, 69, 97–8.
[132] Thrupp 1948: 127, 106, 222–3, 256–7; Willan 1953: 51–2, 72–3; 1959: 203; McGrath 1949: 93–6; *John Isham*, pp. xxxi–xxxii; Habakkuk in Goodwin 1953: 15–16; Stephens 1958: 154; Lang 1963: 8, 353; 1974: 40, 41.

country estate near London or a provincial town with part-time municipal residence and an active business.[133] Sometimes a merchant would purchase a seat for his son, but not live there himself.[134] The transition to the gentry usually occurred in three stages; first urban property, then agricultural land and then an estate. County families were often founded on land originally acquired for other reasons.

By the end of the century, the financial innovations of the 1690s had created the institutional framework for a monied elite. The stock and money markets were, however, still speculative and required as much professional expertise as lending on mortgage. Tallies had an uncertain date of payment and could only be liquidated at a discount before maturity. The government debt was not initially funded, but consisted of annuities and lotteries which were hard to sell and which were more appropriate for short and medium than for long-term capital.[135] Although secured by taxation, 40 per cent of the public debt, in 1714, was still funded by three Companies. A National Debt of easily negotiated instruments really dates from the conversion of 1717.[136] When peace reduced the yield on government loans and the Bubble discredited the stock market, land once more became an attractive option.

A distinct move from leases, ships and mortgages into stocks can, nevertheless, be discerned in the 1690s; only 6 per cent of assets in the Orphans' inventories were invested in leasehold property and 6 per cent in mortgages.[137] Company stocks and the Funds offered competitive forms of passive investment; Sir William Hedges' bequests to his children, in 1701, were all in the Funds.[138] The long-term debt was held predominately by London merchants, office-holders and self-made men who dominated the money market and government finance.[139] The directors of the public Companies were drawn primarily from an interlocking group of City families and, by the 1740s, an indigenous and permanent bankocracy had emerged in the financial world.[140]

The long-term public debt which evolved after 1690 did offer merchants a high return in relation to risk and a more easily managed income for retirees and dependants and those who sought freedom from the need to earn their livelihood. The Funds were particularly well suited to first-

[133] Bod. Eng. Lett. MS C.192, letter 27 May 1700; Whiting 1939; BL Add. MS 4224; Priestley 1951: 208–12; Shropshire RO, Betten-Strange MSS; Keeler 1954: 364–7; Stephenson 1977: 286; Ellis 1981a: 8; Hall 1949; 111–12; Som. RO, Hylton MSS, memorandum book; Bouch & Jones 1961: 86–7.

[134] Stone 1964a: 246; Lincs. AO Ancaster MSS; Kirby 1986: 163; Wilson 1988: 87.

[135] Neal 1990: 13.

[136] Habakkuk 1979: 207, 30; 1980: 206.

[137] D. W. Jones in Clark & Slack 1972: 327; 1988: 264 ff; Earle 1989a: 367 also found that mortgages were held by 7 per cent of his sample.

[138] Dickson 1967: 30.

[139] Holmes 1967: 159–61; Pope, *Prose Works*, iii. 123; Dickson 1967: 260–6, 279–81.

[140] Rogers 1979: 443, 450, as modified by Andrew 1981; Corfield 1982: 50.

generation fortunes and to alien merchants who had no roots in English society. They were held primarily as a reserve by active businessmen and could not have supported a leisure class large enough to challenge the landed interest. But the greater choice and availability of rentier investments did diminish the functional distinctiveness and continuity of the business community.

Social ambivalence

Merchants always had an incentive to reject a social order whose hierarchy of estates could not easily accommodate business and which favoured agriculture and those bred to conspicuous leisure.[141] As early as the fifteenth century, Richard Hill rated the merchant after Masters in Chancery, but before gentlemen.[142] Thomas Deloney's dialogue between a citizen and his wife convincingly voiced the claims of merit against birth.[143] The clothiers of Wiltshire held their ground against the gentry and the ebullience and self-assertiveness of the Bristol merchants were notorious.[144] The preambles to wills display self-confidence and independence; the great merchants used their marks like coats of arms blazoned on their funeral monuments, almshouses, bed-posts, ceilings, windows, door jambs, fireplaces and carriages, their pewter, glass, embroidery and token coins.[145]

The business community on occasion closed its ranks defensively and asserted its collective claim to recognition. Pride in commercial achievement was expressed in the legends and myths which embellished the splendour and reputation of the merchant princes. Merchants felt that they had earned their wealth and they were aware of the utility and productivity of their occupation; those who ventured overseas belonged to an international community whose sophistication was in marked contrast to the parochialism of country life in England. Puritan reformism and religious persecution also created a potential basis for solidarity and new reasons for hostility to the patrimony of landed society. The moral pride which apologists like Hall and Stow attributed to the London citizenry was associated with Protestantism. After the Restoration, the isolation of Dissent by the Clarendon Code created a distinct social group, cut off from the life of rural society and identified with business.

But businessmen usually suffered from a sense of social inferiority.

[141] *English Winding Sheet*, pp. 5–6; Clark 1983: 142, 184–5.

[142] Hanham 1985: 3. [143] Deloney, *Works*, p. 112.

[144] Ramsay 1969: 45–6; Conder & Were 1907: 273–82; Hall 1944: 139; *Bristol Worthies* 1886.

[145] Elmhirst 1964: viii; Manship, *Great Yarmouth*, pp. ii. 98; Keynes 1966: 128; Gray 1965: 103; Cotton 1872: 47.

'Look not in amitie with too many men that are above thy calling', wrote Browne.[146] Lewis Roberts, Thomas Mun and Henry Robinson recognized that merchants had a poor self-image.[147] The social illusions and insecurities of men of business were the stock-in-trade of Restoration Comedy; Molière was translated into English and propagandists played on social pretences.[148] Businessmen lacked that innate sense of superiority and self-assurance which centuries of supremacy conferred on the landed class and which successfully masked its personal inadequacies and commanded loyalty and respect. Merchants were often obsequious towards the gentry and the Court; their subordinate position was ritualized by many symbolic survivals of acts of domination and service.[149] A merchant who had married his daughter to a lord stood bareheaded in her presence until given leave to cover.[150] Since wealth and 'worship' did not precisely coincide, there was status inconsistency. Magistrates were not the social equals of the landed knights and esquires, nor were ordinary merchants on par with country gentlemen who always took precedence over the urban gentry.[151]

The self-respect of businessmen was continuously undermined by anticipatory socializing; they tended to adopt, not the values and manners of the community to which they belonged, but those of the genteel society to which they aspired. The merchant who 'speaks ill of gentlemen', wrote Gainsford, 'committeth an error when all that he labours for is to be esteemed so, or at least to leave his son so'.[152] They were ambivalent towards a society whose norms were disregarded but whose acceptance was craved. If they sought emancipation from communal traditions which impeded acquisition, they did not wish to cut themselves off from their own society. They accepted conventional values and the social hierarchy, provided that sufficient provision was made for their own mobility and advancement. Merchants imitated the etiquette of the courtesy books, infiltrated county families and acquired country houses and life styles.[153]

Even Non-Conformists betrayed a touch of wishfulness about their social origins. Oliver Heywood wrote: 'tis possible we might spring from some younger brother of the house of Heywood of Heywood an ancient

[146] Browne, *Marchant's Avizo*, p. 63.
[147] *Select Collection Early Tracts Commerce*; Jordan 1942: 218.
[148] Ravenscroft, *Citizen Turned Gentleman*.
[149] Ellis 1981a: 213.
[150] Wedgwood 1955: 53.
[151] Chalklin 1965; 8; Kirby 1983: 33; Cressy 1976b: 30; Hexter 1968: 52; Squibb 1981: 45; Stone in Forster & Greene 1970: 62.
[152] Gainsford, *Rich Cabinet*, p. 90v°.
[153] Whigham 1984: 5; Curtin 1985: 422; Palliser 1979: 99; Goring in Ives 1978: 214; Plumb 1967: 141; Gleason 1969: 195; Samaha 1974: 70; Everitt 1961: 40; *Banks Family Letters*, v; Stone in Aydelotte *et al.* 1972: table 7, as revised by Spring 1985: 153–4.

Esq.'.[154] Defoe wrote effusively about the conflict between godliness and acquisition, but his characters were more interested in gentility than in wealth.[155] The merchants of the Chesapeake and the Caribbean were driven by profit, often uncivilized and not committed to permanent settlement; in New England there was resistance to commercial initiatives and the abundance of land gave it less cachet.[156] But English merchants were still attracted to Virginia by the prospect of large estates and the great planters of Barbados and the Chesapeake adopted a sedentary life and vestiges of an aristocratic style; Samuel Shrimpton of Boston lived like a gentleman.[157]

Businessmen avidly sought titles of honour. It was extremely rare for an active merchant to be made a peer, as this was considered too high an honour, though the second generation was sometimes elevated.[158] It was more common for both London and provincial merchants to purchase baronetcies; of 417 baronets, 1611–49, 49 were merchants and 21 sons of merchants.[159] Knighthoods were easily acquired by performing a stint of public service, though some had links with adventuring overseas: Edward Des Bouverie was knighted on board ship, in 1685.[160] Le Neve could not resist the occasional disparaging comment, such as that on Sir Richard Ryves: 'his father was a tradesman in Shaftsbury of no family'.[161] Heraldry was the ritual language of power and grants of arms continued to recite the qualities of virtue and courage, though they in practice recognized wealth and political importance.[162] The Livery Companies and Corporations were obsessive about their arms and paid heavily for confirmation.[163] In Norwich, aldermen who were armigerous emphasized this distinction; Ralph Starkey, merchant of London, made a hobby of collecting the pedigrees and coats of London merchants.[164] Sir Edward Barkham's funeral monument depicted him in a gown over knightly armour.[165]

Often merchants simply borrowed their plumage; as Henry Dethick commented, 'all have arms, though few are Gentlemen'.[166] The Visitations of the Heralds reveal that merchants frequently assumed titles,

[154] Heywood, *Autobiography*, i. 17. [155] Shinagel 1968: 125–6; Earle 1976: 159.

[156] Brindenbaugh 1972: 345; Dunn 1972; Green 1988: 26–7, 36; Breen 1975: 27; Quinn and Dunn in Quinn 1982: 127, 243–5; Jeaffreson, *Papers*, i. 16; Puckrein 1984: 27, 65; Atherton 1939: 30–1; Bailyn 1964: 102–3.

[157] Bailyn 1964: 192; Craton in Bailyn & Morgan 1991: 327; Lockridge 1970: 157–61; Bushman in Greene & Pole 1984: 345–83; MacCusker & Menard 1985: 10; Middlekauf 1976. [158] *Gent. Mag.* (1732), p. 1014; Ramsay 1975: 155.

[159] Stone 1964a: 190; 1958: apps. 1–2; Eerde 1961: 145; *Leicester Roll Mayors*, p. 98.

[160] Shaw 1906: ii. 264. [161] Le Neve, *Pedigrees Knights*, p. 177.

[162] Sayer 1979: 6; MacCulloch 1986: 119.

[163] Peele 1947–8: 240; GLL MS 3342; Bromley & Child 1960.

[164] Evans 1979: 51; Bod. Eng. Misc. MS C.14. [165] Peck in Orgel & Lytle 1981: 143.

[166] Styles 1978: 147.

invented pedigrees and usurped arms, sometimes for use at the funerals of their wives.[167] Dugdale noted that usurpation was more likely to occur 'if their name doth sound anything like that of a gentleman'.[168] Humphrey Chetham procured a coat of arms which unfortunately belonged to another family.[169] The Heralds usually upheld merchants who served in municipal office or married into ancient families and they often conspired to ignore fictitious ancestry. The English system always condoned the elevation of rich men over time through appropriate channels if they accepted the ruling value system.

The social ambitions of merchants were inspired as much by family loyalty as by individual vanity. Like landed families, they respected their ancestors and they used their wealth to perpetuate and advance the status of their line. Pride in family, instead of reinforcing their sense of identity and occupational self-worth, encouraged social climbing and imitation.[170] Since daughters had a better chance than sons of improving a family's status through marriage, merchants were often tempted to produce large portions at the expense of the family business and of the sons, who alone could continue the family name. This desire for emulation did reinforce the acquisitive instinct, but it also weakened the capacity of business to resist absorption.

Even when they intended their eldest for the gentry, merchants could still place their younger sons in business. Indeed, by favouring primogeniture, they faced the same problem of provision as did landed families. Families with several sons did try to place one in trade and the majority of sons of Bristol merchants were still apprenticed after grammar school.[171] George Wansey, in 1713, was thought 'well suited for academical studies for which he was pretended . . . but my father wanting him at home, it was judged best that he should be with him in the business'.[172] But trade was risky and had limited opportunities, especially for children of mediocre talent. Some sons were simply put out to grass or allowed to pursue their fancies.[173] Lodge, who inherited £300 per annum from his father, a Leeds merchant, went to Cambridge and on a tour of Venice with Thomas Belassis and became an artist.[174]

But most chose to educate and train their offspring for a career, rather than simply settling annuities on them. Sons were educated for a

[167] Latimer 1904; MacCaffrey 1958: 279–80; Wagner 1975: 46–7; Ryan 1981: 532; Squibb 1978: 12–25; *Heraldic Cases*, pp. 106, 110; *Cely Letters*, p. x.

[168] Dugdale, *Antient Usage Arms*.

[169] Raines & Sutton 1903: 102.

[170] Dyer 1972: 187.

[171] Holmes 1977: 88–9; Barry in Reay 1985a: 65; Ellis 1981a: 197; Cooper 1992: 292.

[172] *Wiltshire Documents Textile Industry*, p. xiii.

[173] Kirby 1983: 42; Walmsley 1991: 3.

[174] Vertue, *Notebooks*, pp. 74–5; Atkinson 1885: 159.

profession, even by an illiterate father like Robert Brerewood.[175] Thomas Pitt wished to 'render them more acceptable in the world . . . and able to get their livelyhood for which I will stand noe charge'.[176] Although admission to the Universities and Inns, after 1603, was theoretically limited to gentlemen, the educational system provided an avenue of mobility for the sons of businessmen; colleges in practice drew the line at husbandmen and registered plebeians as *generosi*.[177] The notables of London and York sent their children to university, often via urban schools like St Paul's and Manchester Grammar School.[178] Sons of merchants certainly constituted a substantial proportion of undergraduates; at Caius, Cambridge, they rose from 6 per cent in the 1600s to 23 per cent in the 1620s before falling to 16 per cent in the 1630s.[179]

Sons of merchants were outnumbered at the Inns by the gentry. Only 108 were admitted, 1590–1630, and usually they were eldest sons; they constituted only 7 per cent of barristers and 11.9 per cent of Benchers compared with 55 per cent from the gentry.[180] There was, however, an increase in the 1630s and a change after 1680, when overall numbers of admissions fell; the proportion of entrants from business (mainly eldest sons) rose to 6 per cent and, when the urban gentry are disregarded, an increase in plebeians becomes apparent.[181] Four merchants and thirty-four citizens also became civil lawyers.[182]

Merchants, concerned about the risks of business, had always spread their younger children between the professions.[183] The law was usually the first choice; Peter King, son of an Exeter grocer, was apprenticed to business, but sent to read law at Leiden on the advice of Locke and ultimately became Lord Chancellor.[184] Many children pursued careers in both central and local government; Etherege was the son of a London vintner and was originally apprenticed to a glass-seller, but he became a

175 Woodward 1967: 103. 176 Hedges, *Diary*, ii. p. lxix.

177 MacConica 1977: 124–7.

178 Palliser 1979: 176; Mumford 1919: 48; *St Paul's School Register*, p. xxiii; Goring in Ives 1978: 221; *Liverpool in Reign Anne*, p. 140; Harte & Ponting 1973: 145; Stratford 1867: 9; Whitelocke, *Liber Famelicus*, pp. 4–6; Heywood, *Autobiography*, p. 21.

179 Stone 1974: 20; Curtis 1959: 60–1; MacConica 1986: 729; 1973: 547; Cressy 1970: 115; Simon 1963: 63.

180 Prest 1972; 1986: table 4.1; Stone & Stone 1984: fig. 7.7; Stone 1964: 58–9, table 4.

181 See table 12.1. Lemmings 1990: 163, table 1.1–1.2, 6.2 a–b; businessmen are not clearly distinguished in the data from other plebeians. Lucas 1974: 239 underestimates the plebeians. 182 Levack in Prest 1981: table 5.2; 1973: 11, 16.

183 Defoe, *Novels and Selected Writings*, viii. 9; Bramston, *Autobiography*, p. 106; Robinson, *Autobiography*, p. 5; Ferguson 1972: 199; Clode 1872: 11, 391; Lincs. AO Holywell MSS; *Durham Wills*, iv. 160; Cholmely, *Memoirs*, p. 7.

184 Shropshire RO 1224, letter of William Sharpe to Mary Brooks, 12 Oct. 1664; Mousley 1958–9: 477; Harrison 1920: 692; Yonge, *Diary*, p. ix; Jacobsen 1932: 36; Ryder, *Diary*, p. 4; Greene, *Diary*, p. 386; Hoskins 1935: 193, 99; Cranston 1957: 3–5.

Table 12.1. *Sons of merchants admitted to the Middle Temple, 1620–1719*

	No.	Total entry	%	No. called	Percentage (no.) who were eldest sons	
1620–29	4	520	0.77	1	50	(2)
1630–39	7	560	1.25	0	57	(4)
1640–49	3	460	0.65	0	33	(1)
1650–59	8	570	1.40	3	37	(3)
1660–69	13	680	1.91	3	69	(9)
1670–79	11	700	1.57	3	45	(5)
1680–89	37	700	5.29	11	73	(27)
1690–99	57	810	7.04	13	49	(28)
1700–09	39	800	4.88	8	77	(30)
1710–19	38	760	5.00	10	63	(24)
Total	217	6560	3.31	52	61	(133)

Note: The parents include 20 aldermen and 118 merchants of London, 12 from Ireland, 13 from across the Atlantic, 7 from Bristol, 38 from other provincial towns, 1 from Edinburgh and 4 foreigners. Eight had distinguished legal careers. The number of sons of merchants is understated because many described themselves as gentlemen. Many families sent more than one son and others appear in the register of more than one Inn.
Source: Calculated from *Middle Temple Register of Admissions*.

proctor in the Court of Arches and eventually a diplomat.[185] The highest positions in the Church were occasionally within reach; four Jacobean bishops were sons of merchants and 2.6 per cent of the bishops, 1660–88, were sons of farmers, craftsmen and tradesmen.[186] Others joined the Puritan ministry and even went to New England.[187] Although soldiering was infrequently chosen as a career before the 1690s, many famous naval officers were sons of merchants or ship-masters.[188] Others became physicians, scholars, schoolmasters and even playwrights and actors.[189]

Mobility and integration

Some historians have disputed that England was an open society.[190] One consequence of the Civil War was that institutions were fossilized for two centuries and there does seem to have been less movement between the aristocracy (as distinct from the gentry) and business in the eighteenth century.[191] The division between propertied society and the masses was certainly a permanent fault line and there was always social tension between businessmen and other groups.[192] The free movement of individuals, whether within or from outside society, was widely feared, because it threatened social homogeneity and created instability. The preachers had long associated social climbing with covetousness and each generation of writers lamented the decay of old families.[193] Contemporaries were wary of change and clung to the fiction of an organic and static social structure in which everyone had a predetermined place.[194]

185 Lehmberg 1964: 4; Alsop 1979a: 33; Etherege, *Letter Book*, p. 2; Coleman 1963: 132; Corie, *Correspondence*, p. 7.

186 Brook 1962: 1; Carlton 1987: 3; Fincham 1990: 19; Simon 1968: 48; Holmes 1982: 90. See also p. 274.

187 Waterhouse 1975a: 473; *Yorkshire Diaries*, p. 24.

188 Healey 1992: 22; Williamson 1969: chap. 2; Willan 1959: 203; Patterson 1976: 39; Andrews 1991: 142; Holmes 1982: 269.

189 Birken 1987: 205; Burnby 1983: 108; Feingold 1990; Lawson 1963: 81; Cressy 1980: 36; Lawless 1977: 515; Forse 1990: table 1; Hodges 1941: 5.

190 Advocates of the view that England was a closed society similar to other *anciens régimes* include Cannon 1984; 1988; Bush 1984; Colley 1986: 369. Stone & Stone 1984: 403 regard an open gentry as a 'hoary myth'; they accept the integration of the landed interest with the professions, but not with business, though their porous generalizations frequently contradict each other. The reverse view is argued by Perkin 1969: chap. 2; 1985; Spring 1986; 1985; Beckett 1986. See also Kaniss 1981; Neale 1981: 8. Only patrilinear extinction, new creations and intermarriage can prevent rigidification of an hereditary estate. But the acid test of an open society is the degree of downward mobility, without which upward mobility can only dilute the exclusiveness of an established elite which, by definition, must represent a small percentage of the population. England had a unified elite, but not a 'classless society', an idea which can be traced back to Maitland; see Pollock & Maitland 1968: ii. 274. Anti-business snobbery does appear to have been much more characteristic of Victorian than of seventeenth-century England.

191 Kenyon 1988: 246; Habakkuk in Baugh 1975: 12.

192 Supple in Ives 1968.

193 Crowley, *Way to Wealth*.

194 Tillyard 1947: 94; Benbow 1980: 112.

Other historians have emphasized the conflict between the landed and monied interests.[195] Friction between the gentry and the merchants was certainly generated by jealousy of new wealth and by the fact that land bore the burden of direct taxation.[196] Landowners feared that City lenders would exploit their need for loans and that the monied interest would reduce the value of land.[197] The landed interest felt sufficiently aggrieved to pass the Game Laws and the Property Qualification Bill of 1711.[198] But the most successful businessmen were confidants of the Court and the nobility and, even if a merchant, turned landowner and gentleman, faced some snobbery and other difficulties of adjustment to rural life, his children could marry into the gentry and were easily absorbed. It was the directors of the Bank and the Companies, the government financiers and the Wilhelmite civil and military officers whom the gentry feared and attacked, not the commodity traders and manufacturers. In 1696, the property qualification proposed for Parliament was £5,000, excluding stocks, for bona fide merchants who had traded for at least seven years. Landowners did not feel threatened by social dilution or vulnerable to business wealth, because merchants were relatively few in number and anxious to enter, not to destroy, the privileged world of landed society.[199]

There remained a surprising ease of communication and frequency of contact between land and trade. The gentry maintained regular and friendly relations with the civic elites and with business families of comparable wealth, even if they did not concede complete equality; in 1698, peers walked in procession at the funeral of Alderman Sir Thomas Fowke.[200] Country gentlemen mixed freely with the merchants in the towns and they maintained houses in London, Lincoln, York and Durham, though not in other towns like Bristol.[201] Their children went to the same schools in the towns.[202]

As many pamphleteers pointed out, 'trade and land go hand in hand as to their interest'.[203] As agricultural producers, landowners had always been involved with the commodity markets of the regional towns and,

[195] Holmes 1967: 159–61; Speck 1966: 127; Holmes & Speck 1967, as modified in Holmes 1969: 135; Speck 1970: 6; Holmes in Cannon 1981: 19, 23; Namier 1957: chap. 1.

[196] Whetstone, *Mirour for Magistrates*, p. 12. The epithets were subdued: the usurer was called a 'trim merchant' and the landed rascal a 'jolly gentleman'. On Bolingbroke's diatribe against the merchant interest see Burtt 1993: 100–1.

[197] Dickson 1967: 29.

[198] Wren, *Considerations Harrington's Oceana*, pp. 14–15, 86–9; Munsche 1981: 18.

[199] Ascending individuals and groups always have the choice of fighting or joining those above them: see Sorokin 1927: 133–4.

[200] MacCaffrey 1958: 279; Stone & Stone 1984: 240; A. H. Smith 1974: 15.

[201] Everitt 1973: 57; Holmes 1980a: 15.

[202] O'Day 1982: 37; Pound 1986a.

[203] Cary, *Essay on Trade*, p. 20; *England's Great Happiness*, pp. 10–13; Wright, *Passion of Minde*, p. 304.

since the heyday of the Staple, had an economic stake in foreign trade. Their borrowing needs brought them into close and regular contact with the London merchants, and their methods of estate management both drew from and contributed to business. The gentry could not sensibly despise merchants or ignore merit, when business provided employment for their children and financial services for their estates. There was much truth in Bethel's claim that the apprenticeship of younger sons allowed landed families to concentrate their estates.[204] The legal and commercial training of younger sons of the gentry helped families to adjust to a new economy; they provided important advice on the purchase of urban property and served as marketing agents for estate produce and minerals.[205] The business community, for its part, did not regard the gentry as an economic threat, because gentility was personal rather than legal and conferred no fiscal privileges which would have created unfair competition. As the more dynamic towns aggressively colonized their hinterland, merchants formed matrimonial and business alliances with gentry families.[206]

The mutual conversion of gentlemen and merchants was a self-perpetuating and self-maintaining process.[207] Continuous interaction, in turn, accelerated the rate of migration and cross-fertilization. Mobility reduced regional differences; the clergy for example did not usually acquire livings in the parish of their birth.[208] From the Elizabethan, William Harrison, to the Stuart tycoon, Sir Josiah Child, a series of commentators noted that reciprocal advantage governed the mutual exchange of men, habits and ideas between business and landed society.[209] Waterhouse maintained that 'as all Sumptuary Laws are vanished by the mixture of gentry with the plebs in Corporations; so ought all grudges between the Court and the City gentry to be cessated'.[210] Foreign observers commented on this unusual alliance between noble and bourgeois which has also perplexed Marxist historians.[211]

The assimilation of all potential rivals by the landed gentry created a united propertied interest which embraced business, agriculture and the professions.[212] Similar and complementary ambitions and needs allowed

204 Bethel, *Interest of Princes*, p. 8. 205 Roper 1946: 47.
206 Clark 1981: 6; Chalklin in Chalklin & Worden 1989: 102, 115; Chalklin & Havinden 1974: 247–8.
207 Defoe, *Novels and Selected Writings*, viii. 9; Coade, *Letter Commissioners of Trade*, p. 21.
208 Cornwall 1967: 11–12.
209 Harrison, *Description of England*, p. 115; he put the merchants after the gentry and the phrase 'mutual conversion' does not occur in the first edition. Defoe, *Compleat English Gentleman*, p. 262; Pocock 1972a; Lucas 1973; 92.
210 Waterhouse, *Gentleman's Monitor*, p. 71.
211 Mousnier 1955: 8; Dobb 1946: 120; K. G. Davies 1962; MacKeon 1987: 166.
212 Fletcher & Stevenson 1985: 4.

both merchants and gentry to compromise, co-operate and harmonize their family and regional interests.[213] What linked and bound both parties was the migration of younger sons, who took up residence in the towns either as businessmen or as professionals. Mobility was downward as well as upward.[214] Many scions of the gentry did not return to the land because they lacked either the means or the desire, and through marriage and business connections they became indistinguishable from other city men. But urban gentlemen remained an integral part of the county families from which they sprang and registered their children in the Visitations. Networks of kin crossed occupational barriers and created a hybrid society in which money served as a neutral and universal standard. The movement between town and country was so continuous that the distinctions of social terminology became blurred.[215] It is noteworthy that tragedy, which flourishes in a poorly integrated society, was relatively unimportant in England.

The degree of mobility should not be exaggerated. The range of individual choice was always limited by birth, kinship and patronage. All trades and professions had vested interests and corporate traditions and retained strong hereditary features. Although traditional rather than traditionalist, the system had inherent oligarchic tendencies.[216] Sectors of the elite periodically attempted to curb or reverse social fluidity and to create greater uniformity and rigidity by raising barriers to mobility. But continual infusions of new blood did counter hardening of the social arteries and change was not limited to circular short-term movements between elite groups. The system was sufficiently flexible and fluid to admit new talent without undermining the hierarchical structure of power, which was in fact strengthened by temporary reversals.[217] In England no profession, with the possible exception of the Army, was monopolized by one section of propertied society. Although the law and office had their own networks of patronage, neither developed, as in the continental monarchies, into a new caste distinct from both the landed class and the business community.[218]

English society was not universalistic, specific or closely knit, but particularist, diffuse and heterogeneous. There was a complex plurality of separate subcultures, each with its own peer group, which overlapped but which were never completely integrated. Within and between the numerous economic and functional groups, which were fragmented by mobility

[213] Clark 1962: 42. [214] Macintosh 1978: 280. [215] Le Neve, *Pedigrees Knights*.

[216] Hoselitz in Braibanti 1961: 111. 'Traditional' here refers to the value system of the previous century; as Pococke points out in Dunn 1989: 123, when equated with 'pre-industrial' it describes 98 per cent of human history.

[217] Turner 1969: 176. [218] Trevelyan 1930–4: i. 33; Anderson 1971: 61.

and differentiated by background, wealth and religion, there were finely graded differences of manners and attitude.[219] After 1660, Dissent formed a legally distinct group, and Catholics never enjoyed full civil status.[220] Alien minorities retained a separate identity and did not marry outside their group; the Protestant refugees were slow to assimilate and there was rivalry between Walloons and Huguenots.[221] Very few Jews lived outside their communities.[222] The Quaker merchants were set apart by their costume, group residence, speech, and refusal to take oaths, bear arms or recognize the authority of the law.[223] But once they had won limited toleration, Non-Conformists acquiesced in maintaining the prevailing social order; businessmen found ways to minimize the effects of exclusion and isolation. Flemish and Dutch residents acquired freedom of the City and were ultimately absorbed after immigration slackened.[224]

Diversity did not lead to divergence. English society may not have been organic, but it was symbiotic. Differences were bridged by compromise, by multiple loyalties and by face-saving rituals.[225] Co-operation was a preferred alternative to institutionalization.[226] There were many conflicts of interest, but conflict occurs even in static societies and is frequently aggravated by artificial efforts to restore harmony.[227] Functionally independent and specialized occupational groups successfully combined and consolidated into a relatively stable structure, which survived the potential destabilization of religion, taxation and politics. Pressure from the subcultures gradually modified the social hierarchy without undermining the stability of the whole system. By constant adjustment towards equilibrium, English society was slowly but steadily transformed without radical disruption.

The value system

Business did have some distinctive values. Merchants tended to adopt a rational empiricism and their habits were learned rather than instinctively assumed. Their sense of justice and mutual responsibility was based on reasoning and conscience, not on residual notions of chivalry. Peter Delaval, a younger son turned merchant, did return to fight a duel on family grounds and one merchant found himself in the Court of Chivalry; but merchants did not usually subscribe to heroic concepts of honour and settled their disputes by litigation.[228] They regarded their success as a sign

219 Corfield 1987. 220 Spurr 1991: 165.
221 Pettigree in Chartres & Hey 1990: 302; Vane 1984: 138.
222 Hyamson 1951–2: 99.
223 Vann 1969a: 98; Lloyd 1950: 77. 224 Grell 1989: 27; Roker 1965–70: 24–9.
225 Goffman 1967: 12. 226 Braddick 1991: 2. 227 Stone 1972: intro.
228 Stone 1964a: 246; *Reports Heraldic Cases*, p. 49; Charlton 1965: x.

of virtue, whereas gentlemen considered their endowment of property as an injunction to abstain from work.

Businessmen were more willing to recognize merit, to seek independence and to tolerate greater freedom of choice. Some can be credited with greater respect for the inner self and with hostility towards external symbols of success in a society which rewarded the unproductive. They denounced violence, frivolity and dissoluteness in favour of propriety, respectability, personal rectitude, moderation and decency.[229] They protected their ancient urban way of life and they developed their own business and family networks.[230] It is also possible that businessmen differed from the gentry in their bearing, posture and forms of speech.[231]

The Humanists had borrowed from the Stoics the ideal of *mediocratas* which the Puritan theorists identified with those of the 'middling station' who were not tempted away from God by riches; many contemporaries chose to describe those who were neither poor nor gentlemen as the 'better sort'.[232] Non-Conformist theology did in certain respects devalue the importance of birth and constitute an alternative culture.[233] The Dissenters and other outsiders – the aliens, Jews, Huguenots, Quakers and other voluntary and involuntary migrants – were prepared to reject received wisdom and the primacy of descent, to emphasize alternative signs of success and to seek the respect of those who could see the quality of the inner man.

The Puritan ethic was, however, as much anti-business as it was opposed to landed society.[234] The preachers were suspicious of the educational system and feared change and the wilderness.[235] Their definition of the duties of a calling ignored the new structure of an expanding economy; Towerson argued that each should only acquire what was necessary to maintain life in his station.[236] The General Baptists Assembly, in 1656, discouraged members from leaving their calling or undertaking more business than they could manage personally.[237] The preachers of all denominations emphasized the transitory nature of earthly pleasure and the futility of human desires and achievements.

Protestantism could not serve as the ideology of business, because the preachers denounced materialism and spoke primarily to the artisan

[229] Earle 1989a: 10; Smith, *Theory Moral Sentiments*, part i, ser. 3; chap. 3; Andrews 1988: 161. [230] Small 1992a: 29.

[231] Despite numerous studies of *langue et parole*, such as Corfield 1991, there is little hard evidence about differences of dialect, accent and phrasing which in later periods became a badge of class. [232] Todd 1987: 130; Wrightson in Corfield 1991: 50–1.

[233] Georges 1961: 170, n.165 with reservations, 171; Greaves 1985.

[234] See pp. 295–7. [235] Greene 1988: 19; Butts 1982: 673.

[236] Heywood, *Autobiography*, i. 22–3; Schlatter 1940; 119.

[237] Jackson, *Pious Prentice*, p. 115; Watts 1978: 368; Hanham 1985: 20.

tradesman.[238] Business was closely associated with individualism which, if pursued too vigorously, could undermine communal ideals and lead to disruption and fanaticism. The pursuit of gain beyond the needs of life was still branded as morally reprehensible and strenuous efforts were made to control the selfish passions by either internal or external coercion. By emphasizing a particular calling and the dignity of work, in contrast to the capitalist practices of speculation and usury, the preachers reinforced a fundamental division within the business community between those who were willing to scramble for profit and those who favoured security and fraternal values. The businessmen, unlike the majority of tradesmen, chose to interpret the doctrine of a calling in a positive sense; they rejected the static concept of a society based on consensus and co-operation, in which the place of every man was predetermined by inheritance rather than earned by achievement.

Business values could not seriously challenge or compete with the dominant ethos of landed society, which commanded widespread, if not universal, acceptance. It was a world of insiders in which power and inherited status, rather than function or the economic substructure, defined the elite.[239] A few assertive iconoclasts, either by choice or through default, set themselves apart and rejected the values of landed society. But most businessmen were as socially conservative as the gentry, because their status was subject to constant uncertainty and change. Driven by social anxiety, they accepted and imitated the dominant culture with different degrees of enthusiasm and compliance. Businessmen might claim moral superiority, but they still felt insecure and ill at ease. They adopted genteel standards in order to defend themselves against charges of mercenary behaviour and because social acceptance depended not on native ability, but on breeding and refinement.

Nor could business compete with the *esprit de corps* of the professions, which were beginning to acquire their own identity. They also demanded and rewarded skill; status was conferred by position rather than by birth. But, unlike business, their values were bureaucratic. They were all self-maintaining and self-validating; office made the man, rather than vice versa. Each profession was identified with a specialized area of knowledge and organized into a monopolistic institution which had a pyramidical structure co-ordinated by vertical lines of authority. Although none had yet rigidified into an exclusive academic discipline and although there was no equivalent to the theoretically meritocratic examination system of the Chinese *literati*, a university education and literacy in Latin did serve as

[238] Seaver 1980: 45–6.

[239] Clifford-Vaughan 1960: 320. Mousnier 1969: 20–1 draws heavily on American sociology which some regard as dated: see Ariazza 1980: 56.

paper qualifications.[240] In public offices, incumbents were assigned precise responsibilities and could obtain appointments without demonstrating specific expertise.

The aristocracy and their champions arrogantly decried the values of the marketplace and the corruption of wealth; to counter the pretensions of the citizenry, there was a libertine reaction against self-control and respectability at the Restoration Court and a self-conscious concern for etiquette.[241] The higher echelons of society constantly discarded practices, which they had introduced, as soon as widespread acceptance and popularity made them less exclusive. Theoretically they pursued an Aristotelian concept of leisure, based on freedom from the need to earn. Many cultivated a courteous, well-bred ignorance and stubbornly retained their amateur status; they declined to increase their capacity by training when they served in public office.[242]

At the same time, landed society shared many of the extrinsic and intrinsic values of businessmen. The Court was not isolated from the City and there was no unified country culture.[243] Most gentlemen lived by relatively simple rural standards and all were preoccupied with extending their assets.[244] In practice, those who entered politics or administered their own estates had little opportunity for leisure and inevitably adopted a utilitarian approach and quietly acquired professional skills. Their financial behaviour was as rational and as open to moral objections as those of the business world.[245] The conduct books, written for landed and commercial families, do differ in emphasis and mannerisms. But their authors borrowed from each other, emphasized reciprocal duties, promoted educational and moral values and offered similar advice on the husbanding of revenues.

The conventional middle-class virtues were diffused throughout landed society by the pervasive influence of London, by economic pressures and by social mobility.[246] The heroic and military ideal, first challenged by the Humanists, was steadily undermined by philosophers like Hobbes and Pascal and by the greater sophistication of military organization.[247] Human appetites were analysed more objectively; interest was accorded priority over passion and duty, provoking nostalgic complaints about the decline of grandeur.[248] After 1660, the towns were gentrified and the doctrine of estates was superseded by a concept of Civil

[240] Chan 1977: 60–1; Teng 1943. [241] Bryson in Gert & Llewellyn 1990: 152.
[242] Coleman 1973: 93; Ustick 1932a: 153–7; Noyes 1937: 3; Wisdon in Borger & Cioffi 1970: 284–5; Allen in Coates & Hillard 1986. [243] Smuts 1987: 3, 54.
[244] Thompson 1963: 22. [245] Barnard 1941.
[246] Wrigley 1967a: 226; Gellner 1988: 35; Coleman 1966: 176.
[247] Thomas in Brown 1965: 198; Wood 1980: 442.
[248] Hirschman 1977: 117; Lovejoy 1961: 215.

Society with a single hierarchy.[249] The courts increasingly emphasized the sanctity of contract, which steadily replaced status as an organizing principle. The duel provided for disputes of honour to be settled not by random feudal violence but in an orderly manner between individuals contracting on equal terms.[250]

Although not ranked on an equal footing, the codes of behaviour characteristic of business and landed society were able to co-exist and were both complementary and mutually dependent. Conflicts between opposites is normal in societies; the process of acculturation is a conjunction of autonomous systems.[251] Conflicting attitudes tended to neutralize each other and the values of propertied society became relative rather than absolute. Businessmen and landowners differed more in degree than in kind, as both modified their allegiance to old customs and traditions and disengaged from ascriptive ties. Neither could sustain an independent ideology and both had to compromise their higher principles in the face of a pecuniary culture.[252]

To protect the fabric of society, provide time for adjustment and minimize disruption, contemporaries often chose to camouflage innovations as a return to the status quo ante. The impact of change was cushioned by continuity of forms, if not of substance. Changes in function and relative importance were concealed by similarities in nomenclature. Many archaic customs outlived the conditions which had created them and created, *ipso facto*, the illusion of permanence.[253] They were allowed to slowly atrophy until they were ultimately superseded or persisted only as symbols. Change can occur even without a change of direction; like recycled paper, the revival of old forms creates something new. It takes energy to maintain the status quo; custom should not be equated with inertia.[254] New incongruences appeared as internal features of the social system were displaced without corresponding alterations in the overall structure.

The formal system of authority, however, remained intact and the new functional elite legitimized itself by continuing to acknowledge a disinterested ideal and to rely on the presumptions of birth and breeding. The criteria for social differentiation did not change, but the operational system became more flexible and complex. The old order was perpetuated by an innovative compromise between continuity and change. Landowners did not take their supremacy for granted and they reconstituted their culture according to need. They were prepared to validate retrospectively economic and social realities and, *mutatis mutandis*,

[249] Borsay 1989: 312; Benedict 1989: 30; Bossy 1982: 51; Cooper 1978: 22.
[250] Ashton 1969b: 14; Kiernan 1988: 16.
[251] Cust & Hughes 1989: 17; Ponsioen 1962: 53. [252] Abramovitz 1989: 101.
[253] Thomas 1983a; Geertz 1988.
[254] Burke in Burke 1979: 7; Medick & Sabean 1984: 7; Basu *et al.* 1987: 17.

rationalize change by revising their mythology. Because it retained its exclusive aura and because new wealth was accorded an appropriate descent, the hierarchy was not demythologized, despite a substantial number of segmental changes in the normative structure and individual roles. Social deviance was accommodated and the claims of business did not provoke a crisis, because the basic premises of landed society were not threatened. These changes did, however, cumulatively represent a fundamental break with the past and were more than transitions or diversions. Once new values were adopted, they rapidly became the norm.[255]

The polarization of aristocratic and bourgeois values is a false dichotomy, which has been perpetuated by a modern fondness for categorization and by the pleasure which observers of the social scene derive from dissecting the anatomy of snobbery.[256] Within the dominant system, there were variations. The Court stood apart as the only national centre for the elite and there were fundamental differences between town and country and between the propertied and the populace.[257] The extraordinary growth of London, which was large enough to accommodate every interest and small enough for those attracted by its unusual opportunities to meet face to face, concentrated talent and money and created a metropolitan culture.[258] But a bilateral process of acculturation within propertied society created a relatively homogeneous system. The nobility abandoned its feudal past and absorbed the acquisitive and cosmopolitan values of an urban culture. The wealthier merchant families gradually eliminated the peculiar customs which separated them from landed society and over several generations merged into the rural landscape. In the towns, businessmen shared the same milieu as the resident and visiting gentry. They were too few in number and wealth and too ambivalent about their role to found a new self-supporting culture, which requires continuity of adherents over several generations.

Business remained an economic function and generated no self-conscious class with its own *mentalité*.[259] Merchants did not have a

[255] Herskovits in Braibanti 1961: 115.

[256] The old view is most clearly stated by Strauss 1952: 127–8 and MacPherson 1962 and discredited by Berlin 1964: 454 and Daunton 1989: 133.

[257] Smuts in Peck 1991: 111.

[258] Wrigley 1967a: 8.

[259] Both liberal and Marxist theories of the development of the bourgeoisie are untenable. The former is well represented by Jordan 1960a: 49, who argues that merchants formed a homogeneous group with common modes of conduct and founded a liberal society with new values. The Marxists divide into those who believe that a self-conscious class developed, those who argue that the bourgeoisie existed before it had been recognized and named and those who have transferred the historical role of the bourgeoisie from business to agriculture. See Tawney 1944: 208; Rosen 1981: 25; George 1971: 410; Milner 1981: 51, 62; MacNally 1988: xi, 9; Wood 1991: chap. 1; Tribe 1981: chap. 1; Laski 1936: chap. 2; Rollson 1987: 311; Lis & Soly 1979: 71; Hobsbawm 1971: 37; Wallerstein 1974: i. 352; Lowr 1982: 28; Ryan 1965: 229; Hill in Pococke 1980: 111, 130; Wood 1984: 13; Gould 1987: 253; Maddison 1982: 15.

particular attitude of mind, as Sombart and Weber thought, or a consistent attitude on any issue, as implied by the concept of *mentalité*.[260] The cohesion of the business community was constantly undermined by internal divisions, by lack of continuity, by a rentier mentality, and by emigration to the gentry and the professions. Because businessmen and their children could move upwards and sidewards in English society, they never constituted a permanently frustrated and alienated, separate group. The liquidity of mercantile wealth made it a ready instrument for satisfying social aspirations, and because business fortunes were fragile, finite and closely tied to the established order, they could not act as a social leveller or create new social institutions. The evolution from communal to private business management, from *Gemeinschaft* to *Gesellschaft*, occurred slowly over the centuries; despite obvious tensions, elements of both co-existed in pre-industrial England.[261]

The transition in Marxist theory from feudalism to capitalism (whether bourgeois, proto-industrial or agrarian) barely deserves the description of a model and is little more than rhetoric.[262] Contemporary businessmen had no ideology and were not aware of any historical obligation to develop into a bourgeoisie.[263] Ultimately that role would be filled in the post-industrial world not by private business, but by the professions, with their collegiate and bureaucratic mentality, their pluralistic, tenured and self-regulating institutions, their universal norms, community of interest, corporate identity and romantic reformism, and their cult of collective loyalty divorced from social origins.[264] The principal obstacle to the emergence of a business society was not the *trahison de la bourgeoisie* but the *trahison des clercs*.

260 Cooper 1978: 22.

261 Hirschman 1980: 125 points out that the concepts of feudal shackles and *doux commerce* were both anti-capitalist.

262 Tonnies 1957: 165. Pocock 1975 attempts to construct a bourgeois ideology out of civic humanist values, denoting the expansion of credit as the catalyst, but he simply repeats the rarified musings of intellectuals and never examines the attitudes of actual businessmen. He also appears, p. 460, to embrace the notion of agrarian capitalism whose fundamental inconsistencies are exposed by Appleby 1975a: 592 and Ormrud 1988: 12, 45. On the equally dubious notion of proto-industrialization see Coleman 1983: 446. On the abuse of the terms 'bourgeois' and 'feudalism' see Corcoran 1980: 301–3; Brown 1974: 1063–88; Heers 1974: 646, 652.

263 MacFarlane 1977; Bailyn 1964: 190; Johnson 1981: 415; MacIntyre in Wilson 1970: chap. 6.

264 Thompson 1969; Maude 1953: 27; Gellner 1965: 13; Parry 1976: 24; Bousma 1975: 324; Bledstein 1976.

Conclusion: Private enterprise in a pre-industrial economy

The English economy in the seventeenth century oscillated between stagnation and spurts of activity and achieved only modest increases in per capita real income and in output per head per man hour.[1] Where quantitative increases in output did occur, they were often due to better harvests, virgin territory or the application of more manpower. Bottlenecks in production, lack of critical skills, unequal income distribution, low productivity, inflexibility of demand and inelasticities of cost all constrained qualitative growth. The rate of investment decelerated whenever saturation of the market reduced the rate of return.

Despite periodic recessions, the momentum of English economic development was sustained as an upward secular trend. The physical size of the market was extended, most obviously in international trade through re-exports and colonial settlement, and its structure changed.[2] London was the most powerful engine of growth but, after 1650, it was equalled by the aggregated activity of the outports and provincial towns.[3] Scarce resources were better allocated and utilized, distribution costs were reduced, products were diversified and new sources of supply and demand were tapped. Although imports often tended to run ahead of exports, a balance was ultimately struck.[4] The productivity of agriculture increased with regional specialization and market integration; domestic industry slowly improved its range and capacity for import substitution.[5]

[1] The model of a stagnant European economy, into which England and Holland never fitted, has been substantially modified: see Léon 1978: ii. 192; 1970: 17–19; Wallerstein 1979: 141; Cameron 1973: 145–8; *Review* 1979; Dillen in Earle 1974; Hartwell 1969: 13; Hobsbawm 1972: 48. The flaws in the model proposed by North & Thomas 1970: 14–16 and 1973 are outlined by Reed 1973: 182–3, 194–6; Rapp 1975: 508 n.23; Ringrose 1973: 287.

[2] R. Davis in Carus-Wilson 1954–66: ii. 257 ff; 1973: table 4; D. W. Jones 1988: fig. 5.1.

[3] Wrigley in Abram & Wrigley 1978: 237–42; Corfield in Coleman & John 1976: 232; Goose 1986: 167; O'Brien & Engerman in Solow 1991: 180.

[4] Taylor 1968: 20; in Kellenbenz 1970: 252–5; 1972: 237; Dietz in Beier & Finlay 1986: 123, table 9; Fisher 1990: 189–90; Suivaranta 1923: 160.

[5] In some respects the rural sector was more dynamic than the urban: see John in Coleman & John 1976: 45–68 and Carus-Wilson 1954–66, ii. 198; E. L. Jones 1967: 56; 1974: 103, 109; Wrigley in Rotberg & Rabb 1986: 138; 1985: 724; Kussmaul 1985: 27; Chartres in Chartres & Hey 1990: 313; Allen 1988a: 141. For a contrary view see O'Brien 1985: 775.

A majority of the population remained poor, but real wages and domestic consumption gradually increased; production of food outstripped demand and disposable income rose within propertied society.[6] Capital was accumulated at a surprisingly high rate and from profits and savings rather than through inflation and expropriation.[7] Despite heavy losses in new ventures and the cost of civil and foreign wars, sufficient domestic and foreign capital was available to fund the trading empires, to rebuild London after the Great Fire and at the same time to lower the natural rate of interest.[8]

Although it is difficult to determine precisely the relative importance of different sectors or whether growth occurred at the margin rather than the centre, the dynamism of the economy is evident.[9] During the century 1590–1690, English merchants reduced the relative share of trade handled by alien merchants, inherited the commercial hegemony of the Italian states in the Mediterranean, drew ahead of the French and ultimately achieved parity with the Dutch.[10] Progress on a wide front and at a level and a pace which was impressive for a pre-industrial economy, occurred both in absolute terms and relative to the past.

Objective factors

It is difficult to account for these changes without descending to tautology and rehearsing the obvious factors of growth in sequential paradigms; models of economic development are designed to explain process rather than origins.[11] It is hard to separate the accidental from the fundamental,

[6] Appleby 1978: 183–4; 1979; 1973: 430–1; Outhwaite 1971a: 401; Walter & Wrightson 1976: 40–2; 1991:34; Schofield 1983: 290; Walter and Wrigley in Walter & Schofield 1989: 70–5, 90, 278; Hoskins 1968: 21; Harrison 1971; Rogers 1887: v. 216–31; Persson 1988: table 5.1; Shammas 1990: 293–6; Clay 1984: ii. 32–3; Thirsk 1978: 175–6; Menard 1980: fig. 2; Weatherill 1988: 93, 195. [7] Spengler 1968: 437.

[8] The rate on government loans fell with peace and cheap money did not in itself promote growth: France had a low interest of rate of 4.5 per cent from 1665 onwards and the rate on state annuities fell from 7 per cent to 5 per cent. See Goubert 1960: 538–40; Dickson 1967: 12, 90–7, 483.

[9] Chambers 1972: 144; O'Brien 1982: 5; in *Intl Cong. Ec. Hist. X 1990*: 171–7; Price in Fohlen & Godechot 1970. On the relative significance of foreign trade, manufacturing and towns see R. Davis 1979: 10; Minchinton 1969: 46; Chartres and Dietz in Beier *et al.* 1986: 130–1, 168–74, 186, 192; Cares 1980; Gomes 1987: 57–8. Industrial growth cannot be aggregated and Europe remained the main market for English exports and re-exports: see Coleman in Harte & Ponting 1973: 20–1; Wilson 1960: 90–7. On the fallacies of the Wallerstein thesis see Ragin & Chinot in Skopcol 1984: 286–8.

[10] Rapp 1976: 95; Divitiis 1986: 147–8; Cipolla in Pullan 1968: 134–6; Mazzei 1979: 199–200; Sella 1969: 236; Krantz & Hohenberg 1975: 13–14; Israel 1989a: 308–10; 1990: 154–9, 375–6; Delumeau 1960: 104–5; Morineau 1970: 169–71; Symcox in Baxter 1985: 172. New rivals, such as Hamburg, also emerged: see Newman 1985.

[11] The main factors are listed in Meier & Baldwin 1957 and Meier 1970; Hartwell in Kindleberger & Tello 1983; Sutch in Ransom *et al.* 1982: 36; Cairncross 1962: 140.

the parameters from the dependent variables, to distinguish between symptoms, causes, conditions and effects. A high correlation coefficient does not necessarily constitute a causal relationship, nor do intentions explain results.[12] Did supply follow or create demand? Were individuals and governments more forced than forcing? Did the market create entrepreneurs or did opportunities languish until the right entrepreneur came on the scene? Given that all factors are interdependent, there is no sure way of weighing their relative importance.[13] Each answer only raises more questions.

At the macro level, objective economic forces, which themselves derived from prior changes, established the framework for business decisions. Thanks to a low level of technology, business operated primarily with given natural resources and it was comparative advantage which dictated the direction and type of growth; the ocean served as an expanding frontier.[14] It was the comparative rate of return in relation to risk which determined levels and choice of investment; irreducible needs limited the degree of experimentation. If economic conditions did not offer realistic prospects of profit, entrepreneurs had no incentive to act. In many respects, businessmen merely accelerated the rate of change which was already in process.

Nor should institutional factors be taken for granted.[15] The market was unified by the state and could not have functioned without representative institutions and a centralized and stable political system.[16] England did not refeudalize and favoured an empirical culture based on case law; without guaranteed property rights, which became more precise as their resource value rose, there would have been no private business.[17] The English state had a poor track record of business development and investment; its ineffective attempts at regulation and its corrupt and fiscal licensing system before 1640 just created additional costs.[18] After 1660, however, there were no industrial monopolies and gradually the administrative machinery was developed to enforce a national economic policy. The government ran large-scale enterprises, like the naval dockyards, regulated the money supply through control of the Mint and defended economic interests through legislation, diplomacy and war. Forced savings were created through taxation; by redistributing revenues

[12] Tully 1988: 107; Cairncross 1989: 182. [13] Martin 1982: 58.

[14] MacLeod 1988: 201; Manley 1974: 389; Thomas 1986: 143; Thom in Tracy 1991: 152; Goldthwaite 1987: 31.

[15] North & Thomas 1970: 14–16 emphasize the decline in transaction costs and the size of market, though (p. 5) they accept that institutions become variables in long-term growth and that productivity gains precede industrialization.

[16] North & Wengart 1989: 806. [17] Proudhon 1866: 146; Libecap 1986: 231.

[18] Coleman 1969b: 14; P. Williams 1979: 172; Aylmer 1990: 92.

through expenditure and by creating fictitious credit through fiduciary orders, the government stimulated intermediate output, if not overall levels of consumption.[19] Businessmen benefited from colonial acquisitions, the Navigation Acts and the exercise of naval power.[20] The economy also benefited indirectly from the unintended consequences of war and persecution, which diffused technology and redistributed skilled manpower.

Growth may also have occurred in spite of, not because of, the efforts of merchants. Fortunes were frequently acquired by a zero-sum game of expropriating a larger percentage of a flat Gross National Product.[21] Most of the territorial states of the period were plunder or rentier economies, in which a fixed quantity of cake was distributed between property-owners and the government; unbridled acquisition and unproductive usury flourish in subsistence economies.[22] Businessmen squeezed the consumer through monopolies and siphoned off government revenues through membership of parasitic tax-exempt bureaucracies, which in turn bled a subsistence peasantry. Economies could stagnate on high profit margins when businessmen neglected to plough back their earnings. In England too, business fortunes were acquired without raising productivity.[23] Merchants sought to profit from the mistakes of others, to benefit their families, not the whole economy.

Nonetheless growth was cumulative and achieved through co-operation as much as by competition; each individual built on the groundwork of his predecessors and overcame obstacles by trial and error. New raw materials were constantly discovered, population growth was regulated by the age of marriage and by emigration, and the importance of silver supplies was diminished by financial instruments. It was businessmen who noticed and exploited opportunities and who cleaned up after disasters. In every crisis – the 1590s, the 1620s, the 1690s – their reaction was positive.[24] When their staple trades declined, the overseas merchants could simply have allowed their market to shrink, but they chose instead to seek new outlets, to infiltrate existing trade networks in Asia and to create new markets and a commercial Empire in the Atlantic.

Broadly speaking, economic factors can be regarded as a necessary prerequisite, institutional factors as a contingent condition and individual enterprise as the sufficient cause of growth. Sir William Temple allocated

[19] Lane 1975: 13; Aylmer 1974: 249; 1973: 324; Coleman 1977: 195; Root 1991: 338 ff; Waquet 1982: 99; Mathias & O'Brien 1976: 639.
[20] Kennedy 1983: 85. [21] Leibenstein 1963: 117.
[22] Kerridge in Anderson & Latham 1986; E. L. Jones 1988: 46, 95, 120; Persson 1988: 3–5.
[23] Ashton 1964: 586. [24] Clark 1988: 71; Andrews 1984: 35.

business aptitude a key role in the Dutch economic miracle.[25] What has still to be asked is whether individual initiative and social values can account for differences in response to economic opportunities in England. Was business performance at the micro level conditioned more by internal dynamics than by external pressures? In order to answer these questions, it is necessary to examine the efficiency with which manpower was utilized, the comparative merits of personal and corporate organization and the conflict between enterprise and bureaucracy.

Human capital

The ability of English society to unearth, train, motivate and employ the talent of its members was a crucial factor in determining its rate of economic growth.[26] Business had to attract able recruits to replace experienced retired merchants.[27] Although the stabilization of the population coincided with colonial expansion, there was never, in fact, any shortage of candidates for business. Because there were no social barriers to restrict occupational and geographical mobility, the labour pool was continually replenished by adolescents from all families which had risen above subsistence level. Only those who lacked the self-confidence vital in business were likely to be deterred by residual social prejudice. The relative deprivation of deviant religious groups diverted additional manpower from agriculture and the professions into business, which was not effectively subject to the Penal Laws. The pool was further enlarged by voluntary and involuntary alien immigrants fleeing persecution or seeking better opportunities.[28] Indigenous and imported candidates multiplied so fast that supply exceeded demand.

It was, however, the quality rather than the quantity of human resources which mattered. The productivity of labour is a function of individual talent and education and, according to the law of error, any growth of numbers leads to a decline in quality. The distribution of entrepreneurial talent is biologically random and is not determined by membership of an elite. Material success does not necessarily perpetuate itself. Enthusiasm is no substitute for ability and many children from propertied society displayed neither. Nor could their suitability be

[25] Temple, *Observations United Provinces*, p. 229 suggested 'a great concurrence of Circumstances'; Haley 1988: 51, 108; Klein 1969: 7–19; in Aymard 1982: 87; Swart 1970: 14.

[26] The same was true of Holland and Scotland: see Vries 1973: 201–2; Smout 1968: 69; in Dyrvik 1979: 23; Whatley 1989: 180; Houston & Whyte 1989: 93; Donaldson 1974: 237.

[27] Kiker 1966: 482; E. L. Jones 1981: 81; Lewis in Agarwala & Singh 1958.

[28] On the mobility of merchants see Flinn 1981: 70.

gauged in advance. Intellectual and moral qualities could be weighed, but no system of examination had been devised which could recognize business ability.[29] There was no autonomous mechanism which put the ablest into business or endowed minority groups or the needy with the greatest talent. Families were also reluctant to accept the logic and pain of natural selection. Social mobility benefits the underdog, but selection by merit hurts individuals and conflicts with family loyalties. Nepotism was consequently widely practised and patronage carried greater weight than qualifications.[30] Propertied families did not rush to embrace equality of opportunity; business was regarded as a support for the gentry, not vice versa.[31] Because fashion often dictated choice, many areas of business were starved of new recruits.

Imperfections in the selective process were, however, rectified over time by sheer numbers; some talent was bound to surface in business, which needed NCOs as well as officer material.[32] Outbreeding tends to release energy and favours the introduction of new ideas.[33] The high turnover in the Companies introduced new blood and the pressure on places drove new recruits into unpopular trades. Those insulated or excluded from traditional society and trades became innovators from necessity. The competitiveness of business acted as a self-selecting mechanism; it was the marketplace which ultimately allocated scarce talent between alternative ends.[34] The weakest went to the wall and, because many parents were willing to accept the downward mobility of their children, there was a constant shakeout of the incompetent.[35] Second sons sometimes had more options than their eldest brothers; merchants favoured their ablest children.[36] Parents were prepared to shoulder the costs of training and compensate for earnings foregone by their children.[37] Because only the fittest survived, the elite became more meritocratic; labour and skill were distributed voluntarily without the inefficiencies and costs of forced allocation.

The service industries did, of course, compete for the same talent; they were socially and economically attractive and, in some respects, parasitic. Contemporaries were well aware of the siren call of office and the professions, and that they drained talent from business.[38] But the

[29] Bowman in Anderson & Bowman 1965: 96. [30] Rappaport 1989: 309.
[31] Robinson, *England's Safety*, pp. 48–9; Petty, *Economic Writings*, i. 312.
[32] MacKendrick *et al.* 1982: 192–3; R. S. Smith 1989.
[33] Darlington 1978; Perkin 1968: 136.
[34] Lipson 1944: 88. For an opposite view see Hintze 1929: 506. [35] Sharpe 1974: 42.
[36] R. Davis 1967a: 13; Cooper 1992: 289. [37] Becker 1975: 24.
[38] *Britannia Languens*, pp. 302, 375; Wilson, *Treatise of Revenues* in Columbia Univ. Lib. Seligman MS 1625; BL Lans. MS 891, fo. 94; Hunt. Lib. MS 1264, fos, 169–72; Johnson 1937: chap. 7; Shelton 1981: 101; Hall, *Advancement of Learning*, p. 17.

professions were indirectly accountable and it was inevitable that they would expand with the economy. The contemporary labour theory of value underestimated the contribution of the tertiary sector, which had no measurable output, but which provided essential support facilities. A richer, more complex and better-integrated economy needed more lawyers, physicians, fighting-men and administrators. Their functions were not antagonistic so long as their respective demands on manpower were not excessive.

What did distort the distribution of talent was the desire for security and regularity of income.[39] It was a rational response to a world in which no man was immune from disaster and there was no safety net apart from the family. It was the uncertainties of business rather than social prejudice which attracted many to salaried positions which combined tenure with prestige and opportunities for corruption. The bureaucracies of the state and of monopolistic enterprises had greater appeal than private firms because they were not governed by market risk and discipline and because their goals were not exclusively economic and could be manipulated. Incomes were not necessarily related even to performance, because it was difficult without objective tests to measure productivity; only private business had the ultimate sanction of the bottom line. Salaried employees were often jealous of businessmen, whose incomes appeared to be much higher, but they conveniently ignored the ratio between risk and reward. Salaries did not confer the independence of private property, but a businessman could lose all his capital; factors who worked on commission starved if they were unable to purchase and sell.

The independent firm

The seventeenth-century economy was neither dominated nor led by big business or by corporate management, but by small firms whose capital financed both production and distribution.[40] The fundamental unit was still the partnership, usually dominated by one individual.[41] The Newcastle coal trade, the Bristol slave trade and ultimately Lloyd's were run

[39] For a similar argument advanced in the debate over Victorian entrepreneurship see Rubinstein 1988: 54. For alternative views see Lewis 1978: 129; MacCloskey 1973; Wiener 1981; Palmade 1972: 11; Bruchey 1960: 497; Wilson, *Discourse upon Usury*, p. 366.

[40] R. S. Smith 1967: 127; Whetter 1974: 164; Gough 1967: 125; Donald 1961: 35; Hammersley 1973a: 612; Lewis 1966: 214–16; Godfrey 1976: 168, 175, 255; Minchinton in Butel 1979: 194; Willan 1956: 40, 78; Nef 1940: 34; Chapman 1979: 205.

[41] Lane in Riemersma 1953: 87, 100; Postan 1973b: 17–21, 68–70; Pryor 1973: 35–7; Day 1987; Phillips 1979: 332, 339. Aitken 1963–4: 5–6 argues that entrepreneurship is indistinguishable from the firm, but one person was always dominant.

by interlocking partnerships. Independent businessmen were the prime movers and managers who alone could vent goods and who both controlled output and created and sustained the market.[42] It was the *Verlagssystem*, rather than guild organization, which sustained the small craft producers. Merchants were essential to finance and sustain colonial development and they stimulated the growth of the service industries.[43] The interests and functions of the great businessmen remained relatively unspecialized and they shouldered the vital task of co-ordinating the functions of different sectors of the economy.[44]

The firm did slowly acquire a legal personality distinct from the sum of the partners.[45] But typically it had an informal and non-bureaucratic structure with little division of labour. Ownership and management were combined in what is best described as household government. Merchants did not delegate decision-making to subordinates or diffuse their personal control. The agents and attorneys, whose services they utilized, were really self-employed and only in a handful of industries was it necessary to organize large groups of workmen.[46] Firms were run as an extended family; the uncertainties of the market were countered by the combined resources of kinship groups. Partnerships were, of course, subject to fraud and disputes; kinsmen could be a liability and patriarchal direction could fossilize techniques and policy. But small firms usually demonstrated flexibility of response and their innovations were more effective because they were introduced at the grass roots, not imposed from the top by administrative fiat.

Family businesses were, of course, limited in size by the numbers, ability and lifespan of their members.[47] They could survive the death of their founder only if the second generation possessed talent and interest. Many did not last even one lifetime. Although some businessmen chose to die in harness and carefully picked and trained their successors, many disinvested in order to retire or secure their dynasty through landholding. It is noteworthy that no business was ever sold as a unitary asset in the seventeenth century and that no value was placed on goodwill. The three-generation cycle, initially categorized by Pirenne, did frequently fracture private enterprise.[48] The first generation created a business, the second

[42] Morriss 1914: 95–101. [43] Martin 1991: 294.
[44] Wilson in Rich & Wilson 1977: 12; Fisher 1990: 198; Supple 1970: 13.
[45] Maitland 1957: 14. [46] Pollard 1965.
[47] On the theoretical limits to the size of the firm see Coase 1936; P. L. Williams 1978: 13–14; Cochran 1974: 1466; Pollard 1990: 158–9; Herbert & Link 1982: chap. 9; Galambo 1966: 14; Penrose 1959; Cyert & Hedrick 1972: 407–9.
[48] Pirenne in Bendix & Lipset 1966: 502; 1939: ii. 104. The debate on Pirenne continues: see Braudel 1979: ii. 429; Hibbert in Abram & Wrigley 1978: 101–2; Herlihy 1974: 641. Rostow 1971: 72 offers a variant of this triad – creation, organization and committees.

consolidated and the third dissipated the gains. Each generation reacted against the habits and values of its predecessor and short life expectancy limited the size of groups of mature coevals.[49] Only when fathers married early and died late did different generations have the opportunity to interact and share ideas over a long period. Mobility and liquidity aggravated these tendencies. Aliens and Dissenters often had little choice but to plough back their profits, but the Jews and the Huguenots constantly changed their place of residence and those who had no roots in the culture had less incentive to commit their capital permanently.[50]

The disadvantages of discontinuity can, however, be exaggerated. When planning for the future, it is not always best to be guided by past experience. Undying corporations perpetuated old shibboleths and antiquated practices. In a family business, in contrast, the traditional authority of age was weakened by generational rivalry and conflict of egos. Continuity through kinship was probably more effective in harnessing talent than continuity through direct descent. The withdrawal of families from business also recirculated wealth, weakened oligarchy and redistributed manpower without destabilizing the social and political order. Continuous turnover increased both equality of opportunity and the likelihood of productive change. Young and hungry migrants tend to be energetic and willing to innovate; each new trade had a different set of entrepreneurs.

Family continuity was, moreover, less important than the transfer of skills; each generation draws on the intellectual capital and practical experience accumulated over the past.[51] Superficially, business methods might appear primitive in the seventeenth century; merchants did not jettison obsolete knowledge or relearn their skills. Management functions were still not clearly defined; advances in accounting theory had little effect on actual practice and information systems were fragmented, instinctive and haphazard. There was undoubtedly a world market with an international nexus of commerce and banking, but its coherence and degree of integration can be exaggerated.[52] To fault seventeenth-century businessmen by applying inappropriate standards would, however, be a presumptuous error. They were less concerned with obtaining more for the same effort than with increasing output without reducing quality. Their goal was optimal utilization of energy and manpower, not optimal efficiency.[53] Merchants recognized the cost-effectiveness of simplicity and their style of management was closely related to the risks and actual

[49] Redlich 1971: 307.
[50] Hoselitz 1960: 67.
[51] Nakamura 1981: 265; Bowman & Arnold in *Intern. Conf. Ec. Hist. IV* 1973: 247 ff; Kaniss 1981: 13.
[52] Jeannin 1964: 60–1; Richard 1968.
[53] Dovring 1987: 15.

needs of trade. Had they calculated the odds more accurately, they might have eschewed investments which proved beneficial in the long run.

Because it was not feasible to introduce too many changes at once, businessmen had to concentrate on reforming those procedures which malfunctioned or had obvious disutility. Competition forced them to revise backward techniques and they did not shrink from radical experimentation or plagiarism. As business expanded, the informal networks of communication and distribution were systematized and regularized and they functioned remarkably well. Craft skills were nursed in the towns, which had to retrain migrants from the countryside.[54] In order to compete with hardened veterans, a young businessmen did not need to be a technocrat, but he could not survive as an amateur.

The chartered Companies

A corporate structure was essential to guarantee perpetual succession and continuity of management, to maintain and protect the sea lanes and the forts and factories established on foreign territory.[55] A single institution with fixed assets could co-ordinate shipping, regulate the flow of goods, purchase in advance and sell in bulk, cope with slow turnover, avoid wasteful multiplication of services and lobby for diplomatic and military and naval support.[56] There was anarchy when two alternative Companies competed in India. Monopolistic privileges had some justification in the first phase of expansion, when transaction costs were high and Companies were required by the state to assume unprofitable responsibilities.[57] Interlopers might protest their exclusion, but they sought to enjoy the benefits without contributing to the substantial costs. The chartered Companies emerged in response to genuine business needs and they failed to survive in areas, like the Atlantic, where their services were superfluous.

The regulated Companies represented a compromise between individual and group organization.[58] They were the preferred choice of merchants, because they provided an institutional framework, while leaving individual members free to exercise their own initiative and

[54] Everitt 1978: 100; Wrigley 1991: 118. Bridbury 1972: 51 argues incorrectly that trade was not a recondite skill.

[55] Steensgaard & Klein in Blusse & Gaastra 1981: 23–4, 241; Schnutthoff 1939; Silva in *Intern. Conf. Ec. Hist. III* 1968: 66ff; Scott 1910–12: i. 227. Anderson *et al.* 1983: 565 make the obvious point that the Companies wished to exclude interlopers, but this does not negate the argument that forts were necessary and expensive.

[56] Chaudhuri 1985: 232; Carter & Nicholas 1988: 418.

[57] K. G. Davies 1974: 315.

[58] Hickson & Thompson 1991: 167.

employ their own capital.[59] Merchants were reluctant to fund permanent stocks and indeed abandoned them in the Levant and Muscovy Companies.[60] The joint-stock Companies traded on borrowed capital, through issuing bonds, not on their paid-up share capital.[61] The 1698 Act was a compromise between a regulated and joint-stock Company in the East India trade and, as late as 1733, efforts were made to convert the East India Company into a regulated Company.[62] Many joint-stock Companies were also small, informal concerns with unlimited liability and a short life.[63] Although a fundamental distinction remained between corporate and unincorporated business, partnerships often developed into a joint-stock organization. The New River Company was a hybrid and the Tobacco Adventure to Russia had five active managers and numerous sleeping partners.[64] Even in the great Companies, ownership was in practice still combined with management, because merchants remained the primary shareholders and retained control.

By institutionalizing their goals, however, the chartered Companies became inflexible and acquired a greater interest in continuity and stability than in growth. Their primary objective was the protection of the institution from external and internal predators, to distribute rather than to promote business. By artificially restricting competition and manipulating prices, they sought, like the guilds, to reduce friction between their members and control the market.[65] The major joint-stock Companies introduced bureaucracy into business. As Adam Smith later pointed out, their operational system became a formal system of ordered principles which governed all specific cases and could be administered in an exact, repetitive and predictable way through printed orders.[66] Despite some contingency planning, precedent and standard procedures were preferred to new options.

Operating a business through a board of directors and paid servants proved to be wasteful, cumbersome and inefficient. The early industrial

59 Ashley in Ollard & Tudor-Craig 1986: 204. Ekelund & Tollison 1981: 136–7 misinterpret the differences between the regulated and joint-stock Companies.

60 Blake in Cronne *et al.* 1948: 103; Steensgaard 1973: 56–8; Willan 1955: 406; 1956: 273; MacKenney 1987: chap. 6.

61 Reeder 1973: 487ff.

62 D. W. Jones in Clark & Slack 1972: 344; Horwitz 1977: 11; Coornaert in Rich & Wilson 1967: 252.

63 See p. 219.

64 Scammel 1972: 401; Price 1961a: 83; Pollet 1973: 30–1; Rudden 1985: 3.

65 Klein in Blusse & Gaastra 1981: 26. Fisher in Minchinton 1969: 74 equates regulated trades with established markets and settled prices.

66 Carlos & Nicholas 1988: 419; Anderson *et al.* 1983: 221ff; Chaudhuri in Chaudhuri & Dewey 1979: 152; 1978: fig. 1, 21, 69; 1985: chap. 15. Chaudhuri exaggerates the extent to which the Company adopted modern principles of systems analysis: see Massarella in C. Jones *et al.* 1986: 159; Basset 1981; Smith, *Wealth Nations*, ii. 756; Anderson & Tollison 1982: 1242.

Companies squandered capital on monopolies instead of technology. Management by committee in the Africa and Russian Companies proved disastrous and reinforced institutional drift.[67] The Hudson's Bay Company tried formal contracts and higher and graduated salaries; it imposed oaths and demanded sureties, searched letters and checked invoices, but still could not eliminate private trading.[68] Supervision and control of employees was equally difficult for absentee owners and for the Dutch and Portuguese.[69]

The classic case is the East India Company. Except when dominated by a single man, like Josiah Child, the primacy of procedure over substance created inertia and indecision, inevitable compromises and delays. It was no accident that the concept of 'unripe time' should be invented by the Company's historian.[70] The directors were afraid to delegate responsibility to their agents, but without rapid communications, decisions at the centre had to be made *ex post facto* on information which had usually been overtaken by events. Those at the top were only told what they wanted to hear. Authoritarian controls failed with monotonous regularity to close loopholes or counter the centrifugal tendencies of the market. The chain of command was weak and the records confused; costs were hidden and employees were rewarded for discharging fixed responsibilities, rather than for merit, initiative and effort.[71] Although high mortality weakened the stranglehold of patronage, one result of the struggle for place was that talent stagnated in low-level positions.

What made the East India Company profitable for its employees and directors, if not for the minority of passive shareholders, was corruption and the private trade. A few incumbents took pride in their work, but most developed no *esprit de corps*.[72] The senior officers responsible for enforcing Company policy were themselves dishonest; the private trade could not be eliminated and indeed was necessary to maintain the flow of

[67] Merrit 1960: 2; Willan 1956: 259–61; Carlos & Nicholas 1990: 863; Watt & Zimmermann 1983: 613–14. Galenson 1986: 144–7 presents a vigorous, if rather laboured defence of the Company's management. But the degree of sophistication of the market is exaggerated and the poor performance of the Company cannot simply be blamed on slow communications, pressure from planters, military obligations and interlopers. Carlos & Nicholas 1988: 417–19 also exaggerate the role of Companies.

[68] *Hudson's Bay Company Letters Outward 1680–7*, p. 74; Carlos & Nicholas 1990: 874.

[69] Galenson 1985: 233–4; Bennett 1966: 117; Disney 1977: 251; Hamilton 1948: 44; Glamman 1958: 2–49; Prakash 1985: 83–5; Roorda & Huvssen 1977; Steensgaard in Tracy 1990: 113, 127. For a contrary view that the VOC (Dutch East India Company) had a more explicit political structure see Meilink-Roelofsz 1976; Massarella in C.Jones *et al.* 1986: 147; Israel 1989a: 16, 412; Williamson 1985: chap. 2; Boyajian 1993: 123, 168; Patterson 1990: 168; Clarke & MacGuinness 1987: 19.

[70] Parkinson 1937.

[71] Cyert & March 1963; Arrow in Pratt & Zeckausen 1984: 49–50.

[72] Furber 1977: 93.

goods.[73] The joint-stock Companies succeeded precisely because they were not, in Weberian terms, legal-rational entities which enforced universal, impersonal rules, but a coalition of individual merchants who identified for their own personal gain the areas of greatest profit.

The East India Company did not initially have imperial ambitions, but by classifying its servants into graded ranks with defined duties and setting up a system of promotion based on seniority, it anticipated the future structure of the departments of state.[74] The professions and the government bureaucracy, which never went out of business, could afford to adopt as a value system those anti-acquisitive qualities of gentility which many gentlemen chose to ignore.[75] The notion of trusteeship, that public service was a duty, was appropriate for preserving and administering existing assets, for distributing wealth and for running a government or an empire. But, in pre-industrial England, economic growth was promoted by private business not by institutional loyalty or by enlightened bureaucracy.[76]

Entrepreneurs and rentiers

The optimal deployment of human resources depends on the relative weight of two related, but different, factors – the willingness to take risks and the impulse to innovate.[77] There was no clear division in English society between entrepreneurs and rentiers. Payment by fees and the private trade blurred the distinction between public careers and private business. The former cannot be identified with altruism, nor the latter with profit maximization. Some lawyers, doctors and clergymen were entrepreneurs and many a salaried employee aspired to run his own business. From the medieval Chamber to the modern kitchen cabinet, decision-makers have always felt obliged to bypass the bureaucrats and rely on their own intimate advisers. Small firms were often highly conservative and entrepreneurs usually sowed the seeds of their own destruction; a business which succeeded would eventually reach a size

[73] Watson 1980a: 111, 184; Chaudhuri 1965: 46; Anderson *et al.* 1983: 229; Carlos 1991: 143.

[74] See p. 106. Fry 1969. The French tobacco monopoly was run along similar bureaucratic lines: see Price 1973.

[75] Coleman 1987b: 148; Checkland in *Intern. Conf. Ec. Hist. III* 1968: ii. 72; Duman 1979; Elliott 1972: 47, 55–6; Reader 1966: 202–4; Rothblatt 1968: 91; Perkin 1989; Wiener 1981; Armstrong 1973: 49; Spangenberg 1976: 16.

[76] It is noteworthy that Tawney never asked why growth occurred: see Chambers 1971: 357.

[77] Ashton in Hayek 1954: 59–61; Sabel 1988: 35–7. Hobsbawm, on the other hand, in Aston 1965 summarily dismisses 'autonomous vagaries in businessmen's states of mind' and equates enterprise with the spirit of capitalism.

which could only be administered by an impersonal organization.[78] In a post-industrial world, the visible hand of the bureaucrat would become as necessary in business as in government.[79]

There was, however, a fundamental difference of attitude between the self-employed of every occupation, who had to generate their own income, and those living on salaries or passive, unearned income from property.[80] The former assumed risk in the expectation of profits and initiated change whereas the latter institutionalized their activity and favoured stability.[81] Even in profit-based corporations, managers could acquire an aversion to risk and novelty and place more emphasis on control of income than on maximization of profits.[82] The organization man, whether in business or government, tended to husband rather than to augment resources, to consolidate not to create, to plan but not originate.[83] Businessmen who played safe and clung to well-worn routines could miss opportunities and fall behind their more enterprising competitors.[84] There was always a danger that a comfortable managerial ideology would supersede egotism and the pursuit of profit.[85]

No progress would have been achieved, had men of property invested solely in assets with minimum risk. The rentier spirit always inclined to reduce the supply of venture and working capital. In most European states, surplus capital was invested in land, heritable offices, *rentes constituées*, and perpetual and life annuities from either the state or from private individuals.[86] There was a genuine danger that capital in England would also be diverted from productive business to underwrite the military expenditure of the government and the social costs, portions and consumption of the landowners.[87] Although several distinct capital markets emerged, they were all imperfect and geared primarily to the needs of the state. Public investment in business was hampered by

[78] Mommsen 1980: 167.

[79] Pollard 1965: 13–14; Dingwall & Lewis 1983: 47; Williamson 1981: 1537–8; Chandler 1979; Chandler & Daems 1980.

[80] Anderson in Anderson & Latham 1986: 176–7; Perkin 1969: 221–30, 319–23.

[81] This distinction is similar to but not identical with that of Sombart, who distinguished the competitive, acquisitive entrepreneur from the rational, systematic, frugal and disciplined bourgeois.

[82] On the role of entrepreneurship in corporate management of modern firms see Easterbrook 1949: 326; Cole 1968–9: 20–3; Lee 1990; Landes 1986: 616.

[83] Berlin in Warner *et al.* 1969: 23.

[84] Veblen 1904: 380.

[85] Weber 1968: iii. 1393 feared that bureaucracy would stifle capitalism; Mommsen 1974: 95–115.

[86] Roper 1969: 35–6; Hurstfield 1973a: 324; Cowan 1991: 129; Burke 1974: 319; Wolfe 1972; Collins 1988: 218; Schnappen 1957: 108; 1960: 1115–26; Thomson 1982: 129; Richet 1968: 785; Bonney 1980: 379; Tracy 1985: chap. 5; Hurt 1976; *Amterkauflichkeit* 1980.

[87] Habakkuk in Minchinton 1968: 200–1; Supple 1961. Even in the 1670s, contemporaries were afraid that royal borrowing would crowd out business investment: see BL Add. MS 32094, fo. 243v°; Child, *New Discourses*, p. 24; Giesey 1983: 204.

obstacles to sale and transfer of holdings. Capital was immobilized in bad years and investors responded slowly to opportunity. Most personal assets, including the pension funds of retirees, were invested in either real estate or, after 1688, in the Funds. Many landowners restricted their investment in business to providing their younger sons with an apprenticeship and a modest stake.[88]

Merchants acquired real property as a fixed asset, but they had a high liquidity preference. They inevitably concentrated on short-term and easily acquired profits; their life cycle determined the distribution of their investments.[89] The early colonial schemes were under-capitalized as they had no clear economic purpose and merchants were reluctant to invest in the future.[90] It was more prudent for a family to simply set up one or two of each generation in business and to secure their main capital in passive assets. The unincorporated, small-scale businesses which dominated manufacturing and the domestic trades had to rely on short-term and expensive credit, because they had to compete in the capital market with those who could offer land as security.

There were, however, compensating factors. Relatively little capital was immobilized in parasitic offices; assets were used to generate wealth as well as to secure status and stability.[91] Since offices did not confer nobility or tax exemptions, no hereditary office-holding class was created; the lawyers were more interested in founding landed families than judicial dynasties.[92] The elite in England was not simply concerned to maintain its dominance; it was prepared to look ahead and bear the unavoidable losses which accompanied expansion. Landowners invested in their property instead of just drawing rental income. The propensity to invest in risky undertakings remained constant. Despite the absence of limited liability, there was sufficient confidence to launch the voyages of discovery, the fisheries, the plantations, the chartered Companies and a variety of new industries, many floated by landowners who often borrowed their venture funds from more cautious merchants. The Atlantic trades were financed without support from the bankers.[93]

Joint-stocks tapped the accumulated savings of propertied society, not only for the long-distance trades but also for long-term industrial projects.[94] Although subject to calls, stock investments could be made in

[88] The aggregate transfer of capital through premiums was not negligible. In 1710, £3,792 was collected in Stamp Duty, representing *c.* £150,000 in premiums.

[89] This is a feature of modern underdeveloped economies: see Leibenstein 1963: 53, 113.

[90] Pares 1960: 6, 12; Andrews 1964: 360–1; Blake in Cronne *et al.* 1949: 92; Porter 1968: 59.

[91] For the impact of venality on European economies see Beik 1985: 13; Mousnier 1945; Kamen 1964: 69 n.12.

[92] Lucas 1974: 241.

[93] Price 1989: 279–81; 1987: 39–40.

[94] There is rarely a shortage of capital, only of conduits: see Postan 1935–6: 2.

instalments and shares could be bought, assigned, mortgaged, bequeathed and sold without reference to other owners.[95] The pool of investors continuously increased. Only 13 per cent of the Hudson's Bay Company's stock was held by actual traders; an average share in the early joint-stocks of the East India Company was £100–300 and, before 1694, active merchants were minority shareholders in the Company.[96] Despite complete lack of accountability, illiquidity and unlimited liability, the North-west Company attracted numerous small investors who paid 42 per cent of the start-up costs.[97] The great Companies could raise working capital on bond at stable and decreasing rates of interest. New financial intermediaries took deposits from passive investors and channelled them into more speculative ventures.[98] Informal joint-stocks in the shipping industry raised in fixed capital the equivalent of four years' wages per seaman.[99]

The Funds certainly competed with land for those seeking secure income investments, but they did not crowd out the venture capital of those who chose to invest in growth.[100] In fact, the extraordinary level of government borrowing provided an outlet for capital which could not be employed in trade because of the French War; recessions forced capital into riskier enterprises.[101] The English economy suffered more from shortages of opportunity than from shortages of capital. A satisfactory balance was also maintained between savings and investment; the rate of saving may have been low, but what mattered was that surplus capital was productively invested.[102] Its distribution was not perfect, but it was related to real economic needs and financed not just trade and industry but also agricultural improvement, building, utilities, education and the basic infrastructure. Unlike closed societies, like Tokugawa Japan, where restrictions on land purchase dissipated commercial capital, a free market and social competition mobilized both venture and working capital.[103] Risk and opportunity, not social prejudice, regulated investment. The rate of profit determined whether trade could compete with the returns from other investments; decisions were made by individuals, not by central planners.

The character of both the public and private bureaucracy was also different from that of the modern world. Ethical standards were low,

95 Jarvis 1959: 318.
96 Krey 1985: 138; D. W. Jones in Clark & Slack 1972: 343; Chaudhuri 1965: 3.
97 Shammas 1975: 98, 104.
98 See p. 88.
99 R. Davis 1962: 389.
100 Habakkuk 1979: 208.
101 Cullen 1968: 210.
102 Nurske 1964: 156.
103 Sheldon 1958: 85–8; Walker 1979: 8–9. For a different view and an attack on the Kyoto School see Hall 1961; T. C. Smith 1960: 97–102; Shiraishi 1958. Hirschmeier & Yui 1975: 308 show that the merchants later tried to feudalize, whereas the *samurai* industrialized.

office was considered to be private property and uncertified amateurism flourished. Salaried employees did not identify their interests with those of their employers and, despite their authoritarian structure, government and business institutions relied more on persuasion than on coercion. Limited resources imposed a ceiling on the overall size of the service industries. Although corruption and inefficiency in the public sector did raise private costs, business institutions were able to avoid many social costs.

Skills were acquired indirectly through apprenticeship and experience, because the schools were concerned with spiritual indoctrination or with producing scholars and gentlemen. Had a self-perpetuating, formal system of education been devised by academics for business, it would have reinforced bureaucratic tendencies and have stifled innovation. Although many men in government cherished the illusion that commerce could be regulated by statute and manoeuvred like a regiment, England was not hostage, like Colbertian France, to that intellectual and social arrogance which undervalues practical experience and exaggerates the power of reason over economic forces.[104]

Entrepreneurial behaviour is not a cumulative process; it occurs randomly in all societies and is directed towards diverse goals. The frequency of innovation depends on cultural conditioning and expectations, the range of choices and the distribution of rewards. Few businessmen in the seventeenth century resemble the dramatic *persona* conjured up by Schumpeter.[105] Even the more creative ignored obvious possibilities or failed to distinguish between their fruitful and their lunatic ideas. Others overresponded to market stimulus, were overconfident or too volatile or too undisciplined to translate their imaginative concepts into practical and profitable reality. Several ruined their associates and were usually indifferent to the harm inflicted on others by their mistakes. Success also bred complacency and rigidity of behaviour; the innovators of one generation became the conservatives of the next.[106]

The dynamism of the English economy is, however, largely explained by an abundance of creative entrepreneurs, who made a conscious effort to respond aggressively to events, who were committed to change and

[104] Bureaucracy knows no national or cultural barriers: see Kinmonth 1981. On the seventeenth-century debate in France and Holland see Rothkrug 1961: 85–6.

[105] Schumpeter's concept was foreshadowed by Sombart and by Friedrich von Wiesen: see Streisser & Marz 1988: 195, 208; Marz 1991: 20. On the protracted debate over the role of the entrepreneur see Leff 1979: 48–9; Soltow 1968; Gerschenkron 1962: 60; Sawyer 1958: 437–9; Bell 1967: 4; Holmes & Ruff 1975: 33; Kirzner 1989: 174; 1985: 11, 66; Barth 1962: 7–10; Hughes 1973: 2; Binks & Vale 1990: 18–20; Barreto 1989: 15; Casson 1985: 9; MacKendrick in Seldon 1980: 48; Payne 1967: vi; Bruchey 1965: xxii–xxiii; Court in Finberg 1962: 30; Habakkuk 1971: 316; Glade 1967: 246.

[106] Kardiner 1963: 35–8.

oriented towards growth. The active businessman lives in the present; when he develops a sense of history, it is a sign that his commitment and ability has peaked.[107] Instead of relying on old routines and protecting their share of the market by controlling output and sales, English entrepreneurs chose to invest in new concepts and techniques and to expand both extensively and intensively. They adopted an informal, flexible approach to problems and inspired others to follow their example and learn from their failures. Even errors of judgement led to inadvertent discoveries.[108]

The entrepreneur and the bureaucrat have antagonistic personalities and conflicting objectives. Historians, who themselves fall into one of these two categories, incline to value whichever matches their own temperament.[109] They either fault the bureaucrat for his neglect of economic efficiency or the entrepreneur for his indifference to social order. Paradoxically, however, the *modus procedendi* of each overlapped, complemented and reinforced the other.[110] Since wealth has to be created before it can be distributed, there is always a *quid pro quo* between public values and private interests. England never developed into a confiscatory economy, because political and social forces discouraged an excessive disparity between individual goals and collective values. The state bureaucracy acted as self-appointed guardians of the whole nation and the professions mediated between society and the individual. The personal dynamism and originality of the projector introduced change and loosened the dead hand of bureaucracy. The bureaucrats, on the other hand, absorbed and normalized change, slowed its pace in order to allow time for adjustment and moderated any excesses.

To develop the potential of the economy, both personal control and group direction were necessary.[111] Progress was achieved by Lamarckian adaptation as well as by Darwinian selection. Only the unconventional strategy of the entrepreneur could overcome cultural restraints; but only the conservative, systematic tactics of the bureaucrat could shore up and consolidate genuine improvements without alienating the elite. Shock troops were essential to break through the line, but regular divisions were needed to mop up opposition and occupy the ground. The unilateral strengths of each cancelled out their respective weaknesses.

They did not have equal importance. In most societies, entrepreneurs are less common than bureaucrats, who expand to fill any vacuum.

[107] Bourn 1975. [108] Nye 1991: 131ff; Greenfield & Strickon 1981: 490–9.

[109] Modern theories of entrepreneurship usually treat employee-managers as potential entrepreneurs, but Schumpeter 1950 predicted that capitalism would metamorphose into socialist bureaucracy. See Heertje 1981: 103; Clemens 1989: 254–63; Rosovsky in Rosovsky 1966. [110] Abernathy *et al.* 1983; Hirschman 1959: 17.

[111] Burke 1974: 10; Hirschman 1970: 18; Dimock 1960: 1–4; Blau 1963: 9.

Adjustment was also necessary to ensure that the professional and business sectors of the economy developed in tandem. It is difficult to determine how successfully the distribution of talent in pre-industrial England balanced innovation with consolidation. Even modern economies have largely failed to identify the precise mixture of elements which, through controlled combustion, will yield the maximum propulsive power. But where both approaches could be co-ordinated and synthesized, economic change could be reconciled with social stability.

Dynamic equilibrium

Market forces can only operate effectively in an open and integrated society.[112] A totally closed society would have impoverished the landed interest and frustrated the business community.[113] Pre-industrial societies, like *ancien régime* France, could be paralysed by social gridlock, which required a major war or revolution to disentangle.[114] But a permanent equilibrium would have been self-defeating. It was dynamic incongruence which sustained effort, as men wavered between the lure of security and the opportunity to advance. A perfectly adjusted society, which assimilates too efficiently, loses vigour and becomes obsolescent; mature societies, such as China or ancient Rome, fell into the torpor of a high equilibrium trap.[115] Even in an open society, there is always a danger that the newly arrived will succumb to the temptations of oligarchy and throw up new social barriers behind them.

English society had a flexible structure which was at the same time open and closed.[116] Merchants and gentlemen could bypass or ignore the restraints imposed by institutions and by convention without provoking a hostile reaction which might compromise their social objectives. Deviation was tolerated and self-help was encouraged by reduced social control. Merchants could join the elite without becoming office-holding nobles. But community standards were also enforced and social preferment was denied to those whose behaviour failed to conform to accepted patterns of obligation. The difficulty of obtaining social recognition only reinforced its desirability and exclusivity; achievement was legitimized without diluting incentives through saturation. The harmony between landed and business interests constituted a dynamic equilibrium, because it maintained social tension.

The social system also distributed wealth in gradations of inequality

112 Supple 1963: 55; Brown 1973: 65; Moore 1963: 18–21; Leibenstein 1963: 129.

113 Corbet, *Discourse Religion England*, p. 47; Chaussinard-Nogaret 1970: 476.

114 Mendels in Rabb & Rotberg 1981: 72.

115 Needham 1965: 48–9; 1970: 82; Balazse 1960; Kuznets *et al.* 1955: 517, 525.

116 Wrigley in Rabb & Rotberg 1981: 33.

which favoured growth. The primary resources of the country remained in private hands. Primogeniture and intermarriage concentrated capital in the hands of conspicuous investors whilst occupational mobility diffused capital between different sectors. Landholding was not morcellated or unproductively utilized, as in Han China or in those areas of Europe where partible inheritance impoverished more families in the long run than did primogeniture.[117] Large, consolidated estates were run efficiently, like businesses, and managed by professionals.[118] The rich became richer, but at the same time incomes slowly increased among the lesser men of property whose purchasing power was tapped by a network of towns.[119] A national market was created in many commodities; entrepreneurs were encouraged to emphasize volume rather than high profits per transaction.

A similar balance was struck between centralization and decentralization. The scale and distribution of business units were related to need. Although production was still imperfectly geared to distribution, thousands of small-scale and separate units were combined by both vertical and horizontal linkages. England did not have a dual economy; food production, mining, forestry and textiles were all integrated with domestic and foreign trade.[120] If those who paid the land tax and controlled government policy had not comprehended that their economic interests were closely bound up with business, they could have frustrated development. Agricultural productivity and estate management were instead improved by borrowing commercial techniques and by the continual stimulus of access to a larger market. The whole nation participated in expansion without any need for substantial government interference or for reform from the top.

This unusual degree of interaction reflected a healthy compromise between hope and doubt. The speculative excesses of the projectors and the intoxication of credit, which culminated in the Bubble, generated anxiety and hostile legislation.[121] The desire for growth was not universal because it carried heavy social costs and provoked disruption; many feared that they would be numbered the victims.[122] England, like all underdeveloped societies, resisted mobility and individualism which undermined social solidarity.[123] The elite had a vested interest in the status quo and all were aware that economic development has variable

[117] Ho 1964: 167; Firth & Yamey 1964; Nurske 1967: chap. 3. The negative effects of partible inheritance were also offset by earlier mortality and by remarriage.
[118] Thompson 1966: 516–17; Spring 1963.
[119] Eversley in E. L. Jones & Mingay 1967: 216–31.
[120] Dietz 1986: 288; Blanchard 1973: 85.
[121] Hoppit 1990: 309.
[122] Hirsch 1976: 11; Hollinger 1973: 377.
[123] Barbour 1950: 130.

benefits. Concerned about food shortages, external threats and internal dissension, Tudor governments had regarded every deviation from a subsistence economy with suspicion. But, in the seventeenth century, fear of competition and instability declined among the ruling elite and temporary upheavals did not prompt immediate retrenchment into self-sufficiency. Exposure to a wider world, as the economy expanded, encouraged optimism. The fact of growth reinforced belief in its virtues and a more rapid rate of development made it appear more natural and routine. Once it was recognized that all groups in society had a mutual interest in expansion, the notion of linear growth was gradually assimilated into the normative order and the question of distribution became less important.[124]

No phase of economic development can properly be described as revolutionary, except in the sense of accelerated evolution. It is difficult to distinguish in this period, as Adam Smith recognized, between the merely quantitative and the qualitative.[125] The economic developments of the seventeenth century had no *terminus ad quem* and they were both real and irreversible; but they were changes of degree rather than of kind and there was no sharp break with the past.[126] Institutions evolved slowly, because they did not wish to jeopardize the hierarchy of authority or their own internal cohesion. Business did not, like science, develop in great strides following in the footsteps of giants and mavericks. It was fuelled by the energy and input of many thousands of individuals, whose particular contribution was small, but whose cumulative impact was significant in the long run.[127] Economic change was not rectilinear, but multilinear, particularist and fast only in relation to the past. It was an ordered sequence, not of fixed stages, but of small steps and increments, which constituted piecemeal development through adaptation and mutation.[128] It is best described as evolutionary stasis.

This process was continuous and self-renewing. Growth was built into

[124] Genovese 1973: n.18. [125] Skinner 1979: 8.

[126] Gerschenkron 1968: 21; Hirschman 1977: 58.

[127] Jack 1977: 13; Meyer 1975: 56. An exaggerated distinction is sometimes made between on the one hand, the *Fernhandel* and 'high capitalism' and, on the other, the 'peddling' trade or the 'microcapitalisme des boutiques': see Braudel 1985: 60, 66; Rothermund 1988: 8; Wee 1988. Chaudhuri 1985: 82 argues that fear of the sea in agrarian societies excluded them from the long-distance trade. For criticism of these categories see Bentley 1975: 512–18; Meilink-Roelofsz 1962: 119. A more sophisticated distinction is that between the 'gains from trade' merchant and the 'value-added merchant': see Kindleberger in Skinner & Wilson 1976: 5; 1978: 137; Browne, *Works*, iv. 43.

[128] The theory of stages represents a compromise between evolution and revolution. See Supple 1984: 114; Hershlag 1969: 680. On the debate between the neo-functionalists and the evolutionists see Lyman in Brown & Lyman 1978: 69. Evolutionary models can transcend the limitations of regarding prices and markets as merely social mechanisms for transmitting information: see Nelson & Winter 1982: 403.

the system, because each factor was responsive to the movement of other factors in the causal network. Changes in one sector forced sequential changes elsewhere and an imbalance between sectors corrected any tendency towards self-maintenance.[129] Mobility and devotion to business were both a cause and a result of social and cultural integration and of economic development.[130] As Josiah Child put it, 'An Egg is the cause of a Hen and a Hen the cause of an Egg.'[131] The new wealth generated by business necessitated adjustments in the social structure, but the pursuit of that wealth was also conditioned by social ambition. The demonstration effect of expansion through individual effort stimulated others to embrace similar aspirations.

Business provided employment for the gentry and their entry made it more prestigious. Entrepreneurs gravitated towards areas of opportunity which, through further development, widened their comparative advantage. Knowledge begat knowledge and the accretion of new ideas multiplied choices. Urbanization and the continuous division of labour created new specialities. Prosperity generated a greater need for professional skills and further enlarged the market. Increased purchasing power changed the structure of demand and eventually improved productivity. The wealth generated by economic individualism fed the desire and provided the means for individual expression. Because each advance was incomplete or unsatisfactory in some respect, a counter-reaction was provoked which, in its turn, generated further development. Economic change was self-perpetuating and it occurred at an exponentially faster rate.

The pre-industrial English economy was not governed by long-term cycles, but it did tend to oscillate between extremes. Although the process of change was sometimes dialectical or triadic, it was usually dichotomous.[132] The pendulum swung between economic freedom and restriction, between centralization and decentralization, between ascription and achievement, between concentration and dispersion, between formality and informality.[133] Successive reversals of policy arose from a natural tendency to overreact to failure and the improbability that any approach could be totally successful.[134] Although continuous alternation was inherently self-limiting, it was precisely the tension between opposites which maintained dynamism in the economy.

No historicist necessity or inner logic of capitalism decreed that the

129 Hayek 1978; Kirzner 1979: 173.

130 Perkin in Finberg 1962: 66.

131 Child, *New Discourse*, p. 63.

132 Wagener & Drukker 1986: 16.

133 Gay 1923–4; Gras 1933: 311–12.

134 The argument that change develops dialectically rather than incrementally is developed by Kuhn 1970: 193. See also Bronfenbrenner 1971: 136–7.

vicious cycle of underdevelopment would be broken. Growth in England was not predictable or pre-ordained, but depended on a series of historical contingencies. It is true that, *ceteris paribus*, a business either expands or dies. Economic forces determined the fate of businessmen as a species, if not as individuals. But no single factor was completely autonomous and interdependence is very different from determinism. Evolution is governed by the flexibility of the cell as well as by the tyranny of the gene. The direction, speed and pervasiveness of change were all subject to variation, because they reflected individual decisions and individuals differed in their choices. Some ends were sacrificed and some alternatives forgone. Several events were fortuitous, many circumstances were unforeseen, and many of the consequences of human action and thought were unintended.

Historical interpretations have always been subject to cycles of fashion and to the influence of contemporary events. The study of pre-industrial societies has been conditioned by anthropological concepts and by the example of the Third World in the twentieth century. The theory of economic development has often proceeded by analogy and concocted a witches' brew of determinism and probability replete with appropriate ideological incantations. It is, of course, easy to construct plausible explanations *a posteriori*, when the outcome is a matter of record. But even short-term economic projections are invariably inaccurate and the arguments subsequently advanced to account for the discrepancy between prediction and result do not inspire confidence. It is doubtful whether the pattern of economic growth in pre-industrial England was sufficiently uniform to support a general theory of its mechanism.[135] No one hypothesis can accommodate all the evidence and the same factors operated differently at different times and places. Although growth is likely to occur whenever there are no constraints, through most of human history it has been the exception; lack of entrepreneurship can be seen as a consequence as well as a cause of economic backwardness.[136] The extraordinary economic vitality of Stuart England seems to warrant an exceptional theory. Historians always assume that all events have ascertainable causes, but the proposition must at least be entertained that some questions may never be definitively answered.[137]

There is a danger of exaggerating the uniqueness of the English experience and of underestimating the potential of other cultures.[138] England shared many characteristics with other pre-industrial societies

[135] Supple 1960: 554. For a similar conclusion about America see Bruchey 1965: 8; Abramovitz 1989: 82–3.
[136] Hoselitz 1952: 81.
[137] Hayek 1967: 40; Hexter 1955: 423; Heisenbach 1959; Buck & Cohen 1971: 107.
[138] Wrightson in Houston 1989: 249; Checkland 1960: 189; Cameron in Gallman 1977: 294.

and mobility also occurred in *ancien régime* monarchies, like France whose rate of growth was comparable, if not equal.[139] Entrepreneurial ability is found in all societies and it took enormous effort just to maintain even stagnant economies and empires.[140] The Asian merchants could hold their own with the English, African chiefs became important middlemen and the Cambodians were said to equal the Italians in knowledge of commerce; the Spanish Empire was sustained by its merchants as well as by its soldiers.[141] The triumph of Europe in world markets owed as much to firepower as to business skill.

England's rise from obscurity to economic preponderance without social upheaval or political coercion has similarities with the Dutch Republic. It had a comparative, though not an absolute advantage. But what was typical about England's economic performance was not necessarily what was most significant. Its distinctive business identity derived from internal dynamics, from the flexibility of its social structure and the relative mobility of its population. It was no coincidence that talent and commitment to business should emerge in an open society. The more sluggish performance of other European economies reflected their failure to tap efficiently the talent of their populations.

The expansion of the English economy was neither fortuitous nor simply induced by external pressures. Businessmen could of course only respond with the technology available to the specific opportunities presented by an economy, whose size and structure imposed severe limitations. Their methods and attitudes were different in important respects from businessmen in an industrialized world with its greater specialization, technological resources, scale and complexity of operations and its different structure of labour. But their contribution was indispensable. Even though they could not command the economic tides, they managed to overcome many obstacles by sheer resourcefulness and energy, to make the most of scarce resources, diversify the range of options and establish priorities. They were more than passive beneficiaries of favourable circumstances; they were the catalyst of change. It was the human factor which made the crucial difference, which both disturbed and restored equilibrium. In the final analysis, it was the businessman who made the pre-industrial economy work and who ultimately changed the rules of the game.

139 'La mobilité sociale' 1979: 36; Crouzet 1985. 140 Hirschman 1958: 3.

141 Tracy 1990: 10, 82, 95, 383–4; Pines, *Summa Oriental*, p. 41; Phillips 1987: 544; Chaudhuri 1971: 188; Brennig 1977: 338; Daaku 1970: 120–1; Curtin 1975; Subrahmanyam 1990a: 11; 1993.

Bibliography

MANUSCRIPTS

LONDON: PUBLIC ARCHIVES

The British Library

Cotton Charters iii, 13

Cotton Vespasian F. xvi–xvii

Downshire or Trumbull MSS Add. 41, 79, 86, 93–4, 101

Egerton 627, 784, 917, 921, 1049, 1680, 1971–2, 2224, 2395, 2521–4, 2543, 2713–22, 2974

Hargrave 321

Harleian 36, 597, 1231, 1529, 1875, 1898, 2243, 2286, 4354, 6815, 6821, 6837, 6949, 7021, 7497, 7525, 7601

King's 40

Lansdowne 162, 241, 683, 691, 768, 1156, 1849

Oriental and India Office Collections

European A.33, D.300, E.192

Court Minutes 31–5, 1678–90

Interest payments 1675–84

Accountant-General's Department, ledgers 1664–1720 (L/A G/1–10)

Stock transfers and dividends, 1681–8

Original correspondence series E/3/26–7, 1659–1712

Private Trade ledgers

Letter Books 1659–97 E/3/84

Factory Records Miscellaneous, 1664–73, 1676–1708, xvi, 1682–3

Factory Records Madras: Masulipatam 1682–3, Fort St George, 1655 and XXVI, 1677 Miscellaneous xii, xvi

Home Letter Series Miscellaneous 1/2, 4/1–2, 7–13, 15/1–3, 16, 23/1, 30, 36/6, 40/3, 40/5, 40/11–12, 44, 78/2

Marine Misc. xxvii/1 Committee of Shipping Minutes, 1685–6

Marine Records lxxix, lxxxix

Sloane 857, 867, 1341, 1425, 1453, 2809, 2902, 3228, 3668, 3670–1, 3675, 3984

Stowe 219–20, 303, 320(i), 324, 327, 554, 670, 745, 759, 993

Additional 2902, 4155, 4224, 5138, 5222, 5488–501, 5540, 5819, 6115, 9365, 10038, 10119–21, 10130, 10616, 11409–411, 12017, 12429, 12496–501, 14031, 14253, 14254, 15640, 15643, 15898, 17478, 17767, 18206, 18913, 19277–81, 19788, 20031, 21133, 21417–26, 21539, 21575, 22183–6, 22781,

22842–56, 22910–14, 22919, 23199, 24107, 24934, 25115, 25494–581, 27462, 27999–28009, 28078–9, 28140, 28714, 29548–96, 29873, 30383, 30494, 31300–2, 32093–4, 32324, 32456, 32504, 32519–20, 32524, 34015, 34123, 34218, 34324, 34799, 36109, 36448, 40696–713, 41613, 42122, 42123, 43730–3, 53725–8, 53782, 54332–4, 61903, 61935, 61989, 70223 (formerly Loan 29/223)

Loan 29/45C, 223; 57/73

Verney family correspondence (microfilm)

Corporation of London Records Office

Letter Books XX, YY, ZZ

Repertories of the Court of Aldermen 81–95

Common Serjeant's Books I–IV; Miscellaneous Inventories, Rolls 52–5, Nos. 15–189, orphanage accounts

Chamber loans and assessments 40/35

Journals of Common Council 49–51, 1678–94

Common Hall minutes 1642–60

Mayor's Court Rolls and Depositions

Session Rolls, Certificates of Convictions

Sheriff Court Rolls of Actions

Assessments under 1 Wm & Mary c. 13

Accounts of committee for compounding

Minutes of committee for registering exchange brokers

Guildhall Library

J. J. Stocken Collection of Biographies to 1700

Noble Collection of Memorials compiled by S. Gregory

D'Aeth papers 204, 507–507A, 1106, 2879, 2909, 2931, 2942, 2988, 3041/1–4, 3118–19, 3181–4, 3283–4, 3324, 3359, 3381, 3465, 3504, 3547, 3613, 3723, 5100–5112A, 5301–5301A, 5576/1–3, 5667–9, 5676, 6112, 6158/1–2, 6372, 6428/1–4, 6430–1, 6642–4, 6647–8, 6653–6, 6665–6, 6680–763, 6784, 6809–18, 6901–7, 6911–15, 7057, 7086–125, 7147–218, 7256, 7294–6, 7301, 7351–9, 7836, 8493A, 10187–8, 10770, 10823, 10835, 10857, 10882, 11311, 11316, 11593/1–3, 11741, 11892–3, 11892A, 11896, 12158, 15892A, 17145, 18760, 29429.

House of Lords Record Office

Correspondence of Robert Gray, 1606–18

Journal of Daniel Bonnel, 1624–9

Main Papers 264, Cary v. White

South Sea Company Papers

Committee Book of Select Committees, 1661–1716

Minute Book for Proceedings of Committee of the whole House, 1675–1714: Original Acts

Public Record Office

High Court of Admiralty: HCA 1/5–17, 22–4, 2/560, 7/75–103, 630, 23/4–23, 30/636

Assizes: ASS I 23/3, 24/19, 24/23
Audit Office: AO 1/3/1, 1/2303/2, 1/3814, 899/42, 1090, 1323, 1382–5, 1409, 1442/2
Chancery: Old Series (Quarles papers) 412; C1/3; C2/L/18/39, M/5/8, N3/39, O2/12, P16/69, R1/2, S5/15, S22/45, T5/48, W11/50; C103/40/168; C104/11–12, 15–16, 44–5, 107–8, 124–31; C105/12, 15, 29; C107/17–18, 20, 70–2, 161; C108/30, 132; C109/19–24; C110/28, 42–3, 81, 140, 151–2, 181; C111/50, 127; C113/11–14, 31, 34–7, 55–8; C114/59, 63, 78, 164–5, 180; C203; C205/10, 12A, 21; C213/473; C214/9; C459/97
Colonial Office: CO 77/49–51, 323/1–6, 324/1–9, 326/2, 388/1–7, 389/1–8, 390/1–2, 6–7, 12–14, 391/1–4, 91–106, 396/6–7
Customs: CUST 1A–1B, 64/55–6, 65/39, 72/71A, 89/37, 96/130, 97/74A
Exchequer: E101/63–5, 127/10, 520/24–5, 521/10,15, 634/4–13, 33–4, 635/39–41, 637/4, 668/4; E114; E122/17, 29, 31, 38, 44, 122, 196/30, 230/25, 237–40; E134/5; E154/3/35–4/40; E159; E178/2035, 4105, 4118, 4182, 4200, 4807, 5450, 5455–6, 5458, 5467, 7099; E190/53–6, 58, 62, 73–6, 78, 79, 80, 83; E209; E351/2966–7; E390/1–2, 13; E407/33; E520/24–5; E521/100; E.522/3
Prerogative Court of Canterbury: PROB 4, 5 (inventories); 11 (copies of wills)
Privy Council: PC1/1; 2/40–85
Court of Requests: REQ 2/295–7, 300, 302, 307, 308/27, 309, 312, 331, 387–90, 393, 397, 408, 417, 595, 669
State Papers: SP 9/91, 96, 106, 202, 247/54, 248/76–7; 14/26, 70, 81, 88, 102, 124; 16/155/57; 29/247; 31/5; 44/13, 18, 33, 37, 46, 54–5, 61, 71; 46/13, 83–8, 101–3; 71/22–7; 97/18–21; 105/108–9, 112–15, 143–68, 173–216, 332–8, 341, 343; 110/10–59, 67–9, 73, 76, 88–9; Misc. 15, 165
Treasury: T1/1, 130; T4/2–5; T11/8–11; T27/6–11; T40/1c; T48/7, 23; T70/76–82, 100–1, 107–9, 125–6, 163, 169, 1433; T64302

LONDON: PRIVATE ARCHIVES

Leathersellers Company of London
Court Minutes
Register of Bindings
Estate Records
Charitable Trusts
Wardens' Accounts

Lincoln's Inn
Hale XII, Collectanea Seldeni, xxxvii, lxxvii
Hargrave MSS
Maynard MSS, lix

Mercers Company
Court Minutes
Registers of Bindings

Religious Society of Friends Library
Autobiographical MSS 74

University of London, Palaeography Room
Nos. 59, 62, 265, 401–2, 553, 655

Westminster Abbey Muniments
Nos. 417–18, 683–704, 906–40, 10377, 11348–9, 54114, 54982, 58137

Dr William's Library
Baxter MSS

THE PROVINCES: PUBLIC ARCHIVES

Bristol City Record Office
Accessions 1087, 10531, 12964/1, 4281710
Ashton Court papers, AC C1–5, B.64, John King papers
Court of Orphans, 04426
Freke and Eston MSS

Bristol Reference Library
Jefferies MSS

Bedfordshire County Record Office
Harvey MSS, Trevor Wingfield MSS, Wynne MSS

Berkshire Record Office
Add. 41, 79, 86, 93–5, 101; D/EBUF/13, D/EDB1, 2, D/EDF/41, D/EEZ/31, D/ENF 611, D/EZ5/B1–6, 6/1–2, D/EHR/B1–3, D/EHY/36–4; Craven MSS F1–2

Buckinghamshire Record Office
Towne 7/11/191–8, R. H. Way

Cambridge University Library
DD ii. 13, iii. 84, vii. 26, ED iii. 70, EE ii. 32, iv. 18, 22, GG v. 8, 18, MM vi. 50, 57, OO vi. 114; Add. 91C, 3303 (9), 4858–9, 4873; Houghton MSS; Baumgartner papers

Cambridgeshire Record Office
L 95/12

Chester City Record Office
C/B/166

Cornwall Record Office
Ledger of Samuel Enys

Derbyshire Record Office
Gell MSS

Devon Record Office
Business papers of Leonard Yeo
61/6/1 Thomas Jeffery's ledger

Dorset Record Office
910, 2693e–2694, 10447

Essex Record Office
D/ENF/ D/DBA, D/DDC/A 1–2,5–5,F3,F7, D/DU 457/7; D/DEL F4, 7846
Papillon MSS

Gloucestershire Record Office
D.1086–7, 1799/247

Manchester Central Library
Accounts of Abraham Rodes

Hampshire Record office
Heathcote of Hursley and Richards papers

Hereford Record Office
F/iv/c, Business papers of John Foley

Hertfordshire Record Office
Panshanger Collection, papers of Robert Booth

Humberside County Archives Office
Lawley, DDFA 3713–17 (Thompson papers)

Centre for Kentish Studies
Q/SPd, U.22/E7, U.119/A1, C1–4, 7, U.133/B1–11, U.145/B2, C1, U.480/F1–2, U.593, 1301, 4466, U.1015/020, U.1515/1–2; Aylesford, Tufton and Lennard MSS

Lancashire Record Office
DDCa1/105, DDB/56(1), 58(4,12), 59(6,10), 61(1–21), 62(101,145,147), 64(3–4), DDCa/146, DDHp/38–9, DDK3, DDPd, DDR, DDTo, DDX/43, 312; Blundell MSS

Leicestershire Record Office
4 D 42/165
23 D57/2238–2370, 6332(46)

Lincolnshire Archives Office
Ancaster-Heathcote, 8/1, 9A/1–19, 9B/1–11, 9/D/1–17, 9/E/1–11, 10/A/13, 10/28, 11/A/4, 12/C/51; Holywell, 93/21; Massingberd of Gunby (Thomas Meux and Sir Burrell Massingberd); Monson and Eyre, 3/9–11, 28, 7/17/1–50, B/5, Misc. Books 21, CCIII; Nelthorpe 4/21/3, 7/17/1–50, 9/A–B, 9/D/

169/; Pearson-Gregory (Walter and William Williams papers) 2PG 121; Trollope-Bellew (John & Anthony Trollope papers); Whichcote 1/16–17, 1/B/48–51, 2/11/27, 2/28, 41–43, 2/56, 66–7, 77, 114/5; Sheffield MSS D/1–3, 6, D/2/28, 32, D/3/18–19

Diocesan Archives, Probate Inventories, Nos. 169/97, 172/202, 173/253

Norfolk Record Office

Inventories

Northamptonshire Record Office

Cokayne C.2438, 2482, 2531–2, 2537, 2562, 2575–6, 2581, 2592–4, 2596–2658, 2690, 2701, 2711–17, 2775, 2804, 2807, 2815, 2821–2, 2858–9, 2871–2, 2882, 2898, 2902, 2922–3, 3218; IL 438, 3136–8, 3145–6, 3166, 3173, 3182

Bodleian Library

Add. A.56, C.267; Ashmole 1809; Ashurst C.1, DD cl; Aubrey 10; Carte 81, 216; Ch. London & Middlesex 501; Dashwood/A1–2; Dep. C.231; Don. C.61; Eng. Hist. B.122, C.44, 63, 236, D.156–63; Eng. Lett. C.192, D.195; Eng. Misc. C.14, 260, 292, D.12–13, F.78; Fr. C.28; Jones 17, Locke C.5, C.30; Malone 2; Perrott 2; Radcl. dep. deeds 68; Rawl. A.21, 82, 303, 315, 414, 478, C.395/37, 745–7, 861, D.23, 745–7, 1114, 1483; Rawl. Lett. 66; Rylands E.17; Smith Newsb. C.10; Tanner clxxx, 287; top. Kent a. 1, 913

Shropshire Record Office

Attingham (Richard Hill papers) 112/1924–44, 1948, 1969, 2866; Brooke (Forester) 1224 (William Sharpe papers); Plymley, Acc. 567; Scott, 49/602, 633–4; Whitmore MSS, Walcott & Bitterley MSS; Shrewsbury Drapers Company records

Somerset Record Office

Dickinson of Kingweston (Prankard & Dickinson), Trollope-Bellew and Carew of Crowcombe papers; Hylton (Amerdown Park) MSS

Staffordshire Record Office

Wombourne Wodehouse, Bundle 46/2

Suffolk Record Office (Ipswich Branch)

Barnes 359/785/XIX, 4090/VII; Beccles Borough Records A.34, Misc.4, D.2; Blois HE30, 312/178, 369/25, 34, 154, 207, 223, 336, 407; Marnock SI/13/6/1–2, 1318; Mills GB1/8/1–4; Tollemache B.4,7, L.J.V (28); Tooley Acc. 2672; Eye Borough Court papers, Bundle B

Surrey Record Office

Bray (540) 85/15/1, More MS

Ledger of John Yeamans

Somers MSS, E.23, H.1–5, K.18, L.10, N.3, O.1–7

East Sussex Record Office

145/1–8, 145/11

West Sussex Record Office
Add. 194–5, 346, 507, 523, 834, 864; Cowdray papers (Newdigate Owsley)

Warwickshire Record Office
Alsop MSS, CR. 314/114–57, 721

Wiltshire Record Office
Wansey papers

North Yorkshire County Record Office
Z.C.Q., Acc. ZCG 1–8; ZK 11125–55 (Turner-Newcomen papers)

Sheffield Archives
Barker Bright BR.184 (JO6); FitzWilliam, Letter Book 9; Pye, 1–2; Spencer Stanhope (William, Benjamin and John Spencer papers); Tibbetts T.C. 58, 382, 515–16 (Samuel and Aquila Dawson)

West Yorkshire Archive serving Leeds
NH 2183, 2191, 2193A, 2277, 2292, 2365, 2438–40, 2444, 2448, 2492, 2513, 2638–42, 2644–9, 2650–95, 2724, 2735, 2737, 2739–40 (22/1–9), 2758A, 2760, 2762–3, 2767–8, 2774, 2841, 2845, 2854, 2859–60, 2863, 2900, 2911–13, 2922, 2926, 2949, 2954, 2960–1, 2962 (K.13); DB/36, 129, 204/2; PO/6–10; Bilton Park HC

National Library of Wales
Bodewyd 3; Myddelton 721–31, 732, 734–5, 1208, 1210, 1297, 3247, 3367, 3666, 3670, 4740, 5609, 12540; Wynn, 473, 696, 789, 865, 883, 895–6, 964, 1013, 1023, 1078, 1083, 1088, 1132, 1154, 1205, 1558–9, 1561, 1952, 2602, 5830, 9685B; Add. 465

Birmingham City Archives
Zachary Lloyd Collection, Hampton MSS, Coventry MSS

Coventry City Record Office
MS A.105, Account book of Company of Corvisiers

THE PROVINCES: PRIVATE ARCHIVES

Bristol University Library
Pinney papers, Society of Merchant Venturers

Cambridge, Trinity College
O 11 e. 3; 710 (R. 515)

Cambridge, Gonville and Caius College
420, 425

Cambridge, St John's College
Bb James 613

Nantwich Parish Church
Accounts of Tench family

Chetham's Library
Raines MSS, vol. xi
MS Mun A.2.137, A.3.123

John Rylands University Library of Manchester
Clark papers; Crutchley MSS, no. 180

Liverpool Record Office
Norris papers

Liverpool University Library
Moore papers

Nottingham Library Archives Department
Mellish of Hodsock, B.1., LBJ/176–1151, ME 151–90; Myddelton MS

Oxford, Worcester College
B.2.19

William Salt Library (Staffordshire Record Office)
HM 37/36, SMS 1(i–ii); Chetwyn MS 110; Dartmouth MSS; Hand Morgan MS 24/1, 27/329/8

Hall MSS (privately owned)
Commercial correspondence, 1688–1703

Leeds University Libraries
Brotherton Collection, LTQ Tempest, Aptall

West Yorkshire Archive Service, Yorkshire Archaeological Society
Grantley MSS 323

FOREIGN ARCHIVES: USA

William Andrews Clark Library
Account book of Rebecca Steel (M.3 M 531)

Huntington Library, San Marino
Ellesmere, 34/C/34, 35/B/34, 2373, III (6959–68A, 8508–17), V (9873–81), xviii, xxi, xxxiii-vi, HM 17, 821, 1264, 2509, Almanack 1652–8, Blathwayt 9625, Stowe MSS

Beinecke Library, Yale University
Chardin MSS

Boston Public Library
Acc. 284/C.1.24, K.53

Harvard University Library, Kress Library
Seligman MS 1625 E.W 69; 96, 106, 123, 138, 148, 787 (Foxwell)

New York Public Library
Hall MSS

FOREIGN ARCHIVES: FRANCE

Archives Nationales
AQ^{62}; Sous Series B^1 76–7, 376–89, 1042–3; B^3 1, 33–9, 234–5, 244, 249, 301; E 2664; G^7 1518, 1521, 1684–1703, 1893; V^7 27–32/400
Affaires Etrangères, correspondence politique 208–10, 2000–3; Fonds divers Angleterre 35–6

Archives Départementales
Bouches du Rhône
IX B 171–2, 174–5; E.2664 (Mélanges); xxxix E. 29, 35, 47, 53
Gironde
7 B. 2020
Ille-et-Vilaine
4 FC
Lot-et-Garonne
E. 41–8, 4 J. 20
Rhône
Fonds B

Archives de la Seine
Ser. B^6, 1/32–6, 4/1–5, 5/2923

Bibliothèque Nationale
Anc. franc MS 18592

Bibliothèque Sainte Geneviève
MS 1052

ALPHABETICAL LIST BY NAME OF PRIVATE BUSINESS RECORDS

This list includes English families active in every type of business between the mid sixteenth century and 1720, whose private papers have survived in more than fragmentary form. The majority of records relate to the second half of the seventeenth century. Some of them appear in more than one archive and many names have variant spellings. The size and scope of the individual collections vary enormously. A few contain thousands of letters and whole sets of ledgers, but most consist of individual account books; journals are more common than ledgers and letter books. New private collections constantly come to light and there are numerous caches among the records of the law courts. Some examples (John Kendricke, Sir William Cranmer, Thomas Carew, Thomas Evans, Thomas Lewes and John Wise) have surfaced briefly in sales of manuscripts. Several personal papers, like those of the Hudleston family, also remain in private hands.

The following categories have been excluded: alien merchants who were temporarily resident in England and merchants native to other countries whose home and base of operations were permanently abroad; the official correspondence and business records of the factors and agents of the joint-stock Companies and of employees of central and local government and the guilds; logs and journals of travellers, ship captains and pursers unless they are combined with account books, as is the case with Bryan Blundell. Collections which straddle different categories or the terminal date of 1720 have usually been included

Abbott, Robert: GLL 2931
Adams, Richard: PRO E178/4182
Alsopp, Nathaniel: Warws. RO CR 314/114–57
Alvey family: Notts. RO DDA
Anderson family: University of Virginia , McGregor Collection
Archdale, Richard: GLL
Ashe, James, Richard, Edward and Abraham: PRO C107/20; IESRO A.P. S1/177
Ashley, Joseph: Westminster City Archives Acc. 985
Ashton, Matthew: Bod. Eng. Misc. C.602; German c.21
Ashurst, Henry: Bod. Ashurst DD c.1
Attwood, William: PRO C109/19–24
Aylward, John: Bod. Eng. Lett. C.192; Arundel Castle, Aylward MSS
Backwell, Edward: Glynn Mills
Baker, Thomas: Bod. Eng. Hist. C.236
Banks, Sir John: see D. C. Coleman, *Sir John Banks* (Oxford, 1973)
Barcroft, Ambrose: Lancs. RO DD/B/56–64
Best, Thomas: KAO U.480/F 1.2
Blackett, John, William and Michael: CUL Dd vii.26, Add. 91c; Northumberland RO
Blackwell, John: PRO C105/29
Blois, William: IESRO HE 30
Bluett family: Devon RO, Nutcombe and Bluett
Blundell, Bryan and Nicholas: Lancs. RO; see N. Blundell, *The Great Diurnall*, ed. J. S. Bagley (Rec. Soc. Lancs. & Ches., 110, 1968) and *Blundell's Diary and Letter Book*, ed. M. Blundell (Liverpool, 1952)
Blundell, haberdasher: GLL
Blunt, Charles: PRO C114/164–5
Boddington, George and Thomas: GLL 10823
Bolton, Francis: East Sussex RO 145/1–8
Bolton family: in private hands
Bonnell, Daniel: House of Lords RO
Booth, Robert: House of Lords RO; Herts. RO, Panshanger Collection
Bosanquet family: in private hands

Boucher, Benjamin: Lincs. AO Ancaster 9/A/5, 9/D/10, 16a
Boughey, Thomas: GLL 18760
Bowrey, Thomas: GLL 3041/1–4; Lloyd's; BL Add. 5222
Bragg, Giles: PRO SP 46/86–7
Brailsford, Thomas: PRO C142/13, C110/152
Bridgwater family: PRO C104/11–13
Bristow, Robert: Virginia State Library Acc/22953
Broadley, Thomas: Wilberforce House, Broadley MSS
Brooke, William: GLL
Buckeridge, Nicholas: Bod. Eng. Hist. C.63, Rawl. C.395, 746–7; see also N. Buckeridge, *Journal and Letter Book*, ed. J. R. Jensen (Minneapolis, 1973)
Bulmer, Sir Bevis: see H. M. Robertson in *J. Ec. & Bus. Hist.*, 4 (1931–2)
Burlamachi, Philip: see A. V. Judges in *Economica*, 6 (1926)
Burr, Olyff: see J. E. G. Bennell in *Trans. Lond. & Midd. A. S.*, 31 (1980)
Burwell, John: Devon RO
Caillouel family: Dorset RO, Solly MSS
Caldwell, Sir James and Henry: John Rylands Univ. Lib., Bagshaw MS 3/1–3, 12/1/59
Calley, Sir William: in private hands
Campbell, John: Coutts Strange
Carew, Thomas: sold to unknown buyer
Cary, John and Shershaw: Bristol RO 10531; BL Add. 5540, Stowe 670; PRO C459/07, 512/46; Bod. Locke MS C.5, 30, Rawl. A.414
Catchpoole, Allen: Kress Lib. MS 148
Causton, William: PRO E178/4118
Chapman, Sir John: GLL
Chardin, Daniel: PRO 30/26/52, C114/180; Beinecke Lib., Yale
Chetham, George and Humphrey: Chetham's Lib., Raines MSS
Child, Sir Francis: Williams Glynn; Greater London RO Acc. 1128/177–8; see G. H. Price, *The Marygold by Temple Bar* (1902); 'Child and Co.', *Three Banks Review*, 98 (1973); E. R. Samuel, 'Sir Francis Child', *ibid.* 113 (1977)
Child, Sir Josiah: IOL Home Misc. 40/12; PRO C10/161/16, C110/140
Cholmely, Sir Hugh and Nathaniel: N. Yorks. RO ZCG/1–8
Clarke family: BL Sloane 867
Clarke, William and Ralph: Public Record Office of Northern Ireland, Belfast
Clayton, Sir Robert: see F. T. Melton, 'The Clayton papers', *B. I. H. R.*, 52 (1979) and *Sir Robert Clayton* (Cambridge, 1986)
Cocks, Nathaniel: KAO U.22/E7
Cokayne family: Northants. RO C.2438–3218
Coles, Robert: see J. S. Bromley, *Corsairs and Navies 1660–1760* (1987)
Cope, James: PRO C104/45
Corsellis, Nicholas: Essex RO D/DU 45717
Corsini, Nicolas: GLL
Corwin, George: Essex Institute, Salem
Cotesworth family: Gateshead Central Lib. Carr Ellison MSS; see J. M. Ellis, *William Cotesworth* (1981)
Courteen, Sir William: BL Sloane 3515
Cranfield, Lionel: see M. Prestwich, *Lionel Cranfield* (Oxford, 1966)

Cranmer, Sir William: sold to unknown buyer
Craven, Sir William: Berks. RO
Crewsdon, John: Cumbria RO, Crewsdon of Kendal
Crofton family: Manchester Reference Library
Crowley, Ambrose: see M. W. Flinn, *Men of Iron* (Edinburgh, 1962)
Cruttenden, Joseph: Bod.; see *Atlantic Merchant Apothecary*, ed. I. K. Steele (Toronto, 1977)
Cullum, Sir Thomas: see A. Simpson, *The Wealth of the Gentry* (Chicago, 1961)
D'Aeth, Thomas: GLL; see A. E. J. Hollaender in *Archives*, 3 (1957)
Daffy, Anthony: PRO C114/59
Daniel, Alexander, William and John: KAO U.119
Darby, Paul and Roger: PRO C107/158 and in private hands
Dashwood, Sir Francis: Bod. Dashwood A1–2
Davis, Richard: ULL 655
Dawson, Aquilla and Samuel: Sheffield Central Lib. Tibbetts MSS
Day family: Bristol RO
Delafaye, Charles: PRO SP
Dickinson family: Som. RO
Duarte, Manuel Levy: see E. R. Samuel in *T. J. H. S. E.*, 27 (1982)
Du Cane, Peter and Richard: Essex RO D/DDC
Eaton, Prestwick: PRO SP 437
Ebford family: Devon RO
Edge, Ralph: Notts. RO DDE
Edwards, John: Leics. RO 23 D57
Elwes, Jeremiah: PRO C107/161
Enys, Samuel: Cornwall RO
Eston, Thomas: Bristol RO
Evance, Sir Stephan: PRO C110/81, C111/50
Evans, Thomas: sold to unknown buyer
Eyre, John and Thomas: Lincs. AO 28B/5
Ferrar, Nicholas and John: Magdalene College, Cambridge
Fisher, Edward: KAO U.133/B1/1–11
Fisher, Thomas: GLL
Fleming, Sir Daniel: Cumbria RO, Le Fleming of Rydal Hall
Foley, John and Robert: Gloucs. RO D.421/E6; Heref. RO F/iv/c
Fowle, Sir Thomas: PRO C104/107–8, 124–5
Fowney, John: Som. RO, Castle MSS
Fox, Sir Stephen: see C. Clay, *Public Finance and Private Wealth* (Oxford, 1978)
Freeman, William: Institute of Jamaica
Gayer, John: GLL 1525
Gell, Philip: Derbyshire RO, Gell MSS
Gibbs, Robert: Massachusetts Historical Society, Boston, Massachusetts MS
Giesque, Mathias: PRO C104/126–9
Goldney, Thomas: Bath RO
Goodman, Gabriel: Somerset RO, Hylton MSS
Gore, Sir William: BL Loan 29/455
Granthan, Thomas: Lincs. AO, Andrews MSS
Gray, Robert: House of Lords RO

Greene, John: BL Sloane 857

Gresham, Sir Thomas: Mercers Company London; PRO E101/520–1, 14A; see P. H. Ramsey, 'The Merchant Adventurers' (unpub. D.Phil. thesis, Oxford, 1958)

Guy, John: Lambeth Palace 250

Hall, Hugh: New York Public Library

Hall, Seckford: PRO C110/15A–B

Hall family: in private hands; see C. Gill, *Merchants and Mariners* (1961)

Hanmer family: Som. RO, Trollope-Bellew (Carew) MSS

Hardwick, Thomas: Drapers Company of London

Harley, John: Som. RO, Hylton MSS

Harley, Nathaniel: BL Portland MSS; Heref. RO; see HMC, Portland

Hart, Moses: Shropshire RO, Attingham 112/1948

Havilland, James de: see J. de L. Mann in *Trans. Soc. Guérn.*, 21 (1982)

Heathcote, Sir Gilbert and Caleb: Lincs. AO, Ancaster-Heathcote MSS; Hampshire RO, 9A1–19, B1–11, Heathcote of Hursley MSS; Bod. Don. C.61

Hedges, Sir William: IOL Misc. Factory Records

Helyar, Cary: Som. RO; see J. H. Bennett in *Wm & Mary Q.*, 3rd ser., 21 (1964)

Herne, Frederick: GLL 6372

Hibbins family: BL Add. 34273

Hill, John: KAO U.1515/01

Hill, Richard, Samuel, Thomas, Nathaniel and Humphrey: KAO U.1515, U.1451 c. 1; Coventry RO; CUL; BL Add. 5488–9; Shropshire RO Attingham 112–1775; Kress Lib. 148; see also R. H. E. Hill in *Home Counties Mag.*, 6 (1904)

Hoare, Edward and Joseph: PRO 30/70, C104/12–13; in private hands; see also N. K. Woodbridge in *History Today*, 69 (1969)

Hodgkinson, William: in private hands; see P. Riden in *Scand. Ec. H. R.*, 35 (1987)

Hosea, Alexander: see A. Plummer, *London Weavers Company* (1977)

Hoskins, William: ULL 265

Houblon family: Berks. RO; Essex RO, Hallingbury Place MSS

Hovell, William: National Register of Archives, Dublin

Howell, Thomas: Drapers Company of London; see G. Connell-Smith in *Ec. H. R.*, 2nd ser., 3 (1950–1)

Hunter, Henry: Berks. RO D/EZ5

Hutchinson, James: Company of Merchant Adventurers of York

Ingram, Sir Arthur: West Yorkshire Archive Service, Leeds TN EA/1/, PO/LA; see also A. F. Upton, *Sir Arthur Ingram* (1961)

Isham, John: see *John Isham Mercer*, ed. G. D. Ramsay (Northants. Rec. Soc., 21, 1962)

Jacobson, Rimbold: PRO SP Misc. 9/96, 46/88

Jaison, Roger: John Rylands Univ. Lib., Crutchley MSS

Jeake, Samuel: East Sussex RO 145/11, FRE 4870

Jeffery, Thomas: Devon RO 61/6/1

Johnson, Sir Henry: BL Add. 22183–6

Johnson, John: see B. Winchester, *Tudor Family Portrait* (1955)

Jones, Richard: Berks. RO D/EBu/T96

Kendricke, John: PRO Chancery Old Series (Quarles MS) 412
Kendrick, John: see Melton 1986a
King, Sir Andrew: WAM
King, John: Bristol RO
Knight, John: GLL; see also I. V. Hall in *T. B. G. A. S.*, 68 (1949)
Knight, Joseph: PRO C459/97
Knipe, Edward: IOL Misc. Factory Records, Bombay, xii
Knott, Thomas: PRO, Records of the committee for compounding
Kytson, Sir Thomas: CUL Hengrave Hall 78, 81, 88; see P. H. Ramsey in *Produzione Consumo commercio e Consumo dei Panna di Lana* (Prato, 1970)
Lambard, John: Drapers Company of London
Laurence, Thomas and Isaac: PRO E520/24–5, 521/10, 15
Leppington, Lemuel: see D. Dawe, *Stilbeck's Drysalters* (1950)
Liddell family: see *The Letters of Henry Liddell, 1673–1717*, ed. J. M. Ellis (Surtees Soc., 197, 1987)
Lister, John and Samuel: Newcastle upon Tyne Univ. Lib. Caldendale MSS
Lloyd, John: PRO C107/161
Loving, John: BL Add. 12423
Lowther, Sir Christopher: see *Commercial Papers of Sir Christopher Lowther*, ed. D. R. Hainsworth (Surtees Soc., 189, 1977)
Lucas, Thomas: IOL Factory Records, Fort St George
Lyde, Nehemiah: Essex RO D/DDC
Macartney, George, 1660–81: Belfast Linen Hall Lib.
MacFarlane family: GLL
Manifold, John: IOL Home Misc. 40/11
Marigana, Joan: PRO E178/5456
Marnock, Thomas: IESRO SI/13/6/1
Marescoe, Charles (and Jacob David): PRO C114/63–78; see *Markets and Merchants*, ed. H. Roseveare (Oxford, 1987)
Massingbird family: IOL Home Misc. 40/3
Master, Streynsham: IOL Misc. Factory Records
Masters, James, Daniel and Richard: KAO U.119
Mawhood, William: GLL
Mead, John: GLL 11896
Mellish family: University of Nottingham ME 151–90, LBJ/176
Meux, Samuel and Thomas: Lincs. AO, Massingberd of Gunby
Michel, John: GLL
Mills, Thomas: IESRO GB1
Mills family: see D. W. Thoms in *Business History*, 11 (1969)
Mitchell, Samuel: Lincs. AO, Ancaster-Heathcote 9/6–13
Mitford, Michael: GLL 11892–892a
Mohun, Richard: IOL Factory Records, Fort St George, xxxvi
Monson, William: Lincs. AO, Monson MSS
Montague, Charles: Newcastle upon Tyne Univ. Lib.
Moore, Sir John: GLL 507, 507A, 3504; Leics. RO
Moore, Robert: Shropshire RO
Moore family of Liverpool: University of Liverpool Lib.
Morley, John: Som. RO, Hylton MSS

Mosley, Nicholas: CUL Ed iii. 70
Myddelton, Sir Thomas and Richard: National Library Wales, Chirk Castle MSS; see also E. D. Jones in *Nat. Lib. Wales J.*, 1; J. W. Gough, *Sir Hugh Myddelton* (Oxford, 1964)
Narbough, John: BL Add. 21539
Nelmer family: Gloucs. RO D1086
Nelthorpe family: Lincs. AO 4/21/3
Newall, Richard: Bod. Malone 2
Newcombe, Thomas: PRO C104/107–8, 124–5
Newsom family: PRO C104/77–80
Nichols, William, Charles and Thomas: KAO U.133/B1/1–4
Nicholson, Clement: PRO C107/161
Nicholson family: Liverpool RO
Noblet, Ruddock & Co.: Bristol RO
Norris, Richard: Liverpool RO
North, Sir Dudley: see R. Grassby *The English Gentleman in Trade* (Oxford, 1994)
North, Richard: Bod. Rawl. 746
Nutcombe and Bluett: Devon RO
Owsley, Newdigate: West Sussex RO
Oxinden family: BL Add. 27999–8009, 40696–713, 54332–4
Pagnelli family: CUL Add. 4858–9, 4873
Palmer, Thomas: GLL 3723; PRO C114/55–6
Palavicino, Sir Horatio: see L. Stone, *Sir Horatio Palavicino* (Oxford, 1956)
Papillon, Thomas and Philip: KAO U.1015/C20–27; Essex RO, Colchester and North-east Essex Branch
Payne, Charles: GLL 5301–1A
Peers, Sir Charles: GLL 10187
Pengelly, Thomas: Bod. Add. C267 and in private hands
Pepperell, William: see B. Fairchild, *William Pepperell* (Ithaca, 1954)
Phill, Henry: PRO C111/127
Pinney family: University of Bristol Lib.; see also R. Pares, *A West India Fortune* (1950), *Merchants and Planters* (Economic History Review, supplement 4, 1960) and *The Historian's Business*, ed. R. and E. Humphreys (Oxford, 1961)
Pitt, Thomas: BL Add. 22842–56; PRO C110/28, 81
Plymley, Richard: Shropshire RO Acc. 567
Pollexfen family: Devon RO, Drake MSS
Pooley, Giles: Lancs. RO DDC/A
Povey, Thomas: BL Add. 11410–11; Gloucs. RO D 1799/E247
Prankard, Griffin: Som. RO, Dickinson of Kingweston MSS
Prowde, Richard: Shropshire RO Acc. 567
Pye, Thomas: Sheffield Archives Pye 7 (b); National Maritime Museum
Radcliffe family: GLL 6642–4: see also R. Davis, *Aleppo and Devonshire Square* (1967)
Ramstorn, Edwin and William: Essex RO D/DEL/F4; GLL
Rank, Edward: Doncaster Archives Department
Reeve, Thomas: GLL 3181–4
Richards, John: Dorset RO; GLL

Richardson, Thomas: Northants. RO, Misc. 6
Riddell family: Northumberland RO
Robinson, Sir William: West Yorkshire Archive Service, Leeds, Newby Hall MSS
Rodes family: see T. S. Willan, *The Inland Trade* (Manchester, 1976)
Rooke, John: GLL
Sandes, Thomas: Bank of England RO
Sanford, Henry: Bod. Dep. C.231
Schoppens, Edward and John: Leics. RO 23 D57
Scott, Rich and Jonathan: Shropshire RO, Betton-Strange MSS
Sexton family: PRO SP 46/9; see W. Sharp, 'Correspondence of Thomas Sexton' (unpub. M.A. thesis, London, 1953)
Shalcross, Sir Humphrey: see M. Beloff in *E. H. R.*, 54 (1939)
Sharpe, William: Shropshire RO, Brooke (Forester) MSS
Sharpe family, Ireland: Friends Historical Society, Dublin; see O. C. Goodboy, in *J. Friends Hist. Soc.*, 48 (1950)
Shaw, Sir John: BL Add. 23199; Bod. Eng. Hist. C.44
Sherman, Rowland and Edmund: GLL 3547
Simpson, Nathan: PRO C104/13–14
Skilbeck family: GLL 10857
Smith, Francis: see H. M. Colvin in *Warws. Hist.*, 3 (1972)
Smith family of Bideford: PRO C10/181
Smythe, John: Bristol RO 1087; see also *The Ledger of John Smythe*, ed. J. Vanes (Brist. Rec. Soc., 1974)
Smythe, William: Bod. Ashmole 1809
Sneyd, Elizabeth: William Salt Lib. 37/36
Starkey, Ralph: see J. M. Price in *Business in the Age of Reason*, ed. R. T. P. Davenport-Hines and J. Lieberman (1989)
Stoddard, George: PRO SP 46/13/110–43
Strong, Edward: GLL
Sykes, John: Leeds University Libraries, Brotherton Collection
Symons, Robert: Som. RO, Dunster Castle MSS
Tanturier, Florentine: IESRO 359/785, 4090
Thompson, Sir Henry: Humberside County Archives Service, DDFA 37/3–7
Tooley, Henry: IESRO Acc. 2672; see J. G. Webb, *Great Tooley of Ipswich* (Suffolk Record Society, 1962)
Towne, Charles: Bucks. RO 7/11/191–8
Trollope, John: Lincs. AO, Trollope-Bellew MSS
Turgis, Richard: University of Nottingham, Mellish MSS
Turner, Jacob: PRO C104/44–5
Turner, Sir William: GLL 5100–5112A, 10770; North Yorkshire RO ZCQ, ZK 11125–55
Twyford, James: Som. RO, Hylton MSS
Vanderson, Arthur: Bristol RO
Varder, Sir Anthony: Bristol RO, Ashton Court MSS
Vaughan, Stephen: see W. C. Richardson, *Stephen Vaughan* (Baton Rouge, 1953)
Verney, John: Verney MSS at Claydon House on microfilm in BL
Vyner, Robert and Thomas: West Yorkshire Archive Service, Leeds, Newby Hall 2724; see D. K. Clark in *Essays in Honor of W. C. Abbott* (Cambridge,

Massachusetts, 1941)
Walcot, Humphrey: Shropshire RO, Walcott-Bitterley MSS
Wansey, George: Wilts. RO
Warner, George and John: PRO SP 46/83–5; Kress Lib. Foxwell MSS 787
Warren, Sir William: in private hands
Watts, William: PRO C113/31
Weddell, Thomas, Richard and William: West Yorkshire Archive Service, Leeds, NH 2762–8, 2183, 2191
Weston, Richard: PRO E101/634/4
Whalley family: Gloucs. RO D 1086
Whichcote, Henry: Lincs. AO, Whichcote 1/16–17, 1/B/48; Bod. Eng. Misc. C.260
White, Matthew: Northumberland RO, Ridley MSS
Wicks, Paul: PRO C107/70–2
Williams, William: Lincs. AO, Pearson-Gregory MSS
Wilmot, Robert: Offley, Forrester & Co
Wingfield, Ferdinando: Sheffield Archives, Bagshawe MSS
Wise, John: sold to unknown buyer
Wrigley, Henry: Lancs. RO DDHp
Wynne, Maurice: NLW, Wynne MSS
Yale, Elihu: Beinecke Lib., Yale
Yardley, Thomas: Hereford RO
Yeamans, John: Surrey RO, Kingston
Yeo, Leonard: Devon RO
Yeo, Richard: see R. Walters and H. N. W. Toms in *Devon and Corn. N.&Q.*, 30 (1967)

ANONYMOUS BUSINESS RECORDS

PRO C110/15; C103/40, C104/11–12, 15–16, 130–1; C105/12; C107/17–18, 20; C108/203; C109/248; C110/42–3; C114/57–9, 180; C217/74
PRO E101/520/21, 245, 635/39–41; 521/7, 10, 14–15; 522/3, 16–17; E178/5455, 5467
PRO HCA 2/566, 30/636
PRO SP 9/96, 106
CLRO Small MSS, Box 40/108/B, Mayor's Court depositions
GLL 2931, 3613,
BL Cotton Vesp. F xvii, Egerton 2984, Sloane 867, Stowe 320(i), 759, 1578, Add. 61935
Berks. RO D/EBuF1, D/EDB2, D/EEZB13
CUL Add. 3303(9)
Cumbria RO, Kendal draper's journal
Devon RO, Exeter wool merchant's accounts
Essex RO, Cavendish, Russell of N. Ockendon, 7846
Bristol RO, Virginia trader
Bristol University Library, Society of Merchant Venturers
Lancs. RO DDCa/105, DDC, DDCa/45
Leics. RO 6332
Scarborough Corporation, shipowner's accounts

Northants. RO, Newnham
Bod. Rawl. A.21, D. 1483, Rawl. Lett. 66, Add. A.56
Som. RO, Carew of Crowcombe
West Yorkshire Archive Service, Leeds TN/OA/D13
University of York, Borthwick Institute, merchants of the Staple
Coates MSS in private hands

ALPHABETICAL LIST BY NAME OF PERSONAL PAPERS

This includes travelogues, autobiographies, memoirs, family letters, diaries, commonplace books and some inventories of personal effects. The latter, whether taken after death or in response to bankruptcy or a government enquiry, survive in practically every class of record, although the majority occur in the diocesan and archdiocesan archives. Since they are not grouped by occupation, a list is impractical, but the most important single group for businessmen are those deposited in the Orphans Court of London in the CLRO.

Abott, John: Devon RO
Aptall, Cpt. G: Leeds University Libraries, Brotherton Collection
Archer, Henry and Anne: BL Add. 30494
Barnes, Ambrose: BL Stowe 745
Bell, Robert: North Yorkshire RO ZA G7
Boddington, George: GLL 10823/1
Booth, Robert: Herts. RO, Panshanger MSS
Bowrey, Thomas and Mary : IOL Eur. A.33, E.192; GLL 3041/4; see also *The Bowrey Papers*, ed. R. C. Temple (Hakl. Soc., 2nd ser., 58, 1927)
Bufton, John: Leeds University Libraries, Philip Unwin's MS 8–10
Bulman, Thomas: BL Add. 28714
Caunt, John: PRO E178/5450
Chetham, George and Humphrey: Chetham's Lib., Raines MSS; see also F. R. Raines and C. W. Sutton, *Life of Humphrey Chetham* (Cheth. Soc., 49–50, 1903)
Clarke, Richard: GLL
Cogge, John: Bod. Eng. Misc. F. 78
Cox, Richard: BL Add. 31300–1
Crouch, Giles: GLL 5677
Daniel, Alexander: Cornwall RO
Everard, Charles: Bod. Lond. & Midd. 501
Freeman, John: BL Lans. 1156
Fryer, John: GLL 12017
Geckie, John: Leics. RO 4D 42/165
Gilly, William: GLL 6666
Godschall, John: Surrey RO, Guildford, Bray 540, 85/15/1
Green, Thomas: PRO E178/4807
Gwin, Thomas: Religious Society of Friends Lib. 74
Hadley, George: Bod. Eng. Misc. C.292
Harrold, Edmund: Chetham's Lib. Mun. A 2 137

Haynes, John: Devon RO: see T. N. Brushfield, *Diary of a Citizen of Exeter* (Exeter, 1901) and *Trans. Devon Assoc.* 33 (1891)

Jeffries, Joyce: BL Egerton 3054; see also R. G. Griffiths in *Trans. Worcs. A. S.*, NS, 10–12 (1933–5)

Jones, Thomas of Llaneldidyn: NLW, Bodewyd 3

Laurence, Thomas: PRO E178/7099

Le Neve, Peter: BL Add. 61903

Light Bowne, Samuel: Chetham's Lib., Raines MSS

Marniott, Timothy: Bod. Add. A.49

Marsh, Andrew: PRO E178/2035

Masters, John of Poole: Dorset RO 2694

Mawhood, William: GLL

Monteage, Stephen: GLL 205/1

Mundy, Peter: BL Harl. 2286, Add. 19278–81; Bod. Rawl. A.315; see *Travels of Peter Mundy*, ed. Sir R. C. Temple and L. M. Anstey (Hakl. Soc., 2nd ser., 17, 1907; 78, 1936)

Pengelly, Rachel: BL Add. 32456

Ruckle, William: IOL Factory Records, Masulipatnam

Rudstone, Sir John: BL Harl. 1231

Sanderson, John: BL Lans. 241; see *Travels of John Sanderson*, ed. Sir William Foster (Hakl. Soc., 2nd ser., 67, 1931)

Sanderson, William: see R. A. MacIntyre in *Wm & Mary Q.*, 3rd ser. 12 (1956)

Savage, Sarah: Dr William's Lib. 90.4

Scattergood family: BL Add. 42122–3, 43730–3; Bod. Eng. Hist. D.156–63; see also *The Scattergoods*, ed. Sir R. C. Temple, L. M. Anstey and B. P. Scattergood (Harpenden, 1935)

Smythe, William: Bod. Ashmole 1809

Stone, Thomas: PRO E178/4200

Tempest, John: Leeds University Libraries, Brotherton Collection LTQ

Thomas, William: NLW 9685 B

Tilliard, William: in private hands

Twiselton, John: Surrey RO, Guildford, Moore MSS

Uvedale, Edward: IOL Home Misc. 40/5, Marine Records lxxix

Vaux, John: BL Add. 14253

Wallington, Nehemiah: GLL 204; see also P. S. Seaver, *Wallington's World* (1985)

Wansey, George and Hester: Wilts. RO; see J. de L. Mann in *Ec. H. R.*, 2nd ser. 9 (1956–7)

Ward, Sir Patience: BL Add. 4224

Webb, Benedict: Gloucester City Library SZ 23/2/4; Smyth of Nibley MSS; see also E. Moir in *Ec. H. R.*, 2nd ser., 10 (1957)

Whiteway, William: BL Egerton 784; see D. Underdown, *Fire from Heaven* (1992)

Willoughby family: see R. S. Smith in *Ren. & Mod. Stud.*, 11 (1967) and *Trans. Thoroton Soc.*, 65–6 (1961–2)

Wyche, Nathaniel: IOL Home Misc. 40/5, Marine Records lxxix

Wyche, Richard: Bod. Rawl. 4.4

ANONYMOUS AND COLLECTIVE PERSONAL PAPERS

PRO CO 77/50–51
Leeds University Libraries, Brotherton Collection 8–10
Chetham's Lib. Mun A.2.137
Bod. Rawl. A.315, C.861, D.1114
BL Cotton Vesp. F xvi–xvii, Egerton 3054, Lans. 241, Add. 19278–81, Harl. 2286
GLL MS 204
Coventry City RO A.105
Dorset RO 2694

PRINTED PRIMARY SOURCES

'The account book of a Marian bookseller 1553–4', ed. J. N. King, *Brit. Lib. J.*, 13 (1987)
Achelley, T. *The Massacre of Money* (1602)
Adams, E. *A Brief Relation of the Surprising Several English Merchants' Goods* (1664)
Admiralty High Court Depositions 1637–8, ed. D. O. Shilton and R. Holworth (1932)
Advice to the Liverymen of London (1713)
Advice to the Women and Maidens of London (1678)
Aikin, J. *A Description of the Country around Manchester* (1795)
Ailesbury, Thomas, 2nd Earl of, *Memoirs*, ed. W. E. Buckley (Roxburgh Club, 1890), 2 vols.
Albyn, B. *An Appeal to God and King* (1697)
Aliens, Returns of, Henry VIII–James I, ed. R. E. G. and E. F. Kirk (Hug. Soc. Lond. quarto ser., 10, 1900–8), 4 vols.
Aliens. Letters of Denizens and Acts of Naturalisation, 1603–1700, ed. W. A. Shaw (Hug. Soc. Lond. quarto ser., 18, 27, 1911–23)
Aliens. Strangers, Returns of, ed. I. Scouloudi (Hug. Soc. Lond., quarto ser., 57, 1985)
Allen, H. *Caveatt: the Markets of London in 1598*, ed. I. Archer, C. Barron and V. Harding (Lond. Topog. Soc. Pub., 137, 1988)
Allen, W. and J. 'Note from two Plymouth diaries, 1664–71', ed. R. N. Worth, *The Antiquary*, 13 (1886)
Allestree, R. *The Gentleman's Calling* (1687)
Ames, W. *Conscience* (1639)
'An apothecary's cash book, 1706–07', *M & B Pharmaceutical Bulletin*, 5 (1956)
The Art of Thriving (1674)
Ashley, Sir Francis, *Case Book as Recorder of Dorchester, 1614–35* (Dorset Rec. Soc., 1981)
Ashley, R. *Of Honour*, ed. V. B. Heltzel (San Marino, 1947)
Ashwood, B. *The Heavenly Trade* (1678)
Aubrey, J. *Remains of Gentilisme and Judaism, 1686–7*, ed. J. Britton (Folk Lore Soc., 4, 1881)
Idea Of Education, ed. J. E. Stephens (1971)
News from the New Exchange (1650)

Brief Lives, ed. A. Clark (Oxford, 1898)
Brief Lives, ed. O. Dick (Ann Arbor, 1957)
The Aufrère Papers, ed. W. Turner (Hug. Soc. Lond. Pub., 40, 1946)
Awdeley, J. *An Epitaph on Maister Fraunces Benison* (1570)
Aylmer, B. *A Full Account of Dr Assheton's Proposal* (1699)
Bacon, F. *The Works*, ed. J. Spedding, R. L. Ellis and D. D. Heath (1857–94), 7 vols.
Bacon, Sir Nathaniel, *The Papers*. ed. A. H. Smith, G. M. Baker and R. W. Kenny (Norfolk Rec. Soc., 46, 49, 1978)
The Bagford Ballads, ed. J. W. Ebsworth (1878), 3 vols.
Bagnall, R. *The Steward's Last Account* (1622)
Bagshaw, W. *Trading Spiritualised* (1694)
Bagwell, W. *The Distressed Merchant* (1644)
Balsall, J. *The Accounts of, 1480–81*, ed. T. F. Reddaway and A. A. Ruddock (Camd. Misc., 23, 1969)
Banbury. Corporation Records, ed. J. S. W. Gibson and E. R. C. Brinksworth (Banbury Hist. Soc., 1977)
Banbury. Wills and Inventories, ed. J. S. W. Gibson and E. R. C. Brinksworth (Banbury Hist. Soc., 13, 1976; 14, 1985)
Bangs, B. *Memoirs of the Life* (1757)
Bankes, J. *The Memorandum Book, 1586–1617* (priv. pr., 1935)
Bankes Family Early Records, ed. J. Bankes and E. Kerridge (Cheth. Soc., 3rd ser., 21, 1973)
Banks Family Letters and Papers 1704–60, ed. J. W. F. Hill (Lincs. Rec. Soc., 45, 1952)
Barbon, N. *An Apology for the Builder* (1685)
A Discourse of Trade (1690), ed. J. H. Hollander (Baltimore, 1905)
Barcroft, A. *Memorandum Book as High Constable of Blackburn Hundred*, ed. R. S. France (Hist. Soc. Lancs. & Ches., 107, 1956)
Bargrave, Robert, *Travel Diary, 1646–53*, ed. A. Rude (Hamburg, 1905)
Barlow, E. *Journal of his Life at Sea*, ed. B. Lubbock (1934), 2 vols.
Barlow, R. *A Brief Survey of Geography*, ed. E. G. R. Taylor (Hakl. Soc., 2nd ser., 69, 1931)
Barnard, Sir John *A Present for an Apprentice*, 2nd edn (1742)
Barrett, W. *History and Antiquities of Bristol* (Bristol, 1789)
Barrow, I. *Of Industry* (1693)
Battie, J. *The Merchant's Remonstrance* (1648)
Baxter, R. *Christian Directory*, ed. W. Orme (1830)
Faithful Souls shall be with Christ (1681)
Reliquiae Baxteriana (1696)
Calendar of the Correspondence: vol. I, *1638–60*, ed. N. H. Keeble; vol. II, *1660–96*, ed. G. F. Nuttall (Oxford, 1991)
Beake, Robert, *Diary 1655–56*, ed. L. Fox (Dugd. Soc. Misc., 31, 1977)
Bearcroft, P. *An Historical Account of Thomas Sutton* (1737)
Beatson, R. *Political Index*, 3rd edn rev. (1806)
Beddle Wills and Inventories, ed. K. M. Burnstead (Yorks. Arch. J., 57, 1985)
Bedfordshire. Apprentices, 1711–20, ed. A. V. Jenkinson (Bed. Rec. Soc., 9, 1925)
Bedfordshire. The Visitations of 1566, 1582 and 1634, ed. F. A. Blaydes (Harl. Soc., 19, 1884)

Behn, A. *Works*, ed. M. Summers (1915)
Belasyse, H. *An English Traveller's First Curiosity* (1657), in *HMC Var. Coll.*, vol. II
Belle-Guise, A. *Traité de la noblesse et de son origine* (1669)
Bellers, J. *Writings*, ed. A. R. Fry (1935)
Benbrigge, J. *A Ready Way to Rectify Usury* (1646)
Bennett, T. and Clemens, H. *The Notebook, 1686–1719*, ed. N. Hodgson and C. Blagden (Oxford Bibliog. Soc., NS, 6, 1956)
Bethel, S. *The Interest of the Princes and States of Europe*, 3rd edn (1689)
Observations on the Letter Written to Sir Thomas Osborne (1673)
Bevis Marks' Records, ed. L. D. Barnett (Oxford, 1940–9)
Bevys, R. 'The inventory', ed. E. A. Donaldson, *Trans. Devon Assoc.*, 41 (1909)
Bewley, G. *A Narrative of the Christian Experience* (Dublin, 1750)
Biddulph, W. *The Travels of Certayn Englishmen* (1609)
Biggs, A. *A Briefe and Serious Warning* (1678)
Billinghurst, G. *The Judges' Resolutions upon the Several Statutes Concerning Bankruptcy* (1676)
Birch, T. *The Court and Times of James I* (1849), 2 vols.
The History of the Royal Society (1756–7)
Blackstone, Sir William, *Commentaries on the Laws of England*, 16th edn (1825)
Blake Family Records, 1300–1600, ed. M. J. Blake (1902, 1905), 2 vols.
Blakeney: Maritime Trade of the Port, ed. B. Cozens-Hardy (Norf. Rec. Soc., 8, 1936)
Blanch, J. *The Interest of England Considered* (1694)
Bland, J. *Trade Reviv'd* (1659)
Blome, R. *Britannia* (1673)
The Art of Heraldry, 2nd edn (1693)
Blount, T. *The Several Forms of Instruments Relating to the Affairs of Merchants* (1674)
Blundell, N. *The Great Diurnal*, I: *1702–11*, II: *1712–19*, III: *1720–28*, ed. J. S. Bagley and F. Tyrer (Lancs. & Ches. Rec. Soc., 110, 1968; 112, 1970; 114, 1972)
Blundell's Diary and Letter Book, 1702–28, ed. M. Blundell (Liverpool, 1952)
Blundell, W. *Cavalier Letters*, ed. M. Blundell (1933)
Bodin, J. *Methodus ad facilem historiarum cognitionem* (1565)
Bohun, E. *The Diary of Edmund Bohun*, ed. S. W. Rix (Beccles, 1853)
Bohun, W. *Privilegia Londini*, 3rd edn (1723)
The Bolton Letters, 1695–1714, ed. A. L. Simon (1928), 2 vols.
Bolton, E. *The Cities' Advocate*, lst edn (1629)
Bolton, R. *A Short and Private Discourse* (1637)
The Book of Dignities, ed. J. Hayden and H. Ockerby (1890)
A Book of Valuation of all the Ecclesiastical Preferments (1680)
'A bookseller's account book, 1545', ed. L. M. Oliver, *Harv. Lib. Bull.*, 16 (1968)
Borough Customs, ed. M. Bateson (Seld. Soc., 1, 1904; 2, 1906)
Boston, The Port Books of, ed. R. W. K. Hinton (Lincs. Rec. Soc., 50, 1956)
Bourne, H. *The History of Newcastle upon Tyne* (Newcastle, 1736)
Bourne, I. *The Godly Man's Guide* (1620)
Bowles Family, Records of the, ed. W. H. Bowles (priv. pr., Derby, 1918)
Bowrey Papers 1669–1713, ed. Sir R. C. Temple (Hakl. Soc., 2nd ser., 58, 1927)

'The Bowyer ledger', ed. K. I. D. Maslen, *Papers Bibliog. Soc. Amer.*, 82 (1988)
Boyle, R. *Works, with a Life by T. Birch* (1772), 6 vols.
Boyne, W. *Tokens Issued in the Seventeenth Century*, new edn, rev. G. C. Williamson (1889–91)
Bradford, S. *The Honest and Dishonest Ways of Getting Wealth* (1720)
Braithwaite, R. *The English Gentleman* (1630)
A Survey of History (1638)
The Turtles' Triumph (1641)
Bramston, Sir John, *Autobiography*, ed. Lord Braybrook (Camd. Soc., 32, 1845)
Brand, J. *History and Antiquities of Newcastle upon Tyne* (Newcastle, 1789)
Brent, N. A. *A Discourse Consisting of Motives for the Enlargement and Freedom of Trade* (1645), repr. in *Mercantilist Views on Trade and Money* (New York, 1972)
Brereton, W. *Letters and Accounts*, ed. E. W. Ives (Lancs. & Ches. Rec. Soc., 116, 1976)
Breton, N. *The Works*, ed. A. B. Grosart (Chertsey Worthies Lib., 1879)
Brewster, Sir Francis, *Essays on Trade* (1695), with excerpts in *Bull. Bus. Hist. Soc.*, 15 (1941)
Bridges, N. *Vulgar Arithmetique* (1653)
Brinsley, J. *Ludus Literarius or the Grammar School* (1611)
Briscoe, J. *A Discourse of Money* (1696)
Bristol, Africa and the Eighteenth-Century Slave Trade to America, ed. D. Richardson (Bristol Rec. Soc., 38, 1986)
Bristol. Calendar of the Apprentice Book, 1532–42, ed. D. Hollis (Bristol Rec. Soc., 14, 1949); *1542–65*, ed. E. Ralph and N. M. Hardwick (Bristol Rec. Soc., 33, 1980; 43, 1992)
Bristol. Records of a Church of Christ, 1640–87, ed. R. Hayden (Bristol Rec. Soc., 27, 1974)
Bristol. The Deposition Books, 1643–47, ed. H. E. Nott (Bristol Rec. Soc., 6, 1935); *1650–54*, ed. H. E. Nott and E. Ralph (Bristol Rec. Soc., 13, 1947)
Bristol. Documents Illustrating the Overseas Trade in the Sixteenth Century, ed. J. Vanes (Bristol Rec. Soc., 31, 1979)
Bristol. Great White Book, ed. E. Ralph (Bristol Rec. Soc., 33, 1979)
Bristol. The Inhabitants in 1696, ed. E. Ralph and M. E. Williams (Bristol Rec. Soc., 25, 1968)
Bristol. Merchants and Merchandise in the Seventeenth Century, ed. P. McGrath (Bristol Rec. Soc., 19, 1955)
Bristol. Records Relating to the Society of Merchant Venturers, ed. P. McGrath (Bristol Rec. Soc., 17, 1951)
Bristol. Minute Book of the Men's Meeting of the Society of Friends, 1667–86, ed. R. Mortimer (Bristol Rec. Soc., 26, 1971)
Bristol. The Ordinances, 1506–98, ed. M. Stanford (Bristol Rec. Soc., 41, 1990)
Bristol. Company of Soapmakers Proceedings, 1562–1642, ed. H. E. Matthews (Bristol Rec. Soc., 10, 1940)
Bristol. The Staple Court Books, 1509–1678, ed. E. E. Rich (Bristol Rec. Soc., 5, 1934)
Bristol. The Register of Servants Sent to Foreign Plantations, 1654–86, ed. P. W. Coldham (Baltimore, 1988)

Bristol. Tudor Wills, 1546–1603, ed. S. Lang and M. MacGregor (Bristol Rec. Soc., 44, 1992)

Britannia Languens (1680), repr. in *Early English Tracts on Commerce*

The British Book Trade, 1710–77: An Index to the Masters and Apprentices, comp. I. Maxted (Exeter, 1983)

Brittaine, W. de, *Humane Prudence, or the Art by which a Man may raise himself and his fortune*, 9th edn corr. and enlarg. (1702)

Broadside Ballads of the Restoration, ed. F. B. Fawcett (1930)

The Broken Merchant's Complaint (1683)

Browne, J. *The Marchant's Avizo*, ed. P. McGrath (Cambridge, Massachusetts, 1957)

Browne, Sir Thomas, *The Works*. ed. G. Keynes (1964), 4 vols.

Browne, T. *Amusements Serious and Comical*, ed. A. L. Hayward (1927)

Bruer, J. *The Life*, in S. Clark, *The Marrow of Ecclesiastical History* (1675), vol. II

Brugge, P., *Diary*, in *The Elliot Papers*, ed. E. Howard (Gloucester, 1893)

Brydall, J. *Jus Imaginis apud Anglos* (1675)

Camera Regis (1676)

Brydges, C. *Continuation of the History of the Willoughby Family*, ed. A. C. Wood (1958)

Buck, Sir George, *The Third University* (1615)

Buckeridge, B. *The Art of Painting* (1706), transcr. R. de Piles

Buckeridge, N. *Journal and Letter Book, 1651–4* , ed. J. R. Jensen (Minneapolis, 1973)

Buckinghamshire Probate Inventories, 1661–1714 , ed. M. Reed (Bucks. Rec. Soc., 24, 1988)

Bulwer, J. *Chinologie* (1644)

Bunyan, J. *The Life and Death of Mr Badman*, ed. J. F. Forrest and R. Sharrock (Oxford, 1988)

Burn, R. *Ecclesiastical Law*, 9th edn rev., R. Phillimore (1842), 4 vols.

Burrell, T. *Journal and Account Book*, ed. R. W. Blencoe (Suss. Arch. Coll., 3, 1850)

Burton, R. *The Anatomy of Melancholia*, ed. F. Dell and P. Jordan Smith (1931)

Burton, W. *The Christian's Heavenly Treasure* (1608)

Bury, S. *Account of the Life of Elizabeth Bury* (Bristol, 1721)

Butler, S. *Characters and Passages from Notebooks*, ed. A. R. Waller (Cambridge, 1908)

Hudibras, ed. J. Wilders (Oxford, 1973)

Byrd, W. *The Diary and Life of William Byrd II of Virginia, 1674–1744*, ed. K. A. Lockridge (Chapel Hill, 1987)

The Correspondence of Three William Byrds of Westover, 1684–1776, ed. M. Tinling (Charlottesville, 1977)

Caesar, Sir Julius, *The Ancient State of the Court of Requests*, ed. L. M. Hill (1975)

Calamy, E. *A Sermon at the Merchant's Lecture in Salters Hall* (1709)

Calthorpe, Sir H. *Reports of Special Cases Touching Several Customs and Liberties of London* (1655), repr. in *English Reports*, 80.

Calvin, J. *Institutes of the Christian Religion*, ed. J. T. McNeill (Philadelphia, 1960)

'A Cambridge bookseller's accounts', ed. D. Pearson, *Trans. Camb. Bib. Soc.*, 9

(1986–90)
Cambridge. Printers, Abstracts from the Wills, 1504–1699, ed. G. J. Gray and W. M. Palmer (Camb. Bibliog. Soc. 1915)
Campbell, R. *The London Tradesman* (1747)
Canterbury. Roll of the Freemen, 1392–1800, ed. J. M. Cowper (Canterbury, 1903)
Capel, R. *Tentation*, 3rd edn (1636)
Cardiff. The Port Books, ed. E. A. Lewis, *Trans. Cardigan Antiq. Soc.*, 7 (1930), 9 (1933)
The Port of Cardiff 1606–10, ed. W. Rees (S. Wales and Mon. Rec. Soc. 3, 1954)
Carlisle. Municipal Records, ed. R. Ferguson and W. Nanson (Cumb. & West. Antiq. & Arch. Soc. Pub., 1887)
Carpenter, I. *A Most Excellent Instrument for the Exact and Perfect Keeping Merchants Books of Accounts* (1632)
Carpenters Company Records, 1: *Apprenticeship Entry Book 1654–96*, ed. R. Bowen Marsh (Oxford, 1913)
Cary, J. *An Essay on the State of England in relation to its Trade* (Bristol, 1695)
Essay Towards Regulating the Trade and Employing the Poor, 2nd edn (1719)
Catcott, A. *The Antiquity & Honourableness of the Practice of Merchandise* (Bristol, 1744)
Caxton, W. *The Prologue and Epilogues*, ed. W. J. B. Crotch (E. E. T. S., OS, 176, 1928)
Cecil, W. *Certain Precepts or Directions for the Well Ordering of a Man's Life* (1615)
The Cely Letters, ed. A. Hanham (E. E. T. S., OS, 273, 1975)
Chamberlain, J. *The Letters*, ed. N. E. McLure (Philadelphia, 1939)
Chamberlayne, E. *Angliae Notitiae*, 1st edn (1669)
Chancery Reports and Cases in the Reigns of Charles I, Charles II and James II (1715), 3 vols.
Chandler, R. *The History and Proceedings of the House of Commons* (1743–4)
Chappel, S. *A Diamond or Rich Jewel* (1650)
Character and Qualifications of an Honest and Loyal Merchant (1686)
Character Writings of the Seventeenth Century, ed. H. Morley (1891)
Chester. Rolls of the Freemen, 1392–1700, ed. J. H. E. Bennett (Lancs. & Ches. Hist. Soc. Rec. Ser., 51, 1906)
Chester. City Council Minutes, ed. M. J. Groomsbridge (Lancs. & Ches. Hist. Soc. Rec. Ser., 106, 1956)
Chesterfield. Wills and Inventories, 1521–1602, ed. J. M. Bestall and D. V. Fowkes (Derby. Rec. Soc., 6, 1977)
Chesterfield. Records of the Borough 1204–1835, ed. P. Rider and J. Blair (Chesterfield, 1980)
Child Collection of English and Scottish Popular Ballads, ed. H. C. Sargent and G. L. Kittredge (New York, 1932)
Child, J. *Brief Observations Concerning Trade and Interest of Money* (1668), repr. in W. Letwin, *Sir Josiah Child* (Cambridge, Massachusetts, 1959)
The New Discourse of Trade (1693)
Chirk Castle Accounts, ed. W. H. Myddelton, *1606–66* (priv. pr., St Albans, 1908), *1666–1753* (priv. pr., Horncastle, 1931)
Cholmely, Sir Hugh, *Memoirs* (repr. Malton, 1870)

Chubb, T. *The Posthumous Works* (1748)
Church of England, Activities of the Puritan Faction, 1625–33, ed. I. M. Calder (Church Hist. Soc., 1957)
Churchyard, T. *Generall Rehearsall of Warrs* (1579)
The Citizen's Companion or the Tradesman's Mirror (1673)
Clarke, W. 'The Letter Book, 1598–1602', ed. P. R. Harris (unpub. M.A. thesis, London, 1953)
Claver, M. *Diary of a West Country Physician, 1684–1726*, ed. E. Hobhouse (1934)
Claypoole, J. *Letter Book, 1681–4*, ed. M. Balderston (San Marino, 1967)
Clifton & Westbury. Probate Inventories, 1609–1761, ed. J. S. Moore (Bristol & Avon Local History Association, 1981)
Clockmakers Company Register of Apprentices, comp. C. E. Atkins (1931)
The Clothiers Complaint Against the Blackwell Hall Factors (1692)
The Clothiers Reason for Establishing the Company of Merchant Adventurers (*c.* 1690)
Coade, G. *A Letter to the Commissioners of Trade and Plantations* (1747)
Cobbett, W. *The Parliamentary History of England* (1808)
Cocks, R. *Diary, 1615–22*, ed. E. M. Thompson (Hakl. Soc., 66–7, 1883, 1887)
Coke, R. *Reasons of the Increase of the Dutch Trade* (1671)
England's Improvement (1675)
Cole, W. *A Rod for the Lawyers* (1659)
A Collection of the Experiences of the Works of Grace (*c.* 1700)
Collett, J. *The Private Letter Book*, ed. H. H. Dodwell (1933)
Collins, J. *An Introduction to Merchants' Accompts* (1653)
Colsoni, F. *Le Guide de Londres* (1693, repr. Lond. Topog. Soc., 1951)
A Companion for Debtors (1669)
The Complete Solicitor (1683)
The Compton Census in 1676, ed. A. Whiteman (Brit. Acad., 1986)
Congreve, W. *Letters and Documents*, ed. J. C. Hodges (1964)
Considerations Offered to All the Corporations (1681), repr. in *Seventeenth-Century Economic Documents*
Constitution and Canon Ecclesiastical 1604, ed. H. A. Wilson (Oxford, 1923)
The Conway Letters, ed. M. H. Nicolson (1930)
Cony, T. 'Extracts from the Household Book', ed. E. Turner (*Archaeologia*, 11, 1794)
Cook, J. *Unum Necessarium* (1648)
Coole, B. *Honesty, the Truest Policy* (1700)
Miscellanies (1712)
Cooper, T. *The Worldling's Adventure* (1619)
Corbet, J. *A Discourse of the Religion of England* (1667)
Corie, T. *Correspondence, 1664–87*, ed. R. H. Hill (Norfolk Rec. Soc., 1956)
Cornish, J. *Life of Thomas Firmin* (1780)
Courtin, A. de, *Traité de la paresse* (1673)
Cowcher, T. 'Inventory of the goods', ed. R. G. Griffiths *Trans. Worcs. A. S.*, 14 (1937)
Coxere, H. *Adventures by Sea*, ed. E. H. W. Meyerstein (Oxford, 1946)
Cradocke, F. *An Expedient for Taking Away all Impositions* (1660)

Cranfield Papers, HMC Sackville (Knole) MSS: 1. *1551–1612*, ed. A. P. Newton (1940); 2. *1597–1612*, ed. F. J. Fisher (1966)
Crodacott, J. *The Vanity and Mischief of Making Earthly Treasures our Chiefe Treasure* (1655)
Croker, J. *Brief Memoirs of the Life*, ed. W. Barclay, 2nd edn (1839)
Cromwell, O. *Writings and Speeches*, ed. W. C. Abbott (Cambridge, Massachusetts, 1937–47), 4 vols.
Crouch, N. *The Apprentice's Companion* (1681)
Crouch, W. *Posthuma Christiana* (1712)
Crowley, A. *The Law Book of the Crowley Ironworks*, ed. M. W. Flinn (Surt. Soc., 167, 1952)
Crowley, R. *The Way to Wealth* (1550), in *Select Works*, ed. J. M. Cooper (E. E. T. S., extra ser., 15, 1875)
Cruttenden, J. *Atlantic Merchant Apothecary Letters, 1710–1717*, ed. I. K. Steele (Toronto, 1977)
Cruwys, J. 'Diary, 1682–88', ed. M. C. S. Cruwys, *Devon & Corn. N. & Q.*, 18 (1934–5)
Culpeper, Sir Thomas *The Necessity of Abating Usury Reasserted* (1670)
Tracts Concerning Usury Reprinted (1708)
Cust Family Records, 1479–1700, ed. E. and L. Cust (1898–1927)
Dafforne, R. *The Apprentice's Time Entertainer* (1640)
Dallaway, J. *Inquiry into the Origins and Progress of Heraldry* (Gloucester, 1793)
Danvers Family Memorials, ed. F. N. MacNamara (1895)
Davenant, C. *The Political and Commercial Works*, ed. Sir Charles Whitworth (1771, repr. 1967), 5 vols.
Two Manuscripts, ed. A. P. Usher (Baltimore, 1942)
Davies, R. *An Account of the Commencement*, 5th edn (1794)
Defoe, D. *The Compleat English Tradesman* (1727), 2 vols.
The Review, ed. A. W. Secord (New York, 1938), 9 vols.
A Tour through England and Wales, ed. G. D. H. Cole and D. C. Browning (1962), 2 vols.
The Novels and Selected Writings, Shakespeare Head edn (Oxford, 1927–8), 12 vols.
Essay on Projects (1697)
The Compleat English Gentleman, ed. K. D. Bulbring (1890)
The Great Law of Subordination Considered (1724)
Matrimonial Whoredom, repr. in *The Works*, ed. W. Hazlitt (1840–43)
Dekker, T. *Dramatic Works*, ed. F. Bowers (Cambridge, 1953–61), 4 vols.
Non Dramatic Works, ed. A. B. Grosart (New York, 1963), 5 vols.
Dell, W. *Right Reformation* (1646)
Deloney, T. *The Works*, ed. F. O. Mann (Oxford, 1912)
Derby Trade Tokens, ed. T. D. Whittet (Derby. Arch. J., 108, 1988)
Derbyshire. The Visitation, 1662–64, by Sir William Dugdale, ed. G. D. Squibb (Harl. Soc., NS, 8, 1989)
Dering, Sir Edward, *The Parliamentary Diary, 1670–73*, ed. B. D. Henning (New Haven, 1940)
The Diaries and Papers, 1644–84, ed. M. F. Bond (1976)
Desagulier, H. *Traité général de la reduction des charges et monnoyes* (Amsterdam,

1701)
Devon. Inventories of the Sixteenth and Seventeenth Centuries, ed. M. Cash (Devon & Corn. Rec. Soc., NS, 11, 1966)
D'Ewes, Sir Simond, *The Autobiography and Correspondence*, ed. J. O. Hallwell (1845), 2 vols.
The Journal, ed. W. Notestein and W. H. Coate (New Haven, 1923, 1942)
Dickinson, M. *Seventeenth-Century Tokens of the British Isles* (1980)
'Directions for the conduct of a merchant counting house, 1766', ed. J. M. Price, *Bus. Hist.*, 28 (1986)
A Discourse of the Commonwealth of this Realm of England, ed. M. Dewar (Charlottesville, 1969)
A Discourse of the Necessity of Encouraging Mechanic Industry (1690)
Disney, G. *Some Remarkable Passages in the Holy Life and Death* (1692)
Dod, J. and Clever, R. *A Godly Form of Household Government* (1612)
Doderidge, Sir John, *Honour's Pedigree* (1642, repr. 1652)
Doe, C. 'Autobiography', in *Collection of the Experience of the Works of Grace* (*c.* 1700)
Donaldson, J. *The Undoubted Art of Thriving* (Edinburgh, 1700)
Donne, J. *The Sermons*, ed. G. R. Potter and E. Simpson (Berkeley and Los Angeles, 1953–62)
Dorne, J. 'The daily ledger', ed. F. Madan, in *Collectanea*, ed. C. R. L. Fletcher (Oxford Hist. Soc., 5, 1885; 16, 1890)
Dorney, H. *Divine Contemplations* (1684, repr. 1773)
Dorset. Hearth Tax Assessments, ed. C. A. F. Meekings (Dorchester, 1951)
Dorset. Visitation by Sir Edward Bysshe, ed. G. D. Squibb (Harl. Soc., 117, 1977)
Down. Survey History, 1655–1656 (Irish Archaeol. Soc., 1851)
Dryden, J. *The Works*, ed. H. T. Swedenberg (Berkeley, 1956–72)
Dudley. Probate Inventories, 1605–85, ed. J. S. Roper (priv. pr., Dudley, 1966)
Dugdale, Sir William, *Origines Juridicales*, 3rd edn (1680)
The Antient Usage in Bearing of Arms (Oxford, 1682)
The Life, Diary and Correspondence, ed. W. Hamper (1827)
Dugdale's Visitation of Lancaster, 1664–5, ed. F. R. Raines (Cheth. Soc., 84–5, 88, 1872)
Dugdale's Nottingham and Derbyshire Visitation Papers, ed. G. D. Squibb (Harl. Soc., NS, 6, 1987)
Dunton, J, *The Life and Errors* (1705), ed. J. B. Nichols (1818)
Durham. Wills and Inventories, ed. H. M. Wood (Surt. Soc., 112, 1906; 142, 1929)
Dwynn, L. *Heraldic Visitations of Wales, 1586–1613*, ed. Sir S. R. Meyricke (Llandovery, 1846), 2 vols.
Dyke, J. *Counter-poyson against Covetousness* (1619)
Eachard, J. *The Grounds and Occasions of the Contempt of the Clergy* (1670)
Earle, J. *Microcosmography*, ed. A. S. West (Cambridge, 1920)
Early English Tracts on Commerce, ed. J. R. McCulloch (1856, repr. Cambridge, 1954)
East Anglian Pedigrees, ed. A. Campling (Norf. Rec. Soc., 13, 1940)
East India Company. Letters Received, 1600–17, ed. Sir G. Birdwood and Sir W. Foster (1893–1902), 6 vols.

East India Company. The English Factories in India, 1618–69, ed. Sir William Foster (Oxford, 1906–27), 13 vols.
The East India Company. The English Factories in India, 1670–84, ed. Sir C. G. H. Fawcett (Oxford, 1936–55), 4 vols.
East India Company. Calendar of the Court Minutes, 1635–71, ed. E. B. Sainsbury (Oxford, 1907–38), 11 vols.
East India Company's Reply to Allegations of the Turkey Company (1681)
Eastland Company. The Acts and Ordinances, ed. M. Sellers (Camd. Soc., 3rd ser., 11, 1906)
Ecclesiastical Courts in the Diocese of London, Extracts from the Act Books, 1475–1640, ed. W. H. Hale (1847)
Ecton, G. 'Inventory of a potter of Abingdon', ed. D. G. Vaisey and F. S. C. Celonia, *J. Ceramic Hist.*, 7 (1974)
Ecton, J. *Liber valorum et decimarum* (1711)
Edgeworth, R. *Sermons Very Fruitful Godly and Learned* (1557)
Edmundson, W. *A Journal of the Life, Travels and Labours* (Dublin, 1715)
Edward VI. The Chronicle and Political Papers, ed. W. K. Jordan (1960)
Edwards, R. *The Correspondence, 1669–79*, ed. Sir R. C. Temple (Bengal P. & P., 17–20, 1919–22)
The Eliot Papers, ed. H. Eliot (Gloucester, 1893)
Elmhirst, E. M., *Merchants' Marks*, ed. L. Dow (Harl. Soc., 108, 1959)
Elyot, Sir Thomas *The Book Named the Governour*, ed. H. H. S. Croft (1880), 2 vols.
Of the Knowledge which Maketh a Wise Man (1531), ed. E. J. Howard (Oxford, Ohio, 1946)
Emerson, T. *A Concise Treatise of the Courts of Law of London* (1794)
England's Great Happiness (1677)
English Adventurers and Emigrants, 1609–1773, ed. P. W. Coldham (Baltimore, 1984–5)
English Economic Documents, ed. A. E. Bland, P. A. Brown and R. H. Tawney (1914)
The English Reports
An English Winding Sheet (1699)
Ent, Sir George, *Grounds of Unity in Religion* (1679)
Eon, J. *Le Commerce honorable* (1646), ed. Dugast-Matifeux (Nantes, 1857)
Erswicke, J. *A Brief Note of the Benefits of Fish Days* (1642)
Esdaile, K. A., *English Church Monuments, 1510–1840* (1946)
Essex. Farm and Cottage Inventories, 1635–1749, ed. F. W. Steer (Colchester, 1950)
Essex. Gentry and Merchants Wills, ed. F. G. Emmison (Essex Record Office Publications, 71, 1978)
Essex. Early Essex Town Meetings: Braintree, 1619–36; Finchingfield, 1626–34, ed. F. G. Emmison (Chichester, 1970)
Essex. The Visitations in 1552, 1558, 1570, 1612, 1634, ed. W. C. Metcalfe (Harl. Soc., 13–14, 1878–9)
Etherege, Sir George, *The Letter Book*, ed. S. Rosenfield (1928)
The Euing Collection of English Broadside Ballads, ed. J. Holloway (Glasgow, 1971)

Evelyn, J. *Public Employment and an Active Life* (1667)
The Diary, ed. E. S. De Beer (Oxford, 1955), 6 vols.
Navigation and Commerce (1674)
Exeter. Freemen, 1266–1967, ed. M. M. Rowe and A. M. Jackson (Devon & Corn. Rec. Soc., extra series 1, 1973)
Exeter in the Seventeenth-Century. Tax and Rate Assessments, ed. W. G. Hoskins (Devon & Corn. Rec. Soc., NS, 2, 1957)
Exeter. Tax Assessments, 1489–1595, ed. M. M. Rowe (Devon & Corn. Rec. Soc., NS, 22, 1977)
Eyffler, N. *Nicholas Eyffler of Warwick* (Dugd. Soc. Pub., 31, Misc. 1, 1977)
F., J. *The Merchant's Warehouse Laid Open* (1690)
Fairchild, T. *The City Gardener* (1722)
Fairclough, S. *The Saints' Worthiness* (1653)
Favin, A. *The Theatre of Honor and Knighthood* (1623)
Fell, S. *The Household Account Book*, ed. N. Penney (Cambridge, 1920)
Fennor, W. *The Counters' Commonwealth* (1617), repr. in A. V. Judges, *The Elizabethan Underworld* (1930)
Fenton, R. *A Treatise of Usurie* (1612)
Ferne, J. *The Blazon of Gentry* (1586)
The Ferrar Papers, ed. B. Blackstone (Cambridge, 1938)
Fiennes, C. *Through England on a Side Saddle*, ed. C. Morris (1983)
Filmer, Sir R. *Patriarcha and Other Political Works*, ed. P. Laslett (Oxford, 1949)
A Discourse Whether it may be Lawful To Take Use for Money (1653)
Fisher, P. *The Catalogue of Most of the Memorable Tombs in the Churches of London* (1668), rev. and ed. G. B. Morgan (1885)
William Fitzhugh and his Chesapeake World, 1676–1701: The Letters, ed. R. B. Davis (Chapel Hill, 1963)
Fitzwilliam, *The Correspondence of Lord Fitzwilliam and Francis Guybon, 1697–1709*, ed. D. R. Hainsworth and C. Walker (Northants. Rec. Soc., 1990)
Flecknoe, R. *Relations of Ten Years* (1653)
Fleetwood, W. *Chronicon Preciosum or an Account of English Money* (1707)
Two Sermons (1718)
The Flemings in Oxford (1650–80), ed. J. R. McGrath (Oxford Hist. Soc., 1904)
Fletcher, Giles the Elder, *The English Works*, ed. L. E. Berry (Madison, 1964)
Philip Foley: Stour Valley Ironworks, 1668–74, ed. R. G. Schafer (Worcestershire Historical, 9, 1978; 13, 1990)
Fontaine, J. *Mémoires d'une famile huguenote* (Toulouse, 1877, repr. New York, 1954)
Forman, S. *The Autobiography, 1552–1602*, ed. J. O. Hallwell-Phillips (1849)
Founders Company of London. Wardens' Accounts, ed. G. Parsloe (1964)
Fox, G. *A Warning to all the Merchants in London and Such as Buy and Sell* (1658)
The Line of Righteousness and Justice Stretched Forth (1661)
An Epistle by way of Caution to Shopkeepers, Merchants and Factors (1674)
Journal, ed. J. L. Nickalls (Cambridge, 1952)
Foxe, J. *The Acts and Monuments*, 4th edn, rev. J. Pratt and J. Stoughton (1877), 8 vols.
Frampton Cotterel and District Probate Inventories, 1539–1840, ed. J. S. Moore (Chichester, 1976)

Freke, E. *Diary, 1671–1714*, ed. M. Carbery (J. Cork Hist. & Antiq. Soc., 16–19, 1910–13)
Fretwell, J. *The Diary*, repr. in *Yorkshire Diaries* (Surt. Soc., 65, 1877)
Fryer, J. *A New Account of East India and Persia*, ed. E. W. Crooke (Hakl. Soc., 2nd ser., 19, 1909; 20, 1912; 39, 1915)
The Fuller Letters, 1728–55, ed. D. Crossley and R. Saville (Sussex Rec. Soc., 76, 1991)
Fuller, T. *The Holy State and the Profane State*, ed. M. G. Walten (New York, 1938)
The History of the Worthies of England (1657), ed. P. A. Nuttall (1849)
The Church History of Britain, ed. J. S. Brewer (Oxford, 1845), 6 vols.
Gaby, W. 'His book, 1656', ed. E. Coward (Wilts. Arch. & Nat. Hist. Soc., 46, 1932–4)
Gage, J. *The History and Antiquities of Hengrave in Suffolk* (1822)
Gage, T. *A New Survey of the West Indies* (1648), ed. J. E. S. Thompson (1958)
Gainsborough Monthly Meeting of Friends. First Minute Book, 1669–1719, ed. H. W. Brace (Lincs. Rec. Soc., 38, 1948)
Gainsford, T. *The Rich Cabinet* (1616)
Galland, A. *Journal*, ed. C. Schefer (1881)
Gandy, H. 'Inventory', *Western Antiquary*, 7 (1888)
Gardner, R. *Papers*, ed. R. Howell (Soc. Antiq. Newcastle Rec. Ser., 2, 1978)
Gataker, T. *God's Eye on his Israel* (1645)
Gent, T. *History of Hull* (1735, repr. Hull, 1869)
The Gentleman's Companion (1676)
The Gentleman's Magazine (1732) (1829) (1832) (1904)
Gibbon, E. *Memoirs of my Life*, ed. G. A. Bonnard (1966)
Girling, G. F. A. *English Merchants' Marks* (repr. Oxford, 1964)
Gloucester. A Calendar of the Registers of the Freemen, 1641–1838 , ed. A. R. J. Jurica (Gloucs. Rec. Soc., 4, 1991)
Gobain, P. *Le Commerce en son jour* (Bordeaux, 1702)
Godolphin, J. *The Orphans' Legacy* (1674)
Godwin, M. *The Negros' and Indians' Advocate* (1680)
Trade Preferred before Religion (1685)
Goodinge, T. *The Law against Bankrupts*, 3rd edn (1713)
Goodman, G. *The Court of James I*, ed. J. S. Brewer (1839)
The Goods and Chattels of our Forefathers, ed. J. S. Moore (Chichester, 1976)
Gore, J. *Certaine Sermons*, 3rd edn (1636)
Goudet, J. *Case of John Goudet* (1698)
Gouge, W. *Of Domesticall Duties* (1622)
Gouget, T. *The Surest and Safest Way of Thriving* (1673)
Gough, R. *History of Myddle* (1723), ed. D. Hey (Folio Soc., 1983)
The Grand Concern of England explained (1673), repr. in *Harl. Misc.*, vol. VIII
Graunt, J. *Natural and Political Observations on the Bills of Mortality* (1662), ed. W. F. Willcox (Baltimore, 1939)
Gray, W. 'Inventory', *Arch. Aliena*, 11 (1886)
Gray's Inn The Pension Book, 1569–1669, ed. R. J. Fletcher (1901–10), 2 vols.
Gray's Inn Register of Admissions, 1521–1889, ed. J. Foster (1889)
Greene, J. 'Diary 1635–57', ed. E. M. Symonds, in *E. H. R.*, 43–4 (1928–9)

Greene, R. *A Notable Discourse of Coosenage* (1571), repr. in Judges, *Elizabethan Underworld*
The Defence of Conny Catching, repr. in G. Salgado, *The Elizabethan Underworld* (1992)
Grey, A. *Debates of the House of Commons 1667–97* (1768), 10 vols
The Guardian, repr. in *The British Essayists*, ed. A. Chalmers (1823), vols. XIII–XV
Gwin, T. *Journal* (Falmouth, 1837)
H., N. *The Compleat Tradesman* (1684)
Hadley, G. *A History of Kingston upon Hull* (1788)
Haines, R. *The Prevention of Poverty* (1674)
Hakluyt, R. *The Principal Navigations, Voyages and Discoveries of the English Nation* (1589) (repr. Hakl. Soc., extra ser., 39, Cambridge, 1965)
The Original Writings and Correspondence of the Two Richard Hakluyts, ed. E. G. R. Taylor (Hakl. Soc., 2nd ser., 76–7, 1935)
Hale, Sir Matthew, *Works Moral and Religious*, ed. T. Thirwall (1805), 2 vols.
De Successionibus apud Anglos (1700)
Halifax, George Savile Marquess of, *Complete Works*, ed. J. P. Kenyon (1969)
Hall, D. *Some Brief Memoirs of the Life* (1758)
Hall, J. *Advancement of Learning* (1649), ed. A. K. Croston (Liverpool, 1953)
Halyburton's Ledger, 1492–1503, ed. C. Innes (Edinburgh, 1867)
Hampshire, H. 'Inventory', ed. T. N. Brushfield, *Devon & Corn. N. & Q.*, 2 (1902–3)
The Harleian Miscellany, ed. J. Park (1808–11), 12 vols.
Harrington, J. *The Political Works*, ed. J. G. A. Pocock (Cambridge, 1977)
Harris, A. *The Œconomie of the Fleet*, ed. A. Jessopp (Camd. Soc., 2nd ser., 25, 1879)
Harrison, W. *Description of England*, ed. G. Edelen (Ithaca, 1968)
Harrold, E. 'Diary', in *Manchester Collectanea*
Hartlib, S. in *Directions by a Gentleman to his Son* (1670)
Hatton, E. *The Merchant's Magazine or Tradesman's Treasury* (1695)
Haverfordwest. Calendar of the Records of the Borough, ed. B. G. Charles (Cardiff, 1967)
Haward, L. *The Charges Issuing Forth of the Crowns Revenue* (1660)
Hawkins, Sir John, *A General History of the Science and Practice of Music* (1776, repr. New York, 1963)
Hayne, J. *The Financial Diary, 1631–43*, ed. T. N. Brushfield (Exeter, 1901)
Haynes, J. *Great Britain's Glory* (1715)
Hearne, T. *Reliquiae Hearnaniae*, ed. J. Bliss and J. B. Brown (1966)
A Health to the Gentlemanly Profession of Serving Men (1598), in *Inedited Tracts*, ed. W. C. Hazlitt (Roxburgh Club, 1861)
Hedges, Sir Charles, *Reasons for Settling Admiralty Jurisdiction* (1690)
Hedges, Sir William, *Diary, 1681–7*, transcr. R. Barlow, ed. H. Yule (Hakl. Soc., 74, 1886; 75, 1887; 78, 1888)
Henslowe's Diary, ed. R. A. Foakes and R. T. Rickert (Cambridge, 1961)
The Henslowe Papers, ed. R. A. Foakes (1977)
Heraldic Cases in the Court of Chivalry Reports, 1623–1732, ed. G. D. Squibb (Harl. Soc., 107, 1956)
Heriot, G. 'Last will', in *Misc. Maitland Club*, 3 (1843)

Heyward, Sir Rowland, 'Will', ed. R. C. Purton, *Trans. Shrop. Arch. & Nat. Hist. Soc.*, 51 (1941–3)
Heywood, A.'Extracts from the private ledger', ed. H. A. Omerud (Trans. Hist. Soc. Lancs. & Ches., 103, 1951)
Heywood, O. *His Autobiography, Anecdotes and Event Books*, ed. J. H. Turner (Brighouse, 1881–5)
Heywood, T. *The Dramatic Works*, ed. R. H. Shepherd (1874)
Three Heywood Pageants, ed. D. M. Bergeron (New York, 1986)
H(ill), J. *The Exact Dealer* (1688)
Hill, J. *The Interest of these United Provinces* (1673)
Hill, T. *The Art of Vulgar Arithmetick* (1600)
Historical Manuscripts Commission
3rd Report (Part 1)
8th Report (Lords Papers)
9th Report (Part 2)
14th Report, app. 9
15th Report, app. 10
25th Report, app. 10
Finch
Fleming
Fortescue, vol. 1
House of Lords MSS, 1695–1714
Portland, 2
Salisbury, vol. 2
Var. Coll., 2
Hobbes, T. *Behemoth*, repr. in *Select Tracts*, ed. F. Maseres (1815)
Leviathan, ed. W. G. Pogson Smith (Oxford, 1909)
The English Works, ed. Sir William Molesworth (1839–45), 11 vols.
De Cive, ed. S. P. Lamprecht (New York, 1949)
Hobbs, T. 'The household goods', ed. G. C. R. Morris, *Trans. Lond. & Midd. A. S.*, 23 (1972)
Hodder, J. *Hodder's Arithmetic* (1661)
Hodges, R. *Enchiridion Arithmeticon* (1636)
Hoker, J. (alias Vowell) *The Description of the Citie of Excester*, ed. W. J. Harte, J. W. Schopp and H. Tapley-Soper (Devon & Corn. Rec. Soc., 2, 1919)
Holles Family Memorials, 1493–1656, ed. A. C. Wood (Camd. Soc., 3rd ser., 55, 1937)
Holroyd, J. *Letter Books of Joseph Holroyd and Samuel Hill*, ed. H. Heaton (Banksfield Museum Notes, 2nd ser., 3, Halifax, 1900, 1914)
Hornsey Court Rolls, ed. W. M. and F. Marcham (1929)
Houblon, J. *Pious Memoirs being the Substance of Letters Written with his Own Hand* (1863)
Houghton, J. *A Collection of Letters for the Improvement of Husbandry and Trade* (1681–3)
Howell, J. *Epistolae Ho-Elianae*, ed. J. Jacobs (1890)
Londinopolis (1657)
Hudd, A. E. *Bristol Merchant Marks* (Proc. Clifton Antiq. Club, 7, 1910–11)
Hudson's Bay Company. Minutes, 1671–84, ed. E. E. Rich (Champlain Soc. Rec.

Ser., 5, 1942; 8–9, 1945–6)
Hudson's Bay Company. Letters Outward, 1680–7, ed. E. E. Rich (Hudson's Bay Co. Rec. Ser., 11, 1948)
Hudson's Bay Company. Letters Outward, 1688–96, ed. E. E. Rich and A. M. Johnson (Hudson's Bay Co. Rec. Ser., 20, 1957)
An Humble Proposal to Cause Bankrupts to Make Better and More Speedier Payment (1670)
An Humble Representation upon the Perpetual Imprisonment of Insolvent Debtors (1687)
Hume, D. *Writings on Economics*, ed. E. Rotwein (1955)
Hunt, T. *A Defence of the Charter of London* (1682)
The Imprisonment of Men's Bodies for Debt (1641)
'Instructions for an eighteenth-century commercial traveller', ed. D. H. Kennett (Proc. Camb. Antiq. Soc., 67, 1977)
'An insurance agent's account', printed in F. Martin, *The History of Lloyds* (1876)
The Interest of England Considered in an Essay upon Wool (1694)
'An Ipswich merchant's cloth account, 1623–4', ed. J. Webb, (Proc. Suff. Inst. Arch. & Nat. Hist., 37, 1990)
The Ipswich Probate Inventories, 1583–1631, ed. M. Reed (Suff. Rec. Soc., 22, 1981)
Poor Relief in Elizabethan Ipswich, ed. J. Webb (Suff. Rec. Soc., 9, 1966)
Isham, J. *John Isham Mercer and Merchant Adventurer*, ed. G. D. Ramsay (Northants. Rec. Soc., 21, 1962)
Isham, T. *Diary, 1625–81*, transcr. N. Marlow, ed. Sir Giles Isham (Farnborough, 1971)
Diary, ed. W. Rye (Norwich, 1875)
The Italian Relation of England, ed. C. A. Sneyd (Camd. Soc., 37, 1847)
Ivie, John, *A Declaration* (1661), repr. in *Poverty in Early Stuart Salisbury*, ed. P. Slack (Wilts. Rec. Soc., 31, 1978)
J(ackson), A. *The Pious Prentice* (1640)
Jacob, G. *City Liberties* (1732)
Jeaffreson, C. *Papers*, ed. J. C. Jeaffreson as *A Young Squire of the Seventeenth Century* (1878), 2 vols.
Jeake, S. *An Astrological Diary*, ed. M. Hunter and A. Gregory (Oxford, 1988)
A Complete Body of Arithmetick (1701)
Jeffries, J. *Account Book*, ed. J. Webb (Archaeologia, 37, 1857 and Trans. Woolhope Naturalists Field Club, 1921–3)
Johnson, T. *A Discourse consisting of Motives for Enlargement and Freedom of Trade* (1645)
Johnston, N. *The Dear Bargain* (1688)
Jones, E. *Luxury Pride and Vanity the Bane of the British Nation*, 2nd edn (1736)
Jonson, B. *Works*, ed. C. H. Herford, P and E. Simpson (Oxford, 1925–52), 11 vols.
Jordan, T. *The Debtors Apologie* (1644)
Josselin, R. *The Diary, 1614–83*, ed. A. McFarlane (Brit. Acad., NS, 3, 1976)
Jourdain, J. *Journal, 1608–17*, ed. Sir William Foster (1905)
Judges, A. V. *The Elizabethan Underworld: A Collection of Tudor and Early Stuart Tracts and Ballads* (1930)

K., C. *Some Seasonable and Modest Thoughts* (1696)
Keayne, R. *The Apologia*, ed. B. Bailyn (New York, 1965)
Keeling, W. and Bonner, T. *Journal, 1615–17*, ed. M. Strachan and B. Penrose (Minneapolis, 1971)
Kendricke, J. R. *The Last Will and Testament* (1625)
Kent. The Visitation, 1619–21, ed. R. Hovenden (Harl. Soc., 42, 1898)
Kent's Directory (1745)
Keymer, J. *Original Papers Regarding Trade*, ed. M. F. Lloyd Prichard (New York, 1967)
Khan, S. A. *Sources for the History of British India in the Seventeenth Century* (New Delhi, 1978)
Kiffin, W. *Life*, ed. J. Ivimey (1883)
Remarkable Passages, ed. W. Orme (1823)
King, G. 'Notebook 1679–80', in *Historical Collections of Staffordshire*, ed. W. Salt (1919)
Two Tracts, ed. G. E. Barnett (Baltimore, 1936)
Staffordshire Pedigrees based on the Visitation by Dugdale, ed. Sir G. Armytage and W. H. Rylands (Harl. Soc., 63, 1912)
Kingston upon Thames. Register of Apprentices, 1563–1713, ed. A. Daly (Surrey Rec. Soc., 28, 1974)
Kirk, R. *London in 1689–90*, ed. D. Maclean and N. G. Brett James, *Trans. Lond. & Midd. A. S.*, NS, 6 (1929–33)
Kirkman, F. *The Unlucky Citizen Experimentally Described* (1673)
Knapp Family Memorials, in S. Grimaldi, *Miscellaneous Writings* (1874–81)
The Knaving Merchant now turn'd Warehousman Characterised (1661)
Knight, F. *A Relation of Several Years' Slaverie under the Turkes* (1640)
Knox, J. *Works*, ed. D. Laing (Edinburgh, 1846–64), 6 vols.
Laertius Diogenes, *Lives of Eminent Philosophers*, trans. R. D. Hicks (Cambridge, Massachusetts, 1966)
Lancashire and Cheshire. Wills and Inventories, ed. G. J. Piccope (Cheth. Soc., OS, 54, 1861)
ed. G. J. Piccope and J. P. Earwaker (Cheth. Soc., NS 3, 1884)
Lancashire and Cheshire. Wills and Inventories 1572–1696, ed. J. P. Earwaker (Cheth. Soc., NS, 28, 1893)
Lancashire and Cheshire. Wills 1563–1807, ed. J. P. Rylands (Cheth. Soc., NS, 37, 1897)
Cheshire. Wills from the Ecclesiastical Court of Chester, ed. G. J. Piccope (Cheth. Soc., OS, 50, 1857; 53–5, 1860–1)
Lancashire. Probate Records, ed. C. B. Phillips and J. H. Smith (Lancs. & Ches. Rec. Soc., 124, 1985)
Lancashire. Visitation of the County Palatine by Sir William Dugdale, ed. F. R. Raines (Cheth. Soc., 1872)
Lancaster. The Rolls of the Freemen, 1688–1840, ed. T. C. Hughes (Lancs. & Ches. Rec. Soc., 87, 1935)
Laporte, M. de, *Le Guide des négocians et teneurs de livre* (1685)
Laroon, M. *Engravings and Drawings*, ed. S. Shesgreen (1990)
Law Merchant Select Cases: 1270–1638, ed. C. Gross (Seld. Soc., 23, 1908); *1239–1779*, ed. H. Hall (Seld. Soc., 46, 49, 1929)

Law and Custom of the Sea: Documents, 1205–1767, ed. R. G. Marsden (Navy Rec. Soc., 49–50, 1915–16)
Lawrence, W. *The Diary*, ed. G. E. Aylmer (Beaminster, 1961)
Le Neve, J. *Pedigrees of the Knights*, ed. G. W. Marshall (Harl. Soc., 8, 1873)
Fasti ecclesiae Anglicanae, ed. H. P. E. King, J. B. Horn and B. Jones (1962–7)
Monumenta Anglicanae (1715–19), 5 vols.
Lee, J. *A Vindication of a Regulated Enclosure* (1656)
Leicester. Register of the Freemen, 1196–1930, ed. H. Hartopp (Leicester, 1927–31), 2 vols.
Leicester. Roll of the Mayors, 1209–1935, comp. H. Hartopp (Leicester, 1935)
Leland, J. *Itinerary*, ed. T. Hearne (Oxford, 1710–12), 9 vols.
Letters of Medieval Jewish Traders, ed. S. D. Gotein (Princeton, 1973)
Letters from a Subaltern Officer of the Earl of Essex's Army, ed. Sir Henry Ellis (Archaeologia, 35, 1853)
Lettres marchandes, ed. F. Ruiz Martin (1965)
Lever, J. 'Public Diary', *The Antiquary*, 19 (1889)
Lewis, L. 'English commemorative sculpture in Jamaica', *Jamaica Hist. Rev.*, 9 (1972)
Lex Londinensis (1680)
Leybourn, W. *A Platform Guide* (1668)
The Public Markets of London Surveyed 1677, ed. B. R. Masters (Lond. Topog. Soc., 1975)
Lichfield and District Probate Inventories, 1568–1680, ed. D. G. Vaisey (Collections for the History of Staffordshire, 4th ser., 5, 1969)
Liddell, H. *The Letters, 1673–1717*, ed. J. M. Ellis (Surt. Soc., 197, 1987)
Lillo, G. *Merchant of London* (1731), ed. B. Dobrée (1948)
Lilly, W. *History of his Life and Times* (1715)
Lillywhite, B. *London Signs* (1973)
Lincoln. Probate Inventories, 1661–1714, ed. J. A. Johnston (Lincs. Rec. Soc., 80, 1991)
Lincoln's Inn Admissions, 1420–1769 (1896)
Liset, A. *Amphitalami or the Accomptant's Closet* (1660)
The Lisle Letters, ed. M. St. Clare Byrne (Chicago, 1981), 6 vols.
Lister, Joseph, *The Autobiography of*, ed. T. Wright (1842)
Lithgow, W. *The Rare and Painful Peregrinations* (repr. Glasgow, 1906)
Liverpool. Customs Letter Books, 1711–1813, ed. R. C. Jarvis (Cheth. Soc., 6, 1954)
Liverpool in the Reign of Queen Anne, 1705–08, ed. H. Reed, in *Trans. Hist. Soc. Lancs. & Ches.*, 59, (1907)
Locke, J. *Works*, 12th. edn (1824)
The Educational Writings, ed. J. L. Axtell (Cambridge, 1968)
Some Thoughts concerning Education, ed. J. W. and J. S. Yolton (Oxford, 1989)
Travels in France, ed. J. Lough (Cambridge, 1953)
Two Treatises on Government, ed. P. Laslett (Cambridge, 1960)
The Correspondence, ed. E. S. De Beer (Oxford, 1976–89), 8 vols.
Locke on Money, ed. P. H. Kelley (Oxford, 1991), 2 vols.
Lodge, T. *Complete Works* (New York, 1963), 4 vols.
Loe, W. *The Merchants Manuell* (1638)

London. Chamberlain's Accounts, ed. B. R. Masters (London Rec. Soc., 20, 1984)
London. Characters of the Lord Mayors and the Court of Aldermen presented to Charles II, printed in *Gentleman's Magazine*, 39 (1769)
London. Consistory Court Wills, 1492–1547, ed. I. Darlington (London Rec. Soc., 3, 1967)
The Historical Charters and Constitutional Documents of London, ed. W. de G. Birch (1887)
Historical Monuments Commission: London (1924), 5 vols.
'The inhabitants of London in 1638', ed. T. C. Dale (Soc. Genealogists, 1931), 2 vols.
'List of the principal inhabitants of London, 1640', ed. W. J. Hervey (Misc. Genealog. & Herald., 2nd ser., 2, 1880)
'London citizens in 1651', ed. J. C. Whitebrook (1910)
A Collection of the Names of the Merchants Living in and about the City of London (1677)
London Inhabitants within the Walls, 1695, ed. D. V. Glass (London Rec. Soc., 2, 1966, and Supp. in Guild. Stud. Lond. Hist., 2)
The Lists of the Liveries of the Fifty-six Companies of London (1701)
The London Jilt (1683)
Monumental Inscriptions and Heraldry in St Olave's, ed. A. J. Jewers (1929)
London. Calendar of Plea and Memorandum Rolls, ed. A. H. Thomas and P. E. Jones (1926–61)
The Port and Trade of Early Elizabethan London, ed. B. Dietz (Lond. Rec. Soc., 8, 1970)
London Prentices and Trades, A Collection of Songs and Ballads, ed. C. Mackay (Percy Soc., 1, 1841)
London. Sessions Records, 1605–85, ed. H. Bowles (Cath. Rec. Soc., 34, 1934)
London. Visitation of London in 1568, ed. J. J. Howard and G. J. Armytage (Harl. Soc., 1, 1869)
London. Visitation of 1568 with Additional Pedigrees, 1569–90, ed. H. S. London and S. W. Rawlins (Harl. Soc., 109, 110, 1963)
London. Visitation of London Anno Domino 1633, 1634 and 1635 by Sir Henry St George, ed. J. Howard and J. L. Chester (Harl. Soc., 15, 1880; 17, 1883)
London. Visitation Pedigrees, 1664, ed. J. B. Whitmore and A. H. Hughes Clark (Harl. Soc., 92, 1940)
London. Calendar of Wills Proved and Enrolled in the Court of Hustings, vol. II, *1358–1688*, ed. R. R. Sharpe (1889)
Love, C. *Scriptural Rules to be Observed in Buying and Selling* (1653)
Lowe, R. *The Diary, 1663–74*, ed. W. L. Sachse (1938)
Lowndes, W. *Diary, 1679–1709* (Records of Bucks., 12, 1929)
Lowther, Sir Christopher, *Commercial Papers, 1611–44*, ed. D. R. Hainsworth (Surt. Soc., 189, 1977)
Lowther, Sir John, 'Autobiography', repr. in *Lowther Family Estate Book, 1617–75*, ed. C. B. Phillips (Surt. Soc., 191, 1979)
Correspondence in Whitehaven, 1693–8, ed. D. R. Hainsworth (1983)
Luddington, W. R. B. D. 'Robert Luddington', *Trans. Worcs. A. S.*, 25 (1949)
Luttrell, N. *A Brief Relation of State Affairs, 1678–1714* (Oxford, 1857)
The Parliamentary Diary, 1691–3, ed. H. Horwitz (Oxford, 1972)

Lynn. A Calendar of the Freemen of King's Lynn, 1292–1836 (Norf. & Norw. Arch. Soc., 1913)
Lysons, D. *London and its Environs Described* (1792–6), 4 vols.
Machin, H. *Diary, 1550–63*, ed. J. G. Nichols (Camd. Soc., 42, 1847)
Mackenzie, Sir George, *The Moral History of Frugality* (1691)
Mackerell, B. *The History and Antiquities of Kings Lynn* (1736)
Magno, A. *London Journal, 1562*, ed. C. Barron, C. Gobb and C. Coleman, in *Lond. J.*, 9 (1983)
Malynes, G. de, *Consuetudo vel lex mercatoria* (1622)
Free Trade or Means to make Trade Flourish, 2nd edn (1622)
Manchester, Collectanea relating to, ed. J. Harland, (Cheth. Soc., OS, 68, 1866)
Mandeville, B. de, *Free Thoughts on Religion the Church and National Happiness* (1720)
A Modest Defence of Public Stews (1724)
An Enquiry into the Origins of Honour (1732), ed. M. M. Goldsmith (1971)
The Fable of the Bees, ed. F. B. Kaye (Oxford, 1924), 2 vols.
Manley, T. *Usury at Six Per Cent Examined* (1669)
Manningham, J. *Diary*, ed. R. P. Sorlien (Hanover, New Hampshire 1976)
Manship, H. *The History of Great Yarmouth*, ed. C. J. Palmer (Great Yarmouth, 1854–6), 2 vols.
Marchetti, F. *Discourse sur le négoce des gentilhommes de Marseille* (Marseilles, 1671)
Explication des usages et coutumes (Marseilles, 1683)
Marescoe, C. *Markets and Merchants in the Late Seventeenth Century: the Marescoe–David letters, 1668–1680*, ed. H. Roseveare (Brit. Acad. Rec. Social and Econ. Hist., 12, Oxford, 1987)
Marion, E. *Prophetical Warnings* (1707)
Marius, J. *Advice concerning Bills of Exchange* (1651)
Tudor Market Rasen, ed. D. Neave (Hull, 1985)
Markham, F. *The Booke of Honour* (1625)
Markham, G. *The English Housewife* (1613), ed. M. R. Best (Montreal, 1986)
Hobson's Horse-load of Letters (1617)
Marperger, P. J. *Der allzeit fertige Handels Korrespondent* (Hamburg, 1707)
Martindale, A. *The Life of Adam Martindale*, ed. R. Parkinson (Cheth. Soc., OS, 4, 1845)
Martyn, H. *Considerations upon the East India Trade* (1701), repr. in *Early English Tracts on Commerce*
Masons Records, ed. E. Conder (1894)
Master, J. *Expense Book, 1646–76*, ed. M. Dallison and W. A. Scott Robinson (Arch. Cant., 15, 1883)
Master, S. *The Diaries, 1675–80*, ed. Sir R. C. Temple (Indian Rec. Soc., 1911), 2 vols.
Mather, C. *Ornaments for the Daughters of Zion* (Boston, 1691)
May, R. *The Accomplisht Cook*, 2nd edn (1665)
Mellis, J. *Brief Instruction and Maner to Keep Bookes of Accompt* (1588)
Mercers Company of London, Acts of Court, 1453–1527, ed. L. Lyell (1936)
The Merchant Adventurers of England their Laws and Ordinances, ed. W. R. Lingelbach (Philadelphia, 1902)

Merchant Taylors School, Register, 1561–1934, ed. E. P. Hart (1936), 2 vols.
The Merchant's Warehouse Laid Open (1695)
Mesopotamia, Ledgers and Prices and Early Merchant Accounts of, ed. D. C. Snell (New Haven, 1982)
Middle Temple. Register of Admissions, comp. Sir Henry Macgeagh and H. A. C. Sturgess, vol. I, *1501–1781* (1949)
Middlesex County Records, ed. T.C. Jeaffreson and W.J. Le Hardy (Midd. County Rec. Soc., 1886–92), vols. III and IV
Middleton, T. *The Triumph of Honor and Industry* (1617)
A Chaste Maid in Cheapside, ed. R. B. Parker (1960)
Miller, J. *New York Considered and Improved* (1695), ed. V. H. Paltsits (Cleveland, 1903)
Milles, T. *The Misterie of Iniquity Discovered* (*c.* 1611)
The Catalogue of Honour or Treasury of True Nobility (1610)
Milton, J. *The Complete Prose Works*, ed. M. Kelley, rev. edn (New Haven, 1982)
Commonplace Book
Misselden, J. *The Circle of Commerce* (1623)
Misson, Henri de Valbourg, *Mémoires et observations* (The Hague, 1698)
Molloy, C. *De jure maritimo et navali* (1676)
Mons Pietatis (1719)
Monteage, S. *Debtor and Creditor made easy* (1708)
Monumental Brasses 1301–1632: The Portfolio Plates of the Monumental Brass Society, ed. M. W. Norman (Woodbury, 1988)
Monumental Inscriptions Registers (Eng. Mon. Inscr. Lib.)
The Moore Rental, ed. T. Heywood (Cheth. Soc., OS, 12, 1847)
Morant, P. *The History and Antiquities of the County of Essex* (1768), 2 vols.
More, Sir Thomas, *The Complete Works*, ed. E. Surtz and J. H. Hexter (New Haven, 1965)
Morgan, W. *London Actually Surveyed* (1682, repr. Lond. Topog. Soc., 1904)
Moryson, F. *An Itinerary* (1617, repr. Glasgow, 1907)
The Mosley Family, ed. E. Axon (Cheth. Soc., Misc., NS, 47, 1902)
Mulcaster, R. *Positions* (1581), ed. R. H. Quick (1888)
Mun, T. *England's Treasure by Foreign Trade* (1664, repr. 1928)
Mundy, P. *The Travels in Europe and Asia, 1608–67*, ed. R. C. Temple and L. M. Anstey (Hakl. Soc., 2nd ser., 17, 1907; 35, 1914; 45–6, 1919; 55, 1925; 78, 1936)
Muralt, B. L. de, *Lettres sur les Anglois* (Cologne, 1725)
Myddelton, Sir Thomas, 'Inventory', ed. M. A. R. F. Lawes-Wittewronge, *Home Counties Mag.*, 5 (1903)
The Mystery of the New-fashioned Goldsmiths (1676), reprinted in J. B. Martin, *The Grasshopper in Lombard Street* (1892)
Naish, T. *Diary*, ed. D. Slatter (Wilts. Arch. & Nat. Hist. Soc. Rec. Ser., 20, 1965)
Nashe, T. *Works*, ed. R. B. McKerrow and F. P. Wilson (1958), 5 vols.
Nedham, G. *The Politics of a Tudor Merchant Adventurer*, ed. G. D. Ramsay (Manchester, 1979)
New York. Select Cases from the Lord Mayor's Court, 1674–1785, ed. R. R. Morris (Washington, 1935)
Newcastle upon Tyne. Company of Hostmen Records, ed. F. W. Dendy (Surt. Soc.,

105, 1901)
Newcastle. Company of Shipwrights' Records, 1622–1967, ed. D. J. Rowe (Surt. Soc., 184, 1971)
Newcastle. Merchant Adventurers' Records, ed. F. W. Dendy and J. R. Boyle (Surt. Soc., 93, 1895; 101, 1899)
Newcastle. The Register of Freemen (Newcastle Rec. Comm., 1923)
Newcombe, H. *The Autobiography*, ed. R. Parkinson (Cheth. Soc., OS, 26–7, 1852)
Newmarket. Inventories, ed. P. May (Newmarket, 1976)
Newton, J. *The Scales of Interest* (1668)
Newton, S. *Diary of an Alderman of Cambridge*, ed. J. E. Foster (Camb. Antiq. Soc., 23, 1890)
Niccholl, A. *A Discourse of Marriage and Wiving* (1615), in *Harl. Misc.*, vol. II
Nicholas, A. *The Young Accomptant* (1711)
Nichols, S. *The History and Antiquities of the County of Leicester* (1795)
Noble, J. *A Hereford Mercer's Inventory and Accounts*, ed. F. C. Morgan (Hereford, 1947)
Norfolk. Lieutenancy Journal, 1660–76, ed. R. M. Dunn (Norf. Rec. Soc., 45, 1977)
Norfolk. Visitation in 1563, ed. G. H. Dashwood (Norf. & Norw. Arch. Soc., 1878, 1895), 2 vols.
The Norris Papers, ed. T. Heywood (Cheth. Soc., OS, 9, 1846)
North, R. *Lives of the Norths*, ed. E. D. Mackerness (1972)
A Discourse on the Study of the Laws (1824)
North Country Wills, 1558–1604 (Surt. Soc., 121, 1912)
'A Northampton mercer's probate inventory', ed. M. C. Harrison, *Northants. P. & P.*, 6, (1982)
Northampton Records, ed. C. A. Markham and J. C. Cox (1898)
Norwich. The Register of the Freemen, 1548–1713, ed. P. Millican (Norwich, 1934)
Norwich. An Index of Indentures of Apprentices, 1510–1749, ed. W. M. Rising and P. Millican (Norf. Rec. Soc., 29, 1959)
Norwich. Minutes of the Court of Mayoralty, 1630–35, ed. W. L. Sachse (Norf. Rec. Soc., 15, 1942; 36, 1967)
Norwich. Accounts for the Customs of Strangers' Goods, 1582–1610, ed. D. L. Richwood (Norf. Rec. Soc., 39, 1970)
Norwich. Records of Early English Drama, 1540–1642, ed. D. Galloway (Toronto, 1984)
Norwood, R. *The Journal*, ed. W. B. Hayward (New York, 1945)
Nottinghamshire. Household Inventories, ed. P. A. Kennedy (Thoroton Soc. Rec. Ser., 22, 1963)
Nottinghamshire. The Visitation of 1662–3, ed. G. D. Squibb (Harl. Soc., NS, 5, 1986)
Nye, S. *Life of Thomas Firmin* (1698)
Oglander, Sir John, *Commonplace Book*, ed. F. Bamford (1936)
Olearius, *The Travels*, ed. S. H. Baron (Stanford, 1970)
Oliver, V. L. *The Monumental Inscriptions in the Churches of Barbados* (1915)
Onslow Family Memoirs
Original Letters Illustrative of English History, ed. H. Ellis (1846), 4 vols.

Osborne, D. *Letters to Sir William Temple, 1652–4*, ed. K. Hart (Folio Soc., 1968)
Osborne, F. *Advice to a Son* (1656), repr. L. B. Wright (Ithaca, 1962)
Overs, J. *The True History of Old John Overs, the Rich Ferryman of London* (1673)
Ovington, J. *Voyage to Surat*, ed. H. G. Rawlinson (Oxford, 1929)
Owen, T. 'Inventory', in *Trans. Shrop. Arch. & Nat. Hist. Soc.*, 53 (1949–50)
Oxford. City Apprentices, 1697–1800 (Oxford Hist. Soc., NS, 31, 1987)
Oxford. Seventeenth-Century Tokens, ed. J. G. Milne (1935)
Oxford. Visitation of the County, 1566, 1574 and 1634 (Harl. Soc., 5, 1871)
Oxfordshire. Household and Farm Inventories, 1550–90, ed. M. A. Havinden (Oxfordshire Rec. Soc., 44, 1965)
The Oxinden Letters, 1607–42, ed. D. Gardiner (1933)
The Oxinden and Peyton Letters, 1642–72, ed. D. Gardiner (1937)
Oxley, J. *Offering to his Children*, repr. in *A Select Series*, ed. J. Barclay (1839), vol. V
P., J. *Merchant's Daily Companion* (1684)
Page, J. *Jus Fratrum* (1658)
Paige, J. *The Letters, 1648–58*, ed. P. Riden (Lond. Rec. Soc., 21, 1984)
Palmer, T. *Business Diary* (Suss. Arch. Coll., 20, 1867)
Papillon, T. *Memoirs*, ed. A. F. W. Papillon (Reading, 1827)
A Treatise concerning the East India Trade (1677)
Parker, H. *Of a Free Trade* (1648)
Parliament
The Commons Journals
The Lords Journals
The Commons Debates of 1621, ed. W. Notestein, F. H. Relf and H. Simpson (New Haven, 1935), 7 vols.
Proceedings in 1626, ed. W. B. Bidwell and M. Jansson (New Haven, 1992)
The Commons Debates of 1628, ed. R. C. Johnson, M. F. Keeler, M. J. Cole and W. M. Bidewell (1977), 3 vols.
The Commons Debates of 1629, ed. H. Relf and W. Notestein (Minneapolis, 1921)
A Complete Collection of the Protests of the Lords, ed. J. E. T. Rogers (Oxford, 1875)
The Parliamentary or Constitutional History of England, 1066–1660 (1751–71), 24 vols.
The Paston Letters and Papers, ed. N. Davis (1971, 1976), 2 vols.
Paterson, J. *Pietas Londinienses* (1714)
'A pauper's clothmaking account', ed. D. H. Kennett, *Text. Hist.*, 4 (1973)
The Pawson Inventory and Pedigrees, ed. C. B. Norcliffe (Thoresby Soc. Misc., 4, 1892–5)
Peacham, H. *The Art of Living in London* (1642), repr. in *Harl. Misc.*, vol. IX
The Complete Gentleman, ed. V. B. Heltzel (Ithaca, 1962)
Pecunia obediunt omnia (1696)
Peele, J. *The Maner and Fourm How to Kepe a Perfecte Reconying* (1553)
The Path Waye to Perfectnes (1569)
Pemberton, W. *The Godly Merchant* (1613)
Pepys, S. *The Diary*, ed. R. Latham and W. Matthew (1970–1)
The Pepys Ballads, ed. H. E. Rollins (Cambridge, Massachusetts, 1931)

Perkins, W. *The Works*, ed. I. Brewart (Abingdon, 1970)
English Puritanist His Pioneer Works on Casuistry, ed. T. F. Merrill (Nieuwkoop, 1966)
Perry, W. *A Treatise on Trade or the Antiquity and Honor of Commerce*, 2nd edn (1753)
'Sir John Petrie and some Elizabethan tradesmen', ed. A. C. Edwards (Lond. Topog. Soc. Rec. Ser., 23, 1972)
Pett, Sir Peter, *The Happy Future State of England* (1688)
Pett, P. *The Autobiography*, ed. W. G. Perrin (Navy Rec. Soc., 51, 1917)
The Petty Papers, ed. Marquess of Lansdowne (1927), 2 vols.
Petty, Sir William, *The Economic Writings*, ed. C. H. Hull (Cambridge, 1899)
Advice of W.P. to Mr Samuel Hartlib (1647–8), repr. in *Harl. Misc.* vol. VI
Petty–Southwell Correspondence 1676–87, ed. Marquess of Lansdowne (1928)
The Petworth House Archives: A Catalogue, ed. F. M. Steer and N. H. Osborne (Chichester, 1968–)
Philip, H. *Diaries and Letters*, ed. M. H. Lee (1882)
Phillips, G. *Life and Death of the Rich Man* (1600)
Phillips, H. *The Grandeur of the Law* (1684)
The Purchaser's Patterne, 3rd edn (1656)
Pike, J. *Some Account of the Life Written by Himself*, ed. J. Barclay (1837)
Pines, T. *The Summa Oriental*, ed. A. Cortesao (1944)
Pinney, J. *The Letters of John Pinney, 1679–99*, ed. G. F. Nuttall (Oxford, 1939)
Pitt, M. *The Cry of the Oppressed* (1691)
Plain Dealing in a Dialogue between Mr Johnson and Mr Waring (1691)
Platter, T. *Travels in England*, trans. C. Williams (1937)
The Pleasant Art of Money Catching (1684)
Pollexfen, J. *Discourse of Trade and Coyn* (1697)
England and East India Inconsistent in their Manufactures (1697)
The Merchant's Companion (1697)
Pope, A. *The Prose Works of Alexander Pope*, ed. R. Cowler (Oxford, 1986)
The Portledge Papers, 1687–97, ed. P. J. Kerr and I. C. Duncan (1928)
Portsmouth. Borough Sessions Papers, 1653–88, comp. A. J. Willis, ed. M. T. Hoad (Portsmouth Rec. Ser., 1, 1971)
Potenger, J. *Private Memoirs*, ed. C. W. Bingham (1841)
Potter, W. *The Key to Wealth* (1650)
Powell, G. *Theological and Scholastic Positions Concerning Usurie* (Oxford, 1602)
Powell, T. *Tom of All Trades* (1631), ed. F. J. Furnivall (New Shakespeare Soc., 6, 1876)
Poyntz, S. *The Relation of Sydenham Poyntz*, ed. A. T. S. Goodwich (Camd. Soc., 3rd ser., 14, 1908)
The Present State of War (1708)
Preston. Rolls of Burgesses, 1397–1682, ed. W. A. Abram (Lancs. & Ches. Rec. Soc., 9, 1884)
Preston, J. *A Remedy against Covetousness* (1632)
Sin's Overthrow (1633)
Price, D. *The Marchant* (Oxford, 1608)
Price, P. *Gravamina mercatoris* (1694)
Price, R. *The Compleat Cook*, ed. M. Masson (1974)

Prideaux, H. *Letters*, ed. E. M. Thompson (Camd. Soc., NS, 15, 1875)
Primatt, S. *The City and Country Purchaser and Builder* (1667)
Printers and Stationers. Abstracts from Wills, ed. H. R. Plomer (1903)
The Proclamations of the Tudor Kings, ed. R. W. Heinze (1976)
The Proclamations of the Tudor Queens, ed. F. A. Youngs (Cambridge, 1976)
Stuart Royal Proclamations, ed. J. F. Larkin (Oxford, 1983), 2 vols.
Pryme, A. de la, *Diary* (Surt. Soc., 54, 1869)
Purchase, S. *Hakluytis Posthumous, or Purchase his Pilgrim* (Glasgow, 1905–7), 2 vols.
Purser, W. *Compound Interest and Annuities* (1634)
The Pynchon Papers, ed. C. Bridenbaugh (Col. Soc. Mass., 1982)
R., M. *Memoir of the Life of Ambrose Barnes*, ed. W. H. D. Longstaffe (Surt. Soc., 50, 1866)
Raleigh, Sir W. *Works* (Oxford, 1829), 8 vols.
Ravenscroft, E. *The Citizen Turned Gentleman: A Comedy based on Molière* (1672)
Rawdon, Sir Marmaduke, *Memoirs 1582–1646*, ed. H. F. Killick, (Yorks. Arch. J., 25, 1919)
Rawdon, M. *The Life of Marmaduke Rawdon of York* , ed. R. Davies (Camd. Soc., 85, 1863)
Raymond, T. *Autobiography*, ed. G. Davies (Camd. Soc., 28, 1917)
Reasons Humbly Offered against Establishing by Act of Parliament the East India Trade (n.d.)
The Remonstrance of the Apprentices in and about London (1659)
Requests, Select Cases in the Court, ed. I. S. Leadam (Seld. Soc., 1898)
Reresby, Sir John, *Memoirs*, ed. A. Browning, 2nd edn (R. H. S., 1991)
Reynell, C. *The True English Interest* (1674)
Reynolds, E. *Works* (1826), 6 vols.
Rhodes, H. *The Memorandum Book, 1675–1700*, ed. C. Blagden (The Book Collector, 3, 1954)
Ricard, S. *Traité général du commerce*, 2nd edn (Amsterdam, 1705)
The Rich Papers: Letters from Bermuda, 1615–1646, ed. V. A. Ives (Toronto, 1984)
Richards, J. *Country Diary, 1698–1701* (Retrospective Review, NS, 1, 1853)
Richelieu, *Testament Politique*, ed. L. André (1947)
Ridley, T. *A View of the Civil and Ecclesiastical Laws* (1607)
Rigge, A. *Constancy in the Truth Commended*, ed. G. Whitehead (1710)
A Briefe and Serious Warning to Such as are Concerned in Commerce (1678)
Roberts, J. *The Trades Increase* (1615)
Roberts, J. ap., *The Younger Brother his Apologie* (Oxford, 1634; 2nd edn 1671)
Roberts, L. *Merchant's Map of Commerce* (1638)
Robinson, H. *England's Safety in Trades Increase* (1641), repr. in *Select Tracts*, ed. W. A. Shaw (1935)
Robinson, H. *Certain Proposals in Order to the People's Freedom* (1652)
Brief Considerations Concerning the Advancement of Trade (1649)
Robinson, M. *Autobiography*, ed. J. E. B. Major (Cambridge, 1856)
Robinson, T. *The Common Law of Kent* (1741)
Roe, Sir Thomas, *Journal of the Embassy to the Great Mogul* (repr. in Hakl. Soc., 2nd ser., 2, 1899)

Rogers, F. *Diary*, repr. in B. S. Ingram, *Three Sea Journals of Stuart Times* (1936)
Rogers, J. *A Sermon Preached before Trinity House* (1681)
Rogers, J. 'Inventory', *N. & Q. Som. & Dorset*, 28 (1966)
Rogers, R. *A Living Remembrance* (1601)
Roper, I. M., *The Monumental Effigies of Bristol and Gloucester* (Gloucester, 1930)
The Roxburghe Ballads, ed. W. Chappell and J. W. Ebsworth (Ballad Soc., Hertford, 1880, 1884)
Royal Commission of 1552 Report, ed. W. C. Richardson (Morgantown, 1974)
Ryder, D. *Diary*, ed. W. Matthews (1939)
Rye Shipping Records, ed. R. F. Dell (Suss. Rec. Soc., 64, 1965–6)
Saikaku, *The Japanese Family Storehouse*, trans. G. W. Sargent (Cambridge, 1959)
Life of an Amorous Woman, ed. I. Morris (1963)
Saint Paul the Tentmaker (1690)
Saint Paul's School Register, ed. Sir M. McDonnell (1977)
Salisbury. Poverty in early Stuart Salisbury, ed. P. Slack (Wilts. Rec. Soc., 31, 1975)
Salusbury Correspondence Calendar, ed. W. J. Smith (Cardiff, 1954)
Sanderson, J. *The Travels, 1565–1602, with his Autobiography and Selections from his Correspondence*, ed. Sir William Foster (Hakl. Soc., 2nd. ser., 67, 1931)
Sanderson, J. *An Iron Rod for the Naylors* (1655)
Sanford, P. *Letter Book, 1670–85*, ed. H. W. Preston (Providence, 1928)
Santer, D. *The Practise of Bankrupts of these Times* (1640)
Savary, J. *Le Parfait Negoçiant* (1675)
Scarborough. Records, 1600–60, ed. M. Y. Ashcroft (North Yorks. RO Pub. 47, 49, 1991)
Scarletti, J. *Stile of Exchanges* (1682)
The Scattergoods and the East India Company, ed. Sir R. C. Temple, L. M. Anstey and B. P. Scattergood (Harpenden, 1935)
Scott, J. *The Christian Life* (1681)
Scott, W. *An Essay on Drapery*, ed. S. L. Thrupp (Kress Lib. Pub., 9, 1953)
Scriveners Company Papers, 1357–1628, ed. F. W. Steer (Lond. Rec. Soc. Pub., 4, 1968)
Segar, Sir William, *Honor Military and Civil* (1602)
Selden, J. *Table Talk*, ed. Sir Frederick Pollock (1927)
Titles of Honour (1614)
Select Charters of Trading Companies, 1530–1707, ed. C. T. Carr (Seld. Soc., 28, 1913)
Select Tracts and Documents Illustrative of English Monetary History 1626–1730, ed. W. A. Shaw (1935)
Sevenoaks. Wills and Inventories in the Reign of Charles II, ed. H. C. F. Lansberry (Maidstone Arch. Soc., 1988)
Seventeenth-Century Economic Documents, ed. J. Thirsk and J. P. Cooper (Oxford, 1972)
Sexton, T. 'The correspondence of Thomas Sexton 1540–60', ed. W. Sharpe (unpub. M.A. thesis, London, 1953)
Shadwell, T. *Complete Works*, ed. M. Summers (1927), 5 vols.
Sheridan, T. *A Discourse of the Rise and Power of Parliaments* (1677)

Sherley, Sir Anthony, *The Three Brothers or the Travels and Adventures of Sir Anthony, Sir Robert and Sir Thomas* (repr. 1825)

The Shiffren Archives, ed. F. W. Steer (Lewes, 1959)

Shipwrights Company Records, 1428–1780, ed. C. H. Ridge (1939)

The Shirburn Ballads, 1585–1616, ed. A. Clark (Oxford, 1907)

Shrewsbury. Burgess Rolls, ed. H. E. Forrest (Shrewsbury, 1924)

'Shrewsbury drapers' apprentices', ed. M. Peele, *Trans. Shrop. Arch. Soc.*, 50 (1939)

Shropshire. Visitation of 1623, ed. G. Grazebrook and J. P. Rylands (Harl. Soc., 28–9, 1889)

Sidney Ironworks Accounts, 1541–73, ed. D. W. Crossley (Camd. Soc., 4th ser., 15, 1975)

Sitwell, G. *The Letterbook, 1662–66*, ed. P. Riden (Derby. Rec. Soc., 1985)

'Skinners Company apprentices', ed. G. E. Cokayne (Misc. Genealog. & Herald., 3rd ser., 1, 1896)

Skinners Company of London Records, ed. J. J. Lambert (1934)

Slingsby, Sir Henry, *Diary*, ed. D. Parsons (1836)

Smallwood, G. *A Sermon Preached at the Funeral of Sir Abraham Reynardiston* (1661)

Smith, A. *The Wealth of Nations*, ed. R. H. Campbell and A. S. Skinner (Oxford, 1976), 2 vols

The Theory of Moral Sentiments, ed. D. D. Raphael and A. L. MacFie (Oxford, 1976)

Smith, J. *The Berkeley Manuscripts: The Lives of the Berkeleys*, ed. Sir J. Maclean (Gloucester, 1883–5), 3 vols.

Smith, Sir Thomas, *De Republica Anglorum*, ed. M. Dewar (1982)

Smythe, J. *The Ledger, 1538–50*, ed. J. Vanes (Bristol Rec. Soc., 28, 1975)

Smythe Family of Ashton Court: Calendar of the Correspondence, ed. J. H. Bettey (Bristol Rec. Soc., 35, 1982)

Smythe, R. *The Obituary*, ed. Sir Henry Ellis (Camd. Soc., 44, 1849)

Smythies, W. *Advice to Apprentices* (1687)

Some Thoughts on the Interest of Money in General (*c.* 1728)

Somers Tracts, ed. W. Scott (1811)

Somerset. Sale of Wards, 1603–14, ed. M. J. Hawkins (Som. Rec. Soc., 67, 1965)

Somerset. Assize Orders, ed. J. S. Cockburn (Som. Rec. Soc., 71, 1971)

Somner, W. *A Treatise of Gavelkind* (1660)

South Sea Company, the Particulars and Inventories of the late Directors (1721)

Southampton. Assembly Book, 1609–10, ed. J. W. Horrocks (Southamp. Rec. Soc., OS, 20, 1920)

Southampton. Assembly Books, 1611–14, ed. J. W. Horrocks (Southamp. Rec. Soc., OS, 24, 1924)

Southampton. The Book of Examinations and Depositions, 1634–39, ed. R. C. Anderson (Southamp. Rec. Soc., OS, 34, 1934)

Southampton. The Third Book of Remembrance, 1573–89, ed. A. L. Merson (Southamp. Rec. Soc., NS, 10, 1965)

Southampton. Calendar of Apprentices, ed. A. J. Willis and A. L. Merson (Southamp. Rec. Soc., NS, 12, 1968)

Southampton. The Admiralty Court Book, 1566–85, ed. E. Welch (Southamp.

Rec. Soc., NS, 13, 1969)
Southampton. Probate Inventories, 1447–1575, ed. E. Roberts and K. Parker (Southamp. Rec. Soc., NS, 34–5, 1992)
Southampton. Port Books, 1509–10, ed. T. B. James (Southamp. Rec. Soc., NS, 32–3, 1990)
Spain and the Jacobean Catholics, ed. A. J. Loomis (Cath. Rec. Soc., 64, 1973; 68, 1978)
The Spanish Company, ed. P. Croft (London Rec. Soc., 9, 1973)
The Spectator, ed. D. F. Bond (Oxford, 1965)
Spelman, Sir John, *Reports*, ed. J. H. Baker (Seld. Soc., 93–4, 1977–8)
Spinoza, B. de, *The Political Works*, ed. A. G. Wernham (Oxford, 1958)
Sprat, T. *History of the Royal Society*, ed. J. I. Cope and J. W. Jones (1959), 2 vols.
Stafford, the Committee at 1643–5, ed. D. H. Pennington and I. A. Roots (Manchester, 1957)
Staffordshire. Heraldic Visitations of 1614, 1663, 1664, ed. H. S. Grazebrook (Coll. Hist. Staffs., 1884)
Staffordshire. Collections for a History, ed. R. M. Kidson (Staffs. Rec. Soc., 4th ser., 2, 1958)
Stanley, T. *Account Book and Letters*, ed. M. Dalison and W. A. Scott Robinson (Arch. Cant., 17, 1887)
Staple, *Ordinance Book of the Staple*, ed. E. E. Rich (Cambridge, 1937)
State Papers,
Letters and Papers Henry VIII
Calendar of State Papers Domestic
Calendar of Proceedings of the Committee for Compounding 1643–60
Acts of the Privy Council
Calendar of State Papers Venetian
Calendar of State Papers Colonial Series East India, China, Persia, America and West Indies
Stationers Company, 'Apprentices, 1605–40', ed. D. M. MacKenzie, *The Library*, 5th ser., 13 (1958) and *Bibliog. Soc. Univ. Virginia* (1961)
Stationers Company. Records of the Court: 1576–1602, ed. W. W. Greg and E. Boswell (Lond. Bibliog. Soc., 1930); *1602–40*, ed. W. A. Jackson (Lond. Bibliog. Soc., 1957)
Stationers Company. Loan Book, 1592–1692, ed. W. C. Ferguson (Lond. Bibliog. Soc., 1989)
Statutes of the Realm (1810–28)
Steele, R. *The Conscious Lovers* (1722)
Steele, R. *The Religious Tradesman* (1684, repr. 1807)
Stephens, E. *Relief of Apprentices Wronged by their Masters* (1687)
Stockport. Probate Records, 1578–1619, ed. C. B. Phillips and J. H. Smith (Lancs. & Ches. Hist. Soc. Rec. Ser., 124, 1985)
Stoddard, G. 'Account book extracts', printed in H. Hall, *Society in the Elizabethan Age*, 3rd edn (1889)
The Stonor Letters and Papers, 1290–1483, ed. C. L. Kingsford (Camd. Soc., 3rd ser. 29, 1919)
Stoughton, J. *The Arraignment of Covetousness* (1640)
Stout, W. *The Autobiography, 1665–1752*, ed. J. D. Marshall (Cheth. Soc., 3rd

ser., 14, 1967)
Stow, J. *A Survey of London* (1598), ed. J. Strype (1720), 2 vols.
A Survey of London (1598), ed. C. L. Kingsford (1908, repr. Oxford, 1971)
Stowes Memoranda, ed. J. Gairdner (Camd. Soc., NS, 28, 1880)
Strong, W. *Trust and the Account of a Steward* (1647)
Suffolk Tears or Elegies for that Renowned Knight Sir Nathaniel Barnardiston (1653)
Surrey. Apprenticeships, 1711–31, ed. Sir Hilary Jenkinson (Surrey Rec. Soc., 30, 1928–9)
Surrey. Visitations of 1530, 1573, 1623, ed. W. B. Bannerman (Harl. Soc., 43, 1899)
Sussex. Apprentices, 1710–52, ed. R. Grice (Sussex Rec. Soc., 28, 1965)
Sussex. Lay Subsidy Rolls, 1524–5, ed. J. Cornwall (Sussex Rec. Soc., 56, 1956)
Swift, J. *The Prose Works*, ed. H. Davis (Oxford, 1939–74), 16 vols.
Swinburne, H. *A Brief Treatise of Testaments and Last Wills* (1590)
A Treatise of Spousals (1686)
Sydenham, H. *The Rich Man's Warning Peece A Sermon* (1630)
T., R. *The Art of Good Husbandry* (1675), in *Harl. Misc.*, vol. I
The Tatler, ed. G. S. Aitken (1899)
Tavernier, J. B. *The Six Voyages* (1678)
Taylor, J. *Holy Living and Dying* (1650)
The Whole Life of Henry Walker (1642), repr. in C. Hindley, *The Old Book Collector Misc.* (1871–3), vol. III
Works (Spencer Soc., 1870–8), 5 vols.
Taylor, R. *A Discourse of the Growth of England in Populousness and Trade since the Reformation* (1689)
Taylor, S. *History of Gavelkind* (1663)
Telford. Yeomen and Colliers, ed. B. Trinder and J. Cox (Chichester, 1980)
Temple, P. and Heritage, T. *The Account Book*, ed. N. W. Alcock (Brit. Acad. Rec. Soc. & Econ. Hist., NS, 4, 1982)
Temple, Sir William, *Observations on the United Provinces*, ed. G. N. Clark (Cambridge, 1923)
Tennison, E. *The Excellency and Usefulness of Public Spirit* (1711)
Teonge, H. *Diary*, ed. G. E. Manwaring (1927)
Testamenta Leodiensia, 1535–53, ed. G. Lumb (Thoresby Soc., 19, 27, 1913–30)
Thenard, J. F. *Mémoire ou livre de raison d'un bourgeois de Marseille* (1881)
Thomas, D. *A Historical Account of the Rise and Growth of the West India Colony* (1690), in *Harl. Misc.*, vol. II
Thomas, W. *Rayling Rebuked* (1656)
The Case of Richard Thompson and Company with Relation to their Creditors (1678)
Thoresby, R. *The Diary and Correspondence, 1677–1724*, ed. J. Hunter (1830), 2 vols.
Thoresby, R. *Ducatus Leodiensis*, ed. D. Whitaker, 2nd edn (Leeds, 1816)
Tilley, M. P. *A Dictionary of Proverbs in England in the Seventeenth Century* (Ann Arbor, 1950)
Tilliard, W. *Diary*, in *HMC 15th Report*, app. 10 (1899)
Tilney, E. *A Brief and Pleasant Discourse on Duties in Marriage* (1571)
The Trade of England Revived (1681), repr. in *Seventeenth-Century Economic*

Documents
Trades Increase (1615), repr. in *Harl. Misc.*, vol. IV
The Tradesman's Calling (1684)
The Tragic History of the Sea, ed. C. R. Boxer (Hakl. Soc., 2nd ser., 112, 1959)
Traill Family Letters, ed. H. Marwick (Kirkwall, 1936)
Calendar of Treasury Books, 1660–1718, ed. W. A. Shaw *et al.* (1904–23), 32 vols.
Calendar of Treasury Papers, 1557–1696, ed. J. Redington (1868–89), 6 vols.
The Trelawney Papers, 1631–1770, ed. J. P. Baxter (Coll. Mass. Hist. Soc., 2nd ser., 3, 1884)
Trenchfield, C. *A Cap of Grey Hairs for a Green Head* (1671)
Trimmer, Some Account of the Life and Writings, vol. II: *1685–1756*, 2nd edn (1816)
Trinity House of Deptford. Transactions, 1609–35, ed. G. G. Harris (Lond. Rec. Soc., 19, 1983)
Trinity House of Hull. The First Order Book, 1632–65, ed. F. W. Brooks (Yorks. Arch. Rec. Ser., 1942)
Trosse, G. *The Life* (1715), ed. A. W. Brink (Montreal, 1974)
Tryon, T. *Some Memoirs of the Life* (1705), repr. in H. Irving, *The Providence of Wit in the English Letter Writers* (Durham, North Carolina, 1950)
A New Method of Educating Children (1695)
Tse, M. *The Social Teachings*, ed. L. Tomkinson (Trans. Asiatic Soc. Japan, 2nd ser., 4, 1927)
A Tudor Book of Rates, ed. T. S. Willan (Manchester, 1962)
Tudor Economic Documents, ed. R. H. Tawney and E. Power (1929)
Tully I. *Narrative of the Siege of Carlisle in 1644–5*, printed in *Carlisle Municipal Records*
Turner, T. *The Diary, 1754–65*, ed. D. Vaisey (Oxford, 1984)
Vallans, W. *The Honorable Prentice* (1615)
Valor Beneficiorum (1695)
Valor Ecclesiasticus, ed. J. Caley and J. Hunter (1810–34)
Vanity Mischief to make Earthly Treasures our Chief Treasure (1655)
Vaughan, Sir John *The Reports and Arguments* (1677)
Vaughan, W. *The Golden Grove* (1600)
Vega, J. de la, *Confusion de confusiones* (Kress Lib. Pub., 13, 1957)
Venn, H. *Memoirs of the late Sir John Barnard* (priv. pr., 1885)
Verax, P. *The Knavish Merchant* (1661)
Verney Family Memoirs, ed. F. P. Verney (1892–99), 4 vols.
Verney Letters of the Eighteenth Century, ed. M. M. Verney (1930)
Vernon, J. *The Compleat Comptinghouse* (1678)
Vertue, G. *Notebooks* (Walpole Soc., 26, 1938)
Vickaris, A. *An Essay for Regulating of the Coyn*, 2nd edn (1696)
A Vindication of the Degree of Gentry (1663)
Violet, T. *Humble Proposal against Transporting of Gold and Silver* (1661)
Virginia Company Records: The Court Book, 1607–26, ed. S. M. Kingsbury (Washington, 1906–35)
Vox Juvenalis, or the Loyal Apprentice's Vindication (1681)
Vulgar Errors Censured (1659)
Wales. Calendar of Letters relating to North Wales, ed. B. E. Howells (Univ. of

Wales Hist. & Law Ser., 23, Cardiff, 1967)
Walker, Sir Edward, *Historical Discourses upon Several Occasions* (1705)
Wallis, J. *Account of his Own Life*, transcr. T. Hearne (Oxford, 1725)
Walthew, R. R. *Will, Inventory and Account Book*, ed. J. J. Bagley (Lancs. & Ches. Rec. Soc., 109, 1965)
Warburton, J. *London and Middlesex Illustrated* (1749)
Ward, E. *The Reformer or the Vices of the Age Expos'd*, (5th edn, *c.* 1700)
The London Spy, ed. K. Fenwick (Folio Soc., 1955)
The Comforts of Matrimony (1780)
The Wealthy Shopkeeper (1700)
The Modern World Disrob'd (1708)
Ward, J. *The Lives of the Professors of Gresham College* (1740)
W(arre), J. *The Merchant's Handmaide* (1622)
Warwick. The Great Fire of 1694, ed. M. Farr (Dugd. Soc. Pub., 36, 1992)
Warwickshire. Apprentices and their Masters, 1711–60, ed. K. J. Smith (Dugd. Soc. Pub., 29, 1975)
Warwickshire. Ecclesiastical Terriers, ed. D. M. Barratt (Dugd. Soc. Pub., 22, 1955; 27, 1971)
Warwickshire. Quarter Sessions, 1625–96, ed. L. E. Stephen, H. C. Johnson and N. J. Williams (Warwick, 1935–64), 9 vols.
Wase, C. *Considerations Concerning the Free Schools as Settled in England* (1678)
Waterhouse, E. *The Gentleman's Monitor* (1665)
Watts, T. *An Essay on the Proper Method of Forming the Man of Business* (1716), ed. A. H. Cole (Kress Lib. Pub., 1940)
The Way to be Rich according to the Practice of the Great Audley who Began with Two Hundred Pounds (1662)
Weavers Company of London. Extracts from the Court Books, 1610–1730, ed. W. C. Walter (Hug. Soc. Lond. Pub., 33, 1931)
Webb, B., 'Narrative of my employments', in *Seventeenth-Century Economic Documents*
Weever, J. *Ancient Funerall Monuments* (1631)
Welbeck. A Catalogue of the Letters and other Historical Documents Exhibited in the Library, ed. S. A. Strong (1903)
The Welsh Port Books, 1550–1603, ed. E. A. Lewis (Cymm. Soc. Rec. Ser., 12, 1927)
Welsh Tokens of the Seventeenth Century, ed. G. C. Boon (Cardiff, 1973)
Welwood, W. *An Abridgment of all Sea Laws* (1613)
Wentworth, T. *The Office and Duty of Executors*, 4th edn (1656)
The Wentworth Papers 1597–1628, ed. J. P. Cooper (Camd. Soc., 4th ser., 12, 1973)
West, T. *The Accounts of Thomas West of Wallingford*, ed. M. Prior (Oxoniensa, 46, 1981)
Westcote, T. *A View of Devonshire in 1630*, ed. G. Oliver and P. Jones (Exeter, 1845)
Western Circuit Assize Orders, 1629–48, ed. J. S Cockburn (Camd. Soc., 4th ser., 17, 1976)
Westminster, Dean and Chapter. Allegations for Marriage Licences issued 1558 to 1699 and for those issued by the Vicar General of the Archbishop of Canterbury

(Harl. Soc., 23, 1888)
Whately, W. *A Bride's Bush* (1617)
A Caveat for the Covetous (1609)
Wheeler, J. *A Treatise of Commerce*, ed. G. B. Hotchkiss (New York, 1931)
Wheler, Sir George, *A Journey into Greece* (1682)
Whetstone, G. *A Mirour for Magistrates* (1584)
Whiston, J. *The Causes of our Present Calamities* (1695)
Whitelocke, B. *The Diary 1605–75*, ed. R. Spalding (Brit. Acad. Rec. Soc. & Econ. Hist., NS, 13, 1989)
Whitelocke, J. *Liber Famelicus*, ed. J. Bruce (Camd. Soc., 1st ser., 70, 1858)
Whitson, J. *A Pious Meditation*, ed. G. S. Catcott and J. Eden (Bristol, 1829)
The Whore's Rhetoric (1683)
Wilkinson, H. *The Debt Book* (1625)
Wilkinson, R. *The Merchant Royall*, ed. S. Pargellis (Herrin, Illinois, 1945)
Willoughby Letters, ed. M. A. Welsh (Thor. Soc. Rec. Ser., 24, 1967)
Willsford, T. *The Scales of Commerce* (1660)
Wilson, C. *Self Denial* (1625)
Wilson, T. *A Discourse upon Usury*, ed. R. H. Tawney (1925)
Wilson, T. *The State of England, 1600*, ed. F. J. Fisher (Camd. Misc., 16, 1936)
Wiltshire. Apprentices and their Masters 1710–60, ed. C. Dale (Wilts. Rec. Soc., 17, 1961)
Wiltshire. Textile Trades Documents, ed. J. de L. Mann (Wilts. Arch. & Nat. Hist. Soc., 19, 1963)
Wiltshire. Two Sixteenth-Century Taxation Lists, ed. G. D. Ramsay (Wilts. Arch. & Nat. Hist. Soc., 10, 1954)
Wiltshire. Visitation Pedigrees, 1623, ed. G. D. Squibb (Harl. Soc., 105–6, 1953–4)
Winchester. Consistory Court Depositions, 1561–1602, ed. A. J. Willis (Winchester, 1960)
Wingate, E. *Arithmetique Made Easie* (1650)
Winthrop Papers, ed. S. Mitchell and A. B. Forbes (Mass. Hist. Soc., 1929–47), 5 vols.
Witt, R. *Arithmeticall Questions* (1613)
Wood, A. *Atheniae Oxonienses* (repr. 1967)
Woodcock. T. *Extracts from the Papers*, ed. G. C. M. Smith (Camd. Misc., 3rd ser., 13 (11), 1907)
Woodward, J. *An Account of the Societies for Reformation of Manners* (1699)
Woolley, H. *The Gentlewoman's Companion* (1682)
Worcester. The Chamber Book, 1602–50, ed. S. Bond (Worcs. Hist. Soc., NS, 8, 1975)
Worcester. Probate Inventories of Tradesmen, 1545–1614, ed. A. D. Dyer (Worcs. Hist. Soc. Misc., 5, 1967)
Worde, W. de, 'Inventory', ed. H. R. Plomer, *The Library*, 3rd ser., 6 (1915)
Wray, W. 'The account book of William Wray', ed. J. T. Fowle, *The Antiquary*, 32 (1896)
Wren, M. *Considerations on Mr Harrington's Oceana* (1657)
Wright, T. *The Passion of the Minde* (1601)
Wycherley, N. *The Plays*, ed. A. Friedman (Oxford, 1979)

Wynn of Gwydir Papers: Calendar, 1515–1690 (Aberystwyth, 1926)
Wynn, W. *Life of Leoline Jenkins* (1724), 2 vols.
Yarmouth A Calendar of the Freemen of Great Yarmouth, 1429–1800 (Norf. & Norw. Arch. Soc., 1910)
Yarmouth. Assembly Minutes, 1538–45, and Norwich, Accounts for Custom on Strangers Goods 1582–1610, ed. P. Rutledge (Norf. Rec. Soc., 39, 1970)
Yarranton, A. *England's Improvement by Sea and Land* (1677)
Yonge, J. *Plymouth Memoirs*, ed. J. J. Beckenlegge (1951)
The Journal, ed. F. N. L. Poynter (1963)
Yonge, W. *Diary*, ed. G. Roberts (Camd. Soc., 41, 1848)
York. Register of the Freemen, vol. II, *1559–1759* (Surt. Soc., 102, 1899)
York. Mercers and Merchant Adventurers, ed. M. Sellers (Surt. Soc., 129, 1917)
Yorkshire. Abstracts of Wills, ed. J. W. Clay (Yorks. Arch. & Topog. Assoc. Rec. Ser., 9, 1890)
Yorkshire. Abstracts of Abbotside Wills, 1552–1688, ed. H. Twaite (Yorks. Arch. Soc. Rec. Ser., 130, 1967)
Yorkshire. Diaries and Autobiographies in the Seventeenth Century, ed. C. Jackson (Surt. Soc., 65, 75, 77, 1877–86)
Yorkshire. Probate Inventories, 1541–1649, ed. P. C. D. Brears (Yorks. Arch. Soc. Rec. Ser., 134, 1972)
Yorkshire. West Riding Quarter Sessions Records, ed. J. Lister (Yorks. Arch. Soc. Rec. Ser, 54, 1915)
Young, E. *The Poetical Works* (Westport, 1970)
Younge, R. *The Prevention of Poverty* (1660)

SECONDARY SOURCES

Abbott, J. A. R. 1956 'Robert Abbott', *Guild. Misc.*, 7
Abbott, W. C. 1941 *Essays in Modern English History in Honor of W. C. Abbott* (Cambridge, Massachusetts)
Abel, W., Borchardt, K., Kellenbenz, H. and Zorn, W. (eds.) 1966 *Wirtschaft, Geschichte und Wirtschaftsgeschichte* (Stuttgart)
Abernathy, W. J., Clark, K. B. and Kantrow, A. M. (eds.) 1983 *Industrial Renaissance* (New York)
Abrahams, D. 1937 'Jewish brokers of London', *T. J. H. S. E.*, Misc. part 3
Abramovitz, M. (ed.) 1955 *Capital Formation and Economic Growth* (Princeton)
1989 *Thinking About Growth* (Cambridge)
Abrams, P. 1972 'The sense of the past and the origins of sociology', *P. & P.*, 54
1982 *Historical Sociology* (Ithaca)
Abrams, P. and Wrigley, E. A. (eds.) 1978 *Towns in Societies* (Cambridge)
Acres, W. M. 1934–7 'Huguenot directors of the Bank of England', *Proc. Hug. Soc. Lond.*, 15
Acton, H. B. 1971 *The Morals of Markets*
Adair, J. E. 1969 *Roundhead General: A Military Biography of Sir William Waller*
Adam, A. 1951 *History of the Company of Blacksmiths*
Adams, H. H. 1943 *English Domestic or Homilectic Tragedy, 1575–1642* (New York)

Adams, P. 1983 *Travel Literature and the Evolution of the Novel* (Lexington)
Adams, S. and Rodriguez-Salgado, M. J. (eds.) 1991 *England, Spain and the Grand Armada, 1558–1604* (Edinburgh)
Adamson, I. R. 1980 'The administration of Gresham College', *Hist. Educ.*, 9
Addy, J. 1989 *Sin and Society in the Seventeenth Century* (New York)
1992 *Death, Money and the Vultures: Inheritance and Avarice, 1660–1750*
Adey, K. R. 1974 'Seventeenth-century Stafford', *Mid. Hist.*, 2
Agarwala, A. N. and Singh, S. P. 1958 *Economics of Underdevelopment* (Oxford)
Agnew, J.-C. 1986 *Worlds Apart: The Market and the Theatre, 1550–1750* (Cambridge)
Aiken, W. A. and Henning, B. D. (eds.) 1960 *Conflicts in Stuart England: Essays in Honor of W. A. Notestein*
Airs, M. 1975 *The Making of the English Country House, 1500–1640* (Chichester)
Aitken, H. G. J. 1963–4 'The fiction of entrepreneurial research', *Expl. Ent. H.*, 2nd ser., 1
1965 (ed.) *Explorations in Enterprise* (Cambridge, Massachusetts)
Albertson, M. 1932 'London merchants and their landed property during the reigns of the Yorkists' (unpub. Ph.D. thesis, Bryn Mawr)
Albright, E. M. 1927 *Dramatic Publication in England, 1580–1640* (New York)
Album Helen Cam 1960–1 (International Commission for the History of Representative and Parliamentary Institutions, 23–4, Louvain)
Alchan, A. A. 1950 'Uncertainty, evolution and economic theory', *J. Pol. Econ.*, 58
Aldous, V. E. 1989 'The archives of the Freedom of London, 1681–1915', *Genealog. Mag.*, 23
Alexander, C. G. 1923–7 'The ancient custom of the Province of York', *Thoresby Soc. Misc. Pub.*, 28
Alexander, J. 1989 'The economic structure of the City of London at the end of the seventeenth century', *Urban Hist. Year.*
Alford, B. W. E. 1977 'Entrepreneurship, business performance and industrial development', *Bus. Hist.*, 19
Alford, B. W. E. and Barker, T. C. 1968 *History of the Carpenters Company*
Ali, M. A. 1966 *The Mughal Nobility under Auranzeb, 1658–1707*
Alldridge, N. J. 1983a 'House and household in Restoration Chester', *Urban Hist. Year.*
1983b (ed.) *The Hearth Tax: Problems and Possibilities*
Allen, B. H. 1951 'The administrative and social structure of the Norwich merchant class, 1485–1660' (unpub. Ph.D. thesis, Harvard)
Allen, B. S. 1937 *Tides in English Taste* (Cambridge, Massachusetts)
Allen, D. F. 1972 'The role of the London trained bands in the Exclusion Crisis', *E. H. R.*, 87
1976 'Political clubs in Restoration London', *H. J.*, 19
Allen, H. C. and Thompson, R. (eds.) 1976 *Contrast and Connection: Bicentennial Essays in Anglo-American History*
Allen, P. 1946 'Medical education in seventeenth-century England', *J. Hist. Med. & All. Sc.*, 1
Allen, R. C. 1988a 'The price of freehold land and the interest rate', *Ec. H. R.*, 2nd ser., 41

1988b 'The growth of labour productivity in early modern England', *Expl. Ec. H.*, 25
Allen, T. 1828 *The History and Antiquities of London*
Allen, W. R. 1970 'Modern defenders of mercantilist theory', *Hist. Pol. Econ.*, 2
Allison, K. J. 1960–1 'The Norfolk worsted industry in the sixteenth and seventeenth centuries', *Yorks. Bull. Ec. Soc. Res.*, 12–13
Allison, M. 1987 'Puritanism in mid-seventeenth-century Sussex: Samuel Jeake the elder of Rye', *Suss. Arch. Coll.*, 125
Alsop, J. P. 1979a 'The financial enterprises of Jerome Shelton', *Guild. Stud. Lond. Hist.*, 4
1979b 'Gerard Winstanley's later life', *P. & P.*, 82
1989 'Ethics in the marketplace', *J. B. S.*, 28
Alston, L. J. and Schapiro, M. O. 1984 'Inheritance laws across colonies', *J. Ec. H.*, 44
Alter, G. 1983 'Plague and the Amsterdam Annuitants', *Pop. Stud.*, 37
Altman, I. and Horn, J. (eds.) 1991 *To Make America: European Emigration in the Early Modern Period* (Berkeley)
Ambrose, G. P. 1931–2 'English traders at Aleppo, 1658–1756', *Ec. H. R.*, 3
1933 'The Levant Company mainly from 1640 to 1753' (unpub. B.Litt. thesis, Oxford)
Amelang, J. S. 1982 'Purchase of nobility', *J. Eur. Ec. Hist.*, 11
1986 *Honoured Citizens of Barcelona, 1490–1719* (Princeton)
Amterkauflichkeit 1980 *Aspekte sozialen mobilität in Europäischen Vergleich* (Berlin)
Amussen, S. D. 1988 *An Ordered Society: Gender and Class in Early Modern England* (Oxford)
Anderson, A. B. 1977 'A study of the sociology of religious persecution', *J. Rel. Hist.*, 9
1979 'The social origins of the early Quakers', *Quaker History*, 68
Anderson, B. L. 1968 'Provincial aspects of the Financial Revolution', *Bus. Hist.*, 10
1970 'Money and the structure of credit in the eighteenth century', *Bus. Hist.*, 12
Anderson, B. L. and Latham, A. J. H. (eds.) 1986 *The Market in History*
Anderson, C. A. and Bowman, M. J. (eds.) 1965 *Education and Economic Development* (Chicago)
Anderson, G. M. and Tollison, R. D. 1982 'Adam Smith's analysis of joint-stock companies', *J. Pol. Econ.*, 90
1983 'Apologiae for chartered monopolies in foreign trade, 1600–1800', *Hist. Pol. Econ.*, 15
Anderson, G. M., McCormick, R. E. M. and Tollison, R. D. 1983 'The economic organization of the East India Company', *J. Ec. Behav. & Org.*, 4
Anderson, H. H. 1934 'Daniel Defoe', *Univ. Chicago Theses Abstracts*, 9
1942 'The paradox of trade and morality in Defoe', *Mod. Phil.*, 39
Anderson, J. L. 1991 *Explaining Economic Growth*
Anderson, M. 1980 *Approaches to the History of the Western Family, 1500–1914*
Anderson, R. T. 1971 *Traditional Europe: A Study in Anthropology and History*
Anderson, R. V. 1952 *Catalogue of Ship Models* (National Maritime Museum,

Greenwich)
Anderson, S. 1969 'Sir Paul Rycaut', *Proc. Hug. Soc.*, 21
1989 *An English Consul in Turkey: Paul Rycaut at Smyrna, 1667–78* (Oxford)
Anderson, T. L. 1975 'Wealth estimates for New England colonies, 1650–1709', *Expl. Ec. Hist.*, 12
1979 'Economic growth in colonial New England', *J. Ec. H.*, 39
Andreski, S. 1987 'The syphilitic shock', *Encounter*, 58
Andrews, C. M. 1908 *British Committees, Commissions and Councils of Trade and Plantations 1622–72* (Baltimore)
1934–8 *The Colonial Period of American History* (New Haven), 4 vols.
Andrews, D. T. 1979–81 'Aldermen and big bourgeoisie of London reconsidered', *Soc. Hist.*, 4 & 6
1988 'The secularisation of suicide in England, 1600–1800', *P. & P.*, 119
1989 *Philanthropy and Policies* (Oxford)
Andrews, J. H. 1955 'English merchant shipping in 1701', *Mar. Mirr.*, 41
1956–7 'Two problems in the interpretation of the Port Books', *Ec. H. R.*, 2nd ser., 9
Andrews, K. R. (ed.) 1959 *English Privateering Voyages to the West Indies, 1585–95* (Hakl. Soc., 2nd ser., 111)
1964 *Elizabethan Privateering during the Spanish War, 1585–1603* (Cambridge)
1967 *Drake's Voyages* (New York)
1972 'Sir Robert Cecil and Mediterranean plunder', *E. H. R.*, 77
1974a 'English voyages to the Caribbean 1596–1604', *Wm & Mary Q.*, 3rd ser., 31
1974b 'Caribbean rivals and the peace of 1604', *History*, 69
1978 *The Spanish Caribbean, 1530–1630* (New Haven)
1984 *Trade Plunder and Settlement* (Cambridge)
1991 *Ships, Money and Politics* (Cambridge)
Andrews, K. R., Canny, N. P. and Hair, P. E. H. (eds.) 1979 *The Westward Enterprise: English Activities in Ireland, the Atlantic and America, 1480–1656* (Detroit)
Anglin, J. P. 1980 'The expansion of literacy', *Guild. Stud. Lond. Hist.*, 4
1985 *The Third University* (Norwood)
Anspach, R. 1972 'The implication of the theory of Moral Sentiments', *Hist. Pol. Econ.*, 4
Anstey, L. M. 1905 'William Jearsen', *Indian Antiquary*, 34
1931 'The library of a London merchant', *N. & Q.*, 160
Anstey, R. and Hair, P. E. H. (eds.) 1976 *Liverpool: The African Slave Trade and Abolition* (Hist. Soc. Lancs. & Ches. Occ. Ser., 2)
Antler, S. D. 1972 'Quantitative analysis of the Long Parliament', *P. & P.*, 56
Applebee, J. H. 1979 'Dr Arthur Dee, merchant and litigant', *S. E. E. R.*, 57
Appleby, A. B. 1973 'Disease or famine', *Ec. H. R.*, 2nd ser., 26
1975a 'Agrarian capitalism, or seigneurial reaction', *A. H. R.*, 80
1975b 'Nutrition and disease: the case of London 1550–1750', *J. I. H.*, 6
1978 *Famine in Tudor and Stuart England* (Stanford)
1979 'Grain prices and subsistence crises, 1590–1746', *J. Ec. H.*, 39
1988 'The disappearance of the plague', *Ec. H. R.*, 2nd ser., 33
Appleby, J. O. 1978 *Economic Thought and Ideology in Seventeenth-Century*

England (Princeton)
Appleton, W. W. 1956 *Beaumont and Fletcher*
Arasaratnam, S. 1966 'Indian merchants and their trading methods', *Ind. Ec. & Soc. Hist. Rev.*. 3
1986 *Merchant Companies and Commerce on the Coromandel Coast, 1650–1740* (Oxford)
Archdeacon, T. J. 1976 *New York City, 1664–1710* (Ithaca)
Archer, I. W. 1988 'The London lobbies in the late seventeenth century', *H. J.*, 31
1991a *The Pursuit of Stability: Social Relations in Elizabethan London*
1991b *The History of the Haberdashers Company* (Chichester)
Architects and Craftsmen in History 1956 (Tübingen)
Ariazza, A. 1980 'Mousnier and Barber', *P. & P.*, 89
Aries, P. 1967 *Centuries of Childhood: A Social History of Family Life*, trans. R. Baldick (New York)
Arkel, T. 1987 'The incidence of poverty in England', *Soc. Hist.*, 12
Arkin, M. 1955 'A neglected forerunner of Adam Smith', *South African J. Econ.*, 23
Armour, D. A. 1980 *The Merchants of Albany, New York, 1686–1766* (New York)
Armstrong, J. A. 1973 *The European Administrative Elite* (Princeton)
Arnett, M. 1937 'Chamberlayne', *B. I. H. R.*, 15
Arnold, A. P. 1970 'Apprentices of Great Britain, 1710–73', *T. J. H. S. E.*, 22, Misc. 7
Arrow, K. J. 1974 *Essays on the Theory of Risk Bearing* (Amsterdam)
Arup, E. 1907 *Studier i Engelsk og Tyck Handels Historie* (Copenhagen)
Ascoli, G. 1930 *La Grande Bretagne devant l'opinion française au XVIIe siècle*, 2 vols.
Ashcraft, R. 1972 'Marx and Weber on liberalism as a bourgeois ideology', *Comp. Stud. Soc. Hist.*, 14
1986 *Revolutionary Politics and John Locke's Two Treatises on Government* (Princeton)
Ashley, M. P. 1962 *Financial and Commercial Policy under the Cromwellian Protectorate*, 2nd edn
Ashman, P. M. 1988 'Heraldry and the law of arms in England', *J. Legal Hist.*, 9
Ashton, J. 1937 *Social Life in the Reign of Queen Anne*
1969 *The History of Gambling in England* (Montclair)
Ashton, R. 1955–6 'Revenue farming under the early Stuarts', *Ec. H. R.* 2nd ser., 8
1957 'The Disbursing Official under the Early Stuarts', *B. I. H. R.*, 30
1957–8 'Deficit finance in the reign of James I', *Ec. H. R.*, 2nd ser., 10
1960a *The Crown and the Money Market*
1960b 'Usury and high finance', *Ren. & Mod. Stud.*, 4
1964–5 'Puritanism and progress', *Ec. H. R.*, 2nd ser., 17
1967, 1969a 'Parliament and free trade', *P. & P.*, 38, 43
1969b 'Aristocracy in transition', *Ec. H. R.*, 2nd ser., 22
1969c 'Cavaliers and capitalists', *Ren. & Mod. Stud.*, 5
1978 'Stow's London', *Trans. Lond. & Midd. A. S.*, 29
1979 *The City and the Court 1603–43* (Cambridge)
1983 'Popular entertainment and social control', *Lond. J.*, 9

1989 *The English Civil War*, 2nd edn
Ashton, T. S. 1958 'Business history', *Bus. Hist.*, 1
1964 *An Economic History of England in the Eighteenth Century*
Ashtor, E. 1975 'Profits from trade in the Levant', *Bull. Soc. Orient. Afr. Stud.*, 38
1983 *Levant Trade in the Later Middle Ages* (Princeton)
Ashworth, G. J. 1969 'Some uses of apprenticeship records', *Loc. Hist.*, 8
Aspetti e causa della decadenza economica venezia nel secolo XVII 1961 (Civilita Veneziana Studi, 9)
Aston, M. 1984 *Lollards and Reformers*
Aston, T. (ed.) 1965 *Crisis in Europe, 1560–1660* (New York)
Aström, S.-E. 1963 *From Cloth to Iron: The Anglo-Baltic Trade in the Late Seventeenth Century*, trans. D. Coleman and M. Webster (Helsingfors)
1968 'The reliability of the port books', *Scand. Ec. H. R.*, 16
Atherton, L. E. 1939 *The Pioneer Merchant in Mid-America* (Univ. Missouri Stud., 14)
Atiyah, P. S. 1971 *An Introduction to the Law of Contract*, 2nd edn Oxford
1979 *The Rise and Fall of Freedom of Contract* (Oxford)
Atkinson, D. H. 1885–7 *Ralph Thoresby the Topographer* (Leeds), 2 vols.
Atkinson, J. W. 1957 'Motivational determinants of risk-taking behaviour', *Psych. Rev.*, 64
(ed.) 1958 *Motives in Fantasy Action and Society* (Princeton)
Atkinson, T. 1963 *Elizabethan Winchester*
Attman, A. 1981 *The Bullion Flow between Europe and the East, 1000–1750* (Acta Regiae Societatis Scientiarum et Litterarum Gothoburgensis, 20)
1986 *American Bullion and the European Woollen Trade, 1600–1800* (Acta Regiae Societatis Scientiarum et Litterarum Gothoburgensis, 26)
Aubrey, C. L., Land, A. C., Carr, L. G. and Papenfuse, E. C. (eds.) 1977 *Law, Society and Politics in Early Maryland* (Baltimore)
Aungier, C. J. B. 1924 'Gerard Aungier and the East India Company', *N. & Q.*, 146
Austen, B. 1978 *English Provincial Posts, 1633–1840: A Study Based on Kentish Examples*
Austern, L. 1989 'Female musicians and sexual enchantment', *Ren. Q.*, 42
Auwers, L. 1978 'Fathers, sons and wealth in colonial Windsor', *J. Fam. Hist.*, 3
Aveling, J. C. H. 1966 *Northern Catholics: The Catholic Recusants of the North Riding of Yorkshire 1558–1790* (New York)
1967 'Yorkshire recusants, 1558–1791', *Studies in Church History*, 4
1970 *Catholic Recusancy in the City of York, 1558–1791* (Cath. Rec. Soc. Monog. Ser., 2)
1976 *The Catholic Recusants in England from Reformation to Emancipation*
Avery, E. L. 1966 'The Restoration audience', *Phil. Quart.*, 45
Axtell, J. L. 1970 'Education and status in Stuart England', *Hist. Educ. Q.*, 10
Ayal, E. B. (ed.) 1973 *Micro Aspects of Development* (New York)
Aydelotte, F. 1913 *Elizabethan Rogues and Vagabonds* (Oxford)
Aydelotte, W. O., Bogue, A. G. and Fogel, R. W. (eds.) 1972 *The Dimensions of Quantitative Research in History* (Princeton)
Ayers, R. W. 1967 'Robinson Crusoe', *P. M. L. A.*, 77
Aylmer, G. E. 1957 'Attempts at administrative reform, 1625–40', *E. H. R.*, 72

1957–8 'The last years of purveyance, 1610–1660', *Ec. H. R.*, 2nd ser., 10
1959 'Office holding as a factor in English history', *History*, 44
1965 'Place bills and the separation of powers', *T. R. H. S.*, 5th ser., 15
1970 'Gentlemen Levellers', *P. & P.*, 49
1973a *The State's Servants: The Civil Service of the English Republic, 1649–60*
(ed.) 1973b *Interregnum: The Quest for Settlement, 1646–1660*
1974 *The King's Servants*, 2nd edn
(ed.) 1975 *The Levellers and the English Revolution*
1980 'The meaning and definition of Property', *P. & P.*, 86
1990 'Peculiarities of the English state', *J. Hist. Sociol.*, 3
Aymard, M. (ed.) 1982 *Dutch Capitalism and World Capitalism* (Cambridge)
Babb, L. 1959 *Sanity in Bedlam* (East Lansing)
Babel, A. 1963, *Mélanges d'histoire économique et sociale en homage* (Geneva)
Backscheider, P. R. 1986 *Daniel Defoe* (Lexington)
Badiane, E. 1968 *Roman Imperialism in the Late Republic* (Ithaca)
Bagley, J. J. 1958 'Matthew Markland', *Trans. Hist. Soc. Lancs. & Ches.*, 18
Bahlman, D. W. R. 1968 *The Moral Revolution of 1688* (New Haven)
Bailyn, B. 1953 'Communications and trade', *J. Ec. H.*, 13
1959 *Massachusetts Shipping, 1697–1714* (Cambridge, Massachusetts)
1964 *The New England Merchants in the Seventeenth Century*, 2nd edn (New York)
1982 'The challenge of modern historiography', *A. H. R.*, 87
1986 *Voyagers to the West* (New York)
Bailyn, B. and Morgan, P. D. (eds.) 1991 *Strangers within the Realm* (Chapel Hill)
Bainton, R. H. 1936 'Changing ideas and ideals in the seventeenth century', *J. M. H.*, 8
Baker, A. R. H., 1964 'Open fields and partible inheritance', *Ec. H. R.*, 2nd ser., 17
Baker, C. H. C. and M. I. 1949 *James Brydges, First Duke of Chandos* (Oxford)
Baker, J. H. 1977 'Male and married spinsters', *Amer. J. Legal Hist.*, 21
(ed.) 1978 *Legal Records and the Historian* (R. H. S.)
1979 'The law merchant and the common law', *Camb. Law J.*, 38
1986 *The Legal Profession and the Common Law*
1990 *An Introduction to English Legal History*, 3rd edn
Baker, J. H. and Milsom, S. F. C. (eds.) 1986 *Sources of English Legal History*
Bal, K. 1924 *Commercial Relations between India and England, 1601–1757*
Balazse, E. 1960 'Birth of capitalism in China', *J. Ec. & Soc. Hist. Orient*, 3
Baldwin, F. E. 1926 *Sumptuary Legislation and Personal Regulation in England* (Baltimore)
Baldwin, T. W. 1943 *William Shakespeare's Petty Schools* (Urbana)
Ball, J. N. 1977 *Merchants and Merchandise: The Expansion of Trade in Europe, 1500–1630* (New York)
Ball, R. M. 1990 'Tobias Eden', *J. Legal Hist.*, 11
Ballagh, J. C. 1895 *White Servitude in Virginia* (Baltimore)
Banac, I. and Bushkovitch, P. (eds.) 1983 *The Nobility in Russia and Eastern Europe* (New Haven)
Bank of England Catalogue of Engravings, Drawings and Paintings 1928
Bankes, J. H. M. 1943 'James Bankes', *Trans. Lancs. & Ches. Hist. Soc.*, 94
Banks, C. E. 1961 *The Planters of the Commonwealth, 1620–40* (Baltimore)

Barber, B. 1957 *Social Stratification: A Comparative Analysis of Structure and Process* (New York)
Barber, C. L. 1957 *The Idea of Honour* (Göteborg)
Barbieri, G. 1940 *Ideali economici degli italiani* (Milan)
Barbour, H. 1964 *The Quakers in Puritan England*
Barbour, V. 1928 'The consular service in the reign of Charles II', *A. H. R.*, 33
1929 'Marine risks and insurance', *J. Ec. & Bus. Hist.*, 1
1950 *Capitalism in Amsterdam in the Seventeenth Century* (Baltimore)
Barbu, Z. 1960 *Problems of Historical Psychology* (New York)
Bard, N. P. 1977 'The ship money case', *B. I. H. R.*, 50
Barder, R. C. R. 1983 *English Country Grandfather Clocks* (Newton Abbot)
Barish, J. 1981 *The Anti-theatrical Prejudice* (Berkeley)
Barker, A. 1942 *Milton and the Puritan Dilemma* (Toronto)
Barker, R. H. 1958 *Thomas Middleton*
Barker, T. C. 1957 *The Girdlers Company*
Barker, T. C., Campbell, R. H. and Mathias, P. G. 1960 (eds.) *Business History* (Hist. Assoc.)
Barker, T. M. 1982 *Army, Aristocracy, Monarchy* (Boulder)
Barley, M. W. 1955 'Farmhouses and cottages, 1550–1725', *Ec. H. R.*, 2nd ser., 7
Barley, M. W. and L. B. 1959 'Lincolnshire shopkeepers in the seventeenth and eighteenth centuries', *The Local Historian*, 2
Barlow, F. 1980 'The King's Evil', *E. H. R.*, 95
Barnard, E. A. B. 1944 *A Seventeenth-century Country Gentleman* (Cambridge)
Barnard, F. P. 1916 *The Casting Counter and the Counting Board* (Oxford)
Barnard, T. C. 1973 'Planters and policies in Cromwellian Ireland', *P. & P.*, 61
Barnes, H. E. 1948 *Historical Sociology: Its Origins and Development* (New York)
Barnes, T. G. 1961 *Somerset, 1625–1640*
1970 'The prerogative and environmental control', *California Law Review*, 58
Barnet, M. C. 1968 'The barber surgeons of York', *Med. Hist.*, 12
Barnett, R. C. 1969 *Place, Profit and Power* (Chapel Hill)
Baron, S. H. 1980 *Muscovite Russia*
Barratt, D. M. 1953 'The Bankes papers', *Bod. Lib. Rec.*, 4
Barreto, H. 1989 *The Entrepreneur in Micro-economic Theory*
Barrett, J. M. 1968 'Bunyan and the autobiographer's artistic purpose', *Criterion*, 10
Barrie-Curien, V. 1977 'La prohibition du commerce avec la France', *Revue du Nord*, 59
1988 'The English clergy, 1560–1620', *Hist. Eur. Ideas*, 9
Barron, C. 1990 'London and Parliament in the Lancastrian period', *Parl. Hist.*, 9
Barron, O. 1906 *Northamptonshire Families*
Barth, F. 1962 *The Role of the Entrepreneur in Social Change* (Bergen)
Barton, A. 1978 'London comedy and the ethos of the city', *London J.*, 4
Barty-King, H. A. 1991 *A Country Builder*
Bary, W. T. de (ed.) 1970 *Self and Society in Ming Thought* (New York)
Basset, D. K. 1981 Review of Chaudhuri, *Bull. Sch. Orient. & Afr. Stud.*, 44
Basu, K., Jones, E. L. and Schlicht, E. 1987 'The growth and decay of custom', *Expl. Ec. H.*, 24
Bate, F. 1908 *The Declaration of Indulgence, 1672*

Battick, J. F. A. 1972 'A new interpretation of Cromwell's Western Design', *J. Barb. Mus. & Nat. Hist. Soc.*, 34

Baugh, D. A. 1965 *British Naval Administration in the Age of Walpole* (Princeton)

(ed.) 1975 *Aristocracy, Government and Society in Eighteenth-century England* (New York)

Bauman, W. R. 1990 *The Merchant Adventurers and the Continental Cloth Trade* (New York)

Baumann, G. (ed.) 1986 *The Written Word: Illiteracy in Transition* (Oxford)

Baxter, S. B. 1957 *The Development of the Treasury, 1660–1702*

(ed.) 1983 *England's Rise to Greatness, 1660–1783* (Berkeley)

Baxter, W. T. (ed.) 1950 *Studies in Accounting*

Baxter, W. T. and Davidson, S. (eds.) 1962 *Studies in Accounting Theory*

Beamish, D. 1976 *Mansions and Merchants of Poole* (Poole)

Bean, J. M. W. 1968 *The Decline of English Feudalism, 1215–1540* (Manchester)

Beattie, H. 1979 *Land and Lineage in China* (Cambridge)

Beattie, J. M. 1967 *The English Court in the Reign of George I* (Cambridge)

1981 *Crime and the Courts in England, 1660–1800* (Princeton)

Beaty, N. L. 1970 *The Craft of Dying* (New Haven)

Beaven, A. 1908–13 *The Aldermen of the City of London*, 2 vols.

Bebb, E. D. 1935 *Non Conformity and Social and Economic Life, 1660–1800*

Bec, C. 1967a 'Mentalités et vocabulaires des marchands florentins', *Annales*, 22

1967b *Les marchands écrivains: affaires et humanisme à Florence, 1375–1434*

Becker, G. S. 1975 *Human Capital*, 2nd edn (New York)

Becker, M. 1967 *Florence in Transition* (Baltimore)

Beckett, J. V. 1977 'English landownership in the late seventeenth and eighteenth centuries', *Ec.H.R.*, 2nd ser., 30

1981 *Coal and Tobacco: The Lowthers and the Economic Development of West Cumberland, 1660–1760* (Cambridge)

1980 'The disinheritance of Sir Christopher Lowther', *Trans. Cumb. & West. Antiq. & Arch. Soc.*, 80

1984 'The pattern of landownership, 1660–1880', *Ec. H. R.*, 37

1985 'Land tax or excise', *E. H. R.*, 100

1986 *The Aristocracy in England, 1660–1914* (Oxford)

Beckett, J. V. and Turner, M. 1990 'Taxation and economic growth in eighteenth-century England', *Ec. H. R.*, 2nd ser., 43

Beckles, H. M. 1981 'Sugar and white servitude', *J. Barb. Mus. & Hist. Soc.*, 36

Beddard, R. 1967 'The Commission for Ecclesiastical Promotions, 1681–4', *H. J.*, 10

1988 *A Kingdom Without a King* (Oxford)

Bedell, J. 1990 'The gentry of Huntingdonshire', *Loc. Pop. Stud.*, 44

Beecheno, F. R. 1919 'The Sucklings' house at Norwich', *Norf. Arch.*, 20

Behrens, B. 1941 'The Whig theory of the Constitution in the reign of Charles II', *C. H. J.*, 7

Beier, A. L. 1974, 1976 'Vagrants and the social order', *P. & P.*, 64, 71

1975 'Industrial growth and social mobility', *Brit. J. Sociol.*, 26

1978–9 'Social problems in Elizabethan London', *J. I. H.*, 9

1983 *The Problem of the Poor in Tudor and Stuart England*

1985 *Masterless Men: The Vagrancy Problem in England, 1560–1640*

Beier, A. L. and Finlay, R. (eds.) 1986 *London, 1500–1700: The Making of the Metropolis*

Beier, A. L., Cannadine, D. and Rosenheim, J. M. (eds.) 1989 *The First Modern Society: Essays in Honour of Lawrence Stone* (Cambridge)

Beier, L. M. 1987 *Sufferers and Healers: The Experience of Illness*

Beik, W. 1985 *State Power and Provincial Aristocracy in Languedoc* (Cambridge)

Belasco, P. S. 1925 'John Bellers', *Economica*, 5

Belcher, V. 1986 'A London attorney of the eighteenth century', *Lond. J.*, 12

Beljame, A. 1948 *Men of Letters and the English Public, 1660–1744*, trans. E. V. Lorimer, ed. B. Dobrée

Bell, G. M. 1980 'Sir Thomas Chaloner's diplomatic expenses in Spain', *B. I. H. R.*, 53

1981 'Elizabethan diplomatic compensation', *J. B. S.*, 20

1990 *A Handlist of British Diplomatic Representatives, 1509–1688* (R. H. S.)

Bell, H. E. 1953 *An Introduction to the History of the Court of Wards and Liveries* (Cambridge)

Bell, H. E. and Ollard, R. L. (eds.) 1963 *Historical Essays, 1600–1750, Presented to David Ogg*

Bell, M. 1989 'Hannah Allen', *Pub. Hist.*, 26

Bell, P. F. 1967 'The direction of entrepreneurial exploration', *Expl. Ent. H.*, 2nd ser., 5

Bell, W. G. 1910 'An old City merchant's house', *The Pall Mall Mag.* (March)

1920 *Unknown London*

1923 *The Great Fire of London in 1666*, 2nd edn

1924 *The Great Plague of London in 1665*

Bellah, R. N. 1957 *Tokugawa Religion* (Glencoe, Illinois)

Bellamy, J. G. 1989 *Bastard Feudalism and the Law*

Bellasis, A. F. 1931 'Old tombs in the cemeteries of Surat', *J. Bombay Branch Roy. Asiatic Soc.*, NS, 6

Bellot, H. L. 1910 'The exclusion of the attorneys from the Inns', *Law Q. R.*, 26

Beloff, M. 1939 'Humphrey Shalcross and the Civil Wars', *E. H. R.*, 54

1942 'A London apprentice's notebook, 1703–5', *History*, 27

Ben Amos, I. K. 1988 'Service and the coming of age of young men', *Cont. & Ch.*, 3

1991a 'Failure to become freemen', *Soc. Hist.*, 16

1991b 'Women apprentices in early modern Bristol', *Cont. & Ch.*, 6

Benbow, R. M. 1980 'The Court of Aldermen and the Assizes', *Guild. Stud. Lond. Hist.*, 4

Bendix, R. 1959 *Max Weber: An Intellectual Portrait*

Bendix, R. and Lipset, S. M. (eds.) 1966 *Class Status and Power*, 2nd edn (New York)

Benedict, P. (ed.) 1989 *Cities and Social Change in Early Modern France*

Beneviste, E. 1951 'Sur l'histoire du mot negotium', *Annali della Scuola Normale Superiore di Pisa*, 2nd ser., 20

Bennell, J. E. G. 1980 'A businessman in Elizabethan Southwark', *Trans. Lond. & Midd. A. S.*, 31

Bennett, A. 1985 'The Mangies of Hull', *Yorks. Arch. J.*, 57

1988 'The Goldsmiths in Church Lane, Hull, 1527–1784', *Yorks. Arch. J.*, 60

Bennett, E. *The Company of Carmen of London*, rev. edn
The Company of Wheelwrights, 1670–1970 (Newton Abbot)
Bennett, H. S. 1965 *English Books and Readers, 1558–1603* (Cambridge)
1970 *English Books and Readers, 1603–40* (Cambridge)
Bennett, J. A. 1962 *Sir Thomas Browne* (Cambridge)
1986 'The mechanics philosophy', *Hist. Sc.*, 24
Bennett, J. H. 1964 'Cary Helyar', *Wm & Mary Q.*, 3rd ser., 21
1966 'William Whaley', *Agric. Hist. Rev.*, 40
Bennetton, N. A. 1938 *Social Significance of the Duel* (Baltimore)
Bentley, G. E. 1941–68 *The Jacobean and Caroline Stage* (Oxford), 7 vols.
(ed.) 1968 *The Seventeenth-century Stage* (Chicago)
1971 *The Profession of Dramatist in Shakespeare's Time* (Princeton)
1984 *The Profession of Player, 1590–1642* (Princeton)
Berckman, E. 1979 *Victims of Piracy, 1575–1678*
Berengo, M. 1956 *La societa veneta alla fine del settecento* (Florence)
1965 *Nobili e mercanti nella lucca del cinquecento* (Turin)
Beresford, M. W. 1958 'The common informer', *Ec. H. R.*, 2nd ser., 10
1979 'The Decree Rolls of Chancery', *Ec. H. R.*, 2nd ser., 32
1985–6 'East End, West End: the face of Leeds, 1684–1842', *Proc. Thores. Soc.*, 60–1
Berg, M. (ed.) 1991 *Markets and Manufactures in Early Industrial Europe*
Bergasse, L. and Rambert, G. 1954 *Histoire du commerce de Marseille*
Berger, R. M. 1980 'The development of retail trade in provincial England', *J. Ec. H.*, 40
1981–2 'Thomas Atheral, a Coventry apothecary', *Warws. Hist.*, 5
1982 'Mercantile careers in the early seventeenth century', *Warws. Hist.*, 5
1993 *The Most Necessary Luxuries: The Mercers Company of Coventry, 1550–1680* (University Park, Pennsylvania)
Bergeron, D. M. 1967 'Anthony Munday's pageant', *H. L. Q.*, 30
1971 *English Civic Pageantry, 1558–1642*
Berkner, L. K. 1975 'The use and misuse of census data', *J. I. H.*, 5
Berkowitz, D. S. 1988 *John Selden's Formative Years* (Cranbury, New Jersey)
Berlatsky, J. 1978 'Marriage and family in a Tudor elite', *J. Fam. Hist.*, 3
Berlin, I. 1961 'The concept of scientific history', *Hist. & Theory*, 1
1964 'Hobbes, Locke and MacPherson', *Pol. Q.*, 35
Berlin, M. 1986 'Civic ceremony in early modern London', *Urban Hist. Year.*
Bernard, G. W. 1982 'The fortunes of the Greys', *H. J.*, 25
Berner, S. 1972 'The Florentine patriciate, 1530–1609', *Stud. Med. Ren. Hist.*, 9
Bernong, R. H. 1991 'Changing attitudes towards material wealth in Sydney's Arcadia', *Sixt. Cent. J.*, 22
Berry, B. M. 1974 'The first English pediatricians', *J. H. I.*, 35
Berry, C. J. 1989 'Luxury and the politics of need and desire', *Hist. Pol. Thought*, 10
Berry, G. 1988 *Seventeenth-Century England, Traders and their Tokens*
Berry, L. E. and Crummey, R. O. (eds.) 1968 *Rude and Barbarous Kingdom* (Madison)
Bertaux, D. (ed.) 1982 *Biography and Society: The Life History Approach in the Social Sciences*

Besnard, P. 1970 *Protestantisme et capitalisme*
Best, E. E. 1982 *Religion and Society in Transition* (New York)
Best, G. F. A. 1964 *Temporal Pillars* (Cambridge)
1982 *Honour Among Men and Nations* (Toronto)
Betteridge, A. 1976 'Early Baptists of Leicestershire and Rutland', *Bapt. Q.*, 26
Bettey, J. H. 1975 'Portland: partible inheritance on the island', *N. & Q. for Som. & Dorset*, 30
1978 *The Rise of a Gentry Family: The Smyths of Ashton Court, 1500–1642* (Bristol Hist. Assoc., 43)
1982 'Land tenure and manorial custom in Dorset, 1570–1670', *South. Hist.*, 4
Beutin, L. K. J. 1963 *Gesammelte Schriften zur Wirtschafts- und Sozial-geschichte*, ed. H. Kellenbenz (Cologne)
Bézard, Y. 1931 'Deux hommes d'affaires sous Louis XIV', *Rev. Quest. Hist.*, 3rd ser., 19
1932 *Fonctionnaires maritimes et coloniaux sous Louis XIV. Les Bégon*
Bhattacharyya, 1954 *The East India Compnay and the Economy of Bengal*
Bieber, R. P. 1919 *The Lords of Trade and Plantations, 1675–96* (Allentown)
Bielenstein, H. 1980 *Bureaucracy of Han Times* (Cambridge)
Biemer, L. 1982 'Business letters of Alice Livingstone, 1680–1726', *New York Hist.*, 63
Bill, P. A. 1965–6 'The medieval parochial clergy of Warwickshire', *Univ. B'ham H. J.*, 10
Billet, J. 1976 'The just economy', *Rev. Soc. Econ.*, 34
Bindoff, S. T. 1944 'Clement Armstrong', *Ec. H. R.*, 4
1982 *The House of Commons, 1509–58*
Bindoff, S. T., Hurstfield, J. and Williams, C. H. 1961 (eds.) *Elizabethan Government and Society: Essays Presented to Sir John Neale*
Bingham, H. 1938 *Elihu Yale* (Worcester, Massachusetts)
Binks, M. and Vale, P. 1990 *Entrepreneurship and Economic Change*
Biraben, J. N. 1975–6 *Les hommes et la peste*
Bird, J., Chapman, H. and Clark, J. (eds.) 1978 *Collecteana Londiniensia: Studies in London Archaeology and History presented to Ralph Merrifield* (Lond. & Midd. Arch. Soc,)
Birken, W. F. 1987 'The social problem of the English physician', *Med. Hist.*, 31
Birks, M. 1960 *Gentlemen of the Law*
Bittle, W. G. and Lane, R. T. 1976 'Inflation and philanthropy in England', *Ec. H. R.*, 2nd ser., 29
Blackmore, H. L. 1986 *A Dictionary of London Gunmakers, 1350–1850* (Oxford)
Blackwood, B. G. 1970 'The marriages of the Lancashire gentry', *Genealog. Mag.*, 16
1976 'The economic state of the Lancashire gentry', *North. Hist.*, 12
1977 'The Catholic and Protestant gentry of Lancashire', *Trans. Hist. Soc. Lancs. & Ches.*, 126
1978 *The Lancashire Gentry and the Great Rebellion, 1640–60* (Cheth. Soc., 3rd ser., 25)
Blagden, C. 1957 'The English joint-stock', *The Library*, 5th ser., 12
1958a 'The Stationers Company in the Civil Wars', *The Library*, 5th ser., 13
1958b 'The distribution of almanacks', *Stud. in Bibliog.*, 11

1960 *The Stationers Company: A History, 1403–1959*
Blair, W. J. 1975 'Cradlers, 33/5 street, Leatherhead', *Proc. Leatherhead & District Loc. Hist. Soc.*, 3
Blanchard, I. S. W. 1973 'Commercial crisis and change', *North. Hist.*, 8
1978 'Labour productivity and work psychology in the English mining industry, 1400–1600', *Ec. H. R.*, 2nd ser., 31
Blanchard, R. 1901 *Gentilhommes verriers italiens* (Vannes)
Bland, D. S. 1978 'Learning exercises and readers at the Inns of Chancery', *Law Q. R.*, 95
Blau, P. M. 1963 *The Dynamics of Bureaucracy* (Chicago)
Bledstein, B. J. 1976 *The Culture of Professionalism* (New York)
Blench, J. W. 1964 *Preaching in England in the Late Fifteenth and Sixteenth Centuries* (Oxford)
Bliss, R. M. 1990 *Revolution and Empire* (Manchester)
Bloch, M. 1961 *Feudal Society*, trans. L. A. Manyon
Bloom, E. A. and L. D. 1971 *Joseph Addison: Sociable Animal in the Marketplace* (Providence)
Bloom, J. H. and James R. R. 1935 *Medical Practitioners in the Diocese of London, 1529–1725* (Cambridge)
Bloom, R. 1980 'Reflections on uncertainty in Accounting', *Acc. Hist. Journ.*, 4
Blouin, F. X. 1979 'A new perspective on the appraisal of business records', *Amer. Archiv.*, 42
Blusse, L. and Gaastra, F. (eds.) 1981 *Companies and Trade* (Leiden)
Boas, F. S. 1950 *Thomas Heywood*
Boas, G. 1966 *The Cult of Childhood*
Boddington, R. S. 1880 *Pedigree of the Gould Family*
Bog, I. (ed.) 1971 *Der Aussenhandel Ostmitteleuropas* (Cologne)
Bogucka, M. 1971 'Merchants' profits in Gdansk foreign trade', *Acta Polon. Hist.*, 23
Boisrouvray, A. du, 1936 'Un exemple de l'esprit commerciale des français sous l'ancien régime', *Rev. Quest. Hist.*, 64
Boiteux, L. A. 1968 *La Fortune de mer: le besoin de securité et les débuts de l'assurance maritime*
Bolton, J. L. 1990 'Dick Whittington', *Lond. J.*, 15
Bond, S. and Evans, N. 1976 'The process of granting charters to English boroughs', *E. H. R.*, 91
Bonfield, L. 1979–80 'Marriage settlements and the rise of the great estate', *Ec. H. R.*, 2nd ser., 32–3
1983a *Marriage Settlements, 1601–1740* (Cambridge)
1983b 'Marriage, property and the affective family', *Law & Hist. Rev.*, 1
1988 'Strict settlement and the family', *Ec. H. R.*, 2nd ser., 41
Bonfield, L., Smith, R. M. and Wrightson, K. (eds.) 1986 *The World We Have Gained* (Oxford)
Bonnell, V. E. 1980 'The uses of theory', *Comp. Stud. Soc. Hist.*, 22
Bonney, R. J. 1979 'The failure of the French Revenue farms', *Ec. H. R.*, 2nd ser., 32
1980 'English and French civil wars', *History*, 65
1981 *The King's Debts: Finance and Politics in France, 1589–1661* (Oxford)

Bordonove, G. 1963 *Les Templiers*
Borger, R. and Cioffi, F. 1970 (eds.) *Explanations in the Behavioural Sciences* (Cambridge)
Borsay, P. 1977 'The English urban renaissance', *Soc. Hist.*, 5
1982 'Culture status and the English urban landscape', *History*, 67
1989 *The English Urban Renaissance, 1660–1770* (Oxford)
Bosher, R. S. 1951 *The Making of the Restoration Settlement*
Bossy, J. 1962 'The character of Elizabethan Catholicism', *P. & P.*, 21
1982 'Social England', *Encounter*, 59
(ed.) 1983 *Disputes and Settlements* (Cambridge)
Bottigheimer, K. S. 1971 *English Money and Irish Land* (Oxford)
Bottrall, M. 1958 *Every Man a Phoenix*
Bouch, C. M. L. and Jones, G. P. 1961 *A Short Economic and Social History of the Lake Counties, 1500–1830* (Manchester)
Boulton, J. P. 1984 'The limits of formal religion', *Lond. J.*, 10
1986 'Residential mobility in seventeenth-century Southwark', *Urban Hist. Year.*
1987 *Neighbourhood and Society: A London Suburb of the Seventeenth Century* (Cambridge)
1989 'Economy of time', *Loc. Pop. Stud.*, 43
1990 'London widowhood revisited', *Cont. & Ch.*, 5
1991 'Itching after private marrying', *Lond. J.*, 16
Boulton, W. B. 1901 *The Amusements of Old London*
Bourdieu, P. 1972 'Les stratégies matrimoniales', *Annales*, 27
Bourn, A. M. 1975 'Business history and management education', *Bus. Hist.*, 17
Bourne, H. R. F. 1866 *English Merchant Memoirs*
1876 *The Life of John Locke*, 2 vols.
1890 *Famous London Merchants*
Bousma, W. J. 1975 'Lawyers', *A. H. R.*, 78
Boutruche, R. 1963 *La Crise d'une société*
Bowden, P. J. 1971 *The Wool Trade in Tudor and Stuart England*, 2nd edn
Bower, J. 1991 'Probate accounts', *Arch. Cant.*, 109
Bowley, M. 1973 *Studies in the History of Economic Theory before 1870*
Bowman, M. J. 1951 'The consumer in the history of economic doctrine', *Amer. Ec. Rev. Papers & Proc.*, 41
Bowyer, T. H. 'The published forms of Josiah Child's *A New Discourse*', *The Library*, 5th ser., 11
Boxer, C. R. 1957 *Dutch in Brazil* (Oxford)
1965 *The Dutch Seaborne Empire, 1600–1800*
1969 *The Portuguese Seaborne Empire, 1415–1825*
Boyajian, J. C. 1993 *Trade in Asia under the Hapsburgs, 1580–1640* (Baltimore)
Boyce, B. 1947 *The Theophrastan Character in England to 1642* (Cambridge, Massachusetts)
1953 *The Polemic Character, 1640–1660* (Lincoln)
Bradbrook, M. C. 1961 'The status seekers', *H. L. Q.*, 24–5
1962 *The Rise of the Common Player*
Braddick, M. J. 1991 'State formation and social change', *Soc. Hist.*, 16
Braddock, R. C. 1975 'The rewards of office-holding', *J. B. S.*, 14

Bradfer-Lawrence, H. L. 1929 'The merchants of Lynn', in *A Supplement to Blomefield's Norfolk*, ed. C. Ingelby
Bradley, R. D. 1982 'The failure of accommodation', *J. Rel. Hist.*, 12
Brady, C. and Gillespie, R. A. 1986 (eds.) *Natives and Newcomers* (Dublin)
Braibanti, R. J. (ed.) 1961 *Tradition, Values and Socio-economic Development* (Durham, North Carolina)
Brailsford, D. 1969 *Sport and Society: Elizabeth to Anne*
Brailsford, M. R. 1915 *Quaker Women, 1650–90*
Braithwaite, W. C. 1919 *The Second Period of Quakerism*
Brandon, W. 1845 *The Customary Law of the City of London*
Brashear, J. H. and L. 1969 'Economic theory reflected in George Lillo', *Appalachian State Univ. Fac. Pub.*, 66
Bratchell, M. E. 1978 'Italian merchant organization in early Tudor London', *J. Eur. Ec. Hist.*, 7
1980 'Regulation and group consciousness', *J. Eur. Ec. Hist.*, 9
1983 'Germain Cioll', *B. I. H. R.*, 56
1984 'Alien merchant colonies', *J. Med. & Ren. Stud.*, 14
Braubach, M. 1964 *Spiegel der Geschichte: Festgabe für Max Braubach*, ed. K. Repgen and S. Skalweit (Munich)
Braudel, F. 1966 *La Méditerranée et le monde méditerranéen*, 2nd edn, 2 vols.
1973 *Histoire économique du monde méditerranéen, 1450–1650: mélanges en l'honneur de Fernard Braudel* (Toulouse)
1979 *Civilisation, matérielle économie et capitalisme, XVe–XVIIIe siècles*, 3 vols.
1985 *La dynamique du capitalisme*
Brauer, G. C. 1959 *The Education of a Gentleman, 1660–1775* (New York)
Bray, A. 1988 *Homosexuality in Renaissance England*, 2nd edn
Bredvold, L. I. 1962 *The Natural History of Sensibility* (Detroit)
Breen, T. H. 1966 'The non-existent controversy', *Ch. Hist.*, 35
1975 'Persistent localism', *Wm & Mary Q.*, 3rd ser., 22
(ed.) 1976 *Shaping Southern Society: The Colonial Experience* (New York)
1980 *Puritans and Adventurers: Change and Persistence in Early America* (Oxford)
1985 *Tobacco Culture* (Princeton)
1986 'An empire of goods', *J. B. S.*, 25
Breen, T. H. and Foster, S. 1973 'Moving to the New World', *Wm & Mary Q.*, 3rd. ser., 30
Brenner, R. 1993 *Merchants and Revolution* (Princeton)
Brennig, J. J. 1977 'Chief merchants and the European enclave of Coromandel', *Mod. Asian Stud.*, 2
Brent, C. E. 1975 'Urban employment and population in Sussex, 1550–1660', *Suss. Arch. Coll.*, 113
(ed.) 1981 *The Maritime Economy of Eastern Sussex, 1550–1700* (Lewes)
Breslow, B. 1977 'Richard de Refhan', *J. Med. Hist.*, 3
Brett-James, A. 1962 'The Levant Company factory in Aleppo', *Hist. Tod.*, 12
Brett-James, N. G., 1929–33a 'The London bills of mortality', *Trans. Lond. & Midd. A. S.*, NS, 6
1929–33b 'A speculative London builder', *Trans. Lond. & Midd. A. S.*, NS, 6
1935 *The Growth of Stuart London*

Breward, I. 1972 'The abolition of Puritanism', *J. Rel. Hist.*, 7
Brewer, J. 1989 *Sinews of Power: War, Money and the English State, 1688–1783*
Bridbury, A. R. 1972 *Historians and the Open Society*
Bridenbaugh, C. 1938 *Cities in the Wilderness, 1625–1742* (New York)
1968 *Vexed and Troubled Englishmen, 1590–1642* (Oxford)
Bridenbaugh, C and R. 1972 *No Peace Beyond the Line* (New York)
Brief, R. P. 1991 'Accounting errors as a factor in business history', *Accounting, Business and Financial History*, 1
Brigden, S. 1982 'Youth and the English Reformation', *P. & P.*, 95
1984 'Religion and social obligation in early sixteenth-century London', *P. & P.*, 103
1989 *London and the Reformation* (Oxford)
Bright, J. B. 1858 *The Brights of Suffolk* (Boston)
Brimble, M. C. 1971 'Monumental inscriptions', *Genealog. Mag.*, 16
Bristol Worthies, reprinted from the *Bristol Times and Mirror* (1886)
Britnell, R. H. 1986 *Growth and Decline in Colchester, 1300–1525* (Cambridge)
1991 'The towns of England and North Italy', *Ec. H. R.*, 2nd ser., 44
Broad, J. 1979 'Gentry finances and the Civil War', *Ec. H. R.*, 2nd ser., 32
1983 'Sir John Verney', *B. I. H. R.*, 56
Brochett, A. 1962 *Non-conformity in Exeter, 1650–1845* (Manchester)
Brodsky, G. W. S. 1988 *Gentlemen of the Blade* (New York)
Brodsky, V. 1980 *Single Women in the London Marriage Market: Age, Status and Mobility, 1598–1619* (Newberry Lib.)
Bromley, J. and Child, H. 1960 *Armorial Bearings of the Guilds of London*
Bromley, J. S. (ed.) 1970 *The New Cambridge Modern History* (Cambridge), vol. VI, *The Rise of Great Britain and Russia*
1987 *Corsairs and Navies, 1660–1760*
Bromley, J. S. and Kossmann, E. H. (eds.) 1960 *Britain and the Netherlands*, vol. I
1964 *Britain and the Netherlands*, vol. II (Groningen)
1968 *Britain and the Netherlands*, vol. III, *In Europe and Asia*
1971 *Britain and the Netherlands*, vol. IV, *Metropolis, Dominion and Province* (The Hague)
Bronfenbrenner, M. 1971 'The structure of revolutions and economic thought', *Hist. Pol. Econ.*, 3
Brook, F. W. 1945–7 'The social position of the parson', *J. Brit. Arch. Assoc.*, 3rd ser., 10
Brook, T. 1981 'The merchant network in sixteenth-century China', *J. Ec. & Soc. Hist. Orient*, 24
Brook, V. J. K. 1962 *Archbishop Parker* (Oxford)
Brooke, C. N. L. 1964 *Europe in the Central Middle Ages, 962–1154*
Brooke, I. 1958 *Dress and Undress*
1972 *A History of English Costume*, 4th edn
Brooks, C. 1974 'Public finance and political stability', *H. J.*, 17
1982 'Projectors, political arithmetic and the Act of 1695', *E. H. R.*, 97
Brooks, C. W. 1984 'The country persuasion in the 1690s', *Parliament Estates and Representation*, 4
1986 *Pettyfoggers and Vipers of the Commonwealth* (Cambridge)
Brown, E. A. R. 1974 'The tyranny of a construct', *A. H. R.*, 79

Brown, F. E. 1986 'Continuity and change in the urban house', *Comp. Stud. Soc. Hist.*, 28
Brown, K. C. (ed.) 1965 *Hobbes Studies* (Oxford)
Brown, N. O. 1959 *Life Against Death* (New York)
Brown, P. 1967 'The later Roman Empire' *Ec. H. R.* , 2nd ser., 20
Brown, R. (ed.) 1968 *A History of Accounting and Accountants* (repr. New York)
Brown, R. H. 1973 'Social mobility and economic growth ', *Brit. J. Sociol.*, 34
Brown, R. H. and Lyman, S. M. (eds.) 1978 *Structure, Consciousness and History* (Cambridge)
Browne, R. B. and Fishwick, M. F. (eds.) 1972 *Heroes of Popular Culture* (Bowling Green, Kentucky)
Browning, A. 1944–51 *Thomas Osborne, Earl of Danby* (Glasgow)
Bruce, A. P. C. 1980 *The Purchasing System in the British Army, 1660–1871* (R. H. S.)
Bruce, J. 1818 *Annals of the East India Company*, 3 vols.
Bruchey, S. 1960 'Inadequacy of profit maximization', *Bus. Hist. Rev.*, 34
1965 *The Roots of American Economic Growth, 1607–1861* (New York)
Brulez, W. 1959 *De firma della faille en de internationale handel* (Brussels)
1981 'Shipping profits in the early modern period', *Acta Hist. Neer.*, 14
Brunschvig, R. 1962 'Métiers vils en Islam', *Studia Islamica*, 16
Brunskill, R. W. *Illustrated Handbook of Vernacular Architecture*, 3rd edn
Brunt, P. A. 1967 'Les equités romains', *Annales*, 22
1971 *Social Conflicts in the Roman Republic*
1983 Review of D'Arms in *J. Ec. H.*, 43
Brunton, D. and Pennington, D. H. 1954 *Members of the Long Parliament*
Bruster, D. 1990 'Cuckoldry and capital', *Stud. Eng. Lit.*, 30
1992 *Drama and the Market in the Age of Shakespeare* (Cambridge)
Bruyn, J. R. 1978 'Dutch privateers during the Second and Third Anglo-Dutch Wars', *Acta Hist. Neer.*, 11
Bryant, M. E. 1986 *The London Experience of Secondary Education*
Bryson, W. H. 1975 *The Equity Side of Exchequer* (Cambridge)
Buck, A. 1976 'Dress as a social record', *Folk Life*, 14
Buck, P. 1977 'Seventeenth-century political arithmetic', *Isis*, 68
Buck, R. C. and Cohen, R. S. (eds.) 1971 *Boston Studies in the Philosophy of Science*, vol. VII (Dordrecht)
Buckatsch, E. J. 1948–9 'Occupations in the parish registers of Sheffield', *Ec. H. R.*, 2nd ser., 1
1949–50 'Places of origin of immigrants into Sheffield', *Ec. H. R.*, 2nd ser., 2
Buisseret, D. 1986 *Tools and Maps* (Newberry Library, Chicago)
Buisseret, D. and Pawson, M. 1975 *Port Royal, Jamaica* (Oxford)
Bumstead, K. M. 1985 'Wills and inventories', *Yorks. Arch. J.*, 57
Bunn, J. H. 1980 'Aesthetic of British mercantilism', *New Lit. Hist.*, 11
Bunskill, R. W. 1987 *Illustrated Handbook of Vernacular Architecture*, 3rd edn
Burford, E. J. 1976 *Bawds and Lodging*
Burgess, C. F. 1967 'Further notes for a biography of George Lillo', *Phil. Quart.*, 46
Burgon, J. W. 1839 *The Life and Times of Sir Thomas Gresham*, 2 vols.
Burke, P. 1974 *Venice and Amsterdam*

1975 'Some reflections on the pre-industrial city', *Urban Hist. Year.*
1977 'Popular culture in seventeenth-century London', *Lond. J.*, 3
1978 'Reflections on the historical revolution in France', *Review*, 1
(ed.) 1979 *The New Cambridge Modern History* (Cambridge), vol. XIII
1980a *Sociology and History*
1980b 'The history of *mentalités* in Great Britain', *Tijd. v. Gesch.*, 93
(ed.) 1985 *Early Central Europe in Transition* (Cambridge)
1986a 'Strengths and weaknesses of the history of mentalités', *Hist. Eur. Ideas*, 7
1986b *The Italian Renaissance*, 2nd edn (Cambridge)
(ed.) 1991 *New Perspectives on Historical Writing* (Cambridge)
Burley, G. H. C. 1961 'Andrew Yarranton', *Trans. Worcs. A. S.*, 38
Burley, K. H. 1957 'The economic development of Essex in the late seventeenth and early eighteenth centuries' (unpub. Ph.D. thesis, London)
1958–9 'An Essex clothier', *Ec. H. R.*, 2nd ser., 11
Burn, J. F. 1938 *A Dictionary of Low Dutch Elements in the English Vocabulary* (Oxford)
Burn, R. 1842 *Ecclesiastical Law*, 9th edn corr. by R. Phillimore
Burnby, J. G. L. 1983 *A Study of the British Apothecaries 1660–1760* (Med. Hist. Supp., 3)
Burns, T. and Saul, S. B. (eds.) 1967 *Social Theory and Economic Change*
Burrage, M. C. and Corry, D. 1981 'At sixes and sevens', *Amer. Sociol. Rev.*, 46
Burton, A. 1989 'Looking foward from Aries', *Cont. & Ch.*, 4
Burton, I. F., Riley, P. W. J. and Rowlands, E. 1968 'Political parties in the reigns of William III and Anne', *B. I. H. R.*, Supp. 7
Burtt, S. 1992 *Virtue Transformed: Political Argument in England, 1688–1740* (Cambridge)
Bury, J. B. 1960 *The Idea of Progress* (repr.)
Bush, M. L. 1975 *The Government Policy of Protector Somerset*
1983 *The European Nobility* (Manchester)
1984 *The English Aristocracy* (Manchester)
1988 *Rich Noble, Poor Noble* (Manchester)
(ed.) 1992 *Social Orders and Social Classes in Europe since 1500*
Bushell, T. L. 1967 *The Sage of Salisbury* (New York)
Bushkovitch, P. 1980 *The Merchants of Moscow* (Cambridge, Massachusetts)
Bushman, R. L. 1967 *From Puritan to Yankee* (Cambridge, Massachusetts)
Butcher, A. F. 1974 'The origins of Romney Freemen, 1433–1525', *E. H. R.*, 2nd ser., 27
Butel, P. (ed.) 1979 *Sociétés et groupes sociaux en Aquitaine et en Angleterre* (Bordeaux)
Butel, P. and Cullen, L. M. (eds.) 1986 *Cities and Merchants, 1500–1900* (Dublin)
Butler, E. H. 1951 *The Story of British Shorthand*
Butler, M. 1984 *Theatre and Crisis, 1632–42* (Cambridge)
Butters, H. 1986 *Governors and Governed in Early Sixteenth-century Florence* (Oxford)
Butts, F. T. 1982 'The myth of Perry Miller', *A. H. R.*, 87
Bynum, W. F. and Porter, R. (eds.) 1991 *Living and Dying in London*
Bynum, W. F. and Shepherd, M. 1985 *The Anatomy of Madness*

Bywater, M. F. and Yamey B. S. 1982 *History of Accounting Literature*
Cain, L. P. and Uselden, P. J. (eds.) 1973 *Business Enterprise and Economic Change* (Kent, Ohio)
Cain, P. 1987 'Robert Smith and the archives of London', *Lond. J.*, 13
Cain, P. J. and Hopkins, A. G. 1986 'Gentlemanly capitalism and British expansion overseas 1688–1850', *Ec. H. R.*, 2nd ser., 39
Cairncross, A. K. 1962 *Factors in Economic Development*
1989 'In praise of economic history', *Ec. H. R.*, 2nd ser., 42
Caldicott, C. E. J., Gough, H. and Pittion, J.-P. (eds.) 1987 *The Huguenots and Ireland: Anatomy of an Emigration* (Dublin)
Caldwell, P. 1983 *The Puritan Conversion Narrative* (New York)
Callahan, W. J. 1972 *Honoring Commerce and Industry in Eighteenth-century Spain* (Boston)
Calvert, H. 1965 'Some speculations about the law of business association', *Amer. J. Legal Hist.*, 9
Calvert, H. 1978 *A History of Kingston upon Hull*
Cam, H. M. 1960–1 *Album. Helen Maud Cam* (Louvain)
Cambridge Legal Essays 1926 (Cambridge)
Cameron, A. 1970 'Sir Henry Willoughby', *Trans. Thor. Soc.*, 74
Cameron, H. C. and Wall, C. 1963 *A History of the Society of Apothecaries*, vol. I, *1617–1815*, ed. and rev. by E. A. Underwood (Oxford)
Cameron, R. 1973 'The logistics of European economic growth', *J. Eur. Ec. Hist.*, 2
Cameron, W. J. 1964 'The Company of white paper makers', *Univ. Auckland Bull.*, 68
Camp, A. J. 1974 *Wills and their Whereabouts*, 4th edn, rev.
Camp, C. W. 1924 *The Artisan in Elizabethan Literature* (New York)
Campbell, A. E. 1976 'The London parish and the London precinct, 1640–60', *Guild. Stud. Lond. Hist.*, 2
Campbell, Sir Duncan, 1925 *Records of Clan Campbell in the Military Service of the East India Company, 1600–1858*
Campbell, G. A. 1961 *William Fuller, 1670–1733*
Campbell, Lord John, 1874 *The Lives of the Chief Justices of England*, 3rd edn, 4 vols.
Campbell, L. 1989 'Wet nurses', *Med. Hist.*, 33
Campbell, M. 1960 *The English Yeoman under Elizabeth and the Early Stuarts*
Campbell, P. F. 1974 'The merchants and planters of Barbados', *J. Barb. Mus. & Hist. Soc.*, 34
Canard, M. 1913 'Essai de sémantique: le mot bourgeois', *Rev. Philol. Franc. et Litt.*, 27
Cannadine, D. 1978 'The theory and practice of the English leisure classes', *H. J.*, 21
Cannon. J. A. (ed.) 1981 *The Whig Ascendancy*
1982 'The isthmus repaired', *P. B. A.*, 68
1984 *Aristocratic Century: The Peerage in Eighteenth Century England* (Cambridge)
Canny, N. P. 1973 'The ideology of English colonisation', *Wm & Mary Q.*, 3rd ser., 30

1975 *The Formation of the Old English Elites in Ireland* (Dublin)
Canny, N. P. and Pagden, A. (eds.) 1987 *Colonial Identity in the Atlantic World, 1500–1800* (Princeton)
Capkora, D. 1978 'The education plan of Comenius', *Hist. Educ.*, 8
Capp, B. S. 1975 'Will formularies', *Loc. Pop. Stud.*, 14
1979 *Astrology and the Popular Press: English Almanacks, 1500–1800*
1989 *Cromwell's Navy* (Oxford)
Caracciolo, F. 1966 *Il Regno di Napoli* (Rome)
Cares, R. E. 1980 'Exports and economic growth', *Expl. Ent. H.*, 17
Carlos, A. M. 1991 'Agent opportunism and the role of company culture', *Bus. & Econ. Hist.*, 2nd ser., 20
Carlos, A. M. and Nicholas, S. 1988 'Giants of an earlier capitalism', *Bus. Hist. Rev.*, 62
1990 'Agency problems in the early chartered companies', *J. Ec. H.*, 50
Carlton, C. H. 1971 'The administration of London's Court of Orphans', *Guild. Misc.*, 4
1973 'John Hooker and Exeter's Court of Orphans', *H. L. Q.*, 36
1974a *The Court of Orphans* (Leicester)
1974b 'Changing jurisdictions', *Amer. J. Legal Hist.*, 18
1978 'The widow's tale', *Albion*, 10
1987 *Archbishop Laud*
1992 *Going to the Wars: The Experience of the British Civil Wars, 1638–51*
Carpenter, C. 1992 *Locality and Polity: A Study of Warwickshire Landed Society, 1401–1499* (Cambridge)
Carr, G. 1990 *Residence and Social Status: The Development of Seventeenth-century London*
Carr, L. G. and Jordan, D. W. 1974 *Maryland's Revolution in Government, 1689–92* (Ithaca)
Carr, L. G. and Walsh, L. 1977 'A planter's wife', *Wm & Mary Q.*, 34
Carr, L. G., Morgan, P. D. and Russo, J. B. (eds.) 1988 *Colonial Chesapeake Society* (Chapel Hill)
Carrère, C. 1967 *Barcelone, centre économique, 1380–1452*
Carrière, C. 1973 *Negoçiants Marseillais au XVIIIe siècle* (Marseilles), 2 vols.
Carroll, J. 1981 'The role of guilt, 1350–1800', *Brit. J. Sociol.*, 32
Carroll, R. 1968 'Yorkshire parliamentary boroughs', *North. Hist.*, 3
Carson, E. A. 1971a 'The custom records of the Kent ports', *J. Soc. Archiv.*, 4
1971b 'Custom bills of entry', *Mar. Hist.*, 1
1977a 'The customs records of Portsmouth', *J. Soc. Archiv.*, 5
1977b 'Customs records as a source', *Archives*, 13
Carson, G. M. 1991 'The Wisemans', *Fam. Hist.*, NS, 16
Carsten, F. L. 1954 *The Origins of Prussia* (Oxford)
(ed.) 1961 *The New Cambridge Modern History*, vol. V, *The Ascendancy of France* (Cambridge)
Carswell, J. P. 1960 *The South Sea Bubble*
Carter, A. 1901 'Early history of the law merchant in England', *Law Q. R.*, 17
Carter, A. C. (Le Mesurier) 1934–5 'The Orphans Inventories', *Ec. H. R.*, 5
1959 'Financial activities of the Huguenots', *Proc. Hug. Soc. Lond.*, 19
1964 *The English Reformed Church at Amsterdam* (Amsterdam)

1975 *Getting, Spending and Investing*, ed. J. de Vries (Assen)

Carus-Wilson, E. M. 1934 'The origin and early development of the Merchant Adventurers', *Ec. H. R.*, 3

1949–50 Review of S. L. Thrupp, *Ec. H. R.*, 2nd ser., 2

(ed.) 1954–66 *Essays in Economic History*, 3 vols.

1954 *Medieval Merchant Venturers*

Casey, J. 1979 *The Kingdom of Valencia in the Seventeenth Century*

Casey, J. 1989 *History of the Family* (Oxford)

Caspari, F. 1954 *Humanism and the Social Order in Tudor England* (Chicago)

Cassedy, J. H. (ed.) 1973 *Mortality in Pre-industrial Times*

Casson, M. 1982 *The Entrepreneur: An Economic Theory* (Oxford)

Castells, F. de P. 1931 *English Freemasonry, 1600–1700*

Catheart, C. D. 1969 'Doubting consciences', *Diss. Abstr.*, 29

Cauwenberghe, E. von, 1975 *Structures et mobilité nobiliaires aux Pays Bas méridonaux, 1425–1795* (Leuven)

Cave, C. H. 1899 *A History of Banking in Bristol, 1750–1899* (Bristol)

Cave, R. 1973 'Thomas Craddock's books', *Bull. Jamaica Lib. Assoc.*

Cecil, E. 1895 *Primogeniture*

Cell, G. T. 1965 'The Newfoundland Company', *Wm & Mary Q.*, 3rd ser., 22

1969 *English Enterprise in Newfoundland, 1577–1660* (Toronto)

Cernovodeanu, P. 1972 *England's Trade Policy in the Levant, 1600–1700* (Bucharest)

Chalk, A. F. 1951 'Natural law and the rise of economic individualism', *J. Pol. Econ.*, 59

1966 'Mandeville's Fable', *South. Econ. J.*, 33

Chalklin, C. W. 1965 *Seventeenth-Century Kent*

1974 *The Provincial Towns of Georgian England*

Chalkin, C. W. and Havinden, M. A. (eds.) 1974 *Rural Change and Urban Growth, 1500–1800: Essays in Honour of W. G. Hoskins*

Chalkin, C. W. and Worden, J. R. (eds.) 1989 *Town and Countryside: The English Landowner in the National Economy, 1660–1860*

Chaloner, W. H. 1949–50 'The Egertons in Italy and the Netherlands', *B. J. R. L.*, 32

Chaloner, W. H. and Ratcliffe, B. M. (eds.) 1977 *Trade and Transport: Essays for T. S. Willan* (Manchester)

Chambers, D. S. (ed.) 1966 *Faculty Office Registers, 1534–49: A Calendar* (Oxford)

(ed.) 1970 *Patrons and Artists in the Italian Renaissance*

Chambers, J. D. 1966 *Nottinghamshire in the Eighteenth Century*, 2nd edn

1971 'The Tawney tradition', *Ec. H. R.*, 2nd ser., 24

1972 *Population, Economy and Society in Pre-industrial England*

Chambers, R. J. 1966 *Accounting, Evaluation and Economic Behaviour*

Champness, R. 1966 *The Company of Turners*

Chan, A. 1982 *The Glory and Fall of the Ming Dynasty* (Norman, Oklahoma)

Chan, W. K. K. 1977 *Merchant Mandarins and Modern Enterprise* (Cambridge, Massachusetts)

Chance, I. O. 1971 'The auction', *J. Roy. Soc. Arts*, 119

Chandaman, C. D. 1975 *The English Public Revenue, 1660–88* (Oxford)

Chandler, A. D. 1977 *The Visible Hand* (Cambridge, Massachusetts)
Chandler, A. D. and Daems, H. (eds.) 1980 *Managerial Hierarchies* (Cambridge, Massachusetts)
Chandler, F. W. 1907 *The Literature of Roguery* (Boston)
Chandler, G. 1965 *Liverpool under Charles I* (Liverpool)
Chandler, M. J. 1979 'Emigrants from Britain to the colonies', *J. Barb. Mus. & Hist. Soc.*, 36
Chandra, S. 1959 'Commercial activities of the Moghul emperors', *Bengal P. & P.*, 78
1966 'The growth of a money economy in India', *Indian Ec. & Soc. Rev.*, 3
Chang, C.-L. 1955 *The Chinese Gentry* (Seattle)
1962 *The Income of the Chinese Gentry* (Seattle)
Chapman, A. 1980 'Barter as a universal mode of exchange', *L'Homme*, 20
Chapman, S. D. 1972 'The genesis of the British hosiery industry', *Text. Hist.*, 3
1979 'British marketing enterprise', *Bus. Hist. Rev.*, 53
Charles, L. and Duffin, L. (eds.) 1985 *Women and Work in Pre-industrial England*
Charlton, K. 1960–1 'Liberal education and the Inns of Court', *Brit. J. Educ. Stud.*, 9
1965 *Education in Renaissance England*
1969 'The professions in the sixteenth century', *Univ. B'ham H. J.*, 12
Chartier, R. (ed.) 1989 *The Culture of Print* (Cambridge)
Chartres, J. A. 1977a 'The capital's provincial eyes', *Lond. J.*, 3
1977b *Internal Trade of England 1500–1700*
1977c 'Road carriage in England in the seventeenth century', *Ec. H. R.*, 2nd. ser., 30
1980a 'Trade and shipping in the port of London', *J. Trans. Hist.*, 3rd ser., 1
1980b 'Road Carriage', *Ec. H. R.*, 33
Chartres, J. A. and Hey, D. (eds.) 1990 *English Rural Society, 1500–1800: Essays in Honour of Joan Thirsk* (Cambridge)
Chaudhuri, K. N. 1965 *The English East India Company, 1600–40*
1978 *The Trading World of Asia and the English East India Company* (Cambridge)
1985 *Trade and Civilisation in the Indian Ocean* (Cambridge)
Chaudhuri, K. N. and Dewey, C. J. (eds.) 1979 *Economy and Society* (Delhi)
Chaudhuri, S. 1971 'Bengal merchants and commercial organization', *Bengal P. & P.*, 90
1975 *Trade and Commercial Organization in Bengal, 1650–1720* (Calcutta)
Chaunu, P. 1967 'Structure sociale et représentation littéraire', *Rev. Hist. Ec. & Soc.*, 52
1984 *Rétrohistoire*
Chaussinard-Nogaret, G. 1970 'Capital et structure sociale sous l'Ancien Régime', *Annales*, 25
Checkland, S. G. 1960 'Theories of economic and social evolution', *Scot. J. Pol. Econ.*, 7
Chiat, M. J. and Reyerson, K. L. (eds.) 1988 *The Medieval Mediterranean: Cross-cultural Contacts* (St Cloud, Minnesota)
'Child and Company: three hundred years', *Three Banks Rev.*, 98 (1973)
Childs, J. C. R. 1976 *The Army of Charles II*

1980 *The Army of James II and the Glorious Revolution* (Manchester)
1987 *The British Army of William III, 1689–1702* (Manchester)
Childs, W. R. 1978 *Anglo-Castilian Trade* (Manchester)
Chilton, C. W. 1979 'A provincial bookseller's stock', *Library*, 1
Chinnery, V. 1979 *Oak Furniture: The British Tradition*
Christensen, P. P. 1989 'Hobbes and the physiological origins of economic science', *Hist. Pol. Econ.*, 21
Christianson, J. R. 1981 'The reconstruction of the Scandinavian aristocracy', *Scandinavian Studies*, 53
Cioni, M. L. 1985 *Women and Law in Elizabethan England* (New York)
Cioranescu, A. 1963 *Thomas Nichols* (La Lagune de Teneriffe)
Clagett, M. 1959 (ed.) *Critical Problems in the History of Science* (Madison)
Clark, A. 1919 *Working Life of Women in the Seventeenth Century*
Clark, A. B. 1931 'Notes on the mayors of Nottingham', *Trans. Thor. Soc.*, 41
Clark, A. M. 1931 *Thomas Heywood* (Oxford)
Clark, C. E. 1970 *The Eastern Frontier: The Settlement of North New England, 1610–1763* (New York)
Clark, G. 1989 'London nurses', *Genealog. Mag.*, 23
Clark, Sir George, 1923 *The Dutch Alliance and the War against French Trade, 1688–97* (Manchester)
1928 'War trade and trade war', *Ec. H. R.*, 1
1938 *Guide to English Commercial Statistics, 1696–1782*
1944 'The Barbary corsairs', *C. H. J.*, 8
1949 *Science and Social Welfare in the Age of Newton*, 2nd edn (Oxford)
1950 *The Seventeenth Century*, 2nd edn (Oxford)
1954 'The Nine Years War, 1688–97', *C. H. J.*, 11
1958 *War and Society in the Seventeenth Century* (Cambridge)
1962 *Three Aspects of Stuart England* (Oxford)
1966 *A History of the Royal College of Physicians* (Oxford), 2 vols.
Clark, P. A. 1976a 'Popular protest and disturbances in Kent', *Ec. H. R.*, 2nd ser., 29
(ed.) 1976b *The Early Modern Town*
1977 *English Provincial Society from the Reformation to the Revolution* (Hassocks)
1978 'Thomas Scott and the growth of urban opposition', *H. J.*, 21
1979 'Migration in England', *P. & P.*, 83
(ed.) 1981 *Country Towns in Pre-industrial England* (Leicester)
1983 *The English Alehouse, 1200–1800*
(ed.) 1984 *The Transformation of English Provincial Towns, 1600–1800*
(ed.) 1985 *The European Crisis of the 1590s*
1987 'Planters and Plantations', *Irish Econ. & Soc. Hist.*, 14
Clark, P. A. and Slack. P. (eds.) 1972 *Crisis and Order in English Towns 1500–1700* (Toronto)
(eds.) 1976 *English Towns in Transition, 1500–1700*
Clark, P. A. and Souden, D. (eds.) 1987 *Migration and Society in Early Modern England*
Clark, P. A., Smith, A. G. R. and Tyacke, N. (eds.) 1979 *The English Commonwealth, 1547–1640: Essays Presented to Joel Hurstfield* (Leicester)

Clark, P. P. 1978 'Newspapers and novels', *Studies in Novel*, 7

Clark, R. A. 1980 'Good and sufficient maintenance', *Derby. Arch. J.*, 100

Clark, S. 1983 *The Elizabethan Pamphleteers*

Clarke, H. F. 1940 *John Hull, a Builder of the Bay Colony* (Portland, Maine)

Clarke, H. F. and Foote, H. W. 1936 *Jeremiah Drummer, Colonial Craftsman and Merchant* (New York)

Clarke, M. L. 1959 *Classical Education in Britain, 1500–1900* (Cambridge)

Clarke, P. 1973 *First House in the City: Child and Company, 1673–1973* (priv. pr.)

Clarke, R. and MacGuiness, T. 1987 *The Economics of the Firm* (Oxford)

Clarkson, L. A. 1965 'English economic policy', *B. I. H. R.*, 38

1966 'The leather crafts', *Agric. Hist. Rev.*, 14

1975 *Death, Disease and Famine*

1989 *Proto-industrialization*

Clawson, M. A. 1980 'Early modern fraternalism', *Fem. Stud.*, 6

Clay, C. G. 1968 'Marriage, inheritance and the rise of the large estate, 1660–1815', *Ec. H. R.*, 2nd ser., 21

1974 'The price of freehold land', *Ec. H. R.*, 2nd ser, 22

1978 *Public Finances and Private Wealth: The Career of Sir Stephen Fox, 1627–1716* (Oxford)

1981 'Property settlements', *J. B. S.*, 21

1984 *Economic Expansion and Social Change: England, 1500–1700* (Cambridge)

Clay, J. W. (ed.) 1894–6 *Familiae Minorum Gentium* (Harl. Soc., 37–8)

Clemence, R. V. and Doody, F. S. 1966 *The Schumpeterian System* (repr. New York)

Clemens, P. G. E. 1976 'Rise of Liverpool, 1665–1730', *Ec. H. R.*, 2nd ser., 29

Clemens, P. G. E., Bogue, A. G. and Fogel, R. W. (eds.) 1980 *The Atlantic Economy and Colonial Maryland's Eastern Shore* (Ithaca)

Cliffe, J. T. 1969 *The Yorkshire Gentry from the Reformation to the Civil War*

1984 *The Puritan Gentry*

1988 *Puritans in Conflict*

Clifford, J. L. (ed.) 1968 *Man versus Society in Eighteenth-century Britain* (Cambridge)

Clifford-Vaughan, M. 1960 'Some French concepts of elites', *Brit. J. Sociol.*, 11

Clifton, R. 1984 *The Last Popular Rebellion: The Western Rising 1685*

Clode, C. M. 1875 *Memorials of the Merchant Taylors*

1888 *The Early History of the Merchant Taylors of London*

1892 *London During the Great Rebellion, being a Memoir of Sir Abraham Reynardiston*

Clough, C. H. 1982 (ed.) *Profession, Vocation and Culture in Late Medieval England* (Liverpool)

Clowes, G. S. L. 1932 *Sailing Ships: Their History and Development*, 2 vols.

Coase, R. 1936 'The nature of the firm', *Economica*, 16

Coate, M. 1963 *Cornwall in the Great Civil War*, 2nd edn (Truro)

Coates, D. and Hillard, J. (eds.) 1986 *The Economic Decline of Modern Britain* (Brighton)

Coats, A. W. 1960–1 'Economic thought and Poor Law policy', *Ec. H. R.*, 2nd ser., 13

1962 'Adam Smith', *Ren. & Mod. Stud.*, 6

1973 'The interpretation of Mercantilist economics', *Hist. Pol. Econ.*, 5
1976 'The relief of poverty', *Intl Rev. Soc. Hist.*, 21
1980 'The historical context of the new economic history', *J. Eur. Ec. Hist.*, 9
Cobb, H. S. 1978 'Cloth exports from London and Southampton', *Ec. H. R.*, 2nd ser., 31
Cochran, T. C. 1947 'A plea for the study of business thinking', *Pol. Sc. Q.*, 62
1964 *The Inner Revolution* (New York)
1973 'History and cultural crisis', *A. H. R.*, 78
1974 'The business revolution', *A. H. R.*, 79
Cockburn, J. S. 1969 'The clerk of assize', *Amer. J. Legal Hist.*, 13
1972 *A History of English Assizes, 1558–1714* (Cambridge)
(ed.) 1977 *Crime in England, 1550–1800*
Cockburn, J. S. and Green, T. A. (eds.) 1988 *Twelve Good Men and True* (Princeton)
Cockerell, H. A. L. and Green, E. 1976 *The British Insurance Business, 1547–1970*
Cohen, C. L. 1986 *God's Caress: The Psychology of Puritan Religious Experience* (New York)
Cohen, J. 1953 'The idea of work and play', *Brit. J. Sociol.*, 4
Cohen, J. 1982 'The history of imprisonment for debt', *J. Legal Hist.*, 3
Cohn, B. S. 1980 'History and anthropology', *Comp. Stud. Soc. Hist.*, 22
Cokayne, A. E. 1873 *Cokayne Memoranda* (priv. pr.)
Cokayne, G. E. 1877 *Some Account of the Lord Mayors and Sheriffs of London, 1601–25*
1900–6 *Complete Baronage, 1611–1800* (Exeter)
Cole, A. 1956 'The social origins of the early Friends', *J. Friends Hist. Soc.*, 48
Cole, A. H. 1949 *Change and the Entrepreneur* (Cambridge, Massachusetts)
1957 *The Historical Development of Economic and Business Literature* (Kress Lib. Pub., 12)
1959 'The tempo of mercantile life', *Bus. Hist. Rev.*, 33
1968 'Meso-economics', *Expl. Ent. H.*, 2nd ser., 6
Cole, A. T. 1961 'The anonymous Iamblich', *Harv. Stud. Class. Phil.*, 55
Cole, C. R. and Moody, M. E. (eds.) 1975 *The Dissenting Tradition: Essays for Leland H. Carson* (Athens, Ohio)
Coleby, A. M. 1987 *Central Government and the Localities: Hampshire, 1649–89* (Cambridge)
Coleman, A. and Hammond, A. (eds.) 1981 *Poetry and Drama, 1570–1700: Essays in Honour of H. F. Brooks*
Coleman, D. C. 1953 'Naval dockyards under the later Stuarts', *Ec. H. R.*, 2nd ser., 6
1958 *The British Paper Industry, 1495–1860* (Oxford)
1959 'Technology and economic history, 1500–1750', *Ec. H. R.*, 2nd ser., 11
1963 *Sir John Banks* (Oxford)
1966 'The gentry controversy', *History*, 51
1969a 'An innovation and its diffusion: the new draperies', *Ec. H. R.*, 2nd ser., 22
(ed.) 1969b *Revisions in Mercantilism*
1972a *What Has Happened to Economic History* (Cambridge)
1972b 'Early modern economy of England', *Ec. H. R.* 2nd ser., 25

1973 'Gentlemen and players', *Ec. H. R.*, 2nd ser., 26
1977 *The Economy of England, 1450–1750* (Oxford)
1978 'Philanthropy deflated', *Ec. H. R.*, 2nd ser., 31
1980 'Mercantilism revisited', *H. J.* , 23
1983 'Proto-industrialization', *Ec. H. R.*, 2nd ser., 36
1987a 'The uses and abuses of business history', *Bus. Hist.*, 29
1987b *History and the Economic Past* (Oxford)
1988 'Adam Smith', *Hist. Eur. Ideas*, 9
Coleman, D. C. and John, A. H. (eds.) 1976 *Trade, Government and Economy in Pre-industrial England: Essays Presented to F. J. Fisher*
Coleman, D. C. and Mathias, P. G. (eds.) 1984 *Enterprise and History: Essays in Honour of Charles Wilson* (Cambridge)
Colley, L. 1986 'The politics of eighteenth-century British history', *J. B. S.*, 25
Collier, S. 1991 *Whitehaven, 1600–1800* (HMSO)
Collinge, T.M. (comp.) 1978 *Navy Board Officials, 1660–1832* (IHR)
Collins, J. B. 1988 *Fiscal Limits of Absolutism* (Berkeley)
Collins, R. 1986 *Weberian Sociological Theory* (Cambridge)
Collinson, P. 1982 *The Religion of Protestants* (Oxford)
1983 *Godly People*
1988a *The Birthpangs of Protestant England*
1988b 'Puritan men of business', *Parlt. Hist.*, 7
'La Colloquie démographie historique de Cambridge', *Annales*, 24 (1969)
Colman, J. 1972 'Mandeville and the reality of virtue', *Philosophy*, 47
1983 *John Locke's Moral Philosophy* (Edinburgh)
Colvin, H. M. 1954, 1978 *Biographical Dictionary of English Architects, 1600–1840*
1972 'Francis Smith', *Warws. Hist.*, 2
Colvin, H. M. and Wodehouse, L. M. 1961 'Henry Bell', *Arch. Hist.*, 4
Colvin, H. M., Summerson, J., Biddle, M., Hale, J. R. and Merriman, M. (eds.) 1982 *The History of the King's Works* (HMSO), vol. IV, *1485–1660*
Colyer, R. J. Moore, 1988 'The Welsh cattle trade', *Nat. Lib. Wales J.*, 25
Cominos, P. T. 1963 'Late Victorian sexual respectability', *Intl Rev. Soc. Hist.*, 8
Commons, J. 1968 *Legal Foundations of Capitalism* (Madison)
Conder, E. and Were, F. 1907 'The heraldry of some citizens of Bristol', *T. B. G. A. S.*, 30
Condon, T. J. 1968 *New York Beginnings* (New York)
Connell-Smith, G. 1950–1 'Ledger of Thomas Howell', *Ec. H. R.*, 2nd ser., 3
Consitt, F. 1933 *The London Weavers Company* (Oxford)
Constant, J. T. 1973 'L'enquête de noblesse de 1667', *Bull. Soc. d'Hist. Mod.*, 5
Cook, A. J. 1981 *The Privileged Playgoers of Shakespeare's London, 1576–1642* (Princeton)
1991 *Making a Match* (Princeton)
Cook, H. J. 1986 *The Decline of the Old Medical Regime in Stuart London*
1987 'The Society of Chemical Physicians', *Bull. Soc. Hist. Med.*, 61
1990 'The Rose Case reconsidered', *J. Hist. Med. & All. Sc.*, 45
Cook, M. A. (ed.) 1970 *Studies in the Economic History of the Middle East*
Cooke, C. A. 1950 *Corporation Trust and Company* (Manchester)
Cooke, R. I. 1974 *Bernard Mandeville*

Coombs, D. 1957 'Dr Davenant', *Ec. H. R.*, 2nd ser., 10
Cooper, C. R. H. 1984 'The archives of London livery companies', *Archives*, 16
Cooper, J. P. (ed.) 1970 *The New Cambridge Modern History* (Cambridge), vol. IV, *The Decline of Spain*
1978 'In search of agrarian capitalism', *P. & P.*, 80
1983 *Land, Men and Beliefs*, ed. G. E. Aylmer and J. S. Morrill
Cooper, S. M. 1986 'Family household and occupation', *Diss. Abstr.*, 46
1992 'Intergenerational social mobility', *Cont. & Ch.*, 7
Coornaert, E. 1930 *Un centre industriel d'autrefois: la Draperie-Sayetterie d'Hondschoote*
Cope, J. I. 1956 'Seventeenth-century Quaker style', *P. M. L. A.*, 71
Cope, S. R. 1978 'The Stock Exchange revisited', *Economica*, 45
Copeman, W. S. C. 1968 *The Company of Apothecaries*
Coppel, S. 1988 'Willmaking on the deathbed', *Loc. Pop. Stud.*, 40
Corcia, J. de, 1978 'Bourg, bourgeois', *J. M. H.*, 50
Corcoran, P. E. 1977 'The bourgeois and other villains', *J. H. I.*, 38
1980 'The bourgeois in Marxist rhetoric', *Hist. Pol. Thought*, 1
Corfield, P. J. 1982 *The Impact of English Towns, 1700–1800* (Oxford)
1987 'Class by name and number', *History*, 122
1989 'Dress for deference and dissent', *Costume*, 23
(ed.) 1991 *Language, History and Class* (Oxford)
Corfield, P. J. and Keene, D. (eds.) 1990 *Work in Towns, 850–1850* (Leicester)
Corfield, P. J. and Priestley, V. 1982 'Rooms and room use in Norwich houses', *Post Med. Arch.*, 16
Cornish, P. J. 1981 *The Catholic Community in the Seventeenth and Eighteenth Centuries* (Dublin)
Cornwall, J. C. K. 1962–3 'English country towns in the 1520s', *Ec. H. R.*, 2nd ser., 15
1964–5 'The Early Tudor gentry', *Ec. H. R.*, 2nd ser., 17
1967 'Evidence of population mobility', *B. I. H. R.*, 40
1976 'Sussex wealth and society', *Suss. Arch. Coll.*, 64
1988 *Wealth and Society in Early Sixteenth-century England*
Corry, J. and Evans, J. 1816 *History of Bristol*
Costello, W. T. 1958 *The Scholastic Curriculum in Seventeenth-century Cambridge* (Cambridge, Massachusetts)
Cotterell, M. 1968 'Interregnum law reform: the Hale Commission of 1652', *E. H. R.*, 83
Cotton, R. W. 1889 *Barnstable*
Cotton, W. 1872 *An Elizabethan Guild of Exeter: The Society of Merchant Adventurers* (Exeter)
Cottrell, P. L. and Aldcroft, D. H. (eds.) 1981 *Shipping Trade and Commerce: Essays in Memory of Ralph Davis* (Leicester)
Cottret, B. J. 1991 *The Huguenots in England: Immigration and Settlement* (New York)
Coulton, B. 1989 'Tern Hall and the Hill family', *Trans. Shrop. Arch. & Nat. Hist. Soc.*, 66
Coumet, E. 1970 'La théorie du hasard', *Annales*, 25
Council, N. 1973 *When Honour's at the Stake*

Court, W. H. B. 1953 *The Rise of the Midland Industries* (Oxford)
Coutau-Bégarie, H. 1989 *Le phénomène Nouvelle Histoire*, 2nd edn
Cowan, A. F. 1986 *The Urban Patriciate: Lubeck and Venice, 1580–1700* (Cologne)
1991 'Urban elites in early modern Europe', *Hist. Res.*, 64
Coward, B. 1971 'Disputed inheritances', *B. I. H. R.*, 44
1983 *The Stanleys, 1385–1672* (Cheth. Soc., 3rd ser., 30)
1988 *Social Change and Continuity, 1550–1750*
Cowell, J. B. 1984 'Anglesey shops and shopkeepers', *Trans. Anglesey Antiq. Soc. & Field Club*
Cowgill, U. M. 1967 'Life and death in the sixteenth century', *Pop. Stud.*, 21
1970a 'Marriage and its progeny', *Kroeber Anthrop. Soc. Papers*, 42
1970b 'The people of York, 1538–1812', *Scient. Amer.*, 222
Cowie, L. W. 1949 'The conflict of political, religious and social ideas in English education', *B. I. H. R.*, 22
1973 'Bridewell', *Hist. Tod.*, 23
Cox, A. 1982 *Sir Henry Unton* (Cambridge)
Cox, M. 1975 *History of Sir John Deane Grammar School* (Manchester)
Cox, N. and J. 1984 'Probate inventories: the legal background', *Loc. Hist.*, 16
Cox, W. 1897 *Annals of St Helen's, Bishopsgate*
Cragg, G. R. 1957 *Puritanism in the Period of the Great Persecution* (Cambridge)
1960 *The Church in the Age of Reason*
Craig, Sir John 1946 *Newton at the Mint* (Cambridge)
Cranston, M. 1957 *John Locke*
Crawford, A. 1977 *A History of the Vintners Company*
Crawford, M. A. 1987 'Instrument makers in the London guilds', *Ann. Sc.*, 44
Crawford, P. 1984 'Printed advertisements for women medical practitioners', *Bull. Soc. Hist. Med.*, 35
1986 'The sucking child', *Cont. & Ch.*, 1
Cresswell, B. F. 1930 *A Short History of the Company of Weavers, Fullers and Sheremen of Exeter* (Exeter)
Cressy, D. 1970 'The social composition of Caius College, 1580–1640', *P. & P.*, 47
1974 'Literacy in pre-industrial England', *Societas*, 4
1975 *Education in Tudor and Stuart England*
1976a 'Educational opportunities in Tudor and Stuart England', *Hist. Educ. Q.*, 16
1976b 'Describing the social order', *Lit. & Hist.*, 3
1979 'School and college admission age', *Hist. Educ.*, 8
1980 *Literacy and the Social Order* (Cambridge)
1986 'Kinship and kin interaction', *P. & P.*, 113
1987 *Coming Over: Migration and Communication between England and New England* (Cambridge)
1989 *Bonfires and Bells*
1990a 'The Protestant calendar', *J. B. S.*, 29
1990b 'Death and the social order', *Cont. & Ch.*, 5
Croft, M. E. F. 1962–72 *Decorative Painting in England, 1537–1837*, 2 vols.
Croft, P. 1972 'Englishmen and the Spanish Inquisition', *E. H. R.*, 87

1975 'Free trade and the Commons, 1605–06', *Ec. H. R.*, 2nd ser., 28
1983 'English mariners trading to Spain', *Mar. Mirr.*, 69
1987a 'Fresh light on Bate's Case', *H. J.*, 30
1987b 'Parliament, 1605', *Parlt. Hist.*, 6
1987c 'The rise of the English stocking export trade', *Text. Hist.*, 18
1989 'Trading with the enemy, 1585–1604', *H. J.*, 32
Crofts, J. E. V. 1967 *Packhorse, Waggon and Post*
Cronne, H. A., Moody, T. W. and Quinn, D. B. (eds.) 1949 *Essays in British and Irish History in Honour of J. E. Todd*
Crosfield, H. G. 1913 *Margaret Fox*
Cross, M. C. 1960 'Noble patronage in the Elizabethan Church', *H. J.*, 3
1966 *The Puritan Earl* (New York)
1967 'Supervising the finances of the Earl of Huntingdon', *B. I. H. R.*, 40
1976 *Church and People, 1450–1660*
1982 'The development of Protestantism in Leeds and Hull', *North. Hist.*, 18
1985 *Urban Magistrates and Ministers* (Borthwick Paper, 67)
1987 'Northern women', *Yorks. Arch. J.*, 59
Cross, M. C., Loades, D. and Scarisbrick, J. J. (eds.) 1988 *Law and Government under the Tudors: Essays Presented to Sir Geoffrey Elton* (Cambridge)
Crossley, D. W. 1966 'The management of a sixteenth-century ironworks', *Ec. H. R.*, 2nd ser., 19
1972 'The performance of the glass industry', *Ec. H. R.*, 2nd ser., 25
Crossley, F. H. 1951 *Timber Building in England*
Crouzet, F. 1985 *De la supériorité de l'Angleterre sur la France*
Crowhurst, P. 1977 *The Defence of British Trade, 1689–1815* (Folkestone)
Cruickshank, C. G. 1966 *Elizabeth's Army*, 2nd edn (Oxford)
Cruickshank, E. 1989 (ed.) *By Fault and By Default* (Edinburgh)
Crummey, R. O. 1983 *Aristocrats and Servitors* (Princeton)
Crummy, P. and Moyer, R. H. 1976 'Post Reeve's house, Colchester', *Post. Med. Arch.*, 10
Crump, C. G. and Jacob, E. F. (eds.) 1951 *The Legacy of the Middle Ages* (Oxford)
Crump, H. J. 1931 *Colonial Admiralty Jurisdiction in the Seventeenth Century*
Crump, W. B. and Ghorbal, G. 1935 *History of the Huddersfield Woollen Industry* (Huddersfield)
Cuisenier, J. and Segalen, M. (eds.) 1977 *The Family Life Cycle in European Societies*
Cullen, L. M. 1968 *Anglo-Irish Trade, 1660–1800* (Manchester)
1987 *An Economic History of Ireland since 1660*, 2nd edn
Cullen, L. M. and Smout, T. C. (eds.) 1977 *Comparative Aspects of Scottish and Irish Economic and Social History, 1600–1900* (Edinburgh)
Cuming, G. J. (ed.) 1967 *Studies in Church History, IV* (Leiden)
Cumming, G. V. 1984 *The Seventeenth Century* (New York)
Cunnington, C. W. and P. 1966 *Handbook of English Costume*
Cunnington, P. and L. C. W. 1967 *Occupational Costume in England*
Currer-Briggs, C. N. 1969 *Virginia Settlers and English Adventurers*
Curry, P. 1987 *Astrology, Science and Society* (Woodbridge)
1989 *Prophecy and Power: Astrology in Early Modern England* (Princeton)
Curtin, M. 1985 'A question of manners', *J. M. H.*, 57

Curtin, P. D. 1975 *Economic Change in Pre-colonial Africa* (Madison)
Curtis, L. A. 1981 'A case study of Defoe's domestic conduct manuals', *Stud. Eight. Cent. Cult.*, 10
Curtis, M. H. 1959 *Oxford and Cambridge in Transition, 1558–1642*
1962 'The alienated intellectuals of early Stuart England', *P.& P.*, 23
1964 'Education and apprenticeship', *Shakes. Surv.*, 17
Curtis, T. C. and Speck, W. A. 1976 'The societies for reformation of manners', *Lit. & Hist.*, 3
Cussans, J. E. 1877–81 *History of Hertfordshire*, 4 vols.
Cust, R. 1987 *The Forced Loan and English Politics, 1626–8* (Oxford)
1992 'Anti-Puritans and urban politics', *H. J.*, 35
Cust, R. and Hughes, A. (eds.) 1989 *Conflict in Stuart England*
Custance, R. (ed.) 1982 *Winchester College Sixth Centenary Essays* (Oxford)
Cuvillier, J. P. 1970 'La noblesse catalan et le commerce', *Mélanges de la Casa de Velásquez*, 6
Cyert, R. M. and Hedrick, C. L. 1972 'Theory of the firm: past, present and future', *J. Ec. Lit.*, 10
Cyert, R. M. and March, J. G. 1963 *A Behavioural Theory of the Firm*, 2nd edn (Cambridge, Massachusetts)
Daaku, K. Y. 1970 *Trade and Politics on the Gold Coast, 1600–1720* (Oxford)
Daeley, J. I. 1967 'Plurality in the diocese of Canterbury, 1559–75', *J. Eccles. Hist.*, 18
Daems, H. and Wee, H. van der (eds.) 1974 *The Rise of Managerial Capitalism* (Leuven)
Dahlerup, T. L. and Jorgensen, J. 1965 'The old Danish aristocracy', *Scand. Ec. H. R.*, 13
Dale, M. K. 1932–4 'A study of the London silkwomen of the fifteenth century', *Ec. H. R.*, 4
Dalton, Sir Cornelius, 1915 *Thomas Pitt* (Cambridge)
Dalton, R. J. 1991 'Gerard Winstanley', *H. J.*, 34
Daly, J. 1979 *Sir Robert Filmer* (Toronto)
Darlington, C. D. 1978 *The Little Universe of Man*
D'Arms, J. H. 1981 *Commerce and Social Standing in Ancient Rome* (Cambridge, Massachusetts)
D'Arms, J. H. and Kopff, E. C. (eds.) 1980 *The Seaborne Commerce of Ancient Rome* (Amer. Acad. Rome)
Daube, D. 1969 *Roman Law* (Edinburgh)
Daunton, M. J. 1988 'Inheritance and succession in the City of London', *Bus. Hist.*, 30
1989 'Gentlemanly capitalism and British India', *P. & P.*, 122
Davenport-Hines, R. T. P. (ed.) 1990 *Capital, Entrepreneurs and Profits*
Davenport-Hines, R. T. P. and Lieberman, J. (eds.) 1986 *Business in the Age of Reason*
David, F. N. 1962 *Games, Gods and Gambling*
Davies, A. G. 1988 *The Landed Gentry of Hertfordshire, 1580–1688* (Hertford)
Davies, C. S. L. 1964–5 'Provisions for armies, 1509–50', *Ec. H. R.*, 2nd ser. 17
1966 'Slavery and Protector Somerset' *Ec.H.R.*, 2nd ser., 19
Davies, D. W. 1961 *A Primer of Dutch Overseas Trade in the Seventeenth Century*

(The Hague)
1967 *Elizabethan Errant* (Ithaca)
Davies, J. C. (ed.) 1957 *Studies Presented to Sir Hilary Jenkinson*
Davies, J. D. 1991 *Gentlemen and Tarpaulins: The Officers and Men of the Restoration Navy* (Oxford)
Davies, J. H. 1948 *The Worship of the Puritans*
1970–6 *Worship and Theology in England* (Princeton), vols. I–III
Davies, K. G. 1952a 'Joint-stock investment in the late seventeenth century', *Ec. H. R.*, 2nd ser., 4
1952b 'The origins of the commission system', *T. R. H. S.*, 5th ser., 2
1957 *The Royal Africa Company*
1962 'Mess of the middle class', *P. & P.*, 22
1974 *The North Atlantic World in the Seventeenth Century* (Minneapolis)
Davies, K. M. 1977 'The sacred condition of equality', *Soc. Hist.*, 5
Davies, M. G. 1956 *The Enforcement of English Apprenticeship, 1563–1642* (Cambridge, Massachusetts)
1971 'Country gentry and payments to London', *Ec. H. R.*, 2nd ser., 24
1978 'Country gentry and falling rents in the 1660s and 1670s', *Mid. Hist.*, 4
Davies, R. R. (ed.) 1984 *Welsh Society and Nationhood: Historical Essays Presented to Glamnor Williams* (Cardiff)
Davis, D. 1966 *A History of Shopping*
Davis, J. C. 1962 *The Decline of the Venetian Nobility as a Ruling Class* (Baltimore)
1975 *A Venetian Family and its Fortune, 1500–1900* (Amer. Phil. Soc.)
1976 'Gerard Winstanley', *P. & P.*, 70
Davis, N. Z. 1960 'Sixteenth century French Arithmetics', *J. H. I.*, 21
1975 *Society and Culture in Early Modern France*
Davis, R. 1956 'Merchant shipping in the economy', *Ec. H. R.*, 2nd ser., 9
1962 *The Rise of the English Shipping Industry*
1964 *The Trade and Shipping of Hull 1500–1700* (East Yorks. Loc. Hist. Soc., 17)
1965 *History and the Social Sciences* (Leicester)
1966a 'Shipping records', *Archives*, 7
1966b 'The rise of protection in England, 1669–1786', *Ec. H. R.*, 2nd ser., 19
1967a *A Commercial Revolution* (Hist. Assoc.)
1967b *Aleppo and Devonshire Square*
1967c 'Untapped sources' (Marine Historical Association, Mystic, Connecticut)
1973a *The Rise of the Atlantic Economy*
1973b *English Overseas Trade, 1500–1700*
1979 *The Industrial Revolution and British Overseas Trade* (Leicester)
Davis, R. B. 1955 *George Sandys, Poet-Adventurer*
Davis, W. 1969 *Idea and Act in Elizabethan Fiction* (Princeton)
Davison, L., Hitcock, T. and Keirns T. (eds.) 1992 *Stilling the Grumbling Hive, 1689–1750* (New York)
Davity, W. 1985 'The numbers game and the profitability of the British trade in slaves', *J. Ec. H.*, 45
Davril, R. 1954 *Le Drame de John Ford*
Dawe, D. A. 1950 *Skilbeck's Drysalters, 1650–1950*

Dawes, N. H. 1949 'Titles and symbols of prestige in seventeenth-century New England', *Wm & Mary Q.*, 3rd ser., 6
Dawson, G. E. and Skipton, L. K. 1966 *Elizabethan Handwriting, 1500–1650*
Day, J. 1987 *The Medieval Market Economy* (Oxford)
Day, J. F. R. 1987 'Trafficking in honor', *Renaissance Papers*, 33
1990 'Primers of honor', *Sixt. Cent. J.*, 21
Day, L. F. 1911 *Penmanship of the Sixteenth, Seventeenth and Eighteenth Centuries*
Deakin, Q. E. 1980 'John Hooker's description of Exeter', *Devon N. & Q.*, 6
Dean, D. M. 1988 'Public and private: the leather industry in Elizabethan England', *H. J.*, 31
1989 'London lobbies', *Parlt. Hist.*, 8
1991 'Pressure groups and lobbies', *Parliaments, Estates and Representation*, 11
Dean, D. M. and Jones, N. L. 1990 (eds.) *The Parliaments of Elizabethan England* (Oxford)
Deane, P. and Cole, W. A. 1967 *British Economic Growth, 1688–1955*, 2nd edn (Cambridge)
Debien, G. 1952 *Les Engagés partis pour les Antilles, 1634–1715*
Dechêne, L. 1974 *Habitants et marchands de Montreal au XVIIe siècle* (Montreal)
Delaney, P. 1969 *British Autobiography in the Seventeenth Century* (New York)
Delumeau, J. 1966 'Le commerce extérieure français', *XVIIe Siècle*, 70–1
1969 *Histoire de la Bretagne*
Delzell, C. F. (ed.) 1977 *The Future of History* (Nashville)
Demos, J. 1968 'Families in colonial Bristol', *Wm & Mary Q.*, 5th ser., 25
1971 'Developmental perspective on the history of children', *J. I. H.*, 2
Denholm-Young, N. 1937 'En remontant le passé de l'aristocratie anglaise', *Annales*, 9
1965 *History and Heraldry, 1254–1310* (Oxford)
1969 *The Country Gentry in the Fourteenth Century* (Oxford)
Dermigny, L. 1964 *La Chine et l'Occident*
Dessert, D. L. 1979 'Le laquais financier', *XVIIe Siècle*, 125
1984 *Argent, pouvoir et société au Grand Siècle*
Detweiler, D. R. 1971 'Was Richard Hakluyt a negative influence?', *N. Carolina Hist. Rev.*
Devine, T. M. 1975 *The Tobacco Lords: The Merchants of Glasgow, 1740–90* (Edinburgh)
Devyver, A. 1973 *Le Sang épuré* (Brussels)
Dewar, M. 1964 *Sir Thomas Smith: A Tudor Intellectual in Office*
1970 'A question of plagiarism', *H. J.*, 22
Dewhurst, K. 1975 *Dr Thomas Sydenham* (repr.)
Dewhurst, K. and Doublet, R. 1974 'Thomas Dove', *Med. Hist.*, 18
Deyon, P. 1967 *Amiens, capitale provinicale*
1972 'La concurrence internationale des manufactures', *Annales*, 27
Deyon, P. and Jacquart, J. (eds.) 1978 *Histoire économique et sociale du monde*, vol. II, *1580–1740*
Diamond, A. S. 1974 'The community of the Resettlement', *T. J. H. S. E.*, 24
Diamond, S. 1958 'From organization to society: Virginia', *Amer. J. Sociol.*, 63
1967 'Values as an obstacle to economic growth', *J. Ec. H.*, 27
Dias, J. R. 1981 'Lead, society and politics', *Mid. Hist.*, 6

Dickens, A. G. 1959 *Lollards and Protestants in the Diocese of York, 1509–58* (Oxford)
Dickinson, H. T. 1977 *Liberty and Property: Political Ideology in Eighteenth Century Britain*
1988 'How revolutionary was the Glorious Revolution', *Brit. J. Eight. Cent. Stud.*, 11
Dickinson, M. 1986 *Seventeenth-century Tokens of the British Isles*
Dickson, P. G. M. 1954 'The South Sea Bubble 1720', *Hist. Tod.*, 4
1967 *The Financial Revolution in England*
Dietz, B. 1986 'The North-east coal trade, 1550–1756', *North. Hist.*, 22
1991 'The Royal Bounty and English shipping', *Mar. Mirr.*, 77
Dijk, H. van, and Roorda, D. S. 1976 'Social mobility under the Regents', *Acta Hist. Neer.*, 9
Dijkstra, B. 1987 *Defoe and Economics* (Basingstoke)
Dimock, M. E. 1960 *Administrative Vitality: The Conflict with Bureaucracy*
Dingwall, R. and Lewis, P. (eds.) 1983 *The Sociology of the Professions*
Dion, R. 1959 *Histoire de la vigne et du vin en France*
Disney, A. R. 1977 'The first Portuguese India Company', *Ec. H. R.*, 2nd ser., 30
Divitiis, G. P. de, 1986 'L'Espansione commerciale Inglese', *Studi Storici*, 27
1990 *Mercanti inglesi nell'Italia dei seicento*
Dobb, M. 1946 *Studies in the Development of Capitalism*
Dobson, R. B. 1973 'Admission to the Freedom of York', *Ec. H. R.*, 2nd ser., 26
Dodd, A. H. 1952 *Studies in Stuart Wales* (Cardiff)
Dodge, M. H. 1944 'The financial affairs of a Jacobean gentleman', *Arch. Aliena*, 31
Dodwell, B. 1967 'Holdings and inheritance', *Ec. H. R.*, 2nd ser., 20
Doerflinger, T. H. 1986 *A Vigorous Spirit of Enterprise* (Chapel Hill)
Donagan, B. 1981 'Providence, chance and explanation', *J. Rel. Hist.*, 11
1984 'Puritan ministers and laymen', *H. L. Q.*, 47
Donald, D. 1989 'Mr Deputy Dumpling', *Burl. Mag.*, 131
Donald, M. B. 1961 *Elizabethan Monopolies: The History of the Company of Mineral and Battery Works, 1565–1604* (Edinburgh)
1965 *Elizabethan Copper: The History of the Company of Mines Royal, 1568–1605*
Donaldson, G. 1974 *Scotland: The Shaping of a Nation*
Donnen, E. 1931 'Micajah Perry', *J. Ec. & Bus. Hist.*, 4
Doolittle, I. G. 1975 'The effect of the plague on a provincial town', *Med. Hist.*, 19
1982 *The City of London and its Livery Companies* (Dorchester)
1983 'The City of London's debt to its orphans', *B. I. H. R.*, 56
Doran, S. 1988 'The finances of an Elizabethan nobleman', *Hist. Res.*, 61
Dore, R. P. 1962 'Talent and the social order in Tokugawa, Japan', *P. & P.*, 21
Dorsten, J. van (ed.) 1974 *Ten Studies in Anglo-Dutch Relations*
Dosi, G., Giannetti, R. and Toninelli, P. A. (eds.) 1992 *Technology and Enterprise in a Historical Perspective* (Oxford)
Douch, H. L. 1969 'Cornish potters and pewterers', *J. Roy. Inst. Corn.*, NS, 6
Doursther, H. 1840 *Dictionnaire universel des poids et mesures* (Brussels)
Dovring, F. 1960 *History as a Social Science* (The Hague)

1987 *Productivity and Value: The Political Economy of Measuring Progress* (New York)
Dow, F. D. 1985 *Radicalism in the English Revolution* (Oxford)
Dow, J. 1965 'Sixteenth-century Scania merchants', *Scot. Hist. Rev.*, 44
Downie, J. A. 1979 *Robert Harley and the Press* (Oxford)
Downs, N. (ed.) 1953 *Essays in Honour of Conyers Read* (Chicago)
Dray, W. 1957 *Laws and Explanation in History* (Oxford)
Drummond, J. C. and W. A. 1958 *The Englishman's Food*, rev. D. Hollingsworth
Dublin, L., Lotka, A. J. and Spiegelman, M. 1949 *Length of Life* (New York)
Dubois Rouray, A. 1936 'Un exemple de l'esprit commerciale', *Rev. Quest. Hist.*, 24
Duby, G. 1968 'The diffusion of culture patterns in feudal society', *P. & P.*, 39
1988 *La société dans la Région Maçonnaise aux XIe et XIIe siècles*
Duffy, I. P. H. 1980 'English bankrupts, 1571–1861', *Amer. J. Legal Hist.*, 24
Dugmore, C. W. L. and Duggan, C. (eds.) 1964 *Studies in Church History*, vol. I
Duke, A. C. and Tamsk, C. A. (eds.) 1977 *Britain and the Netherlands*, vol. VI, *War and Society* (The Hague)
Duman, D. 1979 'The creation and diffusion of a professional ideology', *Soc. Res.*, 27
1980 'Pathway to professionals', *J. Soc. Hist.*, 13
Dumbauld, E. 1973 'Legal records', *Amer. Archiv.*, 36
Dummelow, J. 1973 *The Wax Chandlers of London*
Duncan, G. I. O. 1971 *The High Court of Delegates* (Cambridge)
Duncan, T. B. 1975 'Niels Steensgaard and the European–Asian trade', *J. M. H.*, 47
1977 *Atlantic Islands* (Chicago)
Duncan-Jones, R. 1990 *Structure and Scale in the Roman Economy* (Cambridge)
Dunlop, O. J. 1912 *English Apprenticeship and Child Labour*
Dunlop, W. R. B. 1949 'Robert Luddington', *Trans. Worcs. A. S.*, 35
Dunn, J. 1906 *The Reformed Library Keeper* (Chicago)
Dunn, J. 1969 *The Political Thought of John Locke* (Cambridge)
(ed.) 1989 *The Economic Limits to Modern Politics* (Cambridge)
Dunn, R. S. 1962 *Puritan and Yankee: The Winthrop Dynasty* (Princeton)
1963 'The downfall of the Bermuda Company', *Wm & Mary Q.*, 20
1969 'The Barbados census of 1680', *Wm & Mary Q.*, 26
1972 *Sugar and Slaves* (Chapel Hill)
1974 'The Barbados census of 1650', *J. Barb. Mus. & Hist. Soc.*, 34
Dunn, R. S. and M. M. (eds.) 1986 *The World of William Penn* (Philadelphia)
Dures, A. 1983 *English Catholicism, 1558–1642* (Harlow)
Durston, C. G. 1981 'London and the provinces', *South. Hist.*, 3
Durtnell, C. S. 1974 'The unusual archives of Richard Durtnell & Sons', *Bus. Arch.*, 40
Dutton, R. 1948 *The English Interior, 1500–1900*
Dworzaczek, W. 1977 'La mobilité social de la noblesse polonaise', *Acta Poloniae Historica*, 36
Dyer, A. D. 1965–6 'The economy of Tudor Worcester', *Univ. B'ham H. J.*, 10
1972 *The City of Worcester in the Sixteenth Century* (Leicester)
1977 'English town chronicles', *Loc. Hist.*, 12

1978 'The influence of bubonic plague in England', *Med. Hist.*, 22
1979a 'Northampton in 1524', *Northants. P. & P.*, 6
1979b 'The market towns of southern England', *South. Hist.*, 1
1979c 'Growth and decay of English towns', *Urban Hist. Year.*
1981 'Urban housing', *Post Med. Arch.*, 15
1991 *Decline and Growth of English Towns, 1400–1640* (Basingstoke Stud. Econ. & Soc. Hist.)
Dyrvik, S., Mykland, K. and Oldervoll, J. (eds.) 1979 *The Satellite State in the Seventeenth and Eighteenth centuries* (Bergen)
Earle, P. (ed.) 1974 *Essays in European Economic History, 1500–1800* (Oxford)
1976 *The World of Defoe*
1977 *Monmouth's Rebels*
1989a *The Making of the English Middle Class, 1660–1730*
1989b 'The female labour market in London', *Ec. H. R.*, 2nd ser., 42
Easterbrook, W. T. 1949 ' The climate of enterprise', *Amer. Ec. Rev. Papers & Proc.*, 39
Eberhard, W. 1962 *Social Mobility in Traditional China* (Leiden)
1967 *Guilt and Sin in Traditional China*
Ebner, D. 1971 *Autobiography in Seventeenth-century England* (The Hague)
Edie, C. A. 1966–7 'New building, new taxes and old interests', *J. B. S.*, 6
1970 *The Irish Cattle Bills* (Trans. Amer. Phil. Soc., NS, 60)
1987 'London's gift to Charles II', *H. L. Q.*, 50
Edler, F. 1934 *Glossary of Medieval Terms of Business* (Cambridge, Massachusetts)
Edmond, M. 1978–80 'Limners and picturemakers', *Walpole Soc.*, 47
1987a *Sir William Davenant* (New York)
1987b 'Bury St. Edmunds', *Walpole Soc.*, 53
Edwards, J. D. 1960 'Early book-keeping and its development into accounting', *Bus. Hist. Rev.* 34
Edwards, J. R., Hammersley, G. and Newell, E. 1990 'Cost accounting at Keswick *c.* 1598–1615', *Acc. Hist. Journ.*, 17
Edwards, P. R. 1981 'The cattle trade of Shropshire', *Mid. Hist.*, 6
Eeckaute, D. 1965 'Le commerce russe', *Rev. Hist.*, 233
Eerde, K. S. van, 1961 'The Jacobean baronets', *J. M. H.*, 33
Ehrenberg, R. 1895 *Hamburg und England im Zeitalter der Königin Elisabeth* (Jena)
1963 *Capital and Finance in the Age of the Renaissance* (repr. New York)
Ehrman, J. P. 1953 *The Navy in the Wars of William III* (Cambridge)
Eisenach, E. J. 1981 *Two Worlds of Liberalism* (Chicago)
Eisenstadt, S. N. (ed.) 1968 *The Protestant Ethic and Modernization* (New York)
Eisenstein, E. L. 1979 *The Printing Press as an Agent of Change* (Cambridge), 2 vols.
Eister, A. W. (ed.) 1974 *Changing Perspectives in the Scientific Study of Religion* (New York)
Ekelund, R. B. and Tollison, R. D. 1981 *Mercantilism as a Rent-seeking Society* (College Station, Texas)
Elias, N. 1989 *The Civilising Process*, trans. E. Jephicott (Oxford)
Elliot, J. H. 1963 *The Revolt of the Catalans* (Cambridge)

1971 *The Old World and the New, 1492–1650* (Ithaca)
1989 *Spain and its World, 1500–1700* (New Haven)
Elliot, J. H. and Koenigsberger, H. G. (eds.) 1970 *The Diversity of History: Essays in Honour of Sir Herbert Butterfield* (Ithaca)
Elliott, B. 1984 'The Nevilles', *Rec. Hist.*, 17
Elliott, B. B. 1962 *A History of English Advertising*
Elliott, D. C. 1981 'Elections to Common Council in 1659', *Guild. Stud. Lond. Hist.*, 4
1984 'Thomas Andrews' *H. L. Q.*, 47
Elliott, P. 1972 *The Sociology of the Professions* (New York)
Ellis, F. H. 1965 'The background of the London Dispensary', *J. Hist. Med. & All. Sc.*, 20
1969 *Twentieth Century Interpretations of Robinson Crusoe* (Englewood Cliffs)
Ellis, I. P. 1970 'The archbishop and the usurers', *J. Eccles. Hist.*, 21
Ellis, J. M. 1981a *A Study of the Business Fortunes of William Cotesworth, 1688–1726*
1981b 'A bold adventurer', *North. Hist.*, 17
Elton, C. I. and Mackay, H. J. H. 1897 *Robinson on Gavelkind*, 5th edn
Elton, G. R. 1961 'Stuart government', *P. & P.*, 20
1967 *The Practice of History* (Sydney)
1973 *Reform and Renewal: Thomas Cromwell and the Commonweal* (Cambridge)
1976 'Tudor government III: the Court', *T. R. H. S.*, 5th ser., 26
1977 'The historian's social function', *T. R. H. S.*, 5th ser., 27
1986 *The Parliament of England, 1559–81* (Cambridge)
1991 *Return to Essentials* (Cambridge)
Eltringham, G. J. 1953 'The timber wharf of the Carpenters Company', *Guild. Misc.*, 1
Elvin, M. 1973 *The Pattern of the Chinese Past*
Emmer, P. C. (ed.) 1986 *Colonialism and Migration* (Higham)
Emmison, F. G. (ed.) 1973 *Elizabethan Life: Morals and the Church Courts* (Chelmsford)
(ed.) 1980 *Elizabethan Life: Wills of Essex Gentry and Yeomen* (Chelmsford)
Endrei, W. and Egan, G. 1982 'The sealing of cloth', *Text. Hist.*, 13
Englefield, W. A. D. 1923 *The History of the Painter Stainers Company*
English, B. 1990 *The Great Landowners of East Yorkshire, 1530–1910*
English, B. and Saville, J. 1980 'Family settlements', *Ec. H. R.*, 2nd ser., 33
1983 *Strict Settlements. A Guide for Historians* (Hull)
The Entrepreneur 1957 (Papers published by the Econ. Hist. Soc., Cambridge)
Epstein, S. A. 1988 'Business cycles and a sense of time', *Bus. Hist. Rev.*, 62
Erickson, A. L. 1990 'Common law versus common practice', *Ec. H. R.*, 2nd ser., 43
Erickson, E. H. 1959 *Identity and the Life Cycle: Selected Papers* (New York)
1963a *Identity, Youth and Crisis* (New York)
1963b *Childhood and Society*, 2nd edn (New York)
Erikson, K. T. 1966 *Wayward Puritans* (New York)
Erlington, C. R. 1965 'Church livings in Gloucestershire, 1650', *T. B. G. A. S.*, 83
1966 'The records of the Cordwainers Society of Tewkesbury', *T. B. G. A. S.*, 85

Esdaile, K. A. 1946 *English Church Monuments* (New York)
Esherick, J. W. and Rankin, M. B. (eds.) 1990 *Chinese Local Elites and Patterns of Dominance* (Berkeley)
Esmonin, E. 1913 *La Taille en Normandie en temps de Colbert*
Esper, T. 1967 'The *odnodvortsy* and the Russian nobility', *S. E. E. R.*, 45
Evans, E. J. 1970 'Tything customs and disputes', *Agric. Hist. Rev.*, 18
Evans, F. M. G. 1920 'Emoluments of the Principal Secretaries', *E. H. R.*, 35
1923 *The Principal Secretary of State* (Manchester)
Evans, J. T. 1974 'The decline of oligarchy', *J. B. S.*, 14
1979 *Seventeenth-century Norwich: Politics, Religion and Government, 1620–90* (Oxford)
Evans, N. 1985 *The East Anglian Linen Industry, 1500–1850* (Aldershot)
Evans-Pritchard, E. E. 1937 *Witchcraft, Oracles and Magic among the Azande* (Oxford)
1961 *Anthropology and History* (Manchester)
1962 *Essays in Social Anthropology*
Everitt, A. M. 1957 *The County Committee of Kent in the Civil War* (Leicester)
1960 *Suffolk and the Great Rebellion* (Suff. Rec. Soc., 3)
1961 *The Community of Kent and the Great Rebellion* (Leicester)
1962–3 Review of W. K. Jordan, in *Ec. H. R.*, 2nd ser., 16
1965 'Social mobility', *P. & P.*, 32
1968a 'Urban growth and inland trade, 1570–1770', *The Local Historian*, 8
1968b 'The peers and the provinces', *Agric. Hist. Rev.*, 16
1969 *Change in the Provinces* (Leicester)
(ed.) 1973 *Perspectives in English Urban History*
1975 'The primary towns of England', *Loc. Hist.*, 11
1978 'Courts, country and town', *T. R. H. S.*, 5th ser., 29
1985 *Landscape and Community in England*
Ewald, W. B. 1956 *The Newsmen of Queen Anne* (Oxford)
Ewen, C. H. L'Estrange 1932 *Lotteries and Sweepstakes*
Fairbank, J. K. 1953 *Trade and Diplomacy on the China Coast* (Cambridge, Massachusetts)
Fairchild, B. 1954 *Messrs William Pepperell* (Ithaca)
Fairholt, F. W. 1834–44 *Lord Mayors' Pageants* (Percy Soc., 10)
Fanfani, A. 1951 'La préparation intellectuelle et professionnelle', *Le Moyen Age*, 57
Faraday, M. A. 1976 'The returns of the Ludlow poll tax return of 1667', *Trans. Shrop. Arch. & Nat. Hist. Soc.*, 59
Farnell, J. E. 1963–4 'The Navigation Act of 1651', *Ec. H. R.*, 2nd ser., 16
1967 'The usurpation of honest London householders: Barebones Parliament', *E. H. R.*, 82
1977 'The social and intellectual basis of London's role in the Civil War', *J. M. H.*, 49
Farnie, D. A. 1962–3 'Commercial empire of the Atlantic, 1607–1783', *Ec. H. R.*, 2nd ser., 15
Faroqhi, S. 1984 *Towns and Townsmen of Ottoman Anatolia, 1520–1650* (Cambridge)
Farr, M. W. 1968 *The Fetherstons of Packwood* (Dugdale Soc. Occ. Papers, 18)
Farrer, E. 1908 *Portraits in Suffolk Houses*

Farrington, A. 1991 *The English Factory in Japan, 1613–23*
Feather, J. 1979 'Country Book Trade Apprentices, 1710–60', *Pub. Hist.*, 6
Febvre, L. 1911 *Philip II et la Franche-Comté* (thèse, Paris)
1948 'Travail', *J. Psych. Norm. & Path.*
(ed.) 1973 *A New Kind of History*, ed. P. Burke, trans. K. Folca
Fedorowicz, J. K. 1976 'Anglo-Polish commerce', *J. Eur. Ec. Hist.*, 5
1980 *England's Baltic Trade in the Early Seventeenth Century* (Cambridge)
(ed.) 1982 *A Republic of Nobles* (Cambridge)
Feigl, M. and Brodbeck, M. (eds.) 1953 *Readings in the Philosophy of Science* (New York)
Feiling, Sir Keith, 1955 *Warren Hastings*
Feingold, M. 1984 *The Mathematician's Apprenticeship: Science, Universities and Society in England, 1560–1640* (Cambridge)
(ed.) 1990 *Before Newton: The Life and Times of Isaac Barrow* (Cambridge)
Ferber, M. 1990 'The ideology of "The Merchant of Venice"', *Eng. Lit. Ren.*, 20
Ferguson, A. B. 1960 *The Indian Summer of English Chivalry* (Durham, North Carolina)
1965 *The Articulate Citizen of the English Renaissance* (Durham, North Carolina)
Ferguson, W. C. 1976 'Stationers Company Poor Book, 1608–1700', *The Library*, 31
Ferguson, W. S. 1972 'Mathew Springham', *Trans. Lond. & Midd. A. S.*, 23
Ferrier, R. W. 1970 'The trade between India and the Persian Gulf', *Bengal P. & P.*, 89
Ferris, J. P. 1965 'The gentry of Dorset', *Geneal. Mag.*, 15
Feyerhaven, W. R. 1976 'The status of the schoolmaster', *Hist. Educ.*, 5
Ffoulkes, C. J. 1969 *The Gunfounders of England*, 2nd edn (York)
Fideler, P. A. and Mayer, T. F. (eds.) 1992 *Political Thought and the Tudor Commonwealth*
Field, A. J. (ed.) 1989 *The Future of Economic History* (Boston)
Fielder, K. 1968 'Samuel Smiles and self help', *Victorian Studies*, 12
Fieldhouse, R. and Jennings, B. 1978 *A History of Richmond and Swaledale* (Chichester)
Fildes, V. 1986 *Breast, Bottles and Babies* (Edinburgh)
1988 'The English wet nurse, 1538–1800', *Med. Hist.*, 32
(ed.) 1990 *Women as Mothers in Pre-industrial England*
Finberg, H. P. R. 1956 *The Gostwicks of Willington* (Beds. Hist. Soc., 36)
(ed.) 1957 *Gloucestershire Studies* (Leicester)
(ed.) 1962 *Approaches to History: A Symposium*
Finch, M. E. 1956 *The Wealth of Five Northamptonshire Families, 1560–1640* (Northants. Rec. Soc., 19)
Fincham, K. 1990 *Prelate as Pastor: The Episcopate of James I* (Oxford)
Finkelpeare, P. J. 1990 *Court and Country Politics in the Plays of Beaumont and Fletcher* (Princeton)
Finlay, R. 1980 *Politics in Renaissance Venice*
Finlay, R. A. P. 1979 'Population and fertility in London, 1580–1650', *J. Fam. Hist.*, 4
1981 *Population and Metropolis: The Demography of London, 1580–1650* (Cambridge)

Finlayson, M. G. 1973 'Puritanism and Puritans: labels on libels', *Canad. J. Hist.*, 8
1983 *Historians, Puritans and the English Revolution* (Toronto)
Finley, M. I. 1970 'Aristotle and economic analysis', *P. & P.*, 47
(ed.) 1974 *Studies in Ancient Society*
(ed.) 1976 *Studies in Roman Property* (Cambridge)
1985 *The Ancient Economy*, 2nd edn
Firebrace, C. W. 1932 *Honest Harry*
Firth, Sir Charles, 1907 *Notes on the Diplomatic Relations of England and Germany* (Oxford)
1932 'Macaulay's third chapter', *History*, 17
Firth, R. 1944 'Anthropological background to work', *Occ. Psych.*, 22
1964 *Elements of Social Organization* (repr. Boston)
Firth, R. and Yamey, B. S. 1964 *Capital Saving and Credit in Peasant Societies*
Fischer, D. H. 1970 *Historical Fallacies* (New York)
1989 *Albion's Seed* (Oxford)
Fisher, F. J. 1936 *A Short History of the Company of Horners* (pr. print.)
(ed.) 1961 *Essays in the Economic and Social History of Tudor and Stuart England* (Cambridge)
1990 *London and the English Economy, 1500–1700*
Fisher, H. E. S. 1968 *The South West and the Sea* (Exeter)
1971 *The Portuguese Trade, 1700–70*
(ed.) 1989 *Innovations in Shipping and Trade* (Exeter Maritime Studies, 6)
Fishlow, A. 1974 'The new economic history revisited', *J. Eur. Ec. Hist.*, 3
Fissel, M. C. (ed.) 1991 *War and Government in Britain, 1598–1650* (New York)
Fitch, D. E. 1965 'London merchants on Bristol Bridge', *T. B. G. A. S.*, 74
Fitch, N. 1984 'Statistical fantasies and historical facts', *Hist. Meth.*, 17
Fitzhugh, T. 1981 'The India Office records', *Fam. Hist.*, NS, 12
1983 'East India Company families', *J. Fam. Hist.*, 12
Fitzmaurice, E. G. 1895 *Sir William Petty 1623–87*
Flaherty, D. H. (ed.) 1969 *Essays in the History of Early American Law* (Chapel Hill)
Flandrin, J. L. 1977 'Repression and change', *J. Fam. Hist.*, 2
Flaningham, J. 1977 'The Occasional Conformity controversy', *J. B. S.*, 17
Fleming, D. 1979 'The gentry in Stuart Leicestershire', *Leics. Hist.*, 2
Fletcher, A. 1975 *A County Community in Peace and War: Sussex, 1600–60*
1981 *Outbreak of Civil War*
1988 *Reform and the Provinces* (New Haven)
Fletcher, A. and Stevenson, J. (eds.) 1985 *Order and Disorder in Early Modern England* (Cambridge)
Fletcher, G. P. 1975 'The metamorphosis of larceny', *Harvard Law Review*, 89
Flinn, M. W. 1962 *Men of Iron: The Crowleys in the Early Iron Industry* (Edinburgh)
1981 *The European Demographic System, 1500–1820* (Brighton)
Flinn, M. W. and Smout, T. C. (eds.) 1974 *Essays in Social History* (Oxford)
Floud, R. 1973 *Introduction to Quantitative Methods for Historians*
(ed.) 1974 *Essays in Quantitative Economic History* (Oxford)
Fogel, R. W. and Elton, G. R. 1983 *Which Road to the Past?* (New Haven)
Fohlen, C. and Godechot, J. (eds.) 1979 *La Revolution américaine et l'Europe*

Foister, S. 1981 'Paintings in sixteenth-century English inventories', *Burl. Mag.*, 123
Forbes, T. R. 1971 *Chronicles from Aldgate* (New Haven)
1976 'By what disease or casualty', *J. Hist. Med.*, 31
1980 'Weavers and cordwainers', *Guild. Stud. Lond. Hist.*, 4
Forman, R. and Turner, M. 1980 'There is no future for business history', *Bus. Hist.*, 22
Forrest, H. E. 1911 *The old houses of Shrewsbury* (Shrewsbury)
Forse, J. H. 1990 'Art imitates business', *J. Pop. Cult.*, 24
Forster, G. C. F. 1983 'Government in provincial England', *T. R. H. S.*, 5th ser., 33
Forster, R. 1960 *The Nobility of Toulouse in the Eighteenth Century* (Baltimore)
1961 'The noble wine producers of the Bordelais', *Ec. H. R.*, 2nd ser., 14
1978 'The achievements of the *Annales* school', *J. Ec. H.*, 38
Forster, R. and Greene, J. P. 1970 *Pre-conditions of Revolution in Early Modern Europe* (Baltimore)
Fortescue, Sir J. W. 1910 *History of the British Army*, vol. I
Fortune, S. A. 1984 *Merchants and Jews* (Gainesville)
Foss, E. 1848–64 *The Judges of England*
1870 *Biographia Juridica, 1066–1870*
Foster, F. F. 1972 'Merchants and bureaucrats in Elizabethan London', *Guild. Misc.*, 4
1977 *The Politics of Stability: A Portrait of the Rulers of Elizabethan London* (R.H.S.)
Foster, I. L. and Alcock. L. (eds.) 1963 *Culture and Environment: Essays in Honour of Sir Cyril Fox*
Foster, M. 1978 'Sir Richard Foster', *Rec. Hist.*, 14
Foster, S. 1971 *Their Solitary Way* (New Haven)
Foster, Sir William, 1924 *The East India House*
1926 *John Company*
Fowkes, J. W. 1965 'The minute book of York Court of Quarter Sessions', *Yorks. Arch. J.*, 163
Fox, D. R. 1926 *Caleb Heathcote, Gentleman Colonist, 1692–1721* (New York)
Fox, F. F. 1880 *Some Account of the Merchant Taylors of Bristol* (Bristol)
Fox, H. S. A. and Butler, R. A. (eds.) 1979 *Change in the Countryside: Essays on Rural England, 1500–1900*
Fox, L. (ed.) 1956 *English Historical Scholarship in the Sixteenth and Seventeenth Centuries*
1962 'The Coventry guilds', *Trans. B'ham A. S.*, 78
Foxon, W. 1963 'Libertine literature in England, 1660–1745', *Book Collector*, 12
Francis, A. D. 1972 *The Wine Trade*
Francis, C. W. 1983 'The structure of juridical administration', *Columbia Law Rev.*, 83
Francois, M. E. 1966 'The social and economic development of Halifax, 1558–1640', *Proc. Leeds Phil. & Lit. Soc.*, 11
Frank, C. M. 1984 'The early hostmen', *Arch. Aliena*, 5th ser., 12
Frank, C. M. and Einsley, K. 1971 'Some early recorders of Newcastle, *Arch. Aliena*, 4th ser., 49

Frank, J. 1955 *The Levellers* (Cambridge, Massachusetts)
Frappel, L. O. (ed.) 1979 *Principalities, Powers and Estates* (Adelaide)
Fraser, C. M. and Emsley, K. 1978 'Newcastle Merchant Adventurers from West Yorkshire', *Arch. Aliena*, 5th ser., 6
Fraser, D. (ed.) 1980 *A History of Modern Leeds* (Manchester)
Fraser, D. and Sutcliffe A. I. 1983 *The Pursuit of Urban History*
Fraser, J. A. 1935 *Spain and the West Country*
Fraser, P. 1956 *The Intelligence of the Secretaries of State, 1660–88* (Cambridge)
Freeman, G. 1967 'A Lord Mayor's autobiography: John Fryer, 1671–1726', *Hist. Tod.*, 17
Freeman, K. B. 1976 'The significance of MacClelland's variables', *Ec. Dev. & Cult. Ch.*, 24
French, A. 1964 *The Growth of the Athenian Economy*
French, C. J. 1992 'Crowded with traders', *Lond. J.*, 17
French, D. 1972 'A sixteenth-century English merchant in Anatolia', *Anatolian Stud.*, 22
Freudenberger, H. 1977 *The Industrialisation of Brno, a Central European City*, Pasold Pub. vol. VI (Edington)
Freund, E., Mitchell, W. E. and Wigmore, J. H. (eds.) 1907–9 *Select Essays in Anglo-American Legal History* (Boston), 3 vols.
Friis, A. 1927 *Alderman Cokayne's Project and the Cloth Trade 1603–25*
Frijhof, W. T. M. 1981 *La Société néerlandaise et ses gradués, 1575–1814* (Amsterdam)
Fromm, E. 1932 *Die Psychoanalytische Charakterologie* (Zeitschrift für Sozialforschung, 1)
Fry, A. R. 1935 *John Bellers, 1654–1725*
Fry, F. M. 1907 *The Pictures of the Merchant Taylors Company*
Fry, G. K. 1969 *Statesmen in Disguise*
Fryde, E. B. 1983 *Studies in Medieval Trade and Finance*
1988 *William de la Pole*
Fuhrmann, J. T. 1972 *The Origins of Capitalism in Russia* (Chicago)
Fujimura, T. H. 1952 *The Restoration Comedy of Wit* (Princeton)
Fumenton, P. 1991 *Cultural Aesthetics* (Chicago)
Furber, E. C. (ed.) 1966 *Changing Views of British History*
Furber, H. 1951 *John Company at Work* (Cambridge, Massachusetts)
1977 *Rival Empires of Trade in the Orient, 1600–1800* (Oxford)
Furet, F. 1971 'Quantitative history', *Daedalus*, 100
Furniss, E. S. 1920 *The Position of the Labourer in a System of Nationalism* (New York)
Fussner, F. S. 1962 *The Historical Revolution, 1580–1640*
Gage, J. 1822 *The History and Antiquities of Hengrave in Suffolk*
Gair, W. R. 1982 *The Children of Pauls* (Cambridge)
Galambo, L. 1966 'Business history', *Expl. Ent. H.*, 2nd ser., 4
Gale, G. F. and Lawton, G. H. (eds.) 1969 *Settlement and Encounter: Geographical Studies Presented to Sir Grenfell Price*
Galenson, D. W. 1978–9 'Middling people', *Wm & Mary Q.*, 3rd ser., 35–6
1981 *White Servitude in Colonial America* (Cambridge)
1985 'Population turnover in the English West Indies', *J. Ec. H.*, 45

1986 *Traders, Planters and Slaves* (Cambridge)
(ed.) 1989 *Markets in History: Economic Studies of the Past* (Cambridge)
Gallman, R. E. 1977 (ed.) *Recent Developments in the Study of Business and Economic History: Essays in Memory of H. E. Knooss* (Greenwich, Connecticut)
Gammon, S. R. 1977 *Statesman and Schemer: William First Lord Paget* (Newton Abbot)
Garcia-Valdecasas, A. 1948 *El Hildago y el honor*, 2nd edn (Madrid)
Gardiner, J. K. 1977 'Elizabethan psychology', *J. H. I.*, 38
Gardiner, P. 1952 *The Nature of Historical Explanation* (Oxford)
Garnier, S. P. 1954 *Evolution of Cost Accounting to 1925* (Montgomery, Alabama)
Garnsey, P., Hopkins, K. and Whittaker, C. R. (eds.) 1983 *Trade in the Ancient Economy*
Garrard, R. P. 1980 'English probate inventories and the English interior', *A. A. G. Bijdragen*, 23
Garrard, T. 1852 *Edward Colston*, ed. S. G. Tovey (Bristol)
Garrett, C. H. 1938 *The Marian Exiles* (Cambridge)
Garrett, K. I. 1977 'Marie Hackett, Crosby Hall and Gresham College', *Guild. Stud. Lond. Hist.*, 3
Gascoigne, J. 1985 'The Universities and the Scientific Revolution', *Hist. Sc.*, 23
Gascon, R. 1971 *Lyons et ses marchands: Grand Commerce et vie urbaine au XVIe siècle, 1520–80*, 2 vols.
Gatrell, V. A. C., Lenman, B. and Parker, G. (eds.) 1980 *Crime and the Law* (Princeton)
Gaunt, J. L. 1978 'Popular fiction and the ballad market', *Bibliog. Soc. Amer. Papers*, 72
Gautier, D. P. 1966 'The role of inheritance in Locke's political theory', *Canad. J. Econ. & Pol. Sc.*,
Gay, E. F. 1923–4 'The rhythm of history', *Harv. Grad. Mag.*, 32
1928–9 'Letters from a sugar plantation in Nevis, 1723–32', *J. Ec. & Bus. Hist.*, 1
1932 *Facts and Factors in Economic History* (Cambridge, Massachusetts)
1939 'The Temples of Stowe and their debts', *H. L. Q.*, 2
Gayley, C. M. 1914 *Francis Beaumont, Dramatist*
Geertz, C. 1980 *The Interpretation of Cultures* (Cambridge)
Geiger, E. 1976 *Die soziale Elite der Hansestadt Lemgo* (Detmold)
Gellner, E. 1965 *Thought and Change* (Chicago)
1988 *Plough, Sword and Book*
Gemery, H. A. 1980 'Emigration from the British Isles to the New World, 1630–1700', *Res. Ec. Hist.*, 5
Gemery, H. A. and Hogendorn, J. S. (eds.) 1979 *The Uncommon Market*
Génichot, L. 1962 'La noblesse au Moyen Age dans l'ancienne Francie', *Annales*, 16
Genovese, E. F. 1973 'The many faces of moral economy', *P. & P.*, 58
Gent, L. and Llewellyn, N. (eds.) 1990 *Renaissance Bodies: The Human Figure in English Culture, c.1540–1660*
Gentles, I. J. 1973 'The sales of Crown land during the English Revolution', *Ec. H. R.*, 2nd ser., 26

1976 'The purchasers of Northamptonshire Crown lands, 1649–60', *Mid. Hist.*, 3
1978 'London Levellers and the English Revolution', *J. Eccles. Hist.*, 29
1980 'The sale of bishops' lands, 1646–60', *E. H. R.*, 95
1983 'The struggle for London in the Second Civil War', *H. J.*, 26
1991 *The New Model Army in England, Ireland and Scotland, 1645–53*
Gentles, I. J. and Sheils, W. J. 1981 *Confiscation and Restoration: The Archbishopric Estate and the Civil War* (Borthwick Inst., 59)
George, C. H. 1957 'English Calvinist opinion on usury, 1600–40', *J. H. I.*, 18
1968 'Puritanism as history and historiography', *P. & P.*, 41
1971 'The making of the English bourgeoisie', *Sc. & Soc.*, 35
1976 'Hill's century', *Sc. & Soc.*, 40
George, C. H. and K. 1961 *The Protestant Mind of the English Reformation, 1570–1640* (Princeton)
George, E. and S. 1988 *Guide to the Probate Inventories of the Deanery of the Diocese of Bristol, 1542–1804* (Bristol Rec. Soc.)
George, R. H. 1936 'Parliamentary elections and electioneering', *T. R. H. S.*, 4th ser., 19
Georgescu-Roegen, N. 1971 *The Entropy Law and the Economic Process* (Cambridge)
Gerbet, M.-C. 1970 *La Noblesse dans le royaume de Castile, 1454–1516*
Gerhard, P. 1960 *Pirates of the West Coast of New Spain* (Glendale)
Gerschenkron, A. 1962 *Economic Backwardness in Historical Perspective* (Cambridge, Massachusetts)
1968 *Continuity in History and Other Essays* (Cambridge, Massachusetts)
Gervais, C. 1870–3 'Sur des verreries de la Normandie', *Bull. Soc. Antiquaires de Normandie*, 6
Gibb, M. A. 1947 *John Lilburne the Leveller*
Gibbon, J. S. W. 1980 'Inventories in the records of the P.C.C.', *Loc. Hist.* 14
Gibbons, B. 1980 *Jacobean City Comedy*, 2nd edn
Giesey, R. E. 1977 'Rules of inheritance', *A. H. R.*, 82
1983 'State building in early modern France', *J. M. H.*, 55
Gilchrist, J. 1969 *The Church and Economic Activity in the Middle Ages* (New York)
Gill, C. 1930 *Studies in Midland History*
1952 *History of Birmingham* (Oxford), vol. I
1961 *Merchants and Mariners of the Eighteenth Century*
Gill, E. 1935 *Work and Leisure*
Gill, M. A. V. 1980 'The Newcastle goldsmiths and the capital', *Arch. Aliena*, 5th ser., 8
Gillespie, H. G. 1944 'The rediscovery of an Elizabethan Merchant Adventurer', *Genealog. Mag.*, 9
Gillespie, J. E. 1920 *The Influence of Overseas Expansion on England to 1700* (New York)
Gillespie, R. 1985 *Colonial Ulster, 1600–1641: The Settlement of East Ulster* (Cork)
Gillett, E. 1970 *A History of Grimsby*
Gillett, E. and MacMahon, K. A. 1980 *A History of Hull* (Oxford)

Gilmore, W. J. 1984 *Psychohistorical Inquiry* (New York)
Giner, S. 1968 *Continuity and Change: The Social Stratification of Change* (Reading)
Girouard, M. 1990 *The English Town* (New Haven)
Girtin, T. 1958 *The Golden Ram: A Narrative History of the Clothworkers Company, 1528–1958*
1964 *The Triple Crowns: The Drapers Company, 1364–1964*
1975 *The Mark of the Sword*
Gittings, C. 1984 *Death, Burial and the Individual in Early Modern England*
1991 'Probate accounts, a neglected source', *Loc. Hist.*, 21
Given-Wilson, C. 1987 *The English Nobility in the Late Middle Ages*
Glade, W. P. 1967 'Approaches to a theory of entrepreneurial function', *Expl. Ec. H.*, 2nd ser., 4
Glamann, K. 1958 *Dutch Asiatic Trade, 1620–1740* (Copenhagen)
Glasgow, T. 1970 'Maturing of naval administration, 1556–64', *Mar. Mirr.*, 56
Glass, D. V. 1968 'Notes on the demography of London', *Daedalus*, 97
Glass, D. V. and Eversley, D. E. C. (eds.) 1965, 1974 *Population in History: Essays in Historical Demography*
Glass, D. V. and Revelle, R. (eds.) 1972 *Population and Social Change*
Gleason, J. H. 1969 *The Justice of the Peace in England, 1558–1640* (Oxford)
Glinski, G. von, 1964 *Die Königsberger Kaufmannschaft des 17 und 18 Jahrhundert* (Marburg)
Gloag, J. 1964 *The Englishman's Chair*
Glover, M. 1980 'The purchase of commissions', *J. Soc. Army Hist. Res.*, 58
Godelin, M. 1966 *Rationalité et irrationalité en économie*
Godfrey, E. S. 1976 *The Development of English Glassmaking, 1560–1640* (Oxford)
Goffman, E. 1967 *Interactive Ritual: Essays in Face to Face Behaviour*
Goitein, S. D. 1956–7 'The rise of the Near Eastern bourgeoisie', *Cahiers d'Hist. Mond.*, 3
1966 *Studies in Islamic History and Institutions* (Leiden)
Goldberg, P. J. (ed.) 1992 *Woman is a Worthy Wight: Women in English Society, 1200–1500*
Goldie, M. 1980 'Roots of true Whiggery', *Hist. Pol. Thought*, 1
1983 'John Locke and Anglican Royalism', *Pol. Stud.*, 31
1992 'John Locke's circle and James II', *H. J.*, 35
Goldsmith, M. M. 1976 'Public virtue and private vices', *Eight. Cent. Stud.*, 9
1977 'Mandeville and the spirit of capitalism', *J. B. S.*, 17
Goldstone, J. A. 1991a *Revolution and Rebellion in Early Modern Europe* (Berkeley)
1991b 'The causes of long waves', *Res. Ec. Hist. Supp.*, 6
Goldthwaite, R. A. 1968 *Private Wealth in Renaissance Florence* (Princeton)
1972 'Schools and teachers of commercial arithmetic', *J. Eur. Ec. Hist.*, 1
1987 'The Medici bank and Florentine capitalism', *P. & P.*, 114
1994 *Wealth and the Demand for Art in Italy, 1300–1600*
Gollard, J. 1989 'The apprenticeship system', *Genealog. Mag.*, 23
Gomes, L. 1987 *Foreign Trade and the National Economy*
Goodbody, O. C. 1956 'Arthur Sharp, wool merchant, 1643–1707', *J. Friends*

Hist. Soc., 48
1978 'Inventories of five Dublin Quaker merchants', *Irish Ancestor*, 10
Goodfriend, J. D. 1992 *Before the Melting Pot: Society and Culture in Colonial New York, 1664–1730* (Princeton)
Goodman, W. L. 1972 'Woodworking apprentices', *Ind. Arch.*, 9
1974 'Bristol apprenticeship registers, 1532–1658', *Mar. Mirr.*, 60
Goodwin, A. C. (ed.) 1953 *The European Nobility in the Eighteenth Century*
Goody, J. R. 1962 *Death, Property and the Ancestors* (Stanford)
(ed.) 1968 *Literacy in Traditional Societies* (Cambridge)
1970 'Marriage prestations', *Comp. Stud. Soc. Hist.*, 1
1973 'Strategies of heirship', *Comp. Stud. Soc. Hist.*, 15
1976 *Production and Reproduction* (Cambridge)
1986 *The Development of the Family and Marriage in Europe* (Cambridge)
1990 *The Oriental, the Ancient and the Primitive* (Cambridge)
Goody, J. R., Thirsk, J. and Thompson, E. P. (eds.) 1976 *Family and Inheritance* (Cambridge)
Goose, N. R. 1980 'Household size and structure in early Stuart Cambridge', *Soc. Hist.*, 5
1982a 'The Dutch in Colchester', *Imm. & Min.*, 1
1982b 'England's pre-industrial urban economies', *Urban Hist. Year.*
1984 'Decay and regeneration in seventeenth-century Reading', *South. Hist.*, 6
1986 'In search of the urban variable, 1500–1650', *Ec. H. R.*, 2nd ser., 39
Gordon, B. J. 1974 *Economic Analysis before Adam Smith*
Gordon, D. H. 1970 'The book collector', *Harv. Lib. Bull.*, 18
Gordon, G. and Dicks, B. (eds.) 1983 *Scottish Urban History* (Aberdeen)
Goreau, A. 1980 *Reconstructing Aphra* (New York)
Goring, J. 1975 'Social change and military decline in mid Tudor England', *History*, 60
Goss, C. W. F. 1929–33 'Sir Paul Pindar', *Trans. Lond. & Midd. A. S.*, NS, 6
1932 *The London Directories, 1677–1855*
John Goswell and Company Limited, 1677–1947 (1947)
Gottfried, R. S. 1978 *Epidemic Disease in Fifteenth-century England* (Leicester)
1982 *Bury St Edmunds and the Urban Crisis, 1290–1539* (Princeton)
Gottschalk, L. (ed.) 1963 *Generalization in the Writing of History* (Chicago)
Goubert, P. 1959 *Familles marchandes sous l'ancien régime*
1960 *Beauvais et le Beauvaisis de 1600 à 1730*
1969 *L'Ancien Régime*, vol. I, *La Société*
1991 *Louis XIV et vingt millions de France*, rev. edn
Gough, B. M. 1970 'The Adventurers of England trading into Hudson Bay', *Albion*, 2
Gough, J. W. 1932 *The Superlative Prodigal: A Life of Thomas Bushell* (Bristol)
1950 *John Locke, Political Philosopher* (Oxford)
1964 *Sir Hugh Myddelton* (Oxford)
1967 *Mines of Mendip*, rev. edn (Newton Abbot)
1969 *The Rise of the Entrepreneur*
Gould, J. D. 1954–5 'The trade depression of the early 1620s', *Ec. H. R.*, 2nd ser., 7
1955, 1958 'The trade crisis of the early 1620s', *J. Ec. H.*, 15 and 18

1964–5 'The price revolution reconsidered', *Ec. H. R.*, 2nd ser., 17
1969 'Hypothetical history', *Ec. H. R.*, 2nd ser., 22
1978 'Bittle and Lane on charity', *Ec. H. R.*, 2nd ser., 31
Gould, M. 1987 *Revolution in the Development of Capitalism* (Berkeley)
Grace, F. 1989 'The administration of a will', *Suff. Rev.*, 12
Gragg, L. D. 1991 'Shipmasters in early Barbados' *Mar. Mirr.*, 77
Grampp, W. D. 1948 'Adam Smith and Economic Man', *J. Pol. Econ.*, 56
1950–1 'The Moral Hero and the Economic Man', *Ethics*, 61
1965 *Economic Liberalism* (New York)
Grant, J. 1962 'The gentry of London in the reign of Charles I', *Univ. B'ham H. J.*, 8
Gras, N. S. B. 1933 'Economic rationalism in the late Middle Ages', *Speculum*, 8
1971 *Business and Capitalism* (repr.)
Grassby, R. B. 1958 'Die letzen Verhandlungen zwischen England und die Hanse', *H. Gbl.*, 76
1960 'Social status and commercial enterprise under Louis XIV', *Ec. H. R.*, 2nd ser., 13
1969 'The rate of profit in seventeenth-century England', *E. H. R.*, 84
1970a 'The personal wealth of the business community', *Ec. H. R.*, 2nd ser., 23
1970b 'English merchant capitalism', *P. & P.*, 46
1994 *The English Gentleman in Trade: The Life and Works of Sir Dudley North, 1641–91* (Oxford)
Gravil, R. 1968 'Trading to Spain and Portugal, 1670–1700', *Bus. Hist.*, 10
Gray, I. E. 1945 'Merchants at Alexandretta', *Genealog. Mag.*, 9
1965 'Some seventeenth-century token issues', *T. B. G. A. S.*, 74
Greaves, R. L. 1969 *The Puritan Revolution and Educational Thought* (New Brunswick)
1975 'John Bunyan's Holy War', *Bapt. Q.*, 26
1981a 'The origins of English Sabbatarianism', *Sixt. Cent. J.*, 12
1981b *Society and Religion in Elizabethan England* (Minneapolis)
1985 'The Puritan Nonconformist tradition in England, 1560–1700', *Albion*, 17
1990 *Enemies under his Feet, 1664–77* (Stanford)
Green, I. M. 1978 *The Re-establishment of the Church of England, 1660–63* (Oxford)
1979 'The persecution of scandalous and malignant parish clergy', *E. H. R.*, 94
1981 'Career prospects and clerical conformity', *P. & P.*, 90
Greene, E. 1974 'The Vintners lobby, 1552–68', *Guild. Stud. Lond. Hist.*, 1
1975 'The location of historical records of insurance', *J. Chart. Inst. Ins.*, 72
Greene, J. P. 1988 *Pursuits of Happiness* (Chapel Hill)
Greene, J. P. and Pole, J. R. (eds.) 1984 *Colonial British America* (Baltimore)
Greenfield, L. 1987 'Science and national greatness', *Minerva*, 25
Greenfield, S. A. (ed.) 1986 *Entrepreneurship and Social Change* (Lanham, Maryland)
Greenfield, S. A. and Strickon, A. 1981 'A new paradigm for the study of entrepreneurship and social change', *Ec. Dev. Cult. Ch.*, 29
Greenough, C. N. 1947 *A Bibliography of the Theophrastan Character in English* (Cambridge)
Greenwood, M. 1948 *Medical Statistics from Graunt to Farr* (Cambridge)

Gregg, P. 1961 *Free-born John*
Gregory, T. E. 1921 'The economics of employment', *Economica*, 1
Grell, O. P. 1987 'French and Dutch congregations in London', *Proc. Hug. Soc. Lond.*, 24
1989 *Dutch Calvinists in Early Stuart London* (New York)
Grell, O. P., Israel, J. and Tyacke, N. (eds.) 1991 *From Persecution to Toleration* (Oxford)
Greven, P. J. 1966 'Family structure in seventeenth-century Andover', *Wm & Mary Q.*, 23
1970 *Four Generations: Population, Land and Family in Colonial Andover* (Ithaca)
Greyerz, K. von (ed.) 1984 *Religion and Society in Early Modern Europe, 1500–1800*
Grierson, P. and Perkins, J. W. (eds.) 1956 *Studies in Italian Medieval History Presented to E. M. Jamison* (Papers of the Brit. Sch. Rome, 24)
Griffiths, G. M. 1954 'The Castle Hill Collection', *Nat. Lib. Wales J.*, 8
Griffiths, J. 1972 'Of Plymouth Plantation', *Arizona Q.*
Griffiths, R. G. 1933–5 'Joyce Jeffries of Ham Castle', *Trans. Worcs. A. S.*, NS, 10–11
Grimaud, J. 1983 'Les Port Books anglais', *Canad. J. Hist.*, 18
Grimelet, M. 1957 *Thomas Heywood et le drame domestique Elisabéthain*
Gross, C. 1966 *A Bibliography of British Municipal History*, 2nd edn (Leicester)
Grubb, F. 1992 'Fatherless and friendless', *J. Ec. H.*, 52
Grubb, I. 1930 *Quakerism and Industry before 1800*
Gruenfelder, J. K. 1991 'Nicholas Murford salt producer', *Norf. Arch.*, 41
Gueneau, L. 1919 *L'Organisation du travail à Nevers* (thèse, Paris)
Guilday, P. 1914 *The English Catholic Refugees on the Continent, 1559–1795*
Gunn, J. A. W. 1968 'The civil politics of Peter Paxton', *P. & P.*, 40
1969 *Politics and the Public Interest in the Seventeenth Century*
Gurney Read, J. 1989 *Trades and Industries of Norwich* (Norwich)
Gurvitch, G. D. 1957 'Continuité et discontinuité en histoire', *Annales*, 12
1964 *The Spectre of Social Time* (Dordrecht)
Guth, D. J. and MacKenna, J. W. (eds.) 1982 *Tudor Rule and Revolution: Essays for G. R. Elton* (Cambridge)
Gwynn, R. D. 1976 'The distribution of Huguenot refugees', *Proc. Hug. Soc. Lond.*, 22
1983 'The number of Huguenot immigrants', *J. Hist. Geog.*, 9
1985 *Huguenot Heritage*
Habakkuk, H. J. 1940 'English landownership, 1680–1740', *Ec. H. R.*, 10
1950 'Marriage settlements in the eighteenth century', *T. R. H. S.*, 4th ser., 32
1952–3 'The long-term rate of interest and the price of land', *Ec. H. R.*, 2nd ser., 5
1965 'Landowners and the Civil War', *Ec. H. R.*, 2nd ser., 18
1971 'Economic history and economic theory', *Daedalus*, 100
1978 'The Land Settlement and the Restoration', *T. R. H. S.*, 5th ser., 28
1979–81 'The rise and fall of landed families', *T. R. H. S.*, 5th ser., 29, 30, 31
Hacking, I. 1975 *The Emergence of Probability* (Cambridge)
Hadden, R. W. 1988 'Social relation and the content of early modern science',

Brit. J. Sociol., 39
Hadley, G. 1976 *Citizens and Founders*
Hadwin, J. F. 1978 'Deflating philanthropy', *Ec. H. R.*, 2nd ser., 31
Haffenden, P. S. 1974 *New England and the English Nation, 1689–1713* (Oxford)
Hagen, E. E. 1969 *On the Theory of Social Change*, (Homewood, Illinois)
Haigh, C. 1975 *Reformation and Resistance in Tudor Lancashire* (Cambridge)
1977 'Puritan Evangelicism in the reign of Elizabeth I', *E. H. R.*, 92
(ed.) 1984 *The Reign of Elizabeth I*
(ed.) 1987 *The English Reformation Revised* (Cambridge)
Haines, C. R. 1899 *A Complete Memoir of Richard Haines*
Hainsworth, D. R. 1985 'The essential governor', *Hist. Stud. Univ. of Melbourne*, 21
1988 'The Lowthers' younger sons', *Trans. Cumb. & West. Antiq. & Arch. Soc.*, 88
1993 *Stewards, Lords and People* (Cambridge)
Halcrow, E., Harbottle, B. and Slipper, J. 1952 'Merchant charities of Newcastle', *Arch. Aliena*, 30
Hald, A. 1990 *History of Probability and Statistics and their Application before 1750*
Hale, J. R. (ed.) 1973 *Renaissance Venice* (Totowa, New Jersey)
Haley, K. H. D. 1986 *An English Diplomat in the Low Countries: Sir William Temple and John de Witt, 1665–72* (Oxford)
1988 *The British and the Dutch*
Halfpenny, E. 1959 'The cities' loyalty', *Guild. Misc.*, 10
Hall, A. R. 1965 'The Scientific and Puritan Revolution', *History*, 50
Hall, B. 1933 'The trade of Newcastle upon Tyne and the North-east coast, 1600–40' (unpub. Ph.D. thesis, London)
1934 'The trade of Newcastle', *B. I. H. R.*, 12
Hall, H. and Nichols, F. J. 1929 (eds.) *Select Tracts and Table Books relating to English Weights and Measures, 1100–1742* (Camd. Misc. 3rd ser., 15)
Hall, I. V. 1944 'Whitson Court sugar house', *T. B. G. A. S.*, 65
1949 'John Knight, sugar refiner', *T. B. G. A. S.*, 68
1951 'The Grant of Arms to the Cary family', *T. B. G. A. S.*, 70
1957 'Temple St. sugar house', *T. B. G. A. S.*, 76
1965 'The Daubenys', *T. B. G. A. S.*, 74
Hall, J. R. 1980 'The time of history', *Hist. & Theory*, 19
Hall, J. W. 1961 *Japanese History: New Dimension of Approach* (Washington)
Hall, J. W. and Jansen, M. B. (eds.) 1968 *Studies in the Institutional History of Early Modern Japan* (Princeton)
Hall, M. G. 1960 *Edward Randolf* (Chapel Hill)
Hallan, H. A. N. 1967 'Lamport Hall revisited', *The Book Collector*, 16
Haller, W. 1938 *The Rise of Puritanism, 1570–1643*
Halls, Z. 1970 *Men's Costume, 1580–1750* (HMSO)
Halperin, J. 1945 *Le role des assurances dans le capitalisme moderne* (Neufchatel)
Hamard, J. 1965 'Le drame bourgeois: l'influence de Lillo', *Rev. Litt. Comp.*, 39
Hambrick-Stowe, C. E. 1982 *Practice of Piety* (Chapel Hill)
Hamilton, B. 1951–2 'The medical profession in the eighteenth century', *Ec. H. R.*, 2nd ser., 4

Hamilton, E. J. 1929 'American treasure and the rise of capitalism', *Economica*, 9
1948 'Role of monopoly in overseas enterprise', *Amer. Ec. Rev.*, 38
Hammer, C. J. 1978 'Anatomy of an oligarchy: the Oxford Town Council', *J. B. S.*, 18
Hammersley, G. 1973a 'The early English copper industry, *c.*1580–1650', *Bus. Hist.*, 15
1973b 'The charcoal iron industry and its fuel, 1540–1740', *Ec. H. R.*, 2nd ser., 26
Hammond, E. A. 1960 'Incomes of English medieval doctors', *J. Hist. Med.*, 17
Hampshire, S. 1983 *Morality and Conflict* (Oxford)
Hanawalt, B. A. (ed.) 1986 *Women and Work in Pre-industrial Europe* (Bloomington)
Hands, A. P. and Scouloudi, I. 1971 'French Protestant refugees relieved', *Proc. Hug. Soc. Lond.*, 49
Hanham, A. 1972 'Some fraudulent accounts in the Cely papers', *Speculum*, 48
1979 'A medieval Scots merchant handbook', *Scot. Hist. Rev.*, 50
1982 'Profits on English wool exports, 1472–1544' *B. I. H. R.*, 55
1985 *The Celys and Their World* (Cambridge)
Hannah, L. 1983 *Entrepreneurship and the Social Sciences*
Hans, N. 1966 *New Trends in English Education in the Eighteenth Century* (Cambridge)
Hanson, C. A. 1981 *Economy and Society in Baroque Portugal, 1668–1703* (Minneapolis)
Hanson-Jones, J. A. 1977 *American Colonial Wealth* (New York), 3 vols.
1982 'Estimating the wealth of the living', *J. I. H.*, 13
Harbage, A. 1935 *Sir William Davenant, Poet Venturer, 1606–68* (Philadelphia)
1941 *Shakespeare's Audience* (New York)
1968 *Shakespeare and the Rival Tradition*, 2nd edn (New York)
Hardenberg, H. 1970 'English history in Dutch archives', *J. Soc. Archiv.*, 4
Harding, V. 1989 'Location of burials', *Lond. J.*, 14
1990 'The population of London, 1500–1700', *Lond. J.*, 15
Hardy, E. G. 1899 *Jesus College, Oxford*
Hare, S. M. 1984 'The records of the Goldsmiths Company', *Archives*, 16
Harford, A. (ed.) 1909 *Annals of the Harford Family*
Harley, S. B. and Yamamura, K. (ed.) 1977 *Economic and Demographic Change in Pre-industrial Japan* (Princeton)
Harlow, V. T. 1926 *A History of Barbados, 1625–85* (Oxford)
Harper, L. A. 1939 *The English Navigation Laws* (New York)
Harper-Bill, C. and Harvey, R. (eds.) 1986 *The Ideas and Practice of Medieval Knighthood* (Woodbridge)
Harpham, E. J. 1984 'Liberal civic humanism and Adam Smith', *Amer. Pol. Sc. Rev.*, 78
1985 'Class commerce and the state', *West. Pol. Q.*, 38
Harré, R. (ed.) 1986 *The Social Construction of Emotions* (Oxford)
Harris, B. J. and McNamara, J. K. (eds.) 1984 *Women and the Structure of Society* (Durham, North Carolina)
Harris, G. G. 1969 *The Trinity House of Deptford, 1514–1660*
Harris, J. 1960 *English Decorative Ironwork, 1610–1836*

Harris, J. R. (ed.) 1969 *Liverpool and Merseyside*
Harris, M. and Lee, A. J. (eds.) 1986 *The Press in English Society*
Harris, O. 1983 'Households and their boundaries', *Hist. Work. J.*, 13
Harris, P. R. 1960 'An Aleppo merchant's letter book', *Brit. Mus. Q.*, 22
Harris, S. E. (ed.) 1951 *Schumpeter, Social Scientist*
Harris, T. 1987 *London Crowds in the Reign of Charles II* (New York)
1988 'Was the Tory reaction popular', *Lond. J.*, 13
1989 'The problem of popular political culture in seventeenth-century London', *Hist. Eur. Ideas*, 10
Harris, T., Seaward, P. and Goldie, M. (eds.) 1990 *The Politics of Religion in Restoration England* (Oxford)
Harrison, C. J. 1971 'Grain price analysis and harvest qualities, 1485–1634', *Agric. Hist. Rev.*, 19
Harrison, F. 1919 *The Virginia Carys* (New York)
1920 *The Devon Carys* (New York)
Hart, A. T. 1955 *The Eighteenth-century Country Parson* (Shrewsbury)
1958 *The Country Clergy, 1558–1660*
1968 *Clergy and Society, 1600–1800*
Hart, W. G. 1930 'Roman Law and the custom of London', *Law Q. R.*, 46
Harte, N. B. 1971 (ed.) *The Study of Economic History*
Harte, N. B. and Ponting, K. G. (eds.) 1973 *Textile History and Economic History: Essays in Honour of Miss J. de L. Mann* (Manchester)
Hartley, J. M. (ed.) 1986 *The Study of Russian History from British Archival Sources* (New York)
Hartwell, R. M. 1969 'Economic growth in England before the Industrial Revolution', *J. Ec. H.*, 29
Harvey, J. H. 1972 *Early Gardening Catalogues*
Harvey, R. 1979 'English poverty and God's providence, 1675–1725', *The Historian*, 41
Hasan, F. 1991 'Conflict and co-operation in Anglo-Mughal trade', *J. Ec. & Soc. Hist. Orient*, 34
Hasebroek, J. 1933 *Trade and Politics in Ancient Greece*, trans. L. M. Fraser and D. C. MacGregor
Haselgrove, D. 1989 'The seventeenth-century ale house', *Trans. Lond. & Midd. A. S.*, 37
Hasler, P. W. (ed.) 1982 *The House of Commons, 1558–1603*, 3 vols.
Hatcher, J. and Barker, T. C. 1974 *A History of British Pewter*
Hatton, R. and Anderson, M. S. (eds.) 1970 *Studies in Diplomatic History: Essays in Honour of D. B. Horn*
Hatton, R. and Bromley, J. S. 1968 (eds.) *William III and Louis XIV: Essays 1680–1720 by and for M. A. Thomson* (Liverpool)
Hauser, A. 1951 *The Social History of Art*, 2 vols.
Hauser, W. B. 1974 *Economic Institutional Change in Tokugawa, Japan*
Hausman, W. J. 1977 'Size and profitability of English colliers', *Bus. Hist. Rev.*, 51
Haveren, T. K. 1975 'Household and family process', *Hist. & Theory*, 14
Havinden, M. (ed.) 1973 *Husbandry and Marketing in the South West, 1500–1800* (Exeter Papers in Ec. Hist.)

Hawkins, M. J. 1982 'Wardship, Royalist delinquency and too many children', *South. Hist.*, 4
Hawthorne, G. 1976 *Enlightenment and Despair: A History of Sociology*
Hay, C. 1980 'Historical theory and historical confirmation', *Hist. & Theory*, 19
Hay, D. 1958 *Polydore Vergil* (Oxford)
(ed.) 1975 *Albion's Fatal Tree: Crime and Society in Eighteenth Century England*
Hayami, A. 1983 'The myth of primogeniture', *J. Fam. Hist.*, 8
Hayden, R. 1970 'Broadmead, Bristol', *Bapt. Q.*, 23
Hayek, F. A. von, 1942–3 'Scientism and the study of society', *Economica*, NS, 9–10
(ed.) 1954 *Capitalism and the Historians* (Chicago)
1966 'Dr Bernard Mandeville', *P. B. A.*, 52
1967 *Studies in Philosophy, Politics and Economics*
1978 *New Studies in Philosophy, Politics, Economics and the History of Ideas* (Chicago)
Hayes, S. P. 1950 'Some psychological problems of economics', *Psych. Bull.*, 47
Haynes, A. 1992 *The Invisible Power: The Elizabethan Secret Services, 1570–1603*
Haynes, J. 1992 *The Social Relations of Jonson's Theatre* (Cambridge)
Hayton, D. 1988 'Sir Richard Cocks', *Albion*, 20
1990 'Moral reform and country politics', *P. & P.*, 128
Heal, Sir Ambrose 1924 *London Tradesmen's Cards of the Seventeenth Century*
1931 *The English Writing Masters and their Copy Books, 1570–1800* (Cambridge)
1935 *The London Goldsmiths, 1200–1800* (Cambridge)
1947 *The Signboards of Old London Shops*
Heal, F. 1973 'Economic problems of the bishops', *Ec. H. R.*, 2nd ser., 26
1980 *Of Prelates and Princes* (Cambridge)
1981 *The English Church 1500–1800*
1990 *Hospitality in Early Modern England* (Oxford)
Heal, F. and O'Day, R. (eds.) 1977 *Church and Society in England, Henry VIII to James I*
Healey, E. 1992 *Coutts and Company, 1692–1992*
Hearder, H. and Loyn, H. R. 1974 (eds.) *British Government and Administration: Studies Presented to S. B. Chrimes* (Cardiff)
Hearne, J. 1967 'The naked footprint', *Rev. Eng. Lit.*, 8
Hearnshaw, L. S. 1954 'Attitudes to work', *Occ. Psych.*, 28
Heath, J. B. 1869 *Some Account of the Grocers Company*, 3rd edn
Heath, P. 1969 *The English Parish Clergy on the Eve of the Reformation*
Heathcote, E. D. 1899 *An Account of Some Families Bearing the Name of Heathcote* (Derby)
Heaton, H. 1965 *The Yorkshire Woollen and Worsted Industries*, 2nd edn (Oxford)
Hecht, J. 1964 'La querelle de la noblesse commerçante', *Population*, 19
Hector, L. C. 1966 *The Handwriting of English Documents*, 2nd edn
Heers, J. 1961 *Société et économie à Genes*
1963 *L'Occident aux XIVe et XVe siècle*
1974 'The feudal economy and capitalism', *J. Eur. Ec. Hist.*, 3
Heertje, A. 1981 (ed.) *Schumpeter's Vision* (Eastbourne)
Heilbronner, R. 1956 *The Quest for Wealth* (New York)

Heinemann, M. 1980 *Puritanism and Theatre: Thomas Middleton and Opposition Drama* (Cambridge)
Heisenberg, W. 1959 *Physics and Philosophy: The Revolution in Modern Science*
Helleiner, K. F. 1951 'The moral conditions of economic growth', *J. Ec. Hist.*, 11
Hellie, R. 1978 'Stratification of Muscovite society', *Russian History*, 5
Hembry, P. 1967 *The Bishops of Bath and Wells, 1540–1640*
Hemmeon, J. C. 1912 *A History of the British Post Office* (Cambridge, Massachusetts)
Hemphill, C. D. 1982 'Women in court', *Wm & Mary Q.*, 3rd ser., 39
Henderson, E. G. 1974 'Relief from bonds', *Amer. J. Legal Hist.*, 18
Hennetta, J. A. 1965 'Economic development and social structure in colonial Boston', *Wm & Mary Q.*, 3rd ser., 22
Henning, B. D. (ed.) 1983 *The House of Commons, 1660–90*
Hepburn, A. C. 1978 (ed.) *Minorities in History*
Herbert, R. F. and Link, A. N. 1982 *The Entrepreneur: Mainstream Views and Radical Critiques*
Heriot, G. 1822 *Memoirs with an Historical Account of the Hospital Founded by Him* (Edinburgh)
Herlan, R. W. 1976 'Social articulation', *Guild. Stud. Lond. Hist.*, 2
1977 'Poor relief in Budge Row, 1638–64', *Guild. Stud. Lond. Hist.*, 3
1978 'Poor relief in London during the Puritan Revolution', *J. B. S.*, 18
1980 'Aspects of population history, 1645–67', *Guild. Stud. Lond. Hist.*, 4
Herlihy, D. O. 1969 'Vieillir au Quattrocento', *Annales*, 24
1972 'Raymond de Roover', *J. Eur. Ec. Hist.* 1
1974 'Three patterns of social mobility in medieval history', *J. I. H.*, 3
1981 'Numerical and formal analysis in European history', *J. I. H.*, 12
Herr, R. 1958 *The Eighteenth Century Revolution in Spain* (Princeton)
Herringham, Sir Wilmot, 1932 'Dr William Harvey', *Ann. Med. Hist.*, 3rd ser., 4
Herrup, C. B. 1984 'New shoes and mutton pies', *H. J.*, 27
1987 *The Common Peace* (Cambridge)
Herschlag, Z. Y. 1969 'Theory of stages of economic growth', *Kyklos*, 22
Herskovits, M. J. 1952 *Economic Anthropology*, 2nd edn (New York)
1955 *Man and his Works* (repr. New York)
Hertzler, J. R. 1971 'The abuse and outlawing of sanctuary for debt', *H. J.*, 14
Hetherington, N. S. 1975 *Almanacks and the Extent of Knowledge of the New Astronomy* (Proc. Amer. Phil. Soc., 119)
Heward, E. 1972 *Matthew Hale*
Hexter, J. H. 1955 'A new framework for social history', *J. Ec. H.*, 15
1961 *Reappraisals in History*
1967 'The rhetoric of history', *Hist. & Theory*, 6
1968 'The English aristocracy, 1558–1660', *J. B. S.*, 8
1971 *Doing History* (Bloomington)
1979 *On Historians* (Cambridge, Massachusetts)
Hey, D. G. 1974 *An English Rural Community Myddle under the Tudors and Stuarts* (Leicester)
Heyrman, C. L. 1984 *Commerce and Culture* (New York)
Hibbard, C. M. 1980 'Early Stuart Catholics', *J. M. H.*, 52
Hicks, Sir John R. 1969 *A Theory of Economic History* (Oxford)

1983 *Classics and Moderns: Collected Essays on Economic Theory* (Oxford)
Hicks-Beach, S. E. 1909 *A Cotswold Family: Hicks and Hicks-Beach*
Hickson, C. R. and Thompson, E. A. 1991 'A new theory of guilds', *Expl. Ec. H.*, 28
Higgins, L. M. 1980 'The apostatized apostle', *Quaker History*, 69
Higgs, L. 1991 'Wills and religious mentality in Tudor Colchester', *Essex Arch. & Hist.*, 22
Higham, C. S. S. 1921 *Development of the Leeward Islands, 1660–88* (Cambridge)
Hill, A. O. and B. H. 1980 'Marc Bloch and comparative history', *A. H. R.*, 85
Hill, B. W. 1971 'The change of government and the loss of the City', *Ec. H. R.*, 2nd ser., 24
Hill, C. E. J. 1956 *The Economic Problems of the Church from Archbishop Whitgift to the Long Parliament* (Oxford)
1964 *Society and Puritanism in Pre-revolutionary England*
1980a *Some Intellectual Consequences of the English Revolution* (Madison)
1980b 'Robinson Crusoe', *Hist. Work. J.*, 10
1986 *The Collected Essays* (Amherst)
Hill, C. E. J., Reay, B. and Lamont, W. 1983 *The World of the Muggletonians*
Hill, C. P. 1951 *History of Bristol Grammar School* (Bristol)
Hill, J. W. F. 1956 *Tudor and Stuart Lincoln*
Hill, L. M. 1977 'Continuity and discontinuity', *Albion*, 9
1988 *Bench and Bureaucracy: The Public Career of Sir Julius Caesar, 1580–1636* (Stamford)
Hill, R. H. E. 1904 'Thomas Hill, a London merchant', *Home Counties Mag.*, 7
1907 'Richard Hill of Moreton', *Devon & Corn. N. & Q.*, 4
Himmelfarb, G. 1987 *The New History and the Old* (Cambridge, Massachusetts)
Hinton, R. W. K. 1955 'The mercantile system in the time of Mun', *Ec. H. R.*, 2nd ser., 7
1959 *The Eastland Trade and the Commonweal* (Cambridge)
Hintze, O. 1929 'Der moderne Kapitalismus', *Hist. Zeit.*, 139
Hirsch, F. 1976 *Social Limits to Growth* (Cambridge, Massachusetts)
Hirschberg, D. R. 1980 'The government and church patronage in England, 1660–1760', *J. B. S.*, 20
Hirschman, A. O. 1959 *The Strategy of Economic Development* (New Haven)
1970 *Exit Voice and Loyalty* (Cambridge, Massachusetts)
1977 *The Passions and the Interests* (Princeton)
1980 *Rival Views of Market Society*
Hirschmeier, J. 1964 *The Origins of Entrepreneurship in Meji Japan* (Cambridge, Massachusetts)
Hirschmeier, J. and Yui, T. 1975 *The Development of Japanese Business, 1600–1973* (Cambridge, Massachusetts)
Hirst, D. 1975 *The Representative of the People* (Cambridge)
Hirst, H. C. M. 1927 'A seventeenth century house in Bristol', *T. B. G. A. S.*, 49
Historical Monuments Commission. London, vol. IV, *The City* (1929)
Hizigrath, H. 1912 *Die Handelsbeziehungen zwischen Hamburg und England, 1611–60* (Hamburg)
Ho, P.-T. 1959 'The salt merchants of Yang-Chou', *Harv. J. Asiat. Stud.*, 17
1962 *The Ladder of Success in Imperial China: Aspects of Social Mobility, 1368–*

1911 (New York)
Hoare, E. 1883 *Some Aspects of the Families of Hore and Hoare*
Hoare, H. P. R. (ed.) 1955 *Hoare's Bank: A Record, 1673–1955* (repr.)
Hobsbaum, P. 1972 'Calvinism in action', *Hudson Review*, 25
Hobsbawm, E. J. 1971 'From social history to the history of society', *Daedalus*, 100
Hobsbawm, E. J. and Ranger, T. (eds.) 1983 *The Invention of Tradition* (Cambridge)
Hobson, R. 1954 *Navaho Acquisitive Values* (Peabody Museum Arch. and Anthrop. Papers, 42)
Hodgdon, G. E. 1918 *Reminiscences of the Vaughan Family of New Hampshire* (Rochester)
Hodge, H. S. V. 1953 *Sir Andrew Judd* (Tonbridge)
Hodgen, M. T. 1964 *Early Anthropology in the Sixteenth Century* (Philadelphia)
Hodges, G. R. 1986 *New York City Cartmen, 1667–1850* (New York)
Hodges, J. C. 1941 *William Congreve* (New York)
Hoffer, P. C. and Hull, N. E. H.1981 *Murdering Mothers: Infanticide in England and New England, 1558–1803* (New York)
Hoffman, R. and Carson, C. 1987 (eds.) *Of Consuming Interest*
Hogben, L. (ed.) 1938 *Political Arithmetic*
Holden, J. M. 1951 'Bills of exchange during the seventeenth century', *Law Q. R.*, 67
1955 *The History of Negotiable Instruments in English Law*
Holden, W. P. 1954 *Anti-Puritan Satire, 1572–1640* (New Haven)
Holderness, B. A. 1970 'Elizabeth Parker and her investments', *Trans. Hunter A. S.*
1972 'Rural tradesmen, 1660–1850', *Lincs. Hist. & Arch.*, 7
1974 'The English land market in the eighteenth century', *Ec. H. R.*, 2nd ser., 27
1975 'Credit in a rural community' *Mid. Hist.*, 3
1976a *Pre-industrial England: Economy and Society, 1500–1750*
1976b 'Credit in rural society, 1650–1720', *Agric. Hist. Rev.*, 24
Holdsworth, Sir William, 1914 'The rules of venue and the beginning of the commercial jurisdiction of the Common Law courts', *Columbia Law Rev.*, 14
1924–5 'Defamation in the sixteenth and seventeenth centuries', *Law Q. R.*, 40–1
1925 *Sources and Literature of English law* (Oxford)
1956 *History of the English Law*, 7th edn, rev. A. L. Goodhart and H. G. Hanbury
Hole, C. 1953 *The English Housewife in the Seventeenth Century*
Hollaender, A. E. J. 1957 'A London merchant's letter book' *Archives*, 3
Hollaender, A. E. J. and Kellaway, W. (eds.) 1969 *Studies in London History Presented to P. E. Jones*
Hollaender, S. 1977 'Adam Smith and the self-interest axiom', *J. Law Econ.*, 20
Hollinger, D. A. 1973 'Kuhn's theory of science', *A. H. R.*, 78
Hollingshead, J. E. 1990 'The gentry of south-west Lancashire', *North. Hist.*, 26
Hollingsworth, T. H. 1965 *The Demography of the British Peerage* (Pop. Stud. Supp. 18)

1969 *Historical Demography* (New York)
Hollingsworth, T. H. and M. F. 1971 'Plague mortality rates, *Pop. Stud.*, 25
1977 'Mortality in the British peerage families', *Population*, 32
Holman, J. R. 1975 'Orphans in pre-industrial towns', *Loc. Pop. Stud.*, 15
1977 'Some aspects of higher education in Bristol and Gloucester', *T. B. G. A. S.*, 95
1979 'Apprenticeship as a factor in migration', *T. B. G. A .S.*, 97
Holmes, C. 1974 *The Eastern Association in the English Civil War*
(ed.) 1978 *Immigrants and Minorities in British Society*
1980a *Seventeenth Century Lincolnshire* (Lincoln)
1980b 'The county community', *J. B. S.*, 19
Holmes, G. and Ruff, H. 1975 'The perils of entrepreneurial history', *Bus. Hist.*, 17
Holmes, G. A. 1973 'The emergence of an urban ideology at Florence', *T. R. H. S.*, 5th ser., 22
Holmes, G. S. (ed.) 1969 *Britain after the Glorious Revolution, 1689–1714*
1977 'Gregory King and the social structure', *T. R. H. S.*, 5th ser., 27
1981 'The professions and social change in England, 1680–1730', *P. B. A.*, 65
1982 *Augustan England: Professions, State and Society, 1680–1730*
1986 *Politics, Religion and Society in England, 1679-1742*
1987 *British Politics in the Age of Anne*, 2nd edn
Holmes, G. S. and Speck, W. A. (eds.) 1967 *The Divided Society, 1694–1716: Parties and Politics in England*
Holmes, P. J. 1981 *Elizabethan Casuistry* (Cath. Rec. Soc., 67)
Holt, J. C. 1972 'Politics and property in early medieval England', *P. & P.*, 57
Holt, P. M., Lambton, A. K. S. and Lewis, B. (eds.) 1977 *The Cambridge History of Islam* (Cambridge), 2 vols.
Homans, G. C. 1937 'Partible inheritance of village holdings', *Ec. H. R.*, 8
1940 'The Puritans and the clothing industry', *New Eng. Q.*, 16
Homer, S. 1963 *A History of Interest Rates* (New Brunswick)
Hone, C. R. 1950 *John Radcliffe, 1652–1714*
Honigmann, E. A. J. (ed.) 1986 *Shakespeare and his Contemporaries* (Manchester)
Hoon, E. E. 1938 *The Organisation of the English Customs System, 1696–1786* (New York)
Hope, V. M. 1989 *Virtue by Consensus: The Moral Philosophy of Hutcheson, Hume and Adam Smith* (Oxford)
Hopper, K. T. 1976 'The early Royal Society', *Brit. J. Hist. Sc.*, 9
Hoppit, J. 1987 *Risk and Failure in English Business, 1700–1800* (Cambridge)
1990 'Attitudes to credit in Britain, 1680–1796', *H. J.*, 33
Horle, C. W. 1982 'John Camm', *Quaker History*, 71
1988 *The Quakers and the English Legal System, 1660–88* (Philadelphia)
Horn, D. B. 1932 *British Diplomatic Representatives, 1689–1789* (Camd. Soc., 3rd ser., no. 46)
1959 'Rank and emolument', *T. R. H. S.*, 5th ser., 9
1961 *The British Diplomatic Service, 1689–1789* (Oxford)
Horn, J. P. P. 1981 'The distribution of wealth in the vale of Berkeley', *South. Hist.*, 3
Hornbeak, K. G. 1934 *The Complete Letterwriter in English, 1568–1800*

Horne, D. M. 1952 *George Peele* (New Haven)
Horne, T. A. 1978 *The Social Thought of Bernard Mandeville* (New York)
Hornstein, S. R. 1991 *The Restoration Navy and English Foreign Trade, 1674–88*
Horsefield, J. K. 1957 'The financial organization of a company', *Acc. Res.*, 8
1977 'The beginnings of paper money in England', *J. Eur. Ec. Hist.*, 6
1982 'The Stop of the Exchequer', *Ec. H. R.*, 2nd ser., 35
1983 *British Monetary Experiments, 1650–1710* (repr.)
Horton, R. and Finnegan, R. (eds.) 1973 *Modes of Thought*
Horwitz, H. 1968 *Revolution Politics: The Career of Daniel Finch* (Cambridge)
1977 'The East India trade', *J. B. S.*, 17
1984 'Testamentary practice, family strategies and the Custom of London', *Law & Hist. Rev.*, 2
1987 'The mess of the middle class revisited', *Cont. & Ch.*, 2
Hoselitz, B. F. (ed.) 1951 *The Progress of Underdeveloped Areas* (Chicago)
1960 *Sociological Aspects of Economic Growth* (Chicago)
(ed.) 1961 *Theories of Economic Growth* (Glencoe, Illinois)
1963 'Entrepreneurship and traditional elites', *Expl. Ent. H.*, 2nd ser., 1
Hoselitz, B. F. and Moore, W. E. (eds.) 1963 *Industrialization and Society*
Hoskins, W. G. 1935 *Industry, Trade and People in Exeter, 1688–1800* (Manchester)
1946 'Devonshire gentry in Carolean times', *Devon & Corn. N.& Q.*, 22
1950 *Essays in Leicestershire History* (Liverpool)
1956 'English provincial towns in the sixteenth century', *T. R. H. S.*, 5th ser., 6
1963 *Provincial England*
1968 'Harvest fluctuations and English economic history, 1620–1759', *Agric. Hist. Rev.*, 16
1972 *Devon*, new edn
1976 *The Age of Plunder, 1500–47*
Hoskins, W. G. and Finberg, H. P. R. 1952 *Devonshire Studies*
Hotson, L. 1928 *The Commonwealth and Restoration Stage* (Cambridge)
Houblon, A. A. 1907 *The Houblon Family*, 2 vols.
Houghton, W. E. 1938 *The Formation of Thomas Fuller's Holy and Profane States* (Cambridge, Massachusetts)
1941 'The history of trades', *J. H. I.*, 2
1942 'The English virtuoso in the seventeenth century', *J. H. I.*, 3
Houlbrooke, R. 1972 'Persecution of heresy', *Norf. Arch.*, 35
1984 *The English Family, 1400–1700*
1985 'The making of marriage in mid-Tudor England', *J. Fam. Hist.*, 10
(ed.) 1988 *English Family Life, 1576–1716* (Oxford)
(ed.) 1989 *Death, Ritual and Bereavement*
Houston, R. A. 1982a 'Illiteracy in the diocese of Durham', *North. Hist.*, 18
1982b 'The development of literacy in northern England', *Ec. H. R.*, 2nd ser., 35
1982c 'The literacy myth', *P. & P.*, 96
1988 *Literacy in Early Modern Europe, 1500–1800*
Houston, R. A. and Whyte, I. D. (eds.) 1989 *Scottish Society, 1500–1800* (Cambridge)
Houtte, J. A. van, 1977 *An Economic History of the Low Countries, 800–1800* (New

York)
Howarth, D. 1984 'Merchants and diplomats', *Furn. Hist.*, 20
Howell, C. 1983 *Land, Family and Inheritance in Transition: Kibworth-Harcourt* (Cambridge)
Howell, R. 1967 *Newcastle upon Tyne and the Puritan Revolution* (Oxford)
1979 'The structure of urban politics', *Albion*, 11
1980 'Newcastle and the nation' *Arch. Aliena*, 5th ser., 8
1984 *Puritans and Radicals in North England* (Lanham, Maryland)
Howell, W. S. 1956 *Logic and Rhetoric in England, 1500–1700* (Princeton)
Hsu, F. L. K. 1949 'Social mobility in China', *Amer. Sociol. Rev.*, 14
Hudleston, C. R. 1978 'Non-resident clergy of Bristol', *T. B. G. A. S.*, 96
Hudson, A. 1988 *The Premature Reformation* (Oxford)
Hudson, J. 1983 'The marriage duty Acts and Shrewsbury, 1695–8', *Loc. Pop. Stud.*, 31
Hufton, O. 1984 'Women without men', *J. Fam. Hist.*, 9
Hughes, A. 1986 'Reproductive success and occupational class', *Soc. Biol.*, 33
1987 *Politics, Society and Civil War in Warwickshire, 1620–60* (Cambridge)
Hughes, D. O. 1975 'Urban growth and family structure', *P. & P.*, 66
Hughes, E. 1952a *North Country Life in the Eighteenth Century* (Durham), 2 vols.
1952b 'The professions in the eighteenth century', *Durham Univ. J.*, NS, 13
Hughes, G. 1991 *Swearing: A Social History* (Oxford)
Hughes, H. S. 1926 'The middle class reader and the English novel', *J. E. G. P.*, 25
Hughes, J. 1973 *The Vital Few: American Economic Progress and its Protagonists*
Hughes, P. and Williams, D. (eds.) 1971 *The Varied Pattern* (Toronto)
Hughes, R. 1974 'Samuel Osborne, 1674–1731', *J. Barb. Mus. & Hist. Soc.*, 34
Hugo, T. 1862 *An Illustrated Itinerary of the Ward of Bishopsgate*
Huizinga, J. 1955 *Homo Ludens* (Boston)
Hull, D. 1979 'In defence of presentism', *Hist. & Theory*, 18
Hull, S. W. 1982 *Chaste, Silent and Obedient* (San Marino)
Hume, R. D. 1976 *The Development of English Drama in the Late Seventeenth Century* (Oxford)
Humpherus, H. 1887 *History of the Company of Watermen and Lightermen, 1514–1859*
Hundert, E. J. 1972 'The making of homo faber', *J. H. I.*, 33
Hunt, M. L. 1911 *Thomas Dekker* (New York)
Hunt, R. W., Philip, I. G. and Roberts, R. J. (eds.) 1975 *Studies in the Book Trade in Honour of Graham Pollard* (Oxford Bibliog. Soc., 18)
Hunt, W. 1887 *Bristol*
Hunt, W. 1983 *The Puritan Moment: The Coming of Revolution in an English County* (Cambridge, Massachusetts)
Hunter, J. P. 1966 *The Reluctant Pilgrim*
Hunter, M. 1975 *John Aubrey and the Realm of Learning*
1982 *The Royal Society and its Fellows, 1660–1700*
Hunter, M. and Schaffer, S. (eds.) 1989 *Robert Hooke: New Studies* (Woodbridge)
Hunter, R. and MacAlpine, I. 1963 *Three Hundred Years of Psychiatry, 1535–1860*
Hunter, Sir William, 1961 *A History of British India* (repr.), 2 vols.

Huppert, G. 1977 *Les Bourgeois Gentilhommes* (Chicago)
Hurstfield, J. 1967 'Political corruption in modern England', *History*, 53
1973a *The Queen's Wards*, 2nd edn
1973b *Freedom, Corruption and Government in Elizabethan England*
Hurt, J. 1976 ' Les offices au parlement de Bretagne', *Rev. Hist. Mod. & Cont.*, 23
Hurwich, J. J. 1970 'Social origins of early Quakers', *P. & P.*, 48
1976 'Dissent and Catholicism in English society: Warwickshire, 1660–1720', *J. B. S.*, 16
1977 'A fanatic town: the political influence of Dissenters in Coventry', *Mid. Hist.*, 4
Husbands, C. 1980 'Gravestones and local history', *Loc. Hist.*, 14
1981 'Standards of living in north Warwickshire', *Warws. Hist.*, 4
1987 'Regional change in a pre-industrial society', *J. Hist. Geog.*, 13
Hutchinson, M. B. 1904 'The Ipswich Apprentices Book', *N.& Q.*, 10
Hutchinson, T. W. 1988 *Before Adam Smith* (Oxford)
Hutson, L. 1989 'The displacement of the market in Jacobean city comedy', *Lond. J.*, 14
Hyamson, A. M. 1928 *History of the Jews in England*
1952 *The Sephardim of England*
Hyde, F. E. 1962 'Economic theory and business history', *Bus. Hist.*, 5
1971 *Liverpool and the Mersey, 1700–70* (Newton Abbot)
Ibbetson, D. 1982 'Assumpsit and debt', *Camb. Law J.*, 41
1983 'Sixteenth-century contract law', *Oxford J. Legal Stud.*, 4
Imbert, G. 1959 *Des Mouvements à longue durée Kondratieff* (Aix)
Impey, O. and MacGreggor, A. 1985 *The Origins of Museums* (Oxford)
Imray, J. 1968 *The Charities of Richard Whittington*
Inalcik, H. 1969 'Capital formation in the Ottoman Empire', *J. Ec. H.*, 29
Ingram, M. 1987 *Church Courts, Sex and Marriage in England, 1570–1640* (Cambridge)
Ingram, W. 1978 *Francis Langley, 1548–1602* (Cambridge, Massachusetts)
Inkeles, A. and Smith, D. M. 1974 *Becoming Modern* (Cambridge, Massachusetts)
Innis, H. A. 1954 *The Cod Fisheries*, rev. edn (Toronto)
International Congress of Economic History I 1960 (Stockholm)
International Congress of Economic History III 1968 (Munich)
International Congress of Economic History IV 1973 (Bloomington)
International Congress of Economic History IX 1986 (Stuttgart)
International Congress of Economic History X 1990 (Stuttgart)
International Congress of Studies of Underdeveloped Areas 1954 (Milan)
Irwin, D. A. 1991 'Mercantilism as strategic trade policy' *J. Pol. Econ.*, 99
Irwin, R. 1958 *The Origins of the English Library*
Israel, J. T. 1989a *Dutch Primacy in World Trade, 1585–1740* (Oxford)
1989b *European Jewry in the Age of Mercantilism, 1550–1750*, 2nd edn (Oxford)
1990 *Empire and Enterprise*
(ed.) 1991 *The Anglo-Dutch Moment* (Cambridge)
Ives, E. W. 1959–60 'The reputation of the common lawyer, 1450–1550', *Univ. B'ham H. J.*, 7
1964 'The law and the lawyers', *Shakes. Surv.*, 17

1967 'The Statute of Uses', *E. H. R.*, 82
(ed.) 1968 *The English Revolution*
1983 *The Common Lawyer in Pre-Reformation England* (New York)
Ives, E. W. and Manchester, A. H. (eds.) 1983 *Law Litigants and the Legal Profession*
Ives, E. W., Knecht, R. J. and Scarisbrick, J. J. (eds.) 1978 *Wealth and Power in Tudor England: Essays Presented to S. T. Bindoff*
Jack, S. M. 1977 *Trade and Industry in Tudor and Stuart England*
Jackson, G. 1972 *Hull in the Eighteenth Century* (Oxford)
1978 *The British Whaling Industry*
Jackson, P. A. 1970 *Professions and Professionalisation* (Cambridge)
Jacob, J. R. 1975 'The origins of the Royal Society', *Hist. Sc.*, 13
Jacob, M. 1981 *The Radical Enlightenment* (Winchester)
Jacob, M. C. 1977 *The Newtonians and the English Revolution, 1689–1726* (Hassocks)
Jacobsen, G. A. 1932 *William Blathwayt* (New Haven)
Jago, C. 1973 'The influence of debt', *Ec. H. R.*, 2nd ser., 26
Jaher, J. C. (ed.) 1973 *The Rich and the Well Born and the Powerful Elites in History* (Urbana)
James, F. G. 1948 'Charity endowments as a source of local credit', *J. Ec. Hist.*, 8
James, G. F. and Shaw, J. J. S. 1936–8 'Admiralty jurisdiction and personnel, 1619–1714', *B. I. H. R.*, 14–16
James, M. 1941 'The political importance of the tithes controversy in the English Revolution', *History*, 26
James, M. E. 1973 'The concept of order', *P. & P.*, 60
1974 *Family Lineage and Civil Society, 1500–1640* (Oxford)
1978 *English Politics and the Concept of Honour, 1485–1642* (Oxford)
1983 'Ritual drama and the social body', *P. & P.*, 98
1986 *Society, Politics and Culture* (Cambridge)
James, M. K. 1956 'A London merchant of the fourteenth century', *Ec. H. R.*, 2nd ser., 8
1971 *Studies in the Medieval Wine Trade*, ed. E. M. Veale (Oxford)
Jamieson, A. G. (ed.) 1986 *People of the Sea: The Maritime History of the Channel Islands*
Jancey, E. M. 1955–6 'Richard Hill of Hawkstone, 1655–1727', *Trans. Shrop. Arch. & Nat. Hist. Soc.*, 55
Jann, R. 1983 'From amateur to professional', *J. B. S.*, 22
Jansen, M. B. and Stone, L. 1966–7 'Education and modernisation', *Comp. Stud. Soc. Hist.*, 9
Janssens, P. 1974 'Histoire économique ou économie rétrospective', *Hist. & Theory*, 13
1975 *Coûts et bénéfices des structures nobiliares aux Pays Bas* (Leuven)
Jardine, L. 1975 *Francis Bacon* (Cambridge)
Jarvis, R. C. 1954 'Customs, Port of Liverpool', *Cheth. Soc.*, 16–19
1957–8 'Sources for the history of shipping', *J. Trans. Hist.*, 3
1959 'Fractional shareholders in British merchant ships', *Mar. Mirr.*, 45
1977a 'Books of rates', *J. Soc. Arch.*, 5
1977b 'The metamorphosis of the port of London', *Lond. J.*, 3

Jay, W. 1933 'Sir Roland Hayward', *Trans. Lond. & Midd. A. S.*, 6
Jeannin, P. 1957 *Les Marchands au XVI siècle*
1964 'Les comptes du Sund', *Rev. Hist.*, 231
1968 'En Europe de Nord', *Annales*, 23
1969 *L'Europe du Nord Ouest et du Nord au XVIIe siècle*
Jefferies, P. 1979 'The Medieval Use as family law', *South. Hist.*, 1
Jeffreys, M. V. C. 1967 *John Locke: Prophet of Commonsense*
Jenkins, D. 1975 (ed.) *Legal History Studies* (Cardiff)
Jenkins, P. 1982 'The rise of a graduate clergy in Sussex, 1540–1640', *Suss. Arch. Coll.*, 120
Jenkins, P. 1983 *The Making of a Ruling Class: The Glamorgan Gentry, 1640–1790* (Cambridge)
Jenkinson, Sir Hilary, 1926 'The teaching and practice of handwriting in England', *History*, 11
Jennings, J. M. 1977 'The distribution of landed wealth in the wills of London merchants, 1400–50', *Medieval Studies*, 39
Jensen, A. L. 1963 *The Maritime Commerce of Colonial Philadelphia* (Madison)
Jensen, J. V. 1976 'The staff of the Jacobean Privy Council', *H. L. Q.*, 40
Jessup, F. 1965 *Sir Roger Twysden, 1597–1672*
Johansson, B. 1966 *Law and Lawyers in Elizabethan England* (Stockholm)
John, A. H. 1958 'The London Assurance Company', *Economica*, NS, 25
1961 'Aspects of economic growth', *Economica*, NS, 28
Johnson, A. H. R. 1914–22 *The History of the Company of Drapers*, 5 vols. (Oxford)
Johnson, B. 1949 *Acts and Ordinances of the Company of Merchant Taylors in York*
Johnson, B. H. 1952 *Berkeley Square to Bond Street*
Johnson, B. L. C. 1951–2 'The Foley partnerships', *Ec. H. R.*, 2nd ser., 4
Johnson, D. J. 1969 *Southwark and the City* (Oxford)
Johnson, E. A. J. 1932a *American Economic Thought in the Seventeenth Century*
1932b 'Unemployment and consumption: the mercantilist view', *Q. J. Econ.*, 46
1937 *Predecessors of Adam Smith* (New York)
1964 'The place of learning, science, vocational training and art', *J. Ec. H.*, 24
Johnson, F. R. 1950 'Notes on English retail book prices', *The Library*, 5th ser., 5
Johnson, H. A. 1963 *The Law Merchant and Negotiable Instruments in Colonial New York* (Chicago)
Johnson, H. T. and Kaplan, R. S. 1987 *Relevance Lost: The Rise and Fall of Management Accounting* (Boston)
Johnson, J. T. 1970 *A Society Ordained by God* (Nashville)
Johnson, R. R. 1981 *Adjustment to Empire: The New England Colonies, 1675–94* (New Brunswick)
1986 'The imperial Webb', *Wm & Mary Q.*, 3rd ser., 43
Johnson, T. J. 1972 *Professions and Power*
Johnston, F. A. 1971 'Parliament and the protection of trade, 1689–94', *Mar. Mirr.*, 57
Johnston, J. A. 1971 'The probate inventories and wills of a Worcestershire parish', *Mid. Hist.*, 1
1978 'Worcestershire probate inventories, 1699-1716', *Mid. Hist.*, 4

Jones, A. H. M. 1955 'The social structure of Athens', *Ec. H. R.*, 2nd ser., 8
1964 *The Later Roman Empire, 284–600* (Oxford)
1974 *The Roman Economy*, ed. P. A. Brunt (Oxford)
Jones, A. S. E. 1968 'The Port of Ipswich', *Suff. Rev.*, 3
Jones, C. (ed.) 1984 *Party and Management in Parliament, 1660–1784*
(ed.) 1987 *Britain in the First Age of Party, 1684–1750. Essays Presented to Geoffrey Holmes*
1989 'The Harley family and papers', *B. L. J.*, 15
Jones, C. and Jones D. L. (eds.) 1986 *Peers, Politics and Power: The House of Lords, 1603–1911*
Jones, C., Newitt, M. and Roberts, S. (eds.) 1986 *Politics and People in Revolutionary England: Essays for Ivan Roots* (Oxford)
Jones, D. W. 1972 'The Hallage receipts', *Ec. H. R.*, 2nd ser., 25
1988 *War and Economy in the Age of William III* (Oxford)
Jones, E. 1953 *Life and Work of Sigmund Freud* (New York)
Jones, E. 1980 'London in the early seventeenth century', *Lond. J.*, 6
1981 'The Welsh in London', *Welsh Hist. Rev.*, 10
1982 'The first West End comedy', *P. B. A.*, 68
Jones, E. D. 1939–40 'An account book of Sir Thomas Myddelton', *Nat. Lib. Wales J.*, 1
Jones, E. L. (ed.) 1967 *Agriculture and Economic Growth in England*
1974 *Agriculture and the Industrial Revolution* (New York)
Jones, E. L. 1981 *The European Miracle* (Cambridge)
1984 *A Gazetteer of English Urban Fire Disasters, 1500–1900* (Norwich)
1988 *Growth Recurring: Economic Change in World History* (Oxford)
Jones, E. L. and Falkus, M. E. 1979 'Urban improvement and the English economy', *Res. Ec. Hist.*, 4
Jones, E. L. and Mingay, G. E. (eds.) 1967 *Land, Labour and Population in the Industrial Revolution: Essays in Honour of J. D. Chambers*
Jones, G. L. 1969 *History of the Law of Charity, 1532–1827* (Cambridge)
Jones, G. P. 1967 'The commercial interests of Wilfrid Hudleston', *Trans. Cumb. & West. Antiq. & Arch. Soc.*, NS, 67
Jones, G. S. 1976 'From historical sociology to theoretical history', *Brit. J. Sociol.*, 27
Jones, H. G. 1975 *An Introduction to Modern Theories of Economic Growth*
Jones, I. F. 1938–9 'Apprenticeship books of Bristol', *Genealog. Mag.*, 8
Jones, J. G. 1983 'The Merioneth gentry, 1540–1640', *J. Merion. Hist. & Rec. Soc.*, 9
1989 *Wales and the Tudor State, 1534–1640* (Cardiff)
Jones, J. R. 1972 *The Revolution of 1688 in England*
1978 *Court and Country: England, 1658–1714*
(ed.) 1979 *The Restored Monarchy, 1660–88*
Jones, N. and Dean, D. 1989 'Interest groups and legislative activity in Elizabethan Parliaments', *Parlt. Hist.*, 8
Jones, P. E. 1943 'The City Courts. IV: Mayor and Sheriff's Courts', *Law J.*, 43
1965 *The Company of Poulterers*, 2nd edn (Oxford)
1976 *The Butchers of London*
Jones, P. E. and Judges, A. V. 1936 'London population in the late seventeenth

century', *Ec. H. R.*, 6
Jones, P. J. 1980 *Economie e societa nell'Italia medievale* (Turin)
Jones, R. D. 1990 *Structure and Scale in the Roman Economy* (Cambridge)
Jones, R. F. 1930 'Science and English prose style', *P. M. L. A.*, 45
Jones, T. 1909–30 *A History of Brecknock* (Brecknock), 4 vols.
Jones, W. J. 1959 'Elizabethan marine insurance', *Bus. Hist.*, 2
1967 *The Elizabethan Court of Chancery* (Oxford)
1971 *Politics and the Bench*
1979 *The Foundations of English Bankruptcy* (Trans. Amer. Phil. Soc., 69)
Jones, W. R. 1971 'Actions for slander', *Q. J. Speech*, 57
Jones, W. R. D. 1970 *The Tudor Commonwealth, 1529–59*
Jones-Davies, M. T. 1958 *Thomas Dekker*, 2 vols.
Jordan, W. K. 1932–40 *The Development of Religious Toleration in England*, 4 vols.
1942 *Men of Substance* (Chicago)
1959 *Philanthropy in England, 1480–1660*
1960a *The Charities of London, 1480–1660*
1960b *The Forming of the Charitable Institutions of the West of England* (Trans. Amer. Phil. Soc., NS, 50)
1961a *The Charities of Rural England, 1480–1660*
1961b *The Social Institutions in Kent 1480–1660* (Arch. Cant., 75)
1962 *The Social Institutions of Lancashire* (Cheth. Soc., 3rd ser., 11)
Jorgensen, J. 1957 *Det kobenhavnske patriciat* (Copenhagen)
1963 'Denmark's relations with Lübeck and Hamburg', *Scand. Ec. H. R.*, 11
Jouanna, A. 1968 'Recherches sur la notion d'honneur', *Rev. Hist. Mod. et Cont.*, 15
1976 *L'Idée de race en France, 1498–1614* (Lille), 3 vols.
Joyce, P. 1982 *The History of Morden College* (Henley)
Judd, J. 1971 'Frederick Philipse and the Madagascar trade', *New York Hist. Soc.*, 55
Judges, A. V. 1925 'Philip Burlamachi', *Economica*, 18
1931 'The origins of English banking', *History*, 16
1938–9 'History and business records', *Genealog. Mag.*, 8
Judson, M. A. 1949 *The Crisis of the Constitution, 1603–45* (New Brunswick)
Kadish, A. 1989 *Historians, Economists and Economic History*
Kahl, W. F. 1956 'Apprenticeship and the Freedom of the London Livery Companies, 1690–1750', *Guild. Misc.*, 7
1960 *The Development of the London Livery Companies* (Kress Lib. Pub., 15)
Kakagawa, K. (ed.) 1977 *Third International Conference on Business History*, vol. II, *Social Order and Entrepreneurship* (Tokyo)
Kamen, H. 1964 'The decline of Castile', *Ec. H. R.*, 2nd ser., 17
1971 *The Iron Century: Social Change in Europe, 1550–1660*
1980 *Spain in the Late Seventeenth Century*
1984 *European Society, 1500–1700*
Kamenka, E. and Neale, R. S. 1975 *Feudalism, Capitalism and Beyond*
Kammen, M. G. 1970 *Empire and Interest: The American Colonies and the Politics of Mercantilism* (Philadelphia)
Kaniss, P. C. 1981 *Evolutionary Change in Hierarchical Systems* (Ithaca)
Kaplan, L. 1976 *Politics and Religion during the English Revolution* (New York)

Kardiner, A. 1939 *The Individual and his Society* (New York)
1963 *The Psychological Frontiers of Society* (New York)
Kargon, R. 1963 'John Graunt, Francis Bacon and the Royal Society', *J. Hist. Med.*, 18
Katz, D. S. 1982 *Philo-Semitism and the Re-admission of the Jews to England, 1603–55* (Oxford)
Kaufmann-Rochard, J. 1969 *Origines d'une bourgeoisie russe, XVIe–XVIIe siècles*
Kautsky, J. H. 1982 *The Politics of Aristocratic Empire* (Chapel Hill)
Kavka, G. 1986 *Hobbesian Moral and Political Theory* (Princeton)
Kea, R. A. 1982 *Settlement, Trade and Politics in the Seventeenth-century Gold Coast* (Baltimore)
Kearney, H. 1964 'Puritanism, capitalism and the Scientific Revolution', *P. & P.*, 28
1970 *Scholars and Gentlemen: Universities and Society in Pre-industrial Britain, 1500–1700*
Kedar, B. Z. 1976 *Merchants in Crisis: Genoese and Venetian Men of Affairs* (New Haven)
Keeble, N. H. 1987 *The Literary Culture of Non-Conformity* (Leicester)
Keeler, M. F. 1954 *The Long Parliament, 1640–41* (Philadelphia)
Keen, M. H. 1965 *The Laws of War in the Later Middle Ages*
1984 *Chivalry* (New Haven)
Keeton, G. W. 1958 *Social Change in the Law of Trusts*
1960 *The Norman Conquest and the Common Law*
1965 *Lord Chancellor Jeffries and the Stuart Cause*
1967 'George Jeffries' *Trans. Cymm. Soc.*
Keirn, T. 1988 'Daniel Defoe and the Africa Company', *Hist. Res.*, 61
Keirn, T. and Melton, F. T. 1990 'Thomas Manley and the rate of interest debate', *J. B. S.*, 29
Kellaway, W. 1961 *The New England Company, 1649–1776*
Kellenbenz, H. 1953–4 'German aristocratic entrepreneurship', *Expl. Ent. H.*, 6
1957 'Die unternehmerische Betätigung', *V. J. S. W.*, 44
1965 *Die Merkantilismus und die soziale Mobilität in Europa* (Wiesbaden)
(ed.) 1970 *Fremde Kaufleute auf der Iberischen Halbinsel* (Cologne)
1976 Review of Wallerstein, *J. M. H.*, 48
1982 'Fritz Redlich', *J. Eur. Ec. Hist.*, 11
Kellett, J. R. 1952 'The cause and progress of the financial decline of the Corporation of London, 1680–94' (unpub. Ph. D. thesis, London)
1957–8 'The breakdown of Guild and Corporation control', *Ec. H. R.*, 2nd ser., 10
1963 'The financial crisis of the Corporation of London', *Guild. Misc.*, 11
Kelly, P. H. 1984 'Between politics and economics', *Studi Settecenteschi*, 5
Kelly, T. 1966 *Early Public Libraries*
Kelsall, A. F. 1974 'The London house plan', *Post Med. Arch.*, 8
Kelso, R. 1929 *The Doctrine of the English Gentleman in the Sixteenth Century* (Urbana)
Kemp, B. 1980 *English Church Monuments*
Keniston, K. 1971 'Psychological development and historical change', *J. I. H.*, 2.
Kennedy, D. E. 1962 'The Jacobean Episcopate', *H. J.*, 5

Kennedy, P. 1983 *The Rise and Fall of British Naval Power*
Kennedy, W. 1913 *English Taxation, 1640–1799*
'The Kennon family' 1905–6, *Wm & Mary Q.*, 14
Kenny, C. S. 1879 *History of the Law of England as to the Effect of Marriage on Property*
Kenny, C. S. and Laurence, P. M. 1878 *Two Essays on the History of the Law of Primogeniture in England* (Cambridge)
Kent, A. 1975 'Probability and statistics in genealogy', *Genealog. Mag.*, 18
Kent, J. R. 1973 'Attitudes of members of the Commons to regulation of personal conduct', *B. I. H. R.*, 46
1981 'Population mobility and Alms', *Loc. Pop. Stud.*, 27
Kenyon, G. H. 1955 'Kirkford inventories, 1611–1776', *Suss. Arch. Coll.*, 93
1958, 1960 'Petworth town and trades', *Suss. Arch. Coll.*, 95, 98
Kenyon, J. P. 1972 *The Popish Plot*
1986 *The Stuart Constitution, 1603–88* (Cambridge)
1988 *The Civil Wars of England*
Kepler, J. S. 1973 'Value of ships gained and lost, 1624–30', *Mar. Mirr*, 59
1975 'The operating potential of London marine insurance', *Bus. Hist.*, 17
1976 *The Exchange of Christendom* (Leicester)
1979 'The maximum duration of trading voyages', *Mar. Mirr.*, 65
Kermode, J. P. 1982 'The flight from office', *Ec. H. R.*, 2nd ser., 35
Kerridge, E. 1985 *Textile Manufacture in Early Modern England* (Manchester)
1988 *Trade and Banking in Early Modern England* (Manchester)
Kessler, L. D. 1976 *K'ang-Hsi and the Consolidation of Ch'ing rule, 1661–1684* (Chicago)
Keswani, D. G. 1971 'Western commercial enterprise in the East', *Indian Archives*, 20
Ketton-Cremer, R. W. 1944 *Norfolk Portraits*
Keynes, Sir Geoffrey, 1937 *John Evelyn* (Cambridge)
1966 *William Harvey* (Oxford)
Keynes, Sir Geoffrey and R. A. Skelton (eds.) 1940 *The Library of George Gibbon*
Keynes, J. M. 1934 *A Treatise on Money* (New York), 2 vols.
1939 *General Theory of Employment, Interest and Employment*
Khan, S. A. 1923 *The East India Trade in the Seventeenth Century*
1978 *Sources for the History of British India* (repr. Delhi)
Kidson, R. M. 1958 *The Gentry of Staffordshire, 1662–3* (Staffs. Rec. Soc., 4th ser., 2)
Kiernan, V. G. 1988 *The Duel in European History* (Oxford)
Kierner, C. A. 1991 *Trade and Gentlefolk: The Livingstones of New York, 1675–1790* (Ithaca)
Kiker, B. F. 1966 'The historical roots of the concept of human capital', *J. Pol. Econ.*, 74
Kilby, P. (ed.) 1971 *Entrepreneurship and Economic Development* (New York)
Killeen, J. 1976 'Restoration and early eighteenth-century Drama', *Sociological Review*, 24
Kindleberger, C. P. 1978a *Manias, Panics and Crashes*
1978b *Economic Response* (Cambridge, Massachusetts)
Kindleberger, C. P. and Tella, G. di (eds.) 1982 *Economics in the Long View:*

Essays in Honour of W. W. Rostow (New York)
King, P. 1968 'The Episcopate during the Civil Wars', *E. H. R.*, 83
King, P. and Parekh, B. C. 1986 (eds.) *Politics and Experience* (Cambridge)
Kingdon, J. A. 1901 *Richard Grafton, Citizen and Grocer of London*
Kingman, M. J. 1978 'Markets and marketing in Tudor Warwickshire', *Warws. Hist.*, 4
Kingsford, C. L. 1925 'A London merchant's house, 1310–1614', *Archeologia*, 74
Kinmonth, E. H. 1981 *The Self-Made Man in Meiji Japanese Thought* (Berkeley)
Kiralfy, A. K. 1951 *The Action on the Case*
Kiralfy, A. K., Slatter, M. and Virgoe, R. (eds.) 1985 *Custom, Courts and Counsel*
Kirby, C. 1931 'The Stuart game prerogative', *E. H. R.*, 46
1933 'The English game law system', *A. H. R.*, 38
Kirby, D. A. 1970 'The radicals of St Stephens' Coleman Street, 1624–42', *Guild. Misc.*, 3
Kirby, E. W. 1942 'The lay feofees', *J. M. H.*, 14
Kirby, J. W. 1983 'The rulers of Leeds', *Thoresby Soc. Pub.*, 59
1986 'Restoration Leeds', *North. Hist.*, 22
Kirchner, W. 1956 'Entrepreneurial activity in Russian–Western trade', *Expl. Ent. H.*, 8
1966 *Commercial Relations between Russia and Europe, 1400–1800* (Bloomington)
Kirkman, F and Head, R. 1935 *The English Rogue*, rev. edn
Kirzner, I. M. 1979 *Perception, Opportunity and Profit* (Chicago)
1985 *Discovery and the Capitalist Process* (Chicago)
1989 *Discovery, Capitalism and Distributive Justice* (Oxford)
Kisch, B. 1965 *Scales and Weights*
Kishlanski, M. A. 1986 *Parliamentary Selection* (Cambridge)
Kissack, K. E. 1975 *Monmouth: The Making of a County Town*
Kitching, C. J. 1976 'Probate during the Civil War and Interregnum', *J. Soc. Archiv.*, 5
1989 'Fire disasters and fire relief', *B. I. H. R.*, 54
Klassen, P. J. 1964 *The Economics of Anabaptism, 1525–60* (The Hague)
Kleim, C. R. 1968 'Primogeniture and entail in Colonial Virginia', *Wm & Mary Q.*, 3rd ser., 25
Klein, B. 1991 'Civic pageantry', *Lond. J.*, 17
Klein, P. W. 1969 'Entrepreneurial behaviour and the economic rise and decline of the Netherlands', *Ann. Cisalp. Hist. Soc.*, 1
Kluchevsky, V. 1958 *Peter the Great,* trans. L. Archibald
Knafla, L. A. 1969 'The law studies of an Elizabethan student', *H. L. Q.*, 32
Knappen, M. M. 1963 *Tudor Puritanism* (Gloucester, Massachusetts)
Knight, F. H. 1921 *Risk, Uncertainty and Profit* (New York)
1935 *The Ethics of Competition*
Knights, L. C. 1937a *Drama and Society in the Age of Johnson*
1937b 'Restoration comedy', *Scrutiny*, 6
Knoll, R., Ashcraft, R. and Zagorin, P. (eds.) 1992 *Philosophy, Science and Religion in England, 1640–1700* (Cambridge)
Knoop, D. and Jones, G. P. 1932 'Masons and apprenticeship in medieval England' *Ec. H. R.*, 3

1935 *The London Masons in the Seventeenth Century* (Manchester)
Knorr, K. E. 1963 *British Colonial Theories, 1570–1850* (Toronto)
Knorr, R. B. (ed.) 1977 *Reformation, Conformity and Dissent: Essays in Honour of G. Nuttall*
Knowles, C. C. 1972 *The History of Building Regulation in London, 1189–1972*
Knowles, D. 1948–59 *The Religious Orders in England* (Cambridge, 4 vols.)
Knox, N. 1961 *The Word 'Irony' and its Context, 1550–1755* (Durham, North Carolina)
Knox, S. J. 1962 *Walter Travers*
Kocher, P. H. 1953 *Science and Religion in Elizabethan England* (San Marino)
Kolko, G. 1961 'Weber on America', *Hist. & Theory*, 1
Koot, G. H. 1980 'English historical economics', *Hist. Pol. Econ.*, 12
Kooy, M. (ed.) 1972 *Studies in Economics and Economic History in Honour of H. M. Robertson*
Kooy, T. P. van der, 1931 *Hollands Stapelmarkt en haar verval* (Amsterdam)
Korner, M. H. 1980 *Solidarités financières suisses au seizième siècle* (Lausanne)
Kousser, J. M. 1984 'The revivalism of narrative', *Soc. Sc. Hist.*, 8
Kracke, E. A. 1947 'Family and merit in the examination system', *Harv. J. Asiat. Stud.*, 10
Kramer, S. 1927 *The English Craft Gilds* (New York)
Krammick, I. 1972 'Reflections on revolution', *Hist. & Theory*, 11
Krantz, F. and Hohenberg, P. M. (eds.) 1975 *Failed Transitions to Modern Industrial Society* (Montreal)
Kreager, P. 1988 'New light on Graunt', *Pop. Stud.*, 42
Krey, G. S. de, 1985 *A Fractured Society: The Politics of London, 1688–1715* (Oxford)
Krishna, B. 1924 *Commercial Relations between India and England, 1601–1757*
Kroeber, A. L. and Kluckhorn, C. 1952 *Culture. A Critical Review of Concepts and Definitions* (Cambridge, Massachusetts)
Kroef, J. V. 1961 'The acquisitive urge', *Soc. Res.*, 28
Kruger, L., Daston, L. J. and Heidelberger, M. 1987 (eds.) *The Probabilistic Revolution* (Cambridge, Massachusetts)
Kuehn, G. W. 1940 'The novels of Thomas Deloney', *J. Pol. Econ.*, 48
Kuhn, T. S. 1970 *The Structure of Scientific Revolutions*, 2nd edn (Chicago)
Kumar, D. (ed.) 1981 *The Cambridge Economic History of India* (Cambridge), vol. I
Kunze, B. Y. 1989 'Poore and in necessity', *Albion*, 21
Kunze, B. Y. and Brautigam, D. D. 1992 (eds.) *Court, Country and Culture: Essays in Honour of Perez Zagorin* (Rochester, New York)
Kupperman, K. O. 1984 'Fear of hot climates', *Wm & Mary Q.*, 3rd ser., 41
Kussmaul, A. 1981 *Servants in Husbandry in Early Modern England* (Cambridge)
1985 'Agrarian change in seventeenth-century England', *J. Ec. H.*, 45
Kuznets, S. S., Moore, W. E. and Spengler, J. S. 1955 (eds.) *Economic Growth: Brazil, India, Japan*
Labatut, J. P. 1978 *Les Noblesses européennes*
Labib, S. Y. 1969 'Capitalism in medieval Islam', *J. Ec. H.*, 29
Labrot, G. 1977 'Le comportement collectif de l'aristocratie napolitaine', *Rev. Hist.*, 258

Lachs, P. S. 1965 *The Diplomatic Corps under Charles II and James II* (New Brunswick)

Lake, P. 1982 *Moderation, Puritans and the Elizabethan Church* (Cambridge)

1988 *Anglicans and Puritans*

Lake, P. and Dowling, M. (eds.) 1987 *Protestantism and the National Church in Sixteenth Century England*

Lamb, R. B. 1974 'Adam Smith's system', *J. H. I.*, 35

Lambert, B. 1806 *The History and Survey of London and its Environs*

Lambley, K. 1929 *The Teaching and Cultivation of the French Language in England* (Manchester)

Lammens, H. 1924 *La Mecque à la veille de l'Hégire* (Beirut)

Lamont, W. M. 1979 *Protestant Imperialism and the English Revolution*

Lancashire Record Office Archivist's Report (1963, 1966)

'Lancashire miscellany' 1965 *Hist. Soc. Lancs. & Ches. Rec. Ser.*, 109

Lancaster, J. C. 1966 *A Guide to Lists and Catalogues in the India Office Records*

Land, A. C. 1972 'The planters of colonial Maryland', *Maryland Hist. Mag.*

(ed.) 1977 *Law, Society and Politics in Maryland* (Baltimore)

Lander, J. R. 1980 *Government and Community: England, 1450–1509*

Landes, D. S. 1983 *Revolution in Time* (Cambridge, Massachusetts)

1986 'What do bosses really do', *J. Ec. H.*, 46

Landreth, H. 1975 'The economic thought of Bernard Mandeville', *Hist. Pol. Econ.*, 7

Lane, F. C. 1944 *Andrea Barbarigo, 1418–49* (New Brunswick)

1975 'The role of governments in economic growth', *J. Ec. H.*, 35

1987 *Studies in Venetian History*

Lane, F. C. and Riemersma, J. C. (eds.) 1953 *Enterprise and Secular Change*

Lane, J. 1973 'The household of a Stuart physician', *Med. Hist.*, 17

1977 'The Warwickshire attorney', *Warws. Hist.*, 3

1988 'Provincial medical apprentices and masters', *Eight. Cent. Life*, 12

Lane, M. 1927 'The Diplomatic Service under William III', *T. R. H. S.*, 4th ser., 10

Lang, J. 1956 *Rebuilding St Paul's after the Great Fire*

Lang, R. G. 1963 'The Greater Merchants of London in the early seventeenth century' (unpub. D. Phil. thesis, Oxford)

1969 Review of B. W. E. Alford and T. C. Barker, *Ec. H. R.*, 2nd ser., 22

1971 'London aldermen in business', *Guild. Misc.*, 3

1974 'Social origins and aspirations of Jacobean London merchants', *Ec. H. R.*, 2nd ser., 27

Langbein, J. H. 1983 'Albion's fatal flaw', *P.& P.*, 98

Langdale, A. B. 1937 *Phineas Fletcher* (New York)

Langton, J. 1979 *Geographical Change and the Industrial Revolution* (Cambridge)

1982 'The behavioural theory of evolution', *Sociology*, 17

Lapeyre, H. 1955 *Une famille de marchands: les Ruiz*

Larminie, V. 1984 'Marriage and the family', *Mid. Hist.*, 9

1987 'Settlement and sentiment', *Mid. Hist.*, 12

Larmour, R. R. 1966 'Business investment and social attitudes', *Bus. Hist. Rev.*, 40

1967 'The grocers of Paris', *Ec. H. R.*, 2nd ser., 20

Laski, H. 1936 *The Rise of Liberalism* (New York)
Laslett, P. 1948a 'Sir Robert Filmer', *Wm & Mary Q.*, 3rd ser., 5
1948b 'The gentry of Kent in 1640', *C. H. J.*, 9
1964 'Market society and political theory', *H. J.*, 7
1969 'Size and structure of the household', *Pop. Stud.*, 22
1974 'Parental deprivation', *Loc. Pop. Stud.*, 13
1976 'The wrong way through the telescope', *Brit. J. Soc.*, 27
1977 *Family Life and Illicit Love* (Cambridge)
1983 *The World We Have Lost. Further Explorations*, 3rd edn
Laslett, P. and Runciman, W. G. (eds.) 1962 *Philosophy, Politics and Society, II* (Oxford)
Laslett, P. and Wall, R. (eds.) 1972 *Household and Family in Past Time* (Cambridge)
Laslett, P., Oosterveen, K. and Smith, R. M. (eds.) 1980 *Bastardy and its Comparative History*
Laslett, P., Runciman, W. G. and Skinner, Q. (eds.) 1974 *Philosophy, Politics and Society, IV* (Oxford)
Latham, R. C. 1941 'Roger Lowe', *History*, NS, 26
Latimer, J. 1900 *Annals of Bristol in theSeventeenth Century* (Bristol)
1904 'The alleged Arms of Alderman Whitson', *Proc. Clifton Antiq. Club*, 5
Laurence, A., Owens, W. R. and Sim, S. (eds.) 1990 *John Bunyan and his England, 1628–88*
Lauterbach, A. T. 1954 *Man, Motives and Money* (New York)
Lavin, J. A. 1969 'William Barley', *Bibliog. Soc. Univ. Virg.*, 22
Lawless, D. S. 1977 'Robert Daborne Senior', *N. & Q.*, 222
Lawlis, M. E. 1960 *Apologist for the Middle Class: The Dramatic Novels of Thomas Deloney* (Bloomington)
Lawson, J. 1963 *A Town Grammar School through Six Centuries*
Lawton, H. 1988 *The Psychohistorian's Handbook*
Lea, P. A. 1966 'The ideal of the English gentleman', *Diss. Abstr.*, 28
Leader, R. E. 1901 *Sheffield in the Eighteenth Century* (Sheffield)
1905–6 *History of the Company of Cutlers in Hallamshire* (Sheffield)
Lears, J. 1985 'The concept of cultural hegemony', *A. H. R.*, 90
Leatherbarron, J. S. 1947 *Lancashire Elizabethan Recusants* (Manchester)
1982 'Financing the eighteenth-century clergy', *Trans. Worcs. A. S.*, 8
Leder, L. H. 1961 *Robert Livingstone, 1654–1728, and the Politics of Colonial New York* (Chapel Hill)
Leder, L. H. and Carosso, V. P. 1956 'Robert Livingstone', *Bus. Hist. Rev.*, 30
Lee, C. H. 1990 'Corporate behaviour in theory and history', *Bus. Hist.*, 32
1991 'Fanatic magistrates', *H. J.*, 35
Lee, G. A. 1975 'The concept of profit in British accounting', *Bus. Hist. Rev.*, 49
1980 'Historical business accounting records', *Bus. Arch.*, 46
Lee, M. 1967 'The Jacobean Diplomatic Service', *A. H. R.*, 72
Lee, P. A. 1969 'Play and the English gentleman', *The Historian*, 31
Lee, W. 1869 *Daniel Defoe*, 3 vols.
Lees, R. M. 1933 'The constitutional importance of commissioners', *Economica*, 13
1939 'Parliament and the proposal for a Council of Trade', *E. H. R.*, 54

Leff, N. H. 1979 'Entrepreneurship and economic development', *J. Ec. Lit.*, 17
Lefroy, J. A. P. 1972 'The British factory at Leghorn', *Proc. Hug. Soc. Lond.*, 22
1980 'Anthony Lefroy', *Proc. Hug. Soc. Lond.*, 23
Leftwich, B. R. 1930 'The later history and administration of the Customs Revenue', *T. R. H. S.*, 4th ser., 13
Leggatt, A. 1973 *Citizen Comedy in the Age of Shakespeare* (Toronto)
1988 *English Drama: Shakespeare to the Restoration*
LeGuin, C. A. 1967 'Sea life in seventeenth-century England', *Amer. Nept.* (April)
Lehman, W. C. 1960 *John Miller, 1735–1801* (Cambridge)
Lehmberg, S. E. 1960 *Sir Thomas Elyot, Humanist* (Austin)
1964 *Sir Walter Mildmay and Tudor Government* (Austin)
Leibenstein, H. 1963 *Economic Backwardness and Economic Growth* (New York)
Leighton-Boyce, J. A. S. 1958 *Smith the Bankers, 1658–1958*
Leinwand, T. B. 1982 'London *triumphans*', *Clio*, 2
Leites, E. 1974 'Conscience, casuistry and moral decision', *J. Chin. Phil.*, 2
1982 'The duty to desire', *J. Soc. Hist.*, 15
1986 *The Puritan Conscience and Modern Sexuality* (New Haven)
(ed.) 1988 *Conscience and Casuistry in Early Modern France* (Cambridge)
Lemmings, D. 1985 'The student body of the Inns, 1688–1714', *B. I. H. R.*, 58
1990 *Gentlemen and Barristers: The Inns of Court and the English Bar, 1680–1730* (Oxford)
Lenman, B. R. 1990 'The English and the Dutch East India Companies', *Eight. Cent. Stud.*, 14
Lennard, R. 1931 (ed.) *Englishmen at Rest and Play, 1558–1714* (Oxford)
Léon, P. 1954 *La Naissance de la Grande Industrie en Dauphiné* (Univ. of Grenoble Pub., 9)
1970 *Economies et sociétés préindustrielles, 1650–1789*
(ed.) 1978 *Histoire économique et sociale du monde*, vol. II, *Les hésitations de la croissance, 1580–1740*
Léonard, E. G. 1961 *A History of Protestantism*, trans. R. M. Bethell, 2 vols.
Leonard, E. M. 1900 *The Early History of English Poor Relief* (Cambridge)
Leonard, H. H. 1978 'Distraint of knighthood', *History*, 63
Le Play, F. 1956 *Recueil d'études sociales publié à la mémoire de Frédérick Le Play*
Le Roy Ladurie, E. 1981 *La Territoire de l'historien*, trans. B. and S. Reynolds (Brighton)
Lestocquoy, J. 1952 *Aux origines de la bourgeoisie. Les villes de Flandres et d'Italie*
Letwin, S. R. 1981 'Idea of a gentleman', *Encounter*, 57
Letwin, W. 1959 *Sir Josiah Child, Merchant Economist* (Kress Lib. Pub., 14)
1963 *The Origins of Scientific Economics: English Economic Thought, 1660–1776*
Levack, B. P. 1973 *The Civil Lawyers in England, 1603–41* (Oxford)
Levenson, J. R. 1958–65 *Confucian China and its Modern Face*
1967 *European Expansion and the Counter Example of Asia, 1300–1600* (Englewood Cliffs)
Leverenz, T. 1988 *The Language of Puritan Feeling* (New Brunswick)
Lévi-Strauss, C. 1963 *Structural Anthropology* (New York)
Levin, J. 1969 *The Charter Controversies in London, 1660–88*
Levine, G. 1973 'Some Norwich goldsmith wills', *Norf. Arch.*, 35

Levinthal, L. E. 1919 'The early history of English bankruptcy', *Univ. Penn. Law. Rev.*, 67
Levy, A. 1954 'Economic views of Hobbes', *J. H. I.*, 15
Levy, F. J. 1982 'How information spread among the gentry', *J. B. S.*, 21
Levy, R. 1962 *The Social Structure of Islam* (Cambridge)
Lévy-Leboyer, M. 1970 'L'Héritage de Simiand', *Rev. Hist.*, 243
Lewis, G. R. 1966 *The Stannaries* (repr. Truro)
Lewis, M. A. 1939 *England's Sea Officers*
1969 *The Hawkins Dynasty*
Lewis, P. S. 1968 *Late Medieval France: The Polity*
Lewis, W. A. 1955 *The Theory of Economic Growth*
1978 *Growth and Fluctuations, 1870–1913*
Leyden, W. von, 1982 *Hobbes and Locke*
Leys, M. D. R. 1961 *Catholics in England, 1558–1629*
Libecap, G. D. 1986 'Property rights in economic history', *Expl. Ec. H.*, 23
Lillywhite, B. 1963 *London Coffee Houses*
Limon, J. 1985 *Gentlemen of a Company: English Players in Central and Eastern Europe, 1590–1660* (Cambridge)
Lincolnshire Archivist's Report (1968–9)
Lindeboom, J. 1950 *Austin Friars, 1550–1950*, trans. D. de Long (The Hague)
Lindert, P. H. 1980 'English occupations, 1670–1811', *J. Ec. H.*, 40
1981 'An algorithm for probate sampling', *J. I. H.*, 11
1986 'Unequal English wealth since 1670', *J. Pol. Econ.*, 94
Lindert, P. H. and Williamson, J. G. 1980 *American Inequality* (New York)
1982 'Revising England's social tables, 1688–1812', *Expl. Ec. H.*, 19
Lindley, E. S. 1962 *Wootton-under-Edge*
Lindley, K. J. 1983 'Riot prevention and control', *T. R. H. S.*, 5th ser., 33
1991 'The maintenance of stability in early modern London', *H. J.*, 34
Lingelbach, W. E. 1902 'Internal organisation of the Merchant Adventurers', *T. R. H. S.*, 2nd ser., 16
1903 *The Internal Organisation of the Merchant Adventurers of England* (Philadelphia)
1903–4 'The Merchant Adventurers of Hamburg', *A. H. R.*, 9
Lipson, E. 1931 *The Economic History of England*, 3 vols.
1944 *A Planned Economy or Free Enterprise*
Lis, C. and Soly, M. 1979 *Poverty and Capitalism in Pre-industrial Europe* (Brighton)
Litchfield, R. B. 1969a 'Demographic characteristics of Florentine families', *J. Ec. H.*, 29
1969b 'Les investissements commerciaux des patriciens florentins', *Annales*, 24
1986 *Emergence of a Bureaucracy: The Florentine Patriciate, 1530–1796* (Princeton)
Litten, J. 1991 *The English Way of Death*
Little, B. 1956 *The Monmouth Episode*
Littleton, A. C. 1933 *Accounting Evolution to 1900* (New York)
1961 *Essays on Accountancy* (Urbana)
Littleton, A. C. and Yamey, B. S. 1956 (eds.) *Studies in the History of Accounting*

(Homewood)
Liu, T. 1978 'The founding of the London Provincial Assembly', *Guild. Stud. Lond. Hist.*, 3
1986 *Puritan London* (Newark)
Livi-Bacci, M. 1983 'The nutrition–mortality link', *J. I. H.*, 14
Llewellyn, N. 1991 *The Art of Death: Visual Culture in the English Death Ritual,* c. *1500–1800*
Lloyd, A. 1950 *Quaker Social History*
Lloyd, C. 1978 'Elizabethan prize money', *Mar. Mirr.*, 44
1981 *English Corsairs on the Barbary Coast*
Lloyd, C. 1986 *Explanation in Social History* (Oxford)
Lloyd, H. 1975 *The Quaker Lloyds*
Lloyd, H. A. 1968 *The Gentry of South-West Wales, 1540–1640* (Cardiff)
Lloyd, N. 1949 *A History of the English House*, new edn
Lloyd, T. H. 1982 *Alien Merchants in England in the High Middle Ages* (Brighton)
1991 *England and the German Hanse* (Cambridge)
Lloyd-Jones, H., Pearl, V. and Worden, B. (eds.) 1981 *History and Imagination: Essays in Honour of H. R. Trevor-Roper*
Loach, J. 1986 *Parliament and the Crown in the Reign of Mary Tudor* (Oxford)
1991 *Parliament under the Tudors* (Oxford)
Loach, J. and Tittler, R. 1980 (eds.) *The Mid-Tudor Polity,* c. *1540–60*
Locke, A. A. 1916 *The Hanbury Family*
Lockridge, K. A. 1970 *A New England Town: Dedham, Massachusetts* (New York)
1974 *Literacy in Colonial New England* (New York)
Loewe, K. von, 1973 'Commerce and agriculture in Lithuania, 1400–1600', *Ec. H. R.*, 2nd ser., 26
Lofthouse, S. 1976 'David Hume and achievement motivation', *Rev. It. de Sci. Econ.*, 23
Loftis, J. 1959 *Comedy and Society from Congreve to Fielding* (Stanford)
Lohmann Villena, G. 1968 *Une famille d'homme d'affaires en Espagne. les Espinosa*
London, H. S. 1947 'John Philpot', *Arch. Cant.*, 60
London and Middlesex Archaeological Society, report to the Twentieth General Meeting, 12 April 1860, printed in *Trans. Lond. & Midd. A. S.*, 2 (1864)
Longfield, A. K. 1929 *Anglo-Irish Trade in the Sixteenth Century*
Loomie, A. J. 1963a *Toleration and Diplomacy* (Trans. Amer. Phil. Soc., 53)
1963b 'Sir William Semple', *T. B. G. A. S.*, 82
1972 'Thomas James, the English consul of Andalucia', *Rec. Hist.*, 11
1973, 1978 (ed.) *Spain and the Jacobean Catholics* (Cath. Rec. Soc. Pub., 64 & 68)
Lopez, R. S. 1937 'Aux origines du capitalisme génois', *Annales*, 9
1938 *Storia delle colonie genovesi nel Mediterraneo* (Bologna)
1958 'Le marchand génois: un profil collectif', *Annales*, 13
1969–70 'Stars and spices', *Expl. Ec. H.*, 7
Lopez, R. S. and Irving, W. B. (eds.) 1955 *Medieval Trade in the Mediterranean World*
Lorwin, V. R. and Price, J.M. (eds.) 1972 *The Dimensions of the Past* (New Haven)
Loschky, D. J. and Krier, D. F. 1969 'Income and family size', *J. Ec. H.*, 29

Lourie, E. 1966 'A society organized for war: medieval Spain', *P. & P.*, 35
Louw, H. J. 1981 'Anglo-Netherlandish architectural interchange, *c.* 1600–60', *Arch. Hist.*, 24
1989a 'Demarcation disputes of Newcastle', *Arch. Aliena*, 5th ser., 17
1989b 'Demarcation disputes between carpenters and joiners', *Constr. Hist.*, 5
Love, H. 1987 'Scribal publications in seventeenth-century England', *Trans. Camb. Bib. Soc.*, 9
Love, H. D. 1913 *Vestiges of Old Madras, 1640–1800*, 4 vols.
Lovejoy, A. O. 1936 *The Great Chain of Being* (Cambridge, Massachusetts)
1961 *Reflections on Human Nature* (Baltimore)
Lovett, A. A., Whyte, I. D. and Poisson, K. A. 1985 'Regression analysis and migration fields', *Trans. Brit. Instit. Geog.*, 10
Lowe, D. M. 1982 *History of Bourgeois Perception* (Brighton)
Lowe, N. 1972 *The Lancashire Textile Industry in the Sixteenth Century* (Cheth. Soc. Pub., 3rd ser., 20)
Lowry, S. T. 1974 'The archaeology of the circulation concept', *J. H. I.*, 35
(ed.) 1987 *Pre-classical Economic Thought* (Boston)
Lucas, C. 1973 'Nobles, bourgeois and the origins of the French Revolution', *P. & P.*, 60
Lucas, P. 1962 'Blackstone and the reform of the legal profession', *E. H. R.*, 77
1974 'A collective biography of students of Lincoln's Inn', *J. M. H.*, 46
Luetic, J. 1978 'English mariners and ships in seventeenth-century Dubrovnik', *Mar. Mirr.*, 64
Lukes, S. 1973 *Individualism* (Oxford)
Lütge, F. 1966 *Deutsche Sozial und Wirtschaftsgeschichte*, 3rd edn (Berlin)
Luzzatto, G. 1937 'Les activités économiques du patriciat vénétien', *Annales*, 9
Lyman, D. B. 1935 *The Great Tom Fuller* (Berkeley)
Lynam, E. (ed.) 1946 *Richard Hakluyt and his Successors*
Lynch, K. M. 1926 *The Social Mode of Restoration Comedy* (New York)
Lynch, M. 1981 *Edinburgh and the Reformation*
(ed.) 1987 *The Early Modern Town in Scotland*
Lynch, M. and Spearman, M. (eds.) 1988 *The Scottish Medieval Town* (Edinburgh)
Lysons, S. 1860 *The Model Merchant*
MacArthur, E. A. 1928 'Sir Edmund Berry Godfrey', *E. H. R.*, 43
MacCaffrey, W. T. 1968 *The Shaping of the Elizabethan Regime* (Princeton)
1976 *Exeter, 1540–1640*, 2nd edn (Cambridge, Massachusetts)
MacCampbell, A. E. 1976 'The London parish and the London precinct', *Guild. Stud. Lond. Hist.*, 2
MacClelland, D. C. 1961 *The Achievement Society* (Princeton)
MacClelland, D. C. and Winter, D. G. 1969 *Motivating Economic Achievement* (New York)
MacClelland, P. D. 1975 *Causal Explanation and Model Building in History* (Ithaca)
MacClenaghan, B. 1924 *The Springs of Lavenham* (Ipswich)
MacCloskey, D. N. 1973 *Economic Maturity and Entrepreneurial Decline* (Cambridge, Massachusetts)
1976 'English open fields', *Res. Ec. Hist.*, 1

MacConica, J. K. 1973 'The prosopography of the Tudor university', *J. I. H.*, 3
1977 'The social relations of Tudor Oxford', *T. R. H. S.*, 5th ser., 27
(ed.) 1986 *The History of the University of Oxford*, vol. III (Oxford)
MacCracken, C. 1983 'The exchange of children in Tudor England', *J. Fam. Hist.*, 8
MacCullagh, C. B. 1984 *Justifying Historical Descriptions* (Cambridge)
1987 'Representation of historical events', *Hist. & Theory*, 26
MacCulloch, D. M. 1986 *Suffolk and the Tudors, 1500–1600* (Oxford)
MacCusker, J. J. 1978 *Money and Exchange in Europe and America, 1600–1789*
1983 'European bills of entry', *Harv. Lib. Bull.*, 31
1985 *European Bills of Entry and Marine Lists* (Cambridge, Massachusetts)
1986 'The business press in England', *Library*, NS, 8
1991 'The early history of Lloyds List', *Hist. Res.*, 64
MacCusker, J. J. and Gravesteijn, C. 1991 *The Beginning of Commercial and Financial Journalism* (Amsterdam)
MacCusker, J. J. and Menard, R. R. 1985 *The Economy of British America, 1607–1789* (Chapel Hill)
MacDonald, A. 1979 'Wallerstein's world economy' *J. Asian Stud.*, 38
MacDonald, D. 1964 *The Johnsons of Maiden Lane*
MacDonald, H. 1944 'The law and defamatory biographies in the seventeenth century', *Rev. Eng. Stud.*, 20
MacDonald, M. 1981 *Mystical Bedlam* (Cambridge)
1986 'The secularization of suicide', *P. & P.*, 111
1987 'An early seventeenth-century defence of usury', *Hist. Res.*, 60
MacDonald, M. and Murphy, T. R. 1990 *Sleepless Souls: Suicide in Early Modern England* (Oxford)
MacDonald, R. 1976 'The creation of an ordered world in Crusoe', *Dalhousie Review*, 66
MacDonnell, M. F. J. 1909 *A History of St Paul's School*
MacFarlane, A. 1970 *The Family Life of Ralph Josselin* (Cambridge)
1977 'Historical anthropology', *Soc. Hist.*, 5
1978 *The Origins of English Individualism* (New York)
1979 'The family, sex and marriage', *Hist. & Theory*, 18
1983 *A Guide to English Historical Records* (Cambridge)
1985 *Marriage and Love in England, 1300–1840* (Oxford)
1987 *The Culture of Capitalism* (Oxford)
MacFarlane, K. B. 1957 'The investment of Sir John Falstaff's profits of war', *T. R. H. S.*, 5th ser., 7
1965 'The English nobility in the Later Middle Ages' (Congrès de Comité Intern. des Sc. Hist., Vienna)
1973 *The Nobility of Late Medieval England* (Oxford)
1981 *England in the Fifteenth Century: Collected Essays*, ed. G. L. Harriss
MacFie, A. L. 1967 *The Individual in Society*
MacGee, J. S. 1976a 'Conversion', *J. B. S.*, 15
1976b *The Godly Man in Stuart England, 1620–70* (New Haven)
MacGrath, P. 1949 'The wills of Bristol merchants in the Great Orphans Book', *T. B. G. A. S.*, 68
1954 'Merchant shipping in the seventeenth century', *Mar. Mirr.*, 40

1970 *John Whitson and the Mercantile Community of Bristol* (Bristol Hist. Assoc. Pamph., 25)
1975 *The Merchant Venturers of Bristol* (Bristol)
(ed.) 1985 *A Bristol Miscellany* (Brist. Rec. Soc.)
MacGrath, P. and Cannon, J. (eds.) 1976 *Essays in Bristol and Gloucestershire History* (Bristol)
MacGreggor, A. 1983 *Tradescant's Rarities* (Oxford)
MacGregor, F. and Wright, N. 1977 *European History and its Historians* (Adelaide)
MacHattie, M. 1951 'Mercantile interests in the House of Commons, 1710–13' (unpub. M.A. thesis, Manchester)
MacHenry, R. W. 1984 'Dryden's history', *H. L. Q.*, 47
Machin, R. 1977 'The Great Rebuilding: a reassessment', *P. & P.*, 77
Machlud, F. (ed.) 1976 *The Political Economy of Freedom: Essays on Hayek* (New York)
MacInnes, A. 1982 'When was the Revolution', *History*, 67
1988 'Emergence of a leisure town: Shrewsbury, 1660–1760', *P. & P.*, 120
MacInnes, C. M. 1939 *Bristol, a Gateway to Empire* (Bristol)
MacInnes, C. M. and Whittard, W. T. 1955 *Bristol* (Bristol)
MacIntosh, A. W. 1982 'The number of the English regicides', *History*, 67
Macintosh, M. K. 1977 'Some new gentry', *Essex Arch. & Hist.*, 9
1978 'The fall of a gentle family', *H. L. Q.*, 41
1984 'Servants and the household', *J. Fam. Hist.*, 9
1988a 'Local responses to the poor', *Cont. & Ch.*, 3
1988b 'Money-lending on the periphery of London', *Albion*, 20
1991 *A Community Transformed: The Manor and Liberty of Havering, 1500–1626* (New York)
MacIntyre, A. 1984 *After Virtue: A Study in Moral Theory* (Notre Dame)
MacIntyre, R. A. 1956 'William Sanderson', *Wm & Mary Q.*, 3rd ser., 12
1963 *Debts Hopeful and Desperate* (Plymouth)
MacKay, A. 1977 *Spain in the Middle Ages*
MacKendrick, N. 1970 'Josiah Wedgwood and cost accounting', *Ec. H. R.*, 2nd ser., 23
MacKendrick, N. and Outhwaite, R. B. (eds.) 1986 *Business Life and Public Policy* (Cambridge)
MacKendrick, N., Brewer, J. and Plumb, J. H. (eds.) 1982 *The Birth of a Consumer Society*
MacKenney, R. 1987 *Tradesmen and Traders: The Worlds of the Guilds in Venice and Europe* c.*1250–1650*
1990 'Letters from the Venetian archives', *B. J. R. L.*, 72
MacKenzie, D. M. 1958 'Apprentices to the Stationers Company', *The Library*, 5th ser., 13
MacKeon, M. 1975 *Politics and Poetry in Restoration England* (Cambridge, Massachusetts)
1987 *The Origins of the English Novel* (Baltimore)
Mackerness, E. D. 1963 *A Social History of English Music*
MacKinley, R. A. 1980 'Social class and the origin of surnames', *Geneal. Mag.*, 20
Mackinnon, F. D. 1936 'Origins of commercial law', *Law Q. R.*, 52

MacKisack, M. 1932 *The Parliamentary Representation of the English Boroughs*
MacKittrick, D. 1990 'John Field in 1668', *Trans. Camb. Bib. Soc.*, 9
MacLachlan, H. J. 1931 *English Education under the Test Acts* (Manchester)
MacLachlan, J. O. 1940 *Trade and Peace with Old Spain, 1667–1750* (Cambridge)
MacLaren, A. 1984 *Reproductive Rituals*
MacLaren, D. 1978 'Fertility, infant mortality and breast feeding', *Med. Hist.*, 22
Macleod, C. 1983 'Henry Martyn', *B. I. H. R.*, 56
1986 'The 1690s patents boom', *Ec. H. R.*, 2nd ser., 39
1988 *Inventing the Industrial Revolution* (Cambridge)
MacLure, M. 1958 *The Paul's Cross Sermons, 1534–1642* (Toronto)
MacMillan, D. S. (ed.) 1977 *Canadian Business History: Select Studies 1497–1971* (Toronto)
MacMullan, J. L. 1982 'Criminal organization in sixteenth- and seventeenth-century London', *Soc. Prob.*, 29
1984 *The Canting Crew: The London Criminal Underworld, 1550–1700* (New Brunswick)
MacMullen, N. 1977 'The education of English gentlewomen, 1540–1640', *Hist. Educ.*, 6
MacNally, D. 1988 *Political Economy and the Rise of Capitalism* (Berkeley)
MacPherson, C. B. 1962 *The Political Theory of Possessive Individualism* (Oxford)
MacVeagh, J. 1981 *Tradeful Merchants: The Portrayal of the Capitalist in Literature*
Maddison, A. 1982 *Phases of Capitalist Development* (Oxford)
Madjarian, G. 1982 'Hobbes et la société marchande', *Temps Moderns*, 39
Magalhaes-Godinho, V. 1969 *L'Economie de l'empire portugaise aux XV et XVIe siècles*
Mahoney, M. 1979 'Presbyterians in London, 1643–7', *H. J.*, 22
Maidy, L. G. de, 1885 *De la prétendue noblesse des gentilhommes verriers en Lorraine* (Nancy)
Main, G. L. 1975 'Probate records as a source', *Wm & Mary Q.*, 3rd ser., 32
1982 *Tobacco Colony: Life in Early Maryland, 1650–1720* (Princeton)
1983 'The standard of living in colonial Massaschusetts', *J. Ec. H.*, 43
Maine, Sir Henry 1906 *Ancient Law*, ed. Sir Frederick Pollock (New York)
Maistrov, I. E. 1974 *Probability Theory* (New York)
Maitland, F. W. 1957 *Selected Historical Essays*, ed. H. M. Cam (Cambridge)
Malament, B. C. (ed.) 1980 *After the Reformation: Essays in Honour of J. H. Hexter* (Manchester)
Malcolm, N. 1981 'Hobbes, Sandys and the Virginia Company', *H. J.*, 24
Malinowski, B. 1960 *A Scientific Theory of Culture* (Oxford)
Malone, J. 1972 'England and the Baltic naval stores trade', *Mar. Mirr.*, 58
Malowist, M. 1957 'Frage des Handelspolitik des Adels', *H.Gbl.*, 79
1959 'The economic and social development of the Baltic countries', *Ec. H. R.*, 2nd ser., 12
Man, M. 1986 *The Sources of Power* (Cambridge)
Manchée, W. H. 1936–7 'Some Huguenot smugglers', *Proc. Hug. Soc. Lond.*, 15
Mander, C. H. W. 1931 *The Guild of Cordwainers of London*
Manders, F. W. D. 1973 *A History of Gateshead*
Mandrou, R. 1961 *Introduction à la France moderne, 1500–1640*

Manley, G. 1974 'Central England temperatures', *Q. J. Roy. Meteor. Soc.*, 100
Mann, J. de L. 1956–7 'A Wiltshire family of clothiers', *Ec. H. R.*, 2nd ser., 9
1971 *The Cloth Industry of the West of England, 1640–1880* (Oxford)
1982 'A Guernsey merchant of the Commonwealth period', *Soc. Guérn. Rep. & Trans.*, 21
Manning, R. B. 1988 *Village Revolts* (Oxford)
Manuel, F. E. 1971 'The use and abuse of psychology in history', *Daedalus*, 100
Marambaud, P. 1973 'William Byrd I', *Virginia Mag. Hist. Biog.*, 81
Maravall, J. A. 1979 *Poder, Honor y Elites* (Madrid)
Marchant, R. A. 1960 *The Puritans and the Church Courts in the Diocese of York, 1560–1640* (Cambridge)
1969 *The Church under the Law* (Cambridge)
Maré, E. S. de, 1958 *London Riverside*
Margolies, D. 1985 *Novel and Society in Elizabethan England* (Totowa, New Jersey)
Markham, Sir C. R. 1870 *The Great Lord Fairfax*
Marley, D. de, 1979 'Fashionable suppliers, 1660–1700', *Antiq. J.*, 58
Marriner, S. (ed.) 1978a *Business and Businessmen* (Liverpool)
1978b 'Accounting records in English bankruptcy proceedings', *Acc. Hist. Journ.*, 3
1980 'English bankruptcy records', *Ec. H. R.*, 2nd ser., 33
Marsh, R. H. 1961 *The Mandarins and the Circulation of Elites in China, 1600–1900* (Glencoe, Illinois)
Marshall, A. 1961 *Principles of Economics*, 9th edn
Marshall, D. 1937–8 'The Old Poor Law, 1662–1795', *Ec. H. R.*, 8
Marshall, G. 1980 *Presbyteries and Profits, 1560–1707* (Oxford)
Marshall, J. D. 1975a *Kendal, 1660–1801* (Kendal)
1975b 'Kendal', *Trans. Cumb. & West. Antiq. & Arch. Soc.*, 75
1980 'Agrarian wealth and social structure', *Ec. H. R.*, 2nd ser., 33
1983 'The Cumbrian market towns', *North. Hist.*, 19
Marshall, P. J. 1976 *East India Fortunes* (Oxford)
Marshall, S. 1987 *The Dutch Gentry, 1500–1650* (New York)
Marshall, T. H. 1950 *Citizenship and Social Class* (Cambridge)
Marston, J. G. 1973 'Gentry honor and royalism', *J. B. S.*, 13
Martin, F. 1876 *The History of Lloyds*
Martin, G. and Bezançon, M. 1911 *L'Histoire du Crédit en France*
Martin, I. 1980 'John Crane', *Med. Hist.*, 24
Martin, J. 1979 'Estate Stewards, 1660–1760', *Morganweg*, 23
Martin, J. B. 1892 *The Grasshopper in Lombard Street*
Martin, J. F. 1991 *Profits in the Wilderness*
Martin, J. M. 1977 'An investigation into the small size of the household', *Loc. Pop. Stud.*, 19
1982 'Stratford', *Mid. Hist.*, 8
Martin, R. 1977 *Historical Explanation, Reenactment and Practical Inference* (Ithaca)
1982 'Causes, conditions and causal importance', *Hist. & Theory*, 21
Martinez, L. 1963 *The Social World of the Florentine Humanists*
1979 *Power and Imagination* (New York)

Martiny, F. 1938 *Die Adelsfrage in Preussen vor 1806* (Berlin)
Marvyama, M. 1974 *Studies in the Intellectual History of Tokugawa Japan* (Princeton)
Marz, E. 1988 'The economic system of J.A. Schumpeter', *J. Eur. Ideas*, 9
1991 *Joseph Schumpeter* (New Haven)
Mason, J. 1982 'Accounting records and business history', *Bus. Hist.*, 24
Mason, J. E. 1935 *Gentlefolk in the Making* (Philadelphia)
Mason, T. A. 1985 *William Juxon, 1586–1663*
Massarella, D. 1990 *A World Elsewhere: Europe's Encounter with Japan* (New Haven)
Masson, P. 1896 *Histoire du commerce français dans le Levant*
Master, G. S. 1874 *Some Notes on the Family of Master* (priv. printed)
Masters, B. 1988 *The Origins of Western Economic Dominance in the Middle East, 1600–1786* (New York)
Masters, B. R. 1975 'The Corporation of London Record Office', *Archives*, 12
1988 *The Chamberlain of the City of London, 1237–1987*
Mathers, C. J. 1988 'Family partnerships and international trade', *Bus. Hist. Rev.*, 62
Mathew, D. 1948 *The Social Structure in Caroline England* (Oxford)
1951 *The Age of Charles I*
Mathew, S. 1968 *The Court of Richard II*
Mathias, P. G. 1957–8 'The social structure in the eighteenth century', *Ec. H. R.*, 2nd ser., 10
1959 *The Brewing Industry in England, 1700–1830* (Cambridge)
(ed.) 1972 *Science and Society* (Cambridge)
1975 'Business history and managerial education', *Bus. Hist.*, 17
Mathias, P. G. and O'Brien, P. 1976 'Taxation in Britain and France, 1715–1810', *J. Eur. Ec. Hist.*, 5
Mathias, P. G. and Pearsall, A. W. H. (eds.) 1971 *Shipping: A Survey of Historical Records* (Newton Abbot)
Matthews, A. G. 1934 *Calamy Revised* (Oxford)
1948 *Walker Revised* (Oxford)
Matthews, L. G. 1962 *History of Pharmacy in Britain*
1964 'Royal apothecaries', *Med. Hist.*, 8
1974 'London immigrant apothecaries', *Med. Hist.*, 18
Matthews, W. 1950 *An Annotated Bibliography of British Diaries, 1442–1942*
1955 *British Autobiographies* (Berkeley)
Maude, A. 1953 *Professional People in England* (Cambridge, Massachusetts)
Mauro, F. 1958 'La bourgeoisie portuguaise', *XVIIe Siècle*, 40
1983 *Le Portugal et l'Atlantique, 1570–1670*, new edn
Mause, L. de (ed.) 1974 *The History of Childhood* (New York)
May, P. 1984 *The Changing Face of Newmarket, 1660–1760* (Newmarket)
Mayhew, G. 1989 *Tudor Rye* (Falmer)
1991 'Life cycle service and the family unit', *Cont. & Ch.*, 6
Mayo, C. H. 1922 'The social status of the clergy', *E. H. R.*, 37
Mayo, R. 1970 'The Bristol Huguenots', *Proc. Hug. Soc. Lond.*, 21
Mayr, E. 1976 *Evolution and the Diversity of Life* (Cambridge, Massachusetts)
1982 *The Growth of Biological Thought* (Cambridge, Massachusetts)

Mazzei, R. 1979 'The decline of the city economies of Italy', *J. It. H.*, 2
Medick, H. and Sabean, D. W. 1984 (eds.) *Interest and Emotion* (Cambridge)
Medlycott, M. T. 1977 'The London Freedom Registers', *Geneal. Mag.*, 19
Meehan-Waters, B. 1982 *Autocracy and Aristocracy* (New Brunswick)
Meek, R. L. 1950 *Studies in the Labour Theory of Value*
Meier, G. M. 1970 *Leading Issues in Economic Development*, 2nd edn (New York)
Meier, G. M. and Baldwin, R. E. (eds.) 1957 *Economic Development: Theory, History, Policy* (New York)
Meilink-Roelofsz, M. A. P. 1962 *Asian Trade and European Influence* (The Hague)
1976 'Eeen vergelijkend onderzoek', *Bijd. en mededelingen betreffende de gesch. de Nederland*, 91
Melis, F. 1972 *Documenti per la storia economica dei secolo xiii–xiv* (Florence)
Melling, J. and Barry, J. (eds.) 1992 *Culture and History: Production, Consumption and Value in Historical Perspective* (Exeter)
Melton, F. T. 1977 'Sir Robert Clayton's building projects', *Guild. Stud. Lond. Hist.*, 3
1978 'Absentee land management', *Agric. Hist. Rev.*, 52
1979 'The Clayton papers', *B. I. H. R.*, 52
1986a *Sir Robert Clayton* (Cambridge)
1986b 'Deposit banking in London, 1700–90', *Bus. Hist.*, 28
Menard, R. R. 1973 'Immigration to the Chesapeake colonies', *Maryland Hist. Mag.*, 68
1974 'Opportunities and equality', *Maryland Hist. Mag.*, 59
1980 'The Chesapeake tobacco industry', *Res. Ec. Hist.*, 5
Menard, R. R., Carr, L. G. and Walsh, L. S. 1983 'A small planter's profit', *Wm. & Mary Q.*, 40
Mendel, F. F. 1978 'Notes on the age of maternity', *J. Fam. Hist.*, 3
Mendelson, S. H. 1979 'The weightiest business', *P. & P.*, 85
1987 *The Mental World of Stuart Women* (Brighton)
Mendenhall, T. C. 1951 'The social status of Shrewsbury drapers', *Trans. Shrop. Arch. & Nat. Hist. Soc.*, 54
1953 *The Shrewsbury Drapers and the Welsh Wool Trade* (Oxford)
Mendle, M. 1989 'The ship money case', *H. J.*, 32
Meredith, R. 1964 'The Eyres of Hassop, 1470–1640', *Derby. Arch. J.*, 74–75
1965 'A Derbyshire family in the seventeenth century', *Rec. Hist.*, 8
Merle, L. and Debien, G. 1954 *Au commencement d'une fortune coloniale*
Meroney, G. 1968 'The London entrepôt merchants', *Wm & Mary Q.*, 3rd ser, 25
Merrit, J. E. 1960 'The triangular trade', *Bus. Hist.*, 3
Merton, R. K. 1964 *Social Theory and Social Structure*, rev. edn (Glencoe, Illinois)
Metcalf, P. 1977 *The Halls of the Fishmongers*
1984 'Living over the shop', *Arch. Hist.*, 27
Metzger, T. A. 1973 *The Internal Organization of Ch'ing Bureaucracy* (Cambridge, Massachusetts)
Mews, H. 1935 'Middle-class conduct books', *B. I. H. R.*, 13
Meyer, J. 1960 *La Noblesse bretonne au XVIIIe siècle*, 2 vols.

1975 'Le XVIIe siècle', *XVIIe Siècle*, 106–7
Meyer, W. R. 1981 'English privateers in the war of 1688–97', *Mar. Mirr.*, 67
1983 'English privateers, 1702–13', *Mar. Mirr.*, 69
Michael, I. L. 1987 *The Teaching of English* (Cambridge)
Michel, R. H. 1978 'English attitudes towards women, 1640–1700', *Canad. J. Hist.*, 13
Middlekauf, R. 1976 *The Mathers, 1596–1728* (New York)
Milbourne, T. 1888 *The Vintners Company*
Miles, M. 1986 'A haven for the privileged', *J. Soc. Hist.*, 11
Milford, E. 1990 'The Navy at peace, 1603–18', *Mar. Mirr.*, 76
Mill, J. S. 1911 *Principles of Political Economy*, repr.
Millard, A. M. 1956 'The import trade of London, 1600–40' (unpub. Ph.D. thesis, London)
Miller, A. C. 1963 *Sir Henry Killigrew* (Leicester)
Miller, D. 1980 'Hume and possessive individualism', *Hist. Pol. Thought*, 1
Miller, E. 1952 'The state and landed interests', *T. R. H. S.*, 5th ser., 2
Miller, E. A. 1946 'Some arguments concerning a standing army', *J. M. H.*, 18
Miller, E. H. 1959 *The Professional Writer in Elizabethan England* (Cambridge, Massachusetts)
Miller, H. K., Rothenstein, E. and Rousseau, G. S. (eds.) 1970 *The Augustan Milieu: Essays Presented to L. A. Landa* (Oxford)
Miller, J. L. 1973a *Popery and Politics in England, 1660–88* (Cambridge)
1973b 'Catholic officers in the late Stuart army', *E. H. R.*, 88
1983 *The Glorious Revolution*
1985 *Restoration England: The Reign of Charles II*
Miller, K. A. 1985 *Emigrants and Exiles: Ireland and the Exodus to North America* (Oxford)
Miller, L.R. 1926 'The shipping and imports of London, 1601–2', *Q.J.Econ.*, 41
Miller, P. and Johnson, T. H. (eds.) 1938 *The Puritans* (New York)
Miller, W. L. 1980 'Primogeniture, entails and endowment', *Hist. Pol. Econ.*, 12
Milles, C. W. 1969 'Benjamin Franklin's "Way to Wealth"', *Papers Bibliog. Soc. Amer.*, 63
Milne, D. J. 1951 'The results of the Rye House Plot', *T. R. H. S.*, 5th ser., 1
Milner, A. 1981 *John Milton and the English Revolution*
Milsom, S. F. C. 1969 *The Historical Foundations of the Common Law*
1976 *The Legal Framework of English Feudalism* (Cambridge)
John Milton and his Commonplace Book 1969 (New York)
Mimardiere, A. M. 1964 'The finances of a Warwickshire gentry family', *Univ. B'ham H. J.*
Minchinton, W. E. 1957 *The Trade of Bristol in the Eighteenth Century* (Bristol Rec. Soc., 20)
1962 *Politics and the Port of Bristol* (Brist. Rec. Soc., 25)
(ed.) 1968 *Essays in Agrarian History* (Newton Abbot)
(ed.) 1969 *The Growth of Overseas Trade in the Seventeenth and Eighteenth Centuries*
1978 *Capital Formation in South-west England* (Univ. of Exeter Dept. Ec. Hist.)
(ed.) 1988 *Britain and the Northern Seas* (Pontefract)
Mingay, G. E. 1963 *English Landed Estate in the Eighteenth Century*

1976 *The Gentry: The Rise and Fall of a Ruling Class* (Harlow)
Mirowski, P. 1982 'Adam Smith's empiricism and the rate of profit', *Hist. Pol. Econ.*, 14
Mises, L. von, 1949 *Human Action* (New Haven)
Mish, C. C. 1952 *English Prose Fiction, 1600–1700* (Bibliog. Soc. Univ. Virg.)
Miskimin, H. A., Herlihy, D. and Udovitch, A. L. (eds.) 1977 *The Medieval City* (New Haven)
Mitchell, N. H. 1986 'John Locke and the rise of capitalism', *Hist. Pol. Econ.*, 18
Mitchell, R. J. and Leys, M. D. R. 1958 *A History of London Life*
Mitchell, W. 1904 *Essay on the Early History of the Law Merchant* (Cambridge)
Mitchell, W. F. 1932 *English Pulpit Oratory from Andrews to Tillotson*
Mitchison, R. 1962 'Pluralities and the poorer benefices in eighteenth-century England', *H. J.*, 5
Mitchison, R. and Roebuck, P. 1988 (eds.) *Economy and Society in Scotland and Ireland, 1500–1939* (Edinburgh)
Mitzman, A. 1970 *The Iron Cage* (New York)
'La mobilité sociale au XVIIe siècle', *XVIIe Siècle*, 122 (1979)
Modern Reports, King's Bench
Mohl, R. 1933 *The Three Estates in Medieval and Renaissance literature* (New York)
Moir, E. 1957–8 'Benedict Webb, clothier', *Ec. H. R.*, 2nd ser., 10
Moir, T. L. 1938 *The Addled Parliament of 1614*
Molen, R. L. de, 1974 'Richard Mulcaster and the profession of teaching', *J. H. I.*, 35
1976 'Age of admission', *Hist. Educ.*, 6
Mollat, M. 1952 *Le Commerce maritime normand à la fin du Moyen Age*
(ed.) 1970 *Sociétés et compagnies de commerce en Orient et dans l'Océan Indien*
Mommsen, W. J. 1974 *The Age of Bureaucracy* (New York)
1980 'Towards the iron cage of serfdom', *T. R. H. S.*, 5th ser., 30
Monicat, J. 1955 'Les archives notariales', *Rev. Hist.*, 214
Monier-Williams, R. H. 1970 *The Tallow Chandlers of London*
Monroe, H. 1975 *The Ambivalence of Bernard Mandeville* (Oxford)
Moody, T. W. 1939 *The Londonderry Plantation, 1609–41* (Belfast)
Moore, Sir Edward, 1899 *Liverpool in King Charles II's Time*, ed. W. Ferguson (Liverpool)
Moore, J. R. 1935 *Defoe and Modern Economic Theory* (Indiana Univ. Stud., 104)
Moore, J. S. 1993 'Jack Fisher's flu', *Ec. H. R.*, 46
Moore, P. 1972 'An Aleppo merchant's letters', *Morganweg*, 8.
Moore, W. E. 1963 *Social Change* (Englewood Cliffs)
Moran, J. A. H. 1979 *Education and Learning in the City of York* (York)
1981 'Literacy and education in northern England', *North. Hist.*, 17
1985 *The Growth of English Schooling, 1340–1548* (Princeton)
Morazé, C. 1957 'Origines de gentilhommes verriers', *Chercheurs et Curieux*, 71
Moreton, C. E. 1991 'A social gulf', *J. Med. Hist.*, 17
Morgan, E. S. 1966 *The Puritan Family* (New York)
1971a 'The first American boom', *Wm & Mary Q.*, 28
1971b 'The labour problem at Jamestown', *A. H. R.*
Morgan, J. 1986 *Godly Learning, 1560–1640* (Cambridge)

Morgan, J. H. 1940 'John Watson, painter, merchant and capitalist', *Proc. Amer. Antiq. Soc.*, 50

Morgan, P. 1970 'South Warwickshire clergy', *Warws. Hist.*, 1

1978 *Warwickshire Apprentices in the Stationers Company, 1573–1700* (Dugdale Soc., Occ. Papers, 25)

Morineau, M. 1970 'Flottes de commerce et trafics français en Méditerranée', *XVIIe Siècle*, 86–7

Morison, S. E. 1930–2 'William Pynchon', *Proc. Mass. Hist. Soc.*, 64

Morrill, J. S. 1974 *Cheshire, 1630–60* (Oxford)

1976 *The Revolt of the Provinces, 1630–50*

1977 'Provincial squires and middle sort', *H. J.*, 20

1979 'The Northern gentry and the Great Rebellion', *North. Hist.*, 15

(ed.) 1982 *Reactions to the English Civil War, 1642–9*

Morrill, J. S., Slack, P. and Woolf, D. (eds.) 1993 *Public Duty and Private Conscience in Seventeenth-Century England: Essays Presented to G. E. Aylmer* (Oxford)

Morris, G. C. R. 1972 (ed.) 'Thomas Hobbs, surgeon', *Trans. Lond. & Midd. A. S.*, 23

Morris, J. N. 1966 *Versions of the Self* (New York)

Morrison, J. J. 1977 'Strypes Stow: the 1720 edition', *Lond. J.*, 3

Morriss, M. S. 1914 *Colonial Trade of Maryland, 1689–1713* (Baltimore)

Morrow, R. B. 1978 'Family limitation in pre-industrial England', *Ec. H. R.*, 2nd ser., 31

Morse, H. B. 1921 'The supercargo in the China trade', *E. H. R.*, 36

1926 *The Chronicles of the East India Company Trading to China, 1635–1834* (Oxford), 5 vols.

Mortimer, R. S. 1953 'Bristol Quaker merchants', *J. Friends Hist. Soc.*, 45

Morton, T. N. 1889 'Family of Moore in Liverpool', *Trans. Hist. Soc. Lancs. & Ches.*, 38

Mossner, E. C. 1954 *David Hume* (Edinburgh)

Motley, M. 1990 *Becoming an Aristocrat* (Princeton)

Mousley, J. E. 1958–9 'The fortunes of some gentry families of Elizabethan Sussex', *Ec. H. R.*, 2nd ser., 11

Mousnier, R. 1945 *La Vénalité des offices sous Henri IV et Louis XIII* (Rouen)

1951 'L'évolution des publique finances en France', *Rev. Hist.*, 205

1955 'L'opposition politique bourgeoise', *Rev. Hist.*, 213

(ed.) 1966 *Problèmes de stratification sociale. Actes du colloque internationale*

1969 *Les Hierarchies sociales de 1450 à nos jours*

1974 *Les Institutions de la France sous la monarchie absolue*, vol. I, *Société et état*

Muchmore, L. 1969 'Gerard de Malynes', *Hist. Pol. Econ.*, 1

1970 'A note on Thomas Mun', *Ec. H. R.*, 2nd ser., 23

1971 'The project literature', *Bus. Hist. Rev.*, 45

Muldrew, C. 1993 'Credit and the courts', *Ec. H. R.*, 46

Mullett, C. F. 1946 *Public Baths and Health in England* (Bull. Hist. Med. Supp. 5)

Mullett, M. 1972 'The politics of Liverpool', *Trans. Hist. Soc. Lancs. & Ches.*, 124

1975 'Preston politics, 1660–90', *Trans. Hist. Soc. Lancs. & Ches.*, 125

1983 'Elections in Lancashire, 1660–88', *North. Hist.*, 19

Mulligan, L. 1977 'Winstanley', *J. Eccles. Hist.*, 28
1983 'The religious roots of William Walwyn', *J. Rel. Hist.*, 12
Mulligan, L. and G. 1981 'Reconstructing Restoration science', *Social Studies of Science*, 11
Mumby, F. A. 1949 *Publishers and Booksellers*
Mumford, A. A. 1919 *The Manchester Grammar School, 1515–1913*
Munby, L. M. (ed.) 1991 *All My Worldly Goods: An Insight into Family Life from Wills and Inventories, 1447–1742* (Bricket Wood)
Munday, R. 1977 'Legal history of the factor', *Anglo Amer. Law Rev.*, 6
Munk, W. 1878 *The Roll of the Royal College of Physicians*, vol. I, *1518–1700*, 2nd edn
Munsche, P. B. 1981 *Gentlemen and Poachers: The English Game Laws, 1671–1831* (Cambridge)
Munter, R. L. and Grose, C. L. 1986 *Englishmen Abroad* (New York)
Murphy, A. E. 1986 *Richard Cantillon* (Oxford)
Murphy, G. 1925 *A Bibliography of English Character Books, 1608–1700* (Oxford)
Murphy, K. 1989 'Analysis of a cesspit', *Bull. Board Celt. Stud.*, 36
Murphy, T. R. 1986 'Suicide in children and adolescents, 1507–1710', *Sixt. Cent. J.*, 17
Murray, D. 1930 *Chapters in the History of Bookkeeping and Accountancy* (Glasgow)
Murray, E. F. C. 1962 *Decorative Painting in England, 1537–1837*, 2 vols.
Murray, J. 1988 'Kinship and friendship', *Albion*, 20
Murray, J. T. 1910 *English Dramatic Companies, 1558–1642*, 2 vols.
Murray, Sir O. A. R. 1937–9 'The High Court of Admiralty', *Mar. Mirr.*, 33–5
Mustazza, L. 1989 'Thomas Deloney's Jack of Newbury', *J. Pop. Cult.*, 23
Mutch, R. E. 1980 'Colonial America and the debate about transition to capitalism', *Theory and Society*, 9
Myers, M. L. 1972 'Philosophical anticipation of laissez faire', *Hist. Pol. Econ.*, 4
1983 *The Soul of Economic Man*
Myers, R. 1983 'The records of the Stationers', *Archives*, 16
Myers, R. and Harris, M. (eds.) 1985 *Economics of the British Book Trade, 1605–1939* (Cambridge)
Nadelhaft, J. 1982 'The Englishwoman's sexual civil war', *J. H. I.*, 43
Nakamura, J. I. 1981 'Human capital accumulation in pre-modern Japan', *J. Ec. H.*, 41
Namier, Sir Lewis, 1939 *In the Margin of History*
1957 *The Structure of Politics at the Accession of George III*, 2nd edn
1961 *England in the Age of the American Revolution*, 2nd edn
1962 *Crossroads of Power*
Namier, Sir Lewis and Brooke, J. 1964 *House of Commons, 1754–90*
Narrett, D. E. 1993 *Inheritance and Family Life in Colonial New York City*
Naughton, K. S. 1976 *The Gentry of Bedfordshire in the Thirteenth and Fourteenth Centuries* (Leicester)
Neale, Sir John, 1948 'The Elizabethan political scene', *P. B. A.*, 34
1950 *Elizabethan House of Commons* (New Haven)
Neale, L. 1988 'The rise of a financial press', *Bus. Hist.*, 30

1990 *The Rise of Financial Capitalism* (Cambridge)
Neale, R. S. 1981 *Class in English History* (Oxford)
Neave, D. 1988 *The Dutch Connection: The Anglo-Dutch Heritage of Hull and Humberside* (Hull)
Needham, N. J. T. M. 1954 *Science and Civilisation in China* (Cambridge)
1965 'Time and Eastern Man', *Royal Anthrop. Instit. Occ. Papers*, 21
1970 *Clerk and Craftsman in China and the West* (Cambridge)
Nef, J. U. 1932 *The Rise of the British Coal Industry*, 2 vols.
1940 *Industry and Government in France and England, 1560–1640* (Amer. Phil. Soc. Mem., 15)
Nelson, B. N. 1969 *The Idea of Usury*, 2nd edn (Chicago)
Nelson, R. R. and Winter, S. G. 1982 *An Evolutionary Theory of Economics* (Cambridge, Massachusetts)
Nethercot, A. H. 1938 *Sir William Davenant* (Chicago)
Nettels, C. P. 1934 *The Money Supply of the American Colonies* (Univ. of Wisconsin Stud., 20)
Neumann, J. von, and Morgenstern, O. 1964 *Theory of Games and Economic Behaviour*, new edn (Princeton)
Nevinson, J. L. 1974 'Crowns and garlands', *Guild. Stud. Lond. Hist.*, 1
New, J. F. H. 1963 'The meaning of Harrington's Agrarian', *P. & P.*, 25
Newdigate, B. H. 1961 *Michael Drayton and his Circle* (Oxford)
Newey, V. (ed.) 1980 *'The Pilgrim's Progress': Critical and Historical Views* (Liverpool)
Newman, K. 1983 'Financial advertising, past and present', *Three Banks Review*, 140
Newman, K. 1985 'Hamburg and the European economy', *J. Eur. Ec. Hist.*, 14
Newman, P. R. 1979 'Roman Catholics in pre-Civil War England', *Rec. Hist.*, 15
Newton, A. P. 1914 *The Colonising Activities of the Early Puritans* (New Haven)
Newton, S. C. 1966 'The gentry of Derbyshire', *Derby. Arch. J.*, 86
Nicholl, J. 1851 *The Company of Ironmongers*
Nicholls, J. F. 1870 *Bristol Biographies* (Bristol)
Nicholls, M. 1992 'As Happy a Fortune as I Desire', *Hist. Res.*, 65
Nichols, G. O. 1971 'English government borrowing, 1660–88', *J. B. S.*, 10
1985 'The development of English repayment and interest rates', *Rev. Intl Hist. Banque*, 30–1
1987 'Intermediaries and borrowing: the development of English government, 1675–79', *Bus. Hist.*, 29
Nichols, J. G. 1863 'Gerard Legh', *Herald & Genealogist*, 1
Nicolas, J. 1978 *La Savoie au XVIIIe siècle*, 2 vols.
Nieli, R. 1981 'Commercial society and Christian virtue', *Rev. Politics*, 51
Nierop, H. K. van, 1993 *The Nobility of Holland from Knight to Regent, 1500–1650* (Cambridge)
Nietkiewicz, M. 1989 'James Howell', *Canad. J. Hist.*, 25
Nightingale, P. 1989 'Capitalist crafts and constitutional change', *P. & P.*, 124
1990 'Monetary contraction', *Ec. H. R.*, 2nd ser., 43
Nockolds, H. (ed.) 1977 *History of the Company of Coachmakers*
Noonan, J. T. 1957 *The Scholastic Analysis of Usury* (Cambridge, Massachusetts)
Norman, P. 1935 *Watermen of London after the Great Fire*

North, D. C. 1973 *The Rise of the Western World. A New Economic History* (Cambridge)
North, D. C. and Thomas, R. P. 1970, 1973 'An economic theory of the growth of the Western world', *Ec. H. R.*, 2nd ser., 23, 26
North, D. C. and Wengart, B. R. 1989 'Constitutions and commitment', *J. Ec. H.*, 49
North, M. 1984 'Elbing in the sixteenth century', *J. Eur. Ec. Hist.*, 13
Notestein, W. 1954 *The English People on the Eve of Colonisation, 1603–30* (New York)
1956 *Four Worthies*
Novak, M. E. 1962 *Economics and the Fiction of Daniel Defoe* (Berkeley)
1963 *Defoe and the Nature of Man*
1970 'A whiff of scandal', *H. L. Q.*, 34
Noyes, G. E. 1937 *Bibliography of Courtesy and Conduct Books in Seventeenth Century England* (New Haven)
Nungezer, E. 1929 *A Dictionary of Actors* (New Haven)
Nurske, R. 1967 *Problems of Capital Formation in Underdeveloped Countries* (New York)
Nuttall, G. F. and Chadwick, W. O. (eds.) 1976 *From Uniformity to Unity, 1662–1962*
Nye, J. V. 1991 'Lucky fools and cautious businessmen', *Res. Ec. Hist.*, Supp. 6
Oakeshott, M. J. 1962 *Rationalism in Politics* (New York)
Oates, J. C. T. 1986 *Cambridge University Library: A History* (Cambridge)
O'Brien, P. K. 1982 'European economic development', *Ec. H. R.*, 2nd ser., 35
1985 'Agriculture and the home market for British industry', *E. H. R.*, 100
1988 'The political economy of British taxation', *Ec. H. R.*, 2nd ser., 41
O'Brien, P. K., Griffith, T. and Hunt, P. 1991 'Political components of the Industrial Revolution', *Ec. H. R.*, 2nd ser., 44
O'Day, R. 1975a 'The law of patronage', *J. Eccles. Hist.*, 26
1975b 'Cumulative debt', *Mid. Hist.*, 3
1976 'Immanuel Bourne', *J. Eccles. Hist.*, 27
1979 *The English Clergy: The Emergence of a Consolidated Profession, 1558–1642* (Leicester)
1982 *Education and Society, 1500–1800*
O'Day, R. and Heal, F. (eds.) 1976 *Continuity and Change* (Leicester)
1981 *Princes and Paupers* (Leicester)
Oden, B. 1960 *Kopparhandel och statsmonopol* (Stockholm)
O'Donoghue, E. G. 1929 *Bridewell*
O'Driscoll, G. P. and Rizzo, M. J. 1985 *The Economics of Time and Ignorance* (Oxford)
O'Dwyer, M. 1980 'Some Essex recusants of the professional classes', *Essex Recusants*, 21
Ogden, H. V. S. 1955 *English Taste in Landscape in the Seventeenth Century* (Ann Arbor)
Ogg, D. 1955 *England in the Reigns of James II and William III* (Oxford)
1967 *England in the Reign of Charles II*, 2nd edn (Oxford)
Ogilvie, Sir Charles, 1958 *The King's Government and the Common Law, 1471–1641* (Oxford)

O'Hara, D. 1991 'Ruled by my friends', *Cont. & Ch.*, 6
Okin, S. M. 1983 'Patriarchy and married women's property', *Eight. Cent. Stud.*, 17
Oldham, J. B. 1952 *History of Shrewsbury School, 1552–1952* (Oxford)
Oliveira, A. H. de, 1971 *Daily Life in Portugal in the Middle Ages* (Madison)
Ollard, R. 1969 *Sir Robert Holmes and the Restoration Navy*
Ollard, R. and Tudor-Craig, P. 1986 (eds.) *For Veronica Wedgwood*
Olson, A. G. 1980 'The Board of Trade and London-American interest groups, 1690–1790', *J. Imp. and Comm. Hist.*, 8
1983 'The Virginia merchants of London', *Wm & Mary Q.*, 40
1992 *Making the Empire Work: London and American interest groups, 1690–1790* (Cambridge, Massachusetts)
O'Malley, L. S. S. 1965 *The Indian Civil Service, 1601–1930*, 2nd edn
Oman, Sir Charles, 1965 *English Domestic Silver*, 6th edn
O'Neill, B. H. S. 1953 'Some seventeenth-century houses in Great Yarmouth', *Archaeologia*, 95
Ong, W. J. 1959 'Latin language study', *Stud. Phil.*, 56
Oosterveen, K. 1970 'Deaths by suicide, drowning and misadventure', *Loc. Pop. Stud.*, 4
Oppenheim, M. 1896 *History of the Administration of the Royal Navy, 1509–1660*
Orgel, S. and Lytle, G. F. 1981 *Patronage in the Renaissance* (Princeton)
Origo, I. 1957 *The Merchant of Prato*
Orme, N. 1989 *English Schools in Medieval and Renaissance England*
Ormerod, H. A. 1951 'The private ledger of Heywood', *Trans. Hist. Soc. Lancs. & Ches.*, 103
Ormrod, D. 1973 *The Dutch in London*
1985 *English Grain Exports and the Structure of Agrarian Capitalism* (Hull Univ. Occ. Papers Ec. & Soc. Hist., 12)
Orpen, P. K. 1977 'Schoolmastering as profession', *Hist. Educ.*, 6
1979 'Recruitment patterns of the schoolmasters', *Warws. Hist.*, 4
Ortiz, A. D. 1963 *La sociedad espanola en el siglo XVI* (Madrid)
Osborn, J. M. 1960 *The Beginnings of Autobiography in England* (Los Angeles)
Ostrander, G. M. 1973 'The making of the triangular trade myth', *Wm & Mary Q.*, 30
Otsuka, H. 1982 *The Spirit of Capitalism* (Tokyo)
Outhwaite, R. B. 1966a 'A note on the practice of the Exchequer Court', *E. H. R.*, 81
1966b 'The trials of foreign borrowing', *Ec. H. R.*, 2nd ser., 19
1971a 'Who bought Crown lands?', *B. I. H. R.*, 44
1971b 'Royal borrowing in the reign of Elizabeth I', *E. H. R.*, 86
1971c 'Dearth and government intervention', *Ec. H. R.*, 2nd ser., 24
1973 'Age at marriage in England', *T. R. H. S.*, 5th ser., 23
(ed.) 1981 *Marriage and Society*
1982 *Inflation in Tudor and Stuart England*, 2nd edn
1991 *Dearth and Public Policy*
Overton, M. 1977 'Computer analysis of an inconsistent data source', *J. Hist. Geog.*, 3
1983 *A Bibliography of British Probate Inventories* (Newcastle)

Owen, A. E. B. 1980 'A scrivener's notebook', *Archives*, 61
Owen, D. E. 1964 *English Philanthropy, 1660–1960* (Cambridge, Massachusetts)
Owen, G. D. 1962 *Elizabethan Wales: The Social Scene* (Cardiff)
1988 *Wales in the Reign of James I*
Owen, H. G. 1959 'Parochial curates in Elizabethan London', *J. Eccles. Hist.*, 10
1960 'The episcopal visitation in Elizabethan London', *J. Eccles. Hist.*, 11
Owen, J. H. 1938 *War at Sea under Queen Anne, 1702–08* (Cambridge)
Owen, W. S. 1991 *Richard Baxter, 1615–91*
Owst, G. R. 1961 *Literature and Pulpit in Medieval England* (repr. Oxford)
Oxley, G. W. 1974 *Poor Relief in England and Wales, 1601–1834* (Newton Abbot)
Ozment, S. E. 1983 *When Fathers Ruled* (Cambridge, Massachusetts)
Pachzs, P. 1966 'En Hongrie au XVIe siècle', *Annales*, 21
Pagan, A. C. 1985 'William Paggen of London, brewer', *Fam. Hist.*, NS, 13
Pagan, J. R. 1979 'Growth of the tobacco trade, 1614–40', *Guild. Stud. Lond. Hist.*, 3
Pagden, A. 1986 'The impact of the New World', *Ren. & Mod. Stud.*, 30
(ed.) 1987 *The Languages of Political Theory in Early Modern Europe* (Cambridge)
Pailin, D. A. 1984 (ed.) *Attitudes to Other Religions: Comparative Religion in Seventeenth and Eighteenth Century Britain* (Manchester)
Palliser, D. M. 1973 'Epidemics in Tudor York', *North. Hist.*, 8
1978 'A crisis of English towns: the case of York', *North. Hist.*, 14
1979 *Tudor York* (Oxford)
1982a 'Civic mentality and the environment in Tudor York', *North. Hist.*, 18
1982b 'Tawney's century', *Ec. H. R.*, 2nd ser., 35
1985 'A regional capital as magnet, 1477–1560', *Yorks. Arch. J.*, 57
Palmade, G. P. 1972 *French Capitalism in the Nineteenth Century* (Newton Abbot)
Palmer, A. N. 1902 'The adventures of a Denbighshire gentleman in the East Indies', *Arch. Cambr.*, 6th ser., 2
Palmer, R. 1981 'A Stratford on Avon wigmaker's diary', *Warws. Hist.*, 4
Palmer, V. V. 1989 'The history of privity', *Amer. J. Legal Hist.*, 33
Palmer, W. C. 1933–4 'The activities of the East India Company in Persia', *B. I. H. R.*, 11
Pape, T. 1938 *Newcastle under Lyme in Tudor and Early Stuart Times* (Manchester)
Papworth, J. W. 1961 *Ordinary of British Armorials* (repr. with an intro. by G. D. Squibb and Sir Anthony Wagner)
Pardailhé-Galabrun, A. 1988 *La Naissance de l'intime*
Parel, A. (ed.) 1983 *Ideology, Philosophy and Politics*
Pares, R. 1950 *A West India Fortune*
1954 *George III and the Politicians* (Oxford)
1956 *Yankees and Creoles*
1956–7 'The London Sugar Market, 1740–69', *Ec. H. R.*, 2nd ser., 9
1960 *Merchants and Planters* (Ec. H. R. Supp. 4)
1961 *The Historian's Business and Other Essays*, ed. R. A. and E. Humphreys (Oxford)
Parker, C. 1990 *The English Historical Tradition since 1850* (Edinburgh)
Parker, G. 1972 *The Army of Flanders and the Spanish Road, 1567–1659*

(Cambridge)
1977 *The Dutch Revolt* (Ithaca)
1979 *Spain and the Netherlands, 1559–1659*
1988 *The Military Revolution, 1500–1800* (Cambridge)
Parker, J. (ed.) 1965a *Merchants and Scholars* (Minneapolis)
1965b *Books to Build an Empire* (Amsterdam)
Parker, K. L. 1988 *The English Sabbath* (Cambridge)
Parker, R. A. C. 1975 *Coke of Norfolk* (Oxford)
Parker, R. H. (ed.) 1980 *Bibliography for Accounting Historians* (New York)
1982 *History of Accounting Literature*
1991 'Misleading accounts', *Bus. Hist.*, 33
Parker, V. 1971 *The Making of King's Lynn* (Chichester)
Parkes, J. 1925 *Travel in England in the Seventeenth Century* (Oxford)
Parkinson, C. N. 1937 *Trade in the Eastern Seas, 1703–1813* (Cambridge)
1952 *The Rise of the Port of Liverpool* (Liverpool)
Parks, G. B. 1928 *Richard Hakluyt and the English Voyages* (New York)
Parks, S. 1976 *John Dunton and the English Book Trade* (New York)
Parry, G. 1967 'Performatic utterance obligation in Hobbes', *Phil. Quart.*, 17
Parry, J. H. 1954 'The Patent Offices in the British West Indies', *E. H. R.*, 69
Parry, N. J. 1976 *The Rise of the Medical Profession*
Parsons, T. 1961 *Theories of Society* (Glencoe, Illinois), 2 vols.
Paterson, J. 1982 'Salvation from the sea', *J. Rom. Stud.*, 72
Patten, J. H. C. 1971a 'Freemen and apprentices', *Loc. Hist.*, 4
1971b 'The hearth taxes', *Loc. Pop. Stud.*, 7
1977 'Urban occupations in pre-industrial England', *Trans. Instit. Brit. Geog.*, NS, 2
1978 *English Towns, 1500–1700* (Folkestone)
(ed.) 1979 *Pre-industrial England: Geographical Essays*
Patterson, A. T. 1966 *A History of Southampton, I: 1700–1835* (South. Rec. Soc., 11)
1976 *Portsmouth: A History* (Bradford on Avon)
Patterson, M. and Reiffen, D. 1990 'The effect of the Bubble Act', *J. Ec. H.*, 50
Pauling, N. G. 1957 'The employment problem in pre-classical economic thought', *The Economic Record*, 27
Payling, S. J. 1992 'Social mobility, demographic change and landed society', *Ec. H. R.*, 45
Payne, P. L. 1967 (ed.) *Studies in Scottish Business History*
Pearl, V. 1961 *London and the Outbreak of the Puritan Revolution* (Oxford)
1979a 'John Stow', *Trans. Lond. & Midd. A. S.*, 30
1979b 'Change and stability in seventeenth-century London', *Lond. J.*, 5
Pears, I. 1988 *The Discovery of Painting* (New Haven)
Pearsall, A. W. H. 1989 'The Royal Navy and trade protection, 1688–1714', *Ren. & Mod. Stud.*, 30
Pearson, G. H. J. (ed.) 1958 *Adolescence and the Conflict of Generations* (New York)
Pearson, K. 1978 *The History of Statistics in the Seventeenth and Eighteenth Centuries*
Peck, L. L. 1982 *Northampton Patronage and Policy at the Court of James I*

1986 'Perspective on Court patronage', *J. B. S.*, 25
(ed.) 1991 *The Mental World of the Jacobean Court* (Cambridge)
Peele, M. 1939 'Shrewsbury drapers apprentices', *Trans. Shrop. Arch. & Nat. Hist. Soc.*, 50
Peju, A. 1900 *La Course à Nantes aux XVIIe et XVIIIe siècles*
Peller, S. 1947 'Studies on mortality since the Renaissance', *Bull. Hist. Med.*, 21
Pelling, M. 1982 'Occupational diversity: barber-surgeons and the trades of Norwich', *Bull. Hist. Med.*, 56
1983a 'Apothecaries in Norwich, *circa* 1600', *Pharm. Hist.*, 13
1983b 'Medical practice in the early modern period', *Bull. Soc. Hist. Med.*, 32
1987 'Medicine and economic incentives', *Bull. Soc. Hist. Med.*, 41
Penn, C. D. 1913 *The Navy under the Early Stuarts* (Manchester)
Penn, S. A. C. 1986 'A fourteenth-century Bristol merchant', *T. B. G. A. S.*, 104
Pennington, R. R. 1973 *Stannary Law* (Newton Abbot)
Penrose, E. 1959 *The Theory of the Growth of the Firm* (Oxford)
Penson, L. M. 1924 *The Colonial Agents of the British West Indies*
Pepys, W. D. 1965 'My friend the merchant', *Hist. Tod.*, 15
Perceval, C. H. 1893 'Jeake's Diary', *N. & Q.*, 8th ser., 4
Pérez, J. I. F. 1981 *Córdoba en el siglo XVI* (Cordoba)
Pérez-Ramos, A. 1988 *Francis Bacon's Idea of Science* (Oxford)
Peristiany, J. G. (ed.) 1965 *Honour and Shame: The Values of Medieval Society*
Perkin, H. J. 1968 'The social causes of the British industrial revolution', *T. R. H. S.*, 5th ser., 18
1969 *The Origins of Modern English Society, 1780–1880*
1985 'An open elite', *J. B. S.*, 24
1989 *The Rise of a Professional Society*
Perkins, E. J. 1989 'The entrepreneurial spirit in colonial America', *Bus. Hist. Rev.*, 62
Perotta, C. 1991 'Is the mercantilist theory of the favourable balance of trade really erroneous?', *Hist. Pol. Econ.*, 23
Perroy, E. 1961 'La noblesse des Pays Bas', *Revue du Nord*, 43
1962 'Social mobility among the French noblesse', *P. & P.*, 21
Perry, N. 1977 'Voltaire's view of England', *J. Eur. Stud.*, 7
Persson, K. S. 1988 *Pre-industrial Economic Growth* (Oxford)
Petersen, E. L. 1967 *The Crisis of the Danish Nobility* (Odensee)
1968 'La crise de la noblesse danoise', *Annales*, 23
Petter, H. M. 1974 *The Oxford Almanacks* (Oxford)
Pettigree, A 1986 *Foreign Protestant Communities in Sixteenth-Century London* (Oxford)
Phelps, W. H. 1978 'The will of Randall Taylor', *Bibliog. Soc. Amer. Papers*, 72
Phelps-Brown, E. H. and Hopkins, S. V. 1981 *A Perspective of Wages and Prices*
Philip, I. G. 1983 *The Bodleian Library in the Seventeenth and Eighteenth Centuries* (Oxford)
Phillips, C. R. 1979 *Ciudad Real, 1500–1750* (Cambridge, Massachusetts)
1983 'Spanish merchants and the wool trade', *Sixt. Cent. J.*, 14
1987 'Time and duration', *A. H. R.*, 92
1982 'The Spanish wool trade, 1500–1780', *J. Ec. H.*, 42
Phillips, G. B. 1970 'County committees and local government, 1642–60', *North.*

Hist., 5
Phillips, J. 1973 *The Reformation of Images, 1535–1665* (Berkeley)
Phillips, J. D. 1979 'The theory of small enterprise', *Expl. Ec. H.*, 16
Phillips, J. M. 1959 'Between conscience and the law', *Ch. Hist.*, 28
Phillips, M. and Tompkinson, W. S. 1927 *English Women in Life and Letters* (Oxford)
Phillips, P. A. S. 1935 *Paul de Lamerie, Citizen and Goldsmith of London*
Phipps, G. M. 1983 *Sir John Merrick* (Newtonville)
1990 'The Russian Embassy to London, 1645–6', *S. E. E. R.*, 68
Phythian-Adams, C. 1971 'Records of the craft guilds', *Loc. Hist.*, 9
1977 *The Traditional Community under Stress* (Milton Keynes)
1979 *Desolation of a City: Coventry and the Urban Crisis* (Cambridge)
Piaget, J. 1971 *Structuralism*
Pijassou, R. 1974 'Le marché de Londres et la naissance des grands crus médocains', *Rev. Hist. Bordeaux*, NS, 23
Pike, R. 1965 'The Sevillian nobility and trade', *Bus. Hist. Rev.*, 39
1966 *Enterprise and Adventure: The Genoese in Seville* (Ithaca)
Pilgrim, J. E. 1940 'The cloth industry of Essex and Suffolk, 1558–1640', *B. I. H. R.*, 8
1959 'The rise of the new draperies in Essex', *B. I. H. R.*, 7
Pillorget, R. 1979 *La Tige et le rameau*
Pinchbeck, I. and Hewitt, M. 1969 *Children in English Society*, vol. I
Pinkus, S. C. A. 1992 'Popery, trade and universal monarchy', *E. H. R.*, 107
Piper, D. 1982 *Artists' London*
Piquet, J. 1930 *Des banquiers au Moyen Age*
Piquet-Marchal, M. O. 1965 'Gregory King', *Rev. Econ.*, 16
Pirenne, H. 1939 *Les Villes*
1953 *Histoire de Belgique*, 4th edn (Brussels)
1958 *Economic and Social History of Medieval Europe*, trans. I. E. Clegg
Plant, M. 1974 *The English Book Trade*, 3rd edn
Platt, C. 1973 *Medieval Southampton: The Port and Trading Community, 1000–1600*
1976 *The English Medieval Town*
Platt, E. M. 1902 *Sir Thomas Johnson* (Liverpool)
Plomer, H. R. 1968 *A Dictionary of the Printers and Booksellers at Work in England, 1668–1725*, ed. A. Esdaile (repr. Bibliog. Soc.)
Plucknett, T. F. T. 1956 *A Concise History of the Common Law*, 5th edn
Plumb, J. H. (ed.) 1955 *Studies in Social History: A Tribute to G. M. Trevelyan* (Cambridge)
(ed.) 1964 *Crisis in the Humanities*
1967 *The Growth of Political Stability in England, 1675–1725*
1975 'The new world of children', *P. & P.*, 67
Plummer, A. 1972 *The London Weavers Company, 1600–1970*
Plummer, A. and Early, R. E. 1969 *The Blanket Makers, 1669–1969*
Pocock, J. G. A. 1972a 'Virtue and commerce in the eighteenth century', *J. I. H.*, 3
1972b *Politics, Language and Time* (Oxford)
1973 *Obligation and Authority in Two English Revolutions* (Wellington)

1975 *The Machiavellian Moment* (Princeton)
1979 'To market, to market', *J. I. H.*, 10
(ed.) 1980 *Three British Revolutions* (Princeton)
1982 'The limits and divisions of British history', *A. H. R.*., 87
1986 *Virtue, Commerce and History* (Cambridge)
Polányi, K., Arensberg, C. M. and Pearson, H. W. (eds.) 1957 *Trade and Markets in the Early Empires* (Glencoe, Illinois)
Pollak, E. 1989 'Moll Flanders', *The Eighteenth Century*, 30
Pollard, G. 1978 'The English market for printed books', *Pub. Hist.*, 4
Pollard, S. 1954 *Three Centuries of Sheffield Steel* (Sheffield)
1965 *The Genesis of Modern Management*
1990 'Reflections on entrepreneurship and culture', *T. R. H. S.*, 5th ser., 40
Pollard, S. and Crossley, D. W. 1969 *The Wealth of Britain, 1085–1966* (New York)
Pollet, R. 1973 'John Hawkins' troublesome voyage', *J. B. S.*, 12
Pollins, H. 1982 *Economic History of the Jews in England* (Rutherford)
Pollock, Sir Frederick, and Maitland, F. W. 1968 *The History of English Law before Edward I*, 2nd edn, rev. S. F. C. Milsom (Cambridge)
Pollock, L. A. 1983 *Forgotten Children: Parent–Child Relationships from 1500 to 1900* (Cambridge)
1987 'Courtship and marriage', *H. J.*, 30
1989a 'The making of women in the upper ranks', *Cont. & Ch.*, 4
1989b 'Younger sons in Tudor and Stuart England', *Hist. Tod.* , 39
Ponko, V. J. 1964–5 'N. S. B. Gras and Elizabethan corn policy', *Ec. H. R.*, 17
Ponsioen, J. A. 1962 *Analysis of Social Change Reconsidered* (The Hague)
Ponting, K. 1965 'A clothier's pattern book', *J. Ind. Arch.*, 2
1971 *The Woollen Industry of South-western England* (Bath)
Pool, B. 1966 *Navy Board Contracts, 1660–1832*
Poole, B. 1962 'Liverpool trade in the reign of Anne' (unpub. M.A. thesis, Liverpool)
Popofsky, L. S. 1990 'Tonnage and poundage in 1629', *P. & P.*, 126
Popper, K. R. 1957 *The Poverty of Historicism*
Porter, H. 1968 'The Crispe family and the African trade', *J. Afr. Hist.*, 9
Porter, K. W. 1937 *The Jacksons and the Lees* (Cambridge, Massachusetts)
Porter, R. 1987 *Disease, Medicine and Society in England, 1550–1860*
1989 *Health for Sale: Quackery in England, 1660–1850* (Manchester)
Porter, S. 1973 'Fires in pre-industrial towns', *Loc. Hist.*, 10
1976 'The making of probate inventories', *Loc. Hist.*, 12
1984 'Property destruction in Civil War London', *Trans. Lond. & Midd. A. S.*, 35
1986 'Property destruction in the English civil war', *Hist. Tod.*, 36
Portman, D. 1966 *Exeter Houses, 1400–1700* (Exeter)
Postan, M. M. 1935–6 'Recent trends in the accumulation of capital', *Ec. H. R.*, 6
1942 'Some social consequences of the Hundred Years War', *Ec. H. R.*, 12
1964 'The costs of the Hundred Years War', *P. & P.*, 27
1971 *Facts and Relevance: Essays on Historical Method* (Cambridge)
1973a *Essays in Medieval Agriculture and General Problems of the Medieval Economy* (Cambridge), 2 vols.

1973b *Medieval Trade and Finance* (Cambridge)

Postan, M. M. and Power, E. 1933 *Studies in English Trade in the Fifteenth Century*

Postan, M. M. and Rich, E. E. (eds.) 1952 *Cambridge Economic History of Europe* (Cambridge), vol. II, *Trade and Industry in the Middle Ages*

Postan, M. M., Rich, E. E. and Miller, E. (eds.) 1963 *Cambridge Economic History of Europe* (Cambridge), vol. III, *Economic Organization and Policies*

Posthumous, N. W. 1946 *Inquiry into the History of Prices in Holland* (Leiden), 2 vols.

Pound, J. F. 1962 'An Elizabethan census of the poor', *Univ. B'ham. H. J.*, 8

1966 'The social and trade structure of Norwich', *P. & P.*, 34

1976 'Vagrancy and the social order', *P. & P.*, 71

1981 'The validity of the freemen lists', *Ec. H. R.*, 2nd ser., 34

1986a 'Clerical poverty in early seventeenth-century England', *J. Eccles. Hist.*, 37

1986b 'The social and geographical origins of the English grammar school pupil', *Bull. Hist. Educ. Soc.*, 37

1986c *Poverty and Vagrancy in Tudor England*, 2nd edn (New York)

Powell, C. L. 1917 *English Domestic Relations, 1487–1653* (New York)

Powell, J. W. D. 1930 *Bristol Privateers and Ships of War* (Bristol)

Power, Sir Darcy, 1909 'The fees of our ancestors', *Janus*

Power, E. 1941 *The Wool Trade in English Medieval History* (Oxford)

Power, M. J. 1978 'A London suburban community: Shadwell', *Lond. J.*, 4

1985 'London and the control of the crisis of the 1590s', *History*, 70

1986 'A crisis reconsidered', *Lond. J.*, 12

Powicke, F. J. 1924–7 *The Life of the Rev. Richard Baxter, 1615–91*, 2 vols.

Powicke, M. 1962 *Military Obligation in Medieval England* (Oxford)

Poynter, F. N. L. and Bishop, W. J. 1951 *A Seventeenth-Century Doctor and his Patients: John Symcotts, 1592–1662* (Beds. Hist. Rec. Soc., 31)

Prakash, O. 1985 *The Dutch East India Company and the Economy of Bengal, 1630–1720* (Princeton)

Prange, R. 1963 *Die Bremische Kaufmannschaft des 16. und 17. Jahrhunderts* (Bremen)

Pratt, J. and Zeckhausen, R. (eds.) 1984 *Principals and Agents: The Structure of Business* (Boston)

Pressnell, L. S. and Orbell, J. 1985 *A Guide to the Historical Records of British Banking* (New York)

Prest, W. R. 1967 'Legal education of the gentry', *P. & P.*, 38

1972 *The Inns of Court under Elizabeth I and the Early Stuarts*

(ed.) 1981 *Lawyers in Early Modern Europe and America*

1986 *The Rise of the Barristers, 1590–1640* (Oxford)

(ed.) 1987 *The Professions in Early Modern England*

1991 'Law and women's rights', *The Seventeenth Century*, 6

Prestwich, M. 1950 'Diplomacy and trade in the Protectorate', *J. M. H.*, 22

1966 *Lionel Cranfield: Politics and Profit under the Early Stuarts* (Oxford)

(ed.) 1985 *International Calvinism, 1541–1715* (Oxford)

Prestwich, M. 1972 *War, Politics and Finance under Edward I* (Totowa, New Jersey)

Priaulx, T. F. 1961 'The Guernsey stocking export trade', *Trans. Soc. Guérn.*

Price, F. G. H. 1875 *Account of Ye Marygold*

1891 *A Handbook of London Bankers*, 2nd edn

Price, J. M. 1954–5 'Note on some London price currents', *Ec. H. R.*, 2nd ser., 7

1961a *The Tobacco Adventure to Russia* (Trans. Amer. Phil. Soc., NS, 51)

1961b 'Multilateralism and/or bilateralism', *Ec. H. R.*, 2nd ser., 14

1962 'Who was John Norden', *Wm & Mary Q.*, 19

1973 *France and the Chesapeake, 1674–1791* (Ann Arbor), 2 vols.

1980 *Capital and Credit in British Overseas Trade, 1700–1776* (Cambridge, Massachusetts)

1989 'What did merchants do', *J. Ec. H.*, 49

1992 *Perry of London* (Cambridge, Massachusetts)

Price, J. M. and Clemens, P. G. E. 1987 'A revolution in scale', *J. Ec. H.*, 47

Price, W. H. 1906 *The English Patents of Monopoly* (Boston)

Prichard, M. F. L. 1960 'The significant background of the Stuart Culpepers', *N. & Q.*, 7

Prideaux, Sir Walter S. 1896–7 *Memorials of the Goldsmiths*

Priestley, M. 1951 'Anglo-French trade, 1660–85', *Ec. H. R.*, 2nd ser., 4

1956 'London merchants and opposition politics', *B. I. H. R.*, 29

Priestley, U. 1985a *Shops and Shopkeepers of Norwich* (Norwich)

1985b 'The fabric of stuffs', *Text. Hist.*, 16

Prince, J. 1810 *Danmonii orientales illustres, or The Worthies of Devon*

Prior, M. (ed.) 1985 *Women in English Society, 1500–1800*

Pritchard, J. E. 1922 'The Great Plan of Bristol by Jacobus Millerd', *T. B. G. A. S.*, 44

Produzione, commercio e consumo dei Panna di Lana 1976 (Prato)

Property: Its Rights and Duties, with an Introduction by the Bishop of Oxford 1915

Proudhon, P.-J. 1866 *Théorie de la propriété*, 2nd edn

Prouty, C. T. 1942 *George Gascoigne* (New York)

Pruett, J. H. 1975 'Career patterns among the clergy', *Ch. Hist.*, 44

1978 *The Parish Clergy under the Later Stuarts* (Urbana, Illinois)

Pryce, G. 1854 *Memorials of the Canynges Family* (Bristol)

Pryor, J. H. 1977 'The origins of the Commenda contract', *Speculum*, 52

'The publication of business records', *Archives*, 5 (1951)

Puckrein, G. A. 1984 *Little England: Plantation Society and Anglo-Barbadian Politics 1627–1700* (New York)

Pugh, R. B. 1978 'Newgate between two fires', *Guild. Stud. Lond. Hist.*, 3

Pullan, B. 1964 'Service to the Venetian state', *Studi Secenteschi*, 5

(ed.) 1968 *Crisis and Change in the Venetian Economy*

1971 *Rich and Poor in Renaissance Venice* (Oxford)

1976 'Catholics and the poor', *T. R. H. S.*, 5th ser., 26

Pulling, A. 1842 *A Practical Treatise on the Laws and Customs of London*

Purver, M. 1962 *The Royal Society*

Quiason, S. D. 1966 *English Country Trade with the Philippines, 1664–1724* (Quezan City)

The Quiet Conquest: The Huguenots, 1685–1985 1985

Quiller, D. E. 1961 *The Office of Ambassador in the Middle Ages* (Princeton)

Quiney, A. 1979 'Thomas Lucas, bricklayer, 1662–1736', *Archaeol. J.*, 136

Quinn, D. B. 1966 'Advice for investors', *Wm & Mary Q.*, 3rd ser., 23
(ed.) 1974 *The Hakluyt Handbook* (Hakl. Soc., 2nd ser., 144–5)
1976 'Renaissance influences on English colonization', *T. R. H. S.*, 5th ser., 26
(ed.) 1982 *Early Maryland in a Wider World* (Detroit)
1983 *England's Sea Empire, 1550–1642*
Quistnell, B. 1988 'Charles I and his Navy in the 1630s', *Seventeenth Century*, 3
Quitt, M. H. 1988 'Immigrant origins of the Virginia gentry', *Wm & Mary Q.*, 45
Raasch, J. H. and Wall, R. C. B. 1962 *A Directory of English Country Physicians, 1603–43*
Rabb, T. K. 1964 'Sir Edwin Sandys and the parliament of 1604', *A. H. R.*, 69
1968a *Enterprise and Empire, 1575–1630* (Cambridge, Massachusetts)
1968b 'Free trade and the gentry' *P. & P.* 40
1974 'The expansion of Europe and the spirit of capitalism', *H. J.*, 17
1979 'The stirrings of the 1590s', *T. J. H. S. E.*, 26
Rabb, T. K. and Rotberg, R. I. (eds.) 1981 *Industrialization and Urbanization* (Princeton)
(eds.) 1982 *The New History: The 1980s and Beyond* (Princeton)
Rabb, T. K. and Seigel, J. E. (eds.) 1969 *Action and Conviction in Early Modern Europe: Essays in Memory of E. H. Harbison*
Rabe, H. 1962 'Aktienkapital und Handelsinvestitionen im Ubersiehandel', *V. J. S. W.*, 49
Radcliffe-Brown, A. R. 1957 *A Natural Science of Society* (Glencoe, Illinois)
Raeff, M. 1983 *The Well-ordered Police State, 1600–1800* (New Haven)
Raftis, J. A. 1980 *Godmanchester, 1278–1400* (Toronto)
1990 *Early Tudor Godmanchester* (Toronto)
Ragin, C. C. 1987 *The Comparative Method: Moving Beyond Qualitative and Quantitative Strategies*
Raines, F. R. and Sutton, C. W. 1903 *Life of Humphrey Chetham* (Cheth. Soc., 49–50)
Raistrick, A. 1950 *Quakers in Science and Industry*
Ralph, E. 1988 *Guide to the Archives of the Society of Merchant Venturers of Bristol*
Ralph, P. L. 1947 *Sir Humphrey Mildmay, 1633–52* (New Brunswick)
Ramsay, G. D. 1952 'The smuggler's trade', *T. R. H. S.*, 5th ser., 2
1957 *England's Overseas Trade during the Centuries of Emergence*
1965 *The Wiltshire Woollen Industry in the Seventeenth and Eighteenth Centuries*, 2nd edn (Oxford)
1975a *The City of London in International Politics* (Manchester)
1975b 'Industrial discontent in early Elizabethan London', *Lond. J.*, 1
1977 'Clothworkers, Merchant Adventurers and Richard Hakluyt', *E. H. R.*, 92
1978 'The recruitment and fortunes of some London freemen', *Ec. H. R.*, 2nd ser., 31
1982a 'Thomas More at Mercers Hall', *E. H. R.*, 97
1982b *The English Woollen Industry, 1500–1750*
1985 'Victorian historiography and the guilds of London', *Lond. J.*, 10
1986 *The Queen's Merchants and the Revolt of the Netherlands* (Manchester)
Ramsey, P. H. 1958 'The Merchant Adventurers in the first half of the sixteenth century' (unpub. D. Phil. thesis, Oxford)

(ed.) 1971 *The Price Revolution in Sixteenth-century England*
Ramsey, R. W. 1930 *Studies in Cromwell's Family Circle*
1949 *Henry Ireton*
Ramsey, W. 1898 *The Company of Glass-sellers of London*
Ransom, R. L., Sutch, R. and Walton, G. M. (eds.) 1982 *Explorations in the New Economic History: Essays in Honor of D. C. North* (New York)
Ransome, D. R. 1964 'Artisan dynasties in London', *Guild. Misc.*, 2
Ranum, O. 1979 *Paris in the Age of Absolutism* (Bloomington)
Ranum, O. and P. (eds.) 1972 *Popular Attitudes towards Birth Control* (New York)
Rapp, D. 1974 'Social mobility in the eighteenth century', *Ec. H. R.*, 2nd ser., 27
Rapp, R. T. 1975 'The unmaking of the medieval trade hegemony', *J. Ec. H.*, 35
1976 *Industry and Economic Decline in Seventeenth-century Venice* (Cambridge, Massachusetts)
1979 'Real estate and rational investment in early modern Venice', *J. Eur. Ec. Hist.*, 8
Rappaport, S. 1983–4 'Social structure and social mobility', *Lond. J.*, 9–10
1989 *Worlds within Worlds: Structures of Life in Sixteenth-century London* (Cambridge)
Rappaport, S., Monfasani, J. and Musto, R. G. (eds.) 1991 *Renaissance Society and Culture: Essays in Honour of E. F. Rice* (New York)
Rattinger, H. 1973 '"Die Tradition" 1956 bis 1971', *Tradition*, 18
Raven, J. 1989 'British history and the enterprise culture', *P. & P.*, 123
Ravitch, N. 1965 'The social origins of the French and English bishops', *H. J.*, 8
1966 *Sword and Mitre* (The Hague)
Rawcliffe, C. 1988 'The profits of practice', *J. Soc. Hist. Med.*, 1
Rawley, J. A. 1981 *The Trans-Atlantic Slave Trade* (New York)
Rawlinson, H. G. 1920 *British Beginnings in Western India, 1579–1657* (Oxford)
1921 'Life in an English factory', *Proc. Indian Hist. Rec. Comm.*, 3
Raymond, S. A. 1986 'On the editing of probate inventories', *Archives*, 17
Read, C. 1925 *Mr Secretary Walsingham*, 3 vols.
Reader, W. J. 1966 *Professional Men: The Rise of the Professional Classes*
Reavis, W. A. 1957 'The Maryland gentry and social mobility', *Wm & Mary Q.*, 14
Reay, B. G. 1976 'The Muggletonians', *J. Rel. Hist.*, 9
1978 'The Quakers, 1659', *History*, 63
1981 'The social origins of early Quakers', *J. I. H.*, 11
(ed.) 1985a *Popular Culture in Seventeenth-century England*
1985b *The Quakers and the English Revolution*
Reay, B. G. and MacGregor, J. F. (eds.) 1984 *Radical Religion in the English Revolution* (Oxford)
Reddaway, T. F. 1940 *The Rebuilding of London after the Great Fire*
1963 'Goldsmiths' Row, 1558–1645', *Guild. Misc.*, 2
1966 'The livery companies and Tudor London', *History*, 51
Redlich, F. 1956 *Looting and Booty: De Praeda Militari, 1500–1800*
1957 'Academic education for business', *Bus. Hist. Rev.*, 31
1958 'Der deutsche fürstliche Unternehmer', *Tradition*, 3
1964–5 *The German Military Enterpriser and His Workforce* (Wiesbaden), 2 vols.

1966 'Some English Stationers of the seventeenth and eighteenth centuries', *Bus. Hist.*, 8
1968 'Pitfalls in economic history', *Expl. Ent. H.*, 2nd ser., 6
1971 *Steeped in Two Cultures* (New York)
Reed, C. G. 1973 'Transaction costs and differential growth', *J. Ec. H.*, 33
Reeder, J. 1973 'Corporate loan financing', *Anglo Amer. Law Rev.*, 2
Rees, J. A. 1923 *The Company of Grocers, 1345–1923*
1934 *The English Tradition: The Heritage of the Venturers*
Rees, W. 1968 *Industry before the Industrial Revolution* (Cardiff), 2 vols.
Reeves, D. D. 1956 'Sir Richard Gough and his broadside collection', *Harv. Lib. Bull.*, 10
1960 'Sixteenth-century writings on bookkeeping', *Bus. Hist. Rev.*, 34
Reeves, P. 1966 '"The Pilgrim's Progress" as a precursor of the novel', *Georgia Review*, 20
Reichard, H. M. 1952 'Pope's social satire', *P. M. L. A.*, 67
Reid, G. L. 1989 *Classical Economic Growth* (Oxford)
Reid, R. P. 1921 *The King's Council in the North*
Reid, W. 1966 'Commonwealth supply departments within the Tower', *Guild. Misc.*, 2
Reisman, D. A. 1976 *Adam Smith's Sociological Economics*
1982 *State and Welfare*
Reissmann, M. 1975 *Die hamburgische Kaufmannschaft des 17. Jahrhunderts* (Hamburg)
Reitan, E. A. 1966 'The Civil List in eighteenth-century British politics', *H. J.*, 9
1970 'From Revenue to Civil List', *H. J.*, 13
The Renaissance: A Symposium 1953 (New York)
Rendel, R. 1975 'The true identity of George Ravenscroft', *Rec. Hist.*, 13
Renouard, Y. 1949 *Les hommes d'affaires italiens du moyen âge*
1968 *Etudes d'histoire médiévale*
'The representation of historical events' 1987 *Hist. & Theory*, 26
Reyerson, K. L. 1985 *Business Banking and Finance in Medieval Montpellier* (Toronto)
Reynolds, S. 1977 *An Introduction to the History of Medieval English Towns* (Oxford)
Ribalta, M. 1985 *La burguesia mercantil en la Espana* (Madrid)
Ribeiro, A. and Cumming, V. 1989 *The Visual History of Costume*
Rich, E. E. 1949–50 'The population of Elizabethan England', *Ec. H. R.*, 2nd ser., 2
1957 'Shaftesbury's colonial policy', *T. R. H. S.*, 5th ser., 7
1958 *The History of the Hudson's Bay Company, 1670–1763* (Hudson's Bay Rec. Soc., pub. 21)
Rich, E. E. and Wilson, C. H. 1967 (eds.) *Cambridge Economic History of Europe* (Cambridge), vol. IV, *The Economic Expansion of Europe*
(eds.) 1977 *Cambridge Economic History of Europe* (Cambridge), vol. V, *The Economic Organization of Early Modern Europe*
Richard, G. 1958 'La noblesse commerçante à Bordeaux et à Nantes', *Inf. Hist.*, 20
1960 'Un aspect de politique économique et sociale', *XVIIe Siècle*, 49

Richard, R. 1976 'Comptes et profits de navires', *Rev. Hist. Ec. & Soc.*, 54
Richards D. S. 1970 (ed.) *Islam and the Trade of Asia* (Oxford)
Richards, G. R. B. 1932 *Florentine Merchants in the Age of the Medicis* (Cambridge, Massachusetts)
Richards, R. D. 1926 'Early history of the term capital', *Q. J. Econ.*, 40
1928 'Edward Backwell', *Ec. J. Supp.*, ser. 3
1965 *The Early History of Banking* (repr. New York)
Richardson, D. 1985 *The Bristol Slave Traders: A Collective Portrait* (Bristol)
Richardson, N. 1930 'Early advertising', *Discovery*, 17
1936 'Early commercial advertising', *J. Roy. Soc. Arts*, 81
Richardson, R. 1962 *Coutts and Company, Bankers*
Richardson, R. C. 1972a 'Wills and willmakers', *Loc. Pop. Stud.* 9
1972b *Puritanism in North-west England* (Manchester)
1974 'The diocese of Chester', *Loc. Hist.*, 11
(ed.) 1992 *Town and Countryside in the English Revolution* (Manchester)
Richardson, R. C. and Ridder, G. M. (eds.) 1986 *Freedom and the English Revolution* (Manchester)
Richardson, W. C. 1953 *Stephen Vaughan* (Baton Rouge)
1961 *History of the Court of Augmentations, 1536–54* (Baton Rouge)
Richet, D. 1968 'Croissance et blockage', *Annales*, 23
Richetti, J. J. 1975 *Defoe's Narratives* (Oxford)
Richmond, C. 1981 *John Hopton* (Cambridge)
Rickwood, D. L. 1984 'The Norwich Strangers, 1565–1643', *Proc. Hug. Soc. Lond.*, 24
Riden, P. 1981 *Cowbridge: Trades and Tradesmen, 1660–1750* (Cardiff)
1984 *History of Chesterfield*, vol. II, *Tudor and Stuart Chesterfield* (Chesterfield)
(ed.) 1985 *Probate Records and the Local Community* (Gloucester)
1987 'An English factor at Stockholm in the 1680s', *Scand. Ec. H. R.*, 35
Rieber, A. J. 1982 *Merchants and Entrepreneurs in Imperial Russia* (Chapel Hill)
Riemersma, J. C. 1950 'Government influence on company organization', *J. Ec. H.*, 10
1952 'Usury restrictions in a mercantile economy', *Canad. J. Econ. & Pol. Sc.*, 18
(ed.) 1953 *Enterprise and Secular Change*
1968 *Religious Factors in Early Dutch Capitalism, 1500–1650* (The Hague)
Riesman, D. 1954 *Individualism Reconsidered and Other Essays* (Glencoe, Illinois)
Riis, T. (ed.) 1986 *Aspects of Poverty in Early Modern Europe* (Odensee)
Ringrose, D. R. 1973 'European economic growth', *Ec. H. R.*, 2nd ser., 26
1983 *Madrid and the Spanish Economy, 1560–1850*
Rink, O. A. 1986 *Holland on the Hudson* (Ithaca)
Ripley, P. 1976 'Trade and social structure of Gloucester, 1600–40', *T. B. G. A. S.*, 94
1980 'The economy of Gloucester, 1660–1740', *T. B. G. A. S.*, 98
1984 'Village and town', *Agric. Hist.*, 32
Rivington, C. 1981 'Sir Thomas Davies', *The Library*, 6th ser., 3
Roach, J. H. 1965 'Five early seventeenth-century English country physicians', *J. Hist. Med. & All. Sc.*, 20

Roake, M. 1970 'Gavelkind', *Cantium*, 2
Robbins, C. 1967 'William Popple, 1638–1708', *Wm & Mary Q.*, 3rd ser., 24
1972 'State oaths in England, 1558–1714', *H. L. Q.*, 35
1982 *Absolute Liberty*, ed. B. Taft (Hamden)
Robbins, W. G. 1969 'The Massachusetts Bay Company', *The Historian*, 22
Roberts, C. 1977 'The constitutional significance of the financial settlement in 1690', *H. J.*, 20
1985 *Schemes and Undertakings* (Columbus)
Roberts, D. 1989 *The Ladies: Female Patronage of Restoration Drama* (Oxford)
Roberts, J. D. 1968 *From Puritanism to Platonism* (The Hague)
Roberts, M. 1964–5 *Gustavus Adolphus* (repr.), 2 vols.
1967 *Essays in Swedish History*
(ed.) 1973 *Sweden's Age of Greatness, 1632–1718*
Roberts, R. S. 1962a, 1964 'The personnel and practice of medicine', *Med. Hist.*, 6 & 8
1962b 'The apothecary in the seventeenth century', *Pharm. J.*, 188
Roberts, W. I. 1965 'Samuel Storke', *Bus. Hist. Rev.*, 39
Robertson, H. M. 1931 'Sir Bevis Bulmer', *J. Ec. & Bus. Hist.*, 4
Robertson, J. 1942 *The Art of Letter Writing* (Liverpool)
Robertson, J. C. 1990 'Caroline culture', *History*, 75
Robinson, A. (ed.) 1987 *Economic Progress*, 2nd edn (New York)
Robinson, D. E. 1963 'The importance of fashion and taste', *Bus. Hist. Rev.*, 37
Robinson, F. J. G. and Wallis, P. J. 1975 'Some early mathematics schools in Whitehaven', *Trans. Cumb. & West. Antiq. & Arch. Soc.*, 75
Robinson, H. 1948 *British Post Office* (Princeton)
Robinson, J. 1958 *The Accumulation of Capital*
Robinson, S. 1972 'Theories of economic growth', *Ec. Dev. & Cult. Ch.*, 21
Robson, R. 1959 *The Attorney in Eighteenth-century England* (Cambridge)
Roderick, A. J. (ed.) 1960 *Wales Through the Ages* (Llandybie)
Rodway, A. 1972 'Restoration comedy re-examined', *Ren. & Mod. Stud.*, 16
Roebuck, P. 1979 'Post-Restoration landownership', *J. B. S.*, 18
1980 *Yorkshire Baronets, 1640–1760* (Oxford)
Rogal, S. J. 1974 'John Vanbrugh and the Blenheim Palace controversy', *J. Soc. Arch. Hist.*, 33
Rogers, C. D. 1971 'Education in Lancashire and Cheshire, 1640–60', *Trans. Hist. Soc. Lancs. & Ches.*, 123
Rogers, J. E. T. 1887 *A History of Agriculture and Prices* (Oxford), vol. V, *1583–1702*
Rogers, K. M. 1966 *The Troublesome Helpmate* (Seattle)
Rogers, M. 1983 *William Dobson, 1611–46*
Rogers, N. 1979 'Money, land and lineage', *Soc. Hist.*, 4
Rogers, P. 1971 'Defoe in the Fleet', *Rev. Eng. Stud.*, 20
1972–3 'Literary art in Defoe's "Tour"', *Eight. Cent. Stud.*, 6
1975 'Defoe at work', *B. N. Y. P. L.*, 78
Rohde, E. S. 1924 *The Old English Gardening Books*
Roker, L. F. 1965–70 'The Flemish and Dutch community in Colchester', *Proc. Hug. Soc. Lond.*, 21
Rollson, D. 1987 'The bourgeois soul of John Smythe', *Soc. Hist.*, 12

Ronald, P. 1978 *The Basketmakers Company* (priv. pr.)
Roncaglia, A. 1985 *Petty: The Origins of Political Economy* (Armonk, New York)
Roorda, D. J. and Huvssen, A. H. 1977 'Bureaucratie en bureaucratisering', *Tijd. v. Gesch.*, 90
Roosegaard, B. W. 1910 *The Rise of the London Money Market*
Root, H. L. 1991 'The redistributive role of government', *Comp. Stud. Soc. Hist.*, 33
Roover, R. de, 1949 *Gresham on Foreign Exchange* (Cambridge, Massachusetts)
1953 *L'Evolution de la lettre de change, XIVe–XVIIIe siècle*
1957 'Thomas Mun in Italy', *B. I. H. R.*, 30
1958 'The concept of the just price', *J. Ec. H.*, 18
1963 *The Rise and Decline of the Medici Bank, 1397–1494* (Cambridge, Massachusetts)
1974 *Business Banking and Economic Thought*, ed. J. Kirshner (Chicago)
Roper, H. R. T., Baron Dacre, 1946 'The bishopric of Durham', *Durham Univ. J.*
1953 *The Gentry, 1540–1640* (Ec. H. R. Supp. 1)
1962 *Archbishop Laud*, 2nd edn
1972 *Religion, the Reformation and Social Change*, 2nd edn
Roper, I. M. 1931 *The Monumental Effigies of Bristol and Gloucester* (Gloucester)
Rordorf, W. 1968 *Sunday*, trans. A. A. K. Graham
Roscoe, E. S. 1924 *A History of the English Prize Court*
1931 *The Admiralty Jurisdiction*, 5th edn
Rose, E. 1975 *Cases of Conscience* (Cambridge)
Rosen, M. 1981 'The dictatorship of the bourgeoisie in England, 1688–1721', *Sc. & Soc.*, 45
Rosenberg, H. 1958 *Bureaucracy, Aristocracy and Autocracy* (Cambridge, Massachusetts)
Rosenberg, N. 1962 'Mandeville and *laissez faire*', *J. H. I.*, 24
Rosenfeld, P. 1959 'The provincial governors', *Anciens Pays et Assemblées*, 17
Rosenthal, J. T. 1972 *Gift Giving and the Aristocracy, 1307–1485*
1984 'Heirs, age and family succession', *Yorks. Arch. J.*, 56
1991 *Patriarchy and Families of Privilege* (Philadelphia)
Roseveare, H. G. 1973 *The Treasury, 1660–1870*
1991 *The Financial Revolution, 1660–1760*
Roskell, J. S. 1954 *The Commons in the Parliament of 1422* (Manchester)
Rosovsky, H. 1966 *Industrialization in Two Systems: Essays in Honor of A. Gerschenkron*
Ross, J. F. 1941 *Swift and Defoe* (Berkeley)
Ross, R. P. 1975 'The social and economic causes of the revolution in mathematical sciences', *J. B. S.*, 15
Rostenberg, L. 1965 *Publishers printers and booksellers in England, 1551–1700* (New York), 2 vols.
1989 *The Library of Robert Hooke*
Rostow, W. W. 1971 *Stages of Economic Growth*, 2nd edn (Cambridge)
Røstvig, M.-S. 1962 *The Happy Man*, rev. edn (New York)
Rotberg, R. I. and Rabb, T. K. 1986 (eds.) *Population and Economy* (Cambridge)
Roth, C. 1959 *A History of the Marranos* (repr. New York)

1964 *A History of the Jews in England*, 3rd edn
Roth, C. and Schluchte, N. 1979 *Max Weber's Vision of History* (Berkeley)
Roth, G. 1976 'History and sociology', *Brit. J. Sociol.*, 27
Rothbard, M. N. 1979 *Individualism and the Philosophy of the Social Sciences* (San Francisco)
Rothblatt, S. 1968 *The Revolution of the Dons* (New York)
Rothenberg, M. 1975 'The Protestant ethic', *Brit. J. Sociol.*, 26
Rothermund, D. 1988 *Asian Trade and European Expansion* (New Delhi)
Rothkrug, L. 1961 'Critique de la politique commerciale', *Rev. Hist. Mod. & Cont.*, 8
1965 *Opposition to Louis XIV* (Princeton)
Rothstein, N. 1989 'Canterbury and London', *Text. Hist.*, 20
Rougé, J. 1966 *Recherches sur l'organisation du commerce maritime en Méditerranée*
Routh, E. M. G. 1912 *Tangiers, 1661–89*
Rowe, M.M. and Trease, G.E. 1971 'The 1572 bill of an Exeter apothecary', *Devon and Corn. N. & Q.*, 32
Rowland, A. L. and Manhart, G. B. 1924 *Studies in English Commerce and Exploration in the Reign of Elizabeth* (Philadelphia)
Rowlands, M. B. 1975 *Masters and Men in the West Midlands*
1977 'Society and industry in the West Midlands', *Mid. Hist.*, 4
Rowse, A. L. 1941 *Tudor Cornwall*
1950 *The England of Elizabeth*
Roy, I. and Porter, S. 1980 'The tything at Worcester', *B. I. H. R.*, 53
Rubini, D. 1967 *Court and Country, 1688–1702*
1970 'Politics and the battle for the banks, 1688–97', *E. H. R.*, 85
Rubinstein, W. D. 1981 *Men of Property*
1988 'Social change, social attitudes and British business life', *Oxford Rev. Econ. & Pol.*, 4.
1993 *Capitalism, Culture and Economic Decline in Britain, 1750–1990*
Rubinstein, W. D. and Duman, D. H. 1974 'Probate records as a tool', *Loc. Hist.*, 11
Rudden, B. 1985 *The New River* (Oxford)
Ruddock, A. A. 1949 'The earliest records of the High Court of Admiralty', *B. I. H. R.*, 22
1951 'Italian merchants and shipping at Southampton, 1270–1600' (South. Rec. Soc.)
Ruegg, W. 1986 'The academic ethos', *Minerva*, 24
Runciman, W. G. 1984 'Accelerated social mobility', *P. & P.*, 104
Runyan, W. M. 1982 *Life Histories and Psychobiography* (New York)
Rushton, P. 1991 'The matter of variance', *J. Soc. Hist.*, 25
Russell, C. 1979 *Past and Present Politics* (Oxford)
1990 *The Causes of the English Civil War* (Oxford)
Russell, E. 1977 'The influx of commoners into the University of Oxford', *E. H. R.*, 92
Russell, P. 1950 *Dartmouth: A History of the Port and Town*
Russell, W. H. 1893 'The laws of the Mercers Company of Lichfield', *T. R. H. S.*, 2nd ser., 7

Russian Institutions and Culture up to Peter the Great 1975
Rüstow, A. 1945 *Das Versagen des Wirtschaftsliberalismus* (Istanbuler Schriften, 12)
Rutman, D. B. 1965 *Winthrop's Boston, 1637–49* (Chapel Hill)
Ryan, A. 1965 'Locke and the dictatorship of the bourgeoisie', *Pol. Stud.*, 13
Ryan, C. C. 1981 'The fiends of commerce', *Hist. Pol. Econ.*, 13
Ryan, M. T. 1981 'Assimilating new worlds', *Comp. Stud. Soc. Hist.*, 23
Ryland, J. P. 1888 *A List of Persons Disclaimed as a Gentleman of Coat Armour by the Heralds* (Guildford)
Sabel, C. F. 1988 'Proto-industry and the problem of capitalism as a concept', *Intl Labour & Working Class Hist.*, 33
Sachse, W. L. 1947–8 'The migration of New Englanders to England, 1640–60', *A. H. R.*, 53
1956 *The Colonial American in Britain* (Madison)
1973 'England's Black Tribunal', *J. B. S.*, 12
Sacks, D. H. 1985 *Trade, Society and Politics in Bristol, 1500–1640* (New York)
1986a 'The corporate towns and the English state', *P. & P.*, 110
1986b 'The demise of the martyrs, 1400–1600', *Soc. Hist.*, 11
1987 *The Widening Gate: Bristol and the Atlantic Economy, 1450–1700*
Sahlin, S., Marshall, D. and Service, E. (eds.) 1960 *Evolution and Culture* (Ann Arbor)
Sainty, J. C. 1961 'A reform in the tenure of offices', *B. I. H. R.*, 41
1965 'The tenure of offices in the Exchequer' *E. H. R.*, 80
Sakula, A. 1980 'The Betchworth portraits', *Med. Hist.*, 24
Sale, J. H. 1990 'Goldsmiths of Gloucester, 1500–1800', *T. B. G. A. S.*, 108
Salerno, A. 1979 'The social background of seventeenth-century emigration to America', *J. B. S.*, 19
Salgado, G. 1992 *The Elizabethan Underworld* (repr.)
Salingar, L. 1987 *Dramatic Form in Shakespeare and the Jacobeans* (Cambridge)
Salisbury, W. 1966–7 'Early tonnage measurements', *Mar. Mirr.*, 52–3
Salmon, J. H. M. 1975 *Society in Crisis: France in the Sixteenth Century*
Salmon, M. 1986 *Women and the Law of Property in Early America* (Chapel Hill)
Salomon, N. 1964 *La Campagne de Nouvelle Castille à la fin du XVIe siècle*
Salter, J. 1976 'Wills and inventories of Warwickshire clergy, 1660–1720', *Warws. Hist.*, 3
Saltzman, L. T. 1931 *English Trade in the Middle Ages* (Oxford)
Salzman, P. 1985 *English Prose Fiction, 1558–1700* (Oxford)
Samaha, J. 1974 *Law and Order in Historical Perspective*
Sampson, M. 1990 'Thomas Hobbes', *Hist. Pol. Thought*, 11
Samuel, E. R. 1958 'Portuguese Jews in Jacobean London', *T. J. H. S. E.*, 18
1977 'Sir Francis Child's jewellery business', *Three Banks Rev.*, 113
1982 'Manual Levy Duarte', *T. J. H. S. E.*, 27
1988–90 'Readmission of the Jews', *T. J. H. S. E.*, 31
Samuelsson, K. 1961 *Religion and Economic Action*, trans. E. G. French and D. C. Coleman (Stockholm)
Sanborn, F. R. 1930 *Origins of the Early English Maritime and Commercial Law* (New York)
Sanderson, H. E. 1943 'An Elizabethan economist's method of literary compo-

sition', *H. L. Q.*, 6
Sapori, A. 1955 *Studi di storia economica secoli XIII, XIV, XV*, 3rd edn (Florence)
1957 *Studi in onore di Armando Sapori* (Milan)
1970 *The Italian Merchant in the Middle Ages* (New York)
Sargeaunt, J. 1898 *Annals of Westminster School*
Saul, A. 1981 'English towns in the late Middle Ages', *J. Med. Hist.*, 8
Saul, N. G. 1981 *Knights and Esquires: The Gloucestershire Gentry in the Fourteenth Century* (Oxford)
Savidge, A. 1955 *The Foundation and Early Years of Queen Anne's Bounty*
1964 *The Parsonage in England*
Sawyer, J. E. 1958 'Entrepreneurial studies', *Bus. Hist. Rev.*, 32
Sayer, M. J. 1975 'Norfolk visitation families', *Norf. Arch.*, 36
1979 *English Nobility* (Norfolk Heraldry Society)
Sayous, P. A. 1936 'Le genèse du système capitaliste', *Annales*, 8
1940 'Le patriciat d'Amsterdam', *Annales*, 2
Scammel, G. V. 1970 'Manning the English merchant service', *Mar. Mirr.*, 56
1972 'Shipowning in the economy', *H. J.*, 14–15
1989 *The First Imperial Age* c. *1400–1715*
Scammel, J. 1974 'Freedom and marriage in medieval England', *Mar. Mirr.*, 27
Scartlebury, J. 1978 'John Rashleigh of Fowey', *J. Roy. Inst. Corn.*, 8
Schaeper, T. J. 1983 *The French Council of Commerce, 1700–15* (Columbus)
Schafer, J. 1971 'When they marry they get wenches', *Shakes. Q.*, 22
Schafer, R. G. 1971 'Genesis and structure of the Foley ironworks partnership', *Bus. Hist.*, 13
Schalk, E. 1986 *From Valor to Pedigree* (Princeton)
Schatz, S. P. 1965 '*N* achievement and economic growth' *Q. J. Econ.*, 80
Schelling, F. E. 1908 *Elizabethan Drama, 1558–1642* (Boston), 2 vols.
Schenk, W. 1944 'A seventeenth century radical', *Ec. H. R.*, 14
Scherichaven, H. D. J. van (pseud. Larwood, J.) and Hotten, J. C. 1900 *The History of Signboards*, 11th edn
Schlatter, R. B. 1940 *Social Ideas of the Religious Leaders, 1660–88* (Oxford)
1954 'The higher learning in Puritan England', *Hist. Mag. Prot. Episc. Ch.*, 23
(ed.) 1984 *Recent Views on British History* (New Brunswick)
Schnapper, B. 1957 *Les Rentes au XVIe siècle*
1960 'Vente de rentes en vieille Castille', *Annales*, 15
Schneider, D. M. and Gough, K. 1961 (eds.) *Matrilinear Kinship* (Berkeley)
Schnucker, R. V. 1975 'Elizabethan birth control', *J. I. H.*, 4
Schnutthoff, M. 1939 'The origins of the joint-stock company', *Univ. Toronto Law J.*, 3
Schochet, G. J. 1967 'Thomas Hobbes on the family', *Pol. Sc. Q.*, 82
1969 'Patriarchalism, politics and mass attitudes in Stuart England', *H. J.*, 19
1975 *Patriarchalism in Political Thought* (New York)
Schofield, J. 1984 *The Buildings of London*
Schofield, R. S. 1965 'The geographical distribution of wealth in England', *Ec. H. R.*, 2nd ser., 18
1983 'The impact of scarcity and plenty', *J. I. H.*, 14
1985 'English marriage patterns revisited', *J. Fam. Hist.*, 10

Schucking, L. L. 1929 *The Puritan Family* (Leipzig)
Schulin, E. 1969 *Handelstaat England* (Wiesbaden)
Schultz, H. C. 1943 'The teaching of handwriting', *H. L. Q.*, 6
Schulz, F. 1954 *Classical Roman Law* (Oxford)
Schumpeter, J. 1950 *Capitalism, Socialism and Democracy* (New York)
1989 *Essays and Entrepreneurs*, ed. R. V. Clemens (New Brunswick)
1991 *The Economics and Sociology of Capitalism*, ed. R. S. Wedberg (Princeton)
Schuyler, R. L. 1931 *Josiah Tucker* (New York)
Schwartz, S. B. 1979 'New World mobility', *Studies in Mediterranean Culture*, 13
Schwarz, L. 1987 'London apprentices in the seventeenth century', *Loc. Pop. Stud.*, 38
Schwoerer, L. G. 1974 *No Standing Armies* (Baltimore)
1986 'Women and the Glorious Revolution', *Albion*, 18
(ed.) 1992 *The Revolution of 1688–89: Changing Perspectives* (Cambridge)
Scott, J. 1988a *Algernon Sidney and the English Republic* (Cambridge)
1988b 'Radicalism and Restoration', *H. J.*, 31
Scott, T. and Kouri, E. I. (eds.) 1986 *Politics and Society in Reformation Europe: Essays for G. R. Elton*
Scott, W. H. 1910–12 *The Constitution and Finance of English, Scottish and Irish Joint Stock Companies to 1720* (Cambridge)
Scouller, R. E. 1966 *The Armies of Queen Anne* (Oxford)
Scouloudi, I. 1937–41 'Alien immigration into London, 1558–1640', *Proc. Hug. Soc. Lond.*, 16
1947 'Thomas Papillon', *Proc. Hug. Soc. Lond.*, 18
(ed.) 1987 *The Huguenots in Britain, 1550–1800* (Totowa)
Seaver, P. S. 1970 *The Puritan Lectureships* (Stanford)
1980 'The Puritan work ethic revisited', *J. B. S.*, 19
1985 *Wallington's World: A Puritan Artisan in Seventeenth Century London*
1989 'A social contract, master against servant', *Hist. Tod.*, 39
Seaward, P. 1988 'The House of Commons' committee of trade, 1664', *H. J.*, 30
1989 *The Cavalier Parliament, 1661–7* (Cambridge)
Seddon, P. R. 1981 'Marriage and inheritance in the Clifton family', *Trans. Thor. Soc.*, 84
Sedgwick, R. (ed.) 1970 *The House of Commons, 1715–54*
Seldon, A. (ed.) 1980 *The Prime Mover of Progress* (Lond. Instit. Ec. Aff.)
Seliger, J. M. 1968 *The Liberal Politics of John Locke*
Sella, D. 1969 'Industrial production in seventeenth-century Italy', *Expl. Ent. H.*, 2nd ser., 6
1977 Review of I. Wallerstein in *Peasant Studies*, 6
1979 *Crisis and Continuity: The Economy of Spanish Lombardy* (Cambridge, Massachusetts)
Sena, J. F. 1973 'Melancholic madness', *Harvard Theological Review*, 66
Senior, C. M. 1976 *A Nation of Pirates* (Newton Abbot)
Senning, C. F. 1983 'Piracy, politics and plunder under James I', *H. L. Q.*, 46
Sergeantson, M. S. 1935 *A History of Foreign Words in English*
Seybolt, R. F. 1917 *Apprenticeship in Colonial New England* (New York)
Seyer, S. 1821 *Memoirs of Bristol, Historical and Topographical* (Bristol), 2 vols.
Shackle, G. L. S. 1961 *Decision, Order and Time in Human Affairs* (Cambridge)

Shammas, C. 1975 'The Invisible Merchant and property rights', *Bus. Hist.*, 17
1977 'The determinants of personal wealth', *J. Ec. H.*, 37
1980 'The domestic environment in early modern England and America', *J. Soc. Hist.*, 14
1987 'English inheritance law', *Amer. J. Legal Hist.*, 31
1990 *The Pre-industrial Consumer in England and America* (Oxford)
Shammas, C., Salmon, M. and Pahlin, M. (eds.) 1987 *Inheritance in America from Colonial Times to the Present*
Shanley, M. L. 1979 'Marriage contract and social contract', *West. Pol. Q.*, 32
Shapin, S. 1991 'A scholar and a gentleman', *Hist. Sc.*, 29
Shapiro, B. J. 1975a 'Science, politics and religion', *P. & P.*, 66
1975b 'Law reform in the seventeenth century', *Amer. J. Legal Hist.*, 19
1980 'Sir Francis Bacon', *Amer. J. Legal Hist.*, 24
1983 *Probability and Certainty in Seventeenth Century England* (Princeton)
Sharp, B. 1980 *In Contempt of all Authority* (Berkeley)
1989 'Popular political opinion in England, 1660–85', *Hist. Eur. Ideas*, 10
Sharpe, A. 1974 'Waterhouse's views of social change', *P. & P.*, 62
Sharpe, J. A. 1980a 'Defamation and sexual slander in early modern England', *Borthwick Papers*, 58
1980b 'Plebeian marriage in Stuart England', *T. R. H. S.*, 5th ser., 36
1981 'Domestic homicide in early modern England', *H. J.*, 24
1984 *Crime in Early Modern England, 1550–1750*
1987 *Early Modern England: A Social History, 1350–1760*
Sharpe, K. (ed.) 1978 *Faction and Parliament*
1984 'Thomas Witherings', *B. I. H. R.*, 57
1987 *Criticism and Compliment* (Cambridge)
1989 *Politics and Ideas in Stuart England*
Sharpe, K. and Zwicker, S. N. (eds.) 1987 *Politics of Discourse* (Berkeley)
Sharpe, R. R. 1894–5 *London and the Kingdom*
Shashko, P. 1966–7 'Nikolai Alexandrovich Mel'gunov', *Comp. Stud. Soc. Hist.*, 9
Shaw, L. M. E. 1989 *Trade, Inquisition and the English Nation in Portugal, 1650–90* (Manchester)
Shaw, W. A. 1900 *History of the English Church, 1640–1660*
1906 *The Knights of England*, 2 vols.
Sheail, J. 1972 'The distribution of taxable population and wealth in England during the early sixteenth century', *Trans. Instit. Brit. Geog.*, 55
Sheavyn, P. A. B. 1967 *The Literary Profession in the Elizabethan Age*, 2nd edn, rev. J. W. Saunders (Manchester)
Sheehan, M. M. 1963 *The Will in Medieval England* (Toronto)
Sheils, W. J. (ed.) 1984 *Persecution and Toleration* (Eccles. Hist. Soc.)
(ed.) 1985 *Monks, Hermits and the Ascetic Tradition* (Eccles. Hist. Soc.)
Sheils, W. J. and Wood, D. (eds.) 1986 *Voluntary Religion* (Eccles. Hist. Soc.)
Sheldon, C. D. 1958 *The Rise of the Merchant Class in Tokugawa, Japan, 1600–1868* (New York)
Shelton, G. 1981 *Dean Tucker and Eighteenth-century Economic and Political Thought*
Shennan, J. H. 1969 *Government and Society in France, 1461–1661*

Shepherd, J. F. and Walton, G. M. 1972 *Shipping, Maritime Trade and the Economic Development of Colonial North America* (Cambridge)
Sheppard, E. M. 1983 'The Reformation and the citizens of Norwich', *Norf. Arch.*, 38
Sheppard, F. H. W. (ed.) 1966– *The Survey of London* (Greater London Council)
Sheridan, R. B. 1951 'The sugar trade of the British West Indies, 1660–1756' (unpub. Ph.D. thesis, London)
1960–1 'The rise of a colonial gentry', *Ec. H. R.*, 2nd ser., 13
1965, 1968 'The wealth of Jamaica', *Ec. H. R.*, 2nd ser., 18 and 20
1974 *Sugar and Slavery: An Economic History of the British West Indies, 1623–1775* (Barbados)
Sherman, A. A. 1976 'Pressure from Leadenhall', *Bus. Hist. Rev.*, 50
Sherwell, J. W. 1937 *The Saddlers of London*, 3rd edn, rev. K. S. Laurie and A. F. G. Everitt (Chelmsford)
Sherwin, O. 1950 'Thomas Firmin', *J. M. H.*, 22
Shinagel, A. 1968 *Defoe and Middle Class Gentility* (Cambridge, Massachusetts)
Shipley, N. R. 1973 'Thomas Sutton and his landed interests in Essex', *Essex J.*, 8
1975a 'The history of a manor, 1580–1629', *B. I. H. R.*, 48
1975b 'The foundation of Charterhouse, 1610–16', *Guild. Stud. Lond. Hist.*, 1
1976 'Thomas Sutton', *Bus. Hist. Rev.*, 50
Shiraishi, B. 1958 'The merchants of Osaka', *Japan Q.*, 5
Shoemaker, R. B. 1991 *Prosecution and Punishment, c. 1660–1785* (Cambridge)
Short, J. F. (ed.) 1981 *The State of Sociology: Problems and Prospects* (Beverley Hills)
Shorter, A. H. 1957 *Paper Mills and Paper Makers in England, 1495–1800* (Hilversum)
Shrewsbury, J. F. D. 1970 *History of Bubonic Plague in the British Isles* (Cambridge)
Shumaker, C. W. *English Autobiography: Its Emergence, Materials and Form* (Berkeley)
Sievekin, G. H. 1907 *Studio sulle finanze genovesi* (Atti della Società Lìgure di Storia Patria, 35)
Silberner, E. 1939 *La Guerre dans la pensée économique du XVIe aux XVIIIe siècles*
Silva, J. G. de, 1962 'Richesse et enrichissement', *Annales*, 17
1964 'Au XVIIe siècle: la stratégie du capital florentin', *Annales*, 3
Silvette, H. 1967 *The Doctor on the Stage* (Knoxville)
Simiand, F. 1987 *Méthode historique et science sociale*, ed. M. Cedronio
Simms, J. G. 1965 'Dublin in 1685', *Irish Hist. Stud.*, 14
Simon, A. L. 1906–9 *History of the Wine Trade*
(ed.) 1953 *Bibliotheca Gastronomica*
Simon, J. 1963 'The social origins of Cambridge students, 1603–40', *P. & P.*, 26
1966 *Education and Society in Tudor England* (Cambridge)
(ed.) 1968 *Education in Leicestershire, 1540–1940*
Simon, J. B. 1964 *Robert Burton et 'l'Anatomie de la melancholie'*
Simon, W. G. 1965 *The Restoration Episcopate* (New York)
Simpson, A. 1958–9 'Thomas Cullum, draper', *Ec. H. R.*, 2nd ser., 11
1961 *Wealth of the Gentry* (Chicago)

Simpson, A. W. B. 1961 *An Introduction to the History of Land Law*
1966 'The penal bond with conditional defeasance', *Law Q. R.*, 82
1979 'The Horwitz thesis', *Univ. Chicago Law Rev.*, 46
Simpson, E. 1985 'Understanding Inventories', *Fam. Hist.*, 13
Sisson, C. J. (ed.) 1933 *Thomas Lodge and Other Elizabethans* (New York)
Sitwell, G. R. 1902 'The English gentleman', *The Ancestor*, 1
Skeel, C. A. J. 1916 'The Canary Company', *E. H. R.*, 31
Skilliter, S. A. 1977 *William Harborne and the Trade with Turkey, 1578–82* (Brit. Acad.)
Skinner, A. S. 1979 *Adam Smith: A System of Social Science* (Oxford)
Skinner, A. S. and Wilson, T. (eds.) 1976 *The Market and the State: Essays in Honour of Adam Smith* (Oxford)
Skinner, G. W. (ed.) 1977 *The City in Late Imperial China* (Stanford)
Skinner, Q. 1974 'Some problems in the analysis of political thought', *Pol. Theory*, 2
Skocpol, T. 1977 'Wallerstein's world capitalist system', *Amer. J. Sociol.*, 82
(ed.) 1984 *Vision and Method in Historical Sociology* (Cambridge)
Slack, P. 1971 'The disappearance of plague', *Ec. H. R.*, 24
1974 'Vagrants and vagrancy in England, 1598–1664', *Ec. H. R.*, 2nd ser., 27
1980 'Book of Orders', *T. R. H. S.*, 5th ser., 30
(ed.) 1984 *Rebellion, Popular Protest and the Social Order in Early Modern England* (Cambridge)
1985 *The Impact of Plague in Tudor and Stuart England*
1988 *Poverty and Policy in Tudor and Stuart England*
1989 *The English Poor Law, 1530–1782*
Slater, M. 1984 *Family Life in the Seventeenth Century: The Verneys of Claydon House*
Slatter, M. D. 1953 'The records of the Court of the Arches', *J. Eccles. Hist.*, 4
Slaughter, M. 1966 *Politics and Profit: A Study of Sir Ralph Sadler, 1507–47* (Cambridge)
1982 *Universal Language and Scientific Taxonomy in the Seventeenth Century* (Cambridge)
Slights, C. 1981 *The Casuistical Tradition in Shakespeare, Donne, Herbert and Milton* (Princeton)
Sloane, W. 1955 *Children's Books in England and America in the Seventeenth Century* (New York)
Small, J. 1992a 'The Stansfields of Halifax', *Albion*, 24
1992b 'Manufacturers and artisans', *J. Soc. Hist.*, 25
Smart, T. W. W. 1861 'A biographical sketch of Samuel Jeake, Senior', *Suss. Arch. Coll.*, 13
Smedt, H. de, 1973 'Methode rot reconstructie', *Hist. Ec. Belg.*, 2
Smedt, O. de, 1950 *De Engelse Natie te Antwerpen in de 16de eeuw, 1496–1582* (Antwerp)
Smelser, N. J. and Lipset, S. M. 1966 *Social Structure and Mobility in Economic Development*
Smiles, S. 1884 *Characters* (New York)
Smith, A. 1974 'Samuel Ogden', *Derby. Arch. J.*, 94
Smith, A. E. 1947 *Colonists in Bondage* (Chapel Hill)

Smith, A. G. R. 1968 'The secretariat of the Cecils, 1580–1612', *E. H. R.*, 83
(ed.) 1973 *The Reign of James VI and I*
Smith, A. H. 1974 *Country and Court: Government and Politics in Norfolk, 1558–1603* (Oxford)
Smith, D. M. 1990 *Guide to the Archives of the Company of Merchant Adventurers of York* (Borthwick Inst.)
Smith, D. S. A. 1973 'Parental power and marriage patterns', *J. Marr. & Fam.*, 35
Smith, G. C. M. 1936 *The Family of Withypoll*
Smith, H. L. 1982 *Reason's Disciples* (Urbana)
Smith, J. M. (ed.) 1959 *Seventeenth Century America: Essays in Colonial History* (Chapel Hill)
Smith, L. B. 1953 *Tudor Prelates and Politics, 1536–58* (Princeton)
1976 'The gage and the land market', *Ec. H. R.* 29
Smith, L. W. 1972 'Daniel Defoe, incipient pornographer', *Lit. & Psych.*, 22
Smith, R. (comp.) 1962 *Ceremonials of the Corporation of London*
Smith, R. (ed.) 1984 *Land, Kinship and Life Cycle* (Cambridge)
Smith, R. J. 1960 'Pre-industrial urbanism in Japan', *Ec. Dev. & Cult. Ch.*, 9
Smith, R. J. 1974 'Bureaucracy in Elizabethan England: the office of naval ordnance', *Albion*, 6
Smith, R. S. 1961–2 'A wood growing project', *Trans. Thor. Soc.*, 65–7
1967 'Sir Francis Willoughby's ironworks, 1570–1616', *Ren. & Mod. Stud.*, 11
1989 *Early Coal Mining around Nottingham, 1500–1650* (Nott. Univ. Dept. Adult Educ.)
Smith, S. R. 1972 'The apprentices parliament of 1647', *Hist. Tod.*, 22
1973a 'The social and geographical origins of the London apprentices, 1630–60', *Guild. Misc.*, 4
1973b 'The London Apprentices', *P. & P.*, 61
1974–5 'Religion and the conception of Youth', *History of Childhood*, 2
1976 'Growing old in early Stuart England', *Albion*, 8
1978–9 'The London apprentices during the Civil Wars', *H. L. Q.*, 43
1981 'The ideal and the reality: apprentice-master relationships', *Hist. Educ Q.*, 21
Smith, T. C. 1959 *The Agrarian Origins of Modern Japan* (Stanford)
1960 'Landlords' sons in the business élite', *Econ. Dev. & Cult. Ch.*, 9
1973 'Pre-modern economic growth: Japan and the West', *P. & P.*, 60
Smith, W. D. 1984 'The function of commercial centers in the modernization of Europe', *J. Ec. H.*, 44
Smithers, P. 1968 *The Life of Joseph Addison*, 2nd edn (Oxford)
Smout, T. C. 1960a 'Scottish commercial factors in the Baltic', *Scot. Hist. Rev.*, 39
1960b 'The development of enterprise in Glasgow, 1556–1707', *Scot. J. Pol. Econ.*, 7
1961 'The early Scottish sugar houses, 1660–1720', *Ec. H. R.*, 2nd ser., 14
1963 *Scottish Trade on the Eve of Union, 1660–1707* (Edinburgh)
1968 'The Glasgow merchant community in the seventeenth century', *Scot. Hist. Rev.*, 47
1969 *A History of the Scottish People*

(ed.) 1979 *The Search for Wealth and Stability: Essays Presented to M. W. Flinn*
Smuts, R. M. 1987 *Court Culture and the Origins of a Royalist Tradition* (Philadelphia)
1991 'The Court and its neighbourhood', *J. B. S.*, 30
Smyth, W. D. 1905a *The Company of Girdlers of London*
1905b *The Company of Saddlers*
Snyder, F. and Hay, D. (eds.) 1987 *Labour, Law and Crime*
Snyders, R. 1965 *La Pédagoge en France aux XVIIe et XVIIIe siècles*
Solomons, D. 1952 (ed.) *Studies in Costing*
Solow, B. (ed.) 1991 *Slavery and the Atlantic System* (Cambridge)
Solt, L. F. 1967 'Puritanism, capitalism, democracy and the New Science', *A. H. R.*, 73
Soly, H. 1975 'The betrayal of the sixteenth-century bourgeoisie: a myth', *Acta Hist. Neer.*, 8
1977 *Urbanisme en kapitalisme te Antwerpen in de 16de eeuw* (Brussels)
Sombart, W. 1913 *Der Bourgeois* (Munich)
Sommerville, C. J. 1976 'Religious typologies and popular religion', *Ch. Hist.*, 45
1981 'The anti-Puritan work ethic', *J. B. S.*, 20
1992a *The Discovery of Childhood* (Athens)
1992b *The Secularisation of Early Modern England* (New York)
Sorokin, P. 1927 *Social Mobility* (New York)
Sosin, J. M. 1985 *English America and Imperial Inconstancy, 1696–1715* (Lincoln)
Souden, D. 1978 'Indentured servant emigrants', *Soc. Hist.*, 3
Souers, P. W. 1931 *The Matchless Orinda* (Cambridge)
Soustelle, J. 1959 *La Vie quotidienne des Aztecs*
Southern, R. W. 1968 (ed.) *Essays in Medieval History*
South Sea Company. Particulars and Inventories of the late Directors (1721)
Spalding, R. 1975 *Improbable Puritan: A Life of Bulstrode Whitelocke, 1605–75*
Spangenberg, B. 1976 *British Bureaucracy in India*
Spear, T. G. P. 1932 *The Nabobs*
Spearman, D. 1966 *The Novel and Society*
Speck, W. A. 1966 'Social status in late Stuart England', *P. & P.*, 34
1970 *Tory and Whig, 1701–1715: The Struggle for the Constitution*
1988 *Reluctant Revolutionaries: England and the Revolution of 1688* (Oxford)
Speck, W. A. and Gray, W. A. 1975 'Londoners at the polls', *Guild. Stud. Lond. Hist.*, 1
Spengler, J. J. 1959 'Veblen and Mandeville', *Welt. Arch.*, 82–3
1968 'Demographic factors and early modern economic development', *Daedalus*, 98
Sperling, J. 1961–2 'The international payments mechanism in the seventeenth and eighteenth centuries', *Ec. H. R.*, 2nd ser., 14
Spooner, F. C. 1983 *Risks at Sea* (Cambridge)
Spring, D. 1963 *The English Landed Estate in the Nineteenth Century* (Baltimore)
1985 'The English landed élite', *Albion*, 17
Spring, D. and E. 1983 'The family, strict settlement and historians', *Canad. J. Hist.*, 18
1986 'Social mobility and the English landed élite', *Canad. J. Hist.*, 21
1988 'The strict settlement', *Ec. H. R.*, 2nd ser., 41

Sprinzak, E. 1975 'Weber's thesis as an historical explanation', *Hist. & Theory*, 11
Sprunger, K. 1982 *Dutch Puritanism* (Leiden)
Spufford, M. 1979 'First steps in literacy', *Soc. Hist.*, 4
1981 *Small Books and Pleasant Histories*
1984 *The Great Reclothing of Rural England*
Spufford, P. 1973–4 'Population mobility in pre-industrial England', *Genealog. Mag.*, 17
Spurling, Sir Stanley, 1955 *Sir Thomas Smythe* (New York)
Spurr, J. 1988 'Latitudinarianism in the Restoration Church', *H. J.*, 31
1991 *The Restoration Church in England* (New Haven)
Squibb, G. D. 1959 *The High Court of Chivalry* (Oxford)
1977 *Doctors' Commons* (Oxford)
1978 *Visitation Pedigrees and the Genealogist*, 2nd edn
1981 *Precedence in England and Wales* (Oxford)
Starkey, D. (ed.) 1987 *The English Court*
Starr, G. A. 1965 *Defoe and Spiritual Autobiography* (Princeton)
1967 'From casuistry to fiction', *J. H. I.*, 28
1971 *Defoe and Casuistry* (Princeton)
Statt, D. 1990 'The City of London and the controversy over immigration', *H. J.*, 33
Stauffer, D. A. 1930 *English Biography before 1700* (Cambridge, Massachusetts)
Staves, S. 1989 'The secrets of genteel identity', *Stud. Eight. Cent. Cult.*, 19
1990 *Married Women: Separate Property in England, 1660–1833* (Cambridge)
Stearns, P. N. and C. Z. 1985 'Emotionology', *A. H. R.*, 90
Steckley, G, F, 1978 'Merchants and the Admiralty Court', *Amer. J. Legal Hist.*, 22
1980 'The wine economy of Teneriffe', *Ec. H. R.*, 2nd ser., 33
Steele, I. K. 1968 *Politics of Colonial Policy, 1696–1720* (Oxford)
1977 'Joseph Cruttenden, apothecary, 1710–1717', *Wm & Mary Q.*, 3rd ser., 24
1986 *The English Atlantic, 1675–1740* (Oxford)
Steensgaard, N. 1965 'Freight costs in the English East India trade, 1601–57', *Scand. Ec. H. R.*, 13
1973 *The Asian Trade Revolution of the Seventeenth Century*
Steer, F. W. (ed.) 1964 *The Lavington Estate Archives*
1973 *History of the Company of Scriveners*
Stein, R. L. 1979 *The French Slave Trade in the Eighteenth Century* (Madison)
Stephens, J. N. 1983 *The Fall of the Florentine Republic, 1512–30* (Oxford)
Stephens, W. B. 1954 'Merchant companies in Exeter, 1625–88', *Trans. Devon Assoc.*, 86
1957 'Roger Mallock', *Trans. Devon Assoc.*, 88
1958 *Seventeenth-century Exeter* (Exeter)
1960 'Roger Mallock, merchant and royalist', *Trans. Devon Assoc.*, 92
1968 'The overseas trade of Chester in the early seventeenth century', *Trans. Hist. Soc. Lancs. & Ches.*, 120
1969a 'The cloth exports of the provincial ports, 1600–40', *Ec. H. R.*, 2nd ser., 22

1969b 'The Exchequer Port Books', *Text. Hist.*, 1
1969c 'The trade of Plymouth', *Trans. Devon Assoc.*, 100
1971 'Further observations on English cloth exports', *Ec. H. R.*, 2nd ser., 24
1974 'Trade trends at Bristol, 1600–1700', *T. B. G. A. S.*, 93
Stephenson, D. 1977 'The Myddeltons of Stansted Mountfield', *Essex Arch. & Hist.*, 8
Stern, W. M. 1956 'The trade of silk throwers', *Guild. Misc.*, 6
1960 *The Porters of London*
1979 'The Cheesemongers of London', *Lond. J.*, 5
1981 'The Company of Watermen', *Guild. Stud. Lond. Hist.*, 5
Steven, J. 1969 'Prince's "Worthies of Devon"', *Devon & Corn. N. & Q.*, 31
Stevenson (O'Connell), L. C. 1974 'Anti-entrepreneurial attitudes', *J. B. S.*, 15
1984 *Praise and Paradox: Merchants and Craftsmen in Elizabethan Popular Literature* (Cambridge)
Stevenson, S. J. 1987–8 'The rise of suicide verdicts in South-east England, 1530–90', *Cont. & Ch.*, 2
Stevenson, W. H. and Salter, H. E. 1939 *The Early History of St John's College, Oxford* (Oxford)
Steward, J. H. (ed.) 1946 *Handbook of South American Indians* (Smithsonian Institution, Bureau of American Ethnology, 143)
Stewart, G. 1881 *Curiosities of Glasgow Citizens* (Glasgow)
Stieg, M. F. 1982 *Laud's Laboratory* (Lewisburg)
Stitt, F. B. 1973 'Midland archive collections', *Mid. Hist.*, 2
Stoianovich, T. 1974 *French Historical Method: The Annales Paradigm* (Ithaca)
Stoker, D. 1980 'Doctor Collinge and Norwich city library', *Lib. Hist.*, 5
Stone, L. 1956 *Sir Horatio Palavicino* (Oxford)
1958 'The inflation of honours', *P. & P.*, 14
1964a *The Crisis of the Aristocracy, 1558–1641* (Oxford)
1964b 'The educational revolution in England, 1560–1640', *P. & P.*, 28
1967 'Office under Queen Elizabeth', *H. J.*, 10
1968 'Literacy and education in England, 1640–1900', *P. & P.*, 42
1972 *The Causes of the English Revolution, 1529–1642*
1973 *Family and Fortune* (Oxford)
(ed.) 1974 *The University in Society* (Princeton)
1977a *The Family, Sex and Marriage in England, 1500–1800*
1977b 'Age of admission to educational institutions', *Hist. Educ.*, 6
(ed.) 1978 *Schooling and Society* (Baltimore)
1979 'The revival of narrative', *P. & P.*, 85
1980 'The age of admission to college', *Hist. Educ.*, 9
1981 'Family history in the 1980s', *J. I. H.*, 12
1983 'Interpersonal violence in English society, 1330–1980', *P. & P.*, 101
1987 *The Past and the Present* (Boston)
1990 *Road to Divorce: England, 1530–1987* (Oxford)
1992 *Uncertain Unions. Marriage in England 1660–1753* (Oxford)
1993 *Broken Lives: Separation and Divorce in England, 1660–1857* (Oxford)
Stone, L. and Everitt, A. 1965 'Social mobility', *P. & P.*, 32
Stone, L. and J. F. C. 1984 *An Open Elite? England, 1540–1880* (Oxford)
Stonex, A. B. 1916 'The usurer in Elizabethan drama', *P. M. L. A.*, 31

Storey, A. 1967 *Trinity House of Kingston upon Hull* (Hull)
Stout, H. S. 1974 'University men in New England, 1620–60', *J. I. H.*, 4
Stoye, J. W. 1952 *English Travellers Abroad, 1504–1667*
Strachan, M. 1989 *Sir Thomas Roe, 1581–1644* (Salisbury)
Strachey, R. C. C. 1916 *Keigwin's Rebellion, 1683–4* (Oxford)
Straker, E. 1960 *Wealden Iron* (repr. Newton Abbot)
Stratford, J. 1867 *Good and Great Men of Gloucester* (Cirencester)
Stratton, J. M. 1969 *Agricultural Records, 220–1968*, ed. R. Whitlock
Strauss, L. 1952 *The Political Philosophy of Hobbes* (Chicago)
Streeter, B. H. 1931 *The Chained Library*
Streisser, E. and Marz, E. 1988 'The intellectual and political impact of the Austrian school', *J. Eur. Ideas*, 9
Strong, R. C. 1958 'The popular celebration', *J. Warburg & Court. Inst.*, 21
1969 *Tudor and Jacobean Portraits*, 2 vols.
Strout, C. 1968 'Ego psychology and the historian', *Hist. & Theory*, 7
'Studies in quantitative history and the logic of the social sciences', *Hist. & Theory*, 9 (1969)
Stump, W. 1974 'An economic consequence of 1688', *Albion*, 6
Styles, P. 1951 'A census of a Warwickshire village', *Univ. B'ham H. J.*, 3
1962 'The social structure of Kineton Hundred', *Trans. B'ham A .S.*, 78
1978 *Studies in Seventeenth-century West Midland History* (Kineton)
Subrahmanyam, S. 1990a *The Political Economy of Commerce: Southern India, 1550–1650* (New York)
(ed.) 1990b *Merchants, Markets and the State* (Delhi)
1993 *The Portuguese Empire in Asia, 1500–1700*
Suckling, A. 1848 *The History and Antiquities of Suffolk*
Suivaranta, B. 1923 *The Theory of the Balance of Trade* (Helsinki)
Summerson, J. N. 1970a *Architecture in Britain, 1530–1830*, rev. edn
1970b *Georgian London* (repr. New York)
Sundstron, R. A. 1976 'Huguenots and the Civil List, 1696–1727', *Albion*, 8
Supple, B. E. 1957–8 'Currency and commerce in the early seventeenth century', *Ec. H. R.*, 2nd ser., 10
1959 'From business to government', *Bus. Hist. Rev.*, 33
1960 'Economic history and economic growth', *J. Ec. H.*, 20
1961 'Economic history and underdevelopment', *Canad. J. Econ. & Pol. Sc.*, 27
1961–2 'The uses of business history', *Bus. Hist.*, 4
1963 'The great capitalist manhunt', *Bus. Hist.*, 6
1970 *Commercial Crisis and Change in England, 1600–42*, new edn (Cambridge)
1984 'Revisiting Rostow', *Ec. H. R.*, 2nd ser., 37
Surfield, G. 1986 'Seventeenth-century Sheffield', *Yorks. Arch. J.*, 58
Surry, N. W. 1981 'Hampshire apprentices to the Painters Stainers Company, *c.* 1660–1795', *Proc. Hants. Field Club & Arch. Soc.*, 37
Sutherland, J. 1950 *Daniel Defoe*, 2nd edn
1986 *The Restoration Newspaper* (Cambridge)
Sutherland, L. S. 1934 'The law merchant in England', *T. R. H. S.*, 4th ser., 17
1935–6 'The use of business records', *B. I. H. R.*, 13
1952 *The East India Company in Eighteenth-century Politics* (Oxford)
1962 *A London Merchant, 1695–1774* (Oxford)

Sutherland, N. 1974 *Tudor Darlington*
Sutton, A. F. 1986 'William Shore, merchant of London and Derby', *Derby. Arch. J.*, 106
Sutton, S. C. 1967 *A Guide to the India Office Library*, new edn
Swain, J. T. 1986 *Industry before the Industrial Revolution: North-east Lancashire, 1500–1646* (Cheth. Soc., 32)
Swales, R. J. W. 1977 'The ship money levy', *B. I. H. R.*, 50
Swanson, H. 1988 'The illusion of economic structure', *P. & P.*, 121
1989 *Medieval Artisans: An Urban Class* (Oxford)
Swart, K. W. 1949 *Sale of Office in the Seventeenth Century* (The Hague)
1970 *The Miracle of the Dutch Republic*
Swetz, F. J. 1987 *Capitalism and Arithmetic: The New Maths of the Fifteenth Century*
Sykes, N. 1962 *William Wake, 1657–1737* (Cambridge), 2 vols.
1967 *Church and State in England in the Eighteenth Century* (repr. Hamden)
Syme, Sir Ronald, 1986 *The Augustan Aristocracy* (Oxford)
Symonds, R. W. 1955 *Furniture Making in Seventeenth- and Eighteenth-century England*
Syrett, H. C. 1954 'Private enterprise in New Amsterdam', *Wm & Mary Q.*, 3rd ser., 11
Szeftel, M. 1936 'La règle de vie exemplaire des nobles', *Rev. Inst. Sociol.*, 16
Takenaka, Y. 1969 'Endogenous formation and the development of capitalism in Japan', *J. Ec. H.*, 29
Talbot, G. 1986 'Worcester as an industrial and commercial centre, 1660–1750', *Trans. Worcs. A. S.*, 10
Tate, T. W. and Ammerman, D. L. (eds.) 1979 *The Chesapeake in the Seventeenth Century* (Chapel Hill)
Tatlock, J. S. P. 1950 *The Legendary History of Britain* (Berkeley)
Tattersfield, N. 1991 *The Forgotten Trade*
Tawney, R. H. 1921 *The Acquisitive Society*
1944 *Religion and the Rise of Capitalism*
1958 *Business and Politics under James I* (Cambridge)
1978 *History and Society Essay*, ed. J. M. Winter
Taylor, E. G. R. 1956 *The Mathematical Practitioners of Tudor and Stuart England* (Cambridge)
Taylor, G. A. 1938 'A list of London merchants and traders trading to New England 1716', *Genealog. Mag.*, 8
Taylor, G. L. 1964 *Silver through the Ages*
Taylor, G. R. 1958 *The Angel Makers*
Taylor, H. 1968 'Price revision or price revolution', *Ren. & Mod. Stud.*, 12
1972 'Trade neutrality and the English road, 1630–48', *Ec. H. R.*, 2nd ser., 25
Taylor, J. G. M. 1949 'The civic government of Gloucester, 1640–46', *T. B. G. A. S.*, 77
Taylor, J. S. 1976 'The impact of pauper settlement, 1691–1834', *P.& P.*, 73
Taylor, L. 1983 *Mourning Dress*
Taylor, O. H. 1955 *Economics and Liberalism: Collected Papers* (Cambridge, Massachusetts)
Taylor, R. 1974 'Town houses in Taunton, 1500–1700', *Post Med. Arch.*, 8

Taylor, R. M. and Crandale, R. J. (eds.) 1986 *Generation and Change: Genealogical Perspectives in Social History* (Macon)
Taylor, S. 1945 'Daily life and death', *Trans. Cumb. & West. Antiq. & Arch. Soc.*, NS, 44
Taylor, W. L. 1965 *Francis Hutcheson and David Hume* (Durham)
Tedder, A. W. 1916 *The Navy of the Restoration* (Cambridge)
Temperly, H. 1977 'Capitalism, slavery and ideology', *P. & P.*, 75
Temple, Sir Richard, 1922 'A factor's complaint', *Indian Antiquary*, 51
Teng, S. 1943 'Chinese influence on the western examination system', *Harv. J. Asiat. Stud.*, 7
Terrill, R. J. 1981 'Humanism and rhetoric in legal education: Sir John Dodderidge', *J. Legal Hist.*, 2
Thirsk, J. 1952–3 'The sale of Royalist land during the Interregnum', *Ec. H. R.*, 2nd ser., 5
1955 'The content and sources of English agrarian history after 1500', *Agric. Hist. Rev.*, 3
1963 'Unexplored sources in local records', *Archives*, 6
1969 'Younger sons in the seventeenth century', *History*, 54
(ed.) 1970 *Land, Church and People: Essays Presented to H. P. R. Finberg* (Reading)
(ed.) 1971, 1978 *The Agrarian History of England and Wales* (Cambridge), vols. IV and V
1984 *The Rural Economy of England: Collected Essays*
1988 *Economic Policies and Projects: The Development of a Consumer Society in Modern England* (Oxford)
1990 'The fashioning of the Tudor and Stuart gentry', *B. J. R. L.*, 72
Thomas, B. 1986 'Was there an energy crisis in the seventeenth century?', *Exp. Ec. H.*, 23
Thomas, D. 1972 'The social origins of marriage', *Pop. Stud.*, 26
Thomas, D. 1977 'Leases in reversion on the Crown lands, 1558–1603', *Ec. H. R.*, 2nd ser., 30
Thomas, Sir Keith, 1964 'Work and leisure in pre-industrial society', *P. & P.*, 29
1971 *Religion and the Decline of Magic*
1976a 'Age and authority in early modern England', *P. B. A.*, 62
1976b *Rule and Misrule in the Schools* (Reading)
1977 'The place of laughter in Tudor and Stuart England', *T. L. S.*, 21 January
1983a *The Perception of the Past in Early Modern England*
1983b *Man and the Natural World: Changing Attitudes in England, 1500–1800*
1987 'Numeracy in early modern England', *T. R. H. S.*, 5th ser., 37
Thomas, Sir Keith, and Pennington, D. 1978 (eds.) *Puritans and Revolutionaries: Essays Presented to Christopher Hill*
Thomas, R. P. 1968 'The sugar colonies of the old Empire', *Ec. H. R.*, 2nd ser., 21
Thompson, E. P. 1972 'Anthropology and the discipline of historical context', *Mid. Hist.*, 1
Thompson, F. M. L. 1962 *English Landed Society in the Nineteenth Century*
1966 'The social distribution of landed property', *Ec. H. R.*, 2nd ser., 19
(ed.) 1983 *Horses in European Economic History* (Reading)
1990 'Life after death', *Ec. H. R.*, 2nd ser., 43

Thompson, I. A. A. 1979 'The purchase of nobility in Castile, 1552–1760', *J. Ec. H.*, 8
1985 'Neo-noble nobility', *Eur. Hist. Quart.*, 15
Thompson, R. 1974 'Seventeenth-century English and colonial sex ratios', *Pop. Stud.*, 27
1979 *Unfit for Modest Ears*
Thompson, R. C. 1966 'Officers, merchants and foreign policy in the Protectorate', *Hist. Stud. Aust. & New Zeal.*
Thompson, T. 1870 'The Herrick portraits', *Trans. Leics. Archit. & Arch. Soc.*, 2
Thompson, V. A. 1969 *Bureaucracy and Innovation*
Thoms, D. W. 1969a 'The Mills family, London sugar merchants', *Bus. Hist.*, 11
1969b 'Slavery in the Leeward Islands', *B. I. H. R.*, 42
Thomson, H. W. and Yamey, B. S. (eds.) 1968 *Bibliography of Foreign Books on Bookkeeping and Accounting, 1494–1750* (Inst. Chartered Accountants)
Thomson, J. A. F. 1965 'Piety and charity in late medieval London', *J. Eccles. Hist.*, 16
Thomson, J. K. J. 1982 *Clermont de Lodère, 1633–1789* (Cambridge)
Thomson, M. A. 1932 *The Secretaries of State, 1681–1782* (repr.)
Thorne, S. E. 1959 'English feudalism and estates in land', *Camb. Law J.*, 38
1985 *Essays in English Legal History*
Thornton, A. P. 1952 'Sir Andrew King', *Jamaica Hist. Rev.*, 7
1956 *West India Policy under the Restoration* (Oxford)
Thornton, P. 1978 *Seventeenth-century Interior Decoration*
1984 *Authentic Decor*
Thorp, M. R. 1976 'The anti-Huguenot undercurrent in seventeenth-century England', *Proc. Hug. Soc. Lond.*, 22
Thrupp, S. L. 1933 *A Short History of the Bakers Company*
1948 *The Merchant Class of Medieval London, 1300–1500* (Chicago)
1965 'The problem of replacement rates', *Ec. H. R.*, 2nd ser., 18
Thwaites, W. 1984 'Women in the market-place: Oxfordshire, 1690–1800', *Mid. Hist.*, 9
Tibbetts, G. R. 1977 'Lysons and the model merchant', *Genealog. Mag.*, 19
Tierney, B. 1959 *The Medieval Poor Law* (Berkeley)
Tilly, C. (ed.) 1978 *Historical Studies of Changing Fertility* (Princeton)
Tilly, L. A. and Cohen, M. 1982 'Does the family have a history?', *Soc. Sc. Hist.*, 6
Tillyard, E. M. W. 1947 *The Elizabethan World Picture*
Tilmouth, M. 1972 'Music on the travels of an English merchant', *Music and Letters*, 53
Tipping, H. A. 1920–37 *English Homes*, 9 vols.
Tiryakian, E. A. (ed.) 1963 *Sociological Theory Value and Sociocultural Change: Essays in Honor of P. A. Sorokin* (Glencoe, Illinois)
Tittler, R. 1977a 'The English fishery industry in the seventeenth century', *Albion*, 9
1977b 'The incorporation of boroughs, 1540–58', *History*, 62
1985a 'The economy of Poole, *c.* 1500–1600', *South. Hist.*, 7
1985b 'The building of civic halls in Dorset', *B. I. H. R.*, 58
1987 'The end of the Middle Ages in the English country town', *Sixt. Cent. J.*, 18

1989 'Elizabethan towns and the points of control', *Parlt. Hist.*, 8
1991 *Architecture and Power: The Town Hall and the English Urban Community, 1500–1640* (Oxford)
1992 'Seats of honour', *Albion*, 24
Todd, M. 1986 'Providence, chance and the new science', *H. J.*, 29
1987 *Christian Humanism and the Puritan Social Order* (New York)
Todd, T. 1952 *William Dockwren: The Story of the Penny Post, 1680–82* (Edinburgh)
Tolles, F. B. 1948 *Meeting House and Counting House, 1682–1763* (Chapel Hill)
Tolmie, M. 1977a 'Thomas Lambe', *Bapt. Q.*, 27
1977b *The Triumph of the Saints* (Cambridge)
Tomlinson, H. C. 1974 'Place and profit: the Ordnance Office, 1660–1714', *T. R. H. S.*, 5th ser., 24
1979 *Guns and Government: The Ordnance Office under the Later Stuarts*
Tonnies, F. 1957 *Gemeinschaft und Gesellschaft*, ed. C. P. Loomis (East Lansing)
Tonomura, H. 1992 *Community and Commerce in Late Medieval Japan* (Stanford)
Torrey, G. C. 1892 *The Commercial Technical Terms in the Koran* (Leiden)
Tournier, C. 1912 ' Le commerce d'un gentilhomme toulousan', *Rev. des Pyrenées*, 24
Tout, T. F. 1934 *The Collected Papers* (Manchester)
Tracy, J. D. 1985 *A Financial Revolution in the Hapsburg Netherlands, 1515–65* (Berkeley)
(ed.) 1990 *The Rise of Merchant Empires, 1350–1750* (Cambridge)
(ed.) 1991 *The Political Economy of Merchant Empires*, (Cambridge)
Travers, B. 1990 'Trading patterns in the east Midlands, 1660–1800', *Mid. Hist.*, 15
Travers, T. H. E. 1977 'Samuel Smiles and the origins of "Self Help"', *Albion*, 9
Treadwell, J. M. 1976 'Swift and William Wood', *J. B. S.*, 15
Trease, G. E. 1964 *Pharmacy in History*
1965 'Apothecaries and their tokens, 1648–79', *Pharm. J.*, 25
1972 'Devon apothecaries', *Devon & Corn. N. & Q.*, 32
Trenerry, C. F. 1926 *The Origins and Early History of Insurance*
Treppo, M. del, 1972 *I mercanti catalani è l'espansione della Corona d'Aragona* (Naples)
Tresham-Lever, Sir J. P. 1947 *The House of Pitt*
Trevelyan, G. M. 1930–34 *England under Queen Anne* 3 vols.
Tribe, K. 1981 *Genealogies of Capitalism*
Trinterud, L. J. and Hudson, W. S. 1971 *Theology in Sixteenth and Seventeenth Century England* (Los Angeles)
Troeltsch, E. 1931 *The Social Teachings of the Christian Churches*
Tronrud, T. J. 1985a 'Dispelling the gloom', *Canad. J. Hist.*, 20
1985b 'The resistance to poverty in three English towns', *Histoire Sociale*, 35
Troyer, H. W 1946 *Ned Ward of Grubstreet, 1671–1731* (Cambridge, Massachusetts)
Trumbach, R. 1977 'London sodomites', *J. Soc. Hist.*, 11
1978 *The Rise of the Egalitarian Family*
Truxes, T. M. 1989 *Irish American Trade, 1671–1783* (Cambridge)

Tuck, R. 1979 *Natural Rights Theories: Their Origins and Development* (Cambridge)
Tucker, E. F. J. 1984 *Intruders into Eden* (Columbia, South Carolina)
Tucker, G. S. L. 1960 *Progress and Profits in British Economic Thought, 1650–1850* (Cambridge)
Tucker, N. 1961 'Sir Richard Wynn of Gwydir', *Trans. Caern. Hist. Soc.*, 22
Tully, J. 1980 *A Discourse on Property: John Locke and his Adversaries* (Cambridge)
(ed.) 1988 *Meaning and Context: Quentin Skinner and His Critics* (Cambridge)
Tuma, E. H. 1971 *Economic History and the Social Sciences* (Berkeley)
Turnbull, G. H. 1947 *Hartlib Drury and Comenius* (Liverpool)
Turner, H. D. 1965–6 'Charles Hatton', *Northants. P. & P.*, 3
Turner, J. A. 1973 'Mathematical instruments and the education of gentlemen', *Ann. Sc.*, 30
Turner, R. W. 1931 *The Equity of Redemption* (Camb. Stud. Eng. Legal Hist.)
Turner, V. W. 1969 *The Ritual Process: Structure and Anti-structure* (Chicago)
Twigg, J. 1987 *History of Queens' College Cambridge, 1448–1986*
Twitchett, D. C. 1963 *Financial Administration under the T'ang Dynasty* (Cambridge)
Tyack, N. C. P. 1981 'English exports to New England', *New Eng. Hist. & Genealog.*, 135
Tyacke, N. 1987 *Anti-Calvinists: The Rise of the English Arminians, 1590–1646* (Oxford)
1991 'The ambiguities of early modern English Protestants', *H. J.*, 34
Tyacke, S. 1978 *London Map Sellers, 1660–1720* (Tring)
Tyacke, S. and Wallis, H. 1973 (eds.) *My Head is a Map: Essays in Honour of R. V. Tooley*
Tyler, P. 1969 'The church courts at York, 1567–1640', *North. Hist.*, 4
Udovitch, A. L. (ed.) 1981 *The Islamic Middle East, 700–1900* (Princeton)
Ufford, H. Quarles van, 1983 *A Merchant Adventurer in the Dutch Republic* (Amsterdam)
Ulrich, L. T. 1982 *Good Wives: Image and Reality* (New York)
Underdown, D. 1957 *Etherege and the Seventeenth-Century Comedy of Manners* (New Haven)
Underdown, D. 1992 *Fire from Heaven*
Unwin, G. 1904 *Industrial Organisation in the Sixteenth and Seventeenth centuries* (Oxford)
1927 *Studies in Economic History*, ed. R. H. Tawney
1938 *The Guilds and Companies of London*, ed. F. J. Fisher, 3rd edn
Upton, A. F. 1961 *Sir Arthur Ingram*
Usher, A. P. 1943 *The Early History of Deposit Banking in Mediterranean Europe* (Cambridge, Massachusetts)
Usher, R. G. 1913 *The Reconstruction of the English Church*, 2 vols.
Ustick, W. L. 1932a 'Changing ideals of aristocratic character and conduct', *Mod. Phil.*, 30
1932a 'Advice to a son', *Stud. Phil.*, 29
Vale, M. 1977 *The Gentleman's Recreation* (Totowa)

Vale, V. 1956 'Clarendon, Coventry and the sale of naval offices, 1660–88', *C. H. J.*, 12

Valentine, J. L. and Mennis, E. 1980 *Quantitative Techniques for Financial Analysis*

Vance, J. E. 1990 *Capturing the Horizon: The Historical Geography of Transportation* (Baltimore)

Vane, C. M. 1984 'The Walloon community in Norwich', *Proc. Hug. Soc. Lond.*, 24

Vanes, J. M. 1977 *The Port of Bristol in the Sixteenth Century* (Bristol Hist. Assoc.)

1982 *Education and Apprenticeship in Sixteenth-century Bristol* (Bristol Hist. Assoc.)

Vann, R. T. 1969a *The Social Development of English Quakerism, 1655–1755* (Cambridge, Massachusetts)

1969b 'Quakerism and the social structure of the Interregnum', *P. & P.*, 43

1979 'Wills and the family', *J. Fam. Hist.*, 4

Vann, R. T. and Eversley, D. E. C. 1992 *Friends in Life and Death: The Demography of the British and Irish Quakers* (Cambridge)

Vaughn, K. I. 1980 *John Locke: Economist and Social Scientist* (Chicago)

Veale, D. 1970 *The Popular Movement for Law Reform, 1640–60* (Oxford)

Veale, E. M. 1966 *The Fur Trade in the Later Middle Ages* (Oxford)

Veblen, T. 1904 *The Theory of Business Enterprise* (New York)

1935 *The Theory of the Leisure Class*

Veda, T. 1956 'Saikakuku's Economic Man', *Annals of the Hitotsubashi Academy*, 7

Veeser, H. (ed.) 1989 *The New Historicism* (New York)

Venturi, F. 1985 *Eta dei lumi Studia Storici sul settecento Europeo in honore F. Venturi* (Naples)

Verdera, F. 1989 'Smith on the falling rate of profit', *Scot. J. Pol. Econ.*, 39

Verlinden, C. 1970 *The Beginnings of Modern Colonisation* (Ithaca)

Vernon, P. M. 1962 'Marriages of convenience', *Essays in Criticism*, 12

Victoria County History of Derbyshire, vol. II (1907)

Victoria County History of the City of Gloucester, ed. N. Herbert, vol. IV (1988)

Victoria County History of Leicestershire, ed. R. A. MacInley, vol. IV (1958)

Victoria County History of Middlesex, ed. T. F. T. Baker, vol. V (1976)

Victoria County History of Wiltshire, vol. VI (1962)

Victoria County History of the City of York, ed. P. M. Tillcot and C. G. F. Forster (1961)

Victoria County History of Yorkshire, East Riding, ed. K. J. Allison (1969)

Vincent, W. A. L. 1950 *The State and School Education, 1640–60*

1969 *The Grammar Schools, 1660–1714*

Viner, J. 1937 *Studies in the Theory of International Trade*

1958 *The Long View and the Short* (Glencoe, Illinois)

1962 'Relative abundance', *Indian Ec. J.*, 9

1972 *The Role of Providence in the Social Order* (Proc. Amer. Phil. Soc., 90)

1978 *Religious Thought and Economic Society*, ed. T. Melitz and D. Winch (Durham, North Carolina)

Vinogradoff, Sir Paul (ed.) 1913 *Essays in Legal History*

Vives, J. V. 1969 *An Economic History of Spain* (Princeton)
Vogler, B. (ed.) 1979 *Les Actes notariés* (Strasburg)
Vries, J. de, 1973 'On the modernity of the Dutch Republic', *J. Ec. H.*, 33
1974 *The Dutch Rural Economy, 1500–1700* (New Haven)
1984 *European Urbanisation, 1500–1800* (Cambridge, Massachusetts)
Wachter, K. W. (ed.) 1978 *Statistical Studies of Historical Structure* (New York)
Waddel, D. 1958–9 'Charles Davenant', *Ec. H. R.*, 2nd ser., 11
Wadmore, J. F. 1903 *The Company of Skinners of London*
Wadsworth, A. P. and Mann, J. de L. 1931 *The Cotton Trade and Industrial Lancashire, 1600–1780* (Manchester)
Wagener, H. J. and Drukker, J. W. 1986 (eds.) *The Economic Law of Motion* (Cambridge)
Wagner, Sir Anthony, 1939 *Heralds and Heraldry in the Middle Ages*
1951 *Heralds of England* (Baltimore)
1961 *English Ancestry* (Oxford)
1967 *A History of the Office and College of Arms*
1975 *Pedigree and Progress*
1983 *English Genealogy*, 3rd edn (Oxford)
1985 'Idleness and the ideal of the gentleman', *Hist. Educ. Q.*, 25
Wagner, D. O. 1937 'The common law and free enterprise', *Ec. H. R.*, 7
Wake, C. H. H. 1979 'Changing pattern of European pepper and spice imports, 1400–1700', *J. Eur. Ec. Hist.*, 8
Wake, J. 1953 *The Brudenells of Deane*
Wakeman, F. E. 1985 *The Great Enterprise: The Manchu Reconstruction of the Imperial Order* (Berkeley)
Walcott, R. 1956 *English Politics in the Early Eighteenth Century* (Oxford)
Walker, C. F. 1938 *Young Gentlemen: The Story of Midshipmen*
Walker, D. P. 1964 *The Decline of Hell*
Walker, J. 1948 'The English exiles in Holland', *T. R. H. S.*, 4th ser., 30
Walker, J. 1979 *The Japanese Novel of the Meiji period* (Princeton)
Walker, R. B. 1973 'Advertising in London newspapers, 1650–1750', *Bus. Hist.*, 15
Wall, M. 1958–9 'The rise of a Catholic middle class', *Irish Hist. Stud.*, 11
Wall, R. 1978 'The age of leaving home', *J. Fam. Hist.*, 3
Wall, R., Robin, J. and Laslett, P. (eds.) 1983 *Family Forms in Historical Europe* (Cambridge)
Wall, R. E. 1972 *Massachusetts Bay, 1640–50* (New Haven)
Wallerstein, I. 1974, 1980 *The Modern World System* (New York), 2 vols.
1979 'Y a-t-il une crise du XVIIe siècle?', *Annales*, 34
Wallis, P. J. 1983 'Thomas Watts' academy', *Bull. Soc. Hist. Educ.*, 32
Walmsley, J. 1991 *John Reynolds* (Lampeter)
Walsh, E. and Forster, A. 1969 'Recusancy of the Brandlings', *Rec. Hist.*, 10
Walsh, J. D. and Bennett, G. V. 1966 *Essays in Modern English Church History*
Walter, J. and Schofield, R. (eds.) 1989 *Famine, Disease and the Social Order* (Cambridge)
Walter, J. and Wrightson, K. 1976 'Dearth and the social order', *P. & P.*, 71
Walter, K. and Toms, H. N. W. 1967 'An Exeter merchant in Spain', *Devon & Corn. N. & Q.*, 30

Walton, C. 1894 *History of the British Army, 1660–1700*
Walton, J. C. 1978 'The household effects of a Waterford merchant', *J. Cork Hist. & Antiq. Soc.*, 83
Walton, K. M. 1973 'The Company of Upholders of London', *Furn. Hist.*, 9
Walzer, M. D. G. 1965 *The Revolution of the Saints* (Cambridge, Massachusetts)
Wanklyn, M. D. G. 1979a 'Landownership, political authority and social status', *West Midland Stud.*, 40
(ed.) 1979b *Landownership and Power in the Regions* (Wolverhampton)
Waquet, J. C. 1982 'Who profited from the alienation of public revenues?', *J. Eur. Ec. Hist.*, 11
Warburton, J. C. 1929 *Chief Justice Coke*
Ward, I. 1991 'Settlement, mortgage and aristocratic estates, 1649–60', *J. Legal Hist.*, 12
Ward, J. R. 1978 'The profitability of sugar planting, 1650–1834', *Ec. H. R.*, 2nd ser., 31
Ward, J. T. and Wilson, R. G. 1974 (eds.) *Land and Industry* (Newton Abbot)
Ward, W. R. 1953 *The English Land Tax in the Eighteenth Century* (Oxford)
1955 'The English revenue commissioners', *E. H. R.*, 70
Wardle, A. C. 1938 'Sir Thomas Johnson', *Trans. Hist. Soc. Lancs. & Ches.*, 90
Wardle, D. 1967 'Education in Nottinghamshire', *Trans. Thoroton Soc.*, 71
Wareing, G. J. 1978 'The emigration of indentured servants from London, 1683–6', *Genealog. Mag.*, 18, 20
1980 'Changes in the geographical distribution of the apprentices to London Companies, 1486–1750', *J. Hist. Geog.*, 6
1981 'Migration to London and trans-atlantic emigration, 1683–1775', *J. Hist. Geog.*, 7
Wark, K. R. 1971 *Elizabethan Recusancy in Cheshire* (Cheth. Soc., 3rd ser., 19)
Warner, A. W., Morse, D. and Cooney, T. E. (eds.) 1969 *Environment of Change* (New York)
Warnicke, R. M. 1974 'A dispute among the Freemen of the Drapers', *Guild. Stud. Lond. Hist.*, 1
1984 'John Lambarde', *Indiana Soc. Stud. Q.*, 36
Warrender, H. 1961 *The Political Philosophy of Hobbes* (Oxford)
Waterhouse, E. K. 1953 *Painting in Britain, 1530–1790*
Waterhouse, R. 1975a 'Reluctant emigrants', *Hist. Mag. Prot. Episc. Ch.*, 44
1975b 'England, the Caribbean and South Carolina', *J. Amer. Stud.*, 9
Waterman, A. S. 1984 *The Psychology of Individualism* (New York)
Watkins, J. W. N. 1965 *Hobbes' System of Ideas*
Watkins, O. C. 1972 *The Puritan Experience*
Watney, Sir John 1914 *The Mercers of London*
Watson, C. B. 1960 *Shakespeare and the Renaissance Concept of Honour* (Princeton)
Watson, F. 1899 'The teaching of arithmetic and writing', *Genealog. Mag.*, 287
1900 'The curriculum and text books', *Trans. Bibliog. Soc.*, 6
1908 *The English Grammar Schools to 1600* (Cambridge)
1909 *The Beginnings of the Teaching of Modern Subjects in England*
Watson, I. B. 1980a *Foundation for Empire: English Private Trade in India, 1659–1760* (New Delhi)

1980b 'Fortifications and the idea of force', *P.& P.*, 88
Watson, J. S. 1963 *A History of the Salters Company* (Oxford)
Watson, R. C. 1989 'According to the custom of the Province of York', *Lancs. Loc. Hist.*, 5
Watt, I. P. 1967 *The Rise of the Novel* (Berkeley)
Watt, R. and Zimmermann, J. 1983 'Agency problems and the theory of the firm', *J. Law & Econ.*, 26
Watt, T. 1991 *Cheap Print and Popular Piety, 1550–1640* (Cambridge)
Watt, W. M. 1961 *Islam and the Integration of Society* (Evanston)
Watts, C. T. and M. J. 1983 'Company records', *Genealog. Mag.*, 21
Watts, M. R. 1978 *The Dissenters* (Oxford)
Watts, S. J. 1975 *From Border to Middle Shire* (Leicester)
Weatherill, L. 1971 *The Pottery Trade of North Staffordshire, 1660–1760* (Manchester)
1986 'A possession of one's own', *J. B. S.*, 25
1988 *Consumer Behaviour and Material Culture in Britain, 1660–1760*
Webb, J. 1955 'William Salwyn', *Mar. Mirr.*, 41
1960 'Apprenticeship in the maritime occupations at Ipswich, 1596–1651', *Mar. Mirr.*, 46
1962 *Great Tooley of Ipswich* (Suff. Rec. Soc.)
Webb, J., Yates, N. and Peacock, S. (eds.) 1981 *Hampshire Studies Presented to D. Dymond*
Webb, S. S. 1968 'William Blathwayt, imperial fixer', *Wm & Mary Q.*, 3rd ser., 25
1979 *The Governors-General* (Chapel Hill)
Weber, M. 1968 *Economy and Society* (New York)
Webster, C. (ed.) 1974 *The Intellectual Revolution of the Seventeenth Century*
1975 *The Great Instauration, 1621–60*
(ed.) 1979 *Health, Medicine and Mortality in the Sixteenth Century* (Cambridge)
1982 *From Paracelsus to Newton* (Cambridge)
Wedgwood, C. V. 1955 *The King's Peace*
Wee, H. van der, 1963 *The Growth of the Antwerp Market and the European Economy* (The Hague), 3 vols.
1967 'Anvers et les innovations', *Annales*, 22
1972 *Historische aspecten van de economische groei* (Antwerp)
1978 'Prices and wages as developmental variables', *Acta Hist. Neer.*, 10
(ed.) 1988 *The Rise and Decline of Urban Industry in Italy and the Low Countries* (Leuven)
Wee, H. van der, and Pieters, F. 1970 'Un modèle de croissance', *Annales*, 25
Weed, K. K. and Bond, R. R. 1946 *Studies of British Newspapers and Periodicals* (Chapel Hill)
Weigall, D. 1975 'Sir Robert Filmer', *Arch. Cant.*, 91
Weinstein, A. L. 1981 *Fictions of the Self, 1550–1800* (Princeton)
Weinstein, F. and Platt, G. M. 1973 *Psychoanalytic Sociology* (Baltimore)
1975 'The coming crisis in psychohistory', *J. M. H.*, 47
Weinstock, R. 1986 'The making of a Lord Mayor', *Proc. Hug. Soc. Lond.*, 24
Weir, D. R. 1984 'Rather never than late', *J. Fam. Hist.*, 9

1989 'Tontines', *J. Ec. H.*, 49

Weisskopf, W. A. 1951 'Hidden value conflicts in economic thought', *Ethics*, 61

Welch, C. 1902 *History of the Company of Pewterers of London*

1909 *History of the Company of Paviours of London*

1916–23 *History of the Cutlers Company of London*, 2 vols.

Welford, R. 1885 'Cuthbert Gray', *Arch. Aliena*, 11

1895 *Men of Mark twixt Tyne and Tweed*, 3 vols.

Weller, T. de, 1988 'Sex and sexual attitudes', *Ren. & Ref.*, 24

Wells, R. V. 1975 *The Population of the British Colonies in America before 1776* (Princeton)

Wells, S. 1981 'Jacobean city comedy', *J. Eng. Lit. Hist.*, 48

Wellwarth, G. E. 1970 'George Lillo', *Proc. Leeds Phil. & Lit. Soc.*, 14

Welsby, P. A. 1962 *George Abbot*

Wentworth, M. 1986 *Thomas Heywood: A Reference Guide* (Boston)

Wenzel, S. 1960 *The Sin of Sloth* (Chapel Hill)

Wermel, M. T. 1939 *The Evolution of the Classical Wage Theory* (New York)

Wernham, R. B. 1980 *The Making of Elizabethan Foreign Policy, 1558–1603* (Berkeley)

Wertenbaker, T. J. 1922 *The Planters of Colonial Virginia* (Princeton)

1959 *Patrician and Plebeian in Virginia* (New York)

West, S. G. 1954 'Members of the Lisbon factory', *Ann. Rep. Hist. Assoc. Lisbon*

Westerfield, R. B. 1915 *Middlemen in English Business, 1660–1760* (Trans. Conn. Academy Arts & Sciences, 19)

Western, J. R. 1972 *Monarchy and Revolution: The English State in the 1680s*

Westrupp, J. A. 1942 'Domestic music under the Stuarts', *Proc. Music Assoc.*, 68

Whalley, J. I. 1969 *English Handwriting, 1540–1853*

Wharton, D. P. 1979 *Richard Steere, Colonial Merchant Poet*

Whatley, C. 1989 'Economic causes and consequences of the union', *Scot. Hist. Rev.*, 68

Wheaton, R. 1974–5 'Family and kinship in Western Europe', *J. I. H.*, 5

Wheaton, W. 1907 *Knaresburgh and its Rulers* (Leeds)

Whetter, J. A. C. 1974 *Cornwall in the Seventeenth Century* (Padstow)

Whigham, F. 1984 *Ambition and Privilege* (Berkeley)

Whinney, M. D. and Millar, O. 1957 *English Art, 1625–1714* (Oxford)

Whitaker, W. B. 1933 *Sunday in Tudor and Stuart Times*

Whitbrook, T. C. 1938–9 'Sir Thomas Andrews', *Congreg. Hist. Soc. Trans.*, 2nd ser., 13

White, B. R. 1983 *The English Baptists in the Seventeenth Century*

White, C. M. 1992 'The proper concern of economic history', *Scand. Ec. H. R.*, 40

White, H. C. 1931 *English Devotional Literature, 1600–1640* (Madison)

1944 *Social Criticism in Popular Religious Literature* (New York)

White, H. V. 1987 *The Content of the Form* (Baltimore)

White, P. O. G. 1992 *Predestination, Policies and Polemic* (Cambridge)

White, S. D. 1979 *Sir Edward Coke* (Manchester)

Whiteman, A., Bromley, J. S. and Dickson, P. G. M. (eds.) 1973 *Statesmen, Scholars and Merchants: Essays Presented to Lucy Sutherland* (Oxford)

Whitford, H. C. 1967 'Exposed to sale.', *B. N. Y. P. L.*, 71

Whiting, C. E. 1931 *Studies in English Puritanism* (New York)

1939 'Sir Patience Ward', *Yorks. Arch. J.*, 34
Whiting, J. R. S. 1971 *Trade Tokens: A Social and Economic History* (Newton Abbot)
Whitlocke, B. W. 1955 'The orphanage account of John Donne', *Guild. Misc.*, 4
Whitney, D. W. 1963 'London Puritanism: the Haberdashers Company', *Ch. Hist.*, 32
Whittet, T. D. 1964 'The apothecary in provincial gilds', *Med. Hist.*, 8
Wickham, G. 1963 *Early English Stage, 1300–1660*, 2 vols.
Wiener, C. Z. 1975 'Sex roles and crime', *J. Soc. Hist.*, 8
Wiener, M. J. 1981 *English Culture and the Decline of the Industrial Spirit* (Cambridge)
Wilber, C. K. 1974 'R. H. Tawney', *Amer. J. Econ. Sociol.*, 33
Wiles, P. 1972 'The necessity and impossibility of political economy', *Hist. & Theory*, 11
Wiles, R. C. 1974 'Mercantilism', *Eight. Cent. Stud.*, 8
Wilkes, D. L. 1991 'James II's religious indulgence', *Mid. Hist.*, 16
Wilkins, H. J. 1920 *Edward Colston, 1631–1721* (Bristol)
Wilkinson, H. C. 1958 *The Adventurers of Bermuda*, 2nd edn
Willan, T. S. 1953 *The Muscovy Merchants of 1555* (Manchester)
1955 'Some aspects of English trade with the Levant', *E. H. R.*, 70
1956 *The Early History of the Russia Company, 1553–1603* (Manchester)
1959 *Studies in Elizabethan Foreign Trade* (Manchester)
1967 *The English Coasting Trade, 1600–1750* (repr. Manchester)
1976 *The Inland Trade* (Manchester)
1979 'Manchester clothiers', *Text. Hist.*, 1
1980 *Elizabethan Manchester* (Cheth. Soc., 3rd ser., 27)
Willcox, W. B. 1946 *Gloucestershire, 1590–1640* (New Haven)
Willen, D. 1984 'Guildwomen in York, 1560–1640', *The Historian*, 46
Williams, B. 1913 *Life of William Pitt*, 2 vols.
1932 *Stanhope* (Oxford)
Williams, D. A. 1955 'Puritanism in City government, 1610–40', *Guild. Misc.*, 1
Williams, G. 1962 *The Welsh Church* (Cardiff)
(ed.) 1974 *Glamorgan County History*, (Cardiff), vol. IV *Early Modern Glamorgan*
Williams, G. A. 1963 *Medieval London from Commune to Capital*
Williams, M. I. 1978 'Carmarthen Maritime Trade', *Trans. Carmarthen. Antiq. Soc.*, 14
Williams, N. J. 1956 'The London port books', *Trans. Lond. & Midd. A. S.*, 18
1961 *Contraband Cargoes* (Hamden)
1988 *The Maritime Trade of the East Anglian Ports, 1550–90* (Oxford)
Williams, O. C. 1954 *The Clerical Organisation of the House of Commons, 1661–1850* (Oxford)
Williams, P. 1958 *The Council in the Marches of Wales under Elizabeth I* (Cardiff)
1979 *The Tudor Regime* (Oxford)
Williams, P. L. 1978 *The Emergence of the Theory of the Firm*
Williams, R. 1983 *Key Words*, rev. edn
Williams, S. 1959 'Lord Mayor's Show', *Guild. Misc.*, 10
Williams, W. O. 1948 'The Anglesey gentry as businessmen', *Trans. Anglesey*

Antiq. Soc. & Field Club
1967 'The social order in Tudor Wales', *Trans. Cymm. Soc.*
Williamson, G. C. 1889 *Trade Tokens Issued in the Seventeenth Century*
Williamson, J. A. 1969 *Hawkins of Plymouth*, 2nd edn
Williamson, O. E. 1981 'The modern corporation', *J. Ec. Lit.*
1985 *The Economic Institutions of Capitalism* (New York)
Wilson, A. 1980 'The infancy of the history of childhood', *Hist. & Theory*, 19
Wilson, A. and Ashplant, T. G. 1988 'Whig history and present-centered history', *H. J.*, 31
Wilson, A. L. 1972 'Richard Norwood, 1590–1675', *Bermuda Hist. Q.*, 29
Wilson, B. R. (ed.) 1970 *Rationalism* (Evanston)
1971 'Sociological method and the study of history', *T. R. H. S.*, 5th ser., 21
Wilson, C. 1984 'Natural fertility in pre-industrial England', *Pop. Stud.*, 38
Wilson, C. H. 1957 *Profit and Power: A Study of England and the Dutch Wars*
1958 *Mercantilism* (Hist. Assoc.)
1960 *Anglo-Dutch Commerce and Finance in the Eighteenth Century* (repr. Cambridge)
1969 *Economic History and the Historians*
1970 *Queen Elizabeth and the Revolt of the Netherlands* (Berkeley)
1972 'Twenty years after', *J. Eur. Ec. Hist.*, 1
Wilson, F. P. 1927 *The Plague in Shakespeare's London* (Oxford)
1960 *Seventeenth-century Prose* (Berkeley)
Wilson, G. 1963 'Mun and specie flows', *J. Ec. H.*, 18
Wilson, G. W. 1975 'The economics of the just price', *Hist. Pol. Econ.*, 7
Wilson, R. G. 1967 'Records for a study of the Leeds woollen merchants', *Archives*, 8
1971 *Gentlemen Merchants: The Merchant Community of Leeds, 1700–1830* (Manchester)
1988 'Merchants and land: the Ibbetsons', *North. Hist.*, 24
Wilson, W. 1808–14 *The History and Antiquities of Dissenting Churches in London*, 4 vols.
Winch, D. 1978 *Adam Smith's Politics* (Cambridge)
1992 'Adam Smith', *H. J.*, 35
Winchester, B. 1955 *Tudor Family Portrait*
Winder, W. H. D. 1936 'The Courts of Requests', *Law Q. R.*, 52
Winfrey, J. C. 1981 'Charity versus justice in Locke's theory of property', *J. H. I.*, 42
Winn, J. A. 1987 *John Dryden and His World* (New Haven)
Winstanley, D. A. 1935 *Unreformed Cambridge* (Cambridge)
Wiseman, T. P. 1971 *New Men in the Roman Senate, 139 B.C.–A.D. 14* (Oxford)
Wither, H. E. 1943 *The Property Qualification of Members of Parliament* (New York)
Withington, R. 1920 *English Pageantry* (Cambridge)
Wojcik, M. 1979 'Zur interpretation des Robinson Crusoe', *Zeit. für Anglistik und Amerikanistik*, 27
Wolf, E. R. 1951 'The social organisation of Mecca', *South-west Journal of Anthropology*, 7
Wolfe, L. 1934 *Essays in Jewish History*, ed. C. Roth

Wolfe, M. 1972 *The Fiscal System: Renaissance France* (New Haven)
Wolff, C. G. 1968 'Literary reflections on the Puritan character', *J. H. I.*, 68
Wolfran, S. 1987 *In Laws and Out Laws: Kinship and Marriage in England*
Wood, A. C. 1935 *A History of the Levant Company* (Oxford)
Wood, E. M. 1991 *The Pristine Culture of Capitalism*
Wood, J. B. 1980 *The Nobility of the Election of Bayeux* (Princeton)
Wood, N. 1980 'Thomas Hobbes and the crisis of the English aristocracy', *Hist. Pol. Thought*, 1
1984 *Locke and Agrarian Capitalism* (Berkeley)
Wood, T. 1950 'The eighteenth-century English casuists', *Ch. Q. Rev.*, 149
1952 *English Casuistical Divinity during the Seventeenth Century*
1966 'Seventeenth-century moralists', *Trivium*, 1
Wood-Jones, R. B. 1963 *Traditional Domestic Architecture* (Manchester)
Woodbridge, K. 1969 'Accounts rendered: the letters of Sir Richard Hoare', *Hist. Tod.*, 19
Woodcock, B. L. 1952 *Medieval Ecclesiastical Courts in the Diocese of Canterbury* (Oxford)
Woodfill, W. L. 1950 'Education of professional musicians in Elizabethan England', *Med. & Hum.*, 6
1969 *Musicians in English Society from Elizabeth I to Charles I* (New York)
Woodford, 1600–1836 (Proc. Woodford Hist. Soc., 10, 1950)
Woodhead, J. R. 1965 *The Rulers of London, 1660–89* (Trans. Lond. & Midd. A. S.)
Woodhouse, A. S. P. 1974 *Puritanism and Liberty*, 2nd edn
Woodruffe, W. 1956 'History and the businessman', *Bus. Hist. Rev.*, 30
Woodward, D. M. 1965 'The foreign trade of Chester in the reign of Elizabeth I' (unpub. M.A. thesis, Manchester)
1967 'The Chester leather industry 1558–1625', *Trans. Hist. Soc. Lancs. & Ches.*, 119
1969 'The assessment of wages', *Loc. Hist.*, 8
1970a *The Trade of Elizabethan Chester* (Hull)
1970b 'The port books', *History*, 55
1970c 'Freemen rolls', *Loc. Hist.*, 9
1973 'The port books of England and Wales', *Mar. Hist.*, 3
1977a 'Anglo-Scottish trade', *Scot. Hist. Rev.*, 56
1977b 'Ship masters and shipowners of the Wirral', *Mar. Mirr.*, 63
1980 'The background to the Statute of Artificers', *Ec. H. R.*, 2nd ser., 33
1981 'Wages rates and living standards', *P. & P.*, 91
Woolf, M. 1974 'Foreign trades of London Jews in the seventeenth century', *T. J. H. S. E.*, 24
Woolf, S. J. 1964–5 'Economic problems of the nobility', *Ec. H. R.*, 2nd ser., 17
1970 'The aristocracy in transition', *Ec. H. R.*, 2nd ser., 23
Woolrych, A. 1982 *Commonwealth to Protectorate* (Oxford)
Worden, B. 1974 *The Rump Parliament, 1648–53* (Cambridge)
1985 'Providence and politics in Cromwellian England', *P. & P.*, 99
Wordie, R. 1982 *Estate Management: The Building of the Leveson-Gower Fortune in Eighteenth-Century England* (R. H. S.)
Woude, A. van der, and Schyuurman, A. (eds.) 1980 *Probate Inventories* (A. A. G.

Bijdragen, 23)
Wren, M. C. 1948 'The Chamber of London in 1633', *Ec. H. R.*, 2nd ser., 1
Wretts-Smith, M. 1920 'The English in Russia', *T. R. H. S.*, 4th ser., 3
1963 'The business of the East India Company, 1680–81', *Indian Ec. & Soc. Hist. Rev.*, 1
Wright, A. 1987 *R.H. Tawney* (Manchester)
Wright, C. and Fayle, C. E. 1928 *A History of Lloyds*
Wright, L. B. 1940 *The First Gentlemen of Virginia* (San Marino)
1947 *The Atlantic Frontier, 1607–1763* (New York)
1957 *Cultural Life of the American Colonies, 1607–1763* (New York)
1958 *Middle-class Culture in Elizabethan England* (repr. Ithaca)
1974 *Religion and Empire, 1558–1625* (repr. Chapel Hill)
Wright, L. M. 1932 *The Literary Life of the Early Friends, 1650–1725* (New York)
Wright, L. R. 1969 'The military orders in Spanish society', *P. & P.*, 43
Wright, S. M. 1983 *The Derbyshire Gentry in the Fifteenth Century* (Derby. Rec. Soc., 8)
Wrightson, K. 1981 'Household and kinship', *Hist. Work. J.*, 12
1982 *English Society, 1580–1680*
Wrightson, K. and Levine, D. 1979 *Poverty and Piety in an English Village*
Wrigley, E. A. (ed.) 1966a *An Introduction to English Historical Demography*
1966b 'Family limitation in pre-industrial England', *Ec. H. R.*, 2nd ser., 19
1967a 'A simple model of London's importance', *P. & P.*, 37
1967b 'London and the great leap forward', *The Listener* (6 July)
1969 *Population and History*
1973a 'Clandestine marriages in the late seventeenth century', *Loc. Pop. Stud.*, 10
(ed.) 1973b *Identifying People in the Past*
1973c Review of H. J. Habakkuk in *Ec. H. R.*, 2nd ser., 26
1977 'Reflexion on the history of the family', *Daedalus*, 106
1985 'Urban growth and agrarian change', *J. I. H.*, 15
1987 *People, Cities and Wealth* (Oxford)
1991 'City and country in the past', *Hist. Res.*, 64
Wrigley, E. A. and Schofield, R. S. 1981 *The Population History of England, 1541–1871* (Cambridge, Massachusetts)
1983 'English population history from family reconstruction', *Pop. Stud.*, 37
Wroth, L. C. 1954 'An Elizabethan merchant and man of letters', *H. L. Q.*, 17
Wunderli, R. M. 1990 'Evasion of the office of Alderman of London, 1523–1672', *Lond. J.*, 15
Wunderli, R. M. and Broce, G. 1989 'The final moment before death', *Sixt. Cent. J.*, 20
Wyatt, T. 1952–8 'Aliens in England before the Huguenots', *Proc. Hug. Soc. Lond.*, 19
Yamamura, K. 1968 'A re-examination of entrepreneurs in Meiji Japan', *Ec. H. R.*, 2nd ser., 21
1971 'The increasing poverty of the Samurai, 1606–1868', *J. Ec. H.*, 31
1974 *A Study of Samurai Income and Entrepreneurship* (Cambridge, Massachusetts)
Yamey, B. S. 1949 'Scientific bookkeeping and the rise of capitalism', *Ec. H. R.*,

2nd ser., 1
1959 'Some seventeenth- and eighteenth-century double entry ledgers', *Acc. Rev.*, 34
1960 'A seventeenth-century double entry journal', *Accountancy*, 71
1963 Review of G. D. Ramsay in *Accountancy*, 74
1968 *Foreign Books on Bookkeeping, 1494–1750*
1989 *Art and Accounting* (New Haven)
Yamey, B. S. and Bywater, M. F. 1982 *Historic Accounting Literature: A Companion Guide*
Yamey, B. S., Edey, H. C. and Thomson, H. W. (eds.) 1963 *Accounting in England and Scotland, 1543–1800*
Yarbrough, A. 1979 'Apprentices as adolescents in sixteenth-century Bristol', *J. Soc. Hist.*, 13
1980 'Geographical and social origins of Bristol apprentices', *T. B. G. A. S.*, 98
Yogev, G. 1978 *Diamonds and Coral* (Leicester)
Yolton, J. W. 1969 (ed.) *John Locke: Problems and Perspectives* (Cambridge)
Youings, J. 1968 *Tuckers Hall, Exeter* (Exeter)
Young, M. B. 1979 'Cranfield and the Ordnance', *H. J.*, 22
1986 *Servility and Service: The Life and Work of Sir John Coke*
Young, S. 1889 *Annals of the Barber Surgeons of London*
1913 *History of the Company of Glass-sellers of London*
Youngson, J. (ed.) 1972 *Economic Development in the Long Run*
Yule, H. and Burnell, A. C. 1968 *Hobson-Jobson*, 2nd edn (Delhi)
Yver, J. 1966 *Egalité entre héritiers et exclusion des enfants dotés*
Zagorin, P. 1969 *The Court and the Country*
1982 *Rebels and Rulers, 1500–1600* (Cambridge), 2 vols.
1990a 'Historiography and post-modernism', *Hist. & Theory*, 29
1990b *Ways of Lying* (Cambridge, Massachusetts)
Zahedieh, N. 1986a 'Trade plunder and economic development in Jamaica, 1655–89', *Ec. H. R.*, 2nd ser., 39
1986b 'The merchants of Port Royal, Jamaica', *Wm & Mary Q.*, 3rd ser., 43
Zajaczkowski, A. 1963 'Cadres structurels de la noblesse', *Annales*, 18
Zakai, A. 1991 *Orthodoxy in England and New England* (Proc. Amer. Phil. Soc., 135)
Zaller, R. 1986 'What does the English revolution mean', *Albion*, 18
1987 'The debate on capital punishment', *Amer. J. Legal Hist.*, 31
Zanetti, D. E. 1972 *La demografia del patriziato milanese* (Ann. Cisalp. Hist. Soc., 2)
Zaniewicki, W. 1967 *La Noblesse populaire en Espagne et en Pologne* (Lyons)
Zaozerskaza, E. I. 1965 'Le salariat dans les manufactures textiles russes', *Cahiers du monde russe et soviétique*, 6
Zaret, D. 1980 'Ideology and organization in Puritanism', *Eur. J. Sociol.*, 21
1985 *The Heavenly Contract* (Chicago)
Zeldin, T. 1976 'Social history and total history', *J. Soc. Hist.*, 10
1982 'Personal history', *J. Soc. Hist.*, 15
Zell, M. L. 1979 'Fifteenth- and sixteenth-century wills', *Archives*, 14
1981 'The Exchequer lists of provincial clothmakers', *B. I. H. R.*, 54
1984 'The social parameters of probate records', *B. I. H. R.*, 57

Zeuner, F. E. 1963 *A History of Domesticated Animals*
Zimanyi, V. 1987 *Economy and Society in Sixteenth- and Seventeenth-century Hungary* (Budapest)
Zins, H. 1973 *England and the Baltic in the Elizabethan Era*
Zlatar, Z. 1975 'The crisis of the patriciate in Dubrovnik', *Balcanica*, 6
Znaniecki, F. 1969 *On Humanistic Society*, ed. R. Bierstadt (Chicago)
Zschocke, A. 1984 'Kondratieff cycles in the pre-industrial period', *Hist. Soc. Res.*, 31
Zupco, R. E. 1985 *British Weights and Measures* (Madison)

Index

Made in the USA
Middletown, DE
16 August 2022